DATE DUE

Encyclopedia of Women and World Religion

Encyclopedia of Women and World Religion

Edited by

Serinity Young

Volume 2

Macmillan Reference USA
New York

Macmillan Reference USA
1633 Broadway, New York, NY 10019-6785

Printed in the United States of America

Printing Number

2 3 4 5 6 7 8 9 10

Library of Congress Cataloging-in-Publications Data

Encyclopedia of women and world religion / Serinity Young, editor in
   chief.
     p. cm.
    Includes bibliographical references and index.
    ISBN 0-02-964608-8 (set). — ISBN 0-02-864859-5 (vol. 1). — ISBN
0-02-864860-9 (vol. 2)
    1. Women and religion—Encyclopedias. I. Young, Serinity.
BL458.E53   1998
200′.82—dc21   98–39292
                                                 CIP

Laity

The term and the concept *laity* is rooted in European Christianity, specifically Roman Catholicism, where it refers to persons who have not taken the vows of a priest, monk, or nun. In more general terms, laypersons are those who can be distinguished from individuals who have renounced ordinary life in the world in order to follow a religious vocation. Such a distinction can be found in the Buddhist, Jain, and Taoist traditions, but it is less meaningful in other religious contexts. Even in traditions where the distinction between lay and monastic is clearly defined, the boundary may be blurred in practice. This seems to be the case particularly for women. There are many women—like the Christian lay sisters of medieval Europe, the Buddhist "precept women" of contemporary Southeast Asia, or female ascetics in Hinduism—who occupy a borderline status. Many other women have combined in a single life the roles of family woman and renunciant. And in many contexts there has been a shared religious culture among laywomen and nuns: in eighteenth-century China and India, nuns and female ascetics had access to the women's quarters in elite homes, while in the same period in Italy, aristocratic laywomen were frequent visitors to cloistered convents.

When we speak, therefore, of laywomen's religious activities, we are concerned with virtually the entirety of women's religious lives. Laywomen's religious activity encompasses private devotion and communal celebration, domestic observances and public practices. Among the many aspects of this activity are prayer, singing, dancing, the recitation of sacred stories, receiving religious instruction, study, writing (the composition of Yiddish prayer books, the translation of Christian religious works, the copying of Buddhist sutras), the performance of vows, food preparation, feasting, undertaking fasts and other austerities, life-cycle ceremonies, worship, visiting the graves of relatives and saints, pilgrimage, participation in festivals, and religious patronage. It is the last of these activities that is the focus of the remainder of this article.

Religious giving—alms-giving, charity, sponsorship of religious activities, persons, and institutions—is regarded by virtually all traditions as an important religious activity that benefits both the community, allowing other members of society to observe the faith, and the donor, who is able through giving to practice compassion, generosity, and renunciation and to receive blessings or religious merit, or to fulfill a religious duty. We are increasingly coming to appreciate the extent to which women have been active as donors, in the whole range of forms of religious giving. Much of women's patronage and sponsorship of religious activity in the domestic or community setting—a Buddhist, Jain, or Hindu woman's offering of food to a mendicant at her doorstep, a Muslim woman's distribution of alms during Ramadan or her hosting of a gathering of women in her home to hear the stories of saints, a Jewish woman's visit to a sick person or her embroidering of Torah covers for the synagogue, a Christian woman's mending and laundering of the clothes of the poor—goes virtually unnoticed. Yet such activities are frequently highly significant inasmuch as the spiritual benefit arising from them extends beyond the individual woman to her household and to the entire community.

Women have not, however, been confined in their religious giving only to providing services, cooking and

A laywoman gives alms to Buddhist monks, Nong Khai, Thailand, 1991 (Michael S. Yamashita/Corbis).

sewing, and donating their handiwork. They have also had access to wealth that they have used for religious purposes. Art historical and inscriptional evidence shows that women acted as patrons to a much greater extent than we would expect, given the restrictions on their economic autonomy and access to resources suggested by normative religious texts. The women of ruling families are particularly famed as generous donors: women of the Chinese and Japanese imperial courts built Buddhist monasteries; Byzantine royal women commissioned churches adorned with rich mosaics; medieval Christian queens made gifts of sumptuous altar-cloths and stained-glass windows to European churches; women of the families of the Abbasid caliphs and successive Muslim rulers built mosques and tombs and supported saints and scholars; while royal women in medieval South India sponsored the building of Hindu temples and donated precious jewels to adorn the images of the deities. But countless other women have also had the means and the motivation to make religious gifts, commissioning books and works of art, sponsoring religious services, and endowing places of religious scholarship, charity, and worship.

Women's religious patronage, in various traditions and throughout history, has brought not only spiritual benefits to themselves and their families, but has provided them with the opportunity to exert influence over the institutions and activities that they have supported. In addition, women's choices about the kind of patronage they wish to extend, and the symbolic and stylistic qualities of the objects they have created or commissioned, have allowed women's concerns and interests to be represented in the religious life of their communities.

BIBLIOGRAPHY

Baskin, Judith R., ed. *Jewish Women in Historical Perspective.* 1991.

Brooten, Bernadette J. *Women Leaders in the Ancient Synagogue: Inscriptional Evidence and Background Issues.* 1982.

Buitelaar, Marjo. *Fasting and Feasting in Morocco: Women's Participation in Ramadan.* 1993.

Cavallo, Sandra. *Charity and Power in Early Modern Italy: Benefactors and Their Motives in Turin, 1541–1789.* 1995.

Clark, Elizabeth A. "Patrons, Not Priests: Gender and Power in Late Ancient Christianity." *Gender and History* 2, no. 3 (1990): 253–273.

Falk, Nancy Auer, and Rita M. Gross, eds. *Unspoken Worlds: Women's Religious Lives.* 1989.

Findly, Ellison Banks. "Women's Wealth and Styles of Giving: Perspectives from Buddhist, Jaina, and Mughal Sites." In *Women, Patronage, and Self-Representation.* Edited by D. Fairchild Ruggles. 1998.

Keddie, Nikki R., and Beth Baron, eds. *Women in Middle Eastern History: Shifting Boundaries of Sex and Gender.* 1991.

Kendall, Laurel. *Shamans, Housewives, and Other Restless Spirits: Women in Korean Ritual Life.* 1985.

King, Catherine. "Women as Patrons: Nuns, Widows and Rulers." In *Siena, Florence and Padua: Art, Society and Religion, 1280–1400.* Vol. 2. Edited by Diana Norman. 1995.

Mann, Susan. *Precious Records: Women in China's Long Eighteenth Century.* 1977.

McCash, June Hall, ed. *The Cultural Patronage of Medieval Women.* 1996.

Orr, Leslie C. "Women's Wealth and Worship: Female Patronage of Hinduism, Jainism, and Buddhism in Medieval Tamilnadu." In *Captive Subjects: A Social and Cultural Casebook on the Women of India.* Vol. 2, *The Medieval Period.* Edited by Mandakranta Bose. 1998.

"Patronage by Women in Islamic Art." Special issue. *Asian Art* 6, no. 2 (1993).

Prochaska, F. K. *Women and Philanthropy in Nineteenth-Century England.* 1980.

Reynell, Josephine. "Women and the Reproduction of the Jain Community." In *The Assembly of Listeners: Jains in Society.* Edited by M. Carrithers and C. Humphrey. 1991.

Sered, Susan Starr. *Women as Ritual Experts: The Religious Lives of Elderly Jewish Women in Jerusalem.* 1992.

Weidner, Marsha, ed. *Flowering in the Shadows: Women in the History of Chinese and Japanese Painting.* 1990.

See also Craft; Fasting; Food; Patronage; Pilgrimage; Ritual.

LESLIE C. ORR

BIBLIOGRAPHY

Kumar, P. Pratap. *The Goddess Lakṣmī: The Divine Consort in South Indian Vaiṣṇava Tradition.* 1997.

Narayanan, Vasudha. "Śrī: Giver of Fortune, Bestower of Grace." In *Devi: Goddesses of India.* Edited by John Stratton Hawley and Donna Marie Wulff. 1996.

VASUDHA NARAYANAN

Lakṣmī

Śrī, more popularly known as Lakṣmī (Lakshmi), is perhaps the best-known goddess in the Hindu and Jain traditions of India. Considered to be the goddess of wealth and good fortune, she is pictured standing or seated on a resplendent red lotus. This image graces millions of homes, shops, and businesses. She is said to shower wealth and salvific grace just by glancing at a person. Her right hand points to the ground; in Hindu iconography this is said to be the *varada* or giving position. In art, one sees her giving wealth to her devotees: gold coins emanate and shower from her hand. Sometimes, her palm is uplifted, facing the viewer; this is the *abhaya* position, symbolic of her granting fearlessness in this life.

While she is depicted as an independent goddess in pictures and has her own shrine in many temples, Lakṣmī is also portrayed in temples and in theology as inseparable from Vishnu. This inseparability is iconographically depicted through her dwelling on the chest of Vishnu.

In the *Śrī Sukta*, or Hymn to Śrī, found in some later sections of the *Ṛgveda* (c. 1000 B.C.E.), Lakṣmī is praised as the wife of Vishnu and as one who dwells on the lotus flower. However, it is in the Purāṇas (first millennium C.E.) that she emerges with a distinct personality; here she is extolled through several hymns. She appears in architecture around the third century B.C.E. and later in Kausambi and on coins issued during the Gupta dynasty around the fourth century C.E. Separate shrines to Lakṣmī within the precincts of Vishnu temples were built only after the tenth century. Separate shrines are particularly popular in the temples built or managed by the Śrī Vaiṣṇava community of south India.

Prayers in honor of Lakṣmī have been written for more than two thousand years. Friday evenings are considered to be particularly sacred to Lakṣmī as she is said to be in the flame of lamps lit then. There are many rituals for Lakṣmī, and the most important festival is on the tenth day of the fall *navaratri* ("nine nights") festival, which occurs roughly in September–October.

Lands, Mythic

Legends about all-women societies abound in ancient ethnography, along with tales of half-human, half-animal hybrid creatures like dog-headed humans and other fabulous beings dwelling in distant lands. Such fantastic legends of cultural Others have been read as the royal road to the collective unconscious of dominant male cultures and subcultures (Lederer, 1968). Whether they are to be read as indications of a universal gynophobia or simply as windows onto the ambivalent psyches of those individual sailors, geographers, ethnographers, and other bards who told such tales, the fantasy content of such legends begs for feminist analysis. They are full of what Susanne Kappeler would classify as "pornographic" representations of the feminine, whereby women are objectified by the very structure of the narratives in which they appear (Kappeler, 1986). Tales of legendary women are not *their* stories but rather those of the men who set foot on their mythic "lands." If we watch the plot of the typical land-of-women story unfold through the eyes of the protagonist, we are positioned by the framing of the narrative as a male subject with no direct access to the thoughts of the women we meet. These are narratives about a man's experience of "virgin territory" in which the subjectivity of the women thus encountered is presented at one remove.

The Amazons of Greek legend, for example, were depicted as a society of warrior women who got along without marriage and essentially without men. Said to live on the edge of the known world (their homeland is variously located in Asia Minor and North Africa), the Amazons were said to have been formidable fighters against such Greek heroes as Theseus and Heracles (Hercules). Like other fabulous beings living beyond the pale of the ancient Greco-Roman world, Amazons stand as figures of reversal whose abnormality yields insight into the norms of Greco-Roman culture. Their highly transgressive female world in fact delineates the very patriarchal cultural norms they overturn.

An Amazon armed with an axe rides on horseback (Leonard de Selva/Corbis).

A common feature of legends about exclusively female societies is the tendency to locate such societies on extraordinary, distant islands in the sea. These legends, fantastic and dreamlike in their expression of male fears and desires, are found in much of Asia, the Middle East, the Pacific Islands, and Native North America (Ishida, 1964). They say a great deal about the regime of repression and symbolic expression that governs the psyches of those who transmitted the tales. An Arabo-Islamic example with many fascinating variants is the island of Al Waqwāq, where women grow on trees, ripe for the taking. Although dubious as sources of geographic or ethnographic knowledge, accounts of Al Waqwāq are invaluable as psychobiographies, maps of the mind or psychodynamic processes. In Al Waq-wāq—a major trope in medieval Arabo-Islamic writing (Malti-Douglas, 1991)—the female fruits resembling human women hang from the branches by their hair, continually crying out, "Wak-Wak!" If someone should come along and "harvest" the fruit of a certain type of woman-bearing tree, the fruit would die within a day or so. He who did the cutting, however, could enjoy her sexually and would experience intense pleasure with her beyond that experienced with a normal woman.

Although many tales of female societies resemble legends of Al Waqwāq in catering to male sexual fantasies,

others take the form of cautionary tales warning men of the catastrophic consequences of allowing women to take the upper hand, especially through traditionally female forms of empowerment such as sexual captivation. Wish-fulfillment surely plays a role in Buddhist cautionary tales circulated by South Asian merchants (Lewis, 1994; Wilson, 1996), in which the women are, as a literary rule, sweet-sixteen and ever so available. But ultimately it is the fear of being cannibalized that predominates in these tales: the nubile, sexually voracious women encountered by shipwrecked men on distant shores are also voracious for flesh. They have an urgent need to feed, and although they appear to be attractive young women, they are in actuality hideous shape-shifting ogresses, vampires whose diet consists of castaway men. In the end, the men must escape or be devoured by these femmes fatales, just as in Native American and Asian legends men must beware of the hidden dangers of consorting with women who have toothed vaginas (*vagina dentata*).

In the legends discussed above, distant lands of women serve as incarnations of anomaly in which the alterity of the Other and the transgression of norms are emphasized. Tantric Buddhist references to Odiyana, the realm of the *ḍākinīs* or sky-walking female deities, suggest that the all-female locale of the *ḍākinīs* is both a locus of otherness and an idealized potential within the self—the enlightened mind inherent in all sentient beings. Odiyana is, then, not a distant land in which a man finds himself stranded and eaten alive but a region in which the impure mind (that generates such desire- and fear-based fantasies) is transcended.

BIBLIOGRAPHY

Burton, Richard F. *The Book of a Thousand Nights and a Night.* 10 vols. 1885–1887.

Dharmalabhda Jātaka. In *Mahāvastu.* Edited by Émile Senart. 3 vols. 1882–1897. Vol. 3, pp. 286–300. Translated from the French by J. J. Jones as *The Mahāvastu.* 3 vols. 1949–1956. Vol. 3, pp. 274–287.

Ishida, Ei'ichiro. "Mother-Son Deities." *History of Religions* 4, no. 1 (Summer 1964): 30–52.

Kappeler, Susanne. *The Pornography of Representation.* 1986.

Lach, Donald F. *Asia in the Making of Europe.* Vol. 1, *The Century of Discovery,* Book 1. 1965.

Lewis, Todd. "Newar Tibetan Trade and the Domestication of the Siṃhalasārthabāhu Avadāna." *History of Religions* 33 (1994): 135–160.

Malti-Douglas, Fedwa. *Woman's Body, Woman's Word: Gender and Discourse in Arabo-Islamic Writing.* 1991.

Rothery, Guy C. *Amazons in Antiquity and Modern Times.* 1910.

Sutherland, Gail Hinich. *The Disguises of the Demon: The Development of the Yakṣa in Hinduism and Buddhism.* 1991.

Tyrrell, William Blake. *Amazons: A Study in Athenian Mythmaking.* 1984.

Valāhassa Jātaka. In *Jātakāṭṭhakathā* (The Jātaka together with its commentary). Edited by V. Fausboll. 1877–1896. Vol. 2, p. 127. Translated by R. Chalmers, W. H. D. Rouse, H. T. Francis, and R. A. Neil as *The Jātaka or Stories of the Buddha's Former Births.* 1895–1907. Vol. 2, p. 89. Reprint, 1962–1964.

White, David Gordon. *Myths of the Dog-Man.* 1991.

Wilson, Liz. *Charming Cadavers: Horrific Figurations of the Feminine in Indian Buddhist Hagiographic Literature.* 1996.

LIZ WILSON

Language

As a number of anthropologists, psychologists, and historians have noted, the different ways in which women and men use language is intimately connected to the different ways in which women and men relate to others, understand their moral lives, and, at its most basic level, experience the world. Poststructuralist thinkers such as Jacques Lacan and Julia Kristeva have even gone so far as to suggest that language itself is intrinsically male. Two approaches may illuminate how language, and women's particular relationships to particular languages, relates to women and religion. The first is to examine the ways in which women's relations to the sacred languages of various religious traditions are related to women's access to religion. The second is to examine the significant changes in Jewish and Christian liturgical practice since the 1970s that attempt to adopt inclusive language and the ensuing debates over that language.

Many of the world's great religions have historically excluded women from religious life precisely by denying them access to the sacred texts of those traditions. This restriction has of course literally been a question of language. Without being taught Arabic, Greek, Hebrew, or Sanskrit, women could have no intimate connection to or experience of the sacred texts of Islam, Christianity, Judaism, Hinduism, or Buddhism. The male world, which meant religious education, schools, scholarship, and houses of worship, was often connected with the holy tongue. The female world of family life, the home, and intimate relationships was often linked to vernacular languages.

The relation between sacred and vernacular languages is one of social hierarchy but also one that has transformative possibilities. An instructive example is the relation between Hebrew, the holy tongue (*Loshn-kodesh*), and Yiddish, the vernacular, "mama-language" (*mame-loshn*). Historically, Hebrew represented the male world and Yiddish the female one, a distinction that by the early modern period was institutionalized ritually. Since women had no access to the holy tongue, Rabbi Jacob Ashkenazi in the early seventeenth century published women's prayers (*Tehinot*) so that women would know how to conduct themselves ritually. The Yiddish vernacular became increasingly associated not only with women but also with ignorant men, and hence the Jewish masses. What was originally a language written only for women and then ignoramuses, became in the early twentieth century a national, often secular, literary language that transformed the hierarchical religious and social relations within the Jewish community itself.

The replacement of the sacred for the vernacular has also been a major vehicle for transforming Christian liturgy and practice, particularly in America in the late twentieth century. At stake in the gendered biases of a liturgy are at least two theological issues: the impact of perceiving God as either masculine or feminine, and the impact of the community's participating together in either exclusive or inclusive prayer. Concerned more with the latter issue, and contending that Christianity was always a religion that insisted on the primacy of the vernacular, some Christian feminists such as Gail Ramshaw suggest that it is precisely the task of feminists to expand the intrinsically inclusive language of Christianity to embrace those who have been historically excluded: women. More conservative positions put less weight on social concerns and more on doctrinal ones by contending that feminine language has the potential to erode a truly Trinitarian conception of God into a secular ideology.

Within the Jewish community, attempts to use more inclusive language have been met with a host of responses, some of which retain and at times augment the sacred Hebrew language, others of which turn almost completely to the vernacular English. Both within the conservative and liberal branches of Judaism, the trend has gone from eliminating specifically masculine language to returning to some use of the masculine pronouns and explaining the original context of their use. In an attempt to transform both Jewish theology and society, Reconstructionist Judaism has turned toward the Jewish mystical tradition, and in particular to the notion of Shekhinah, God's feminine emanation, for a greater model of gender inclusivity. However, scholars

A Jewish woman covers her face with her prayerbook at the women's area of the Western Wall, where women are expected to pray quietly (Annie Griffiths Belt/Corbis).

Gupta, Lina, "Kali the Savior." In *After Patriarchy: Feminist Transformation of the World Religions.* Edited by Paula Cooey, William Eakin, and Jay McDaniel. 1991.

Hassan, Riffat. "Muslim Women and Post-Patriarchal Islam." In *After Patriarchy: Feminist Transformations of the World Religions.* Edited by Paula Cooey, William Eakin, and Jay McDaniel. 1991.

Kristeva, Julia. *Language—the Unknown: An Initiation into Linguistics.* Translated by Anne M. Menke. 1989.

Ragland-Sullivan, Ellie, and Mark Bracher, eds. *Lacan and the Subject of Language.* 1991.

Ramshaw, Gail. *God beyond Gender: Feminist God-Language.* 1995.

Robinson, Sandra. "Hindu Paradigms of Women." In *Women, Religion, and Social Change.* Edited by Yvonne Haddad. 1985.

Seidman, Naomi. *A Marriage Made in Heaven: The Sexual Politics of Hebrew and Yiddish.* 1997.

Spender, Dale. *Man Made Language.* 1980.

Wolfson, Elliot R. *Through a Speculum that Shines: Vision and Imagination in Medieval Jewish Mysticism.* 1994.

See also Deconstruction; Literature; Postmodernism.

LEORA BATNITZKY

such as Elliot Wolfson, though not denying the possibility of a feminist reinterpretation of Jewish mysticism, have raised questions about the historical accuracy of an uncritical feminist portrayal of the Jewish mystical tradition.

Within the Islamic tradition, some feminist attempts at transformation have also come through a redefinition of language. Muslim feminists such as Riffat Hassan have emphasized the interpretative aspect of all scriptural exegesis and have attempted to retranslate parts of the Qur'an to point out where equality between men and women is in fact advocated by the tradition. Lina Gupta, a Hindu feminist, has attempted similarly to discard Hinduism's patriarchal framework and to thereby revalue various linguistic descriptions of the Hindu goddess Kālī.

It is in the relation between the authority of the past and the need for meaning in the present that theological and social issues intersect; and it is here that the question of language becomes most vexing.

BIBLIOGRAPHY

Falk, Nancy Auer, and Rita M. Gross, ed. *Unspoken Worlds: Women's Religious Lives.* 1989.

Law

Law, like religion, is a distinct cultural form that is found in all human society. Law may be defined along a continuum ranging from a broad encompassing of all rule making and conflict resolution, formal and informal, within a society, to a narrow reference to that which is state promulgated and enforced. Legal scholars have found law in cultural forms such as the rubrics of religious ritual, the rules of monastic life, manuals of etiquette, the informal formation of queues in supermarkets, vodou trance, and in local forms of mediation as well as in the formal acts of kings, judges, and legislators. Religious cosmologies profoundly shape the anthropology that underlies all legal forms; legal concepts are frequently based on religious concepts. Secular legal ritual, legal specialists, and legal institutions and texts frequently find their origins in religious ritual, priesthoods, institutions, and texts. Conversely, it can be said that the various forms of religious life are largely determined by law.

Although women throughout history have both created and been created by law and religion, until the twentieth century—and in many cases during it—most women have had limited legal capacity to contract, hold property, sue, vote, or hold public office. Sustained and increasingly sophisticated feminist critiques of the role of both law and religion in women's lives have, in the last quarter of the twentieth century, radically altered understanding of these areas. Key contemporary figures in the feminist critique of Anglo-American law include Herma Hill Kay, Catherine MacKinnon, and Robin West. Their critiques share the conviction that Anglo-American law and legal institutions are fundamentally unjust because of their patriarchal history, location, language, and structure. Key figures in the feminist critique of Christianity include Mary Daly, Elisabeth Schüssler Fiorenza, and Rosemary Radford Ruether. Although most legal feminism, like most contemporary legal scholarship, has shown a marked lack of interest in religion, some legal historians and anthropologists have studied the ways in which religious understandings of the individual and the family, of women, and of women's bodies have fundamentally shaped the language and culture of the law and of women's lives. Because there is enormous variety in women's lives with respect to law and religion, understanding the precise relationship of women, religion, and law must be grounded in the historical and socioeconomic location of particular women.

COSMOLOGY AND LAW

Legal cultural forms are significantly shaped by the religious cosmologies that support them. In most cases those cosmologies, as enacted in legal systems, construct a reality that denies women equality and burdens women's differences; but all religious systems also contain countervailing and subversive cosmologies that provide a basis for challenging the dominant legal order.

Before the modern secularization of law, religious cosmologies were a source of explicit references for legal understandings of the human person, male and female. In legal systems arising in communities formed by Judaism, Christianity, and Islam, legal understandings of the nature and status of women are profoundly and variously shaped by Biblical and Qur'anic accounts of God as male and of the events of creation and the nature of the family as modeled on patriarchal society. Women are frequently portrayed as incomplete and subordinate. In the traditional legal systems of South Asia, law (dharma) incorporates a Vedic identification of women with samsara (the repeated cycles of birth, misery, and death caused by karma), an identification that supports a view of women's marginal place in the cosmic and natural order. Confucian law is based in a religio-philosophical system that divides the universe into a dark, female force, yin, and a light, male principle, yang. While there are also resources supporting gender equality in all these religious traditions, secular legal systems that have succeeded these traditional legal systems continue, in many ways, to be founded in cosmological constructions that limit women and women's lives.

RELIGIOUS LAW

Prior to the distinctively modern differentiation of social forms, religion and law, though distinct, were frequently conjoined in the same institutions and texts. All premodern law might be loosely termed religious law. Theology and law were both found in such texts as the Laws of Manu (Hindu) and the Torah (Judaic), and the law found therein might be enforced by religious or political authorities. Within this religious law contract law, laws of evidence, family law—marriage, divorce, and inheritance—and laws governing ecclesiastical office and ritual purity all constructed women as legally less than whole persons.

Women, like men, were also, however, subject to public law—including constitutional and international law—which was distinct from private and family law and responded to the needs of religious pluralism and the demands of international commerce. Both public and private law with respect to laypersons were also distinct from canon law and the rule of monastic orders. The law with respect to laywomen in Buddhist legal systems, for example, had sources and, in the premodern period, institutions different than those of the *sangha* (ascetic order), although both might be termed religious law. Both women and men were subject to plural and overlapping legal jurisdictions, which varied depending on their social location.

SECULAR LAW

In modern secular states the influence of religious cosmologies on secular law persists, as does the continued enforcement of religious law in some jurisdictions. Disestablishment, liberalism, and the Enlightenment have all contributed to the creation of new forms of law, which, though historically indebted to forms of law explicitly created in the context of religious cosmologies and found in religious texts, have come to be justified in secular positivist terms. Family law concepts such as those governing marriage and divorce, which are central to Western legal systems, can be traced to Christian theological reflection on sexuality and sexual difference, for example, but are now explained in terms of utilitarian and scientistic understandings of law. On the other hand, secular notions of gender equality in liberal

Western law have been criticized by some feminist legal scholars (Robin West, for example) as being founded in a secular notion of the autonomous individual that recognizes women as equal in legal status but slights the real difference between men's and women's experience—a difference that may be acknowledged in traditional religious cosmologies. In this view, liberal law has solved the problem of traditional patriarchal legal orders by making women into men.

In secular societies members of women's religious orders and women in positions of religious leadership may also continue to participate formally in internal ecclesiastical legal orders, as, for example, the synodal governing structure of the Presbyterian Church. Lay women may be subject to the operation of religious law both through consensual participation in and submission to the norms of religious communities. Religious law may also indirectly govern women through secular laws dependent on its anthropology, such as in the case of protectionist labor laws.

Finally, women may be caught in the unwieldy constitutional struggles of secular democracies to disestablish religion while guaranteeing the free exercise of religion. Women living in secular states may find that secular law provides a refuge from oppressive religious law, such as that limiting divorce; but they may also find that compliance with religious law is confined by secular law, such as in the case of U.S. laws prohibiting Mormon polygyny or French and Turkish laws prohibiting the wearing of head scarves by Muslim women. The human rights movement and the creation of international law promote feminist consciousness about the role of religion and law in women's lives, leading, not infrequently, to a conflict between local cultural and religious ways of imagining women's lives and universalist articulations of the rights of women. Women may find a conflict between a desire to affirm a religious identity through, for example, the support of autonomous customary family law systems, as is the case in the Muslim community in South Africa, and a desire to critique that religious identity through the use of either subversive religious or universalist discourse about women's rights. In the postmodern context increased legal and religious pluralism has rendered the interrelationship of different forms of law immensely complicated.

BIBLIOGRAPHY

Broadly understood, religion and law threaten to swallow each other up as intellectual categories. Furthermore, there is not a great deal of sophisticated theoretical writing explicitly treating women and religion and law, particularly in the academic legal community. The work of anthropologists and historians tends to have a more subtle understanding of the importance of the interrelationship of religion and law. Finally, virtually all writing on women and religion touches on law, particularly in the more legalistic traditions such as Judaism and Islam. The works listed here address all three factors.

Abu-Odeh, Lama. "Post-Colonial Feminism and the Veil: Considering the Differences." *New England Law Review* 26 (1992): 1527–1537.

Bartholomeusz, Tessa. *Women Under the Bo Tree: Buddhist Nuns in Sri Lanka.* 1994.

Biale, Rachel. *Women and Jewish Law: The Essential Texts, Their History, and Their Relevance for Today.* 1984.

Brundage, James A. *Law, Sex and Christian Society in Medieval Europe.* 1990.

Callaway, Barbara, and Creevey Lucy. *The Heritage of Islam: Women, Religion and Politics in West Africa.* 1994.

Cohen, David William. *Burying SM: The Politics of Knowledge and the Sociology of Power in Africa.* 1992.

Dayton, Cornelia. *Women Before the Bar: Gender, Law and Society in Connecticut, 1639–1789.* 1995.

Delaney, Carol. *Abraham on Trial: The Social Legacy of Biblical Myth.* 1998.

Esposito, John. *Women in Muslim Family Law.* 1982.

Hay, Margaret Jean, and Marcia Wright, eds. *African Women and the Law: Historical Perspectives.* 1982.

Kawanami, Hiroko. "The Religious Standing of Burmese Buddhist Nuns." *Journal of the International Association of Buddhist Studies* 13 (1990): 16–39.

Kuehn, Thomas. *Law, Family and Women: Toward a Legal Anthropology of Renaissance Italy.* 1991.

Mir-Hosseini, Ziba. *Marriage on Trial: A Study of Islamic Family Law; Iran and Morocco Compared.* 1993.

Moors, Annelies. *Women, Property and Islam.* 1995.

Norton, Mary Beth. *Founding Mothers and Fathers: Gendered Power and the Forming of American Society.* 1996.

Nussbaum, Martha. "Religion and Women's Human Rights." In *Religion and Contemporary Liberalism.* Edited by Paul J. Weithman. 1997.

Obiora, Leslye. "The Issue of Female Circumcision: Bridges and Barricades: Rethinking Polemics and Intransigence in the Campaign against Female Circumcision." *Case Western Reserve Law Review* 47 (1997): 275–378.

Paul, Diana. *Women in Buddhism: Images of the Feminine in the Mahayana Tradition.* 1985.

Raming, Ida. *The Exclusion of Women from the Priest-hood: Divine Law or Sex Discrimination? An Histori-cal Investigation of the Juridical and Doctrinal Foun-dations of Canon Law, Canon 968, 1.* 1976.

Wegner, Judith Romney. *Chattel or Person: The Status of Women in the Mishnah.* 1988.

West, Robin L. "Jurisprudence and Gender." In *Femi-nist Jurisprudence.* Edited by Patricia Smith. 1993.

WINNIFRED FALLERS SULLIVAN

Leadership

When a new religious movement is initiated by a founder, women are typically prominent as converts, proselytizers, financial benefactors, and leaders, since a new religious movement will not turn away dedicated workers and leaders due to their sex. Thus women's sta-tus is usually higher in the early stages of a religious movement. This was the case with the great religious traditions initiated by Gautama Buddha, Jesus, and Muhammad. A new religion in a patriarchal culture in-creasingly excludes women from leadership as it be-comes institutionalized.

A similar process of exclusion from religious leader-ship occurs in indigenous (nonfounded) religions. Women experience greater equality when societies are relatively simple. Women have status in hunting and gathering bands, and in matrilineal and matrilocal hor-ticultural (farming with a hoe) groups, because they make direct contributions to subsistence. The change to plow agriculture marks a shift to male ownership of land, patrilineal inheritance that excludes daughters, and patrilocal families in which new brides become members of their husbands' families. Women living in this "classic" patriarchy have few opportunities to be independent. This type of family unit has been the building block of complex class-stratified cultures with men dominating the political order and religion. The process takes many centuries, but as the culture be-comes more complex and patriarchal, women are ex-cluded from religious leadership. Classic patriarchies practice sex segregation; males and females work in separate spheres—men outside the home and women inside the home. In patriarchal sex-segregated cul-tures, women may form separate religious groups in which they exercise religious leadership, but women are excluded from leadership in the dominant religious institutions.

As a culture becomes patriarchal, women's role be-comes restricted to that of wife and mother. Buddhism and Christianity are notable in offering the alternative role of celibate religious to women. Many women have led fulfilling lives as Buddhist and Christian nuns but the patriarchal cultures have resulted in nuns being subordinated to and supervised by their male counter-parts.

As the patriarchal understanding of gender as dictat-ing separate roles for males and females is breaking down due to women making gains in a variety of fields, women are moving into roles of religious leadership. Correspondingly, women are reevaluating and reimag-ining patriarchal scriptures and theologies to create re-ligious worldviews that empower women.

CHARISMATIC LEADERSHIP, POSSESSION, AND SHAMANISM

Charisma, defined as direct contact with the divine, cuts through patriarchal restrictions on a woman and enables her to establish for herself a sphere of greater freedom. Shamanism, usually involving possession, is the earliest type of charisma available to women.

Women who are diagnosed by a shaman as possessed are typically "called" by the spirits by experiencing a great deal of misfortune, or they become severely ill, and after all medical treatments fail are diagnosed as being possessed. This diagnosis rallies family support to placate the possessing deity or ancestor so that the woman can become well. The only way for the woman to be healed is to become a shaman. In her new role as shaman, the woman may gain a means of economic in-dependence by treating the ailments of others. She may become regarded as a prophet and found a new reli-gion. Within women's possession groups, such as the *zar* cult among Muslim women in Sudan, individual women take on leadership roles and adopt new identi-ties. Separate women's rituals involving *zar* possession permit these women to articulate and negotiate prob-lems of which they are otherwise not permitted to speak.

SAINTS

Charisma can impel exceptional women to revered sta-tus as saints, even in patriarchal cultures. Interestingly, both exceptional medieval Christian and Hindu women were considered saints because they claimed to be married to God and therefore could not be married to mere human men. These women were not viewed as good role models for the majority of women to follow, but by their exceptional sanctity and devotion to God, they became revered spiritual guides.

WOMEN'S RITUALS

Women living in sex-segregated patriarchal societies often develop their own religious rituals. In Hinduism,

Frances Willard (1839–1898), American educator and reformer, leader of the National Woman's Christian Temperance Union (Library of Congress)

women perform ritual worship to secure the well-being of the members of their family, especially the men on whom they are dependent, their husbands, brothers, and sons. These rituals are often performed by groups of women who sing devotional songs, dance, and act out mythical episodes. Muslim women may spend hours or even days in the sanctuaries surrounding saints' tombs. They go there to cry, tell their troubles to the saint, pray for assistance, and be comforted by other women. Like the *zar* possession rituals, women's rituals in patriarchal societies permit women to come together, socialize, express themselves, and support each other, and they provide means by which women can actively attempt to control their circumstances.

WOMEN FOUNDERS OF RELIGIONS

Charisma empowers women to inspire or found religious organizations. Some examples are Mother Ann Lee (Shakerism), Miki Nakayama (Tenrikyo), Ellen G. White (Seventh-Day Adventist Church), Nao Deguchi (Omoto), Helena P. Blavatsky (Theosophical Society), Mary Baker Eddy (Church of Christ, Scientist), Alma White (Pillar of Fire; first American woman bishop, consecrated in 1918), Sayo Kitamura (Tensho-kotai-jingu-kyo), Mother Leafy Anderson (Spiritual churches in New Orleans), Aimee Semple McPherson (International Church of the Foursquare Gospel), and Elizabeth Clare Prophet (Church Universal and Triumphant). These women are considered by their followers to be prophets, and sometimes, messiahs. Charismatic women founders are not necessarily feminists. They are likely to teach patriarchal gender roles, and they are likely to prepare men, rather than women, to succeed them in leadership after their deaths. During their lifetimes, charismatic women may rely on men to be the administrators of their religious organizations.

WOMEN'S ORDAINED MINISTRIES AND ALTERNATIVE MINISTRIES

Ordained ministry represents a routinized form of religious leadership, which in the modern era is based more on professional training than on charisma. In Christianity, however, charisma continues to be linked to the ordained ministry. The Christian concept of being "called" to the ministry empowered women to preach even prior to women's access to seminary education. This was especially true in the nineteenth-century Holiness movement in which women such as Phoebe Palmer, Amanda Berry Smith, and others were evangelists.

Biblical passages have been cited to exclude Christian women from ordained ministry as well as to urge the ordination of women. What Rosemary Radford Ruether terms the "theology of subordination" is found in Genesis 2–3, 1 Corinthians 11:2–12, 1 Corinthians 14:34–35, and 1 Timothy 2:12–15. Ruether points out that a "theology of equivalence" is found in Genesis 1:27, Galatians 3:28, and Acts 2:17–18.

In the United States, the Protestant denominations with congregational polities were the first to ordain women as ministers. But the ordained ministry has never been the sole form of religious leadership exercised by women. Pastors' wives have exercised ministries. The Protestant women's missionary societies were important arenas for women's leadership in the nineteenth and early twentieth centuries as was the deaconess movement, the women's suffrage movement, and the Woman's Christian Temperance Union. Sociologist Paula Nesbitt cautions, however, that alternative ordination or leadership tracks often work to deflect women from the prestigious ordination tracks.

FEMINIST SPIRITUALITY

In the late twentieth century, there is a broad feminist spirituality movement in which women are creating feminist liturgies and theologies, where the divine is seen as female and women's bodies and sexuality are affirmed. Feminist wicca (benevolent witchcraft) returns to indigenous animistic traditions. The broad Women-Church movement includes Protestant and Catholic women. Women rabbis are creating feminist rituals within Judaism.

Women exercise religious leadership in diverse ways. Charisma remains an important legitimation of women's religious authority. Steadily women are moving into routinized forms of leadership such as the ordained ministry and rabbinate. As they do so, they are introducing changes in leadership styles, liturgies, and theologies. Separate women's religious groups remain important sources of women's spiritual nurturance as they work to change the patriarchal mainstream religions. Many women choose to leave the patriarchal religions to create alternative women-affirming traditions, where women either predominate in leadership roles or leadership is shared equally with men. Whether women are inside or outside the patriarchal religious traditions, there is a remarkable similarity among the various women's religions. Feminist theologies emphasize the immanence of the sacred and the sacrality of the feminine, honor important spiritual foremothers, and affirm that women can be more than solely wives and mothers.

BIBLIOGRAPHY

Boddy, Janice. *Wombs and Alien Spirits: Women, Men, and the Zar Cult in Northern Sudan.* 1989.

Bynum, Caroline Walker. "Women Mystics in the Thirteenth Century: The Case of the Nuns of Helfta." In *Jesus as Mother: Studies in the Spirituality of the High Middle Ages.* 1982.

Ehrenberg, Margaret. *Women in Prehistory.* 1989.

Falk, Nancy Auer, and Rita M. Gross, eds. *Unspoken Worlds: Women's Religious Lives.* 1989.

Friedl, Ernestine. *Women and Men: An Anthropologist's View.* 1975.

Greenberg, Blu. "Feminism Within Orthodoxy: A Revolution of Small Signs." *Lilith* 17 (Summer 1992): 11–17.

Hackett, Rosalind I. J. "Sacred Paradoxes: Women and Religious Plurality in Nigeria." In *Women, Religion, and Social Change.* Edited by Yvonne Yazbeck Haddad and Ellison Banks Findly. 1985.

Haddad, Yvonne Yazbeck, and Ellison Banks Findly, eds. *Women, Religion and Social Change.* 1985.

MacHaffie, Barbara J. *HerStory: Women in Christian Tradition.* 1986.

Manushi. Tenth Anniversary Issue, nos. 50, 51, 52 (January–June 1989).

Ruether, Rosemary Radford. "Christianity." In *Women in World Religions.* Edited by Arvind Sharma. 1987.

Ruether, Rosemary, and Eleanor McLaughlin, eds. *Women of Spirit: Female Leadership in the Jewish and Christian Traditions.* 1979.

Tsomo, Karma Lekshe. "Tibetan Nuns and Nunneries." In *Feminine Ground: Essays on Women and Tibet.* Edited by Janice D. Willis. 1989.

Tsomo, Karma Lckshe, ed. *Sakyadhita: Daughters of the Buddha.* 1988.

Wessinger, Catherine, ed. *Religious Institutions and Women's Leadership: New Roles Inside the Mainstream.* 1996.

———. *Women's Leadership in Marginal Religions: Explorations Outside the Mainstream.* 1993.

Winter, Miriam Therese, Barbara Hargrove, and Adair T. Lummis. *Defecting in Place: Women Claiming Responsibility for Their Own Religious Lives.* 1994.

See also Authority; Charisma; Ordination; Wicca.

CATHERINE WESSINGER

Lee, Ann

Ann Lee (c. 1736–1784) was the primary founder of Shakerism (the United Society of Believers in Christ's Second Appearing) in the United States, the movement that produced the longest-lived communal religious organization in U.S. history. The daughter of a blacksmith, Ann Lee (originally Lees) grew up without schooling, working in a textile mill in Manchester, England. She married Abraham Standerin, also a blacksmith, in January 1762, and, according to Shaker tradition, the couple had four children, all of whom died in infancy.

In 1758 Ann Lee had become a member of a small dissenting religious society headed by tailors Jane and James Wardley. Jane Wardley acted as mother of the sect, hearing religious confessions of sin and leading meetings at which shaking and shouting out against sin were seen as ecstatic bodily expressions of spiritual fervor. Schooled in the Wardley society's traditions of Protestant mysticism and pietism, as well as female religious leadership, Ann Lee experienced intense visionary and ecstatic "gifts," including a striking revelation in 1770 that celibacy was a precondition for a life modeled on Christ's. Lee now became the acknowledged leader of the Shaking Quakers, as the Wardley society came to be called. The Shakers' verbal attacks on the churches and clergy for failing to teach what was necessary for salvation in the approaching day of judgment led to mob attacks, arrests, and jail sentences. This "persecution," along with a schism within the Wardley society's ranks, likely prompted Ann Lee and a small number of followers to migrate to the American colonies in 1774.

Within a few years the English Shakers had established their church on a tract of land in Niskeyuna (later Watervliet) near Albany, New York. As in England, the Shakers' unconventional religious behavior and uncompromising antichurch public testimony brought them to the attention of civil authorities. Their militant pacifism and English origins led to the jailing of Lee and members of her inner circle as possible British sympathizers in July 1780. The following year, Ann Lee, along with her brother, William, and a third British Shaker leader, James Whittaker, began a two-year missionary tour through Massachusetts and Connecticut, which laid the basis for the founding of the first New England Shaker communities in the years immediately following Lee's death. Within a year after returning to Niskeyuna, both Ann and William Lee died.

Ann Lee's charismatic authority is amply documented in an oral-historical volume based on the memories of her American followers and designed to preserve her sayings and doings as a kind of sacred scripture. She was remembered as an awe-inspiring, even frightening figure of power—one who, as seer, could reveal the spiritual condition of the living and the dead, and who, as spiritual mother, displayed her devotion to her children through often harsh punishments or threats designed to help them put away soul-killing sin.

The Shaker religion and culture that flourished and evolved after Lee's death was not entirely her own creation, but in many of its practices and values it embodied her spirit. Its religious-based celibacy honored her visionary understanding of sexuality as sin. The requirement that Shaker brethren and sisters confess their sins to their religious elders recalled the practice of Jane Wardley. The governance structure of the society of communities, in which equal numbers of male and female leaders oversaw both spiritual and industrial and domestic work, is certainly a legacy of Ann Lee's foundational leadership.

It seems unlikely from the surviving evidence that she herself claimed to be the "second appearing of Christ in the female," an event deemed necessary to complete the redemptive process begun when Christ appeared in male form. This was a claim made for her in 1808 by a few of her influential followers. By the midnineteenth century, a four-part, gender-balanced godhead, including Holy Mother Wisdom and Ann Lee as aspects of divinity, had been theorized by male Shaker theologians.

Ann Lee herself spent only ten years on U.S. soil, conducting a public ministry during just the last four and never writing a line. Yet her spiritual experience and ability to communicate it were the driving force behind a complex religious dissent movement. After her death, this movement crystallized into a religious communal organization that has existed for over two hundred years. In the last decade of the twentieth century, a small number of believers remains at Sabbathday Lake, Poland Spring, Maine.

BIBLIOGRAPHY

Andrews, Edward Deming. *The People Called Shakers.* 1963.

Garrett, Clarke. *Spirit Possession and Popular Religion from the Camisards to the Shakers.* 1987.

Humez, Jean M. *Mother's First-Born Daughters: Early Shaker Writings on Women and Religion.* 1993.

———. "Ye Are My Epistles: The Construction of Ann Lee Imagery in Early Shaker Sacred Literature." *Journal of Feminist Studies in Religion* 8, no. 1 (Spring 1992): 83–103.

Marini, Stephen A. *Radical Sects of Revolutionary New England.* 1982.

Mercadante, Linda. *Gender, Doctrine, and God: The Shakers and Contemporary Theology.* 1990.

Morse, Flo. *The Shakers and The World's People.* 1980.

Procter-Smith, Marjorie. *Women in Shaker Community and Worship: A Feminist Analysis of the Uses of Religious Symbolism.* 1985.

"The Shakers—Hands to Work, Hearts to God." Directed by Ken Burns and Amy Stechler Burns. Florentine Films. 1984.

Stein, Stephen J. *The Shaker Experience in America.* 1992.

Testimonies of the Life, Revelations, and Doctrine of Our Ever Blessed Mother Ann Lee. 1816.

JEAN M. HUMEZ

Lenshina, Alice

Alice Lenshina Mulenga (c. 1920–1978), Zambian religious leader and prophetess, founded the Lumpa Church in 1953. Alice belonged to the dominant ethnic group, the Bemba, of the Northern Province of Zambia.

The granddaughter of a minor Bemba chief and daughter of a local Native Administration messenger, she received little formal education. As a young woman she underwent religious training to become a member of the local Presbyterian mission church at Lubwa in Chinsali District. Though she was illiterate and failed to complete her training, she became familiar with biblical texts, and some of her followers claimed that she could in fact read the Bible.

Alice was the mother of five children; her husband had worked at Lubwa as a carpenter. Women have played important roles within Christian religious movements in central, southern and eastern Africa. Historically, they have been the mainstay of congregations, occupying prominent positions within African churches. Their contribution to the spread of Christianity has not been restricted to nor contained within Christian missions and African independent churches. They have also founded new religious movements of which the Lumpa Church is an example. Alice's spiritual experiences are typical of male and female leaders of southern and central African prophetic movements. After experiencing serious bouts of illness, probably malaria, she met with the Rev. Fergus Macpherson of Lubwa mission and claimed to have died four times, met with Jesus, and risen from the dead. She said that Jesus had taught her hymns, shown her special religious texts (the Book of Life), and given her spiritual powers. As her reputation spread, she left the Presbyterian church altogether and founded her own. She became known as Alice Lenshina, *lenshina* being the Bemba pronunciation of *regina* (queen). The Lumpa Church swept through northern and eastern Zambia and along the rail lines into the urban centers of the copper belt. By 1959 the membership was estimated at between fifty and a hundred thousand, with an untold number of persons from central and southern Africa having visited Alice's church at Kasomo.

In 1964 Zambia was scheduled to gain its independence from British rule. Church members attempted to withdraw from all secular activities, antagonizing both the colonial government and the main African political party. In the months prior to Zambian independence, Lumpa and non-Lumpa engaged in fierce battles, resulting in the death of more than seven hundred Zambians. Government troops quelled the disturbances, detained the Lumpa in prison camps, and banned the church. Alice and her husband were arrested. She was released in 1975 and placed under house arrest in Lusaka, where she died in 1978.

BIBLIOGRAPHY

Bond, George C. "A Prophecy That Failed." In *African Christianity.* Edited by George Bond et al. 1978.

Hinfelaar, Hugo. "Women's Revolt: The Lumpa Church of Lenshina Mulenga in the 1950s." *Journal of Religion in Africa* 21, no. 2 (1991): 99–129.

Ipenburg, At. *All Good Men: The Development of Lubwa Mission, Chinsali, Zambia, 1905–1967.* 1991.

Oger, L. "Le movement lenshina en Rhodesie du Nord." In *Église vivante.* Vol. 14. Paris, 1962.

Roberts, Andrew. "The Lumpa Church of Alice Lenshina." In *Protest and Power in Black Africa.* Edited by R. Rotberg and A. Mazrui. 1970.

Rotberg, R. "The Lenshina Movement of Northern Rhodesia." *The Rhodes-Livingston Journal* 29 (1961).

Van Binsbergen, W. *Religious Change in Zambia.* 1981.

See also **Christianity: In Africa.**

GEORGE BOND

Lesbianism

A Classical View

The modern meaning of *lesbianism* did not gain currency until late in the nineteenth century when introduced by the early sexologists to represent love between women as a pathology. (In the ancient world *lesbian* referred to fellatio, not to female homosexuality.) Originally a label applied by others, it has become a name many contemporary women proudly claim. Because it invokes a historical Greek woman, Sappho of Lesbos, who serves as a near-mythical prototype of a woman-loving woman, the term, like a rich, open-ended metaphor, allows room for understandings that are primarily sexual, erotic, cultural, or political. Some understand *lesbianism* to signify a commitment to women—a rejection of a heterosexist, male-dominated society and a celebration of the intimacy, emotional closeness, and full mutuality possible among women—at least as much as the particular pleasures associated with lesbian sexuality. For others, to minimize the importance of the sexual dimension of lesbianism is to deny its most vital aspect. The disagreement has led to the notion of a continuum of passionate connections among women resisting patriarchy and compulsory heterosexuality. In this sense lesbian relationships may be viewed as an ordinary part of most women's experience and central to the lives of some. Thus it may be more appropriate to speak of *lesbianisms* in the plural.

Serious concerns have also been raised about the cross-cultural and transhistorical application of the term. Is imposing the notion that there have always been lesbians imperialist, essentialist, disrespectful of cultural diversity? Are there lesbians in societies that have no equivalent concept, or where there are no sexually specific identities? The wish to learn as much as possible about the many forms that women's love of women has assumed while paying careful attention to cultural and historical specificities leads to an understanding of the term *lesbian* as a linguistic convenience, as a metaphor, for referring to a continuum of intimate connections between women.

Part of the interest in lesbian history arises out of a longing for images and language that may help illuminate the experience of contemporary lesbians. Learning about women in other times and places for whom the love of women was a central force in their lives challenges and enriches present self-understanding. However, the general difficulty of access to female experience because of the patriarchal suppression of women's voices is compounded in the case of lesbians, who are so often invisible, their very existence denied. Erotic or sexual relations among women seem always to have received less attention than such relations among men, perhaps because a sexuality without penile penetration seems almost unimaginable to the male writers who have been our primary historical sources.

Because women's love of women, particularly if given sexual expression, is ignored or castigated in most religious traditions, lesbians have rarely received religious validation for their most important emotional experience. Classical Greece, however, offers glimpses of a society where same-sex love was not only accepted but given religious validation and important educational and social functions. Though there is much less historical evidence about erotic relationships among Greek women than among Greek men, there are many Greek myths testifying to the joys and difficulties associated with such experience. However, in looking at how Greek mythology might deepen understanding of women's love of women, one quickly discovers that there are almost no written accounts by women of their own experience of such love or of its mythical representation.

The exception, of course, is the poetry of Sappho, the first extant testimony coming directly from a woman of a woman's experience of love and of what women mean to one another. The poems present Sappho as associated with a circle of women companions to some of whom she was passionately attached and some of whom she regarded as rivals. Many scholars believe that ritualized initiatory homosexuality, designed to help prepare a young girl for marriage, may have played an important role in Sappho's circle.

In the *Symposium* Plato invents a myth (put in the mouth of Aristophanes) describing how the primordial "round people" (some of whom were male, some fe-

The poet Sappho, who wrote in the early sixth century B.C.E., is depicted in a statue in Mytilene on the island of Lesbos, Greece (Dave Bartruff/Corbis).

male, some hermaphrodite) were cut in two as punishment for daring to challenge the authority of the gods, leaving "each half with a desperate yearning for the other." The tale gives equal value to heterosexual, homosexual, and lesbian longing.

The Amazons, whether historical or purely mythic women, were said to live out their sexuality primarily with one another; once a year, however, solely for the sake of reproduction, they had intercourse with the men of neighboring tribes (Keuls, 1985).

Maenads, some of whom also appear in myth, actually participated in Dionysian rituals and practices; these rites may have had a sexual dimension representing an initiation of women by women into women's own sexuality, into arousal for its own sake (Burkert, 1985). The Thesmophoria, the most important ritual celebrated in honor of the goddess Demeter, provided an occasion for married women to gather together to indulge their own capacity for sexual desire and pleasure.

When one looks at the traditions about the Greek goddesses primarily for stories of overtly sexual connections with women, one finds little; but neither are they shown as fitting easily into the normative pattern of heterosexual relationships. However, these traditions communicate a great deal about the multidimensional and diverse erotic relationships between women. The emotional bond that connects Demeter and her daughter Persephone evokes the intense intimacy characteristic of lesbian erotic attachments. Fiercely independent, passionately virginal Artemis shuns the world of men and spends her time alone in the wild or in the company of her nymphs (with some of whom, the myths hint, she may be sexually involved). Scholars such as Eva Cantarella believe that at Artemis's temple in Brauron pubertal girls were initiated into the mysteries of their own sexuality by her priestesses. Aphrodite was associated with all lovemaking dedicated to mutual enjoyment (rather than domination or procreation), whether marital or adulterous, heterosexual, homosexual, or lesbian. She models women's affirmation of their own sexuality as powerful, beautiful, and sacred.

BIBLIOGRAPHY

Boswell, John. "Concepts, Experience, and Sexuality." In *Forms of Desire: Sexual Orientation and the Social Constructionist Controversy.* Edited by Edward Stein. 1992.

Burkert, Walter. *Greek Religion.* 1985.

Cantarella, Eva. *Bisexuality in the Ancient World.* 1992.

Card, Claudia. *Lesbian Choices.* 1995.

Cavin, Susan. *Lesbian Origins.* 1985.

Dover, K. J. *Greek Homosexuality.* 1978.

Downing, Christine. *Myths and Mysteries of Same-Sex Love.* 1989.

Faderman, Lilian. *Surpassing the Love of Men: Romantic Friendship and Love between Women from the Renaissance to the Present.* 1983.

Foucault, Michel. *The History of Sexuality.* Vol. 1, *An Introduction.* 1978; Vol. 2, *The Use of Pleasure.* 1986.

Fuss, Diana. *Essentially Speaking: Feminism, Nature, and Difference.* 1989.

Grahn, Judy. *Another Mother Tongue: Gay Words, Gay Worlds.* 1984.

Keuls, Eva C. *The Reign of the Phallus.* 1985.

Raymond, Janice. *A Passion for Friends: Toward a Philosophy of Female Friendship.* 1986.

Rich, Adrienne. "Compulsory Heterosexuality and Lesbian Existence." In *On Lies, Secrets and Silence.* 1979.

See also **Sappho.**

CHRISTINE DOWNING

In the West

Are lesbians by definition Western? Is the West defined by the existence of lesbians? Given the complexity of the relevant conceptual terrain, what can be said about the relation between "lesbian," "religion," and the "West"? For some, phrases like lesbian religion or religious lesbian are inherently contradictory; many religious figures view lesbianism as anathema, and many lesbians see religion and homosexuality as mutually exclusive. Frequently, these views rest on a presumed historical antagonism between religion (often equated with Christianity) and homosexuality. Yet there has emerged, since the 1970s, a literature of personal narrative and polemic, arguing that religious lesbians do exist, as well as a scholarly literature about Western religion and lesbianism; this literature has developed in complex tension with feminist inquiry as well as gay or queer scholarship.

Judaism and Christianity turn to Biblical sources to articulate current understanding of the ethical and ritual significance of lesbians and gay men. Various interpretive strategies have been used to bring Biblical texts into connection with contemporary life. More conservative approaches have adopted "literal" readings. On the more progressive or liberal theological end, efforts have focused on contextualizing texts and clarifying their referents, emphasizing linguistic concerns as well as authorial intent, and comparing various Biblical cultures to cultures currently seeking to use the Bible to inform ethical and moral judgment.

No text in the Hebrew Bible specifically prohibits lesbianism. The sole source in the Christian Bible that does so is Romans 1: 26–27. Some additional texts have also been understood as relevant to lesbians either because they have been read as about male homosexuality and extended to lesbians (e.g., Lev. 18:22 or the Sodom and Gomorrah story) or because they portray female-female relationships (e.g., Ruth). In the case of Romans 1: 26–27, Bernadette Brooten has sought to understand its inclusion by locating the verses in relation to such contemporaneous material as cemetery inscriptions pairing two women, astrological texts, and Jewish and Roman references to lesbianism. In doing so, Brooten has shown that lesbianism was situated differently from male homosexuality in early Christianity and provided an understanding of the gender dynamics of Biblical material addressing homosexuality.

The Qu'ran likewise serves as a key resource for reflection on sexuality. Homosexuality is specifically prohibited; it is discussed, as well, in stories regarding Lot. The Hadith also harshly condemns homosexuality. While heterosexuality is positively affirmed, homosexuality is depicted as an aberration, with repentance urged and punishment, while harsh, requiring multiple eye witnesses.

Intervening between the cultures of the three scriptures and today are years of interpretation and history. In Judaism, subsequent interpretations beginning with the Talmud reiterate the Biblical rejection of male homosexuality while reducing the punishment. Despite relatively little attention to lesbianism, Ellen Umansky (and others) note an early rabbinic reference in the Sifra commentary on Leviticus 18:3 in which lesbian activity is characterized as a lesser offense than male homosexuality, a view confirmed by various later authorities such as Maimonides. Reasons offered for the lesser attention to lesbian activity in historical sources include, according to Rachel Biale, the possibility that women did not pursue such activities, that rulings on this topic did not survive, and that male authorities were so unaware of female lives as to miss lesbianism.

Efforts to locate lesbianism with reference to Christianity recognize its embeddedness in Christian antagonism to (nonprocreative) sex. Conventional overviews provide a history of homosexuality moving from sin to crime to illness to minority group identity. Such a narrative obscures the place of lesbians; indeed, it equates secularization with liberation (thereby reinforcing views of religion and homosexuality as antagonistic) and simplifies the complex historical and cultural variation of Christianity. Having said this, Augustine's elevation of celibacy and equation of acceptable sex with procreation, Aquinas's subsequent identification of homosexuality as particularly sinful within the context of natural law, the elaborate specification of sin within medieval penitentials, the incorporation of negative views within canon law, and the impact of Protestant reformers (e.g., Luther) who reiterated historic antagonism to homosexuality eventually influenced the construction of legislation criminalizing homosexuality (and sometimes lesbianism).

Judith C. Brown's book *Immodest Acts* exemplifies problems involved in generalizing about historical relations between lesbianism and Christianity. Brown identifies a "lesbian nun" in Renaissance Italy and asserts that lesbianism has existed over time and within the dominant religious framework of Christianity. In drawing on trial testimony to do so, Brown makes evident Christianity's role in constraining sexuality as well as resistance to hegemonic organizations of sexuality. Yet the question of whether the individuals involved were or were not lesbian remains controversial.

Like post-Biblical Judaism and Christianity, developments in post-Qu'ranic Islam vary by historical era and region. While schools differ somewhat, early development of Shari'a (religious law) makes homosexuality a punishable offense. Commentaries dispute appropriate punishment and continue to emphasize the need for multiple eye witnesses to attest to the crime. Khalid Duran emphasizes the gap between the punitive orientation of Shari'a and cultural acceptance of discretely practiced homosexuality. Little specifically is known regarding lesbianism.

Current debates regarding the place of lesbians within Western religion take place within these complex historical fields and in the context of social and political movements in Europe and North America. These include the homophile movement of the 1950s (e.g., Daughters of Bilitis), the women's liberation and gay rights movements of the 1960s and 1970s, and queer activism in the 1980s and thereafter.

Within the cumulative traditions of Judaism, institutional change has focused on support for gay and lesbian civil rights and discussion of the appropriateness of gay and lesbian rabbis. While much current discussion continues to see homosexuality as wrong, non-Orthodox Judaism has been increasingly supportive of gay and lesbian Jews. For example, Reform Judaism has adopted resolutions supporting civil rights and supported gay and lesbian rabbis. Reconstructionist organizations followed. Conservative Judaism has affirmed the Jewish tradition's emphasis on heterosexuality and prohibits commitment ceremonies for same-sex couples but has also supported civil rights and admission to rabbinical and cantor's assemblies. The development of specifically gay and lesbian synagogues like Beth Chayim Chadashim (Los Angeles) and Beth Simcha Torah (New York City) as well as the creation of the World Congregation of Gay and Lesbian Jewish Organizations in the early 1980s is also relevant. Alongside these institutional developments has come religious reflection posed against traditionally antigay positions. Among others, Ellen Umansky, Judith Plaskow, and Rachel Alpert have critiqued antilesbian views and argued for the legitimacy of Jewish lesbian partnerships. In *Like Bread on the Seder Table,* for example, Alpert offers a Jewish lesbian interpretation of Torah.

Within Christianity, concerns about civil rights and more specifically religious concerns around ordination and commitment (or marriage) ceremonies have been increasingly important across denominations. After substantial study, a variety of denominations have affirmed civil rights (beginning in the United States with the Unitarian Universalist Association and the Lutheran Church in America in 1970). Ordination remains problematic for most mainstream denominations, though in 1976 the Episcopal bishop of New York City (illegally) ordained an openly lesbian priest, Ellen Barrett, and in 1988 the Assembly of the United Church of Canada voted favorably for ordination. Additional institutional changes include the development of denominational caucuses including, for example, Dignity (Roman Catholic); Integrity (Episcopalian), Affinity (Mormon); and Evangelicals Concerned. In response to negative views of homosexuality within the fundamentalist and evangelical wings of Protestantism, the Metropolitan Community Church was founded in 1968. Beyond such developments, the rise of feminist Christian and post-Christian theologies has been coterminous with the articulation of specifically lesbian theologies. Exemplary figures include Carter Heyward (an Episcopalian priest) and Mary Daly, who began within the context of Roman Catholicism and moved increasingly out of Christianity to articulate a lesbian metaphysics.

The situation in Islam is substantially less developed. Hostile regimes have targeted homosexuals for persecution (e.g., Iran, 1979–1984) and, while Duran reports requests received by Muslim theologians to address relevant concerns, he also notes that a "theological coming-to-terms with this issue has not even made a start." Locating this within the context of ideological equations of homosexual identity politics with Western (colonialist) decadence, Duran notes that unofficial tolerance characterizes some Muslim countries and argues that the principal route to change may rest with Sufi (mystical) traditions. European and American converts as well as diaspora Muslims in the West are, however, pushing for change.

In addition to these developments within the cumulative traditions of Western religions, further possibilities abound. Beyond post-Christian developments like those articulated by Mary Daly, thinkers like Christine Downing have drawn upon psychology, feminism, and Greco-Roman mythology to develop a religious affirmation of lesbians. Likewise, neopagan and New Age religious practices, while controversial, have been attractive to some lesbians in Europe and North America, particularly as they trace their mythic roots to witchcraft and matriarchal goddess religions. Others have moved toward religions such as Buddhism. Both within and beyond traditional religion, theorists have also drawn on the notion of female-female friendship predating twentieth century lesbianism to argue for a spiritual or ontological foundation for lesbianism (e.g., Mary Hunt, Janice Raymond).

In sum, lesbians in the West face a complex world when it comes to religion. Much of traditional Judaism, Christianity, and Islam remains hostile or wrestles with

The medieval theologian Thomas Aquinas strongly condemned homosexuality as a contravention of natural law. Aquinas, depicted in a fresco by Fra Angelico, was very influential in Western Christianity (Corbis-Bettmann).

concerns about homosexuality. Yet lesbian and gay Jews, Christians, and, more rarely, Muslims are articulating their presence and their right to religious freedom. If not entirely secular, those who reject these traditions, whether modified by lesbian critiques or not, create and participate in a wide range of religious alternatives. What such movements and thinkers share is the assumption that religion (variously understood) is important, that homophobia and heterosexism must be resisted, and that lesbians have been and are worthy contributors to Western religion, traditional and alternative.

BIBLIOGRAPHY

Anthologies of experientially based narratives that focus on lesbians (and sometimes gay men) and religion include: Christie Balka and Andy Rose, eds., *Twice Blessed: On Being Lesbian or Gay and Jewish* (1989); Evelyn Torton Beck, ed., *Nice Jewish Girls: A Lesbian Anthology* (1982); Robert Nugent, ed., *A Challenge to Love: Gay and Lesbian Catholics in the Church* (1989); Ron Schow, *Peculiar People: Mormons and Same-Sex Orientation*, edited by Wayne Schow and Mary Beth Raynes (1993); Barbara Zanotti, ed., *A Faith of One's*

Own: Explorations by Catholic Lesbians (1986); and the special issue "Lesbians and Religion," *Sinister Wisdom* 54 (Winter 1994/95). Others, organized around different themes, also attend to relevant issues. See, for example, Juanita Ramos, ed., *Campaneras: Latina Lesbians* (1987); and Carla Trujillo, ed., *Chicana Lesbians: The Girls Our Mothers Warned Us About* (1991). For a set of reflections from gays and lesbians coming to terms with religions in various ways, see David Shallenberger, *Reclaiming the Spirit* (1998).

For basic background on homosexuality and Western religious traditions, see the chapters on Judaism, Roman Catholicism, Protestantism, and Islam in Arlene Swidler, ed., *Homosexuality and World Religions* (1993). For a collection of an array of material at the intersection of lesbian and gay studies and religious studies, see Gary David Comstock and Susan E. Henking, *Que(e)ry ing Religion: A Critical Anthology* (1997). For background documents, see J. Gordon Melton, ed., *The Churches Speak on Homosexuality: Official Statements from Religious Bodies and Ecumenical Organizations* (1991). On Catholicism see Jeannine Gramick and Pat Furey, eds., *The Vatican and Homosexuality: Reactions to the "Letter to the Bishops of the Catholic Church on the Pastoral Care of Homosexual Persons"* (1988); Jeannine Gramick, "Social Discrimination of Lesbians and the Church," *Concilium* 194 (1987): 72–78; and Mary E. Hunt, "On Religious Lesbians: Contradictions and Challenges," in *Homosexuality, Which Homosexuality?* International Conference on Gay and Lesbian Studies (1989). On Judaism, see especially Rebecca T. Alpert, *Like Bread on the Seder Table* (1997); and Ellen Umansky, "Jewish Attitudes Towards Homosexuality: A Review of Contemporary Sources," in *Que(e)rying Religion: A Critical Anthology*, edited by Gary David Comstock and Susan E. Henking (1997). On Islam, see also Everett K. Rowson, "The Effeminates of Early Medina," and Shahid Dossani, "Being Muslim and Gay," in *Que(e)rying Religion: A Critical Anthology*, edited by Gary David Comstock and Susan E. Henking (1997).

Key historical sources on religion and homosexuality create a backdrop against which lesbians—as a group that both shares the fate of gay men and differs significantly from them—must be understood. In this regard, important resources are Derrick Sherwin Bailey, *Homosexuality and the Western Christian Tradition* (1955); John Boswell, *Christianity, Social Tolerance, and Homosexuality: Gay People in Western Europe from the Beginning of the Christian Era to the Fourteenth Century* (1980); and David Greenberg and Marcia H. Bystryn, "Christian Intolerance of Homosexuality," *American Journal of Sociology* 88 (1982): 515–548.

Bernadette Brooten's work is crucial in complicating these perspectives and specifically locating lesbians in relation to Christianity. See especially her article, "Paul's Views on the Nature of Woman and Female Homoeroticism," in *Immaculate and Powerful: The Female in Sacred Image and Social Reality*, edited by Clarissa Atkinson, Constance H. Buchanan, and Margaret R. Miles (1985); and her book, *Love between Women: Early Christian Responses to Female Homoeroticism* (1996).

For the historical example cited, see Judith C. Brown, *Immodest Acts: The Life of a Lesbian Nun in Renaissance Italy* (1986), and such responses to it as E. Ann Matter, "Discourses of Desire: Sexuality and Christian Women's Visionary Narratives," in *Que(r)rying Religion: A Critical Anthology*, edited by Gary David Comstock and Susan E. Henking (1997); and Rudolph Bell, "Renaissance Sexuality and the Florentine Archives: An Exchange," *Renaissance Quarterly* 40 (1987): 485–511.

On lesbian theology, see, for example, Carter Heyward and Mary E. Hunt, Bernadette Brooten, Clare B. Fischer, Delores Williams, and Evelyn Torton Beck, "Roundtable Discussion: Lesbianism and Feminist Theology," *Journal of Feminist Studies in Religion* 2 (Fall 1986): 95–106. Of particular importance are such works as Mary Daly, *Beyond God the Father* (1973) and *Gyn/Ecology: The Metaethics of Radical Feminism* (1978); Christine Downing, *Myths and Mysteries of Same-Sex Love* (1989); and Carter Heyward, *Touching Our Strength: The Erotic as Power and the Love of God* (1989).

On contemporary issues of controversy, see, for example, Robert Williams, "Toward a Theology for Lesbian and Gay Marriage," *Anglican Theological Review* 72 (Spring 1990): 134–157 (with responses, 158–174); and Ann Brenoff, "Jewish Paper in San Diego Tackles a Difficult Subject," in *Que(e)rying Religion: A Critical Anthology*, edited by Gary David Comstock and Susan E. Henking (1997). Though not focused on lesbians per se, Keith Hartman's journalistic book, *Congregations in Conflict: The Battle Over Homosexuality* (1996), provides insight into a variety of Christian denominations. For an important resource focusing on what gays and lesbians contribute to churches, see Gary David Comstock, *Unrepenting, Self-Affirming, Practicing: Lesbian/ Bisexual/Gay People within Organized Religion* (1996).

On lesbian spirituality, Wicca, and related phenomena, see "Lesbians and Religion," *Sinister Wisdom* 54 (Winter 1994/95), edited by Elana Dykewoman; and Charlene Spretnak, ed., *The Politics of Women's Spirituality* (1982). See also, in *Que(e)rying Religion: A Critical Anthology*, edited by Gary David Comstock and Susan E. Henking, Micaela di Leonardo, "Warrior Virgins and Boston Marriages" on female friendship across cultures; and on separatism and related matters, Nancy R. Howell, "Radical Relatedness and Feminist Separatism" and L. J. "Tess" Tessier, "Feminist Separatism—The Dynamics of Self-Creation."

SUSAN E. HENKING

In Asia

The field of Asian lesbianism in relation to religion is virtually nonexistent; consequently, we do not have even basic terms with which to proceed in investigating it. In the absence of substantial information about Asian lesbianism, such an investigation must proceed out of the conviction that "lesbians," or their regional Asian counterparts, must exist, interfacing with the particular religions in which they were born or chose to practice—that is, out of the a priori conviction that lesbianism is "universal" (Ng, 1996).

In this article the word *lesbianism* is used as a tentative term not only for an actual sexual exchange between two women involving physical and genital contact, which may or may not be accompanied by emotional or affectional bonding or commitment; but also for a primary emotional and affectional bond between two adult women that makes them more aware of themselves as embodied sexual beings, even though it may or may not include physical contact, especially genital contact, between them. In the absence of relevant terms and appropriate perspectives and tools, we may be more successful in identifying environments supportive of female homoeroticism—that is, social and cultural environments that would be conducive to the above two forms of exchange and relation between two women—than in identifying actual narratives of female homoeroticism within communities.

HINDUISM

Ancient Hindu temple carvings, texts, and myths depict same-sex affection and sexual relations. Vatysyana's *Kama* sutra, a systematic study of erotic practices (fourth century B.C.E.–fourth century C.E.), is a repository of a much older Indian tradition that sees *kāma*, desire, as the vehicle through which the continuation of the human species is ensured. The *Kama* sutra devotes a whole section to the "virile behavior of women," which mostly describes modes of uninhibited sexual expression between women lovers.

In Manu's *Dharmashastra* (c. second century C.E.), the representative text of the ancient Hindu tradition of *dharma*, or social ethics, lesbian relations carry a severe penalty: "A damsel who pollutes [another damsel] must be fined two hundred panas, pay the double of her nup-

tial fee and receive ten [lashes with a] rod" (VIII:369). "But a woman who pollutes a damsel shall instantly have [her head] shaved, or two fingers cut off, and be made to ride [through the town] on a donkey" (VIII: 370). (Quoted in Buhler, 1967, p. 466).

The term *svairini* (from *svaira*, following one's own will, uncontrolled, independent), which appears in the *Kama* sutra, has been translated by Eva Neumaier-Dargyay as "one who makes love with her own kind." She argues that the reluctant acceptance of *svairini* in the *Kama* sutra and its condemnation in the *Dharmashastra* could be read as an acknowledgment of a class of Hindu women who asserted their right to the expression of their homoerotic feelings and an independence from heterosexual norms or behavior. Whether these Hindu women also had a religious culture—myths, rituals, beliefs that affirmed their life-styles—is yet to be researched.

Patanjali's *Yoga* sutra (compiled 300–500 C.E.), the text concerned with *kaivalya*, spiritual liberation, advocates celibacy or continence (*brahmacarya*) for the practitioner of yoga. What the soul seeks in sexual intimacy is to be found in the practice of yoga. Sexual desire as a subcategory of desire, *raga*, and sexual involvement lead to suffering rather than pleasure. Beyond the recommendation of celibacy the *Yoga* sutras do not comment further on either hetero- or homosexuality.

The consequence of practicing *brahmacarya* is claimed to be strength and virility. Preservation of the vital semen within the male body and avoidance of its loss through ejaculation is a common theme in many Indian texts concerned with *mokṣa*, or spiritual liberation. As lesbian lovemaking does not involve the loss of semen, can it be said not to break the vows of *brahmacarya*? In the context of the ancient discussions on *brahmacarya*, this question would be inapplicable since only men were expected to practice yoga. Though yoga is primarily for the celibate renunciates, there is today an increasing community of householders who claim to base their yoga practice in the *Yoga* sutras. They understand *brahmacarya* as allowing for limited heterosexual expression within a monogamous marriage. Yet the householder yoga communities in India, like other Hindu communities, tend to be homophobic.

BUDDHISM

In Buddhism, as in Hindu yoga, the general issue is not homosexuality versus heterosexuality but rather sexuality versus celibacy. For the most part Buddhism has been neutral on the issue of homosexuality; when homosexuality is condemned, it is more because of the sex act per se than because it involves same-sex partners. Condemnation has never led to persecution. Buddhist tradition ranks celibate monastic life over the lay noncelibate life, and the lay Buddhist was not expected to abide by strict or high standards of heterosexual monogamy. One finds prohibition of male and female homosexuality in the Vinaya (rules and discipline of monastic life), but it is difficult to ascertain how prevalent lesbianism was in the Buddhist monastic communities.

In *Pitying the Fragrant Companion*, a play by Li Yu (China, 1611–1680), a young married woman falls in love with a woman two years her junior in a Buddhist convent, takes vows with her as lovers before an image of the Buddha, and eventually convinces her husband to take her lover into their household as a second wife. In the nineteenth century, Buddhist convents in China gave rise to the Golden Orchid Association, a movement of marriage resisters who lived together in communities similar to the Buddhist convents. In general, however, there is a denial of the existence of lesbians and a concomitant homophobic attitude. Some claim that this homophobia was learned from contact with Western Christian missionaries.

ISLAM

The Qur'an asserts the immorality and therefore the illegality of male homosexual behavior, but there is no clear textual evidence of strictures against female homosexual behavior. Two Qur'anic verses are sometimes cited as prohibiting female homosexual behavior; they are, in fact, ambiguous as to the nature of the offense and the gender composition of the couple: "And those among your women who are guilty of lewdness, take the evidence of four witnesses from among you against them and if they testify then confine them to houses until death claim them or God make another way for them" (IV:15). "And if two persons among you are guilty of lewdness punish them both. If they repent and amend leave them alone for God is Oft Forgiving, Most Merciful" (IV:16). Whereas in the earliest extant commentaries of the Qur'an (c. 688 C.E.), these verses are understood to refer to heterosexual couples, in the twentieth century the verses have been cited as providing the textual evidence needed unequivocally to condemn female homosexual behavior.

A case cited in Shiite juristic texts functions similarly to condemn female homosexuality in the absence of clear Qur'anic injunctions. The case, claimed to have been ruled upon by Hasan ibn 'Ali (624–669 C.E.), Muhammad's grandson, and Jafar al-Sadiq (700–765 C.E.), Hasan ibn 'Ali's grandson, involves a woman who subsequent to having sexual intercourse with her husband engages in sexual activity with a virgin slave, transferring her husband's semen to her female sexual partner, thus causing her partner to become pregnant

with the husband's child. Both judges rule that the married woman is to be stoned to death; the child is to be returned to the father and the slave woman flogged. The same punishment is meted out for female homosexual acts as is prescribed by Islamic law for extramarital heterosexual acts. Regardless of whether the case is a juristic fiction or an actual case, the fact that it is quoted in several Shiite texts is a recognition both of the reality of female homosexuality and of the intent to condemn and control it.

The current regime in Iran, which claims to be enforcing Shiite law, is actually much harsher in its treatment of women accused of being deviant, including lesbians, than the classical Shiite law permits. The requirement of evidence to establish sexual misconduct—three adult male eyewitnesses of high moral standing—practically rules out the possibility of any individual being found guilty. However, in many Muslim countries at the end of the twentieth century, religious fanatics and extremists, individuals as well as some governments, exhibiting their ignorance of Islamic law, disregard due process and use the prohibition against sexual misconduct to persecute women suspected of same-sex affections.

Whereas the religious texts of high Islam have historically condemned homosexuality, the literary and mystical texts have preserved a male homoerotic and homosexual tradition. *The Book of Songs* by the literary historian of the Arabo-Muslim renaissance, Abul Farraj al-Isbahani (c. 897–967 C.E.), contains references to female homoeroticism among the court poets and singers. In contemporary literature by Asian Muslim women an implicit but undeniable theme of female homoeroticism can be found, for example, in the short stories of the Pakistani writer Khalida Hussain. It is not clear, however, whether Hussain is aware of the undercurrent of female homoerotic engagement in some of her writing. In the provocative fiction of the acclaimed Indian writer Ismat Chughtai, one finds a frank exploration of both hetero- and homosexuality. In general, the emotion and expression of homoeroticism among Asian Muslim women remains unnamed for fear of reprisals.

BIBLIOGRAPHY

Aguilar-San Juan, Karin. "Landmarks in Literature by Asian American Lesbians." *Signs* 18, no. 4 (1993): 936–938.

Anwar, Ghazala. "Female Homoeroticism in Islam." In *Encyclopedia of Homosexuality*. Volume on lesbianism, edited by Bonnie Zimmerman. 1990.

Barnes, Nancy Schuster. "Buddhism." In *Women and World Religions*. Edited by Arvind Sharma. 1987.

Buhler, G., trans. *The Laws of Manu.* Delhi, 1886, 1967.

Cabezón, José Ignacio. "Homosexuality and Buddhism." In *Homosexuality and World Religions.* Edited by Arlene Swidler. 1993.

Crompton, Louis. "Homosexuality in Imperial China." Paper delivered at the Conference on Homosexuality: Which Homosexuality? Amsterdam, 1987.

Daniélou, Alain, trans. *The Complete Kama Sutra.* 1994.

Duran, Khalid. "Homosexuality and Islam." In *Homosexuality and World Religions.* Edited by Arlene Swidler. 1993.

Kase, Alleson. "Asian Lesbians Speak: A Conference Report." In *Off Our Backs* 22, no. 8 (1992).

Neumaier-Dargyay, Eva. "Querying/Queering Buddhist Text." Paper presented at the American Association of Religions annual meeting. 1994.

Ng, Vivien. "Looking for Lesbians in Chinese History." In *New Lesbian Studies.* Edited by Bonnie Zimmerman and Toni McNaron. 1996.

Rakesh, Ratti, ed. *A Lotus of Another Color: An Unfolding of the South Asian Gay and Lesbian Experience.* 1993.

Sharma, Arvind. "Homosexuality and Hinduism." In *Homosexuality and World Religions.* Edited by Arlene Swidler. 1993.

Swidler, Arlene, ed. *Homosexuality and World Religions.* 1993.

Takarazuka. *Sexual Politics and Popular Culture in Modern Japan.* 1998.

Topley, M. "Marriage Resistance in Rural Kwangtung." In *Women in Chinese Society.* 1975.

Woods, James Houghton. *The Yoga-system of Patanjali.* Delhi, 1988 [1914].

Zwilling, Leonard. "Homosexuality as Seen in Indian Buddhist Texts." In *Buddhism, Sexuality and Gender.* Edited by José Ignazio Cabézon. 1992.

GHAZALA ANWAR

In Microhistorical Traditions

Lesbianism has been and continues to be a reality in many small-scale societies. Relying on the Human Relations Area Files, a collection of cross-cultural ethnographic data, Clellan S. Ford and Frank A. Beach (1951) reported that of the seventy-six societies for which information about homosexuality was available, evidence of lesbianism was found in seventeen of them. These seventeen societies were the Aranda, Aymara, Azande, Chiricahua, Chukchee, Crow, Dahomeans, Haitians, Manus, Mbundu, Nama, Ojibwa, Quinault, Samoans, Sanspoil, Tswana, and Yuma. However, Evelyn Blackwood (1985), whose work has for many years focused on lesbianism cross-culturally, found evidence of lesbian and female cross-gender behavior in ninety-five cultures. In another study (1984) she reported that thirty-three North American indigenous nations recognized a female cross-gender role, which meant, according to Blackwood, that these females had the opportunity to assume a male role permanently and marry women. These and other sources reveal the presence of same-sex sexuality in many small-scale societies prior to significant outside influence, particularly by the West.

Several factors make even a basic understanding of female same-sex sexual intimacy difficult. Use of Western concepts, such as "lesbian" and "lesbianism," for instance, carries implications that are inaccurate when applied in non-Western contexts. Who "counts" as a "lesbian" or what qualifies as "lesbian" behavior is also a matter of debate. In some Native American nations, historically the female partner of a cross-gender female was not a "lesbian"; she was a woman in the traditional sense understood by that society and could have married a man or a woman. And in some African tribes, same-sex sexual intimacy between girls was tolerated or even expected as a stage in their preparation for adult heterosexual life.

Lack of information is another problem in this area of study. Developing a valid survey of female homosexuality in indigenous traditions is difficult, whether because of the often private nature of sexuality, the reluctance of informants to discuss homosexuality, the heterosexual bias of the researcher, the fact that most research has been conducted by men who worked with male informants, or any of several other factors. What information there is is generally found in the reports of missionaries, travelers, colonists, and anthropologists. These sources have often been influenced by bias, such as the misconceptions of the "primitive" nature of indigenous cultures, the abnormality of homosexuality, and the inferiority of women.

There is also a lack of information about whether indigenous practices and beliefs continue to the present day. Scholars must often use the past tense in describing the cultures of small-scale societies because updated information is not available. This use of the past tense, however, supports the mistaken assumption that indigenous people are a "dying breed" and obscures the degree to which traditional ways of life continue.

Moreover, the religious import of lesbianism is difficult to determine. Much of the evidence about homosexuality focuses on sexual behavior, not on the meaning assigned to it or ritual dimensions of it. Because of the lack of information and the nature of the sources, blanket statements about a society's disapproval of homosexuality must be evaluated with a healthy dose of skepticism. It should be pointed out, as well, that Ford and Beach showed that of the seventy-six small-scale societies for which information was available, 64 percent of them considered homosexuality socially acceptable for some members of their societies. Despite these and other problems in the literature, a few examples of female same-sex sexuality in indigenous contexts give a sense of some of its religious aspects.

The Santals of India, according to Charulal Mukherjea (1962), engaged in the practice of "flower friendships," in which two girls of approximately the same age pledged life-long friendship. In a ceremony recognizing their relationship, each placed a particular flower in the hair of the other and from that time forward addressed the other by her "flower name." The Santals denied the involvement of homosexuality in such relationships. However, the pair formed a strong emotional bond, eating, talking, and, if possible, sleeping with each other.

The Dahomey of West Africa brought girls aged nine to eleven together to form "schools" consisting of approximately ten girls. As described by Melville J. Herskovits (1938), these girls gathered in the evenings along with their adult female caretaker to engage in *axoti*, the massaging and enlarging of the vaginal lips. While it was said that having "thin" lips was less attractive than "thickened" lips, the girls themselves were not aware that the purpose of the *axoti* was to enhance sexual pleasure of their future male partners. Homosexuality among adolescent boys was permitted. Herskovits makes no mention of it among adolescent girls, but he does acknowledge that some adult females found their "most valid sex experiences" with other females, despite the risk of public derision (1932).

Among the Mohave Indians of the American Southwest, homosexuals are thought to have dreamt of their role change within the womb (Devereux, 1967). As they neared adolescence their gender roles became more definite, females choosing the dress and implements of men, and males that of women. If the community could not dissuade a female child from her role change, she was given the status of a *hwame*, or female homosexual. It was also the case that a chief's spiritual power could change a person's gender role.

In regard to ceremonialism, Walter L. Williams (1986) refers to a transformation ceremony held by the Kaska Indians of subarctic North America in which a girl was changed into a boy. Because of the importance of sons to a family for the purpose of hunting, if a family had only daughters, one of them would be selected to "be like a man." The ceremony involved the tying of dried bear ovaries to a belt the girl always wore, a practice intended to prevent menstruation and pregnancy and to make her a lucky hunter. Thereafter, she dressed like a man and assumed men's duties.

E. E. Evans-Pritchard (1970) documented the existence of female same-sex sexuality in the culture of the African Azande people. Such relationships usually took place between women in a polygynous household. It was also the case that two women friends, with the permission of their husbands, could formalize their bond with a *bagburu* ceremony. Azande men suspected such friendships were a cover for their wives' sexual intimacy. For an Azande man to witness sexual expression between women was particularly inauspicious, even potentially lethal, according to Evans-Pritchard (1937). Although the reasons for this belief are unclear, it should be pointed out that female homosexuals were suspected to be witches.

Some homosexual individuals in indigenous cultures were considered to be supernaturally powerful. A Kutenai woman of the North American Plateau region, for instance, was known for her abilities in prophecy and healing (Williams, 1986). And it seems that the Mohaves believed that homosexuals were intended at the beginning of the world to be spiritual practitioners (Devereux).

These few examples only begin to sketch the religious dimensions of female homosexuality in indigenous cultures. Without a doubt, more research is needed into the religious significance of same-sex sexuality in small-scale societies, not only historically but also in the present.

BIBLIOGRAPHY

Baum, Robert M. "Homosexuality and the Traditional Religions of the Americas and Africa." In *Homosexuality and World Religions.* Edited by Arlene Swidler. 1993. Notable for its emphasis on the religious aspects of homosexuality; somewhat limited in its treatment of lesbianism in particular.

Blackwood, Evelyn. "Breaking the Mirror: The Construction of Lesbianism and the Anthropological Discourse on Homosexuality." *Journal of Homosexuality* 11, nos. 3 and 4 (1985): 1–17. A critical survey of anthropological assumptions about homosexuality and of relevant theoretical approaches employed in the field.

———. "Sexuality and Gender in Certain Native American Tribes: The Case of Cross-Gender Females." *Signs* 10, no. 1 (1984): 27–42. An excellent resource on the female "cross-gender" role, especially in western North America and the Plains.

Devereux, George. "Homosexuality among the Mohave Indians." In *The North American Indians: A*

Sourcebook. Edited by Roger C. Owen, James J. F. Deetz, and Anthony D. Fisher. 1967. A relatively detailed discussion of both male and female homosexuality, relying heavily on statements by a ceremonial leader who knew "transvestite" initiation songs; originally published in 1937.

Evans-Pritchard, E. E. "Sexual Inversion Among the Azande." *American Anthropologist* 72, no. 6 (1970): 1428–1434. Valuable for its focus on homosexuality among the Azande.

———. *Witchcraft, Oracles and Magic among the Azande.* 1937. An extensive ethnographic study based on fieldwork; little about homosexuality.

Ford, Clellan S., and Frank A. Beach. *Patterns of Sexual Behavior.* 1951. A cross-cultural survey of human sexual behavior with a useful chapter on homosexuality.

Herskovits, Melville J. *Dahomey: An Ancient West African Kingdom.* 2 vols. 1938. A detailed description of Dahomean society based on fieldwork; little about homosexuality.

———. "Some Aspects of Dahomean Ethnology." *Africa* 5, no. 1 (1932): 266–296. Focuses on the organization of Dahomean economic, social, and religious life; limited in its treatment of homosexuality.

Jacobs, Sue-Ellen, Wesley Thomas, and Sabine Lang. *Two-Spirit People: Native American Gender Identity, Sexuality, and Spirituality.* 1997. An essential work for the study of contemporary American Indian homosexuality.

Mukherjea, Charulal. *The Santals.* 2d ed. 1962. An ethnographic monograph on an important aboriginal tribe in India.

Roscoe, Will. "Bibliography of Berdache and Alternative Gender Roles among North American Indians." *Journal of Homosexuality* 14, nos. 3 and 4 (1987): 81–171. Includes a list of tribes in which the existence of same-sex sexuality has been documented.

Roscoe, Will, ed. *Living the Spirit: A Gay American Indian Anthology.* 1988. A collection of articles and creative writing by contemporary gay and lesbian American Indians.

Weston, Kath. "Lesbian/Gay Studies in the House of Anthropology." In *Annual Review of Anthropology.* Vol. 22. 1993. An assessment of the status of lesbian and gay studies in anthropology highlighting problems in the anthropological study of homosexuality.

Williams, Walter L. *The Spirit and the Flesh: Sexual Diversity in American Indian Culture.* 1986. The most thorough study of Native American same-sex sexuality to date; only one chapter is devoted exclusively to females, however.

Woodsum, Jo Ann. "Gender and Sexuality in Native American Societies: A Bibliography." *American Indian Quarterly* 19, no. 4 (1995): 527–554. Good bibliography on Native American women in general; includes several entries on same-sex sexuality and a list of films and videos, some of which concern homosexuality.

MARY C. CHURCHILL

Lesbian Studies

In 1982, Margaret Cruikshank's groundbreaking anthology, *Lesbian Studies: Present and Future,* defined the multidisciplinary field of lesbian studies, which had grown out of a decade of feminist activism and women's studies scholarship. Founded on the theoretical interventions of lesbian feminism, lesbian studies attempted to theorize beyond the inadequacies perceived in academic feminism and women's studies. A major objective of lesbian studies was to reveal the ideological heterosexism and homophobia of academic discourse (including that arising from the more established women's studies), which both perpetuated lesbian invisibility and distorted lesbian realities. In the context of lesbian and gay politics after Stonewall, the 1969 monumental protest of a police raid on a gay bar in New York City that marked the birth of the modern lesbian and gay movement, lesbian theorists began to reclaim lesbian history and culture. During the 1970s and 1980s lesbian theorists offered critical perspectives on the attitudes toward lesbians in various cultures and in various historical periods.

The mid-1990s saw lesbian studies become an innovative and expanding academic enterprise in most U.S., Canadian, and European universities. As lesbian scholarship has earned its place among such disciplines as literature, history, anthropology, and psychology, the number of courses offered has increased considerably. The field has produced anthologies, articles, and books, offering critical perspectives on lesbians in various social contexts and their contributions.

The sense of lesbian self-understanding derives from knowledge of how the stigmatization of lesbians is connected with issues of gender, the family, public speech, consumption and desire, nature and culture, racial and national fantasy, class identity, censorship, intimate life and social display, terror and violence, health care, and strong cultural norms about the female body. Differences in age, immigrant status, ethnic and racial identities, and geographical locales reveal the untenable and naive position of an essential lesbian self.

The questions and methodologies posed by queer theory have challenged lesbian studies; in their quest to undermine the notion of a static, unified identity or self, queer theorists question the very existence of categories, identities, and labels, including that of lesbian. Although some lesbians participate in queer theory and activism, many lesbian feminists debate the merit of applying the term *queer* to lesbian realities, arguing that it represents a false unity of women and men and often collapses the experiences of women into the experiences of men. The term is used in different ways depending on who puts it forth, thus excluding certain groups and creating an impossible conflict between racial, ethnic, or religious affiliation and sexual politics. Traditionally many feminist lesbians have drawn upon the works of Adrienne Rich and Audre Lorde; those influenced by queer studies cite such scholars as Eve Kosofsky and Judith Butler.

LESBIAN STUDIES AND RELIGION

The success of lesbian scholarship in many humanistic and social scientific fields has not been fully matched in the religious discipline. With a few notable exceptions, religious studies departments continue to deny the place and role of lesbians in religious traditions; the theoretical perspectives emerging from lesbian religious scholars are still marginalized. In spite of the attempts of some women's studies departments, the rich feminist and lesbian contributions to religious studies remain invisible within academe.

Certain religious scholars have achieved prominence on the topic of spirituality conjoined with lesbian studies. Mary Daly's historical and political analysis in *Beyond God the Father* (1969; 1985) helped to spur interest in women-centered religiosity. In Daly's religious and philosophical canon, as in lesbian feminism in general, one finds variations on such themes as the repression of difference, the Other, and the subversion of authority as traditionally known. In *Gyn/Ecology* (1978) and *Pure Lust* (1984), Daly redefined femaleness by subverting accepted language and conventional rationality and producing new meanings and new subject positions for women. Women's new identity is founded upon "true" femaleness, based in women's biological nature. The process of achieving a new identity is often conceived as a journey, which involves breaking with patriarchal perspectives, confronting the horrific violence of patriarchy, and developing and celebrating new forms of female creativity—for which Daly uses the image of "spinning" in a new space. Daly's lesbian separatism suggests that the new woman-identified environment enables the realization of women's true

The work of poet and author Adrienne Rich has been important to the growth of lesbian studies (UPI/Corbis-Bettmann).

selves, which patriarchy distorts, fragments, and denies.

Carter Heyward, a lesbian Episcopal priest and theologian, is another important figure who has advanced lesbian issues in religious scholarship. In *Touching Our Strength* (1989), Heyward envisions a sexual theology in which sex and God are seen as empowering sparks of humans in relationship with others. Heyward affirms the experiences of lesbians and gays as sexual, erotic beings, whose experience of the sacred is part of the larger liberationist movement aimed at analyzing and eradicating the interworkings of sexism, racism, homophobia, and heterosexism found in religious institutions and the wider culture. To speak of the erotic or of God is to speak of power in right relations. The erotic symbolizes the yearning for mutuality and justice; it is the shape of God in a life shared as particular selves in proper relation. Mutuality empowers people to experience one another as intrinsically valuable, irreplaceable. Elsewhere in her writings Heyward affirms the intersections of lesbian desire, ethical reflections, and transformative faith.

WOMEN'S SPIRITUALITY

In spite of the lack of attention to lesbian religious faith and spirituality in much lesbian theory, some isolated studies have shown the impact of the contemporary women's spirituality movement on lesbian spirituality.

Reacting against oppressive forms of religion, the women's spirituality movement has become a noninstitutionalized, syncretistic, and gynocentric movement that is gradually spreading worldwide. The women's spirituality movement emphasizes and celebrates different manifestations and practices of sexuality, even though lesbians predominantly organize and attend the various festivals and gatherings. The symbolism and images celebrated in lesbian women's spirituality derive from the Goddess, eco-feminist, New Age, Christian, Jewish, Native American, Afro-Caribbean, pagan, and metaphysical traditions.

BIBLIOGRAPHY

Brooten, Bernadette. *Love Between Women: Early Christian Responses to Female Homoeroticism.* 1996. Historical study of the early church's views and doctrinal stance on sexuality and homoeroticism among women.

Eller, Cynthia. *Living in the Lap of the Goddess.* 1993. Traces the development and unique aspects of the contemporary feminist spirituality movement.

Garber, Linda. *Tilting the Tower.* 1995. Addresses issues related to the institutionalization of lesbian studies, and to lesbian pedagogy in the United States.

Griffin, Gabriele, and Sonya Andermahr. *Straight Studies Modified.* 1987. Essays assessing the impacts lesbians as activists, teachers, and researchers have had and continue to have on changing disciplines and the academy.

Henking, Susan, and Gary D. Comstock. *Que(e)rying Religion.* 1996. Collection of essays featuring insights emerging from the intersection of religious studies, queer theory, and lesbian and gay studies.

Hunt, Mary. *Fierce Tenderness.* 1991. Explores religious and ethical implications of friendships between lesbians and among women.

Jay, Karla, ed. *Lesbian Erotics.* 1995. Essays on lesbian sexuality.

Rothblum, Esther D. *Classics in Lesbian Studies.* 1997. Collection of previously published articles in lesbian studies that addresses erasure of lesbians, lesbian health, and lesbian feminism.

Zanotti, Barbara. *A Faith of One's Own: Explorations by Catholic Lesbians.* 1986. Personal narratives of lesbians raised in Catholicism and their search for a meaningful spiritual life.

See also **Gender Studies; Heterosexism; Queer Theory; Women's Contemporary Spirituality Movement; Women's Studies.**

CAROL WAYNE WHITE

Liberation Theologies

Liberation theologies emerged in the social movements of the late 1960s in both developing countries and North America. Challenging the domination of Eurocentric, middle-class, male heterosexual theologies, theologies of liberation represent the theological voices of the poor, the marginalized, and the colonized. Liberation theologies in developing countries arose in the sociopolitical struggles against colonialism, militarism, economic oppression, cultural hegemony of the West, and ecological degradation. In North America, liberation theologies are rooted in the civil rights movement, women's movement, gay and lesbian struggles, and indigenous peoples' struggle for sovereignty rights.

Although diverse contexts give rise to different liberation theologies, these theologies share some common presuppositions: 1) theology is a reflection on concrete sociopolitical struggles to bring about justice and peace; 2) God is on the side of the marginalized and disfranchised; 3) sin is not only personal but also systemic; 4) salvation in Christ means not only personal reconciliation with God but also liberation from social and political oppressions; 5) people are subjects of history and have moral agency to effect social change; and 6) the reign of God is here and now and not just in the world to come.

In Asia, major issues of liberation theologies include the relation between gospel and culture; religious pluralism; the struggle for democracy; neocolonialism; and Asian spirituality. In *Waterbuffalo Theology*, Japanese theologian Kosuke Koyama argues that Christianity must be indigenized in Asian soil, using Asian idioms and languages. Korean *minjung* theology (theology of the masses) emphasizes people as the subjects of history and reinterprets the Bible through the *minjung* perspective. Indian theologians have focused on dialogues between Christianity and Hinduism, while recent discussions include *dalit* (untouchables) theology. In the Philippines, theologians reflect on the political significance of people's movements in social change.

Latin American liberation theologians use Marxist social analysis to critique the economic oppression by the industrial nations and unjust class structures within Latin American societies. Gustavo Gutierrez, Leonardo Boff, and José Míguez Bonino have written on God's "preferential option for the poor," the "hermeneutical privilege" of the poor in understanding Scripture, Jesus as the liberator, and the role of the church in social change. These theologians stress the relation between faith and ideology, theology and praxis, and history and

Anglican archbishop Desmond Tutu gives a sermon at the National Cathedral, Washington, D.C., 1984, protesting apartheid in South Africa (UPI/Corbis-Bettmann).

eschatology. More recent writings also include issues such as popular religiosity, ecojustice, and the struggle of women and indigenous peoples.

African theologians discuss inculturation, the legacy of colonialism and neocolonialism, apartheid, and the challenge to Christianity of Islam and traditional religions. Facing famine and dire poverty, theologians challenge the global economic system that threatens the survival of many African people. South African theologians such as Archbishop Desmond Tutu and Allan Boesak have been on the forefront in condemning apartheid. To articulate people's aspiration for justice, theologians turn to people's myths, fables, and folktales to interpret faith and Scripture. Some have also used Marxist hermeneutics to articulate black theology in South Africa.

Liberation theologies in North America include divergent theological currents. Feminist theologies advocate women's dignity and seek full participation of women in church and society. The diversity of women's experiences give rise to white feminist theology, womanist theology, *mujerista* (U.S. Latina women) and mestiza theology, and Asian American feminist theology. Black theology, Hispanic/Latino theology, and Asian American theology focus on racism, the politics of difference, and multiculturalism. Gay and lesbian theologies challenge heterosexism and homophobia. Native Americans reflect on the significance of sovereignty rights and their interdependence with the land. People with disabilities are beginning to articulate a religious vision for a more inclusive church.

Although women have been the poor among the poor, most male liberation theologians have not paid sufficient attention to women's issues, because they are working in male-dominated churches and popular movements, and suspect that feminism is only for middle-class, white women in developed nations. Further, Marxist theory does not adequately analyze oppressions based on sex and gender. Sometimes, patriarchal elements in Christianity are reinforced by indigenous cultures. Also, the liberation of the nation, the poor, or the race can be seen as preceding the liberation of women. Finally, there is fear of a split along gender lines in social movements.

Today, Christian women from all over the world are claiming their authority as theological subjects. Women are no longer passive consumers of theological symbols and doctrines formulated by men but are producers of theological knowledge and active participants in theological discourse. Women in developing nations and minority women in North America challenge both male liberation theologians and white, middle-class feminist theologians to include multiple forms of marginalization of women in their analysis and work for the liberation of all.

BIBLIOGRAPHY

Boesak, Allan A. *Farewell to Innocence: A Socio-ethical Study on Black Theology and Black Power.* 1977.

Chung, Hyun Kyung. *Struggle to Be the Sun Again: Introducing Asian Women's Theology.* 1990.

Cone, James H. *God of the Oppressed.* 1975.

Gutierrez, Gustavo. *A Theology of Liberation.* 1973. Rev. ed., 1988.

Heyward, Carter. *Touching Our Strength: The Erotic as Power and the Love of God.* 1989.

King, Ursula, ed. *Feminist Theology from the Third World.* 1994.

Koyama, Kosuke. *Waterbuffalo Theology.* 1974.

Martey, Emmanuel. *African Theology: Inculturation and Liberation.* 1993.

Oduyoye, Mercy Amba, and Musimbi R. A. Kanyoro, eds. *The Will to Arise: Women, Tradition, and the Church in Africa.* 1992.

Pieris, Aloysius. *An Asian Theology of Liberation.* 1988.

Plaskow, Judith, and Carol P. Christ, eds. *Weaving the Visions: New Patterns in Feminist Spirituality.* 1989.

Russell, Letty M. *Human Liberation in a Feminist Perspective: A Theology.* 1974.

Tamez, Elsa, ed. *Through Her Eyes: Women's Theology from Latin America.* 1989.

See also **African American Churches; Christianity: In Africa; Christianity: In Asia; Christianity: In Latin America and the Caribbean; Mujerista Tradition; Womanist Traditions.**

KWOK PUI-LAN

Lilith

Lilith is a major figure in Jewish demonology with roots in ancient Near Eastern folklore. Mentioned in the Hebrew Bible among the wild beasts and demons who will devastate the world on the day of divine retribution (Isaiah 34:14), Lilith appears in rabbinic literature (first through sixth centuries C.E.) as a female night spirit with a woman's face, long hair, and wings (Babylonian Talmud 'Erubin 100b, Niddah 24b, Shabbat 151b, and Baba Bathra 73b). The *Alphabet of Ben Sira,* a midrashic work of the medieval period (probably eleventh century C.E.), conflated the demonic Lilith with rabbinic traditions about the "first Eve," a being believed to have been created simultaneously with Adam and subsequently rejected by him in favor of a more subservient partner (*Genesis Rabbah* 17:7, 18:4, and 22:7). This exegetical fiction reconciled the contradictions in the two biblical accounts of female creation (Gen. 1 and Gen. 2:4 ff.). According to the *Alphabet,* Lilith was the "first Eve," who would not give up her equality with Adam, refused a subordinate position in sexual intercourse, and ultimately fled her husband, pronouncing the divine name and flying away. Despite pursuit and capture by angels, Lilith refused to return to Adam, asserting her demon status and her intention to harm women in childbirth and kill newborn infants. According to the *Alphabet,* however, Lilith is powerless to injure mothers and infants who are wearing protective amulets. Many Jewish amulets with preventive inscriptions against Lilith survive, indicating both the tenacity of this legend and the perils of childbirth before the modern era. In Jewish mystical literature the demonic Lilith represents the dangers for men of uncontrolled female sexuality. Lilith has been reclaimed by some contemporary Jewish feminists as emblematic of the equality between women and men, which is essential for continued Jewish survival and creativity.

BIBLIOGRAPHY

For comprehensive citation of references to Lilith in classical and medieval Jewish sources, see Louis Ginzberg, *The Legends of the Jews* (1947). Aviva Cantor, "The Lilith Question," in *On Being a Jewish Feminist: A Reader,* edited by Susannah Heschel (1983; rev. ed. 1995), offers a contemporary feminist reading of legends connected to Lilith, while T. Schrire, *Hebrew Magic Amulets: Their Decipherment and Interpretation* (1966; repr. 1982) presents information about amulets used by Jewish women for protection against her.

JUDITH R. BASKIN

Literary Theory and Criticism

Literary texts have historically been central to the religious experience of women as both writers and readers. Significant social control with profound implications for women has been exerted by theorists and critics over publishing, reviewing, anthologizing, and translating. Most recently the globalization of the literary-critical enterprise has been influencing all spheres of human activity around the world, including the religious. Highly educated elites, among them some women, have been the principal participants in this controversial, predominantly secular and Western movement.

"Theory" is understood here to be concerned primarily with reflection on principles and definitions, "criticism" with direct engagement in the interpretation and evaluation of specific, albeit broadly conceived, "texts." Much contemporary theory in the West originated in a fundamental shift from "New Criticism," which held the traditionally defined "literary work" and its "author" to be the sites of critical interest, toward reconceptualization of all productions of writing (and of film and other media) and their producers as being multiply constructed phenomena shaped by a complex of forces—personal, historical, social, political—as well as by linguistic and cultural convention. Thus, the adjective "literary" in the traditional sense lost its usefulness as a descriptor.

The Johns Hopkins Guide to Literary Theory and Criticism (1994) harnesses an otherwise intractable mass of material from the 1950s to the 1990s—the period of theory and criticism's ascendancy—and offers a substantive historical review of the many overlapping areas of inquiry. These areas are not "schools of thought" but groupings of writers with certain affinities and interests. Although pervasively Euro-American and distinctively Western in its perspective, the *Guide* also traces the movement of literary theory and criticism in Arabic countries, Africa, Australia, the Caribbean, China, India, Japan, and Latin America.

The relative brevity in the *Guide* of the "Biblical" and related entries and the virtual absence of reference to religions outside of Judaism and Christianity show the theories' essential secularism. Diverse contributors regularly demonstrate, however, that much of their theory, including such central notions as "canon"—certain texts and authors privileged as "classic" and assigned authority—trace their origins to Biblical hermeneutics (theory of interpretation) and exegesis (practice of interpretation).

For female readers, however, the *Guide* and the original sources it represents should be consulted warily because certain directions in theory have been liberating for women, whereas others have been constraining, often insidiously so. Even theory self-identified as feminist (female-centered, antipatriarchal, committed to equality of females and males) has been challenged for neglect of class, race, and sexual orientation, for ethnocentrism, and for residual adherence to masculinist values and modes of perception and presentation.

U. S. scholar Phyllis Trible's *Texts of Terror: Literary-Feminist Readings of Biblical Narratives* (1984) seemed to provide viable alternatives to traditional interpretations of women's roles in the Bible. Dutch scholar Mieke Bal, however, criticized the work as still dependent on methods of textual analysis that are themselves, like the content they analyze, misogynist. In her own Biblical scholarship, Bal drew on and contributed to narratology: reading narratives not as fictionalized versions of "real" life but as composites of formal elements such as devices, structures, and discourses. Narratology could thus distance female readers from identifying with their representations in texts, helping them to detect and express their marginalization in the "master narratives" of their cultures, which had traditionally confined women to roles of minor, often denigrated subjects.

Such androcentric bias was identified in the scholarship on Christianity by early feminist theologians such as Carol Christ (1976). Christ started with her discovery that novels of spiritual quest by female authors such as Doris Lessing offered women alternatives to male-generic narratives of spiritual development. She advocated "a whole new set of texts written by women and the creation of theories and methods for their interpretation" and sought recovery of lost female views and

texts, a project typical of new historicism. Recognizing that both "history" and "literature" are culturally constructed, new historicists view past aesthetic productions and their transmission over time and across cultures as interwoven with ideologies and power relations of the societies involved. Thus, they seek recuperation from the past of "lost," ignored, neglected, and disparaged texts that frequently turn out to be those by and about women.

New historicists also see race, sexual orientation, and other categories of difference to have been a basis for the devaluation of certain texts and writers. Like women, then, each outsider group debated whether to fit its writing into an existing canon of texts, form their own canon, or do away with the notion of canon entirely. They also questioned whether in theory and criticism to use the dominant discourse selectively and critique it while doing so, engage in oppositional and subversive discourse, or, in African-American scholar Henry Louis Gates's words: "develop criticism indigenous to our own literature (1989, p. 25)." Barbara Smith (1980), self-identified as black and lesbian, argued for a black feminist criticism, claiming that white female academics had already been canonized within a racist and class-based feminism. The voices of excluded others often spurred a fundamental interrogation of the notion and value of theory itself, of the applicability of given critical criteria to texts that emerge from radically different world views.

The *Encyclopedia of Feminist Literary Theory* (1997) actively engages the controversies above through inclusion of Native American, Asian-American, Chicana, and other points of view as well as entries on queer theory (by and about lesbians, gays, and bisexuals), literature of the developing world, and children's literature. Such perspectives, omitted or underemphasized in the mainstream theory and criticism, are considered indispensable in feminist inquiry. The absence of an entry on religion indicates some feminists' continued aversion to traditional religious institutions, which are seen as forms of patriarchal control. Entries on spirituality, mysticism, and the goddess, however, recognize the meaningfulness of these spheres in women's lives when constituted by females out of their own experience. Narrative theory's valorizing of "stories" and storytelling empowers women to tell their own stories, to appreciate and to use noncanonical genres such as letters and diaries, certain forms of biography and autobiography, and the fantastic.

The understanding of women's relation to religion is enriched by those theories, such as deconstruction and structuralism, that challenge tradition and authority, postulate the indeterminacy and undecidability of phe-

Author Doris Lessing has written novels of spiritual quest that offer women an alternative to male-patterned narratives (UPI/Corbis-Bettmann).

nomena previously regarded as fixed, loosen boundaries between the "inside" of a text and its "outside" context and identity, and then reverse or undermine hierarchies and oppositions that seek to determine the status of texts and to set the limits of interpretation.

Reader-response criticism can move women to develop their own productive strategies of reading. It fosters critical self-consciousness because it treats reading as a process of dynamic exchange between reader and text where meaning is not inherent but rather generated through each reader's active engagement with the text.

Women's investigations have been furthered by one standpoint common to various theories: theorizing is always politicized. In the words of Norwegian Toril Moi, textual politics are sexual politics. Thus, feminist approaches in literature and aesthetics foreground the female body and critically examine rape and specifically such female processes as menstruation, childbirth, and lactation (see Suleiman, 1986). In this and other areas, psychological and particularly psychoanalytic theory have had powerful though often negative impacts.

Feminist theory identifies language as a central force in the empowerment or alienation of women, asserting that all language is gender inflected with a bias in favor of maleness. Believing that to name is to gain power over, some feminists have sought creation of a new vocabulary, words such as Ms., thealogy, gynesis, gynocritics, womyn. Further, translation assumes critical importance as a feminist activity. The selections in *An Anthology of Sacred Texts by and about Women* (1993), for example, owe their existence to the capacity of transla-

tors to make accessible women's spiritual stories from diverse cultures.

As feminist revisionism of the great mass of literary theory and criticism moves the undertaking toward much needed interdisciplinarity and internationalism, it can foster the development of new forms, replace the privileging of rationality with an inclusive respect for the female, the subjective, and the sacred, and bring other needed reforms.

BIBLIOGRAPHY

Abrams, M. H. *A Glossary of Literary Terms.* 6th ed. Can serve as an initiation into the history and terminology of literary theory and criticism. 1993.

Bal, Mieke. *Lethal Love: Feminist Literary Readings of Biblical Love Stories.* Translation, by the author, of *Femmes imaginaires.* 1987.

Christ, Carol P. "Feminist Studies in Religion and Literature: A Methodological Reflection." *Journal of the American Academy of Religion* 44 (1976): 317–325.

Gates, Henry Louis, Jr. *Black Literature and Literary Theory.* 1984.

———. "Canon-Formation, Literary History, and the Afro-American Tradition: From the Seen to the Told." In *Afro-American Literary Study in the 1990s.* Edited by Houston A. Baker, Jr. and Patricia Redmond. 1989.

Groden, Michael, and Martin Kreiswirth, eds. *The Johns Hopkins Guide to Literary Theory and Criticism.* 1994.

Hull, Gloria T., Patricia Bell Scott, and Barbara Smith. *All the Women Are White, All the Blacks Are Men, but Some of Us Are Brave.* 1982.

Kowaleski-Wallace, Elizabeth, ed. *Encyclopedia of Feminist Literary Theory.* 1997.

Lauter, Estella. *Women as Mythmakers: Poetry and Visual Art by Twentieth-Century Women.* 1984.

Lauter, Estella, and Carol Schreier Rupprecht, eds. *Feminist Archetypal Theory: Interdisciplinary Re-Visions of Jungian Thought.* 1985. Counters the acknowledged tendency of Jungian thought to be ahistorical and essentialist while preserving Jung's respect for the "feminine" and the "holy" and the potential to enhance women's understanding of their own creative capacities in literature, art, myth, and religion.

O'Flaherty, Wendy Doniger. *Dreams, Illusion and Other Realities.* 1984. An articulation, from a female-inclusive and religion-oriented perspective, of Eastern and Western differences in thought with consequent effects on the translation and cross-cultural transport of theory and criticism.

Rigsby, Roberta K. "Archetypal Criticism." *Encyclopedia of Feminist Literary Theory.* Edited by Elizabeth Kowaleski-Wallace. 1997.

Rupprecht, Carol Schreier. "Enlightening Shadows: Between Feminism and Archetypalism, Literature and Analysis." In *C. G. Jung and the Humanities: Toward a Hermeneutics of Culture.* Edited by Karin Barnaby and Pellegrino D'Acierno. 1990.

Smith, Barbara. *Toward a Black Feminist Criticism.* 1980.

Suleiman, Susan Rubin, ed. *The Female Body in Western Culture: Contemporary Perspectives.* 1986.

Young, Serinity, ed. *An Anthology of Sacred Texts by and about Women.* 1993.

Yue, Daiyun. "Standing at a Theoretical Crossroads: Western Literary Theories in China." *China Exchange News* 21, nos. 3 and 4 (1993): 9–12. A compact historical survey, focusing on the twentieth century, of China's interaction with Western literary theory and criticism.

CAROL SCHREIER RUPPRECHT

Literature

In the East

The production of literature by women can be appreciated only against the background of women's literacy and education. Asian cultures value learning, but religious and social strictures against the formal education of women—particularly for the purpose of public life—have encouraged women to carve out private domains of literary expression. Women's literature frequently makes use of the genres of poetry, fiction, and the diary, which are well suited for private expressions, and it often makes use of vernacular or regional tongues.

Ban Zhao (d. 116), a female historian of Han Dynasty China, authored the *Nu Jie* (Commandments for women), an exhortatory work on female virtues that prefigured literature by and for women for centuries to come. Ban Zhao is an exceptional figure, however, not only for her education but for her public visibility as an official court historian. Unsurprisingly, her literary work is a public document that conforms to didactic Confucian aims. Most literate women of traditional China found an outlet for their talents in poetry. Poetic composition is a long-standing social practice in East Asia that functioned as both private and public expression. It was a means of romantic courtship, but also a staple of polite company, where spontaneous versification marked both private and public (usually court-related) occasions. The Chinese classic novel of the eighteenth century, *The Story of the Stone* (variant title, *Dream of the Red Chamber*) realistically depicts aristocratic life through the female members of the Jia family, who compose poetry as a gay yet skilled form of entertainment at social gatherings.

Private literary expression by Asian women is often religiously inspired and also takes up the poetic form. The *Therīgāthā* (Songs of the elders) of the earliest Indian Buddhist nuns recount the personal tragedies or events that occasioned these women to leave home for the religious life. The poetess saints of Hinduism and Sufism, such as Mirabai, Mahādēviyakka, and Rabi'a, express an intense and personal devotion to God in their regional dialects. The religious sentiments offered by these female voices do not differ substantially from male religious voices. What is significant, however, is that the religious life gave these women the medium to participate in a literary domain that was subject to preservation.

A distinct tradition of female literature can be identified in Japan and Korea, where the impact of Buddhism encouraged use of the vernacular, often for the purpose of disseminating Buddhist texts. As recipients of Chinese culture, Korea and Japan (and Vietnam) adopted Chinese writing early in their respective histories. Chinese became the lingua franca of male scholar-officials who served in government, the structures of which were also adapted from Chinese models. The invention of native phonetic scripts—Japanese *kana* (ninth century) and Korean *han'gul* (fifteenth century)—offered easy-to-learn modes of literacy, but they nevertheless bowed to the higher prestige of Chinese learning. These scripts were therefore relegated to women, who were restricted from Chinese literacy and the pursuit of public official life.

It is an irony of East Asian history that the "female letters," traditionally confined to private, unpublished production and consumption, attracts far greater interest today than its male counterpart. In Japan, the height of this female literary tradition appears between the eighth and twelfth centuries, in the Heian era. The women's court literature of this period produced Lacy Murasaki's novel *Tale of Genji*, Sei Shōnagon's diary *The Pillow Book*, as well as numerous poems collected in the *Manyōshū*, the oldest anthology of Japanese poetry. In addition to the amount of female output, what attracts scholars to these works is their "feminine sensibility." This sensibility is comprised in part by subject matter—often the affairs of the heart—and more substantially by the aesthetic tone, which set the mood for Japanese literature for centuries to come. While Japanese men of court struggled to express public sentiments in a foreign language, with Chinese images and tropes that were not of their own experience, "feminine literature" bent the native tongue to keen reflection upon day-to-day affairs. The woman alone, waiting in vain for her lover; the passage of time and fragility of beauty as expressed through nature imagery; the mundane yet profound glimpses of court life—these variant situations were observed with a refined sensitivity that embodied the Buddhist ideal of acceptance of all affairs as equally illusory and equally deep. The strength of this feminine sensibility is evident in the fact that men at times took on a female literary persona in order to reflect upon private affairs. Ki no Tsurayuki, the author of the *Tosa Diary*, written in 936, writes in a female genre and in a female voice to express his grief at the death of his daughter during a sea journey.

As in Japan, the Korean literary tradition is bifurcated. The Korean *han'gul* script postdates the Japanese syllabary by six centuries. Until the fifteenth century, then, the literary tradition was monopolized by high-born men educated in *hanmun*, or Sino-Korean characters. The promulgation of the Korean script, however, created a writing system capable of expressing both the sounds and sentiments of the native tongue. *Han'gul* was resisted by the learned men who monopolized scholarship and government service but was readily adopted by upper- and middle-class women, earning the script the designation of "female letters."

Two of the most significant works of court literature in Chosŏn dynasty Korea are the *Kyech'uk ilgi* (Diary of the Year of the Black Ox [1613]), written by an unnamed court lady in service to Queen Inmok; and *Hanjung nok* (Records made in distress), the autobiographical memoirs of Lady Hong, of the late eighteenth century. In contrast to the court literature of Japan examined above, these works do not focus on the refined settings and sentiments of court life but rather on the anguished sufferings brought about by palace intrigue. *Kyech'uk ilgi* documents the difficult fate suffered by Queen Inmok at the hands of her stepson, the crown prince Kwanghaegun, including the murder of her son, Prince Yongch'ang, and her long imprisonment. *Hanjung nok* recounts the life of Lady Hong and culminates with the dramatic death in 1762 of her husband, the crown prince of Sado, who was put to death by his father, King Yongjo, by being buried alive in a rice chest. Although both works focus on significant events in the annals of court history, they are told from the female perspectives of mother and wife. They voice the laments of women caught up in external forces and embody the Korean concept of *han,* a sentiment born of distilled bitterness and sorrow.

An illustration of the ghost of Lady Yugao, from chapter 4 of *The Tale of Genji*, woodblock print by Buemon Akiyama Tsukioka Yoshitoshi, 1886 (Asian Art & Archaeology, Inc./Corbis)

Although there is only a handful of published poems by the patrician women of the Chosŏn dynasty, tens of thousands of unpublished *kasa*—a poetic form that originated from song lyrics in the fifteenth century—have come to light during this century. These poems have been dubbed *kyubang kasa*, or "inner room kasa," after the name of the women's quarters in the traditional Korean home. A primary category of composition is songs of admonition by mothers to daughters departing the natal home for marriage. These poems draw formulaically upon Confucian didactic texts, one of the most influential being Queen Mother Sohye's *Naehun* (Admonitory words to women), published in 1475. Although the model for these poems goes back to China's Ban Zhao, the use of idiomatic language allows for the expression of personal concerns. These *kasa*, copied by hand onto paper scrolls, were a bride's prized possession, to be augmented by her own compositions and passed on to her daughter.

The most interesting category of *kyubang kasa* are the *chat'an ka,* or songs of complaint. These songs tell of the personal sufferings caused by social customs. Married women were severely restricted in movement, confined to their husbands' family compound, and restricted from visiting their own family. Women had little say in the choice of their husbands and were also obligated to self-immolation or lifelong chastity and isolation in the event of the husband's death. These songs embody the direct, anguished voice of the woman, comprising a body of literature unique for its intensity in the larger field of Korean classical literature.

Whether the sentiment is the intense bitterness of *han,* or the serene observations derived from a Buddhist aesthetic, the usage of the vernacular (encouraged by Buddhist practice) enabled women's literature in East Asia. This literature, with its "feminine sensibility," has driven the larger literary tradition and given an alternative voice to men. In China the ascendancy of the vernacular and the rise of the novel in the sixteenth century created another genre of private literature. Although its authors are male, its literary voice is female. The nineteenth-century Vietnamese novel *Tale of Kieu* exemplifies the tradition of men and, indeed, of entire nations, taking on a female literary persona. The novel's female protagonist, with her endless tribulations, is embraced today as a gendered symbol of Vietnam's political rape and betrayal at the hands of masculine foreign aggressors. Such narratives have been extended by filmmakers such as Japan's Mizoguchi Kenji and Communist China's Zhang Yimou, who continue the focus on female subjectivity, sublimating real women's sufferings into a personal subjectivity that speaks for entire cultures.

BIBLIOGRAPHY

Cao Xueqin. *Story of the Stone.* Translated by David Hawkes and John Minford. 5 vols. 1977.

Davids, C. A. F. Rhys, trans. *Poems of Early Buddhist Nuns* (Therīgāthā). 1989.

Haboush, JaHyun Kim. *The Memoirs of Lady Hyegyong: The Autobiographical Writings of a Crown Princess of Eighteenth Century Korea.* 1996.

Hawley, Jack S., and Mark Jurgensmeyer. *Songs of the Saints of India.* 1988.

Keene, Donald. "Feminine Sensibility in the Heian Era." In *Appreciations of Japanese Culture.* Tokyo, 1993.

Kim, Kichung. "Kyubang Kasa: The Unpublished Poetry of Chosŏn Dynasty Women." *Korean Culture* 14, no. 1 (1993): 22–31.

———. "Palace Literature: Women Writers of the Chosŏn Dynasty." *Korean Culture* 12, no. 2 (1991): 22–33.

Mair, Victor. "Buddhism and the Rise of the Written Vernacular in East Asia: The Making of National Languages." *Journal of Asian Studies* 53, no. 3 (1994).

Murasaki Shikibu. *Tale of Genji.* Translated by Edward Seidensticker. 1987.

Nguyen Du. *The Tale of Kieu.* Translated by Huynh Sanh Thong. 1983.

Ramanujan, A. K., trans. *Speaking of Śiva.* 1973.

Sung, Marina H. "The Chinese *Lieh-nu* Tradition." In *Women in China.* Edited by Richard W. Guisso and Stanley Johannesen. 1981.

Swann, Nancy Lee. *Pan Chao: Foremost Woman Scholar of China.* 1932.

Waley, Arthur, trans. *The Pillow Book of Sei Shōnagon.* 1960.

See also **Mahādēviyakka**; **Mirabai**; **Rabi'a**.

FRANCISCA CHO

In the West

The imaginative literature written by secular women during the medieval and modern periods in the West, although not overtly religious in the orthodox Christian sense, addresses problems of justice, the inner spiritual life, and ways of achieving an authentic spiritual experience. The creation of a paradise, the quest myth, myths of transformation and resurrection, and metaphors drawn from the world of nature appear in novels and poetry by women. Women outside the mainstream circles of culture in the West—black North American women, for example—are attracted to both the myth of the social quest as integration into a community and to the myth of the spiritual quest as integration with the self, two themes identified by Carol P. Christ in her study of religion and literature, *Diving Deep and Surfacing* (1986). The religious or sacred dimension in the works of contemporary black women writers is based more or less loosely on Christian theology but also on other traditions such as the Yoruba traditions of West Africa.

THE MIDDLE AGES AND RENAISSANCE

The meeting of pre-Christian mythologies and Christian theology has often created a tension of contradictory effects for women seeking alternate ways to achieve authentic religious experience. The genre of the Celtic *lai*, with its journey to the Otherworld where transformation occurs, is the favorite form of Marie de France, the earliest known European woman writer, who wrote between 1155 and 1215. Her total contribution consists of twelve *lais*, 103 fables, and *L'Espurgatoire Seint Patriz* (St. Patrick's purgatory), her most religious piece. The *lais* and the fables are Marie's

The author Toni Morrison, winner of the 1993 Nobel Prize in Literature, weaves both African and Christian religious imagery into her work (Gamma-Liaison, Inc.).

retelling of stories she defines as Celtic and of Latin animal stories set in the context of twelfth-century life. Marie gives herself a spiritual task: to seek authenticity through writing. "Whoever wishes defense from vice must study and understand and begin a difficult work. Through that effort one may distance and deliver oneself from great pain" (*Lais*, Prologue, pp. 23–27). The general amorality of the *lai* suggests that Marie looks for morality of love different from that of the church. In several of the fables (which follow the conventional Aesopian form of moralizing at the end), Marie changes the male god into a female, implying a higher female spiritual power.

The creation of a paradise for women is Christine de Pizan's (c. 1364–c. 1430) chief concern. Educated by her father and married at an early age, she found herself fatherless and husbandless at the age of twenty-five. Then, she writes in *Le Livre de la Mutacion de Fortune*, Fortune made her a man when she began to earn her living as a writer, composing twenty-three

works altogether. This psychological change in perception complicates her feminism as she seeks female sources of inspiration. Religion colors her work in her use of the Trinitarian doctrine of Christianity, for example, in the title of *Le Livre des trois vertus* (1405, The Book of the Three Virtues, sometimes called The Treasury of the City of Ladies). Her *Le Livre de la cit'aae des dames* (1405, The Book of the City of Ladies) portrays a fortressed female paradise as a refuge for women from misogynist male teachings, which female saints enter led by the Virgin Mary. In the book three goddesses appear to the narrator—Raison (Reason), Droitture (Rectitude), and Justicia (Justice)—and command her to build the city. They are modeled on the three angels who appear to Abraham to tell him his wife, Sarah, would bear a son. The goddesses here seem to provide an alternative to the three forms of the Christian godhead. Religion acts with the power of myth as Christine creates her imaginary city, challenging Augustine's vision in *The City of God*.

Women writers who describe a spiritual journey or write about religious subjects and who are not confined to convents or monasteries are rare in the following centuries. They are aristocrats, well educated, and pursue the vocation of writing. At the same time, they are not included in male circles interested in similar pursuits of the spiritual life. Like Marie de France and Christian de Pizan, they find themselves at the margin of the intellectual life of their times, subject to criticism from the male establishment. In France, Madeleine de Roches (1520–1587) and her daughter Catherine des Roches (1542–1587) work as a team and together write a play on a biblical subject, the story of Sarah and Tobias. Catherine never married, choosing chastity instead; she defined marriage as servitude. Catherine created a myth of origin for women's writing and inspiration in the story "L'Agnodice" (The Unknown). Agnodice is a gentle young woman, beautiful, wise, and subtle, who disguises herself as a man in order to study medicine. But when she attempts to help women, they refuse her offer because she looks like a man. These women have suffered not only pains from childbirth and illness but also the ridicule of their husbands. When she uncovers her breasts and shows herself to them, they accept her help and recover their own beauty. She continues to exhort them to study, a discipline she offers as the path to inner integration. Catherine des Roches presents Agnodice as a healer not only of physical ills but also of spiritual pain (Sankovitch, 1988, pp. 43–71).

Mary Herbert, Countess of Pembroke (1561–1621), was Sir Philip Sidney's sister and enjoyed the reputation of a poet. When Sir Philip was killed, he left an unfinished manuscript of his translation into English of the first forty-three Psalms of David. Mary Herbert completed the translation of the remaining 107 in 1599, a collection praised in her day by John Donne, perhaps for the intensity of feeling her translations convey.

THE TWENTIETH CENTURY

Although the twentieth century provides quite different models of female spirituality than those of earlier ages, women's writing continues to contour their interior life. One document that might be called religious is Etty Hillesum's diary, *An Interrupted Life*, written during the years 1941–1943. In addition to entries detailing her daily life and her fears as the lives of Jews in Amsterdam were more and more curtailed, she described her growing awareness of her love for God: love letters to God are the "only love letters one ought to write" (p. 193). On 26 August 1941, Hillesum wrote in her diary: "There is a really deep well inside me. And in it dwells God. Sometimes I am there too. But more often stone and grit block the well, and God is buried beneath. Then He must be dug out again" (p. 36). Etty Hillesum died in Auschwitz on 30 November 1943.

"Letters to God," written by Celie the narrator, begin Alice Walker's novel *The Color Purple* (1982); they propose direct access to the divine through means other than orthodox Christianity. Celie, a victim of childhood rape, does not attend any church. Her letters illustrate the continuing need for recording spiritual growth either through the diary or letter.

The literary traditions of black American women writers provide ample evidence of rich interior lives of women alienated from the world around them yet striving to become moral agents and to find interior freedom when the exterior world denies them freedom to make choices compatible with their desire. Black American women writers who, whether religiously observant or not, seek ways of creating a spiritual life for their women characters, find the genre of the novel most convenient. Individual freedom, no matter how determined, remains the primary value. In this literature religious experiences are of the folk variety, grounded in remembrances of the Yoruba rituals of West Africa, with Christian symbols of the resurrection playing an important part in the transformation of personalities. In Zora Neale Hurston's *Jonah's Gourd Vine* (1934), a mother on her deathbed advises her nine-year-old daughter, "Don't you love nobody better'n you do yo'-self. Do, you'll be killed 'thout being struck uh blow'" (p. 130). The self-love advocated here is the essence of survival and a pointer on the way to achieving individ-

ual authenticity in the spiritual quest. To ignore such self-preservation is death.

Delores S. Williams argues that Margaret Walker's *Jubilee* (1966) is a novel of transformations wrought by slavery. The characters Hetta and Vyry represent negative personal transformation; yet Vyry experiences a positive transformation by the end of the work, although she endures cruel treatment from the slave master's wife. Tribulations and wrongful mistreatment act as the fiery furnace through which female characters pass into the new, transformed self, resilient and powerful. Celie in *The Color Purple* is another such example. Celie is aided in her transformation from acquiescent female into independent woman by another woman, Shug Avery, the liberated singer described as a queen honey bee. Shug tells Celie, "God ain't a he or a she, but a It. . . . God is inside you and inside everybody else. . . . God is everything." Similarly, Ntozake Shange, in *for colored girls who have considered suicide / when the rainbow is enuf* (1977), the Lady in Red reveals that she has found god in herself and loves her, fiercely. Such a definition owes something to the idea that "the kingdom of God is within you," and so may be classified as a Christian one.

In many novels, transformation is aided by a mentor or "wise woman," the reworking of the "conjure woman" as spiritual guide. This figure, famous from Charles Waddell Chestnutt's stories in *The Conjure Woman* (1899), is refigured as a positive mentor, as a source of power, for women's spiritual journeys. Toni Cade Bambara's *The Salt Eaters* (1980) depicts female solidarity that aids transformation when Minnie Ransome assists Velma Henry to emerge from the cocoon of depression into which she has retreated. Minnie herself is helped by her spirit guide, Karen Wilder. Here the butterfly is the main symbol as Velma takes the first steps toward health. Minnie is a practitioner of herbal medicine, in direct opposition to the medicine practiced at the local clinic, and Bambara compares her to the spider, a popular metaphor in black American writing. (Ananse, the Yoruba spider god, crossed the Atlantic with the slaves from Africa's west coast, and he figures as an agent of transformation in the novels of Gail Jones [*Corregidora*, 1975] and Toni Morrison [*Sula*, 1974].) Gloria Naylor's *Mama Day* (1988) centers on the family relations of a powerful conjure-woman.

The serpent represents both madness and transformation (because it sheds its skin) in Walker's *Meridian* (1976), Eva Jones's *Eva's Man* (1976), and *The Salt Eaters*. The snake metaphors represent the hidden work of the soul's renewal as the women characters move toward self-healing. Meridian experiences ecstasy in the great Serpent Mound in Ohio, entering the serpent and emerging with new insights. Her release from the confines of depression is likened to the raising of Lazarus from the dead. In *Eva's Man,* Eva sees herself as the Medusa who petrifies men's penises.

Paule Marshall has addressed the theme of illness as the agent of transformation from one spiritual state to another in two novels, *The Chosen Place, The Timeless People* (1969) and *Praisesong for the Widow* (1984). In the former novel, Merle's illness is the cleansing and transforming agent that moves her from victim to moral agent. The latter novel is structured on the ritual of cleansing and transformation based on the presence of Legba, the Yoruba god of crossroads. The novel is also a reinterpretation of the quest myth, as Avatara Johnson, whose name, based on the word *avatar,* means "manifestation of a released soul" or "reincarnation." It also appears as "Avey," the shortened form, throughout the work.

Another revision of the quest myth is Octavia Butler's *Patternmaster* (1976), which, Thelma J. Shinn suggests, is a reworking of the grail quest. Butler's *Survivor* (1978) follows the pattern of rebirth and transformation aided by the "wise woman" or the "conjure woman," who also plays an important part in Butler's other novels, *Kindred* (1979) and *Wild Seed* (1980). Generally viewed as a witch in mainstream writing, this figure is revealed as a spiritual mentor in Circe from Toni Morrison's *Song of Solomon* (1977); and in Ntozake Shange's *Sassafras, Cypress and Indigo* (1982), where Sassafras undergoes Yoruba rituals that promise a vision of the god. The poet Audre Lorde marries two mythologies when she claims the West African thunder god, Shango, as her inspiration even as she insists that as warrior woman she has sprung from the dragon's teeth of Greek myth.

Fragmentation by the social community leads to estrangement and withdrawal into a more private sphere where growth toward wholeness can occur. Avey's transformation in *Praisesong for the Widow* takes place on the island of Carriacou, an island not found on any map but existing just off Grenada. Similarly, Walker's Meridian and Bambara's Velma withdraw from the civil rights movement for a period of hibernation through illness, and Morrison's Sula withdraws from the community when it does not accept her. During this period of isolation, the women find themselves. Sula tells her friend Nell, "I got me," as she lies ill in her room (*Sula,* p. 143). The heroes of these novels begin the spiritual journey in solitude, aided by instinctual forces represented by insects and serpents; in this they come full circle to the solitude of medieval women mystics and secular women writers.

Women writers, from the twelfth to the twentieth centuries, rewrite pagan as well as Christian myths to suit the exigencies of their existence. In all these examples, the spiritual life thrives, most often outside the particular confines of orthodox Christianity. Tilde A. Sankovich (1988) points out that women mythmakers of every time "take patriarchal myths and stories apart, as one would a confining, unbecoming, ill-fitting garment, and reassemble them so that the new myths fit *their* particular specifications and individual forms" (p. 154). Writing becomes a spiritual tool in the work of achieving an authentic self.

BIBLIOGRAPHY

Bambara, Toni Cade. *The Salt Eaters.* 1980.

Blumenfeld-Kosinski, Renate. "Christine de Pizan and Classical Mythology." In *The City of Scholars: New Approaches to Christine de Pizan.* Edited by Margarete Zimmerman and Dina de Rentiis. 1994.

———. "'Femme de Corps et Femme par Sens': Christine de Pizan's Saintly Women." *The Romantic Review* 87 (1996): 157–175.

Butler, Octavia. *Kindred.* 1979.

———. *Mind of My Mind.* 1977.

———. *Patternmaster.* 1976.

———. *Survivor.* 1978.

———. *Wild Seed.* 1980.

Chestnutt, Charles Waddell. *The Conjure Woman.* 1899.

Christ, Carol P. *Diving Deep and Surfacing: Women Writers on Spiritual Quest.* 2d ed. 1986.

Christian, Barbara. "Ritualistic Process and the Structure of Paule Marshall's *Praisesong for the Widow.*" *Callaloo* 6 (1983): 74–84.

Coleman, James. "The Quest for Wholeness in Toni Morrison's *Tar Baby.*" *Black American Literature Forum* 20 (1986): 63–73.

de Pizan, Christine. *The Book of the City of Ladies.* Translated by Earl Jeffrey Richards. Foreword by Marina Warner. 1982.

———. *The Letter of Othea to Hector.* Translated with introductory notes and interpretative essay by Jane Chance. 1990.

———. *Le livre de la mutacion de Fortune.* Edited by Suzanne Solente. 4 vols. 1959–1966.

———. *The Treasure of the City of Ladies, or The Book of the Three Virtues.* Translated with introduction by Sarah Lawson. 1985.

de Weever, Jacqueline. *Mythmaking and Metaphor in Black Women's Fiction.* 1991.

Hillesum, Etty. *An Interrupted Life: The Diaries of Etty Hillesum, 1941–1943.* Introduction by J. G. Gaarlandt. Translated by Arno Pomerans. 1983.

Huot, Sylvia. "Seduction and Sublimation: Christine de Pizan, Jean de Meun, and Dante." *Romance Notes* 25 (1985): 361–373.

Hurston, Zora Neale. *Jonah's Gourd Vine.* 1934. Reprint, 1990.

Jones, Gayl. *Corregidora.* 1975.

———. *Eva's Man.* 1976.

Lourde, Audre. *Chosen Poems: Old and New.* 1982.

Marie de France. *Fables.* Edited and translated by Harriet Speigel. 1987.

———. *Lais.* Translated with introduction and notes by Robert Hanning and Joan Ferrante. 1978.

Marshall, Paule. *The Chosen Place, the Timeless People.* 1969.

———. *Praisesong for the Widow.* 1984.

McDowell, Deborah E. "The Self in Bloom: Alice Walker's *Meridian.*" *CLA Journal* 24, no. 3 (1981): 262–275.

Morrison, Toni. *Song of Solomon.* 1977.

———. *Sula.* 1974.

Naylor, Gloria. *Mama Day.* 1988.

Quilligan, Maureen. *The Allegory of Female Authority: Christine de Pizan's* Cité des Dames. 1991.

Royster, Philip M. "A Priest and a Witch Against Scorpions and Snakes: Scapegoating in Toni Morrison's *Sula.*" *Umoja* 2 (1978): 149–168.

Sankovitch, Tilde A. *French Women Writers and the Book: Myths of Access and Desire.* 1988.

Shange, Ntozake. *for colored girls who have considered suicide / when the rainbow is enuf.* 1977.

———. *Sassafrass, Cypress and Indigo.* 1982.

Shinn, Thelma J. "The Wise Witches: Black Women Mentors in the Fiction of Octavia E. Butler." In *Conjuring: Black Women, Fiction, and Literary Tradition.* Edited by Marjorie Pryse and Hortense J. Spillers. 1985.

Sidney, Philip. *The Psalms of Sir Philip Sidney and the Countess of Pembroke.* Edited with introduction by John C. A. Rathmell. 1963.

Walker, Alice. *The Color Purple.* 1982.

———. *Meridian.* 1976.

Walker, Margaret. *Jubilee.* 1966.

Weisenfeld, Judith, and Richard Newman, eds. *This Far by Faith: Readings in African-American Women's Religious Biography.* 1996.

Willard, Charity Cannon. *Christine de Pizan: Her Life and Works, a Biography.* 1984.

Williams, Delores S. "Black Women's Literature and the Task of Feminist Theology. In *Immaculate and Powerful: The Female in Sacred Image and Social Reality.* Edited by Clarissa W. Atkinson, Constance H. Buchanan, and Margaret R. Miles. 1985.

See also Images of Women: Literary Images of Human and Divine Women

JACQUELINE DE WEEVER

Liturgy

The term *liturgy* derives from the Greek words for "people" and "work"; frequently mistranslated as "the work of the people," it originally referred to a public work on behalf of the people—an act of noblesse oblige, a civic service. By around the first century B.C.E., the term had come to be applied, in early Greek versions of the Hebrew scriptures, to the services of the Temple in Jerusalem, where priests performed sacrifices and other ceremonies for the sake of the entire Jewish community. Eventually, with the ascendency of Christianity, the term was associated with the Eucharist (Mass), the chief service of public worship, and is still used this way in both the Eastern Orthodox and Roman Catholic traditions.

Since the mid-nineteenth century, the word *liturgy* has also been applied to the study of religious ritual, a field variously called liturgy, liturgics, or liturgiology. Interest in the systematic investigation of the development and practices of liturgy led, during the middle of the twentieth century and particularly in Roman Catholicism and Anglicanism, to a widespread renewal of interest in worship called the Liturgical Movement. Characterized by extensive research into early sources and a searching reexamination of the principles underlying corporate worship, the movement focused on restoring the laity to an active role in religious observances. In consequence, Vatican II (1962–1965) authorized a sweeping revision of Roman Catholic liturgical practice, Anglican churches developed a new Book of Common Prayer, and Lutherans, Presbyterians, and other Protestants also produced revised manuals of worship. Today, the study of liturgy is understood to encompass such diverse factors as the analysis of ancient texts, liturgical history, theology, performance theory, popular religiosity, and social scientific approaches.

Every religion has liturgy. Even those traditions that consider themselves to be nonritualistic incorporate ritual elements: Buddhists meditate, Baptist services follow an order of worship, Pentecostals receive the gifts of the Spirit according to fairly well defined patterns. Indeed, any repeated, symbolic, meaningful activity, public or private, related to communion with the transcendent can be liturgy. A Muslim praying toward Mecca five times daily, a Native American sweat lodge ceremony, a Santeria drumming are all liturgy as surely as is the Catholic Mass. Like all ritual, liturgy is about relationships, whether between the transcendent and the worshiper or among a group of worshipers. The critical element in distinguishing liturgy from other ritual is a concern with ultimacy and the relations which that implies.

Like all ritual, liturgy is constructive of social categories, not the least of which is gender. Rituals, because they are dependent on powerful symbols that can create as well as reflect reality, are not merely models or paradigms; rather, they are among the constitutive elements of reality itself, and help to construct how it is experienced and expressed. Communities of believers use liturgy in various ways, one of the most important of which is to define reality in accordance with their own values. Thus, in the West, the liturgical structures and practices of hegemonic Roman Catholicism throughout the Middle Ages contributed to an acceptance of the scriptural mandate and theological necessity of male predominance and female weakness—that is, to the spiritual and intellectual foundations of Western patriarchy. Today's familiar gender ascriptions—for example, that women must be either virgins, wives, or harlots, or that men are rational thinkers while women are earthy and sexual—are rooted in and justified by the liturgical praxis of the past.

One result of that development has been resistance to the full incorporation of women in religious ceremonies, particularly as worship leaders. In many tribal religions, religious leadership is vested in a shaman, an individual whose spiritual credentials are established by the ability to personally journey into the spirit world in what appears outwardly as a trance state, and to return with a boon—healing, prophecy, ritual instructions to ensure good fortune. In most such cultures, shamans can be either women or men. In organized and proselytizing religions, however, the leadership model is the priest, an official representative of the institution, whose authority is delegated rather than personal. The priest is meant to image the ideal of religious society—a role seldom deemed fitting for women until recently.

In the twentieth century, an increasing number of Protestant Christian churches, as well as some branches of Judaism, have struggled with the issue of women's leadership and, with no little controversy, have allowed women into the ranks of priests, ministers, and rabbis. The Vatican, however, remains firmly opposed to such a move (as have the Eastern Orthodox churches), and has pronounced male-only ordination an infallible doctrine.

Another issue that has put liturgy at the center of concerns about women and religion has been the use of exclusive male language to describe both the worshiping community and the deity. Dialogue is continually advancing on removing gender-specific pronouns from religious ritual. While the furor over inclusive language for describing people has largely abated, discussion of the gender of God and appropriate references to God in the liturgy remain unresolved.

Such issues have driven many women out of established religious organizations and into cooperative worshiping communities in which they are actively engaged in creative ritualizing, devising their own liturgical patterns and principles. Whether these groups remain connected with traditional Christianity or Judaism, branch out ecumenically, adopt devotion to a female deity, or practice witchcraft, many are intentionally feminist in their principles, values, and methods, and feminist liturgy has become an active subfield of study in itself. Numerous feminist liturgists, including Marjorie Procter-Smith, Starhawk, Theresa Berger, and Dianne Neu, have begun to map out the genre of feminist liturgy, identifying its characteristic features—particular ritual images, activities, and presuppositions that typically occur in rituals developed by women. Among these are the predominance of horizontal over vertical imagery, the use of circular and spiral patterns in symbolism and movement, the incorporation of natural and domestic objects and activities, an appreciation of the body (including women's sexuality and reproductive capacity), an emphasis on community and shared leadership, and the central use of personal narrative. While none of these features is found in all women's worship, and no community seems to incorporate every one, they are characteristic of women's worship wherever it may arise. Specifically feminist liturgy may also include an intentionally political facet.

While feminist liturgy is perhaps the most visible manifestation of what women do when they worship together, women predominate in a variety of lesser-known religions in such places as Burma (spirit worship), Muslim countries (*zar* cults), Okinawa (shamanism), Thailand (matrifocal kinship religion), and the United States (American Spiritualism). These religions, too, often exhibit the common liturgical features found in women's ritualizing.

The development of ritual communities specifically by and for women, whether they are supported by or stand in judgment against the prevailing culture, appears to be a growing phenomenon. Nonetheless, the majority of religious women continue to worship comfortably in established religions with familiar liturgical structures. It remains to be seen if the development by women of new forms of liturgy will influence, supplant, or succumb to these majority practices.

BIBLIOGRAPHY

Caron, Charlotte. *To Make and Make Again: Feminist Ritual Thealogy.* 1993. In this useful synthetic work, Caron sketches an outline of emerging feminist liturgy.

Falk, Nancy Auer, and Rita M. Gross, eds. *Unspoken Worlds: Women's Religious Lives.* 1989. One of the earliest works on women and religion geared to both a general and an academic audience, this book provides a series of essays on the religious experience of women in a variety of cultures, returning repeatedly to the theme of the importance of liturgical activity in their lives.

Neu, Dianne L., and Mary E. Hunt. *Women-Church Sourcebook.* 1993. Pp. 14–16. This booklet, published by the Women's Association for Theology, Ethics, and Ritual, is a guidebook for groups of women wishing to put together their own liturgies.

Northup, Lesley A. *Ritualizing Women: Patterns and Practices.* 1997. This comprehensive overview of the emerging subfield of women's ritualizing discusses common patterns in women's liturgies, key themes and topics in the field, and the political implications of women's worship.

Northup, Lesley A., ed. *Women and Religious Ritual.* 1993. Northup presents a collection of essays on liturgical issues affecting women, from considerations of current rituals in established traditions to feminist alternatives.

Procter-Smith, Marjorie. *In Her Own Rite: Constructing Feminist Liturgical Tradition.* 1990. This is an earlier book on the development of feminist Christian liturgy from the leading writer in the field.

———. *Praying with Our Eyes Open: Engendering Feminist Liturgical Prayer.* 1995. In her most recent work, Procter-Smith explores the political and theoretical aspects of feminist liturgy.

Procter-Smith, Marjorie, and Janet R. Walton. *Women at Worship: Interpretations of North American Diversity.* 1993. A fine collection of essays on women's ritualizing, this book covers a broad spectrum of liturgical situations.

Ruether, Rosemary Radford. *Women-Church: Theology and Practice.* 1985. Ruether's groundbreaking book set in motion Women-Church, a growing movement—primarily among Roman Catholic women, but including others—that established independent groups of worshiping women. It provides not only the rationale for separate women's liturgies, but offers suggestions on how to devise them.

Walker, Barbara. *Women's Rituals.* 1990. Walker provides a popular collection of liturgical activities for women.

Wessinger, Catherine, ed. *Women's Leadership in Marginal Religions: Explorations Outside the Mainstream.* 1993. Wessinger's book contains useful and fascinating discussions of numerous religions led by women.

See also **Language; Ordination: An Overview; Prayer; Ritual; Women's Religions; Worship.**

LESLEY A. NORTHUP

Love

In the world's religious traditions, love is commonly identified as an attribute of the divine, or as having a divine origin. In the West, God is described above all as a loving God. The Psalms of the Hebrew Bible recall again and again God's loving kindness. In the Christian canon, according to 1 John (4:17) "God is love; he who dwells in love is dwelling in God and God in him." Sura 5:59 of the Qur'an likewise rejoices in the love that Allah shares with humankind. The young French nun Thérèse of Lisieux (1873–1897) was convinced that God alone was the source of all love: "If I am to love You as You love me, I must borrow Your love" (*The Autobiography of St. Thérèse of Lisieux: The Story of a Soul,* 1957, p. 147).

In the polytheistic traditions, specific gods and goddesses are associated with love: The Yoruba goddess Osun, found also in the New World tradition of Santeria, is a goddess of love. Manifest as the river, her rhythmic dance recalls the beauty of sensual love. Indians celebrate the goddess Rādhā especially because of her ecstatic passion for the god Krishna. Her longing for reunion with the god of love is the subject of the *Gîtâ Govinda,* a devotional poem written in Sanskrit by the poet Jayadeva (twelfth century). In Chinese popular religion, Kuan Yin has come to represent the compassion that overcomes all suffering. The Semitic goddess Ishtar—perhaps the most powerful deity of the ancient Near East until the establishment of Islam—was associated with both erotic love and compassion. Other goddesses of the ancient world came to be identified with Ishtar as goddesses of erotic and compassionate love: notably, the Greek Aphrodite, the Egyptian Isis, and the Roman Venus.

Worship with acts of love is fundamental in all religious traditions. In devotion, the human being experiences the divine within the framework of intimacy and personal relationship. The human creature often imagines the creator as a loving parent. For example, figurines found in homes and graves of prehistoric Mesopotamia depict a mother goddess who is half human and half snake; she holds an infant at her breast. An ancient Egyptian image shows the goddess Isis as a sycamore tree suckling Thutmose III as a young boy. In China, Wu-sheng Lao-mu (Eternal Mother) is both creator and savior. Full of a mother's love, she sends help to her troubled offspring through inspired leaders and revealed books. Even a male god may evoke maternal imagery: The Vīraśaiva poet Basava (c. 1150) envisioned Lord Siva as a loving mother:

> As a mother runs
> close behind her child
> with his hand on a cobra
> or a fire,
> the lord of the meeting rivers
> stays with me
> every step of the way
> and looks after me.
>
> (Ramanujan, trans. p. 71)

Erotic love between the divine and the human is another common theme. In the shamanic traditions of Siberia, the shaman often has a celestial wife or husband, who serves as teacher and guide. Spirit marriages between humans and "saints" are common in American Vodou. Karen McCarthy Brown, author of *Mama Lola: A Vodou Priestess in Brooklyn* (1991) joins in marriage with the warrior spirit Papa Ogou. As a result, she spends one night a week in his company alone.

Sacred marriage (involving at least one divine partner) has a long and complex history in the West. In ancient Mesopotamia the king sometimes participated in a ritual marriage with the Queen of Heaven in order to legitimate his rule. Hosea interprets the covenant between Yahweh and Israel as a marriage covenant, emphasizing the unfaithfulness of Israel and the constancy of a forgiving God. This symbolism appears in Christianity as the marriage between Christ and Ecclesia (the church). The sacred marriage also provides a symbolic framework for mystical experience: In the visions of the medieval mystic Mechtild of Hackborn, God beckons to her as a bridegroom to his bride; "Come, my love, and receive all that the beloved can give to His beloved. . . . Come, My bride, and enjoy My Godhead" (*Liber Specialis Gratiae*, 1.2.1).

When the god or goddess appears to devotees as a human child, this manifestation evokes feelings of love and tenderness. In Egypt a special temple called a *mamessi*, or "birthing house," was dedicated to the divine child. In Idfu, beside the main temple to Horus,

An image of love in Hindu tradition is the god Krishna, depicted as dancing the Dance of Life with his lover Rādhā and her companions (Williams College Museum of Art).

there was a *mamessi* dedicated to Horus as a child. Images of the child-god dancing on a lotus flower decorated the columns of the temple. During the Hellenistic era, Mithra was worshiped as a child of new light emerging from a meteorite. For Christians, the birth of the infant Jesus is a rich theme for celebration and devotion, and Buddhists tell of the miracles surrounding the birth of Shakyamuni, the historical Buddha, who walked and talked within minutes of his birth. As each foot touched the earth, a lotus flower sprang up marking his path.

In addition to knowing their gods as loving gods, people throughout time have believed that they are commanded to love one another. It is not enough to love God alone, as, for example, in the teachings of Leviticus (19:18b): "You shall [also] love your neighbor as yourself." In the writings of Confucius, which have supported the ethical system of China for thousands of years, the most important virtue is empathy, or *jen*. The ideogram for this term comprises the character for *person* and the character for *two*. As a form of love, *jen* cannot exist in isolation but always involves identifying oneself with the other while maintaining a sense of what is just.

Another word commonly used for love in Asian cultures is *karuṇā* (Sanskrit, "compassion"). In Hinduism, the intuition that the divine lives and moves in all creatures is the basis for treating self and others with loving compassion. Ahimsa, the discipline of avoiding acts that cause harm or injury, is a practical outcome of this belief. In Buddhism, it is awareness of universal suffering that evokes this most important of all human qualities. Sutra 129 of the *Dhammapada* records the Buddha as saying, "Since we know that all beings tremble before danger and all fear death, how can we not feel and act out of compassion."

BIBLIOGRAPHY

Aronson, Harvey B. *Love and Sympathy in Theravada Buddhism.* 1980.

Flacelière, Robert. *Love in Ancient Greece.* Translated by James Cleugh. 1962.

McGinn, Bernard. "Love, Knowledge, and Mystical Union in Western Christianity: Twelfth to Sixteenth Centuries." *Church History* 56 (March 1987): 7–24.

Nygren, Anders. *Agape and Eros: The Christian Idea of Love.* 1982.

Palmer, Martin, and Jay Ramsey with Kwok Man-Ho. *Kuan Yin: Myths and Prophecies of the Chinese Goddess of Compassion.* 1995.

Ramanujan, A. K., trans. *Speaking of Siva.* 1973.

Rao, K. L. Seshagiri, and Henry O. Thompson, eds. *The Love of God in the World's Religions.* 1994.

Rougemont, Denis de. *Love in the Western World.* Rev. ed., 1956.

Yao, Xinzhong. "Jen, Love, and Universality: Three Arguments Concerning Jen in Confucianism." *Asian Philosophy* 5 (October 1995): 181–195.

See also **Aphrodite (Venus); Compassion; Desire; Divine Child; Ishtar and Anat; Isis; Kuan Yin (Kannon); Sacred Marriage.**

BEVERLY MOON

Lying and Dissimulation

Lying is contextual; a lie functions across the religious spectrum from taboo to sacred imperative. Lying includes intentional falsehood; dissimulation and fooling; silence; shape-shifting and disguise; sacred stories; and the creative aspect of language that brings the nonexistent to the tongue and therefore to life. Liar's error may

be teller's truth: cultures tell themselves into existence with a skein of make-believe and authenticating action.

Why are women so often the mythic deceivers? It is not that lies are the exclusive linguistic property of women, but that dissembling is given a feminine cast. Why, in many cultures, is deceptive language gendered feminine? Specious lore is called old wives' tales; in Chinese, the ideograph for gossip is written by doubling the character for woman. Why, in traditional tales, do deceitful women spin themselves into both ruin and success?

In the Hebrew Scriptures, history and meaning turn on great feminine deceptions. Women who betray the Israelites (Delilah or Potiphar's wife), or who work for the Israelites (Rahab or the Hebrew midwives in Egypt), do their political and divine work by lying. The covenant itself is perpetuated by stories of feminine deceit coiled with uncertain fertility (Rachel or Tamar), suggesting that disguise can be necessary to reveal truth and bring it into being by way of promised sons. Sarah lies about laughing, yet gives birth to Isaac, the covenantal child, whose name means laughter. Perhaps for a woman to speak in the ancient world (for object to act as subject), she must lie; that is, she must speak against patriarchs, perhaps against God, and therefore against truth.

The biblical model of feminine deception devolves to a medieval stereotype of mere women and their runaway tongues. Chaucer's Wife of Bath perversely brags, "Deceite, weping, spinning God hath yive / To wommen kindely" (lying, weeping, and weaving are natural to women); spinning and crying are metaphorically associated with feminine guile. The Wife of Bath refers to Aesop's fable of the lion who saw a painting of a man killing a lion. The lion told a man that if lions painted, the story would be different. The Wife of Bath, who does not lie, paints an alternative view within the misogynist one. She tells on herself (by implication, on all women) and tells on lies—that truth has to do with perspective: "By God! if wommen hadde writen stories . . . They wolde han writen of men more wikkednesse / Than al the mark of Adam may redresse."

Folk tales and jokes exploit the metaphorical correlation between the feminine and guile. A medieval jest tells of a palmer (pilgrim) who challenges a pardoner, an apothecary, and a peddler to tell the greatest lie. The palmer then says that in all his travels he has never seen an impatient woman. The other three immediately concede the contest.

Lacking authoritative voice in a patriarchal context, women may find silences to be the foundational deceptions by which they live. Culture critics investigate a vast range of feminine silences: the psychoanalytic (as with Freud speaking for the young woman he called Dora); racial or sexual (as in the poet Maya Angelou's five years of silence after she was raped); legal (as revealed by attorney Patricia J. Williams's study of rhetoric and race and gender in culture; written (as noted by Helene Cixous, French feminist theorist, who said that women have been kept in the dark even about themselves and have interpreted their own desire to write as madness); and biological (the genitals and estrus of human females are hidden; thus their sexuality and fertility are metaphorically implicated in silence and deception). In every dimension of culture, women have been silenced.

In sacred and traditional literature, feminine characters are often not what they seem. Asian stories abound with fox women appearing as beautiful mortals to doom ill-fated men. Pandora, according to Hesiod, is a woman-shaped snare sent from the gods to humans. Melusina, in a long European tradition, slips back into her serpentine form, leaving behind her children and mournful husband. A jealous Haida husband spies on his wife copulating with a whale, dresses up like his wife, tricks the whale, and feeds his wife the whale's penis. The woman, who is a whale herself, leaps into the water becoming a reef. That shaky reef is called Woman. A Korean shaman's successful trance and healing powers depend on her masquerade, her understanding that "the gods want to play." In the Japanese cosmogony, Amaterasu, the sun goddess, makes excuses for her chaotic, furious brother, by telling little polite lies. He behaves so shockingly Amaterasu strikes herself in the genitals with her weaving shuttle and dies, withdrawing her light into a cave. The innumerable gods gather for the crisis, hanging a mirror and beads on a tree and setting up a drum. One of the goddesses dances before them, pulling up her garment, causing all of the gods to laugh. Amaterasu, curious, demands to know what is going on. The gods lie to her, saying they have replaced her with someone even more beautiful. She rolls toward her own brilliant reflection in the mirror and is recaptured. With a cosmic lie, all life is saved.

Lying is a linguistic continuum that ranges from the destructive to the creative, from the comic to the cruel, from the loathsome to the sublime. A traditional story that blurs the edges between truth and lying tells of a man who sought truth. After a long time the man climbed a tall mountain, where in a deep cave he found Truth. She had only one tooth left in her ancient mouth, and her bones nearly poked through her old parchment skin. The man stayed with her for a year and a day until he knew everything Truth could tell. Before he left, he

asked her, When the people back home ask me about Truth, what shall I tell them about you? Tell them, she whispered, that I am young and beautiful.

Language itself is metaphorical: it is, in a sense, based on lies. Any report of the real includes the unreal; and though the world relies on the word, even the plainest language is partial, positioned, and shaped, therefore unable to achieve truth if the physical world is its only measure. Feminist critiques of objectivity (e.g., philosophers of science Sandra Harding and Evelyn Fox Keller) consider the ways in which a gendered culture invents the world we inhabit. Our ways of knowing are selective and constructive—we make up the world we inhabit, even a world that claims to know an easy distinction between truth and lie.

If lying and dissimulation are gendered feminine, then the cosmogonic power of language itself is as untrustworthy and seductive as a woman. As Emily Dickinson advised, "Tell all the truth but tell it slant."

BIBLIOGRAPHY

Bok, Sissela. *Lying: Moral Choice in Public and Private Life.* 1978. Bok insists that fiction and lying are separate, although she cites the confusion between fiction and deception back to Plato. Beginning with the premise of a truth as well as the ethical obligation to that truth, she claims, "Lying requires a reason, while truth-telling does not" (p. 22).

Dinesen, Isak. *Last Tales.* 1955. A now classic tale, "The Blank Page" weaves lies and silence, blood and its absence. Contemporary novels also investigate the multiplicity of truths and generative qualities of lying. See Ann Patchett, *The Patron Saint of Liars* (1992) and Kirsten Bakis, *Lives of the Monster Dogs* (1997). Film portrays the deceitful woman in classics from screwball comedy to film noir; popular films of the 1990s play with disguise, self-deception, or the notion that lies conquer all. See *Princess Caraboo*, directed by Michael Austin (1994); *Secrets & Lies*, directed by Mike Leigh (1996); and *While You Were Sleeping*, directed by Jon Turteltaub (1995).

Harding, Sandra, and Merrill B. Hintikka, eds. *Discovering Reality: Feminist Perspectives on Epistemology, Metaphysics, Methodology and Philosophy of Science.* 1983.

Kendall, Laurel. *The Life and Hard Times of a Korean Shaman: Of Tales and the Telling of Tales.* 1988. Kendall has also produced a video of a ritual *kut.* In her analysis, the anthropologist reflects her own ambiguous participation in the events she is observing.

Rich, Adrienne. *On Lies, Secrets, and Silence: Selected Prose, 1966–1978.* 1979. In her 1975 aphoristic essay,

"Women and Honor: Some Notes on Lying," she says that in the breaking of the silences imposed on women, women will "extend the possibilities of truth between us. The possibility of life between us."

Yolen, Jane, ed. *Favorite Folktales from around the World.* 1986. In her introduction Yolen relates a version of "The Old Lady in the Cave" to describe the significance of story as permissible lies.

See also **Amaterasu; Language; Speech; Truth.**

LYNDA SEXSON

Machig Labdron

Machig Labdron (c. 1055–c. 1149) was one of many extraordinary female meditators active in Tibet during the eleventh and twelfth centuries, a key period for the establishment of Buddhism there. But unlike other meditators, whose names are now known only from lineage lists or brief biographical notes, Machig (The One Mother) is widely remembered by virtue of a plethora of legends, paintings, statues, rituals, and, especially, several long versions of her biography. Traditionally said to be the only Tibetan whose Buddhist teachings were transmitted to India (instead of vice versa), one can add from a feminist perspective that she is the only historical Tibetan woman who has achieved prominence as the initiator of a major meditative practice.

Attracting the notice of her elders for her precocity at reading texts, she received Buddhist training but boldly took up with an Indian yogin, with whom she bore several children. Enduring criticism for her nonmonastic, tantric life-style, she later parted ways with her mate and occasionally also left her children so as to continue her Buddhist studies. After she took up residence on Mt. Zangri Karmar, her children were among her principal disciples. Machig's most significant contribution to Tibetan Buddhism is her "Cutting" (*gcod*) teaching, which provides a means to experience through visualization a startlingly violent but efficacious ritual process. The meditator goes to a cemetery or haunted place, visualizes her body as being chopped up, boiled, and then offered to the summoned ghouls and demons, thereby "cutting" off all attachment to the ego and its possessions, but meanwhile enabling a moment of transcendence and unification with the *ḍākinī* Vajravarāhī. Although the sources maintain that Machig learned this technique from her Indian master Phadampa Sangye, there is no independent evidence of the existence of Cutting in India, nor in the materials specifically connected with Phadampa and his "Pacifying" (*zhi-byed*) tradition. It is likely that Cutting was largely codified by Machig herself. The success of Cutting is seen in its great popularity among practitioners of all Tibetan religious schools today. Machig herself continues to serve as one of the few female figures who are said to reincarnate as living female teachers.

BIBLIOGRAPHY

Edou, Jérôme. *Machig Labdrön and the Foundations of Chöd.* 1996

Gyatso, Janet. "The Development of the gCod Tradition." In *Soundings in Tibetan Civilization.* Edited by Barbara Nimri Aziz and Matthew Kapstein. Delhi, 1985.

Roerich, George, trans. *The Blue Annals.* 2d ed. Delhi, 1976.

JANET GYATSO

Maenads

Maenads, from the Greek *mainomai,* meaning to rave or become insane, were female worshipers of the Greek god Dionysos (also called Bacchus). According to Euripides' *Bacchae* (405 B.C.E.), the first maenads engaged in ecstatic rites under compulsion, as punishment for the failure of Dionysos' maternal (human) relatives to believe that his father was Zeus. Temporarily possessed by Dionysos, women abandoned their homes and nursing infants, donned animal skins and leafy crowns, fled

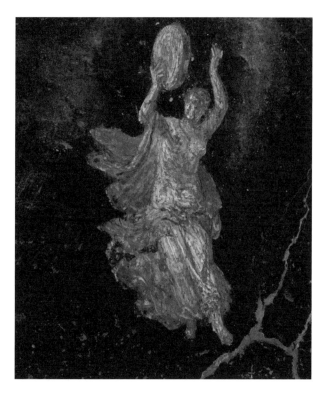

A fresco painting from Pompeii of a dancing Maenad
(Mimmo Jodice/Corbis)

dancing to the mountains, consumed honey, wine, and milk welling up from the ground, and with their bare hands rent apart wild animals and consumed them.

It remains uncertain whether the *Bacchae* reflects what devotees did in Euripides' own time, or whether the play formed the basis for subsequent rituals. By the third century B.C.E. inscriptions testify to maenadic associations in western Asia Minor, including private rites of women's initiation. Hellenistic authors describe maenadic rites in various Greek cities, and the Roman historian Livy provides a hostile narration of the importation of Bacchanalian practices to Rome in the early second century B.C.E. The membership and practices of maenadic associations probably differed from place to place and over time. Some ancient writers suggest that only married women could perform certain rites, but other evidence points to the participation of unmarried women of various social statuses.

Numerous explanations have been proposed for the functions of ecstatic maenadic practices and their attractions for women. Following the work of anthropologist I. M. Lewis on trance possession cults, Dionysian rites may be understood as affording women a strategy of indirect aggression against their constricted roles in society. Compelled by the god to abandon, temporarily, their

homes, babies, and household obligations—that is to say, their gendered identities—women could attain limited but sufficient redress in a supportive ritual community of other women. Lewis has suggested that men acquiesce to possession rites partly out of shared beliefs about the existence and power of possessing deities, and partly out of tacit recognition of underlying gender inequities. Such dynamics may have accounted for male tolerance of women's participation in ancient Dionysian practices.

BIBLIOGRAPHY

Kraemer, Ross S. "Ecstasy and Possession: Women of Ancient Greece and the Cult of Dionysus." In *Unspoken Worlds: Women's Religious Lives.* Edited by Nancy Auer Falk and Rita M. Gross. 1989.

———. "Women's Devotion to Dionysos." In her *Her Share of the Blessings: Women's Religions Among Pagans, Jews and Christians in the Greco-Roman World.* 1992.

Kraemer, Ross S., ed. *Maenads, Martyrs, Matrons, Monastics: A Sourcebook of Women's Religions in the Greco-Roman World.* 1988.

Lewis, I. M. *Ecstatic Religion: An Anthropological Study of Spirit Possession and Shamanism.* 1971. Reprint, with a new introduction, 1989.

See also **Possession Cults**.

ROSS S. KRAEMER

Magic

The word *magic* comes from the Latin *magie* and the Greek *magikē*, both of which derive from the Persian word *magi*, meaning priest. This etymology introduces an almost universal idea about magic, that it is something foreign or at least marginal—an idea most often represented by geography (that is, magic performed by a foreigner, e.g. Medea, or someone living at the margins of society, e.g. Circe), or by gender (magic as something done by women or through the agency of goddesses such as Diana, Hecate, Māyā, or Durgā). The religions of the world present vivid portrayals of male magicians such as Zoroaster, Moses, Solomon, Jesus, and so on; but their activities are described in relationship to the "true" god and characterized as theurgy, philosophically grounded magic as practiced by Neoplatonists such as Plotinus and Porphyry. Equally famous female practitioners are described in more sinister terms, usually in the context of undoing men, such as Lilith and Adam, the Queen of Sheba and Solomon, Morgan Le Fay and Merlin.

This positioning of women with magic parallels their exclusion from the most sacred aspects of male-dominated religions. A South Asian folktale brings out some of these issues. The male hero, Gopi Chand, goes to Bengal, one of the Indian equivalents of Greek Thessaly, the land of witches and magic, where he successfully battles a band of female magicians (*jādūgāriyāṃ*) through his superior yogic, that is male, religious powers (Gold, 1991). The association of women with magic is so pervasive that in some societies, such as Nepal, male magicians dress and wear their hair like women (Allen, 1992). Yet Asian tantric traditions positively incorporate the connections between women and magic in the figure of the *ḍākinī* or *shakti*, who confers magical powers (*siddhi*), though mostly on male practitioners (Sanford, 1991). Most essentially, magic is about power, and whether it is spiritual or secular power, it is illegitimate for women to have it, unless like the *ḍākinī*s they use it to serve men. The rhetoric on women and magic concerns the male fear of powerful women and ancient ideologies about the inherent malevolence of women's nature.

From its very beginnings, the academic study of religion has been compromised in its attempts to distinguish religion from magic by an older Christianized scholarship that located religion among Christians and a few other high cultures, whereas magic was practiced among "primitives" and other outsiders. In other words, "we" have religion while "they" have magic; magic is what the "other" does. Two leading examples are the demonization of classical paganism and of the religious practices of colonized subjects. In point of fact, there is no objective way to distinguish magic from religion that will hold up in a variety of cultural settings (Lighstone, 1985). Except for the intent, little difference can be perceived between sticking pins in a "voodoo doll" in order to harm an enemy and honoring a statue of a saint or god. Is the faithful Hindu who presents the goddess with a new sari and parades her around town performing magic or maintaining a benevolent relationship with the deity? In Santeria such distinctions are particularly fluid because the *orisha* (spirits) represent both African deities and Christian saints who can perform good or ill. Upon scrutiny, ideas about religious versus magical language do not hold up either: uses of the imperative such as "deliver us from evil" and "grant us this day our daily bread" seem appropriate to Western ears, while examples from so-called magical texts seem rude, if not delusional: "Spirits I command thee!" The point is that magic and religion are essentially the same thing.

Simcha Fishbane (1993) brings out some interesting Talmudic aspects of the relationship of women and

Female practitioners of magic have been characterized in sinister terms usually in the context of undoing men, such as the Queen of Sheba depicted meeting Solomon in this fresco by Piero Della Francesca, painted 1452–1466 (David Lees/© Corbis).

magic that are also true in non-Jewish contexts, such as women slipping magical potions into food; the belief in sororities of sorceresses or witches, as well as an intriguing argument for its historical reality in the Greco-Roman world; and the association of magic particularly with old women. This last notion needs to be balanced with images of younger, sexually intoxicating women such as Circe and Morgan Le Fay, who charm men, exercise their glamour on them, and weave spells that entrap them. In other words, women use sexual magic in their love struggles with faithless men, especially through love potions, hence male fears about food as something women control and men internalize and the characterizations of women as poisoners. Such ideas are widespread in the literary texts of the ancient world, in which practical magic is presented almost exclusively as the province of women. In contrast, scientific and philosophical texts present men as doing theurgy, theoretical magic. Yet the archaeological evidence of tablets that contain spells and texts reveal practical magic to have been predominantly for and by men, especially sexual magic (Betz, 1992). This is not to deny that women utilize such practices—they do, especially in societies where they experience high rates of dependency on male favor combined with low rates of control over men (Golomb, 1993)—but to highlight male misrepresentations of men's own activities.

In the modern West the nineteenth-century English magical Order of the Golden Dawn has had a lasting impact on the practice of magic. Women were prominent members from its inception (Greer, 1991) along with such luminaries as the poet William Butler Yeats and the scholar of religion Evelyn Underhill. Dion Fortune (1890–1946), an influential English occultist, was also briefly a member. She wrote numerous, highly regarded books on the occult and magic, including popular novels that contain fictionalized descriptions of magical practices and theory.

Another member's name, that of Aleister Crowley, is synonymous with magic, especially magical practices of the darker sort. Crowley (1875–1947) was a significant figure not only in occult circles but in the larger world as well, owing to his erratic and eccentric behavior, flashes of brilliance, and general showmanship. He remains, however, an elusive figure. His writings are purposely obscure and even dedicated followers disagree as to what should be taken seriously and what was meant ironically. Crowley left the Golden Dawn when he was unable to take control of it and began traveling with his wife, Rose. In Egypt, while Crowley was performing a ritual to the Egyptian god Thoth, Rose went into a trance and dictated *The Book of the Law*, which convinced Crowley he was the Antichrist. He then founded his own magical order and began to write extensive commentaries on the revelation that came through Rose and about magic in general. Despite the importance of Rose in his life and work, Crowley left some very damning statements about women (in his *The Book of Wisdom or Folly*) and it is his name, not hers, that is remembered.

Modern feminist magic is most popularly represented by Starhawk, who defines it as "changing consciousness at will." Throughout North America and Europe mostly middle-class women have embraced magic as a form of spirituality that affirms and empowers women (Luhrmann, 1989; Pahnke, 1995). Donate Pahnke's analysis of Starhawk's writings, as well as those of Heide Göttner-Abendroth (a leading figure in the women's spirituality movement in German-speaking countries), brings one back to the ever-illusive distinction between religion and magic. Both Starhawk and Göttner-Abendroth conflate these terms, most often in their references to ancient goddess *religions*, although they are both opposed to patriarchal religions, and in representing *magic* as a spiritual path for women. Pahnke's point is that these were and remain politically loaded terms that must be used with a fuller understanding of their complexity and entwined history.

BIBLIOGRAPHY

Adler, Margot. *Drawing Down the Moon: Witches, Druids, Goddess-Worshippers, and Other Pagans in America Today.* 1979; rev. ed., 1986.

Allen, Michael R. *The Cult of Kumari: Virgin Worship in Nepal.* 1975; 3d ed., Kathmandu, 1992. See pp. 68–69 for his discussion of male transvestite sorcerers, their ritual dances in which they become goddesses, and their rumored sacrifice of premenarcheal girls whose ashes they use for sorcery.

Apuleius. *The Golden Ass.* Translated by Robert Graves. 1954. An amusing presentation of various aspects of sexual magic by the second-century C.E. author. Interestingly, in his own life, after he married an older, wealthy woman, Apuleius was accused by her former in-laws of having won her love by magic. He was put on trial but successfully defended himself.

Betz, Hans Dieter. *The Greek Magical Papyri in Translation.* 1986. Reprint, 1992. Originally published as *Papyri Graecae Magicae* in 1928 in Germany. This is a collection of magical spells and formulas, hymns, and rituals from Greco-Roman Egypt. As the title implies, these texts were written on papyrus, mostly in Greek, which was the language of the educated no matter what their religion.

"The Biography of Lilith." Produced by Women Make Movies, New York, 1997. A fascinating film about the use of amulets to protect girls and women from the influence of Lilith, a powerful female manipulator of magic in Jewish lore from the most ancient period to the present.

Crowley, Aleister. *The Book of Wisdom or Folly.* N.d.

Euripides. *Medea.* Translated by F. L. Lucas. Oxford, 1924.

Fishbane, Simcha. " 'Most Women Engage in Sorcery': An Analysis of Sorceresses in the Babylonian Talmud." *Jewish History* 7, no. 1 (Spring 1993): 27–42.

Fortune, Dion. *The Sea Priestess.* 1938. Reprint, 1978, 1991). While accepting prevailing ideas about men being active and women passive in the ordinary world, Fortune emphasizes women's occult powers on the "astral," the realm where the magician does her or his work and where gender roles are reversed. She expresses these ideas through her heroine, Vivien Le Fay Morgan, an incarnation of Morgan Le Fay whom Fortune traces back to the legendary land of Atlantis.

Gager, John G. "A New Translation of Ancient Greek and Demotic Papyri, Sometimes Called Magical." *The Journal of Religion* 67, no. 1 (January 1987): 80–86. A thoughtful review of the Greek magical papyri texts; discusses them within the context of the religious life of the period.

Gold, Ann. "Gopi Chand." In *Gender, Genre, and Power in South Asian Expressive Traditions*. Edited by Arjun Appadurai et al. 1991.

Golomb, Louis. "The Relativity of Magical Malevolence in Urban Thailand." In *Understanding Witchcraft and Sorcery in Southeast Asia*. Edited by C. W. Watson and Roy Ellen. 1993.

Gonzalez-Wippler, Migene. *Santeria: African Magic in Latin America*. 1973. Reprint, 1981.

Greer, Mary K. "Women of the Golden Dawn." *Gnosis Magazine* no. 21 (Fall 1991): 56–63.

Homer. *The Odyssey*. Translated by Robert Fitzgerald. 1961. Book Ten tells the story of Circe.

Luhrmann, T. M. *Persuasions of the Witch's Craft: Ritual Magic in Contemporary England*. 1989.

Pahnke, Donate. "Religion and Magic in the Modern Cult of the Great Goddess." In *Religion and Gender*. Edited by Ursula King. 1995.

Sanford, James H. "The Abominable Tachikawa Skull Ritual." *Monumenta Nipponica* 46, no. 1 (Spring 1991): 1–20. Describes a Japanese Buddhist tantric rite that identifies some magical appropriations of women.

Starhawk. *Dreaming the Dark: Magic, Sex and Politics*. 1982.

GENERAL WORKS ON MAGIC

Frazer, James. *The Golden Bough* (1890–1915; single condensed vol., 1923). This is a dated but still essential source on the study of magic and religion. Frazer follows the male literary tradition of classical Greek and Roman literature in associating women with magic, though he does present some fascinating data on women from the folk tradition. Because of his reliance on dated and problematic secondary sources combined with his highly imaginative approach to the study of religion, caution is required before accepting these examples as fact.

Lighstone, Jack N. "Magicians, Holy Men and Rabbis: Patterns of the Sacred in Late Antique Judaism." In *Approaches to Ancient Judaism,* vol. 5. Edited by William Scott Green. 1985. This essay is a thoughtful discussion of how classifying terms such as *magician* and *holy man* functioned among both Jews and Christians in the Greco-Roman world, keeping the former at the boundaries of society and the latter at the center. See also Lee Siegel, *Net of Magic: Wonders and Deceptions in India* (1991), for a provocative discussion of these cross-overs in modern India (especially pp. 147–171), beginning with his own early inability to distinguish between magicians and holy men (p. 331); and Ann Gold, "Devotional Power or Dangerous Magic? The Junghi Rani's Case." In *Listen to the Heron's Words: Reimagining Gender and Kinship in North India*, edited by Gloria Goodwin Raheja and Ann Grodzins Gold. (1994), which contrasts women's devotional powers with dangerous female magic.

Ray, Reginald. "Introduction" *The History of the Sixteen Karmapas of Tibet*. By Karma Thinley, 1980. For a well-thought-out discussion of the function of magic in Buddhist tantric biographies, see pp. 9–18.

Thorndike, Lynn. *A History of Magic and Experimental Science*. 8 vols. 1923–1958. This voluminous historical study of magic in the Western world remains invaluable.

See also **Alchemy**; **Maya**; **Tantra**; **Witchcraft**.

SERINITY YOUNG

Mahādēviyakka

The sole woman among the twelfth-century Vīraśaiva saints of the Kannada country of South India, Mahādēviyakka considered herself betrothed to the god Śiva. Compelled to marry a local chieftain, her lyrics written in free verse reveal the ambiguity of her relationship with Śiva, who is sometimes her illicit lover, at other times her only legitimate husband:

> Husband inside,
> lover outside.
> I can't manage them both.
>   This world
>   and that other,
>   cannot manage them both. (Ramanujan, p. 127)

When her inner conflicts became unbearable, she left her husband, choosing the life of a homeless, unclad wanderer. She walked toward the town of Kalyana, center of the Vīraśaiva saints, where she had to prove herself in a long trial by dialogue to gain acceptance among the coterie of males. Asked by their leader, Allama, why she wandered about without clothes and yet clad herself, in false modesty, in her long tresses, she replied:

> I'd a feeling it would hurt you
> if I displayed the body's seals of love....
>   When all the world is the eye of the lord,
>   onlooking everywhere,
>   what can you cover and conceal? (Ramanujan, p. 131)

Acceptance into the company of the saints did not satisfy her for long; soon she felt the call of the holy mountain of Srisaila, where she wandered in her god-intoxicated state, finding Siva only to lose herself. It is believed that she was barely in her twenties when Siva accepted her into oneness with him. Her poems poignantly express the difficulties of being a woman in her agonized lovelorn quest for ecstatic union.

BIBLIOGRAPHY

Basavaraju, L., ed. *Akkana Vacanagalu.* Mysore, 1966.

Ramanujan, A. K., trans. *Speaking of Siva.* 1979.

VIDYA DEHEJIA

Mahāprajāpatī

Mahāpajāpatī Gotamī was the maternal aunt and foster-mother of Siddhartha Gautama, the historical Buddha (Awakened One). She was instrumental in founding the first order of Buddhist nuns (*bhikshunī-sangha*), although there is some debate that suggests Yaśodharā, the Buddha's wife, was the first nun. Narrative and hagiographical accounts of the life of Mahā-pajāpatī are given in the *Gotamī-apadāna* (Story of Go-tamī), which was composed during the second and first centuries B.C.E. and is found in the *Khuddakanikāya* (Miscellaneous Division), and the *Therīgatha* (Lives of the Nuns), which is found in the *Sutta Piṭaka* (Book of Discourses) and dates to the First Council in the fourth century B.C.E. Accounts are also recorded in the Cullavagga and Bhikṣuṇīkarmavācāna portion of the *Vinaya Piṭaka* (Book of Discipline). Other testimonial accounts are preserved in various retellings of the story.

According to these traditional accounts, Mahāpajā-patī was born in Devadaha to Sulakkhanā and a Śakyan nobleman named Añjana. She, and her older sister Māyā, married Suddhodhana, the king of Kapilavastu. Māyā gave birth to a son named Siddhartha, and then died seven days later. According to ancient Indian social custom, Mahāpajāpatī became the infant's surrogate mother—hence, mother of the Buddha.

After Suddhodhana died, Mahāpajāpatī accepted the guardianship of her son and followed the Buddha as a mendicant. According to traditional accounts, Mahā-pajāpatī asked the Buddha three times to establish an order of nuns, and each time the Buddha denied her request. Ānanda, the Buddha's disciple and personal secretary, interceded on her behalf by asking the Buddha if women could obtain the fruits of dharma (teachings of the Buddha). The Buddha answered yes unhesitatingly, at which time Ānanda requested that the Buddha found an order of nuns for Mahāpajāpatī and her delegation of five hundred Śakyan women. The Buddha agreed on the condition that the women accept eight chief rules (*gurudharma*). These rules, however, placed the nuns in a subordinate position to the monks and have been cited as the primary reason for the disappearance of the nuns' order in India. Finally, the *Gotamī-apadāna* narrates that at the end of her life, as an accomplished practitioner and teacher, Mahāpajāpatī, like the Buddha, attained *parinirvāna* (the great going out).

Mahāpajāpatī's life is significant for several reasons. She is revered as the mother of the Buddha. She was the first, and founding, Buddhist nun. Her accomplishments, such as the attainment of the six higher knowledges, *siddhis* (special powers), and so forth, as narrated in the *Gotamī-apadāna*, are paradigmatic particularly for laywomen and nuns on the Buddhist path, and offer proof of the equal capacity of women to attain the fruits of dharma. After her *parinirvāna*, she is revered by the *sangha* (Buddhist community) as a female counterpart to the Buddha. In sum, her story provides evidence of the achievements that some of the nuns realized in the patriarchal socio-religious milieu of ancient Indian society, while also raising important questions concerning the androcentrism, and possible misogyny, in early Indian Buddhism.

BIBLIOGRAPHY

Gross, Rita M. *Buddhism after Patriarchy: A Feminist History, Analysis, and Reconstruction of Buddhism.* 1993.

Horner, I. B. *Women under Primitive Buddhism.* 1930.

Lilley, Mary E., ed. *The Apadāna of the Khuddakanikāya.* Vol. 2. 1927.

Paul, Diana Y. *Women in Buddhism: Images of the Feminine in Mahāyāna Tradition.* 1979.

Rhys Davids, C. A. F., trans. *Poems of Early Buddhist Nuns.* Reprint, 1989.

Rhys Davids, C. A. F., and Hermann Oldenberg, trans. *Vinaya Texts.* 1885.

Walters, Jonathan S. "The Buddha's Mother's Story," *History of Religions* 33 (1994): 350–379.

———. Gotamī's Story. In *Buddhism in Practice.* Edited by Donald S. Lopez, Jr. 1995.

See also **Monasticism: In the East; Ordination: In Buddhism.**

ELLEN GOLDBERG

Mammy Wata

Mammy Wata is a water goddess worshiped by both men and women across central and western Africa. The goddess promises well-being, health, and wealth to her worshipers, and poverty, illness, or other misfortune to those who displease her.

Mammay Wata is often portrayed as a long-haired mermaid of fair skin, sometimes holding a mirror and accompanied by a snake. The origins of the multivalent qualities of the deity are complex. Her water goddess images may have developed originally from ships' figureheads encountered by Africans when European traders arrived on African shores in the fifteenth century. This imagery combined with the European mermaid image, and in later centuries was modified again by way of the circulation and distribution throughout sub-Saharan Africa of an image copied from a German chromolith of circa 1885 showing a female snake charmer. The name "Mammy Wata" is Pidgin English for "mammy water," or "water mother/woman," revealing its extra-African origins. Yet Mammy Wata arises from African roots, including the association of female sexuality with long hair and whiteness with purity. In Eastern Zaire the deity is called Mamba Muntu (crocodile person); there she holds the ambivalent qualities associated with crocodiles. Mammy Wata is also associated with Indian deities and other images conveyed to Africa since the early twentieth centuries on European and Indian prints.

Mammy Wata conveys power, sexuality, and independence. She is irrevocably associated with modernity. She symbolizes both the independence achieved by women who leave their home communities to work in urban areas (with the ambiguous status this conveys) as well as the unpredictability of the modern urban world and status achieved within it. Mammy Wata may be associated with a rise in fortune, particularly for men; yet, she also represents the caprice and unpredictability experienced by men in economic and political life. Both the protected white woman of colonial times and the independent urban black prostitute can be seen as prefigured in Mammy Wata: as a mermaid she is a half-woman, separated from her devotees and therefore powerfully different from them; yet she sometimes carries jewels, a watch, and a comb and may wear glasses, elements associated with the fatefully alluring and independent female of the urban areas.

Mammy Wata worship, though partaking of traditional African religious expression including divination, possession, and dreams, has many modern expressions. Worshipers may offer perfume and talcum powder along with sweet food and drink, and when possessed smoke cigarettes. Mammy Wata's high popularity was given expression in a high-life hit song of the 1960s by Victor Uwaifo (from Benin City). In Zaire she is often pictured on murals, paintings, and record covers. Mammy Wata's complex female attributes—her allure, power, and danger—express both enduring African social realities and the paradoxes and tensions of social change.

BIBLIOGRAPHY

Drewal, Henry John. "Mermaids, Mirrors, and Snake Charmers: Igbo Mami Wata Shrines." *African Arts* 21, no. 2 (1988): 38–45.

———. "Performing the Other: Mami Wata Worship in Africa." *The Drama Review* 32, no. 2 (1988): 160–185.

Fabian, Johannes. "Popular Culture in Africa: Findings and Conjectures." *Africa* 48, no. 4 (1978): 315–334.

———. *Remembering the Present: Painting and Popular History in Zaire*. 1966.

Gore, Charles. "Mami Wata: Western Africa." In *Encyclopedia of Africa South of the Sahara*. Edited by John Middleton. 1997.

Jewsiewicki, Bogumil. "Mami Wata: Zaire." In *Encyclopedia of Africa South of the Sahara*. Edited by John Middleton. 1997.

Olanlokun, Olajire. *Mammy Water and Other Stories*. 1993.

Salmons, Jill. "Mammy Wata." *African Arts* 10, no. 3 (1977): 8–15.

NANCY G. WRIGHT

Mandaean Religion

The Mandaeans (from Aramaic *manda,* knowledge) seem to have arisen in the Jordan area in the first century C.E. and soon found refuge in Iraq and Iran, where they still survive. Especially since the wars beginning in 1980, Mandaeans have emigrated individually and in groups to other countries. With their numbers at fewer than 100,000, these sole remaining ancient Gnostics subscribe to a tempered dualism in which the heavenly, preexistent Lightworld and its denizens retain a constant connection with the lower worlds of earthly, concrete life. Thus, present and future life is made possible, and the soul, captive in the human body, may achieve knowledge, *gnosis,* of its Lightworld origin and at the end of its imprisoned life ascend home.

Human beings, of both genders, are divided into three forces: soul, spirit, and body. The two upper elements are female—sisters who merge at the body's death to rise as one into the Lightworld, the body being of no further account. This arrangement, then, implies no model of holy marriage (*hieros gamos*) in which a female joins a male in salvation; instead, the salvation image is thoroughly female. Thus, the souls and spirits of both men and women rise to a Lightworld populated by lightbeings of both genders. A pervasive gender balance reigns in Mandaean symbolism, with right, light, and gold being male; and left, darkness/earth, and silver being female. Mandaeism insists on the necessity of the female, not to be overcome or abolished here on earth or in the Lightworld. Imitating its Lightworld models and abhorring asceticism, Mandaeism advocates marriage and fertility.

Even John the Baptist, the Mandaean prophet par excellence, was married. Mandaeans practice repeated baptism in running fresh water (*yardna*), for water is the form by which the Lightworld manifests itself on the earth. Complex rituals, vast mythologies, and extensive ritual-exegetical commentaries continue to sustain the religion, which has remained remarkably consistent for nearly two thousand years. Dependent on texts meticulously copied throughout the ages in its own Eastern Aramaic language, Mandaeism is hierarchical, with priests as leaders in matters religious, legal, and communal, and learned lay people, *yalufas*, as ritual helpers, teachers, and mediators situated between priests and the regular lay population. Today, there are more than twenty priests in Baghdad, at least three in Ahwaz, Iran, and two recently emigrated priests serving the Australian congregation. (The North American continent still has no priests.)

Historically, Mandaean women owned libraries, copied texts, and were priests. Theoretically, nothing prevents a Mandaean woman from becoming a priest, though none seem to have existed for the past century. The earliest copyist of one of the oldest Mandaean texts, the *Left Ginza,* was a woman, Shlama, daughter of Qidra (c. second century), and women copyists' names appear throughout history.

A few European scholars have studied Mandaeism during the past few hundred years. In this century the most prominent scholars are Mark Lidzbarski, Lady Ethel S. Drower, Kurt Rudolph, and Rudolf Macuch. Many Mandaean texts still remain to be translated, and some are unknown to the West. Mandaeans today take a keen interest in scholarly studies of their traditions.

BIBLIOGRAPHY

Mark Lidzbarski translated *Das Johannesbuch* (1915) from the Mandaean *Drasa D- Yahia* (or Book of John) and the Mandaean holy text *Ginza: Der Schatz oder das grosse Buch der Mandäer* (1925), which is separated into a right and a left part. For a full field account, see E. S. Drower, *The Mandaeans of Iraq and Iran* (1937; 2d ed., 1962). Kurt Rudolph's *Die Mandäer I: Prolegomena: Das Mandäerproblem* and *Die Mandäer II: Der Kult* (1960–1961) offer a thorough, scholarly presentation. Rudolf Macuch's theory on the origins and early history of the Mandaeans is set forth in "Anfänge der Mandäer," in *Die Arber in der alten Welt II,* edited by F. Altheim and R. Stiehl (1965).

JORUNN JACOBSEN BUCKLEY

Manfreda, Sister

For English-speaking readers, the legendary Pope Joan is more likely to be familiar than the historical Sister Manfreda of Pirovano, who was elected pope by the Lombard sect of Guglielmites and subsequently condemned to be burned at the stake by the Inquisition in 1300.

Building on the prophecies of the Calabrian visionary Joachim of Fiore (d. 1202) that a new Age of the Holy Spirit was approaching in which the church would be transformed, the Guglielmites took the novel line that this transformation would involve women replacing men as popes and cardinals in the religious hierarchy; priests could be of either sex. Their founder was one Guglielma of Bohemia, who settled in Milan circa 1271. Her followers claimed that she had the stigmata and performed miraculous cures, while an inner circle of disciples believed that she was the incarnation of the Holy Spirit.

After Guglielma's death in 1281, the Cistercian monastery of Chiaravalle outside Milan became the center of a conventional saint cult for her. Behind the usual trappings, however, heresy lurked. Guglielma's followers believed that she would return to earth at the feast of the Pentecost in 1300 to open the new age, when Sister Manfreda (or Maifreda) who had been chosen to be the first of the new line of female popes, would be enthroned at Rome.

Little is known of Sister Manfreda herself. She was a nun of the Umiliati order and a cousin of Matteo Visconti, the first Duke of Milan. While awaiting the return of Guglielma, she celebrated Mass, consecrated hosts, and wrote litanies and prayers for the use of the new church.

Members of the sect belonged to Milan's well-to-do, as evidenced by the handsome gifts made in anticipation of Manfreda's elevation: gold-embroidered silks, pearls, sacred vessels. Unfortunately for the Guglielmites, their hopes also found expression in indiscreet utterance, and the Inquisition finally took action in 1300. Sister Manfreda was consigned to the pyre that autumn; Guglielma's bones were exhumed and burned.

Most versions of the Pope Joan legend also condemn their protagonist to a public death, after the added humiliation of being unmasked by giving birth in public. Certain details vary (Joan is also known as Jutta, Glancia, and sundry other names, and different centuries are given as the setting), but the essential story line is fairly consistent. A talented woman who is disguised as a man goes from a brilliant career as a student to election as pope, only to be undone by biology.

With the exception of Mario Equicola of Alvito (d. 1525), who, according to J. N. D. Kelly, "argued that Providence has used Joan's elevation to demonstrate the equality of women with men" (p. 329), the traditional point of the story tended to be satirical of women or the church, or both. It is representative of social changes in the twentieth century that, whereas previously the idea of a female pope was freighted with negative assumptions, now it has become an attractive notion inspiring novels and even a musical; Pope Joan has been transformed from a justly punished upstart to a tragic heroine.

BIBLIOGRAPHY

"Guglielmiti." In *Enciclopedia italiana di scienza, lettere ed arti.* 1929–1938.

Helder, Ebba M. van der. *Pope Joan in Legend and Drama: A Case Study in Medieval German Drama.* 1987.

Kelly, J. N. D. *The Oxford Dictionary of Popes.* 1986.

Lambert, Malcolm. *Medieval Heresy.* 1977.

Lea, Henry C. *A History of the Inquisition of the Middle Ages.* 1887.

Wessley, Stephen E. "The Thirteenth-Century Guglielmites: Salvation Through Women." In *Medieval Woman.* Edited by Derek Baker. 1978.

CHARLOTTE W. BOYNTON

María de Santo Domingo

María de Santo Domingo (c. 1485–c. 1524), also known as the Beata de Piedrahita, was a Spanish mystic and prophetess. Details about the early life of this illiterate peasant remain sketchy. According to some sources, María began a life of charity, intense prayer, and penance as a child in her native village of Aldeaneuva, in the bishopric of Avila in central Castile.

As a teenager she began a lifelong association with the Dominican friars of the nearby town of Piedrahita, becoming a tertiary between 1502 and 1504. By 1507 María had acquired a reputation as a charismatic holy woman. Stories circulated of a young tertiary who prophesied the future, experienced trances and bodily signs, and received mystical visions and voices from God. Many, however, were scandalized by this woman who conversed with friars and presumed to speak out publicly, exhorting sinners to repent and promoting ascetic reform within the Order of Preachers.

María de Santo Domingo, upon being summoned to the royal court, greatly impressed King Ferdinand of Aragon and the head of the Catholic Church in Spain, Cardinal Cisneros. Nevertheless, the Rome-based Dominican hierarchy grew concerned about reports of bodily contortions, ecstatic pronouncements, spontaneous (some said lewd) dancing, and close (some said too close) relations with confessors. Eventually a full-fledged investigation was launched into María's lifestyle and teachings. Four trials took place between 1508 and 1510, after which a panel of Dominican judges, essentially hand-picked by Cisneros, not only exonerated the Beata of charges of fraudulent sanctity and lascivious behavior but declared that her "exemplary life and doctrine" were "very useful and to be highly recommended."

In an extraordinary instance of social mobility, María de Santo Domingo subsequently took up the position of prioress of a convent founded for her by her feudal lord and patron, the Duke of Alba, in her hometown of Aldeaneuva. The Beata apparently remained there until her death. Her extant dictated works—two letters, an unpublished set of revelations, and *The Book of Prayer,* published around 1520—provide insights into the charismatic discourse of one of the earliest of Spain's women mystics.

BIBLIOGRAPHY

Libro de la oración de Sor María de Santo Domingo, edited by Jose Manuel Blecua (Madrid, 1948) is a fascimile edition of María's own work that also includes transcriptions of the Beata's two extant letters. For an English translation, with an extensive introductory essay, see Mary E. Giles, *The Book of Prayer of Sor María of Santo Domingo: A Study and Translation* (1990).

The fullest account—although a hostile one—of the Beata's career, along with partial trial transcriptions, can be found in Vicente Beltrán de Heredia, *Historia de la Provincia de España 1450–1550* (Rome, 1939). Several studies reassess this figure and her works in light of feminist scholarship in history, literary studies, and religion: Jodi Bilinkoff, "Charisma and Controversy: The Case of María de Santo Domingo," *Archivo Dominicano* 10 (1989): 55–66, reprinted in *Spanish Women in The Golden Age: Images and Realities,* edited by Magdalena S. Sánchez and Alain Saint-Saëns (1996), pp. 23–35; Jodi Bilinkoff, "A Spanish Prophetess and Her Patrons: The Case of María de Santo Domingo," *Sixteenth Century Journal* 23 (1992): 21–34; Jodi Bilinkoff, "Establishing Authority: A Peasant Visionary and Her Audience in Early Sixteenth Century Spain," *Studia Mystica* 18, no. 3 (1997): 36–59; Mary E. Giles, "The Discourse of Ecstasy: Late Medieval Spanish Women and Their Texts," in *Gender and Text in the Later Middle Ages,* edited by Jane Chance (1996); Mary E. Giles, "Holy Theatre/Ecstatic Theatre," in *Vox Mystica: Es-*

says on Medieval Mysticism in Honor of Professor Valerie M. Lagorio, edited by Anne Clark Bartlett et al. (1995); Ronald E. Surtz, *Writing Women in Late Medieval and Early Modern Spain: The Mothers of Saint Teresa of Avila* (1995), ch. 4.

JODI BILINKOFF

Marriage and Singleness

An Overview

The ideals of marriage and singleness display a nexus of religious values orchestrated in concert with a society's most intricate arrangements of sexuality, political order, and domestic economy. Heterosexual pairing is set forth as normative in most human societies, with the languages of religion proclaiming the primordially given necessity of marriage as the link between the order of the cosmos and the order of society.

Religion offers marriage a supernatural sanction: in many societies the event of marriage is highly ritualized, with weddings performed by religious leaders, though arranged through economic and political negotiations. Religious discourse naturalizes heterosexual marriage, defining which and whose sexual practices are moral through doctrine and primordial myth. Polytheistic pantheons pair gods and goddesses in heterosexual union; abstract cosmologies posit the marriage of such gendered entities as earth and sky; the creation narratives of the Bible (Gen. 2–4) and the *Bṛhadāraṇyaka* upanishad (1.4.3–4) portray the primordial person as a singular man, from part of whose divided body a woman was created, after which they reunited in heterosexual intercourse that resulted in the procreation of humanity. Religious narratives present marriage as a primordial paradigm for humans to emulate as a religious practice, instituting social norms in terms of cosmic structures.

Marriage domesticates sexuality and biological reproduction, producing not just new human lives but persons to be socialized within the family system, persons whose family socialization trains them to perform their class and gender roles within the larger social system. Marriage produces heirs to a society's property, ideals, politics, and religion, and is often the crux for the perpetuation of asymmetrical power relations between men and women. Men exercise control of the means of the reproduction of society by implicit and explicit requirements that women be sexually, economically, and socially subordinate to them in marriage: while women bear its heirs, those children are fully accepted by society only if they were produced within its construct of acceptable union.

Although women's subordination in marriage is ubiquitous in human societies, women across cultures manage what power they have artfully. Contemporary feminist ethnographies show that women in many societies are not passive but outspoken, self-assured actors in the social life of their communities. Yet social status and the ability to exercise agency often depend upon women fulfilling the requirement of marriage and childbearing; not doing so commonly results in social and economic marginalization. Women may exercise degrees of power and resistance within patriarchal marriage, but their privilege is usually at the price of supporting the social order that systematically subordinates them to men.

Where marriage is the condition of women's access to social agency, religions can pose marriage as a woman's access to the divine: some Muslim, Hindu, and Christian traditions direct women's devotion toward the deity through or solely for the sake of her husband. According to the *Laws of Manu*, a Hindu women's deity is her husband, and marriage is her religious practice: "A virtuous wife should constantly serve her husband like a god, even if he behaves badly, freely indulges his lust, and is devoid of any good qualities" (5.154). While Paul implies that Christian marriage recreates primordial union when he says "A man shall... be joined to his wife and the two shall become one flesh" (Eph. 5:31), he also defines marriage as a hierarchical arrangement: "the head of every man is Christ, the head of a woman is her husband" (1 Cor. 11:3; c.f. Eph. 5:23); the seventeenth-century poet John Milton reflects Paul when he describes the religious structure of Adam and Eve's marriage: "Hee for God only, shee for God in him" (*Paradise Lost* II:299).

TYPES OF MARRIAGE

Common forms of marriage are monogamy, the union of one woman and one man; polygyny, where one man has multiple wives; and polyandry, where one wife has multiple husbands. The term polygamy, commonly used to mean polygyny, actually means both polygyny and polyandry.

Polygyny occurs in African, Hindu, Islamic, pre-eleventh-century Jewish (and subsequently among some North African Jewish), Native American, and some Mormon societies. Many polygynous societies use men's, and especially kings', accumulation of wives as displays of wealth and power. Solomon reportedly had seven hundred wives (1 Kgs. 11:3); Muslim Sudanese and Bedouin men make their economic stature known by the number of wives they support. Women's status in polygynous marriages depends on factors of seniority, production of sons, and favoritism of the husband. Younger co-wives are often expected to perform the bulk of household labor in service of older wives.

A Muslim Uighur man rests with his two wives and their six children in front of their house at the Buzak Commune in Xinjiang Province, China (Earl Kowall/ Corbis).

Polyandry is known to occur in Tibet, Burma, the Himalayan plateau, and some tribes of India. Nancy Levine's study of polyandry among Tibetan Nyinba of Nepal shows them practicing fraternal polyandry, where a group of brothers marries one wife, and where the eldest brother, who holds authority over wife and younger brothers, has priority of sexual relations early on in the marriage so as to father the first-born children. Some Nyinba practice polyandrous polygyny: a group of brothers, married to one woman, will jointly marry another woman, ideally, her sister.

SINGLENESS AND MONASTICISM

Many religious traditions reflect a deep ambivalence toward marriage and sexuality by sanctioning both marriage and celibacy as competing religious ideals. Paul enjoins Christians to resist marriage if they can, saying "those who marry will have worldly troubles" (1 Cor. 7:28) which distract from their religious work; he considers marriage a concession: "it is better to marry than to be aflame with passion" (1 Cor. 7:9). Although women are generally enjoined to marry, women who avoid or leave marriages in order to devote themselves more fully to religious devotion have also been enshrined as demonstrating a religious ideal, as with, for example, Rabi'ah al-'Adawiyya of eighth-century Basra, Margery Kempe in medieval England, or Mīrābāī of sixteenth-century India. In societies that support monastic institutions, virginity is often an ideal. Yet unmarried women (or formerly married, as with widows) may be seen as threatening to the social and religious order. Some religions afford women an avenue of singleness through monastic life, sometimes defining a woman's monastic vocation as marriage to the deity. Where celibate women's religious communities have shown great independence and growth, there have often been movements to suppress them—as with the Beguines in medieval Europe—or to bring them under the care of

men's authority. Women may not always have the choice of whether they marry a man or join a monastic community. Christian convents have functioned as depositories for women whose families considered them unmarriagable for reasons such as deformity (as was the case for the Italian nun Archangela Tarabotti), and women longing for monastic life have likewise been forced to marry.

SAME-SEX UNIONS

While there is compelling historical evidence of the practice of same-sex sexual activity across many cultures through millennia, evidence of same-sex marriage—where a same-sex couple's publicly established sexual, economic, and domestic union is accorded the same social and religious status as heterosexual marriage—is historically sparse. Historian John Boswell argues, by reconstructing evidence of medieval Christian ceremonies solemnizing same-sex unions, that same-sex couples' unions were accorded the status of marriage in certain parts of medieval Europe. Same-sex marriage has been the focus of intense debate in the United States. While public rituals that pronounce and celebrate same-sex relationships hold a deep appeal to many lesbians, the emulation of the institutional structures of marriage in these relationships enjoins much controversy.

BIBLIOGRAPHY

There is a rich history of scholarship on marriage, much of which expresses theoretical assumptions about gender organization that accept without question the idea that women are naturally, even biologically, driven to marry a man, depend on him economically, and bear children—that marriage is a given female need rather than a result of elaborate historical socialization. The following sources, in varying ways, engage and challenge this assumption in their analyses of marriage as a complex social practice and institution.

Boddy, Janice. *Wombs and Alien Spirits: Women, Men, and the Zār Cult in Northern Sudan.* 1989.

Boswell, John. *Same-Sex Unions in Premodern Europe.* 1994.

Brown, Peter. *The Body and Society: Men, Women, and Sexual Renunciation in Early Christianity.* 1988.

Fernea, Elizabeth W. *Guests of the Sheik: An Ethnography of an Iraqi Village.* 1965. Gives an intimate portrait of Iraqi women's lives in segregation from men.

Gillison, Gillian. *Between Culture and Fantasy: A New Guinea Highlands Mythology.* 1993. This ethnography analyzes the inter-relation of myth-telling and gender organization.

Leslie, Julia I. *The Perfect Wife: The Orthodox Hindu Woman According to the Stridharmapaddhati of Tryambakayajvan.* 1989. Within its focus on an eighteenth-century Sanskrit treatise on women's religious and marital propriety, this offers a thorough analysis of marriage and women's social and religious status according to a wide span of Brahmanical Hindu literature.

Levine, Nancy E. *The Dynamics of Polyandry: Kinship, Domesticity, and Population on the Tibetan Border.* 1988.

Murphy, Yolanda, and Robert F. Murphy. *Women of the Forest.* 1974. This is a clearly written, nonromantic ethnography of the social and marital life of Brazilian Mundurucú women.

Sullivan, Andrew, ed. *Same-Sex Marriage: Pro and Con.* 1998. These essays give voice to the panorama of positions on same-sex marriage.

KAREN LEE ANDERSON

In Microhistorical Traditions

In the microhistorical traditions nearly everyone enters into a socially approved sexual and economic union with another person at least once in a lifetime. Prior to modernization it would be rare to find a woman who did not marry, but there are numerous instances of men who, for social or religious reasons, remained single. For example, among the Huli of Papua New Guinea some men became permanent members of the *haroli* bachelor cult. In kin-based societies seeking to expand their membership, society would expect that adults play their part in bearing and raising children. Although colonialism, modernization, and urbanization have given individuals more options, it is still the case that nearly all indigenous women enter into marriage of a traditional, transitional, or modern type. Entry into marriage takes myriad forms and usually involves exchange of goods (variously called bride wealth, bride price, bride service, or marriage goods). In some groups the process of marriage is not considered to be complete until a child is born. Then, too, many societies require that affinal payments be made at the birth of the child to compensate the side of the family that forgoes adding the child to its membership. Thus, in a patrilineal society the mother's family would receive gifts from the father's family.

Many of the microhistorical traditions permit polygyny, but polyandry is restricted to a few groups in Tibet and Nepal, southern India and Sri Lanka, and northern Nigeria and northern Cameroon. Less common is the pattern of group marriage reported in the nineteenth century of the Nayar, a caste group in southern India whose men were hired soldiers. The Nayar did not enter into permanent marriages but, after a ritual marriage in which the "groom" placed a gold ornament around the neck of the "bride," the woman joined a large household where she was visited by many "husbands." Her children were provided for by her blood relatives. In traditional small-scale and kin-based societies, single women include those waiting to enter into marriage, those whose husbands have died, and those who have divorced (or been divorced by) their husbands. As Diane Bell's work on the religious life of Warlpiri and Kaititja women in central Australia has shown, mature women not attached to men may bear a particular responsibility for women's rituals, through which ties to land and kin are renewed and transformed, and for providing a place of refuge and female sociality for married women seeking respite from spouses and male-dominated contexts.

In the worldviews of indigenous traditions the sexual relationship of woman and man is often seen as homologous with that of land and gardener or land and hunter. A sense of the fruitfulness of male-female conjunctions informs ritual and myth. Moreover, social and economic exchanges may be conceived of as "marriages," and the partners, whether male or female, may be referred to as "mother" and "father." Hence marriage, with its reciprocal rights and obligations, is not only a social institution but also a metaphor for conceptualizing life-giving relationships. No society leaves sexuality to nature; all have rules and most have religious sanctions for the breach of rules. For example, it is common that sexual relations be prohibited before activities such as hunting, fishing, fighting, planting, brewing, and iron smelting. The understanding is that energy and potency should not be expended in sex when they are required elsewhere. Similarly, taboos may apply during menstruation, pregnancy, and mourning.

The microhistorical traditions vary in their attitudes toward homosexuality. The Siwan of North Africa and the Kaluli of Papua New Guinea expect all males to engage in homosexual activities for a period of their lives, while traditionally the Cheyenne of the Great Plains allowed married men to take on berdaches (male transvestites) as second wives. Prior to the establishment of British rule in Sudan, temporary homosexual marriages occurred among the Azande, with warriors who could not afford wives taking on "boy wives." Some theorists suggest that homosexuality, as a permanent status, is more acceptable in societies that, because of resource limitations, wish to limit population. Female-female marriages are reported to have occurred in a number of African societies but it is thought that they did not involve sexual relationships. Rather, they were a socially approved way for a woman to assume what were usually male roles such as those of trader, political leader, or religious officiant.

Even in matrilineal societies men usually occupy the positions of political and religious leadership, but some

A Mendi woman is dressed in a headdress of leaves and shells for a bridewealth ceremony, Mount Hagen, Papua New Guinea, 1994 (Chris Rainier/Corbis).

sharing of responsibilities may occur. For example, among the Haudenosaunee (People of the Longhouse, also known as the Iroquois or Six Nations) the clan mothers appointed and could remove the chiefs, all of whom were men. The Onondaga still observe this system today, whereas other nations have adopted an elective system for appointing chiefs. Haudenosaunee women serve as members of the medicine societies, and the clan mothers have responsibility for naming the newborn. In many traditions public ritual is presided over by men, and in some cases, such as in the male cults of New Guinea in which men celebrate their relationship with ancestors and enlist their help to ensure the fecundity of the land and community, women are excluded. Nevertheless, women in the microhistorical traditions engage in many rituals for securing and restoring health and wealth, for connecting with ancestors, and for engaging with cosmic powers. Practical activities such as gardening often have a symbolic counterpart. In storytelling and song making women and men transmit their community's worldview and also seek to reimagine and reconstruct it. In some societies there are gender-based rules about who may tell which stories.

Since 1800 particularly, and for longer in some regions of the world, the microhistorical traditions have come under the domination of colonial powers and have been influenced by the missionary religions of Christianity and Islam. Christianity has required that

its converts maintain monogamous marriages. The combination of missionary religion and rapid social change has in many cases resulted in a more individualistic ethos; it has also encouraged the development of the nuclear family. Today in Africa, Oceania, and the Americas there are mature women from indigenous communities who, in assuming professional positions, have placed themselves outside traditional expectations. Sometimes it is said in their communities that they have "become men." They may or may not marry. A significant number of Catholic women in these areas have joined religious orders. Moreover, both Catholic and Protestant women have played active roles in the development of indigenous styles of Christianity. They serve as teachers, prayer leaders, evangelists, and musicians. Women of indigenous communities have been ordained in some Protestant churches, but other local churches have preserved a traditional exclusion of women from such leadership roles.

Unfortunately, most of the study of the microhistorical traditions has been done from a male point of view. Male ethnographers have been restricted in their access to women's knowledge and, until the late twentieth century, even women anthropologists have been trained to expect a society's significant myths and rituals to be under male control. Ethnographies tend to characterize women as producers and reproducers in the domestic sphere and men as transactors in the social and political sphere. However, the entry of women into the disciplines that study the microhistorical traditions has provided more direct information on women's religious lives and challenged assumptions such as that ritual is the preserve of men. With the development of feminist perspectives in anthropology and the study of religion, and with the inclusion of indigenous scholars in academic ranks, these will be new assessments of the religious worlds that, in the present state of scholarship, are referred to as "local," "indigenous," and "microhistorical."

BIBLIOGRAPHY

Bell, Diane. *Daughters of the Dreaming.* 1983.

Brown, Judith K. "Economic Organization and the Position of Women among the Iroquois." *Ethnohistory* 17 (1970): 151–167.

Brown, Paula, and Georgeda Buchbinder, eds. *Man and Woman in the New Guinea Highlands.* American Anthropological Association special publication, no. 8, 1976.

Comaroff, John, ed. *The Meaning of Marriage Payments.* 1980.

Gleason, Judith, and Elissa Tesser. "Becoming a Woman in Okrika." Follows five young women as they undergo the traditional rite of passage that is a prelude to marriage in the Okrika community of the Niger River delta. Videocassette, 27 minutes. 1990.

Herdt, Gilbert. *Sambia: Ritual and Gender in New Guinea.* 1987.

Krige, Eileen J., and John Comaroff, eds. *Essays on African Marriage in Southern Africa.* Cape Town, 1981.

Lewis, Ariane, Jon Jerstad, and Gilbert Lewis. "Garden Days." An account of women's lives in the Sepik area of Papua New Guinea, with an emphasis on gardening and ritual. Videocassette, 25 minutes. 1988.

Marksbury, Richard A., ed. *The Business of Marriage: Transformations in Oceanic Matrimony.* 1993.

O'Brien, Denise. "Female Husbands in Southern Bantu Societies." In *Sexual Stratification: A Cross-Cultural View.* Edited by Alice Schlegel. 1977.

Parkin, David, and David Nyamwaya, eds. *Transformations of African Marriage.* 1987.

Strathern, Marilyn. *The Gender of the Gift: Problems with Women and Problems with Society in Melanesia.* 1988.

MARY N. MACDONALD

In Asian Religions

The state of marriage is an ideal in Asian religious traditions, and it is expected that nearly everyone—that is, most men, but virtually all women—aspire to marriage as the most appropriate and perhaps the only life-style. Singleness is considered an aberration tolerated only under specific circumstances.

In Hindu India people of every distinction adhere to four basic goals in life: *kāma* (pleasure), *artha* (material wealth), *dharma* (appropriate behavior, religious responsibility), and *mokṣa* (liberation). The first three goals are "this-worldly," whereas the fourth is the transcendent ideal. Although India has many ascetics in active pursuit of spiritual liberation, most people live within the realm of the first three goals, and this plays out most specifically in the stage of life known as *gṛhastya*, or that of the householder. The householder is responsible for maintaining the workings of ordinary life and helping the family, and, by extension, the community, to flourish. The community is understood to include the living, the deceased ancestors, and the gods. The emphasis on performing one's worldly duties well, and even beautifully and aesthetically, falls specifically on women in their roles as householders. In Hindu India, as in much of Asia, it is married women who are considered to be responsible for general well-being in life.

Why women and why must they be married? In the Hindu worldview, all women are understood to be em-

bodiments of *shakti*, or divine, primordial life-energy. The concept of *shakti* is personified as a goddess, and by extension all women are considered to be earthly manifestations of the goddess and her primordial power. Women are therefore understood to possess the magical power of creation—the other side of this being that they carry the power to destroy. The maintenance and possible dissolution of a prosperous and harmonious household lies with the woman, just as those activities on a cosmic scale lie with the goddess. The most fearsome goddesses, such as Durgā or Chinnamastā, are understood to be able to wreak such destruction precisely because of their singleness; they are unhindered by all of the restraints that marriage entails—the restraints on time, space, and freedom of voice and activity.

Because women's roles and responsibilities are so complex in themselves and constitute an intrinsic aspect of Hindu society, there developed in India the concept of *strīdharma*, that is, appropriate behavior and responsibilities of women, which all Hindu women are expected to follow. By following *strīdharma*, a Hindu woman lives according to the paradigms established in the personas of the Hindu goddesses of auspiciousness. By directing their natural *shakti* in scripturally sanctioned ways, women are considered to carry on the auspicious responsibility of life itself. The application of *strīdharma* varies from caste to caste. In general, the higher the status of the woman, whether by caste (religious demarcation) or class (social and economic demarcation), the more stringent the rules that apply to her. The choice of mate and even the choice to divorce are similarly more rigid as the caste becomes higher.

In the latter part of the twentieth century, arranged marriages continue to be the norm. In India, for the most part it remains the dharma of Hindu parents to arrange the marriage of their children. Traditional Chinese marriages were arranged, whereas in Burma this custom has only been followed by a small minority from among the upper-class elite. There are usually specific groups from which to choose an appropriate prospective spouse. Whereas South Asian Muslims may, like Muslims elsewhere, marry their cousins, such endogamous practices are strictly interdicted in Hindu marriages. Rather, the choice must be made from within one's *gotra*, a designation of appropriate caste and clan; that is, it indicates someone close enough in family status yet far enough from bloodlines. The chosen mate must also, in most cases, come from outside of one's natal village. Upon her marriage the bride goes to live with her husband's family in his extended household. As the newcomer, the young woman (often in her teens) is immediately at a disadvantage in terms of exerting her own personality, desires, or opinions. Although out-lawed, dowry is still quite common, and the custom does much to perpetuate the notion that the young woman is something of a handicap. Etiquette, that is, *strīdharma*, dictates that the bride honor her husband's family, and foremost this entails a very specific relation-ship with her mother-in-law. Thus two women, both pivoting around the same man, are set at potential odds with each other. The bride's requisite qualities of mod-esty, humility, and self-effacement are immediately put to the test in the way in which she interacts with her mother-in-law.

In Hindu India the married woman exhibits the cre-ativity of life and its beneficent nourishment and bounty through her accoutrements: in a traditional con-text, the married woman adorns herself with brightly colored jewelry, red powder for her hair and a bright red dot on her forehead, and intricate saris.

Because there is no official status of divorce in the Hindu law books, although it is allowed constitutionally in the secular Indian government, officially a high-caste Hindu woman loses her husband only through death. The widow is feared, abhorred, and shunned as inauspiciousness incarnate. She must wear simple clothing and keep her head shaved. She is considered a burden to her family and to society. If a husband dies before his wife, it is on some level believed to be her fault for not having performed the *vratas*, or personal rituals, for the well-being of her husband and family correctly or often enough.

Indian women such as twelfth-century Mahādevī-yakka of South India and sixteenth-century Mīrābāī of Rajasthan, as well as numerous well-known female spiritual leaders of the twentieth century, have gained renown and respect as religious mendicants. Such sta-tus as a renunciant, even when elevated to recognition as a "saint," requires a particular understanding of the Asian context. Those who have made a full-time com-mitment to a religious life-style are indeed free of fam-ily and of householder status. They are not, however, single in a Western understanding of the term—that is, they are not unattached. If the traditionally married woman maintains a sacred allegiance to her husband, and by extension, to his family, the ascetic woman bears a sacred allegiance to her concept of God, and by exten-sion, to God's family, that is, to those who would come for her blessings and her teachings. These women have often described themselves as married to God; whether bound in matrimony to an earthly spouse or to God, the individual in most traditional Asian cultures operates within a vast web of allegiances.

In Confucian China, such allegiances formed the ba-sis of one's identity, which was determined by a com-

The bride at a Muslim wedding enters on horseback covered with an embroidered red shawl with money stuffed in her costume. Her face is shrouded with garlands of flowers, Delhi, India, 1994 (Zen Icknow/ Corbis).

plex structure of hierarchical relationships. Marriage customs in China have entailed a variety of systems, which have undergone different kinds of transforma-tions from the ancient, to the early imperial, and to the late imperial periods, and even more so into the mod-ern period. In addition, such customs in the premodern period varied according to status, whether of the impe-rial family, the educated elite, or ordinary people.

Despite these variations in the specifics of customs, marriage has been and continues to be an essential in-stitution, foundational to society. Entrance into the state of marriage is synonymous with achieving adult status: the state of singleness is seen as an uncomfortable, inap-propriate, and undesirable extension of childhood.

In premodern China, the Confucian ideal of filial piety entailed a patriarchal family structure that elaborately venerated previous generations through ancestor worship. A woman gained status and power primarily through her husband. Marriages among the imperial family were arranged for the purpose of powerful allegiances and dominance. Wives in certain ways participated in this power, but often the mother and sisters of the emperor wielded more influence than did the wife of the regent. Women who married into the educated elite did so through arrangements made by their fathers. Women in these positions shared more of the power with their husbands. But in so doing they were required to personify the honor of their family by demonstrating chastity and virtue.

Men often had more than one wife. Women's roles, therefore, could fall into several categories. These included wife; secondary wife, who might be a younger relative of the wife and who was legally married to the husband; concubine, whose function was similar to that of the second wife, except that she was not officially married to the husband during periods where the law prescribed monogamy; and second wife, a subsequent wife after divorce or the death of the first wife.

Traditionally, little or no choice existed in the selection of mate. After marriage, at the onset of which the woman went to live in the home of her husband, she enjoyed little personal freedom. The extreme pressures under which many women lived led to an expectation of high suicide rates among them.

The Communist Family Law of 1 May 1950 set forth new guidelines for marriage in modern China, although it essentially codified a change in attitudes that had already begun in the early part of the twentieth century. The new law sought to undo the hierarchical attitudes both between the sexes and between the generations, in which the parents decided upon their children's marriage partners. Marriage was now to be based solely on love, and the exchange of money, whether as a dowry or as bride-price, was prohibited. Even as early as 1931, the state officially withdrew its financial support of ancestor worship, which has been foundational to the Confucian-based familial hierarchy.

Although contemporary China has radically changed its political structure, and the large extended family as an idea has disappeared with the imperial families that fostered it, marriage continues as a priority in contemporary China. In certain ways, the face of the family has changed completely, as in the "one couple, one child" mandate. In addition, it has become increasingly necessary for spouses to live apart because of employment; in 1998 an estimated fifty million people were living in this situation. However, in what may seem to be a natural holdover of ancient allegiances to family, the law requires adult children to care for their aging parents. Even under such changing circumstances, however,

the single person—whether male or female—continues to be an unusual exception in Asian cultures.

BIBLIOGRAPHY

Bumiller, Elisabeth. *May You Be the Mother of a Hundred Sons: A Journey Among the Women of India.* 1990.

Chao, Paul. *Chinese Kinship.* 1983.

Croll, Elisabeth. *The Politics of Marriage in Contemporary China.* 1981.

Goode, William J. *World Revolution and Family Patterns.* 1970.

Hanchett, Suzanne. *Coloured Rice: Symbolic Structure in Hindu Family Festivals.* Delhi, 1988.

Harlan, Lindsey, and Paul B. Courtright, eds. *From the Margins of Hindu Marriage: Essays on Gender, Religion, and Culture.* 1995.

Jacobson, Doranne, and Susan S. Wadley. *Women in India: Two Perspectives.* 1992.

Leslie, Julia. *The Perfect Wife: The Orthodox Hindu Woman According to the "Stridharmapaddhati" of Tryambakayajvam.* Delhi, 1989.

Leslie, Julia, ed. *Roles and Rituals for Hindu Women.* 1991.

Mace, David, and Vera Mace. *Marriage: East and West.* 1960.

Spiro, Melford E. *Kinship and Marriage in Burma: A Cultural and Psychodynamic Analysis.* 1977.

UNESCO. Principal Regional Office for Asia and the Pacific. *Women in Asia: Beyond the Domestic Domain.* Bangkok, 1989.

Watson, Rubie S., and Patricia Buckley Ebrey. *Marriage and Inequality in Chinese Society.* 1991.

CONSTANTINA RHODES BAILLY

In Judaism, Christianity, and Islam

Marriage in Judaism, Christianity, and Islam has traditionally been based on a heterosexual contract in which a person secures sexual and reproductive rights to the body of another person. Procreation, kinship, and transfer or conservation of property have all been core issues in marriage in each of these traditions to varying degrees in different times and places.

JUDAISM

Heterosexual marriage in Judaism is the normative state for adult men and women, based on the example of Adam and Eve in Genesis. The first divine commandment after creation is to be fruitful and multiply (Gen. 1:28); later in the narrative, companionship is added to the advantages of the male-female bond (Gen. 2:18). For the Hebrew prophets, marriage is a potent metaphor for God's relationship to Israel (Hos. 2:21–22; Isa. 61:10, 62:5; Ezek. 16).

Although these prophetic texts clearly reveal a monogamous expectation for the marital state, polygyny was known and acceptable in Judaism until the eleventh century C.E., when Rabbi Gershom b. Judah banned it for Jews of the West (Ashkenazim). For Jews of the East (Sephardim), polygyny continued to be permitted except in those countries where it was prohibited by civil law, although this practice was restricted by the requirement that each wife be provided with equivalent levels of material maintenance and conjugal attention. Concubinage, the keeping of an unmarried woman by a man who acknowledges her offspring as his own, occurs in the Bible (and occurred sometimes in medieval Judaism also), but most rabbinic authorities prohibit the practice today. A married woman is forbidden to have sexual relations with anyone besides her husband.

Throughout Jewish history certain marriages have been prohibited, usually based on consanguinity and affinity (Lev. 18, 20), and endogamous marriages within the Jewish group have always been strongly preferred. Fruitfulness, from Biblical times, has been a sign of blessedness, and barrenness of shame and favor withheld by God. After ten years barren marriages may be dissolved; in earlier times a man could take a second wife.

Rabbinic Judaism frowns upon singleness and celibacy (Kid. 29b; Yeb. 63a–64a) and views sexual desire as the source of creativity and drive in human beings (Gen. Rab. 9:7).

Jewish marriage is a sacred relationship, expressed in the term *Kiddushin*, derived from the Hebrew word for "holiness." In Jewish marriage the wife is consecrated to her husband and forbidden to cohabit with anyone else (Kid. 2a–b), but he may cohabit with other women as long as they are not married. The husband acquires exclusive rights to his wife's sexuality and reproductivity, though he also incurs the obligation to satisfy her need for food, clothing, and conjugal activity. Divorce, which may be given only by the husband, is permitted but discouraged. Both parties may remarry after a divorce. Whether or not there is a formal Jewish divorce decree, a man is permitted by Jewish law to remarry and father more children, but without this decree, called a *get*, his first wife may not. Under Jewish law the children born to a woman who cohabits with another man while she is still technically married to her first husband are branded *mamzerim*. According to the Bible, *mamzerim* and their offspring for ten generations are banned from the community of Israel (Deut. 23:2); they may not marry other Jews or participate in ritual activities.

Abuses of the husband's exclusive right to grant divorce have, in modern times and among Orthodox

Bride and groom joined in marriage by a rabbi, depicted in illustrated medieval Biblical manuscript (Biblioteca Palatina, Parma Italy)

Jews, created an abused class of women called *agunot*, or "chained" women, whose husbands refuse to give them a Jewish divorce decree. In earlier times social pressure from rabbinic authority or within the tightly knit Jewish community was enough to encourage the husband to free his wife. Today, Orthodox Jewish feminists are challenging Orthodox rabbis who have been reluctant to censure men who withhold the divorce decree out of spite or in order to coerce the wife to capitulate on contested issues of property division or child custody.

CHRISTIANITY

Catholic marriage is seen as a permanent bond between members of a legally competent, baptized heterosexual couple with the primary purpose of bearing and raising children within the Catholic Church. Divorce is not permitted. In the New Testament, Paul encourages wives to be subservient to their husbands in Jesus' name (Eph. 5:22), and even in the modern period Catholic wives are seen as having their highest vocation expressed inside the home; any public activity by women should enable them to "join in stemming the tides which threaten to engulf the home," as Pope Pius XII wrote in his 1945 encyclical.

Most Protestant Christian churches allow remarriage after divorce or the death of a spouse, as do Eastern rite Catholics. However, for Roman Catholics, marriage is the seventh sacrament and the symbol on the earthly plane of the heavenly unity between Christ and the Church. The marital union is consecrated by a permanent sacrament that the bride and groom administer to and receive from each other, as they acknowledge their mutual consent to enter into the state of matrimony. For Catholics the symbolic reality of the unity of Christ and Church as expressed in the unity of husband and wife is permanent until the death of one of the marriage partners. Catholic marriage is conceived as being exclusive and permanent. Therefore, concubinage, which is considered adultery, is officially forbidden.

Not everyone is obligated to enter the marital state, according to Catholic doctrine. Anyone, male or female, is free to withhold the power of their bodies to generate offspring by refraining from marriage. But once marriage is freely chosen, then the sacramental joining of the couple signifies that they have entered into a marriage contract that consists of yielding permanent and exclusive power over their bodies to their partner with the specific view of engaging in procreative acts. Catholic theologians regard marriage as a vocation, to which the majority of human beings are called by God.

Within the Abrahamic traditions, the practice of celibacy is an almost exclusively Catholic institution. Beginning in the New Testament, virginity is presented as an earthly expression of the heavenly state (Luke 20:36, Matt. 22:30, Mark 12:25) and a powerful means of worshiping God. Celibacy in Catholic canon law is a freely undertaken renunciation of marriage in order to practice perfect chastity and dedication to God's service. Celibacy and consecrated virginity are considered even higher vocations than is the vocation of marriage (1 Cor. 7:26–35). Although married male clergy were permitted in early Catholicism in the Roman rite and are so even today in the Eastern rite at the lowest hierarchical levels, all Roman Catholic clergy today must be celibate. For women, virginity and the consecration of one's life to God transcends physical motherhood as a vocation, representing as it does a public affirmation of God's transcendence and the primacy of the Kingdom of Heaven (Matt. 19:11–12).

The Protestant Reformation abolished celibacy, terming it a human institution and not divinely decreed. In 1522, several years after his break with the Catholic Church, Martin Luther condemned celibacy and was himself married on 13 June 1525. Although John Calvin did not condemn it, in 1561 he wrote that celibacy was not to be preferred over the married state.

Christian feminists today are focusing on the mutuality of the marriage bond that has been traditional in their religion, emphasizing individual personal and sexual fulfillment more than the primarily procreative emphasis of earlier times.

ISLAM

In Islam the extended family is the central economic, social, and political unit, and marriage, with its profound impact on family relationships, is the peak experience of an individual's life cycle. Marriage in Islam is regarded as a universal obligation, the appropriate state for every mentally and physically competent person. Temporary celibacy is advocated by some in Islamic mystical traditions as a way of purifying oneself and enhancing self-control and spiritual receptivity. Permanent celibacy, however, is viewed by Muslims as a violation of the Qur'an and was rejected by the prophet Muhammad.

Marriage in Islam is a bilateral contract between the bride's family or guardian and the groom. The bride's consent is generally required, although, in the case of a virgin, silence may be taken to signify consent, and some interpretations allow her to be coerced into her first marriage. All women are expected to be virgins the first time they marry. Islamic law sets no minimum age for the marriageability of either men or women, though civil laws in some areas do. Also required in Islamic marriage is the cooperation of the bride's guardian and the payment of a bride price, called *mahr*, for the rights that the husband acquires over the wife. Often the contract stipulates that only part of the bride price is to be paid upon marriage, the remainder to be paid to the wife in the event of divorce. Marriage does not result in community of property between husband and wife, and the woman retains ownership of her bride price. The husband is obliged to maintain the household and support his wife in a particular manner befitting her status or she may demand dissolution of the marriage. If the wife is not obedient and prepared to meet her husband's conjugal needs, she loses her claim to support. A husband is forbidden to take vows of celibacy.

Pre-Islamic society permitted temporary marriage in which a man and woman cohabit for a fixed period mutually stipulated in a marriage contract. At the end of the stipulated period, the husband declares the divorce formula and the marriage is over. Some Muslims adduce Qur'anic evidence that Muhammad permitted his devotees to contract temporary marriages, termed *mut'a*, especially on lengthy expeditions (4:28). After the prophet's death, this practice was prohibited by the early caliph Omar, who regarded it as fornication, although some factions of Islam still permit it today.

Islamic marriage is endogamous within the community of believers, based on Qur'anic stipulation (2:200). According to some interpretations, Islamic men may marry women of other "scriptural" religions such as Jews, Christians, and Zoroastrians (5:7), though Muslim women may marry only Muslim men. In general practice marriages are made within the even narrower confines of tribe, clan, and extended family and are frequently arranged by the bride's male relatives or another intermediary.

Marriages are forbidden among certain degrees of affinity and consanguinity (4:26–28), though often the preferred marriage is of a daughter to her father's brother's son, who, in some Islamic circles, must renounce his right to marry his paternal cousin, termed a *bint amm,* before she can be betrothed to another suitor. This form of marriage serves to build the extended family and ensure loyalty to the father's house. Polygyny is permitted in Islam, though the Qur'an stipulates that a man may marry no more than four wives and must undertake to treat them equally (4:3).

Divorce is permitted in Islam, and remarriage after divorce is common for both men and women. Both men and woman have the right to initiate divorce, but it has generally been the prerogative of the male. He can do this by simply pronouncing a formula stating his intention, although civil law in different regions often requires more procedural formality. The woman receives that portion of her bride price that was reserved, in her marriage contract, for payment in case of divorce.

BIBLIOGRAPHY

CHRISTIANITY

Brown, Peter. *The Body and Society: Men, Women and Sexual Renunciation in Early Christianity.* Lectures on the History of Religion, vol. 13. 1988.

Heyward, Carter. *Touching Our Strength: The Erotic as Power and the Love of God.* 1989.

Pantel, Pauline Schmitt, ed. *From Ancient Goddesses to Christian Saints.* Vol. 1 of *A History of Women in the West.* Translated by Arthur Goldhammer. 1992.

Pellauer, Mary D. "The Moral Significance of Female Orgasm: Toward Sexual Ethics That Celebrates Women's Sexuality." *Journal of Feminist Studies in Religion* 9, no. 1/2 (1993): 161–182.

ISLAM

Ahmed, Leila. *Women and Gender in Islam: Historical Roots of a Modern Debate.* 1992.

Sabbah, Fatna A. *Woman in the Muslim Unconscious.* Translated by Mary Jo Lakeland. 1984.

Young, Serinity, ed. *An Anthology of Sacred Texts by and About Women.* 1994.

JUDAISM

Baskin, Judith R., ed. *Jewish Women in Historical Perspective.* 1991.

Biale, Rachel. *Women and Jewish Law: The Essential Texts, Their History, and Their Relevance Today.* 1984. Reprint, 1995.

Greenberg, Blu. *On Women and Judaism: A View from Tradition.* 1981.

Mann, Denese Berg. *The Woman in Judaism.* 1979.

Stowasser, Barbara Freyer. *Women in the Qur'an, Traditions, and Interpretation.* 1994.

Wegner, Judith Romney. *Chattel or Person? The Status of Women in the Mishnah.* 1988.

DIANE M. SHARON

Martyrdom

Martyrdom, from the Greek *martyria,* meaning "witness," connotes the death, understood by those who champion it as a willing death, of an individual on behalf of a belief or principle. Its earliest emergence in the West occurs in the Apocrypha to the Hebrew Bible, in the account of the persecutions of the Jews by the Seleucid ruler Antiochus IV Epiphanes at the beginning of the second century B.C.E. Already these early sources display the particular magnetism of gender in the context of martyrdom: the texts emphasize the heroism of a mother and her seven sons, in terms that underline the outrage the reader should feel at the suffering and heroism of women and children (2 Macc. 7:20ff). The peculiar narrative magnetism of female suffering recurs in a variety of religious contexts: the persecution of Fāṭimah and her sons, for example, serves as the foundation myth for Shiite Islam.

The conjunction between the perceived heroism of unjust suffering and the narrative magnetism of female suffering raises important theoretical issues. The social meaning of acts of religious heroism can shift dramatically according to the socially constructed connotations imposed by the gender of the agent (Saiving, 1992). Thus, self-sacrifice would have a different meaning for women—assuming a social context in which women are exhorted to engage in self-abnegating behaviors—than it would for men. Where gendered social constraints play a coercive role, as in the case of sati, the self-immolation of Hindu widows, it may be impossible to uncover the "voice" or intention of the woman in question; and the interpreter is left to adjudicate among the assertions of those who would claim to speak on behalf of the dead. A particularly well-documented case is the competition among rival groups over the memory of Roop Kanwar, a twenty-year-old Rajput who died in 1987 (Harlan, 1992). Those who defend sati argue that it is a symbol not only of a woman's boundless devotion to and unity with her husband, but a blessing on the wider community, and an emblem of indigenous tradition besieged by Western colonial powers and Western-educated elites. Contemporary Indian feminists, by contrast, struggle to assess the competing concerns for women's human rights as against the post-colonial need for cultural autonomy.

A debate over gender dynamics has emerged in the case of the early Christian martyrs. The sources (second to fourth centuries C.E.) record dramatic gender reversals; while at the same time taking an interest in a heroine's bodily suffering in a way that can only be described as pornographic. The early-third-century martyr Perpetua records in her prison diary a dream in which she is transformed into a man and bests the devil in gladiatorial combat (*Acts of Perpetua and Felicitas* 10), while the diary's (presumably male) editor appends an epilogue describing her actual death in the arena in terms, drawn from contemporary romances, with emphasis on torn garments, flowing hair, and ladylike modesty. In the second-century *Acts of the Martyrs of Lyons,* it is the anonymous author of the text who juxtaposes the feminine qualities of the slave-girl Blandina, "tiny, weak, and insignificant" (*Martyrs of Lyons* 42), with her prowess as "a noble athlete," whose stamina under torture leaves her torturers weary and exhausted, while she, though "her entire body was broken and torn" (*Martyrs of Lyons* 18), is refreshed by the opportunity to assert her faith and emerges as an explicitly Christlike figure (*Martyrs of Lyons* 41). Another second-century work, the fictional *Acts of Paul and Thecla,* suggests that the women of the ancient Mediterranean converted to Christianity as a gesture of solidarity with the heroism of the female martyrs (MacDonald, 1983), but the voyeuristic depiction of both historical and fictional heroines suggests that the martyr texts may have been aimed at a specifically male readership (Cooper, 1996).

The suffering of a woman serves to confer legitimacy on religious groups in a variety of ways. The victim's vulnerability and moral superiority are understood as representing the fragile preciousness of a faith to be defended, while in narrative terms, women have stood since earliest epic as the paradigmatic rallying point for a shared cause.

BIBLIOGRAPHY

The Acts of the Early Christian Martyrs. Edited by Herbert Musurillo. 1972.

Ayoub, M. *Redemptive Suffering in Islam: A Study of the Devotional Aspects of Asura in Twelver Shiism.* 1978.

Baumel, Judith Tydor, and Jacob J. Schacter. "The Ninety-Three Bais Yaakov Girls of Cracow: History or Typology?" In *Reverence, Righteousness, and Rahamanut: Essays in Memory of Rabbi Dr. Leo Jung.* Edited by Jacob J. Schachter. 1992.

Castelli, Elizabeth. "Visions and Voyeurism: Holy Women and the Politics of Sight in Early Christianity." *Protocol* of the Seminar at the Center for Hermenutical Studies, Berkeley, CA. 1995.

Cooper, Kate. *The Virgin and the Bride: Idealized Womanhood in Late Antiquity.* 1996.

———. "The Voice of the Victim: Gender, Representation and Early Christian Martyrdom." In *Religion, Gender and Representation.* Edited by Grace Jantzen. 1998.

Harlan, Lindsey. *Religion and Rajput Women: The Ethic of Protection in Contemporary Narratives.* 1992.

Harlan, Lindsey, and Paul B. Courtright, eds. *From the Margins of Hindu Marriage: Essays on Gender, Religion, and Culture.* 1995.

Hawley, John Stratton. *Sati: The Blessing and the Curse.* 1994.

Hinson, E. Glenn. "Women Among the Martyrs." *Studia Patristica* 25 (1993): 423–428.

Jelsma, Anke. "Women Martyrs in a Revolutionary Age: A Comparison of Books of Martyrs." In *Church, Change and Revolution.* Edited by J. Berg and P. Hoftijzer. 1991.

Lewis, Bernard. *Origins of Ismailism.* 1940.

Mani, Lata. "Contentious Traditions: The Debate on Sati in Colonial India." In *Recasting Women: Essays in Indian Colonial History.* Edited by Kumkum Sanga. 1989.

Saiving, Valerie. "The Human Condition: A Feminine View." In *Womanspirit Rising: A Feminist Reader.* Edited by Carol P. Christ and Judith Plaskow. 1992.

Shaw, Brent. "The Passion of Perpetua." *Past and Present* 139 (1993): 3–45.

van Henter, J. W. *The Maccabean Martyrs as Saviours of the Jewish People: A Study of 2 and 4 Maccabees.* 1997.

Waddy, Charis. *Women in Muslim History.* 1980.

Young, Robin Darling. "The 'Woman with the Soul of Abraham': Traditions about the Mother of the Maccabean Martyrs." In *"Women Like This": New Perspectives on Jewish Women in the Greco-Roman World.* Edited by Amy-Jill Levine. 1991.

See also **Perpetua and Felicity.**

KATE COOPER

Marxism

Women's protests over the exploitation of their bodies and their labor have long resonated with Marxist concerns over the exploitation of the working classes. Although gender never displaced class as the primary category of oppression in socialist analysis, Marxists nonetheless identified with the plight of women, as they did with racial, colonized, or other oppressed groups, and associated themselves with these struggles for justice. The source for this frequently tumultuous and controversial alliance between socialism and feminism can be found in the origins of Marxism itself, intertwined with its analysis of religion in a patriarchal social order.

In the work of Karl Marx and Fredrich Engels, prehistoric religion functioned as an explanation for and a bulwark against the forces of nature. Magical incantations that orchestrated the powers of fantasized deities alleviated human helplessness. In ancient, medieval, and modern societies, religion likewise played a significant role by legitimating the power of the ruling class and comforting its victims, be they slave, serf, or proletarian. Under capitalism, faith narcotized the masses, rendering them insensate to the suffering they bore and offering them hope in a heavenly Kingdom of God (*Contribution to the Critique of Hegel's Philosophy of Law*). Even the free-thinking bourgeoisie, whose rebellion against the feudal order was predicated on skepticism and the scientific revolution, acquiesced to the mutually beneficial marriage of religion and capital. Both religion and capitalism thrived on fetishism that rendered the inanimate animate (gods or commodities) and objectified human beings as things (pawns in the divine order or labor-power sold in the marketplace) (*Capital*, vol. 1). In place of the fantasized reality of cult and commodity, Marx and Engels theorized the possibility of a realized fantasy, a Kingdom of Freedom in which human beings would both master nature and collectively control their own destiny.

True human history would only begin with the revolution that promised to eliminate class, the key obstacle to human progress. Class was foreshadowed by a gendered division of labor, founded upon child-bearing (*The German Ideology*) and reinforced by patriarchy's overthrow of humanity's matriarchal origins (*The Origins of the Family, Private Property, and the State*). This social stratification was further enhanced by the historical development of property relations under ancient, feudal, and capitalist social orders. As Marx and Engels argued in the *Communist Manifesto*, the male bourgeois exploited not only proletarian women through prostitution but also women of his own class through the institutions of marriage and family. Like Engels and her father, Eleanor Marx Aveling advocated free love in her pamphlet *The Women Question;* however, since ownership of the means of production was the key to revolutionizing social relations, only the expropriation of the capitalist class would liberate women—a sentiment shared by August Bebel, leader of Germany's turn-of-the-century Social Democratic Party and author of *Women in the Past, Present, and Future*. To such Marxist leaders as Angelica Balabanoff, Clara Zeitkin, and Rosa Luxemburg, those who campaigned for women's rights alone ignored the origin of women's oppression and were thus regarded as bourgeois reformers rather than true progressives. The Soviet experiment, however, was perhaps no more successful in liberating women from patriarchal institutions than it was in suppressing religion.

Outside of the Soviet bloc, a rapprochement of Marxism and religion emerged in the development of a feminist Christian Marxism and liberation theology. Like Marx himself, the German Christian Marxist theologian Dorothee Soelle sees religious suffering, for example, Christ's passion, as emblematic of real suffering; yet, unlike Marx, she reads the Christian kerygma as a sign that empowers the oppressed to build the Kingdom rather than as a symbol of acquiescence to an unjust social system. To Soelle religion itself may be the very basis for resistance to a postmodern consumerist society, infused with the values of commodity fetishism. Similarly, the North American feminist socialist theologian Beverly Wildung Harrison urges the adoption of a neo-Marxist socioeconomic approach that incorporates both antiracist and feminist analyses. In Latin America, male liberation theologians have theorized a postmillennial peasant worker–governed society, growing out of urban and rural base communities and nurtured by the crossfertilization of Christian faith and Marxist economic analysis. However, their female counterparts, such as Elsa Tamez, found that the question of gender was rarely explored and developed a specifically feminist liberation theology. In light of the fall of the Berlin Wall and the collapse of Nicaragua's Sandinista government marking the end of socialist experiments in Europe and Central America, European, Latin American, and North American feminist theologians of the 1990s are being challenged to retheorize the relationship between women, religion, and capitalist society.

BIBLIOGRAPHY

Amanecida Collective. *Revolutionary Forgiveness: Feminist Reflections on Nicaragua.* 1987.

Aveling, Eleanor Marx. *The Woman Question.* 2d ed., 1987.

Balabanoff, Angelica. *My Life as a Rebel.* 1938.

Bebel, August. *Women in the Past, Present and Future.*
  1886.
Eagleson, John, trans. and ed. *Against Machismo: Interviews by Elsa Tamez.* 1987.
Florence, Ronald. *Marx's Daughters: Eleanor Marx,
  Rosa Luxemburg, Angelica Balabanoff.* 1975.
Gutiérrez, Gustavo. *A Theology of Liberation.* 1973.
Harrison, Beverly Wildung. *Making the Connections:
  Essays in Feminist Social Ethics.* Edited by Carol S.
  Robb. 1985.
Hewitt, Marsha Aileen. *Critical Theory of Religion: A
  Feminist Analysis.* 1995.
Irigaray, Luce. *Sexes and Genealogies.* Translated by
  Gillian C. Gill. 1987.
Lukács, Georg. *History and Class Consciousness.*
  Translated by Rodney Livingstone. 1968.
Luxemburg, Rosa. *Politische Schriften.* Vols. 1–3.
  Edited by Ossip K. Flechtheim. 1966–1968.
Marx, Karl, and Engels, Fredrich. *Collected Works.*
  Vols. 1–6. 1974–1976.
Miranda, José Porfirio. *Marx and the Bible: A Critique
  of the Philosophy of Oppression.* 1974.
Soelle, Dorothee. *Revolutionary Patience.* Translated
  by Rita and Robert Kimber. 1977.
Scott, Hilda. *Does Socialism Liberate Women?* 1974.
Tamez, Elsa, ed. *Through Her Eyes: Women's Theology
  from Latin America.* 1989.

See also Economics; Liberation Theologies.

JAMES MCBRIDE

Mary

See Virgin Mary.

Maryam (Mary)

Maryam, mother of the prophet Jesus (Isa), is the female figure to whom the greatest attention is given in the Qur'an and the only one identified by name. Some seventy verses refer to her, in thirty-four of which she is named. The Qur'an treats her nativity, her retreat into the temple (probably in Jerusalem) and life of piety, the announcement by the angel Gabriel that though a virgin she will bear a son, the birth of Jesus, and Jesus' defense of her virtue when she is accused of wrongdoing by her people. The traditions have developed these themes at length, giving special attention to such matters as the mode of Jesus' conception and Mary's exceptional piety and virtue.

The purest of women, Maryam is said by some both to have been virginal throughout her life and never even to have had the defilement of menstruation. As the model of the true believer she has been heralded in theological treatises, popular piety, and Sufi devotional literature. Some exegetes have speculated that as the recipient of a message from Gabriel she might fall into the category of prophet, although this is generally not accepted. Considerable debate has been held as to whether Maryam or the Prophet's daughter Fāṭimah is preeminent in the Garden of Paradise, Sunni Muslims generally assigning the honor to Maryam. In some parts of the world Mary is venerated by Muslims and Christians together, in mutual respect for her status as a woman of purity and piety and as the virginal mother of Jesus.

BIBLIOGRAPHY

McAuliffe, Jane D. "Chosen of All Women: Mary and
  Fatima in Qur'anic Exegesis." *Islamo* 7 (1981):
  19–28.
Schimmel, Annemarie. *Mystical Dimensions of Islam.*
  1975.
Smith, Jane I., and Yvonne Y. Haddad. "The Virgin
  Mary in Islamic Tradition and Commentary." *The
  Muslim World* (July-October 1989): 161–187.
Spellberg, D. A. *Politics, Gender and the Islamic Past.*
  1994.
Stowasser, Barbara F. *Women in the Qur'an: Traditions
  and Interpretation.* 1994.

See also Virgin Mary.

JANE I. SMITH

Mary and Martha

Mary and Martha, named as followers of Jesus in the New Testament, are frequently remembered through a short exemplary story in Luke 10:38–42 that pits the two women against each other. When Martha complains of the burden of serving the meal, Jesus defends and affirms the silent Mary who "sat at the Lord's feet and listened to what he was saying" (10:39). Traditional interpretation made Mary represent the contemplative life and Martha the "lesser" active life; tried to identify the "better part" Mary chose (10:42); or discussed whether the original text proclaimed "one" or "few" things necessary (10:42). Further, Mary was often confused with the anonymous penitent who washes and anoints Jesus' feet in Luke 7:36–50 or with Mary Magdalene, disciple and witness to the Resurrection.

"At his feet" in Luke 10:39 has been reinterpreted as a term for discipleship (compare Acts 22:3, where Paul claims to have been educated "at the feet of" the famous teacher Gamaliel). Jesus' rebuke to Martha is then read as affirming the right of women to be disciples. But this reading further denigrates the Marthas who work at sustaining life. Another reading recognizes that the words translated as "tasks" and "to do work" (*diakonia, diakonein*) convey a double-reference to table service and Christian ministries (2 Cor. 3:4–11, 4:1; Mark 10:41–45; Acts 6–7) and so celebrate Martha as a minister (*diakonos;* cf. Rom. 16:1). But the approval Jesus gives to Mary seems to discourage women from ministry. Unfortunately, this reading fits Luke's interest in including women while restricting their roles.

The more complex stories in John 11:1–12:19, bound together by the characters Mary, Martha, and Lazarus, represent the two women differently. Here they act in concert on behalf of their brother. Martha dominates John 11:1–44, initiating the dialogue with Jesus, professing her belief in Jesus, and instigating Mary's encounter with Jesus. Mary takes center stage in the anointing scene (12:1–8).

The two different versions of Luke and John have only few common features. In both, Martha is said to serve and to minister (*diakonein*, Luke 10:39–40, John 12:1), and Mary is called "sister"; Martha as the householder welcomes Jesus (Luke 10:38, John 11:20). These features seem to reflect communal memories of the two women's roles in the (post-Resurrection) early Christian mission. Martha was remembered as the *diakonos* (minister, cf. Rom. 16:1: "Phoebe the (*diakonos*) minister"). Perhaps, like Prisca and Aquila (Rom. 16:3–5), Philemon (Philem. 1), and Nympha (Col. 4:15), Martha the *diakonos* hosted a house-church with "Mary the sister." *Sister* can indicate kin, erotic partner, female Christian, or a role in the mission. Like Paul with his missionary companions (e.g., Paul the *apostolos* and Sosthenes the brother in 1 Cor. 1:1), Martha and Mary worked as missionary partners. Romans 16 includes male and female pairs who may have been spouses (Prisca and Aquila, 3–5; Junia and Andronicus, 7; Julia and Philologus, Nereas and his "sister," 15), and a pair of women, Tryphaena and Tryphosa (16:12). Thus sisterhood can represent not blood relationship but partnership in the mission. Partnership may have involved a commitment to each other as well as to the mission; perhaps Martha and Mary should be located in a "lesbian continuum," a prehistory of women's same-sex commitments.

BIBLIOGRAPHY

D'Angelo, Mary R. "Women Partners in the New Testament." *Journal of Feminist Studies in Religion* 6 (1990): 65–86.

———. "Women in Luke–Acts: A Redactional View." *Journal of Biblical Literature* 109 (1990): 441–461 (esp. 453–455).

Reinhartz, Adele. "From Narrative to History: The Resurrection of Mary and Martha." In *"Women Like This": New Perspectives on Jewish Women in the Greco-Roman World.* Edited by Amy-Jill Levine. 1991.

Schüssler Fiorenza, Elisabeth. *But She Said: Feminist Practices of Biblical Interpretation.* 1992. Pp. 0–76.

———. "A Feminist Critical Interpretation for Liberation: Martha and Mary: Luke 10:38–42." *Religion and Intellectual Life* 3 (1986): 21–35.

MARY ROSE D'ANGELO

Mary Magdalene

The four Gospels contain twelve references to Mary Magdalene, a woman from Galilee who became a disciple of the teacher Jesus of Nazareth. Luke 8:2–3 reports the "Mary who is called Magdalene" was the woman from whom Jesus cast out seven demons. She is listed among the faithful present at the Crucifixion (Matt. 27:56; Mark 15:40; John 19:25), her presence is noted at the entombment (Matt. 27:61; Mark 15:47), and yet again on Easter Sunday among the women who return to the sepulcher (Matt. 28:1; Mark 16:1; John 20:1). Upon hearing of the Resurrection, she and the women hasten to tell the other disciples (Luke 24:10). According to Mark 16:9, Mary Magdalene received the Paschal privilege of seeing the risen Christ first. The final and most extended treatment of this female disciple is in John 20:18. As she stands weeping at the sepulcher, a man she mistakes for the gardener approaches, calling out her name. Recognizing his voice, she turns and addresses him in Hebrew. Although Jesus rebuffs her touch, he nevertheless entrusts her to announce the Good News of his Resurrection to the other disciples (John 20:18). This compelling image, the "apostle of the apostles," is Scripture's final witness of Mary Magdalene.

In the early medieval period Pope Gregory the Great transformed Mary Magdalene's identity, establishing a new Magdalene for Western Christendom. He collapsed into one individual the identities of three distinct women described in the Gospels: first, an unnamed female sinner who anointed Jesus' feet with perfumed oils and dried them with her hair (Luke 7:37–50); second, Mary of Bethany, sister of Martha (John 11:1–45; 12:1–8; and third, the demonically possessed Mary called Magdalene (Mark 16:9). Mary Magdalene thus gained a preconversion identity as a prostitute, acquired siblings, and became associated with the contemplative life. Gregory the Great's composite figure was largely accepted in the West; the Greek Church, however, never accepted the Gregorian saint.

The composite Magdalene's first *vita*, a homily based on selected Gospel passages, appeared in tenth-century Burgundy. Other legends emerged to relate more fanciful events of her life. A ninth-century southern Italian *vita* incorporated an episode from the life of Mary of Egypt recounting how the saint spent the last years of her life in eremitical reclusion. An eleventh-century *vita* claimed that Mary Magdalene and a cohort of disciples evangelized the pagans of southern Gaul. These two *vitae* soon merged to form a new legend that related how, after evangelizing, the Magdalene withdrew to the "desert" to live out her life in ascetical contemplation. Appended to her various *vitae* are a number of miracles: spectacular cures, assistance with matters of fertility and childbirth, the liberation of prisoners, and the raising of the dead. The saint's major pilgrimage sites, where these miracles were performed or recorded, are in Burgundy and Provence: the Romanesque church at Vézelay, the Gothic basilica of Saint-Maximin, and La Sainte-Baume, the cave outside Aix-en-Provence, where, according to legend, the saint retired from the world.

Through the liturgy, preaching, devotional literature, sacred plays, and the fine arts—her visual attribute is an alabaster of oil—Mary Magdalene's legend was disseminated throughout Christendom. Preachers and moralists turned each symbolic aspect of her life toward didactic ends. Her preconversion sinfulness was used to warn against the sins of vanity and lust. Consequently, Mary Magdalene became the patron saint of repentant prostitutes. The Magdalene's great penitential conversion at Jesus' feet taught an important lesson to sinners about the sacrament of penance. In Italy, confraternities devoted to the penitential discipline of self-flagellation made her their patron. Cloistered nuns dedicated their convents to the contemplative aspect of the saint. Conversely, the Magdalene's role as herald of the Resurrection, along with her legendary apostolate in Provence, was regarded as a model for active engagement in the world. Catherine of Siena, among others, praised Mary Magdalene's preaching and took the saint as a model for her own mission in the world.

Since 1969 the Roman liturgical calendar has venerated Mary Magdalene under the title "disciple of Christ;" nonetheless the enduring image of the saint is Luke's sinner, now glorified in heaven. As such she is

An engraving by Gustave Doré, *Mary Magdalene Repentant*, 1866 (Chris Hellier/Corbis)

the paradigmatic symbol of hope: through penitential conversion a great sinner became a great saint. However, the Magdalene's role in Christian salvation history is equally important: the risen Christ appeared to her first. Mary Magdalene was doubly privileged, therefore, when Christ then entrusted her to proclaim the Resurrection, the central tenet of the Christian faith.

BIBLIOGRAPHY

Beriou, Nicole. "La Madeleine dans les sermons parisiens du XIIIe siècle." *Mélanges de l'école française de Rome (moyen age)* 104, no. 1 (1992): 269–340.

Duperray, Eve, ed. *Marie Madeleine dans la mystique: Les arts et les lettres.* Actes du colloque international, Avignon, 20-21-22 juillet, 1988. Paris, 1989.

Faillon, E.-M. *Monuments inédits sur l'apostolat de Sainte Marie-Madeleine en Provence et sur les autres apôtres de cette contrée, Saint Lazare, Saint Maximin, Sainte Marthe.* 2 vols. Paris, 1859.

Fiorenza, Elisabeth Schüssler. *In Memory of Her: A Feminist Theological Reconstruction of Christian Origins.* 1983.

Garth, Helen Meredith. *Saint Mary Magdalene in Medieval Literature.* 1950.

Hänsel, Hans. *Die Maria Magdalena Legende: Eine Quellen Untersuchung.* In *Greifswalder Beiträge zur Literatur und Stilforschung* XVI/ 1. Greifswald, 1937.

Haskins, Susan. *Mary Magdalen: Myth and Metaphor.* London, 1993.

Jansen, Katherine Ludwig. "Maria Magdalena: Apostolorum Apostola." In *Women Preachers and Prophets through Two Millennia of Christianity.* Edited by Beverly M. Kienzle and Pamela Walker. 1997.

———. "Mary Magdalen and the Mendicants: The Preaching of Penance in the Middle Ages." *Journal of Medieval History* 21, no. 1 (1995): 1–25.

———. *Mary Magdalen in the Middle Ages.* 1999.

Karras, Ruth Mazo. "Holy Harlots: Prostitute Saints in Medieval Legend." *Journal of the History of Sexuality* 1, no. 1 (1990): 3–32.

LaRow, Magdalen. "The Iconography of Mary Magdalen: The Evolution of a Western Tradition until 1300." Ph.D. diss., New York University, 1982.

Malvern, Marjorie. *Venus in Sackcloth: The Magdalen's Origins and Metamorphoses.* 1975.

Saxer, Victor. *Le Culte de Marie-Madeleine en occident dès origines à la fin du moyen-âge.* 2 vols. Cahiers d'archéologie et d'histoire, 3. Auxerre-Paris, 1959.

Szövérffy, Joseph. " 'Peccatrix quondam femina': A Survey of the Mary Magdalen Hymns." *Traditio* 19 (1963): 79–146.

Wilk, Sarah. "The Cult of Mary Magdalen in Fifteenth-Century Florence and Its Iconography." *Studi Medievali* II, 3d series, 26 (1985): 685–698.

See also **Prostitution**; **Saints.**

KATHERINE LUDWIG JANSEN

Material Culture

Material culture consists of all the tangible things made and used by people. Archaeologists use these material remains of ancient cultures—their tools, utensils, buildings, graves, roads, and other landform modifications—to reconstruct the behavior of ancient peoples. Archaeologists generally classify items of material culture as features, artifacts, or ecofacts. Features—items that cannot be moved without destroying some part of their functional integrity—include all types of build-ings (domestic structures, palaces, temples, shrines), walls, agricultural terraces, statues, holes (e.g., storage pits), and graves. Artifacts—portable, intentionally modified objects—include pottery, stone or metal vessels, stone tools, figurines, clothing, and jewelry. Ecofacts—natural items that reflect human activities—include such things as remnants of food items (bones and plants) and fuel. Archaeologists generally consider items of material culture to have utilitarian, social, or ideological functions or roles in the societies that made them, although items might perform several functions simultaneously—for example, a ceramic pot might be used to cook special food for a ritual meal—and functions can change over time. It is the ideological function, which serves to symbolize and communicate the ideological rationalizations for the social system and represent relationships with the supernatural, that is most often used in studies of ritual and religion.

The most important elements of interpretation of material culture are context and association. The context consists of the medium surrounding an object and the object's physical location in a room, site, or other locality. Association consists of physical occurrence with other items of material culture (which things are found together). Both context and association are critical to interpretation of how objects and buildings are used and what they meant to ancient peoples.

Early archaeological studies (nineteenth and most of the twentieth centuries) of women by archaeologists such as Etienne Renaud, Maria Gimbutas, Sir Arthur Evans, and Ann Barstow and religion focused primarily on identifying the presence of women and particularly "goddesses." Among the earliest-made items of material culture traditionally interpreted as religious are the small, generally nude female figurines, often referred to as Venus figures, from Upper Paleolithic (c. 30,000–17,000 B.C.E.) Europe. These have been variously interpreted as early goddess figures, fertility amulets, and erotic ideals. Maria Gimbutas interpreted female figurines and other geometric designs found in Neolithic Europe (c. 6000–3000 B.C.E.) as representing an early cult of goddess worshipers. Although these and similar studies have gained an enormous popular following, much of the early work has been discredited on theoretical and methodological grounds by feminist scholars, many of whom point out that the studies generally ignore context and association, use argument by assertion, and present a normative framework.

In the 1980s and 1990s, feminist archaeologists such as Sarah Nelson, Pamela Russell, and Diane Bolger have intensified and reoriented the study of material culture in order to investigate the roles of women in ancient religions. The most common objects of study are figurines, figurative representations carved in various media or painted on ceramic vessels and walls, and the contents of burials. The goal is no longer simply to engender religion by "discovering" the presence of females in religious practice. Rather, the objective of current scholars is to use interpretation of material culture to understand how religion functioned to structure the social and political orders and, by extension, the status of women in ancient societies.

BIBLIOGRAPHY

Claassen, Cheryl. *Exploring Gender Through Archaeology.* 1992.

Ehrenberg, Margaret. *Women in Prehistory.* 1989.

Gero, Joan, and Margaret W. Conkey, eds. *Engendering Archaeology: Women and Prehistory.* 1991.

Nelson, Sarah M. *Gender in Archaeology: Analyzing Power and Prestige.* 1998.

Wright, Rita P., ed. *Gender and Archaeology.* 1996.

See also Archaeology; Gimbutas, Marija.

CATHY LYNNE COSTIN

Matriarchy

Perhaps the most interesting feature of matriarchy is that no one agrees on how to define it. In fact, most people who study the concept of societies in which women are central, have power, or are equal to men are eager to supply words other than *matriarchy* to describe them. Thus there is a proliferation of terms: gynocratic, matricentric, glyanic, matrifocal, gynocentric, partnership, sex equalitarian, mother-right, goddess-worshiping, and so on. Anthropologists seeking analytic precision have generally described matriarchy as a social form that is the mirror image of patriarchy: women have social dominance over men or pronounced institutional power based on their sex alone. *Matrilineality* is then defined as a practice under which name, inheritance, clan membership, or some such feature is passed through the mother's line, and *matrilocality* is defined as a practice under which husbands either live in their wives' homes or villages or come there only as visitors, remaining for the most part in the homes of their mothers or sisters.

Most anthropologists agree that no known societies, past or present, are matriarchal in the sense described above, and that matrilineal and matrilocal societies may give women a relatively high status or a relatively low one but never one higher than that given to men. Matrilineal and matrilocal societies also do not necessarily have a religious focus on goddesses, though they may—as may patrilineal, patrilocal, or patriarchal societies.

Matriarchy has had a beleaguered and complex history in the Western world (notwithstanding the anthropological consensus of the late twentieth century), especially since many contemporary feminists, unlike their mainstream anthropologist peers, believe that there have been societies that are truly matriarchal or that, failing this, there have been societies in which women are not in any way oppressed. The dream of a nonpatriarchal society has fascinated not only feminists but people of all political and ideological stripes, in many different cultures, and from the beginnings of written Western history. Interestingly, this dream is almost always depicted as a golden age, even by those who believe that the patriarchy which ended it was an important or necessary step forward for humanity.

Several tribal cultures (most notably in South America and New Guinea) have myths that state that social dominance was women's province before men stole it from them. In classical Greece numerous texts refer to cultures (such as Egypt) where women rule, or relate details about Amazon cultures where men are either absent or enslaved. In the West the idea of matriarchy was revived in the nineteenth century by J. J. Bachofen in his *Das Mutterrecht* (Mother-right), published in 1861. According to Bachofen, women were prominent in prehistory owing to the fact that kinship was necessarily traced through mothers alone, because sexual relations were promiscuous and thus individual fathers could not be determined for individual children. However, Bachofen also claimed that women were so offended by the excessive sexual demands of men in this promiscuous state that they introduced monogamy, and with it, matriarchy.

The late nineteenth century brought burgeoning interest to the topic of matriarchy from a great many directions. Bachofen had followers, especially on the European continent, but there were also British and American anthropologists and intellectuals who advanced ideas similar to Bachofen's, some without any prior familiarity with his work (for example, John Ferguson McLennan and Lewis Morgan). Unlike Bachofen, the British matriarchalists were inclined to believe that women's centrality in prehistoric or "savage" societies was not accompanied by high status for women: they viewed these societies as matrilineal and matrilocal, but not matriarchal. Their ideas were picked up by feminist and communist scholars of the same era, and these writers made stronger claims for women's social dominance. Several feminists (among them Matilda Joslyn Gage and Elizabeth Cady Stanton) in the late nineteenth and early twentieth centuries lamented the downfall of "the matriarchate" at the hands of patriarchs. Friedrich Engels brought the concept of matriarchy—including the social dominance of women—fully into the communist movement. His version of prehistoric matriarchy was the reigning dogma in Soviet anthropology for decades (at least into the 1960s) and was later resurrected in the West as socialist feminists began to rework Engels's ideas in the 1970s.

Those who today seek to reconstruct, record, or imagine matriarchy are unanimous in giving women in these societies (or, alternatively, "femininity" or "the female principle") a slight advantage over men (or "masculinity"). Still, there is a huge distance between those who envision matriarchies as sexually egalitarian societies whose central deity happens to be a bit more female than male in its attributes, and those who believe that prior to a worldwide cataclysm in 3000 B.C.E., all societies were basically owned and operated by women via a global religion of the goddess, while men played only subsidiary roles.

Speculation about the religious practices of such societies abounds, a few key assumptions being: (1) that goddesses were more numerous or powerful than gods; (2) that women were seen as embodiments of the divine; (3) that women had special female-only rituals; (4) that nature and the body (seen to be connected to women or the feminine) were highly valued by the entire society; and (5) that societies practicing these goddess-oriented religions were unusually peaceable and sexually unrepressed.

BIBLIOGRAPHY

For concise definitions of *matriarchy, matrilineality,* and *matrilocality,* see Robert H. Lowie, *The Matrilineal Complex* (1919) and W. H. R. Rivers, *Social Organization,* edited by W. J. Perry (1924). Descriptions of myths of matriarchy from tribal societies can be found in Robert F. Murphy, "Social Structure and Sex Antagonism," *Southwestern Journal of Anthropology* 15, no. 1 (1959): 89–98; Anne MacKaye Chapman, *Drama and Power in a Hunting Society* (1982); and Anna S. Meigs, *Food, Sex, and Pollution* (1984). Discussions of classical Greek materials on Amazonism and matriarchy can be found in Simon Pembroke, "Women in Charge: The Function of Alternatives in Early Greek Tradition and the Ancient Idea of Matriarchy," *Journal of the Warburg and Courtauld Institutes* 30 (1967): 1–35; and William Blake Tyrrell, *Amazons, a Study in Athenian Mythmaking* (1989).

Important nineteenth-century sources on matriarchy include: Matilda Joslyn Gage, *Woman, Church, and State: A Historical Account of the Status of Woman through the Christian Ages, With Reminiscences of the Matriarchate* (1900; repr., 1972); and Lewis H. Morgan, *Ancient Society* (1878). For a discussion of nineteenth-century male matriarchalists see Elizabeth Fee, "The Sexual Politics of Victorian Social Anthropology," in *Clio's Consciousness Raised: New Perspectives on the History of Women,* edited by Mary S. Hartman and Lois W. Banner (1974).

For information on the concept of matriarchy in Soviet ethnography, see Ernest Gellner, "The Soviet and the Savage," *Current Anthropology* 16 (1973): 595–617. For recent feminist reworkings of Engels, see Christine Ward Gailey, "The State of the State in Anthropology," *Dialectical Anthropology* 9 (1985): 65–89. For an overview of the use of matriarchy in contemporary feminist spirituality, see Cynthia Eller, "The Rise and Fall of Women's Power," chapter 8 of *Living in the Lap of the Goddess* (1995) and references therein.

See also **Amazons**; **Goddess**.

CYNTHIA ELLER

Maya

Most often translated into English as "illusion," the feminine Sanskrit noun *maya* is an important concept in Hinduism. Maya first appeared in Hinduism's earliest scriptures, the Vedas (c. 1200–700 B.C.E.). Eventually maya passed into Buddhism (from the fifth century B.C.E.) with slightly altered implications. Maya's root meanings in Sanskrit have to do with creation, construction, or most concretely with craft. Maya thus comprises a generative power that is more than reproductive. In later speculations beginning with the Upanishads (c. 800 B.C.E.–400 B.C.E.)—philosophical teachings understood as the culmination of Vedic revelations—maya retained this fertile potency. It also came to be identified as the principle or process intervening between a singular, undifferentiated reality and the multiple, proliferated worlds of impermanent appearances. It is "illusion" because it does not look like ultimate reality; however, some Hindu nondualistic philosophical schools held this created and creative multiplicity to be continuous with, rather than separate from, cosmic truth. Buddhism, by contrast, denying any real cosmic ground, pushed the concept of maya to one of starker deception, or delusion masking emptiness.

As the principle or source for multiplicities of name and form exuberantly emerging from a monistic base, maya is closely allied with two other Sanskrit nouns of decidedly feminine character: *prakriti,* often translated "nature"; and *shakti*, often translated "power." In the Puranas (c. 300 C.E.–900 C.E.), Hinduism's mythological texts, maya, like *shakti*, appears as a name for the Goddess or Devī. The *Devīmāhātmya* (Greatness of the Goddess, c. 550 C.E.) exalts her creative power as "Great Maya" (Mahāmāyā).

Within the vernaculars, the semantic domain of maya links its captivating potency with ordinary sources of attachment to the apparent world, on the one hand; and with extraordinary magical capacity to transform appearances, on the other. The "net of maya" (*māyājāl*) may accordingly refer to all that people find valuable in life, or to a "magic show."

Maya is often identified with the two most powerful sources of human illusions: love and money. In several South Asian vernacular tongues, including notably Bengali and Nepali, maya is used casually to refer to the sweet attachments engendered in domestic life, compelling familial bonds. Sometimes maya also means wealth and property, or names a particular goddess associated with material prosperity. Wealth is not only a commanding object of desire, but eminently transformable. In the more specialized context of magical arts, maya's special associations are with shape-shifting, and by extension with sleight-of-hand trickery.

Thus creative grace, binding attachments, and delusive skills are all encompassed in the concept of maya. Maya is a gendered term, not merely formally but in its semantic domain. Most especially, maya is female through its identification with the Goddess, and its close affinities with *shakti* and *prakriti*. As profuse creativity, maya's female identity is a positive recognition of limitless power. In popular thought, maya is not necessarily associated with women, but rather with the power of love that causes persons of both sexes to form attachments to impermanent bodies. For men attempting to free themselves from attachments, beloved women as hindrances may seem to be embodiments of maya.

BIBLIOGRAPHY

Coburn, Thomas B. "Devī: The Great Goddess." In *Devī: Goddesses of India*. Edited by John S. Hawley and Donna M. Wulff. 1996. A concise and helpful discussion of the Goddess as glorified in the *Devīmāhātmya* including her nature as Mahāmāyā.

Gold, Ann Grodzins. "Gender and Illusion in a Rajasthani Yogic Tradition." In *Gender, Genre, and Power in South Asian Expressive Traditions*. Edited by Arjun Appadurai, Frank Korom, and Margaret Mills. 1991. Two views of maya—as love for women and as women magicians' spells—in a Rajasthani oral epic of renunciation.

Goudriaan, Teun. *Māyā Divine and Human*. 1978. A book-length study of the Sanskrit concept.

Lamb, Sarah. "Growing in a Net of *Māyā*: Persons, Gender and Life Processes in a Bengali Society." Ph.D. diss., University of Chicago. 1993. A revealing ethnography based on fieldwork in rural India, focused on the ways Bengalis understand maya as a compellingly valuable attachment they must noneheless prepare to sever as part of the aging process.

O'Flaherty, Wendy Doniger. *Dreams, Illusion and Other Realities*. 1984. A delightful exploration of illusion in Hindu mythic understandings of reality expressed through complex narratives.

See also **Prakriti**; **Shaktism**.

ANN GRODZINS GOLD

Mazu (Tianhou)

A popular Buddho-Taoist deity whose cult originated in China's southeast coastal province of Fujian during the Sung dynasty (960–1279 C.E.), devotion to Mazu gradually spread outward via migration and trade routes to Korea, Japan, Taiwan, Southeast Asia, and, more recently, to the Americas. As a female object of devotion in ethnic Chinese communities, Mazu ranks second only to the bodhisattva Kuan Yin, with whom she is sometimes identified. Annual pilgrimages to important temples draw huge numbers of followers.

Standard hagiographies assert that Lin Moniang ("the silent one") was born on the 23d day of the third lunar month in 960 C.E. on the island of Meizhou. She was renowned as a young girl for her filial devotion to her parents and her knowledge of Buddhist sutras, and was later said to be able to exorcise demons using a Taoist talisman. Popular legends describe her salvific powers. In one, Lin, who had fallen into a trance at her loom, plucked the fishing boats of her family members from the water, saving them from calamity during a fierce storm. Lin Moniang died a young woman, unmarried and childless. Since her death, she has been associated with the protection of people in maritime and riverine communities.

Miracles attributed to her resulted in the granting of posthumous imperial titles, culminating with the bestowal of *tianhou* (empress of heaven) by the Kang Xi emperor in 1693; she is officially and widely worshiped by this appellation. Fujianese and Taiwanese, however, prefer the affectionate term Mazu, meaning mother ancestor. Tianhou is symbolic of Chinese patriarchal order and is approached for general blessings of peace and harmony; yet as a female, Mazu symbolizes the potential subversion of that order—and is frequently approached for personal requests that favor the recipient over others within the community.

The Mazu cult was suppressed in China after 1949; since the late 1980s, temple reconstruction has begun, largely financed by Taiwanese and other overseas donors. In Taiwan, the goddess' cult has shown increasing vigor and is a highly visible and contested symbol of local identity.

BIBLIOGRAPHY

Huang Meiying. *Taiwan mazu de xianghuo yu yishi* [Mazu incense offerings and ceremonies in Taiwan]. 1994.

Li Hsien-chang. *Boso Shinkô no Kenkyû* [Research on Mazu beliefs]. 1979.

Nyitray, Vivian-Lee. "Becoming the Queen of Heaven: The Life and Bureaucratic Career of Mazu." In *Goddesses of Sovereignty.* Edited by Beverly Moon and Elizabeth Benard. 1998.

Sangren, P. Steven. "Female Gender in Chinese Religious Symbols: Kuan Yin, Ma Tsu, and the 'Eternal Mother'." *Signs* 9 (1983): 4–25.

———. "The Ma-Tsu Cult of Taiwan." *Comparative Studies in Society and History* 30 (1988): 674–697.

VIVIAN-LEE NYITRAY

McPherson, Aimee Semple

Popular evangelist, author, and founder of the International Church of the Foursquare Gospel, Aimee Semple McPherson (1890–1944), was born on a farm near Ingersoll, Ontario, Canada, and named Aimee Elizabeth Kennedy. She was the daughter of James Kennedy, a Methodist, and his second wife, Mildred "Minnie" Pearce, a member of the Salvation Army. "Sister," as she would be called, was influenced in her teens by the newly forming Pentecostal movement. In 1908 she was converted and baptized. She then married Irish evangelist Robert Semple, and in 1910 they traveled to Hong Kong, where Robert was to be a missionary. He died three months after their arrival. Their daughter, Roberta, was born one month after his death. After her return to the United States Sister married Harold McPherson, with whom she had a son, Rolf, born in 1913. Her marriage to McPherson ended in divorce, as did a third marriage. Those divorces, along with her mysterious disappearance for several weeks in 1926, added elements of scandal to her public life. She died after an overdose of sleeping pills, which was ruled accidental.

Although her stormy personal life sometimes complicated her ministry, she was a remarkably popular evangelist. Her dramatic style, enthusiasm, and energy carried her through preaching and revival tours from Florida to California, where she built the Angelus Temple in Los Angeles in the early 1920s. Her Christ-centered message of salvation, baptism in the Spirit, healing, and the return of the Savior appealed to many. Having had a following of over 35,000 during her lifetime, McPherson's church continues today.

BIBLIOGRAPHY

Blumhofer, Edith L. *Aimee Semple McPherson: Everybody's Sister.* 1993.

Epstein, Daniel Mark. *Sister Aimee: The Life of Aimee Semple McPherson.* 1993.

McPherson, Aimee Semple. *This Is That.* 1919. 2d. ed., 1923.

ALEXANDRA F. GRISWOLD

Mead, Margaret

Margaret Mead (1901–1978) was perhaps the best-known anthropologist, American or otherwise, of the twentieth century. Her career as an anthropologist and later as a public figure and intellectual took her all over the world; but her early fieldwork focused on research in the Pacific, specifically in American Samoa, four different cultures in Papua New Guinea, and the tiny Indonesian island of Bali. For most of her career, Mead was a curator at the American Museum of Natural History in New York City. She also taught anthropology for many years at Columbia University.

Mead is best known for her research on female adolescence (*Coming of Age in Samoa*, 1928), gender and sexuality (*Sex and Temperament in Three Primitive Societies*, 1935; *Male and Female*, 1949), socialization (*Growing Up in New Guinea*, 1930), and cultural change (*New Lives for Old*, 1956). Much of Mead's research focused on the analysis of women's roles. In *Coming of Age in Samoa*, for example, she describes the ceremonial role of a village *taupou* or princess whose virginity symbolizes her high rank and the honor of the community. In *Sex and Temperament in Three Primitive Societies*, she was the first anthropologist to argue that gender roles are socially rather than biologically determined. In all these works, Mead also dealt with religious beliefs, ritual, supernaturalism, magic, and healing. Thus, for example, in *Growing Up in New Guinea*, a study of the socialization of Manus children, Mead sought to explain why adults in Manus believed in ghosts and other forms of supernatural beings while

Margaret Mead (1901–1978) was an important American cultural anthropologist. She wrote several books about her fieldwork in Samoa, Bali, and New Guinea including *Coming of Age in Samoa* (Library of Congress/Corbis).

Manus children did not. In doing so, she described the role such supernatural beliefs played in the moral lives of the Manus.

In the 1930s, Mead studied the practice of trance among the Balinese, including the role of women in trance dances. Trance behavior is associated with Hindu-Balinese religious practices. Mead analyzes the religious significance of Balinese trance ritual in the film "Trance and Dance in Bali," which depicts an evil female witch (Rangda) in battle with a benign male dragon (Barong). Their struggle represents the forces of good and evil that are constantly in conflict in the world.

Like her mentor, anthropologist Ruth Benedict, Mead felt that anthropology offered scientific insight into the spiritual dimension of the human condition. Moreover, science and religion could, and must, she felt, work together to solve humanity's problems; they would do so utilizing the diversity of cultures in order to make the world anew.

Awed but not overwhelmed by the power of the atomic bomb, at the end of World War II Mead combined her belief in the efficacy of science with her faith in the love of God to form a religious and ethical system she felt appropriate to the postwar world. In *Twentieth-Century Faith* (1973), she articulated her vision and the hope for survival it offered. As a young woman, Mead had converted to the Episcopal Church, and she remained an active participant in the church throughout her life. She participated for many years in National and World Council of Churches conferences, spoke to religious groups of diverse faiths, and wrote in the popular press and women's magazines such as *Redbook* on ethical issues such as abortion, birth control, euthanasia, and sexual mores (Mead, 1974; 1980).

BIBLIOGRAPHY

WORKS ON MEAD

Bateson, Mary Catherine. *With a Daughter's Eye: A Memoir of Margaret Mead and Gregory Bateson.* 1984.

Howard, Jane. *Margaret Mead: A Life.* 1984.

Lutkehaus, Nancy. Introduction to *Blackberry Winter: My Earlier Years.* By Margaret Mead. 1972. Repr., 1995.

———. "Margaret Mead and the 'Rustling-of-the-Wind-in-the-Palm-Trees' School of Ethnographic Writing." In *Women Writing Culture.* Edited by Ruth Behar and Deborah Gordon. 1995.

WORKS BY MEAD

Aspects of the Present. With Rhoda Metraux. 1980.

Blackberry Winter: My Earlier Years. 1972.

Coming of Age in Samoa. 1928.

Growing Up in New Guinea: A Comparative Study of Primitive Education. 1930.

Male and Female: A Study of the Sexes in a Changing World. 1949.

The Mountain Arapesh. Vol. 2: *Arts and Supernaturalism.* 1942.

New Lives for Old: Cultural Transformation—Manus, 1928–1953. 1956.

Sex and Temperament in Three Primitive Societies. 1935.

To Love or to Perish: The Technological Crisis and the Churches. Edited by Mead, J. Edward Carothers, Daniel D. MacCracken, and Roger L. Shinn.

"Trance and Dance in Bali." Directed by Mead and Gregory Bateson. American Museum of Natural History Film and Photography Archives. 1952.

Twentieth Century Faith: Hope and Survival. 1973.

A Way of Seeing. With Rhoda Metraux. 1974.

See also **Benedict, Ruth.**

NANCY C. LUTKEHAUS

Mechtild of Magdeburg

Mechtild of Magdeburg (c. 1207–c. 1282) was the author of the first great work of religious literature in the German language. She received her first vision at age twelve and, about twenty years later, migrated to Magdeburg, where she adopted the life of a Beguine. (Beguines were women who lived religious lives of prayer and chastity but remained in the world and did not take formal vows.) About 1250, with the support of her confessor, she began to write down revelations, poems, and dialogues on random sheets in Low German. A certain Henry, possibly the learned Dominican Henry of Halle, organized these writings as *The Flowing Light of the Godhead* and circulated five or six books of them during her lifetime. Courageous in castigating the corruption of her clerical contemporaries and audacious in her erotic description of mystical encounter, Mechtild garnered criticism. In 1270, old and nearly blind, she retreated to the convent of Helfta, where she composed a seventh book of the *Flowing Light* and influenced two younger nuns, Gertrude the Great and Mechtild of Hackeborn, whose revelations, composed in Latin in the 1280s and 1290s, are also among the great works of women's mysticism.

The *Flowing Light* survives only in a Latin version made shortly after Mechtild's death and in a High German translation from fourteenth-century Basel, where it circulated widely. Forgotten from the fifteenth to the nineteenth centuries, its rediscovery in 1861 was a major scholarly event. Mechtild's spirituality represents a confluence of courtly love poetry with a theological sophistication learned from Dominican preaching. Earlier scholarship questioned whether her emphasis on the soul's deification verged on heresy. Recent work has stressed her role in creating both religious literature in the vernacular and a tradition of affective female mysticism.

BIBLIOGRAPHY

The best edition of Mechtild's work is Hans Neumann, ed., *Das fliessende Licht der Gottheit: nach der Einsiedler Handschrift in kritischem Vergleich mit der gesamten Überlieferung* (1990). For an English translation, see Susan Clark, ed., and Christiane M. Galvani, trans., *Flowing Light of the Divinity* (1991). On the three Helfta mystics, see Caroline Bynum, "Women Mystics in the Thirteenth Century: The Case of the Nuns of Helfta," in her *Jesus as Mother: Studies in the Spirituality of the High Middle Ages* (1982). The best studies are Jeanne Ancelet-Hustache, *Mechtilde de Magdeburg (1207–1282): Étude de psychologie religieuse* (1926), and Amy M. Hollywood, *The Soul as Virgin Wife: Mechtild of Magdeburg, Marguerite Porete, and Meister Eckhart* (1995).

CAROLINE WALKER BYNUM

Media and Religion

Complex religious commitments, disagreements, and conflicts are woven into the fabric of human lives. Yet few subjects are as sensitive and volatile as that of religion in public discourse and media. On the one hand, contemporary Western print and broadcast journalism adheres to a tradition that at least nominally ascribes to an ideal standard of skeptical inquiry in the interest of objective "fact" or "truth." On the other hand, a richly diverse range of religious institutions and communal traditions employs elaborate patterns of ritual, symbol, belief, and practice in the service of faith commitments or the pursuit of enlightenment. Ultimately human faith is as elusive and intangible as that toward which it purports to direct itself; similarly, the enlightenment of nirvana or satori cannot adequately be conveyed by the positivistic discourse of mainstream news reporting. It is not hard, then, to understand why mainstream news coverage of religion is criticized as poor in quality and substance.

Nevertheless, in spite of this seeming epistemological divide, a considerable amount of information and knowledge about religion is produced and conveyed regularly through the interpretive lens of mass media. This information is marked by discursive and institutional norms through which circulate definitions of what various religions "really" are, as well as how they are to be valued and located within society as a whole.

Part of the problematic nature of media coverage lies in its too-frequent employment of paradigmatic frameworks within which religion and religion-related news is easily cast. Examples include recurrent "feel-good" holiday themes, the pageantry of a papal visit, bizarre scandals, superstitious or naive irrationality, political and military menace, and deviancy. Very real institutional constraints operate upon both print and broadcast media formats, including imposed deadlines, space and time limitations, and the need to appeal to a wide audience for sales and ratings. Only a small percentage of daily newspapers employ full-time religion reporters, and the situation is even worse in broadcasting. That media coverage of religion so often appears—to insiders and outsiders alike—superficial and shallow, infused with stereotypes, misconceptions, inaccuracies, and seemingly deliberate distortions stemming, in part, from sheer ignorance, should come as no surprise.

Within such standard coverage, women's active participation in religious traditions and religiously influenced events, when not invisible, tends to fall into three basic formats: women as obedient supporters of male leadership and initiatives; women as passive victims; and women raising a ruckus on the fringe of "organized" religion. A 1995 study found that male bylines on religion stories appeared twice as often as female bylines, while within these stories, on average, references to men occurred around four times more than to women. The study suggested both an overreliance on male religious leaders as the authoritative basis of stories and an underrepresentation of women that is particularly noteworthy given the higher rate of member-

The Dalai Lama holds a press conference, New York City, 1994 (Mitchell Gerber/© Corbis).

ship and active participation of women over men in many religious organizations. Nor are these observations an isolated finding. A similar content analysis of mainstream press coverage of Pope John Paul II's October 1995 visit to the United States found that men, both expert and lay, were quoted far in excess of women. Of related significance is the fact that when women were quoted, it was most often in relation to stories about dissent from Vatican policies.

Both locally and nationally, the Christian tradition, which holds dominance in the United States, receives more coverage than other traditions. Even so, such coverage is far from complete. Coverage of Catholicism centers around papal initiatives and pronouncements, while Mother Teresa serves as a familiar icon of approved self-sacrificing femininity. Protestantism, with its wide variety of denominations, receives more uneven coverage. Many groups receive little or no media attention at all; others receive a disproportionate amount, as has been the case with politically conservative religious groups. Often feminist issues serve as the target of the so-called religious right. The upshot of standard coverage has been an exaggeration of the tensions between faith traditions and modern secularity such that it often appears as if religious folk are all on one side of an issue and secular folk all on the other. Such an impoverished presentation obscures the wide range of moral and religiously informed stances taken in support of a diverse range of positions on issues like abortion rights, birth control, homosexuality, so-called family values, and the ordination of women.

The theme of women making trouble on the fringe of organized religion has a long history, of which media coverage is only one small part. But it can be argued that standard coverage helps to sustain the status quo

of male power and visibility. For example, when it is through institutional hierarchies—dominated by men— that religions are presented in their ostensibly truest form, then the role played by women is inevitably marginalized. Emphasis on the communal practices and struggles of the laity, by contrast, would almost certainly elevate recognition of women's roles and voices. The 1979 excommunication of Sonia Johnson, a fifth-generation Mormon from the Church of Jesus Christ of the Latter-day Saints, because of her feminist stance in public support of the passage of the Equal Rights Amendment was treated more or less sympathetically by the press. Media coverage reinforced the impression that in the face of male power, women's proper role is to be invisible and silent or to be ousted. When women do come together authoritatively in religious forums, they are still likely to suffer media marginalization. For example, when the media covered a 1993 ecumenical conference held in Minneapolis—"RE-Imagining: A Global Theological Conference by Women"—it focused primarily on exaggerated and distorted claims that the conference had been dominated solely by themes of heresy, paganism, blasphemy, and lesbianism—attention-grabbing claims that had been made by conservative religious groups within two of the sponsoring mainline denominations.

Counter-cultural new religious movements are often labeled pejoratively by the press as sects or cults and linked to such loaded terms as brainwashing and deprogramming. Groups like the Unification Church or the Church of Scientology are often treated as affronts to the social order and cast in a simplistic duality of normalcy versus deviance. Tragedies such as the 1978 mass suicide in Jonestown, Guyana, or the destruction of the Branch Davidian compound in Waco, Texas in 1993, evince representations of women as gullible victims of false prophets.

Immense problems surface in terms of media coverage of non-Christian religions as well. Here a distinction must also be drawn between coverage of national and international issues and events. When not being covered in terms of Middle Eastern events, Judaism often tends to be absorbed under the highly problematic rubric of "Judeo-Christian" norms; Jewish women achieve about the same level of visibility as do Christian women. Other traditions are subject to media stereotyping of the sort that equates Muslim with terrorist, Buddhist with bald male pacifist, and Hindu with Gandhi.

There is probably no better example of egregious treatment of a non-Christian tradition than that extended to Islam. Muslim women, when presented at all, appear as projections of Western ideas and impressions. Edward Said has long argued that Western media treatment of Islam is shaped by a mixture of ignorance, enduring Orientalist stereotypes, and the geopolitical concerns of foreign policy and oil interests. He points to the 1980 PBS broadcast of "Death of a Princess," which recounts the execution of a Saudi Arabian princess and her commoner lover. The docudrama was made by a non-Muslim and broadcast in a conflated context of anti-Islamic and anti-Arab feelings that had reemerged in the wake of the Iranian revolution and the holding of American hostages (from late 1979 until early 1981). The film reflects Western culture's longstanding historic and political interest in attributing fanatical barbarity to the Islamic tradition as a whole. Islam is one of the fastest-growing religions around the world and in the United States, yet the images of Islam in mainstream press and broadcast coverage continue to cast all Muslims as Arabs and all Arabs as terrorists. The veiled Muslim woman repeatedly crops up as the image of the tragic victim of Islamic fundamentalism run amok. Some women, indeed, are coerced into wearing the head or full body veil; but other women choose to do so as an expression of their faith commitments, or as a form of resistance to the colonizing imperatives of Western cultures. That there are also Muslim feminists tends to be little noted.

Clearly, the task of evaluating media coverage of women in world religions requires a subversive interpretive strategy that attempts to see through the normative procedures, power relations, and biases that pervade and shape the news deemed fit to print or broadcast.

BIBLIOGRAPHY

Bates, Stephen. "Separation of Church and Press." *Forbes Mediacritic* (Summer 1994): 48–55.

Buddenbaum, Judith M. "Network News Coverage of Religion." In *Channels of Belief: Religion and American Commercial Television.* Edited by John P. Ferré. 1990.

"By Men, For Men, and About Men: Media Coverage of the Visit of Pope John Paul to the U.S. in October of 1995." Catholics for a Free Choice, Washington, D.C., March, 1996. Content analysis, including media coverage of women and religion.

Dart, John, and Jimmy Allen. *Bridging the Gap: Religion and the News Media.* Freedom Forum First Amendment Center. 1993.

"Death of a Princess." Directed by Anthony Thomas. WBGH. 1980.

"Faith vs. Fact: Press Images of Religion in the United States." University of Rochester. 1995. Study of seven major American newspapers.

FitzSimon, Martha. *Religion and the News: A Conference Report.* Freedom Forum Media Studies Center. 1994.

Ghareeb, Edmund. *Split Vision: The Portrayal of Arabs in the American Media.* American-Arab Affairs Council. 1983.

God in the Newsroom: Fifteen Articles on Coverage of Religion. Nieman Reports at Harvard University. 1993.

Said, Edward. *Covering Islam: How the Media and the Experts Determine How We See the Rest of the World.* 1981.

Silk, Mark. *Unsecular Media: Making News of Religion in America.* 1995.

"Through Ignorance or Design: A Discussion of Stereotypes." Directed by Kathleen Shannon. National Film Board of Canada. 1990. Discusses the effects on women of others' misconceptions of customs and beliefs.

See also **Film and Video.**

JESSICA G. GUGINO

Meditation in Asian Traditions

Although the word *meditation* does not correspond to a single term across Asian traditions or even within a single tradition, it is generally described as a disciplined activity of destroying unwholesome mental states and initiating wholesome states. It is a systematic methodology for transforming the practitioner's understanding of herself and the world, and accomplished meditators are sometimes believed to develop supernormal powers.

Although many Vedic women in early India were educated in scripture and ritual, women's access to orthodox religion eventually declined. The growth of Buddhism in India offered women and men salvation through the same specialized meditation techniques, involving imaginative visualization, concentration on the mind and the breath, recitation, and gestures. Over the centuries, Buddhist literature throughout Asia describes influential, respected nuns who taught and wrote, although little survives of their teachings or of how their experiences were shaped by their gender. While Buddhist monks in Tibet studied philosophy, art, and sciences, nuns in Tibet were for the most part limited to the practice of meditation and ritual. Tibetan texts identify daily practices for women, such as visualization of deities, scriptural recitation, and fasting. Stories of great nuns report meditative accomplishments

A Buddhist nun meditates inside the Long San Pagoda temple, Nha Trang, Vietnam, 1993 (Owen Franken/ Corbis).

such as breath control and inner heat generation, and rigorous fasting programs, such as long-term isolation retreats or the practice of "essence extraction," subsistence on herbal pellets.

In classical Hinduism, because spiritual advancement by meditation or study was denied to women, the Indian woman's primary religious practice was ritualized worship of her husband, even after his death. Beginning in eighth-century India, Hindu women worshiped with purificatory baths, fasting, recitations, and reenactments of the deities' activities. Using the model of marriage, the Hindu bhakti movement taught that salvation comes through intense dedication to a deity. Through love of her deity, a woman could obtain the meditative state of blissful awareness described by philosophers. For serious devotees, such a deep meditative experience could result in the rejection of family life. Chinese, Korean, and Japanese texts document

spiritually accomplished women whose meditative experiences led them toward careers as shamans.

Turning to the symbolic realm, feminine imagery is widely utilized in Asian meditative practices where meditators identify themselves with feminine forces; the complex use of such imagery emphasizes the fact that meditation is not limited to a ritualized seated position. Taoist teachings rely on feminine symbols such as water, while the female body represents the creative force of the Tao and feminine behavior is the model for all Taoists. Buddhism and Hinduism offer myriad female deities as visualization objects for female and male meditators. In some Taoist and tantric traditions, symbolic practices of uniting feminine and masculine forces became explicitly sexual, and marginal groups of practitioners engaged in ritualized intercourse, described in meditation manuals.

BIBLIOGRAPHY

Denton, Lynn, "Varieties of Female Asceticism." In *Roles and Rituals for Hindu Women.* Edited by Julia Leslie. 1991.

Havnevik, Hanna. *Tibetan Buddhist Nuns: History, Cultural Norms and Social Reality.* 1989.

Ray, Reginald A. "Accomplished Women in Tantric Buddhism of Medieval India and Tibet." In *Unspoken Worlds: Women's Religious Lives.* Edited by Nancy Falk and Rita Gross. 1989.

Tsai, Kathryn. *Lives of the Nuns: Biographies of Chinese Buddhist Nuns from the Fourth to Sixth Centuries.* 1994.

See also Asceticism; Emptiness; Monasticism: In the East; Mysticism; Prayer; Sexuality; Tantra; Wisdom: Prajñā and Prajñāpāramitā.

FRANCES M. GARRETT

Memory

As a category in religion, memory is related to issues of knowledge, tradition, history, religious identity, and religious practice. Investigation of women's memory in religion is guided initially by two central questions. What is women's memory? Is it authentic? The first question leads to uncovering and exploring women's histories and experiences. The second asks for an evaluation of available memories. Memory is both a problem and a resource for those who deal with such questions of availability and of authenticity. Given that memory is often viewed as essential for identity, both personal and social, the recognition that theologies, traditions, and religious practices are androcentric raises questions about women's experiences and their sense of place and role in religion. Memory is viewed as a problem in two senses. A study of religious traditions reveals the lack, silencing, erasure, and distortion of women's experiences and of women's histories. Additionally, women's access to religious memory, to knowledge and full participation in religious traditions, is often limited or indirect. As a resource, the search for memory reclaims women's experiences and histories as necessary both for understanding the exclusion and oppression of women and for finding alternative approaches to women's lives and religious experiences. Women's memories are understood to be a necessary resource for religious identity, authentic practice, and empowerment.

A third question then emerges: how is remembering a religious practice that enhances women's religious experience? This question is especially important in those religious expressions such as Judaism and ancestor worship, in which remembering the past and locating oneself in the present by means of memorative practices are central.

WOMEN'S MEMORY

Simone de Beauvoir, whose groundbreaking feminist work has influenced decades of scholarship, wrote in *The Second Sex* (1961) that women "have no past, no history, no religion of their own" (p. xix). This charge—essentially, that women have no memory of their own—rendered women's lives and experiences as a problem of lack. Feminist scholars and writers responded by launching a search for women's memory, history, religious experience, and sources of power.

This search has proceeded in multiple directions. One direction has reexamined and reconstructed religious traditions in order to add or insert women's stories. Jewish theologian Judith Plaskow and Christian theologian Elisabeth Schüssler Fiorenza both assume 1) that the Jewish and Christian traditions, as formulated and passed down, exclude women; and 2) women were and are active participants in those traditions. Therefore, the traditions, as memory, are not only incomplete, but distorted; they need to be transformed to include women's experiences and women's lives. Yet questions remain: should women's lives in religious traditions be viewed primarily through a lens of suffering and oppression, a lens of forgotten leadership and agency, or one of resistance and struggle? Was there a pristine golden age before patriarchal distortion; is there an authentic strain by which the rest of tradition might be assessed and corrected; or are the distortions fundamental to the entire religious tradition? Emphasis

Holocaust memory is incomplete without attention to women's experiences, such as childbirth, forced prostitution, and subjection to reproductive experimentation. These women and children were liberated from Lambach Concentration Camp in Austria, 7 May 1945 (The National Archives/Corbis).

on one or another approach suggests different strategies and practices for retrieval and change.

Some scholars and investigators have suggested that there is a forgotten, other realm of women's experiences that ought to be uncovered and recovered if women are to have a past and authentic memory. Such experiences are both ontological and historical. Women's true being is not manifest within patriarchal history. Women's memories are to be discovered in lost gynocentric or matriarchal practices and traditions. Alternatively, they are to be found in what may be considered folk practices and customs that are marginalized, disapproved of, or unrecognized by institutionalized religions. Those searching for such memories either use historical methods to uncover forgotten pasts or they suggest an imaginative reconstruction of a female past. Some cite from Monique Wittig's work, *Les Guerilleres* (1971): "There was a time when you were not a slave, remember that. . . . Make an effort to remember. Or, failing that, invent" (p. 89). This approach may draw upon ideas of the unconscious storage of memories or a collective unconscious that may be retrieved or revealed through changing one's consciousness.

AUTHENTIC MEMORY

The search for memory raises questions regarding authentic memory for women. Debates abound about whether women's lives in the major religious traditions constitute false consciousness and, if so, whether authentic memory must be found elsewhere. There are also debates about both the status of women's oppression and leadership within those traditions, and the tendency either to valorize women's past or to focus on women's suffering. Underlying these various perspectives are questions about difference and whether women's lives are historically distinct or ontologically different. Two examples from European history illustrate these differences. During the late Middle Ages and Reformation, large numbers of women were killed as witches. Should these women be remembered as victims of a patriarchal Christianity intent on destroying women? Or should they be viewed as the defeated practitioners of alternative religious and folk practices in a war for religious control? In other words, were they helpless victims or defeated heroines? Another example concerns Jewish women in the Holocaust: are women to be considered a special case in Holocaust remembrance? Early research by Joan Ringelheim claimed that women survived better because of certain female traits and behaviors. Later Ringelheim herself questioned this argument and its presuppositions. Issues remain about the different experiences of women during the Holocaust and whether such differences ought to carry special status or demand separate attention. Holocaust memory is arguably incomplete without attention to women's particular experiences, such as childbirth, forced prostitution, and subjection to reproductive experimentation.

REMEMBERING AS RELIGIOUS PRACTICE

Many religions understand remembering as a religious practice carrying salvific significance: remembering re-members persons and communities through changing consciousness or mediating the revelatory past to the present. Given this central role accorded to remembering, how are women present or represented in such practices? Some argue that the story of the Exodus must recall Miriam's role as well as Moses' and that female ancestors ought to be accorded as much power as male ancestors. Further arguments suggest that religion ought to incorporate not only the memory of women, but women's distinctive and marginalized experiences and practices. In some cases, investigations reveal alternative or hidden religious practices that are transmitted by women's memories through generational and relational female networks. Religious traditions, such as Buddhism, in which memory relates both to practice of mindfulness and to the recollection of past lives, suggest other and distinctive questions about memory. How are these practices gendered ones and what impact does that have on women's memory? At-

tending to such arguments and questions may reform religious traditions and communities that have been not only incomplete, but harmful to women's lives. Remembering of and by women emerges as a complex process of retrieval and transformation.

BIBLIOGRAPHY

For theoretical and theological considerations of women's historical memory in Christianity and Judaism, see Elisabeth Schüssler Fiorenza's *In Memory of Her: A Feminist Theological Reconstruction of Christian Origins* (1983; 2d ed., 1994) and Judith Plaskow's *Standing Again at Sinai: Judaism from a Feminist Perspective* (1990). Mary Daly's *Gyn/Ecology: The Metaethics of Radical Feminism* (1978; 2d ed., 1990) offers an overview of her approach to women's true ontological memory and the false memories instilled by patriarchy. For an introduction to selected arguments for women's alternative, lost, or hidden traditions, see Charlene Spretnak, ed., *The Politics of Women's Spirituality: Essays on the Rise of Spiritual Power within the Feminist Movement* (1982), especially Part I and Appendix II. Anne Llewellyn Barstow's *Witchcraze: A New History of the European Witch Hunts* (1994) presents a feminist interpretation of the witch-hunts. For issues regarding women and the Holocaust, see Carol Rittner and John K. Roth, eds., *Different Voices: Women and the Holocaust* (1993), which includes a selection by Joan Ringelheim that reviews her reconsideration of her own arguments; Myrna Goldenberg, "Different Horrors, Same Hell: Women Remembering the Holocaust," in *Thinking the Unthinkable: Meanings of the Holocaust*, edited by Roger S. Gottlieb (1991); and Sara R. Horowitz, "Memory and Testimony of Women Survivors of Nazi Genocide," in *Women of the Word: Jewish Women and Jewish Writing*, edited by Judith R. Baskin (1994). Memoirs and autobiographies, as well as particular historical studies, also offer rich resources and reflections on women's memory and religion.

See also **Ancestor Worship; Goddess: History of Study.**

FLORA A. KESHGEGIAN

Menarche

In all gathering-hunting and horticultural traditions, menarche (first menstruation) rituals are of utmost importance not only for women but for the culture as a whole. These rituals mark not simply the physical maturity of the females of the communities but their becoming one with cosmic spirits, particularly Earth and

Moon, and manifesting the fertile potentiality of the female, both human and divine. Hence, the ritual celebrates the spiritual unfolding of the female for the good of the entire community. These cultures, which can be matrilineal and matrilocal, are egalitarian from the sociopolitical standpoint. As among the Hopi of the American Southwest, both males and females acknowledge the superior importance (but not superiority) of females. There is no male equivalent to this physical-spiritual marking of the human female's coming of age.

GATHERING-HUNTING CULTURES

Menarche is the first time that a young woman sequesters herself from males in cultures where hunting is an important male activity; this is to prevent powerful pheromones that can be smelled by animals for miles from becoming attached to hunters and their implements. Simultaneously, this is the time of her first major vision-quest, when spirit(s) come to her to provide her with spiritual power for the rest of her life. Hence, menarche denotes the female's coming into her spiritual powers as she bonds herself to the spirit realm through the flow of her blood onto Earth; through the paralleling of the flow of her blood and the flow of the waters, the blood of Earth; and through matching the cycles of Moon.

In at least some native Australian traditions, a young women's menstrual blood was rubbed on her body during the menarche ritual, and young males had ritual penile subincision during their initiation rites in order to approximate a bleeding vagina. In the continuing Algonkian-speaking traditions of northern North America, both young boys and girls begin fasting for visions from an early age; while the major fast for young girls is at the menarche, for males it can take place any time during adolescence. Contemporary traditionalist Anishnabe (Ojibwe, Odawa, Potowatami) women speak of gaining not only spiritual empowerment but a strong sense of self-worth at this time. In the northern Athabaskan-speaking traditions (Dené), young women may be sequestered for up to a year at this time; but it is acknowledged by men that at the conclusion of the menarche separation and rituals, women may gain spiritual power stronger than those available to males.

HORTICULTURAL TRADITIONS

In horticultural (here defined as nonintensive agricultural) traditions menarche is more important with regard to the manifesting of a young woman's fertility, both in the sense of women's ability to produce children and women's virtual monopoly on the fertility of the horticultural fields, symbolized through blood. Accordingly, the celebration is more communal or family-oriented, and the ritual may be delayed until after the menarche when sufficient resources have been gathered for a major ceremonial.

For example, among the Yoruba of Nigeria, Benin, and Togo, an elaborate menarche ritual begins on a major market day, a day special to women who control the markets, and lasts for nine days. These rituals, through special exorcisms and mock betrothals and marriages, transform the girl into a woman. The dangers of uncontrolled power of the first menstruation is replaced by the controlled power of the mature woman. Through the spiritual connections she develops, the new adult is ready to take up the traditional triple female roles of wife, mother, and trader.

In the neighboring Akan culture of Ghana, when a young woman first menstruates her mother places her on a white stool of honor in front of the dwelling entrance. This important news is then announced to the entire village, and the old women gather to sing ritual songs and beat a drum before her. A week of symbolically rich and elaborate rituals take place—involving special foods, rites performed alongside rivers, the wearing of fine clothing, and the linking of the young woman to the fertility of Earth—after which, owing to the new relationship between her and the spirit realm, she is recognized as a mature member of the community.

Among the Diné (Apache and Navajo of the southwestern United States), a fusion of the Dené focus on the spiritual potentiality of the menarche and Pueblo horticultural traditions has led to perhaps the most impressive menarche rituals in the world: the menarche ritual has become the major ceremony of the tradition and the focus of the entire community. Particularly among the Apache, the ceremony awaits the gathering of resources to arrange for masked dancers, feasting by the entire community, and many guests for several days. During this elaborate ceremonial, the young woman incarnates (becomes) the Earth Mother herself. Her touch can heal the sick and promote the growth of young children. For the four days of the ritual, she is utterly holy, for she is the deity herself. At the end of the ritual, she is transformed into an adult. Every woman who has had this experience will remain empowered for the rest of her life. Those who have not, because of modern lifestyle changes, often express a lifelong regret.

AGRICULTURAL-INDUSTRIAL CULTURES

It is only in the patriarchal, agricultural-industrial cultures that women tend to lose not only their public roles but also ceremonial acknowledgment of the power, made manifest at menarche, that is exclusively female. In Jewish, Christian, and Muslim cultures menstruation is understood to be polluting rather than powerful, and menarche is hidden and shameful rather than celebrated. Unfortunately, this essentially misogynist attitude permeates ethnological and religious studies literature, which tends to ignore or misconstrue menarche and menstruation rituals and reflect Western rather than indigenous understandings.

BIBLIOGRAPHY

For more detailed religious, cultural, and methodological perspectives, see Jordan Paper, *Through the Earth Darkly: Female Spirituality in Comparative Perspective* (1977), which covers cultures discussed here and also Saami, Hopi, Chinese, Japanese, Korean, and other cultures. Further material on Anishnabe menarche rituals can be found in Ron Geyshick, *Te Bwe Win (Truth)* (1989); on Athapaskan traditions, in June Helm, *Prophecy and Power Among the Dogrib Indians* (1994). Limited material on Yoruba menarche rituals can be found in Jacob Kehinde Olupona, *Kingship, Religion and Rituals in a Nigerian Community: A Phenomenological Study of Ondo Yoruba Festivals* (1991). Regarding the Diné, a fuller description of the Navajo menarche ritual can be found in Charlotte Johnson Frisbie, *Kinaaldá: A Study of the Navajo Girl's Puberty Ceremony* (1967); of an Apache menarche ritual, in Morris Edward Opler, *An Apache Life-Way: The Economic, Social, and Religious Institutions of the Chircahua Indians* (1941).

See also Blood; Menopause; Menstruation; Rites of Passage.

JORDAN PAPER

Menchú, Rigoberta

Guatemalan indigenous woman, political activist, and human rights champion Rigoberta Menchú was awarded the Nobel Peace Prize in 1992. Born in 1959, she grew up in the mountain village of Chimel in north central Guatemala. Like many other Indian families with too little land, the Menchús spent part of each year working for cash on large plantations (where one brother died of malnutrition and another of pesticide poisoning). She did not attend school and only learned Spanish as an adolescent in order to communicate with other Indians (the Quichés are one of around twenty ethnic groups in Guatemala) and other Guatemalans.

Menchú's community activism began when she was a catechist. She learned much accompanying her father, Vicente Menchú, who for many years led a struggle to protect the community from those who would take their land, often traveling to other villages and to government offices in regional towns and Guatemala City. At one point he was jailed for over a year for his organizing efforts. In the late 1970s, Vicente Menchú became affiliated with a new peasant organizing effort, the CUC (Committee for Peasant Unity), and Rigoberta also became a CUC organizer. Priests and sisters in her local parish and from Guatemala City were key figures in Menchú's emergence as a leader. While giving due credit to Catholic Church pastoral workers, she also defends the legitimacy of traditional indigenous religion, which the Catholic Church historically opposed and despised.

As existing political conflicts became more open in the late 1970s and early 1980s, Menchú was swept into public events. Responding to a perceived guerrilla threat, the Guatemalan army increased its attacks on Indian villages and organizations such as the CUC. In 1979 her younger brother Petrocinio was captured, brutally tortured, and then publicly burned alive along with others that the army had accused of subversion. In January 1980, a group of people from Quiché went to Guatemala City seeking to draw attention to the repression and occupied the Spanish embassy; the police attacked, a fire broke out, and thirty-nine people, including Vicente Menchú, were burned alive. In April the army abducted her mother, Juana Tum, and slowly tortured her to death. Menchú continued as a CUC organizer but finally had to flee Guatemala, like many other activists, in 1981.

In 1982 she and Venezuelan anthropologist Elisabeth Burgos-Debray collaborated to produce her autobiography, *I, Rigoberta Menchú*, which was then translated into over a dozen languages. In the book she celebrates the beauty and joy of the Indian way of life and customs and denounces the oppression under which indigenous people live (describing, for example, the humiliations she endured as a maid in Guatemala City). The book also chronicles her growing political awareness. For example, initially *ladinos* (non-Indians) are portrayed exclusively as evil exploiters of the Indians, but over time she (and her father) discover that many *ladinos* are also poor and exploited. Similarly, she credits priests and sisters with crucial help and recognizes that many church people were martyrs, while also noting that institutional representatives of the Catholic Church continued to support the army.

During the 1980s Menchú became part of a five-member team that had nongovernmental status at the United Nations, where each year they lobbied to have human rights violations in Guatemala censured by the General Assembly (a sober estimate is that fifty thousand to seventy-five thousand people were murdered by the army or death squads in the 1978–1985 period). Being in effect a diplomat, while constantly traveling and lecturing, she continued her political education. In 1987 she returned to Guatemala for the first time, in a high-level delegation and under the glare of the international press as protection. Her visits became more frequent until she moved back to Guatemala permanently in 1994. Rigoberta Menchú was awarded the Nobel Peace Prize in 1992, the International Year of Indigenous People.

BIBLIOGRAPHY

Menchú, Rigoberta. *I, Rigoberta Menchú: An Indian Woman in Guatemala.* 1984.

"Rigoberta Menchú: Broken Silence." Films for the Humanities, 1993.

See also Christianity: In Latin America and the Caribbean; Liberation Theologies.

PHILLIP BERRYMAN

Menopause

Unlike menarche, which receives ceremonial recognition in numerous societies, menopause, an event that can only be identified retrospectively, is not marked by ritual. It is not, however, without spiritual significance, nor is menopause overlooked in the belief systems of nonindustrial societies. Thus, for example, there is the Caribbean belief that the end of menstruation is the result of impregnation by a supernatural being. And menopause is not without its secular myths, largely medical in industrial societies, such as the physical and psychological consequences attributed to "the change."

In the nonindustrial world, menopause ushers in two major changes in women's lives: First, in some societies, the end of childbearing signals the elimination of a variety of strictures and taboos. Women are freed from observing menstrual customs, cumbersome restrictions that are often motivated by fear of the supernatural evil contained in menstrual blood. Menopause also frees women from the customs pertaining to pregnancy and lactation, which are regarded as necessary for the spiritual welfare, health, or physical appearance of the unborn or very young child. In some societies, in the Muslim world and in South Asia, where religious restriction limit women to life within the household and its courtyard during childbearing years, menopause frees a woman to move about without chaperonage. The middle-aged woman is also relieved of a variety of religious rules about comportment and modesty and the need to exhibit subservient and elaborate deferential behavior toward her husband and specified members of the ascending generation, such as the mother-in-law.

Second, the end of childbearing also ushers in the possibility that a woman's special spiritual gifts and ritual knowledge receive recognition beyond the household. In many societies postmenopausal women are eligible for special status, such as being a healer or a midwife. Such is the case among Maya villagers in Mexico (Beyenne, 1989) and in Korea (Kendall, 1985). In some cases, ritual activity that a woman may have been taught earlier in life may be practiced only after menopause, as among the North American Comanche (Jones, 1984). Among the Kiliai of Papua New Guinea, postmenopausal women are allowed to enter the men's house, handle sacred paraphernalia, and participate in men's ritual, all of which are totally forbidden to younger women (Counts, 1992). Older women's central role in ritual is also reported among the Garifuna, also known as Black Caribs (Kerns, 1983).

The following example, taken from the account by Meigs (1984) of the Hua of Papua New Guinea, illustrates how one particular religion constructs a complex developmental sequence for women's spiritual condition. Meigs reports that Hua women look forward to menopause because they then become "like a man." In this society, menstruation and childbirth are viewed as unclean and degrading, and menstrual blood and the fluids expressed at childbirth are the most feared as being polluting to men. A woman's pollution makes her less vulnerable to disease and as her pollution diminishes, her invulnerability diminishes also. Through birth, the male becomes slightly polluted by his mother, but this is removed by the rituals of initiation. The mature man is vulnerable and becomes polluted by each sexual act. By old age, he is truly polluted but virtually invulnerable. Postmenopausal women, on the other hand, have become cleansed by the act of giving birth at least three or more times, by sexual intercourse, and by menstruation. Such women are initiated and shown the secrets of the men's society, after which they take up residence in the men's house, where they observe the prohibitions and food avoidances practiced by men. However, those postmenopausal women who have given birth to fewer than three children do not receive this changed status and are viewed as polluted. Among the Hua, pollution, vulnerability, maleness and femaleness, the postmenopausal status of women, and women's relationship to the sacred are all interrelated, negotiable, and far from static.

As this example illustrates, although menopause may not receive ritual recognition, it may nevertheless enjoy a prominent place in a people's belief system and may exert a profound influence on the spiritual (as well as secular) life of women. In some societies menopause opens up to older women a variety of opportunities—to heal, to deliver babies, to make contact with the supernatural, to have the sacred revealed to them—that are denied to that society's women of childbearing age.

BIBLIOGRAPHY

Beyenne, Yewoubdar. *From Menarche to Menopause: Reproductive Lives of Peasant Women in Two Cultures.* 1989.

Brown, Judith K. "Cross-cultural Perspectives on Middle-Aged Women." *Current Anthropology* 23, no. 2 (1982): 143–156.

Counts, Dorothy A. "*Tamparonga:* The Big Women of Kaliai (Papua New Guinea)." In *In Her Prime: New Views of Middle-Aged Women,* 2d ed. Edited by Virginia Kerns and Judith K. Brown. 1992.

Davis, Donna. *Blood and Nerves: An Ethnographic Focus on Menopause.* 1983.

Jones, David E. *Sanapia: Comanche Medicine Woman.* 1984.

Kaufert, Patricia A. "Midlife in the Midwest: Canadian Women in Manitoba." In *In Her Prime: A New View of Middle-Aged Women.* Edited by Judith K. Brown and Virginia Kerns. 1985.

Kendall, Laurel. *Shamans, Housewives, and Other Restless Spirits: Women in Korean Ritual Life.* 1985.

Kerns, Virginia. *Women and the Ancestors: Black Carib Kinship and Ritual.* 1983.

Kerns, Virginia, and Judith K. Brown, eds. *In Her Prime: New Views of Middle-Aged Women.* 2d ed., 1992.

Lock, Margaret. *Encounters with Aging: Mythologies of Menopause in Japan and North America.* 1993.

Meigs, Anna S. *Food, Sex, and Pollution: A New Guinea Religion.* 1984.

See also **Fertility and Barrenness**; **Menstruation**.

JUDITH K. BROWN

Men's Spirituality Movement

The men's spirituality movement, often referred to simply as the men's movement, is more accurately viewed as a constellation of movements that have come into being, mostly in North America, since the late 1970s. Covering "a spectrum from pro-gay activist to anti-liberal 'save the family' positions" (Doty, 1993, p. 5), men's spirituality movements encompass the "queer," neopagan Radical Faeries (described as "profeminist and prowomanist" by Gorsline in Krondorfer, 1996, p. 128); the weekend-retreat coteries of drum-beating, self-styled "wild men" (a cultural fad of the late 1980s and early 1990s); and the antifeminist, antigay Promise Keepers, an evangelical Christian organization whose revival-like meetings were filling football stadiums in the mid-1990s. All these movements are historically linked by the fact that they have arisen in the wake of second-wave feminism and can, at least in part, be understood as responses to or reactions against it.

In the popular mind, men's spirituality is probably most closely identified with figures such as the poet Robert Bly (1990), the theologian Sam Keen (1991), and a host of other writers, lecturers, and workshop leaders (including, to name a few, Michael Meade, Robert Moore, Malidoma Somé) who represent what has come to be called the mythopoetic branch of the men's movement.

Heavily influenced by Jungian psychoanalysis (especially the work of latter-day Jungians such as James Hillman) and by the archetypal interpretations of world mythologies put forth by the late historian of religions Joseph Campbell (see Campbell, 1949), this loosely organized faction of the men's movement appeared, by the late 1990s, to have passed its heyday. The aims of its lecture-circuit gurus are several: (1) to limn a crisis of masculinity in contemporary society, which is accused of systematically robbing men of the opportunity for spiritually wholesome self-realization; (2) to rediscover mythic role models, folkloric narratives, and ritual lifeways that define and nurture a vital, life-affirming masculinity; and (3) to deploy this reclaimed knowledge in the creation of new forms of male initiation, mentoring, and sociality that will rescue men from the depersonalizing, spiritually desiccating effects of industrial and postindustrial civilization and, in the bargain, do much to rectify the currently strained relations between men and women.

In its aims of cultural analysis, spiritual reclamation, and ritual (re)invention, the mythopoetic men's movement owes much to the feminist and women's spirituality movements that preceded and have grown up alongside it. (Indeed, the men's movement finds one of its origins in the small, local men's groups that emulated women's consciousness-raising groups of the early 1970s [see Driver in Krondorfer, 1996].) This debt has often been acknowledged and lip-service paid to feminist goals of gender equality, but the theorists of this branch of the men's movement concur that men are ill served by woman-centered spirituality and that feminism, if inadvertently, has contributed to the emasculation—the "softening" (Bly)—of contemporary males. In general, men's movement theorists have indulged in a highly essentializing ideology of masculinity that parallels essentialist conceptions of femaleness postulated by some (especially earlier) proponents of women's spirituality but that diverges sharply from views that stress the historically and culturally differential, socially constructed character of gender (see Mirsky in Krondorfer, 1996).

The mythpoetic men's movement possesses a mixed agenda that is, by turns, conservative and progressive. For example, the desire to regain "lost" male power is to some extent counterbalanced by the recognition that men's experiences are inevitably perspectival and nongeneric. Similarly, a genuine openness to other cultural patterns must be set against a tendency—which the men's movement has shared with other New Age movements—to "exoticize" and coopt non-Western spiritual traditions. The mythopoetic men's movement has thus earned both condemnation and a smattering of (partial and highly tentative) approval from feminist observers (see Hagan, 1992). But the "men's responsibility" movements of the mid-1990s, including the October 1995 Million Man March on Washington, D.C., organized by Nation of Islam leader Louis Farrakhan, and the Promise Keepers, who organized their own march on the capital in the fall of 1997, are much more unambiguously reactionary in temper, reasserting the man's "natural, God-given" status as head of family, community, and society.

BIBLIOGRAPHY

The men's movement and the related academic discipline of men's studies have spawned a vast literature, which ranges from pop-psychological self-help books to an academic quarterly, *The Journal of Men's Studies,* which commenced publication in 1992. For the uninitiated (pun intended) reader, a good place to begin is the men's movement's best-selling manifestos, Robert Bly's *Iron John: A Book About Men* (1990) and Sam Keen's *Fire in the Belly: On Being a Man* (1991). (Both Bly and Keen were the subjects of Public Broadcasting System programs hosted by the mytho-poetaster journalist Bill Moyers.) Of the scores (hundreds?) of books produced by men's movement gurus and wannabe-gurus, one of the most affecting is Malidoma Patrice Somé's memoir of his life as a shaman of the Dangara people of Burkina Faso, *Of Water and the Spirit: Ritual, Magic, and Initiation in the Life of an African Shaman* (1994).

One of the deepest intellectual taproots of the contemporary men's movement is the work of Joseph Campbell, especially *The Hero with a Thousand Faces* (1949 and many subsequent editions). An updated version of the Campbellian quest for spiritually restorative mythic models is William G. Doty's *Myths of Masculinity* (1993), worthwhile especially for Doty's critical questioning of essentializing tendencies in the men's movement. The impact of the men's movement on liberal Christianity in the United States may be assessed by glancing at Stephen B. Boyd's *The Men We Long to Be: Beyond Domination to a New Christian Understanding of Manhood* (1995).

The diversity of feminist viewpoints on the men's movement is well represented by *Women Respond to the Men's Movement: A Feminist Collection* (1992), edited by Kay Leigh Hagan. The increasingly self-critical and theoretically sophisticated stances of at least some (male) men's studies scholars is exhibited in the excellent collection *Men's Bodies, Men's Gods: Male Identities in a (Post-) Christian Culture* (1996), edited by Björn Krondorfer and containing, among many others, essays by Robin Gorsline, Tom Driver, and Seth Mirsky. The men's studies subdiscipline of religious studies has, thus far, produced one masterpiece, Howard Eilberg-Schwartz's *God's Phallus and Other Problems for Men and Monotheism* (1993), which uncovers the inherent anxieties attending male identity and sexuality in ancient Israelite religion and modern Judaism—that is, in monotheistic religious systems that are male-dominated and heterosexually structured.

The burgeoning literature on gay men's spirituality includes spiritual autobiography and confession. *Wrestling with the Angel: Faith and Religion in the Lives of Gay Men* (1995), edited by Brian Bouldrey, is a superb anthology as is feminist-influenced, gay-male theological reflection such as Gary David Comstock's *Gay Theology without Apology* (1993) and Richard Cleaver's *Know My Name: A Gay Liberation Theology* (1995). Randy P. Conner's ambitious study of "gender-variant" men's roles in world religious traditions, *Blossom of Bone: Reclaiming the Connections Between Homoeroticism and the Sacred* (1993), is marred by a New Age approach that facilely equates widely divergent cultural phenomena.

See also **Queer Theory.**

JAMES C. WALLER

Menstruation

Early anthropological accounts of menstruation presupposed the existence of a universal menstrual taboo. But later studies from the 1970s to 1990s indicate that the ritual proscriptions that surround menstruation vary greatly among religious traditions. And even some previously perceived menstrual taboos have been reappraised as menstrual celebrations (Buckley and Gottlieb, 1988). In many cultures, however, an ambivalent attitude greets menstruation, with ceremonial rites simultaneously regulating and endorsing the power of the menstruating woman.

In the Sioux tradition, menarche (first menstruation) is celebrated with ritual seclusion, ceremonial instruction, and a special feast and gift-giving ceremony (Black Elk, [Joseph Epes Brown, ed.] in *The Sacred Pipe*, pp. 116–126). The young girl is treated as sacred and powerful and is honored by her community. The Yurok of California believe that a woman has supernatural or extraspiritual abilities during her menses. The menstruating woman takes part in ritual seclusion in a number of different traditions, such as the natives of Momog Island (Pacific), the Djuka (Guiana), the Warao (Venezuela), the Kaska (western Canada), and the Yurok (California), among others. Though some view this segregation from daily life as restrictive, others see it as an opportunity for the menstruating woman to be free from traditional domestic chores, to socialize with other women, to cook special meals, to weave, to meditate and worship, to participate in women-only rituals, songs, myths, and prayers, or even to take part in extramarital affairs (Buckley and Gottlieb, "A Critical Appraisal of Theories of Menstrual Symbolism" in *Blood Magic*, pp. 1–50).

The belief in the life-affirming powers of menstrual blood is widespread. Many traditions including the Kwakiutl (Pacific Northwest) and the Asante (Ghana) use menstrual blood in fertility and planting rituals, or in protective ceremonies to ward off evil forces. The powerful life-giving properties of menstrual blood are likely responsible for the prohibitions in most hunting cultures against menstruating women touching the hunting equipment or taking part in the hunt itself.

In Hinduism menstruation is thought to purify a woman's body, ridding her of the dangers caused by excess blood; yet the process of menstruation itself is said to be polluting. Menarche is treated as an auspicious event, marked by ritual seclusion, special dietary restrictions, and a ceremonial bath at the end of the menses (on the seventh day). The *Law of Manu* state that menstrual blood is unclean (*ashaucha*), and that a menstruating woman should be treated, for a total of four days, as if she were an "untouchable." Theoretically there are many restrictions that must be observed during a woman's menses: a menstruating woman is not permitted to perform religious worship or devotion; she must remain secluded from other members of her family during this time, in a special corner or section of the household, and is not to communicate with others; touch or play with children; cook; bathe or change her clothing; or wear jewelry, or oil or brush her hair. A man who touches a menstruating woman is defiled by her polluted state, and a man who has sex with a menstruating woman will lose his health, wisdom, and energy. On the fourth day of her menses, a woman must perform an ablution that will allow her to interact nor-

Young Kalash women perform a purification dance after going through menstruation, part of rites that must be performed after menstruation or childbirth. According to Kalash belief, women must live separately when "impure," Bumburet Valley, North-West Frontier Province, Pakistan (Earl Kowall/ Corbis).

mally with others once again. Yet, there are festivals such as Raja Samkranti (eastern India) that celebrate the menstruation of the goddess whose stained menstrual cloths are said to be highly valued by her devotees. During this festival, women undergo the same ceremonial restrictions as if they were menstruating.

In the Hebrew Bible (Leviticus 15 and 18) a menstruating woman is described as impure and unclean, and for a period of seven days must follow a number of prohibitions, including a ban on sexual relations. The Talmud extended the period of impurity to an additional seven days after the cessation of menstrual flow, followed by immersion in a pool of water (mikveh). This applies only to married women and does not affect any other aspects of religious practice, such as attending a synagogue. Sexual relations may resume after the ablution has been completed. The ritual separation (niddah) of the menstruating woman is today upheld by Orthodox Jews as part of the family purity laws. Most non-Orthodox Jews have rejected niddah although some Jewish feminists have revived immersion in the mikveh as an empowering women's ritual.

Early rabbinic and Christian commentaries extended the statement in Genesis (3:16) to include menstruation along with the pangs of childbirth as women's punishment for the sins of Eve, hence the common Western name for menstruation as "the curse" (Delaney, pp. 33–48; Buckley, p. 32; Shuttle, p. 138, 306). Christian patristic writers, such as Augustine, maintained the Levitical prohibitions regarding menstruation as literal and not figurative prescriptions (*Forgiveness*, 21, XII). Extreme negative views of menstruation put forth in Pliny's *Natural History* and Aristotle's *The Generation of Animals* (Book II, 3+4; Book IV, 1+2) in addition to other Hebrew Bible references to menstruation as polluting (Esther 14:16; Isaiah 30:22; Ezekiel 36:17; Lamentations 1:17), often informed theologians and philosophers on the topic of female sexuality generally. While a number of contemporary Christian traditions no longer accept Levitical prohibitions and menstrual taboos, there are still many denominations that maintain a negative view of menstruation. Views of menstruation from the Hebrew Bible have been used as an argument against the ordination of women in the Catholic faith. The Greek Orthodox Church continues to restrict the religious practices of menstruating women, such as communion. In some areas of Greece today (particularly in the rural regions), menstruating women are not permitted to touch religious icons or light votive candles. However, a New Testament passage (Mark 5; Matthew 9; Luke 8) tells of a woman with a menstrual disorder who was cured by Jesus; for some commentators this has suggested a positive valence for menstrual health in the Christian tradition (Buckley and Gottlieb, p. 258; Delaney, p. 36).

The Qur'an of the Islamic faith states that a menstruating woman is polluted and should be ritually secluded from her husband until the cessation of her menses. She should then undergo a cleansing to be free from impurities, after which sexual relations may resume (Qur'an 2:223). Hadith literature further states that a menstruating woman is not permitted to fast, recite her daily prayers, take part in religious ritual, enter a mosque or touch the Qur'an. (These prohibitions do not apply during the Hajj.) The Islamic creation story, however, states that menstrual blood was the material from which humankind was formed.

In Buddhist tradition menstrual blood is considered to be highly polluting and a menarcheal girl is said to be a danger to those around her, particularly to men. Buddhist women of menstruating age are restricted from a number of religious ceremonies and duties, and a menstruating woman is prohibited from entering a temple or undertaking a religious pilgrimage. Yet Buddhists in Sri Lanka perform complex menarcheal rituals that indicate that menstruation is an important and sacred event for both a young woman and her community (Winslow, 1980).

BIBLIOGRAPHY

Sources on menstruation are few in number. Probably the most important anthropological work to date that discusses the menstrual practices, rites, and beliefs of a wide selection of cultures, and the first to reject the assumption of a universal menstrual taboo, is Thomas Buckley and Alma Gottlieb, eds., *Blood Magic: The Anthropology of Menstruation* (1988). Equally important

to an anthropological investigation of menstruation is Chris Knight, *Blood Relations: Menstruation and the Origins of Culture* (1991), which argues that menstruation was the event from which all cultural constructions, including religious rituals, were originally established. Unfortunately this work is flawed by its vast scope (the origin of culture itself) and its often intrusive Marxist bias and dense theoretical language.

Some of the most important work on menstruation comes from those sources that focus on specific cultural and religious traditions. Yewoubdar Beyene's *From Menarche to Menopause: Reproductive Lives of Peasant Women in Two Cultures* (1989) is a succinct examination of the menstrual beliefs and practices of Maya and Greek rural women. Beyene's ethnographic approach is markedly different from other anthropological studies of menstruation, since she gives equal consideration to biological information (dietary habits, fertility cycles, aging patterns) and psychological and cultural responses to menstruation. Deborah Winslow's "Rituals of First Menstruation in Sri Lanka" (*Man* 15 [1980]: 603–625) details the surprising similarities found between the menstrual ceremonies of Buddhists, Catholics, and Muslims living in Sri Lanka. In "Menstruation and Reproduction: An Oglala Case" (*Signs* 6, no. 1 [1980]: 54–65) Marla N. Powers offers a positive interpretation of the menstrual practices of the Oglala Sioux, while at the same time providing a critical analysis of the methodology employed in previous anthropological interpretations of menstruation. In "Purity and Piety: The Separation of Menstruants from the Sancta," Shaye J. D. Cohen (pp. 103–115 in Susan Grossman and Rivka Haut, eds., *Daughters of the King: Women and the Synagogue,* 1992) offers a clear and concise historical survey of the prohibitions surrounding menstruation in the Ashkenazi and Sephardic Jewish traditions, concluding that the exclusion of menstruating women from the synagogue is not to be found in Jewish law but solely from isolated historic and geographic customs.

On a more general and accessible level, *The Curse: A Cultural History of Menstruation,* by Janice Delaney, Mary Jane Lupton, and Emily Toth (1976; 2d ed., rev. and enl., 1988) provides interpretations of menstrual taboos as they have existed in a number of different religious traditions and historical periods. Two other important crosscultural studies of menstruation are Deana Dorman Logan, "The Menarche Experience in Twenty-Three Foreign Countries" (*Adolescence* 15, no. 57 [1980]: 247–256) and Rita E. Montgomery, "A Cross-Cultural Study of Menstruation, Menstrual Taboos, and Related Social Variables" (*Ethos* 2, no. 1 [1974]: 137–170). Logan concentrates on the emotional reception of menarche by young girls in relation to their respective cultural views of menstruation; Montgomery establishes a complex relationship between men's roles in creation stories or childbirth with existing menstrual restrictions and taboos.

Of the texts that focus on mythology and menstruation, *The Wise Wound* by Penelope Shuttle and Peter Redgrove (1978; 2d ed., rev. and enl., 1986), is the most encompassing and informative, offering a Jungian analysis of Western mythology and religious symbology in relation to menstrual blood and providing a positive, spiritual interpretation of the powers of menstruation. An important analysis of ancient Greek medical texts, mythology, and goddess worship as they relate to menstruation is provided by Helen King, "Bound to Bleed: Artemis and Greek Women," in *Images of Women in Antiquity*, edited by Averil Cameron and Amélie Kuhrt (1983). Barbara Walker's *The Woman's Encyclopedia of Myths and Secrets* (1983) includes compelling though controversial readings of a number of early goddess mythologies from various regions and traditions (Babylonian, Maori, Hindu, African, and South American), which indicate that menstrual blood was the primary material used by the goddess for the creation of the world or humankind. Similarly, Judy Grahn's *Blood, Bread, and Roses: How Menstruation Created the World* (1993) offers nothing less than, in the author's own word's, a "new myth of origin" (p. 7) for humankind, based on menstrual blood. Grahn demonstrates that the process of menstruation has established a kind of "logic" which constitutes the foundation for science, mathematics, temporal measurement, and by extension, all human developments. Grahn, a poet with the scope of a visionary, does not allow the burden of proof to interfere with her sweeping hypothesis, but instead weaves together anthropological, mythological, biological, and archaeological data as elements in her myth-making.

Finally, for an exhaustive bibliography of menstruation sources on the Internet see Paula Wansbrough and Kathleen O'Grady, "Menstruation: A List of Sources" (1995) at *www.inform.umd.edu/EdRes/Topic/Womens Studies/Bibliographies/menstruation*. Another interesting Web resource is the controversial Museum of Menstruation, run by Harry Findley, *www.mum.org*.

See also **Blood**; **Menarche**; **Menopause**; **Rites of Passage**.

KATHLEEN O'GRADY

Mesoamerican Religions

The geographical term "Mesoamerica" has historical and cultural connotations. As such, it refers to the cultures of an area of mid-Mexico that includes some of northern Central America. In this region, complex and sophisticated civilizations attained a peak in religion, art, architecture, agriculture, medicine, and calendaric knowledge.

Data about the earliest periods of Mesoamerican religions are basically archaeological. Iconographic studies, interpretation of hieroglyphs, and examination of mural painting and sculpture have revealed the importance of feminine presences in myth and ritual during those periods. The first written records properly speaking about Mesoamerican peoples and religion are from the contact period of the early sixteenth century. They consist mostly of transcriptions of poetry, chants, and mythic narratives belonging to the period immediately prior to the European invasion of the territory then ruled by the Aztecs. These primary sources are generally called codices and are either pictograms or alphabetical Nahuatl (Aztec language) or Spanish. Spanish chroniclers seldom displayed the sensibility of Fray Bernardino de Sahagún. With the help of indigenous assistants, the Spanish cleric interviewed the elders of three communities in the area of Tenochtitlán, the Aztec capital, and composed the most reliable document—now known as the *Florentine Codex*—on the ancient Mexicans, their beliefs, rituals, gods-goddesses, and myths. Other key early Spanish sources (Olmos, Molina) provide basic references to a world decimated not only physically but also culturally.

A search of these texts for women's voices and ritual practices relies heavily on Spanish sources and translations of the sixteenth century. Consisting mainly of the work of (male) Catholic clerics and conquerors, these sources are of limited bearing to the presence and contributions of women in myth and ritual. Even Sahagún often translates pictograms, which unambiguously represent women acting as doctors, midwives, or ritual practitioners, into a Spanish generic masculine that erases women from agency and preeminence. Critical reinterpretations of pictographic codices (Berlo, 1983; Brown, 1983; Ichon, 1973; Hellbom, 1967) as well as recent Spanish retranslations from the original Nahuatl documents (for instance, those by Lopez Austin, León Portilla, or Willard Gingerich) have brought new insights into women's participation (Quezada, 1997; Marcos, 1989, 1991, 1995, 1996).

Combining records of the contact period with archaeological findings of previous periods, it is possible to elaborate on a commonality of certain Mesoamerican generative roots. Most scholars indeed assume a common cultural core, manifest in similarities of symbolic meanings, rituals and social practices, medical knowledge, architectural forms, iconographies, writing systems (hieroglyphs, pictograms), and measurement of time (calendars) among the diverse peoples of Mesoamerica (Gossen, 1986; Kirchoff, 1968; Lopez Austin,

1988; León-Portilla, 1987). Some even affirm the existence of one broad "Mesoamerican religious armature" (Hunt, 1977). Duality, equilibrium, as well as body concepts, seem to bear a particular weight on gender constructions within Mesoamerican beliefs (Marcos, 1996).

PERIODS IN MESOAMERICAN RELIGIONS

Through several millennia (6500–2500), complex forms of belief and ritual developed, but we can speak properly of a Mesoamerican religion only from about 2500 B.C.E.

Many clay figurines from the Preclassic or Formative period (1500 B.C.E.–200 C.E.) have been found, specially in Tlatilco, a site in the Valley of Mexico. Consisting mostly of representations of women, the Tlatilco figurines date from 1200 to 600 B.C.E. and attest to the beauty and the important place of women. Excavations in Xochitecatl (600 B.C.E.–200 C.E.), a site in the state of Tlaxcala, have revealed a feminine ceremonial center (Serra Puche, 1996). The abundant quantities of figurines, although different in style from those of Tlatilco, show women in every moment of their life cycle and with attires that express their place in that society: they are priestesses, governors, and "queens."

During this period, the Olmecs were the high civilization of Mesoamerica. Sacral objects for agricultural cults abound in archaeological findings. Although these findings are mainly concentrated along the Gulf of Mexico and the southern state of Tabasco, Olmec religious architecture and sculpture spread through a good part of Mesoamerica (Coe, 1968). Traces of this diffusion abound, particularly on the Central Plateau, along the Pacific coast, in Oaxaca, and in territories later identified as Mayan. The Olmecs have been considered the mother culture of Mesoamerica, and the core of the Mesoamerican pantheon was already formed in their time.

During the Classic period (c. 200 C.E.–900 C.E.) exquisite architecture, bas-relief, mural painting, and sculpture developed. Numerous sites attest to that period's creativity. Besides the Teotihuacanos, the Mayans, and the Toltecs, several other peoples are representative of this period: the Tlaxcalans, the Mixtecs, the Tarascans, the Zapotecs, and the Totonacs.

In the ancient city of Teotihuacán in the Central Plateau, temples and palaces formed the largest urban ceremonial center of the time. The two big pyramids dedicated to the Sun and the Moon are surrounded by buildings and palaces where some mural paintings have been restored. In the mural of Tepantitla, the main deity has been found to be a male-female deity with no exclusive feminine or masculine characteristics (Pasztory, 1976).

Stone statue of an Aztec goddess (Gianni Dagli Orti/ Corbis)

The most impressive archaeological sites of the Maya region are Palenque, Uxmal, and Chichén Itzá in Mexico, Tikal in Guatemala, and Copán in Honduras. In Palenque, as recently as 1994, an archaeological finding challenged opinions about the position of women in Maya society. Since its discovery in 1952, the great Templo de las Inscripciones had been believed to be the tomb of King Pacal of the Classic Maya period. The striking discovery was that the pyramid was in fact hosting also the tomb of a woman, called the Red Queen by its discoverers. All Mayan classical sites reveal a mastery of architecture, bas-relief carvings, sculpture, and mural painting. The Mayans were knowledgeable about the technique of corbelled vaulting. As with other Mesoamerican peoples of the Classic period, their artistic, calendaric, and hieroglyphic sophistication was imbued with sacred and divine meanings (León-Portilla, 1973; Thompson, 1970).

The life-size terra-cotta sculptures of *cihuateteo* (divine women) found in El Zapotal, the Totonac area of southern Vera Cruz is an expression of divinized femaleness of the period (Heyden, 1987).

The Post-Classic period (c. 900–1519) is marked by the decline of the cultural centers of the previous area and by the rise of the Mexica or Aztecs. Their mythology traces their origins back to a place in the north, from where they came in a long exodus. Chimalma or Teomama ("woman bearer of God") is a central figure of this myth of origin.

The Aztecs built their city on islands of the shallow lake that occupied most of the Valley of Mexico and called it Tenochtitlán. They situated in the neighboring ancient site, Teotihuacán, the cosmological center of their religio-political world. In what was their city, the impressive ceremonial complex called the Templo Mayor has been unearthed.

DUALITY IN MESOAMERICAN RELIGIONS

Everywhere, the Mesoamericans constructed their beliefs and practices around a dual feminine-masculine deity called Ometeotl, literally "Two-God." Ometeotl was conceived as Omecihuatl and Ometecuhtli, Lady and Lord of Duality, the creative heavenly pair who dwelt in the innermost part of the cosmos, at the ultimate celestial level. The early manuscript *Historia de los Mexicanos por sus Pinturas,* attributed to Andrés de Olmos by Garibay, depicts a mythical universe in which the pervading divine dual unity unfolded in almost endless multiplicities. For gods as for humans, there was no masculine without its feminine. Among the dual divinities we find: Mictlantecuhtli-Mictecacihuatl, Lord and Lady of Mictlan ("land of the dead"), Tlaloc-Chalchiuhticue, Lord and Lady of the waters; Quetzalcoatl-Cihuacoatl, feathered serpent and female serpent; Tezcatlipoca-Tezcatlanextia, mirror that obscures things and mirror that makes them brilliant.

With slight variations, all other Mesoamerican peoples constructed their pantheon around dual gods-goddesses. For example, the Maya called this dual divinity E Quahalom (begetter of children)-E Alom (conceiver of children). Among the Zapotecs, the supreme dual god was Pitao Cozaana-Pitao Cochaana. He-she was also called *Pije-Tao* and was, as such, the deity of time.

The idea of a divine duality was deeply rooted in Mesoamerican thought, as was a fusion of feminine and masculine, in one bipolar principle. The nonhierarchical organization of this duality (Marcos, 1996) certainly bears an impact on how gender duality was conceived. The feminine-masculine dual unity was fundamental to the creation of the cosmos, its (re)generation and sustenance. This principle is manifested by representations of gods in pairs.

The gods-goddesses possessed few attributes that were exclusively and unambiguously theirs. Although scholars have attempted to structure the various gods-goddesses of the Mesoamerican pantheon into clear orderings (Caso, 1968; Nicholson, 1971) with evolutionary or theogonic approaches, it is virtually impossible to portray them as discrete, nonoverlapping categories. The gods did not have fixed unitary meaning.

The pervasive concept of duality permeated all reality in Mesoamerica. Death and life, evil and good, above and below, far and near were but two aspects of one dual reality. Not mutually exclusive, not static, not hierarchically organized, all elements and natural phenomena were construed as having a "gender weight" that made them masculine, feminine, or both (Lopez Austin, 1988). Another key characteristic of Mesoamerican religious thought is that dualities were not fixed and static, but fluid and constantly changing. Deities, people, plants, animals, space, time, and the cardinal directions all had a gender identity that shifted constantly along a continuum. Gender, the primordial duality, was itself dynamic: alternating female and male valences manifested themselves in religious and in everyday life (Marcos 1991; Karttunen, 1986).

SACRIFICE AND BODILY CONCEPTS

In Mesoamerican religions, both humans and divinities were interlocked in mutual need for each other. Human beings were defined as "those made worthy by Divine Sacrifice" (León-Portilla, 1993). Their gods-goddesses sacrificed themselves, offering their blood. This sacrifice of the deities was the primeval act that had to be reenacted by humans in order to renew the sacred powers bequested to their bodies. In return for their sacrifice, the gods-goddesses expected to be sustained by human sacrifices. Besides this, auto-sacrifices, such as the piercing of the tongue and the bleeding of other body parts, were also ritually performed. All these sacrifices expressed a reciprocity of obligations between deities and humans.

In the descriptions of sacrifices found in primary sources, women are neither absent nor prevalent. Depending on calendaric dispositions, they participated both as ritual specialists and as sacrificial objects. Sacrifices were offered as much to gods as to goddesses.

Corporeality is not only acknowledged but conceived of as intertwined with the circumscribing universe. The body could not be extracted from the fabric of the cosmos within which all human activities acquired meaning. It was a body that echoed the cosmic forces and fused with them physically as well as nonphysically. There was no ontological disjunction between mind and body. It can be said that the person was indissolubly a bodily and animic entity (Lopez Austin, 1988). No binary oppositions dividing reason from passion, or culture from nature, or even self from other, appear in this religion.

CALENDARS

Mesoamericans, since the Olmec period, showed great concern for the precise measurement of time. Their calendaric knowledge brings duality into the construction of temporality. As there was a sacred ritual calendar, there was a solar calendar. Correspondingly, there were two counts: the long count (solar calendar) was of 365 days, and the short count (sacred calendar) was 260 days. Schultze Jena correlates this sacred calendar with the nine full moons that elapse during the human gestation period (Furst, 1986).

Although still controversial, this hypothesis is supported by contemporary field data from the Mayan region. Mayan women count their gestation period in nine full moons and not in the days since impregnation. As their Mesoamerican ancestors, these women intimately connect human physiology and day signs.

This fits with the relevant religious role of pregnancy and childbirth in Mesoamerica. For the Aztecs, the woman delivering a baby was a warrior bringing a valuable "prisoner" to the community. Those who died in childbirth were honored as warriors fallen on the battlefield: they became *cihuateteo,* goddesses in charge of carrying the sun from zenith to dusk. The midwives, likewise, were considered preeminent ritual specialists. They contributed to childbirth with their skills as well as with their knowledge of sacred orations and rites.

The ritual relationship that Mesoamericans had with their bodies expresses the explicit connection they established between the external cosmos and the internal human microcosm.

MORAL PRECEPTS: *ILAMATLATOLLI* AND *HUEHUETLATOLLI*

Sahagún's *Florentine Codex* contains transcriptions of the moral precepts predicated by the elders. The Aztecs referred to these precepts as "a scattering of jades" (Sullivan, 1986). These words—as with other ritual words—were considered as permanent and as valuable as jade. A recent (re)translator (Gingerich, 1988) restores from oblivion the term *ilamatlatolli,* literally, orations of the wise old women. This proves that those revered verbal traditions were also expressed in women's voices. Historical writings generally refer only to the term *huehuetlatolli,* which means the sayings of old wise men (León Portilla, 1988; Sullivan, 1986). Both *ilamatlatolli* and *huehuetlatolli* are sacred orations that, in a dense metaphoric language, ensure the transmission of gendered behavior norms. Didactic and rhetorical, they were ritually uttered by the elders in the religious ceremony marking the coming of age of boys and girls.

Seldom do primary sources give such a clear, detailed, and homely presentation of the ancestors' ethical ideas.

In these precepts, erotic pleasure was not only appreciated but considered an essential part of experiencing life on earth. The portrait of everyday life that can be gained from these orations is one in which gender equity was prevalent (Marcos, 1991).

BIBLIOGRAPHY

Brown, Betty Ann. "Seen But Not Heard: Women in Aztec Ritual: The Sahagun Texts." In *Art and Image in Pre-Columbian Art.* Edited by J. C. Berlo. 1983.

Caso, Alfonso. "Religión o religiones Mesoamericanas?" *Verhandlungen des XXXVIII. Amerikanistenkongresses* 3 (1968).

Coe, Michael D. *America's First Civilization.* 1968.

Furst, Peter T. "Human Biology and the Origin of the 260-day Sacred Almanac: The Contribution of Leonhard Schultze Jena (1872–1955)." In *Symbol and Meaning Beyond the Closed Community: Essays in Mesoamerican Ideas.* Edited by Gary H. Gossen. 1986.

Gingerich, Willard. "Chipahuacanemiliztli, 'The Purified Life,' in the Discourses of Book VI, Florentine Codex." *In Smoke and Mist: Mesoamerican Studies in Memory of Thelma D. Sullivan.* Edited by J. K. Josserand and K. Dakin. 1988.

Gossen, Gary H. "Mesoamerican Ideas as a Foundation for a Regional Synthesis." In *Symbol and Meaning Beyond the Closed Community.* Edited by Gary H. Gossen. 1986.

Hellbom, Ana Britta. *La participación cultural de las mujeres indias y mestizas en el México precortsesiano y post-revolucionario.* 1967.

Heyden, Doris. "Mesoamerican Religious Classic Cultures." In *The Encyclopedia of Religion.* Edited by Mircea Eliade. Vol. 9, pp. 409–419. 1987.

Hunt, Eva. *The Transformation of the Hummingbird.* 1977.

Ichon, Alain. *La religión de los Totonacas de la Sierra.* 1973.

Karttunen, Frances. *In Their Own Voices: Mesoamerican Indigenous Women Then and Now.* 1986.

Kirchoff, Paul. "Mesoamerica: Its Geographic Limits, Ethnic Composition and Cultural Characteristics." In *Heritage of Conquest: The Ethnology of Middle America.* Edited by Sol Tax. 1952. Reprint, 1968.

Leacock, Eleanor, and June Nash. "Ideologies of Sex: Archetypes and Stereotypes." In *Cross-Cultural Research at Issue.* Edited by Leonore Loeb Adler. 1982.

León-Portilla, Miguel. *Huehuetlatolli: Testimonios de la antique palabra.* Facsimile repro. and intro. Comisión Nacional Conmemorativa del V. Centenario del Encuentro de Dos Mundos, Instituto de Investigaciones Antropológicas, México. 1988.

———. "Mesoamerican Religions: Pre-Columbian Religions." In *The Encyclopedia of Religion*. Edited by Mircea Eliade. Vol. 9, pp. 390–406. 1987.

———. "Those Made Worthy by Divine Sacrifice: The Face of Ancient Mexico." In *South and Mesoamerican Native Spirituality*. Edited by Gary Gossen. 1993.

———. *Time and Reality in the Thought of the Maya*. 1973.

Lopez Austin, Alfredo. *The Human Body and Ideology*. 2 vols. 1988.

Marcos, Sylvia. "Embodied Thought: Concept of the Body in Mesoamerica." In *Healing and Power*. Vol. 1. 1996.

———. "Gender and Moral Precepts in Ancient Mexico: Sahagun's Texts." *Concilium* 6 (1991): 60–74.

———. "Mujeres, Cosmovisión y Medicina: Las Curanderas Mexicanas. *In Trabajo, Poder y Sexualidad*. Edited by Orlandina de Oliveira. 1989.

———. "Sacred Earth: Mesoamerican Perspectives." *Concilium* 5, no. 261 (1995): 27–37.

Molina, Fray Alonso de. *Vocabulario en lengua Castallana y Mexicana*. 1944.

Nicholson, H. B. "Religions in Pre-Hispanic Central Mexico." In *Archeology of Northern Mesoamerica*, vol. 10 of *Handbook of Middle American Indians*. Edited by R. Wanchope. 1971.

Olmos, Andrés de (attributed to). "La Historia de los Mexicanos por sus pinturas." In *Teogonia e historia de los Mexicanos: Tres opusculos del siglo XVI*. Edited by A. Garibay. 1533. Reprint, 1973.

Pasztory, Esther. *The Murals of Tepantitla, Teotihuacan*. 1976.

Quezada, Noemi. *Sexualidad, amor y erotismo: Mexico prehispanico y Mexico colonial*. 1997.

Sahagún, Fray Bernardino de. *Florentine Codex: General History of the Things of New Spain*. Trans. of original Nahuatl text by A. Anderson and C. Dibble. 1969.

Serra Puche, Maria del Carmen. "The Concept of Feminine Places in Mesoamerica: A Case of Archaeological Evidence on the Site of Xochiecatl, Tlaxcala, Mexico." Presentation at the Recovering Gender in the Pre-Hispanic America symposium, Dumbarton Oaks, Washington, October 1996.

Sullivan, Thelma. "A Scattering of Jades: The Words of the Aztec Elders." *In Symbol and Meaning Beyond the Closed Community: Essays in Mesoamerican Ideas*. Edited by Gary H. Gossen. 1986.

Thompson, Eric S. *Maya History and Religion*. 1970.

SYLVIA MARCOS

Mesopotamian Religions

Mesopotamia (Greek for "between the rivers") strictly speaking is the area between the Tigris and Euphrates River valleys (occupied today by Iraq, eastern Syria, and southern Turkey), but at various times cities and regions to the west of the Euphrates and to the east of the Tigris were also part of a Mesopotamian cultural continuum.

The richest source of information about ancient Mesopotamia comes from textual remains. Evidence for writing first appears in the mid-fourth millennium B.C.E. The first written language of Mesopotamia was Sumerian, spoken in southern Mesopotamia (from Babylon to the Persian Gulf). In the mid-third millennium a Semitic people began to infiltrate Sumerian territory from the north and west. They, along with their language, Akkadian, came to dominate Mesopotamia early in the second millennium. Sumerian survived as a prestigious but dead language reserved for religious and literary genres. The Persian conquest of the last native Babylonian kingdom in 539 B.C.E. and the arrival of Alexander the Great in 331 B.C.E. precipitated the slow decline and death of the Mesopotamian civilization.

The earliest cuneiform ideogram for "woman" was the pubic triangle, denoting "woman" or "vulva." As a symbol of female sexual potency, the vulva always had overwhelmingly positive connotations. The goddess Inanna's vulva was "holy," for example, whereas the penis of Enki (the god of fresh water, who personified male reproductive power and creative intelligence) was not. Nevertheless, the ideogram expresses clearly enough the aspect of women most highly valued in the culture. Sumerian also had a special gender-driven dialect called *emesal*, literally "tongue of women," which in some texts was used for the speech of female protagonists (usually goddesses) and in Laments (almost universally a female genre.)

Cuneiform, the wedge-shaped script of Sumerian and Akkadian, required years of study to master. Consequently, only elite men and women had access to reading and writing. The divine patron of scribes, Nidaba, was female, and there are occasional references to female scribes. The first named author in history may be the Akkadian princess Enheduanna (twenty-third century B.C.E.), daughter of King Sargon. Her father appointed her En-Priestess (High Priestess) of the Moon God at Ur in southern Babylonia. Enheduanna's poetry, a collection of temple hymns, and two hymnal prayers to Inanna (goddess of sexuality and warfare and her father's patron deity) very early entered the canon of Mesopotamian religious literature.

Marble statue of female orant (praying figure), in marble with shell and black limestone inlay, 2700–2600 B.C.E. (Gianni Dagli Orti/Corbis)

OFFICIAL AND POPULAR RELIGION

For over three millennia the city temple was the principal center of Mesopotamian religious practices. During the earliest phases of the Sumerian temple economy, both women and men were the chief administrators of some temples, and both presided over a mixed staff. Mesopotamian mythology explains that the gods created the human race to serve them. Gods and goddesses were represented in their temples by their statues. Throughout Mesopotamian history, male and female clergy brought the deities daily meals, washed and dressed them, and took them to visit their divine relatives and friends in other temples. Priestly duties also included prayer—usually on behalf of the ruler and the city—and divination in connection with animal sacrifice (e.g., omen reading from entrails) or, especially in the case of priestesses, via dreams or ecstatic trances.

Because the bulk of the evidence comes from the ruins of palaces and temples, most of what is known about Mesopotamian religion pertains to the religious practices of the upper strata of society. Texts and images attest most often to official, state-centered cults. As a rule, only royalty and upper-level clergy could actually enter a sanctuary.

Of the religious practices of ordinary men and women, so-called popular religion, only little is known. Practices and concepts pertinent to the religiosity of Mesopotamian women such as the form and function of prayer, votive gestures, and taboos remain obscure. The largest source of information on private religion mainly concerns magical rituals, rather than private devotions, although these two modes of religious practice need not be mutually exclusive. There is some evidence for niches in private houses and on street corners. Apparently from the late third millennium onward most people—male and female, sovereign and slave—venerated a personal god or goddess whose good offices were courted and whose wrath was assiduously avoided. A personal deity could intercede on one's behalf among more powerful gods.

Data on private piety may be eked out indirectly, for example, in studies of theophoric (referring to a deity) personal names, such as the Sumerian names, "The (divine) Lady Has Compassion," or "I Have Turned My Eyes to My (divine) Lady." Frequently names express the divine-human relationship in terms of parent and child. However, the extent to which gender determined the choice of personal name or personal deity is unclear.

THE EARLY PANTHEON

During the proto-urban Uruk period (3500–3000 B.C.E.) the head of the Sumerian pantheon was probably Enki. Goddesses, however, dominated the Sumerian pantheon, in control of all essential aspects of life. Ninhursag, Nintu, and Gatumdug were birth goddesses. Nisaba and Ninsud as grain goddesses ensured abundant harvests. Ninsu was the cattle goddess, Nanshe, the fish and water-fowl goddess, and Inanna presided over the sex drive. Gula healed, and Ereshkigal was the death specialist. Water rather than earth was the element most often associated with mother-goddess symbolism in a region where earth is only fertile when irrigated.

Over the course of the third millennium a number of prominent Sumerian goddesses disappeared or were eclipsed by male deities—particularly warrior gods. Sumerian social organization may have changed, and contact with the Akkadians to the north, where male deities had always dominated, may also have been a factor. In the Babylonian creation epic, the *Enuma Elish*, from the late second millennium, the only active female figure is the evil mother goddess and chaos dragon, Tiamat; her destruction is the signature victory of the Babylonian warrior god Marduk.

Surviving female deities include Nidaba, goddess of scribal skills, Ningal, goddess of dream interpretation, and Gula/Bau, goddess of medicine and healing. Sumero-Akkadian goddesses generally conform to the streotypically female roles, most notably mother, queen, wise mother-in-law, loyal sister, and faithful, fertile wife. The exception is Inanna (Ishtar in Akkadian), goddess of sexuality and war, who remained a significant presence from the mid-third millennium into the Hellenistic period. Inanna's uniquely multifaceted character transcended and transgressed Mesopotamian social and gender boundaries on a spectacular scale. She is a proper young lady, but she rejects all female domestic duties; she represents a force of fertility but does not concern herself with birth; the patron goddess of prostitutes, she embodies a prostitute's *hi-li* (sex-appeal); like a man, she can be called "hero" and may seek out lovers for herself; enthusiastic in war, she is "the destroyer of foreign lands, foremost in battle." At her festivals men dressed as women and women as men.

In the visual art of Mesopotamia, women appear in only a limited number of roles; indeed, this is also the case in Mesopotamian literature, such as the "Epic of Gilgamesh," where women serve most often as catalysts in the story of a male protagonist. Small clay figurines of nude female figures with pronounced hips and pudenda appear at archaeological sites of all periods. While they may attest to continuing veneration of a mother goddess, explanations of their function remain speculative.

SACRED MARRIAGE

Sacred marriage, a ritual in which the goddess engaged in sexual intercourse either with the reigning king or, in later periods, with another deity, is contested. Early scholarship on the sacred marriage was strongly influenced by the fertility theories of Sir James Frazer (*The Golden Bough*, 1911–1915). Today, however, there is no consensus on the exact nature of the ritual; it probably served primarily to promote the proper relationships between humans and gods necessary for social cohesion and prosperity.

Some Assyriologists still feel that the evidence suggests that in the third millennium, an act of sexual intercourse took place between the king and a woman respresenting the goddess. Equally respected scholars believe instead that the encounter was purely symbolic, pointing to the impossibility of identifying a plausible human candidate as Inanna's stand-in. In later periods the sacred marriage ritual was unambiguously centered upon sacred statues of the deities in question.

Evidence for this ritual is strongest from the Ur III/Isin-Larsa Sumerian Renaissance (c. 2000 B.C.E.) when the unusual (for Mesopotamia) concept of divine kingship prevailed. By mating (whether symbolically or actually) with Inanna, the most powerful goddess in the pantheon, the kings of Ur sought to secure legitimacy and divine blessings; they also became the sons-in-law of the chief god of Ur, the moon god Nanna. Thus the sacred marriage is functionally comparable to the appointment of Mesopotamian princesses as priestesses who also mediated between the divine and human realms on behalf of the kingdom.

According to an Ur III text describing the sacred marriage of King Iddindagan (1950 B.C.E.), women of all ages joined musicians and cross-dressing male functionaries of Inanna in a parade. Old women prepared enormous amounts of food for the evening's celebration, and husbands and wives were encouraged to engage in conjugal sex.

FEMALE CLERGY

Seals and other artistic media depict women serving the temples as priestesses, cult participants, musicians, dancers, and servants. The earliest clear evidence for Sumerian women serving as priestesses comes from the Early Dynastic III period (2500–2300 B.C.E.), when royal women as mothers and wives first figure in claims of dynastic legitimacy. At Lagash, rulers' wives administered the temples of the chief goddess of the city.

In the ensuing Sargonic Age (2300–2150 B.C.E.), Akkadian royal princesses—among them Enheduanna—were installed as *En*-priestesses in the principal temples of male Sumerian deities. (Female deities were serve by male *En*s.) Before Sargon the *En*-ship may have been reserved for Sumerian kings alone, representing their control over religious matters. Hence these royal appointments by King Sargon may attest to his wish to assert control over Sumerian cities. On the other hand, Enheduanna's poetry expresses a spirituality that belies suspicions that her appointment was purely political. For five hundred years (c. 2280–1800 B.C.E.) royal priestesses held office, even when a priestess's father fell from power. Some of these women also functioned as oneiromancers (dream interpreters). One of these priestesses was Ninshatapada, a scribe whose written appeal to a conquering king on her city's behalf subsequently served as a copy-text in scribal schools.

There are a number of terms for priestesses in the second and first millennia. For example, *Entu* and *naditu* priestesses were nobly-born virgins dedicated to the service of a deity; they lived out their lives in a semi-cloistered state. They made offerings to their god(s) and intoned prayers on behalf of the king. Whether these priestesses freely chose a religious vocation or were summarily "volunteered" by their parents is unclear. The office of *naditu* early in its history probably provided an alternative to marriage, and the *naditu*'s dowry ensured a measure of independence. Later, the institution's function became largely economic, and the legal right of the *naditus* to buy, sell, and own property was exploited to enhance the landholdings of their families.

At the other extreme, it was long assumed, again under the influence of Frazer's *Golden Bough,* that male and female prostitutes ensured the fertility of the land by engaging in sexual intercourse with strangers in or near a sanctuary. Assyriologists in the late 1990s acknowledge the difficulty both of translating the titles (*qadishtu, ishtaritu,* and *kezertu*) and of interpreting the duties of those supposed cult functionaries. They appear consistently in some texts as prostitutes, in others as wives, midwives, and wet nurses. When prostitution is mentioned in connection with a Mesopotamian cult, it should probably be understood as prostitution organized for the economic benefit of a particular cult. It is also possible that a woman might resort to prostitution to pay a religious vow.

The town of Mari on the middle Euphrates during the Old Babylonian period (c. 2081–1576 B.C.E.) is unusual in Mesopotamian history for the prominence and relative freedom of its women (at least of the upper class) in legal, social, and religious contexts. All the officially designated prayer representatives of the king appear to have been women. Women and men alike made official sacrifices. Women were also professional and lay prophets. The former were attached to a temple and communicated the will of the temple deity. The latter, whose information came via dreams or ecstatic utterances, came from all social levels. At Mari, women, like men, made sacrifices on their own initiative for a variety of reasons. Shattamkiyazi of Mari, for example, had ignored the advice of a liver omen and was suffering an illness that could be cured only by sacrifice.

THE WITCH

Witchcraft was feared as one of several possible causes of misfortune. Incantations against witches (usually, but not always, female) reveal little about female practitioners of malevolent magic; rather, they reveal the range of dangers ordinary Mesopotamians feared and tended to blame on "the Other."

Witches seem to be associated with female members of certain groups and persons whose activities did not conform to social norms, such as prostitutes, actors and snake charmers, and foreigners. To counteract the effects of witches and other dangers, wealthier people hired the services of a socially sanctioned *ashipu* or incantation priest (always a man) whose techniques were themselves magical. The goddess Ishtar (Inanna) is one of the major deities called upon in *ashipu* texts to ward off evil.

There are no textual references to anyone accused of witchcraft, but ordinary women and men clearly had access to similar, if less costly, magic and could resort to a male or female practitioner for a charm, amulet, or spell.

POPULAR RELIGION AND RITES OF PASSAGE

Heightened interest in the role of women in ancient societies has led scholars to look for traces of popular religion, such as rites of passage, in which women may have participated to a greater degree. This avenue of inquiry remains in its early stages.

In Mesopotamia girls apparently married soon after reaching menarche. Law codes and contracts indicate that institutionally marriage functioned largely as a transfer of property in the form of carefully specified bride gifts, a dowry, and the bride herself. For betrothal ceremonies and weddings, however, one may look cautiously to literary texts (admittedly, often from upper social strata) such as the Sumerian Bridal Songs (third millennium) usually involving the goddess Inanna. One finds here references to the ritual bathing and dressing of the bride and to the ceremonial roles of the bride's mother and brother (ritually, the bride's father seems a marginal figure).

Mesopotamian incantation texts lay out the full range of potential ills and dangers caused by demonic powers (both male and female) over the lifetime of an "everyday" Mesopotamian. Supernatural influences—whether of high-ranking deities or "low-level" demons—affected three areas in particular: birth, sexual vigor (i.e., female fertility and male sexual prowess), and death.

Over the course of a year, one may suppose the "average" Mesopotamian woman would participate in various public festivals and make periodic offerings to her dead relatives and to her personal god(s). She might also hire an omen-taker to discover the supernatural cause of and magical cure for illness or bad luck, buy an amulet or figurine for as-yet-undetermined purposes, attend or be the subject of a rite of passage, or lead a lament for a family member.

BIBLIOGRAPHY

GENDER STUDIES AND SURVEYS FOCUSING ON WOMEN

Dalley, Stephanie. *Mari and Karana, Two Old Babylonian Cities.* 1984. See esp. the chapters "Woman" and "Cults and Belief."

Goodnick-Westenholz, Joan. "Towards a New Conceptualization of the Female Role in Mesopotamian Society." *Journal of the American Oriental Society* 110 (1990): 510–521. Draws attention to both useful and outmoded methodology in Assyriology as it pertains to women's studies.

Harris, Rivkah. "Women, Mesopotamia." In the *Anchor Bible Dictionary.* Edited by David N. Freedman et al. 1992.

Kramer, Samuel Noah. "Poets and Psalmists: Goddesses and Theologians." In *The Legacy of Sumer (Bibliotheca Mesopotamica).* Vol. 4. Edited by Denise Schmandt-Besserat. 1976. A relatively early essay about women in Sumerian religion.

Lambert, Wilfred G. "Goddesses in the Pantheon: A Reflection of Women in Society?" In *La femme dans le proche-orient antique (Compte rendu de la XXXIII rencontre assyriologique internationale).* Edited by Jean-Marie Durand. 1987.

Leick, Gwendolyn. *Sex and Eroticism in Mesopotamian Literature.* 1994. Wide-ranging, rich in insights from anthropology and sociology; contains a useful bibliography.

FEMALE CLERGY

Asher-Greve, Julia M. *Frauen in altsumerischer Zeit (Bibliotheca Mesopotamica 18).* 1985. Evaluation of the role of women in earliest Sumerian times based primarily on Sumerian sculpture, especially seals; much attention to evidence for female religious functionaries; valuable for its photographic plates.

———. "The Oldest Female Oneiromancer." In *La femme dans le proche-orient antique (compte rendu de la XXXIII recontre assyriologique internationale).* Edited by Jean-Marie Durand. 1987. Analysis of one intriguing cylinder seal includes discussion of female clerical roles in Sumer.

Batto, Bernard F. *Studies on Women at Mari.* 1974. A classic work, focusing systematically on royal women and on specific priestly titles.

Fleming, Daniel. *The Installation of Baal's High Priestess at Emar.* 1992. Texts from Emar, a city on the eastern periphery of Mesopotamia, provide a more vivid than usual picture of religious ceremonial.

Hallo, William W. "Women of Sumer." In *The Legacy of Sumer (Bibliotheca Mesopotamica).* Vol. 4. Edited by Denise Schmandt-Besserat. 1976.

Harris, Rivkah. *Ancient Sippar: A Demographic Study of an Old-Babylonian City (1894–1595 B.C.).* 1975. Harris was a trail-blazer in her study of the *Naditu* women's role in Sippar.

Jeyes, Ulla. "The Naditu Women of Sippar." In *Images of Women in Antiquity.* Edited by Averil Cameron and Amélie Kuhrt. 1983. The basics about *Naditu* priestesses at Sippar.

Oppenheim, A. Leo. *The Interpretation of Dreams in the Ancient Near East.* 1956. Still the classic introduction to a religious institution with many female practitioners.

Winter, Irene J. "Women in Public: The Disk of Enheduanna, the Beginning of the Office of EN-Priestess and the Weight of Visual Evidence." In *La femme dans le proche-orient antique (Compte rendu de la XXXIII rencontre assyriologique internationale).* Edited by Jean-Marie Durand. 1987. Examines a famous representation of the poet-priestess, Enheduanna.

SACRED MARRIAGE

Cooper, Jerrold S. "Sacred Marriage and Popular Cult in Early Mesopotamia." In *Official Cult and Popular Religion in the Ancient Near East.* Edited by Eiko Matsushima. 1993.

Kramer, Samuel Noah. *The Sacred Marriage Rite.* 1969. The basic texts in translation.

Sweet, R. F. G. "A New Look at the 'Sacred Marriage' in Ancient Mesopotamia." In *Corolla Torontonensis: Studies in Honor of Ronald Morton Smith.* Edited by Emmet Robbins and Stella Sandahl. 1994.

Wolkstein, Diane, and Samuel Noah Kramer. *Inanna Queen of Heaven and Earth: Her Stories and Hymns from Sumer.* 1983. A useful introduction to the goddess. Well-chosen and annotated illustrations from Sumerian art, commentaries, and indices.

PRIVATE RELIGION: RITES OF PASSAGE

Edzard, Dietz O. "Private Frömmigkeit in Sumer." In *Official Cult and Popular Religion in the Ancient Near East.* Edited by Eiko Matsushima. 1993.

Farber-Flügge, Gertrud. "Another Old Babylonian Childbirth Incantation." *Journal of Near Eastern Studies* 43, no. 3 (1984): 311–316.

Geller, M. J. "Taboo in Mesopotamia." *Journal of Cuneiform Studies* 42, no. 1 (1990): 105–117.

Greengus, Samuel. "Old Babylonian Marriage Ceremonies and Rites." *Journal of Cuneiform Studies* 20 (1966): 55–72.

Rollin, Sue. "Women and Witchcraft in Ancient Assyria." In *Images of Women in Antiquity.* Edited by Averil Cameron and Amélie Kuhrt. 1983.

See also **Inanna; Ishtar and Anat; Witchcraft: Witchcraft and Magic in the Ancient Near East and the Bible**.

MARY JOAN WINN LEITH

Miaoshan

Miaoshan is a legendary human manifestation of the bodhisattva Kuan Yin (Avalokiteśvara) in China. The third daughter of King Zhuang, Miaoshan refused to obey her father's demand that she marry. Furious over her disobedience and unfilial behavior, King Zhuang ordered the nunnery to which she had retreated burnt and the nuns killed. Miaoshan miraculously escaped, and when her father was afflicted with a horrible skin disease as punishment for his deeds, Miaoshan gave her arms and eyes, which were needed to cure him. When her grateful parents repented, Miaoshan revealed herself as Kuan Yin.

The earliest written version of Miaoshan's story dates from 1100, although the original is not extant. There are numerous versions of story from the following centuries, including the popular *Xiangshan Baojuan*. Miaoshan was first identified with the thousand-armed and -eyed (*Dabei*) Kuan Yin; over time this changed and Miaoshan was portrayed as a woman with two arms holding a green willow branch and a bottle of pure water or nectar.

Devotees have made pilgrimages to sites honoring Miaoshan since medieval times. Fragrant Mountain in Hebei, the site of Miaoshan's stupa, or shrine, was a major pilgrimage center in medieval China, and pilgrimages were made there especially in the second month of the lunar year. It has since declined in importance; instead another historically important site for the cult at the Upper Tianzhu Monastery in Hangzhou has become the object of yearly pilgrimages. In their devotion to her, pilgrims praise Miaoshan for her religious devotion in the face of her parents' disapproval, and admire her life free from the ties of society and family.

BIBLIOGRAPHY

The classic work on the history of the Miaoshan story and its sources is Glen Dudbridge, *The Legend of Miaoshan* (1978). For the general history of the Miaoshan cult, as well as songs of contemporary women pilgrims honoring Miaoshan, see Chün-fang Yü, "Women's Songs for Guanyin," in *Buddhism in Practice*, edited by Donald S. Lopez, Jr. (1995). On the transformation of Avalokiteśvara into the female bodhisattva Kuan Yin, including in the form of Miaoshan, see Chün-fang Yü, "Feminine Images of Kuan-yin in Post-T'ang China," *Journal of Chinese Religions* 18 (1990): 61–89. For stories of Miaoshan in *baojuan* ("precious scroll") literature, see Li Shiyu, *Baojuan zonglu* (1961).

See also Body: Female Body as Text in Imperial China; Kuan Yin (Kannon); Mutilation.

JENNIFER OLDSTONE-MOORE

Minerva

See Athena (Minerva).

Ministry

The most basic meaning of *ministry* in Christianity derives from the Greek word *diakonia* (service) and its cognates, used in the New Testament to denote cultic and table service and, later, office within and for early Christian communities. Initially, the gifts (charisms) of ministry were shared by all, not reserved to designated leaders. The egalitarianism of Christian ministries eventually gave way to male clerical office modeled after the Roman patriarchal household; by the end of the fourth century C.E., women were effectively excluded from ordained ministry. Although the sixteenth-century reformers taught the priesthood of all believers, mainline Protestant churches maintained a sharp distinction between clergy and laity and continued to reserve ordained ministry to men for several centuries.

Despite their nonclerical status, women missionaries played an important role in the late-nineteenth- and early-twentieth-century missionary movement among Protestant churches, and many more supported them through mission societies in their home churches. Particularly in the United States, Protestant women were mainstays of Christian education through the Sunday School movement; they were responsible for most of the churches' benevolence work and were leaders in social reforms such as the Temperance movement. Among Roman Catholics, women's religious communities were active in missionary endeavors, as well as in charitable works, health care, and education in their home countries. Although none of these groups of women were likely to have considered their work ministry as such, it would be adjudged so today.

Since the mid-twentieth century, women have both contributed to and been affected by important shifts in the practice and theory of ministry. First, although some women had been ordained in Protestant churches in the nineteenth century or even earlier, most Protestant churches began to ordain significant numbers of women ministers in the 1950s; churches in the Anglican communion first recognized women priests in the 1970s (though a woman had been ordained in the diocese of Hong Kong and South China in the 1940s); the Roman Catholic and Orthodox churches continue to regard the ordination of women to the priesthood as impermissible. Second, ecumenical conversations among Christian churches have broadened the focus of discussions of ministry and recalled attention to the ministry of Christians in general. Third, increased commitment on the part of churches to addressing issues of social justice has led to the creation of numerous church-sponsored justice ministries, usually led and staffed by

Deaconess Phyllis Edwards was one of the first women ordained as a deacon. She is pictured here at the Church of the Good Samaritan in San Francisco, April, 1965 (Ted Streshinsky/Corbis).

lay women and men. Fourth, professional lay ministry has burgeoned in the Roman Catholic church in particular, but also in Protestant and, to a lesser extent, Orthodox churches; volunteer ministries abound. Fifth, there is a continuing movement for the ordination of women in the Roman Catholic church, despite papal pronouncements to the contrary.

Across the spectrum of Christianity, therefore, women engage in a full range of ministries. Whether ordained or not, women serve formally in ministries of Christian education, music, liturgy, and social justice, in hospital and other chaplaincies, in campus ministries, and in denominational boards and agencies. Many more also undertake political, organizing, social service, justice, or educational work out of an explicit commitment to ministry but not as institutional representatives of a church or churches. Women's participation in nonor-

dained and ordained, individual and institutional ministries embodies their spirituality and expresses their agency as Christians. It challenges the predominance of men in ordained ministries, extends the meaning of Christian vocation and ministry, and often (but not always) acts in solidarity with the poor, the oppressed, and the disenfranchised in both church and society.

Feminist and womanist theologies and practices of ministry have developed critiques of the concepts of service, servanthood, and related terms, as well as of authoritarian leadership and hierarchical theories of ordination. They point to the damaging effects of differential notions of service as applied to women (particularly, in the U.S. context, to African-American women) and to men, and they draw explicit connections to negative experiences of slavery and servitude based on race, class, and ethnicity. In contrast, women practitioners and theologians propose such models of church as a discipleship of equals, church in the round, or women-church. They conceive of ministry in terms such as mending, empowerment, partnership, bridge building, co-creation, and inclusive discipleship, and they construct collaborative, nonauthoritarian, and participative practices of ministry.

BIBLIOGRAPHY

For an overview of women's ministry in early Christianity, see Francine Cardman, "Silence in the Churches: Women, Ministry and Church Order in Early Christianity," in *Women and Christian Origins: A Reader*, edited by Mary Rose D'Angelo and Ross Shepard Kraemer (1999); much of the textual evidence is assembled and analyzed by Roger Gryson, *The Ministry of Women in the Early Church* (1976).

Contemporary feminist understandings of church and ministry can be found in Lynn N. Rhodes, *Co-Creating: A feminist Vision of Ministry* (1987); Rosemary Radford Ruether, *Women-Church: Theology and Practice* (1985); Letty M. Russell, *Church in the Round: Feminist Interpretations of the Church* (1993); Elisabeth Schüssler Fiorenza, *Discipleship of Equals: A Critical Feminist Ekklesia-logy of Liberation* (1993).

Womanist critiques of service and servanthood are developed particularly by Jacquelyn Grant, "The Sin of Servanthood and the Deliverance of Discipleship," in *A Troubling in My Soul: Womanist Perspectives on Evil and Suffering*, edited by Emily M. Townes (1993); Clarice Martin, "The *Haustafeln* (Household Codes) in African American Biblical Interpretation: 'Free Slaves' and 'Subordinate Women'," in *Stony the Road We Trod: African American Biblical Interpretation*, edited by Cain Hope Felder (1991); Delores S. Williams, *Sisters in the Wilderness: The Challenge of Womanist God-Talk* (1993).

For women's leadership in ordained and lay ministries see *Religious Institutions and Women's Leadership: New Roles Inside the Mainstream,* edited by Catherine Wessinger (1996); *In Search of a Round Table: Gender, Theology and Church Leadership,* (Geneva, 1997). Dana L. Robert, *American Women in Mission: A Social History of Their Thought and Practice* (1996) is a recent study of women and the missionary movement.

See also the succinct entries and bibliography in the *Dictionary of Feminist Theologies,* edited by Letty M. Russell and J. Shannon Clarkson (1996), *"Diakonia"* (Mary Rose D'Angelo), pp. 66–67; "Ministry" (Gail Lynn Unterberger), pp. 183–184; and "Servant/Slave" (Angela Bauer), pp. 255–256.

See also Authority; Christianity; Community; Ethnicity; Monasticism: In the West; Racism; Womanist Traditions.

FRANCINE CARDMAN

Minoan (Cretan) Religion

The religion of the late Bronze Age (second millennium B.C.E.) Minoan peoples of Crete has, since its discovery by Sir Arthur Evans at the end of the nineteenth century, captured the imagination of serious students of religion and of laypeople alike. This is largely because of the provocative nature of the archaeological evidence and the ways it has been sometimes interpreted (Marinatos, 1993; Gimbutas, 1989) as proof of worship of the Greek goddess and female preeminence (or at least equality) in religion and society. Minoan religion can only be known through archaeological remains because written evidence is either undecipherable or inconclusive. These circumstances restrict the amount of secure knowledge than can ever be recovered about Minoan religious rites or rituals, gods, or goddesses. Nevertheless, scholars have compared archaeological remains with evidence from Neolithic Crete, written records of the Mycenaeans (a mainland Greek people contemporaneous with the Minoans who would eventually supercede them at many sites on Crete), accounts of Minoan practices by later classical Greeks, and ethnographic analogy. The results have yielded numerous studies (Nilsson, 1968; Warren, 1988) that lay out, sometimes in great detail, the nature of Minoan religion, its rituals, calendar, theological structure, and even social frameworks.

According to the original excavator of Knossos, Arthur Evans, and most succeeding scholars, a great goddess is at the head of the Minoan pantheon. Her presence is evidenced by several female figurines found in what appear to be cultic contexts at a number of sites on the island. The figurines are in general small and often depict a woman with bare breasts, her hands raised, and wearing a great full skirt. A connection has been made between her and a possible nature cult, since so many Minoan ritual sites seem to have been situated outdoors (some located high on mountain peaks or in caves or near trees). The illustration of similarly dressed women is common in other media, especially frescoes and stamp seals. As Minoan civilization became more sophisticated, evidence of religious activity such as the figurines, small (obviously symbolic) double axes, horns of consecration, conical libation vessels, and "lustral basins" are found at large sites such as Knossos, Mallia, and Zakros. Also found at these sites are numerous wall paintings, some of which seem to depict rituals in which women are seated upon a dais and others where women dance before an audience. It has even been suggested that the centers, usually called palaces, were wholly temple complexes in which women were the high priestesses.

Elaborate ritual is another important component of Minoan religion, and in most representations of such activity women seem to be key participants. A number of tantalizing images are featured on the Ayia Triada sarchophagus, found in a looted tomb dated to the early fourteenth century B.C.E. On this piece of funerary furniture at least four important rituals are illustrated: animal sacrifice, presentation of goods at an altar, presentation of goods to a female cult statue, and a pouring ritual. In three of these four rites women are the primary officiating officers, thus illustrating the prominent role of women in the religion of this culture.

BIBLIOGRAPHY

Evans, Sir Arthur J. *The Palace of Minos.* 4 vols. 1921–1936. These four volumes are the report of the excavation of Knossos, the first fully explored and potentially most important Minoan site on the island of Crete. Alongside Evans's interpretations of the palace is a vivid picture of Minoan culture and religion in which women held high social status and religious power. Although many of Evans's hypotheses have been challenged, the volumes remain an invaluable resource of raw material about Minoan culture.

Gimbutas, Marija. *Language of the Goddess.* 1989. In this book Gimbutas attempts to demonstrate the existence of matriarchal societies and a generic goddess-based religious orientation in Europe during the period prior to 3500 B.C.E. Based on a rich array of iconography from the Paleolithic through the Copper ages, she argues the existence of four focal points of this religion: life-giving orientation, renewing and eternal earth, death and regeneration, and energy and unfolding. Problems arise, however, in her lack of an explicit analytical approach and specific hypothesis testing.'

Kokkinidou, Dimitria, and Marianna Nikolaïdou. *'Η Αρχαιολογία και ἡ Κοινωνική Ταγτότητα του Φύλου: Προσεγγισεῖς την Αγαιακή Προϊστορια* (Archaeology and Gender: Approaches to Aegean Prehistory). 1993. This singular book looks at Bronze Age Greece from the theoretical perspective of feminism and gender studies. Kokkinidou and Nikolaïdou discover gender parity in their study of evidence of Aegean social power structures and offer evidence for increased diversity in the roles of men and women from the Neolithic to the late Bronze Age.

Marinatos, Nanno. *Minoan Religion: Ritual, Image and Symbol.* 1993. In this work Marinatos outlines what she believes to be the major focal points of Minoan religion: a cult of the dead, palace temples, rites of passage rituals, and symbolic systems in art. Within the religious system that Marinatos configures women play major roles as priestesses and goddesses. Two major problems plague the book: first, her use of the evidence is totally uncritical, despite the ambiguous nature of much of it, and, second, there exists a lack of integration with a large body of secondary literature on political and social organization.

Nilsson, Martin, P. *The Minoan-Mycenaean Religion and its Survival in Greek Religion.* 1968. This book is the first on the subject of Bronze Age religion and for this reason has ever since colored attitudes about the topic. Using much of Evans's evidence from Knossos and a large body of stamp seal imagery, Nilsson recreates Bronze Age Greek religion largely as cults focused around celebrated objects evidenced from the archaeological record such as double axes, sacrificial vessels, idols, and pillars. Many of these cults, Nilsson argues, were practiced to honor goddesses and were officiated by priestesses. Nilsson also enriches many of his theories with later Greek myth such as the birth of the child Zeus on Crete.

Ruud, Inger Marie. *Minoan Religion: A Bibliography.* 1996. This book is an important resource tool for the study of Minoan religion. Citations are divided under the headings: Cult Places, Cult Practices, Cult Symbols and Equipment, Deities, Epigraphic Evidence, Iconography/Seals and Sealings, Priesthood and Sacral Kingship, Relation to Greek and Mycenaean Religion, Relation to Other Religions, Relation to Thera, Sacred Animals and Demons, Tombs and Burial Customs.

Warren, Peter. *Minoan Religion as Ritual Action.* 1988. Warren's book presents a configuration of the archaeological evidence of Minoan religion into a coherent structure of five principal aspects of ritual cults: dance, sacred stones, sacred garments, nature (plants and animals), and sacrifice. Interestingly (although Warren makes little of this point), women are most often illustrated officiating in these rituals. Warren proposes that these ritual cults were practiced in order to communicate with the divine, who he suggests was likely a goddess.

See also **Archaeology**; **Goddess**.

SENTA C. GERMAN

Mirabai

Mirabai (born c. 1500) was a sixteenth-century poet-saint living in Rajasthan, India, who was utterly devoted to Krishna. She is immensely popular, and multiple tellings of her story exist today, though there is little historical documentation of her life. Her story is compelling, and many try to draw on her absolute devotion for their own cause. Yet, her devotion to none but God and the resistance so fundamental to her character mitigate against her full incorporation into any social, political, or religious agenda. No identifiable authentic collection of her devotional songs exists, either. Many people have composed in her name over the centuries, singing of their own devotion, suffering, and resistance, and the traditions surrounding her have largely been preserved in the fluid realm of oral tradition.

According to hagiography and legend, Mirabai was married to a prince (many say against her will), but she refused to behave as a royal wife should, dancing and singing in temples and conversing with holy men and people of all castes instead of remaining in seclusion. Her husband or her in-laws tried to kill her by various methods but to no avail. Hindu–Muslim tensions sometimes enter the tale with the emperor Akbar coming in disguise to see her, and some say she became the disciple of the low-caste leather worker Raidas. After her husband's death (some say before) she left her marital home to become a wandering singer-saint. She met Jiv Goswami (a great religious leader in Krishna devotion) in Vrindavan, but only after she countered his refusal to see her with the reminder that all lovers of this decidedly male god are "women." In another episode a lustful holy man claimed Krishna had directed him to make love to her. Setting up a bed amid the company of devotees, she suggested that there should be no shame in carrying out the act publicly if it were Krishna's command. Begging forgiveness, he became her disciple. Eventually she reached Dwarka, but Brahmin priests arrived, demanding that she return to her marital home. When she refused to go, they vowed to fast to the death. Asking to take leave of Krishna, she entered the temple where she merged with her Lord and was seen no more.

Devotees portray Mirabai as one who miraculously survived repeated attempts on her life and whose songs speak of the purest and sweetest love. Low-caste singers stress her rejection of all that her royal husband represented and her choice to live in solidarity with the socially outcaste. Attempting to remove any challenge to gender and caste hierarchies, nationalists made her over into an obedient wife who turned to devotion in sorrow after her husband's death, and movies, comic books, novels, and school textbooks do likewise. Is Mirabai an example for women's empowerment or an exception that proves the rule for women's subordination? Her name is used alternately to curse and praise independent, religious, or talented women, and her life's story has become an interpretive frame for the self-understanding and social acceptance of women who choose to live outside the paradigm of marriage. Both love and ambivalence continue to mark attitudes toward Mirabai, and she remains both popular and controversial.

BIBLIOGRAPHY

Harlan, Lindsey. *Religion and Rajput Women.* 1992.

———. "Abandoning Shame: Mira and the Margins of Marriage." In *From the Margins of Hindu Marriage.* Edited by Lindsey Harlan and Paul B. Courtright. 1995.

Hawley, John Stratton. "The Saints Subdued: Domestic Virtue and National Integration in *Amar Chitra Katha.*" In *Media and the Transformation of Religion in South Asia.* Edited by Lawrence A. Babb and Susan S. Wadley. 1995.

Hawley, John Stratton, and Mark Juergensmeyer. *Songs of the Saints of India.* 1988.

Kishwar, Madhu, and Ruth Vanita. "Poison to Nectar: The Life and Work of Mirabai." *Manushi* 50–52 (1989): 74–93.

Martin-Kershaw, Nancy M. "Mirabai: Inscribed in Text, Embodied in Life." *Journal of Vaisnava Studies* 3, no. 4 (1995): 5–44.

Mukta, Parita. *Upholding the Common Life: The Community of Mirabai.* 1994.

Sangari, Kumkum. "Mira and the Spiritual Economy of Bhakti." *Economic and Political Weekly* (1990) nos. 25, 27: 1464–1475; nos. 25, 28: 1537–1552.

NANCY M. MARTIN

Miriam

According to the Bible, Miriam is the sister of Moses and Aaron. In Exodus 15:20–21 she is called a prophet and is also described as leading the women of Israel in dance and singing a hymn after God's victory over the Egyptians at the Reed (Red) Sea. The prophet Micah lists Miriam together with Moses and Aaron as the leaders who brought Israel to the Promised Land (6:4).

Yet the Bible is not unambivalent in its portrayal of Miriam. In Numbers 12:1–16 she is depicted as challenging Moses' authority, and although she acts together with Aaron, only she is punished. Moreover, although she is presumably the sister who watches over the baby Moses as he floats in a papyrus basket in the reeds of the Nile and who sees him safely delivered into the hands of Pharaoh's daughter (Exod. 2:1–10), she is unnamed in the episode and thus rendered less significant. Finally, the victory song attributed to her in Exodus 15:21 is elsewhere put in the mouth of Moses (Exod. 15:1). Given that typically in the biblical record it is women who are the singers of Israel's victory songs (e.g., Judg. 5:1–31), the attribution of the song to Miriam is probably the older tradition. The subsequent ascription to Moses, like Miriam's condemnation in Numbers 12 and her anonymity in Exodus 2, is thus an example of the way a male-dominated tradition comes to favor its heroes over its heroines.

BIBLIOGRAPHY

Burns, Rita J. *Has the Lord Indeed Spoken Only Through Moses? A Study of the Biblical Portrait of Miriam.* Society of Biblical Literature Dissertation Series 84. 1987.

Cross, Frank, and David Noel Freedman. "The Song of Miriam." *Journal of Near Eastern Studies* 14 (1955): 237–250.

Trible, Phyllis. "Bringing Miriam Out of the Shadows." *Bible Review* 5 (February 1989): 14–25, 34.

SUSAN ACKERMAN

Misogyny

Misogyny, hatred of women, is evident throughout the world's religious traditions. Many scholars have commented on the pervasive cultural tendency to associate women with chaotic sexuality, pollution, and evil. Theories about the cause of misogyny range from the anthropological (a response to the threat of increasing female social rights in a patriarchal culture) to the psychological (conflicts arising from the complexities of the mother-child relationship). In many traditional belief systems, women are portrayed as morally and spiritually weaker than men, less rational, more lustful and promiscuous, and less capable of exercising authority or handling leadership positions. They have therefore frequently been excluded both from religious education and theological discourse. Sacred texts depict acts of physical, sexual, and emotional humiliation and violence against women, sometimes as a result of divine command. Religious institutions support cultural practices that are painful, degrading, and dangerous to women; these practices derive from theologies that elevate sacrifice, suffering, and powerlessness. Misogyny also takes less overt forms such as attitudes of patronizing superiority, the trivializing of women's concerns, the use of seductive patterns of control, and the romanticizing or idealizing of women who conform to a submissive ideal.

Theorists differ as to whether antiwoman attitudes, rituals, and writings are an integral component of religious theologies and institutions or are a result of patriarchal misinterpretations and manipulations. Feminist theory is the scene of debate over whether particular cultural and religious practices—such as sati (widow-burning), female circumcision (clitoridectomy or infibulation), marriage at puberty (with betrothal sometimes preceding puberty), menstrual taboos that isolate women from the general culture, and foot-binding—should be respected as expressions of individual religious faith or resisted as misogynistic.

The radical feminist philosopher Mary Daly, for example, has analyzed some of these customs as evidence of rampant misogyny in all major societies; she asserts that woman-hating is at the foundation of all patriarchal religious institutions. Feminist liberation theologians such as Letty Russell, Rosemary Ruether, and Carter Heyward maintain that the core of religious traditions is a relationship with the sacred which can be equally available to both sexes. These scholars suggest alternative theological interpretations that focus on liberation for all people and resistance to all forms of violence and oppression.

In Western monotheism, misogynistic beliefs and practices have been frequently associated with philosophical systems viewing the world in terms of oppositional dualism based on domination and submission. Men are to rule over women as God over humanity and humans over animals and nature. The elevation of spirit and reason over nature and the body, accompanied by a strong association between women and the physical realm, has led to the degradation of women and the natural world. God is said by religious authorities to reinforce authority of husband over wife, and women are counseled to be silent and submit to their husbands.

Some Eastern religious traditions justify misogynistic practices by associating women with temptations of the physical and carnal realm; women are too tainted to be capable of enlightenment and pose too great a temptation for men seeking to transcend the material. Lorna Rhodes AmaraSingham notes the tendency in Buddhism to view women as barriers to salvation, since their physical sensuality and their association with the household and childbirth tie them too closely to the world of attachments. Many Hindu texts elevate the ideal of the docile and subservient wife and express the view that women cannot attain enlightenment while in female form.

BIBLIOGRAPHY

Works by Mary Daly, especially *Gyn/Ecology* (1978), describe multiple forms of misogyny in religious practice. Beverly Harrison's *Making the Connections* (1985) connects misogyny with other forms of oppression such as homophobia. For discussion of misogynistic practices incorporated in a general discussion of women and world religions, see Denise Carmody's *Women and World Religions* (2d ed., 1989). Phyllis Trible's *Texts of Terror* (1984) includes a discussion of misogynistic biblical texts. For discussion of Christian theology in relation to violence against women, see Joanne Carlson Brown and Carole R. Bohn's *Christianity, Patriarchy and Abuse* (1989). Rita Gross (*Buddhism After Patriarchy,* 1977) and Miranda Shaw (*Passionate Enlightenment,* 1994) discuss misogyny in Buddhism, and Judith Hoch-Smith and Anita Spring consider misogyny in Eastern religious traditions in their introduction to *Women in Ritual and Symbolic Roles* (1978).

See also **Hierarchy**; **Patriarchy**; **Sexism**.

L. J. "TESS" TESSIER

Monasticism

In the East

The term *monasticism* comes from the Greek word *monadzein,* meaning "to live alone." It refers to a way of life distanced from worldly concerns and exclusively devoted to religious pursuits. In the East monasticism has rested on vows of celibacy, renunciation of possessions, restraint of sense-pleasures, and refraining from all work to attain one's livelihood. Monasticism for women in the East has required distancing oneself from one's former household and family, but not cloistering or isolation from the rest of society. Most Eastern monastics, particularly women, remain near to population centers and build close ties to lay communities on which their livelihood depends (Tsai, 1994).

Monasticism for women has been important in Jainism, Buddhism, and in indigenous Asian religions influenced by Buddhism, namely Bonpo in Tibet (Havnevik, 1989) and Taoism in China. The renunciant tradition of India has been the fountainhead of all monasticism in Asia, including women's monasticism. Typical vows include non-injury (ahimsa), truthfulness, not taking anything not given, renunciation of possessions, and celibacy.

Renunciation of household life in India among Buddhists, Jains, and Hindus took different forms, including studying with a guru at an ashram, wandering mendicancy, and living together with others under a rule in a cenobitic mendicant order. It is this last form that closely resembles the tradition of monasticism in the West.

THE ASHRAM

In India, Vedic and Hindu traditions did not early develop the institution of communal monasticism. For instance, the Upanishads emphasize renunciation of the world and the pursuit of spiritual practice and meditation. But the central institution for this was the ashram, a spiritualized family (*gurukula*) under the guidance of a spiritual father, the guru, and his wife; it was not in the full sense a monastery, although it might require celibacy of disciples (Goldman, 1991).

WANDERING MENDICANCY: BUDDHISTS AND JAINS

The tradition of wandering mendicancy, as practiced by Jains, Buddhists, and Hindus of later periods, is the tradition from which true cenobitic monasticism developed in the East. Beginning in the sixth century B.C.E., Jains and then Buddhists both accepted women into their wandering mendicant orders. Hindus, when they later developed such orders, did not. Rather, Hindu Brahmanical society made marriage mandatory for all women (Young, 1987; Jaini, 1991). In Buddhist and Jain texts one can find considerable disagreement about what women can attain through the renunciant life. The wandering mendicant in India, whether Jain, Hindu, or Buddhist, is expected to give up home, household, and property; to beg all sustenance; to vigorously avoid doing harm to any other living thing; and to spend the greater part of his or her life wandering on foot from place to place, alone or in small groups.

The doctrine and rhetoric of the renunciant communities of Buddhism and Jainism stress the avoidance of family ties, emotional bonds, and the pleasures of the senses. In the minds of the men who have dominated these movements, all of these are associated with women. In Buddhist and Jain scriptures and doctrinal debates, the problem is then constructed in terms of the degree to which women are able to make the same sort of renunciatory commitment and spiritual progress as men (Goldman, 1991). In the Buddhist case the Buddha said, when questioned, that women are as capable as men of leading the renunciant life and of attaining its goal, nirvana (Falk, 1980; Jaini, 1991).

JAINS

The major sects of Jainism, the Digambara and the Śvetāmbara, remain deeply divided both on the question of whether it is appropriate for a woman to take up the monastic life and on the question of whether a woman can enter the state of spiritual liberation. The Digambaras argue that women are incapable of keeping the vows of the renunciant in sufficient degree to attain spiritual liberation (Jaini, 1991). Women inevitably kill living organisms contained in various locations in their bodies, and thus cannot perfect the vow of nonharming (ahimsa). Further, modesty, concerns for safety, and their menses prevent them from wandering completely naked as male Digambaras do, and thus they cannot attain complete nonpossession. The Śvetāmbaras believe that one can wear a single robe without any spiritually contaminating inner sense of possession, and deny that the Digambaras' arguments prove that women cannot attain liberation.

Nuns may always have outnumbered monks in the Jain tradition. The Jain canon claims that at the death of Mahāvīra (b. 599 B.C.E. [trad.]), the founder of the Jain movement as we know it today, his *sangha* consisted of fourteen thousand monks and thirty-six thousand nuns. Today, Śvetāmbara women monastics (*sādhvīs*) considerably outnumber their male counterparts (*munis*) by at least two to one. Even the Digambaras have a small number of women renunciants (*āryikās* and *kṣullikā*s), although they are technically regarded as laywomen. Jain nuns act as guides and teachers to laywomen, leading them in ascetic practices (Jaini, 1991).

CENOBITIC MENDICANCY: HINDUS AND BUDDHISTS

Beginning in the ninth century cenobitic monasticism developed for men in Hinduism, but only since the "Hindu renaissance" of the late nineteenth and twentieth centuries have Hindu leaders been interested in establishing monastic orders for women (King, 1984; Young, 1994).

From the very beginning of the Buddhist tradition, the life of the monks and nuns combined two modes: eremitic (solitary wandering) and cenobitic (settled communities). Over time the cenobitic element has predominated; it was as a cenobitic order that Buddhism spread to Central Asia, China, and the rest of Asia. Cenobitic renunciant orders of Buddhists certainly resembled Western monasteries in key respects: practitioners of a spiritual path made vows and lived together under a rule acceptable to the tradition as a whole, deliberately cutting themselves off from any possible involvement in the structure of family ties and the transfer of wealth across generations.

According to Buddhist scriptures, the *bhikshuni sangha* (order of female mendicants or nuns) was founded along with the *bhikshu sangha* (male order) by the Buddha early in his career as a religious teacher. Nuns and monks live as renunciants seeking enlightenment and liberation (nirvana) from pain-bringing attachment to worldly life. Buddhist nuns and monks practice restraint of the senses and contentment with whatever is given in the way of food, clothing, and shelter. Meditation, the cultivation of penetrating wisdom, and moral discipline are the positive elements of the path to self-knowledge and liberation. Monks and sometimes nuns preach the Buddha's doctrines (dharma) to lay devotees, and are in turn supported by their donations of food, clothing, and other necessities (Tsomo, 1996). Within the Mahayana, nuns and monks also perform priestly functions at ceremonies to benefit laypersons.

MONASTIC RULES AND PRECEPTS: THE VINAYA

The ideal against which *bhikshuni*s measure their practice and their institutional life is the body of precepts known as the Vinaya. Different versions of the Vinaya were preserved in different early Buddhist schools, but variations are minor. They contain precepts for *bhikshu*s (fully ordained monks); *bhikshuni*s (fully ordained nuns); *śikṣamāṇā*s (probationary nuns), *śrāmaṇeras* (male novices), *śrāmaṇerikā*s (female novices), laymen and laywomen (Wijayaratna, 1990). A Buddhist woman set upon the renunciant path would first take lay precepts, then probationary precepts (established primarily to create a waiting period to make sure that a woman who wanted to become a *bhikshuni* was not pregnant), then novice precepts, then the more than three hundred *bhikshuni* precepts (Tsomo, 1996).

There are five categories of precepts according to different levels of seriousness and types of correction or punishment. The first category, the *pārājika*, is for precepts whose infraction brings expulsion from the order. There are four precepts in this class for monks, eight

Tibetan Buddhist nuns together sit in the Gaden Cholin Monastery in Dharamsala, India, 1991 (Allison Wright/Corbis).

for nuns. Both orders place in this category 1) sexual intercourse; 2) lying about one's spiritual attainments; 3) taking what is not given; and 4) taking a human life. The rules for nuns also place in this category 5) having bodily contact with a man whose mind is tainted by desire; 6) arranging to meet a man, and so on, who has amorous intentions; 7) concealing a *pārājika* fault committed by another *bhikshuni*; 8) following and obeying a *bhikshu* who has been expelled from the *sangha* (Tsomo, 1996). Thus whereas *bhikshu*s are expelled for actual sexual intercourse, *bhikshuni*s are expelled for acts that risk, encourage, or even appear to encourage sexual intercourse with a man as well as for sexual intercourse itself.

According to the Vinaya, judicial responsibility for interpreting the precepts rests in the hands of local *sangha* communities, which function independently and make decisions as a group on the basis of consensus.

The *bhikshuni sangha* was accorded lower status than, and subordinated to, the *bhikshu sangha*, as reflected in the "eight chief rules" (*gurudharmas*) traditionally believed to have been laid down by the Buddha as a condition for allowing the formation of a renunciant *sangha* for women. These specify, for example, that any nun, however senior, must bow to any monk, even if he has just been ordained that day. These rules also require that communities of nuns maintain ties to communities of monks and involve them in the supervision of their important rites. Ku Cheng-mei (1984) has shown convincingly that these "eight chief rules" do not belong to the earliest stratum of the Vinaya texts, but were an innovation by a particular early school that was hostile to the idea of women as renunciants.

The *bhikshuni sangha* flourished in India for some centuries and then declined in numbers and activity. Meanwhile, the order had been established in Sri

Lanka by Indian nuns around 250 B.C.E. Sinhalese nuns carried it on to China in 433 or 434 C.E., and later to Burma. From China the transmission of the order continued to Korea, Japan, and Vietnam. Eventually the order disappeared completely from India, Sri Lanka, Nepal, and Burma. It has continued to thrive in China and the Chinese diaspora to the present day, as well as in Korea, Japan, and Vietnam (Barnes, 1996).

Ordination of *bhikshunis* according to the Vinaya is still carried out today in China, Korea, and Vietnam. It is a two-step process: novice ordination, possible as early as age eight, though the order recommends that one wait till age twenty; and full ordination after age twenty. At novice ordination a novice takes ten precepts; at full ordination a woman takes more than three hundred precepts. A third bodhisattva ordination based on the precepts of the Brahmajala sutra is specifically Mahayana and carried out in Taiwan, Hong Kong, China, Korea, and Vietnam. Nuns in Tibet commonly adopt both the *śrāmaṇerikā* (probationer's) precepts of the Prātimokṣa and the Bodhisattva precepts of the Bodhisattvabhūmi sutra (Tsomo, 1996; Havnevik, 1989).

In China, Korea, and Vietnam, nuns—though often not receiving as much respect or support from laypersons as did monks—nonetheless enjoyed the same privileges and powers as monks. There were no ceremonies or practices that monks could do from which nuns were excluded. Monastic education was theoretically as open to nuns as to monks. The model for the renunciant life as laid down in the Vinaya has been altered in important respects: nuns now labor for their livelihood in that they often grow their own food, and, because they live in societies where daily begging is impractical, now handle money and make use of bank accounts. Abbesses, nuns, and their *sanghas* practice with more autonomy and independence from the order of monks than envisioned by the "eight chief rules" (Levering, 1994; Barnes, 1996). *Bhikshunis* recently have taken up activities in the fields of education and social service, fields that were not explicitly envisioned in the Vinaya ideal.

In Tibetan Buddhism, where there apparently never was a *bhikshuni sangha*, the probationer nuns, who have considerable freedom and resemble the more numerous monks in lifestyle and dress, have not enjoyed anything like the same access to monastic education, ceremonies, and practices as monks. This is beginning to change among Tibetan exiles in India.

LAY NUNS

The order of fully ordained *bhikshuni* nuns never did spread to other Buddhist countries including Thailand, Cambodia, Laos, Tibet, or the Himalayan kingdoms of Bhutan and Sikkim. However, women have lived as Buddhist renunciants in those countries (as well as in Nepal, where the *bhikshuni* order may once have existed) under lay or probationer vows, taking the eight or ten basic lay precepts (or, in the case of Tibet and other smaller countries under its influence, probationer's precepts), shaving their heads like *bhikshunis* and living a celibate, renunciant life. Bartholomeusz terms these women "lay nuns" (Bartholomeusz, 1994). In some countries such as Thailand and Sri Lanka, these lay nuns live in communities fully separated from household life (Kabilsingh, 1991); in others, such as Bhutan and Ladakh, lay nuns, though celibate and dedicated to religious life, still have to spend the majority of their time performing work and other forms of service in their natal families. Full ordination is not available to many lay nuns, and they are regarded legally by their male-dominated societies as pious laywomen. Many of these probationers or lay nuns regard their religious vocation as making it possible for them to be men and monks in their next rebirths. They do not enjoy high social status. However, in some countries many have time to devote to meditation for the sake of spiritual development.

In Japan monks and nuns both receive a short version of the bodhisattva precepts only, and not the Prātimokṣa precepts. Thus from the standpoint of followers of the traditional Vinaya, monks and nuns in Japan are not really fully ordained *bhikshus* and *bhikshunis*. Nevertheless, until the twentieth century most monks and all nuns in Japan lived a fully renunciant life, and in recent centuries at least the precepts received by both were the same (Arai, 1998). Monks in Japan have returned to married life, but nuns have remained celibate; most receive income from performing ceremonies for laypersons, and from teaching traditional Japanese arts such as flower arranging and tea ceremony.

TAOIST NUNS

The study of Taoist nuns is in its infancy. Taoism was not originally a renunciant or monastic religion; Taoist nuns appeared in the Tang dynasty (618–907 C.E.), when a number of court ladies became nuns (Despeux, 1990). Tu Kuang-t'ing (850–933), a Shang-ch'ing Taoist of the late Tang period, compiled a hagiographical collection devoted entirely to the lives and legends of mortal Taoist women and female Taoist immortals. This work, entitled *Records of the Assembled Transcendents of the Fortified Walled City*, contains biographies of twenty-eight mortal women (Cahill, 1993). Tu wrote that marriage could be a path to perfection and immortality. However, in his view the preferred path involved sexual abstinence and fasting.

Poems written on the occasion of elite Tang women taking vows and becoming Taoist nuns show many resemblances between the Buddhist and Taoist rites of ordination for a woman: shaving off her hair, giving up finery for plain monastic garb, changing her secular name to a religious one, departing from household life and living in a temple or monastery, taking vows of obedience and compassion. But the goals of immortal transcendence, astral travel, and an office in the celestial hierarchy are distinctly Taoist, and it is not clear that celibacy was regarded by all Tang Taoist women as a requirement of the path. Many poems, written by men, express the poet's fantasy of transcendent immortality attained through sexual union with an accomplished Taoist nun.

The Quanzhen order, which emphasized monastic life for men and women and placed considerable emphasis on celibacy, meditation, and a process of inner transformation known as inner alchemy, was founded in the twelfth century. This order is widespread in China, where nuns (*kundao* or *daogu*) as well as monks (*qiandao* or *daoshi*) are trained at a number of monasteries. The government of the People's Republic of China has not allowed full Taoist ordinations of new *kundao* or *qiandao*. Inner alchemy practices continue that are specifically designed to transform a woman's body as well as her spirit (Despeux, 1990; Levering, 1994).

BIBLIOGRAPHY

The study of women and monasticism in the East began with I. B. Horner, *Women Under Primitive Buddhism* (1930), and Carolyn A. F. Rhys Davids, *Psalms of the Sisters* (1909), a translation of the *Therīgatha*, a collection of poems by early Buddhist nuns. The latter has been translated more recently by K. R. Norman (1971) and made more readable for an American audience by Susan Murcott in *The First Buddhist Women* (1991). A pioneering article expressing a view now controversial is Nancy Auer Falk, "The Case of the Vanishing Nuns: The Fruits of Ambivalence in Ancient Buddhism," in *Unspoken Worlds: Women's Religious Lives in Non-Western Cultures*, edited by Nancy Auer Falk and Rita Gross (1980). Gregory Schopen, in "On Monks, Nuns, and 'Vulgar' Practices: The Introduction of the Image Cult into Indian Buddhism," in his *Bones, Stones and Buddhist Monks* (1997), offers evidence to counter the view expressed in Falk's article that the nuns' order declined and vanished in India before the order of monks.

On Hindu women and renunciation, see Katherine K. Young, "Hinduism," in *Women in World Religions*, edited by Arvind Sharma (1987). On the interest shown in Hindu monasticism for women by leaders of the Hindu renaissance, see Ursula King, "The Effect of So-cial Change on the Religious Self-understanding of Women Ascetics in Modern Hinduism," in *Changing South Asia: Religion and Society*, edited by K. Ballhatchet and D. Taylor (1984); and Katherine K. Young "Women in Hinduism," in *Today's Woman in World Religions*, edited by Arvind Sharma, 1994. On the Jain view of women and renunciation, see Padmanabh S. Jaini, *Gender and Salvation: Jaina Debates on the Spiritual Liberation of Women* (1991); the forword by Robert P. Goldman is also valuable. On the historical origins of the eight *gurudharmas*, see Ku Cheng-mei, "The Mahayanic View of Women: A Doctrinal Study," Ph.D. diss., University of Wisconsin (1984). On the struggles to restore the Buddhist order of nuns in Asian countries, see Nancy J. Barnes, "Buddhist Women and the Nuns' Order in Asia," in *Engaged Buddhism: Buddhist Liberation Movements in Asia*, edited by Christopher S. Queen and Sallie B. King (1996).

Studies of Buddhist nuns in various countries include: Paula Arai, *Women Living Zen: Soto Buddhist Nuns in Japan* (1998); Tessa Bartholomeusz, *Women Under the Bo Tree: Buddhist Nuns in Sri Lanka* (1994); Hanna Havnevik, *Tibetan Buddhist Nuns: History, Cultural Norms, and Social Reality* (1989); Chatsumarn Kabilsingh, *Thai Women in Buddhism* (1991); and Pao Chang, *Lives of the Nuns: Biographies of Chinese Buddhist Nuns from the Fourth to the Sixth Centuries*, translated by Kathryn Ann Tsai (1994). A good short article that gives the flavor of nun's practice in the Himalayan kingdoms is Kim Gutschow, "Reflections from a Nunnery Rooftop," *Sakyadhita* 6, no. 2 (Fall 1995); 9–11.

Mohan Wijayaratna, *Buddhist Monastic Life* (1990), focuses on Buddhist monastic life for men, but gives an excellent account of the outlines and intentions of the Buddhist renunciant life as described in the early Buddhist texts; this account applies in fact to both men and women. It is a useful supplement to recent studies of the monastic rules and precepts for women, which include the scholarly study by Chatsumarn Kabilsingh, *A Comparative Study of Bhikkunī Pātimokkha* (1984), and Karma Lekshe Tsosmo, *Sisters in Solitude: Two Traditions of Buddhist Monastic Ethics for Women* (1996). This last gives materials that illuminate the question of whether Tibetan nuns should be allowed to restore full ordination through a Chinese ordination lineage.

On Taoist nuns see Suzanne E. Cahill, *Transcendence and Divine Passion: The Queen Mother of the West in Medieval China* (1993); Catherine Despeux, *Immortelles de la Chine Ancienne* (1990), and Miriam Levering, "Women, Religion and the State in the People's Republic of China," in *Today's Woman in World Religions*, edited by Arvind Sharma (1994).

See also **East Asian Religions: New Buddhist Movements; Ordination: In Buddhism.**

MIRIAM LEVERING

In the West

In the first century of the common era, women in various regions of the Roman Empire were determined to resist the bonds of matrimony in favor of an autonomous celibate life. As widows or virgins, they vowed themselves to permanent chastity and a life of religious and philanthropic service. In Palestine, a few such women have been identified among the Essenes, a radical Jewish colony that produced the Dead Sea Scrolls. In Egypt, Philo Judaeus described the Therapeutae, Jewish women and men who formed a community of chaste celibates devoted to study and prayer. No monastic tradition proceeded from this root, however. Most dramatically, unmarried women joined the disciples who gathered around Jesus and formed a core of "widows" in the early Christian communities. Wealthy women supported the original group and headed many of the "house churches" that appear in the Pauline letters. Peter directed the communities to support three groups of "widows" in return for their prayers, the revelations of their prophetic experiences, and their charitable services to the sick and the needy. Some of them were among the first martyrs put to death in Rome under Nero.

Later sources took various stances in relation to such women. The apocryphal gospels of the second and third centuries fictionalized the development of a cult of chaste celibacy. They depicted various apostles converting women to chastity in defiance of lustful husbands and suitors. Women in third-century Africa were criticized by Tertullian for emulating Thecla, the virgin apostle converted by Paul who challenged the sacramental monopoly of the emerging priesthood by baptizing herself when she was about to be executed for her refusal to marry. Gnostic writings suggest that women who transcended their sexual existence would become men and therefore eligible for the full benefits of spiritual immortality. Despite these views, communities of virgins coalesced in urban settings living in their own homes or with friends, with husbands whom they had converted to a vow of chastity, or as *syneisactics*, women and men who lived together without a sexual relationship. Fearful of scandal and alarmed by the threat to the gender system, enforced by the male clerical monopoly, Christian bishops produced a variety of disciplinary prescriptions concerning the dress, living conditions, and public activity of virgins. Around 200, Tertullian introduced the concept of "brides of Christ," which subjected virgins to the traditional restrictions of married women but also assured their status at the top of a feminine hierarchy of virgins, widows, and wives. Virgins became the prototypical martyrs of the Great Persecution that ended with the legalization of Christianity by the Roman Empire in 313 C.E..

In the fourth and fifth centuries, communities of virgins, widows, and celibate men flourished throughout the empire. In Cappadocia, Macrina and her mother, Emilia, formed a community of women and men on their country estate that was idealized in the writings of Macrina's brothers Basil of Caesarea and Gregory of Nyssa. Marcella and Paula, aristocratic Roman widows, organized study groups of widows and virgins who assisted Jerome in his biblical exegesis. With her daughter Eustochium, Paula founded a monastery of two hundred women in Bethlehem. A similar foundation was established by Melania in Jerusalem. Her granddaughter, Melania the Younger, redistributed one of the greatest fortunes in the empire to support monasteries throughout the Mediterranean. All of these women traveled among the communities of women and men who established the monastic ideal in the deserts of Egypt and Syria. Rules, inspirational precepts, exemplary stories of heroic ascetics, and theological tracts on the principle of virginity guided them in the establishment of the monastic life.

Households of virgins formed in Roman Gaul and also in Spain, and mixed communities of women and men took refuge from the invading barbarians on the island of Lérins off of present-day Cannes. In Marseilles, John Cassian and his sister trained a generation of monastics in the rules and ideals of the eastern deserts. One of these novices was Caesaria, who headed a large community of virgins in Arles under a rule composed for her by her brother the bishop in 506. Situated within the city walls, like most sixth-century monasteries, Saint John of Arles formed a small village community securely enclosed within its own walls. The monastery opened onto the church, which, in turn, provided the only access to the streets. The sisters contributed their own fortunes and their labor for the community's support. Arles may have been the first monastic community to undertake the copying of manuscripts, which the rule suggests as an enterprise compatible with their prayerful life. Caesaria sent the Rule with a letter of spiritual guidance to the Queen of the Franks, Radegund, who had separated from her brutal and polygamous husband to found a large monastery in the city of Poitiers. The principle of enclosure as a protection for religious women was spread with the Rule of Arles during the invasion period. Priests and workmen, however, were always present within the walls, and the nuns remained in constant contact with relatives and patrons by writing or receiving visits. Women's monasteries, like men's, became influential centers of religious teaching. They provided worship and social service to the surrounding community, beggars on the road, and suppliant pilgrims at their shrines.

In the seventh century, monasticism became rural, and the Benedictine Rule, which required stability in the community without enclosure, generally superseded the Rule of Arles. Women of the Frankish aristocracy gave their fortunes to endow communities in the uncleared wilderness, where conversion spread with the establishment of religious centers. Their monasteries offered hospitality to travelers and care for the sick, and they provided capital for agricultural settlements. Under the influence of Irish spirituality, they embraced a variety of penitential principles, including frequent (nonsacramental) confession to the abbess and a series of liturgies designed to amass a treasury of grace for the support of weaker Christians in their struggle for salvation. In the early Middle Ages, therefore, monasticism flourished without regard for gender differences. Although women and men segregated their living arrangements, they maintained the syneisactic principle of joint spiritual effort in a united drive on the frontiers of Christianity in the British Isles and Germany.

With the ninth century, the "reformer" Benedict of Aniane, under imperial patronage, began to impose restrictions on nuns, including forms of enclosure designed to separate them from their male partners. Canonesses, communities of women who lived on their private incomes under temporary vows of chastity, and Benedictine women, who took permanent vows of chastity and shared their property in common, were subjected to the enclosure provisions of the Rule of Arles. In the tenth century, they were excluded from the powerful reforming networks inspired by the abbots of Cluny. Where Benedict had advised against ordination for monks, the Cluniacs increasingly became priests, giving them a strong competitive edge against women's spiritual services, which increasingly depended on their claims to individual sanctity.

With the twelfth century, monasticism became only one alternative for women who pursued the religious life. Papal legislation, culminating in *De Periculoso* in 1298, insisted on strict enclosure for women religious that only obscured the distinction between cloistered nuns devoted to prayer and mystical contemplation and women active in charitable service. Through the Reformation and the early modern period the church officially maintained this position. Monastic women developed complex and heroic spiritualities, most powerfully inspired by Teresa of Avila. They presented themselves for martyrdom in the period of the democratic revolu-

Benedictine nuns of the Convent of Perpetual Adoration, Kansas City, Missouri, gather in a room and read from their devotional books (Ted Spiegel/Corbis).

tion and braved the American frontiers to establish new monastic outposts. Inspired by Thérèse of Lisieux's missionary devotion, expressed through the power of the hidden life, they have spread throughout the world. Today, while the religious orders devoted to social service and teaching are shrinking as women enter the secular professions, the religious appeal of the cloistered life remains powerful and continues to grow in every part of the world.

BIBLIOGRAPHY

Religious women speak eloquently for themselves across the ages. This is a brief sample of biographies (sometimes by men), autobiographies, and other personal accounts of their experience.

Arenal, Electa, and Stacey Schlau. *Untold Sisters: Hispanic Nuns in Their Own Works, 16th–18th Centuries.* 1989.

Brock, Sebastian P., and Susan Ashbrook Harvey, eds. *Holy Women of the Syrian Orient.* 1987.

Gregory of Nyssa. *Ascetical Works: On Virginity, Life of Saint Macrina, On the Soul and the Resurrection.* Translated by Virginia W. Callahan. 1967.

Hildegard of Bingen. *Letters.* Edited by Joseph L. Baird and Radd K. Ehrman. 1994.

Hroswitha. *The Non-Dramatic Works.* Translated and edited by Sr. M. Gonsalva Wiegand. 1937.

———. *Plays.* Translated by Christopher St. John. 1966.

Lewis, Gertrud Jaron. *By Women, for Women, and about Women: The Sister-Books of Fourteenth Century Germany.* 1996.

McNamara, Jo Ann, John E. Halborg, with Gordon Whatley. *Sainted Women in the Dark Ages.* 1992.

Stein, Edith. *Collected Works.* Edited by L. Gelber and R. Leuven. 1986.

Teresa of Avila. *The Life of Saint Teresa of Avila.* Translated by J.M. Cohen. 1957.

Thérèse de Lisieux. *The Story of a Soul.* Translated by John Beevers. 1957.

Weisner-Hanks, Merry, and Joan Skocir. *Convents Confront the Reformation: Catholic and Protestant Nuns in Germany.* 1996.

An extensive bibliography of further primary sources and secondary works can be found in Jo Ann Kay McNamara, *Sisters in Arms: Catholic Nuns Through Two Millennia.* 1996.

See also Asceticism; Community; Seclusion.

JO ANN KAY MCNAMARA

Monotheism

Monotheism is the belief that there is only one God. It is associated particularly with Judaism, and the two monotheistic faiths rooted in Judaism, Christianity and Islam. But the definition and development of monotheism in these traditions is complex. The God of Hebrew Scripture was originally more henotheistic than monotheistic; that is, Hebrew faith prescribed the exclusive worship of the God of Israel, without claiming that gods of other peoples did not exist or that the God of Israel rules all people and the whole earth.

A process of universalization of the God of Israel as the entire world's creator and ruler took place over time, but Hebrew monotheism, and its heirs in Christianity and Islam, maintain the element of God's special relationship to a chosen ethnic or religious group. The universalization of an originally tribal God can be contrasted with a philosophical way of arriving at monotheism found in Greek philosophy. Here the many gods of different peoples are seen as manifestations or cultural expressions of an underlying ontological unity that derives from one Supreme Being.

The idea that the manyness of visible things manifests one underlying ontological unity is associated with pantheism, or the belief that the divine is in and through all things. But this term can be misleading. Platonic and Aristotelian philosophies distinguish in various ways between a transcendent unitary Being and derivative plural manifestations in a differentiated world. Greek philosophy grappled with the relation of the one and the many, transcendent unity and derivative plurality. This became an issue for Hebraic monotheism in its own philosophical expression. The Christian notion of the Trinity is one way of bridging the belief in a transcendent unity of the divine and its immanent expressions in creating, sustaining, and redeeming the world, as Word and Spirit.

Feminists have questioned Hebraic monotheism for its androcentrism, anthropocentrism, ethnocentrism, and kyriarchy; that is, for its identification of God with maleness, humanness, a special relation with one ethnic or religious group, and the rulers or lords of that group. They have sought a more inclusive understanding of the divine that is equally present in women, in nature, and in the many peoples and cultures of the earth, across race and class divisions.

Feminist theology has an affinity with polytheistic ways of approaching divine unity. For instance, God is present and manifest in women as much as in men, and in animals, plants, rivers, and mountains as much as in humans. In additions, feminist theology accepts the validity of different experiences of the divine, rather than construing one religious culture as having a privileged monopoly on revelation of the "true" God. But the Hebrew understanding of God as a God of justice is also important for feminists, without privileging the dominant group, and supporting the struggles of those disprivileged by patriarchy for the equal flourishing of life for all earth beings together.

BIBLIOGRAPHY

Daly, Mary. *Beyond God the Father: Toward a Philosophy of Women's Liberation.* 1973

Heyward, Carter. *The Redemption of God.* 1982.

McFague, Sallie. *Models of God: Theology for an Ecological Nuclear Age.* 1987.

Plaskow, Judith. *Standing Again at Sinai: Judaism from a Feminist Perspective.* 1990.

Ruether, Rosemary. *Sexism and God-talk: Toward a Feminist Theology.* 1983.

See also Christianity: Religious Rites and Practices; Islam: Religious Rites and Practices; Judaism: Religious Rites and Practices; Theology: Feminist Theology.

ROSEMARY RADFORD RUETHER

Moon

One might expect the moon to be an essentially feminine symbol, ascribing a parallel between women's and the moon's monthly cycles. Yet, notions of the moon are as diverse as the peoples holding them. Even within a single tradition associations between women and the moon can be mixed. Several examples show that no simple generalizations can be made.

To start with not all representations of the moon are female. In Japan's Shinto pantheon, Tsukiyomi, the moon god, is the lesser-known brother of Amaterasu, the sun goddess. He is entrusted with the domain of night, she the domain of the "high heavens" (Yusa, 1994). The Akan of Ghana have a deity named Nyame, a sometimes male, sometimes female aspect of a bisexed deity. When female, Nyame is a creator goddess, the lunar goddess who gave birth to the universe without male participation. However, Nyame is also symbolized in the waning moon as "killer-mother." Linkage between life and death can be seen in two Nyame statues: one given to barren women that they may bear children, the other placed on the graves of clan head-women. Both symbolize life-giving power called the lunar *kra*. Mbuti Pygmies also have a goddess, Matu, who is associated with the moon. Her attributes likewise involve what Rosalind Hackett calls an "ambiguity of power." She possesses fire and provides forest animals. However, her name means Night-Hag, Mistress or Mother of the Dead and signifies genital, especially menstrual blood (Hackett, 1994). Associations between women and the moon in these contexts interface with various institutional patterns, configuring opportunities for or prohibitions against women participating ritually, culturally, or politically in their communities. For example, the positions and life-giving abilities of the Akan queen-mother and clan headwomen are culturally, ritually, and politically identified with that of the moon, Nyame (Hackett, 1994, p. 68, 70).

In the Hebrew Bible (Numbers 10:10) the Israelites are told to sound the trumpets on new moon days. Although never static, rituals of lunar renewal (Rosh Hodesh) have been celebrated since the time of David (c. 1030 B.C.E.). Rabbinic commentaries (c. 70–630 C.E.) associate the moon and its rituals with women. Kabbalah, a Jewish mystical tradition begun in the twelfth century, links notions of the feminine with the moon through Rosh Hodesh reflections on the Shekhinah, the Divine Presence figured as female. In Talmudic story the sun and moon were once equal in the sky, then the moon questioned this arrangement, whereupon God reduced its size. Yet Isaiah 30:26 says that there will come a day when the Lord will return them to a balance. Historically this has often been interpreted as a renewal of Israel or the Jewish people. Some modern Jews, especially feminists, appeal to this story as they create Rosh Hodesh rituals reimagining traditional power relationships.

In what have been primarily North American, western European, and Euro-Australian movements, feminist spirituality circles and modern-day pagans usually invoke the moon as female—as Maiden, Mother, or Crone. For them, the moon exhibits a potent cycle of birth, growth, fullness, decline, and death. These loosely networked groups tend to focus on female imagery, often in deliberate countermeasure to what they perceive as male-dominated religion in the West. Honoring the moon becomes a way of celebrating women's bodily phases and all of life's ebbs and flows.

BIBLIOGRAPHY

Adler, Margot. *Drawing Down the Moon: Witches, Druids, Goddess-Worshippers, and Other Pagans in America Today* Rev. ed., 1986.

Eller, Cynthia. *Living in the Lap of the Goddess: The Feminist Spirituality Movement in America.* 1993.

Falk, Marcia. *The Book of Blessings: New Jewish Prayers for Daily Life, the Sabbath, and the New Moon Festival.* 1996. Valuable for contemporary Jewish ritual and theological construction around the moon.

Green, Arthur. "Bride, Spouse, Daughter: Images of the Feminine in Classical Jewish Sources." In *On Being a Jewish Feminist: A Reader.* Edited by Susannah Heschel. 1983.

Hackett, Rosalind I. J. "Women in African Religions." In *Religion and Women.* Edited by Arvind Sharma. 1994. Hackett cites Eva L. R. Meyerowitz's *The Akan of Ghana* (1959) on the female aspect of Nyame.

Shur, Fanchon. "Rosh Chodesh, New Moon Ritual of Renewel." In *Moon, Moon.* Edited by Anne Kent Rush. 1976. Though not particularly full of research data, a great collection of moon references and a springboard for further research.

Spiegel, Marcia Cohn. "Spirituality for Survival: Jewish Women Healing Themselves." *Journal of Feminist Studies in Religion* 12, no. 2 (Fall 1996): 121–137.

Trepp, Leo. *The Complete Book of Jewish Observances: A Practical Manual for the Modern Jew.* 1980.

Waskow, Arthur I. "Feminist Judaism: Restoration of the Moon." In *On Being a Jewish Feminist: A Reader.* Edited by Susannah Heschel. 1983.

Weissler, Chava. "Four *Tkhines*." In *Four Centuries of Jewish Women's Spirituality: A Sourcebook.* Edited by Ellen M. Umansky and Dianne Ashton. 1992.

———. "Religious World of Ashkenazic Women." In *Jewish Women in Historical Perspective.* Edited by Judith R. Baskin. 1991.

Yusa, Michiko. "Women in Shinto: Images Remembered." In *Religion and Women.* Edited by Arvind Sharma. 1994.

See also Sun.

PAM A. DETRIXHE

Morality

Because the moral codes of many religious traditions center around the family, it is only logical that these codes would be replete with gender distinctions. The obvious biological differences in male and female sexuality and early parenting and the subsequent impact on the structure of families provide a context for the emergence of gender differences on moral issues. These differences can be expressed through crucial questions about the family: How is the family arranged? What are the various roles and responsibilities? How is power distributed? How is sexuality understood and controlled? How are family members and those without families cared for? What are the transgressions within the family and how are they punished? What is surprising, especially to the sensibilities of the modern West, are the glaring gender inequities within these codes. Furthermore, because of the prominent inequities, it is easy to miss some underlying strands of gender equity.

Though tensions between equity and inequity remain, the inequities are the most glaring to the modern eye. This history of gender inequities in the moral systems of many religions is, to amend the words of Thomas Hobbes, nasty, brutish, and long. Women are often more restricted than men in matters as diverse as sexuality, education, and property ownership. In many traditions, including Islam, Confucianism, and Judaism, husbands have had greater freedom than wives to initiate divorce. Within Christianity women have been seen as less rational beings and hence less reliable moral actors.

These glaring inequities make it easy to overlook the more equitable side of much religious history. Many religious traditions explicitly affirm the universal moral value and responsibilities of both men and women. For example, charity is held up as a virtue for Christian women and men alike. Moral righteousness and compassion for the poor are expected of both Jewish men and women. Confucianism enjoins care of and obedience to parents for males and females. Moreover, major traditions affirm, either explicitly or implicitly, that women do have moral agency. By uplifting virtues and giving moral commands, these traditions assume that women have the capacity to follow them.

Most traditions also affirm the inherent value of all people, female or male. Judaism and Christianity, for example, insist that all are valuable children of God, made in God's image. The Christian scriptures proclaim that gender differences are obliterated and all are made "one" in Christ. Buddhist teachings have been applied to both men and women from its earliest days; all have the capacity for enlightenment.

A scene of Eve (as temptress) offering the apple to Adam is carved on the wooden doors of the sixteenth-century Church of the Birth of the Virgin, Vetheuil, France (Marc Garanger/Corbis).

Differences in roles and responsibilities are often cast in positive ways, with differences seen in terms of complementarity—both sides of the divide are good and supplement the other. In Confucianism and Taoism, for example, women and men are understood to have a different yet complementary nature. The woman is yin (more passive); the man is yang (more active). Different responsibilities, obligations, and expectations are rooted in this fundamental difference of nature. But complementarity is not necessarily equality: in many cases one side (the male) is judged superior and the other side (the female) inferior.

The claim of gender difference and complementarity is also found in Western feminist scholarship. Some feminists suggest that many women and men have different styles of moral reasoning. Carol Gilligan, for example, contends that men (at least in Western culture) are more often concerned with the fair application of abstract rights and principles, whereas women are more likely to focus on caring for others and nurturing relationships. Others have suggested that this female "ethic of care" is not universal to all women but is, instead, a feature of European-American culture. Womanist ethicist Katie Cannon insists that African-American women have a distinct style of moral reasoning and practice, which she calls a pragmatic, survivalist ethic.

Many of the gender-differentiated rules center on setting boundaries for the family—especially sexual boundaries. Many traditions enact strict restraints on sexual activity outside of marriage; because sexual fidelity for women is so crucial in many of these traditions, chastity and sexual purity become primary virtues for women. Although sexual fidelity is often prescribed for men as well, it is rarely given the same emphasis, and its transgression often carries a lesser penalty.

The need to control women's sexuality may be rooted in the common idea of women as the source of evil and temptations. Many traditions speak of women as sexual temptresses. Throughout Christian history, Eve's choice to eat the apple is seen as the source of sin and the Fall. In contrast, in some forms of eighteenth- and nineteenth-century Protestantism, women were romanticized as more ethically pure than men, who are tainted in their external struggles in the public world, making women the source and protectors of moral purity.

Another crucial component of many moral codes is the responsibility to care for others. In many traditions the responsibilities for child care, daily chores, and management of the household often fall to women, whereas the broader oversight of the family and the larger world more often falls to men. This difference, entailing male leadership, emerges from a strict hierarchy that many traditions use to specify the roles of family members. In the view of many Christian theologians, for example, God placed men over women in a larger chain or hierarchy of being. This is the root (or ground) of male leadership.

Concomitant with male leadership is male responsibility. In many traditions, male heads of families are expected not only to make decisions but to provide for the needs and protection of their families and even to sacrifice for them. In Christianity, for example, husbands are often admonished to love and serve their wives as Christ loves and serves the church.

Because of these so-called natural gender inequalities and hierarchies that are affirmed in some traditions, a central part of a woman's moral obligation is obedience. Yet women are not always submissive, and men are not always dominant. In Confucianism, mothers and wives of older brothers have authority over younger women. Men are expected to obey their rulers, fathers, and older brothers. Thus, obedience and submission are in fact a part of every person's life.

In the belief systems of many traditions, women's lesser rational capacities to understand moral principles and to make good decisions render them submissive. Women are also thought to be deficient in their moral capacities to resist temptation; they are more easily duped or misled.

Repeatedly in the moral codes and stories of many religious traditions we see gender differentiation and the interplay of gender equity and inequity. Most remarkable, however, is the glaring silence and the underlying neglect of these themes in the academic field of ethics. Perhaps as the study of women and religion gains greater ascendancy in academic institutions, this aspect of religious ethics will receive greater attention.

BIBLIOGRAPHY

Andolsen, Barbara H., Christine Gudorf, and Mary Pellauer, eds. *Women's Consciousness, Women's Conscience: A Reader in Feminist Ethics.* 1985.

Cannon, Katie Geneva. *Black Womanist Ethics.* 1988.

Daly, Lois. *Feminist Theological Ethics: A Reader.* 1994.

Gilligan, Carol. *In a Different Voice.* 1982.

Harrison, Beverly Wildung. *Making the Connections: Essays in Feminist Social Ethics.* 1985.

Noddings, Nel. *Caring: A Feminine Approach to Ethics and Moral Education.* 1984.

Ruether, Rosemary Radford. *New Women/New Earth: Sexist Ideologies and Human Liberation.* 1975.

Sharma, Arvind, ed. *Today's Women in World Religions.* 1994.

———, ed. *Women in World Religions.* 1987.

Sharma, Arvind, and Katherine Young, eds. *The Annual Review of Women in World Religion.* 4 vols. 1991–1994.

REBEKAH L. MILES

Mormons

The Church of Jesus Christ of Latter-day Saints (LDS or Mormon) was established in April 1830 at Fayette, New York. Though its membership grew rapidly, its detractors refuted the claims of founding prophet Joseph Smith that he was personally commissioned by God to restore the pristine gospel in its fullness in preparation for the second coming of Jesus Christ. Persecution followed, forcing Joseph Smith and his followers to move from New York to Ohio, west to Missouri, and then to

Nauvoo, Illinois, where they remained for seven years (1839–1846) before making permanent headquarters in Salt Lake City, Utah.

Before his assassination in 1844, Joseph Smith revealed the "plan of salvation," which rests on the concept of the eternity of life and the eternal duration of family relationships. Marriage is a sacred covenant; when performed in a temple, the holiest of LDS sacred places, by one holding appropriate keys of priesthood authority, it is not only eternally binding but a sacrament of salvation. Neither the woman nor the man can reach the highest order in God's kingdom without the other. Moreover, they can anticipate a relationship in the afterlife of full equality. After receiving the priesthood saving ordinances (rituals) for themselves, women may administer designated ordinances to other women when called to be temple officiators, a sacred liturgical calling.

To be temple-worthy, men and women must have incorporated into their lives the religion's highest ideals, which include faith in Jesus Christ, honesty and charity in one's social and business relationships, fidelity to one's family, moral rectitude, a willingness to tithe, and loyalty to Church leaders.

Joseph Smith also organized the women of the Church into the Relief Society (RS), giving them an ecclesiastical identity that in many ways paralleled male priesthood quorums. With its own presiding officers, the RS was commissioned to guard the morals and succor the needy of the LDS community. In its formative years the Relief Society gave women administrative experience, autonomy within the institution, and latitude in developing programs to benefit church members, many of which continue today. It also served as a spiritual resource for women's participation in the charismatic gifts, a practice that declined in the twentieth century. While continuing to provide opportunities for spiritual and personal development and service, the Relief Society has necessarily adapted to changing organizational patterns and institutional objectives. Correlation policies in the 1970s brought all church departments under male priesthood supervision, diminishing some of women's autonomy and responsibilities.

Another principle introduced by Joseph Smith was plural marriage (polygyny), which was declared unconstitutional in 1879 and which fostered the impression of subjugation of plural wives. This impression was offset by the enfranchisement of plural wives in 1870; publication of their journal the *Women's Exponent*, (1872–1914); their association with the national suffrage movement in 1879; and their activism in rallying and petitioning Congress and the President in support of their religion. Church president Brigham Young (served 1845–

Mormon women sing in the Mormon Tabernacle Choir, Salt Lake City, Utah, 1974 (James L. Amos/Corbis).

1877) contributed to this expansive role of women by engaging the Relief Society in his economic program of self-sufficiency and urging women to learn office skills, study medicine, and attend college.

Today, women continue to vote for their ecclesiastical leaders, speak and pray in Church services, including the semiannual conferences of the Church, and conduct their own semiannual general meetings. They preside over the Relief Society, the Young Women's organization, and the Primary (children's) Association. Though only male members are ordained to the priesthood and serve in ecclesiastical office, women serve jointly with men in fulfilling the threefold mission of the Church: as missionaries in preaching the gospel of Jesus Christ to all the world; as teachers and leaders in uplifting and perfecting the members; and as proxies in performing ordinances of salvation to redeem the dead.

Though they have not been official keepers of the historical record of the church or major subjects of historical attention, women have been avid record keepers of their own organizations and have also contributed to a vast archive of diaries, letters, and journals. This rich source of documents has generated new fields of inquiry on LDS women, drawing the interest of both scholars and church women.

BIBLIOGRAPHY

Early studies of LDS women are Edward M. Tullidge's *Women of Mormondom* (1877), a highly eulogistic but informative overview to 1877, and an unpublished master's thesis by Ileen Waspe LeCheminant, "The Status of Women in the Philosophy of Mormonism, 1830–1845" (Brigham Young University, 1942). Later studies include Leonard J. Arrington, "The Economic Role of Mormon Women," *Western Humanities Review* (Spring 1955): 145–164; Claudia Bushman, ed., *Mormon Sis-*

ters: *Women in Early Utah* (1976), a collection of essays describing LDS women's experience in the nineteenth century; and Vicky Burgess-Olson, ed., *Sister Saints* (1978), a compilation of biographical studies on LDS women. More recent analytical studies include *Sisters in Spirit: Mormon Women in Historical and Cultural Perspective*, edited by Maureen U. Beecher and Lavina F. Anderson (1987), and a collection of essays edited by Maxine Hanks, *Re-emerging Mormon Feminism* (1992) which deals with Mormon women's relationship to religious hierarchy. An overview of the Relief Society and history of Mormon women is *Women of Covenant: The Story of Relief Society*, by Jill Mulvay Derr, Janath Russell Cannon, and Maureen Ursenbach Beecher (1992). *Mormon Enigma, Emma Hale Smith*, by Linda King Newell and Valeen Tippetts Avery (1984), examines the life of the wife of Joseph Smith. Mormon doctrine and procedure are contained in the *Doctrine and Covenants*, one of four volumes that form the Mormon scriptural canon (with the Bible, the Book of Mormon, and the Pearl of Great Price). For a full discussion of Mormonism see *Encyclopedia of Mormonism*, 4 vols. (1992). Sonia Johnson's *From Housewife to Heretic: One Woman's Spiritual Awakening and Her Excommunication from the Mormon Church* (rev. ed., 1989) is a controversial autobiography of a woman who left LDS.

CAROL CORNWALL MADSEN

Mother Divine

Mother Divine is the religious leader of the International Peace Mission Movement founded in the first two decades of the twentieth century by the Reverend Major J. Divine, better known as Father Divine (1877–1965). She was born Edna Rose Ritchings in Vancouver, British Columbia, in 1925. In 1940, she encountered the teachings of Father Divine in Vancouver and quickly came to a conviction of his godhood and a belief that ultimate peace in the world was attainable only through living every day inspired by Jesus Christ and Father Divine. In June 1945 she moved to Philadelphia, which had become the headquarters of the church in 1942, and inspired to take the name Sweet Angel, became one of Father Divine's secretaries. In 1946, at age 21, she declared to Father Divine that she wanted to marry the African-American religious leader some fifty years her senior, for the sole reason that she knew that he was God. They were legally married on 29 April in Washington, D.C., where interracial marriages were permitted.

Father Divine's first wife and loyal follower, Peninnah (1865?–1943) was also called Mother Divine. Their marriage date is noted within the Movement as 6 June 1882. Peninnah's recognition of Father as God, her consecration to his mission, and her example of celibate marriage were all significant spiritual milestones in the promulgation of Father Divine's teachings. Father Divine explained that it had been Peninnah's desire to give up her physical form for a younger more active body, and that Sweet Angel was the reincarnation of Peninnah Divine, as well as the reincarnation of the Virgin Mary.

This second marriage of Father Divine as God to a human being had universal, international, and interracial meanings for the movement. Universally, it illustrated God's union with humanity and the gradual transformation of human nature into the divine or spiritual nature. Internationally, it joined an American and a Canadian to exemplify a new age of earthly cooperation. Interracially, it showed the true harmony of the races. The celibate nature of the marriage exemplified the purity of their spiritual union. Though the interracial marriage was publicly controversial, it deeply affected and proved to be an important event in the history of the Peace Mission. It marked the fulfillment of the book of Revelation (19:7–9) and the start of a new dispensation, or era of profound spiritual understanding.

Since Father Divine's physical passing in 1965, Mother Divine has presided over the Peace Mission, and the Movement has developed a matriarchal quality, with Mother maintaining her husband's moral and religious standards as she looks after the spiritual and temporal needs of their "children" or followers. Though the membership is dwindling, Mother Divine sees the activities of the communitarian group continuing into future generations and dispensations through the rein-

Father Divine and Mother Divine at their wedding anniversary banquet service at Unity Mission Church in Philadelphia c. 1950 (Peace Mission Archives)

carnation of former members and the transformation of world consciousness into greater harmony with Father Divine's teachings.

BIBLIOGRAPHY

Mother Divine. *The Peace Mission Movement.* 1982. No biography of Mother Divine has yet been written, but this volume serves as an indispensable explanation of the Peace Mission Movement and its principles.

Mrs. M. J. Divine (Mother). "The Peace Mission Movement in Philadelphia." In *Invisible Philadelphia: Community Through Voluntary Organizations.* Edited by Jean Barth Toll and Mildred S. Gillam. 1995.

The New Day. 57 (1996) Commemorative issue observing the fiftieth anniversary of the marriage of Father and Mother Divine.

Watts, Jill. *God, Harlem USA: The Father Divine Story.* 1992.

Weisbrot, Robert S. *Father Divine and the Struggle for Racial Equality.* 1983. Like Watts, a scholarly examination of Father Divine not endorsed by followers because of the emphasis on Father Divine's humanity over his divinity.

LEONARD NORMAN PRIMIANO

Motherhood and Grandmotherhood

Motherhood is a central concern of religion. The way in which motherhood is presented and understood, however, depends on whose concerns are made central. In patriarchal religious traditions, concerns about motherhood focus on ensuring correct paternity, which in turn is thought to ensure the perpetuation of a correct religio-ethical order. As such, men are made central while women are made peripheral to an ideological construction of biological processes. Within religions dominated by women as well as those religious practices governed by and centered around women, motherhood and grandmotherhood are removed from this process of male jurisprudence to reflect directly the concerns and experiences of women.

MOTHERHOOD AND WOMEN'S RELIGIOSITY

Clearly, religious ideologies work to legitimate particular social configurations; when these ideologies are grounded in patriarchy they reinforce a process of social marginalization for women. But women do not remain marginal to their own religious lives, for religion also functions as a means to transcend oppression and provides the opportunity to define oneself in direct relation to the divine. Historically this has occurred as women, both individually and communally, have chosen particular religious symbols and rituals that directly reflect their concerns and experiences. As motherhood, defined not only as a biological but also as a nurturing process, reflects a central experience of a vast array of women, it naturally comprises a crucial component of women's religiosity, wherein motherhood is regarded as a source of authority, community, and self-expression.

As anyone who has ever participated in the raising of a child knows, mothering can never be reduced to a socially established role. It is crucial, however, to note the ways in which motherhood, as a form of women's religiosity, works within a larger social context. As the following examples show, motherhood ranges in function from a means of centralizing oneself within the parameters of a socially established role to a means of enacting a radical departure from such a role.

HOUSEHOLD RITUALS

Historically, women have been discouraged from pursuing spiritual paths that negate the role of mother; often women's most vocal opponents have been their own mothers. Hindu mythology tells the story of the goddess Pārvatī, who garners the attention of the ascetic god Śiva by practicing a regimen of severe asceticism herself. Her mother attempts to dissuade her from her course and renames her Umā, which translated from Sanskrit means "Oh Don't!" Tsultrim Allione (1984) records the following verse in which a Tibetan mother warns her daughter against pursuing an independent spiritual path within the Vajrayana Buddhist tradition:

> Do not try to do what you are not capable of doing,
> Practicing the Dharma.
> Do what you know how to do,
> Be a housewife.

For those whose spiritual path necessitates a detachment from society, the role of mother and housewife will serve as an obstacle rather than an opportunity. The role of housewife, however, does not preclude a woman's religiosity, for within a wide variety of cultural settings the home is a locus of religious activity in which the mother is crucial and all-powerful. In northern India, for example, only the mother of the house is thought to be efficacious in enacting household rituals designed for the protection of family members and securing prosperity for the coming year.

As women are primarily responsible for the well-being of children, ritual practices are often devoted to the prevention of sickness and the promotion of healing. In the New Territories of Hong Kong, female diviners are charged with curing infant soul loss. As anthropologist Jack Potter (1974) has observed, these women not only correct the immediate problem by entering into a trance to diagnose both physical and spiritual imbalances but they also may ritually adopt the child and become the child's lifelong protector. This practice of ritual adoption points to an important fact: women-centered religiosity involves, recognizes, and validates not merely the mother as biological generatrix but also those women who nurture a child's development. As anthropologist Susan Starr Sered (1994) has noted, in the Black Carib religion of Belize, grandmothers and maternal aunts often participate in the raising of children. Within the feminist spirituality movement in North America, lesbian couples share the responsibilities of child-rearing. Black Womanist theologians have long recognized that mothering is a communal rather than a biological process and have incorporated these symbols of communal nurturing into strong statements of liberation theology.

GRANDMOTHERS

Patriarchal religious traditions often demonize and isolate older women no longer tied down by domestic responsibilities. By contrast, within forms of religiosity centered around women, grandmothers and older women are regarded as those best suited to leadership positions, what with their experiential, ritual, and theological knowledge. Among the Oglala of South Dakota, primarily grandmothers are responsible for instructing children, especially girls, in moral values and spiritual responsibilities. In the urban centers of Iran, grandmothers as well as older childless women conduct classes in their homes, enabling young women to receive ready instruction in the reading of the Qur'an and the fundamentals of Islam. In the Sande Secret Society of West Africa, the passing down of embodied knowledge allows women to practice a certain degree of control over their own reproductive processes through laws governing menstruation, intercourse, and lactation. The older women within the Sande also enforce such practices as clitoridectomy, a fact showing that in a variety of cultural settings grandmothers and older women are instrumental in restricting the choices of younger women and barring deviation from tradition.

The strong link between mother and child leads to religious practices designed to preserve natal bonds, regardless of geographical or sometimes metaphysical boundaries. In northern India, where daughters must often marry outside of their natal villages, rituals such as Brothers Second (enacted to preserve the health and

Ancient Greek relief depicts a mother, child, and grandmother (David Lees/© Corbis).

safety of an escort, usually a brother) are carried out to ensure a daughter's annual visit to her mother's home. In such diverse geographic areas as Belize, Korea, and Haiti, women ritual specialists act as mediators to link maternal ancestors with living relatives.

The convergence of motherhood and spirituality is not a static experience, but one that develops and changes as one takes on new roles and responsibilities within a matrix of relationality. Motherhood, as it encompasses experiences perceived as ultimately meaningful, comprises a central component in the religious lives of women.

BIBLIOGRAPHY

Allione, Tsultrim. *Women of Wisdom.* 1984.

Atkinson, Clarissa, Constance Buchanan, and Margaret Miles, eds. *Immaculate and Powerful: The Female in Sacred Image and Social Reality.* 1985.

Boddy, Janice. *Wombs and Alien Spirits: Men, Women and the Zār Cult in Northern Sudan.* 1989.

Brown, Karen McCarthy. *Mama Lola: A Vodou Priestess in Brooklyn.* 1991.

Carroll, Theodora Foster. *Women, Religion, and Development in the Third World.* 1983.

Cohler, Bertram J., and Henry U. Grunebaum. *Mothers, Grandmothers and Daughters.* 1981.

Falk, Nancy Auer, and Rita M. Gross, eds. *Unspoken Worlds: Women's Religious Lives.* 1989.

Fineman, Martha Albertson, and Isabel Karpin, eds. *Mothers in Law: Feminist Theory and the Legal Regulation of Motherhood.* 1995.

Glenn, Evelyn Nakano, Grace Chang, and Linda Rennie Forcey, eds. *Mothering: Ideology, Experience, and Agency.* 1994.

Krause, Corinne Azen. *Grandmothers, Mothers and Daughters.* 1991.

Potter, J. M. "Cantonese Shamanism." In *Religion and Ritual in Chinese Society.* Edited by Arthur P. Wolf. 1974.

Powers, Marla N. *Oglala Women: Myth, Ritual, and Reality.* 1986.

Ruether, Rosemary Radford. *Womanguides: Readings Toward a Feminist Theology.* 1985.

Sered, Susan Starr. *Priestess, Mother, Sacred Sister: Religions Dominated by Women.* 1994.

LAURIE COZAD

Mother Teresa

Mother Teresa (1910–1997), a Roman Catholic nun, was born Agnes Gonxha Bojaxhiu in Skopje, capital of present-day Macedonia. At the age of eighteen Agnes joined the Order of the Sisters of Loreto in Ireland, later taking the name Teresa in honor of Thérèse of Lisieux, the patron saint of missionaries. Mother Teresa came to embrace suffering as the primary means of salvation and based her life's work on that ideal.

As a result of an inner calling to serve the poor, in 1950 Mother Teresa established the Order of the Missionaries of Charity in Calcutta, India. The Missionaries of Charity was designed to provide education to disadvantaged children, shelter for the homeless, and care for the sick. Within three years of its founding a home for the dying and an orphanage were opened. The Missionaries of Charity now operate over five hundred missions worldwide.

Mother Teresa received the 1979 Nobel Peace Prize, among several other awards, for her charitable accomplishments. She became well known for her work among victims of leprosy and AIDS. Although Mother Teresa has received three esteemed awards from India, natives of West Bengal have expressed concern over western perceptions of Calcutta created by the emphasis on the poor and destitute. In 1982 Mother Teresa was credited with negotiating the release of thirty-seven children held captive in a Beirut hospital.

During her career Mother Teresa met with many world leaders and high-profile figures, including some of controversial reputation. Both her fundraising efforts and the use of funds have come into question. There has been criticism of the methods in which the Missionaries of Charity has been run and issues have been raised about the quality of care provided in the homes.

Controversy also surround Mother Teresa's stance on women's role in society. She maintained a strong pro-life, profamily position, speaking against the use of birth control and abortion; women were encouraged to have many children—including women of impoverished developing-world societies. It has also been noted that the nuns in t-he Missionaries of Charity order lead an obsequious life with minimal emphasis on education.

Beyond the criticism, Mother Teresa's charitable efforts and unwavering dedication remain difficult to ignore. She made a significant impact on many lives and seemed to embody the Indian concept of karma yoga, yoga in action and service. Throughout her life, the energetic, strong-willed nun remained determined to spread her simple message of love.

Mother Teresa holds a child at an orphanage in Calcutta, India, December 1979, shortly before she accepted the Nobel Peace Prize (UPI/Corbis-Bettmann).

BIBLIOGRAPHY

BOOKS BY MOTHER TERESA

My Life for the Poor. 1996.

A Simple Path. 1995.

Total Surrender. 1990.

Works of Love are Works of Peace: Mother Teresa of Calcutta and the Missionaries of Charity. 1996.

BOOKS BY OTHER AUTHORS

Allegri, Renzo. *Teresa of the Poor: The Story of Her Life.* 1996.

Chawla, Navin. *Mother Teresa: The Authorized Biography.* 1996.

Le Joly, Edward. *Mother Teresa of Calcutta: A Biography.* 1977.

Rai, Raghu, and Navin Chawla. *Faith and Compassion: The Life and Work of Mother Teresa.* 1997.

Sebba, Anne. *Mother Teresa: Beyond the Image.* 1997.

Spink, Kathryn. *Mother Teresa: A Complete Authorized Biography.* 1997.

Zambonini, Franca, and Jordan Aumann, trans. *Mother Teresa of Calcutta: A Pencil in God's Hand.* 1993.

USEFUL WEBSITES

<http://www.ascension-research.org.teresa.html>

<http://www.lifetimetv.com/tv/intimate/teresa.htm>

<http://www.cnn.com/WORLD/9708/9/mother.teresa/index.html>

FILMS

"Mother Teresa of Calcutta." Directed by Malcolm Muggeridge. Time-Life Media, 1971.

"Mother Teresa—Work of Love." Directed by William Livingston. Ikonographics, Inc., 1982.

"World of Mother Teresa." Directed by Jan Petrie. Ann Petrie Productions, Films, Inc., 1981.

VANESSA NASH

Mourning and Death Rites

Women are almost universally more closely associated with rituals surrounding death and bereavement than men. Their role in these rituals is prominent in two separate and potentially contradictory spheres. In the first, as handlers of the corpse in the period immediately following death, women assume a role that men avoid as a dangerous source of pollution. In the second, through their preeminence as the makers of laments—ranging from stylized weeping, through tearful recitative to song—women take on the role of chief mourners and mediators between this world and the next. In many parts of the world women are also responsible for tending the graves of the dead, the offerings made to the dead and, in cultures where exhumation is practiced, the washing of the bones before they are reinterred.

Various explanations have been offered for the prominence of women in the ritual care of the corpse before burial, some based on the apparently obvious link between caring for the body after death and womens' role as mothers and principal caregivers, others seeing a link between female sexuality and the pollution of the corpse. Trying to account for the fact that women's sexuality appears to play a part in many funeral customs, Bloch and Parry (1982) argue that flesh and the decomposition of the polluting corpse are linked to the untamed sexuality of women, while the tomb and bones symbolize ancestral fertility. More recently women scholars have pointed out the necessity for examining the role of women in death rituals from a female perspective, and noting the way women may use contradictions in the ideological system to their own benefit (Martin, 1988).

As handlers and dressers of the corpse, women's role in the rituals of death offers them little opportunity for exercising power. In their role as lamenters, however, women have historically and cross-culturally used the occasion of death to express a variety of otherwise unacceptable sentiments. In societies where there is no other outlet for public speech, women have turned laments into vehicles for opposing mean husbands, mothers-in-law, male authority, and established religion. In many cultures, lamentation is a part of the official funerary ritual. In others it is seen as having a peripheral role or as conflicting with the prevailing religion. In countries such as Ireland and Greece, where the established religion has decried the practice of women's laments, particularly the use of professional keeners, the practice has continued in defiance of edicts and imprecations against it. The survival of lament suggests that it represents deeply held beliefs about women's association with death.

ANTIQUITY

Evidence for women's participation in death rituals in the ancient world comes from a variety of sources, archaeological and literary. From the Homeric epics on, there is ample literary evidence for the prominence of women in death rituals, particularly in lamenting the dead. In archaic Greece, death on the battlefield brought honor to the warrior but lasting reknown was achieved through the laments sung after his death by his women kin and by professionals. To die unwept was a fate as unfortunate as to die unburied. As Alexiou (1974) notes, the singing of laments accompanied each stage of Greek death rituals, from the laying out and viewing of the corpse to the burial and after. The practice of hiring or compelling strangers to lament at funerals is attested from the archaic period into the classical era (Holst-Warhaft, 1992). The custom of using professional dirge singers is not unique to Greece. Greeks regarded women lamenters from Asia Minor as having superior skill in the art. Women were also employed to lead funeral processions and chant dirges in the early Jewish community (Bade Ajuwon, 1981).

Legislation was introduced at Athens and other city states in the sixth century B.C.E. restricting elaborate funeral rites. Women lamenters, particularly professionals, appear to have been a principal target of Solon's laws that forbade "laceration of the cheeks, singing of composed dirges and lamentation at other people's tombs" (Plutarch, *Solon* 21). In the same laws where he forbade their laments, Solon restricted women's participation in religious festivals. The laws confirm the prominence of women in the ritual life of the early Greek city and dramatize the connection between mourning and renewed fertility in women's festivals.

The *Epitaphios Logos* or funeral oration for those who died in the war substituted a public male encomium for the private grief of female kin, but the issue of women's control over the rituals of death is one that Attic tragedy repeatedly explores. Perhaps the most famous collision of civic (male) authority and the traditional authority of female kin over the rituals of death and burial occurs in Sophocles' *Antigone*. Antigone's insistence on her right and duty to bury her brother in defiance of Creon's edict pits religious belief against secular law, honor against obedience, ties of blood against those acquired by marriage, women's traditional control of death against men's.

SURVIVAL OF LAMENT

The early Christian church absorbed many of the ritual practices of antiquity, including the laying out of the corpse. Accounts from the fourth century indicate that women continued the traditional practice of washing the body, wrapping it in a winding sheet, strewing it with herbs, and covering it with their shorn hair. Men and women both lamented, but women, especially professional mourners, were the target of severe criticism by the early church fathers for the violence of their mourning (Alexiou, 1974). As the Church began to develop its own forms of lamentation, substituting the singing of psalms and hymns for pagan laments, women continued the practice. Imprecations against women lamenters from the medieval period until the end of the nineteenth century are an important source of evidence for the persistence of laments. In the more remote rural areas of Europe where laments have survived into living memory, ethnographic studies provide detailed information on women's role as chief mourners. The picture that emerges from these studies is remarkably consistent. In Ireland, Greece, the Balkans, and many parts of the former Soviet Union, women lay out corpses and sing laments. Lamenters may be hired to perform, but more often they are discreetly rewarded for their services. Most lamenters are older women, usually past the age of childbearing, and skilled in their art. They occupy a marginal status in the community and are considered suited to the magico-religious function of lament. Women often use a secret or disguised form of language to sing the laments, one that only women are said to understand. Not only do the laments frequently delineate an eschatology that conflicts with the teaching of the Christian church, there is seldom any reference to paradise or salvation. In areas of Europe where laments have survived, women use them as vehicles to express not only the pain of bereavement but a range of other concerns, even as a means to instigate revenge for a slain relative (Holst-Warhaft, 1992). In Ireland women's dramatic performance of lament was accentuated by their wild and disheveled appearance and by the practice of drinking the blood of the corpse before howling their laments.

ASIA

Like their counterparts in Europe, Chinese women have been the traditional handlers of the dead and singers of laments. As in many societies, the corpse is considered highly polluting. Chinese funerary rituals are concerned with removing the polluting flesh of the corpse (*yin*) from contact with the living and reducing it to clean bones (*yang*) (Martin, 1988). Historical and contemporary ethnographic accounts suggest that lamenting has always been a feature of Chinese funerary ritual. The practice of composing laments for the dead is disappearing in modern China, but the Hakka women of Hong Kong continue to sing them. As in Ireland and Greece, lament singers use the opportunity of performing a ritual lament to focus on their own problems and anger (Johnson, 1988). Kim (1989) has shown that in Korea, women shamans, who are believed to communicate with the dead through lamentation, are the instrument of memory, preserving the otherwise repressed history of violent political oppression.

ARAB COUNTRIES

In Islamic societies as in Christian, some of the evidence for women's prominence as lamenters of the dead comes from condemnation and attempts to reduce their participation in funeral ritual. The Islamic book *al-Hadith* condemns wailing at funerals as incompatible with true faith (Racy, 1986). Dirge singing is common among Lebanese Christians and Druze. Druze women, who gather around the corpse to chant dirges, are often reprimanded for singing too loudly during a funeral. In Lebanese villages, funerals are regarded as the special domain of women. Among the Bedouin, men are enjoined to exercise restraint, while women "cry" for the dead (Abu-Lughod, 1986). Like their European counterparts, Bedouin women make veiled references to otherwise forbidden topics in their laments.

AFRICA AND BEYOND

Studies of death rituals in various regions of Africa support the evidence from Europe and Asia of the prominence of women in the preparation of the corpse for burial and the singing of laments. For instance, Bloch and Parry's study of death rituals among the Merina people of Madagascar underlines the prominence of women in mourning, and their association with the pollution of death, which they acquire not only by washing the corpse but by throwing themselves on it. As they carry the corpses to their tombs during the ceremony or second burial, women are driven along by the men and forced to dance with the corpses. Among the Akpafu of Ghana, the "mothers" sing dirges as they carefully prepare the body (Agawu, 1988). Among the Ga of Ghana, the elaborate rituals of music and dance at the wake are performed by women. It is regarded as unmanly for Ga men to weep, so women sing and perform funeral music, learning their skills from "matrikinswomen" (Hampton, 1982, pp. 75–79). Women are also the dirge singers among the Akan people of the Gold Coast. As in other parts of Africa, the Akan believe in the visitations of the dead and their participation in life. Funeral rites, especially the ritual wailing of women, are a means of communicating with dead ancestors and placating their spirits (Nketia, 1969).

Among the Warao people of Venezuela, *sana* (ritual wailing) led by women kin of the deceased provides the first public announcement of the cause of death. Claiming that they lose conscious control as they sing, women can overcome shame and express anger and even use lewd epithets in their laments.

The Kaluli people of the highlands of New Guinea make subtle distinctions between types of weeping, and between male and female weeping (Feld, 1982). Weeping for the dead is the major expressive form of Kululi women, as song is for men. In the elaborate taxonomy of structured weeping among the Kululi, women's laments are not only considered more moving, but more controlled than men's.

Additional studies of death and mourning suggest that women have always played a prominent role in the rituals surrounding death. These studies also provide evidence that women have used lament to focus on broader issues and express personal grievances.

While mourning her husband, a Mendi widow paints her face with clay and wears many necklaces, called "Job's tears," which are shed for his death. Each day she will remove one necklace until all are gone. Mendi, Papua New Guinea, 1984 (Brian Vikander/Corbis)

BIBLIOGRAPHY

Abu-Lughod, Lila. "Honor and Sentiments of Loss in a Bedouin Society." *American Ethnologist* 12, no. 2 (1986): 159–168.

Agawu, V. Kofi. "Music in the Funeral Traditions of the Akpafu." *Ethnomusicology* 32, no. 1 (1988): 75–105.

Alexiou, Margaret. *The Ritual Lament in Greek Tradition*. 1974.

Bade Ajuwon, Ile Ife. "Lament for the Dead as a Universal Folk Tradition." *Fabula* 22 (1981): 272–283.

Bloch, Maurice, and Jonathan Parry. *Death and the Regeneration of Life*. 1982.

Briggs, Charles L. "Personal Sentiments and Polyphonic Voices in Warao Women's Ritual Wailing." *American Anthropologist* 95 (1993): 929–957.

Feld, Steven. "Wept Thoughts: The Voicing of Kululi Memories." *Oral Tradition* 5 (1990): 2–3.

Hampton, Barbara. "Music and Ritual Symbolism in the Ga Funeral." *Yearbook of the International Folk Music Council.* 1982. Pp. 75–105.

Holst-Warhaft, Gail. *Dangerous Voices: Women's Laments and Greek Literature.* 1992.

Johnson, Elizabeth L. "Grieving for the Dead, Grieving for the Living: Funeral Laments of Hakka Women." In *Death Ritual in Late Imperial and Modern China.* Edited by James Watson and Evelyn Rawski. 1988.

Kim, Seong Nae. "Lamentations of the Dead: The Historical Imagery of Violence of Cheju Island, South Korea." *Ritual Studies* 3, no. 2 (1989): 251–285.

Martin, Emily. "Gender and Ideological Representations of Life and Death." In *Death Ritual in Late Imperial and Modern China.* Edited by James Watson and Evelyn Rawski. 1988.

Nketia, J. H. Kwabena. *Funeral Dirges of the Akan People.* 1955. Reprint, 1969.

Racy, Ali Jihad. "Lebanese Laments: Grief, Music and Cultural Values." *World of Music* 28, no. 2 (1986): 27–40.

Tolbert, Elizabeth. "Magico-religious Power and Gender in Karelian Lament." In *Music, Culture and Gender.* Edited by Marcia Herndon and Suzanne Ziegler. 1990.

See also Death.

GAIL HOLST-WARHAFT

Mugai Nyodai

Mugai Nyodai (d.c. 1298) was a Rinzai Zen nun and abbess in thirteenth-century Japan. A dharma heir of the Chinese emigré monk Wuxue Zuyuan (1226–1286), Mugai was one of the first known women in Japanese history to receive transmission in a Zen lineage. She founded several temples in Kyoto, most notably the convent of Keiaiji, which subsequently became the highest-ranking institution among the association of government-affiliated convents known as the *ama-gozan* or Five Mountain Convents. A stunningly lifelike proxy statue carved prior to her death has survived until the present at Hōji'in, a former subtemple of Keiaiji.

Virtually all of the available biographical information derives from primary sources produced several hundred years after her death. According to these sources, Mugai was born into the politically powerful Adachi family, who served in the shogunate at Kamakura. She married into another warrior family, the Kanesawa of Miura, and had one daughter. Upon the exile of her husband and the destruction of her natal family in the Shimotsyki Uprising, Mugai took the tonsure and embarked on a course of intensive meditation and study. Her accomplishments went unrecognized, however, until her encounter with Wuxue, who gave her his surplice and willed her a portion of his relics, traditional symbols of religious authority that signified her status as a master.

Mugai became the subject of legend and a symbol of feminine religious authority and accomplishment after her death. She figures in a wealth of Buddhist folktales as well as secular and clerical diaries, regional gazetteers, collections of clerical biographies, and koan collections from the fourteenth through the nineteenth centuries.

BIBLIOGRAPHY

Ruch, Barbara. "The Other Side of Culture in Medieval Japan." In *The Cambridge History of Japan.* Vol. 3, *Medieval Japan.* Edited by Kozo Yamamura. 1990.

Tokuda, Kazuo. "Chusei nyonin shukkebanashi 'Chiyono monogatari' ni tsuite." *Kokugo Kokubun ronshu* 23 (1995): 25–63.

Yambe, Hiroaki. "Mugai Nyodai no soken jiin." *Miura Kobunka* 53 (1993): 1–14.

ANNE DUTTON LAZROVE

Mujerista Tradition

Latina women living in the United States who are keenly aware of how sexism, ethnic prejudice, and economic oppression subjugate them, and who are willing to struggle against such oppression, call themselves *mujeristas*. The term *mujerista* has emerged to provide a conceptual framework, a point of reference, a mental construct based on Latinas' interpretations of reality; they use this framework to think, understand, and relate to persons, ideas, and movements, as well as to identify explanations of their faith and its role in their struggle for liberation.

Mujeristas engage in liberative praxis: reflective action that has as its goal liberation. To accomplish this *mujeristas* work to develop a strong sense of moral agency and to make clear the importance and value of who they are, what they think, and what they do. *Mujeristas* seek to influence Latino culture as well as the dominant culture and particularly to influence Christian theology and church practices—particularly Roman Catholicism, which is so important in their culture.

Mujeristas struggle to enable Latinas to understand the many oppressive structures that control their daily lives, to enable them to understand that the goal of their struggle should be not to participate in or benefit from these structures but to change them radically. Second, *mujeristas* insist that Latinas define their preferred future and help them do so: what will a radically different society look like? what will be its values and norms? *Mujeristas* work to help their communities understand how much they have acceded to the prevailing systems in society, including the religious systems, and thus have internalized their own oppression; structural change, the *mujeristas* maintain, cannot happen unless radical change takes place in each person. According to *mujerista* theology, these understandings will help Latinas discover and affirm the presence of God in the midst of their communities and the revelation of God in their daily lives. The goal is for Latinas to recognize what the *mujeristas* see as the sinful nature of many social structures and to find ways of combating it; the theology also entails the centrality of eschatology, the full realization of the "kin-dom" of God, in the life of every Christian. (The word *kingdom* is rejected as being both sexist and classist. *Kin-dom* brings into light an understanding of extended family that is central to Latinas' culture.) The future envisioned by Latinas breaks in upon the present oppression they suffer, offering them eschatological glimpses that they work to turn into their whole horizon. *Mujerista* theology assists Latinas in the process of conversion, helping them to see the reality of sin in their lives. Further, it enables them to understand that to resign themselves to what others tell them is their lot and that passively to accept suffering and self-effacement is not necessarily virtuous.

The contemporary *mujerista* tradition is rooted in the central roles Latinas have traditionally fulfilled in their communities: in struggling against oppression, in religion, and transmitting their culture. Some foremothers from various Latinas' ancestral countries are Sor Juana Inés de la Cruz (Mexico, seventeenth century), Ana Betancourt and Mariana Grajales (Cuba, nineteenth century), and Lola Rodríguez de Tío and Mariana Bracetti (Puerto Rico, nineteenth century). Among influential contemporary Latinas in the United States who embody the *mujerista* tradition, even though they might not use this term, are Dolores Huerta (Mexican-American agricultural workers' organizer and leader), Antonia Pantoja (Puerto Rican, founder of ASPIRA, an organization that promotes education among her people), and Gloria Estefan (Cuban-American popular composer and singer).

BIBLIOGRAPHY

Estefan, Gloria. *Mi tierra.* Audiocassette. 1993.

Isasi-Díaz, Ada María. *Mujerista Theology: A Theology for the Twenty-First Century.* 1996.

Sojo, Ana. *Mujer y política.* 1985.

Tamez, Elsa, ed. *El rostro femenino de la teología.* 1986.

Zárate, Rosa Marta. *Profetiza y cántico de mujer.* Audiocassette. 1991.

See also **Ethics: Feminist Ethics; Liberation Theologies; Theology: Feminist Theology; Womanist Traditions.**

ADA MARÍA ISASI-DÍAZ

Muses

According to the seventh-century B.C.E. poet Hesiod's *Theogony,* the Muses (the Reminders) are daughters of Zeus and Mnemosyne (Memory), who is herself the daughter of Cronus whose gift of remembrance and recollection makes human culture possible. For nine successive nights Zeus slept with the goddess at Pieria, and nine daughters were brought forth. Said to reside either on Mount Helicon in Boeotia or at Pieria near Mount Olympus in Thessaly, the Muses' primary function in earliest Greek poetry was singing and dancing at the celebrations of the gods of Olympus and at the festivities of mortals; but the Homeric Hymn to Apollo and the Muses recognizes them as the source of the creative power of poetry and song: "Blessed are the ones whom the Muses love, sweet is the sound that flows from their lips." Hesiod himself invoked them as inspiration at the beginning of his poem: "Let us begin our song with the Heliconian Muses, whose home is high and holy Mount Helicon, who with soft feet dance around the violet spring and the altar of the almighty son of Cronus. . . . These Muses once taught beautiful singing to Hesiod as he was pasturing his lambs at the foot of holy Helicon." Poetry is thus seen as the product of divine possession by the goddess, who uses the voice of the poet to reveal knowledge otherwise unattainable or unknowable to mortals. Homer calls upon them in the opening lines of the *Iliad:* "Sing, goddess, of the anger of Achilles," and the words of the poet are then seen to contain divinely inspired truth and wisdom.

There are few myths about the Muses, although the Thracian poet Thamyris is said to have lost both his sight and his ability to sing when he challenged them to a contest. Often portrayed in Greek myth as a collective entity in the company of Apollo, the god who is the patron of the inspired arts and prophecy, in the Roman period each became associated with particular areas of the performing arts and intellectual pursuits: Clio (history), Euterpe (the flute), Thalia (comedy), Melpomene (tragedy), Terpsichore (choral dancing), Erato (the lyre), Polyhymnia (sacred hymns), Urania (astronomy), and Calliope (epic poetry).

Because of their connection with the various realms of human knowledge, the Muses played a role in the history of Greek philosophy. The sixth century B.C.E. Pythagoras posited that the movement of the planets in concentric circles, each governed by one of the Muses, created a celestial harmony that demonstrated the orderly arrangement of the cosmos. Plato and Aristotle organized their schools as associations for the cult of the Muses to whom prayers and sacrifices were offered on a regular basis; the earliest museums were actually shrines to these goddesses.

The rediscovery of the classical tradition during the European Renaissance drew upon these ancient intellectual and artistic interpretations of the Muses, who were now portrayed as the handmaidens of the arts and sciences. For examples, the sixteenth-century Raphael attempted to demonstrate the profound spiritual kinship between the classical world, scholasticism, and the Church in his depiction of Apollo surrounded by the Muses in a library of the Vatican. The Renaissance representation of the Muses as allegorical embodiments of human artistic achievement found its later expression in seventeenth- and eighteenth-century English poetry, especially the words of Dryden, Pope, and Milton.

BIBLIOGRAPHY

Bush, Douglas. *Mythology and the Romanic Tradition in English Poetry.* 1963.
Mayerson, Philip. *Classical Mythology and Literature, Art, and Music.* 1971.
Seznec, Jean. *The Survival of the Pagan Gods.* 1961.

TAMARA M. GREEN

Music

An Overview

Most religions use the power of music as a constituent component of ritual. A duality inherent in music that exists between its abstract, technical details—linked in literate traditions from China to Greece with mathematics and cosmology—and its sensuous, affective qualities provides a pivot on which some religious traditions have sought to regulate it. In places where religious authorities fear music as a corrupter of morals or distraction from spiritual concerns restrictions fall disproportionately on women, whose musical activities are interpreted as a double dose of sensual depravity.

The cross-cultural study of women in music, however, would be severely impoverished if it were not considered in religious contexts. Exclusion from participation has been met with strong musical resistance from women. From convents to spirit possession, blues joints to funerals, women musicians have seized religious opportunities for music making.

MYTHOLOGY OF MUSIC

Many legends connect female deities and powers to music. In the Emergence Myth of the Acoma of the North American Southwest, the creator goddess Tsichtinako brought the first humans, the sisters Uchtsiti and Nautsiti, into existence through song and taught them the necessary ritual cycle of songs. In a key musical story among the Ojibwas of the Lake Superior region of North America, Tailfeathers Woman is granted the vision and possession of the Dream Drum of Peace by the Great Spirit.

Perhaps the most prominent goddess of music is Sarasvatī, a pan-Asiatic goddess worshiped by Hindus and Buddhists. Known by her attributes of book and *vinā* (an Indian string instrument), she is linked to the flowing nature of water, words, and music, as well as the origins of ritual and speech.

Music figures prominently in the founding myth of the Shinto tradition, in which the sun goddess Amaterasu encloses herself in a cave to protest the outrageous behavior of her brother, Susano. To coax her out the female *kami*, Ame-no-Uzume, improvises wild music while dancing suggestively. Similar elements of love, joy, and music manifest themselves in the Egyptian goddess Hathor.

In Greek mythology the Nine Muses are minor deities born of Zeus' nine-day affair with Mnemosyne. Later European traditions evoked them allegorically. Christian mythology created the virgin martyr Saint Cecilia who reputedly played the organ all night in praise of God rather than submit to sexual intercourse with a pagan husband.

RITUAL AND RELIGIOUS INSTITUTIONS

Shamanism and spirit possession are dependent on the rituals of music and dance; in places where these functions are controlled by female ritual officiants, women are the primary musicians. Ranging from Korean shamans to the oracle of Apollo at Delphi, women's enunciation of a divinely inspired voice—heightened through music—has endowed them with great power.

Among the Mapuche of Argentina communication with ancestors is mediated through the performance of songs known as *tayil*. Only older women, known as *entendidas* (comprehenders), can serve as mediums for this type of music, which is necessary for life-cycle rituals. In contrast, while it is principally men who are the recipients of dream-songs from spirit-guides among the Temiar of Malaysia, the songs must be received and repeated by a female chorus, who absorb the wisdom of the supernatural songs and share it with the rest of the community.

Examples of the persistent association of women and music in funerary rites are prevalent in Africa, Oceania, northern Europe, and the Mediterranean. Having women as chief vocal mourners suggests a sonic preference for women's voices at this function and also highlights gendered conceptions of death, body, pollution, domesticity, and the family. Scholars trace an unbroken continuity in women's laments from the Homeric era to modern Greek villages, presuming that women's public involvement in mourning is an extension of their domestic role. However, ranging from the slave-girl Briseis in the *Iliad* (Book 19: 332–358) to women in modern villages caught up in civil wars, women have used "public mourning as a protected vehicle through which they pronounce moral judgments with political immunity" (Sultan 92). Male authorities have noted this implicit protest disapprovingly: Plato wanted to restrict women's keening to the home (*Republic* 3:395d–e; *Laws* 12.960a).

The Hebrew Bible records similar mourning practices (Jer. 9:17–18; Ezek. 32:16) and also gives evidence of a parallel function—an ensemble of women musicians and singers welcoming victorious warriors (Judges 4, 11:34; 1 Sam. 18:6; and Jer. 31:4), as when Miriam leads a female ensemble of frame-drum players in celebrating the Red Sea's parting (Ex. 15:20–21).

The extremes and contradictions of religious authority restricting women's musical participation were apparent in Catholic tradition. By the fourth century, women were prohibited from singing publicly in churches. Within convents, however, liturgical singing was the most common activity of nuns: they sang the Divine Office and Mass, played instruments, acted as choral directors, and demonstrated the technical and philosophical expertise necessary for composition. Their oeuvre constitutes a rich chapter in the history of women and music, including Kassia (ninth century), Thekla (ninth century) Hroswitha (tenth century), and the celebrated Hildegard of Bingen (1098–1179).

The Council of Trent (1563) attempted to smother the convents' musical flowering by severely curtailing nuns' musical lives: prohibitions were promulgated against playing instruments, adopting new polyphonic styles, and employment of secular music teachers. But these regulations were not universally imposed and met a good deal of creative resistance, both overt and indirect, from nuns. For instance, the Italian convent of San Vito's noted instrumental ensemble continued to perform into the early 1600s, and the earliest printed collection of sacred music by a woman was Raffaella Aleotti's *Sacrae cantiones* in 1593. The Council's decrees did have some impact, however: by effectively forbidding female opera singers, the church validated the creation of male *castrati*.

The *devadāsī* tradition in India in which women were anointed as temple dancers and singers, grew to prominence in medieval Hinduism. Based on the concept that they were married to the divinity of the temple, these women were considered 'ever-auspicious' because their husband could never die. These women were ritual, dance, and music experts, exploring a wide latitude in developing and conveying their traditions. When the British dismantled this tradition because of its sacred sexual component, the *devadāsīs* had become mediators of sacred musical traditions from Sanskrit rituals to popular devotional and festival music in half a dozen vernacular languages.

NEW RELIGIOUS MOVEMENTS AND EXPRESSIVE FREEDOM FOR WOMEN

Radical religious movements create opportunities for women's sacred musical expression. Women *bhaktas* of India ecstatically sang their love for their chosen deity; their public performance broke social norms, but they consciously reconfigured their transgression into devotion. Protestant revival movements in nineteenth-century North America gave women increased prominence in upholding moral values and fostered a new genre called "sacred song," which was to be played and sung around the piano. The many women composers of this genre extended their evangelical fervor to social causes, writing anthems for the temperance movement.

African-American music provides the paradigmatic example of radical religious movements leading to women's musical creativity. The exigencies of slave religion did not encourage strict functional divisions by gender: women were involved in all aspects, including the singing of spirituals. After Emancipation, the earliest black music ensembles, such as the Fisk Jubilee Singers, included both men and women.

Two major vocal genres of black music in the twentieth century—gospel and the blues—featured women at their fount. Lucie E. Campbell (1885–1963) was an influential composer and musical organizer in the National Baptist Convention for over forty years. Thomas Dorsey fostered the careers of talented women composers such as Roberta Martin (1907–1969) and Sallie Martin (1896–1988). Gospel singers Aretha Franklin (b. 1942) and Mahalia Jackson (1911–1972) crossed over into the mainstream to achieve commercial success.

Because African-American religion did not succumb to body-denying dualism, women's musical expression flourished. But as the black church became more institutionalized, women were sometimes excluded from positions of authority, and the spiritual power of sexuality was demonized. Angela Davis and others have surmised that the blues, especially in the voices of women like Gertrude "Ma" Rainey, constituted a resistance to Christian and bourgeois assimilation, drawing on West African philosophical notions of transformation and self-consciousness.

MUSICAL PERFORMANCE AND PIETY

Religious authorities throughout history have discouraged professional public performance by women on the grounds of its affront to morality, family duty, and modesty. This has made it difficult for women to attain specialized professional training. The result has been for women to use piety as a strategy to hallow their entry into the public arena. The first major ensemble piece to be premiered by an American woman composer was a Mass setting by Mrs. H. H. A. Beach in 1892. Popular recording artists in Tunisia display their religiosity by making the 'umra, or minor pilgrimage to Mecca, and by recording Muslim devotional songs in addition to their secular ones. The prominent South Indian vocalist, M. S. Subbalakshmi, has supplemented her classical recordings with massive compendiums of chanted deity names.

Some contemporary performers use the tropes of religion as a critical backdrop for their feminism. The American pop singer Madonna has built the power of religious icons into her self-mythologizing. Contemporary women whose musical projects are overtly connected to spirituality draw from eclectic sources. The compositions of Pauline Oliveros function as "sonic meditations" rooted in Buddhist philosophy. New Age feminist composer-performers Kay Gardner and Layne Redmond attempt to construct and reconstruct female-centered spiritual musics. Bernice Johnson Reagon's vocal ensemble, Sweet Honey in the Rock, draws on sacred musics from the African diaspora, combining politics and spirituality.

BIBLIOGRAPHY

Feminist scholarship on music was slow to emerge compared with other disciplines. Much of the early scholarship was compensatory in nature, searching for lost women composers and performers. Scholarship on music and religion from a religious studies perspective has been woefully small and has rarely addressed gender directly. *Enchanting Powers: Music in the World's Religions*, edited by Lawrence Sullivan (1997), marks a change in this regard.

Two major anthologies adopt a feminist ethnomusicological stance: Ellen Koskoff's *Women and Music in Cross-Cultural Perspective* (1987) is an excellent, balanced volume, and Kimberly Marshall's *Rediscovering the Muses: Women's Musical Traditions* (1993) is especially rich in detail on religiously based women's traditions. The devadasi tradition of India is thoroughly examined by Saskia C. Kersenboom-Story in *Nityasumangalī: Devadasi Tradition in South India* (1987). The myth of Tailfeathers Woman can be found in Thomas Vennum's *The Ojibwa Dance Drum* (1982).

The search for women composers in western art music tradition quickly uncovered women's music making in religious settings. Judith Tick's landmark *American Women Composers before 1870* (1983) and her edited volume with Jane Bowers, *Women Making Music: The Western Art Tradition* (1986) are supplemented by *Women and Music: A History*, edited by Karin Pendle (1991), and *Cecelia Remembered: Feminist Perspectives on Gender and Music*, edited by Susan Cook and Judy Tsou (1994). Valuable bibliographic information, including lists of compositions, can now be easily obtained in *The Norton/Grove Dictionary of Women Composers* (1995), edited by Julie Ann Sadie and Rhian Samuel. Robert Kendrick presents evidence of nuns' resistance to the Council of Trent in *Celestial Sirens: Nuns and Their Music in Early Modern Milan* (1996).

By the early 1990s, new musicology incorporated social perspectives, including feminist theory. Susan McClary's *Feminine Endings: Music, Gender, and Sexuality* (1991) deconstructed music's claims to transcendence and detached objectivity; she also analyzes Madonna's music. Other scholars who have feminist cultural critiques of music include Eva Rieger's "'Dolce semplice'? On the Changing Role of Women in Music," in *Feminist Aesthetics*, edited by Gisela Ecker (1985), and Marcia Citron's *Gender and the Musical Canon* (1993). An intriguing interplay of religion and music surfaces in Corinne Blackmer's study of the refracted cultural image of Saint Teresa of Avila in musical and literary productions by gay men and lesbians in "The Ecstasies of Saint Teresa: The Saint as Queer Diva from

Crashaw to *Four Saints in Three Acts,*" in *En Travesti: Women, Gender, Subversion, Opera,* edited by Corinne E. Blackmer and Patricia Juliana Smith (1995).

Studies of women's lamenting traditions are especially deep in southeastern Europe. Margaret Alexiou's *The Ritual Lament in Greek Tradition* (1974) is extended in a musicological direction by Nancy Fultan's "Private Speech, Public Pain: The Power of Women's Laments in Ancient Greek Poetry and Tragedy" (1993) in Marshall (above), and Susan Auerbach's "From Singing to Lamenting: Women's Musical Role in a Greek Village" (1987) in Koskoff (above). Steven Feld's *Sound and Sentiment: Birds, Weeping, Poetics, and Song in Kaluli Expression* (1982) presents a gender-sensitive structural analysis of weeping in relation to music. Elizabeth Tolbert's work draws parallels between shamanism and women's laments; see her "The Voice of Lament: Female Vocality and Performative Efficacy in the Finnish-Karelian *itkuvirsi,*" In *Embodied Voices: Representing Female Vocality in Western Culture.* Edited by Leslie C. Dunn and Nancy A. Jones (1994).

African-American music scholarship has never neglected religion. Bernice Johnson Reagon's edited volume on gospel composers, *We'll Understand It Better By and By: Pioneering African-American Gospel Composers* (1992) and Angela Davis's *Blues Legacies and Black Feminism: Gertrude "Ma" Rainey, Bessie Smith, and Billie Holiday* (1998) feature thick dialectic readings of religion, spirituality, sexuality, and class. Susan Cavin's "Missing Women: On the Voodoo Trail to Jazz," *Journal of Jazz Studies,* 3, no. 1 (1975): 4–27, speculates that women's interracial participation and justification of vodou established the necessary conditions for the development of jazz.

Studies of Madonna address her manipulation of religious codes, as in Ronald B. Scott's "Images of Race and Religion in Madonna's Video *Like a Prayer:* Prayer and Praise," in *The Madonna Connection: Representational Politics, Subcultural Identities, and Cultural Theory,* edited by Cathy Schwichtenberg (1993) and Nancy Vickers's "Maternalism and the Material Girl" in *Embodied Voices: Representing Female Vocality in Western Culture,* edited by Leslie C. Dunn and Nancy A. Jones (1994). Jennifer Rycenga examines religious thought in the music of Tori Amos and P. J. Harvey in "Sisterhood: A Loving Lesbian Ear Listens to Progressive Heterosexual Women's Rock Music," in *Keeping Score: Music, Disciplinarity, Culture,* edited by David Schwarz, Lawrence Siegel, and Anahid Kassabian (1997). Pauline Oliveros describes her theories of music in *Software for People* (1984).

DISCOGRAPHY

Beach, Mrs. H. H. A. *Mass in E-flat for Orchestra and Chorus, Op. 5.* Stow Festival Orchestra and Chorus, Barbara Jones, conductor. Albany Records #TROY 179.

Begum Akhtar. *Ghazals.* EMI #ECSD2486. 1971. An excellent collection by the premier North Indian woman vocalist specializing in this Muslim poetic genre of human and divine longing.

Bombay Sisters. *Enchanting Devi Krithis.* Pyramid #CD PYR 7024. 1996. This compilation features fourteen Karnatic (South Indian) compositions about goddesses, including pieces in praise of Sarasvatī, Kamakshi, Meenaskshi, and Lakshmi.

Canti nel chiostro: Musica nei monasteri feminili de Bologna, 1580–1680. Cappella Artemisa. Tactus #TC 600001.

Gardner, Kay. *A Rainbow Path.* 1984. Ladyslipper Records #LRCD103.

Madonna. *Like a Prayer.* 1989. Sire #925844-2.

Oliveros, Pauline. *The Roots of the Moment for (Electronically) Expanded Accordian.* Hat Hut "Now" Series #CD6009.

Regon, Bernice Johnson, ed. *African-American Gospel: The Pioneering Composers. Wade in the Waters,* vol. 3. 1994. Smithsonian/Folkways.

Subbulakshmi, M. S. *Music Recital by M. S. Subbulakshmi at the United Nations on Sunday 23 October 1966.* Odeon #MOAE 5001, 5002, 5003.

———. *Bhaja Govindam and Vishnu Saharasnamam.* Odeon #MOAE 5011.

See also **Amaterasu**; **Bhakti**; **Devadāsīs**; **Hildegard of Bingen**, **Sarasvatī**.

JENNIFER RYCENGA

Instruments and Voices

Women have participated in the making of music as composers, vocalists, and instrumentalists throughout history. Judging from the data supplied in Aaron I. Cohen's important catalogue, the *International Encyclopedia of Women Composers,* women have most consistently been involved in the production and performance of vocal music, with 110 women composers of vocal music listed from the thirtieth century B.C.E. through the sixteenth century C.E., and hundreds more from the seventeenth to the twentieth centuries. Indeed, the scholarship to date that seeks to identify women who have contributed to music is dominated by a focus on women's songs, from the hymns of Christian women in medieval Europe to women's marriage songs of traditional cultures in Asia and Africa. A major theme in studies of women's songs is the understanding of messages in their lyrics, with particular interest in the ways their words question or even reverse the prevailing cultural relations of power between masculine and feminine.

A less well-developed field is the study of women as instrumentalists. The history of women instrumentalists may be more difficult to recover than that of women vocalists because of the relatively low numbers of the former prior to the historic explosion of women instrumentalist composers in the nineteenth and twentieth centuries, in whose works the piano has been a dominant instrument. A possible explanation for these low numbers is that historically, women's access to instruments has been limited. If instruments are understood as representing a kind of technology, involving knowledge of the instrument's cultural significance, material construction, and skilled use, then their production and use can be seen as part of a larger cross-cultural pattern of men claiming these domains for themselves, while severely limiting women's access. In contrast, vocal music, and for that matter dance, though requiring skill, do not involve access to materials and modes of production beyond one's own body. Consequently, the role of women in making musical instruments is also an underdeveloped field in scholarship, save for scant references to women who make folk instruments such as hand-held percussion instruments fashioned from gourds.

WOMEN'S INSTRUMENTS

Conventional wisdom in eighteenth-century Europe held that brass, reeds, and complex percussion instruments are associated with males, while strings and flute are associated with females. An older, cross-cultural traditional wisdom tended to dichotomize the strings and flute based on sexual imagery: the former represented the female sexual organ, and the latter, the male.

Strings

Cohen's *Encyclopedia* lists more than a dozen women as composers who used stringed instruments from ancient times up to and including the sixteenth century, making this the second-largest category of women composers after those who wrote vocal music. The woman believed to have been the first female composer, Iti, an Egyptian songstress from the V Dynasty (2563–2424 B.C.E.), is pictured in a frieze at her gravesite accompanied by a female harpist. In many traditions, divine patrons of music and dance have been female and are pictured with stringed instruments, including the Shinto

Benten, the Egyptian Bes, the Greco-Roman Terpsichore, and the Christian Saint Cecilia.

Early women composers using stringed instruments generally achieved prominence in their own time and have contributed to the development of music in many cultures. Ts'ai Yen (c. 162–239) was the daughter of Chinese poet and scholar Ts'ai; she composed the *Eighteen Verses* on war and grief, set to the lute and Tatar horn. Bridget (Saint Bridget of Kildare, 435–525) was an Irish harpist and nun. Habbaba (d. 724) was an Arabian songstress, who sang accompanied by an orchestra of fifty women playing the lute and sang. Ubaida was a ninth-century Arabian tunbur (a lyre of the Islamic period) player, who was acknowledged in her lifetime to be the best. Qasmuna was an eleventh-century Spanish-Jewish woman who wrote women's love songs that were set to the lute by Arabian-Spanish women. Saint Hildegarde (Hildegard of Bingen, 1098–1179) was a German nun who called herself the Harp of the Holy Spirit; her choral music is performed today. Tarquinia Molza (Molsa da Modena) was a sixteenth-century composer for the lute, violin, harp, and voice, who performed with her own three-woman group at the Italian court of Modena. Mirabai was a sixteenth-century saint of north India who composed sacred songs to Lord Krishna, accompanied by tambura and drum. Anne Boleyn (1507–1536), second wife of Henry VIII, played the lute and sang; one of her songs, "O death, rock me asleep," is famous for its innovative separation of accompaniments from the vocal line.

Flutes

In contrast, Cohen lists no women composers using the flute prior to the eighteenth century. Granted, this does not mean that women did not play it; historical evidence from Greece to China suggests that women played the flute at private parties. However, it is the case that very early on the flute—taken at its most generic—was associated with both the development of musical theory and with the imagination of the cosmos; both of these domains, scholarship and public ritual practice, were usually reserved for men. The classic Chinese encyclopedia, *Ch'un-ch'iu* (Spring and Autumn), composed by Lü Pu-wei circa 239 B.C.E., provides an example. He states that the first note sounded from a pitch pipe, the *huang-chung* or "yellow bell," became the first note of the entire Chinese musical system, with one set of six notes rising in perfect fifths, and another set descending in perfect fourths. The notes of the upper series were considered to embody the cosmic male force, yang; those of the lower series were considered the cosmic female force, yin. The significance of the flute in these domains suggests that though its voice might be deemed the essence of the feminine, its form and cultural significance were masculine.

Flutes are exclusively used by men in the Papua New Guinea Highlands, where they are used in sacred rituals for growth and fertility. Significantly, the themes of growth and fertility are centered not on women but on young men during initiation rituals, and on men's prosperity and status during pig festival rituals. The flutes are played in pairs during the ritual, with one viewed as masculine and the other feminine; playing them is like an act of intercourse. Women, who are forbidden to see the flutes, are purposely intimidated by men during these rituals, the flutes becoming instruments of both fear and dominance.

WOMEN AND MUSIC IN TAMIL SOUTH INDIA

A brief discussion of women in music within one cultural tradition may illuminate issues women of many cultures have faced in their pursuit of music making.

The state of Tamil Nadu lies on the eastern coast of the southernmost portion of India. Tamil, as an ethnic and linguistic identity, has its roots in ancient history and boasts a 2,000-year-old continuous literary tradition. The earliest stratum of literature in Tamil, the Cankam (Academy) poems of about 300 B.C.E. to 200 C.E., associate specific melodies (*pans*) and various forms of the ancient stringed instrument, the *yāl*, with each of five landscapes; the pastoral landscape is associated with the flute as well as the *yāl*. The poems mention male and female singers (*pānan* and *pātini*), as well as women dancers (*viraliyar*), and male percussionists.

An early Tamil epic, the *Cilappatikāram* (c. third to fifth centuries C.E.), has provided scholars with a wealth of information on music. Throughout the text are interludes in which themes of the narrative are carried forward through scenes of women singing and dancing. For example, in Canto 17 the cowherd woman Mātari arranges seven maidens in a circle, naming each of them one of the notes in Tamil music, and they dance while singing an invocation to the Lord for the protection of the epic's hero. The epic and its commentaries offer information on the origin, nature, and interrelationships of notes; breathing techniques for singing; the five, seven, and twelve tones; stringing the *yāl*; modulation; and the classification of *pans*.

The first known composer of Tamil hymns was a woman saint, Kāraikkāl Ammaiyār, (c. sixth century C.E.). Her hymn in praise of Lord Siva, the "Tiruvālankāṭṭu Mūtta Tiruppatikankal" (The Ancient Sacred Verses on Tiruvālankātu), is set to the *intalam pan*. In the ninth century the woman saint Āṇṭāḷ wrote the *Tiruppāvai* (Sacred Vow), a song she devoted to the Lord Krishna.

In subsequent centuries women's participation in music and dance was primarily through the Hindu tradition of temple *devadasis* (servants of God), women "married" only to the Lord, ritually employed in singing and dancing his praises. In the late nineteenth century, Veena Dhanammal (1867–1938), a hereditary member of the *devadasi* community, became a disciple of the son of renowned composer Syāma Śāstri and studied the vina, a fretted stringed instrument associated with Sarasvatī, the Goddess of Learning and the Arts, which replaced the *yāl* in Tamil music. It was considered disreputable at the time for a woman to perform in public; although recognized as a virtuoso vina player, Dhanammal was forbidden by male musicians to play at public performing venues, such as the prestigious annual festival to celebrate renowned composer Tyāgarāja. (In contrast, just a few decades later Dhanammal's granddaughter, Balasaraswati (1920–1984), achieved international acclaim for her dancing.)

The careers of women in Dhananmmal's family are emblematic not only of the talent and persistence of women musical performers but also of the changing social composition of and attitudes toward the performing arts. As more upperclass and urban people, including women, became interested in the performing arts, a new class of patrons was created that lent a new respectability—especially for women performers—to what had traditionally been devotional arts, as well as a secular venue for their performance. By the mid-1960s, Madras women vina players constituted 44 percent of concert-level vina players (in contrast to 40 percent of concert vocalists during the same period); 90 percent of concert vina players were of the brahmin (highest) class. Today, the vina is a very popular musical instrument for women to study, in contrast to the traditionally male drums (*mridangam*). Contemporary virtuosos such as female vina player E. Gayatri have their pick of concert venues.

BODY SYMBOLISM

A legend from Greek mythology tells us that the goddess Athena once tried playing the aulos (the major wind instrument of ancient Greece), but when she discovered that doing so distorted her facial features, she threw it away. The idea that instruments appropriate to women were only those that enhanced their feminine beauty and grace has persisted through history. Indeed, in nineteenth-century America, the piano, harp, and guitar were deemed the instruments most appropriate for women, since they were suited to domestic entertainment and required no facial or other movements that interfered with a lady's natural grace.

Similarly, a woman's beauty could provide the metaphor for describing the beauty or sanctity of stringed instruments. A metaphor in medieval Sanskrit poetry from India casts the erotic lovemaking between the Lord Krishna and the cowherd Rādhā as the Lord playing his lover like a lute. The Fang Bwiti of Gabon, Africa, view the voice and body of the *ngombi*, an eight-stringed harp used in Bwiti ritual, as a manifestation of Nyingwan Mbege, the Sister of God. Her face is carved at the top of the harp; the neck and tuning pegs are her spine and ribs, the strings her tendons and sinews, the resonator her stomach and womb, the sound holes her breasts and birth orifice. Her voice represents both feminine compassion and the power to communicate with the unseen world.

BIBLIOGRAPHY

For overviews of regional musical traditions as well as entries on instruments, see Stanley Sadie, ed., *The New Grove Dictionary of Music and Musicians*, 20 vols. (1980), and Don Randel, ed., *The New Harvard Dictionary of Music* (1986). Critically important comparative studies in ethnomusicology are in Bruno Nettl and Philip V. Bohlman, eds., *Comparative Musicology and Anthropology of Music: Essays on the History of Ethnomusicology* (1991).

For sources on musical instruments, see: Stanley Sadie, ed., *The New Grove Dictionary of Musical Instruments*, 3 vols. (1984), and Curt Sachs, *The History of Musical Instruments* (1940). An excellent discussion of the sacred meanings of instruments is Sue Carole DeVale, "Power and Meaning in Musical Instruments," in *Music and the Experience of God*, edited by Mary Collins, David Power, and Mellone Burnim (1989), pp. 94–110. A source on Greek music that includes some gender-specific discussion is Martha Maas and Jane McIntosh Snyder, *Stringed Instruments of Ancient Greece* (1989).

For a comprehensive review of women in music, see Aaron I. Cohen, *International Encyclopedia of Women Composers*, 2 vols., 2d ed. (1987). Diane Apostolos-Cappadona, *Encyclopedia of Women in Religious Art* (1996), reviews the link between goddesses and music in pictorial representation. An early comparative discussion that remains a classic in spite of the low number of citations by today's standards is Sophie Drinker, *Music and Women: The Story of Women in Their Relation to Music* (1948).

Jane Bowers and Judith Tick, eds., *Women Making Music: The Western Art Tradition, 1150–1950* (1986) is a comparative study of women in Western music; see especially the editors' "Introduction," pp. 3–14; Anne Bagnall Yardley, " 'Ful weel she soong the service dyvyne': The Cloistered Musician in the Middle Ages," pp. 15–38; and Judith Tick, "Passed Away Is the Piano Girl: Changes in American Musical Life, 1870–1900," pp. 325–348.

In Ellen Koskoff, ed., *Women and Music in Cross-Cultural Perspective* (1987), see especially the editor's "An Introduction to Women, Music, and Culture," pp. 1–23, and Jennifer Post, "Professional Women in Indian Music: The Death of the Courtesan Tradition," pp. 97–109.

For an overview of music in Tamil South Indian tradition, see "Tamil Music: A Survey," in the *Encyclopedia of Tamil Literature*, 10 vols., Vol. 1: *Introductory Articles* (Madras, 1990), pp. 175–186. An important sourcebook is P. Sambamurthy, *History of Indian Music*, 3d ed. (Madras, 1994). Two excellent articles on gender in Tamil music performance are T. Sankaran and Matthew Allen, "The Social Organization of Music in South India," in *The Garland Encyclopedia of World Music*, Vol 6: *South Asia* (1996–), and Matthew Harp Allen, "Rewriting the Script for South Indian Dance," *The Drama Review*, 41 (Fall, 1997): 63–100. Data on performance in mid-1960s Madras are from Kathleen L'Armand and Adrian L'Armand, "Music in Madras: The Urbanization of a Cultural Tradition," in *Eight Urban Musical Cultures: Tradition and Change*, edited by Bruns Nettl (1978), pp. 115–145.

Discussions of regional traditions that raise important theoretical issues are: Carol Ann Weaver, "Kenyan Women's Music: An Agent of Social, Cultural Change?" *The Conrad Grebel Review* 12 (Spring 1994): 113–130; Terence E. Hays, "Sacred Flutes, Fertility, and Growth in the Papua New Guinea Highlands," *Anthropos* 81 (1986): 435–453; and Gloria Goodwin Raheja, " 'Crying When She's Born, and Crying When She Goes Away': Marriage and the Idiom of the Gift in Pahansu Song Performance," in *From the Margins of Hindu Marriage: Essays on Gender, Religion, and Culture*, edited by Leslie Harlan and Paul B. Courtright (1995).

See also **Devadāsīs; Hildegard of Bingen; Sarasvatī.**

KAREN PECHILIS PRENTISS

Mutilation

Because the body is an important symbol of cultural, religious, and individual identity, mutilation is a powerful means of reshaping it to accord with various ideals of the self. Religious acts of mutilation may be divided into those that are primarily intended to mark the body visibly, and those that center on the inward experience and endurance of pain. The internal and the external need not be mutually exclusive, however, and are often found in the same tradition, as both the endurance of pain and bodily inscription identify individuals as part of larger social and religious orders. It is also important to distinguish between self-inflicted acts of mutilation and those that are inflicted by others, for the question of agency may determine the significance of mutilation within a particular cultural context.

Ascetic acts of self-mutilation performed to demonstrate pain endurance are found in different religious traditions and are usually associated with the religious devaluation of the body. In medieval Christianity, self-mutilation functioned primarily to demonstrate religious penitence, devotion, and martyrdom. Practices such as flagellation, restriction, burning, and other bodily mortifications were believed to increase spiritual merit through the endurance of suffering and the degradation of the flesh.

With its emphasis on female virginity as necessary for sanctification, medieval Christianity also fostered extreme acts of self-mutilation and even suicide on the part of many religious women faced with sexual assault. The hagiographic lore is full of female saints legendary for grossly disfiguring themselves in an effort to repel potential rapists and to thus avoid the shame and defilement that followed a woman's loss of chastity. Perhaps the best known is the ninth-century legend of Saint Ebba, abbess of the monastery of Coldingham (Scotland). Fearing attack by barbarian invaders, Ebba gathered her virginal charges around her and, taking a razor, cut off her nose together with her upper lip to the teeth. She urged the sisters to do the same, counseling them that this drastic measure alone would preserve their chastity. Similar acts of self-mutilation are recorded in England, France, Germany, and Spain throughout the medieval period. In an era where a woman's honor and spiritual integrity were tied to her virginity, self-mutilation not only may have prevented the loss of a woman's chastity, it powerfully inscribed her commitment to these ideals upon her own flesh.

Mutilation was not limited solely to religious contexts in the medieval period, but was also a common judicial punishment for women who had transgressed the norms of sexual behavior, especially in cases of adultery and prostitution. According to an eleventh-century law code, the punishment for an adulterous woman was the severance of her nose and ears. As a judicial punishment, mutilation marked a woman's transgression of social and religious mores, rather than her adherence to them. Thus, the very same practice of mutilation communicated opposite meanings depending upon the agency of the actor, yet both are intimately linked with Christian standards of female sexuality.

The ancient Amazons were alleged by the Greeks to practice a form of self-mutilation that also inscribed gendered ideals upon the female flesh. The Greek term

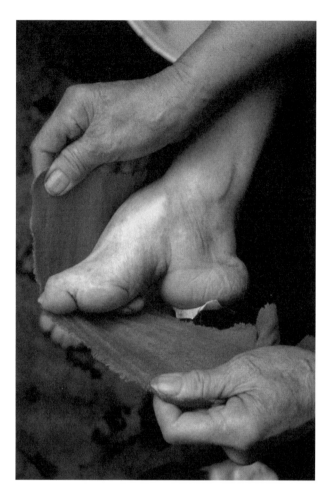

The foot of a Chinese woman, deformed by the practice of footbinding (Photo Researchers, Inc.)

Amazon was commonly, if incorrectly, interpreted to mean "one without a breast." The Amazon was described in a Greek treatise as a member of a race of warrior women whose right breasts had been cauterized in order that their right arms be strengthened for martial combat. In this Greek account, the breast, symbolic of moistness and inferiority, was transformed through the application of heat into a dryness whose superiority and strength flowed to the right shoulder and arm. Thus, in the Greek imagination, the strength and martial ability of Amazon women could only be purchased by the destruction of the breast and the feminine weakness that it symbolized. By mutilating their breasts, Amazon women were believed to transform feminine frailty into martial superiority.

Another example of mutilation as a practice associated with gendered ideals is the Han Chinese custom of footbinding. Lasting from the tenth century to the early twentieth, footbinding radically reshaped women's feet to accord with Chinese standards of beauty. The goal of the process was to force the four smaller toes to curl under the sole of the foot, thus breaking the bones, and then to bring the heel and sole together as closely as possible. The result was a foot between three and five inches long, and an unsteady gait that was considered quintessentially feminine. A widespread phenomenon, footbinding cannot be separated from its larger philosophical and religious context that valorized heaven over earth and men over women. Within this context, footbinding came to symbolize women's subservience to, and control by, men. The bound foot was the subject of much erotic literature, where it was the focal point of male arousal.

As these examples suggest, mutilation is intimately linked with hierarchical constructions of gender that define women as inferior, weak, and sexually threatening. Whether employed as a strategy of self-defense, required as a punishment, or compelled by standards of beauty or frailty, practices of mutilation render visible the religious and cultural ideals of femininity, powerfully inscribing them upon the flesh of the female body itself.

BIBLIOGRAPHY

On Chinese footbinding, the classic account is Howard S. Levy's *Chinese Footbinding: The History of a Curious Erotic Custom* (1966). Levy provides ample documentation of the custom drawn from literature, poetry, and ethnographic interviews with elderly footbound women. Alison Drucker's "The Influence of Western Women on the Anti-Footbinding Movement, 1840–1911," in *Women in China: Current Directions in Historical Scholarship* (1981), edited by Richard Guisso and Stanley Johannesen, draws extensively on Levy's account and traces the origins of the movement of resistance that developed. On facial mutilation among medieval Christian women, see Jane Tibbetts Schulenburg's "The Heroics of Virginity: Brides of Christ and Sacrificial Mutilation," in *Women in the Middle Ages and Renaissance: Literary and Historical Perspectives* (1986), edited by Mary Beth Rose. Schulenberg explores how social and ecclesiastical preoccupations with virginity often had tragic consequences for the lives of medieval women. For a succinct account and interpretation of Amazonian breast mutilation see Bruce Lincoln, "Debreasting, Disarming, Beheading: Some Sacrificial Practices of the Scyths and Amazons," in his *Death, War, and Sacrifice* (1991).

See also **Mutilation, Genital**; **Self**.

KELLY E. HAYES

Mutilation, Genital

Female genital mutilation is a complex and ancient tradition. It has frequently been misnamed "female circumcision," which incorrectly equates it with male circumcision, a procedure that does not limit or damage the function of the penis, does not curtail sexual pleasure, and is not life-threatening. Female genital mutilation is found traditionally among many but not all ethnic groups across some twenty-odd African countries, as well as in some Middle Eastern and South Asian countries and among Australian Aboriginal groups. International migration has brought this custom to Europe and North America. According to the World Health Organization (1994), this centuries-old ritual continues to affect more than 100 million women annually.

The custom is often erroneously associated (by most research and media coverage) with Islam. To the contrary, it preceded that religion, as well as Judaism and Christianity, by several millennia. Apparently it was incorporated from ancient indigenous practices in the above-named regions. Many attribute the continuation of this custom among some practitioners of these faiths to the Hebrew Scriptures, interpreting the Abrahamic injunction that all who believe in the one God should be circumcised to include all people rather than just males.

In all countries and ethnic groups where female genital mutilation is practiced, circumcision of males is also the norm. In these societies genital circumcision is a mark of group identity and one of many steps required in the preparation of girls and boys to become responsible adults in their communities. Female genital mutilation became known to Westerners only in the 1980s through a variety of means, including international women's conferences (Nairobi in 1985, Beijing in 1995); the international human rights and women's movements; great increases in the numbers of refugees and immigrants arriving in the West; and an increase in research on this topic. The practice has since been well publicized by the media. (American sociologist Hanny Lightfoot-Klein (1989) has pointed out that genital mutilation was practiced in the United States on American women in mental hospitals until World War II.) The ritual's specifics vary from one ethnic group to another in terms of the girl's age when it is performed, the place where it is performed, the type of practitioner, and specific genital areas cut. Such variations may also be affected by the social environment (for example, the dominance of circumcising groups in the area; whether it is an urban or rural location; the education level of the girl and her parents and the degree of their Westernization; and the status of civil society and its institutions (e.g., hospitals, courts, etc.).

Most often female genital mutilation is performed on a seven-day-old infant (as with some male circumcisions), or at some age before puberty. However, one eastern Nigerian group customarily subjects its women to this ritual during the seventh month of their first pregnancy. Many nomadic groups, such as the Masai of East Africa, traditionally circumcised older adolescent girls prior to marriage.

There are several variations of this ritual surgery. Some cut the tip of the clitoris; others entirely remove it. Much more severe, as surgery and in terms of the possible consequences, is the removal of the labia minora and the labia majora. In some cases the labia are stitched together, leaving only a tiny opening for urine and menstrual blood; this is known as infibulation.

Approximately 15 percent of women who undergo genital mutilation experience the more severe forms of this practice and have a much greater possibility of medical and emotional complications such as shock, septicemia, infections, hemorrhaging, tetanus, and sometimes death. Additionally, some women experience chronic incontinence, chronic uterine and vaginal infections, long and obstructed labor, severe dysmenorrhea, obstructed menstrual blood, difficult and painful sex, scarring, infertility, and increased risk of pregnancy and childbirth complications (United States Agency for International Development; Women in Development). Other factors contribute to the extent of such complications. They include the physical and emotional state of the girl prior to cutting; the skill of the practitioner; the condition and sterility of the instruments used; the climate and physical environment; the care and support given to the girl after cutting; and the availability of medical care should complications arise. A medical officer from central Africa reports that, in one ethnic group that traditionally circumcises both boys and girls (in separate groups), the cutting used to take place deep in the forest at the beginning of the group's intense three-week socialization process for responsible adulthood. It traditionally involved severe genital cutting and bodily scarification and was conducted solely by the elders. The group, now more urban, has become aware of the possible medical complications of their traditional initiation cutting and has modified it accordingly. It is now performed at the end of the three-week socialization period, at the beginning of school holidays, in an area closer to town, and, most important, with symbolic letting of blood instead of actual cutting. A medical officer (female for the girls' group and male for the boys' group) is always present.

Groups that practice genital cutting state various purposes for it. The cutting is an ordeal in a series of programs preparing young girls to become strong, responsible women and mothers. Beth Ahlberg (1991) has written that some Kenyan groups think that cutting away the "hard" clitoris makes the girl soft and fully feminine. In male circumcision the "soft" foreskin of the penis is cut away, making the boy fully hard and truly male. The surgery is also deemed necessary for a girl to be clean or fit for marriage. Infibulation, in particular, is thought to protect a girl from premarital sex and unwanted, illegal pregnancies. After the engagement or at the time of the marriage the girl's infibulation stitching is opened a bit to permit consummation. Before the birth of the first child she is further opened.

Over one-third of the African nations where such practices flourish have passed laws modifying or opposing the practice as a result of efforts by women's legal and human rights groups. Legislation prohibiting genital mutilation has been passed in several European nations, including Sweden, Denmark, France, and England, and in Ontario, Canada. In the United States, Wisconsin, Rhode Island, North Dakota, Tennessee, New York, Illinois, Delaware, California, and Minnesota have passed laws prohibiting the practice, and legislation is pending in New Jersey (Center for Reproductive Law and Policy).

In 1996 the United States Congress passed legislation on female genital mutilation. Practicing it on a minor was made a federal criminal offense, unless necessary to protect the girl's health. The Department of Health and Human Services is required to compile data on this custom and to engage in outreach to and education of the relevant communities. The United States Immigration and Naturalization Service must provide information to all aliens issued U.S. visas on both the health and psychological effects of female genital mutilation as well as on its legal consequences under criminal or child protection statutes. U.S. executive directors of international financial institutions are required to oppose nonhumanitarian loans to countries that have not begun education programs designed to prevent the practice. Finally, on September 30, 1996, the U.S. Congress passed a law criminalizing as of April 1, 1997, the practice of genital mutilation as part of the Illegal Immigration Reform and Immigrant Responsibility Act of 1996. It calls for fines or sentences of up to five years in prison for anyone who "knowingly circumcises, excises or infibulates the whole or any part of the labia major or labia minora or clitoris of anyone under age 18."

Genital mutilation continues to be practiced on millions of girls around the world as it has been for thou-

An adolescent African girl screams and struggles as she is held down during a female genital mutilation ritual (© Stephanie Welsh/Gamma-Liaison, Inc.).

sands of years. In the 1980s and 1990s well-organized local, national, and international groups and individuals working to eradicate this harmful tradition have had some success both in Africa and in overseas immigrant communities. Of course, a custom so entrenched cannot easily be eliminated; but the greatest success has been to involve the affected groups themselves, including both their leaders and grass-roots organizations, in reform, as has been attempted in Uganda, Eritrea, and Burkina Faso.

BIBLIOGRAPHY

Abdallah, Raquiya Haji Dualeh. *Sisters in Affliction: Circumcision and Infibulation of Women in Africa.* 1992.

Ahlberg, Beth M. *Women, Sexuality and the Changing Social Order.* 1991.

Ashur, D. *Silent Tears.* 1989.

Center for Reproductive Law and Policy. *Legislation on Female Genital Mutilation in the United States.* 1997.

Cisse, B. P. "International Law Sources Applicable to Female Genital Mutilation: A Guide to Adjudicators of Refugee Claims Based on Fear of FGM." *Columbia Journal of Transnational Law* 35, no. 2 (1997).

El Darrer, Asma. *Women, Why Do You Weep? Circumcision and Its Consequences.* 1996.

Kassindja, Fauziya T., and Layli M. Bashir. *Do They Hear You When You Cry?* 1998.

Lightfoot-Klein, Hanny. *Prisoners of Ritual.* 1989.

Magwero, C. *Program to Combat Genital Mutilation (FGM) in Kisii, Kenya, Nairobi.* 1997.

Samad, Asha A. "Female Genital Surgery: Shifting Grounds for Political Asylum." *Columbia Human Rights Law Journal* 5 (1998).

———. "Overview—Afterword." *Natural History Magazine* 5, no. 8 (1996). Special issue on circumcision/genital mutilation.

———. "The Unkindest Cut: Female Genital Cutting/Circumcision." *Whole Life Times* 7 (1996).

Sillah, Memuna. "Bundu Trap." *Natural History Magazine* 5, no. 8 (1996).

Toubia, Nahid. *Female Genital Mutilation.* 1994.

See also **Mutilation; Violence.**

M. ASHA SAMAD

Myerhoff, Barbara

An American anthropologist, Barbara Gay Myerhoff (1935–1985) was a pioneer in work on women and religion, as well as ritual, narratives, and aging. Born in Cleveland, Ohio, she received her Ph.D. in anthropology from the University of California at Los Angeles in 1968 and spent her entire academic career as a faculty member at the University of Southern California.

Myerhoff's initial scholarship was devoted to the developing field of ritual and symbolic studies. Her book *Peyote Hunt: The Sacred Journey of the Huichol Indians* (1974), was a highly regarded work of scholarship about pilgrimages and the religious life of a Mexican Indian group. Myerhoff was the first non-Huichol to participate in the sacred annual pilgrimage.

She explored similar themes in her innovative study of elderly Jews who met at a senior center in Venice, California (*Number Our Days,* 1979). She demonstrated the ways in which rituals, both traditional and invented, gave the aged the visibility that society and family had deprived them of, a theme she initially explored in *Secular Ritual* (coedited with Sally Falk Moore, 1977).

In her study of the elderly, Myerhoff developed important ideas about women and religion based on her observation that women's practice of Judaism is a "domestic religion"; she challenged the notion that religion can only or best be understood from an elite, usually male, perspective.

Myerhoff's work on religion spoke not only to scholars but to men and women throughout the world engaged in trying to understand sacred experience.

BIBLIOGRAPHY

OTHER WORKS BY MYERHOFF

"Bobbes and Zeydes: Old and New Roles for Elderly Jews." In *Women in Ritual and Symbolic Roles.*

Edited by Judith Hoch-Smith and Anita Springs. 1978.

Changing Images of the American Family: A Multidisciplinary Perspective. Coedited with Virginia Tufte. 1979.

Number Our Days. With Lynn Littman. Direct Cinema, 1977.

Symbol and Politics in Communal Ideology: Cases and Questions. Coedited with Sally Falk Moore. 1975.

WORKS ON MYERHOFF

Frank, Gelya. "The Ethnographic Films of Barbara G. Myerhoff: Anthropology, Feminism and the Politics of Jewish Identity." In *Women Writing Culture.* Edited by Ruth Bhear and Deborah A. Gordon. 1995.

In Her Own Time. With Lynn Littman. Direct Cinema, 1985.

Kaminsky, Mark. Introduction to *Remembered Lives: The Work of Ritual, Storytelling and Growing Older,* by Barbara Myerhoff. 1992.

Kirshenblatt-Gimblett, Barbara. Foreword to *Remembered Lives: The Work of Ritual, Storytelling and Growing Older* by Barbara Myerhoff. 1992.

Prell, Riv-Ellen. "The Double Frame of Life History in the Work of Barbara Myerhoff." In *Interpreting Women's Lives: Theory and Personal Narratives.* Edited by Personal Narratives Group. 1989..

RIV-ELLEN PRELL

Mystery Religions

The term *mystery religions* applies to a disparate group of voluntary religious associations in the Greco-Roman world. Individuals who sought membership in these cultic communities were called *mustai* (initiates), and the initiatory rite, conducted in secret, was called *muesis* or *musterion,* hence our word *mystery.* Ancient vows of silence concerning the holy rites have ensured that precise ritual details remain unknown. We do know, however, that all mystery cults shared a common belief that the experience of *muesis,* which the individual elected for him- or herself, conferred upon initiates a specialized knowledge, or *gnosis.* The content of this *gnosis* is also unclear; we cannot assume that the *mustai* completed their initiations with any belief in immortality, as some have argued. Although the popularity of the mystery religions peaked during the Roman Empire, they also played an important role in the religious culture of the Greek city-states during the archaic, classical, and Hellenistic periods. The cult of Demeter at Eleusis, the initiations on the island of Samothrace, the Bacchic mysteries of Dionysos, and the cult of Cybele (or Magna Mater) were established by the end of the classical period in Greece; Rome provided the foundations for the cults of Isis and Mithras.

The experience and position of women in the mystery religions varied from one cult to another. Some divinities worshiped by the *mustai* were female: Demeter and Persephone at Eleusis; Cybele in Asia Minor; Isis in Rome. Birth and rebirth were common symbols at Eleusis, and at the taurobolium of Cybele. Women initiates had more power in some of the mystery associations than they had in the spheres of worship required by membership in the ancient city: at Eleusis and probably Samothrace female *mustai* were on an equal footing with male initiates, and the Bacchic mysteries perhaps provided women with a temporary opportunity to

Mystery religions played an important role in the religious culture of the Greek city-states. This Etruscan statue (sixth century B.C.E.) depicts Magna Mater (Cybele) whose cult was established by the end of the classical period in Greece (Gianni Dagli Orti/Corbis).

invert gender relationships. Worship of Isis was open to all, and was especially attractive to upper-class Roman women. In contrast, initiates to Cybele seem to have been primarily male, and the cult of Mithras was an exclusively male religious association comprised primarily of Roman soldiers.

The shared culture of the mystery cults left a deep impression on the imagination of ancient writers of every generation and background. Language and imagery of the mystery religions can be found in classical Greek tragedies and comedies, in the dialogues of Plato, in treatises of Greek medical writers, in the Roman poets Virgil and Catullus, in the work of the first-century Jewish philosopher Philo, in the New Testament, and in the writings of the Christian Fathers. Fictional accounts of conversion and subsequent initiation into a mystery religion became common in novels from late antiquity, for example Lucius's well-known initiation into the mysteries of Isis as depicted in Apuleius's *The Golden Ass*, and the lesser-known "mystery initiation" into Judaism experienced by the Egyptian princess Aseneth, as depicted in *Joseph and Aseneth* (see the Pseudepigrapha). By the fifth century C.E., the pagan mystery cults had been successfully suppressed by the Christian church, but not before elements of the mysteries had been transformed into some of the Christian sacraments.

BIBLIOGRAPHY

Bianci, Ugo. *The Greek Mysteries.* 1976.

Burkert, Walter. *Ancient Mystery Cults.* 1987.

Foley, Helene. *The Homeric Hymn to Demeter: Translation, Commentary and Interpretive Essays.* 1994.

Martin, Luther. *Hellenistic Religions.* 1987.

Meyer, Marvin, ed. *The Ancient Mysteries: A Sourcebook: Sacred Texts of the Mystery Religions of the Ancient Mediterranean World.* 1987.

Nock, Arthur Darby. "Hellenistic Mysteries and Christian Sacraments." In *Essays on Religion and the Ancient World.* Edited by Zeph Stewart. Vol. 2. 1972.

See also **Cybele; Demeter and Persephone; Isis.**

NANCY A. EVANS

Mysticism

The term *mysticism* reflects several layers of conceptual accretion. It ultimately derives from the Greek verb *muein* (to close [the eyes]), employed in reference to the prohibition laid on initiates from divulging the rites of mystery cults, thus acquiring connotations of silence and secrecy. Later, in second- and third-century Alexandria, the adjective *mustikos* metaphorically signaled difficult or arcane inquiry. It specified "veiled" knowledge or understanding. The Greek Christian fathers used the term when describing allegorical, as opposed to literal, interpretation or knowledge of the spiritual as opposed to the carnal. Only in the medieval period, after assimilating Augustine's influence, does the Latin cognate *mysticus* also serve to denote a rich but peculiar state of mind conveying private, interior, intuitive, higher knowledge. For approximately a millennium thereafter, "mystical" theology designated the supernaturally bestowed experiential union of love with God. Varieties of supernatural visions usually accompanied mystical proficiency. Several divergent but overlapping traditions flourished, captured in testimonies, devotional texts, and manuals of spiritual discipline. Self-conscious tensions, particularly in sixteenth-century Spain and seventeenth-century France, arose between more rational and more experiential methods of theological inquiry. In the seventeenth century substantive, *mysticism,* belatedly appears.

In the nineteenth century the scope of mysticism underwent an enormous expansion. Increasing exposure to the world's diversity of religious beliefs, practices, and texts in conjunction with apologetic or ecumenical efforts to find something universal in religion led to mysticism becoming a broad category term or rubric pertinent to a whole class of literature found in many, if not most, of the world's religious traditions. In this modern usage mysticism refers to a type or several types of experience that seem to defy characterization in language and feature a collapse of all distinctions in consciousness. Because of asseverations in many "mystical" texts about the inability to adequately express the experience, one could, at a sufficiently general level and despite diverse descriptions, conveniently assimilate mystical experiences to one another. Mysticism thus became central to the early, theologically inspired comparative study of religion because it enabled the scholar to view disparate religions as sharing an essence. Despite incompatible beliefs and practices, one could assert that all religions develop from the same ineffable experiences. Because allegedly anterior to language, these originary experiences, furthermore, seemed unassailable by and orthogonal to Enlightenment criticism of religion. A dialectical relationship between mysticism and Romanticism also accounts for its prestige in the nineteenth century. The Romantic aspiration to locate a higher synthesis between spirit and nature found both inspiration and support in the mystical union of opposites. Even the profoundly Romantic anti-Romantic, Friedrich Hegel, observed similarities between his thought and mysticism. Later in the century, mysticism appealed to the Victorian taste for the paranormal.

WOMEN AND MEDIEVAL CHRISTIAN MYSTICISM

Interest in Christian mysticism has grown apace with the burgeoning of women's studies because women command a prominent position in its history, most notably during the medieval period. Many of these women mystics tropologically interpret the biblical Song of Songs. The governing conceit, Spiritual Marriage between the Soul (conceived as feminine) and its Bridegroom, Christ, appears quite commonly, however, in mystics of both sexes. The rigidly circumscribed roles permitted for women in the medieval church probably contributed to the prevalence of women mystics. Invoking Paul's stricture (1 Cor. 14: 34–35) enjoining silence on women in church, medieval church institutions forbade women to preach or expound on scripture and discouraged their learning Latin. After experience of loving union with Christ, many women (Teresa of Avila, d. 1582, and Beatrijs of Nazareth, d. 1268, for instance) felt literally inspired with Christ's masculine strength to exert an influence on the affairs of the world. Similarly, claims of divine inspiration allayed the resistance to female authorship.

The received view of women as weaker and less rational than men paradoxically functioned both to certify the authority of women mystics and to impugn it. God, as the Gospels attest, chooses to address himself to the humble and poor of spirit. Many believed it congruous, therefore, that God would grant extraordinary experience to women. Women's physical and intellectual frailty, however, mean that natural infirmity or the devil can readily deceive them. It remains an open question to what extent one can ascribe these views to the women mystics who avow them and to what extent they voice them strategically to appease male superiors. The threat of heresy continually (though to greater or lesser extents) exercised the church. In the hagiographies and testimonies of the later medieval period, evidence of women mystics' sanctity marks their bodies. Extreme asceticism and miraculous symptoms signal the mystic's legitimacy. That women comprised such a sizable proportion of mystics may have ironically contributed to a leniency toward mysticism, because it ensured that mystics occupied subordinate positions within the church hierarchy.

MYSTICISM AND FEMINISM

Some feminists find the reported collapse of distinctions in mystical consciousness suggestive. The mystical movement toward the union of opposites in a crisis of language and from there to a new relationship to language and culture appears isomorphic to feminine liberation from patriarchy. Carol Christ and Luce Irigaray among others have borrowed conceptually from existentialism and post-structuralism to describe this liberation. After a vertiginous and discomfiting descent into an existential abyss where one recognizes the contingency of language and its power structure reality, one transcends the set of hierarchically ordered dualisms on which patriarchy purportedly depends (transcendence superior to immanence, eternity superior to time, soul superior to body, culture superior to nature, reason superior to emotion, masculine superior to feminine) and arrives at a new relationship to language and culture. The gender confusions in many mystical texts (e.g., references to Jesus' lactating breasts) seem especially salient in this regard as overcoming the devalued feminine in gender duality.

Both Christ and Irigaray repudiate traditional notions of transcendent divinity, and neither evinces real interest in the lives or texts of actual mystics, though both trade on the language of mysticism by reinterpreting it to serve in the recovery of a primordial feminine self. At bottom they aim to provide paradigmatic feminist testimonies or manuals of feminist discipline as a means of liberating oneself from patriarchy. Christ even documents how she employs her text to guide women on "spiritual" quest. This emphasizes mysticism's tendency toward essentialism. To wit, it suggests the possibility of access to some primal essence outside culture and beyond the structuring influence of language. Contact with this ur-femininity or ur-experience beneath the constructions of language and culture represents a source of liberation.

Although most theorists now acknowledge the constitutive role of inherited concepts and language in mystical experience, it remains a potent metaphor for liberation. Simone de Beauvoir, conversely, recognized the conservative elements of mysticism and disparaged the mystics because, like ordinary oppressed women, they define themselves through loving union with a masculine figure. In a similar vein, some feminists celebrate mysticism as exemplary of feminine styles of knowing, while others deplore as sexist the longstanding association between private, experiential, connected, intuitional knowledge and the feminine. Many read Irigaray, for instance, as linking deliverance from patriarchy to the body and thereby reintroducing the same hierarchal dualisms (but with their values inverted).

Paradoxically, however, they thereby sometimes tend to erect a dualism between the conventional and the essential. Many twentieth century thinkers reject this dualism as perhaps the most basic and pernicious one.

BIBLIOGRAPHY

Beauvoir, Simone de. "The Mystic." In *The Second Sex*. Translated by H. M. Parshley. 1952. Classic "second wave" feminism.

Bynum, Caroline Walker. *Fragmentation and Redemption: Essays on Gender and the Human Body in Medieval Religion*. 1991. Clear and compelling discussions of the self, the body, and visionary experience in medieval Christianity.

Christ, Carol. *Diving Deep and Surfacing: Women Writers on Spiritual Quest*. 1980 (preface 1986; afterword 1995). Christ explores common patterns in twentieth-century fiction by women.

Hollywood, Amy. *The Soul as Virgin Wife*. 1996. A historically astute feminist carefully reads three late medieval mystics.

Irigaray, Luce. "La Mystérique." In *Speculum of the Other Woman*. Translated by Gillian C. Gill. 1985. Irigaray's work alludes and reacts to the psychoanalytic theories of Jacques Lacan. She rejects Lacan's exclusive association of language and culture with the masculine and exploits an ambiguity in the work cited below to insist on a sort of archaic femininity beyond the castration imposed by male language. Whereas Lacan implicitly assumes the primacy of the masculine because of its relation to language, Irigaray locates a primal femininity related to the body.

Katz, Steven T. "The 'Conservative' Character of Mystical Experience." In *Mysticism and Religious Traditions*. 1983. Katz points to the culturally conditioned nature of mystical experience.

Kristeva, Julia. "A Pure Silence: The Perfection of Jeanne Guyon." In *Tales of Love*. Translated by Leon S. Roudiez. 1987. A practicing psychoanalyst influenced by Lacan (and less overtly political than Irigaray), Kristeva attempts to explain mysticism. Like Sigmund Freud, she considers it an atavism surviving from infancy.

Lacan, Jacques. "God and the *Jouissance* of The Woman." In *Feminine Sexuality*. Translated by Jacqueline Rose. 1985. A turbid and jargon-laden but suggestive work, it inspired much of the contemporary feminist interest in mysticism. Lacan situates mysticism in relation to language and feminine sexuality.

Matter, E. Ann. *The Voice of My Beloved: The Song of Songs in Western Medieval Christianity*. 1990. A brief but comprehensive history of commentaries on the Song of Songs.

Petroff, Elizabeth Alvilda. *Medieval Women's Visionary Literature*. 1986. A useful anthology spanning ancient and medieval Christian visionary and mystical testimonies.

MATTHEW C. BAGGER

Mythology

An Overview

A myth is a sacred narrative, usually set in a time-before-time and enacted by divine or semidivine beings, that describes or defines the origin of a ritual, custom, or natural phenomenon. Until relatively recently, mythology was not separated from theology, which—whether Christian, Buddhist or other—privileged one set of myths as universally true while sometimes demonizing myths of other eras or areas. Since the nineteenth century, comparative religion, psychology, and folklore studies have challenged the hegemony of theology in the analysis of myths. Today, theology continues to study established, usually patriarchal, religions, whereas the study of mythology occupies itself with the narrative framework of these religions as well as suppressed or ethnic and tribal traditions.

HISTORICAL BACKGROUND

Mythology as a distinct formal discipline dates back only to the early nineteenth century, and for its first century the new discipline examined nonmonotheistic religious systems. Earlier, scholarship about myths was linked to political and cultural expansion. In Europe, Africa, and the Americas, Christian clerics recorded myths and rituals as part of a process of extirpation. In these areas the clarity of the record is sometimes in doubt, as important but less-objectionable myths were ignored while others were elevated, usually for condemnation. Even more questionable are sources that, like some records of Native American mythology, draw suspiciously close connections between an indigenous mythology and that of the colonizing missionaries.

An interesting example of the way in which clerics saved—while also distorting—mythologies can be found in Ireland, where the illuminated manuscripts of Christian monks provide virtually the only written sources for many Celtic myths, the same cultural information existing only in folklore and occasional inscriptions on the island of Britain and on the continent. There was no obvious political agenda involved in the recording— pagan Celts were not martyred for their faith in Ireland—yet the female figures are interpreted through a screen of patriarchal ideals, which especially rejected feminine sexuality (Dexter, 1997).

In the Middle East and Asia, a similar process occurred whenever monotheism displaced polytheistic faiths. Monotheism being invariably centered on a male godhead, its proponents—whether Islamic, Buddhist, Christian or Jewish—interpreted the myths they were supplanting entirely within the new framework, leading to the suppression, misinterpretation, or demonization of many female mythic figures. Not only were individual female figures and their myths erased or defamed, but heterodox visions of maleness and masculinity were also subject to suppression.

Yet many myths endured, often told by mother to child at peasant hearthsides or sung in old ballads. In the nineteenth century, European mythographers engaged in folklore studies, which interpreted fairy and folk-tales as ancient religious stories diminished into childhood entertainments or parables. Often impelled by nationalistic sentiments, folklorists such as the Grimm brothers (in Germany) and Elias Lonrott (in Finland) collected and transcribed European oral literature. Although often tainted by centuries of Christian influence, such collections are valuable for the vestiges of ancient tradition that they include; a sterling example can be found in the *dainas* or folksongs of the Baltic area, where ancient myths are preserved as if in amber. Such collection and recording of folkloric myths continues in some areas, such as Armenia and the Ukraine, today.

In the Americas, collection of oral literatures did not begin in earnest until the twentieth century; thus, some important American myth cycles have been lost, others surviving extinction only through the efforts of a single narrator or transcriber. Some collectors of folklore offered thematic or geographical interpretations of their materials, usually reflecting the cultural or theological predispositions of the researchers. Others merely catalogued motifs without commenting on probable meanings. Although such cataloguing might seem objective and without cultural bias, the analytic categories themselves often revealed implicit but unexamined assumptions.

As emphasis on theological argumentation diminished in the study of myth from the nineteenth century onward, it might be expected that suppression of non-patriarchal material would similarly diminish. But this has not always been the case. Various theoretical constructs have been proposed and material selected that best exemplifies these theories; the fact that most theorists have been male and have functioned from a patriarchal perspective has led to a continued suppression of competing visions. Among the theories that have been used to define and describe myths is the now-discredited "nature mythology" theory, which hold that myth emerges when metaphoric speech about natural,

often celestial, phenomena decays into narrative. Later came Sigmund Freud's use of Greek myth to elucidate the psychological states of his contemporaries and Carl Jung's concept of the archetype, an inner image arising from the collective unconscious that transcends all attempts to encapsulate it. Bronislaw Malinowski offered a functionalist approach to myth, which suggested that such narratives are designed to uphold claims to status and power. At midcentury and later, structuralism—especially linked with the works of Claude Lévi-Strauss—held that myth is a kind of Platonic ideal structure that finds expression in narrative, especially through binary oppositions. At approximately the same time, Paul Ricoeur and other literary critics began to apply thematic, semiotic, and deconstructive approaches to the study of myth as narrative. In the late twentieth century, other literary scholars and poets—most prominently Robert Graves and Joseph Campbell, whose concepts of the "white goddess" and the heroic "monomyth," respectively, have been influential—have melded archetypal psychology with close textual reading to create popularized analyses of significant, usually European, myths.

RECENT APPROACHES TO MYTH

These varying theories generally assume that myth expresses unchanging, universal realities. It was only with the advent of feminist approaches to mythology, in

Statue of Hera and Zeus enthroned, fifth to fourth centuries, B.C.E. (Mimmo Jodice/Corbis)

the mid-twentieth century, that this underlying assumption has been questioned. One common feminist contention is that myth can be read as historical record—although not in the way meant by the ancient Greek Euhemerus, who believed that gods were merely canonized heroes. Rather, some contemporary feminist mythographers such as Merlin Stone and Charlene Spretnak argue that certain myths are cautionary descriptions of the fate of womanist peoples under newly established patriarchies; the "marriages" of the Greek god Zeus to innumerable "nymphs" and goddesses, even including the powerful pre-Hellenic goddess Hera, are read as recording the actual subjugation of the cults devoted to these deities. Another undergirding assumption is that myth is not simply a religious artifact but an indication of the potential (as well as culturally defined proper) roles that actual women may play. Exploration of the image of the earth-mother-goddess, for instance, may illuminate possibilities in the actual role of mother that cultural constraints discourage.

Feminist scholars have also explored biblical and Christian traditions in terms of the narrative framework provided for women's lives. Some argue that Christianity has always given harbor to what Marla Selvidge calls "notorious voices," practicing Christians who envisioned the divine in less than orthodox ways. Such mystics as Julian of Norwich and Hildegard of Bingen are held up as examples of how the limiting and patriarchal imagery of monotheism can be translated to become more inclusive and woman-honoring. Feminine biblical figures such as Judith and Miriam are examined, as Elisabeth Schüssler Fiorenza does, in terms of the richness and relevance of their narratives. Finally, researchers such as Rafael Patai deconstruct biblical texts to reveal suggestions of vestigal paganism and hidden goddesses within them.

THE USES OF SOLAR IMAGERY: A CASE HISTORY

The question of the gender of the heavenly bodies serves to point up the ways in which patriarchal and monotheistic visions of the feminine have resulted in the suppression of alternative information. Pervading much published work on mythology (especially that by writers influenced by Jung) is the assumption that the sun is everywhere a masculine symbol, the moon everywhere a feminine one. Such writing typically describes the masculine sun as representing intellect and consciousness, while the feminine moon is said to rule emotion and the unconscious. The division can be traced to the Greek Orphics, who imagined the soul as separate from the body, associating the former with purity and goodness and the latter with everything dross

and material. The Orphics further associated their purely spiritual male divinities with the solar force; there, no feminine stain was permitted, for goddesses were said to be connected only with the moon or with the earth.

However neat this division, it is not upheld by cross-cultural study of solar myths. Rather, the sun was envisioned as a feminine force, usually a goddess, in a great many cultures, including those of Japan, Korea, Siberia, Egypt, Britain, Scotland, Ireland, Lithuania, Latvia, Finland, Russia, Germany, Scandinavia, northern California, southeastern North America, the Amazon basin, Argentina, Sri Lanka, India, Australia, the Arctic, and Anatolia. Despite the wealth of evidence that the sun has frequently been defined as feminine, dualistic thinking that upholds male-female and sun-moon hierarchies has led to the suppression of information about this mythic motif.

Such suppression began, in Europe, as early as the aforementioned Orphics. It continued as Roman legions redefined indigenous sun goddesses as aspects of the healing goddess Minerva, who was not borne in the solar vehicle; they then imposed on the regions they occupied their own Mithraic religion, with its masculine sun whose influence on the Christian vision of the redeemer is noted especially in the latter's "nativity" on winter solstice. Through the European Middle Ages, imposition of this masculine vision of the sun continued, although remote regions continued to honor a feminine sun. Rediscovered by nineteenth-century folklorists—who often expressed surprise at the deviation from the alleged norm that the sun goddess represented—the image of the solar feminine was available to Jung, who ignored it when he articulated his vision of the human self, as well as to the religious scholar Mircea Eliade, who wrote important treatises on shamanism while suppressing the information that many shamanic religions are centered on a female sun figure.

This suppression of the feminine sun was not limited to Europe or to modern scholarship. As early as the Pyramid Texts in Egypt, we find evidence of the suppressing of the female sun by a male solar figure. In Asia the sun goddess Amaterasu-omi-Kami was "redefined" in the eighth century as a male manifestation of the Buddhist bodhisattva Vairochana; in the thirteenth century Hirata Atsutan, a Japanese theologian, announced that the sun was not really a feminine force but was ruled from a distance by a (male) north-star deity. Similarly, in the Americas colonial Europeans misinterpreted obvious feminine solar symbolism to uphold their preconceptions of the binary division between male sun and female moon. In the 1950s an important study of southeast American myths asked respondents to identify the stars and moon as male or female, but about the sun asked only if it was male.

Feminist scholarship has examined the ways in which this overly neat division of sun and moon echoes the Cartesian mind-body dichotomy and has found in the image of the feminine sun an emblem of suppressed potentialities denied actual women. Feminist scholars such as Paula Gunn Allen, Marina Warner, Charlene Spretnak, Marija Gimbutas, Lucy Goodison, Merlin Stone, and others have questioned underlying assumptions of previous mythographers and have opened the way to new interpretations of mythic material from many cultures.

BIBLIOGRAPHY

GENERAL SURVEYS

Bulfinch, Thomas. *Bulfinch's Mythology.* 1978.

Hastings, James, ed. *Encyclopedia of Religion and Ethics.* 1924.

PSYCHOLOGICAL APPROACHES

Freud, Sigmund. *The Basic Writings of Sigmund Freud.* Translated and edited, with an introduction, by A. A. Brill. 1938.

———. *Civilization and its Discontents.* Translated and edited by James Strachey. 1962.

———. *Totem and Taboo: Some Point of Agreement Between the Mental Lives of Savages and Neurotics.* Authorized translation by James Strachey. 1950.

ARCHETYPAL APPROACHES

Campbell, Joseph. *The Hero with a Thousand Faces.* 1968.

——— *The Masks of God (Oriental Mythology, Primitive Mythology, Occidental Mythology, Creative Mythology).* 1969.

———. *The Way of the Animal Powers.* 1983.

Eliade, Mircea. *Shamanism: Archaic Techniques of Ecstasy.* Translated from the French by Willard R. Trask. 1964.

Graves, Robert. *The White Goddess: A Historical Grammar of Poetic Myth.* 1966.

Jung, Carl Gustav. *Essays on a Science of Mythology: The Myth of the Divine Child and the Mysteries of Eleusis.* Translated by R.F. C. Hull. 1969.

———. *Jung on Alchemy.* Selected and introduced by Nathan Schwartz-Salant. 1995.

———. *Man and His Symbols.* 1964.

Patai, Rafael. *The Hebrew Goddess.* 1967.

FOLKLORIC STUDIES AND ORAL LITERATURE

Duncan, Anthony Douglas. *The Elements of Celtic Christianity.* 1992.

Gifford, E. W. *Culture, Element Distributions XII: Apache-Pueblo.* 1940.

Grimm, Jacob. *Grimms' Fairy Tales.* Translated by Alice Lucas. 1945.

Lonrott, Elias. *The Kalevala: Epic of the Finnish People.* Translated by Eino Friberg. 1988.

Sharkey, John. *Celtic Mysteries: The Ancient Religion.* 1981.

Sprung, Joseph. *Index to Fairy Tales.* 1994.

Thompson, Stith. *Motif-index of Folk-literature: A Classification of Narrative Elements in Folktales, Ballads, Myths, Fables, Medieval Romances, Exampla, Fabliaux, Jest-Books and Local Legends.* 1955.

STRUCTURALIST AND ANTHROPOLOGICAL APPROACHES

Bonnefoy, Yves. *Mythologies.* 1991.

Dumézil, Georges. *Archaic Roman Religion.* Translated by Philip Krapp. 1970.

Dundes, Alan. *The Study of Folklore.* 1965.

Frazer, James George, Sir. *The Golden Bough.* Two volumes in one, with a new foreword. 1981.

Lévi-Strauss, Claude. *The Elementary Structures of Kinship.* Translated from the French by James Harle Bell et al. 1969.

———. *The Raw and the Cooked.* Translated from the French by John and Doree Weightman. 1969.

Littleton, C. Scott. *The New Comparative Mythology: An Anthropological Assessment of the Theories of Georges Dumezil.* 1973.

Malinowski, Bronislaw. *Magic, Science and Religion, and Other Essays.* 1954.

———. *Sex and Repression in Savage Society.* 1953.

Ricoeur, Paul. *The Philosophy of Paul Ricoeur.* 1996.

FEMINIST APPROACHES

Allen, Paula Gunn. *The Sacred Hoop: Recovering the Feminine in American Indian Traditions.* 1986.

Dexter, Miriam Robbins. "The Brown Bull of Cooley and Matriliny in Celtic Ireland." In *From the Realm of the Ancestors: An Anthology in Honor of Marija Gimbutas.* Edited by Joan Marler. 1997.

———. *Whence the Goddess: A Source Book.* 1990.

Fiorenza, Elisabeth Schüssler. *But She Said: Feminist Practices of Biblical Interpretation.* 1992.

Frymer-Kensky, Tiva. *In the Wake of Goddesses: Women, Culture and the Biblical Transformation of Pagan Myth.* 1992.

Gimbutas, Marija. *The Goddesses and Gods of Old Europe, 6500–3500 B.C.: Myths and Cult Images.* 1982.

———. *The Language of the Goddess: Unearthing the Hidden Symbols of Western Civilization.* 1989.

Goodison, Lucy. *Moving Heaven and Earth: Sexuality, Spirituality and Social Change.* 1992.

Paper, Jordan. "The Post-Contact Origin of an American Indian High God: The Suppression of Feminine Spirituality." *American Indian Quarterly* (Fall, 1983): 1–24.

Ruether, Rosemary Radford. *Religion and Sexism: Images of Woman in the Jewish and Christian Traditions*. 1974.

Rutledge, David. *Reading Marginally: Feminism, Deconstruction and the Bible*. 1996.

Selvidge, Marla. *Notorious Voices: Feminist Biblical Interpretation, 1500–1920*. 1996.

Spretnak, Charlene. *The Politics of Women's Spirituality: Essays on the Rise of Spiritual Power Within the Feminist Movement*. 1982.

Warner, Marina. *Alone of All Her Sex: The Myth and the Cult of the Virgin Mary*. 1976.

SOURCES ON SOLAR MYTHOLOGY

Bleeker, C. J. *Hathor and Thoth: Two Key Figures in the Ancient Egyptian Religion*. 1973.

Gimbutas, Marija. *The Balts*. Ancient People and Places Series. 1963.

Goodison, Lucy. *Women, Death and the Sun*. 1989.

Herbert, Jean. *Shinto: At the Fountainhead of Japan*. 1967.

Katzenelenbogen, Uriah. *The Daina: An Anthology of Lithuanian and Latvian Folksongs*. 1935.

Lichtheim, M. *Ancient Egyptian Literature: A Book of Readings*. Vol. 2, *The New Kingdom*. 1976.

Mason, J. W. T. *The Meaning of Shinto*. 1967.

Neuland, Lena. *Motif-Index of Latvian Folktales and Legends*. 1981.

Stone, Merlin. *When God Was a Woman*. 1976.

Troy, Tina. *Patterns of Queenship in Ancient Egyptian Myth and History*. 1986.

Ward, Donald. "Solar Mythology and Baltic Folksongs." In *Folklore International*. Edited by D.K. Wilgus and Carol Sommer. 1967.

See also **Graves, Robert Ranke; Moon; Sun.**

PATRICIA MONAGHAN

Feminist Uses of Mythology about Goddesses

In the early 1970s feminist students of religion, inspired in part by Mary Daly's critique of the patriarchal biases and exclusively masculine theological symbolism of Judaism and Christianity, began searching for evidences of religious traditions more sympathetic to women's needs. They soon discovered the relevance to their own work of the early-twentieth-century classicist Jane Ellen Harrison, who recognized that her interest in the emotional rather than the intellectual aspects of Greek religion, in ritual more than myth, in archaic chthonic cult rather than Olympian religion, reflected a distinctively female perspective. Harrison accepted J. J. Bachofen's thesis that the first period of human history was matriarchal, but unlike Bachofen insisted on the superiority of matriarchy to patriarchy, perhaps in part because of her own longing for a world that values women and their nurturing capacity.

Also rediscovered was the Jungian analyst Esther Harding, who hoped that ancient Near Eastern goddess myths might help contemporary women move beyond identification with either traditionally feminine or masculine roles and attributes. Harding was especially interested in the one-in-selfness of virgin goddesses whose identity was not defined by relationships to men, be they fathers, husbands, or sons.

The most influential contemporary investigator of ancient goddess religion is Marija Gimbutas, whose work combines archaeology, comparative mythology, and folklore. Her sensitivity to analogies and transformations enabled her to read the "language" of shards and figurines and to reconstruct what these artifacts meant to their makers and users and how they might relate to ritual, belief, and social organization. Impressed by the enormous preponderance of female figurines found at worship sites and graves in Neolithic Old Europe, she concluded that, despite the great variety of forms, all were aspects of One Great Goddess, worshiped not as an erotic object but as the parthenogenetic source of all life.

Younger, more self-consciously feminist scholars have tended to write more directly about the relevance of goddess mythology to the religious and psychological needs of contemporary women. Merlin Stone analyzes the process whereby goddess-centered religions in the ancient Near East were violently suppressed by patriarchal religion and argues for the close relation between changes in familial and sociopolitical organization and changes in mythology and theology. Consequently, she believes that changing contemporary patriarchal society requires remembering and recreating a nonpatriarchal mythology.

Carol Christ's "Why Women Need the Goddess" describes what it means to women to grow up in a culture that sees the divine only in male terms and the joy of discovering an alternative. We need the goddesses, she affirms, because they exemplify female power as independent, legitimate, and beneficent, and because they affirm the sacrality of the female body. Goddess worship implies a nonhierarchical vision of the relation among the divine, natural, and human realms; the sacred is viewed as immanent not transcendent; rhythm and change rather than stasis, harmony rather than domination and control, are the dominant values. Christ supports the importance of discovering as much as we can about ancient traditions where the divine was imaged in female form and the importance of women attending to their own deepest experiences of spirituality.

In *Lost Goddesses of Early Greece* Charlene Spretnak presents her recreations of the lost oral traditions about the goddesses of archaic Greece. Her work was not intended as the rediscovery or prehistoric structures but as the transmission of possibilities. Her anthology, *The Politics of Women's Spirituality*, makes even more evident her point that recovery of prepatriarchal myth is the discovery of a history that is politically empowering.

Christine Downing explores how the myths about the Greek goddesses can help women see their own lives more richly and how their own experience can help them enter more deeply into the myths. Downing begins with the highly differentiated goddess of classical literature and then moves backward to uncover earlier versions and to discover what these goddesses might have meant to the women who worshiped them as powerful forces active in their own lives. Downing goes on to explore the relevance of mythic figures to contemporary women's experience of menopause, of sister–sister relationships, and of same-sex love.

Significant work has also been done on non-Western cultures. Rita Gross has made visible the importance of still living goddess religions, such as Hinduism, which have never attempted to exclude female symbolism; Wendy Doniger O'Flaherty frames Indian myths about gender and male–female relationships in ways that serve to challenge Western understandings of divinity; Judith Gleason's study of Oya presents an African goddess's history in the old and new worlds; while Karen Brown's study of Haitian vodou bears witness to the role that friendship plays in her consciously feminist approach to ethnographic research.

BIBLIOGRAPHY

Bachofen, Johann Jakob. *Myth, Religion, and Mother Right*. 1861. Reprint, 1973.

Brown, Karen McCarthy. *Mama Lola: A Vodou Priestess in Brooklyn*. 1992.

Christ, Carol P. *The Laughter of Aphrodite: Reflections on a Journey to the Goddess*. 1987. Contains the essay "Why Women Need the Goddess."

———. *Odyssey to the Goddess: A Spiritual Quest in Crete*. 1995.

Downing, Christine. *The Goddess: Mythological Images of the Feminine*. 1981. Reprint, 1996.

Gimbutas, Marija. *Goddesses and Gods of Old Europe: Myths and Cult Images*. 1982.

———. *The Language of the Goddess*. 1989.

Gleason, Judith. *Oya: In Praise of the Goddess*. 1987.

Gross, Rita. "Hindu Female Deities as a Resource for the Contemporary Rediscovery of the Goddess." In *The Book of the Goddess: Past and Present*. Edited by Carl Olson. 1983.

Harding, M. Esther. *Woman's Mysteries: Ancient and Modern*. 1934. Reprint, 1973.

Harrison, Jane Ellen. *Prolegomena to the Study of Greek Religion*. 1903. Reprint, 1957.

O'Flaherty, Wendy Doniger. *Women, Androgynes, and Other Beasts*. 1982.

Spretnak, Charlene. *Lost Goddesses of Early Greece: A Collection of Pre-Hellenic Myths*. 1978.

———. *The Politics of Women's Spirituality: Essays on the Rise of Spiritual Power Within the Feminist Community*. 1982.

Stone, Merlin. *When God Was a Woman*. 1976.

See also **Gimbutas, Marija; Goddess: History of Study; Harrison, Jane Ellen; Warriors.**

CHRISTINE DOWNING

Native American Religions

The study of religion in Native American societies raises numerous cultural, political, and hermeneutical issues. Without due awareness of such issues, the study of Native American religions, and women's roles in them, will lead to serious misunderstandings. These problems have been aggravated by widespread exploitation and abuse of native traditions by late-twentieth-century non-natives, who are now being denounced for exacerbating the cultural genocide of native peoples (Rose; Clifton; Irwin, 1996).

Some problems in studying religion in traditional cultures are obvious. First, those cultures were generally nonliterate, so there are no classic explanations from past ages. In addition, native cultures are, on many levels, conquered cultures. That conquest has affected, in ways that are sometimes extremely subtle, both the religious life of Native Americans and our ability—as non-natives and postconquest natives—to comprehend it. Of course, some entire cultures were virtually exterminated ages ago. Many other cultures survived, but the effects of the arrival of Europeans were so far-reaching that it is impossible to discuss religion in such cultures without discussing those effects. Anyone seeking a simple exposition of the "original" religious culture of native societies will inevitably be frustrated or deluded. Not only were all native cultures affected by that contact, but our acquisition of information about those cultures is inevitably affected by historical and interpretive realities that shape how we—native and non-native—perceive that data and the nature of the data itself.

Given these interpretive problems, the roles that women played in the religious life of native societies are sometimes clear and at other times barely perceptible. Modernity has often reduced the traditional roles of women, in ways that may or may not ever be reversed. Various twentieth-century renewal movements have begun to restore some women's roles. But the disruption of indigenous traditions was so severe that we may never be able to perceive with precision the true place of women in many cultures.

DATA, INTERPRETATION, AND TRUTH

Written history concerning Native Americans dates back only five hundred years, and was generally produced by members of an alien society (including a number of women anthropologists) whose firsthand knowledge resulted from colonization. Archaeological data is different, but many native sites now lie buried under American civilization, and today's native leaders are sometimes understandably reluctant to sanction excavation of remaining sensitive sites. And although archaeology provides accurate data on many subjects, it often sheds little light on what went on inside the minds of the people involved. The religions of the prehistoric mound-builders, for instance, remain murky, and their relationship to modern cultures remains poorly understood.

Another important source of data is the accounts given to non-natives by natives of past generations. From the earliest European contacts, certain newcomers endeavored to understand the native cultures, and some, often respectfully, sought information from native informants. Such information has furnished much of our knowledge of precontact religions. But we are now beginning to learn that such "knowledge" is to some extent questionable. Naturally, premodern interpreters had their biases: many were Christian missionaries or government agents, who had their own agendas. But

A young Apache girl prepares to enter womanhood during this puberty ceremony (Bill Gillette/Stock Boston).

even the most conscientious and "unbiased" observers were often simply in a poor position to see native cultures accurately (Gill; Sullivan). For instance, the fact that in many native societies women played crucial roles often did not register on European or American observers: virtually all early observers gravitated toward the males in the native societies, assuming them to be the natural "leaders," who could best provide information. For many societies, however, such assumptions were quite false, and the data acquired in such ways is sometimes misleading.

For example, for decades a celebrated portrait of Native American religion was John G. Neihardt's formulation of the life and teachings of the Lakota holy man Black Elk (1863–1950). In many quarters, Neihardt's book *Black Elk Speaks* became a "gospel": It became not merely a representation of the experience of one contact-era native but for many, native and non-native alike, a definitive expression of the essentials of life among all precontact natives. Indeed, even today one often sees words from Neihardt's book repeated as a universal summary of all native religion. Yet scholars have now compared Neihardt's presentation to the actual records of Black Elk's life and words, and have found that presentation to have been deeply skewed (DeMallie). Not only did Neihardt put words into Black Elk's mouth, including many of the most moving and revered passages (Chief Seattle's famous soliloquy is another such literary creation), but one can now see that Black Elk had his own agenda, shaped by his

decades of life as a Catholic—a fact that both he and Neihardt concealed from the public.

Scholars are now learning to read such "classic" accounts much more carefully. It was long assumed that well-intentioned visitors, from missionaries to anthropologists, were given accurate data by their native informants. But research has begun to reveal that some famous authors (such as Carlos Castaneda and Lynn Andrews) simply invented their "informants," and in other cases (e.g., the Navajo "Old Man Hat") informants apparently lied: they did not share the visitors' interests, assumptions, or values, and sometimes simply invented data, playing their scribes for fools. Other native societies, such as certain Pueblo peoples, have resolutely refused outsiders access to information about certain religious activities. More often, because native informants were too polite to say nothing, they would answer questions about religion more incompletely and elliptically than the visitor suspected. And certain "native" expositors (such as Jamake Highwater and Hyemeyohsts Storm) were actually non-natives whose knowledgeability regarding native traditions has been hotly debated. Scholars must thus be very careful regarding both data and interpretations.

DO NATIVE AMERICANS HAVE "RELIGION"?

Another interpretive problem is that Native American societies past or present seldom display a cultural complex that corresponds to what Europeans or Americans tend to consider "religion." Some might say that there are really no "native American religions." There has certainly never been any coherent "Native American Religion," despite tendencies to assume that certain cultural phenomena, such as sweat lodges and vision quests, were standard features of preconquest life.

To some extent, it might be useful to compare indigenous American traditions to the Celtic traditions of pre-Christian Europe, or to the pre-Buddhist traditions of lands such as Japan or Tibet. In each case "religion" is generally diffused throughout the culture, not a separate component of human life that is marked off from "secular" affairs, such as by the institution of a central temple, an organized priesthood, or a uniform pattern of practice. A partial exception might have been the Natchez or the earlier agricultural kingdoms of the Mississippi valley, such as the builders of the city of Cahokia, which may have been influenced by Mesoamerican civilizations. But otherwise Native Americans have generally disdained centralization and have usually been content to maintain traditional practices, with little abstract conceptualization.

Most Native Americans have also felt their relationship to nonhuman beings—both other living things and nonembodied forces (manitus, kachinas, etc.)—to be a matter of direct social and personal interaction. For Native Americans, relating to what non-natives might call "the divine" is not reducible to "worship." The spiritual beings of the world are virtually never "creators" in a Judeo-Christian sense. Many societies do tell of mythic figures of the distant past who instituted basic elements of life as we know it, such as Raven among Northwestern peoples; Nanabozho among the Ojibwa/Anishnaabeg; or the *Divin dine'é,* "the holy people," among the Navajo. But such figures are seldom regarded as rulers of the world, to whom humans owed formal obedience. In fact, nonhuman beings, animal or spiritual, are generally not regarded as different in kind from human beings, and humans owe both animal and spiritual beings respectful interaction in a pattern of economic, moral, and spiritual reciprocation.

Most native conceptions of the world are holistic: unlike modern Westerners, who assume a radical qualitative distinction between "matter" and "spirit," "human" and "nonhuman," or even "life" and "death," Native Americans traditionally felt that (1) the world and all that is in it is continuous, and (2) a fundamental responsibility of humans is to display a respectful awareness of that fact. Animals are not despised inferiors, the natural world is not disdained as insensate, and departed human spirits continue to have a meaningful reality (sometimes as both natural and spiritual forces, like the Pueblo kachinas).

Most native societies have also made little distinction between religious leaders and laypeople. In general, all members of the community play important roles in its religious life. Those roles are often differentiated by age, gender, or occupation; but there is seldom any "class" that holds special social standing. Generally, such standing, for men and women alike, has been accorded by consensus to individuals who undertook to serve the community in a special way. For instance, in most societies healers, male and female, are highly respected, and their activities are generally seen in terms of the holistic patterns of respectful reciprocation that we today might call "religious." Some societies traditionally had what we might call "emergency healers," shamans whose special knowledge of and ability to use uncommon powers from the nonhuman dimensions enabled them to serve the community by rescuing victims of trauma, including misuse of similar powers by evildoers (generally mislabeled "witches"). The natural world is generally seen as full of power, and most societies have honored individuals, female or male, who devote their efforts to learning how to make use of such power for the benefit of society. But in general, because native peoples see no activities as taking place outside of the holistically meaningful patterns of life, no indi-

Hopi kachina doll (Buddy Meyer/Corbis)

vidual—man, woman, or child—is ever regarded as being outside the dimensions of life where its deepest meaning and value are accessed and expressed.

WOMEN IN TRADITIONAL NATIVE RELIGIOUS ACTIVITIES

Native cultures are so diverse—economically, socially, and culturally—that any generalizations about women in religious life are impossible. In some societies, it is sometimes difficult to perceive how women ever played meaningful roles in the community's religious life. The Lakota, for instance, credited the institution of their entire religious complex—the well-known "seven rites"—to a female benefactor, Ptehincalaskawin or White Buffalo Calf Maiden (Hall). But by most accounts Lakota culture was dominated by the male roles characteristic of hunting and war, and women's roles in religious life often seem rather marginal. In Black Elk's accounts, for instance, the girls' puberty rite, *išnati awicalowanpi,* now seldom practiced, seems to have held less meaning than traditional men's rites (such as the vision quest or sweat lodge ceremony) or than community complexes like the so-called Sun Dance, a rite practiced in many Plains societies under various names. But newer research shows that women participated more fully than has often been believed (M. Powers).

A different dynamic is found in other societies. Among the Siksika or Blackfeet, the annual "medicine-lodge ceremony"—their name for what the Lakota called the Sun Dance—was traditionally sponsored by a woman. Each year a woman would volunteer to lead the ceremonies, a role that involved 1) assuming responsibility for the community's *natoas* or "medicine bundle," the embodiment of her people's sacred power, and 2) leading all her people through a series of ritual activities that renewed the sacredness of their relationships to each other, to the higher powers, and to the buffalo, on whom the life of contact-era Plains peoples generally depended. In certain other Plains societies, the annual event reportedly included a real or symbolic ritual marriage, enacted to regenerate the life of all things. Such activities, like those of the Blackfeet medicine-lodge woman, demonstrated to the community the importance of women in maintaining the people's sacred relationship to the economic and spiritual sources of life.

Among the Athabascan peoples of the Southwest, the Apache and Navajo, similar meanings pervade the most important ritual complex. That complex is built around the puberty ceremony by which Navajo and Apache girls enter womanhood (Gill; Frisbie; Schwartz). The ceremonies vary among the different peoples. Among some Apache, masked dancers impersonate the life-giving mountain-spirits (*gan*, analogous to the Hopi kachina). More generally, both the Apache and the Navajo use the girls' rite of passage to bind themselves anew to the economic and spiritual sources of life: corn, the sun, and Asdzáá Nádleehé, Changing Woman. While other societies, such as the Cherokee, associate the origin of corn with a female mythic figure, in perhaps no other culture does that figure play such a central role in a people's religious life. In the Navajo rite, called the *kinaalda*, the celebrant ritually renews the community's sacred relationship to the life-giving sun, embodied in the corn that forms the spiritual and economic basis of Navajo life. She also renews the community's relationship to the "holy people" who had led "the surface-dwelling people" into this world. The celebrant does these things by means of song: within her family home, she sings the world into its proper state of blessed order (*hózhó*) as she ritually transforms into Changing Woman herself. In this way, the girl not only becomes a woman, but she renews the world—physically and sacrally—and demonstrates the ongoing reality of the *Divin dine'é*, the mythic founders of Navajo life.

In the case of other Southwestern peoples, such as the Pueblos, such a complex is absent. The Hopi do have a harvest festival that includes corn rituals similar to those of the Navajo *kinaaldá*. But among no Pueblo people, as far as outsiders know, does a girl's puberty ceremony play a comparable role. However, among the Hopi three of the specialized ritual societies (the Maraw, Lakon, and Owaqöl) are for females (Sullivan, pp. 53–56). Adolescent girls are initiated into the higher-order Maraw (womanhood) society, whose nine-day liturgical rites pertain both to fertility and to war, and sometimes mock men's rites. The middle-order Lakon and Owaqöl, meanwhile, lead a "basket dance" in which they throw gifts to the men; such rites demonstrate the importance of women's productive activity (symbolized by the basketry), and the fact that men are the beneficiaries of that activity. On another level, however, all Hopi children, male and female alike, are initiated into one of the two basic societies, the Kachina or Powamuy; the parents decide which society each child will enter. This complex socioreligious arrangement—linked ritually to the activities of the annual liturgical cycle, and mythically to the beneficent kachinas—weaves women and men together into a set of interactive patterns whereby all take part in maintaining and renewing the fundamental realities of life.

BIBLIOGRAPHY

The literature on religion in Native American cultures is voluminous, and the literature on women in those cultures is growing. The following works are useful starting points.

Bataille, Gretchen, M., and Kathleen M. Sands. *American Indian Women: A Guide to Research*. 1991. A balanced and wide-ranging bibliography of materials pertaining to women in Native American cultures.

Beck, Peggy, Anna Lee Walters, and Nia Francisco. *The Sacred: Ways of Knowledge, Sources of Life*. Rev. ed. 1992. To date, the only general introduction to Native American religions compiled by Native Americans. Not comprehensive, but a valuable counterpoint to presentations by non-natives like Ake Hultkrantz or Joseph Epes Brown.

Clifton, James, ed. *The Invented Indian: Cultural Fictions and Government Policies*. 1990. Includes revealing studies of the exploitation of native religions by non-natives.

Deloria, Vine, Jr. *God is Red: A Native View of Religion*. 2nd ed. 1994. An updated classic; provocative, but always sound, views from a respected Lakota scholar and advocate.

DeMallie, Raymond, ed. *The Sixth Grandfather: Black Elk's Teachings Given to John G. Neihardt*. 1984. A revealing study of the true life and teachings of Black Elk, based on archival sources.

DeMallie, Raymond, and Douglas Parks, eds. *Sioux Indian Religion: Tradition and Innovation*. 1987. A useful collection of essays by scholars and native spokespeople.

Frisbie, Charlotte Johnson. *Kinaalda: A Study of Navajo Girls' Puberty Ceremony.* 1967. A classic study; should now be read in light of Schwarz.

Geertz, Armin. "Contemporary Problems in the Study of Native North American Religions." In *To Hear the Eagles Cry: Contemporary Themes in Native American Spirituality.* Edited by Lee Irwin. 1996. A vital exploration of the cultural and interpretive problems posed by stereotypes.

Gill, Sam D. *Native American Religions: An Introduction.* 1982. A useful introductory text by a knowledgeable historian of religions.

Hall, Robert L. *An Archaeology of the Soul: North American Indian Belief and Ritual.* 1997. A detailed anthropological analysis of a variety of topics from a number of cultures.

Hudson, Charles. *The Southeastern Indians.* 1976. Still a useful exposition of the history and culture of the Southeastern peoples, with much material on Cherokee religion.

Hultkrantz, Ake. *The Religions of the American Indians.* 1979. A dated survey by a Swedish scholar who was regarded as the leading authority of his generation. Though well-intentioned, Hultkrantz was insensitive to many nuances of native cultures and to vital interpretive issues.

Irwin, Lee. *The Dream Seekers: Native American Visionary Traditions of the Great Plains.* 1994. A profound and probing study, with a foreword by Vine Deloria, Jr.

———, ed. *To Hear the Eagles Cry: Contemporary Themes in Native American Spirituality. American Indian Quarterly* 20, nos. 3–4 (1996) and 21, no. 1 (1997). A vital collection of expert articles on the state of the field today, carefully addressing issues of appropriation and representation.

Lobo, Susan, and Steve Talbot. *Native American Voices: A Reader.* 1998. Important materials on current legal and cultural issues, including appropriation and repatriation.

Ortiz, Alphonso. "Ritual Drama and the Pueblo World View." In his *New Perspectives on the Pueblos.* 1972. One of a number of illuminating studies by a leading native interpreter of Southwestern cultures.

Powers, Marla. *Oglala Women: Myth, Ritual, and Reality.* 1986. A challenging reappraisal of women's realities in Lakota (Sioux) culture, by a well-informed scholar.

Powers, William K. *Oglala Religion.* 1977. An impressive study of elements of religion and society among the Lakota, past and present.

Rose, Wendy. "The Great Pretenders: Further Reflections on Whiteshamanism." In *The State of Native America: Genocide, Colonization, and Resistance.* Edited by M. Annette Jaimes. 1992. A restrained yet moving exposition of the abuses of native cultures by self-deceived non-natives. Rose, an honored poet, is Miwok/Hopi.

Schwarz, Maureen Trudelle. *Molded in the Image of Changing Woman: Navajo Views on the Human Body and Personhood.* 1997. A detailed study of Navajo life and beliefs, with rich coverage of the *kinaaldá* and related topics.

Sullivan, Lawrence E., ed. *Native American Religions: North America.* 1989. An indispensable collection of articles from *The Encyclopedia of Religion* (1986), covering major themes and representative peoples and culture areas.

Talamantez, Inez M. "Images of the Feminine in Apache Religious Tradition." In *After Patriarchy.* Edited by P. Cooey et al., 1981. A classic study by a leader of the field today.

Vecsey, Christopher. *Imagine Ourselves Richly: Mythic Narratives of North American Indians.* 1988. Diverse essays by a careful interpreter.

———, ed. *Religion in Native North America.* 1990. Twelve worthwhile essays, including three important studies of the rise of the New Age "Native American Spirituality."

RUSSELL KIRKLAND

Nature

Nature as a concept varies widely in meaning in Western history. Nature can refer to an organizing principle by which something, someone, a class of things, or a class of persons are distinctively what they are, as in, "It is woman's nature to bear children." Nature also refers to the ultimate principle, or system of principles, by which all material reality is organized, as in natural law or the natural order. Nature may simply refer to material reality taken as a whole. Although these definitions appear neutral in value, they are in their application heavily laden with social implications and consequences.

Different models for nature have dominated at different times in Western history. The earliest Near Eastern civilizations, for example, tended to associate nature with vegetative fecundity and human female fertility, as personified by goddesses. This personification of nature as female or feminine is the oldest and most enduring model historically on record.

The metaphorical and conceptual equation of nature with femaleness is also one of the most pervasive and powerful models in the West, attaching easily to later models. These models reflect a highly variable interplay of design, necessity, and chance. The ancient

Greeks and their Roman successors tended to conceptualize nature in atomistic terms, as passive matter animated by dynamic form, or organically in vitalistic terms (as a life force). By contrast, the ancient Hebrews arguably never perceived material reality as a single system, conceptually distinct from the deity or deities who created and preserved it. Later medieval mystics from all three monotheistic traditions viewed nature as a divine creation, filled with hidden meaning crucial to human spiritual transformation. Meanwhile, among their contemporaries, alchemists and folk healers sought to align themselves through magic with nature, conceived vitalistically, as a source of wealth or cure.

From roughly the time of Descartes and Newton until the early nineteenth century, philosophers and the newly emerging scientists modeled nature as machine, determined after initial creation primarily by cause and effect. In the mid-nineteenth century Darwin introduced the principle of natural selection, a concept that presupposes determinism, but includes mutation as a feature. By this time many scientists and philosophers had rejected any concept of design or purposiveness as a feature of nature. In direct reaction to scientific determinism in all its forms, the nineteenth century also saw the rise of Romanticism among philosophers, theologians, preachers, artists, and poets in both Europe and the United States. The Romantics tended to characterize nature as wilderness driven by a vitalistic principle, often feminized, and as a metaphor for artistic creativity and for political, moral, and spiritual freedom. Both scientific and Romantic views continue to coexist into the present. In the early twentieth century, Heisenberg's discovery of the principle of uncertainty—which reintroduces the element of chance at the subatomic level—taken in conjunction with Einstein's theory of relativity—which challenges absolutizing any point in the time–space continuum—not only revolutionized how Westerners conceive nature, but ultimately led to questioning to what extent human intelligence can fully know nature.

Throughout Western history, nature, particularly when characterized by purposiveness or design, often appears paired with a contrasting concept, as in nature and grace, nature and spirit, or nature and culture or society. This characteristic pairing reflects and supports the tendency to attribute feminine gender to nature, the contrasting concept usually being identified with the masculine gender. In her landmark article "Is Female to Male as Nature Is to Culture?", feminist scholar Sherry B. Ortner argues that virtually all cultures distinguish the division of labor between women and men along lines that identify women with nature and men with culture (in *Woman, Culture, and Society*, edited by Rosaldo and Lamphere, 1974). In short, according to Ortner, most cultures have viewed women as, by definition, more natural or closer to nature because of menstruation, gestation, and lactation. By contrast, men, whose bodies are less obviously tied to reproduction and child rearing, are more naturally the makers and preservers of sociocultural life. As Ortner sees it, this "naturalizing" of women's labor across cultures, irrespective of other significant cultural differences, has resulted in the subordination of women's work in value, status, and power in relation to men's work.

Literary and visual evidence does appear across cultures and throughout history justifying the restriction of various tasks along gender lines by linking women to nature and men to culture or society, with the latter most often valued over the former. For example, male theologians and interpreters of the scriptures of Judaism, Christianity, and Islam have tended to identify women more closely than their male counterparts with matter, carnality, and vulnerability to sin. Interpreters from all three traditions have viewed Eve, and by extension all subsequent women, as carriers of sin in the form of temptresses who seduce men away from their proper relation to God. Many Western theologians and other religious authorities have furthermore restricted women to the realm of domesticity and confined their work to the bearing and rearing of children, sometimes romanticized as God's calling and often justified on the grounds of natural law. By identifying masculinity with the realm of spirit, religious authorities have projected masculinity upon the divine. This identification of men with God on the basis of a shared masculinity in turn legitimates the common theological claim that men should assume the role of head of the household and, further, serve exclusively as authoritative institutional representatives of government and of God.

At the same time, many women, past and present, feminist and nonfeminist alike, have affirmed what they have construed as women's unique relation to nature by turning to nature as a resource for their own spirituality. From medieval mystics to modern Wiccans, women have sought to claim power that is distinctively their own by attending to the identification of their own bodily functions with external natural processes as a resource for piety and authority.

This near universal tendency to construe gender difference through the body on the basis of a perceived relation to nature or to culture forces several questions: Is gender difference biologically authorized by a human being's distinctive reproductive functions? Or is gender difference, regardless of whether it gets interpreted positively or negatively, a socially produced strategy, reflecting and justifying sociopolitical power arrangements rather than actual natural differences? To what extent is nature itself a conceptual artifact used to justify elite male interests and power?

Feminists and other scholars continue to dispute these questions. One can nevertheless venture a tentative and qualified "yes" to all three. Biological reproductive capacities do account for different roles; all the same, human beings have little access to the significance of biological differences apart from a heavy overlay of socially generated interpretations. Dominant interpretations, which reflect the past and shape the future, also reflect the interests and values of the interpreters—the power elite—as well. Dominance notwithstanding, the meaning of such fundamental concepts as *nature* and *spirit, woman* and *man*, will likely always vary and be contested, reflecting ongoing struggles and shifts in power.

The ambiguity of the concept *nature* and its further identification with the concept *woman,* nevertheless, seem consistently to reflect serious and enduring ambivalence, shared by men and women alike toward physicality. In the West human vulnerability and finitude have produced ambivalence most especially toward female sexuality and reproduction. This ambivalence appears to arise in part from lack of control in the face of whatever interplay of design, necessity, and chance humans project as nature. This ambiguity and ambivalence underlie the ongoing social construction of gender difference. Regardless of whether nature is viewed positively or negatively in its own right, the concepts *nature* and *woman,* saturated with connotations of fertility and sexuality, seem inevitably to take on secondary status and worth in comparison to *man* and to cultural attempts to transcend the limitations posed by physicality. Furthermore, Western religious institutions have played central roles in reinforcing gender difference in ways that are often oppressive to women. Though feminists continue both to turn to nature as a resource for spirituality and to challenge the social construction of gender difference, it remains to be seen whether these inextricably related concepts can be reconceived and transvalued in lasting ways that are equally beneficial to women and men.

BIBLIOGRAPHY

Bynum, Caroline Walker, Stevan Harrell, and Paula Richman, eds. *Gender and Religion: On the Complexity of Symbols.* 1986. Collected essays addressing the polysemic quality of symbols in relation to the "gendering" of all human experience. See esp. Bynum, "Introduction: The Complexity of Symbols."

Christ, Carol P. "Why Women Need the Goddess: Phenomenological, Psychological, and Political Reflections." In *Womanspirit Rising: A Feminist Reader in Religion.* Edited by Carol P. Christ and Judith Plaskow. 1979. A classic example of a feminist identification of women with nature, divinized as Goddess, as a positive spiritual resource for women's identity as women.

Cooey, Paula M. *Religious Imagination and the Body: A Feminist Analysis.* 1994. Addresses two topics relevant to the significance of nature for gender and religion: the identification of women with physicality and women's use of their spiritual or religious experience, particularly experiences grounded in sentience and emotion, as authoritative alternatives to male-dominated cultural authority.

Daly, Mary. *Gyn/ecology.* 1978. Identifies women with nature through their common oppression and mutilation by patriarchal religious institutions, practices, and world views.

Douglas, Mary. *Natural Symbols: Explorations in Cosmology.* 1973. A classic study in the correlation of views of nature and bodily functions with political ideologies.

Eisenstein, Hester, and Alice Jardine, eds. *The Future of Difference.* 1980. Collected essays taking a spectrum of positions on the origin and significance of, and the role of nature in, gender difference.

Griffin, Susan B. *Woman and Nature, the Roaring inside Her.* 1978. An extended poetic essay that explores both the identification of women with nature in its most oppressive forms and her own anger as a creative response.

Marks, Elaine, and Isabelle de Courtivron, eds. *New French Feminisms.* 1980. Selections from the writings of French feminists, as well as Argentine thinker Luce Irigaray (associated with French feminism).

Suleiman, Susan Rubin. "(Re)writing the Body: The Politics and Poetics of Female Eroticism." In *Poetics Today: International Journal for Theory and Analysis of Literature and Communication* 6, nos. 1–2 (1985): 43–65. Critically assesses female autoeroticism as a strategy for women's liberation; argues for the reconstruction of the concept *androgyny* as transcendence of biology and thus of identification with nature.

Washbourn, Penelope. *Becoming Woman: The Quest for Wholeness in Female Experience.* 1977. A classic expression of early feminist essentialism (attributing nature or biology as "cause" for gender difference) of the second wave.

See also **Animals; Body; Goddess: History of Study; Moon; Romanticism; Sun.**

PAULA M. COOEY

Neith

The goddess Neith, abundantly attested in Egypt's earliest periods, 3000–2575 B.C.E., was the dominant female deity of these times. Appearing in about 40 percent of the theophoric names—names incorporating a deity's name within them—she also played a significant role in relation to royalty. Three queens of the first dynasty bore Neith-related names, and it appears likely that two of them, Neith-hetep and Meret-Neith, ruled for a time as queen regnant. Both women's names appear within royal *serekh*s, the rectangular symbol designating kingship. Significantly, the cult-sign of Neith, the two-lobed object with crossed arrows, surmounts these *serekh*s in place of the Horus falcon that dominates the king's *serekh*s.

The bilobate object with its crossed arrows or simply a pair of crossed arrows, sometimes on a staff, identifies Neith in this earliest time. Soon a third sign, apparently two curved bows tied together, joined the earlier signs to designate the goddess. These bows and arrows earned her the modern epithet of warrior goddess, although no mythology or activity supports this designation.

Neith in a *naos* or temple, depicted in a relief sculpture, first or second century C.E. (Gianni Dagli Orti/ Corbis).

Neith's cult-signs appear on a number of small objects, including ivory labels, jar sealings, jewelry, and bits of furniture from the early periods. Some of these objects relate her to Saïs, the delta town with which she is associated throughout Egyptian history. As a lower (northern) Egyptian deity, Neith was associated with the Red Crown of Lower Egypt, also associated with Saïs, and actually appears coiffed with the Red Crown in the time of Amenemhet III (1844–1797 B.C.E.).

The presence of Neith's bilobate sign on Queen Hetepheres I's carrying chair and on several pieces of jewelry suggests that Neith performed a protective function, an idea confirmed by her presence in later periods on coffins and canopic chests and in birth scenes, usually paired with the scorpion goddess Selket. During the Old Kingdom (2575–2134 B.C.E.) she is also paired with the royal goddess Hathor through the numerous women who served as priestesses of Hathor and Neith.

After the end of the Old Kingdom, Neith's visibility appears to diminish, only to resurface in the Twentieth-Dynasty (1196–1070 B.C.E.) tale describing the contending for the throne by the royal gods Horus and Seth. Her declaration in this tale—that unless her will that Horus sit on the throne be granted "the sky will crash to the ground"—suggests that she, "the great, the divine mother," maintained world order. Later in some second-century C.E. texts from the temples of Esna, Neith appears as the primordial creator, a role she showed less directly in her early associations with the watery-cow goddess Mehet-Weret. In these texts she is hymned as the "original goddess, mysterious and great,/who began to be at the beginning/and inaugurated everything." As a female primordial creator, she is unique in the ancient Near Eastern world, particularly since she is not an earth goddess, but rather is related to water.

Royal goddess, protector goddess, and creator goddess, Neith played an important role in ancient Egypt, a role the Greeks recognized in associating her with Athena.

BIBLIOGRAPHY

Little has been written about Neith, a goddess hardly known outside the field of Egyptology. The only monograph discussing her prior to Ramadan el-Sayed's works is one written in 1888 by D. Mallet, *Le Culte de Neith à Saïs* (Paris). Thus the appearance of el-Sayed's discussions, and particularly the documentation, was most welcome.

Hendrickx, Stan. "Two Protodynastic Objects in Brussels and the Origin of the Bilobate Cult-Sign of Neith." *Journal of Egyptian Archaeology* 82 (1996): 23–41.

Hollis, Susan Tower. "Five Egyptian Goddesses in the Third Millennium BC: Neith, Hathor, Nut Isis, Nephthys." *KMT: A Modern Journal of Ancient Egypt* 5, no. 4 (1994–1995): 46–51, 82–85.

el-Sayed, Ramadan. *La Déesse Neith de Saïs. I: Importance et rayonnement de son culte. II: Documentation.* Cairo, 1982.

———. *Documents relatifs à Saïs et ses divinités.* Cairo, 1975.

Troy, Lana. *Patterns of Queenship in Ancient Egyptian Myth and History.* Uppsala, 1986.

SUSAN TOWER HOLLIS

Neopaganism

Paganism is most commonly associated with the religions of ancient Greece and Rome, and is usually used to refer to these polytheistic religions—or indeed to any polytheistic religion that has not found favor with the dominant monotheistic religions of the West. The prefix *neo* brings paganism into the twentieth century, where it describes a spiritual movement that is to some extent modeled on its Greek and Roman forebears, but is, more accurately speaking, an eclectic blend of classical myths, tribal religions worldwide, folkloric aspects of the major world religions, and the active imaginations of its adherents. The variety in neopaganism is tremendous, and it is difficult to isolate anything that all neopagans agree upon as hallmarks of their spiritual belief and practice. However, common themes include pantheism, polytheism, nature-worship, celebration of solstices and equinoxes, worship of a dominant Goddess, prominence of women in leadership roles, the practice of ritual and magic, and an affinity for activities long designated as occult.

Neopaganism developed most rapidly out of the counterculture of the 1960s in the United States, but its roots go deeper. In fact, some neopagans object to the prefix *neo* and assert that their religion has been handed down to them in an unbroken line from pre-Christian times, having survived underground in Europe for thousands of years while Europe was under the sway of a rigid monotheistic patriarchy. This claim is less frequent today. Neopaganism is still most commonly found in the English-speaking world and practiced mainly by Caucasians who were formerly Jewish or Christian, but it is now as often made up of components from Buddhism, Vodou, or Native American religions as it is of any putatively "authentic" pre-Christian European paganism.

Many neopagans also refer to themselves as witches, and indeed when neopaganism emerged in the middle of the twentieth century, it was in the guise of witchcraft. Gerald Gardner, a British occultist, published several books on witchcraft after the final repeal of England's witchcraft laws in 1951. Gardner claimed to have been initiated into witchcraft by an old woman who had been initiated herself by another, in a long line of occult practice. On this basis, Gardner preached a religion of seasonal celebrations involving dancing, nudity, and chanting, the worship of a Goddess and a God, and the officiation of a high priestess. Gardner initiated many witches himself, several of whom split with Gardner to create their own versions of witchcraft. By the time this witchcraft arrived in the United States, it was hopelessly splintered, becoming even more so as many denizens of the 1960s counterculture created their own versions of witchcraft or paganism, in the process shedding much of the high theater of British witchcraft in favor of free-form rituals and celebrations. Formal initiation gradually became far less important, and most neopaganism today operates without benefit of official training, secrets transmitted ceremonially, and the like.

Contemporary neopagans, like their religions, are a varied lot: some retain the arch-seriousness of the Gardnerian tradition; others are content to attend a festival every year or two, do a little skinny-dipping and candle-burning, and call it their religion. Umbrella organizations for neopaganism tend to be quite welcoming of this variety, and show little interest in imposing dogma upon the neopagan movement. A large number of neopagans are not affiliated with other neopagans with whom they meet regularly: in the movement, such individuals are known as solitaries, and this is as accepted as any other form of neopagan practice. Neopaganism definitely has its serious side, but among new religions, neopaganism is almost unique in its light-heartedness.

Neopaganism has been of crucial importance to feminist religion and theology in the English-speaking world. Feminists created a space within neopaganism by the early 1970s where women could develop a spiritual practice that had no formal connection to male-dominant institutions or patriarchally inspired scriptures. In one step, they were able to do away with all the obstacles that blocked women's progress in the established religions of the West: they could worship a divine female (or many of them); they could serve as priestesses; they could devise rituals that incorporated female-specific imagery or dealt with female-specific issues. In this realm of comparatively enormous freedom, feminist spirituality was born and has continued to grow.

Neopagans were unprepared for much of the feminist interest in goddesses alone or female-only rituals. (This was a source of difficulty especially since Gardnerian witchcraft and many of its heirs were devoted to a complementarity of the sexes that sometimes went so far as to demand equal numbers of women and men for a successful ritual.) Though no important formal splits have occurred in neopaganism, which is surely one of the most tolerant spiritual movements of recent history, there have been tensions between neopaganism proper and feminist spirituality that have tended over the long run to make neopaganism even more tolerant, and feminist spirituality more open (if still somewhat reluctantly) to the religious participation of men in "their" movement.

Neopagan feminist spirituality has also had a profound impact on Jewish and Christian feminism. Efforts to find a home for feminism within established religions have often drawn on spiritual resources first pioneered by neopagan feminists. For example, the unabashed use of the term *goddess*, rituals for female-specific events (e.g., menarche), gatherings of women that include drumming, chanting, use of Tarot cards or the I Ching; all these are now found among feminists in established religions.

Neopaganism does not have an unblemished record where women are concerned. Parts of the movement are paternalistic, sexist, or advocate sexual freedom to a point where it becomes spiritually suspect to refuse sexual activity, and some male leaders have created harems of female followers and assert their spiritual authority over them. But, in the main, neopaganism has been one of the happiest of religious homes for feminists in the twentieth century, providing a strong female deity, and leaving room for women to innovate, participate, and lead in a religion that is not formally or historically—at least within its very brief "neo" history—misogynistic.

BIBLIOGRAPHY

The authoritative source on neopaganism is still Margot Adler's *Drawing Down the Moon: Witches, Druids, Goddess-Worshippers, and Other Pagans in America Today* (2d ed., 1987). A companion piece covering neopaganism in England is T. M. Luhrmann, *Persuasions of the Witch's Craft: Ritual Magic in Contemporary England* (1991). The feminist spin on neopaganism is discussed most extensively in Cynthia Eller, *Living in the Lap of the Goddess: The Feminist Spirituality Movements in America* (1995).

Classics of neopagan literature include Aleister Crowley, *Magick in Theory and Practice* (1976); Dion Fortune, *Sane Occultism* (1967); Gerald Gardner, *Witchcraft Today* (1954); Charles Leland, *Aradia, Gospel of the Witches* (1974); Margaret Murray, *God of the Witches* (1933; repr. 1992); and Doreen Valiente, *Where Witchcraft Lives* (1962). A wealth of sources on neopaganism can be found in the *Circle Guide to Wicca and Pagan Resources*, updated regularly by Circle Sanctuary in Wisconsin.

Classics of feminist neopagan literature include Zsuzsanna Budapest, *Holy Book of Women's Mysteries* (1979); Charlene Spretnak, ed., *The Politics of Women's Spirituality: Essays on the Rise of Spiritual Power Within the Feminist Movement* (1982); Starhawk, *The Spiral Dance: A Rebirth of the Ancient Religion of the Goddess* (1979); and Barbara G. Walker, *The Woman's Encyclopedia of Myths and Secrets* (1983). Additional sources can be found in two bibliographies by Anne Carson, *Feminist Spirituality and the Feminine Divine* (1986) and *Goddesses and Wise Women* (1992).

See also Goddess: Contemporary Goddess Movement.

CYNTHIA ELLER

New Religions

An Overview

What a "new religion" is exactly, and why it is different from an "old" religion, is not without dispute. Academic scholars have reacted to discrimination and bigotry associated with the use of *cult* to indicate a second-class, heretical, or potentially dangerous religion. This use of *cult* became current first in the Evangelical counter-cult movement and later in the secular anti-cult movement arising in the 1960s. As a reaction, scholars have suggested using value-free terms such as *new religious movements* and *new religions*. Some scholars distinguish between new religious movements (the novel groups, comparatively recent and not yet fully institutionalized) and new religions (the older and established alternative religions, once called sects, another word now often avoided for its potential negative associations). Other scholars, however, use the two terms synonymously.

TYPOLOGY

Where does the border lie between new and old religions? Although there is no clear border, and many movements do not remain "new" forever but eventually move into the mainstream, at least in the West one could call "new" those religions groups engaged in proselytization and regarded as marginal by the society. They are not clearly identified with one of the mainline traditions and contradict the historical Western religious paradigm based on a transcendent God, a mediator (Jesus Christ), and a visible, hierarchical church claiming an unbroken continuity from the apostolic age. We could, thus, distinguish three main groups of new religions:

1. Religions with a Christian background, perceived as deviant because of their ecclesiology or theology. Some scholars further distinguish between religions with a Protestant background (theologically Protestant, but with differences in ecclesiology or worship, such as the Pentecostal churches), and religions with a Christian background clearly outside of the mainline Protestant tradition, including the Latter-day Saints (Mormons), Christian Science, the Jehovah's Witnesses, the Unification Church, and The Family (formerly the Children of God).
2. Eastern religions, either novel (the Rajneesh movement) or part of an ancient tradition (the Hare Krishnas, Soka Gakkai) in the East but perceived as deviant or new once they came into the Western society and began to proselytize Westerners.
3. Human potential religions (Scientology) and "ancient wisdom" or magical religions (including religions reappropriating genuine or modified Native American themes), where the element perceived as deviant is a reinterpretation of the definition of religion itself, often not including any reference to a personal or transcendent God.

Although this typology may be helpful, we should keep in mind that such categories are culturally and politically negotiated. Being a new religion or part of the mainline is not a perpetual or essential feature of a religious group but a claim, continuously negotiated with older religious competitors and society at large.

WOMEN AS LEADERS OF NEW RELIGIONS

A number of important sociological and historical works have focused on why women have emerged as founders or leaders of important new religions, such as the Shakers (Mother Ann Lee, 1736–1784), Christian Science (Mary Baker Eddy, 1821–1910), a large wing of New Thought (Emma Curtis Hopkins, 1853–1925), Theosophy (Helena Petrovna Blavatsky, 1831–1891), Japanese new religions including Tenrikyo (Miki Nakayama, 1798–1887) and Oomoto (Nao Deguchi, 1836–1918), and contemporary European additions such as Universal Life (Gabriele Wittek, b. 1933). In other new religions—where a single founder is less easy to identify—women have often emerged as important leaders, as in the case in Pentecostalism, Spiritualism, Afro-

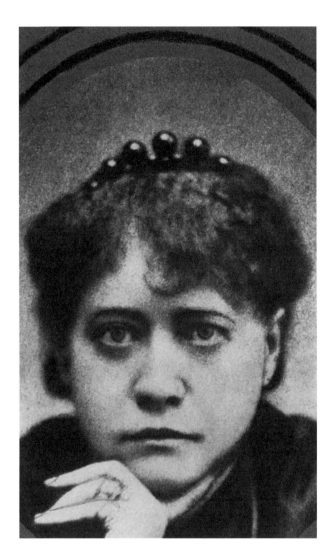

Helena Petrovna Blavatsky (1831–1891) was a spiritualist and promoter of the Theosophy movement (Library of Congress/Corbis).

American syncretistic religions (including Louisiana's Spiritual churches), Wicca, and neopaganism. Scholars of new religions generally agree on two important conclusions. First, the fact that a religion has been founded by a woman is no guarantee that it will remain gynocentric after her death. Even a female image of the divine being or incarnation is not enough when the religion lacks the theoretical tools needed to criticize the patriarchal social structures. The study of Shakers by feminist theologian Marjorie Procter-Smith is a case in point. Second, the fact that a religion is marginal or new does not necessarily mean that it will be antipatriarchal or feminist. Mormons, Jehovah's Witnesses, the Unification Church, and the magical religion of the Ordo Templi Orientis—to name just a few—all subscribe to a rather traditional doctrine of gender relations.

According to an article written in 1980 by historian Mary Farrell Bednarowski, only new religions exhibiting four features become open to a real equality in leadership between men and women: a nonmasculine divine principle; a denial or tempering of the Jewish and Christian doctrine of the Fall; a lack of ordained clergy; and a comparatively nonpatriarchal view of marriage and motherhood. Bednarowski and religious scholar Catherine Wessinger have later emphasized that the four features, of course, do not operate in a vacuum but interact with society at large.

WOMEN AS MEMBERS OF NEW RELIGIONS

Although excellent surveys of women in new religions do exist—such as Canadian sociologist Susan Palmer's *Moon Sisters, Krishna Mothers, Rajneesh Lovers* (1994)—all attempts to build a general model of women's membership in new religions have failed. Since *new religion* is a culturally negotiated label, there are many different new religions, and women's roles range from self-conscious sexual objects in the UFO religion of the Raelian Movement to feminist shamans in some New Age groups or to traditional housewives in the Unification Church. Any distinction of new religions merely in two groups, one patriarchal and the other feminist, would however be misleading. Women have reached leadership positions and considerable power in groups whose teachings and scriptures may seem quite sexist, including the sexually revolutionary Rajneesh tradition and some sexually conservative Pentecostal churches. Palmer also suggests that, given the high defection rates in new religions, joining them may be a rite of passage, offering women a temporary refuge to develop themselves in a chaotic society and to emerge empowered and ready to confront gender relationships as responsible adults. It is, on the other hand, also true that a minority of new religions may simply revictimize women. Any generalization in this field is, by definition, inaccurate.

BIBLIOGRAPHY

General works on new religions, including J. Gordon Melton's *Encyclopedic Handbook of Cults in America* (1986; 2d ed., rev. and updated, 1992), also discuss gender issues. Conversely, general works on women and religion, such as Susan Hill Lindley's *"You Have Stept Out of Your Place": A History of Women and Religion in America* (1996) also discuss nonmainline religions. On women and new religions a seminal article was Mary Farrell Bednarowski's "Outside the Mainstream: Women's Religion and Women Religious Leaders in Nineteenth-Century America," *Journal of the American Academy of Religion* 48 (1980): 207–231. The discussion on female leadership "outside the mainstream" continued inter alia in two 1993 books edited respectively by Catherine Wessinger (*Women's Leadership in Marginal Religions: Explorations Outside the Mainstream* [1993]), and by Elizabeth Puttick and Peter B. Clarke (*Women as Teachers and Disciples in Traditional and New Religions* [1993]); and in Susan Starr Sered's *Priestess, Mother, Sacred Sister: Religions Dominated by Women* (1994). On membership the most important work is Susan Palmer's *Moon Sisters, Krishna Mothers, Rajneesh Lovers: Women's Roles in New Religions* (1994). There is a rich literature of case studies of women in new religions: interesting examples are two studies of Shakerism by Marjorie Procter-Smith, *Women in Shaker Community and Worship: A Feminist Analysis of the Uses of Religious Symbolism* (1985) and *Shakerism and Feminism: Reflections on Women's Religion* (1991); Elaine J. Lawless's *Handmaidens of the Lord: Pentecostal Women Preachers and Traditional Religion* (1988); and, on spiritualism, Ann Braude's *Radical Spirits: Spiritualism and Women's Rights in Nineteenth Century America* (1989), with a British parallel offered by Alex Owen's *The Darkened Room: Women, Power and Spiritualism in Late Victorian England* (1990).

See also **Eddy, Mary Baker**; **Founders**; **Lee, Ann**.

MASSIMO INTROVIGNE

In Europe and the United States

It is often argued that women are more likely to be leaders in new religions (NRs), but such leadership usually relies on charismatic authority and is therefore limited to exceptional individuals. NRs founded for explicitly feminist reasons (e.g., some Goddess groups) are the most likely to treat all women equally; women's roles in other NRs vary considerably.

At one end of the spectrum are NRs whose official teachings support a patriarchal social structure, such as the Mormons and the Unification Church. Both churches affirm the Bible as well as new scriptures revealed by their respective leaders. The Unification Church was founded in South Korea in the 1930s by Rev. Sun Myung Moon. Although God is described as both male and female, the androgynous image reflects a yin-yang polarity that places male and female in a subject-object relationship. Eve is not only blamed for the Fall but is described as having intercourse with Satan before tempting Adam to do the same. As in Mormonism, the traditional family unit is seen as essential to salvation: God wanted Adam and Eve to establish the perfect, God-centered family and felt betrayed when they did not. Jesus could not complete his mission because he was crucified before he could marry. Now God has given humanity one more chance by sending (some Unificationists believe by incarnating Himself in) Rev. Moon and his wife, the "True Parents." Moon matches men and women from many different cultures and conducts mass marriage ceremonies. Such marriages are seen as entrance into a "True Family" that will restore humanity's broken relationship with God, and children born to such families are considered free from original sin. Not surprisingly, such teachings have traditionally been interpreted to mean that a woman's primary role is to be a wife, mother, and homemaker. Nonetheless, women do hold positions of authority in the Unification Church, and unlike the Mormons, both men and women are asked to leave their families temporarily to do missionary work. Unification teachings on gender reflect the patriarchal values of both Korean culture and the Evangelical Christianity Moon was raised in. Yet a vocal feminist movement has arisen within the church to contest the traditional interpretation of their scriptures.

At the other end of the spectrum are NRs whose official teachings seem to challenge patriarchy, such as the Shakers and Christian Science, both founded by women. Mary Baker Eddy, who founded Christian Science in 1875, challenged nineteenth-century gender norms by teaching that God has both masculine and feminine characteristics, explicitly criticizing traditional theology for making God "too manlike." She argued that Eve could not be blamed for the Fall because human suffering is not God's punishment but merely erroneous thinking. Eddy's insistence that only spirit is real and that matter is a product of the human mind decreased the importance of physical differences between the sexes. In contrast to the emerging field of gynecology, in which female patients were expected to passively accept the authority of male doctors, the relationship between patient and Christian Science practitioner was one of equality. And at a time when women were virtually excluded from positions of economic, political, or religious power, each Christian Science church was required to have at least one male and one female reader (worship leader). Yet Eddy never said that she intended to liberate women. Indeed, she created a hierarchical structure that prevented any other women from holding the kind of power she wielded over Christian Science. The Mother Church in Boston was run by men; and given the disproportionate number of women in the movement, the requirement for gender parity among readers ultimately benefitted men. Whatever Eddy's intentions, Christian Science did provide large numbers of educated, middle class women with an alternative to the traditional role of wife and mother in the vocation of practitioner.

The Christian Science Center, the church's headquarters complex, in Boston (Robert Holmes/Corbis).

Finally, some NRs do not explicitly promote any gender norms. The Church of Scientology, founded in the 1950s by L. Ron Hubbard, is an example. Hubbard's wife published a booklet describing the duties of men and women in very traditional ways, but this is not official Scientology doctrine. Scientology teaches that humans are essentially spiritual beings who struggle over many lifetimes to escape the physical body. One's true self, the "OT" (Operating Thetan) remains trapped in "MEST" (matter, energy, space, and time) because "engrams" (unconscious memories of physical or psychological pain) cause one to act irrationally. The goal of Scientology is to bring these engrams into consciousness and thereby diffuse their power, enabling one to become "clear." This is achieved with the help of an "auditor" (a Scientology counselor), who can be either a man or woman. Theoretically, church leadership at all levels is open to everyone, and gender roles in the family are defined by individual practitioners. Yet until a systematic study of gender in Scientology is done, how women actually fare will remain unclear.

The role of women in New Age religions is subject to similar variation. The term *New Age* is problematic because it is yet to be clearly defined. The roots of the New Age movement include Native American and Eastern religions, the Western occult tradition, science fiction, and humanistic psychology. New Age teachers argue that Western culture has been fragmented by a dualistic worldview that separates spirit from matter, male from female, and science from religion. They see the twentieth century as the dawn of a new age that will lead to individual, communal, and planetary wholeness. New Age religions stress the immanence of the divine and practice a variety of techniques (meditation, yoga, drumming, channelling) to reconnect with God, self, and nature. Of course, these are characteristics possessed by many religions, and the New Age label has been applied to traditions as diverse as Theosophy, the Unification Church, Scientology, and feminist spirituality. How women fare in any New Age religion depends on its theological roots and leadership, and ranges from female submission to male gurus to alternative communities that encourage both men and women to develop their feminine characteristics. Although the emphasis on wholeness is consistent with feminist concerns, it is not always applied to gender roles, and feminists have criticized the New Age movement for focusing exclusively on transformation of self while ignoring the need for social and political activism.

As these examples suggest, official gender norms influence but do not fully determine what roles women play in NRs. Although women are more likely to enjoy equality when NR teachings challenge patriarchal norms, it is possible for women to empower themselves even when such teachings are patriarchal.

BIBLIOGRAPHY

The body of literature on women in NRs is small but growing. Most studies of NRs in Europe focus on their struggle for legitimacy in the face of a strong anti-cult movement. In the United States, where the NRs covered in this essay have gained a modicum of legitimacy, more scholars have begun to investigate questions of gender. Thus far, they have tended to focus their analyses on official teachings, which may or may not determine how women actually fare in these groups. There are many excellent studies of Mormonism and the Unification Church that discuss both theological possibilities and historical and sociological realities faced by women. A remarkable development is the emergence of feminist interpretations from within these traditions (for Mormons, see the journal *Dialogue;* for the Unification Church, see sources listed below). With a few exceptions (e.g., Setta below), studies of the Shakers and of Christian Science have tended to focus more on the religions' founders than on ordinary women members. The diffuse nature of New Age religion means scholars refer to it often but shy away from making definitive statements about it. As of this writing, there are no published studies on women in Scientology.

Bednarowski, Mary Farrell. *New Religions and the Theological Imagination in America*, 1989. Does not focus on women, but provides excellent introduction to beliefs and practices of six major NRs, including Scientology, New Age, and the Unification Church. Bibliography lists many sources on women in NRs.

———. "Outside the Mainstream: Women's Religion and Women Religious Leaders in Nineteenth Century America." *Journal of the American Academy of Religion* 48 (June 1980): 207–231.

Beecher, Maureen U., and Lavinia F. Anderson, eds. *Sisters in Spirit: Mormon Women in Historical and Cultural Perspective.* 1987.

James, Gene, ed. *The Family and the Unification Church.* 1983. Though published by Unification Theological Seminary, this book includes several essays that are critical of the church.

Lindley, Susan Hill. "The Ambiguous Feminism of Mary Baker Eddy." *The Journal of Religion* 64 (1984): 318–331.

McDonald, J. "Mary Baker Eddy and the Nineteenth Century 'Public' Woman: A Feminist Reappraisal." *Journal of Feminist Studies in Religion* 2 (1986): 89–111.

Quebedeaux, Richard. *Lifestyles: Conversations with Members of the Unification Church.* 1982.

Setta, Susan. "When Christ is a Woman: Theology and Practice in the Shaker Tradition." In *Unspoken Worlds: Women's Religious Lives.* Edited by Nancy Auer Falk and Rita Gross. 1989.

Warenski, Marilyn. *Patriarchs and Politics: The Plight of Mormon Women.* 1980.

Wessinger, Catherine, ed. *Women's Leadership in Marginal Religions: Explorations Outside the Mainstream.* 1993. Essays cover a broad range of NRs, including the Shakers, Christian Science, Spiritualism, Theosophy, New Thought, Hindu and Buddhist groups, Pentecostalism, African American spiritual churches, Mormonism, and feminist spirituality.

CHRISTEL J. MANNING

In East Asia

The popular religious life of the Chinese, Japanese, and Korean people is characterized by complex, multi-layered belief patterns that incorporate elements of Buddhism, Confucianism, Taoism, Shintoism, and Christianity. In each country, since pre-modern times, women have been thought to possess a strong capability for communication with the divine, and often serve as mediums between humans and divine forces. However with the ascension of Confucianism and institutional Buddhism came a view of women's inferiority and the degradation of both women's religious roles and their possibilities for salvation. Women were largely responsible for domestic religious observances and for supporting religious organizations, with established religion tending to reinforce patriarchal values and social organization. Women's participation in new religious groups in East Asia has been, in part, a response to the male-dominated religious establishment.

In China, participation includes the practice of popular religion, labeled throughout modern history by both Chinese elite and Westerners as superstition. The growth of Marxist thought further hardened this attitude and Communist leaders hoped that religion would disappear with universal education. However, since the 1980s, with the loosening of many restrictions in Chinese society, there has been a resurgence in religious activity, including the building of temples and shrines and more open attitudes toward spiritual practice. In addition, Chinese communities in Taiwan and throughout Southeast Asia have continuously engaged in popular spiritual practice.

In the Chinese traditional patrilineal system, family is the most important concern, and unmarried and infertile women are considered outsiders without a place in the home. Thus, many popular Chinese deities patronized by women are thought to provide assistance with related concerns including fertility, childbirth, and finding a marriage partner. The most popular deity, Kuan Yin, known as the Goddess of Mercy, is worshiped as the giver of male children to the childless and a source of help for worries about children who are ill. The goddess Tianhou, also known as Mazu, is the patron deity of fishermen, but is viewed by women as a maternal protectress who cures barrenness.

The new religions of Japan are salvationist lay movements that are often said to have risen in three stages, the mid to late nineteenth century, the 1890s to 1930s, and post–World War II. The first wave rose in connection with quasi-millenarian movements during the collapse of the shogunate government; in the second stage, in response to rapid industrialization and social change, the new religions were the largest popular movement, with several million adherents. The final period was dubbed "the rush hour of the gods" due to the multitude of sects which arose based on freedom of religion promised by the postwar constitution.

Many of these new religions share certain characteristics, including combinatory doctrines and female founders with similar life cycle patterns who experienced divine possession as a catalyst to their religious activities. Though certain of the sects preferred to identify themselves with Shinto or Buddhist traditions, they were, like those religions themselves, combinatory belief systems. However, they often explicitly rejected and condemned the established religions, particularly Buddhism, for its exclusion of, and discriminating attitudes toward, women.

There have been at least ten different female founders of Japanese new religions. Some of the most well known include Nakayama Miki, founder of Tenrikyo, one of the earliest large and successful groups; Deguchi Nao, founder of the internationalist group Omotokyo, suppressed by the Japanese state for its allegedly treasonous activities; and Kitamura Sayo, the tough-talking founder of Tensho Kotai Jingu Kyo, "the dancing reli-

In China Kuan Yin, known as Goddess of Mercy, is worshiped as the giver of male children (Asian Art & Archaeology, Inc./Corbis).

gion." Most women founders came from poor farm families, had little formal education and were married. They were not allowed to pursue spiritual activity during their childbearing years, but, in keeping with custom, were allowed to participate in socioreligious activities after the age of forty. Many experienced possession by spiritual beings as the initial impetus to their religious life. The role of spirit possession both established a link with traditional folk religious practices, allowing them to assume a legitimate religious role, and provided a supreme authority in the form of a deity, enabling them to criticize society and propose an egalitarian worldview.

Other aspects common to many Japanese new religions include healing, the notion that suffering hardship is a means of strengthening character, and a strong belief in individual self-cultivation. Healing is central to nearly every new religion and provides a concrete means to attract and subsequently convert new followers. Many new religions believe the efficacy of modern medicine is limited, because the cause of disease is in the self, and afflictions can be relieved only with religious devotion to God.

In Japan today, women, particularly, older women, are the strongest supporters of the new religions, which encourage the active participation of women at all levels within the organization and uphold principles of family solidarity, with a clear-cut division of labor between the sexes. Such a division of labor, however, sometimes accounts for the loss of female leadership within the organization. Female founders rely primarily on men for administration and management of sect matters. As a result, subsequent female spiritual heirs may retain religious authority, but sect leadership and management is largely in the hands of a male executive body.

Unlike China and Japan, Korean syncretistic new religions often identify themselves as Christian organizations. As in Japan, new sects arose in Korea at distinct historical junctures. The first stage occurred in relation to the Tonghak popular rebellion in the late nineteenth century. The second stage, under Japanese colonialism in the 1910s to early 1940s, saw the emergence of two types of groups: an unorthodox lay Buddhism, called Won pulgyo, whose early members included widows and Buddhist nuns; and nationalistic religious groups, often gathered around a village called Sindo-an, which was prophesied to be the site of a new dynastic capital. The third stage, following liberation from Japan, featured the establishment of many sects of a Christian type, including Chondo-gwan, a Christian faith healing movement, and T'ongil-gyo, also known as The Unification Church.

While women monopolize the role of shaman in Korean primal religion, in general they play a less important role in domestic and ancestral rites than in either China or Japan. In a strongly Confucian society, their participation in important ancestral rites is limited to the preparation of food offerings. The doctrines of the new religions often stress harmonious family relationships, including normative gender roles. For example, the Unification Church of the Reverend Mun Sonmyong conducts large group weddings after Mun selects suitable marriage partners from among the faithful.

BIBLIOGRAPHY

Ahern, Emily. "The Power and Pollution of Chinese Women." In *Women in Chinese Society*. Edited by Margery Wolf and Roxane Witke. 1975.

Hardacre, Helen. *Lay Buddhism in Contemporary Japan: Reiyukai Kyodan.* 1984.

Hardacre, Helen. *Kurozumikyo and the New Religions of Japan.* 1986.

Kendall, Laurel, and Griffin Dix, eds. *Religion and Ritual in Korean Society.* 1986.

Nakamura, Kyoko. "Revelatory Experience in the Female Life Cycle: A Biographical Study of Women Religionists in Modern Japan." *Japanese Journal of Religious Studies* 8, nos. 3 and 4 (1981): 187–205.

Ooms, Emily Groszos. *Women and Millenarian Protest in Meiji Japan: Deguchi Nao and Omotokyo.* 1993.

Paper, Jordan. *The Spirits are Drunk: Comparative Approaches to Chinese Religion.* 1995.

Reader, Ian. *Religion in Contemporary Japan.* 1991.

NANCY STALKER

In Southeast Asia

In the 1960s new Islamic and Buddhist movements appeared in Southeast Asia. These were primarily urban-based movements led by Southeast Asian intellectuals and university students, who turned to their religious traditions in formulating a response to the effects on their societies of the expanding global economy, particularly the increasing concentration of wealth in fewer hands and the consequent growing gap between the rich and poor, destruction of sustainable local economies, corruption among elites, environmental degradation, and, most important, the erosion of values by Western secularism.

In Indonesia and Malaysia two very different movements arose among university students who turned to Islam with the aim of promoting moral and spiritual development and social justice through a return to Islamic values. In Malaysia the rise of *dakwah* (Arabic *da'wah*, referring to the "call" to Islam) was associated with the Angkatan Belia Islam Malaysia, the Malaysian Islamic Youth League. The Dakwah movement, which is also strong in Indonesia, has been described as fundamentalist or scripturalist because it advocates a return to a literal reading of the scriptures and the hadith (the traditions of the Prophet) and emphasizes meticulous observation of religious obligations as a sign of one's piety and devotion. In Indonesia, Nurcholish Majid, president of Himpunan Mahasiswa Islam, the Association of Islamic Students, emerged as the leading figure in a new stream of modernist Islam known as the Renewal Movement (Pemikiran Pembaruan, literally "new thought"). This movement, which is represented in Malaysia by intellectuals like Naguib Al-Atlas, has been described as modernist because it emphasizes rational critique and *ijtihād,* or the interpretation of scripture in terms of principles rather than prescribed (*halal*) and proscribed (*ḥarām*) practices.

These two movements have very different significance for the role and status of women in Islam. The Dakwah movement, which is generally led by *'ulamā',* the traditional Islamic elite, emphasizes the role of the man as head of the household and the responsibility of women to wear the Islamic headcovering. The more modernist renewal movement, primarily led by Western-educated Islamic intellectuals, is generally favored by the national governments of Indonesia and Malaysia. It takes a more liberal attitude toward women, arguing that Islamic dress codes are more a cultural matter than a religious responsibility. From the interpretationist perspective, the principle that the Qur'an teaches is modesty, and women should be free to decide whether or not this requires them to cover their heads or seclude themselves. Extreme segments of the Dakwah movement, such as Darul Arqam (banned in 1994 in both Malaysia and Indonesia), encouraged polygamy and required women to adopt *hijab*, dress that covers the entire body, often a black *burqa* that covers all but the woman's eyes. The Dakwah emphasis on the authority of men has led to the development of a small but articulate movement of feminist Islamic women in Malaysia, the Sisters in Islam, who work to educate women about their rights under Islamic law and criticize abuses against women sanctioned by Shari'a, the Islamic law code.

In Thailand, Buddhist monks and lay intellectuals also turned to their religious tradition seeking direction in their efforts to combat the social ills that came with modernization and development. The fastest-growing Thai Buddhist movement, Wat Dhammakaya, which was founded in 1978 by Chaiyaboon Sitthiphon (Phra Dhammajayo) and Phadet Phongasawad (Phra Dattajivo) was aimed at introducing meditation practices to the new middle class. This movement, which has received royal patronage and support from the Thai military, has been described as a movement of religious consumerism because of the marketing of meditation retreats, glossy posters of celebrity monks and other Buddhist paraphernalia, the enormous sums of money that have been donated to temples, and costly expenditure on the building and renovation of temples. At the other extreme is Santi Asok, begun by Phra Bodhirak in 1970. Phra Bodhirak and his followers founded a forest retreat where they followed an ascetic regime, in protest against the immorality and corruption of lay society in Thailand. The involvement of Santi Asok monks in politics and the movement's critique of the conservative mainstream *sangha* as being too ritualistic and prone to commercialism and materialism provoked enormous controversy. Phra Bodhirak was disrobed and ordered by the Sangha Council to stop ordaining monks, and in 1989 he was arrested for violation of the 1962 Sangha Act because he refused to comply with the Sangha Council's order to make a formal declaration of leaving the monkhood. More significant for Thai society has been the reform movement associated with activist monks known as "development monks," who began to work with Thai villagers to improve their lives both materially and spiritually, and "forest preservation monks," such as Phra Prachak, Phra Khru Pitak, and Achan Pongsak, who found themselves engaged in a struggle to preserve the habitat in the face of logging and other commercial interests. The activities of these monks were controversial, and the monks were sometimes the target of military reprisals. Nevertheless, they launched a movement that has come to be known as Engaged Buddhism. Bhikkhu Buddhadasa, founder of Wat Suan Mokkh (Garden of Liberation) and Thailand's foremost contemporary philosopher and theologian, is the intellectual leader of the Engaged Buddhist movement in Thailand. His writings, which take a critical view of contemporary society based on the core Buddhist teachings of nonattachment and interdependent coarising, provide the foundation for a critically engaged Buddhist "spiritual politics." The lay intellectual Sulak Sivaraksa has been influential in spreading the teachings of Engaged Buddhism to the West. Engaged Buddhists have supported a greater role for women in Buddhist practice. Some Western women students of Buddhism have become prominent in the Engaged Buddhism movement, such as Joanna Macy, Charlene Spretnak, Nancy Barnes, and Sallie King.

Tradition and the *sangha* have accorded women a subordinate position in Thai society. Women who adopt a religious life, known as *mae chi*, have a much lower status than monks. Efforts by women to reestablish a line of ordained nuns (*bhikkhunis*) have been repulsed by the Department of Religious Affairs and the Council of Elders in charge of all monks. However, in 1957 Voramai Kabilsingh (Bhikkhuni Ta Tao), who was later ordained in a Mahayana lineage of Buddhist nuns, founded Wat Songdharma Kalyani, the first monastery in Thailand established by and for Buddhist women. Her daughter, Chatsumarm Kabilsingh, is the author of the first book on Thai women and Buddhism from a feminist perspective. Also notable are female meditation teachers, such as Achan Naeb and her pupil, Achan Suchin.

In Cambodia, Vietnam, and Burma, monks and nuns have been in the forefront of political struggles to stop the violence that has afflicted their nations. The Cambodian monk Maha Ghosananda and the Vietnamese Zen monk Thich Nhat Hanh have also become known as leaders of the Engaged Buddhist movement. The nun Chân Không (Cao Ngoc Khuong) has written about her role as a woman in the Engaged Buddhist movement in Vietnam.

Vatican II (1965) set the stage for the emergence of liberation theology in the Philippines. In 1970 the

Philippines Bishops Council responded by mandating Social Action Centers in every diocese with the aim of eradicating entrenched injustice and replacing oppressive structures. Under the protection of the Catholic Church and the leadership of activist priests, local grass-roots organizations known as the Basic Christian Community (BCC) organized in support of social justice issues, protested the destruction of the environment by commercial interests, and undertook development projects. Through the BCC structure, women as well as men have found a new role in the Catholic Church of the Philippines.

BIBLIOGRAPHY

Anwar, Zainah. *Islamic Revivalism in Malaysia: Dakwah among the Students.* 1987.

Chân Không. *Learning True Love: How I Learned and Practiced Social Change in Vietnam.* 1993.

De la Torre, Edicio. *Touching Ground, Taking Root: Theological and Political Reflections on the Philippine Struggle.* 1986.

Hassan, Muhammad Kamal. *Muslim Intellectual Responses to "New Order" Modernization in Indonesia.* 1980.

Istiadah. *Muslim Women in Contemporary Indonesia: Investigating Paths to Resist the Patriarchal System.* 1995.

Kabilsingh, Chatsumarn. *Thai Women in Buddhism.* 1991.

Macy, Joanna. *World As Lover, World As Self.* 1991.

Madjid, Nurcholish. "Indonesia in the Future: Sophisticated and Devoutly Religious." *Prisma* 49 (1990).

Muzaffar, Chandra. *Islamic Resurgence in Malaysia.* 1987.

Nagata, Judith. *The Reflowering of Malaysian Islam: Modern Religious Radicals and Their Roots.* 1984.

Phongphit, Seri. *Religion in a Changing Society: Buddhism, Reform and the Role of Monks in Community Development in Thailand.* 1988.

Sisters in Islam. *Are Women and Men Equal Before Allah?* 1991.

Sivaraksa, Sulak. *Seeds of Peace: A Buddhist Vision for Renewing Society.* 1991.

Swearer, Donald, ed. *Me and Mind: Selected Essays of Bhikkhu Buddhadasa.* 1989.

Wazir-Jahan Begum Karim. *Women and Culture: Between Malay Adat and Islam.* 1992.

See also **Buddhism: Modern Movements; Hinduism: Modern Movements.**

ELIZABETH FULLER COLLINS

In Native American Traditions

New religions are emergent, organized, alternative religious movements that are conceived of as separate from the established or existing religious traditions of a given culture (Lucas, 1997). New religious movements have been historically classified according to factors of causation, such as deprivation or disaster, or emphasis, such as apocalypticism, nativism, and revitalization. Although a number of Native American new religious movements have been documented, much about them remains unexplored, particularly in the area of women's participation and contributions. For example, during the Cherokee movement of 1811–1812, two women and a man had a vision calling for a return to traditional ways (Pesantubbee, 1993). Very little is known about the two women or about Cherokee women's involvement in the movement. In another case, Tenskwatawa, a man known as the Shawnee Prophet of 1810–1812, reported revelations from the Master of Life, a male deity, although previous to the movement the creator known as Papoothkwe or Our Grandmother was understood to be female (Clifton, 1984). The effect of this change on women's roles has yet to be studied.

Perhaps the most well-known Native American new religious movement is the Ghost Dance of 1890 begun by the prophet Wovoka, a Paiute man. News of Wovoka's teachings rapidly spread among the Plains people, and as the communities adopted the Ghost Dance they shaped it according to their culture and traditions. Among the various Ghost Dances, common characteristics included a belief in the destruction of whites and a return of the spirits of the deceased ancestors. As with many religious movements, the shape and direction of the movement changed according to visions. Among the Lakota, a woman whose name is not known had a vision in which she saw her friends wearing shirts or dresses with sacred symbols on them. When she awoke from her trance she called the women together and described the garments to them; they began making the ghost skirts, which were believed to protect the dancers from whites' bullets (Mooney, 1896).

Through visions women also introduced new songs and hand games among the Ghost Dancers. A Pawnee woman known only as Mrs. Washington experienced a number of visions that led to new dances and an organization of singers called the Seven Eagle Brothers. The singers dressed in a particular way based on a vision received by another Pawnee woman, Mrs. Goodeagle. She later became known as the Mother of the Seven Eagle Brothers. Following a vision by a male member, Mrs. Cover became the mother of a later group, the Seven Crows (Lesser, 1996).

A wood engraving of Sioux Indians performing the Ghost Dance, 1891 (Library of Congress/Corbis).

Prior to the 1890 Ghost Dance, however, there had been another Ghost Dance, which originated in the late 1860s with a Paiute man named Wodziwob. It is thought that variants of this movement were practiced among several tribes in north-central California. Among these religions was the Bole Maru, which emphasized ethical behavior and the prophetic value of dreams (Du Bois, 1939). Bole Maru Dreamers were predominantly women, who, relying on their dreams, directed the social and political activities of their people (Sarris, 1992). An especially noteworthy example is the twentieth-century Dreamer Essie Parrish of the Kashaya Pomo. Through dreaming, she organized ceremonial dances and songs and designed ritual clothing (Sarris, 1992).

The Ghost Dance of 1890 and its offshoots are only one example of women's involvement in an American Indian new religious movement. In 1799 a Seneca war leader known as Handsome Lake began to have prophetic visions that eventually developed into the *Gaiwiio* or good word. Combining aspects of Iroquoian tradition and Christianity, the *Gaiwiio* is not only history and prophecy but also a ceremonial guide and code of conduct (Wallace, 1972). Native American scholar Paula Gunn Allen (1986) argues that, historically, the Code of Handsome Lake undermined the traditional authority of Iroquois women; however, in the late twentieth century women of the Longhouse religion, as the movement became known, played important organizational and ceremonial roles (Shimony, 1980).

Around 1880 in the Puget Sound area, a movement known as the Indian Shaker religion was founded by John Slocum from the Skokomish tribe. The characteristic trembling of hands and body among Indian Shakers was first experienced by Slocum's wife, Mary Slocum. As she approached her husband's sickbed, she began shaking uncontrollably. He recovered and her shaking was interpreted as a manifestation of divine power. She also had visions in which she received instructions on the special clothing to be worn during curing rites. She continued to instruct Shakers on innovations such as moving clockwise during rituals or arranging tableware in a particular manner (Stowell, 1987).

It is also important to note women's involvement in peyotism. A small cactus that grows in the Rio Grande Valley and to the south, peyote has been used ceremonially for centuries by the Aztec, Huichol, and other Mexican indigenous peoples (La Barre, 1975). During the 1890s peyotism spread northward throughout the plains and developed into what became known in the late twentieth century as the Native American Church. In this form, the peyote religion is a blend of indigenous and Christian elements. Ceremonies or "meetings" regularly last all night and involve singing, praying, and the consumption of peyote. Stories of the origin of peyote vary, but they usually tell of a woman who, while separated from her people, encountered peyote and brought it back to them (Beck and Walters, 1990). Both women and men participate in peyote meetings. While the position of ritual leader or "road man" is reserved for men, the role of "peyote woman" or "water woman," who brings water at dawn, is fulfilled by women. Peyote is also known for its value in relieving the pain of childbirth (Mount, 1993). It was for just this purpose that Mountain Wolf Woman, a Winnebago woman, first used peyote. She tells her life story, including her conversion to the "peyote way," in her autobiography, *Mountain Wolf Woman* (1966).

Women have played and continue to play major roles in Native American new religious movements. Continued research in this area is needed to further scholars' understanding of the nature and extent of this involvement.

BIBLIOGRAPHY

Allen, Paula Gunn. *The Sacred Hoop: Recovering the Feminine in American Indian Traditions.* 1986. An excellent resource for the study of American Indian women.

Beck, Peggy V., and Anna Lee Walters. *The Sacred: Ways of Knowledge, Sources of Life.* 1977. Reprint, 1990. A survey text of Native American religious traditions; notable for its emphasis on American Indian perspectives.

Clifton, James A. *Star Woman and Other Shawnee Tales.* 1984. A collection of oral stories with an introduction about Tecumseh and Tenskwatawa.

"Dream Dances of the Kashia Pomo: The Bole-Maru Religion Women's Dances." Directed by C. B. Smith. University of California Extension Media Center, 1964. An ethnographic video featuring Bole Maru women's dances and a description of the religion by Essie Parrish.

Du Bois, Cora. *The 1870 Ghost Dance.* 1939. A detailed examination of the 1870 Ghost Dance as it was practiced on the West Coast.

La Barre, Weston. *The Peyote Cult.* 1959. Reprint, 1975. A classic study of peyotism in Central and North America including updated surveys of the literature.

Lesser, Alexander. *The Pawnee Ghost Dance Hand Game.* 1933. Reprint, 1996. A detailed ethnography of the rise and development of Pawnee hand games.

Lucas, Phillip C. "Introduction." *Nova Religio* 1, no. 1 (1997): 6–9. Introduces a new journal of alternative and emergent religions.

Mooney, James. "The Ghost-Dance Religion and the Sioux Outbreak of 1890." In *Fourteenth Annual Report of the Bureau of American Ethnology,* part 2. 1896. Reprint, 1973. A study of the Ghost Dance movement based on field investigation among approximately twenty tribes from 1890 to 1894.

Mount, Guy, ed. *The Peyote Book: A Study of Native Medicine.* 1993. A popular introduction to peyotism and the Native American Church emphasizing American Indian perspectives.

Mountain Wolf Woman. *Mountain Wolf Woman, Sister of Crashing Thunder: The Autobiography of a Winnebago Indian.* 1961. Reprint, 1966. Narrates the life of a Winnebago woman who embraced Medicine Lodge, Christian, and peyote religions.

Pesantubbee, Michelene. "When the Earth Shakes: The Cherokee Prophecies of 1811–12." *American Indian Quarterly* 17, no. 3 (1993): 301–317. Examines previous interpretations of the events of 1811–1812 as a Ghost Dance movement.

Sarris, Greg. "Telling Dreams and Keeping Secrets: The Bole Maru as American Indian Religious Resistance." *American Indian Culture and Research Journal* 16, no. 1 (1992): 71–85. An engaging discussion of Dreamer Essie Parrish and the Bole Maru; especially concerned with what is permissible to share with non-Pomo audiences.

Shimony, Annemarie. "Women of Influence and Prestige Among the Native American Iroquois." In *Unspoken Worlds: Women's Religious Lives in Non-Western Cultures.* Edited by Nancy A. Falk and Rita M. Gross. 1980. Disputes the idea of an Iroquois "matriarchy" yet demonstrates the importance of women in Iroquois society historically and into the late twentieth century.

Shanandoah, Audrey. "Women: Sustainers of Life." *Turtle Quarterly* (Summer 1990): 5–10. A discussion of the role of women in the Longhouse religion by a female Longhouse elder.

Stowell, Cynthia D. *Faces of a Reservation: A Portrait of the Warm Springs Indian Reservation.* 1987. A photographic depiction of the various religious traditions among the Warm Springs people with accompanying histories and descriptions.

Wallace, Anthony F. C. *The Death and Rebirth of the Seneca.* 1969. Reprint, 1972. A study of the Handsome Lake movement as a religious and cultural revitalization.

See also **Dreams; Intoxicants and Hallucinogens; Visions.**

MARY C. CHURCHILL
MICHELENE PESANTUBBEE

In Mexico

The ever-growing variety of new religions in Mexico discourages any attempt at definitive classification. Some new religions entrust women with moral authority and effective leadership. Others reinforce women's traditional roles, especially those inspired by a strict interpretation of biblical scriptures. Yet even the new religions that question conventional male dominance are affected by the values of the society in which they are immersed. These values impinge, however marginally, on emerging religious structures and create internal tensions. Such tensions often elicit responses from the devotional feminine community that accommodate innovation—hence a permanent process of internal change.

Three clusters of new religions are particularly illustrative of women's spiritual positions. The first, Espiritualismo Trinitario Mariano, is not a Mexican form of what is called Spiritualism elsewhere, but rather a genuine Mexican figuration. An ecstatic religion that emerged in 1866, Espiritualismo confers leadership on women at all levels of its organization: the *guía* (guide, highest authority), the *pluma de oro* (transcriber of the Lord's word), and the mediums are usually women.

Although Roque Rojas, a former seminarist, was almost certainly the founder, Damiana Oviedo is considered the founder by several of the *templos espiritualistas* (Lagarriga, 1991). A charismatic, divinely-inspired preacher, she is considered the first-ever *pedestal* (the verbal transmitter of the Lord's words and messages). She was not only inspired but influenced the structural shaping of Espiritualismo as it is conceived today (Ortiz, 1990). Other founding priestesses include Apolonia Ortiz, follower of Damiana, who founded today's largest and most influential *templo espiritualista* in Mexico City, El Templo del Medio Día. Its first guide was Manuela Dominguez (Ortiz, 1990).

The cosmology of Espiritualismo implies a gender distinction that precludes gender subordination. Its ethical commands effect considerable changes in gender relations: the male dominance of the outer society is not only strongly discouraged but penalized. Women and men are equal before the Lord. Men should collaborate with women on household chores, be deferential, share responsibility for domestic obligations toward children, and be supportive of the energy and time required—which sometimes verges on total absorption—by women's activities within the temple. It is not rare to observe, among the most devout women and their husbands, an inversion of Mexican gender roles (Marcos, 1991).

The second of the new religions, La Mexicanidad, fuses ancient Mesoamerican religious ideas with contemporary revivals and some Asian influences. It started in 1920 as Movimiento Confederado Restaurador del Anahuac among a select group of intellectuals led by a charismatic figure (generally male) and a council of elders. Believers in La Mexicanidad learn and teach Nahuatl language and philosophy and insist that the history of pre-Hispanic peoples, as presented by scholars, is biased and distorted. Anti-Catholics, they claim that their beliefs are simply a revival of the original Aztec religion. Their knowledge of it is based on revelatory experiences, while their recreated mythology places the Mexica or Aztec culture at the origins of all the other civilizations of the world (Gonzalez, 1996). Unfortunately, their innovative and selective use of Mesoamerican religious ideas tends to dispense with concepts of duality and thus of dual gender configurations. Consequently, the prominence of women in those religions has been minimized.

A new version of La Mexicanidad is known as Reginos. Its central mythic figure is a girl, Regina, who was killed during the student rebellions of 1968 when she allegedly returned to Mexico from Tibet with the mission of raising the spiritual awareness of her country. The Reginos mix Tibetan references with the teachings of the Olmec, Zapotec, Maya, and Nahua Guardians of the Traditions of Mexico. Ascribing to Mexican ancestry a planetary protagonism, they believe that the long-dormant sacred cosmic forces must be awakened in Mexico. Their mythic feminine hero seems to express the aspirations of contemporary women to play an active and leading role.

Finally, several versions of Pentecostalism have brought strict biblical interpretations mainly to Mexico's indigenous and urban poor (Masferrer, 1993). It is clear that women were the founders of this religious movement (Garma, 1992). Romana Valenzuela, who was converted while in Los Angeles, California, founded the first Pentecostal church in the north of Mexico in 1914. The first person to "speak in tongues" was also a woman. Today women are preachers and missionaries but seldom pastors. Regional and ethnic differences impinge on the position of women in Pentecostal churches (Bastian, 1990, De la Torre and Fortuny, 1991). Mayan Pentecostals (with indigenous influences) provide more access for women to positions of authority than do those in El Bajío (a region populated by conservative Catholics). Although some authors have insisted that the regimentation of alcohol consumption within Pentecostalism favors women, it is also true that its strict biblical interpretations limit them in a radical manner by casting them in a subservient, secondary role.

BIBLIOGRAPHY

Bastian, Jean-Pierre. "The Metamorphosis of Latin American Protestant Groups: A Socio-Historical Perspective." *Latin American Research Review* 28, no. 2 (1993): 33–61.

———. *Protestantismos y Modernidad Latinoamericana.* 1994.

De la Torre, Rene, and Patricia Fortuny. "La Mumer en 'La Luz del Mundo'." *Estudios sobre las Culturas Contemporaneas* 4, no. 12 (1991): 125–150.

Finkler, Kaja. *Spiritualist Healers in Mexico.* 1985.

Garma Navarro, Carlos. "Pentecostisme rural et urbain au Mexique: Differences et similitudes." *Social Compass* 39, no. 3 (1992): 389–400.

Goodman, Felicitas, Jeannette Henney, and Esther Pressel. *Trance, Healing, and Hallucination.* 1982.

Gonzalez, Yolotl. "The Revival of Mexican Religious: The Impact of Nativism." *Numen* 43 (1996): 1–31.

Lagarriga, Isabel. *Espiritualismo Trinitario Mariano.* Jalapa, 1991.

Marcos, Sylvia. "Women Healing Rituals and Popular Medicine in Mexico." *Concilium: International Review of Theology* 2 (1991): 108–121.

Masferrer, Elio. "Religious Transformations and Social Change in Latin America." *Religious Transformations and Socio-Political Change.* Edited by Luther Martin. Berlin, 1993.

Ortiz, Silvia. *Una religiosidad popular: El Espiritualismo Trinitario Mariano.* Mexico, 1990.

SYLVIA MARCOS

In South America

The "newness" of new religious movements in South America must be assessed within the context of the continent's complex religious history. This includes not only Catholicism, whose hegemony began with the Spanish and Portuguese conquests in the sixteenth century, but also the indigenous traditions that predated Catholicism in the New World and the African traditions that were introduced as a consequence of prolonged slave traffic. The impact of the nineteenth-century arrivals Protestantism and European Spiritism (which embodies a scientific approach to communication with the spirit world) became significant only in the twentieth century.

The rise of new religious movements has helped make the continent's religious landscape markedly more pluralistic from the late 1960s onward. An underlying cause has been the more tolerant attitude toward non-Catholic religions advocated by the Latin American Bishops' Conference subsequent to the Second Vatican Council (1963–1965). Catholic parishioners have adopted a more favorable view toward such traditions with the lowering of ecclesiastically imposed barriers against interreligious dialogue and experimentation.

Another factor in the rise of new religious movements—an overwhelmingly urban phenomenon—has been accelerating urbanization, as millions of South American women and men have left behind traditional rural ways of life to pursue better economic and educational opportunities in the cities. A minority has indeed achieved upward social mobility and concomitant exposure to new ideas in many spheres, including religion. But the vast majority of rural–urban migrants have found themselves crowded into bleak, impoverished shantytowns with scant hope for improvement in the quality of their lives.

This latter combination of socioeconomic and psychological deprivation has been pivotal for the explosive growth of South America's most widespread new religious movement, Pentecostalism, among the urban lower classes. Despite its traditional Protestant roots, Pentecostalism features a distinctive, exuberant style of worship, with the entire congregation exercising the "gifts of the Holy Spirit"—that is, ecstatic tongues, prophecy, visions, and miraculous healing. Interpretation of such manifestations by church leaders as being both prompted and controlled by the Holy Spirit opens a wider spectrum of participation to women than has been the case in either Catholicism or traditional Protestantism, although female Pentecostal pastors are still the exception. North American denominations such as the Assemblies of God and the Foursquare Gospel span the continent, but the greatest dynamism resides in the hundreds of locally generated Pentecostal churches that are constantly coming into existence.

A more recent addition to the array of new religious movements in South America is a cluster of traditions designated as Japanese New Religions (JNRs), a reflection of their post-1920 eclectic origins in Japan. JNR growth in South America has not been as widespread as that of Pentecostalism; prior to the 1970s their purview was limited to Japanese immigrant communities in Brazil and Peru, but subsequently hundreds of thousands of primarily middle-class members of non-Japanese descent have become affiliated in several countries. The appeal of the more successful JNR traditions, such as Seicho-no-ie (House of Blessing), Mahikari, and Seikai Kyusei Kyo (World Messianity), stems in part from their distinctive bodily rituals for transmitting divine energy for purposes of purification and healing. Lay women as well as men perform these rituals.

Not all new religious movements in South America originated abroad. Many are products of the dynamic interplay among the aforementioned traditions, with additional elements from Western occultism and Oriental traditions being assimilated through the esoteric literature popular in South American capitals since the 1970s. Prominent themes include holistic approaches to healing and the environment, channeling of cosmic energy, and communication with an eclectic array of spirit beings. In Venezuela, for example, the cult of Maria Lionza blends elements from indigenous traditions with European Spiritism, invoking not only the spirits of various national folk heroes but African *orixas* (divine spirits), as well. The Brazilian group Santo Daime focuses on the ritual consumption of *ayahuasca*, a hallucinogenic beverage long utilized by shamans among Amazonian peoples; part of the group's current appeal among the urban elite is its environmentalist aura. The Valley of the Dawn, a spiritualist community founded near Brasilia in the 1960s by a female truck driver, claims to have initiated tens of thousands of male and female mediums; its healing ceremonies draw upon an eclectic melange of symbols, including crosses, the Star of David, and pyramids.

Undoubtedly, this recent flourishing of new religious movements in South America constitutes one of the most innovative chapters in the continent's five-hundred-year saga of interreligious encounters and religious dynamism.

BIBLIOGRAPHY

Brusco, Elizabeth E. *The Reformation of Machismo: Evangelical Conversion and Gender in Colombia.* 1995.

Burdick, John. "Gossip and Secrecy: Women's Articulation of Domestic Conflict in Three Religions of Urban Brazil." *Sociological Analysis* 51, no. 2 (Summer 1990): 153–170.

Clarke, Peter B. "The Cultural Impact of New Religions in Latin and Central America with Special Reference to Japanese New Religions." *Journal of Latin American Cultural Studies* 4, no. 1 (June 1995): 117–126.

García Gacídia, Nelly. *Posesión y ambivalencia en el culto a María Lionza: notas para una tipología de los cultos de posesión existentes en la América del Sur.* Maracaibo, 1987.

Mariz, Cecília Loreto. *Coping with Poverty: Pentecostals and Christian Base Communities in Brazil.* 1994.

Muel-Dreyfus, Francine and Arakcy Martins-Rodrigues. "Reincarnations: note de recherche sur une secte spirite de Brasília." *Actes de la Recherche en Sciences Sociales* 62–63 (June 1986): 118–134.

Pollak-Eltz, Angelina. "Magico-Religious Movements and Social Change in Venezuela." *Journal of Caribbean Studies* 2, nos. 2 and 3 (Fall–Winter 1981): 162–180.

Soares, Luís Eduardo. "O Santo Daime no contexto da nova consciência religiosa." In *Sinais dos tempos: diversidade religiosa no Brasil.* Edited by Leilah Landim. Rio de Janeiro, 1990.

ROBERT T. CARPENTER

Nudity

Nudity is a multivalent symbol, representing both shame and innocence, depravity and fecundity, divine presence and human sinfulness. This variety of meanings depends not only on the gender of the naked body in a specific ritual or text but also on the sociocultural conditions that make possible a range of meanings in a given context.

Archaeological discoveries of naked female figurines with exaggerated reproductive organs (such as the Venus of Willendorf) suggest a link between female nudity and fecundity reaching back to Paleolithic times. But while such figures were believed to promote fertility in ancient Near Eastern cultures, images of a nude woman with a horned cap represented more demonic figures, such as Lilith, the fallen woman of Jewish legend who was said to frighten pregnant women into miscarriage (Apostolos-Cappadona, 1996).

Associations between female nudity and human fecundity are also evident in India, where women employ ritual nudity to increase fertility. At the temple of Hanuman in Bombay, women undress and embrace the monkey god to increase their chances of conception (Phillips, 1983). Ritual nudity is also used to improve agricultural production in India. In Manipur women strip themselves and plough at night in an effort to end a drought. Whereas female nudity is meant to shock Indra (the rain god) into pity in the case of drought, male nudity is typically used to appeal to Indra for restraint in the case of flood. This discrepancy may reflect a broader cultural tendency to associate women with abundance and men with control (Sharma, 1987; Phillips, 1983).

The ritualizing use of nudity to call on supernatural powers is also practiced in magic and witchcraft. Scholars of religion cite myriad examples of the magical uses of female exposure as both a preventative and a remedy for sickness and calamity. Examples range from Pliny's remark (Hist. nat. 28:23) that the course of storms may be altered by women baring themselves, to the case of Russian peasant girls in 1905 ploughing at midnight wearing only their slips in an attempt to ward off cholera (Sharma, 1987; Phillips, 1983). The paucity of examples of male nudity engaged for magical purposes may relate to the symbolic association between the female body and the mysterious powers of the universe. Such meanings are activated in Wiccan rituals, where nudity is used to release the body's magical forces, which clothing ordinarily impedes (Walker, 1983).

The nexus between female nudity and heterodoxy appears in the artistic and literary traditions of Western Christianity. Most visual and verbal images of female nudity draw on the legacy of Eve, whose bare body serves as a literary or iconographical device for tying female nudity to temptation and death. Male authors and artists emphasized Eve's initiative in the Fall, making her not only the mother of sin but also the prototypical woman: seductive and seduced. According to Margaret Miles, female nakedness is the primary artistic convention for signaling the danger of "woman." Unlike the male nude in Christian art, whose body symbolizes power, self-knowledge, and the glory of God, the naked woman frequently becomes a cipher for shame.

The shame associated with female nakedness is both reinforced and contested in the accounts of early Christian martyrs. Whereas male nudity is rarely mentioned in these texts, depictions of women stripped naked before cheering crowds are common (Miles). Such images reflected prominent social views of female bodies as sexual objects. Women in these accounts, however, use their nakedness to resist such meanings and the male authority they presume. The Syrian martyr Mahya tells the ruler who ordered her stripped, "It is to your shame . . . that you have done this; I am not ashamed myself" (quoted in Miles, p. 58). Centuries later, such shamelessness is tamed as male church leaders interpret these accounts in ways that glorify the female martyrs' modesty and sacrifice (Burrus, 1996).

The sexual meanings of female nakedness are simultaneously subverted and reinscribed in another early Christian practice, that of naked baptism. In this rite, the naked body was divested of its sexual meanings and converted into a site of religious subjectivity. For men and women alike, the removal of clothing in baptism symbolized the stripping of one's former socialization and the rebirth into a new life in Christ. The prelapsarian innocence and equality that naked baptism symbolized, however, competed with the ritual's stabilizing function, namely, the maintenance of the early church's patriarchal order. Naked women were not only last to enter the baptismal font (following men and children), but male authorities ordered their hair to be loosened to signify penitence and impurity (Miles).

The connection between nudity and the presumed impurity of the female body is both affirmed and questioned in Jainism. From its beginnings in the sixth century B.C.E., Jainism promoted the pursuit of salvation through extreme asceticism, including the practice of nakedness to signify nonattachment. Though women were attracted to the egalitarian impulses of Jainism, their spiritual status remained in question for reasons that came to the fore in debates about the role of nudity in salvation. By 80 C.E. these debates split Jainism into two groups, the Digambara and the Śvetāmbara. Both groups agreed that ascetic nudity was impossible for women; they disagreed, however, as to whether nudity was required for the attainment of salvation. By insisting that nudity was necessary for achieving spiritual liberation, the Digambaras denied the possibility of female salvation. By asserting that nudity was not essential for the attainment of such release, the Śvetāmbaras left open the possibility of female enlightenment (Balbir, 1994; Jaini, 1991; Dundas, 1992).

BIBLIOGRAPHY

Apostolos-Cappadona, Diane. "Nudity." In *Encyclopedia of Women in Religious Art*. 1996.

Balbir, Nalini. "Women in Jainism." *Religion and Women*. Edited by Arvind Sharma. 1994.

Burrus, Virginia. "Naked Girls, Shame and Shamelessness in Early Christian Martyrdom Tales." Paper presented at the annual American Academy of Religion conference, New Orleans. 1996.

Dundas, Paul. *The Jains*. 1992.

Jaini, Padmanabh S. *Gender and Salvation: Jaina Debates on the Spiritual Liberation of Women*. 1991.

Miles, Margaret R. *Carnal Knowing: Female Nakedness and Religious Meaning in the Christian West*. 1989.

Phillips, David. "Nudity." In *Man, Myth and Magic: The Illustrated Encyclopedia of Mythology, Religion and the Unknown*. Edited by R. Cavendish. 1983.

Pliny the Elder. *Natural History*. With an English translation by H. Rackham. 1938–1963.

Sharma, Arvind. "Nudity." In *The Encyclopedia of Religion*. Edited by Mircea Eliade. 1987.

Walker, Barbara. "Nakedness." In *The Woman's Encyclopedia of Myths and Secrets*. Edited by B. Walker. 1983.

See also Jainism.

MICHELLE LELWICA

Nugua

Also known as Nugua Shi, Nuwa, and Nuxi, Nugua is an important figure in classical Chinese mythology. Nugua is a powerful, independent deity, creator and savior of humankind. In the *Explanations of Social Customs* (*Feng su tongyi*, compiled second century C.E.), Nugua forms humans from earth: she molds the aristocracy from yellow earth and the rest of humankind by dragging a cord through the mud. In the *Huainanzi*, a Taoist text compiled in the second century B.C.E., she brings order to a world in danger of destruction. When the supports holding up the heavens collapsed, rending the sky and threatening annihilation, she melted together the five-colored stones to repair heaven and cut off the feet of a giant sea turtle for props at the corners of the earth. Nugua is depicted as having a woman's head and a long scaly tail instead of legs; she frequently holds the knotted cord and builder's compasses, indicating her creative powers.

Nugua is also the inventer of marriage, instructing humans in that institution after she created them. She and her consort Fuxi are patrons of marriage. A much later source from the ninth century C.E. demotes Nugua from creator goddess to first human: in *A Treatise on Extraordinary and Strange Things* (*Duyi zhi* by Li Rong), Nugua and her brother Fuxi request permission from Heaven to marry and thus become the progenitors of humankind.

Although a powerful deity in ancient times, Nugua's status diminished through the centuries, in part owing to the patriarchal ethic of postclassical China. It appears that by the Tang dynasty (618–907 C.E.) Nugua was not remembered in cults but rather in poetical references and toponymy (place names).

BIBLIOGRAPHY

Anne Birrell, *Chinese Mythology* (1993), presents the various Nugua myths and their sources and analyzes and interprets methodological issues of Chinese myths in general. Edward H. Schafer, *The Divine Woman* (1973), not only provides an excellent account of the various portrayals of Nugua in literature but also traces the change in her status and gradual demotion in Chinese mythology from powerful goddess to subservient woman. A good overview is provided in Derk Bodde, "Myths of Ancient China," in *Essays on Chinese Civilization,* edited by Charles Le Blanc and Dorothy Borei (1981). Also see Chen Tianshui, *Zhongguo gudai shenhua* (1988), pp. 38x–44.

See also **Marriage and Singleness: In Asian Religions**.

JENNIFER OLDSTONE-MOORE

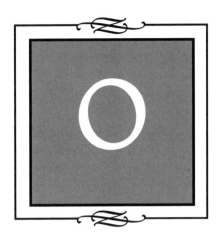

Occultism

Though based on concepts and practices that date from early antiquity, *occultism* as a term used in the West dates from the end of the nineteenth century and refers to a large number of practices ranging from divination and alchemy to magic and occult medicine that are based conceptually on the doctrine of correspondences. According to this principle, the world both visible and invisible is a web of influences, in which like influences like and everything can be manipulated according to one's knowledge and understanding of the nature of the analogies and homologies that make up this web. Today, the distinction is made between esotericism as a philosophy and occultism as the practices based on it.

According to Western occultism, the world is understandable as an interplay of four elements (air, fire, water, earth) and two qualities (male, female) that can be used to define everything else—for example, fire, male, sun, positive, hot, dry; and water, female, moon, negative, cold, wet. Furthermore, human sexuality and sex have served as core metaphors whereby male is active and the agent of change and female is the passive subject acted upon (contrast the Magical and Priestess cards of the tarot). Yet the woman's role does not end there. She is also a metaphor, a tool, an agent, a subject, an initiator, a patron, a muse, a catalyst, and, finally, an occultist in her own right.

From its beginnings, alchemy has been marked by an absence of exclusiveness based on social, professional, or gender differences. Hellenistic Egyptian alchemy was developed by Greek-speaking men and women, of which three human women (Maria Prophetissa, Isis,

and Cleopatra) are identified by name as major authors and inventors of technical equipment. Cleopatra the alchemist, author of *Chrysopeia* (On Gold Making, third–fourth century C.E.) invented the alembic (apparatus for distillation), used the first known representation of the Ouroboros (a snake biting its own tail, which signifies the unity of all matter), and presented in print for the first time the gnostic trinity of father-gold, mother-silver, and son-quicksilver. In later texts this trinity becomes the bases of all alchemical work: the marriage of sun and moon uniting soul and spirit and their subsequent transmutation into the hemaphroditic child realizes the gnostic hermetic goal of wedding Sophia (Wisdom) to her divine lover. In this, women's roles on the symbolic as well as on the physical plane are often equal to those of men, as exemplified by partnerships of married alchemists such as Nicolla and Pernella Flamel of fourteenth-century France.

In the Kabbalah, a system of Jewish mystical thought that originated in southern France and Spain in the twelfth to thirteenth centuries, the greatest catastrophe that can be imagined is the destruction of the unity within the godhead; the separation of the Shekhinah, the female manifestation of God, from her husband. This was precisely the tragic consequence of Adam's original sin in the Garden of Eden. Though undoing that sin is traditionally a male endeavor, women still figure at the level of metaphor in that Kabbalah texts.

In the occult practice known as Ceremonial Magic, the Anima Mundi or World Soul has since the time of Robert Fludd (1574–1637; English physician and Rosicrucian) been considered the female with whom the male magician must interact. It took Dion Fortune (born Violet Mary Firth, 1891–1946; English occultist

A fortune-teller reads the future in the arrangement of tea leaves in the bottom of a cup, Sweden, 1855 (Hulton-Deutsch Collection/Corbis).

and founder of the Fraternity of the Inner Life) to formulate a notion of effective magic as the interplay of male and female energies, in which the female is the operator and the male the anchor and source. In contrast, Aleister Crowley (1875–1947; English occultist who believed that the destiny of man was to engender the gods) perceived women as the channels through which magical power could be accessed by the Magus (master magician); his supreme magical goal, "love under will," is the passionate union of opposites in which magician and scarlet woman beget the divine child through means of transhuman alchemy.

Today, women are often perceived as operators of occult practices (tarot card readers, channels, spirit mediums) and rarely as magicians or theorists of magic. This view of women does not take into account their real numbers and importance within modern magical orders such as Freemasonry, Rosicrucianism, and the Ordo Templi Orientis; the modern magical revival evidenced by Wicca, neowitchcraft, and neopaganism; or their important contributions to New Age formulations of effective visualization and practical magic.

BIBLIOGRAPHY

Bednarowski, Mary Farrell. "Modern Esoteric Spirituality." *Crosscurrents* 43, no. 4 (1993): 549.

Blavatsky, H. P. *Isis Unveiled.* 1877.

Burland, C. A. *The Arts of the Alchemists.* 1967.

Corsetti, Jean-Paul. *Histoire de l'ésotérisme et des sciences occultes.* Paris, 1992.

Couliano, Ioan P. *Eros and Magic in the Renaissance.* Translated by Margaret Cook. 1987.

Crowley, Aleister. *Moonchild.* 1929.

Fortune, Dion. *Moon Magic.* 1976.

———. *The Sea Priestess.* 1938. Reprint, 1978.

Goodison, Lucy. *Moving Heaven and Earth: Sexuality, Spirituality and Social Change.* 1992.

Greer, Mary K. *Women of the Golden Dawn: Rebels and Priestesses.* 1994.

Houque, Patrick. *Eve, Éros, Élohim: La femme, l'érotisme, le sacré.* Paris, 1982.

Hutin, Serge. *Histoire de l'alchimie: De la science archaique à la philosophie occulte.* Verviers, 1971.

Kerr, Howard, and Charles L. Crow, eds. *The Occult in America: New Historical Perspectives.* 1983.

Leek, Sybil. *Diary of a Witch.* 1975.

———. *My Life in Astrology.* 1972.

Luck, George. *Arcana Mundi: Magic and the Occult in the Greek and Roman Worlds.* 1985.

Simon, Sylvie. *The Tarot and Art: Mysticism and Divination.* 1988.

Tertullian. *De Cultu Feminarum.*

Tester, Jim. *A History of Western Astrology.* 1987.

Wissinger, Catherine, ed. *Women's Leadership in Marginal Religions: Explorations Outside the Mainstream.* 1993.

See also **Alchemy; Magic; Neopaganism; Theosophy; Wicca.**

LUCIE DUFRESNE

Oceanic Religions

Polynesia and Micronesia

Most of the islands of Polynesia are located within an immense triangle that stretches out across the Pacific Ocean from the Hawaiian Islands to Easter Island and south to New Zealand. The total population at the time of first contact with Europeans has been estimated at about 520,000. The area of Oceania known as Micronesia is situated to the east and southeast of the Philippines. Its population during the same period was about 180,000. Within each region the cultures and languages, despite much variation, were closely related. There was also a more distant relationship between Polynesia and Micronesia.

POLYNESIA

In societies throughout this region, a basic distinction was made between the state of being *tapu* (sacred, set apart, under religious restriction) and that of being *noa* (ordinary, everyday, profane, unrestricted). These words, or sometimes equivalent terms, were applied in numerous contexts to persons, events, places, and things. In social and political life, and in religious ritual, the conditions of *tapu* and *noa* were complementary and, therefore, of equal importance.

Women were frequently *tapu* for particular reasons, as with women of high rank, or during illness or childbirth, and a married woman was *tapu* in that she could not be approached by men other than her husband. Intrinsically and in general, however, men were *tapu* and women were *noa*. Women's main powers and responsibilities were seen as involving the continuance of life and the patterns of day-to-day existence, that which is *noa,* rather than the more specialized and isolated tasks of men.

In the nature of things everyday life tends to be taken for granted, but nothing in Polynesia was beyond the reach of religion. The condition of being *noa,* as possessed by women, was a powerful religious force. This was revealed on the many occasions when it became necessary to remove a state of *tapu,* or diminish it. In the Marquesas Islands and among the New Zealand Maori, for instance, a newly completed house had to be made safe to use by having some of its *tapu* removed, and for this the ritual participation of a woman was necessary. The Maori procedure was that a high-ranking woman and the officiating priest went into the house together at dawn, appropriate ceremonies were performed, then the waiting people entered with much celebration.

Yet the interplay of male and female powers was more intricate than even this example suggests. Among the Maori (and other Polynesian peoples also), both *tapu* and *noa* were possessed by each person, in that every individual had a *tapu* (male, right) side and a *noa* (female, left) side. On this occasion, therefore, as the priest entered the house he put his left (*noa*) foot over the threshold first. Female powers were so important that men needed to share in them (just as women possessed their share of male powers, located on their right side).

While religious traditions vary from one island group to another, the origins of the universe and humanity always involve the interplay of male and female powers.

Often, as in Tahiti, Hawaii, and New Zealand, sky and earth are persons, with the sky male and the earth female—and since these two are the primal ancestors of all humans, men now are like the sky and women like the earth. While this concept put men in the superior position, it also acknowledged women's fertility and energies as being the basis upon which life depended.

Usually it was men who became religious specialists and performed the rituals that propitiated the gods and ensured people's well-being, but Tongan and Samoan shamans, for instance, could be male or female. And women did in some instances approach female deities on their own behalf. In Tikopia the women performed certain ritual tasks with no men present, being identified on these occasions with Te Atua Fafine, or the Goddess.

In Hawaii, women who beat out tapa cloth had Lauhuki as their patron deity, while those who printed the cloth had La'a-hana. Some women performed rituals to propitiate the fierce Pele, who lived in the volcanic fires on the island of Hawaii. In a building just outside the great ceremonial complexes known as *luakini,* a group of high-born women made offerings to Papa, the first female ancestor, and when appropriate they entered the *luakini* to remove excess *tapu* from warriors returned from battle.

Numerous other women play important parts in religious tradition and are often referred to in ritual chants and songs. The best known is the beautiful Hina, whose adventures in the earliest times reveal the nature of women's roles and responsibilities. Hina was often believed to live in the moon, where she could be seen industriously beating her tapa cloth. Sometimes Hina marries a handsome chief, Tinirau, while in other stories she is seduced by an eel. When this eel is killed, its head grows into the first coconut palm.

MICRONESIA

As in Polynesia, men in Micronesia were intrinsically *tapu* (under religious restriction) while women were intrinsically unrestricted. Most religious experts were men, but women were specialists in healing rituals, rituals to make people fall in love, and rituals to make gardens flourish. Some women were among the mediums that communicated with spirits of the dead.

In myths of origin most ancestors are men, but there are some important women. The different varieties of cultivated plants come directly or indirectly from celestial beings who are usually women. In the Caroline Islands in particular, some societies were organized into totemic clans believed to have been founded by female ancestors who took the form of either animals (such as turtles, porpoises, and owls) or plants (bananas, yams,

Mapuana de Silva performs an ancient hula dance for the goddess Pele at the Halemaumau firepit, Volcanoes National Park, Hawaii, 1991 (Richard A. Cooke/Corbis).

and others). Descent was matrilineal, traced through the female line. Members of the turtle clan, for instance, regarded the turtle as their original ancestor and were strictly forbidden to eat it.

In parts of the Carolines the goddess Ligoupup was thought to have always existed, and to have created the world without a husband. She lies sleeping under the earth, and when she stirs there are earthquakes. Her son is lord of the nether regions and the sea, while her daughter married a god in the sky and had a son who became ruler of heaven and inventor of all knowledge.

BIBLIOGRAPHY

POLYNESIA

Early written records include many accounts by Western voyagers and missionaries, and great numbers of manuscripts written by Polynesians in the nineteenth century. Although a promising start was made by nineteenth-century and early twentieth-century historians, there was later relatively little scholarly interest in this material, and religious ideas have been especially neglected. The many twentieth-century works of ethnography are generally useful, although they describe acculturated societies, and some have little to say about women and religion.

Most of the works listed here have extensive bibliographies.

Beckwith, Martha. *Hawaiian Mythology.* 1940. Reprint, 1970.

Firth, Raymond. *The Work of the Gods in Tikopia.* 1967.

Handy, E. S. Craighill. *The Native Culture in the Marquesas.* 1923.

———. *Polynesian Religion.* 1927.

Herda, Phyllis, Jennifer Terrell, and Niel Gunson, eds. *Tongan Culture and History.* 1990.

Johansen, J. Prytz. *The Maori and His Religion in Its Non-ritualistic Aspects.* 1954.

Oliver, Douglas L. *Ancient Tahitian Society.* 3 vols. 1974.

Orbell, Margaret. *The Illustrated Encyclopedia of Māori Myth and Legend.* 1995.

MICRONESIA

There is no comprehensive study of Micronesian religion. The two authors listed here are the main English-language authorities on the subject. Both give detailed bibliographical information.

Lessa, William A. "Micronesian Religions: An Overview." In *The Encyclopedia of Religion.* Edited by Mircea Eliade. 1987.

Luolama, Katharine. "Micronesian Religions: Mythic Themes." In *The Encyclopedia of Religion.* Edited by Mircea Eliade. 1987.

See also **Hina; Pele.**

MARGARET ORBELL

Australia

In long ago, known as the Dreamtime, the pioneering ancestors, known as Dreamings, traveled across the formless, shapeless, featureless land. At certain places they paused, to rest, eat, make love, fight, confer, give birth, die, perform ceremonies. Their power entered the ground. Their deeds were inscribed on the landscape. Here a pile of rocks indicates the place where the dingo had her pups, while the low-lying hill is the resting body of the ancestral emu. There the red streaks on the cliff recall the blood of the battle between kangaroo and intruders. These sacred sites stand as testimony to the power of the ancestors. All plants and animals, the wind and rain, the stars and sky have a Dreaming, and it is the responsibility of their descendants, as manifest in the many different groups of Aboriginal peoples across Australia, to maintain the law their ancestors established; to keep the stories alive through ceremonial reenactment of the founding drama; and to protect their places.

Nineteenth-century observers of Aboriginal societies such as Baldwin Spencer and F. J. Gillen (*The Native Tribes of Central Australia,* 1899) paid little attention to women and with the notable exceptions of twentieth-century monographs by Phyllis Kaberry (*Aboriginal Woman, Sacred and Profane,* 1939), Catherine Berndt (*Women's Changing Ceremonies in Northern Australia,* 1950), Jane Goodale (*Tiwi Wives,* 1971), and Diane Bell (*Daughters of the Dreaming,* 1983; rev. ed., 1993), Aboriginal religion was treated as the business of men and as an important way in which men exercised power over women. W. Lloyd Warner, for instance, in *A Black Civilization* (1937) wrote of women as making little sacred progress through life but remaining largely profane, while C. W. M. Hart and Arnold Pilling in *The Tiwi of Northern Australia* (1960) wrote of old women as hags and their camps as hotbeds of gossip.

These learned gentlemen, who spent little time working with women and who most certainly never attended any women-only ceremonies, were very sure of their vision. Women's activities were magic, not religion. These writers were little concerned with the micro affairs of hearth and home of woman the gatherer, in favor of the macro concerns of man the hunter. Observations from one region were generalized for the whole continent. However, the actual situation is rather more complex. There is enormous variation in the practices and beliefs from the tropical north to temperate south, through the central deserts to the rich coastal lands. At the time of British settlement in 1788, some three hundred different languages were spoken. Not surprisingly, the way in which the sex division of labor for these hunter-gatherers was represented in religious beliefs and practice varied enormously also.

Unfortunately, little will ever be known of the women's religious lives at the time of first contact. Disease, dispossession, the breakup of families and the heavy hand of missionaries took an enormous toll. But a great deal is known of the women in the north and central regions of Australia through the work of women researchers, and the process of land claims where Aboriginal women have testified regarding their rights and responsibilities in land and in upholding religious values of their societies. It is becoming clear the indigenous women played a vital ceremonial role. For instance, in the desert regions of central Australia, Warlpiri, Pitjantjatjara, Warumungu, and Aranda women have ceremonies that are closed to men, where women teach girls the business of being a woman; where women celebrate in song, body painting, dance, and story their Dreamtime heritage, their rights and responsibilities in land, and their determination to keep their law alive; where women may preempt, thwart, and challenge the activities, decisions, and desires of men. Central themes concern the relations of the living to the ancestors, health, and the management of emotions. In these ceremonies women work to maintain harmonious relations between people and with the land; to "grow up" the land, just as they "grow up" children.

Women also participate in ceremonies where both men and women are present. Here it is apparent that the structuring principles of men's and women's ceremonies rely on the same kin relations to land and the Dreamings. Women also make appearances during male initiation. It is the latter that has been deemed the high point of Aboriginal ceremonial life, but as women field-workers have begun to work with women, it has become apparent that women have a parallel religious life that hitherto has been invisible to male observers and to which Aboriginal men have not called attention, because it is not their business to do so. Each respects what the other knows. Further, it is dangerous to speak of the business of another.

The nature of the relationship between women's ritual knowledge and practices and that of the men has been the subject of lively debate, as has what the existence of women's secret and sacred ceremonies means for the understanding of gender relations in indigenous societies. Here, case material from Australia has been used to make a variety of arguments. There are those, like Eleanor Leacock, who argue that the historical transformation of small-scale societies through incorporation in larger political networks has undermined women's standing; and others, like Nancy Munn in *Walbiri Iconography* (1973), who argue that women, despite their separate and distinctive contribution, remain under the control of men. All agree that there is a degree of complementarity, interdependence, and negotiation in ritual activity. It is perhaps premature and inappropriate to make sweeping generalizations. There is still a great deal of work to be done in the field and a pressing need to pursue serious feminist theorizing of existing research.

Aborigines constitute less than two percent of the Australian population of eighteen million. About two thirds live in cities and country towns. Over the past several decades, in these more settled parts of the country, Aboriginal cultural revitalization is evident. With beneficial legislation in place, people in the longer-settled south have sought protection for their sacred places. However, it has been extremely difficult for women to be taken seriously in this process, and too often they are consulted so late in the planning of development projects that their claims regarding the need to protect their sacred sites are seen as strategic fabrications. Further, because their stories were not recorded in the early days, they have little to substantiate their claims in the written record. If there is one lesson to be learned from the struggles of Aboriginal women to have their religious beliefs and practices acknowledged and respected, it is that they face both sexism and racism from both church and state.

BIBLIOGRAPHY

Bell, Diane. "Aboriginal Women's Religion: A Shifting Law of the Land." In *Today's Woman in World Religions.* Edited by Arvind Sharma. 1993.

———. "Choose Your Mission Wisely: Christian Colonials and Aboriginal Marital Arrangements on the Northern Frontier." In *Aboriginal Australians and Christianity.* Edited by Deborah Bird Rose and Tony Swain. 1988.

———. "In the Tracks of the Munga–Munga." In *Claiming Our Rights: Australian Feminist Essays in Religion.* Edited by Penny Magee and Morny Joy. 1994.

DIANE BELL

Oral Tradition

Oral traditions, most simply, are those traditions communicated by word of mouth; they are most frequently identified in opposition to written traditions. The implication of the term is often that oral traditions belong to nonliterate communities; in this schema, once a verbal tradition is written (whether in composition or for preservation), it is no longer considered oral. This oppositional dichotomy between written and oral, literate and nonliterate texts and performance styles (such as that articulated in Albert Lord's *Singer of Tales,* 1960), is challenged, however, by an examination of verbal traditions in cultures in which oral and written traditions may share a performance repertoire and interwoven histories. The boundaries between the two become blurred with consideration of traditions that are orally composed or performed but written down for preservation, ritual recitation of written texts, and oral traditions (including song, tale, drama, and commentary) that coexist with and interpretively frame written traditions. Texts that exist at one or more of these levels may be identified as oral, along a continuum of oral-written traditions.

The term *tradition* carries different implications in various academic disciplines; it may imply transmission or continuity across generational lines, a shared body of knowledge within a religious community or cultural group in a particular historical time period, or certain features of form and content that identify a verbal, ritual, or artistic genre. Tradition may also carry the implication of a range of related verbal and ritual genres that contextualize each other. Thus we may speak of a Rāmāyaṇa "tradition" in Hinduism (rather than a Rāmāyaṇa "text") that would imply written, oral, and visual variants of the narrative itself, oral communication about the narrative that may be passed down from generation to generation, as well as its various performance genres. Thus, not all oral verbal communication are necessarily traditions, and not all traditions are verbal or oral.

In the study of religion, significant attention has been paid to particular kinds of oral traditions, such as publicly performed (often by males) rituals of religious communities that do not have written sacred texts, or public oral recitation of written sacred texts. Other kinds of oral tradition have, however, until recently, been absent in the study of religion, such as oral commentarial traditions by nonspecialists; performance of folk traditions; and domestic, nonpublic, or informal performance genres. Many of these traditions are performed by women and nonelite men, who may not traditionally have access to literacy or a community's written or oral sacred canonical texts. Their voices have often been ignored in the study of religion because of preconceptions—held both by scholars studying particular religious traditions and by indigenous members of the religious communities themselves—of who and what counts as authoritative, of what kinds of oral traditions are worth listening to and recording.

Oral traditions may or may not reference a written text. Linguist Shirley Heath identifies oral performances in which a written text is integral to the social interactions at hand as "literacy events" (1982). The written text is central in some way, although it may not actually be read. The range of such literacy events includes recitation genres of written sacred texts (such as Qur'anic recitation); sermons and other oral commentarial traditions on a particular text; rituals honoring, worshiping, or otherwise manipulating written texts; dramatic enactments of sacred texts; and oral narratives, proverbs, songs, and conversational genres in which reference to the written text is central. The written text is, in these traditions, interpreted and reshaped in an oral mode; and it is often through this mode that members of a textual religious community come to "know" that text, rather than reading it silently from a book. Scholars of performance are interested in the ways in which the historical, social, and performative contexts of these events frame and shape a particular community's or individual's experiences and interpretations of the written text.

Literacy events are often highly gendered; that is, women's interactions with written sacred texts may differ quite dramatically from men's, depending on levels of literacy and their access to authoritative performances and interpretations of those texts. For example, in women's Rāmāyaṇa singing groups in central India these literacy events feminize the tradition: literate singers through commentary on the written text whose verses they sing, and nonliterate singers through selection of female-centered events and elaboration of female characters in their orally composed songs (Flueck-iger, 1991). Other examples of gendered literacy events are those analyzed by folklorist Elaine Lawless (1988). Her study of sermons and oral life stories of female Pentecostal preachers in Missouri documents the ways in which these women carefully construct (even if unconsciously) both their life narratives and sermons so as to frame positively their activity of public preaching (which, according to Pentecostal literal interpretation of Biblical texts, should be denied to women). Further, Lawless finds that their orally composed sermons share themes and images that characterize particularly female Pentecostal preaching and experience.

In the Hindu tradition a characteristically female ritual and textual event is the reading or oral performance of *vrat kathās*, stories of the power of fasts or vows that are read or told at rituals in which women are keeping the same fast or vow central to the narrative. Whether the texts are oral or written, the performance of *vrat kathās* is a means through which women assert their ritual power to affect their own lives and those of their family. These rituals and orally performed textual traditions are central to Hindu women's lives; however, perhaps because they are so commonplace and are primarily women's traditions, they are rarely included in the study of Hindu sacred texts and tradition.

Other kinds of oral traditions stand independently from written texts. For those religious traditions that do not have a central written sacred text or texts, there may be an authoritative or foundational oral tradition, such as an oral epic for certain African or Central Asian traditions or a genre of shamanistic dream narrative for Native American traditions. These kinds of oral traditions are usually publicly performed, and their significance traditionally has been acknowledged by scholars who study those religious communities. Because traditions are oral, however, does not mean that they are equally accessible to all members of the community as performers or audience members. There are culturally determined rules of performance: who may be the performers or the audience members of what kinds of oral traditions, as well as when, where, and at what time of day, month, and year these may be performed. Women's access to canonical, authoritative oral traditions has often been limited.

Folklorist Marta Weigle (1982) argues, that to learn the perspective and experiences of women (and, it could be added, other nonelite members of a religious community), one may need to look at different kinds of speech genres or oral traditions, whose performances occur in contexts and places different from those of oral traditions identified as authoritative. She quotes the frame of an Inuit woman's life story told to a male an-thropologist in 1931: "I am just an ordinary woman, knowing nothing from myself. I have never been ill and seldom dream. So I have never seen visions. . . . But what you have asked me about . . . is something that is known to every child that has been hushed to sleep with a story by its mother. . . . It is from them we all have our knowledge, for children never forget. And now my story begins" (p. 285). The Inuit woman contrasts two types of knowledge: the authoritative shamanistic dream-vision, access to which is limited to the religious specialist, and the knowledge passed down to every child through his or her mother's bedtime storytelling. These female storytelling traditions also shape religious experience and construct a religious worldview, yet they have often been ignored by scholars of religion.

Feminist scholars of oral tradition (folklorists, anthropologists, and an increasing number of historians of religion) have been particularly interested in women's personal narratives and life histories as sources for understanding women's experiences of and negotiations with, sometimes resistance to, dominant cultural and religious ideologies. Although the content of such narratives may be idiosyncratic or individualistic, their form and general contour is "traditional." That is, there is a cultural construction of what is worth telling and when and where such narratives are appropriately performed; such constructions are passed down across generational lines, even as they shift with each individual telling. Laurel Kendall (1988), Karen McCarthy Brown (1991), and Benedicte Grima (1992) have written excellent studies that focus on women's life histories and personal narratives. Lila Abu-Lughod's (1993) juxtaposition of Bedouin women's personal narratives with "standard" religious prescriptions and images and themes often associated with Muslim Arab society (such as polygyny, patrilineality, honor, and shame) reveals the complex negotiations of individual women's religious lives and practice in their own words.

Finally, other genres of oral tradition that have long been the jurisdiction of folklorists and anthropologists but that have gained the attention of historians of religions are folk songs and narratives. In their study of North Indian women's folksongs, sung in both ritual and nonritual contexts, anthropologists Gloria Goodwin Raheja and Ann Grodzins Gold (1994) found that these women's folk traditions often express alternative or co-existing ideologies of gender and kinship to those articulated in Hindu male-dominated, textual ideologies. The relationship between these songs and women's lived experience is complex; the emphasis of this book is on the multiple and strategic uses and meanings of words by women in various contexts.

To identify and understand multivocality, and to hear women's voices and understand their negotiations within religious traditions, feminist scholars of religion and anthropologists are beginning to take notice of and analyze a wide spectrum of women's oral traditions.

BIBLIOGRAPHY

Abu-Lughod, Lila. "Can There Be a Feminist Ethnography?" *Women and Performance* 5, no. 1 (1990): 7–27.

———. *Writing Women's Worlds: Bedouin Stories.* 1993.

Brown, Karen McCarthy. *Mama Lola: A Vodou Priestess in Brooklyn.* 1991.

Flueckiger, Joyce Burkhalter, and Laurie J. Sears. *Boundaries of the Text: Epic Performances in South and Southeast Asia.* 1991.

Goody, Jack. *The Interface Between the Written and the Oral.* 1987.

Grima, Benedicte. *The Performance of Emotion Among Paxtun Women: "The Misfortunes Which Have Befallen Me."* 1992.

Heath, Shirley. "Protean Shapes in Literacy Events: Ever-Shifting Oral and Literate Traditions." In *Spoken and Written Language: Exploring Orality and Literacy.* Edited by Deborah Tannen. 1982.

Kendall, Laurel. *The Life and Hard Times of a Korean Shaman: Of Tales and the Telling of Tales.* 1988.

Lawless, Elaine. *Handmaidens of the Lord: Pentecostal Women Preachers and Traditional Religion.* 1988.

Ong, Walter. *Orality and Literacy: The Technologizing of the Word.* 1982.

Pearson, Anne MacKenzie. *"Because It Gives Me Peace of Mind": Ritual Fasts in the Religious Lives of Hindu Women.* 1996.

Raheja, Gloria Goodwin, and Ann Grodzins Gold. *Listen to the Heron's Words: Reimagining Gender and Kinship in North India.* 1994.

Seremetakis, C. Nadia. *The Last Word: Women, Death, and Divination in Inner Mani.* 1991.

Tannen, Deborah, ed. *Spoken and Written Language: Exploring Orality and Literacy.* 1982.

Weigle, Marta. *Spiders and Spinsters: Women and Mythology.* 1982.

JOYCE BURKHALTER FLUECKIGER

Ordination

An Overview

Ordination refers to the ritual practices that demarcate leaders within the sphere of a religious tradition. Women are ordained both in male-dominated religions and women-dominated and egalitarian religions. Women-dominated religions are those religious traditions of which the majority of participants and leaders are female (Sered, 1994). When women are ordained within male-dominated religions, rituals of ordination are formal and clearly defined, marking a woman's occupation of a new position and a new status within the religion; these roles are often patterned after positions traditionally reserved for men. The ordination of women in women-dominated or egalitarian religions, by contrast, is generally not as sharply defined or structured. For example, in religious traditions that recognize the power of spirit possession, ordination of women is flexible and reflects the experiences unique to the woman being initiated. Any ritual of ordination, however, invests the ordinand with religious authority according to the particular cosmology and worldview of that tradition.

Much work has been done to document historically the ordination of women in male-dominated religions, in part as evidence to support the ordination of women today. Elisabeth Schüssler Fiorenza (1983) documents the nature of female deacons and presbyters and the larger *ekklēsia* of women in early Christianity; yet it was not until the nineteenth century that the formal ordination of women was advocated. Since then various Protestant Christian denominations have established formal ordination for heterosexual women as priests, ministers, and pastors. Antoinette Brown was the first woman ordained among Congregationalists in 1853; the first woman was ordained in the Lutheran Church of America in 1970; the first seven Episcopalian women ordained to the priesthood in 1974 were ratified in 1976; and the Anglican Church voted to ordain women in 1992. The ordination of lesbians—and gay men—is far from resolved among mainstream Protestant denominations and scarcely an issue in Roman Catholicism, despite testimonies collected by former Roman Catholic nuns Rosemary Curb and Nancy Manahan in *Lesbian Nuns: Breaking Silence* (1985). Metropolitan Community Churches is the only Christian denomination worldwide that has deliberately incorporated lesbians and gay men as both lay and ordained members since its establishment in 1968.

When Henrietta Szold was admitted to study at the Jewish Theological seminary of America in 1903, she had to agree not to pursue ordination. It was not until 1972 that the Reform Jewish seminary ordained Sally Preisand as the first woman rabbi; the Reconstructionist Jewish movement followed in 1974. After much debate, Conservative Judaism admitted Amy Eilberg as the first woman candidate to the Jewish Theological

Minister Kate Latimer wears her clerical robe and stole, Yale University, New Haven, Connecticut (Shelley Gazin/Corbis).

Seminary of America in 1983; she was ordained in 1985. The ordination of women within Conservative Judaism had to be consistent with halakha, or law (arguments for and against the ordination of women may be found in Greenberg, 1988). Orthodox Judaism does not permit the ordination of women.

Similar research has been done in support of the ordination of women in the various branches of Buddhism. Despite documented evidence of *bhikshunis* (nuns) early in the history of South Asian Buddhism, the lineage of Buddhist nuns was broken in Theravada countries by the eleventh century; there are no official nuns in the Theravada Buddhist countries of Burma, Thailand, and Sri Lanka, where formal ordination of women is currently proscribed. Since the late nineteenth century, however, women in Burma, Thailand, and Sri Lanka have followed the precepts, taken the robes, and lived as *bhikshunis* without the official sanction of the government or the *sangha* (ordained monks). In areas where Mahayana Buddhism is practiced, including mainland China, Taiwan, Japan, Southeast Asia, and among Tibetan Buddhists in exile, the lineage has been maintained, and women receive novice, higher, and, if appropriate, bodhisattva ordination among different Buddhist schools.

The ritual of ordination in male-dominated religions actually begins with a period of training in which the initiate cultivates her dedication to the role she is to take on. Jewish and Christian seminaries usually fulfill that role for contemporary ordination. In Buddhism the equivalent of a high-school education is often required, as well as several years of study in the nunnery itself dedicated to those practices characteristic of the particular school of Buddhism, such as *zazen* in Zen and the recitation of the *nembutsu* in Pure Land Buddhism. One formal rite, in which the initiate is established in her role with her new status and authority, consists of receiving the garments and symbols of her new office after proper purification, which involves shaving one's head and a ritual cleansing with water. The formal ritual concludes with the ordinand's acceptance by members of her religious community.

Ordination is less easily recognized in women-dominated or egalitarian religions. For example, a Korean woman who becomes initiated as a shaman first experiences a series of conflicts between her own emerging role as a shaman and her role as a housewife; she senses the onset of an illness and finally recognizes that her illness is due to possession (Harvey, 1979). Rituals of ordination for Korean shamans are loosely structured and unfold in dialogue with one's teacher and, occasionally, with the spirit by whom the ordinand is possessed (Kendall, 1985; Karen McCarthy Brown makes related points about the initiation of a *manbo*, or priestess, in Haitian vodou traditions, in *Mama Lola: A Vodou Priestess in Brooklyn* [1991]). In women-dominated religions, ordination may not always follow a fixed and unvarying formula but is always an investiture of sacred or religious power and authority.

BIBLIOGRAPHY

Bartholomeusz, Tessa. "The Female Mendicant in Buddhist Sri Lanka." In *Buddhism, Sexuality, and Gender.* Edited by José Ignacio Cabezón. 1985.

Carr, Anne E. *Transforming Grace: Christian Tradition and Women's Experience.* 1988.

Chaves, Mark. *Ordaining Women: Culture and Conflict in Religious Organizations.* 1997.

Coleman, Mary Teal. *Monastic: An Ordained Tibetan Buddhist Speaks on Behalf of Full Ordination for Women.* 1995.

Greenberg, Simon, ed. *The Ordination of Women as Rabbis: Studies and Responsa.* 1988.

Harvey, Yongsook Kim. *Six Korean Women: The Socialization of Shamans.* 1979.

Kabilsingh, Chatsumarn. *Thai Women in Buddhism.* 1991.

Kendall, Laurel. *Shamans, Housewives, and Other Restless Spirits: Women in Korean Ritual Life.* 1985.

Maher, Betty. *Called to Be a Nuisance: Reflections from the Fringe.* 1997.

Schüssler Fiorenza, Elisabeth. *In Memory of Her: A Feminist Theological Reconstruction of Christian Origins.* 1983. Reprint, 1994.

Sered, Susan Starr. *Priestess, Mother, Sacred Sister: Religions Dominated by Women.* 1994.

Tsomo, Karma Leshke. *Sakyadhita: Daughters of the Buddha.* 1988.

Wessinger, Catherine Lowman, ed. *Religious Institutions and Women's Leadership: New Roles Inside the Mainstream.* 1996.

CAROL ANDERSON

In Christianity

Ordination in Christianity is an authority of office that derives either from authority of hierarchy or from the authority of representative bodies. Christians believe that the type of authority institutionalized in their respective denominations has Biblical warrant. Authority of office in institutionalized religions is the type of authority that is most difficult for women to gain in patriarchal cultures. Ordination is slowly becoming available to women in denominations with democratic structures able to give the authority of office to qualified women.

The priesthood of the Roman Catholic Church is an example of authority of office derived from authority of a hierarchy. The hierarchical authority is based on the pope's claim to be successor to the authority that Jesus Christ vested in the apostle Peter (Matt. 16:18). Only avowed celibate men are ordained Catholic priests, and ordination is required to become part of the hierarchy that determines the theology, ethics, and policies of the Roman Catholic Church.

Protestant denominations vest authority in individual congregations or in representative bodies. In these denominations, ministers are ordained either by the congregation or by bishops elected by representative bodies. Protestant clergy may be married.

In the United States, the Protestant denominations with congregational polities were the first to ordain women as ministers. Antoinette Brown (Blackwell) became the first ordained woman minister when she was ordained by a Congregational church in 1853. The Universalists began ordaining women in 1863, and the Unitarians in 1871.

Churches governed by representative bodies began to grant ordination to women in the twentieth century. American Methodist women were unlicensed and licensed preachers throughout the nineteenth and early twentieth centuries. The African Methodist Episcopal Church approved the ordination of women ministers in

1948, and in 1956 the Methodist Episcopal Church gave ordained women membership in its General Conference (guaranteeing placement in churches). In 1956, the United Presbyterian Church approved the ordination of women. The Lutheran Church in America and the American Lutheran Church decided to ordain women in 1970.

In 1974 and 1975, fifteen qualified women were "irregularly" ordained Episcopal priests by retired or resigned bishops. This prompted a controversy in the Episcopal Church that was settled when the Episcopal General Convention voted in 1976 to ordain women to the priesthood and the episcopate.

Marjorie Matthews was elected the first mainline Protestant woman bishop in 1980 by the United Methodists. By 1992, the United Methodists had consecrated a total of eight women bishops.

The Episcopal Church is the American branch of the self-governing national churches that form the Anglican communion, with the Church of England as the mother church. In 1989, Barbara Harris was consecrated suffragan (assistant) bishop in the Episcopal Church, the first woman bishop within the Anglican communion. Penelope Ann Bansall Jamieson was elected Anglican bishop in New Zealand in 1990. In 1992, Jane Hart Holmes Dixon was consecrated suffragan bishop in the Episcopal Church. In 1993, Mary Adelia MacLeod was the first woman to be consecrated diocesan bishop in the Episcopal Church. In 1994, the Church of England began ordaining women priests.

Maria Jepsen was elected bishop of Hamburg in 1992, becoming the first Lutheran woman bishop. Also in 1992, April Ulring Larson was elected the first woman bishop of the Evangelical Lutheran Church in America.

The number of ordained women in Protestant denominations is comparatively small. In 1987 clergywomen constituted about 9 percent of United Methodist clergy. In 1992 women pastors constituted 9 percent of all Evangelical Lutheran Church in America pastors. In 1993 ordained women constituted 17.7 percent of the total United Church of Christ clergy, but women constituted 61 percent of UCC seminarians.

The mere ordination of women does not end women's struggle for equality in their denominations. There are the issues of hiring, promotion, and pay in which women ministers experience discrimination. There is what Susie C. Stanley has termed "a stained glass ceiling" in the denominations (Wessinger, 1996, p. 150).

Because of their congregational polity, there are some ordained women in the Baptist denominations in the United States, but their numbers are small, and even fewer are the Baptist ordained clergywomen hired to

Episcopal bishop Barbara Harris celebrates the Eucharist with a priest (left), a deacon (right), and other female clergy (Sygma).

pastor congregations. Baptist women who are ordained are not fully welcomed to minister in their denominations. The majority of American Baptist women serve their churches in nonordained capacities. Those Baptist women have found scope to exercise leadership primarily in women's missionary societies, women's social aid societies, as teachers in denominational schools, Sunday schools, and summer Bible schools, as writers of educational literature, as pastor's wives, as church secretaries, as traveling evangelists, and as missionaries working in the United States or in foreign lands. As missionaries, some Baptist women have found scope abroad to perform many of the functions that ordained ministers perform in the United States.

In the late twentieth century in the Roman Catholic Church in the United States, there are numerous Sisters and laywomen pastoring priestless parishes, but women are excluded from the ordained diaconate and priesthood. Pope John Paul II wanted to simultaneously affirm women's equal human dignity and patriarchally distinct gender roles. In *Mulieris Dignitatum* (1988), he understood women as having only two vocational options determined by their sexual status: 1)

wives and mothers; or 2) celibate women religious. On the basis of his understanding of gender, Scripture, and Catholic tradition, he prohibited women from the ordained priesthood, declaring in *Ordinatio Sacerdotalis* (1994) that this teaching was to be "definitively held" by Catholics. In 1995 the Vatican Congregation for the Doctrine of the Faith declared that the teaching in *Ordinatio Sacerdotalis* had been "set forth infallibly by the ordinary and universal magisterium" (the ordinary teaching authority of the church).

In 1996 some liberal Catholics attempted to exercise democratic power in a nondemocratic church by collecting signatures on a referendum calling for a new church council to make changes in polity and theology including the ordination of women and noncelibate men. Many American Roman Catholic women serve in a variety of fulfilling nonordained ministries. Roman Catholic women today are theologians, social activists, and initiators of new liturgies within the Women-Church movement, which is not separatist and seeks to change the Christian church and theology.

As of the late 1990s women may become ordained ministers in most of the mainline Protestant denominations. But their road remains difficult because of a widespread lack of acceptance of ordained women as equals to ordained men.

BIBLIOGRAPHY

Schmidt, Frederick W., Jr. *A Still Small Voice: Women, Ordination, and the Church.* 1996.

Wallace, Ruth A. *They Call Her Pastor: A New Role for Catholic Women.* 1992.

Wessinger, Catherine, ed. *Religious Institutions and Women's Leadership: New Roles Inside the Mainstream.* 1996.

Winter, Miriam Therese, Adair Lummis, and Allison Stokes. *Defecting in Place: Women Claiming Responsibility for Their Own Spiritual Lives.* 1994.

CATHERINE WESSINGER

In Buddhism

The order of Buddhist nuns (Sanskrit *bhikshuni;* Pali *bhikkuni*) was founded by the Buddha himself, purportedly with some reluctance, and has been supported throughout the following centuries with a great deal of tentativeness. Information about the first ordination of Buddhist women comes from highly problematic textual sources that were written centuries after the fact. The story of the Buddha's initial reluctance to ordain women and his stipulation of eight additional rules for nuns, one of which puts all nuns under the rule of any monk, may say more about later monastic editors than it does about historical fact. This story must be analyzed within the context of the contemporaneous order of Jain nuns and that of other ascetic women in ancient India, as well as related Buddhist literature, especially the rules of the nuns and monks in the Vinaya that paint a more contentious picture. For instance, in exceptional cases the approval of ten *bhikshus* (monks) and ten *bhikshunis* required by code for the ordination of a woman may be unnecessary, and nuns may confer ordination on their own.

Further, if the women involved were indeed members of the Buddha's clan, led by his own stepmother Mahāprajāptī, one has to question the classic story, perhaps in the context of clan dynamics. Whatever the facts of that first ordination, we do know that the ordination lineage of nuns in the Theravada tradition eventually died out in India, Sri Lanka, and most of Southeast Asia, and present-day attempts to renew it are both opposed and supported for complex reasons that vary from region to region.

The first transmission of Buddhism to Sri Lanka in the third century B.C.E. carried with it both the male and female monastic orders, called the *sangha;* both orders were also transmitted to Burma and China, and

from China on to Korea, Japan, and Vietnam. (Little is known about the Buddhist orders in Indonesia in spite of the magnificent Buddhist archaeological remains.) Buddhism went directly to Tibet from India. However, at present, the *bhikshuni sangha* remains intact with its lineage unbroken in China, Taiwan, Korea, Japan, and Vietnam. Karma Lekshe Tsomo in 1989 (see *Sakyadhita*) estimated the number of Buddhists living the life of nuns in the world at sixty thousand, of whom only fifteen thousand were ordained *bhikshuni.* The book of monastic code, the Vinaya, dictates that ten fully ordained *bhikshus* and the same number of *bhikshunis* must be present to give ordination to new nuns; only in East Asia is there a legitimate way to admit women to the monastic path.

However, this technicality has not at all prohibited devoted laywomen from assuming the role of *bhikshuni,* shaving their heads, wearing robes, and taking on the ten precepts of the *sangha.* In Asian countries where there is not a legitimate nuns order, women have come together to function essentially as a disciplined order. This practice has progressively gained much strength and voice, and there is now a movement to reestablish the nuns' order, especially in the West and among Tibetan nuns. This possibility, however, is full of controversy and paradox; not only is there often opposition by monks, but many of the devout who function as nuns are reluctant to put themselves under the auspices of the male *sangha,* even if it means not being fully recognized for their life of devotion.

In Sri Lanka both male and female orders were well established until the eleventh century, when famine and a conquest of the island by the Chola empire in India left few *sangha* members. With the help of Burmese monks, the Sri Lanka monks' *sangha* was reestablished, but the women's order was not. Centuries later, in the wake of the rise of nationalist feelings and independence from European control, Buddhism once again prospered. Female mendicants started to reappear. The optimism of self-rule coupled with a backlash against the West and its religions helped spur the Buddhist revival, and women as the traditional bearers of religion in the home were at the center of this surge.

Where lay Buddhists are required only to take the five precepts (to attempt not to steal, lie, kill, indulge in illicit sex, or drink alcohol), many women took on the ten precepts that were required of male novices. These women are referred to as the *dasa sil mata,* the women of ten precepts. Today this community thrives, with two thousand members in Sri Lanka and some in other parts of Asia and the West. Many Sri Lankans consider the *dasa sil matas* to be much more devout than the monks. However, one cannot gain as much merit by giving to a nun as by giving to a monk, and of renunciates it is mostly monks to whom alms are given and who are asked to take part in religious ceremonies. Though this is the case, most nuns would rather not become fully ordained into the *sangha* and feel that their freedom and devotion would suffer if subjected to government surveillance and the hierarchy set forth in the Vinaya.

Similar movements have occurred in Burma among the *thila-shin,* women who have taken the ten precepts and dress as renunciates, and in Thailand among the *mae ji,* women who as early as the seventeenth century decided to take on more than the prescribed number of precepts and live as nuns, even though Thailand had no previous history of a *bhikshuni sangha* to draw on. The *bhikshuni* order disappeared from Burma sometime around the thirteenth century, but today the *thila-shin* are respected by the community and have a well-organized and -supported system of nunneries. Still, being technically laywomen, they do not receive nearly the same amount of support that monks do and are not seen in the same religious light. Thailand has proved to be very resistant to the presence of female mendicants, and nuns are treated with disrespect and suspicion; whereas monks can depend on financial support and alms from laypeople, the *mae ji* are left to fend for themselves. In recent years the government has taken steps to improve the life of these women by offering education and political support, but they are not yet recognized by the government as renunciates.

The Buddhist kingdom of Tibet, invaded by China in 1950, stands out among South Asian countries as following the Mahayana school of Buddhism. However, Tibetan Buddhism distinguishes itself by its tantric content. Tibetan nuns, called *ani* (aunt), were a strong presence in Tibet before the invasion and have continued to be central to the communities in exile. Nuns as well as monks have been persecuted by the Chinese for their activities in contemporary Tibet.

Although there is no doubt that monks and lamas are given more respect and are the religious authorities in the Tibetan community, the Dalai Lama has actively encouraged the education of nuns and has supported the move toward full ordination, a view most Tibetan nuns seem to accept. The Tibetan communities transposed to Indian and Nepalese soil include nuns and nunneries in sizable numbers, although nothing approaching the 618 nunneries of Tibet prior to occupation. The full ordination of Tibetan nuns in India dates only to 1984, when four nuns received *bhikshuni* precepts in Hong Kong. With the encouragement of the Dalai Lama, this movement is growing.

Buddhist nuns have existed in China since 429 C.E., when a small group of Sri Lankan Theravada *bhik-*

Young nuns study in a monastery, Sagaing, Burma, 1997 (Michael Freeman/Corbis).

*shuni*s arrived. Chinese *bhikshuni*s had a great degree of control over their lives, and their organization sometimes served as a model for non-Buddhist women's movements. Information about ordination in China today is scant, although it is likely the double ordination tradition of a quorum of ten *bhikshu*s and ten *bhikshuni*s was never broken. A few small nunneries have been restored since the Cultural Revolution.

Since the settlement of large numbers of mainland Chinese in Taiwan after 1949, the importance of Buddhism and of the Buddhist orders has grown to great societal as well as religious importance there. Barnes estimates that six to seven thousand women were ordained as *bhikshuni*s between 1952 and 1987. Nuns have founded welfare societies and become respected scholars, artists, and meditation masters. Ten Buddhist colleges in Taiwan provide education for both monks and nuns. Taiwan as well as Hong Kong serves as an important conduit for women from other countries to be ordained as *bhikshuni*s into the *sangha.*

As in other Mahayana regions, the ordination of women has been a continuing tradition in these countries, although there is little material on current practice. In Korea about two hundred nuns receive ordination every year (Tsomo, ed., 1989). All nuns as well as monks attend Buddhist temple schools for three to five years. All together in Korea there are about six thousand *bhikshuni*s and *shramanerika*s (women who are ascetics, perhaps temporarily, but not ordained).

It is estimated that about two thousand nuns live in fifteen hundred temples in Japan, but few young women enter the monastic path. Nuns become priests in these temples, but often they receive little support, and many nuns operate children's schools or teach Japanese traditions such as the tea ceremony to survive (Kondo, in Tsomo, ed., 1989).

Vietnamese Buddhism often combines Theravada and Mahayana traditions. The period of American involvement in Vietnam found many Buddhists in South Vietnam suffering for their protest against the war. At present there is repression of Buddhism to restrict Buddhist political activity or influence against the government. Only a few temples are now actively functioning and the number of monks and nuns is not possible to estimate; most members of the *sangha* are now in exile. There is no report, however, that the ordination tradition has been broken.

In India the *bhikshuni* order was strong for many centuries, but lapsed even as the male order weakened, chiefly because of the resurgence of brahminical Hinduism. By the twelfth century, before the Muslim invasions destroyed monasteries and universities, the nuns order had disappeared, and with it the tradition of ordination. The revival of women's participation in Buddhism has taken three forms: the conversion movement begun by Dr. B. R. Ambedkar in 1956, which brought millions into Buddhism from the previously untouchable caste; the TBMSG (Triloka Bauddh Mahasangha Sahayaka Gana) begun by English Buddhists and now almost wholly Indian, which works primarily among those converted in the Ambedkar movement; and the coming of vast numbers of Tibetan refugees, with the institution of nuns (although not the tradition of ordination) well preserved among them.

Only a handful of women have become nuns in the conversion movement, which has no overarching organization but much local activity. There is no women's order; the remarkable thing about these nuns is that they seek out training in Sarnath or simply put on robes and act as ascetics, with little societal encouragement. There is, however, considerable Buddhist activity among lay women.

In TBMSG there is a single ordination for men and women, based on the Buddhist practices developed by the Venerable Sangarakshita in the Friends of the Western Buddhist Order in England. There is no expectation of a cloistered group or of a robed *sangha*. Retreats, meditation, and dharma (Pali *dhamma*) sessions are paramount in the movement, as is education and social work.

There are areas about which little is known as to the current state of women in the *sangha*, and the explanations for the survival of women's ordination in Mahayana countries but not in Theravada are not completely satisfactory. Nor is there a convincing rationale

behind the lack of ordination from the beginning of Buddhism in Tibet and Thailand. These historical problems may never have a complete answer. Information is also limited about *bhikshuni* orders in East Asia. However, with international conferences of Buddhist women increasingly popular, and the travel of Western women to Asia for ordination, the study of women in Buddhism today in East Asia will surely be forthcoming. Taiwan, Hong Kong, and Korea (and Vietnam of an earlier day) serve as sources for the ordination of both Western and other Asian women, and the vitality of women in Sri Lanka has drawn outsiders to training there. The situation of Cambodian Buddhism is almost totally unknown in the West.

There is considerable ferment in Buddhist countries on the issue of ordination, particularly in Sri Lanka and Thailand. It must be noticed that women act as *bhikshuni*s in great numbers in countries where ordination is not possible.

BIBLIOGRAPHY

Barnes, Nancy. "Buddhist Women and the Nun's Order in Asia." In *Engaged Buddhism: Buddhist Literation Movements in Asia.* Edited by Christopher S. Queen and Sallie B. King. 1996.

Bartholomeusz, Tessa. *Women Under the Bo Tree.* 1994.

Blakiston, Hilary. *But Little Dust: Life Amongst the Ex-Untouchables of Maharashtra.* 1990. Reprinted under the author's Buddhist name of Padmasuri, 1997.

Falk, Nancy. "The Case of the Vanishing Nuns: The Fruits of Ambivalence in Ancient Indian Buddhism." In *Unspoken Worlds: Women's Religious Lives in Non-Western Cultures.* Edited by Nancy Auer Falk and Rita M. Gross. 1980.

Findly, Ellison Banks. "Ananda's Case for Women." *International Journal for Hindu Studies.* Forthcoming.

Horner, I. B. *The Book of the Discipline (Vinaya-Pitaka).* Vol. 5, Cullavagga. 1963.

———. *Women Under Primitive Buddhism.* 1930. Reprint, 1975.

Kabilsingh, Chatsumarn. *Thai Women in Buddhism.* 1991.

Pao-chang. *Lives of the Nuns: Biographies of Chinese Buddhist Nuns from the Fourth to the Sixth Centuries.* Translated by Kathryn Ann Tsai. 1994.

Paul, Diana, ed. *Women in Buddhism: Images of the Feminine in the Mahāyāna Tradition.* 1979. Reprint, 1985. See the important essay by Francis Wilson.

Sponberg, Alan. "Attitudes Toward Women and the Feminine in Early Buddhism." In *Buddhism, Sexuality, and Gender.* Edited by José Ignacio Cabezón. 1992.

Tsomo, Karma Lekshe. "Tibetan Nuns and Nunneries." In *Feminine Ground: Essays on Women and Tibet.* Edited by Janice D. Willis. 1989.

Tsomo, Karma Lekshe, ed. *Sakyadhita: Daughters of the Buddha.* 1989. Especially meaningful for this article are essays by Daw Su Su Sein, Hema Goonatilake, Tessho Kondo, Karuna Dharma, and Tsomo.

Welch, Holmes. *Buddhism Under Mao.* 1972.

ELEANOR ZELLIOT

INGRID KLASS

In Judaism

Semikhah, the Hebrew term for the ordination of rabbis, means laying on of hands. First performed by Moses on Joshua (Number 27:23), it is a symbolic way of passing authority from one leader to the next. Today, a long period of intensive study of Jewish texts culminates in *semikhah.*

Once ordained, a rabbi is authorized to resolve all kinds of disputes between Jews; answer questions about ritual, such as whether a certain food is kosher, fit according to the dietary laws; and evolve new points of Jewish law and practice. The title creates an aura of authority and even a degree of holiness. In the United States today a rabbi is often the spiritual head of a congregation and the representative of the Jewish community to the world at large. In Orthodox circles, a main rabbinic function is responding to queries on Jewish law.

Throughout Jewish history only men served as rabbis. The word *rabbi,* Hebrew for "master" or "teacher," was first used in the first century C.E. to designate a leader of the Jewish community. For as long as there was a cultic center in Jerusalem, *kohanim*—priests, an inherited caste going back to Aaron, the brother of Moses—were Temple functionaries, healers, and also, starting no later than the Hasmonean period, political leaders. With the destruction of the Second Temple in 70 C.E. and the collapse of the Jewish state, *kohanim* passed from the scene and were replaced by rabbis. Any qualified Jewish male could, after years of study and apprenticeship, earn this title. Until the modern era, rabbis, more than any other group in the Jewish community, were the ones who shaped its thinking, behavior, and even political fortunes. One exception to the rule of a male rabbinate was the "maid of Ludomir." Living in nineteenth-century Poland, she functioned as a Hasidic rabbi, teaching and counseling her followers.

Women were not ordained. Positions of leadership and power among the Jews were reserved for the patriarchs. Men viewed women as having limited intellec-

A female Reform rabbi blows a shofar, a ram's-horn trumpet, Greenburg, Mississippi, 1984 (David H. Wells/Corbis).

tual capacities: excluding women from the higher echelons was a sign that their needs were not as important as men's. Indeed, the disabling effect on women of Jewish law, requiring them to remain tied to a husband they were no long living with but unable to divorce, was left unresolved.

Of Judaism's three major branches—Orthodox, which opposes all change in halakhah, or Jewish law; Conservative, which adopts change when necessary; and Reform, which does not view Jewish law as binding and is, therefore, open to reasonable change—it was the Reform movement that first ordained a woman in 1972. The Conservative movement, the largest of the American denominations, debated this issue for years. Finally, in 1983, by a faculty vote at the movement's rabbinical seminary, it approved the ordination of women. By the late 1990s, close to 300 women had become rabbis, while growing numbers of Orthodox women were pressing for an alternative to ordination, for training women to render legal decisions about matters that affect women, such as menstrual impurity and dietary laws. Jews in parts of Europe, even secular ones, resist training and hiring women rabbis.

There are no halakhic problems with a woman fulfilling most tasks of the modern rabbi. A rabbi monitors the prayer services, preaches on sabbaths and festivals, plans and executes life-cycle events, directs children's and adults' formal and informal Jewish education, and counsels individuals and families on Jewish problems. Women are just as suited as men for all of these activities. The obstacle to women's ordination lies in the fact that several key rabbinic duties are off-limits to women: Jewish law prohibits them from counting in the minyan, the quorum of ten needed for public prayer; from acting as *sheliah tzibbur,* prayer leader; and from serving as a witness of life-cycle events, such as weddings, divorces, and conversion ceremonies. For a congregational leader to be barred from these kinds of activities places a great burden on both the rabbi and the community. However, as demonstrated by some of the literature on the subject, (e.g., Greenberg, ed., 1988) women's ability to engage in these practices can be supported by innovative interpretations of traditional legal texts.

Many women and men begin their rabbinic careers as the solo leader of a small congregation or as the assistant rabbi of a large one. Some choose to serve as rabbis in educational institutions or communal organizations. At first, only congregations in out-of-the-way places, which could not attract an outstanding male candidate, would hire a woman. The exigencies of the marketplace, not the ethics of Judaism, led them to prefer a highly talented woman to a man of mediocre skill. As people have grown accustomed to the idea of women as rabbis, larger congregations have begun hiring them. In the Reform movement several women have assumed leadership of premier congregations. Women rabbis seem to have little difficulty in being hired as principals of Jewish schools or heads of Jewish communal organizations.

Although it is too early to measure the full impact of women's ordination on Judaism, it is already evident that more women are being drawn to the synagogue because they find egalitarian Judaism in consonance with their general philosophic outlook. More women are being attracted to the study of Jewish texts. With the structure of the synagogue changing, women are no longer sequestered in auxiliaries or sisterhoods but fully integrated into all synagogue activities. Liturgy is moving toward the standard use of gender-inclusive language. In short, the image of women as competent, knowledgeable, and caring leaders—as role models for girls and boys and men and women alike—is contributing greatly to the ongoing viability of Judaism.

BIBLIOGRAPHY

Berkovits, Eliezer. *Jewish Women in Time and Torah.* 1990.

Greenberg, Simon, ed. *The Ordination of Women as Rabbis.* 1988.

Hauptman, Judith. "Some Thoughts on the Nature of Halakhic Adjudication: Women and Minyan." *Judaism* 42 (Fall 1993): 396–413.

———. "Women and Prayer: An Attempt to Dispel Some Fallacies." *Judaism* 42 (Winter 1993): 94–103.

Heschel, Susannah. *On Being a Jewish Feminist: A Reader.* 1983.

Plaskow, Judith. *Standing Again at Sinai.* 1990.

Wolowelsky, Joel. *Women, Jewish Law and Modernity: New Opportunities in a Post-feminist Age.* 1997.

See also **Jonas, Regina**; **Judaism: Religious Rites and Practices**.

JUDITH HAUPTMAN

Orientalism

The critical concept of "orientalism" was developed by Columbia University literary critic Edward W. Said. Replacing the former sense of orientalism as the scholarly study of Eastern cultures, languages, and peoples, Said, a scholar of Palestinian descent, focused on the role of such scholarship in European colonialism. His 1978 book, *Orientalism,* was a watershed in what is now called postcolonial studies. It focused primarily on the "Muslim orient" rather than the East Asian countries of China, Japan, and Korea, which are more conventionally associated with the Orient and which were more unevenly colonized by Europeans.

Said used a notion of discourse developed by French social theorist Michel Foucault to refer to the connection between orientalist scholarship and power. To create representations of others, he maintained, was to gain power over them. When Europeans described Asians in academic, official, or literary discourse, it had the effect of legitimating European colonial rule. This was so because the representations, even if they were ostensibly positive, made Asians appear to be backward, exotic, and inferior in relation to Western civilization. Moreover, the fact that Asians had little opportunity to represent themselves in European discourse meant that they appeared as mute and hence relatively powerless. Ultimately, then, according to Said, orientalist statements reveal more about the Europeans who made them than about the actual "Orient."

Feminist and other scholars have asserted that Said was inattentive to gender in his analysis of orientalism. What he described as the European voice was a very masculine voice. How women figured in these asymmetrical relations of representation has since been the concern of many scholars inspired by Said. Malek Alloula, an Algerian literary critic, was pivotal in detailing how the colonized other was feminized. In a semiotic study of harem fantasy as revealed in French postcards of colonized Algerian women, Alloula suggested that the control of the camera over these Muslim models, some of whom posed seminude, was a metaphor for the control of France over its colonies. Not only were the women represented as exotic, but they were also made to appear highly erotic, in ways that emphasized their presumed distance from European morals. At the same time, Islamic strictures on women were violated by the access of the camera. This symbolic act of unveiling was, as Frantz Fanon had long ago pointed out, a key to the domination of Muslim men by European men. Contemporary postcolonial extensions of this process of feminizing Asia in relation to the West can be found in analyses by Wilson and Tolentino of mail-order bride catalogues.

Lata Mani looked at the discourse on sati, the Hindu practice of widow-burning, and found that both colonial officials and indigenous scholars were debating whether it should be maintained under colonial rule as a valuable facet of tradition. Mani, noting that women did not enter into this debate at all, concluded that, instead of having a role in the decision that would affect their own lives, women were simply sites on which issues of traditional culture and colonial polity were battled out. What women's interests were, regarding the maintenance or dissolution of Hindu practices, was omitted from the official discourse. Similar processes have been identified within nationalist and fundamentalist movements. Partha Chatterjee demonstrated that India's anticolonial nationalism was premised on the promotion of a new norm of middle-class domestic femininity. Aihwa Ong showed that middle-class anti-Western Islamic revivalism in industrializing Malaysia took the form of anxiety about the changing gender roles of Muslim factory women. All these instances evidence Said's dictum that the represented do not speak for themselves; furthermore, in the case of women, their moral or religious purity becomes a battleground for struggles among men.

Several other approaches demonstrate the centrality of gender to orientalist discourse. Reina Lewis makes the point that European women's roles in orientalism are often overlooked, and that when orientalist images produced by British and French women are taken into account, competing East–West definitions of gender propriety are frequently at issue. Lisa Lowe shows that the French feminism of Julia Kristeva appropriated Chinese revolutionary women for its own purposes. Laura Nader seeks to correct the imbalance in which Europeans do all the representing by looking at the counter-discourse of "occidentalism" produced by Muslim women. Both Nader and Fatima Mernissi make the strong point that Muslim women have their own definitions for the roles of women and their sexuality and that they reject Western critiques of them as oppressed. These rival positions are currently being echoed in debates over female genital mutilation.

BIBLIOGRAPHY

BOOKS

Ahmed, Leila. *Women and Gender in Islam: Historical Roots of a Modern Debate.* 1992.

Alloula, Malek. *The Colonial Harem.* 1986.

Chatterjee, Partha. "Colonialism, Nationalism, and Colonized Women: The Contest in India." *American Ethnologist* 16, no. 4 (1989): 622–633.

Chen, Xiaomei. *Occidentalism: A Theory of Counter-Discourse in Post-Mao China.* 1995.

Chow, Rey. "Where Have all the Natives Gone?" In her *Writing Diaspora.* 1993.

Clifford, James. "On Orientalism." In his *The Predicament of Culture.* 1988.

Fanon, Frantz, "Algeria Unveiled." In his *A Dying Colonialism.* 1967.

Lewis, Reina. *Gendering Orientalism: Race, Femininity and Representation.* 1996.

Lowe, Lisa. *Critical Terrains: French and British Orientalisms.* 1991.

Mani, Lata. "Contentious Traditions: The Debate on Sati in Colonial India." *Cultural Critique* 7 (1987): 119–156.

Mernissi, Fatima. *Beyond the Veil: Male-Female Dynamics in Modern Muslim Society.* 1987.

Nader, Laura. "Orientalism, Occidentalism and the Control of Women." *Cultural Dynamics* 2, no. 3 (1989): 323–355.

Ong, Aihwa. "State Versus Islam: Malay Families, Women's Bodies, and the Body Politic in Malaysia." *American Ethnologist* 17, no. 2 (1990): 258–276.

Tolentino, Roland B. "Bodies, Letters, Catalogues: Filipinas in Transnational Space." *Social Text* 48 (1996): 49–76.

Wilson, Ara. "American Catalogues for Asian Brides." In *Anthropology for the Nineties.* Edited by Johnetta Cole. 1988.

FILMS

"Some Women of Marrakech." Directed by Melissa L. Davies. Granada Television International. 1976.

"Veiled Revolution." Directed by Marilyn Gaunt. Icarus Films. 1982.

See also Colonialism and Postcolonialism; Deconstruction; Women's Religions.

LOUISA SCHEIN

Ornamentation

Embellishment of the human body by means of painting, cutting, or adorning with ornaments is a feature common to all human societies. Some adornments may be temporary, as in the wearing of jewelry or talismans or the application of body paint or makeup; others may be permanent, such as tattooing, scarification (the incision of a knife or other implement to cut the skin), and cicatrization (the precise formation of the scar as the wound heals). Whereas in one culture tattooing, for example, may signal auspiciousness and adhere to the highest ideals of the culture, in another such a technique signals a rebellion, a wish to break away from societal conventions. In any given culture, the human body as a canvas is never neutral.

In preliterate and literate societies, religious practices have dictated specifics of adornment. In societies where the body is not normally clothed, any such covering becomes highly significant. Thus in the headdresses of Borneo, for example, every color, texture, and medium employed conveys a meaning. At the other end of the spectrum, where the body is almost entirely obscured by clothing, the issue of ornamentation again speaks with great significance. Perhaps the most striking example is the adornment of the Muslim bride with elaborate bodily markings in henna. In orthodox Islamic societies, where the only parts of a woman's body that may be exposed to public scrutiny are the hands and the feet, it is just these that become the canvas for intricate, exquisite, red-tinged designs. The leaves of the henna plant are thought to carry *baraka,* or spiritual blessings. Thus the application of significant designs with a significant medium is the most auspicious way to imprint the blessing of the occasion.

The adornment of the bride has great significance, particularly in the cultures bordering the Mediterranean—southern Europe, northern Africa, and the Middle East—as well as throughout Asia. In the Middle East and in much of Asia a bride may be adorned nearly to the point of unrecognizability. The heavy ornamentation serves to deflect some of the magnitude of the event away from the bride herself. Ornamentation, then, can draw attention to a woman's special status, but at the same time it offers prophylaxis. Attraction and repulsion become two sides of the same ornament. Amulets, painting of the body, tattooing, and applying kohl to the eyes are in various cultures understood as armor against negative forces, seen and unseen. In tribal societies, the men paint for war, both to protect themselves spiritually and to frighten their opponents with their unnatural appearance. Extreme actions, such as those in battle, require an extreme psychological component to alter consciousness—to transport all parties involved out of the ordinary mode of being.

Ornamentation in any culture constitutes a method of transcending nature. Military uniforms and the black that football players smear beneath their eyes, ostensibly to guard against the sun, are vestiges of armor and fierce accoutrement. Contemporary women's use of cosmetics continues to reflect the archaic sense of defying nature, covering up as protection before a foray out into the world. Certain expressions, even if uttered only in a mocking sense, can still be heard to describe the process of applying makeup: "I'm putting on my face," or "I'm putting on my war paint." The consciousness of attraction-and-obscuration remains.

The English word *cosmetics* has its etymological root in the Greek term *kosmos,* that is, the "ordered universe," in clear distinction to chaos, or untamed nature. In the Greek view, which in so many ways has continued to be that of the contemporary Western world, the application of cosmetics is understood to be a way of covering up, or improving upon, nature, and in a certain sense a neatly "made up" woman is seen as a reflection of a well-ordered universe—with the attendant virtues of beauty, goodness, and a certain amount of predictability. By contrast, a woman whose face is without makeup and whose hair is uncoiffed represents the uneasy, unrestrained danger of not playing by society's rules. Of course, the too-heavily made-up woman presents problems against the order of society as well.

In classical Greek culture women adorned themselves, and men did not. In an interesting contrast between "civilized" and "uncivilized," the Greek writers noted that one of the signs of the barbarian races was the men's long and unkempt hair and painted, tattooed, or pierced body parts. Although they shared their views about barbarians with the Greeks, the ancient Romans took a slightly different view of cosmetics: they referred to cosmetics as *medicamina,* "medicine," with the im-

An Israeli Jewish bride is heavily veiled in traditional Yemenite wedding attire during the ceremony at a moshav agricultural cooperative in the Negev region, 1988 (Richard T. Nowitz/Corbis).

plication that the female body was something in need of fixing, healing, and changing. The term connoted medicine for the physical body as well as a concoction of a sorcerer's brew for supernatural transformation.

In the Americas, Africa, and the Pacific rim, adornments for men and women are highly specific and recognizable. Women and men each have their own initiations, with accompanying bodily marking and ritual adornment. The ornaments display status in terms of life-cycle and place in the society. To comprehend the rules and to break them is, in a religious context, to upset the ordered universe. Thus the Hindu family that does not provide the appropriate gold ornaments for the bride and the many members of the wedding party may invite scorn, seeming in some way to offend the deities of auspiciousness and augmentation. In contemporary American society, consider the case in which an airline employee risked losing her job for refusing to

wear makeup to work, thereby calling into question the cosmeticized persona of the woman interacting in society. In the 1990s the vigor with which many young people—including a significant number of women—have embraced the permanent alterations entailed in tattooing and body piercing speaks again of the ever-present awareness of the normalization of cosmeticized behavior, and of rebellion against what is seen as an overcosmeticized, oversanitized society. What better way to register such discontent than by means of the subtle yet inescapable language of the ornamented body.

BIBLIOGRAPHY

Biebuyck, Daniel P., and Nelly Van den Abbeele. *The Power of Headdresses: A Cross-Cultural Study of Forms and Functions.* Brussels, 1984.

Ebensten, Hanns. *Pierced Hearts and True Love: An Illustrated History of the Origin and Development of European Tattooing and a Survey of Its Present State.* London, 1953.

Field, Henry. *Body-Marking in Southwestern Asia.* Papers of the Peabody Museum of Archaeology and Ethnology, Harvard University. Vol. 45, no. 1. 1958.

Kapchan, Deborah. "Moroccan Women's Body Signs." In *Bodylore.* Edited by Katharine Young. 1993.

Richlin, Amy. "Making Up a Woman: The Face of Roman Gender." In *Off with Her Head! The Denial of Women's Identity in Myth, Religion, and Culture.* Edited by Howard Eilberg-Schwartz and Wendy Doniger. 1995.

Roach, Mary Ellen, and Joanne Bubolz Eicher, eds. *Dress, Ornament, and the Social Order.* 1965.

Strathern, Andrew, and Marilyn Strathern. *Self-Decoration in Mount Hagen.* 1971.

Vivel, André. *Decorated Man: The Human Body as Art.* 1980.

Vlahos, Olivia. *Body, the Ultimate Symbol.* 1979.

CONSTANTINA RHODES BAILLY

Orthodox Christianity

Until 1054 there had been one official Christian Church, although the Eastern and Western halves had experienced many strains throughout the centuries due to differences of cultures and theological opinion. The Coptic Church and the Syrian Church had split from Rome and Constantinople in 451 over the Christological definition, becoming the Monophysite churches. Except for their Christological definitions, both Orthodox and Monophysite churches have the same ecclesiology and theology. Since the 1980s they have been in full communion with each other. To deal with women in Orthodox Christianity, which includes the Monophysite churches, one must survey both official doctrine and practice.

ORTHODOX THEOLOGICAL ANTHROPOLOGY OF WOMEN

Orthodox theology holds that both genders are created in the image and likeness of God. Gregory of Nyssa (c. 330–395) in *On the Creation of Humanity*, writes that all humans were immortal, just, kind, reasonable, and passionless. But through the devil's temptation first to Eve, then through her to Adam, both disobeyed God. The consequence of their disobedience was to pass on death to all generations. Sexuality and sexual procreation was God's remedy for death, a way to stave off extinction. Consequently both genders are a temporal necessity, unnecessary before the fall.

Christ's coming is the ultimate remediation of human mortality for both genders. Women and men are called to grow in divine life. Both are spiritual equals in Christ, and women's capacity for saintliness is equal to men's.

Despite this theology, Orthodoxy strictly limits women's participation in the leadership of the church. Women are routinely addressed as inferior to men because of the Fall. They have been categorized as morally weaker than men, and, at the worst, depicted as vessels of Satan. Moreover, theologically and in practice in Orthodoxy, women are ritually unclean during their menses.

WOMEN AND CLERICAL ORDINATION

The church has never allowed women to be ordained as clergy for these reasons. Epiphanius (c. 315–403) says women were never chosen to be priest or leaders, while John Chrysostom (c. 344–407), citing 1 Corinthians, Timothy, and Titus, declares that men are naturally the head of women, and women must defer to their authority. Finally this argument is used: Jesus Christ was a male human being, and priests are ordained into his physical "image and likeness." Thus women could never act in the person of Christ. Many contemporary Orthodox writers are challenging these positions in books and at conferences, such as John H. Erickson, in *The Challenge of Our Past* (1991).

MARRIAGE AND DIVORCE

Marriage is highly esteemed by the majority of women in Orthodoxy. As a sacrament of the church, marriage is an eternal bond, which death does not destroy. Hence

A wedding is held in a Greek Orthodox church on the island of Samos, Greece, 1982 (Kevin Fleming/Corbis).

remarriage after a spouse's death is barely tolerated. In marriage the couple becomes the image of God in their union, experiencing a foretaste of the resurrection.

Canonical divorce is permitted to women and men for reasons of desertion, violence, infidelity, or insanity. Either party can initiate divorce proceedings. Remarriage is allowed, although in a penitential service. Theoretically a person can have three divorces and marry four times, although in practice this is quite rare.

MOTHERHOOD

Motherhood is extolled as the natural outcome of marriage. In childbirth a woman brings another life to God's Kingdom, physically participating in Christ's new creation. Motherhood implies the selflessness of Christ, the "divine emptying" or kenosis of Jesus Christ.

Orthodox women venerate the Theotokos, the Mother of God (the Virgin Mary), in marriage and motherhood. The Theotokos protects and nurtures women, their children, and honors their husbands.

MONASTICISM

Monasticism for women has grown tremendously among Orthodox women worldwide since the 1970s. Women can become nuns at three times in their lives: in their teens, in middle age, and as widows. Although each monastery has its own rules, the length of the novitiate is approximately three years. The minimum age for a final profession is sixteen.

No men reside in Orthodox convents. Priests must come from the outside to perform liturgies. The nuns must be completely obedient to the *hegoumene*, the abbess, who is elected by the nuns. She has complete control over the monastery and all the nuns' lives. Life in the monastery is regulated by the cycle of prayer services, physical work, and the liturgical calendar that is punctuated by frequent fasts.

ORTHODOX PRACTICE IN CHURCH LIFE

Women in Orthodox churches participate actively in church life, despite their exclusion from the clergy. They serve as presidents of their communities, readers in some services, and on the parish boards. They direct religious education programs, choirs, and do great physical labor for fund-raising events.

Yet there are practical theological impediments that stultify the theoretical theological equality between the genders. When a woman gives birth to a baby, she is ritually impure for forty days and cannot enter the church. On her fortieth day postpartum, she must go through a penitential service in which she stands at the rear of the church while prayers are read for her. At a female infant's baptism, the infant is not taken into the altar as are male infants. In fact, no women are officially permitted behind the iconostasis, the icon screen in front of the altar. Only elderly women who clean the church are allowed there.

No menstruating woman is allowed to receive the Eucharist. Of course, no one would know, but young girls are taught not to approach the Eucharist at this time. And in predominantly Orthodox societies, menstruating women are taught not to kiss the icons on entering the church, or the priest's hand after the end of the liturgy. Women are also enjoined to cover their heads in church, to stand on the "women's" side of church, the left, and to wear modest clothing that excludes pants and short skirts.

ORTHODOX PRACTICE IN THE HOME

Women in Orthodoxy have a pivotal role to play in creating an Orthodox home and family. It is a woman's responsibility to teach her children daily prayers, Bible stories, and lives of saints. The veneration of icons in the home is a woman's duty. A family's icons are displayed in a corner, and the woman lights an oil lamp before them.

To create an Orthodox home, a woman must know the calendrical cycles for feast days and their required fasts and the level of fasting prescribed for that day or period, be able to teach her family, and then prepare the meals accordingly. Even receiving the Eucharist during regular Sunday liturgy requires abstinence from all animal products on Wednesday, Friday, and Saturday of the week intended. There are four great fasts during the year: Lent, Saints Peter and Paul, The Dormition of the Theotokos (the Assumption of the Virgin), and Advent, in addition to many individual holy days.

BIBLIOGRAPHY

Bishop Nikodim. *Maria of Olonets.* 1987.

Brock, Sebastian, and Susan Ashbrook Harvey, trans. *Holy Women of the Syrian Orient.* 1987.

Durasov, Ghenady. *Beloved Sufferer: Life of Schema-nun Macrina, +1993.* 1994.

Evdokimov, Paul. *Women and the Salvation of the World.* Translated by Anthony P. Gythiel. 1994.

Harrison, Verna. "Male and Female in Cappadocia Theology." *Journal of Theological Studies* 41, no. 2 (1990): 441–471.

Hopko, Thomas, ed. *Women in the Priesthood.* 1983.

Karras, Valerie. "Male Domination of Woman in the Writings of Saint John Chrysostom." *Greek Orthodox Theological Review* 36, no. 2 (1991): 120–140.

———. "Patristic Views on the Ontology of Gender." In *Personhood: Deepening the Connection Between Body, Mind, and Soul.* Edited by J. T. Chirban. 1995.

Laiou, Angeliki. "The Role of Women in Byzantine Society." *Jahrbuch Der Osterreichischen Byzantinistik* 31 (1981): 233–260.

Limberis, Vasiliki. *Divine Heiress: The Virgin Mary and the Creation of Christian Constantinople.* 1994.

Meehan, Brenda. *Holy Women of Russia.* 1993.

Priklonsky, Alexander. *Blessed Athanasia and the Desert Ideal.* Translated by the Nuns of St. Xenia Skete. 1993.

Tripolitis, Antonia. *Kassia: The Legend, the Woman, and Her Work.* 1992.

Senyk, Sophia. *Women's Monasteries in Ukraine and Belorussia to the Period of Suppressions.* 1983.

van Doorn-Harder, Pieternella. *Contemporary Coptic Nuns.* 1995.

Ware, Kallistos. *Orthodox Church.* 1993.

See also Eve; Ordination: In Christianity; Monasticism: In the West; Purification; Virgin Mary.

VASILIKI LIMBERIS

Osun

Osun is an *orisa* (deity) of the Yoruba people of south-western Nigeria. Associated with the Osun River, she is the deity of fresh waters. She is also of one of the most revered deities of the African diaspora religions of Puerto Rico, Cuba, Brazil, Trinidad, Venezuela, and the United States, where the practice of Yoruba religion is growing rapidly.

Osun's cooling, life-giving waters make life not only pleasant but possible. She is hailed as "O re Yeye," the Good Mother, who responds to the needs of her children with healing water and who appears in the bodies of her priestesses and priests in trance, in her animal messengers, in her shrines, and in the power of water itself. In this religion of embodiment, women, most particularly old women, possess *ase,* the power to make things happen. This spiritual authority is exemplified in Osun herself, the perpetually renewing source. Osun images female power and makes that power accessible to her female devotees. The metaphysical power of women, to create or withhold life, as Osun does, gives women authority in the household, the market, and the shrine, and an invisible means of redress against those who would deny them or their children.

Osun is a diviner whose gift of *Merindinlogun,* sixteen-cowrie divination, enables all *orisa* priestesses and priests to reveal the destinies of human beings and the wishes of the deities. She has the extraordinary power to change destiny, and to withhold or allow the blessings of all other deities.

Osun is also an empire builder, and a ruler who "takes the crown without asking." In the Ijesa kingdom, where Osun was a prominent deity, five of the thirty-nine known rulers were women. As the tutelary deity of many towns, she is "a woman with a knife," a warrior and defender of her people. In her most celebrated city, Osogbo, the head priestess of Osun is indispensable for its governance, for Osun granted the first king the right to establish the city. Every year, in one of Nigeria's largest festivals, the king of Osogbo returns to the river and pledges himself to Osun.

Osun is the Iyalode, paramount woman chief and head of the market. The Yoruba market—the meeting place of human beings and spirits—is the sphere of women, the source of their wealth, and a basis of their political power, demonstrated in the mass actions that market women organized against the British colonial powers.

BIBLIOGRAPHY

Abiodun, Rowland. "Women in Yoruba Religious Images." *African Languages and Cultures* 2, no. 1 (1989): 1–18. The most substantial work on the place of Osun in Yoruba religious thought.

Awe, Bolanle. "The Humanity of the Yoruba Goddess Osun: An Introductory Note." Institute for African Studies seminar paper. 1984. This important essay presents Osun as an image of Yoruba women and a figure of immense power.

———. "The Iyalode in the Traditional Yoruba Political System." In *Sexual Stratification.* Edited by Alice Schlegel. 1977. Relevant for its description of the Iyalode (chief of the women), a political title and a praise name of Osun.

Badejo, Deidre L. "Oral Literature of the Yoruba Goddess Osun." In *Religion and Society in Nigeria: Historical and Sociological Perspectives.* Edited by Jacob Olupona and Toyin Falola. 1991. This essay, together with *Osun Segeesi,* makes the point that Osun's gender and political authority are consistent with each other and central to her identity.

———. *Osun Segeesi: The Elegant Deity of Health, Power and Femininity.* 1996.

Cabrera, Lydia. *Yemaya y Ochun: Kariocha, Iyalorichas y Olorichas.* 1974. 2d ed., 1980. Comprehensive study by the premier folklorist of Afro-Cuban religions on Osun (Ochun) in Cuba and her devotees, many of whom are women.

Osun: Her Worship, Her Powers. Directed by Osuntoki Mojisola. Osun Olomitutu Productions. 1994. A film of priestesses of Osun in Osogbo and Ekiti, Nigeria, in ritual performance.

Wenger, Susanne, and Gert Chesi. *A Life with the Gods in Their Yoruba Homeland.* Austria, 1983. An account of Yoruba religion and Osun worship in Osogbo, Nigeria, by Austrian-born artist and priestess of Osun, Susanne Wenger.

MEI-MEI SANFORD

Pacifism and Nonviolence

Pacifism is generally understood to describe a philosophy or ideology whose adherents totally reject war or the use of force as a means of achieving a goal. Nonviolence, if thought of as a philosophy, describes a commitment to a way of life that renounces or resists violence. Nonviolence can also refer to a tactic or technique that may be employed by either pacifists or nonviolent activists to achieve defined goals. According to Mairead Maguire, Nobel Peace Prize laureate and cofounder of the Peace People in Northern Ireland, "Nonviolence is a way of life based on respect for each human person, and for the environment. It is also a means of bringing about social and political change, and resisting evil without entering into evil." Pacifists and advocates of nonviolence may base their philosophy on religio-ethical, humanist, or secular systems.

Nonviolence, often mistakenly thought to have originated as a Western concept, finds its earliest traceable spiritual roots in Eastern thought and religious traditions. Jainism, a predecessor of Buddhism, is a spiritual path that requires from its adherents a total commitment to nonviolence. Ahimsa (nonharming), a teaching of Jainism, Buddhism, and Hinduism, renounces, in different degrees, killing or harming any sentient (living) beings.

A double impediment faces the student of women's participation in the history of pacifism and nonviolence: women have been either entirely excluded or deemphasized in a branch of history that has also been either expunged or overlooked. Peace studies as a field has only recently come into existence, and feminist research into the area is newer still. Certain twentieth-century nonmilitary revolutions, such as those in India, the Philippines, South Africa, Eastern Europe, and the former Soviet Union have opened a new chapter in history that can no longer be ignored.

A brief survey of women's history dating back to the Paleolithic period reveals Goddess-worshiping societies characterized by their life-affirming values. Creation stories from the Americas, Europe, the Middle East, and Asia feature a Goddess-Mother source of all life whose rule emphasized the human connection to, and harmony with, nature. The glorification of weapons of war arose, along with the shift to male dominance, during the transition from the Copper to the Bronze Age between 3500 and 2500 B.C.E. In both Sumerian and later Babylonian legends, the Goddess created men and women simultaneously. A millennia-long tradition of egalitarianism and female divinity was to leave its traces in many ways, including the worship of the Christian Virgin Mary as a compassionate and merciful arbiter many centuries later.

The remaking of myths, legends, and sacred stories placed women in a new role as societies inclined more toward warfare. Take, for example, the serpent, which was a symbol of the prophetic and oracular power of the Goddess. In Greek mythology, it was transformed into a symbol of the dominant power of Zeus, and ultimately in Christian legend it became a symbol of evil.

Athenian democracy (which excluded women and slaves from the right to vote), may have been the setting for the first women's peace movement. Aristophanes' comedy, *Lysistrata*, in which women threaten to withhold sex until men stop making war, is a perfect example of nonviolent resistance. This play, meant to parody women, remains a testament to feminine values that must have prevailed in the fifth century B.C.E.

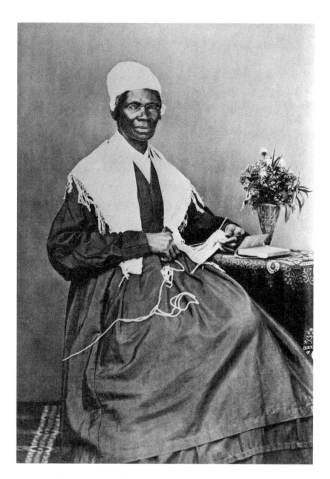

Evangelist and reformer Sojourner Truth (c. 1797–1883) was born a slave and later became a prominent woman suffrage and antislavery preacher (Corbis-Bettmann).

Although many Christian, Jewish, and Muslim adherents of nonviolence credit their religious grounding as the impetus for their beliefs, few female peacemakers or nonviolent activists can be found in the Hebrew Bible, the New Testament, or the Qur'an. A few examples can be noted. There is Abigail (1 Sam. 25: 3–42), who saved the lives of her household after her drunken husband insulted the shepherd David, soon to be king. Abigail cooked up a feast for David and his men and went out to meet the advancing enemy. She apologized for her churlish husband and begged forgiveness, thus preventing a slaughter and winning approval. Her reward was the rapid natural demise of her husband and the invitation (accepted) to become one of David's eight wives. A persistent widow (Luke 18:1–8) in the New Testament wears down a judge by returning over and over to insist on her rights until he finally grants her the justice she deserves. Later Muslim archives reveal the story of Lala Aziza, a fourteenth-century Mo-

roccan saint celebrated for her successful nonviolent encounter with a general who led 6,000 men to conquer her town. She faced him alone and demanded the justice of God for her people, which the amazed general granted.

Countless female activists, named and unnamed, have demonstrated their courage and personal commitment to nonviolent causes throughout history, more often than not as an outgrowth of their religious beliefs or the stirrings of their consciences. Some have given their lives for their beliefs, as in the case of Mary Dyer (1617–1660), who struggled against colonial laws that barred Quakers from freedom of worship. In the nineteenth century, Sarah and Angelina Grimké spoke against slavery before other Quakers were ready to do so. Sojourner Truth, a freed slave, was the first African-American to speak against slavery. Harriet Tubman escaped from slavery and ran an underground railroad to help others to freedom. Lucretia Mott (1793–1880) followed her "inner light" to campaign for the rights of women and Native Americans. Jeanette Rankin (1841– 1973) cast votes against both world wars in the U.S. Congress. Dorothy Day (1897–1980) started the Catholic Worker movement to further "a reconstruction of society."

To these names from American history could be added thousands from around the world. International movements such as the Women's International League for Peace and Freedom, founded in 1915, have empowered women and influenced governments. Spiritually motivated activists have worked in secular and religious organizations across cultures and nationalities. They have entered into dialogue with women from "enemy" camps. They have shared bunkers with women of other races, classes, and cultures. At the Greenham Common Peace Camp in England, women maintained a ten-year presence against militarism. They have stood with "Women in Black" in Jerusalem, Belgrade, Sarajevo, and other cities. They have created effective models of organizing and protesting injustice. Through international conferences and in the expanding world of the Internet, the network of women espousing pacifism and nonviolence is a growing presence on the world stage.

BIBLIOGRAPHY

Baron, Virginia, ed. *Womanspirit Moving: War Resisters League 1997 Peace Calendar*. 1997. Extensive listing of women's nonviolent organizations worldwide.

Cambridge Women's Peace Collective, eds. *My Country Is the Whole World: An Anthology of Women's Work on Peace and War*. 1984.

Dyck, Harvey L., ed. *The Pacific Impulse in Historical Perspective*. 1996.

Eisler, Riane. *The Chalice and the Blade: Our History, Our Future.* 1988.

Holmes, Robert L. *Nonviolence in Theory and Practice.* 1990.

Houver, Gerard. *A Nonviolent Lifestyle: Conversations with Jean and Hildegard Goss-Mayr.* Translated by Richard Bateman. 1989.

Mananzan, Mary John, Mercy Amba Oduyoye, Elsa Tamez, J. Shannon Clarkson, Mary C. Grey, and Letty M. Russell, eds. *Women Resisting Violence: Spirituality for Life.* 1996.

McAllister, Pam. *You Can't Kill the Spirit: Stories of Women and Nonviolent Action.* 1988. Includes a chronology of women's nonviolent actions and list of women's organizations for peace and justice, both international in scope.

Ruether, Rosemary Radford, and Rosemary Skinner Keller, eds. *Women and Religion in America.* Vols. 1–3. 1990.

VIRGINIA OLSEN BARON

Pan Ch'ao

Pan Ch'ao (c. 48–c.112) was a Chinese historian of the Han dynasty (206 B.C.E.–220 C.E.). She was noted for her *Instructions for Women* (*Nu chieh*), a primer of correct behavior, which builds on the ritual decorum for women described in the earlier classic, the *Book of Rites.* It especially outlines appropriate conduct for wives in relation to their husbands and other family members. It also outlines the woman's principal tasks in the household. Pan Ch'ao advocates womanly virtue, womanly words, womanly bearing, and womanly work. Above all a woman is urged to have respect and devotion and to cultivate obedience. Pan Ch'ao based her ideas on the traditional notions of yin (yielding) and yang (strength) as being characteristic of women and men in general. She emphasized the need for humility and acquiescence on the part of women. Yet these ideas also reflect the Taoist notions that in compliance or nonaction there is strength and power. Pan Ch'ao lamented that her own daughters were not as classically educated as she would have liked and encouraged education for young women as well as boys.

Pan Ch'ao was noted for her erudition as the daughter of an eminent scholar, Pan Piao (3–54), who began compiling the *History of the Former Han* (*Han Shu*). This was completed by his son Pan Ku (32–92) and later by Pan Ch'ao herself. She was said to have also served as a tutor to other women at court.

BIBLIOGRAPHY

Baldwin, S. L., trans. *Instructions for Chinese Women and Girls by Lady Tsao.* 1910.

Swann, Nancy Lee. *Pan Chao: Foremost Woman Scholar of China, First Century A.D.* 1932, 1968.

MARY EVELYN TUCKER

Pappenheim, Bertha

Writer and activist Bertha Pappenheim (1859–1936) founded the Jewish feminist movement in Germany and led it for twenty years. She belonged to the German and international women's movements but concentrated on the Jewish women's movement. As a young woman she suffered from severe psychological symptoms after the death of her father. She was treated by Josef Breuer, a colleague of Sigmund Freud, and is known as "Anna O" in their work. After a long convalescence she moved to Frankfurt, where she devoted her intense energy to social welfare. An observant Jew, Pappenheim saw social work as a duty but also as a path to women's emancipation. In 1902 she helped organize Women's Welfare (*Weibliche Fürsorge*), one of the first modern social welfare organizations. Run solely by

Bertha Pappenheim (1859–1936) was the founder of the Jewish feminist movement in Germany and led it for twenty years (Mary Evans Picture Library).

women, the group attempted to transcend "do-gooder" social work, envisaging a broad program of expanded services. It centralized and coordinated social services and merged the concerns of the German women's movement with that of Jewish social work.

In founding the League of Jewish Women (*Jüdischer Frauenbund*) in 1904 and bringing it into the German women's movement, Pappenheim strengthened her commitments to Judaism and to feminism. The League, which became the largest Jewish women's organization in Germany by 1929, fought for women's equality. It demanded women's suffrage within the Jewish community, promoted education for women, combatted white slavery (the white prostitute trade), established a home for unmarried mothers and their children, and set up job counseling centers and home economics schools. In 1933 the League withdrew from the German feminist movement before it disbanded itself rather than be Nazified.

Writing was an integral part of Pappenheim's activism. Beginning in the 1890s she wrote short stories, plays, pamphlets, and books on women's issues. Her best-known book, *Sisyphus Arbeit* (*Sisyphus Work*), described the problem of Jewish prostitution and white slavery. Her translations—the *Tsenerene* (a sixteenth-century Bible for women), the *Mayse Bukh* (a collection of medieval folktales and biblical and Talmudic stories that had been widely read by women), and the eighteenth-century diary of Glückl of Hameln, a businesswoman and mother of twelve—made these classic women's texts available to her contemporaries. Pappenheim died in 1936 before the Nazis destroyed the world she helped to create.

BIBLIOGRAPHY

Kaplan, Marion. *The Jewish Feminist Movement in Germany: The Campaigns of the Jüdischer Frauenbund, 1904–1938.* 1979.
Rosenbaum, Max, and Melvin Muroff, eds. *Anna O: Fourteen Contemporary Reinterpretations.* 1984.

MARION A. KAPLAN

The bodhisattva Kuan Yin (Kannon), beloved as the goddess of mercy by women in the Pure Land sect of Buddhism in Japan, carries the souls of believers to paradise, woodcut by Buemon Akiyama Tsukioka Yoshitoshi, 1888 (Asian Art & Archaeology, Inc./Corbis).

Paradise

In the world's religions paradise often can be said to have two separate though related interpretations. On the one hand it represents the primordial state of innocence before or at the beginning of time. Here woman is represented by Eve, Adam's mate and companion. In Judaism and Christianity Eve generally is assigned responsibility for heeding the serpent's call to disobey God, causing the fall from paradise and the move from the state of original bliss to the condition of travail on earth and in time. The other interpretation of paradise is as the resting place of the righteous after death, present in some form both in traditions that view time as cyclical, such as Hinduism and Buddhism, and in prophetic faiths that understand history to be linear. Synonymous with the idea of heaven, it is a place of reward, whether it is understood to be eternal or temporary, and is believed to be available to both men and women, although the male-gendered language of most classical writings often makes it difficult to discern the intended meaning.

In prophetic traditions such as Judaism, Zoroastrianism, Christianity, and Islam, paradise or heaven is the reward and the abode of those who have lived righteous lives. It is interpreted in various ways in terms of both location and character. Whereas in rabbinical traditions paradise is described as a state of spiritual fulfillment for the righteous, the focus of Jewish thought is less on the reality of paradise than on the importance of living a life of ethical responsibility and ritual purity. Women most certainly share such religious responsibilities with men and sometimes are said to have the fullest capacities for living righteously. Despite the fact that the three specific references to paradise in the New Testament all relate to men, Christians believe that heaven, whether physical or spiritual and wherever its location, is the reward and future dwelling place of those who have faith in the saving grace of Jesus Christ. It is available to both genders, as in Christ there is no male or female. Roman Catholics affirm that Mary the mother of Jesus was taken bodily into heaven, and one of the titles by which she is often identified is "the queen of heaven," a model of piety for all women. Similarly, the Qur'an stresses the ethical responsibilities and future rewards for faithful male and female believers, each on his or her own merits. Unique to Islam is the concept of the maidens of paradise, the pure and sinless Hur, who never inhabit any region but the Garden and are available for the enjoyment of male believers. Though female, the Hur are not to be confused with the believing women in paradise. The Church of Jesus Christ of Latter-day Saints insists that Mormon marriages are "for time and eternity," making access to paradise essential for women as well as men.

For traditions that see time as cyclical, with ages repeating ages, the idea of heaven is temporary rather than eternal. Both Hinduism and Buddhism believe in the existence of many heavens where the dead enjoy the consequences of their good karma, although not even a limited stay in heaven in itself has any liberating value. In the early Vedic tradition the heaven of Yama was described as the realm where the fathers proceed after death to be with the gods. With the advent of the bhakti or devotional aspect of Hinduism came the understanding of the path of devotion as a way of liberation, open to women and outcasts. The abodes of Vishnu and Siva became the goal, with the soul of the devotee carried to paradise. The Indian city of Vrindaban is known as the paradise of Krishna. Only there can the highest degree of devotion be achieved, exemplified by the pure love of the female cowherds for the Lord Krishna, the union of female and male, human and divine.

In Buddhism the ideal of liberation has for the most part been understood to be attainable by both women and men. Whereas early Theravada Buddhism claimed women could not attain liberation, with the development of the Mahayana tradition some women are said to have achieved the status of bodhisattvas (enlightenment beings), working for the salvation of all. Pure Land Buddhism postulates the paradise of Sukhāvatī, abode of the Buddha Amitābha available through faith on the part of men and women. Whether son or daughter, says the text, whoever hears the name of the blessed Buddha and believes will be taken by a host of bodhisattvas into paradise.

BIBLIOGRAPHY

Carmody, Denise Lardner. *Women and World Religions.* 1989.

Holck, Frederick H., ed. *Death and Eastern Thought.* 1974.

Johnson, Christopher Jay, and Marsha G. McGee, eds. *Encounters with Eternity.* 1986.

Klostermaier, Klaus. *In the Paradise of Krishna.* 1969.

JANE I. SMITH

Pārvatī

In Hindu mythology the goddess Pārvatī, whose name means "she who dwells in the mountains," is the daughter of the nymph Menā and the Himalaya mountain; later she becomes the wife of Siva. She is also known as Umā (possibly meaning "mother") and Girijā (daughter of the mountain). Her names, plus the fact that she is not mentioned in the Vedic hymns, the oldest literary strata of Hindu tradition, indicate that she may have originated with the non-Aryan indigenous peoples of India. The Kena Upanishad (third century B.C.E.), one of the mystical treatises composed later than the Vedic hymns, refers to Umā Haimavatī (Umā of the Himalayas) who reveals to the gods the secret knowledge of *brahman*, the supreme reality. Later Shakti (goddess-oriented) traditions identify this goddess as an aspect of the one great goddess (Mahādevī). Pārvatī is also said to be the later incarnation of Siva's wife Satī, who, after immolating herself on her father Daksha's sacrificial fire, was cut up into pieces that then fell on different parts of India as *shakti pīṭhas*, places of power where the Goddess in various manifestations is enshrined.

Among Hindus Pārvatī is best known and loved, however, as the beautiful, devoted, and clever wife and tamer of the rather unruly, hemp-smoking, tiger-skin-wearing, snake-garlanded god Siva. According to the story that appears in numerous written and oral versions, Siva was so engrossed in his severe ascetic meditations that he was oblivious to the charms of the lovely mountain girl who had fallen in love with him. Even the arrow of the god Kāma failed to arouse him; instead, he reduced Kāma to ashes with the flame from his third eye. Pārvatī, after performing severe ascetic austerities of her own for years, finally attracted the attention of Siva and won him as her husband. Their wedding ceremony is widely celebrated in art, songs, and stories, with descriptions often focusing on the incongruity of the wild-looking Siva and his motley retinue with the refined Pārvatī. They have a long and happy marriage, however, making love and matching skills in dance competitions and wits in philosophical debates. Hindus consider them to be Mother and Father of the universe. In a springtime festival throughout India, women and girls reenact their wedding ritually with clay figurines in the hopes of obtaining a good husband and general well-being.

BIBLIOGRAPHY

Kinsley, David. *Hindu Goddesses: Visions of the Divine Feminine in the Hindu Religious Tradition.* 1986.
O'Flaherty, Wendy Doniger. *Asceticism and Eroticism in the Mythology of Siva.* 1973.
———. "The Shifting Balance of Power in the Marriage of Siva and Pārvatī." In *The Divine Consort: Radha and the Goddesses of India.* Edited by John Stratton Hawley and Donna Marie Wulff. 1982.

KATHLEEN M. ERNDL

Patriarchy

In feminist theory patriarchy (rule of the father) refers to a social construction of reality and of thinking that is based on domination of women and also of those groups considered inferior because of race, gender, class, sexual orientation, or disability. The distribution of political, economic, cultural, and intellectual power in society creates a basic structure of injustice and oppression that must be resisted by those committed to the work of mending the creation.

In various forms of patriarchal societies, women are assigned their status according to the race, sex, and class of the men to whom they belong. Fathers, husbands, and sons, by way of a male inheritance system, assume control over women's sexuality and conduct.

Patriarchy is characterized by a dualistic system of thought that divides reality into opposing categories such as men/women, spirit/body, rich/poor, white/black, straight/gay, academic/practical, and so on. It then assigns inferior status, lower value, evil, or sin to the "other" group. In the list given, the latter category in each duality is considered inferior. In North America and Europe this duality supports white, heterosexual, rich male privilege and extends to the white, heterosexual, rich women who share that privilege. It is a self-justifying edifice of oppression that shuts the door on outsiders, the "losers." Unequal access to power to de-termine one's own life and world is a hallmark of women's experience.

Rosemary Radford Ruether has pointed out that although there is no one social system in patriarchal societies, traditional patriarchal societies usually exhibit certain common characteristics. The lineage and inheritance is through the father, and the male children are preferred. The bodies, sexuality, and reproductive capacity of wives belong to husbands. Husbands have the right to use violence against their wives. Women have no public roles and so their education is limited.

Beyond this general description, traditional patriarchal societies vary widely in different historical and geographical settings, as do the many other forms of oppression that are also present in a particular society. Structural analysis by white feminists has often failed to do justice to the interlocking issues of racism, classism, and sexism; their work often fails to acknowledge the white privilege they receive from patriarchal systems. For this reason, womanist theologians such as Delores Williams have rejected the use of the term patriarchy as exclusive of black women's experience of oppression by white women. Racism, colonialism, and many forms of oppression require that we move beyond a perspective that reduces all of women's problems to male domination. To clarify that patriarchy refers to social structures of power and not only to male power, some feminists, such as Elisabeth Schüssler Fiorenza, speak of *kyriarchy*, the rule of the lord. Others, such as Gerda Lerner and Peggy Reeves Sanday have provided historical and contemporary studies of the development of patriarchy.

Islam, Judaism, and Christianity all reinforce patriarchal structures of domination. Yet, in examining how women fare within these religious traditions, attention must also be paid to political and social conflicts and structures of racism and nationalism. To understand points of crisis that spur changes in women's roles, one must first understand how tradition is shoring up the ideological conflicts between larger groups. The scholarship compiled in *After Patriarchy* shows that it is possible to work for transformations of world religions and their teachings about the relationships of women and men. One key to this work of recovery, critique, and transformation is the willingness to use a hermeneutic of suspicion about the cultural and political expressions of patriarchy, and a hermeneutic of commitment to work for transformation of religious beliefs and practices within our traditions.

BIBLIOGRAPHY

Cooey, Paula M., William R. Eakin, and Jay B. Mc-Daniel, eds. *After Patriarchy: Feminist Transformations of the World Religions.* 1991.

Eller, Cynthia. *Living in the Lap of the Goddess: The Feminist Spirituality Movement in America.* 1993.

Lerner, Gerda. *The Creation of Patriarchy.* Vol. 1 of *Women and History.* 1986.

Ruether, Rosemary Radford. "Patriarchy." In *Dictionary of Feminist Theologies.* Edited by Letty M. Russell and J. Shannon Clarkson. 1996.

Sanday, Peggy Reeves. *Female Power and Male Dominance.* 1981.

Schüssler Fiorenza, Elisabeth. "Ties That Bind: Domestic Violence Against Women." In *Women Resisting Violence: Spirituality for Life.* Edited by Mary John Mananzan et al. 1996.

Williams, Delores S. "The Color of Feminism: Or Speaking the Black Woman's Tongue." In *Feminist Theological Ethics: A Reader.* Edited by Lois K. Westminster. 1994.

See also **Misogyny.**

LETTY M. RUSSELL

Patronage

Patronage refers to the encouragement and support that a benefactor makes to an individual or a community. Frequently it involves a financial gift by the patron. Throughout history women have been donors as well as recipients of patronage. Evidence comes from documents and archaeological artifacts, such as inscriptions. Women have financed religious structures; donated ecclesiastical and cultic objects; and promoted religious expression in song, dance, art, and literature.

Prior to World War I, wealthy women tended to come from the elite classes of society, inheriting their riches from fathers or husbands. Since patronage is usually linked to the outlay of money, the historical incidence of women's patronage has been relatively small. Nevertheless, the role of patron has afforded women influence within ancient and modern religious communities, as well as offering the benefactor the prestige and power that accompanies the bestowal of donations.

Patronage was a sophisticated system of influence and honor in the Roman Empire, controlled by favors, social rank, and wealth. Epigraphic evidence from this period indicates that women competed with men in financing the construction of public buildings, including temples richly ornamented with frescoes and mosaics. In addition to donating money for building, women served as patrons of cults, often supplying the funding for religious gatherings such as banquets.

Inscriptions provide clues to patronage by Jewish women during the Second Temple and Mishnaic eras (first century C.E. to third century C.E.). In the catalog of inscriptions compiled by Lifshitz (1967), catalog numbers 29 and 33 specifically mention women, one of whom gave an entire synagogue and the other a marble chancel screen. Another inscription tells of Tation, who built a synagogue from her own funds and is honored by the community with a golden crown and a seat of honor. Donations of the sort mentioned in the epigraphical and literary sources continue today among Jewish women as does patronage in support of song, story, and dance as religious expression.

In the third and fourth centuries ties of patronage between Christian widows, virgins, and deacons on the one hand and male clergy on the other reflected tolerance of the women's almsgiving to the poor and the care of the sick, but alarm that women's influence in the church might grow as a consequence of women's wealth. In the opinion of male authors women's benefaction could safely be bestowed on the poor, but women who used their public status to wield influence in the church were objects of suspicion and scandal. At the same time powerful men influenced the distribution of women's wealth through familial, legal, or religious means. For example, certain Christian bishops positioned themselves as protectors of wealthy widows and virgins, directing these women's energies and money into the service of the church. Since the fourth century there has been a documented tradition of Christian matrons as patron of architecture. The letters of the fourth-century theologian Jerome extol the patronage of the women of his acquaintance. Among the projects sponsored by Christian women are convents, monasteries, and churches.

Carolyn Valone (1992) suggests that sixteenth-century Christian women consciously modeled their patronage of architecture on that of Christian women from late antiquity and the early medieval period. The examples she uses show the striking similarities in women's status and dispersal of wealth in these two historical periods. In addition to donations of monumental gifts, sacristy inventories list crosses for the altar, altar coverings, patens for the chalice, and palliums or banners. As benefactors, these women's names are recorded alongside the names of bishops, cardinals, priors, and important officials of the papal court.

In the pre-Ottoman and Ottoman periods (until the end of World War I), Muslim women from the privileged classes, especially the court of the sultan, sponsored the building of mosques and mausoleums. Structures from the pre-Ottoman period of Islamic Anatolia in what is now Turkey include a large number of tombs commemorating women. One interpretation offered to explain the monumentality of the tombs is that they represent the dominion of Islam over Christianity. It is noteworthy then that women are associated with a large number of these structures.

In the Ottoman period religious institutions such as mosques, schools, *zāwiyahs* (convents for dervishes), and tombs were built under the auspices of wealthy Muslim women. However, the mosque surpasses the mausoleum in association with women's names. Mihrimah Sultan (d. 1578) is unique in Ottoman architecture with two mosques and numerous associated structures attesting to her patronage. The last mosque to have been donated by a female member of the Ottoman court is sited in the Aksaray quarter of Istanbul. Built under the auspices of Pertevniyal, wife of Sultan Mahmud II, the mosque was finished in 1871.

Benefices made by Muslim women are occasionally recorded as *waqf*, which is a religious endowment that produces revenues for the support of a beneficiary, frequently a mosque. In a survey of endowments made by women from the sixteenth century through the nineteenth centuries, women were responsible for between one-quarter and one-third of new *waqfs* in Jerusalem, Jaffa, and Istanbul. One conclusion that might be drawn from this data is that Muslim women were property holders with sufficient power to control their own wealth. However, family pressure by male relatives might have influenced the gifts.

Women's patronage is not confined to western religious traditions. Examples survive in Buddhism where laywomen have been prominent donors, and nuns have also made donations. An inscription from the Kuṣān period (second–third centuries C.E.) tells of the gift of an image by the nun Dhanvatī. Several decades later another nun set up an image, also at Mathurā. At other locations inscriptions record that nuns had parity with monks in their gift giving. The importance of the inscriptions left by donors to Buddhist building projects and monuments attests to the survival of nuns' communities and to the wealth of these women. Though textual evidence states that monks and nuns were to reject material possessions, the archaeological evidence documents donations by both groups. Gifts made by female monastics in northern India decreased in the Gupta period of the fourth and fifth centuries, and the decline continued until the cessation of ordained nuns there.

BIBLIOGRAPHY

Baer, Gabriel. "Women and Waqf: An Analysis of the Istanbul TAHRIR of 1546." *Asian and African Studies.* 17, nos. 1–3 (1983): 9–27.

Bartholomeusz, Tessa. *Women under the Bō Tree: Buddhist Nuns in Sri Lanka.* 1994.

Bates, Ülkü Ü. "Women as Patrons of Architecture in Turkey." In *Women in the Muslim World.* Edited by Lois Beck and Nikki Keddie. 1978.

Collins, Matthew S. "Money, Sex and Power: An Examination of the Role of Women as Patrons of the Ancient Synagogues." In *Recovering the Role of Women: Power and Authority in Rabbinic Jewish Society.* Edited by Peter J. Haas. 1992.

Falk, Nancy Auer. "The Case of the Vanishing Nuns: The Fruits of Ambivalence in Ancient Buddhism." In *Unspoken Worlds: Women's Religious Lives in Non-Western Cultures.* Edited by Nancy Auer Falk and Rita Gross. 1980.

Ilan, Tal. *Jewish Women in Greco-Roman Palestine: An Inquiry into Image and Status.* 1995.

Lifshitz, Baruch. *Donateurs et fondateurs dans les synagogues juives: Repertoire des dedicaces grecques relatives à la construction et à la refection des synagogues.* Paris, 1967.

Plaskow, Judith. *Standing Again at Sinai: Judaism from a Feminist Perspective.* 1990.

Pomeroy, Sarah B. *Goddesses, Whores, Wives, and Slaves: Women in Classical Antiquity.* 1975.

Schopen, Gregory. *Bones, Stones, and Buddhist Monks: Collected Papers on the Archaeology, Epigraphy, and Texts of Monastic Buddhism in India.* 1997.

Van Bremen, Riet. "Women and Wealth." In *Images of Women in Antiquity.* Edited by Averil Cameron and Amelie Kuhrt. 1983.

Valone, Carolyn. "Roman Matrons as Patrons." In *The Crannied Wall: Women, Religion, and the Arts in Early Modern Europe.* Edited by Craig A. Monson. 1992.

Veyne, Paul, ed. *A History of Private Life from Pagan Rome to Byzantium.* 1987.

Willis, Janice D. "Nuns and Benefactresses: The Role of Women in the Development of Buddhism." In *Women, Religion and Social Change.* Edited by Yvonne Yazbeck Haddad and Ellison Banks Findly. 1985.

See also **Art**; **Christianity: Historical Overview from 300 to 1800**; **Monasticism**; **Ordination: In Buddhism**; **Visual Arts.**

DIANE TREACY-COLE

Pazzi, Maria Maddalena de'

Carmelite nun and Italian mystic Maria Maddalena de' Pazzi (1566–1607) was born into the noble Florentine family de' Pazzi and baptized Caterina but took the name Maria Maddalena when she became a nun. When she was still a child, the Jesuits introduced her to their meditation techniques and to some of their basic writings. She joined the convent Santa Maria degli Angeli when she was sixteen (August 1582), taking the veil the following year. Only a few months later she began having daily visions, during which she conversed with the Trinity, and in particular with Christ, whom she generally refers to as the Word. Her visions have a distinctly oral character. The mystic believed that the Word wanted her to summon his being through her voice. Her convent sisters transcribed her monologues and then edited them. The mystic rejected her sisters' writings. Left alone with one of her sisters' texts, she burned it, enraging her confessor. Her visions were her repeated attempts to embody the Word in her voice. Her raptures are often solo mystical plays, which focus on Christ's passion and death. For the mystic, the gospel is a script that allows infinite performances. Christ's blood is the core of Maria Maddalena's mysticism. According to the visionary, the Word's blood is a language that needs to be articulated by every creature. Through the Son's blood the creature can converse with God. Maria Maddalena de' Pazzi was canonized in 1669. Her sisters' manuscripts were edited in seven volumes from 1960 to 1966.

BIBLIOGRAPHY

Catena, Carlo. *Santa Maria Maddalena de' Pazzi: Orientamenti spirituali e ambiente in cui visse.* 1966.

Maggi, Armando. "Blood as Language in the Visions of Maria Maddalena de' Pazzi." *Rivista di letterature moderne e comparate* 3 (1995): 219–235.

Pazzi, Maria Maddalena de'. *Tutte le opere di Santa Maria Maddalena de' Pazzi.* Edited by Carlo Catena and Bruno Secondin. 1960–1966.

Pozzi, Mario. *Le parole dell'estasi.* 1984.

Secondin, Bruno. *Santa Maria Maddalena de' Pazzi: Esperienza e dottrina.* 1974.

ARMANDO MAGGI

Pele

Even now, the Hawaiian goddess Pele is believed by many people to have created the two great volcanoes on the island of Hawaii and to live there in the fiery caldera of Kilauea. Her character has the unpredictability of her chosen home, and she may appear to people as an old woman or a beautiful girl. At intervals she displays her power by sending out lava flows that destroy the fern forests and villages below.

Myths and songs celebrate Pele's early journey to the islands from the distant land of Kahiki, her search for a home, her love affairs, and her battles with rivals. In these stories Pele, her younger sisters, and their friends form a community in which men usually play only a mi-

nor part. The women's passions for each other, both loving and hating, are often the mainspring of the action. In particular there is the love, yet rivalry, between Pele and her favorite little sister, Hiʻiaka.

Soon after Pele's arrival from Kahiki she falls in love with Lohiʻau, a handsome chief living on Kauai island, and after establishing herself in Kilauea she asks Hiʻiaka to fetch him from Kauai. Hiʻiaka "the wise" undertakes this journey, traveling from the southernmost island to the one furthest to the north. At first all goes well, and on the way she composes many hula (songs accompanied by dances) relating to the places she visits. Finding Lohiʻau dead, she restores him to life and takes him to her sister. But Pele has become suspicious that Hiʻiaka herself loves Lohiʻau, and there is a fierce struggle on the brink of the volcano. In the end, though, the two women are reconciled.

Before the arrival of Europeans and Christianity the ritual propitiation of Pele was the main religious activity in the volcanic districts of Hawaii, especially in those at most risk from Pele's streams of molten lava; on the other Hawaiian islands she was known in myths and chants but her propitiation was less important. The many songs attributed to Hiʻiaka are still performed.

BIBLIOGRAPHY

Beckwith, Martha. *Hawaiian Mythology.* 1940. Reprint, 1970.

Emerson, N. *Pele and Hiiaka: A Myth from Hawaii.* 1915.

Nimmo, H. Arlo. "Pele: Ancient Goddess of Contemporary Hawaii." *Pacific Studies* 9, no. 1 (1985): 121–179.

See also **Goddess: Historical Goddesses; Sister.**

MARGARET ORBELL

Performance Art

Performance art is a term that first appeared in North American art discourses in the late 1960s to describe the interdisciplinary, temporal, body- and politically oriented art form developed by conceptual artists exploring the relationship between art and life. Though by nature it resists definition or categorization, performance art (or, more recently, "performance") is a genre that actively blurs the boundaries between the arts and incorporates aspects of theater, sculpture, painting, dance, film, video, music, and poetry. It is influenced by, and in some cases inseparable from, the disparate traditions of European avant-garde (particularly Dada, Futurism, and Surrealism), non-Western art and performance, popular culture, public spectacle, political protest, and religious ritual. The historical emergence of performance as a discrete art form is often thought to mark the shift from modernism to postmodernism. Whereas the artwork of modernity is formal, material (and commodified), bounded, and inscribed with ideological meaning by the individual artist, performance rebels against these exclusive notions of "high art" by alternately creating meaning through diverse forms that are temporal and ephemeral (and therefore neither reproduceable nor commodifiable), collaborative, contingent, and inclusive of the spectator's presence or participation. The late art critic and theorist Craig Owens said that postmodern art is specifically about the act and politics of representing; performance, then, is paradigmatically postmodern.

Historically women's expressions have been excluded from the Western cultural canon and subsumed by the modernist (and androcentric) notion of the universal subject. Not surprisingly, women made up the majority of artists who popularized the deconstructive and self-reflexive art of performance in the 1970s and continued to lead the genre through the 1990s. Women's performances are inherently political since they explore the problematic relationship between women and the Western system of representation. Insofar as feminist theory has demonstrated how meaning is made and how the culturally dominant male attains to subjectivity through the embodied presence of woman as objectified other, feminist performance challenges the discourse of representation not only through its temporal forms and multilayered texts but also by positing the female body as speaking subject.

Feminist performance offers a potentially subversive (and largely untapped) medium for women's expression of religion and spirituality where, through their own words and bodies, women articulate their lived experiences, conceptions of themselves, and the complexity of their sexual, racial, ethnic, class, and religious identities; define their relationships with their bodies, others, and the divine; and assert political, social, and religious ideas and concerns. Using themes of embodiment and mourning, opera-trained performer Diamanda Galas, in her controversial 1989 piece "Plague Mass," used Hebrew Scripture and Christ imagery to witness the pain, suffering, anger, and injustice of people who have died of AIDS, and to condemn the passivity of homophobic culture. In a similar move to give voice to silenced others, Karen Finley, in pieces from the early 1990s, harnessed a form of shamanic trance to channel the words, emotions, and protests of incest survivors. Though widely divergent in their form and content, feminist performances, like ritual, are created in the faith that they will effect change.

BIBLIOGRAPHY

Auslander, Philip. *Presence and Resistance: Postmodernism and Cultural Politics in Contemporary American Performance.* 1992.

Case, Sue-Ellen, ed. *Performing Feminisms: Feminist Critical Theory and Theatre.* 1990.

Dolan, Jill. *Presence and Desire: Essays on Gender, Sexuality, Performance.* 1993.

Hart, Lynda, and Peggy Phelan, eds. *Acting Out: Feminist Performances.* 1993.

Lippard, Lucy R. *Mixed Blessings.* 1990.

Montano, Linda. *Art in Everyday Life.* 1981.

Outside the Frame: Performance and the Object. Cleveland Center for Contemporary Art, 1994.

Owens, Craig. "The Discourse of Others: Feminists and Postmodernism." In his *Beyond Recognition.* 1992.

Phelan, Peggy. *Unmarked: The Politics of Performance.* 1992.

Piper, Adrian. *Talking to Myself: The Ongoing Autobiography of an Art Object.* Brussels, 1974.

Roth, Moira, ed. *The Amazing Decade: Women and Performance Art in America, 1970–1980.* 1983.

Schechner, Richard. *The Future of Ritual.* 1993.

Ugwu, Catherine, ed. *Let's Get It On: The Politics of Black Performance.* 1995.

See also **Performance Theory.**

KIRSTEN STAMMER FURY

Performance Theory

Since the 1960s performance has attracted the attention of scholars in anthropology, religion, sociology, philosophy, theater, and cultural studies. Performance, in contrast to text, involves the body in action. The topic of performance was first treated in the early works of sociologist Erving Goffman, and its discussion encompasses a whole set of phenomena ranging from speech acts and presentations of everyday life to sports, dance, play, and religious rituals. More than diversion, entertainment, and aesthetics, performance is now seen as central to the shaping of culture. Feminist performance theory takes up the task of searching out the contexts, deep structure and process, meanings, and cultural and political power implications of performances.

Performance is acting with the human body that takes place in a public, collective space. This interpretive space is set apart from ordinary space by a frame, such as locale, costumes, masks, and symbols, signaling its extraordinary quality. Crossing the threshold from everyday life into symbolic, imaginary space where the rules and roles of ordinary reality are suspended is highlighted by anthropologist Victor Turner in his concept of liminality. Ritual elders guide the spontaneous flow of affective processes and actions in liminality toward intended goals. A double-edged sword, performance reflects, legitimates, and reinforces the existing cultural hierarchy as well as exposes, questions, reverses, relativizes, and subverts it. Performance that is witnessed by groups and that engages them is an instrument in the social reconstruction of cultural knowledge collectively legitimated.

Whereas rituals effect an intended outcome with active participants, the performing arts like theater engage the audience as spectators. Richard Schechner, trailblazing performance theorist, considers ritual and theater as two "braids" of efficacy and entertainment, one giving rise to the other at different moments. The origins of theater are thought to be in festivals, rites, and ceremonies. On the other hand, magic acts, puppetry, acrobatics, ventriloquism, and other popular entertainments are closely connected to certain shamanic rituals. The boundary between ritual and theater is permeable.

Key to performance is the presence of the body as an elemental vibrating, moving, sweating, vocal organism, with the power to incite deep experiencing. With the body, performance creates an environment for multisensory holistic experience fusing thought and emotion, past and present, mythic and mundane; the site of such dualities, the body is a repository of personal and collective knowledge. The body is necessarily social, inscribed with layers of cultural significations reflected in costumes, gestures, postures, patterns of eye contact, the structure of space, and physical movements.

The socialized body is a genderized body. Philosopher Judith Butler (1990, 1993) contends that gender identity is a performative accomplishment acquired through doing and dramatizing. The body, through stylized repetitive acts over time according to a historical script of two opposing genders, becomes a bearer and reproducer of cultural gender meanings. For Butler, gender and heterosexuality are historical products that have been reified as natural dispositions through performance, on and off stage.

Who were the scriptwriters, directors, actors, and spectators of these genderized performances? Feminist critique of performances in dominant Western and Eastern canonical traditions notes the ostensible absence of women in the production, performance, and reception of theater and religious ritual. Sue-Ellen Case (1988) finds that women disappeared from Greek theater in the fifth century B.C.E., with women relegated to the private sphere and men as the public carriers of power and wealth. In the Elizabethan period in England it was considered immoral for the female body, the custodian of male sexual behavior, to appear on stage. Female roles were played by young boys, scripted from male fantasies, desires, and images of women. Invisibility rendered women insubstantial and an object of male projection. Without a voice, a face, or a body that mattered, women did not really exist.

A similar absence of women characterizes the Asian religio-aesthetic performance traditions of Noh, kathakali, and Chinese opera. Men held a monopoly over the art of these traditions—their prestige, access, and production. It was believed that such practices served to maintain social order and public morality. Institutions of male dominance and lineage upheld militaristic and feudal religious and cultural ideologies.

The anthropologist Elaine Combs-Schilling (1989) demonstrates that in Moroccan Islam, religious and cultural values are inscribed into sexual intercourse, blood spilling, birth, and death through ritual practices. Male and female roles learned and rehearsed during a time of heightened emotions take on the force of universal truth intrinsic to existence. Body, religion, and politics confirm the seamless design of the universal order, with male as divine monarch and creator and female as dependent and peripheral.

Mary Daly (1973) was one of the first women iconoclasts to deconstruct the patriarchal symbols, metaphors, rituals, and organization of the Catholic Church and call women to a spirituality through new female symbols. According to Naomi Goldenberg (1997), it is through the "incessant repetitions" of male-created and directed rituals in Judaism and Christianity that patriarchal values gain the enormous force of historicity that are taken for granted in both religious and secular institutions.

Even when no explicit laws legislate against women's representation in performance, the historicity and prevalence of cultural norms exert powerful sanctions and taboos on women's performability. Contesting and expanding the possibilities of women's representation in the circumscribed space of performance is crucial to redefining women's identity in religious, cultural, and political life.

BIBLIOGRAPHY

Bunch, Ralph, and Mutsuko Motoyama. "Women, Tradition and Politics in Japanese Classical Theatre." *Journal of Asian and African Studies* 22, nos. 1–2 (1987): 80–86.
Butler, Judith. *Bodies that Matter: On the Discursive Limits of "Sex."* 1993.
———. "Performative Acts and Gender Constitution: An Essay in Phenomenology and Feminist Theory."

In *Performing Feminisms: Feminist Critical Theory and Theatre.* Edited by Sue-Ellen Case. 1990.

Case, Sue-Ellen. *Feminism and Theatre.* 1988.

Combs-Schilling, M. Elaine. *Sacred Performances: Islam, Sexuality and Sacrifice.* 1989.

Daly, Mary. *Beyond God the Father: Toward a Philosophy of Women's Liberation.* 1973.

Diamond, Elin. *Performance and Cultural Politics.* 1996.

Dolan, Jill. *The Feminist Spectator as Critic.* 1991.

———. *Presence and Desire: Essays on Gender, Sexuality, Performance.* 1993.

Ferris, Lesley. *Acting Women: Images of Women in Theatre.* 1990.

Gendlin, Eugene. *Experiencing and the Creation of Meaning.* 1962.

Goffman, Erving. *The Presentation of Self in Everyday Life.* 1959.

Goldenberg, Naomi. "A Theory of Gender as a Central Hermeneutic in the Psychoanalysis of Religion." In *Hermeneutical Approaches in Psychology of Religion.* Edited by J. A. Belzen. 1997.

Grimes, Ronald. *Ritual Criticism: Case Studies in Its Practice, Essays on Its Theory.* 1990.

Hanna, Judith Lynne. *Dance, Sex and Gender.* 1988.

MacAloon, John J. *Rite, Drama, Festival, Spectacle: Rehearsals Toward a Theory of Cultural Performance.* 1984.

Phelan, Peggy. *Unmarked: The Politics of Performance.* 1993.

Schechner, Richard. *Performance Theory.* 1988.

Schechner, Richard, and Willa Appel. *By Means of Performance: Intercultural Studies of Theatre and Ritual.* 1990.

Schechner, Richard, and Mady Schuman, eds. *Ritual, Play, and Performances: Readings in the Social Sciences/Theatre.* 1976.

Turner, Victor. *Dramas, Fields and Metaphors.* 1974.

———. *The Ritual Process: Structure and Anti-Structure.* 1969.

Wolff, Janet. *Feminine Sentences: Essays on Women and Culture.* 1990.

Journals to consult in feminist performance include: *Educational Theatre Journal* (predecessor to *Theatre Journal*) 1–30 (1949–1978); *Theatre Journal* 31 (1979–current); *Literature in Performance* (predecessor to *Text and Performance Quarterly*) 1–8 (1980–1988); *Text and Performance Quarterly* 9 (1989–current); *Theatre Topics* 1 (1991–current); and *Women and Performance* 1 (1983–current).

See also **Body**; **Dance and Drama**; **Music**; **Speech**.

BONNIE LEE

Periodization

Ever since Joan Kelly's essay "Did Women Have a Renaissance?" appeared in 1977, scholars of women's history have tried to solve the problem of periodization. If, as Kelly hypothesized, the traditional divisions or breaks in men's history did not apply to women, then where should the divisions be? What were the equivalent defining eras or events for women?

Historians of women did not at first take up Kelly's challenge to find new divisions for history from a female perspective. Instead, in thinking about the intersection of the history of religion and women's history, scholars in the United States and Europe first described women's particular religious experiences and their specific roles in relation to the traditional divisions of men's history. For example, Rosemary Ruether and Eleanor McLaughlin have presented narratives and analyses of women's roles in the evolution of the Jewish and Christian faiths.

Like Kelly, however, women's historians did question the designation of these traditional eras as significant in the same ways for women and men. Kelly's essay had argued that whereas the Italian Renaissance gave men a sense of individualism and new liberties, it reinforced women's subordination and restricted roles within the household. Similarly, studies of the major religions have revolved around the question of whether or not the particular faith was "good" or "bad" for women. Did the doctrine, rituals and practice, and institutional organization promote and value women or suppress and devalue them, their roles, and their potential or actual contributions? For example, Lyndal Roper explains how Protestantism, while apparently liberating, could be manipulated to reaffirm constraints on women's lives. Leila Ahmed shows how religious doctrine and practice reflect a more universal ambivalence about women's nature and appropriate behavior. Lindsey Harlan investigates high-caste women's use of past religious traditions and practice to reconcile contradictions between duties to family and the economic and social changes all around them.

Challenges to traditional periodization came from historians who turned to a more anthropological and sociological approach to the history of women in religion, using belief systems, spaces, and functions specific to women as the defining concepts of their research. Although attentive to chronology, these historians, particularly of Christianity, have not restricted themselves to but rather ranged across traditional divisions of men's religious history. Marina Warner's work became a model for those interested in dissecting ideological aspects of a faith. Caroline Walker Bynum did the same for studies of religious practice. JoAnn McNamara's numerous essays and books about nuns and nunneries presented a continuum of European women's communities related to but not dependent on men's orders.

As studies of women's experiences have been completed for all of the major faiths, a cyclical rather than linear periodization of women's religious history has begun to emerge. Whether in Buddhism, Judaism, Christianity, Hinduism, or Islam, a pattern first hypothesized about European women and religion seems to hold across time and geographical region. In the formative stages women played active, more or less equal roles as disciples, proselytizers, and founders of early religious practices and communities. With the success of the new religion, with political acceptance by dominant male elites and the subsequent institutionalization of the faith, the relatively gender-neutral, egalitarian community of believers was transformed into a hierarchy of authorities with women in clearly differentiated, subordinate roles. As revelation and rituals became dogma, the new faith affirmed rather than contradicted negative views of women's spiritual capabilities and of the female body. Each revival or reform of the faith repeated the cycle.

BIBLIOGRAPHY

Ahmed, Leila. *Women and Gender in Islam: Historical Roots of a Modern Debate.* 1992.

Anderson, Bonnie S., and Judith P. Zinsser. *A History of Their Own: Women in Europe from Prehistory to the Present.* 1988. For a cyclical periodization see vol. 1, sections 1 and 3.

Bynum, Caroline Walker. *Holy Feast and Holy Fast: The Religious Significance of Food to Medieval Women.* 1987.

Haddad, Yvonne Yazbeck, and Ellison Banks Findly. *Women, Religion, and Social Change.* 1985. Useful on women's experiences across time.

Harlan, Lindsey. *Religion and Rajput Women: The Ethic of Protection in Contemporary Narratives.* 1992.

Kelly, Joan. "Did Women Have a Renaissance?" In *Becoming Visible: Women in European History.* Edited by Renate Bridenthal, Claudia Koonz, and Susan Stuard. 2d ed., 1987.

Roper, Lyndal. *The Holy Household: Women and Morals in Reformation Augsburg.* 1989.

Ruether, Rosemary Radford, ed. *Religion and Sexism: Images of Woman in the Jewish and Christian Traditions.* 1974.

Ruether, Rosemary Radford, and Eleanor McLaughlin, eds. *Women of Spirit: Female Leadership in the Jewish and Christian Traditions.* 1979.

Sharma, Arvind. *Today's Woman in World Religions.* 1994. Both collections by Sharma are useful for general descriptions of women's roles and activities according to traditional periodization.

——. *Women in World Religions.* 1987.

Warner, Marina. *Alone of All Her Sex: The Myth and Cult of the Virgin Mary.* 1976.

Young, Serinity. *Sacred Texts.* 1993. Useful on women's experiences across time.

See also **Buddhism: History of Study; Charisma; Christianity: History of Study; Hinduism: History of Study; History; Islam: History of Study; Judaism: History of Study.**

JUDITH P. ZINSSER

Perpetua and Felicity

In the North African city of Carthage in 202–203 C.E., Vibia Perpetua, a well-born woman of twenty-two, was arrested together with Felicity, a slave who may have been her personal servant, and several young men. All were in the process of preparing to become Christians. Perpetua was a nursing mother and Felicity pregnant and near term when the prospective converts were arrested; they were baptized while awaiting imprisonment, jailed, tried, and executed. A third-century account of their deaths, *The Passion of Saints Perpetua and Felicitas*, was compiled by an unknown editor. This *Passio* (suffering or passion, a term for the genre) is remarkable for the "prison journal" of Perpetua at its heart (chaps. 3–10). Although the authenticity of these chapters is disputed, they are probably Perpetua's own work and thus represent the earliest extant writings of a Christian woman.

Perpetua's journal records her fear for her child, conflict with her father, and four dream visions she received at crucial moments in the process leading to her death. The first and last visions depict struggle and victory: a narrow ladder with a dragon at its foot leads to a heavenly garden where a gray-haired shepherd welcomes her; in a wrestling match she becomes a man, defeats her Egyptian opponent, and walks toward the Gate of Life, a woman again. Two other visions are of her dead brother Dinocrates, whose cancerous wounds are finally healed by Perpetua's prayers. Replete with Christian and pagan images, the visions invite multiple interpretations.

Felicity figures only briefly in the narrative, speaking in the editor's voice rather than her own, suffering courageously in labor as well as in the arena where she and Perpetua fight with wild beasts. In asserting their identity as Christians, both women are compelled to abandon their children: Perpetua weans her son and relinquishes him to her non-Christian parents; Felicity prays to give birth early (pregnant women could not be executed) and entrusts her newborn daughter to a woman from the local church. Leaving behind their children and families, they find a new family in the Christian community and a home beyond this world.

Perpetua and Felicity were revered in the North African churches of late antiquity, which celebrated their feast yearly. The two were also commemorated in the Roman calendar of martyrs and in the Roman eucharistic prayer, which kept their names alive in Christian churches in the West.

BIBLIOGRAPHY

The Martyrdom of Saints Perpetua and Felicitas. In *Acts of the Christian Martyrs.* Texts and translations by Herbert Musurillo. 1972. Accessible Greek and Latin texts with English translations.

Cardman, Francine. "The Acts of the Women Martyrs." *Anglican Theological Review* 70, no. 2 (1988): 144–150. Feminist analysis of martyr acts about women.

Franz, Marie-Louise von. *The Passion of Perpetua.* 1980. Classic Jungian interpretation of the visions.

Jensen, Anne. *God's Self-Confident Daughters: Early Christianity and the Liberation of Women.* 1996. English translation of 1992 German original. Locates Perpetua and Felicity in the context of the early Christian experience of martyrdom.

Miller, Patricia Cox. " 'A Dubious Twilight': Reflections on Dreams in Patristic Literature." *Church History* 55, no. 2 (1986): 153–164. Explicates the context of dreams and visions in late antiquity.

Perkins, Judith. *The Suffering Self: Pain and Narrative Representation in the Early Christian Era.* 1995. Uses feminist theory and insights from cultural studies; chap. 4, "Suffering and Power," analyzes sources of power in *The Passion of Saints Perpetua and Felicitas* and other martyr acts.

FRANCINE CARDMAN

Persephone

See Demeter and Persephone.

Phenomenology of Religion

The phenomenology of religion is a descriptive exercise that eschews causal explanations of religious phenomena and seeks instead to understand their meanings as they are understood by the religious actors themselves. Although the discipline has developed independently of Edmund Husserl's philosophical phenomenology, it has been deeply influenced by it. Husserl introduced his philosophy at the turn of the century with the rallying cry "to the things themselves." By this he meant to return philosophy from abstractions and metaphysical presuppositions to concrete experience. His method can be summarized by three terms: intentionality, bracketing, and eidetic vision. By intentionality Husserl means that consciousness is an active, meaning-conferring process. In such a view we do not live in a world of objects but of meanings. Husserl's objective was to uncover the basic structures of experience without any presuppositions. He thus called for the bracketing of all presuppositions on the part of the investigator. Also known as the *epoché* or suspension, this is an attempt to arrive at a detached stance in which all judgments about the truth value or even "real" existence of the phenomena under study are bracketed away. In this way the investigator attempts to neutralize her own cultural presuppositions so as to describe phenomena as experienced by the actors themselves. Finally, phenomenologists seek to arrive at the essence or *eidos* of the phenomenon. Eidetic vision involves the imaginative variation of the structures of a particular experience in order to disclose its invariant, universal, and essential aspects.

Informed by many of these ideas, the pioneers in the phenomenology of religion insisted on the irreducibility of religion to any other aspect of human life and called for a method to study religion on its own terms, apart from what they considered to be the reductive influences of sociology, anthropology, and other fields. Following on these assumptions, scholars such as Rudolf Otto (*The Idea of the Holy*, 1923), Gerardus van der Leeuw (*Religion in Essence and Manifestation: A Study in Phenomenology*, 1938), and Mircea Eliade (*The Sacred and the Profane: The Nature of Religion*, 1957; *The Quest: History and Meaning in Religion*, 1969), posited that religious experience is a universal and essential aspect of all consciousness. Following some of Husserl's insights, these thinkers sought to provide value-free descriptions of religious experience; to search for patterns or structures of religious phenomena across cultural and historical divides; and to discern within these patterns a unique religious meaning beneath its particular cultural manifestations. Eliade's extensive body of work sought to achieve these aims through a study of symbolic systems such as texts, architecture, and art. His approach has often been called hermeneutical, or interpretive, notions that are also current in the phenomenological philosophy of Paul Ricoeur.

The phenomenological attempt to remain truthful to the experience of the other involves a sympathetic understanding or recreation of his or her experience, with the knowledge that the other can never be fully appropriated or fully known. Such an attitude would seem to make it ideal for the study of women's religious experience. And indeed the collection *Women in World Religions* (edited by Arvind Sharma, 1987) stresses its reliance on empathetic understanding as well as an insistence on the irreducibility of religion. However, as Ursula King (1986, 1995) has shown, almost all the pioneering work in the field has ignored not only women's experience but, perhaps most important, the methodological insights that have been developed by studies in feminist thought and gender studies. According to King (1995), a major paradigm shift is taking place within the study of religion that involves the reevaluation and redefinition of methodology and research. In *Transforming Grace: Christian Tradition and Women's Experience* (1990), Anne E. Carr traces three stages in this development: a deconstruction of error in previous research and a suspicion toward the sources traditionally studied; the reconstruction of reality from the perspective of women's experience; and the construction of gender theories, a move that seeks to go beyond an exclusionary focus on women's experience.

In terms of the methodological assumptions within phenomenology of religion, the critique and reconstruction have focused on three issues. The first is the universalist and essentialist claim that religion is sui generis or irreducible to other elements in the social matrix. In its insistence that religion has its own essence, the phenomenology of religion has often ignored the specific social, political, and historical contexts within which religions exist and how these factors shape the experience of concrete embodied individuals. Rosalind Shaw (in King, 1995), suggests that treating religion apart from these factors is irreconcilable with the feminist insight that power relations and social roles fundamentally shape and effect experience. Similarly, in "Women and Religion" (in *The Cross-Cultural Study of Women*, edited by Margot I. Dudley and Mary I. Edwards, 1986), Karen Sinclair calls for an openness to research by social scientists on the way in which religions reflect and perpetuate social values and norms in given societies.

The next area of critique and reevaluation is the field's insistence on understanding meanings. The study of a religion's self-understanding through a "reading" of its symbolic systems overlooks the fact that those systems often perpetuate androcentric normative views. Caroline Walker Bynum (1986) argues for an expansion of the idea that symbols are polysemic in order to explore the way in which they shape women's experience.

Bynum proposes that we need to ask a number of questions: first, how symbols make use of gender; next, in seeking to understand the meaning of religion as the actors themselves understand it, we need to ask whose version or interpretation we are accepting as normative; and further, we need to compare the distinctive ways in which women, as opposed to men in the same cultures, intend and interpret the same symbols. Such an approach is evident in *Immaculate and Powerful: The Female in Sacred Image and Social Reality* (Clarissa Atkinson, Constance Buchanan, Margaret Miles, eds., 1985), a collection of articles that focus on the relation of religious images to the social experience of women.

Finally, scholars have also called into question the ideal of a purely objective descriptive science. In *Buddhism after Patriarchy* (1993), Rita M. Gross questions the possibility of a totally value-free understanding of the other. She argues that the researcher is an embodied individual steeped in the language and culturally shaped values of his or her own world and thus can never totally remove all subjectivity or normative assumptions from research. Gross and other scholars such as Carol P. Christ (1987) and Kim Knott (in King, 1995) address this issue by way of the hermeneutical point that understanding is never totally free of interpretation; and they call for a recognition that the investigator is in a dialogic relationship with the traditions or persons she is studying. Thus the ideal of bracketing away all presuppositions is modified by a self-conscious reflexivity about those presuppositions and how they interact or even clash with the values of the actors, producing a more dynamic and ethical relationship of sympathetic exchange and understanding.

BIBLIOGRAPHY

Herbert Spielberg's *The Phenomenological Movement: A Historical Introduction* (3d rev. and enl. ed., 1982), is perhaps the most comprehensive historical survey of philosophical phenomenology available in English. A more concise overview designed for less specialized readers is provided by Michael Hammond, Jane Howarth, and Russell Keat in *Understanding Phenomenology* (1991). Of the bewildering number of surveys and methodological reflections on the phenomenology of religion, most ignore feminist studies in the field. Of these earlier studies, a particularly exhaustive one is Jacques Waardenburg's *Classical Approaches to the Study of Religion: Aims, Methods and Theories of Research* (2 vols., 1973–1974), which contains selections from major figures and comprehensive bibliographies. Another, shorter collection is provided by Summner B. Twiss and Walter H. Conser, Jr., in *Experience of the Sacred: Readings in the Phenomenology of Religion*

(1992). This includes a valuable introduction to three types of phenomenological analysis: essential, historical-typological, and existential-hermeneutical; it has the merit of including entries by two feminist scholars, Carol P. Christ and Caroline Walker Bynum. Of note also is *The Encyclopedia of Religion,* edited by Mircea Eliade (1987), which contains entries on "Phenomenology of Religion" (Douglas Allen, vol. 11, pp. 272–285); "Androcentrism" (Rosemary Ruether, vol. 1, pp. 272–276); and "Women's Studies" (Constance H. Buchanan, vol. 15, pp. 433–440). A comprehensive reappraisal of phenomenological methodology is provided by the sociologist Louise Levesque-Lopman in *Claiming Reality: Phenomenology and Women's Experience* (1988). Although it does not directly address the phenomenology of religion, its analysis of methodological ideas in phenomenological sociology is relevant to the study of religion. Of special relevance is the work of Ursula King. Her essay "Historical and Phenomenological Approaches to the Study of Religion: Some Major Developments and Issues Under Debate since 1950," in *Contemporary Approaches to the Study of Religion,* vol. 1, edited by Frank Whaling (1983), is an excellent survey, although it does not include feminist developments in the field. Those developments have been addressed in her more recent publications, including "Female Identity and the History of Religions," in *Identity Issues and World Religions,* edited by V. C. Hayes (1986). King has also edited an indispensable collection of essays, *Religion and Gender* (1995), which includes a superb introduction by King ("Gender and the Study of Religion"), as well as a number of methodological and empirical studies. Of particular note are Erin White's "Religion and the Hermeneutics of Gender: An Examination of the Work of Paul Ricoeur," which deals with a major figure in post-Husserlian phenomenology; Rosalind Shaw's "Feminist Anthropology and the Gendering of Religious Studies," and Kim Knott's "Women Researching, Women Researched: Gender as an Issue in the Empirical Study of Religion." Another excellent collection of essays is *Gender and Religion: On the Complexity of Symbols,* edited by Caroline Walker Bynum, Stevan Harrel, and Paula Richman (1986). This contains Bynum's introductory essay, "On the Complexity of Symbols," which lays the foundations for a phenomenology of symbols grounded in women's experience as well as studies of various traditions, including Buddhism, Gnosticism, Hinduism, and Christianity. Carol P. Christ, a major voice in women's feminist theology, provides a critical reading of Eliade's androcentric bias in "Mircea Eliade and the Feminist Paradigm Shift," *Journal of Feminist Studies in Religion* 7, no. 2 (1991), 75–94; as well as a methodological essay, "Toward a Paradigm Shift in the Academy and in Religious Studies,"

in *The Impact of Feminist Research in the Academy,* edited by Christie Farnham (1987). Finally, a useful and detailed survey of research in religious studies conceived from an interdisciplinary and cross-cultural perspective is provided by June O'Connor in "Rereading, Reconceiving and Reconstructing Traditions: Feminist Research in Religion," *Women's Studies* 17, nos. 1–2 (1989): 101–123.

TIRDAD DERAKHSHANI

Philosophy: In the East

The three main schools of Chinese philosophy, Confucianism, Taoism, and Buddhism, speak about women in different ways. Confucianism contextualizes women always in their relationships within state and family. Taoism mostly focuses on the qualities of softness and yielding in the feminine and on the balance between female and male elements; but it also represents women mythologically as primordial teachers and goddesses. Buddhism philosophizes about women in the most complex way, describing them in their various capacities for enlightenment. Although these three branches of Chinese philosophy were distinct and separate, they also influenced and became integrated into each other.

In both classical and neo-Confucianism, women were perceived as naturally belonging to the private realm. The *Shih ching* (Book of Poetry, c. 1000 B.C.E.) includes poems of joy and lamentation by women. The *Li chi* (Book of Rites, c. 500 B.C.E.–100 C.E.) contains two chapters that pertain to women: the "Rituals of Marriage" and the "Rules of the Inner Chambers." Yet another common traditional source, the *Shu ching* (Book of History, c. 500 B.C.E.), states that the dominance of a woman was the foreshadowing of disaster for the family.

These writings formed the foundation for Confucian thinking on women. Women were seen to be the roots of the empire; the relationship between husband and wife was considered to be the most important of the five relationships, which also includes the emperor and the minister, father and son, elder and younger brothers, and friends. A woman's behavior and adherence to her idealized roles, especially as mother and model to her children, was crucial because of the belief that the success of the empire rested on each person's cultivation of him- or herself and harmony within the family.

A woman was expected, above all, to be yielding. Her life had to reflect the ideals of the "three followings" and the "four virtues." In childhood, she was to obey and follow her father; after marriage, she was to do the same for her husband; and after the death of her husband, her son. Moreover, she was to keep her appearance clean and pleasant, but not seductive; she was also to work hard at cooking, weaving, and sewing, thereby providing for the well-being of her family; in speech she was to be gentle, soft, and not aggressive; finally, in action she was to be moral and virtuous.

Taoism, in contrast, has little to say on the mundane details of a woman's life. Instead, much of its earliest efforts were directed by countering the rigidity of Confucian mores. Nondoing (*wei*) or nonbeing (*wu*) was encouraged; natural self-so-ness (*tzu-jan*) and spontaneity were encouraged rather than self-conscious deliberation and cultivation. Furthermore, the Taoist philosopher Chuang-tzu (fourth century B.C.E.) drew from the diversity in nature to expose the myopia of the Confucian vision; and rather than using history, Chuang-tzu used folk beliefs to create fanciful characters like the well-loved goddess Queen Mother of the West.

Whereas Confucians were concerned with harmony and order, the Taoists were preoccupied with the notion of freedom. At the highest level this meant freedom from prescribed roles and, ultimately, freedom from society. Women as well as men were encouraged to pursue this goal. The qualities of softness, gentleness, and yielding so prominently associated with women in Confucianism, are recommended to men in Taoism. By extension, one might conclude that women would be expected to take on some masculine traits; the philosophers, however, are silent on this matter.

Where Confucianism prescribed separate spheres and roles to women and men that were seen as complementary, and where Taoism considered the ultimate goal of liberation to be the same for both sexes (albeit through different paths), Buddhism introduced two radically new ideas. First, some Buddhist writings teach that women are more impure than men. By contrast, the very idea of impurity is antithetical to the Chinese belief that a person's body is sacred, since it is a gift from one's ancestors; a woman's body is especially precious because of its procreative capacity. The second new Buddhist idea was the inferiority of nuns within the community of monks and nuns. This contrasted with *The Book of Rites*, which proscribes women as of equal social rank with their husbands and with the pan-Chinese idea that women are generational seniors to their sons and nephews.

This inferior status of women in Buddhism was balanced by the idea of emptiness: the understanding that all things arise in relationship to other things and are devoid of self-nature, thereby suggesting that women and men are not essentially different. But the notions of impurity, suffering, and karma within Buddhism fed the persistent, though not all-pervasive, belief that women were inferior beings to men. Women are born women as punishment for evil deeds in the past; in order to attain enlightenment, they must first be reborn as men.

All these ideas from the three main schools affected, mostly negatively, the lives of Chinese women. In the 1919 May Fourth Movement's attempt at modernization, Chinese intellectuals used Ibsen's *A Doll's House* to highlight the "failure" of the Chinese philosophical tradition. It remains a point of interest to see how modernization will affect the lives of Chinese women.

In India, women have certainly asked fundamental questions of philosophy and have been concerned with epistemological and soteriological matters. The hymns of Indian women sages, such as Lopāmudrā, Vishvavārā, Sikatā Nivāvari, Ghodā, and Ghoṣhā, among others, are found in the Vedic *Saṃhitās* (recorded by orthodox tradition in the *Sarvānukramaṇikā*, according to A. S. Altekar [1991]), and women such as Maitreyī and Gargī are featured in the Upanishads. A group of women known as *kāśakṛtsnās* studied in the Vedic exegetical tradition of Pūrva Mīmāṃsā. Women teaching in Sanskrit, such as Ātreyī, were called *upādhyāyānīs* or *ācāryās*, and until the fourth century B.C.E. uppercaste women could become life-long *brahmavādinīs* (students of philosophy). The names of women are known to early Indian tradition, yet women did not make contributions comparable to men. Their philosophical engagement was the exception not the rule. It still remains that men are the creators of Indian philosophic discourse, and their names are associated primarily with the principal schools of Indian philosophy. However, if it is true that all Indian philosophical speculation can be traced to the *Ṛgveda* and the Upanishads, then it is significant that women were present in these works.

Eventually, after the institutionalization of Hindu law, the status and dharma (duties) of women in Indian culture were codified. The prescribed legal status of Hindu women, and the tradition of child marriage (c. 300 B.C.E.), contributed to a decline in upper-caste women's pursuit of advanced educational studies. (The duties of women did not include study, philosophy, etc.) Women's duties were primarily the maintenance of home and family, and women were considered the property of the male members of their families. Still, women continued to receive religious education, and in some cases lived such devoted lives practicing austerities (*tapas* and *svādhyāya*) that their philosophic education, or knowledge (*jñāna*), was self-realized. Reading and studying is not the only, or even preferred, way to attain wisdom in Indian thought. The epic *Rāmāyaṇa*, for example, portrays several self-realized women, such as Shabarī and Ahalyā, and in the later medieval period women of extraordinary religious devotion (bhakti), such as Mirabai and Āṇḍāḷ, became saints or hermits and passed on their self-realized knowledge through vernacular mediums such as songs and poetry. The bhakti movement was particularly influential, and its emphasis on spiritual equality between men and women, and castes, opened the way for women to realize the goals of Indian philosophy.

Classical Indian philosophy is a collective and complex discourse whose heroes are men. The six principle schools of Sāmkhya, Yoga, Nyāya, Vaiśeṣika, Mīmāṃsā, and Advaita Vedanta constitute the principle philosophical traditions of Indian thought. Their founders and systematizers, such as Kapila, Patañjali, and Shankara, are men, and the scope of their speculative endeavors probe the very mysteries of the universe. The six systems develop theories on cognition; the forces of nature; the interplay between gross body, subtle body, and mind (delineated as *ahaṃkāra, buddhi, citta,* and *manas*); and the relationships of human beings to ultimate reality. They also speak about the feminine.

Sāmkhya, for example, the oldest of the six schools and possibly the earliest attempt at systematic philosophy in India, is a nontheistic school that influenced Yoga, and the subsequent development of Hindu thought. According to Sāmkhya-Yoga, the world is derived from *prakriti,* a feminine term for original matter or substance. This gendered concept is situated alongside *puruṣa,* a masculine term for pure consciousness or spirit. Herein lies the beginnings of a complex philosophical dialectic between the real (*puruṣa*) and the not-real (*prakriti*). All matter (*prakriti*), consisting of the three *guṇas* (attributes) individuates into elements, mind, and all manifested form, that is, the world as we know it (samsara). The goal of Sāmkhya-Yoga, and Vedanta, is to transcend or annul *prakriti,* in order to realize *puruṣa* (spirit or pure consciousness). In this sense, *puruṣa,* conceived in masculine terms, is portrayed as a higher order of existence. Any identification with *prakriti* is considered *avidyā* (ignorance). Later forms of Yoga, such as tantra, valorize the feminine in ways not found in the earlier, more orthodox schools of Indian philosophy.

In early Indian Buddhism, the admittance of nuns (*bhikshuni*s) into the *sangha,* and the legacy of the Therigatha (Songs of the elder nuns), is evidence of women's presence and accomplishments in the Buddhist Order. The Buddha made no distinction between men and women attaining the fruits of dharma, hence in the Therigatha we hear the voices of Buddhist nuns, such as Mahāprajapatī (the Buddha's foster mother), Kṣhemā, and Sumedhā, singing of their understanding and realization of the philosophical presuppositions of Buddha dharma, such as the four noble truths, the twelve *nidāna* (links) on the wheel of conditioned coarising (*pratītya-samutpāda*). Women were required to live lives of strict asceticism and mental discipline, leading to the same goal as the monks'—that is, the attainment of arhatship and nirvana. Though their status was always subordinate to the monks (*bhikshus*), their education in Buddhist philosophy was provided.

Also, nuns in the Jain Śvetāmbara sect or *sangha* are educated and considered accomplished practitioners of Jain metaphysics and philosophy. Mahāvira, the twenty-fourth *tīrthankara* of Jainism, allowed nuns to fully participate in the Jain monastic community. Jaina religious literature records the contributions of women to Jainism, such as that of Yākinī, who defeated Haribhadra-suri in philosophical debate, and the Śvetāmbara religious canon cites Mallinātha, the daughter of the ruler of Mithilā (modern Bihar), as the nineteenth Tīrthankara. Still, it is their virtues within a patriarchal society, such as chastity for nuns and devotion to husband and children for laywomen, not their contributions to Indian philosophy, that form the basis of women's higher status in Jainism, as well as Buddhism and Hinduism.

BIBLIOGRAPHY

Altekar, A. S. *The Position of Women In Hindu Civilization: From Prehistoric Times to the Present Day.* 1959. English trans., 1991.

Cahill, Suzanne. *Transcendence and Divine Passion: The Queen Mother of the West in Medieval China.* 1993.

Das Gupta, Surendranath. *A History of Indian Philosophy.* 5 vols. 1922–1925.

Ebrey, Patricia. *The Inner Quarters: Marriage and the Lives of Chinese Women in the Sung Period.* 1993.

Jaini, Padmanabh S. *Gender and Salvation.* 1991.

Li, Yo-ning, ed. *Chinese Women: Through Chinese Eyes.* 1992.

Liu, Hsiang. *Lieh-nü chüan.* (The Position of Women in China.) Translated by Albert Richard O'Hara. 1945.

Shih, Po-ch'ang. *Pi-ch'iu-ni chüan.* (Lives of Nuns.) Translated by Katheryn Anu Tsai. 1994.

Majumdar, R. C., and Swami Madhavananda, eds. *Great Women of India.* 1982.

Radhakrishnan, Sarvapalli. *Indian Philosophy.* 2 vols. 1923.

See also **Mahāprajāpatī**; **Prakriti**; **Queen Mother of the West**.

ELLEN GOLDBERG AND TERRY WOO

In the West

Generally recognized as originating in ancient Greece as a systematic discipline, Western philosophy has been implicated in the marginalization and subordination of women since its inception. In his description of the ideal city in the *Republic,* Plato said that women as well as men should be required to take on the role of philosopher-kings or guardians of the state. His position was motivated not by a commitment to equality, nor by any other feminist conviction, but by his belief that the justice of the state should take priority over any individual needs or wants. It is noteworthy that the only female candidates considered capable of ruling in the tripartite class structure that Plato envisaged were those that male philosophers took as wives. The lower classes—the assistants to the guardians, or soldiers (insofar as they were dominated by a spirited temper), and the money-makers, or craftworkers (dominated by appetite or desire)—could not aspire to the rationality of the guardians.

In other works (*Timaeus* or *Symposium*), Plato aligned women with the body, and men with the soul. The effects of this fear of the body (what Spelman calls somataphobia) are still being played out today, even in contemporary feminist theory. The legacy of the Western tradition's denigration of the body and concomitant elevation of the soul is a problem that is sometimes repeated in even the most sophisticated feminist theories, in the eagerness to avoid reducing women to being the material providers or reproductive machines with which they have so often been identified. Plato's elevation of the soul over the body is reworked by the Cartesian mind–body dichotomy, and there is a sense in which the sex–gender distinction that has been so important for feminism is still hampered by its immersion in seventeenth-century Cartesianism. The sexed body is too often viewed as passive and inert, whereas gender is charged with the role of changing or disrupting stereotypical masculine and feminine identifications. Gender is thus conceived as overly intellectualized, as little more than a disembodied will. But instead of Descartes's God being the cause of clear and distinct ideas, and acting as a guarantor of truth, feminism invokes society writ large as the cause of gender—too often leaving unexplained exactly what mechanisms produce gender, and how individuals react to, reinvent, and transform gendered roles. The interactive corporeal dimensions of the processes by which individuals acquire and enact gender, and the ways in which gender intersects with race and class, are engaged with greater precision and efficacy in the work of contemporary feminist theorists such as Butler, De Lauretis, Gatens, Grosz, hooks, and Spivak. It thus becomes clear that gender is not simply chosen by a willful subject, but that it is informed by specific historical situations, and that it is a complex and dynamic interplay in which the subject both constitutes and is constituted by social and cultural expectations, without either being entirely free in regard to them or completely determined by them.

Aristotle, Plato's pupil for twenty years, viewed women as imperfect men. In the *Nicomachean Ethics* Aristotle argued that women, like children, lacked a fully devel-

Virginia Woolf (1882–1941), here in a 1902 photograph, wrote *A Room of One's Own* in 1929 in the modern tradition of feminist philosophy, calling for equal education for women (Hulton-Deutsch Collection/Corbis).

oped deliberative faculty. He thereby established the foundations of a belief that still lingers: women are incapable of full rationality. On this pretext, women have suffered exclusion from the public realm, have been barred from full participation in political life, and have been confined to the domestic sphere where they have been assigned the task of caring for material, rather than intellectual or spiritual, needs. Along with slaves, women played virtually no role in the public life of ancient Greece and were not recognized as citizens in Athenian democracy. The differential political and social treatment of women and men was justified by, and reflected in, Aristotle's differentiation of women from men at the biological level. Aristotle believed that women's menstrual blood was not fully concocted and therefore fell short of men's semen. If Aristotle's biology has been found wanting in this respect, the definition of women as imperfect men that informs it has proved harder to put aside.

The Middle Ages saw little improvement in women's status. Thomas Aquinas, in valorizing Aristotle, did little to displace his belief in the inequality of women and men. Only in the late twentieth century, with the emergence of women's studies as an academic discipline and the appearance of courses on women's history, feminist philosophy, and women and religion, were the likes of Mechtild of Magdeburg (1210–1297) and Julian of Norwich (1343–1413) taken seriously.

Mary Wollstonecraft's *A Vindication of the Rights of Women* (1792) is among the first philosophical texts to be written by a woman that addresses the inequality of the sexes. Strongly influenced by Rousseau, Wollstonecraft (1759–1797) argued that virtue is not innate but a product of reason and knowledge, requiring cultivation. Refuting the separation of virtues doctrine that was popular in the eighteenth century, she maintained that women and men are identical in knowledge and virtue, that both are rational and moral. Wollstonecraft pointed out the logical inconsistency of the popular view that women were amoral but also expected to have the moral ability to teach children to be virtuous. She focused attention on this double standard: that women were assumed to embody superior intuition and sensibility on the one hand yet on the other hand considered deficient in reason and moral character. Maintaining that God could allow only one kind of virtue, and only one kind of reason, Wollstonecraft insisted that the virtues of women cannot be different from those of men. Rather than being treated as vain and frivolous creatures, what women needed was the opportunity to develop and educate themselves.

In 1929 in *A Room of One's Own* Virginia Woolf was still calling for women to be granted an education equal to that of men, and in 1949 Simone de Beauvoir's *The Second Sex* reiterated Wollstonecraft's call for women's financial independence. It is little wonder that until these two demands were met, few women philosophers existed. De Beauvoir deserves credit for appropriating Sartre's existentialist framework and adapting it to the exploration of women's oppression. Given Sartre's belief that freedom is the defining characteristic of individuals, and the extremely voluntaristic flavor with which this belief endowed his early philosophy, de Beauvoir's achievement in shedding light on women's subordination as the other, or second, sex is all the more impressive. Her dictum that one is not born but becomes a woman was taken up by the feminists of the 1970s in terms of the sex–gender distinction. Women were no longer seen as determined by their natural capacity for childbirth, but rather construed in terms of their potential cultural, professional, and artistic equality with men. It is not nature, bodies, or sex that makes women what they are, but nurture, society, or gender.

As feminist theologian Rosemary Radford Ruether argues, if sexism excludes women from social development in the sphere of culture, religion constitutes part of this exclusion. Religion is both shaped by and helps to condone sexist patterns of social behavior. Religion normalizes and even sanctifies sexism. Women's experience has historically been excluded from religion as it is publicly practiced in Judaism and Christianity, and, insofar as God is the patriarch par excellence, religious ideology itself is both informed by, and constitutive of, women's oppression.

Just as for Aristotle women were incomplete men, so for patriarchal religion women reflect the image of God less completely than men. Men are seen as closer to God, and women are seen as more akin to animality; men are more spiritual, whereas women are equated with base materiality. If women have been seen by the tradition of Western philosophy as the dark continent, the mysterious other, they have been viewed by Western religious institutions as the repository of sin, the cause of evil. Especially if they deviate from their traditional roles of mother and housewife, they are liable to be construed as temptresses of the flesh. If they are not virginal, or if they do not embody the virtues of the good mother, they come to embody carnal corruption; if they are not the Virgin Mary, they are the sinful Eve.

Feminists such as Mary Daly and Luce Irigaray have questioned the patriarchal roots that religion shares with philosophy. By returning to ancient mythology and tragedy, invoking in particular figures such as Antigone, Athena, Ariadne, Kore-Persephone, and Clytemnestra, Irigaray asks us to question the foundation of our symbolic order. Providing readings of the ancients, Descartes, Hegel, and Freud, among many other figures, Irigaray has refused to let the gendered blindspots of masculine tradition stand. As Irigaray has breathed new life into an essentially male philosophical tradition, feminist theologians such as Rosemary Radford Ruether have invited us to go back and reexamine the religious representation of women as marginal and domestic figures. Elisabeth Schüssler Fiorenza calls for a feminist hermeneutics of remembrance that does not seek solely to represent the history of patriarchal oppression, but that reconstitutes this heritage as one in which women's freedom and agency is rendered visible.

BIBLIOGRAPHY

Agonito, Rosemary. *History of Ideas on Woman: A Sourcebook*. 1977. A useful historical source for primary texts by philosophers from the Greeks to the present.

de Beauvoir, Simone. *The Second Sex*. Translated by H. M. Parshley. 1954. Lengthy analysis treating Marxism, psychoanalysis, anthropology, philosophy, mythology from an existential perspective.

Butler, Judith. *Bodies That Matter.* 1993. Essays discuss psychoanalysis and race, queer politics, and the materiality of bodies.

———. *Gender Trouble.* 1990. Argues that sex is, like gender, a normative and not a natural category. Part of the normative content that has been prescribed for it in Western culture is heterosexism.

Daly, Mary. *Beyond God the Father: Toward a Theory of Women's Liberation.* 1973. A sequel to *The Church and the Second Sex,* Daly's attempt to take up de Beauvoir's questioning of woman as other in the sphere of religion.

De Lauretis, Teresa. "Upping the Anti [*sic*] in Feminist Theory." In *Conflicts in Feminism.* Edited by Marianne Hirsch and Evelyn Fox Keller. 1990. Lesbian critic raises the issue of essentialism in feminist theory.

Gatens, Moira. *Imaginary Bodies.* 1996. English-born philosopher now resident in Australia discusses the masculinization of metaphors at the heart of political philosophy such as the body politic. Influenced by Spinoza and Deleuze.

Grosz, Elizabeth. *Volatile Bodies: Toward a Corporeal Feminism.* 1994. Australian feminist philosopher takes on the need to address corporeality.

hooks, bell. *Yearning: race, gender, and cultural politics.* 1990. Esp. pp. 57–77 and 89–102. Essays attending to the complexities of race, gender, and class from the perspective of an African-American feminist.

Irigaray, Luce. *Speculum of the Other Woman.* Translated by Gillian C. Gill. 1985. Feminist rereadings of major figures in the history of philosophy, including Plato, Descartes, Hegel, Freud.

Osborne, Martha L. *Woman in Western Thought.* 1978. A collection of primary sources with critical essays.

Ruether, Rosemary Radford. *Sexism and God-Talk: Toward a Feminist Theology.* 1983. A classic text in feminist theology.

Spelman, Elizabeth. *Inessential Woman.* 1990. A monograph that addresses the lacuna that race represents within feminism, discussing figures such as Plato, Aristotle, and de Beauvoir.

Spivak, Gayatri Chakravorty. *In Other Worlds: Essays in Cultural Politics.* 1987. An important collection of essays by an Indian cultural critic, deconstructionist, and Marxist.

Weidman, Judith L., ed. *Christian Feminism: Visions of a New Humanity.* 1984. A collection of essays including contributions by Ruether and Schüssler Fiorenza.

See also **Philosophy of Religion; Thealogy.**

TINA CHANTER

Philosophy of Religion

In the twentieth century, philosophy of religion has been synonymous with empirical realist approaches to the central claims and controversies of the dominant, Western form of theism. The central, theistic claim of Western religion is the existence of God as a personal, bodiless, omnipresent creator and sustainer of the universe, perfectly free, omnipotent, omniscient, perfectly good, and a source of moral obligation; God has these properties eternally and necessarily. The philosophical question is, then, twofold: can a coherent account be given of what it means to say there is such a God, and if so, are there good reasons to show that there is or is not this God?

Any coherent account or proof of God's existence must confront a central controversy concerning God's moral obligation in relation to innocent suffering and evil more generally. If God is all-powerful and perfectly good, why does God not intervene to prevent evil? This question of divine justice results in various theodicies some of which have, as a result of philosophical questioning, proposed new forms of theism. But often the defense of God rests on God's creation of humankind with free will; the possibility of evil is simply a consequence of this good creation. So generally the beliefs and claims of classical theism remain entrenched, determining the main objects of philosophical defense and attack. Atheism is merely the flip side of theism. Here philosophers employ an adversarial method to argue for and against theistic claims. This determines the precise form of philosophical reasoning as well as the strict limits on the form of justified true belief.

Janice Moulton's feminist critique demonstrates that this method of reasoning is only one possible paradigm, arguably a male one, nothing more. The implication is that as long as philosophers of religion remain within the strict parameters of the adversarial method and the empirical-descriptive approach to theistic belief, the status quo in relations between privileged men and others will be maintained. Those who suffer will continue to suffer as far as this conception of philosophy is concerned, since it is merely descriptive and strictly formal without any prescription for change or awareness of the construction of theistic belief as male biased.

Basically contemporary theism and its controversies exclude the specific identity and thinking of women from philosophy of religion as taught and developed in the major Anglo-American academic institutions. Whether in a defense or an attack, the philosophical claims concerning a personal deity conceived as an ideal that supports privileged and powerful men leave women without a personal deity to define their own subjectivity. In the 1970s Mary Daly boldly tried to subvert the dominant form of theism, encouraging many women to separate themselves from men and unite together as sisters with the cosmic dimensions of our world. Daly's efforts were both creative and inspiring, initially "reaching outward and inward toward the God beyond and beneath the gods (divine men) who have stolen our identity." But such separatism cannot remain permanent without resulting in two entrenched forms of sexism. Nevertheless, Daly inspired women to think creatively, to offer something new to philosophy of religion. Not only have her writings in the 1980s and 1990s encouraged new patterns of thinking but they have also suggested new configurations of society.

In various corners, speculation continues concerning the difference that acknowledging women and the sex and gender system could make to philosophy of religion. The classical, theistic God is designed for men; God's existence is necessary for their objectivity as detached thought about the world, and sufficient for the possibility of their representations of an absolute reality. What would a goddess or goddesses be like if conceived as the ideal of female subjectivity? Arguably she would be personally involved with and embodied in the world rather than detached and disembodied or nonembodied. As conceived by man in relation to his God, the contradictory nature of woman supports misogyny. If women were not measured against the divine for men and not used by men, the fundamental contradiction would disappear. In addition, the traditional problem of evil and theodicies would be transformed if women were considered in their own right. In assessing divine goodness, the self-consciously female philosopher of religion would have to account for the unequal suffering of half the human race due to their sex. The argument that God the Father allows evil so that men and women are able to exercise their free will does not justify this masculine God allowing so much more suffering and such long histories of oppression for women. How could it have been necessary to allow an immeasurable amount of sex-specific unfairness? If the male God is all-powerful and all-good, he could have changed the female condition. How could it ever be necessary and, even if necessary, fair that men learn about the consequences of their free will at the expense of women? It seems that the exclusively male God of classical theism and so male subjectivity would have to be rethought at the same time as the divine for women is conceived.

Another major and fundamental weakness of Anglo-American philosophy of religion has been a narrow reading of the history of the arguments of Western philosophers. Much of the apparent strength of the Anglo-American position rests on exclusion of fundamental challenges to their overall approach to philosophy. Among others in the nineteenth century, Ludwig Feuerbach (1804–1872) challenged the idealist and naive realist conceptions of the Christian God as an abstract projection of man; he proposed a new realist form of religious humanism. Building upon the great German philosophies of Immanuel Kant and Georg Wilhelm Friedrich Hegel, Feuerbach's critique had a major impact on post-Hegelian philosophy, as well as on other intellectuals in Europe including theologians, anthropologists, and sociologists. For Feuerbach, religion initially has a positive function. To understand human (male) subjectivity, the essence of religion must be recognized as the projection of man's ideal attributes; and after such recognition, this ideal projection must be taken back from heaven in order for man to become fully himself. Feuerbach gives a major role to love and the wholehearted pursuit of human welfare on this earth.

Notwithstanding Feuerbach's nineteenth-century critique of theism, a central body of twentieth-century Anglo-American philosophers of religion returned to the central tenets of classical theism and, generally, to a naive form of realism. This theism has been built largely upon an empirical or scientific epistemology, undeterred by the fundamental critiques of philosophy that resulted in a separation of science from religion. Empiricist philosophers of religion have tried to stay within certain narrow constraints in order to remain compatible with science. The result is that they not only acquire the male biases of much contemporary scientific method, but their scientism inevitably means bias against other forms of philosophy.

In the 1990s, however, numerous Anglo-American women philosophers heard a new voice in the French philosopher Luce Irigaray. Irigaray picks up on the Feuerbachian challenge, insisting that female subjectivity needs divine women for the possibility of female becoming. Women can only become fully themselves as subjects when they are, first, free to project an ideal for their sex and, second, able to take back their projection and make concrete their ideal. Irigaray refigures Feuerbach's essence of religion by replacing man with woman, and so demonstrating woman's need of a female divine who could serve as the model for becoming fully female. Subsequently, Irigaray moves from concern for the sexually specific identity of female subjectivity to an ethics of sexual difference. Her ethics gives the ground for the mutual recognition of two subjects in love; the divine emerges in the space opened up by the limitations of sexually specific subjects, male and female.

Another area of fruitful discussion involves women's contribution to a philosophical account of spirituality. The work of bell hooks exposes the intertwining of race and sex in conceptions of identity; then to overcome racism, hooks insists upon the unifying ground in spiritual expressions of yearning as a shared space and feeling of possibility. Alternatively a feminist philosophy of religion might confront male philosophers more directly by seeking a new philosophical account of the rationality of religious belief. This account would not deny the content of female desire or the yearning for both spiritual and sexual transformations; but it would target women's fundamental exclusion from Western philosophy more generally as an issue associated with rationality. The contention is that women's exclusion from philosophical reasoning is connected with the fact that the ideal of pure reason has been variously symbolized as male in the history of Western philosophy. What, then, becomes necessary for women's self-identity in philosophy of religion is a critical analysis of the symbolic role given to women and desire in traditional configurations of philosophical reason. In turn, both feminist epistemologies and feminist refigurings of myth can offer new insight concerning reason and belief for a philosophy of religion that includes women and men. The new challenge for philosophers of world religion will be to preserve the multiple identities of women and men who differ by creed, class, gender, and race.

BIBLIOGRAPHY

Adams, Robert, and Marilyn McCord Adams, eds. *The Problem of Evil.* 1990.

Anderson, Pamela Sue. *A Feminist Philosophy of Religion: The Rationality and Myths of Religious Belief.* 1997.

Daly, Mary. *Beyond God the Father: Toward a Philosophy of Women's Liberation.* 1973; 2d ed. with an original reintroduction, 1985.

———. *Gyn/Ecology: The Metaethics of Radical Feminism.* 1978.

———. *Pure Lust: Elemental Feminist Philosophy.* 1984.

Feuerbach, Ludwig. *The Essence of Christianity.* Translated by George Elliot. 1989.

Frankenberry, Nancy. "Introduction: Prolegomenon to Future Feminist Philosophies of Religions," *Hypatia: A Journal of Feminist Philosophy* 9, no. 4 (1994): 1–14. Special issue, "Feminist Philosophy of Religion."

hooks, bell. *Yearning: Race, Gender and Cultural Poetics.* 1990.

Irigaray, Luce. *An Ethics of Sexual Difference.* Translated by Carolyn Burke and Gillian C. Gill. 1993.

———. "Divine Women." In her *Sexes and Genealogies.* Translated by Gillian C. Gill. 1993.

———. "Equal to Whom?" *Differences* 1, no. 2 (1989): 59–76.

Jantzen, Grace. *God's World, God's Body.* 1984.

———. "Feminists, Philosophers and Mystics." *Hypatia* 9, no. 4 (1994): 186–206.

Moulton, Janice. "A Paradigm of Philosophy: The Adversary Method." In *Women, Knowledge and Reality: Explorations in Feminist Philosophy.* Edited by Ann Garry and Marilyn Pearsall. 1989. Contains twenty-one significant essays about women and philosophy, divided into the traditional subfields, including philosophy of religion. Moulton places the male paradigm of adversarial reasoning in perspective, leaving the possibility for other ways of reasoning, evaluating, and discussing philosophy.

Quinn, Phil, and Charles Taliaferro, eds. *The Companion to Philosophy of Religion.* 1996.

Swinburne, Richard. *The Existence of God.* Rev. ed. with appendices, 1991.

See also **Philosophy: In the East.**

PAMELA SUE ANDERSON

Photography

"My aspirations are to ennoble photography and to secure for it the character and uses of High Art by combining the real and the ideal and sacrificing nothing of Truth by all possible devotion to Poetry and beauty." —Julia Margaret Cameron, 1864

Julia Margaret Cameron (1815–1879) may indeed have been the first photographer to articulate the potential of photography to move beyond its prosaic function as the "pencil of nature" and portray the mechanical image as a "peephole" into the imaginary. This marriage of the real and the ideal, of the revealed and the concealed, is still what makes photography such a compelling medium for contemporary women artists working with mythological, ethical, and religious subject matter.

The history of photography shows that women were among those nineteenth-century pioneers actively involved in its formation as an artistic discipline. Still under the influence of nineteenth-century realism, photography was perceived as the "perfect means of reproducing the perfect image" (Clarke, 1997, p. 17); that perfection included a sharp focus, which also served to differentiate it from other visual media. Cameron challenged this and other aesthetic limitations being laid

A photograph entitled "The Hall of the Goddesses" (1989) depicts "women important to the history of photography among goddesses as muses to inspire women photographers" (Ann Pearson).

down by photography's dominant male champions. Her mythological subject matter of Christian saints and Greco-Roman gods and goddesses (with men and women posing in costume) benefited from a soft-focus approach that mimicked the look of dreams, a key reservoir for the imagination. In its early days, the "rhetoric of the real" or the "reality effect" restricted the advance of the art form into more creative applications; however, in its role as the "instrument of Truth," photography became the window of the world's social conscience in the genre known as documentary photography.

The documentary photograph had a "moral and radical vocabulary" (Clarke, p. 147). Here again, women were at the forefront, along with their male colleagues, of a photographic practice dedicated to exposing social injustice. "Truth," for the cameras of women like Dorothea Lange (1895–1965) and Margaret Bourke-White (1904–1971), was to expose the poverty and degradation suffered by millions of Americans during the Depression of the 1930s. Lange's *Migrant Mother* (1934) and Bourke-White's *Sharecroppers Home* (1937) remain two of the most outstanding visual exposés of the period.

Photographs produced in the documentary style, while technically considered evidence of an actual event, are not, however, ideologically neutral. Acknowledging the symbolic impact of these and all photographs, Roland Barthes (1977) characterized photographic images as "myths," while Vicki Goldberg called them "icons." According to Goldberg, secular images

that are saturated with meaning for an entire culture are similar to religious icons in that they "stand for an epoch or a system of beliefs" (Goldberg, 1991, p. 135). A case in point is *Accidental Napalm Attack* (1972), a photograph from the Vietnam War by Hung Cong Ut, which has been reprinted countless times in books on photography. On the other hand, Barthes viewed the power of photographic images as repressing historical truth, transforming history into ideology or mythology (Walker and Chaplin, 1997). Such different modes of analysis of photographs serve pedagogical purposes, and college courses with such titles as Image Ethics examine societal norms and values by "reading" photographs.

Griselda Pollock (1990) has argued that, despite the plethora of photographs of women in advertising, magazines, and books, there are no "images of women" in the dominant culture. Women's bodies, so prevalent in mass media, merely serve as surfaces for exploitation and colonization. The same type of exploitation can be seen in the so-called representations of religious life, popular in geographical and nature magazines of the 1950s, '60s, and '70s. These pictures typically showed seminaked women, especially black or native women from traditional cultures, engaged in various "ritual" activities. This problem of misrepresentation has been addressed by groups like the Native Indian/Inuit Photographers' Association of Canada, whose members have taken up cameras to photograph their own people. Ann Pearson's photograph, *In the Hall of the Goddesses* (1989), also challenges cliché. As the Montreal photographer explains it, she placed images of women important to the history of photography among goddesses as muses to inspire women photographers, just as goddesses have served as muses for various arts.

At the end of the twentieth century, new directions will emerge for women and photography in the age of the digital camera. Given the destabilization of authenticity highlighted by the digitization of images, one can anticipate a cry to return to realism, as digital photography, denatured of light, is no longer considered to be "natural" or photographic. Based on the history of photography, women will be at the forefront of any new artistic turn. How they will figure in the ethical and aesthetic debates about photography and digital imaging will be shaped by a much larger public debate about nature and artifice, as the prevailing cultural norms of "purity and danger" catch up to the values of ecological determinism.

BIBLIOGRAPHY

Arbus, Doon, and Marvin Israel, eds. *.diane arbus.: An Aperture Monograph.* 1972. Examples of images from

America's sub-cultures that have in twenty-five years become "myths" or "icons" in mainstream North American culture.

Barthes, Roland. *Image-Music-Text.* 1977. Among other theoretical notions, Barthes explains the concept of "photograph as myth."

Burnett, Ron. *Cultures of Vision: Images, Media and The Imaginary.* 1995. How perception is shaped by key cultural codes such as gender, ethnicity, class, and sexual preference.

Clarke, Graham. *The Photograph.* 1997. Essays on different genres of photography including "Documentary Photography," "The Body in Photography," and "The Portrait in Photography."

Dickson, Jennifer. *Hospital for Wounded Angels.* Toronto, 1987. A mytho-poetic approach to European gardens and their legendary monuments.

Dorothea Lange: A Visual Life. Directed by Meg Patridge. Pacific Pictures, Valley Ford, Calif., 1994.

Gernsheim, Helmut. *Julia Margaret Cameron: Her Life and Photographic Work.* 1975. Wonderful black and white prints of Cameron's friends and acquaintances posing as religious and mythological personifications.

Goldberg, Vicki. *The Power of Photography: How Photographs Changed our Lives.* 1991. Compares the power of certain photographs to "religious icons" with emphasis on the work of women photographers as the social conscience of a nation.

Heyman, Abigail. *Growing up Female: A Personal Photojournal.* 1974. A dated but still poignant marker of 1970s feminism. Depicts rituals and rites of passage in heterosexual relationships.

Image Bank at the Center for Study of World Religions. Cambridge, Mass. An invaluable source for research.

Langford, Martha. *The Last Silence: Pavane for a Dying World.* Ottawa, 1991.

Mitchell, William J. *The Reconfigured Eye: Visual Truth in the Post-Photographic Era.* 1994. Grapples with the beginnings of a philosophy of image ethics in the age of the digital camera.

Monk, Lorraine. *The Female Eye/Coup d'oeil feminin.* 1975. A survey of photographic images by Canadian women to commemorate International Women's Year. The spiritual heart of the book resides in the concept of women in relationship to others.

Neumaier, Diane, ed. *Reframings: New American Feminist Photographies.* 1995.

Pollock, Griselda. "Missing Women: Rethinking Early Thoughts on Images of Women." In *The Critical Image: Essays on Contemporary Photography.* Edited by Carol Squires, 1990.

Squires, Carol, ed. *The Critical Image: Essays on Contemporary Photography.* 1990. Intelligent essays on gender, photography and social issues, bordering on a moral inquiry into postmodern values.

Thomas, Ann. *Lisette Model.* 1990. "Questions and answers to life" by one of America's foremost female photographers.

Walker, John A., and Sarah Chaplin. *Visual Culture: An Introduction.* 1997.

JANET H. TULLOCK

Pilgrimage

A pilgrimage is a journey to a place with special qualities, qualities that are usually derived from the pilgrimage site's association with a god, saint, spirit, or other form of power. Pilgrimages are found in all major religious traditions and vary from short trips to nearby shrines, to longer journeys to national and international sacred places such as Mecca and Lourdes. However, the term *pilgrimage* itself does not have an exact equivalent in all religions. There may be different terms for different kinds of journeys to special places, or the term for "pilgrimage" may be applied to a broader range of journeys than just sacred ones. A pilgrimage may be undertaken for personal reasons, as when a Greek Orthodox woman goes to a shrine of the Virgin Mary Panayia to pray for a child, or it may be institutionalized, as with the Islamic pilgrimage to Mecca (the hajj). In addition, pilgrimages are often undertaken for transformative purposes, whether this transformation is in the form of a miraculous cure, an elevated ritual status for the pilgrim, or simply an enhancement of one's spiritual state.

Anthropologist Victor Turner viewed pilgrimage as a ritual similar to a rite of passage, in which an individual enters into a liminal state, separated from the routines of daily life and the constraints of normal time. For the pilgrim, this liminality is created by both the physical separation of the pilgrimage journey and the spiritual, nonworldly nature of the time defined by such a journey. In societies in which women's lives are tightly controlled and their movements restricted, the liminal world of pilgrimage can afford women a legitimate reason for travel, an opportunity to escape (for a limited time at least) the routines of their daily lives, and a spiritual and emotional space in which to address their concerns. While women often travel in the company of male family members, especially for longer pilgrimages such as the hajj, they may also make sacred journeys with groups of other women. Such journeys are legit-

A Tibetan Buddhist pilgrim holds a prayer wheel at a memorial *chorten* in Thimbu, Bhutan, 1996 (Alison Wright/Corbis).

imized by their sacred nature and by the fact that women often undertake them in order to secure the welfare of family members or to fulfill family obligations such as those to the dead. Women frequently bring the products of domestic life to pilgrimage shrines, making offerings of food, flowers, clothing, and handicrafts.

Pilgrimage offers women more than a legitimate escape from the routines and strictures of daily life, however, and it is more than simply an extension of domestic duties into a public sphere. For women, who often have little if any formal power within the major world religions, pilgrimage can provide opportunities that are not available in their normal lives. It can give women a space and place in which to express problems and concerns, sometimes in a highly emotional manner. Women visiting the shrine of the Virgin Mary of the Annunciation on the Greek island of Tinos, for example, some-

times crawl on their knees to the church, moaning in obvious pain, and cry out in supplication to Mary as they reach her icon. Women visiting the shrines of saints in Morocco may wail as they tell their troubles at the saint's tomb and receive comfort and advice from the other women gathered there.

Pilgrimage also affords women direct access to the divine and to the power and control over their lives that this provides. Pilgrimage can thus be seen as women's attempts to deal with a material world in which they are often disadvantaged. At the shrine of a saint, an illiterate Moroccan woman can speak directly of her medical problems in her own language rather than having to deal with a medical bureaucracy in which she is subordinate and disadvantaged. In many societies, reproduction, the welfare of children, and relations with husbands are the basis for women's status and power and provide important motivations for pilgrimage. Thus in a Korean town, women make "mountain pilgrimages" to worship the Mountain God and to pray to the Seven Stars in order to conceive and to assure the safety and health of their children. A number of famous pilgrimage sites are dedicated to female divine figures, such as the Virgin of Guadalupe in Mexico City and the Hindu regional goddess Nandadevi in the Himalayas. Rather than simply being reflections of women's domestic gender roles, such female figures may exhibit both male and female characteristics and take an active part in religion and politics (for example, by defending their faith against enemies), thus providing powerful models and protectors for women.

In literate religions in which both religious knowledge and religious institutions are controlled by men, pilgrimage provides women with spiritual legitimation and confirms their identity as religious persons. Pilgrimage is one of the ways in which women perform what has been termed the "domestication" of religion, a process by which women personalize the rituals and even the theology of institutionalized religion in order to make religion more meaningful to them and to safeguard those with whom they are linked in important interpersonal relationships. Through such "domestication," for example, illiterate Jewish women in Jerusalem create their own religious forms within the framework of a highly literate and learned male-oriented Judaism (e.g., Rachel's Tomb, the Wailing Wall).

Pilgrimage sites are sometimes regarded with ambivalence by the officials of institutionalized religion, as they constitute vast popular phenomena only partially controlled by formal authorities. Saints' sanctuaries in North Africa, for example, while often the object of women's pilgrimage, are not official religious sites. Therefore pilgrimage to such sites has an antiestablishment component. Thus for women pilgrimage may offer an opportunity and a framework for resistance to the dominating structures of their society and its religious tradition while at the same time giving them a creative role in shaping the practices of that religion and providing a legitimate space for empowerment. The degree to which such a creative role is possible, however, may depend on the degree of institutionalized male control of a pilgrimage site and its rituals. Muslim pilgrimage, for example, often reinforces gender roles by emphasizing gender segregation, different forms of behavior and dress for men and women, and different access to sacred sites. Thus Turkish village women going on the hajj are symbolically excluded from the ritual of departure and do not have a new social status or new privileges upon their return as do the men. While Turkish women can make the hajj only in the company of a male relative, they can make a *ziyaret* (a journey to pay respects) to saints' shrines in all-female groups. However, such pilgrimages are looked down upon by men, including those of the religious establishment, who consider such faith in the power of the saints inappropriate.

Pilgrimage shows no signs of waning, and indeed in many areas may be growing as increased prosperity and improved means of transportation make pilgrimage to even distant places more feasible for the average person. This, combined with more liberal attitudes toward women's mobility, have also made it possible for more women to undertake pilgrimage. In a study of Muslim pilgrims making the hajj to Mecca from Malaysia, for example, it was found that while before the 1920s there were no references to women making the journey, today half the pilgrims are women, and in some areas, the number of women making the pilgrimage exceeds that of men.

Pilgrimage is both a communal and an individual ritual. Although encapsulated within larger religious traditions and shaped by local custom, it is a flexible practice that not only reflects larger religious values but also accommodates individual needs and desires. It may be for these reasons that it has provided an attractive and powerful religious ritual for women in many regions of the world.

BIBLIOGRAPHY

Betteridge, Anne H. "Specialists in Miraculous Action: Some Shrines in Shiraz." In *Sacred Journeys: The Anthropology of Pilgrimage.* Edited by A. Morinis. 1992. A discussion of the ways in which different shrines meet different needs of pilgrims, including the particular needs of female pilgrims.

Delaney, Carol. "The *Hajj:* Sacred and Secular." *American Ethnologist* 17, no. 4 (August 1990): 513–530.

Contains a discussion of women's roles in the pilgrimage to Mecca from a Turkish village.

Dubisch, Jill. *In A Different Place: Pilgrimage, Gender and Politics at a Greek Island Shrine.* 1995. A study of pilgrimage at a major Greek Orthodox site, with particular attention to Greek women's religious roles.

Gold, Ann Grodzins. *Fruitful Journeys: The Ways of Rajasthani Pilgrims.* 1988. Although not focused on women and pilgrimage, this book contains rich observations on Hindu pilgrimage from the village perspective and includes much information on women.

Kendall, Laurel. *Shamans, Housewives, and Other Restless Spirits: Women in Korean Ritual Life.* 1985. A fascinating examination of the ritual world of women in a Korean town, including the rituals of pilgrimage.

McDonnell, Mary Byrne. "Patterns of Muslim Pilgrimage from Malaysia, 1885–1985." In *Muslim Travellers: Pilgrimage, Migration, and the Religious Imagination.* Edited by D. Eikelman and J. Pescatori. 1990. Contains information on changing patterns of male and female pilgrimage from Malaysia.

Mernissi, Fatima. "Women, Saints, and Sanctuaries." *Signs* 3, no. 2 (1977): 101–112. An evocative description and analysis of women's pilgrimage to saints' tombs in North Africa.

Ross, Ellen. "The Diversity of Divine Presence: Women's Geography in the Christian Tradition." In *Sacred Places and Profane Spaces.* Edited by J. Scott and P. Simpson-Housley. 1991.

Sax, William S. *Mountain Goddess: Gender and Politics in Himalayan Pilgrimage.* 1991. An excellent ethnography of Hindu pilgrimage in the Himalayas, with particular attention to gender and kinship.

Sered, Susan Starr. "The Domestication of Religion: The Spiritual Guardianship of Jewish Women." *Man* 23 (1988): 506–521. Develops the concept of "domestication of religion," which has applications to women's pilgrimage.

———. "Rachel's Tomb and the Milk Grotto of the Virgin Mary: Two Women's Shrines in Bethlehem." *Journal of Feminist Studies in Religion* 2, no. 2 (1986): 7–22. Examines two shrines of particular interest to women.

Tapper, Nancy. "*Ziyaret:* Gender, Movement, and Exchange in a Turkish Community." In *Muslim Travellers: Pilgrimage, Migration, and the Religious Imagination.* Edited by D. Eikelman and J. Pescatori. 1990. A good discussion of the different kinds of "going out" in a Turkish community (including visits to saints' tombs) and their significance for women.

JILL DUBISCH

Places, Sacred

Women and men in all known religions acknowledge certain places as powerful or important, although the meaning of power or importance varies immensely. Some holy sites are powerful or important because a miracle, or miracles, occurred there; some because the religion's founder or leader is associated with the place; some because of the presence of a natural tree, water, or rock formation; others because of rituals that are carried out there. Some sacred places are secret, some are popular, some are restricted to certain groups of people. A typology of gender and sacred places could focus upon access to the site and therefore include categories such as male domination, sexual integration, sexual segregation, and female domination. Or, a typology could focus upon the content of the site, for example, whether the site is associated with a male or female sacred figure.

In many religions men control the official holy places (for example, Buddhist monasteries in Thailand, the important mosques in Mecca, the Vatican). Control of holy places tends to reflect male domination of the religion as a whole—a domination that is reinforced by the power that emanates from the sacred place itself. Male monopoly of sacred sites generally gives expression to ideologies of women as polluted, *other*, or excessively sexual—and therefore unfit to enter the holy site. Throughout the traditional Jewish and Muslim worlds formal holy sites have been controlled by men. For example, in Europe and the United States orthodox Jewish women sit quietly on a balcony behind a curtain while men pray aloud in the main hall of the synagogue; in Asian and North African synagogues, traditionally there was no seating for women.

WOMEN'S ACTIVISM AT SACRED PLACES

Male control of official holy sites does not preclude women from developing their own sacred geography. Thus, traditional Jewish women carry out their most important rituals at home (particularly in the kitchen where through the preparation of kosher and traditional foods they foster the internalization of Jewish culture), the ritual bath, and the cemetery. Although it is possible that some men may view the ritual bath primarily as a place in which menstrual pollution is washed away, for many Jewish women (in particular, North African Jews), the ritual bath serves as a place for women to meet out of view and out of immediate control of men. The cemetery—and the dead who rest there—afford many Jewish women a sense of continuity throughout the generations. The place serves to remind them that they are not alone in bearing the burdens of childrearing—ancestors who understand their problems are looking out for them. These themes emerge clearly in Fatima Mernissi's work among Moroccan Muslim women for whom pilgrimage to shrines is a way both to escape the drudgery of their lives in patriarchal society and to articulate their problems out loud and receive support, advice, and sympathy from other women at the shrine. Some women may become carekeepers of holy tombs, a position of honor and responsibility. (This is in contrast to women's secondary role at the shrines in Mecca.)

The same point can be made regarding Christian churches in the United States and in parts of Europe (such as Spain) where, especially at weekday masses and services, the vast majority of participants are women. In these situations it is clear that despite official male control, the holy site serves as a positive function for women, whether social, spiritual, or both. In fact, it could be argued that the ability to leave the domestic arena and mingle with other women, even in a place under male control, both reflects and enhances a certain degree of female autonomy and cohesion. In many highly patriarchal societies one of the only opportunities that a woman has to leave the house without incurring anger or suspicion is to visit holy places. Jill Dubisch (1995) makes the important point that in Greece religious activities provide an arena for women's performances. Visiting cemeteries, attending church, and going on pilgrimage are legitimate ways for women to move through public space and socialize with other women. According to Dubisch, holy places can be seen as the equivalent of, or a counterpoint to, such public male spaces as the village coffee house. Most important, women are not criticized for their religious excursions because they are not neglecting their duties as wives and mothers but rather engaging in ritual activities on the family's behalf.

Particularly in societies in which women are separated from their natal families upon marriage, visits to holy sites can provide women with opportunities for maintaining both a social connection and a spiritual connection with their own kinfolk. For example, William Sax (1990) has found that in the Garhwal Himalayas, outmarried daughters are required to participate in numerous rituals in their parents' villages. Specifically, women attend pilgrimage rituals to the shrine of Nandadevi, the regional goddess. On the other hand, according to Sax, at the end of the ritual (or, more properly, as the final stage of the ritual), women board busses and return to their husbands' villages, thus acknowledging the legitimacy of virilocality.

CONTROL OF SACRED PLACES

In male-dominated cultures women's control of sacred spaces tends to be tenuous. At the tomb of the biblical matriarch Rachel, located in Bethlehem, Jewish women during the twentieth century have come to pray to "Mother Rachel" for understanding and help with problems of fertility. In the late 1980s the Israeli Ministry of Religion began to prohibit women from lighting candles at the Tomb (lighting candles is a traditional Jewish women's ritual), and approximately ten years later a men's religious seminary moved into the Tomb courtyard. When women in male-dominated religious cultures impinge upon men's space, the result can sometimes be violent. The Western Wall (Wailing Wall) in Jerusalem, Judaism's most holy site, is currently controlled by the orthodox male-dominated Israeli Ministry of Religion. Praying at the Western Wall is sexually segregated, and the men's section is larger, better located, and the main arena for ritual primarily because in traditional Judaism men pray as a group whereas women pray individually. During the past decade a group of women have chosen to pray at the Western Wall, in the women's section, but out loud as a group (in the way that men do). These women have been physically attacked, cursed, and are now involved in a lengthy court case over the right of women to pray aloud as a group, at the Wall.

In some religious situations men and women have equal access to shrines. Good examples are Buddhist and Shinto shrines in Japan. On the other hand, equal access does not necessarily mean equal control. For the most part, Japanese shrines are run (in a sense, owned) by male priests. To what extent the male priests direct women's or men's behavior at the shrines seems to depend, to a great extent, upon the personality of the specific priest. In a study of *mizuko kuya* (rituals for unborn or dead children), Elizabeth Harrison (1995) found that while one priest allowed the woman cultic leader to construct her ritual space as she wished, his successor has had a more interventionist approach.

In certain religious contexts men and women each have their own holy spaces. The best-documented example of this pattern comes from the Australian Aboriginal societies studied by Diane Bell. Women and men each have their own "lines" (geographical-spiritual-historical routes crossing the continent) and their own sacred meeting places. Women's "ring place," located some distance outside of the camp, is where women paint, work on ritual items, discuss grave matters, bring offenders to trial, and carry out rituals. Bell has found that the ring place is understood by both men and women as a place of authority for women, and that men will take circuitous routes to avoid even seeing the ring place. With European domination of Australia, women have lost control over much of their sacred territory, which has meant the loss of crucial economic and spiritual resources and female autonomy.

Jewish women stand by the partition separating the men's and women's sections of the Western Wall, Jerusalem, 1995 (Annie Griffiths Belt/Corbis).

Even in religious contexts that are dominated by women, women's authority over sacred sites tends to be subordinate to political and economic institutions that are dominated by men. For example, in Okinawa (an island chain south of Japan) religious leaders are women, and traditionally only women priestesses could enter the sacred groves. Nowadays, as foreign governments and companies have purchased or leased Okinawan land, women no longer fully control the sacred groves. On one island in Okinawa Prefecture, for instance, the sacred grove is now part of land leased by foreign oil companies, and priestesses must ask the village headman to ask the oil companies for permission to pray at the sacred groves.

GODDESSES AND SACRED PLACES

Some evidence suggests that women are more attracted to sacred sites associated with female figures. Carol Christ, for example, has led and documented pilgrimages in Greece to shrines associated with ancient goddesses. Christ has found that goddess myths and imagery resonate with the inner spiritual lives of the North American feminists who make the pilgrimage. Similarly, the tens of thousands of pilgrims, many or most of whom are women, crawling to the shrine of the Virgin of Guadalupe in Mexico, do seem to offer proof for women's preference for feminine sacred sites. On the other hand, there is substantial evidence showing that in South Asia shrines and temples associated with goddesses are visited more by men than by women. Gananath Obeyesekere (1984), for instance, argues that the cult of the goddess Pattini is oriented to males both in the sense that it addresses men's psychological problems and that women are excluded from the shrine at certain crucial points. What does seem to be the case is that in a variety of cultural contexts holy sites dedicated to female figures serve as national symbols and as rallying points for national liberation. This has been true of the Virgin of Guadalupe, Rachel's Tomb, and the shrine of the Holy Virgin of Saut D'Eau in Haiti.

BIBLIOGRAPHY

Bell, Diane. *Daughters of the Dreaming.* 1983.

Christ, Carol. *Odyssey with the Goddess: A Spiritual Quest in Crete.* 1995.

Christian, William. *Person and God in a Spanish Valley.* 1972.

Dubisch, Jill. *In a Different Place: Pilgrimage, Gender, and Politics at a Greek Island Shrine.* 1995.

Harrison, Elizabeth. "Women's Responses to Child Loss in Japan: The Case of *Mizuko Kuyo.*" *Journal of Feminist Studies in Religion* 11 (1995): 67–94.

Hori, Ichiro. *Folk Religion in Japan.* 1968.

Laguerre, Michel. "Haitian Pilgrimage to Our Lady of Saut d'Eau: A Sociological Analysis." *Social Compass* 33 (1986): 5–21.

Mernissi, Fatima. "Women, Saints, and Sanctuaries." *Signs* 3 (1977): 101–112.

Messiri, Nawal, al-. "The Sheikh Cult in Dahmit." In *Nubian Ceremonial Life.* Edited by John Kennedy. 1978.

Obeyesekere, Gananath. *The Cult of the Goddess Pattini.* 1984.

Preston, James J. *Mother Worship: Themes and Variations.* 1982.

Sax, William. "Village Daughter, Village Goddess: Residence, Gender, and Politics in a Himalayan Pilgrimage." *American Ethnologist* 17 (1990): 491–512.

Sered, Susan Starr. "Rachel's Tomb and the Milk Grotto of the Virgin Mary: Two Women's Shrines in Bethlehem." *Journal of Feminist Studies in Religion* 2 (1986): 7–22.

———. *Women as Ritual Experts: The Religious Lives of Elderly Jewish Women in Jerusalem.* 1992.

Turner, Victor, and Edith Turner. *Image and Pilgrimage in Christian Culture.* 1978.

See also **Geography, Sacred; Pilgrimage; Shrines.**

SUSAN STARR SERED

Political Science

Political science is the academic discipline concerned with the study of politics, that is, the negotiation through the constrained use of power of all aspects of organizations, public activities, and social and cultural practices.

The relationship of religion and political science goes back to the origins of the study of politics in the work of Plato and Aristotle, who understood divine law as intimately connected to the human political institutions they sought to theorize. From the Roman period through the early modern period, the Western study of politics and religion considered both as governed by the natural laws resulting from the divine order of the cosmos. The rise of the more systematic theorization of modern Western polities by Hobbes and Locke, accompanied by the gradual secularization of Western governing institutions, resulted by the early twentieth century in the complete distinction between the two fields.

In twentieth-century political science, religion has been an occasional object of study in terms of its impact upon political behavior. However, religion was often seen as merely historical (and thus a subject for the history of political theory), as a minor institutional actor (the role of the church), or as an "irrational" dimension of individual behavior. For a variety of reasons, in the latter part of the century political science paid more attention to religion: from the increasing visibility of conservative or fundamentalist religious groups throughout the world, to concern within the United States about the nature of a common political morality (communitarianism), to the rising awareness of differing roles of non-Christian religions outside the Western world.

As with religion, the status of women has also come into focus in the field of political science. However, unlike religion, there is no positive historical relationship between the study of politics and of women. The origins of the notions of politics in the fifth century B.C.E. Greek city-states rested upon an idea of politics as public activity among free citizens constructed in contrast with the private, nonpolitical passivity of women and nonfree men. This division of public and private spheres, in different permutations, has haunted the presence of women in Western political thought, especially in the modern period as the emerging notion of citizen was based upon the male head of a household.

Women have found new visibility in political science with the so-called Second Wave of feminism. Many women who were activists in the 1970s found themselves political scientists and theorists in the 1980s. Feminist work began to highlight women's presence in political institutions, giving new attention, for example, in discussions of the "gender gap" to distinctive female voting behavior. Using the insight that "the personal is political," feminist political theorists have broadened the notion of the political, considering the impact of women's experience on basic political categories such as the public and private spheres. Such work has yet to allow for women's religious agency, especially among poor women and women of various racial and ethnic backgrounds as described by feminist liberation theorists, both in the West and in developing countries. Nevertheless, women's experiences and feminist theories are becoming part of the repertoire of political science. On the side of feminist religious scholarship, emerging work in the sociology of religion and religious history may begin to bridge the gap between religious studies and political science as it explores the political dimensions of women's participation in religion. While earlier feminist theologies stressed the political dimension of women's experiences, contemporary theological work engages a variety of disciplines and practices. In Christian feminist ethics, however, the work of feminist political science continues to be an important resource for both critical analyses and constructive proposals.

BIBLIOGRAPHY

Elshtain, Jean Bethke. *Public Man, Private Woman.* 1981.

Harrison, Beverly. *Making the Connections: Essays in Feminist Social Ethics.* 1985.

Tamez, Elsa, ed. *Through Her Eyes: Women's Theology from Latin America.* 1989.

Young, Iris Marion. *Justice and the Politics of Difference.* 1990.

See also Classism; Liberation Theologies; Mujerista Tradition; Social Action; Social Change; Womanist Traditions; Women's Suffrage Movement.

ELIZABETH M. BOUNDS

Polytheism

The word *polytheism*, derived from Greek *poli* (many) and *theos* (god), is the doctrine (*ism*) that there are many gods. By contrast, *atheism* is the belief there is no god, *agnosticism* that if there is a god, god is not knowable; and *pantheism* that god is identifiable with everything. Polytheism is, above all, to be distinguished from *monotheism,* the doctrine that there is only one god, or, more subtly, from *henotheism,* exclusive devotion to one god, without denying the existence of other gods. Henotheism occupies the cusp between monotheism and polytheism.

Theologically, and this is especially the case with Judaism, Christianity, and Islam, one steps out of polytheism, and associated idolatry, into the true faith or belief in one God. In modern times this view becomes more sophisticated, and philosophically polytheism is seen as a step leading up to monotheism in an evolutionary as-cent (polydemonism → polytheism → henotheism → monotheism). The concept of polytheism has suffered theological, philosophical, and religious neglect on account of this stepping-stone status. Such neglect explains the absence of a developed typology of polytheism, although types of it have been identified. R. J. Zwi Werblowsky thus identifies, on the one hand, *pseudo-polytheism,* in which several gods are the "mere manifestations" of an ultimate principle, of a personal or impersonal God, and a *functional polytheism,* on the other, which characterizes systems that practice polytheism but otherwise explicitly or implicitly deny it in theory. To these one can add a third category, *evolutionary polytheism,* in which polytheism evolves into a monotheism or monism.

Reflection on polytheism (polymorphism) of the Indic religious tradition has contributed philosophically to the concept in two ways: by proposing that polytheism may be a means of approaching religious reality rather than stepping away from it, the way a curve might connect discrete points, or by suggesting that polytheism and monotheism may be two separate ways of apprehending the same reality—in parts or as a whole.

Although the Western religious tradition is considered monotheistic, this applies *sensuo stricto* to Islam. Although Biblically both Judaism and Christianity oppose polytheism as false and immoral, theological problems are raised for Christianity by the doctrine of the Trinity and historical problems posed for Judaism by Israelite henotheism. The latent androcentricism of Western monotheism has made feminist and womanist thinking sympathetic to polytheism (and by extension to the Indic and Greek religious tradition in some ways) because of its potential for greater tolerance—where there is much there is room for more—and its gender-inclusivity: polytheism allows room for the flourishing of female divinities, either in their own right or as spouses of male deities.

BIBLIOGRAPHY

Because the topic has been neglected, it is best to start with standard reference books such as the *Encyclopedia of Religion and Ethics,* edited by James Hastings (1917); *Die Religion in Geschichte und Gegenwart,* edited by Hemann Gunkel (1927) and *The Encyclopedia of Religion,* edited by Mircea Eliade (1987). For phenomenological approaches see Gerardus van der Leeuw, *Religion in Essence and Manifestation* (1938); E. O. James, *The Concept of Deity* (1950); and Angelo Brelich, "Der Polytheismus," *Numen* 7 (1960): 123–136. For Eastern approaches see Alain Danielou, *Le Polythisme hindou* (1960) and his *Hindu Polytheism*

(1964); and Pratima Bowes, *Hindu Religious Tradition: A Philosophical Approach* (1978). For modern approaches see David Miller, *The New Polytheism* (1974) and James Hillman, *Re-Visioning Psychology* (1977).

ARVIND SHARMA

Pope Joan

See Manfreda, Sister.

Porete, Marguerite

Marguerite Porete belongs to the circle of Beguines, probably the most creative aspect of the women's movement that emerged on the medieval European scene beginning around the late twelfth or early thirteenth century. Beguines were communities of women, widespread in the urban areas of the Lowlands, northern France, Germany, and extending southward into northern Italy. These communities belonged to no formal, ecclesiastically approved order. The women were committed to poverty, chastity, praying, and service, but they followed no formal rule, which made them automatically suspect in the eyes of some church leaders. Some Beguines lived alone as solitary women; others lived together in groups as small as two or three or as large as three hundred. In France, Beguines were dependent upon regional or local protection, either secular or religious. Perhaps the most famous beguinage was the Great Beguinage in Paris, which was founded by Louis IX in the mid-thirteenth century and housed up to four hundred women.

Marguerite Porete may have been a solitary Beguine, receiving no protection of any kind. She was probably an itinerant teacher and preacher, very likely expounding her teachings contained in her book, *The Mirror of Simple Souls,* to small groups of interested listeners. Word may have reached her of the church hierarchy's displeasure with her views, whereupon she turned to the scholastic theologian Godfrey of Fontaine, who approved the text, although with cautions. Nevertheless, the bishop of Cambrai burned her book in her presence in 1306, with express orders not to teach or write such things ever again, threatening punishment by the secular court. Marguerite Porete did not submit to the bishop's threat, and after being imprisoned for a year and a half she was burned at the stake as a relapsed heretic on 1 June 1310. The excerpts used to condemn Marguerite Porete to the flames were carried to the Council of Vienne in 1311 to support two papal decrees condemning the Heresy of the Free Spirit. One decree, *Cum de quibusdam mulieribus,* explicitly condemned the status of Beguine; the other, *Ad nostrum,* listed eight doctrinal errors of the Beguines. These decrees in effect amounted to an attack on Beguines, especially in Germany, which continued until the Council of Constance in 1417.

The Mirror of Simple Souls enjoyed a fairly wide circulation in the medieval era, according to the manuscript evidence. In addition to the copies in Old French, the text was translated into Latin, Italian, and Middle English. The text of *The Mirror* is, in the traditional format of treatises in Old French on the nature of love, composed as a dialogue among the allegorical figures of Reason, Love, and Soul, as well as others. Theological concepts expressed in courtly language penetrate the nature of the soul in the spiritual ascent to God. *The Mirror of Simple Souls* is a daring attempt to explore the mysteries of humanity in relation to divinity.

BIBLIOGRAPHY

Grundmann, Herbert. *Religious Movements in the Middle Ages.* Translated by Steven Rowan. 1995.

Lerner, Robert E. *The Heresy of the Free Spirit in the Later Middle Ages.* 1972.

Meister Eckhart and the Beguine Mystics. Edited by Bernard McGinn. 1994.

Porete, Marguerite. *La mirouer des simple âmes anienties.* In *Corpus christianorum continuatio mediaevalis* 69. Edited by Romana Guarnieri and Paul Verdeyen. 1986.

———. *The Mirror of Simple Souls.* Translated by Ellen L. Babinsky. 1993.

ELLEN L. BABINSKY

Possession

Possession refers to a widespread set of beliefs to account for changes in an individual's behavior, capacity, or health. A spirit is said to replace temporarily the possessed person's identity. Possession has been reported in 74 percent of preindustrial societies and also appears in segments of industrialized societies (Bourguignon, 1991). Possession experiences have been integrated into larger belief systems and utilized variously for social ends. A society's belief in possession may serve to explain changes in personality and alterations in sensory modalities, including amnesia, anesthesia, speech patterns, voice quality, and so on. Such transformations in behavior and experience may involve an altered state of consciousness, referred to as *possession trance*. Possession trance may be intentionally induced (voluntary) or spontaneous (involuntary). It may be desired (positive) or feared (negative). In the latter case, rituals such as exorcism are likely to exist to compel the possessing entity to depart.

The term *possession* appears in New Testament accounts, and later phenomena in the Christian world have often been patterned on scriptural precedents. Exorcism is still practiced by some Christian churches. Enthusiastic religious behavior, as practiced for example in Pentecostal churches, can also be interpreted as a form of possession—in this case by the Holy Spirit, rather than by harmful beings. Belief in negative possession, and ritual practices associated with such belief, exist in Judaism, Islam, Hinduism, and Buddhism. Such belief and practices often predate the world religion practiced in certain localities and have been integrated into it, frequently rejected by the more sophisticated levels of these complex societies.

A belief in spirit possession in the absence of an altered state, often referred to as *spirit intrusion,* is widely given as an explanation for various types of illness. In the New Testament a spirit causes muteness in a man, excessive menstrual bleeding in a woman, and so on. Among various traditional African societies, such as the Hausa, possession spirits are said to cause sleeping sickness. Many African societies believe in a witchcraft being that dwells in the stomach of the human host and is able to cause harm. When the reputed witch dies, an autopsy can determine the presence of such a witchcraft being. By contrast, some Native Americans believe in a type of power that enters a shaman, giving him the ability to cure.

The identity of the possessed person varies from society to society. The nontrance possessed may be patients or healers, witches or shamans. Persons in trance, believed to be possessed, may be patients or healers but also prophets or politico-religious leaders.

There are no systematic data on the distribution of possession and possession trance by gender, but women generally predominate. However, individual reports give examples of both women and men in each category. In Africa, for example, diviners who use various mechanical devices for diagnosing problems are generally men, whereas diviners who are also mediums are most generally women. Similarly, the Delphic Oracle in ancient Greece was a woman, although her pronouncements were interpreted by male priests. In the European tradition, among both Christians and Jews, the demon-possessed are most frequently women. Other examples include the teenage girls tried for witchcraft in Salem (although said to be possessed by witches, not by de-

A woman in a vodou trance is held by two assistants to the *houngan,* the high priest, who help to guide her through the unseen world, Haiti, c. 1950 (Bradley Smith/Corbis).

mons). Women figure as the possessed nuns of Loudon in seventeenth-century France. There are often-cited cases of possession among women in Hindu India. Women are reported as possessed by fox spirits in Japan.

The classic French cases of possession were studied during the nineteenth century by neurologist Jean-Martin Charcot in connection with his research on hysteria. Charcot found many similarities between hysteric patients and the possessed women described in the literature of past centuries. Clearly, both the hysterics and the nuns had learned their behavior in a cultural context. Hysteria of the type studied by Charcot is no longer seen in clinical settings, and the category has been dropped from medical classifications. Demon-possessed individuals are representative of negative spontaneous possession. Cases of positive spontaneous possession are exemplified by religious leaders such as Mother Ann Lee, the founder of the Shakers, or by the "sleeping" preaching girls of seventeenth-century French Protestantism. There are cases of possession among charismatic leaders in both historic and contemporary (both modern and modernizing) societies. Possessed women appear in various New Age religions in the United States.

The most common remedy for harmful possession is exorcism. In parts of Africa, however, the diagnosis of possession is often considered a step toward accommodation with the possessing spirit. This usually requires membership in a cult group that provides for the periodic "feasting" of the spirits.

Societies vary in the amount of importance given to possession beliefs. Bali, for example, has many different types of such beliefs associated with different social roles. Healers and diviners are usually women. Kris dancers may be both men and women. Masked actors in possession trance dramas are men, although they may impersonate female characters. Hobby horse possession trancers are men. Entranced little girls who, possessed by a village deity, dance on the shoulders of men, are a particularly striking example of Balinese possession trancers.

Why women predominate among possession trancers has been a subject of debate. Suggested reasons include female psychophysiology (hysteria, calcium deficiency), women's conservatism, and their response to an inferior social status. No single explanation accounts for all examples.

BIBLIOGRAPHY

Boddy, Janice. *Wombs and Alien Spirits: Women, Men and the Zar Cult in Northern Sudan.* 1989.

Bourguignon, Erika. *Possession.* 1991.

Brown, Karen McCarthy. *Mama Lola: A Vodou Priestess in Brooklyn.* 1991.

Crapanzano, Vincent, and Vivian Garrison, eds. *Case Studies in Spirit Possession.* 1977.

Garrett, Clarke. *Spirit Possession and Popular Religion: From the Camisard to the Shakers.* 1987.

Lewis, I. M. *Ecstatic Religion: An Anthropological Study of Spirit Possession and Shamanism.* 1971.

Oesterreich, T. K. *Possession, Demoniacal and Other, Among Primitive Races, in Antiquity, the Middle Ages and Modern Times.* Translated by D. Ibberson. 1966.

Ong, Ahiwa. *Spirits of Resistance and Capitalist Work Discipline.* 1987.

Sharp, Leslie A. *The Possessed and the Dispossessed: Spirits, Identity and Power in a Madagascar Immigrant Town.* 1993.

Starkey, Marion. *The Devil in Massachusetts.* 1949.

Suryani, L. H., and G. D. Jensen. *Trance and Possession in Bali: A Window on Western Multiple Personality, Possession Disorder and Suicide.* 1993.

See also **Possession Cults.**

ERIKA BOURGUIGNON

Possession Cults

The term *possession cults* may be said to refer to communities of women and men creating ceremonial opportunities to manifest a spiritual personality through the body of one or several of the participants. *Possession* refers to the interpretation of an altered state of consciousness experienced by a usually trained participant as being the manifestation of the personality of a spirit. *Cult* refers to the communal action usually deemed necessary to manifest and interact with the spiritual person in or through the body of the human participant.

Though the terms *possession* and *cult* have a robust history of usage in social scientific literature, both present barriers to understanding the phenomena they seek to describe. The former has been sensationalized in novels and films to suggest an anomic, pathological, or demonic invasion of the personality, where the latter suggests inauthentic and authoritarian religiosity. Though the phenomena described in scholarly literature as possession cults may not be free of pathology or inauthenticity these religious traditions are characterized by communal, sanctioned action that brings about important, even uplifting, contact with the presence and power of a spiritual person.

To avoid the pejorative associations of both terms we may prefer to privilege the participants' interpretation of the phenomena and speak of spirit "manifestation," "incorporation," or "mediumship." And inasmuch as traditions of spirit manifestation are considered contacts with a sacred world, they may be better termed "religions."

Following the pioneering work of Erika Bourguignon, researchers have organized their interest in these religions in two directions: understanding the state of mind of those experiencing spirit manifestation; and examining the interpretations of their behavior developed by the religious communities concerned with them.

The experience itself has been characterized as trance, dissociation, fugue states, hysteria, hallucinations, catalepsy, epilepsy, hypnosis, and somnambulism. Though attempts have been made to distinguish various types of behavior, researchers have found the distinctions too rigid and the phenomena too fluid for categories to be useful. Bourguignon herself subsumes all related experiences as "altered states of consciousness," while Felicitas Goodman prefers "trance" as a general term.

Certain generalizations can be made about the neurophysiology of spirit manifestation. According to Goodman, those undergoing manifestation are likely to breathe more deeply, perspire more readily, blush, tremble, twitch, and tense their muscles. Their heart rates increase and blood pressures drop. These phenomena are likely occasioned by—though not necessarily caused by—external stimuli such as fasting, exhaustion, or sensory deprivation or overload. In some contexts chemical catalysts may be employed, such as tobacco, cannabis, alcohol, or other psychotropic substances.

It is important to bear in mind that the altered states themselves are conditioned by cultural expectation and that the experiences of those in these states are patterned after the community's interpretation of them. Nowhere is this more important than in the question of the individuals' relative awareness of their own behavior when manifesting spirits. Janice Boddy asked Asia, a medium in the *zar* tradition of Sudan, about her experience while manifesting a spirit and was told: "You forget who you are, your village, your family, you know nothing from your life. You see with the eyes of the spirit until the drumming stops" (Boddy, 1989, p. 350). Karen Brown's Haitian teacher Alourdes told her, "When the spirit in your body, in your head, you don't know nothing. They [the other participants] have to tell you what the spirit say, what message he leave for you" (Brown, 1991, p. 353). Maya Deren refers to her own experience during a Haitian vodou ceremony as "white darkness" (Deren, 1953, p. 247). Each of these examples suggests slightly different kinds of awareness that may serve different purposes for the communities involved. Goodman maintains that the memory of the trance experience is dependent on the expectation of the community rather than the desire of the individual.

Researchers have focused on reports of awareness and amnesia in their interpretations of the function of spirit manifestation and the special prominence of women as mediums and leaders of traditions where it plays a central role. The most influential theory concerning the role of women in religions of spirit manifestation is that of the British social anthropologist I. M. Lewis. Lewis seeks to explain the prevalence of what he terms "ecstatic religion" among marginalized and subordinated groups within a given society, notably women in male-dominated societies. He draws a functional, or in his words "operational," connection between the social and economic deprivation suffered by women throughout the world and their resort to spirit manifestation as compensation for their sufferings. Stemming from his extensive fieldwork among *zar* communities in Somalia, and drawing examples from other traditions worldwide, Lewis argues that spirit manifestation offers women attention, status, catharsis, and redress denied them by male authority and unavailable to them by any other culturally acceptable

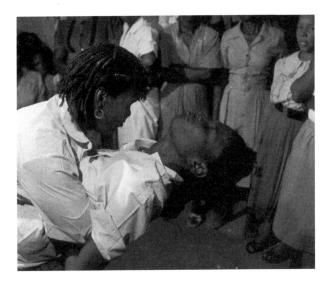

A woman falls into a possession trance during a vodou ceremony, Haiti (Philip Gould/Corbis).

means. When manifesting spirits women receive the elaborate courtesies and respect accorded to sacred beings. Not the least of these perquisites in poor societies is the access to rich and fancy foods appropriate to the spirits. Behaviors usually deemed unacceptable for women, including demands for political, economic, or social power, can be expressed and to a certain extent realized through spirit manifestation.

Basing his generalizations on the *zar* traditions, Lewis concludes that religions of spirit manifestation negotiate power between the genders in male-dominated societies. Spirit manifestation is looked upon by men as a kind of illness requiring the therapy of ceremonial indulgence of the manifested spirit. For women, however, spirit manifestation is seen as a "clandestine ecstasy." It is "an oblique aggressive strategy" carried out by women to compensate for exclusion from male privilege and to redress the imbalance of power.

It is the attribution of "clandestine" and "oblique" functions to religions of spirit manifestation that reveals the limitations of Lewis's approach. It is one thing to demonstrate that the results of the practice of spirit manifestation are compensatory and another to speculate that the participants are acting so as to achieve compensation. Here the awareness of the medium becomes particularly relevant. If the medium's account of her own experience is that she is not self-aware during spirit manifestation, then one must attribute to her unconscious motivations and assume she is gaining unconscious rewards. Finally, Lewis's theories of "oblique" compensation presuppose that women are seeking the kind of power withheld from them by men. Given that spirit manifestation is a global phenomenon in 437 of 488 cultures surveyed by Bourguignon, it ought be argued that it is a normal dimension of religious experience. From this viewpoint it is the lack of spirit manifestation that is more likely to be compensatory rather than its presence. Susan Starr Sered asks if it may be that male socialization prevents such a common cultural experience among men. Goodman is yet more forthright, seeing the ability to manifest spirits as a "genetic endowment" of all human beings.

Compensatory or not, spirit manifestation is a central feature in women's spirituality throughout the world. Sered finds it the key religious experience in nine of the twelve traditions that she documents as "religions dominated by women." She argues that religions of spirit manifestation stress interpersonal and familial relationships, which are of particular relevance and concern to women. The sharing of the medium's body by her own personality as well as that of the spirit parallels the experience of pregnancy and child rearing. Primary relationships are most frequently understood in terms of mothers and daughters, while initiation is seen as giving birth to the spirit as well as the new life of human initiates. The very act of spirit manifestation is a kind of giving birth with its attendant throes, altered states of consciousness, creativity, and nurture.

While spirit manifestation may provide a refuge and protest against restrictive views of gender, it also parallels the ego formation of women in most societies, stressing relatedness and connection over objectivity and separation. Sered argues that this view brings together theories of spirit manifestation among women with participants' explanation of their own experience. In the words of Maria-José, a Brazilian priestess of *macumba*: "From the beginning women are more open to trances—they have fewer obstacles in their minds than men. . . . Women have a much deeper relationship with themselves than men do. A more direct tie—how should I say—to who they really are (Bramly, 1977, p. 117).

Religions of spirit manifestation are traditions throughout the world that have fostered women's creativity and leadership. They have provided access to spiritual power independent of the hierarchical institutions of the world religions and have supported an embodied spirituality that has uniquely reflected women's concerns and hopes.

BIBLIOGRAPHY

Boddy, Janice. *Wombs and Alien Spirits: Women, Men and the Zar Cult in Northern Sudan.* 1989.

Bourguignon, Erika. *Religion, Altered States of Consciousness, and Social Change.* 1973.

Bramly, Serge. *Macumba: The Teachings of Maria-José, Mother of the Gods.* 1977.

Brown, Karen McCarthy. *Mama Lola: A Vodou Priestess in Brooklyn.* 1991.

Deren, Maya. *Divine Horsemen: The Voodoo Gods of Haiti.* 1953. Reprint, 1983.

Goodman, Felicitas D. *Ecstasy, Ritual, and Alternate Reality: Religion in a Pluralistic World.* 1988.

Lewis, I. M. *Ecstatic Religion: An Anthropological Study of Spirit Possession and Shamanism.* 1971.

———. *Religion in Context: Cults and Charisma.* 1986.

Sered, Susan Starr. *Priestess, Mother, Sacred Sister: Religions Dominated by Women.* 1994.

See also **Cults; Self; Shamans.**

JOSEPH M. MURPHY

Postmodernism

Because of the highly contested nature of the term, it is impossible to define *postmodernism*. Its central preoccupations do not constitute a radical break with modernity, but rather a restructuring of many of its elements to bring them to intellectual prominence. Relations between power and knowledge, subjectivity, difference, heterogeneity, fragmentation, and otherness, or "alterity," are key concepts in postmodernist discourse. But these concepts have always been present in discourses of modernity as "counterdiscourses," sometimes subordinate or subterranean to the prevailing discourses where knowledge exercises coercion and conformity to hegemonic norms. Although postmodernism tries to expose the ways in which difference and otherness have been marginalized or rendered deviant in modernist discourses, it is often difficult to distinguish between what Hal Foster (1983) calls a "postmodernism of resistance" and a more reactionary "repudiation of modernism." The distinction is crucial for feminist theory, which remains heavily influenced by postmodernism. Critical theories affirming difference, nonidentity, specificity, and plurality have been used effectively by feminist theorists challenging the androcentric hegemony of academic disciplines that have disregarded or ignored women's contribution to various fields of knowledge. There are conceptual traps for feminist theory within postmodernism, such as the repudiation of notions of the autonomous subject, which, if taken too far, threaten to extinguish the efforts of feminists such as Rosemary Radford Ruether to effect the recognition of the "full humanity of women." The goals of women's liberation are unrealizable in the absence of a situated, contextualized, relational subject capable of forming and exercising her own decisions. The conservativist tendency in postmodernism to erase the subject undermines the emancipatory impulse of feminist theory and practice. In this respect, Craig Owens's speculation that "postmodernism may be another masculine invention engineered to exclude women" ("The Discourse of Others: Feminists and Postmodernism," in Foster, 1983, p. 61) must be taken seriously. Although the feminist theory of Elisabeth Schüssler Fiorenza takes seriously notions of heterogeneity, plurality, and the affirmation of difference among and between women, she does not sacrifice concepts of self or subjective agency. Her work allows the counterdiscourses of modernity to surface without repudiating the emancipatory discourses of modernity that allow for the possibility and legitimacy of feminist struggles for freedom on all levels of human existence.

BIBLIOGRAPHY

Benhabib, Seyla. "Feminism and the Question of Postmodernism." In *Situating the Self: Gender, Community and Postmodernism in Contemporary Ethics.* 1992.

Foster, Hal, ed. *The Anti-aesthetic: Essays in Postmodern Culture.* 1983.

Hewitt, Marsha Aileen. "Cyborgs, Drag Queens and Goddesses: Emancipatory-Regressive Paths in Feminist Theory." *Method and Theory in the Study of Religion* 5, no. 2 (1993): 135–154.

———. "The Eclipse of Subjectivity and Idealizations of the 'Other'." *Journal of Dharma* 22, no. 3 (1997): 323–348.

Ruether, Rosemary Radford. *Sexism and God-talk: Toward a Feminist Theology.* 1983.

Schüssler Fiorenza, Elisabeth. *But She Said: Feminist Practices of Biblical Interpretation.* 1992.

See also **Deconstruction.**

MARSHA AILEEN HEWITT

Prakriti

A Sanskrit and more broadly Hindu concept, *prakriti* denotes matter, materiality, the raw "stuff" of the physical universe. A feminine noun, *prakriti* in early sources is often interchangeable with the neuter *pradhāna*, sometimes in contrast with the masculine *puruṣa* (spirit), but with no larger gender implications. In the late Upanishads and contemporaneous philosophical and popular literature, and subsequently in the Pu-

rāṇas, *prakriti* becomes variously valorized as a gendered concept. Assimilated to the notion of maya (illusion, trick, wiliness), *prakriti* is understood, particularly in more extreme misogynous circles of Advaita Vedanta, as the feminine force that obscures the ultimate reality of the nondual brahman. But when seen as an instance of *shakti* (creative power, energy), *prakriti* is understood, particularly in tantric circles, as the vehicle through which the divine makes itself manifest. Over the past millenium, mythology, iconography, and popular discourse have moved easily and usually unself-consciously between these two poles. Such radically contrasting interpretation of *prakriti* may be seen as paralleling the dramatic differences exhibited by Hindu goddesses. Though possessing distinct individual identities, collectively they are both benign and malevolent, nurturing and murderous, restrained and uncontrolled. Similarly, the ambivalence with which materiality and *prakriti* is regarded in Hindu thought parallels a larger ambivalence toward women and their status. However, contemporary reassessment of traditional scholarly emphasis on the world-renouncing nature of Hinduism is bringing with it new emphasis on the this-worldly nature of the tradition, as also on roles played by women and on the positive functions and aspects of *prakriti*.

BIBLIOGRAPHY

Harzer, Edeltraud. "Prakriti." In *The Encyclopedia of Religion.* Edited by Mircea Eliade. 1987.

Pintchman, Tracy. *The Rise of the Goddess in the Hindu Tradition.* 1994.

THOMAS B. COBURN

Prayer

Prayer is the humble religious approach to the sacred or holy, either for petition, confession, thanksgiving, or praise. As one of the most significant indicators of faith in Judaism, Christianity, and Islam, prayer is a special kind of communication directed to the divine. One takes up the prayer posture mysteriously urged from within to affirm the ever-present power of the Ultimate and to bridge the gap that is sometimes felt between one's daily life on the mundane level and the metaphysical realm of the ultimate on the spiritual level.

Prayer, whether for worship or petition, differs from meditation, a more diffuse and nonverbal form of sacred communication, because it implies an intimate conception of the sacred that can be directly addressed. Prayer is directed to a supernatural being or entity that can intervene on one's behalf and respond to one's request, sometimes in very specific ways. Thus, prayer can be seen as a form of asking that implies that the supernatural entity will hear and can provide some answer.

There are formal, disciplined, ritual prayers, performed invariantly at prescribed times or for specific occasions, as well as informal, spontaneous prayers with a free outpouring of the soul. Both forms can include words, whether in fixed formulas or as an unequivocal kind of petition or loving conversation. The prayer process might also include movements or postures that dramatize it on the outward level and signal acceptance. The sincere effort of communication increases the efficacy of the prayer in direct proportion to one's inner state of belief that a supranatural power can and does intercede in one's affairs.

Supplication or petition can range from the very personal and immediate request to the petition for eternal blessings and benevolence that only the Creator can ultimately bestow. Because no two people have precisely the same life experiences bringing them to the same understanding of the Holy presence, no two people pray in precisely the same manner. The performance of prayer reflects a kind of yearning of the divine spark within humankind to join with more of itself.

The result is that one can use prayer for self-improvement in the task of fulfilling God's will, purpose, or trusteeship on the earth, as variously conceived by the different traditions. Thus, the answer to the prayer may simply be in becoming aware of the gifts and grace provided by God. Hence, prayer serves more than merely as a refuge from responsibility; rather, it gives strength and inspires. It can lead to personal and communal transformation. Prayer that expands the soul is founded upon gratitude.

The more formalized and invariant the prayer rituals have been, the greater the gender hierarchy in a particular denomination. Thus, women have always invoked a more personal communion with God, either before, during, or after the ritual itself, as a means for overcoming this hierarchy, as well as to strengthen the bonds between themselves and God.

JUDAISM

In Judaism the obligation to pray follows the statement in Deuteronomy 6.5, which calls for serving God with the whole heart, soul, and might. The Talmud interprets the "whole heart" here to mean prayer. Prayer is thus prescribed three times throughout the day, to be performed with certain qualifications.

The Shemoneh 'Esreh is at the center of the daily liturgy in Judaism. It consists of nineteen prescribed formulas—three prayers of praise in the beginning, thirteen prayers of petition in the middle, and three prayers of thanks at the end. The performer stands in the direction of Jerusalem and takes three steps forward and three steps back. The body is returned to the original place, as the mind is set right for the prayer state.

The Jewish prayer is not performed aloud; only the lips move. Although these prayers used to be performed exclusively in Hebrew, they are currently also recited in the vernacular by certain branches of Judaism. Although Jews can and do pray anywhere, including in the home or in the marketplace, the synagogue is the formal place of daily worship, with Saturday, the Sabbath, being the most important day.

Prayer links the worshiper with the continuity of history and with a people bounded by the enduring Israel. Most prayers, however, are recited in the present tense, addressed directly to God, with the conviction that the Jewish community and the principles of the Jewish faith live and speak today as they did in the past and as they will in every generation.

Traditionally, the Jewish woman could say the Shemoneh 'Esreh but was not obligated to, since prayer times could interfere with what was thought to be the woman's primary duty to take care of the home. In the Reform and Conservative movements, in which women can become rabbis, the obligation for prayer is now also extended to women, who may also lead the liturgical service and don the prayer garments traditionally worn by men. Women may pray beside, separated from, or dispersed among the men, depending on the particular synagogue.

Through the centuries Jewish women have made particular use of the *techinot* prayers. The *techinot*, originally performed in Yiddish, are personal devotions frequently used for the purpose of pouring out one's heart before the compassionate Father. They can be recited throughout the regular service, for special occasions, on important days of the religious year, or whenever the heart is prompted to offer them.

CHRISTIANITY

In addition to the more significant ritual sacraments in Christianity used to measure the appropriate relationship between humankind and God the Father or Jesus the Son, prayer helps to define the life of the devotee. Here, prayer is not so much an invariant ritual form of worship as it is a form of supplication and thanksgiving. Hence, Christian prayer especially emphasizes the inward power of the Holy Spirit to effect outward and inward change and to guarantee grace. In its communal form, prayer assumes a special power or efficacy signaling mutual understanding of God and a collective acknowledgment of a religious and cultural tradition.

Prayer is a particularly powerful performative that transforms the mood of the worshiper, reorienting him or her toward the direction of the prayer. Thus, the affective and emotive qualities of prayers, whether somber confession, humble petition, or joyous thanksgiving, are a significant dimension of the prayer performance.

With the institutional aspects of the church in the foreground, prayer, especially public prayer, must be seen as a particularly political act. It is constructed within a web of interlocking assumptions about women and men, and about God. Hence, Christian women have benefited from and been limited by prayer. Some of the most outstanding women have made use of prayer as a subversive act empowering them and increasing their efficacy personally as well as within the religious community and in the world at large.

Yet prayer has confirmed the marginalization of women's religious experiences by sustaining the male hierarchy in the church and by privileging the experiences of men in juxtaposition to God. Therefore, some women have directed their prayers toward hope of relief from a particularly abusive private relationship that may be condoned by the church hierarchies. The use of male-identified language when speaking with God can increase ominous feelings of mistrust.

For women to reclaim the power of prayer in both its public and private dimensions might mean first to be granted permission not to pray, to use silence as a way to reclaim the anguish and anger they feel when the church has ignored or condoned relationships that were potentially abusive. This reclaiming allows women to come forth with the urgency and the flaws in the human attempt to address the Ultimate. Feminist prayer, which seeks continually to confirm a particular vantage point with respect to Christian notions of the sacred and to the movement of the holy spirit, has transformation as its goal. Such a transformation leads from awareness that certain relationships of domination function to cut off the full breadth of the religious experiences of women to the resistance to these hierarchies as necessary for the recreation of the church as healthy community for the sake of spiritual well-being.

ISLAM

In Islam the term prayer usually refers to *ṣalat*, the ritual worship performed five times daily that is obligatory for all Muslims, male and female, past puberty. *Ṣalat* is the most distinguishing feature of Islamic practice, with certain prerequisite conditions for its proper performance. After ritual purification the performer stands facing the Kaaba, a cube-shaped structure in

A woman prays over a sacred stone at the entrance of Hazrati Shah-i-Zinda (Shrine of the Living King), Samarkand, Uzbekistan (Francesco Venturi; Kea Publishing Services Ltd./Corbis).

Mecca. For each unit of prayer there are prescribed postures: standing, bowing from the waist, and full prostration, combined with recitation of selections from the Qur'an and other prescribed formulas. The prayer is always recited in Arabic, whether inaudibly during the day or with some portions recited aloud during the predawn and night hours. Women pray separately from men when outside the home, whether above, beside, or behind them as determined by the architectural arrangements of the mosque.

To indicate her immediate state, the worshiper can use at her discretion the *du'ā'*, a personal supplication with no required features. Both the *ṣalat* and the *du'ā'* are significant to the ultimate goal of remembrance of Allah in Islam.

Prayer is part of the diligent search for and delight in the sacred whereby the worshiper opens up her heart and soul to the divine. It is of primary importance to all who have faith in a mysterious presence beyond everyday ordinary life and who long for continual interchange between our lives and the spiritual realm of the holy.

BIBLIOGRAPHY

Denny, Frederick. *An Introduction to Islam,* 2d ed. 1994.

Graham, Maureen. *Women of Power and Presence.* 1990.

Gottlieb, Lynn. *She Who Dwells Within: A Feminist Vision of a Renewed Judaism.* 1995.

Kirzner, Yitzchok, with Lisa Aiken. *The Art of Jewish Prayer.* 1991.

Menzies, Lucy, ed. *Life as Prayer and Other Writings of Evelyn Underhill.* 1946.

Procter-Smith, Marjorie. *Praying with Our Eyes Open: Engendering Feminist Liturgical Prayer.* 1995.

Rappaport, Roy A. *Ecology, Meaning and Religion.* 1979.

Turner, Norma. *A Book of Jewish Women's Prayers: Translations from the Yiddish.* 1995.

See also **Silence.**

AMINA WADUD

Pregnancy

Women's sexual and generative capacities have determined women's primary function and traditional role. In many religious systems for a woman to be childless is a condition of great despair and even greater shame, a denial of her very nature. The sacred texts of such religions offer stern reproaches for childlessness: Rachel cries out to her husband, Jacob, "Give me children, or I shall die!" (Gen. 30:1). Confucian ethics enjoin women to bear children as part of their filial responsibility: since the cosmic order esteemed by the Confucian tradition is radically relational, pregnancy and birth is the essential act that carries the solitary individual into the continuum of this life, another link in the great chain of being. Moreover, it is not uncommon to find in some cultures that once a woman has entered menopause, marking the end of her fertile years, she loses status and value, despite the fact that her body, paradoxically, is becoming similar to the male form.

In the ritualized worship of Paleolithic and Neolithic communities in prehistoric Europe, among others, the pregnant goddess existed as a primary deity, often represented as nude, with engorged breasts and a protruding belly protected by the firm embrace of her own hands. Other, more abstracted, representations of the pregnant goddess included a bulging mound of earth or an oven. The Chinese Tao, itself a highly evocative symbol of the feminine, is often described as the mother of all reality and is often imaged as a womb, valley, or lactating breast; in a similar fashion, Buddhist schools such as the Mahayana Yogācāra speak of the *tathāgata-garbha,* the cosmic womb, the womb of reality.

In many primal societies, the procreative ability of woman was recognized as an aspect of her spiritual strength, perhaps superiority. In fact, for many cultures, such as the Maori of New Zealand, the Buriats of western Mongolia, and tribes in Nigeria, a woman's pregnancy was considered a condition independent of a coital relationship with a male and in no way related to human sexual intercourse; such societies rather believed that impregnation was caused by the moon or by the agency of the Great Moon Mother. The connection between the image of a waning and waxing moon and the physical transformation of the pregnant woman's body is an obvious one; however, it is not uncommon to find in societies well-versed in the physiology of impregnation a latent reliance, albeit symbolic, upon the efficacy of the moon. The image of the crescent moon is especially resonant with symbolism, and in southern Italian communities, for instance, the crescent moon is still worn as a charm to ensure fertility and healthy increase.

Biblical Judaism deconstructs the purely physiological link between human sexual intercourse and the ensuing conception and denies the woman complete personal discretion in her fertility (as well as the man, in fact). Rather, God alone is ultimately responsible for the impregnation and subsequent successful pregnancy (see, e.g., Ps. 139:13–16): it is He who will open and shut wombs, He who will fashion the developing child in the womb, He who will act as midwife, bringing on labor and sending forth the child (see Ps. 139: 13–16; Isa. 46: 3–4; Job 10: 8–11, 18). A fortunate conception, a robust pregnancy, and a favorable delivery (sons) were regarded as tokens of God's approval. Islam also ascribes conception and the development of a woman's pregnancy to the will and mercy of Allah. It is He who molds the fetus from the clot of blood that exists in the woman's womb after the life-giving semen has entered there. Without the decree and knowledge of Allah, no woman can conceive or deliver a child: her womb is the safe place wherein the will of Allah may be realized (see sura 35:11; 39:6; 75:40; 77:22).

Some tribal societies, such as that of the Australian Aborigines, so mythically ground pregnancy and childbirth and deem them events of such formidable mystery that men are excluded from the totemic ceremonial rituals that celebrate the unique experiences of the female anatomy: first menstruation, initial state of pregnancy, labor, and childbirth. Aboriginal belief states that a woman may become pregnant either through the vagina (by squatting at certain springs favored by spirit babies) or through the mouth (by eating food in which the spirit child has settled because it wishes to be born). Chinese folk religion claims that a pregnant woman carries within her a fetus spirit that has the potential to be externally mobile and that family members must be at pains not to offend, lest harm should come to the newborn; for example, cutting with scissors in a room inhabited by the fetus spirit could result in the birth of a child with a missing limb.

Hinduism refers to pregnancy as *garbha-dharana,* womb-possessing, and extols it as the most blessed state of woman. In the ancient and medieval eras, Hindu men and women engaged in various rituals to secure conception and ensure a healthy pregnancy, such as the sacramental *garbha-adhana,* or womb-placing, during which the woman took a "seed-receiving" bath, then awaited her spouse while he spoke verses calling forth his own fertility. Other rites were meant to ensure the birth of a male child and that child's safe and gentle birth. While the Hindu culture, in general, no longer performs such rites, pregnancy and birth are still occasions for ceremonial display and rejoicing.

For centuries, Western Christianity did not divorce itself from ancient Greek and Roman biology, which insisted that while both sexes are necessary for the conception of a child, the female contributes only the material flesh and the area for the growth of the child, the male being the actual source for specific human generation. The female was considered, in fact, a misbegotten male. The male was the standard for humanity and woman was the necessary other, in all ways essentially inferior. Such thinking was compounded by traditional Biblical exegesis of both Catholic theologians as well as Protestant reformers, that woman's experience of pregnancy and the pains attendant upon birthing were her just punishment from God for her role in the Fall of humankind. Reproduction was considered a fact of the natural law of creation and, as such, most Christian denominations inveighed for centuries (some still do) against the prevention or the termination of a pregnancy as an affront to the divine ordering of the cosmos. Islamic law also proscribes the termination of a pregnancy or female sterilization; in many Muslim countries, contraception is rejected. So fundamental is the fact of pregnancy in the life of a mature Arab woman that it defines her spiritually, personally, and so-

cially: she acquires her identity from the birth of her first male child, so that the woman who bore the male child Salamah now becomes Umm Salamah, mother of Salamah, to her family, her community, and in the presence of her God.

BIBLIOGRAPHY

Clark, Gillian. *Women in Late Antiquity: Pagan and Christian Lifestyles.* 1993.

Falk, Nancy A., and Rita M. Gross. *Unspoken Worlds: Women's Religious Lives in Non-Western Cultures.* 1980.

Frymer-Kensky, Tikva. *In the Wake of the Goddesses: Women, Culture and the Biblical Transformation of Pagan Myth.* 1992.

Gimbutas, Marija. *The Goddesses and Gods of Old Europe.* 1982.

Harding, M. Esther. *Woman's Mysteries, Ancient and Modern.* 1990.

Kraemer, Ross Shepard. *Her Share of the Blessings.* 1992.

Trible, Phyllis. *God and the Rhetoric of Sexuality.* 1978.

Ulrich, Laurel Thatcher. "Vertuous Women Found." In *Women in American Religion.* Edited by Janet Wilson James. 1978.

Walker, Benjamin. "Pregnancy." In *The Hindu World,* vol. 2. 1968.

See also **Fertility and Barrenness**; **Vagina**; **Womb**.

JUNE-ANN GREELEY

Prehistoric Religions

Pre-agricultural Peoples

We are modern human beings, Homo sapiens sapiens, and our history is long. Perhaps five to ten million years ago, hominids and apes diverged upon the evolutionary line. Homo habilis appeared perhaps 2.3 million years ago. The hands of Homo habilis were graced with opposable thumbs, enabling those hands to fashion tools of stone. There is no way to know what else they made from other more perishable materials, but we know Homo habilis probably lived in complex, food-sharing bands. Homo erectus appeared in Africa perhaps 1.7 or 1.6 or 1.3 million years ago, and was certainly in China 700,000 years ago or earlier than that. Homo erectus also lived in complex social bands and may have been able to speak. These early humans not only made and used hand tools, they had the use of fire. Indeed, it is possible that as early as 1.5 million years ago Homo erectus could make fire.

The exact relationship of Homo erectus to Homo sapiens sapiens is unclear. For those who subscribe to the single-genesis theory, the movement of Homo sapiens out of Africa is believed to have occurred 150,000 to 200,000 years ago following the earlier movement of Homo erectus out of Africa which occurred perhaps 700,000 to 900,000 years ago. Homo sapiens subsequently populated the entire world, becoming Homo sapiens sapiens. In 1987 scholars announced the discovery of a hypothetical "Eve," an African woman whose mitochondrial DNA 200,000 years ago was said to be the maternal ancestor of all living human beings. Unhappily for single-genesis theorists, the Eve study was later shown to be statistically flawed and has since been set gently aside.

Another equally durable scholarly viewpoint argues for multiple lines of origins for modern humans. Regionalists contend that Homo sapiens arose independently in Africa, Europe, and Asia from Homo erectus and later migrated into the Americas out of Asia. (One version of this viewpoint, the "candelabra" theory, combines both the regionalist and single-genesis viewpoints, arguing Homo erectus originated only in Africa but Homo sapiens appeared elsewhere in multiple sites.)

A most interesting finding supports the regionalists: in 1992, two skulls were found in China displaying features of both Homo erectus and Homo sapiens (*Nature*, June 1992). The skulls are thought to be perhaps 400,000 years old. The mixture of Homo erectus and Homo sapiens characteristics in the same skulls at that time in China could have occurred only in a multigenesis situation. If so, then Homo erectus in Asia did eventually become Homo sapiens sapiens. And if that is so, then there is every reason to assume similar events happened in other places, too.

In the eastern Mediterranean Homo sapiens sapiens was established as Cro-Magnon culture in Israel about 90,000 B.C.E. Neandertal culture did not appear in Israel until 60,000. Both Neandertal and Cro-Magnon sites have been found facing one another across a valley near Mount Carmel and would have been occupied in the same time frame. In China Cro-Magnon is dated at about 80,000 and in Europe appeared about 40,000. Neandertal is dated in Europe to at least 100–130,000, mysteriously disappearing there around 30,000. Neandertal's relationship or possible interrelationship with Cro-Magnon is controversial. The old stories of Sasquatch, Yeti, Big Foot, Windigo, and others told worldwide are persistent and provocative suggestions of interrelations.

The difficulty with all commentary based on events having early dates is that few field researchers claim scholarly certitude for their interpretations. For more than fifty years scholars within and outside the Soviet, Chinese, and Western political spheres could not easily meet, exchange notes, or collaborate. Now, despite the underfunding of field research everywhere, monthly new discoveries, new concordances, and new reckonings are reported. Previously published dates are being shoved backward. Not long ago, for example, the oldest known barbed fishhook was one dated to a Cro-Magnon site in Europe of fourteen thousand years ago. In 1995 a barbed fishhook was discovered in central Africa that could be dated to ninety thousand years ago.

VENUS FIGURES

Our understanding of the justly famed Venus figures of the Cro-Magnon sites is also shifting. The Venus classification is a term devised by Abbé Henri Breuill, one of the earlier French paleontologists, for an all-inclusive category of sculpted feminine figures in a variety of sizes, shapes, and media found in France. The term soon came to be applied to feminine imagery of the Ice Age found everywhere throughout Europe and Central Asia.

The Venus figures vary in size and other features; few have attributes in common other than their femininity. Many of the Venuses appear simply to be human portraits, others hybrid forms whose heads some scholars have described as masked. If so, the hybrid forms may be complex renderings of deities having female human attributes plus phalliform or botanical or animal attributes. The imagery may be even more complicated than that. The Venus of Willendorf, for example, dated to 27,000, was the first of the Venuses to be discovered. She has long been regarded as a masked fertility figure and described as a pregnant woman, yet this interpretive description is not well supported by the physical evidence of the composition itself.

Carved in the round in limestone and 11.5 centimeters tall, Willendorf's fat female torso seems to be surmounted by a nonhuman "head." The head has no facial features and appears to be realistically vegetal or fungous. Masked human heads, minimally, have eyes for seeing, but this Venus has not even that attribute. The arms of the Willendorf Venus are laid over the top of the two very full breasts. This composition emphasizes the importance of the breasts, not the belly. The figure does not appear to be pregnant, but she may be a nursing figure. If so, arms resting atop breasts would be well placed to push and bring down milk. The same arm position may be observed in the Venus of Lespugne of about 18,000 to 25,000, with its birdlike head and tail and phalliform doubling of the image's feminine sexual characteristics. Perhaps the meaning of Willendorf is this: her life-giving milk is deified in combination with a vision-producing potion made of vegetal or fungous matter.

Some of the Venuses are slender, such as the Venus impudique, from about 17,000. Others are clearly pregnant—for example, the Femme au cou perfore from about 28,000, which may have been worn as a pendant, and the Two-headed Lady from Balzi Rossi, also possibly a pendant and dated to 25,000. The artists of the early cultures were also proficient in human portraiture. It is important, therefore, to observe the Venuses closely and see them as physical facts, not as photographs.

Since the discovery of the Venus of Willendorf in 1908, perhaps 12,000 human figures have been discovered dating to the early cultures. That figure does not include the thermally shocked ceramic figures from three Moravian sites. More than 10,000 Moravian fragments have been catalogued to date. One of the best known is the Dolni Vestonice Venus dated to 26,000. Other Moravian fragments include images of dangerous animals. Researchers think the ceramic figures were deliberately broken in a fire-based divinatory practice.

ANIMAL IMAGERY

For years scholars assumed the production of the Venus figures in Europe and Central Asia preceded cave painting by ten to fifteen thousand years. This date has now been revised with the opening in 1994 of the Chauvet cave in the Ardèche region of France. On its rocky walls was found animal imagery more than thirty thousand years old, or contemporaneous with the Venus figures. The Chauvet imagery is every bit as sophisticated in form and color as the Lascaux paintings dated to 17,000. Moreover, their styles are similar, differing mostly in the species of animal portrayed. The animal imagery of Lascaux is of horses, cattle, and bison, whereas Chauvet has images of bears, rhinos, and panthers on its surfaces.

Everywhere in the known cave sites of the Paleolithic, the artists worked rock surfaces into their painted imagery—the thigh of a bison bulges where the rock bulges, for example. Everywhere fragmentary images of animals, anamorphic devices, and abstract glyphs—dots, circles, lines, tectiforms—are more numerous than whole-animal imagery. (John Pfeiffer estimates two or three incomplete images per whole image.) Under the light of a flickering torch, these forms overall were seen as animate, alive, dancing on the surface of rock. The colors are soft, expertly applied, and the effect may have been achieved by spray-painting the images onto the wall. If so, the artist did it this way: the pigment was thoroughly chewed, the saliva-dissolved colors held in the mouth, then spat directly onto the rock walls as Michel Lorblanchet's experiments

Venus figures vary in size and other features. This prehistoric limestone figure, called the Venus of Willendorf (c. 27,000 B.C.E.), has long been regarded as a fertility figure (Francis G. Mayer/Corbis).

have demonstrated. Literally and symbolically, this painting method breathes life into the creator-artist's visionary image.

An additional difficulty facing researchers has been the loss of ancient coastal sites with the rise in sea level. In Europe, between ten and seventy thousand years ago, the sea was nearly 100 meters lower than it is today. Nevertheless, since 1940, when Lascaux was first opened, archaeologists have been finding an average of one new Paleolithic site a year in France.

NEANDERTAL AND CRO-MAGNON

It is not possible to know the beliefs of the peoples of the early cultures in any detail. We know our forebears were dreamers, as human as we are, because we have the records of their dreams in the objects and images they made. We have their footprints and their handprints. We know where they walked and where they gathered to tell their stories, gossip, and plan for the future. We know the peoples of the Neandertal and Cro-Magnon early cultures lived in attractive places that provided clear views of the plains and sky and were near water. In these places people could easily observe the cycles of nature. We have abundant evidence the peoples of the early cultures lived in symbolized, religious worlds. What we do not know is how they interpreted the phenomena around them and within their own psyches. We do not know what stories they told.

Numbering, as Alexander Marshack (1972) argues persuasively, is a time-factored, "storied activity," one which was practiced in the early cultures of both Neandertal and Cro-Magnon, perhaps even by Homo erectus. Examples of numbering systems include schematized bits of very old slate and mammoth horn; the incised horn held in the hand of the Venus of Laussel, dated at twenty-five thousand years ago; a variety of musical instruments dated from seventeen to ninety thousand years ago (including bull roarers, flutes, whistles, drums, clay bells, rattles, conchshell trumpets); and a later series of astronomical henges made of wood and stone, of which the most famous is Stonehenge in England. Henges have been found throughout the world. The earliest in Egypt is dated to eight thousand years ago.

Our ability to think in storied patterns has not changed significantly in the last hundred thousand years because our cognitive skills are essentially the same. This date neatly encompasses possibilities from both the *Neandertal* and *Cro-Magnon* early cultures. Minimally, stories told a hundred thousand years ago were told in both aniconic and iconic images just as we tell them today. Stories were told much earlier, too, as a variety of findings from Homo erectus sites indicates.

The dead of Neandertal and Cro-Magnon were buried in complicated settings. Bodies were often placed in flexed, sideways positions, anointed with ochre, covered with flowers, and buried in earthen mounds. Some scholars have interpreted these descriptions as meaning the human body was being returned to the womb of the earth, the Earth Mother. Unfortunately, it is not known if the earth was understood in feminine terms.

There is a practical consequence obtained when ochre, flowers, and an earth covering are used in combination with a rotting, dead body: ochre is a powerful preservative traditionally used by hunting cultures for tanning animal hides and polishing stone; flowers and an earth covering mask stench; thus, their use in combination hygienically enabled the band to continue caring for the dead body just as they had earlier cared for the dying body. Thus, it is possible to say that the peoples of the early cultures cared for both their dying and their dead. These are quintessentially religious acts.

The peoples of the early cultures also made permanent memorials for their dead, putting into the grave mounds offerings of tools, jewelry, amulets, and other precious goods. Much later, perhaps ten thousand years ago, the people of Jericho began to keep sculptured, naturalistic portraits of the dead in their homes. They made these protosculptures in the simplest possible way: clay was plastered over the severed head of the dead person.

Complex burial mounds are found the world over and have been made in a variety of shapes over a long period of time. Some are mounds of individual burial, some multiple, some built all at one time, some built incrementally. Some are faced with stone, some made entirely of stone. The shapes often reflect the housing patterns observed by the people who built them—dome-shaped, cone-shaped, keyhole-shaped, and sometimes flat-topped. Other burial mounds are shaped into animal effigy figures.

The earliest known earthen grave mound, a meter high, was found in Spain at El Juyo and dated to 14,000 to 20,000. Its patterned surface is decorated with rosettes of colored clay. The mound is surrounded by a dug trench, lined with seashells. Nearby is a stone sculpture of a form both human, a man with mustache and beard, and animal, a toothed carnivore—a shape-shifting one into the other.

Constructed mounds and burial chambers of any sort tell us that for a very long time people have devised "right ways" of caring for the dead and that many solutions involving an earth interment were arrived at in a similar way. No other inferred statement of symbolic meaning is possible without considering the specific context of each site.

The presence of children required complicated social arrangements for the protection and survival of the Paleolithic band. Because food was obtained by foraging, hunting, fishing, and trapping, hunting bands were small and children few. Motherhood was an observably complex event. The fertile women of the band produced babies and the milk to suckle the babies. In hard times, both the babies and the milk may have been food sources ensuring the band's survival, food sources only the women could produce reliably. Were the women of the Neandertal and Cro-Magnon early cultures also hunters and fishers? We do not know.

The presence of fire and of clay effigy figures exploded in fire tells us long-ago peoples wondered, asked questions, attempted to understand the forces of nature and sheer chance in their lives. Further, their understanding of both time and technology was closely based on their observations of nature. They knew that larvae become butterflies, that eggs become birds, that seeds become fruit, that the sea tides are coordinated to the moon's cycles and to women's menstrual cycles, and that other creatures—insects, birds, animals—weave, knot, mold, and shape complicated structures. Our forebears observed these affairs with patience, learning construction and problem-solving techniques from their observations. They told their stories to one another in song, melody, dance, and image. Only site-specific images and bits of material culture survive with their bones.

History is a measure of change over time, not a measure of linear and developmental time with stops and starts that can be demarcated to certain perceived technological shifts—hunting to agriculture (Paleolithic to Neolithic), for example. Thus, it is not possible to speak historically of either pre-history or pre-agriculture, yet commonly we do—forgetting that many nations today were, in the nineteenth century, places anthropologists confidently described as "Stone Age" cultures.

The reason agrarian and pastoral societies do not develop everywhere is because such economies are not everywhere useful. These lifestyles are possible only in a relatively narrow part of the earth's land mass near the equator.

BIBLIOGRAPHY

Archaeology. Bimonthly journal of the Archaeological Institute of America.

Breuil, Henri. *Four Hundred Centuries of Cave Art.* Montignac, 1952. Breuil suggests the Venus figures and cave paintings were used in magical rites for the increase of humans and animals. The interpretations were long influential but have since been discounted as simplistic.

Campbell, Joseph. *The Masks of God: Primitive Mythology.* 1959. Campbell sets up the thesis of "mythogenetic zones," arguing for the diffusion of certain archetypal myths, principally the Great Goddess and the Animal Master. Campbell later expanded this thesis to the five-volume *Historical Atlas of World Mythology* (1989).

Eisler, Riane. *The Chalice and the Blade: Our History, Our Future.* 1987. Recasts much of Marija Gimbutas's work into a speculative and passionate political history of a time when early cultures were based on a linking principle of relationship (the "chalice" model) only to be overthrown by invaders who put in place societies organized on dominating principles (the "blade" model).

Fagan, Brian M. *The Journey from Eden: The Peopling of Our World.* 1990. A balanced argument for the single-genesis theory of world population.

Gadon, Elinor W. *The Once and Future Goddess: A Symbol for Our Time.* 1989. Provides a comprehensive interpretive context for the work of contemporary visual artists sourcing the imagery of early cultures.

Gimbutas, Marija. *The Civilization of the Goddess: The World of Old Europe.* 1991. In a magisterial presentation of primary field data, Gimbutas presents her provocative interpretations of the culture and beliefs of Old Europe, a collection of Neolithic settlements in Eastern Europe.

———. *The Gods and Goddesses of Old Europe, 7,000–3,500 BC.* 1974. Innovative and precedent-setting study that notes that the oldest imagery is the most complicated, even contradictory.

———. *The Language of the Goddess.* 1989. Gimbutas here sets out her interpretation and argument for a series of complex, hybrid, analogical glyphic and iconic images from Eastern Europe, which she interprets in the context of goddess-centered, Neolithic beliefs.

Johnson, Buffie. *Lady of the Beasts: Ancient Images of the Goddess and Her Sacred Animals.* 1988. An artist's thematic study of ancient sacred art—bird, lion, dog, serpent, butterfly, ewe and ram, spider, deer, fish, pig, cow and bull, scorpion, and bear.

Korp, Maureen. "Before Mother Earth: The Ameridian Earth Mound." *Studies in Religion / Sciences Reliqieuses* 19, no. 1 (1990): 17–25. Reviews contemporary misunderstandings of archaic beliefs in terms of the physical evidence presented by the siting of the North American burial mounds.

———. "Bull-Leaping and the Goddess's Powers." *Continuum* 1, no. 3 (1991): 92–103. Argues the relationship of bull and labrys in ancient Crete may have been that of bull and bullroarer, not bull and axe.

———. *Sacred Geography of the American Mound Builders.* 1990. Investigation of ancient Adena and Hopewell mound building sites in North America in terms of a possible alignment to the rising sun as the preeminent sacred direction.

Leroi-Gourhan, André. *Treasures of Prehistoric Art.* 1967. Exploring more than sixty European caves, Leroi-Gourhan concluded the compositions of animal imagery and glyphic forms were based on a system of opposition of female and male symbols and that each site was intended to be a temple symbolizing the cosmos. His discussion continues to be influential.

Levy, Rachel G. *The Gate of Horn* (1948). Reprinted as *Religious Conceptions of the Stone Age and their Influence upon European Thought.* 1963. Important, early interpretive study of Mother Goddess worship of the later European Neolithic period.

Marshack, Alexander. *The Roots of Civilization: The Cognitive Beginnings of Man's First Art, Symbol, and Notation.* 1972. The first scholar to inspect microscopically a wide variety of early artifacts, discovering upon them sequential systems of crosses, lines, and other notational devices. These findings led him to argue there is no essential difference in the thought processes of contemporary humans and those of early Cro-Magnon cultures.

———. "Upper Paleolithic Symbol Systems of the Russian Plain: Cognitive and Comparative Analysis." *Current Anthropology* 20, no. 2 (June 1979): 271–311 (including scholarly responses). Close discussion of the symbol systems of the mammoth-hunting cultures of the Russian plain and those of western Europe, leading to the tentative conclusion that similarities of motifs indicate only that people will think similar thoughts given the opportunity to observe similar phenomena.

Morgan, Elaine. *The Descent of Woman.* 1972. Witty, reasoned, highly influential discussion at the time of why we are so unlike other apes in appearance and manner.

Neumann, Erich. *The Great Mother: An Analysis of the Archetype.* 1955. Thorough discussion of the archetypal feminine and the Great Mother according to classical Jungian lines of investigation.

Pfeiffer, John E. *The Creative Explosion: An Inquiry into the Origins of Art and Religion.* 1982. Valuable introduction for the general reader. New findings, however, have invalidated many of the text dates for Cro-Magnon.

White, Randall. *Dark Caves, Bright Visions: Life in Ice Age Europe.* 1986. Catalogue accompanying the first-time-ever exhibition of important European Paleolithic artifacts in North America.

MAUREEN KORP

Agriculturalists

Some generalizations that have been made about prehistoric agriculturalists include worship of fertility, often in the form of a "mother goddess," a need to predict the change of seasons and therefore an interest in astronomical phenomena, and the general notion that spirits may inhere in natural phenomena. While not necessarily wrong in every case, these formulations tend to overgeneralize the past. More can be learned with site-by-site or region-by-region comparisons of archaeological material.

Prehistoric societies are by definition those without writing. For this reason it is difficult to know with any certainty about the religious beliefs and practices of prehistoric peoples. While archaeologists frequently can reconstruct with a good deal of security the food habits of a group of people from their material remains,

as well as their adaptation to their environment, degree of mobility, and social ranking or lack of it, it is very difficult to reconstruct ideology. Thus, to assert that a given group was composed of agriculturalists is relatively secure, whereas making statements about their religion involves a chain of inferences regarding artifacts and their context that are open to alternative interpretations. One school of archaeology, which emphasizes science and positivism, would suggest that understanding ideology of any kind is fraught with difficulty. In an illustration included in George Gumerman's 1988 work, progressively smaller arrows indicate how much less can be known about social organization than about technology, economy, and subsistence, and still less about systems of thought. Some archaeologists consider any foray into ritual, ceremonial, or spiritual life as merely "paleopsychology," or worse yet inventing "Just So" stories without substance. Others, however, are increasingly optimistic about our ability to recover prehistoric thought. For example, George Cowgill has suggested that archaeologists need to develop a "middle-range theory of the mind," meaning that theoretical formulations based on general studies of human behavior in particular contexts can allow firmer statements about prehistoric thought.

Another problematic aspect of the study of prehistoric religions is the attempt to infer anything about gender—what any society allows and expects women to do as distinct from men. If we wish to avoid making essentialist assumptions about universal qualities of women, it is necessary to examine each region and even each archaeological site for its own evidence of women and religion. Peggy Sanday (1981), by suggesting that creation myths provide gender scripts for the ways women and men should behave, offers an exceedingly useful concept. But the task of learning about prehistoric religions is difficult, and any conclusion may be modified by subsequent excavations.

A SHORT HISTORY OF THE FIELD
Recent discussions about archaeological understandings of the past by a group called the postprocessualists have emphasized the multiple ways in which attitudes and agendas in the present have consciously and unconsciously directed not merely interpretations of the past but also the very questions being posed—which are considered appropriate, what is worth knowing. Although these writings have been more often critiques of nationalism than of sexism, still, there is enough evidence to indict a great deal of archaeology on the grounds of male-centered worldviews, which fail to allow for women to be active participants in the society, perhaps least of all in religion. This archaeological ne-

glect follows on ethnographic accounts of agricultural societies that have been shown to consider only men's activities as important (Wylie, 1991). Thus the post-processual critique applies to many kinds of interpretations, and it is not surprising that archaeological reconstructions based on men's activities and beliefs in the present have been found wanting as a way to understand whole societies in the past.

In the nineteenth century the caveats noted above had not yet arisen, and speculation about prehistoric religion was rife. At that time it was thought that the development of humanity proceeded along similar lines everywhere, according to evolutionary principles, making it possible to consider present-day simple agriculturalists as representatives of prehistoric people. People who did not yet live in cities, who were "uncivilized," were designated "barbarians." Evidence for prehistoric religion was thus not sought in the archaeological record of prehistoric peoples, but rather in the records of civilized people who wrote about barbarians on their borders, and in descriptions of present "survivals" of previous stages.

The first to connect early religions with women was Johann Jakob Bachofen, in *Das Mutterrecht* (1861). Bachofen believed that in early agricultural societies women were the leaders. Like other writers of the time, he relied principally on ethnography and history, as not much archaeological evidence was available for the existence of matriarchies in the past. Although feminists in the 1970s resurrected Bachofen for his insistence on a time when the female point of view dominated, in fact his portrayal of women was not favorable. His intention was to show that rule by women was a lower stage of evolution, not one to return to or emulate. Both Elizabeth Fee (1974) and Rosalind Coward (1983) have exposed the inherent misogyny of Bachofen's writings. Prehistoric agriculturalists would have fallen into his Matriarchal Stage, when "fertility goddesses" were worshiped—a notion that has been well dissected by Jo Ann Hackett in her article titled "Can a Sexist Model Liberate Us?" (1989).

Edward B. Tylor's *Primitive Culture Researches into the Development of Mythology, Philosophy, Religion, Language, Art, and Custom,* (1889), was the first systematic discussion of "primitive" religion. His work is a classic in the field. Basing his work in evolutionary theory, he believed that he had identified laws of human nature that transcended time and place. Tylor formulated a progression in religious thought from simple to complex, developing from animism to polytheism to monotheism. Archaeological sites were irrelevant; the past was extrapolated from the present. In this sequence, Tylor paid no particular attention to women.

Sir James George Frazer (*The Golden Bough,* 1922), on the other hand, postulated that magic was a form of early religion. His work also ranged widely over times, places, and cultures, emphasizing "fertility cults"; but he had nothing specific to say about the religion of prehistoric agriculturalists, although they presumably belong to his Age of Magic. Nor did he specifically consider women in spite of the fact that women are implicated in the notion of fertility. Erich Neumann, in *The Great Mother: An Analysis of the Archetype* (1955), also discusses some prehistoric figurines but considers them in complete isolation from their context. Thus, early answers to the question of the religion of prehistoric agriculturalists would have been animism and belief in magic, with fertility rites as the expression of the need for fruitful agriculture. All of these approaches, when they have anything to do with women, presuppose that the art was made by men and emphasize women as reproducers, as being observed and used, but not as active agents in these religions.

In the twentieth century most theories of primitive religion, such as Émile Durkheim's *Les formes élémentaires de la vie religieuse* (1912), Robert Lowie's *Primitive Religion* (1924), Mircea Eliade's *Shamanism, Archaic Techniques of Ecstasy* (1964) and other works, and E. E. Evans-Pritchard's *Theories of Primitive Religion* (1965) followed the earlier examples in generalizing from cross-cultural samples, without regard to gender perspectives, subsistence base, or archaeological evidence. Frédéric Bergounioux, in *Les Religions des préhistoriques et des primitifs* (1958), made a sketchy attempt to discuss prehistoric religion, describing mortuary ritual, ritual landscapes, and art forms without any general theory of Neolithic religion (by which he meant prehistoric agriculturalists). Joseph Campbell, in *Transformations of Myth through Time* (1990), does include a chapter on the Neolithic period in which he discusses the excavations at Çatal Hüyük, Jericho, southeastern Europe, and Crete, interpreting the female figurines as representations of mother goddesses. Most of his evidence is derived from sculptures and murals, and his interpretation is based on James Mellaart's descriptions (1962) of excavations at Çatal Hüyük and Marija Gimbutas' views (1982, 1991) of archaeological sites in eastern Europe. Although presented in terms of religious belief, these are at least attempts to use primary evidence rather than arrive at an understanding of prehistoric religion through grand evolutionary schemes that work from the present backward or analysis of supposedly pan-human myth.

Again, using archaeological evidence does not guarantee objectivity. An approach to prehistoric religions through the archaeological study of artifacts, their distribution and their context, may conceal a priori notions about "primitiveness," about "fertility," or about women's roles, activities, or behaviors. Two devices that have been used by archaeologists searching for scientific rigor are ethnographic analogy and the direct historical approach. Ethnographic analogy—comparing, for example, a culture known to represent simple agriculturalists with an archaeological site of the same type—is unlikely to lead to any new knowledge of the past, and deciding between competing analogies may not be easy. The direct historical approach uses known religious beliefs and activities to interpret sites left by the ancestors of the same group, and thus is more secure. For example, Patricia O'Brien (1990) used a Pawnee myth to interpret a site from 1,000 years earlier in the region that Pawnees were known to have occupied. Bird bones buried beneath the floor at the entrance to the lodge allowed her to interpret the building as that of a chief, and to identify a scattered burial with many arrows as a sacrifice to the Morning Star. Linda Donley-Reid (1990) considered the ways in which porcelain and beads were used to ward off evil in contemporary Swahili society to interpret their placement in her excavations of earlier Swahili houses. The uses of beads seem to have echoes in Harappan cemeteries of 3,000 and more years earlier (Kenoyer, 1995). Landscape approaches may also be useful, where there is reason to believe that the distribution of natural or artificial features on the landscape may have religious meaning or may have been involved in religious rituals. However, any reconstruction of the religion must be tentative and subject to alternative interpretations. Religion may also be inferred from burials, art, and buildings. Archaeological evidence that can be used to understand prehistoric religions is thus of many kinds.

EVIDENCE OF WOMEN AND RELIGION

Perhaps the earliest evidence yet excavated of women and religion in the neolithic era is Çatal Hüyük, in Turkey. The people who created the mound with their houses and other living debris made figurines of obese women, some of them appearing to be powerful, including one seated on a large chair flanked by animals. In this region similar figurines later indicated deities or rulers. Rooms with mural paintings and bas-reliefs were thought to be shrines. Their symbolism has been interpreted in various ways, including breasts as nurturing and vultures as representing death. Burials in which women appear to be given more important places within the rooms, more grave goods, and more ritual treatment (such as red ocher sprinkling) than men, provide additional data. This leads to the presumption of powerful women, and a religion of a mother goddess or goddesses, based on archaeological evidence. No part of this package has remained uncontested, but the most powerful challenge is that only a small part of the mound has been investigated, that single section being one contiguous area. To generalize from this area to the entire society is unsound; the rest of the mound may present quite different evidence. The site has been recently reopened under the direction of Ian Hodder, and the results are eagerly anticipated.

Marija Gimbutas made a number of claims about the importance of women in eastern European sites from 5000 to 3000 B.C.E. These sites contain large numbers of female figurines (up to one hundred in a single site), many with features such as distorted heads and bodies that make them seem likely to represent the supernatural rather than the natural. Buildings and parts of buildings with artifacts that have no immediate function are interpreted as religious. Gimbutas interprets the figures as goddesses, representing many facets of the world, and the rooms as shrines. She believes the "Prehistoric Great Goddess" had the function of the regeneration of life but was concerned with the cycle of both life and death, and she insists that the underlying notion of the goddess is androgynous. Gimbutas has been criticized for using colorful rather than neutral language to describe the evidence (Tringham, 1993), but her work has received wide attention.

The site of Lepinski Vir, on the Danube river near the "Iron Gates," has been interpreted as having a great deal of religious iconography because of unusual carved boulders with fishlike faces, and trapezoidal houses with burials under and near stone-lined hearths. From this evidence a tale has been spun of a religion of the underworld, in which those buried near the "household sanctuary" (the hearth) are protectors of the dwelling. Triangular projections are interpreted not as female, as Gimbutas finds them, but as representing dead males via the shape of their houses. But who actually made the carved boulders and other art, and for what purposes, remains unclear.

Megalithic monuments in Europe, especially stone constructions made for multiple burials and rings of standing stones called henges, have also been used to interpret the religion of prehistoric agriculturalists. Ian Hodder (1983) has suggested that both houses and burials represent the increasing "taming" of the wild, leading ultimately to the taming of "dangerous" women and the beginnings of patriarchy—a characteristic presentation of only a male point of view. It has been more often suggested that the henge monuments were an agricultural society's way to predict the movement of astronomical bodies, represented as the wishes of the gods, of knowing when to plant. This is yet another example of the possibility of multiple interpretations based on the same evidence.

Because these sites are part of our Western heritage, and because they are well known, they have come to stand for all early agriculturalists and their religions. But there are other varieties of early sites, for which generalizations derived from Europe and southwest Asia may not be appropriate. We need to include these other phenomena in any sweeping statements about early religions.

A recently discovered Neolithic site in northeast China is that of Niuheliang, with mounded stone tombs, jade carvings, and a 27-meter-long building containing life-sized and larger statues of women, as well as part of a pig and a clawed creature (a bird or dragon). The building has been dubbed the Goddess Temple, making the implicit assumption that the unbaked clay statues represent religious figures rather than secular leaders, and that the building had religious purposes (Guo, 1995). This site is a puzzle to its Chinese excavators because it is complex (and therefore ought to be "patriarchal," according to Marxist dogma); but it seems to feature women in its iconography, implying a holdover of the "matriarchal" stage. There are no known local antecedents for the female statues, although pig figurines are common in Neolithic north China.

In Asia agriculture is taken to mean rice growing, so the first farmers who fished or captured wild game in addition to growing millets and vegetables are often described as foragers or hunter-gatherers, although they made pottery and lived in settled villages. In Korea there is very little direct evidence of any kind of religious life at this stage. However, a few crude female figures have been found, made of bone, stone, or pottery (Nelson, 1993). Chinese documents from much later relate that some Korean groups had sanctuaries, marked by bells and drums, and that others celebrated annual sun-worshiping events with singing, dancing, and wine, in a large cave. Still later Korean documents describe animistic beliefs and ancestral goddesses of rivers and mountains (Nelson, 1995). These events and beliefs would not be detectable in the usual archaeological excavation.

Pottery production in Japan is one of the oldest dated ceramic container industries in the world, but the current consensus of scholars in Japan is that the beginning stages, called Jōmon, are not agricultural. Yet there are human figurines beginning in Initial Jōmon, many of which have breasts and are clearly female. By Middle Jōmon there are also stone clubs of a phallic cast, and some of the figurines may be male or at least are not clearly female. The treatment of these sculp-

A fertility sign is painted on rock at the Shelter of Veado, Januaria, Minas Gerais, Brazil, c. 2800 B.C.E. (Pierre Colombel/Corbis).

tures was mixed—many were broken, perhaps ritually, but many were also carefully buried and surrounded by stones (Nagamine, 1986).

Female figurines are widely found in prehistoric agricultural societies in Central and South America as well. Elaborate figurines from the Valley of Mexico are known as "pretty ladies." They are characterized by fat, shapely thighs, which on intact sitting statuettes are spread apart. They are often nude except for elaborate headdresses. Sometimes there is a child or other object in the arms. Anna Roosevelt (1988) has argued that they represent a time period when fertility is valued and represent a pronatalist culture. Some unusual female figurines in Brazil seem to combine the sexes, since the clearly female representations are made in the form of an erect penis and scrotum, with the overall effect that of a kneeling woman.

Region-by-region comparisons are preferable to sweeping generalizations about prehistoric religions, and careful analysis with multiple possible interpretations is better than simply letting the imagination run riot. There is much yet to learn about the religion of prehistoric agriculturalists.

BIBLIOGRAPHY

Sources dealing with specific sites and regions are plentiful. A sample that relates to sites with female figurines and other evidence of women and religion includes the following:

Barstow, Ann. "The Uses of Archaeology for Women's History: James Mellaart's Work on the Neolithic Goddess at Çatal Hüyük." *Feminist Studies* 4, no. 3 (1978): 7–17.

Donley-Reid, Linda W. "The Power of Swahili Porcelain, Beads, and Pottery." In *Powers of Observation.* Edited by S. M. Nelson and A. B. Kehoe. 1990.

Gimbutas, Marija. *The Civilization of the Goddess: The World of Old Europe.* 1991.

———. *The Goddess and Gods of Old Europe: Myths and Cult Images.* 1982.

Guo Dashun. "Hongshan and Related Cultures." In *The Archaeology of Northeast China: Beyond the Great Wall.* Edited by S. M. Nelson. 1995.

Hodder, Ian. "Burials, Houses, Women and Men in the Mesolithic." In *Ideology, Power and Prehistory.* Edited by D. Miller and C. Tilley. 1983.

Kenoyer, Jonathan Mark. "Ideology and Legitimation in the Indus State as Revealed through Public and Private Symbols." *Pakistan Archaeologists Forum* 3 (1995).

Mellaart, James. "Excavations at Çatal-Hüyük." *Anatolian Studies* 12 (1962): 41–65.

Nagamine, Mitsukazu. "Clay Figurines and Jōmon Society." In *Windows on the Japanese Past: Studies in Archaeology.* Edited by Richard J. Pearson. 1986.

Nelson, Sarah M. *The Archaeology of Korea.* 1993.

———. "The Goddess Temple and the Statues of Women at Niuheliang, China." In *The Archaeology of Gender.* Edited by D. Walde and N. Willows. 1991.

———. "Roots of Animism in Korea." In *Korean Cultural Roots.* Edited by Ho-Youn Kwon. 1995.

O'Brien, Patricia J. "Evidence for the Antiquity of Gender Roles in the Central Plains Tradition." In *Powers of Observation.* Edited by S. M. Nelson and A. B. Kehoe. 1990.

Roosevelt, Anna C. "Interpreting Certain Female Images in Prehistoric Art." In *The Role of Gender in Precolumbian Art and Architecture.* Edited by V. E. Miller. 1988.

Srejović, Dragoslav. *Europe's First Monumental Sculpture: New Discoveries at Lepenski Vir.* 1972.

Tringham, Ruth. Review of Gimbutas's *The Civilization of the Goddess. American Anthropologist* 95, no. 1 (1993): 196–197.

Feminist critiques of writings about prehistoric religions include:

Conkey, Margaret W., and Ruth E. Tringham. "Archaeology and the Goddess: Exploring the Contours of Feminist Archaeology." In *Feminisms in the Academy.* Edited by D. C. Stanton and A. J. Stewart. 1996.

Coward, Rosalind. *Patriarchal Precedents.* 1983.

Fee, Elizabeth. "The Sexual Politics of Victorian Social Anthropology." In *Clio's Consciousness Raised.* Edited by M. Hartman and L. W. Banner. 1974.

Hackett, Jo Ann. "Can a Sexist Model Liberate Us? Ancient Near Eastern 'Fertility' Goddesses." *Journal of Feminist Studies in Religion* 5 (1989): 65–76.

Nelson, Sarah M. *Gender in Archaeology: Analyzing Power and Prestige.* 1997.

Sanday, Peggy Reeves. *Female Power and Male Dominance: On the Origins of Sexual Inequality.* 1981.

Wylie, Alison. "Gender Theory and the Archaeological Record: Why Is There No Archaeology of Gender?" In *Engendering Archaeology.* Edited by Margaret Conkey and Joan Gero. 1991.

Other archaeological views cited in the text:

Cowgill, George L. "Distinguished Lecture in Archeology: Beyond Criticizing New Archeology." *American Anthropologist* 95, no. 3 (1993): 551–573.

Gumerman, George J. "A Historical Perspective on Environment and Culture in Anasazi County." In *Anasazi in a Changing Environment.* Edited by G. J. Gumerman. 1988.

See also **Archaeology; Fertility and Barrennesss; Gimbutas, Marija; Goddess: Prehistoric Goddesses; Prehistoric Religions; Pre-agricultural Peoples.**

SARAH MILLEDGE NELSON

Priestess

MESOPOTAMIA

The foundations of ancient Mesopotamian religion were laid by the Sumerians in the beginning of the third millennium B.C.E. Although successive waves of Semites later conquered the region, the Sumerian temple-state structure, with its elaborate priestly hierarchy, persisted until the time of the last Babylonian king, Nabonidus, in the sixth century B.C.E.

Mesopotamian cult was marked by a number of highly specialized roles for both men and women. In the Sumerian period, chief among the priestesses was the Entu, whose name is interpreted to mean "the wife of the god" or "the lady who is a deity." She lived in the god's temple, and her "sacred marriage" to the ruling deity of the city guaranteed the renewed fertility of the land.

Although the office of Entu disappeared with the collapse of Sumerian power at the end of the third millennium B.C.E., other types of priestesses survived. Their role in cult practice is much debated, but it has been suggested that they engaged in sacred prostitution, thus representing the earthly embodiment of Ishtar or Astarte, the great mother goddess.

GREECE AND ROME

Although the lives of women were generally restricted socially and economically in both ancient Greece and Rome, women played an important role in the practice and maintenance of public religion. Many priestly offices, especially but not exclusively those of female deities, were held by women; and these positions carried with them enhanced social and economic status.

In the historical period there is no evidence for the existence of a separate priestly caste, which is perhaps due to the lack of separation between secular and religious life in the ancient Greek and Roman worlds; thus, the duties and obligations of priestesses most often reflect their psychosexual roles in society: that of virgin, wife, and mother.

For both men and women, the performance of priestly duties was seen as a civic obligation, rather than one motivated by religious emotion, and reflected the role of religion in public life; positions were filled by lot or by the choice of elected officials and held for a limited period of time (usually one year). Nevertheless, many priesthoods were hereditary, perhaps a remnant of an earlier stage of political development.

Priesthoods were not generic; rather, a priest or priestess generally served a particular deity in a particular sanctuary and was responsible for the care and upkeep of the sanctuary, in return for a modest fee and a share in the offerings.

Although there is generally a gender correlation between the deity and priest, that is not always the case. There is abundant evidence for priestesses in service not only to the goddesses Demeter, Hera, Athena, Artemis, and Eileithyia (the goddess of childbirth), but to Apollo and Dionysus as well. (Conversely, Athena Polios, the guardian of Athens, was served by a male priest.)

Perhaps the most prominent priestesses in ancient Greece were those at Eleusis, the site of the Eleusinian mysteries, performed yearly in honor of the grain goddess Demeter and her virgin daughter Persephone.

A priestess is shown burning incense in a Minoan fresco painting from the sixteenth century B.C.E. (Gianni Dagli Orti/Corbis).

The office was hereditary, held by the family that had controlled the sanctuary before its capture by the Athenians in perhaps the seventh century B.C.E. The Priestess of Demeter lived at Eleusis in the "Sacred House" and held office for life. Paid an **obol** for each initiate into the mysteries, she participated in the sacred reenactment of Demeter's search for her daughter, playing both the role of the goddess and Persephone. Also at Eleusis were the *panageis*, the all-holy women, who served as ministrants of the cult and who had the right to touch the sacred paraphernalia. Living together in special dwellings at Eleusis, they were allowed no contact with men.

The Pythia at Delphi, the location of the oracle of Apollo, was not really a priestess, for the actual interpreter of the words of the god was a male. Nevertheless, she provides an example of the way in which the psychosexual imagery determined the function of the priestess: possessed by Apollo, she is seen as a hollow vessel, seized by and filled with the god, an inconspicuous instrument of divine revelation. According to ancient sources, the Pythia originally had to be a virgin, but later, after one of them had been seduced by an inquirer, was a woman over 50, who wore, when prophesying, the clothes of a young woman. She had to be of blameless life but could be married and have children; after her appointment, however, she could not live with her husband. She was not selected from any particular family, nor did she have any specific training for the position. In fact, it is her ordinariness that is always emphasized, for it was only under Apollo's influence that she become special.

There is much evidence that the spread and acceptance of Near Eastern cults of the mother goddess (such as Isis and Cybele) into the Greco-Roman world increased the number of women in positions of religious authority, both in the performance of ritual and in the administration of shrines, sanctuaries, and temples. In addition, the names of women are found among the list of public benefactors whose wealth paid for the costs of maintaining and celebrating the rites of individual deities; because no public taxes were demanded of Greek and Roman citizens, this form of patronage was seen both as an expression of piety and of civic pride. Major priestly offices were awarded to those who possessed the resources necessary for cultic responsibilities, and through familial wealth many women enjoyed this privilege.

In the Republican period (509–27 B.C.E.), the majority of priesthoods were held by males organized into *collegia;* the major exception was the office of Vestal Virgin, whose duty it was to care for the public cult of Vesta, goddess of the hearth, and insure that her fire never be allowed to go out. It has been suggested that, in its origin, the position was held by the daughter of the king who also served as chief priest; but, beginning with the republic, it was filled by freeborn women, generally of the upper classes. The office was under the power of the Pontifex Maximus, the High Priest of Rome during the Republican and imperial periods.

The women, who were consecrated to the goddess in childhood and who had to be free from bodily blemishes and other physical defects, served for thirty years (after which they were free to marry, although few did because it was considered unlucky), and enjoyed special privileges, including freedom from male guardianship and the right to make a will and bequeath property. So great was her power that any criminal who accidentally met a Vestal on the way to execution was spared, and anyone who walked beneath her litter was put to death. Although virgins, they wore the garb generally reserved for brides, thus pointing to their function as representing the range of feminine roles. The penalty for breaking the vow of chastity was severe: death by being immured, walled up in a small chamber and left to die.

BIBLIOGRAPHY

Beard, Mary, and John North, eds. *Pagan Priests: Religion and Power in the Ancient World.* 1990.
Foley, Helen, ed. *Reflections of Women in Antiquity.* 1981.
Gardner, Jane. *Women in Roman Law and Society.* 1986.
Hallett, Judith. *Fathers and Daughters in Roman Society: Women and the Elite Family.* 1984.
Kraemer, Ross Shepard. *Her Share of the Blessings.* 1992.
———. "Women in the Religions of the Greco-Roman World." In *Religious Studies Review* 9 (1983): 127–139.
Lefkowitz, Mary, and M. B. Fant. *Women's Life in Greece and Rome.* 1982.
Mylonas, George. *Eleusis and the Eleusinian Mysteries.* 1961.
Pomeroy, Sarah. *Goddesses, Whores, Wives and Slaves in Classical Antiquity.* 1975.
Saggs, H. W. F. *The Greatness that was Babylon.* 1968.
Veyne, Paul. *Bread and Circuses: Historical Sociology and Political Pluralism.* 1990.

See also **Artemis (Diana)**; **Athena (Minerva)**; **Cybele**; **Demeter and Persephone**; **Goddess**; **Hera**; **Isis**; **Shamans**; **Virginity**; **Women's Religions**.

TAMARA M. GREEN

Prophecy

Prophet is a Greek term used by translators of the Bible to mean one who "speaks forth"—that is, a spokesman for a deity. In the Greco-Roman world women often served as priestesses in the sanctuaries of the gods, transmitting and interpreting the messages of deities, as at the famous shrines of Delphi and Didyma where the words of Apollo were delivered. A belief also developed in sibyls, legendary old women whose sayings were recorded in prophetic books; by the second century B.C.E. sibylline writings had even penetrated Jewish circles. Greek prophecies, however, are usually called oracles by scholars so as to distinguish them from Israelite prophecy, which is thought to be more individual and thoroughly ethical.

Five women in the Hebrew Bible are called prophetess (*nabia,* fem. of *nabi*): Miriam, "Aaron's sister," who sang as Pharaoh's army sank into the sea (Ex. 15:20–21); Deborah, the judge, who foretold the victory of the Israelites over the Canaanites and sang her song (Judg. 4 and 5); Huldah, who, when consulted by King Josiah, warned her people of the punishment of the Lord (2

A 1731 engraving by B. Picart of a scene from Homer's *Iliad* depicts Cassandra warning the Trojans of the coming Greek invasion. It was Cassandra's fate that her prophecies, though accurate, would not be believed (Historical Picture Archive/Corbis).

women's prophetic activities were more of an oracular, mantic, or magical kind, or that their utterances were not recorded because they were made by women. Unlike the Biblical text, the *aggadah* (nonlegal rabbinic tradition) focuses on the prophetesses' female sex; thus it says, for instance, that they were extraordinarily beautiful, that their accomplishments made them superior "even" to men, that Deborah judged outdoors so that she would not be alone with a man, that Josiah consulted Huldah rather than Jeremiah because he expected greater compassion from a woman, and that Huldah addressed her reproaches particularly to women.

Women play a distinctive role in Israel's struggle over prophetic authority. In Ezekiel 13:17, the women who falsely prophesy are linked to characteristically female practices (they "sew pillows"), and a kind of female religious specialist called a witch is severely condemned, most famously in Exodus 22:18: "Thou shalt not suffer a witch to live." In common with the earlier Mesopotamian traditions, the Biblical prophets show a special concern for widows—or more accurately, women without husbands and means of financial support. This motif appears in the story of Elijah's miraculous filling of the barrel of meal and cruse of oil for the widow of Zarephath and curing of her son (I Kgs. 17:10–24), and is a recurring theme in ethical pronouncements warning against neglect or oppression of disadvantaged social groups (e.g., 1 Isa. 1:17; Jer. 7:6; Ezek. 22:7; Zech. 7:10).

Until the beginning of the second century C.E., ecstatic prophecy through the Holy Spirit was an active force in the early Christian church. The New Testament itself mentions the names of prophets; among these were the pious and aged Anna, who recognized Jesus as the Messiah (Luke 2:36–38), and Philip the evangelist's "four unmarried daughters," who "possessed the gift of prophecy" (Acts 21:9). The other woman prophet mentioned in the New Testament is a "Jezebel" attached to the church at Thyatira. This woman "[claimed] to be a prophetess" (Rev. 2:20), using her power to tempt church members to fornicate and eat food sacrificed to idols; she and those who follow her are threatened with terrible punishment.

The second half of the second century saw the rise in Asia Minor of the millenarian, ascetic Montanist movement. Opposed by the official church, the Montanists were remarkable not only for their proclamation of a "new prophecy" announcing the imminent second coming of Christ, but also the role of women prophets. Paul, though encouraging prophecy, had tried to regulate it. One of his rules was that women who "pray and prophesy" were to cover their heads, or else "be shorn" (1 Cor. 11: 5–6). Elsewhere he states that women have

Kgs. 2:14–20); Noadiah, apparently regarded by Nehemiah as a false prophetess (Neh. 6:14); and the wife of Isaiah, whom he called prophetess (Isa. 8:3). According to Goitein (1988), mention of these five proves that prophetesses were active for the whole period of Israelite prophecy; he even suggests that Huldah and Noadiah were the chief prophets of their time. Nevertheless, the Hebrew Bible reveals little about their activities. Women in Semitic tribal societies encouraged men to fight through reciting poetry or singing songs. Miriam and Deborah's "prophecy" may have been of this kind, for we are told that Miriam "took a timbrel in her hand, and all the women went out after her with timbrels and with dances" (Ex. 15:20). Huldah's prophecy, on the other hand, is of the ethical or reproving type; speaking in the voice of the "Lord God of Israel," she warns: "because they have forsaken me . . . my wrath shall be kindled against this place [Jerusalem]" (II Kgs. 17). None of the Biblical prophetesses falls into the period of literary prophecy, suggesting either that "no permission to speak" in congregations (1 Cor. 14:34). As church organization became more complex, prophecy, which depended on inspiration and was therefore relatively free and open to women, was further limited and even regarded as heretical. The activity of the Montanist prophetesses Priscilla, Maximilla, and later Quintilla ran counter to this trend. These women asserted that the Spirit spoke again through their persons; "do not hear me, but hear Christ," said Maximilla. Response was vigorous. Their words were written down and circulated, groups called "Priscillianist" and "Quintillianist" appeared, and Montanism, along with regard for female prophecy and the public role of women, appears to have survived in some form into the mid-fourth century. Opposition to the Montanist prophetesses in their lifetimes and in the heresiographies focused on their sex. It was claimed that they were fornicators, the first of them with Montanus himself—though it seems instead that some had dissolved their marriages and were celibate, while others were virgins. Exorcism was used chiefly or exclusively on Montanist prophets, especially females.

The theme of false female prophecy reappears in the early seventh century with the rise of Islam. Following the death of Muhammad, a female prophet named Sajah rose up among the tribes of the Arabian peninsula attempting to throw off the yoke of Islam. Almost nothing is known of her teaching. The sources are dominated by accounts of her association with the "prophet" Musaylimah; the familiar theme of sexual incontinence emerges in some stories. The prophetess returned to her people and later converted to Islam. Female prophets figure less prominently in the Islamic than in the Jewish and Christian scriptures. A minority of commentators on the Qur'an regard Mary as a prophet by virtue of the angel's words to her at the Annunciation (3:42ff.). A few early extremist Shiite traditions mention that Fāṭimah, the daughter of the Prophet, received her own heavenly Tablet either directly or through her husband or father; she is not, however, explicitly credited with prophecy.

It is generally accepted in Judaism that the Holy Spirit departed from Israel and prophecy ceased with the last of the minor prophets. In Islam the belief that Muhammad is the last prophet also prevented subsequent prophetic claims. In Christianity, however, the idea of a present and accessible Spirit left open the possibility of prophecy for Christians, including women—even if prophecy was often suppressed and female prophecy in particular characterized as hysteria, superstition, or demonic delusion. Prophetesses have sometimes arisen as part of a challenge to clerical authority. In 1623 among the Puritans of Massachusetts Bay, Anne Hutchinson declared that she received "immediate revelation" from the Holy Spirit. Her movement attracted many followers, some of them prominent members of the colony, and she was soon tried and banished. Also in the seventeenth century, the Quakers held that the Spirit enlightened every soul and argued in particular for the right of women to speak, although female members were ultimately forced into subordinate, gender-defined roles. Women have also participated in millennial and fulfillment prophecy. In the latter part of the sixteenth century, a certain Lucrecia de Leon related dreams that warned of the destruction of Spain by the Turks; she was disciplined by the Inquisition, which doubted the true prophetic nature of a young girl's visions. In 1625, in the reign of Charles I, Lady Eleanor Davies was inspired by "a voice from heaven" to announce the coming of the Day of Judgment; though imprisoned several times and hindered from publishing her tracts, she insisted to the end on her mission as interpreter of the prophecies of Daniel. A contemporary female prophetic figure is Elizabeth Clare Prophet, spiritual leader of the syncretisic Church Universal and Triumphant, which was founded in 1958 and is based in California and Montana. Mrs. Prophet is a "Messenger" for spiritual beings—including Christ and the Buddha—known as Ascended Masters, whose words come to her through the Holy Spirit. One of the teachings of the church is that females have an equal right with males to religious leadership, since gender is not of the essence of spirit.

Both Muhammad and Jesus have been extolled by members of their communities as liberators of the female sex. On the other hand, the Mormon prophet Joseph Smith and Elijah Muhammad, the prophet of the African-American Nation of Islam, demanded that women resume traditional roles. Reforming prophets have often attempted to reorganize gender relations; women have both gained and lost power at such junctures.

BIBLIOGRAPHY

Barfoot, Charles H., and Gerald T. Sheppard. "Prophetic vs. Priestly Religion: The Changing Role of Women in Classical Pentecostal Churches." *Review of Religious Research* 22, no. 1 (1980): 2–17. Examines the decline of women's charismatic leadership using a Weberian framework.

Bronner, Leila L. "Biblical Prophetesses through Rabbinic Lenses." *Judaism* 40 (1991): 171–183. Presents views of the Hebrew prophetesses and creation of additional "prophetesses" (e.g., Esther, Abigail) in the Talmud.

Cope, Esther M. *Handmaid of the Holy Spirit: Dame Eleanor Davies, Never Soe Mad a Ladie.* 1992. Treats Davies's prophetic career.

————. *Prophetic Writings of Lady Eleanor Davies.* 1995. A selection of thirty-eight tracts.

Goitein, S. D. "Women as Creators of Biblical Genres." *Prooftexts* 8, no. 1 (1988): 1–33.

Huber, Elaine C. *Women and the Authority of Inspiration: A Reexamination of Two Prophetic Movements from a Contemporary Feminist Perspective.* 1985. Treats Anne Hutchinson and the Montanists in comparative perspective. A postscript explores the implications of the tradition of female prophecy for contemporary Christian feminists.

Kagan, Richard L. *Lucrecia's Dreams: Politics and Prophecy in Sixteenth-Century Spain.* 1990. Places Lucrecia's dreams and proceedings of her trial in the context of Spanish society and politics; also discusses her personal and psychological motives as a woman.

Kraemer, Ross Shepard. *Her Share of the Blessings: Women's Religions among Pagans, Jews, and Christians in the Greco-Roman World.* 1992. The chapter "Autonomy, Prophecy, and Gender in Early Christianity" reconstructs women's prophecy in the early community and resistance to it; other chapters, especially "Women's Leadership and Offices in Christian Communities," provide a wider context.

Mack, Phyllis. *Visionary Women: Ecstatic Prophecy in Seventeenth-Century England.* 1992. Presentation of the Quaker case is preceded by consideration of types of female prophecy and reactions.

Trevett, Christine. *Montanism: Gender, Authority, and the New Prophecy.* 1996. Examines the role of women in Montanism in the course of a thorough reassessment of the movement.

Wire, Antoinette Clark. *The Corinthian Woman Prophets: A Reconstruction through Paul's Rhetoric.* 1990. Rhetorical analysis of Paul's speech yields a detailed picture of the prophetic activity of women in first-century Corinth; a model for the uncovering of women's history.

For information on Elizabeth Clare Prophet and the Church Universal and Triumphant, see the website <www.tsl.org>.

L. CLARK

Prostitution

Prostitution is a practice whereby women, children, and, occasionally, men are used for the purpose of male sexual gratification, benefiting both religious and secular institutions. It cannot be argued that prostitution has been documented in every culture, but the practice is geographically widespread and can be found throughout history. Several well-defined schools of thought provide a useful overview of the history of scholarship on the practice.

Classical scholars in the West such as Friederich Engels (1884) and William Sanger (1858) argued in the last century that cultic prostitution (temple or sacred prostitution) in ancient Mesopotamia was the source of commercial prostitution. This conclusion blurs both historical facts and different types of temple prostitution. In ancient Mesopotamia, the gods were considered to actually live in the temples, and the concern for fertility led to the origin of a class of women who offered their sexual services to the gods within the temple. There were a variety of such temple prostitutes in different locations and in different historical periods, such as *en* priestesses in the Old Babylonian period and *nin-dingir* priestesses in ancient Sumer, who were the counterparts of male priests and who participated in the ritual of a sacred marriage between the goddesses and gods. There were also lower class temple servants who served as prostitutes. Gerda Lerner (1986) points out that the conflation of temple prostitution with commercial prostitution failed to recognize the different practices and names for prostituted women and men. Instead, it appears that temple prostitution was located within the temple walls, in contrast to commercial prostitution, which was found outside the temple. Temple prostitution was considered to be socially respectable, whereas commercial prostitution was not. The difference between the two forms of prostitution was one of class, although both forms emerged within the temple's sphere of economic influence at different places and times throughout Near Eastern history.

The argument that temple prostitution gave rise to commercial prostitution also characterizes one well-known study of prostitution in India by S. N. Sinha and N. K. Basu (1933; reprint 1994). Despite the argument drawn from Engels and Sanger, this study documents terms used for prostitution in Indian literature that are not generally available, including the Sanskrit *veśya*, *panyastrī*, *vārāṅganā*, and *vārakanyakā*, which refer to prostituted women in general, and *gaṇikā*, which denotes a narrower class of educated courtesans. Harshad R. Trivedi (1977) focuses on the intersection of caste oppression, economic and religious factors, and sexism that shapes the lives of contemporary *devadāsī*s, women of low caste who are dedicated to a particular temple and god or goddess.

Just as references to prostituted women are found in Jewish and Christian literature, Hindu and Buddhist texts also include numerous references to prostitution. Gautama Buddha, like Christ, is said to have received prostituted women into the *sangha*, the Buddhist order of ordained nuns and monks (*The Elders' Verses II*, 1971). Mary Magdalene is perhaps the most well-

The marble threshold of a first-century C.E. brothel in Ephesus, Turkey, was marked with a carved footprint leading inside, demonstrating the long history of commercial prostitution (Michael Nicholson/Corbis).

known prostituted woman from the New Testament; other widely known prostituted women in Buddhism are Vimalā and Ambapālī, both of whom attained the highest stage of enlightenment. Ambapālī was also an acclaimed supporter of Buddhism. In contrast to the practices of temple prostitution in the ancient Near East and in India, it is striking to note that the emphasis at least in Buddhism and Christianity on prostituted women lies in their conversion to the respective religions; in other words, their fame rests largely in the fact that they stopped practicing as prostituted women once they were welcomed into the religious tradition. Other prostituted women who were widely known during their time, such as Aspasia in fifth century B.C.E. Athens, who made no pretense of leaving prostitution, are not nearly so famous today (Pomeroy, 1975).

Nineteenth century British and American challenges to prostitution are often characterized as moral reforms rooted in Victorian ideals. While such ideals unquestionably determined ideas of gender and sexuality, the analysis of prostitution during this period extended beyond "rescuing fallen women," as Ruth Rosen (1982) documents. In the 1830s Lydia Marie Childs, and other women in the 1870s, worked for solidarity with prostituted women, recognizing that a lack of employment opportunities and education were underlying causes of prostitution. Josephine Butler and other women who opposed the Contagious Disease Acts of 1864 and 1869 in Great Britain were among the first to address traffic in women across European borders. Butler, like her American counterparts, argued that prostitution was supported by governments, police, and the law itself. Traffic in women received international attention in 1877 at a conference in Geneva, Switzerland, that sought to abolish prostitution.

Recent scholarship has extended the analysis of prostitution that emerged 150 years ago. Adding to such goals as solidarity among women, resolving the economic causes of prostitution, and ending traffic in women, Kathleen Barry (1979, 1995) argues that prostitution is an integral part of a larger system of sexual slavery, showing how institutions of slavery and prostitution were closely integrated. The first volume of *Michigan Journal of Gender and Law* (1993) breaks new ground with essays by such scholars and activists as Margaret A. Baldwin, Andrea Dworkin, Evelina Giobbe, Vednita Nelson, and Catharine A. MacKinnon, who argue from different directions that prostitution violates the civil rights of women. There has also been a slight increase in first-person writings by prostituted women that further document the injury of prostitution, such as works by Linda Lovelace (1980), Trudee Able-Peterson (1981), and Toby Summer (1993). Using both feminist and theological arguments, Susan Brooks Thistlethwaite and Rita Nakashima Brock (1996) offer an approach based on (Christian) liberation theology to combat the harms of prostitution in East and Southeast Asia.

Not all recent scholarship is critical of prostitution. Reversing the economic exploitation of prostitution has gained a following since the 1980s; instead of focusing on factors that force women into prostitution, certain scholars and writers have sought to make prostitution profitable for individual women by removing the opprobrium attached to the practice. Critiquing the terms *prostitution* and *prostitute* and arguing that new terms such as *sex-work* and *sex workers* avoid social stigma, essay collections edited by Frédérique Delacoste and Priscilla Alexander (1987) and Gail Pheterson (1989) helped popularize this analysis. While this argument does not address the practice of cultic prostitution, the desire to make sex-work acceptable critically resurrects the difference between temple prostitution, which carried economic, religious, and social value, and commercial prostitution, which was valued economically but not socially, as shown by Lerner.

In light of the harm to women and children documented in recent years, the distinction between one form of prostitution—cultic—that was socially respectable and one that was not—commercial—requires a new comparative analysis that defines more precisely the religious, societal, and economic factors of prostitution. Sociological studies of prostituted women in the United States reveal that incest, battery, rape, coercion, poverty, and lack of education are material factors that predetermine a woman's choice to be prostituted, particularly when the average age of entry into prostitution is as young as fourteen in certain areas (Giobbe, Giobbe and Gibel, and Leidholdt). Similar to Trivedi's analysis of *devadasis*, Rita Rozario (1988) has shown that practices underlying the dedication of women to the service of the gods and goddesses are not fundamentally different than factors that force women into commercial prostitution. These stem from a constraint of women's choices such that prostitution is seen as the most viable option for a woman (economically or religiously): lack of education, poverty, and domestic violence play significant roles in a woman's decision to enter either religious or commercial prostitution.

BIBLIOGRAPHY

Able-Peterson, Trudee. *Children of the Evening.* 1981.

Barry, Kathleen. *Female Sexual Slavery.* 1979. Reprint, 1984.

———. *The Prostitution of Sexuality.* 1995.

Delacoste, Frédérique, and Priscilla Alexander. *Sex Work: Writings by Women in the Industry.* 1987.

Engels, Friedrich. *The Origin of the Family, Private Property, and the State.* 1884. Reprint, 1972.

Giobbe, Evelina. "Juvenile Prostitution: Profile of Recruitment." In *Child Trauma 1: Issues and Research.* Edited by Ann Wolbert Burgess. 1992.

Giobbe, Evelina, and Sue Gibel. "Impressions of a Public Policy Initiative." *Hamline Journal of Public Law and Practice* 16 (Fall 1994).

Horner, I. B. *Women Under Primitive Buddhism.* 1930. Reprint, 1989.

Leidholdt, Dorchen. "Prostitution: A Violation of Women's Human Rights." *Cardozo Women's Law Journal* 1 (1993).

Lerner, Gerda. *The Creation of Patriarchy.* 1986.

Lovelace, Linda. *Ordeal.* 1981.

Norman, K. R., trans. *The Elders' Verses II: Therīgāthā.* 1995.

Mukherji, Santosh Kumar. *Prostitution in India.* 1934. Reprint, 1986.

Pheterson, Gail. *A Vindication of the Rights of Whores.* 1989.

Pomeroy, Sarah B. *Goddesses, Whores, Wives, and Slaves: Women in Classical Antiquity.* 1975.

Richman, Paula. "The Portrayal of a Female Renouncer in a Tamil Buddhist Text." In *Gender and Religion: On the Complexity of Symbols.* Edited by Caroline Walker Bynum, Stevan Harrell, and Paula Richman. 1986.

Rosen, Ruth. *The Lost Sisterhood: Prostitution in America, 1900–1918.* 1982.

Rozario, Rita. *Trafficking in Women and Children in India: Sexual Exploitation and Sale.* 1988.

Rubin, Gayle. "The Traffic in Women: Notes on the 'Political Economy' of Sex." In *Toward an Anthropology of Women.* Edited by Rayna R. Reiter. 1975.

Sanger, William. *A History of Prostitution: Its Extent, Causes and Effects Throughout the World.* 1858. Reprint, 1937.

Sinha, S. N., and N. K. Basu. *A History of Prostitution in India.* 1933. Reprint, 1994.

Summer, Toby [pseudonym]. "Women, Lesbians, and Prostitution." In *Lesbian Culture.* Edited by Julia Penelope and Susan J. Wolfe. 1993.

Thistlethwaite, Susan Brooks, and Rita Nakashima Brock. *Casting Stones: Prostitution and Liberation in Asia and the United States.* 1996.

Trivedi, Harshad R. *Scheduled Caste Women: Studies in Exploitation with Reference to Superstition, Ignorance, and Poverty.* 1977.

Wilson, Liz. *Charming Cadavers: Horrific Figurations of the Feminine in Indian Buddhist Hagiographic Literature.* 1996.

CAROL S. ANDERSON

Protestantism

Protestantism is the branch of Western Christianity that protested against and worked to reform the practices and teachings of the Roman Catholic Church. It emphasizes Biblical authority and justification by faith through grace.

The roots of Protestantism lie in reform movements of the fourteenth and fifteenth centuries. Notable early reformers include John Wycliffe (d. 1384) and the Lollards, who stressed the importance of having translations of the Scriptures in one's own language and concern about the authority of the Pope; and Jan Hus of Bohemia (burned 1415), who stressed that laity be given both bread and wine in communion and the reform of the corrupt practices of the church. It was not until the sixteenth century, however, that a permanent Protestant movement arose with Martin Luther in Germany, John Calvin and Ulrich Zwingli in Switzerland, and a number of reformers in Scotland, England, and the Netherlands.

Women played an important role in this beginning phase as writers and speakers and influential wives of reformers. Wibrandis Rosenblat (1504–1564), after her first marriage to a humanist, subsequently married three reformers, including the famous Martin Bucer. She cared for a large family while supporting the fledgling reform movement in exile. Katherine Zell (1497/8–1562), the wife of Strasbourg reformer Matthias Zell, wrote and published treatises, letters, and speeches. She was an ardent reformer of social conditions. She and her husband worked as a team to reform the church, as did many women and men in this period of the Reformation.

After this initial phase the role of women diminished, and Protestantism itself became rigid and cold in its or-

Barbara Heck (1734–1804) organized the first Methodist society in New York City in 1766, making her the founder of the Wesleyan movement in America. She is shown preaching in this undated woodcut illustration (Corbis-Bettmann).

thodoxy. In England, Puritanism arose as a response to a half-reformed Church of England. The early settlers brought this brand of Protestantism to North America. Women such as Ann Hutchinson (d. 1643) played a part in its beginning fervor but were officially shut out and at times banished for continuing to "preach" and teach and have religious opinions contrary to the elders of the church.

Many continental and North American Protestants were influenced by the rationalism of the Enlightenment, which rejected rigid sectarianism and the religious wars raging on the continent. A renewal movement within Protestantism stressed piety and spirituality to renew the cold churches of the seventeenth century. The largest of these, the Wesleyan or Methodist movement, had women such as Selina, Countess of Huntington (d. 1791), playing a significant role as patrons of reformers, and women preachers and organizers such as Barbara Heck (d. 1804).

The nineteenth century was a time of theological development, especially in Germany, with advances in Biblical scholarship and historical theology. It was also a time of great reform, especially in North America, where the mission movement began in the 1790s. During the 1860s and 1870s, women, moved by the plight of the "heathen" around the world, began organizing on their own for home and foreign missions. This strengthened the position of women in the churches as their or-

ganizational skills and their autonomy sparked a spirit of volunteerism, a developed informational network, and a career choice for the single woman missionary as well as the diaconate. It was theoretically possible for women to be ordained in a few denominations. The nineteenth century is often referred to as the woman's century. This mission movement led Protestants to struggle with the conditions generated by the rise of industrialization and urbanization, either supporting a strong capitalism or its counter, the Social Gospel, which sought to bring the social order into accordance with Christian principles.

The twentieth century has seen the rise of ecumenism, an attempt to heal the division of denominationalism within Protestantism, a rising neo-orthodoxy in theology, and a development of liberation theology, especially among people of color and women, as well as a strong movement for full participation of women in all aspects of religious life.

The early Protestants believed that the Roman Catholic Church had elevated tradition over Biblical authority. The Protestant Reformation occurred in conjunction with the development of the printing press, which put great emphasis on literacy. The Bible was to be translated into everyday language and everyone, including girls, was expected to know how to read it. Biblical authority became the guiding rule for life; this led to a restricting of women's activities as a literal interpretation took sway. All reformers felt that women should be subject to their husbands and that women should remain silent in church. This doctrine of inerrancy of Scripture has lasted into the twentieth century in some sectors of Protestantism. Other denominations have taken a more moderate view, seeing the Bible as the word of God that needs to be interpreted in its many complexities. These denominations (such as the United Church of Christ, and the Methodists) are the ones that slowly began to ordain women and include them in the full life of the church.

Many denominations have creeds that serve to guide them in their daily lives and the development of their theologies. Protestantism remains a religion of the written and preached word.

Many Protestants, especially Lutherans, believe that the heart of the gospel is the free gift of grace, given by God through the life and the atoning death of Jesus Christ. This gift is given to all regardless of merit. One does not earn it. This had vast implications for women in that, spiritually, there was no difference between women and men. Some of the early and nineteenth- and twentieth-century women recognized the full implication of this belief and acted as full participants. The idea of a priesthood of all believers developed from this gift of grace to all. Though in practice this equality has always been a struggle, in theory it is a strong component of Protestantism.

While some denominations such as Anglicans and Lutherans still have bishops and an episcopalian form of government, the Protestant ethos is one that shares the power in local congregations, presbyteries, or conferences depending on the denomination. What is common is the stress on the importance of the laity, though the clergy still tends to be honored because of their role in celebrating the two sacraments, baptism and eucharist, and their role in the preaching of the word. Ordination of women has been a struggle since the beginning. Every reformer in each Protestant movement has faced the challenge from women for preaching rights and responsibilities. The early reformers stressed the importance, indeed, the superiority of marriage. While this raised the role of wife and mother to a Christian vocation it eliminated the important visible official role in the church of the nun. It was not until the mid- and late-twentieth century that women in most Protestant denominations won the right to be ordained.

Since Protestants emphasize the word rather than the Mass, a Protestant worship service culminates in the sermon, with an emphasis on hymn singing and lay participation. In the late twentieth century a movement emerged for inclusive language in Scripture and liturgy. The removal of saints from Protestantism led to a suspicion of art as idolatry, therefore Protestant houses of worship tend to be simple with little art, though some have stained glass windows. The removal of saints also affected women by not allowing them to pray to any kind of female representation. The whole pantheon of female saints with Mary at the fore was replaced solely by the usually male-imaged trinity.

BIBLIOGRAPHY

Most early work done on women and Protestantism took the form of hagiography, model lives of goodly women. In the late twentieth century biographies that took a more critical and analytical approach began to appear. An excellent example of this is the three-volume "Women of the Reformation" series by Roland Bainton: *In Germany and Italy* (1971), *In France and England* (1973), and *From Spain to Scandinavia* (1977). This period also saw the rise of analytical discussions of the role of women in Protestantism in general and in specific movements within Protestantism. The seminal work in this area is Jane Dempsey Douglass, "Women and the Continental Reformation," in *Religion and Sexism,* edited by Rosemary R. Ruether (1974). A selection of writings about and by women during the Reformation is found in Joyce L. Irwin, ed., *Womanhood in Radical Protestantism, 1525–1675* (1979). Sherrin Marshall has edited a collection of essays titled *Women in*

Reformation and Counterreformation Europe: Public and Private Worlds (1989). A collection of essays that spans the history of Protestantism is edited by Richard Greaves, *Triumph Over Silence: Women in Protestant History* (1985). An excellent overview of the history of women in American Protestantism is found in Virginia Lieson Brereton and Christa Ressmeyer Klein, "American Women in Ministry: A History of Protestant Beginning Points," in *Women of Spirit,* edited by Rosemary R. Ruether and Eleanor McLaughlin (1979). An excellent collection of interpretive essays and primary documents, many of which deal with different aspects of Protestantism in North America, is *In Our Own Voices: Four Centuries of American Women's Religious Writing,* edited by Rosemary R. Ruether and Rosemary S. Keller (1995). An important discussion of women in the mission movement is R. Pierce Beaver, *American Protestant Women in World Mission: A History of the First Feminist Movement in North America* (1980). Donna A. Behnke has written a full-length treatment titled *Religious Issues in Nineteenth Century Feminism* (1982), which covers the major issues faced by Protestant women in the nineteenth century such as women as public speakers, ordination, and Biblical exegesis.

See also Ordination: In Christianity.

JOANNE CARLSON BROWN

Psyche

A Greek goddess commonly associated with Eros and Aphrodite, Psyche is best known from the work of the North African philosopher Apuleius, whose *Metamorphoses* recounts the Milesian fairy tale about a beautiful princess who is turned into a goddess so that she can become the wife of Eros, the god of love. In earliest depictions (c. 400 B.C.E.) Psyche appears on sarcophagi, jewelry, and in freestanding sculpture as a young girl, often bearing butterfly wings and usually in the company of Eros.

Psyche's dual nature as both mortal and immortal reflects her history in Greek views of the afterlife and later developments in Greek philosophy. Earliest recorded uses of the term *psykhē* denote an immortal soul that leaves the body at the point of death and flies away to live in the underworld. Although the living person had numerous souls, most of which governed the human being during life, only the *psykhē* survived death of the body. Symbols found in art depicting the Greek afterlife soul include the bird (or bird woman), the bee, the butterfly, and the sometimes-winged eidolon (a diminutive human figure). By 600 B.C.E., astral religion

Psyche riding a camel, c. first century B.C.E.–third century C.E. (Paul Almasy/© Corbis).

from Mesopotamia and Egypt had transformed Greek cosmology, with the result that the heavens rather than the underworld became the dwelling place of the after-life soul in the form of a star.

Greek philosophers identified the *psykhē* as a material component of the biological self. Heraclitus, for example, defined it as the organ responsible for human knowledge. For Plato, *psykhē* is both the afterlife soul and the center of personality. During the lifetime of the individual, the soul is capable of passion and courage as well as knowledge. Beginning with the Jewish Platonist Philo, apologists for all three great Western religions—Judaism, Christianity, and Islam—sought to articulate their religious beliefs within the framework of Greek philosophy, seeing in the *psykhē* both the mortal, biological self and the immortal, afterlife soul.

BIBLIOGRAPHY

Bremmer, Jan. *The Early Greek Concept of the Soul.* 1983.

Claus, David B. *Toward the Soul: An Inquiry into the Meaning of Ψυχή before Plato.* 1981.

Rohde, Edwin. *Psyche: The Cult of Souls and Belief in Immortality among the Greeks.* 8th ed., 1925.

Roscher, W. H. "Psyche." In vol. 3 of his *Ausführliches Lexikon der griechischen und römischen Mythologie.* 1993.

BEVERLY MOON

Psychology of Religion

Psychology of religion draws upon a diverse set of methods and theories to pose interpretive questions about the origins and effects of religion. One branch of the field uses psychoanalytic methods to explore unconscious fantasies underlying religious ideas and practices. Another branch uses sociological methods to study the religious and historical factors underlying the emergence of psychological ideas. Other branches incorporate humanistic and transpersonal approaches, which seek connections between religious experiences and authentic selfhood; "dialogic" approaches, which explore parallels between theology and psychology; comparative approaches, which examine both Western and non-Western traditions; experimental and empirical approaches, which use laboratory or data-based methods to study religious experience; and statistical approaches, which study how social and psychological factors correlate with religious practices.

Scholars using these approaches have made significant contributions to the understanding of religion, but they have not, until recently, raised substantive questions about women or gender. In the last two decades feminists have begun to enact a conceptual shift in the century-old tradition, initiating critiques of androcentrism, incorporating a focus on women's experiences, and analyzing cultural notions of gender and religion. The effects of these feminist projects are most evident in four approaches influenced by Sigmund Freud: psychoanalytic theory, Jungian theory, object-relations theory, and Kristevan theory.

THE FREUDIAN (PSYCHOANALYTIC) THEORY OF RELIGION

Sigmund Freud (1856–1939), the first psychoanalyst, sought the psychological origins of religion in projections of unconscious desires and fears. In *The Future of an Illusion* (1927, 1961) and *Moses and Monotheism* (1939, 1964) he argued that ideas about God and morality are fulfillments of unconscious—primarily oedipal—fantasies. In the "Oedipus complex" the young child expresses incestuous love for the mother and murderous hatred for the father. The father forbids the child to act on these fantasies; the child experiences castration anxiety and renounces the fantasies. This renunciation represents the origin of morality. It also sets the pattern for later relationships to other paternal figures: oedipal fears of divine (paternal) punishment obstruct the emergence of skeptical or atheistic thoughts.

In *Freud on Femininity and Faith* (1982), Judith Van Herik critiques Freud's theory for its androcentrism and its assumption of female inferiority. Freud's emphasis on the cultural and psychological relations between father and son virtually excludes women from the psychoanalytic narrative. And his insistence on the significance of castration anxiety in moral development carries the implication of female moral inferiority. Yet Van Herik's critique does not lead her to dismiss Freud's work. Instead, she uncovers subtle patterns of gender asymmetry in Freud's analysis, showing that he associates illusion, wish-fulfillment, and (Christian) religious belief with femininity, whereas he associates renunciation of illusion, rationality, and (Jewish) morality with masculinity. She asks whether the gendering of belief and morality in Freud's theory might correspond to broader cultural patterns.

Scholars asking related questions have examined the relation of religion to gender in the context of Freud's Jewish background. Jay Geller, in "(G)nos(e)ology: The Cultural Construction of the Other" (1992), and historian Sander Gilman, in *Freud, Race, and Gender* (1993), examine the widespread antisemitic stereotypes in Europe at the turn of the century within which male Jews were perceived as emasculated, homosexual, or feminine. They argue that Freud's theories of gender and sexuality can be understood as a response to the cultural rhetoric of racism.

Others studying women, religion, and psychoanalysis have focused on the women who influenced Freud's theories. British psychoanalyst Estelle Roith, in *The Riddle of Freud: Jewish Influences on His Theory of Female Sexuality* (1987), examines the influences of Freud's mother, Amalie, and his followers Lou Andreas-Salomé, Marie Bonaparte, and Helene Deutsch. In *A Most Dangerous Method: The Story of Jung, Freud, and Sabina Spielrein* (1993), historian John Kerr describes the significant role of a brilliant young Russian woman, Sabina Spielrein, in the troubled friendship between Freud and Jung and in the development of their ideas on religion.

THE JUNGIAN THEORY OF RELIGION

Carl Jung (1875–1961) was Freud's collaborator from 1907 to 1913, but developed an independent theory of psyche and culture in the decades following their break. He sought the origins of religion in the collective unconscious, a vast storehouse of images and symbols shared by all humans, containing "archetypes" or "forms without content." These archetypes, manifested in dreams, myths, and religions, include, among others, the "shadow," the "anima" (the repressed feminine dimension of the male unconscious) and "animus" (the repressed masculine dimensions of the female unconscious), the "Great Mother," the "Wise Old Man," and the "Self." In Jung's view, contemporary religion has become excessively conscious, rational, and masculine, losing touch with the archetypes and the unconscious. In *Psychology and Religion* (1938) he called for a renewal of the connection to the collective unconscious and a reincorporation of the missing feminine archetypes into God-imagery.

Some feminists have found Jung's attention to the feminine archetypes useful in incorporating experiences of women—or, more accurately, images of women—into the psychology of religion. Joan Chamberlain Englesman, in *The Feminine Dimension of the Divine* (1979, 1995), examines the repression and survival of the feminine archetype in Christian Mariology and ecclesiology. Naomi Goldenberg, in *The Changing of the Gods* (1979), draws upon Jung's theory of culture in interpreting a shift toward "feminist religions" in which the authority and divinity of the self are valued. Others, however, have found essentialist and problematic views of women in Jung's thought. In *Returning Words to Flesh* (1990), Goldenberg departs from her earlier acclaim for Jung, arguing convincingly that the theory of the archetypes offers a restrictive version of the feminine based on fantasies of independence from matter and body. Demaris Wehr, in *Jung and Feminism: Liberating Archetypes* (1987), attempts a balanced assessment, acknowledging that Jung's concept of femininity aims to keep women out of the public sphere, although, in her view, his theory as a whole can serve to deconstruct cultural misogyny.

PSYCHOANALYTIC OBJECT-RELATIONS THEORY AND RELIGION

Object-relations theorists such as Margaret Mahler (b. 1908), Melanie Klein (1882–1960), and Donald W. Winnicott (1896–1971), have extended the psychoanalytic inquiry to include a focus on the significance of human interrelatedness in the earliest period of human development. Some scholars of religion, seeking the psychological origins of faith, mysticism, ritual, and God-imagery, have found the hermeneutic centrality of the mother–infant relationship in object-relations theory a rich resource for feminist projects. Mary Ellen Ross and Cheryl Lynn Ross, in "Mothers, Infants, and the Psychoanalytic Study of Ritual" (1982), draw on

Winnicott's notion of "transitional space" (the metaphorical space between infant and mother in which meaning and culture emerge) to develop a feminist theory of the Christian ritual of Holy Communion or Eucharist. Eucharistic symbols of nurturance and unification, they argue, provide worshipers with positive experiences of God as mother. Others drawing upon object-relations theory and the related tradition of "self-psychology" disagree with this analysis. In *Women and Sacrifice: Male Narcissism and the Psychology of Religion* (1992), William Beers maintains that the liturgy of the Eucharist expresses male anxieties about maternal engulfment. In his view, the sacrificial themes of the ritual function to separate men from women, to affirm male power, and to assuage men's narcissistic anxiety.

THE KRISTEVAN THEORY OF RELIGION

French psychoanalyst and linguist Julia Kristeva (b. 1941) introduces a new set of feminist concerns into the psychology of religion. Heavily influenced by poststructuralism, a set of ideas emphasizing the cultural and linguistic construction of knowledge and the effects of language and power on subjectivity, Kristeva brings to the field an emphasis on the subject as a "speaking being." The "speaking being" is always "in process" and always divided between the pull of "the semiotic"—the emotional, bodily, prelinguistic forces—and "the symbolic"—the demands of society and law. In *In the Beginning was Love: Psychoanalysis and Faith* (1987), she interprets religious faith as a subversive irruption by the semiotic of the symbolic order, locating the source of the semiotic in the infant's relation to the body of the mother. The body of the mother is central to other Kristevan texts as well. In *Powers of Horror* (1980, 1982), she undertakes an analysis of the "maternal mytheme" underlying ritual and the sacred, finding a primal abhorrence of the mother, a fear of losing identity by sinking irretrievably into the mother. Kristeva thus discovers an "abject" matriphobia within religious language about defilement, purification, sin, and sacrality. Her work raises important questions about the effects of religion, both liberating and repressive, on psyche, culture, and gender.

WOMEN AND THE PSYCHOLOGY OF RELIGION

Feminist research has led to significant conceptual shifts within some branches of the psychology of religion. Critical projects have taken an oppositional stance toward traditional scholarship, exposing the androcentrism and "womanlessness" of earlier research. Inclusive projects have interpreted women's religious experiences or analyzed women's contributions to theo-

retical developments in the field. And analytic projects have investigated the interdependence of gender, religion, and subjectivity. Although an interest in women and in gender is evident in those approaches influenced by psychoanalysis, most of the other branches of the psychology of religion remain relatively untouched by feminist theory. Much work remains to be done before the psychology of religion is fully attentive to the study of women.

BIBLIOGRAPHY

For research on Freud, gender, and religion, see Daniel Boyarin's important discussion of Judaism, gender, and postcolonialism in the development of Freud's ideas, in "Épater L'embourgeoisement: Freud, Gender, and the (De)Colonized Psyche," *Diacritics* 24, no. 1 (1994): 17–41. Carol Gilligan, in "Conquistadors of the Dark Continent," *Daedalus* 113, no. 3 (1984): 75–95, formulates a valuable critique of Freud's androcentric moral vision and develops a feminist, relational, alternative. Diane Jonte-Pace utilizes Freud to critique cultural misogyny by uncovering in Freud's texts a "counterthesis" analyzing an association linking mothers, death, and fantasies of immortality in "At Home in the Uncanny: Freudian Representations of Death, Mothers, and the Afterlife," *Journal of the American Academy of Religion* 64, no. i 1996: 61–68.

Erich Neumann's *The Great Mother* (1963, 1974) is a massive compendium of myths and symbols of female deities organized according to Jung's archetypal categories. Ann Belford Ulanov's *The Feminine in Jungian Psychology and in Christian Theology* (1971) offers an enthusiastic assessment of Jung's thought from the perspective of Paul Tillich's liberal Protestant theology.

Some feminists draw upon the work of object-relations theorist Melanie Klein for productive analyses of religion. Harriet Lutzky's "Reparation and Tikkun," *International Review of Psychoanalysis* 16 (1989): 449–458, compares Kleinian concepts with concepts from the Jewish mystical tradition. Kelley Raab's "Nancy Jay and a Feminist Psychology of Sacrifice," *Journal of Feminist Studies in Religion* 13, no. 1 (1997): 73–87, utilizes Klein and Mahler to explain and critique the widespread resistance to women's ordination to the sacramental priesthood.

Some recent feminist projects have examined Kristeva's contributions to the psychology of religion. *Body/Text in Julia Kristeva: Religion, Women, Psychoanalysis,* edited by David Crownfield (1992), contains several important essays. *Transfigurations: Theology and the French Feminists,* edited by C. W. Maggie Kim, Susan M. St. Ville, and Susan M. Simonaitis (1993), includes essays examining the contributions of Kristeva and other French feminists to feminist theology as well as to the psychology of religion.

The most comprehensive discussion of the field and its history is David Wulff's *Psychology of Religion: Classic and Contemporary Views* (1991). Peter Homans provides an invaluable introduction to the historical phases of the field in "The Psychology and Religion Movement," in *The Encyclopedia of Religion* (1987).

Although most psychological studies of religion have focused on Judaism and Christianity, a few have addressed other religions. Psychologist David Wulff calls for Jungian and Freudian interpretations of Hindu mother goddesses in "A Prolegomenon to a Psychology of the Goddess," in *The Divine Consort,* edited by John Hawley and Donna Wulff (1982). Psychoanalytic investigations of Indian family patterns and Hindu religious beliefs, with emphases on goddesses, mothers, and women's religious experiences, can be found in the work of psychoanalyst Sudhir Kakar and anthropologist Stanley Kurtz. See Kakar's *The Inner World: A Psychoanalytic Study of Childhood and Society in India* (1978), and Kurtz's *All the Mothers Are One: Hindu India and the Cultural Reshaping of Psychoanalysis* (1993). Fatima Mernissi's *Beyond the Veil: Male-Female Dynamics in Modern Muslim Society* (1975, 1987) brings together psychoanalysis, religion, and gender by contrasting Freud's view of passive, masochistic, female sexuality with an Islamic tradition of active, dangerous, female sexuality. In "Possession Sickness and Women Shamans in Korea," in *Unspoken Worlds,* edited by Nancy Falk and Rita Gross (1980). Youngsook Kim Harvey argues that psychological and interpersonal conflicts precede the onset of "possession sickness" among Korean women who later develop shamanic powers.

See also **Freud, Sigmund**; **Jung, Carl**.

DIANE JONTE-PACE

Purification

Purification is a common and universal preoccupation of religious ritual. Although rites of purification are diverse, a certain thematic consistency among them lends insight into the notion of purity as a religious necessity. Purity is the defining state, the ideal. What is pure is sacred, that is, set apart and differentiated from the banal. By contrast, that which is polluted or defiled is whatever falls outside the boundaries of the sacred. Both purity and pollution are conditions of being with respect to the holy or sacred, and categories of religious experience. Rites of purification aim at restoring per-

son, society, and cosmos to the ideal condition. They are therefore central to the processes of transformation that religions seek to effect: healing, renewal, and transcendence.

Pollution or defilement must be managed ritually. Rituals of purification both protect the individual from the dangers associated with defilement and insulate the community from the contagion that the violating condition presents. Purification restores a person or thing to its proper place within the established order, reintegrates the defiled into a system of meaning, and allows for participation in the sacred.

TYPOLOGIES: SOCIAL AND NATURAL

Purificatory ceremony is necessary on occasions of crisis that threaten sacred order. These crises may be natural (illness or death) or social (initiation or marriage). The natural crisis of puberty is often conflated with a social turning point, initiation, a ritual threshold that signals the assumption of the mature social and spiritual life. Ritual washing typically symbolizes the removal of impurities inherent in the natural condition in preparation for a morally pure life. In Christianity, baptism by immersion or aspersion is such a ritual cleansing. Throughout Africa, initiates are often smeared with white river clay, kaolin, symbolic of the birth caul and evocative of the purity of the newborn.

Social crises occasioned by violation of the moral order, such as in incest or murder, call for ritual purification. These restore sacred order to the community while protecting the culpable individual who may otherwise sustain the symptoms of spiritual retribution. In West Africa murderers are considered vulnerable to persecution by the souls of victims, and the neglect of mandatory purificatory ritual causes madness. Purification ceremonies include entering a state of sympathetic death, signaled by segregation from the community, wearing old clothes, eating from broken vessels, and abstaining from cooked food. Although the spilling of blood through violence is understood to be particularly polluting, blood can also be a cleansing agent. The sacrificial blood of a scapegoat offered by the "unclean" as expiation for an offense restores her to a state of purity and reintegration into communal life. In this way, rituals of purification are the basis for moral systems.

Moral pollution and social defilement are associated with threatening physical states and processes. Purificatory ritual is therefore frequently preoccupied with the maintenance of bodily boundaries. In Islam for example, the chief duty is ritual purity (*tahara*), and washing before prayer is a sign of spiritual cleansing and a pious life. Bodily emissions are potent with vital force when contained within the biological system,

A young woman in a floral headdress holds an offering at a purification ceremony in Kuta, Bali, Indonesia (Nik Wheeler/Corbis).

but upon expulsion become dangerous by-products, charged with power that must be harnessed by social sanction and ritual prescription. Purification demands the appropriate containment of such bodily fluids, the cleansing of the body from the physical impurities of discharges that simultaneously represent an alienation from spiritual integrity. In Islam urine, feces, and intestinal gas are associated with putrefaction and death, and therefore polluting. Contact with such impure matter requires ablution. By contrast, in India, where the cow is sacred, bovine emissions are considered pure. Therefore, cow dung, milk, ghee, curds, and urine are mixed and applied as a purifying balm.

Typically, the uncontrollable shedding of blood in menstruation is identified with a state of ritual pollution. Because menstrual discharge breaches the natural boundaries of the bodily container, it may be coded as polluting. Orthodox Jewish women are required to purify themselves after menstruation at a mikveh, a ritual bath of rainwater, a "natural" cleanser. Substances entering the body may also be considered potentially polluting, and are subject to rules of avoidance, as in the kosher prescriptions of Orthodox Judaism. Hebrew Scripture specifies foods considered clean and those that are abominations, offensive to the Holy. The Hindu practice of vegetarianism is based on the principle of ahimsa, nonviolence, for violence threatens the prescribed order of a sanctified life.

The most polluting natural condition is death. Purification rituals circumscribe defilement associated with death. Funerals demarcate the separate domains of the living and dead and enforce an orderly transition between them. But the close association of the bereaved family with the deceased causes them to be polluted with a "sympathetic befoulment" (Preston, 1987, p. 94). At the end of a period of mourning they must be purified of their contagion. Among the Kuranko of Sierra Leone, widows ritually participate in the death of their husbands by being quarantined for forty days in a state of impurity. Afterward, the widow purges herself of spiritual taint through purifying ablutions, confessing any transgressions against the husband to avoid vengeful attacks by his ghost. Uncontrolled expressions of grief are dangerous, too, for they signify a compromising attachment to the deceased, a dangerous conflation of the domains of living and dead. The flow of tears and ebullient emotions are therefore ritually constrained. The end of funerary rites among the Ndembu is also marked by the ritual washing of the widow or widower, who is then anointed with oil, shaved around the hair line, dressed in a new white cloth, and adorned with white beads. "What is being washed off in these life-crisis rites is the state of ritual death, the liminal condition between two periods of active social life" (Turner, 1967, p. 77).

Rites of purification are considered essential preparation for any sacred undertaking. The North American plains Indians construct a dome-shaped sweat lodge with bent willow branches and bison robes to represent the cosmos. Inside participants bathe in steam vapors created by pouring water over rocks heated in a sacred fire. "The steam, actually conceived as the visible image of the Great Spirit, acts as in an alchemical work to dissolve both physical and psychic 'coagulations' so that a spiritual transmutation may take place" (Gill, 1983, p. 167). A sweat precedes the Vision Quest, a pilgrimage to the sacred center in search of guidance from spiritual guardians. Fire and fumigation are effective means of purification in the Hopi tradition, as well. Ashes are sprinkled on ritual participants to cleanse them of dangerous contact with the spiritual world. The False Face maskers of the Iroquois blow hot ashes to disperse illness and restore healing. In the Indo-Iranian traditions, too, fire is revered for its transformative power. At the Zoroastrian fire temple, practitioners are dedicated to moral purity by meditating in the presence of fire, while the Hindu god Agni is the personification of fire to whom sacrifices are made to purify the whole world.

These examples show that various modes of purification—segregation, the use of water, the control and ritual manipulation of bodily fluids (especially blood), and fire and fumigation—sustain sacred order.

BIBLIOGRAPHY

Buckley, Thomas, and Alma Gottlieb, eds. *Blood Magic: The Anthropology of Menstruation.* 1988.

Douglas, Mary. *Purity and Danger.* London, 1966.

Drewal, Henry, and Margaret Thompson Drewal. *Gelede: Art and Female Power among the Yoruba.* 1983.

Fallaize, E. N. "Purification." In *Encyclopedia of Religion and Ethics,* vol 10. Edited by James Hastings. 1918. Reprint, 1974.

Gill, Sam D. *Native American Traditions: Sources and Interpretations.* 1983.

Jackson, Michael. *Paths Towards a Clearing: Radical Empiricism and Ethnographic Inquiry.* 1989.

Preston, James J. "Purification." In *The Encyclopedia of Religion,* vol. 12. Edited by Mircea Eliade. 1987.

Turner, Victor. *Forest of Symbols: Aspects of Ndembu Ritual.* 1967.

See also Blood; Food; Initiation; Menstruation; Sexuality; Vegetarianism.

LAURA S. GRILLO

Purity and Pollution

Systems of purity within cultures are inseparable from ideas about pollution. If an act or a state is deemed pure, then it is defined with primary reference to a state that is polluted—or not pure. Conversely, concepts of pollution are accompanied by systems that enable an individual to ameliorate that pollution, or in other words, to establish a state of purity. Scholars of religion have been fascinated by systems of purity and pollution within cultures since the nineteenth century, but Mary Douglas (1966) has shown that notions of pollution and purity are fundamentally concepts of order and disorder. An item or an act that is polluted or that causes pollution is "matter out of place," and Douglas rightly illustrates that it is necessary to examine the underlying ideas about order within a culture to understand why the definitions of pollution exist.

Systems of purity and pollution within patriarchal cultures almost always encompass women. Within such cultures, maintaining a state of purity and alleviating pollution is a responsibility of both sexes and is not restricted to either men or women. In general, occasions of change require purification, whether that change is expected (as in life-cycle rituals, such as puberty or marriage) or unexpected (as in instances of illness or death). In these situations women may have particular responsibilities for maintaining purity, but the burden of eradicating pollution is not usually gender specific. In the acts of demarcating the proper boundaries of religious practice, a religious community, or the sacred, the responsibilities of women to maintain purity are not necessarily gendered. In Judaism, for example, it is the traditional responsibility of women to prepare kosher food for everyone to eat, but both sexes are required to follow the laws of *kashrut.*

Within a number of patriarchal cultures, however, certain rituals of purification are designed to eliminate pollution that only women experience: childbirth and menstruation (or problems associated with either). Some rituals are designed to eliminate men's risk of contact with menstruating or pregnant women or women who have just given birth; but women themselves have different and usually more extensive rituals to eliminate the pollution of these experiences. For example, texts that explain the role of women in the ancient Vedic rituals of South Asia indicate that the wife of one who sacrifices could not participate in the sacrificial rites if she was menstruating or if she had recently given birth. Interestingly, the presence of a wife was required during certain other rituals; substitutions for a wife were acceptable, either in the form of another woman or a small image that was placed in the wife's seat (Jamison, 1996).

Rituals that require women's actual separation from the normal run of the household during menstruation are quite common. Historically, Zoroastrian women were required to spend four days in a small stone or concrete enclosure with no windows, to use a special set of utensils, and to wear a set of clothes used only during her menses (Boyce, 1977). She was prohibited from contact, as much as possible, with any of the seven sacred creations: sky, water, earth, plants, animals, men, or fire. More recent traditional Zoroastrian practice requires a woman to remain in one corner of the home, using her own utensils, where she usually catches up on the mending.

Rituals concerning women's reproductive disorders are closely related to the healing practices of a particular culture. For example, among the Ndembu in northwestern Zambia, a woman who has had miscarriages, abortions, or excessive discharges during menstruation is thought to have offended a "shade" who literally occupies her body until restitution is made (Turner, 1967). The woman's mother's mother was by far the most common shade to induce such problems, which Turner found significant in light of the patterns of patrilocality of matrilineal inheritance and succession. A male healer conducts the rituals to restore a woman's reproductive health, a fact that reveals the larger patriarchal context for the eradiation of the pollution in a situation unique to women.

Not all patriarchal cultures consider childbirth and menstruation to be polluting. Mary Douglas has suggested that cultures in which the roles accorded to men and women are clearly defined and directly enforced (often by physical force) have few concepts of sexual pollution, including menstruation. The Walbiri of central Australia, Douglas explains, do not consider menstrual blood to be dangerous or polluting, in part because they do not hesitate to punish deviations from established sex roles.

Susan Starr Sered (1994) has found that female-dominated religions, by contrast, pay little attention to rites of passage or life-cycle rituals, scarcely marking birth, menarche, menstruation, and menopause in their ritual systems. This is not to say that no ideas about purity and pollution surround experiences of childbirth and menstruation within female-dominated religions. In the new Japanese religion Tenrikyo, menstruation is considered a "flowering" rather than a polluting state. Among the African Mende, a menstruating woman is regarded as committed to a supernatural claim that supersedes any claim her husband might have (Harris and Sawyer, 1968). Black Carib women are prevented from eating animals killed in hunting, and are prohibited from any contact with the weapons of the hunters or their dogs. However, these women may use their own menstrual blood in charms or potions that are considered to be more powerful than those made by men (Taylor, 1951). The Tetum in Indonesia regard the umbilical cord and placenta as sacred (Hicks, 1976). It may be the case that among female-dominated religions, as Sered suggests, menstruation and childbirth are more properly considered as providing women with power rather than as polluting experiences.

The means to alleviate states of impurity or pollution—fire, water, dust or sand, potions or detergents, blood, clean clothing—do not appear to be gendered; all are used to restore an individual to a clean state, and there is no evidence that women use any of these more or less often than do men in various cultures. Anne Feldhaus (1995) suggests that the overriding concern with systems of purity and pollution in South Asia has obscured the rich texture of associations between water and fertility in the Indian state of Maharashtra. Some

rituals celebrate the femininity of rivers in Maharashtra, such as one custom that dresses a river in saris; although rivers are said to menstruate in the rainy season (referring to the mud that is carried down during the heavy rains) and to carry away evil and sin, there is a notable lack of any corresponding notion that it is the femininity of the rivers that washes away bad karma. Any association between the femininity of rivers and their ability to purify, Feldhaus suggests, lies in the fact that they are wet and therefore fertile, particularly on the arid Deccan Plateau. Ideas about purity are inseparable from ideas about pollution in religious and cultural systems. In order to determine how such concepts of purity and pollution shape and are shaped by the lives of women in patriarchal traditions, it is necessary to examine how various components of a culture or religion are gendered. Correlations between what is polluting and what is pure rarely fall explicitly and entirely along the lines of gender, but gender remains a category essential to the task of understanding systems of purity and pollution.

BIBLIOGRAPHY

Boyce, Mary. *A Persian Stronghold of Zoroastrianism.* 1977.

Bynum, Caroline Walker. "Women's Stories, Women's Symbols: A Critique of Victor Turner's Theory of Liminality." In *Anthropology and the Study of Religion.* Edited by Frank Reynolds and Robert Moore. 1984.

Choksy, Jamsheed K. *Purity and Pollution in Zoroastrianism: Triumph Over Evil.* 1989.

Douglas, Mary. *Implicit Meanings: Essays in Anthropology.* 1975.

———. *Purity and Danger: An Analysis of the Concepts of Pollution and Taboo.* 1966.

Eliade, Mircea. *Rites and Symbols of Initiation.* 1958.

Falk, Nancy Auer, and Rita M. Gross, eds. *Unspoken Worlds: Women's Religious Lives in Non-Western Cultures.* 1980.

Feldhaus, Anne. *Water and Womanhood: Religious Meanings of Rivers in Maharashtra.* 1995.

Harris, W. T., and Harry Sawyer. *The Springs of Mende Belief and Conduct.* Freetown, Sierra Leone, 1968.

Hicks, David. *Tetum Ghosts and Kin: Fieldwork in an Indonesian Community.* 1976.

Jamison, Stephanie W. *Sacrificed Wife, Sacrificer's Wife: Women, Ritual, and Hospitality in Ancient India.* 1996.

Lincoln, Bruce. *Emerging from the Chrysalis: Studies in Rituals of Women's Initiation.* 1981.

Malkki, Liisa H. *Purity and Exile: Violence, Memory, and National Cosmology among Hutu Refugees in Tanzania.* 1995.

Neusner, Jacob. *The Idea of Purity in Ancient Judaism.* Leiden, 1973.

Parker, Robert. *Miasma: Pollution and Purification in Ancient Greek Religion.* 1983.

Rozario, Santi. *Purity and Communal Boundaries: Women and Social Change in a Bangladeshi Village.* 1992.

Sered, Susan Starr. *Priestess, Mother, Sacred Sister: Religions Dominated by Women.* 1994.

Taylor, Douglas MacRae. *The Black Carib of British Honduras.* 1951.

Turner, Victor. *The Forest of Symbols: Aspects of Ndembu Ritual.* 1967.

CAROL S. ANDERSON

Queen Mother of the West

The Queen Mother of the West (Xiwangmu) is the highest goddess of Taoism, the major religion native to China. Her worship was most widespread during the Middle Ages (c. 300–1100 C.E.). Medieval Chinese Taoists considered her the embodiment of yin, the dark female force. They believed that she, along with other deities, created and maintained the world. Her name reveals she was regal, female, and western. As ruler, she controlled immortality and human contact with deities. As woman, she was ancestress, teacher, and lover to gods and devotees. The *mother* in her name is a ritual title for a powerful ancestress. She is a deity of lineage and dynastic legitimation rather than a great mother goddess. The west is linked in Chinese cosmology with death, afterlife, and paradise. She alone can bestow Taoist teachings, which lead to eternal life; she alone provides the adept with a divine teacher.

Her history is long, her transformations many. Traces of the Queen Mother of the West appear in the archaeological record, Taoist scriptures, and literary and historical texts. She has been revered throughout China for over two millennia. Both elite and popular traditions survive concerning her. Her medieval image combines several earlier figures, both benign and terrifying, foci of cults of shamanism, immortality, alchemy, meditation, and asceticism. Her symbols are the tiger of death and the peaches of immortality. Her worship reaches fullest development in *Shang qing* (Supreme Pure Realm) Taoism after the fourth century C.E. Later, under Buddhist influence, a new version of the goddess emerges, called the Golden Mother of the Turquoise Pond. Her cult is active in Taiwan today.

Xiwangmu, Queen Mother of the West with Divinities. Painting from the Mogao Caves, Dunhuang, Gansu province, China, c. 535–556 C.E. (Pierre Colombel/Corbis)

BIBLIOGRAPHY

Cahill, Suzanne E. *Transcendence and Divine Passion: The Queen Mother of the West in Medieval China.* 1993.

Loewe, Michael. *Ways to Paradise: The Chinese Quest for Immortality.* 1979.

SUZANNE E. CAHILL

Queens, Biblical

Although some of the Hebrew Bible's most memorable characters are queens (e.g., Jezebel), it is nevertheless a fact that the title "queen" is never assigned to a wife of an Israelite king. Instead, the biblical records, especially those from Israel's southern kingdom of Judah, tend to focus on the role of the "queen mother." For example, although the archival records of all but two of the nineteen kings of Judah record the name of the king's queen mother, none mentions the name of a queen. When Judah's King Jehoiachin is taken by the Babylonians into exile, it is his queen mother, not his queen, who is described as being deposed along with him (Jer. 13:18). When Solomon takes over the throne from his father King David, it is his queen mother, Bathsheba, who is described as sitting at his right hand (1 Kings 2:19). Bathsheba, however, is not portrayed as commanding this sort of position before David's death. Even the infamous story of Bathsheba's and David's adultery (2 Sam. 11) does not presume a powerful role for her in David's court. As queen, Bathsheba is insignificant. As queen mother, she is the most important woman in the palace.

There are several reasons for the superior position of queen mothers in Israel. The first concerns the biblical tradition of polygyny, especially royal polygyny. The fact that a king has many wives means it is not immediately obvious which of his royal consorts should be his queen. Only one royal woman, conversely, can be the king's mother, and this affords her a special stature. More significant, though, is the Israelite understanding of the special stature of widows in general, for while biblical law requires that a married woman submit completely to the authority of her husband, it grants this same woman a significant degree of autonomy if that husband dies. Since the queen mother is by necessity a widow, given that it is the death of her husband that has allowed her son to as-

sume the throne, she can assume a position of power that a king's wife cannot. Queen mothers in the south, moreover, assume power based on an understanding that they have a special relationship with the divine, since the southern ideology of kingship holds that God is the king's metaphorical father. This implies a metaphorical divine mother as well, and the actual queen mother seems to represent this heavenly being on earth.

Some other cultures of the biblical world share Israel's stress on the queen mother's dominant role. Yet as the biblical narratives concerning the Queen of Sheba (1 Kings 10:1–13), the Queen of Babylon (Dan. 5:10), the Queen of Ethiopia (Acts 8:27), and various queens of Persia (Neh. 2:6; Esther 1:10–20, 2:17, 5:1–9:32) indicate, powerful queens are not unknown. The Bible's Queen Jezebel, herself of foreign descent, may demonstrate that on occasion this sort of understanding of queenship can be borrowed into Israel.

BIBLIOGRAPHY

Ackerman, Susan. "The Queen Mother and the Cult in Ancient Israel." *Journal of Biblical Literature* 112 (1993): 385–401.

Andreasen, Niels-Erik A. "The Role of the Queen Mother in Israelite Society." *Catholic Biblical Quarterly* 45 (1983): 179–194.

Ben-Barak, Zafrira. "The Status and Right of the *Gĕbîrâ*." *Journal of Biblical Literature* 110 (1991): 23–34.

Berlin, Adele. "Characterization in Biblical Narrative: David's Wives." *Journal for the Study of the Old Testament* 23 (1982): 70–76.

The Queen of Sheba.   Persian miniature, 1600 C.E. (Corbis-Bettman)

Yee, Gale A. " 'Fraught with Background': Literary Ambiguity in II Samuel 11." *Interpretation* 42 (1988): 240–253.

SUSAN ACKERMAN

Queer Theory

Feminist film critic Teresa De Lauretis introduced the term *queer theory* in the pages of *differences: A Journal of Feminist Cultural Studies* in 1991. Generated at a conference discussing new critical work theorizing lesbian and gay sexualities and at another on queer film and video, the term emerged at the same time as *Queer Nation* gave a name to a new generation of political activism in 1990. Queer theory initially was intended to disrupt the reliance on monolithic identity categories and to problematize the multiple differences in the production of dominant categories of sexuality. Attempting to "recast or reinvent the terms of our sexualities, to construct another horizon, another way of thinking the sexual" (De Lauretis, p. iv), queer theorists extended activists' discussions of queer (documented in *Gay Community News* by 1983). Initially influential primarily in literary and film studies, queer theory has grown in importance and has been hotly debated in history and social theory.

Embracing a term originally used as a derogatory label for sexual deviance, *queer* refuses the dominant categories of discourse and challenges assimilationist and liberal-pluralist politics aimed at the legitimization and toleration of excluded groups. Instead, queer theory examines the dominant organization of sexuality and the production of the normal. *Queer* is thus not defined around an identity, but as dissent from and defiance of dominant meanings of sex and gender. As a category of positionality, of resistance to what Michael Warner calls "heteronormativity," "its actual historical forms and positions are open, constantly subject to negotiations and renegotiations" (Duggan, p. 167).

Drawing on poststructuralism, deconstruction, (Lacanian) psychoanalysis, and particularly Michel Foucault's work on sexuality as a modern discursive production, queer theorists examine the production and maintenance of the normal. For example, when dealing with medico-scientific study of "sex variants" in the 1930s, historian Jennifer Terry, instead of attempting to retrieve actors or events elided in official history, explicates precisely the operations that produced those elisions. Placing the production and circulation of sexuality and the emergence of the homo/heterosexual bina-

rism at the core of Western culture, literary theorist Eve Kosofsky Sedgwick argues for the necessity of an antihomophobic stance in any cultural theoretical inquiry. Equally influential at the productive intersection of queer theory with feminist theory are philosopher Judith Butler's works. Examining heterosexual assumptions in theories of gender, Butler analyzes the discursive production of sex and gender and suggests that gender can be understood as a form of "performativity." This approach has been useful to many others in theorizing the production of (gendered) bodies. Butler argues that bodies become intelligible through a citational process that compulsively reinvokes and reiterates norms. Bodies are thus not "natural," but the (material) effect of discursive regulations and normalization. This leads Butler and others to explore how to resist or disrupt such discursive operations.

Queer theory has been criticized by some for reinscribing white gay male dominance by focusing too exclusively on the white male literary canon and by evading specificities of gay, lesbian, bisexual, transgender, sadomasochistic, and other sex-radical identities and communities through a false inclusiveness of *queer* (often used as a summarizing term for the long list of those not conforming to dominant categories of the normal). Yet the multiple differences of race, class, ethnicity, and gender in the production, circulation, and maintenance of heteronormative conceptions of sexuality, and the ways these relate to political strategies, have been and continue to be important issues in queer theory. Already in the 1991 *differences* volume, Tomas Almáguer argues for the inadequacy of identity categories for identifying same-sex behavior in Latino "homosexuality," and Ekua Omosupe problematizes the racially unmarked category lesbian. JanMohamed's work on kinship and sexuality in the context of race shows how regulating sex becomes a way of creating and maintaining the power dynamics of race.

Connections between theory and activism have been crucial in the emergence of queer scholarship and continue to be central to a great deal of it. Cindy Patton's influential work on AIDS and safe-sex education examines representations and cultural shifts in AIDS discourse. She explores the production and contestation of a national AIDS pedagogy that relies on a concept of (compassionate) citizen that is distinct from dangerous bodies. Patton develops a theory of sexual vernaculars linked with space that support dissident pedagogies. Although academic credentials and institutional support have become attached to its mastery, queer theory ideally attempts to maintain this tension between theoretical textual readings and politically relevant and subversive practice. Theorists' work queers various disciplines and fields of normalization. Reminding queers to examine their own production of norms, it understands and enacts queer as resistant relation.

QUEER THEORY AND RELIGION

Some scholars are beginning to use queer theory and explore its implications in the academic study of religion. It is primarily debated within gay, lesbian, and feminist liberation theologies, biblical studies, and ethics dealing with sexuality. It is too early to predict if queer theory will eventually equal the influence of some feminist theories in these and other areas in the study of women and religion.

Because queer theoretical conceptions of power, resistance, or identity may differ greatly from liberationist ones, debates about queer theory's potentials and difficulties and questions regarding agency and social change arise. For example, a queer active opposition to normativity raises questions for feminist ethicists as to how to conceptualize values and norms without relying on reinscribing normativity. How "queering" religion can be subversive and transgressive, and not merely an extension of existing projects, which might reinscribe the normalizing rhetoric they set out to challenge, will continue to be an important question as new sites of queer religious studies are opened up.

Understanding gender as performative and theorizing fluctuating, unstable, and perpetually contested identities and subjectivities raises many questions about the definition of the field "women and religion," or what should be included in a syllabus for such a course. Examining the production of raced and gendered bodies in a number of new and different sites, queer work (in religion) expands and challenges conceptions of what "counts" as the (discipline of) religion. Boyarin's work on Jews in the history of sexuality and Pellegrini and Jakobsen's work at the intersections of cultural studies, religion, feminist theory, and queer theory exemplify the complexity of scholarship in the field.

BIBLIOGRAPHY

Almáguer, Tomas. "Chicano Men: A Cartography of Homosexual Identity and Behavior." *differences: A Journal of Feminist Cultural Studies* 3, no. 2 (1991): 75–100.

Bad Object Choices, eds. *How Do I Look? Queer Film and Video.* 1991.

Butler, Judith. *Bodies that Matter: On the Discursive Limits of "Sex."* 1993.

———. *Gender Trouble: Feminism and the Subversion of Identity.* 1990.

De Lauretis, Teresa. "Queer Theory: Lesbian and Gay Sexualities. An Introduction." *differences: A Journal of Feminist Cultural Studies* 3, no. 2 (1991): iii–xviii.

Duggan, Lisa. "Making It Perfectly Queer." In *Sex Wars: Sexual Dissent and Political Culture.* Edited by Lisa Duggan and Nan D. Hunter. 1995.

GLQ: A Journal of Lesbian and Gay Studies. 1994–.

Halperin, David M. *Saint Foucault: Towards a Gay Hagiography.* 1995.

JanMohamed, Abdul R. "Sexuality on/of the Racial Border: Foucault, Wright and the Articulation of 'Racialized Sexuality'." In *Discourses of Sexuality: From Aristotle to AIDS.* Edited by Domna C. Stanton. 1992.

"More Gender Trouble: Feminism Meets Queer Theory." *differences: A Journal of Feminist Cultural Studies* 6, nos. 2 and 3 (1994).

Omosupe, Ekua. "Black/Lesbian/Bulldagger." *differences: A Journal of Feminist Cultural Studies* 3, no. 2 (1991): 101–111.

Patton, Cindy. *Fatal Advice: How Safe Sex Education Went Wrong.* 1996.

Penn, Donna. "Queer: Theorizing Politics and History." *Radical History Review* 62 (1995): 24–42.

Sedgwick, Eve Kosofsky. *Epistemology of the Closet.* 1990.

Terry, Jennifer. "Theorizing Deviant Subjectivity." *differences: A Journal of Feminist Cultural Studies* 3, no. 2 (1991): 55–74.

Warner, Michael. *Fear of a Queer Planet: Queer Politics and Social Theory.* 1993.

Important work with particular significance to the study of (women in) religion:

Boyarin, Daniel. *Unheroic Conduct.* 1997.

Clark, J. Michael, and Robert E. Goss, eds. *A Rainbow of Religious Studies.* 1996.

Goss, Robert E. *Jesus Acted Up: A Gay and Lesbian Manifesto.* 1993.

Jakobsen, Janet R. *Working Alliances: Diversity and Complexity in Feminist Ethics.* 1996.

Jakobsen, Janet R., and Ann Pellegrini. *Bodies Politic: Contesting Desires in Religious and Cultural Narratives of American-ness.* 1997.

Pellegrini, Ann. *Performance Anxieties.* 1996.

See also **Gender Studies**; **Lesbian Studies**; **Lesbianism**.

CLAUDIA SCHIPPERT

Qur'an and Hadith

The Qur'an, regarded by all Muslims as their divinely dictated scripture, literally means "Recitation." According to Islamic tradition, the Prophet Muhammad

(d. 632) was first ordered by the angel Gabriel to recite in Mecca the revelations sent by the sole and supreme deity Allah. Muhammad's task, according to Muslims, was to deliver the final and perfect message from God to all humanity. The Qur'an explicitly names twenty-four male prophets prior to Muhammad who, as the final monotheistic messenger, completes the Islamic continuum begun with the first prophet Adam. Although the Qur'an does state that not all prophets prior to Muhammad have been revealed (40:78), the gendered Arabic of the scripture specifies that named or unnamed, all prophets are by definition male. The series of 114 suras, or chapters, which form the Qur'an, began in 610 and continued to be revealed until the Prophet's death in 632. These revelations were then collected from written and oral repositories to form a standard version around the year 644.

The Qur'an, as the literal word of God revealed in Arabic, specifically enjoins male and female Muslims to prove their faith through a shared core of ritual acts (33:35). These include proper worship (11:144, 17:78–79); almsgiving (2:43, 4:162); the fast during the month of Ramadan (2:183–185); and the hajj, or pilgrimage to Mecca (2:158, 3:97). These four basic acts, incumbent upon all Muslims, include a fifth and final pillar of Islam, the *shahādah,* or profession of faith that declares: "There is no god but Allah and Muhammad is the messenger of Allah."

Islamists, feminists, and scholars in all cultural contexts agree that Qur'anic precedent formed the basis for the later legal status of women regarding inheritance, marriage, and divorce. Yet it is the later medieval and modern interpretation of these same revelations that is currently an arena for scholarly and religio-political reinterpretation. For example, gender hierarchy and divinely ordained male dominance appear explicit in the Qur'an 4:34: "Men are in charge of women, because Allah made one of them to excel the other." It is in this same verse that men are encouraged to banish and scourge disobedient women. Yet the Muslim female scholar Amina Wadud-Muhsin interprets these verses quite differently and, through philological analysis, asserts a Qur'anic mutuality in male–female relationships aimed at marital accord. Scholars such as Wadud-Muhsin, however, struggle against a long premodern tradition in which such an analysis remains an anomaly. Indeed, only in the modern period have Muslim women begun to interpret the Qur'an, an exclusively male privilege in the premodern period.

In contrast to debates about gender hierarchy in the Qur'an are those revelations which Muslims and many other scholars believe improved the role of women from pre-Islamic standards. The Qur'an designated fixed shares of inheritance to women, including wives,

Students at a school for Muslim girls that offers religious and academic instruction in the Muslim Quarter of Jerusalem's Old City. (Annie Griffiths Belt/Corbis)

daughters, and sisters of the deceased (4:7, 11–12; 2:240). According to the internal evidence of the Qur'an, women could not inherit in Arabia but were themselves considered the property of their husband's surviving male kin (4:19). The Qur'anic system of allotments generally fixed the inheritance proportion at a two-to-one ratio that favored male offspring. The Qur'an also limited the previous Arabian practice of polygyny to four wives (4:3), further diminishing this limit to one in the event that a husband could not do justice to multiple wives. Even theoretically, such a male egalitarian approach to polygyny is deemed impossible in another verse of the Qur'an: "You will never be able to be fair and just between women, even if that were your ardent desire" (4:129). This Qur'anic verse has, with varying success, provided the modern basis for arguments about the establishment of monogamy in Islamic countries. In the premodern period, however, polygyny remained the social norm. It is the husband's exclusive right to initiate divorce proceedings against his wife. A woman's rights to kindness during the divorce process are substantiated in revelation, but her husband's superior social status and power are also reaffirmed (2:228).

Revelations concerning marital arrangements were presumed to regularize unlimited polygyny in Arabia, thus protecting Muslim women, but some scholars, such as Leila Ahmed, have suggested that more fluid pre-Islamic marriage patterns served to enhance female social status. Assertions that the status of Arab women was greater before the advent of Islam, though provocative, are difficult to prove definitively owing to the absence of contemporary written pre-Islamic texts.

Although some Qur'anic injunctions apply directly to all women, others were explicitly enjoined only for the twelve wives of the Prophet. Described as the Mothers of the Believers (33:6), the wives of the Prophet were set apart as "unlike any other women" (33:32). The wives of the Prophet provided the first female models for the Islamic community, and their behavior set precedents that continued to influence succeeding generations of Muslim women. Only the wives of the Prophet were enjoined to stay in their homes (33:33). They were told to speak to men outside the immediate family only from behind a *hijāb*, or curtain (33:53). In the Qur'an, both men and women are enjoined to "lower their gaze and be modest" (24:30–31), yet it is only women whose dress is the subject of comment. They are told to "cover their chests" with a *khimār*, or scarf (24:31) and also "to draw their cloaks around them" to avoid being "recognized" and "annoyed" (33:59). Nowhere in the Qur'an are all Muslim women told to cover their heads or faces explicitly. However, the notion of the *hijāb*, or veiling, and the confinement of women to their houses and away from the public sphere, first applied exclusively to the wives of the Prophet, would later be transformed in post-Qur'anic male interpretation as normative social behavior for all Muslim women.

Although all prophets are male, the Qur'an acknowledges the substantial role of women in their lives: "We have sent messengers before thee [Muhammad], and We appointed for them wives and offspring . . ." (13:38). Of the many women mentioned in the Qur'an, the only one explicitly named is Maryam, or Mary, the mother of the prophet Jesus. She is cited, along with the wife of the Pharaoh in the story of Moses (Āsiya in post-Qur'anic texts) as "an example for those who believe" (66:11). Maryam is lauded for her chastity and obedience (66:12) and described as "chosen," "made pure," and "preferred" by Allah "above all the women of the worlds" (3:42). Her importance in the post-Qur'anic construction of the Islamic feminine ideal affected Islamic historiography profoundly, for the biographies of the women closest to the Prophet, his wives and daughters, would be elaborated based on the precedent of the Qur'anic Maryam.

Other powerful images of women depicted in the Qur'an also resonated in Islamic society. The Queen of Sheba, through her involvement with the prophet Solomon, is portrayed in the Qur'an as a forceful, independent ruler (27:23), a model who might have set a positive political precedent for Muslim women if she had been governing in a monotheistic context (27:24). Issues of female sexuality are raised for all women through the precedent of the wife of 'Azīz, known in the Hebrew Bible as Potiphar's wife and in later Islamic tradition as Zulaykha. Zulaykha's attempted seduction of the prophet Joseph prompts him to de-nounce the *kayd*, meaning wiles or guile, of all women (12:28). Despite the Qur'anic application of this same term to Joseph's brothers (12:5), in post-Qur'anic exegesis, history, and literature to this day the wiles of all Muslim women remain synonymous with a feminine sexuality perceived as dangerous to Muslim men. Although these women and others may seem familiar to those versed in Jewish and Christian scripture, the Qur'an is understood by Muslims as a corrective to these previous (corrupted) monotheist texts.

HADITH

The Qur'an is regarded by Muslims as the literal word of Allah, but in the formation of communal identity and social practice, hadith, the written reports based on the Prophet Muhammad's human example, extended Qur'anic precedent and focused the teachings of Islam. Although the Qur'an would always maintain primacy as a source for religious, social, and political guidance, the preservation of hadith allowed all Muslims to follow the precedent of the Prophet in areas often not covered by revelation. Together, the Qur'an and hadith over a period of roughly two centuries became the basis for male scholars to create the Shari'a, the legal code that determined all aspects of Islamic life.

Hadith, sometimes referred to as traditions, were first recorded orally by women and men who had personally known the Prophet. It is not surprising that many of the Prophet's wives proved excellent points of origin for the transmission of this material. These reports, preserved over generations, passed into written form almost two centuries after the Prophet's death. They were recorded in two parts: the *isnād*, or support, which records the names of the individual transmitters; and the *matn*, the preserved information itself. By the tenth century, male scholars among the Sunni Muslim majority identified six main collections of hadith that would eventually be defined as canonical. Slightly later in the eleventh century, the Shia Muslim minority, relying on distinctly different chains of transmitters that excluded many Sunni authorities as untrustworthy owing to religio-political differences, compiled five separate hadith collections for their own reference.

Although women were active in the oral transmission of these traditions, no female Muslim ever compiled or edited a hadith collection. They remained the passive recipients of these extensive precedents on a wide variety of topics such as medicine, adultery, divorce, marriage, burial, definitions of religious knowledge, and asceticism. Throughout the premodern period, women continued to study hadith. Indeed, they were encouraged to memorize and collect traditions deemed important to their daily lives including *hayd* (menstruation), *ṭahāra* (ritual purity), requisite ablutions, prayer, alms, and fasting. Women might absorb normative knowledge through hadith, but because they were denied access to the exclusively male study of theology and law, they could not determine its practical application to their own lives. They remained the objects of male interpretation, devoid of agency in the formation of premodern religious precedent. Modern Muslim scholars such as Fatima Mernissi have only recently begun to analyze hadith as a male-defined sacred weapon. Such forays, although rare, signal anew the importance of the interpretation of both the Qur'an and hadith. Only in the modern era have Muslim female scholars, whether Islamist or feminist, along with other academics outside the Muslim community, attempted to enter this once exclusively male sphere of religious debate.

BIBLIOGRAPHY

Ahmed, Leila. "Women and the Advent of Islam." *Signs* 11 (1986): 665–691.

Goldman, Shalom. *The Wiles of Women/the Wiles of Men: Joseph and Potiphar's Wife in Ancient Near Eastern, Jewish, and Islamic Folklore.* 1995.

Lassner, Jacob. *Demonizing the Queen of Sheba: Boundaries in Gender and Culture in Postbiblical Judaism and Medieval Islam.* 1993.

Mernissi, Fatima. *The Veil and the Male Elite: A Feminist Interpretation of Women's Rights in Islam.* 1987.

Smith, Jane I. "Women, Religion, and Social Change in Early Islam." In *Women, Religion, and Social Change.* Edited by Yvonne Y. Haddad and Ellison B. Findly. 1985.

Smith, Jane I., and Yvonne Y. Haddad. "Eve: Islamic Image of Woman." In *Women's Studies International Forum* 5 (1982): 135–144.

———. "Women in the Afterlife: The Islamic View as Seen from the Qur'an and Traditions." *Journal of the American Academy of Religion* 43 (1975): 39–50.

Spectorsky, Susan, trans. *Chapters on Marriage and Divorce: Responses of Ibn Ḥanbal and Ibn Rāhwayh.* 1993.

Spellberg, D. A. "Writing the Unwritten Life of the Islamic Eve: Menstruation and the Demonization of Motherhood." *International Journal of Middle East Studies* 28 (1996): 305–524.

Stern, Gertrude. *Marriage in Early Islam.* 1939.

Stowasser, Barbara Freyer. *Women in the Qur'an, Traditions, and Interpretations.* 1994.

Wadud-Muhsin, Amina. *Qur'an and Woman.* 1992.

See also **Islamic Law; Maryam (Mary)**.

D. A. SPELLBERG

Rabi'a

Rabi'a, a Muslim Sufi woman, was born in A.H. 95 or 99 (713–714 or 717 C.E.), at Basra where she spent most of her life and where she was buried in A.H. 185 (801 C.E.). She is known as Rabi'a Basri on account of her birthplace, but also as Rabi'a Al-'Adawiyah or Al-Qaisiya because she belonged to Al-'Atik, a tribe of Qais b. 'Adi.

Rabi'a's image is shrouded in legends including stories of miracles brought about by her intense devotion to God. But as sketchy as the historical details of her life are, they point to an extraordinary personality. Probably a fourth (*rabi'a*) daughter, she was born into extreme poverty. Orphaned at a young age, she was sold into slavery for a paltry sum. She served her master by day but spent most of her nights fasting and praying to God. Once aware of her profound piety, her master released her from bondage.

Among Rabi'a's devotees who lived a celibate, highly austere life were spiritual and temporal leaders of her time. But though many sought her prayers or guidance, she solicited no help from anyone, including God, despite the fact that her life was filled with penury, hardship, and physical afflictions. Her prayers, including the following, reflect an all-consuming passion for God that makes even Heaven and Hell irrelevant: "O my Lord, if I worship Thee from fear of Hell, burn me in Hell, and if I worship Thee from hope of Paradise, exclude me thence, but if I worship Thee for Thine own sake then withhold not from me Thine Eternal Beauty."

Rabi'a, one of the earliest and most outstanding Sufi saints in an age of saints, whose name is used to refer to women who attain the highest spiritual station in any age, has been a source of inspiration to many mystics, including her biographer Farid ud-Din 'Attar who, in his famous poem (*The Conference of the Birds,* pays her the high compliment of being the "Crown of Men" (Taj ar-Rijal).

BIBLIOGRAPHY

The only full-scale biography of Rabi'a in English is Margaret Smith's *Rabi'a, the Mystic* A.D. *717–801 and Her Fellow Saints in Islam* (1928, repr. 1977). Most subsequent writing on Rabi'a in English have borrowed heavily from this book, which has an extensive bibliography of writings on Rabi'a in Western as well as non-Western languages.

Useful sources of biographical information are "Rabi'a Al-'Adwiya," in *Shorter Encyclopedia of Islam,* edited by H. A. R. Gibb and J. H. Kramers (1953); and Annemarie Schimmel, "Rabi'ah Al-'Adawiyah," in *The Encyclopedia of Religion,* edited by Mircea Eliade, vol. 12, 1987, pp. 193–194.

References to Rabi'a may be found in most books on Islamic mysticism or mysticism in world religions. Significant Muslim thinkers such as Al-Ghazali (in *Ihya' 'ulum ad-Din*) or 'Attar (in *Tadkirat al-Awliya*) have written about Rabi'a and her contribution to the history of mysticism in Islam. Rabi'a also figures prominently in biographical books about Muslim women, such as Javad Nurbakhsh, *Sufi Women* (1983), or *Middle Eastern Muslim Women Speak,* edited by Elizabeth Warnock Fernea and Basima Qattan Bezirgan (1977, repr. 1980).

Non-English sources include Al-Hashimi, Talib, "Hazrat Rab'ia Basri," in *Tarikh-e-Islam ki char sau bakamal khwateen,* Lahore, 1996, pp. 108–112, and Jeerajpurai, Aslam, "Hazrat Rab'ia," in *Namwar Musulman Khwateen,* Lahore, 1996, pp. 76–81.

RIFFAT HASSAN

Racism

Understood in its simplest terms, racism refers to the belief in the superiority of one race over another and as a result the right of the superior group to dominate. In the West, white Euro-Americans have typically thought of themselves as the superior race and thus have characterized all people of non-European descent as representatives of so-called inferior groups. The rationale for such beliefs has always been historically conditioned, reflecting prevailing religious, cultural, or scientific justifications for the subordination of the vast majority of the world's nonwhite populations. What has remained constant, however, is the assumption (now largely discounted by most reputable anthropologists) that the worth of human bodies can be quantified according to phenotype, genealogy, and ancestry. Such systems of quantification point to a presumed natural hierarchy of difference in morals, character, and intellectual ability between people.

Racist thought and action has always manifested itself on both a structural as well as individual level. Thus, more than being about the harboring of prejudicial feelings, or even about the complex interaction of various belief systems, racism is about the power of a dominating group to negatively affect the physical, mental, and spiritual well-being of those it has deemed to be in some sense subhuman. Countless well-documented examples exist of the impact dominating racist power has had over the lives of the so-called racially inferior. Most notably, the genocide of various native populations in the Americas and elsewhere, the enslavement and subsequent segregation of Africans in the United States, and the colonization of third world people by European and American countries are but a few of the most extreme cases. In every instance, it is the fullness of the humanity of people of color which has been and continues to be at issue, always with historically devastating political, social, and economic consequences.

Within the field of religion, the theoretical and methodological significance of racism as a concept is difficult to neatly render. This is true because, particularly within the Christian West, religion has functioned as both a justification for racist thinking as well as providing a basis from which to combat it. If one looks, for example, at the history of Eurocentric Biblical interpretation, people of color have either suffered from benign neglect at the hands of scholars (hence the downplaying of the simple fact that the scriptural authors and actors were in fact not white people), or else the sanctioning of racial oppression is thought to reside in the very texts themselves (hence the singling out the Pauline in-junction encouraging slaves to be obedient to their masters). At the same time, racially oppressed people, whose appropriation of scriptural images and themes has traditionally stood in opposition to the dominant opinion, have claimed that in actuality it is the scriptures' essentially liberationist message that has fostered the development of many of their resistance traditions. The reliance by black theologians on the Exodus narratives as well as the employment by other liberation theologians of the words of Jesus in the tradition of the prophet Isaiah that he had come to "proclaim release to the captives," are but two of several examples of the ways religion has functioned to combat racist thinking.

The contradictory nature of racism pertaining to the study of women in religion is no less fraught. For example, during the period of North American chattel slavery, white women of faith figured prominently in the abolitionist movement, even as many of those same women remained uncritical of the supremacist ethos of a society that at least afforded them the opportunity to indirectly benefit from white male privilege. More contemporarily, feminists of color have criticized white feminist scholars of religion for attempting to subsume racial issues under gender ones. Theologically, this tendency has been marked by the claim white women have made to be spiritually linked to vast communities of women through a mythical notion of shared oppression and therefore sisterhood. But where white women have frequently pressed for a universalizing of women's experience based on uncritically accepted white cultural norms, feminists of color have worked hard to put a particular face on women's racial oppression as well as on their resistance to it. Womanist scholars such as Delores Williams, Emilie Townes, and Katie Cannon have offered especially powerful insights in this regard, thereby undermining the totalizing ideology that breeds racist thinking in the first place.

A fuller treatment of the subject would, of course, yield far more examples. What even a cursory glance at this contradictory history does reveal, however, is that like the whole notion of race itself, racism cannot even begin to be adequately defined without reference to a wide cross section of experiences and histories. Insofar as this speaks to the situation of women in religion the task for feminists of all races is clear. Women must be committed to truthfully wading through this difficult history if indeed sisterhood might someday by touted as a realistic spiritual quest.

BIBLIOGRAPHY

Anzaldua, Gloria, ed. *All in Making Faith, Making Soul: Haciendo Caras, Creative and Critical Perspectives by Feminists of Color.* 1990. See Maria Lugones,

"Hablando cara a cara/Speaking Face to Face: An Exploration of Ethnocentric Racism"; Chela Sandoval, "Feminism and Racism: A Report on the 1981 National Women's Studies Association Conference"; and Gloria Yamato, "Something About the Subject Makes It Hard to Name."

Cannon, Katie G. *Black Womanist Ethics*. 1988.

Cassuto, Leonard. *The Inhuman Race*. 1996.

Giddings, Paula. *When and Where I Enter: The Impact of Black Women on Race and Sex in America*. Toronto, 1984.

Lorde, Audre. *Sister Outsider: Essays and Speeches*. 1984.

Mills, Charles W. *Blackness Visible: Essays on Philosophy and Race*. 1998.

Omi, Michael, and Howard Winant. *Racial Formation in the U.S. from the 1960's to the 1990's*. 2d ed., 1994.

Townes, Emilie M. *In a Blaze of Glory*. 1995.

Williams, Dolores. *Sisters in the Wilderness*. 1993.

Wing, Adrien Katherine, ed. *Critical Race Feminism: A Reader*. 1997. See especially Part 7.

LISA ANDERSON

Rādhā

Rādhā is best known in the West as the *gopī* (cowherd woman) especially beloved by the god Krishna, but to many Hindus she is also a goddess. Theologians of the Bengal or Caitanya Vaiṣṇava community have called her Krishna's *hlādinī shakti*, his blissful and bliss-giving energy, and one late mythological work, the *Bramavaivarta Purāṇa* (c. sixteenth century) has even deemed her Mother of the World. Her name is heard as the ubiquitous greeting among devotees at the most important Vaiṣṇava pilgrimage site, Vrindaban (Brindavan), in the Braj region of Uttar Pradesh. Her image is paired with Krishna's in temples and shrines throughout Braj and Bengal, and she is considered by many Vaiṣṇavas to be present with Krishna even when his image stands alone.

It is in poetry, painting, and performance, however, that Rādhā has been most prominent. Composers, artists, musicians, and dancers have depicted every phase of her love with Krishna, from the innocent yearning of its first dawning through the bliss and bewilderment of union, the hurt and jealous anger of betrayal, and the uncomprehending anguish of final separation. Their love is usually considered to be an illicit (*parakīyā*) rather than conjugal (*svakīyā*) union, free from the constraints and tedium of domestic duty. Although this interpretation has created serious difficul-

ties for some Vaiṣṇava theologians, it has rendered Rādhā's love a particularly apt image of the devotee's longing for an absent Lord.

Rādhā challenges conventional Western notions of what a goddess is. Simultaneously human and divine, she is esteemed and loved not because of any supernatural qualities, but rather because of the intensity of her fully human emotions. Yet, however human she may seem, her passionate, selfless devotion to Krishna is held up not as a model of earthly conduct but rather as the highest ideal of religious devotion. For many devotees, this intense, single-minded love in fact renders her superior to Krishna, the Lord of the universe, himself.

BIBLIOGRAPHY

The only sustained book-length treatment of Rādhā is still S. B. Dasgupta's *Śrīrādhār kramabikās darśane o sāhitye* (1952), a comprehensive, well-documented Bengali account of her origins, development, and relations with other goddesses. Certain of Dasgupta's conclusions are available to English readers in his *Obscure Religious Cults* (1969), esp. pp. 122–146. A major treatment of a broader theme, Friedhelm Hardy's *Virahabhakti: The Early History of Kṛṣṇa Devotion in South India* (1983), explores the figure of Rādhā in the context of the developing myths of Krishna and the *gopī*s. Hardy analyzes vernacular sources, beginning with the poems of the Tamil Āḷvārs, as well as the Sanskrit *Purāṇa*s, the writings of Kalidasa, and other works of classical poetry and drama. Barbara Stoler Miller, in an introductory chapter and in her masterful translation of the famous twelfth-century poem celebrating the love of Rādhā and Krishna, *Love Song of the Dark Lord:*

This picture shows the gopī Rādhā being persuaded to meet Krishna. The illustration is from the Sanskrit poem Gita Govi (Angelo Hornak/Corbis).

Jayadeva's Gītagovinda (1977), as well as in a ground-breaking article, "Rādhā: Consort of Kṛṣṇa's Vernal Passion," *Journal of the American Oriental Society* 95 (Oct.–Dec. 1975), has made a major contribution to our understanding of Rādhā's complex history and significance.

The Divine Consort: Rādhā and the Goddesses of India, edited by John S. Hawley and Donna M. Wulff (1982; repr. 1986), contains six essays on her depictions and interpretations in various texts and traditions, along with an extensive annotated bibliography. Donna M. Wulff's "Radha: Consort and Conqueror of Krishna," a revised and expanded version of her essay in that volume, is the sole piece on Rādhā in *Devī: Goddesses of India,* edited by John S. Hawley and Donna M. Wulff (1996), a collection of essays on a diversity of Hindu goddesses. Wulff's "Radha's Audacity in Kirtan Performances and Women's Status in Greater Bengal," on the theme of Rādhā's reproach of Krishna in the broader context of Bengali society, is found in *Women and Goddess Traditions,* edited by Karen L. King (1997). Finally, a growing corpus of work by Sumanta Banerjee considers Rādhā as a representative of two subaltern groups, the lower classes and women. His Marxist interpretation is set forth most clearly in a slim monograph, *Appropriation of a Folk-Heroine: Rādhā in Medieval Bengali Vaishnavite Culture* (1993).

For further references see the bibliographic essay appended to Wulff's article on Rādhā in *The Encyclopedia of Religion,* vol. 12, edited by Mircea Eliade (1987).

Films and CD-Roms include: "The Sword and the Flute," directed by James Ivory, produced by Radim Films, Chicago, Ill., 1959; and a "CD-Rom on the *Gītagovinda,*" produced by the Indira Gandhi Center for the Arts, New Delhi, India.

DONNA MARIE WULFF

Rape

From the point of view of a victim, rape (the forced penetration of the vagina, mouth, or anus by the penis or any other object) is an act of violence rising to the level of terrorism. Rape violates the victim's humanity, security, and sense of self. Given that women have most often been the victims of rape, and that they are often blamed and punished for it, rape is an important element in the control of women's activities and movements.

Women's experience of rape as violent attack belies the general tendency to view it as a primarily sexual event, perpetrated by someone whose sexuality is somehow "out of control." The publication in 1975 of Susan Brownmiller's groundbreaking work *Against Our Will: Men, Women, and Rape* challenged the traditional and widely held belief that rape centers on sexuality and argued powerfully that rape is an instrument of male power and domination. Although Brownmiller's claim that "all men benefit from rape all the time" has been debated, her work marked a sea change in the way rape is understood.

The understanding of rape based on the victim's experiences has arisen primarily in contexts in which victims have been able to come together, tell their stories, and articulate their experiences to a wider audience. But it is often the case that instead the victim is silenced because it is unacceptable, dangerous, or degrading for her to speak. This silencing is an extension of the initial violation and an important aspect of the general context of control of women.

Although religious traditions are unanimous in their condemnation of rape of their own clan members ("for such a thing ought not to be done" [Gen. 34:7]), religious laws and mores are often ambivalent about who should be blamed for rape, whether rape can occur within marriage, and whether it is acceptable to rape persons from other clans, tribes, or races. As a result, religious traditions have at times served to obfuscate the crime and perpetuate the victim's silence. For example, Numbers (31:17–18, 32–35) specifically condones the abduction and rape of virgin women from other tribes during warfare. Events in Bosnia, Algeria, Bangladesh, and the United States (for example, the widespread sexual exploitation of black women by white men during slavery and Reconstruction) testify to the ongoing use of rape as an instrument of war, racism, or "ethnic cleansing." The dehumanization and "sexualization" of the women of an oppressed group by members of a dominant group have allowed territory and status disputes to be played out on women's bodies.

The silencing of victims' experiences of rape has been accomplished in different ways across various religious traditions. In traditional Muslim practice, a woman who was raped might be killed or banished from her family and clan. Vanaja Dhruvarajan reports in *Hindu Women and the Power of Ideology* (1989) that Hindu women are afraid to bring dishonor on their *thavaru,* or household. If they do bring dishonor, they may be considered dead by their family.

Through the lives of such saints as Agnes (who was beheaded rather than sacrifice her virginity), Christian women were enjoined to defend themselves against rape even to the death. Augustine argued in *The City of God* that women who have been raped should not be encouraged to commit suicide; yet his argument is problematic because it maintains that rape is part of God's will, and that suffering is a discipline—either a punishment for sin or a test of faith. In addition, Augustine maintained that the victim remains virtuous if she did not find the sex pleasurable. This, too, is problematic, for, as Fortune comments, "orgasm is a physiological response to fear combined with direct sexual stimulation. . . . The victim is powerless to withhold even sexual response and feels betrayed by her or his own body" (1983, p. 8). As recently as 1950, Maria Goretti, a twelve-year-old Italian girl who was stabbed to death by a would-be rapist after being told to submit or die, was canonized by the Roman Catholic Church as a model of chastity and integrity.

Victims are also silenced when it is difficult or impossible to prove rape, as in the case of Muslim women, who must depend on the confession of the rapist or the testimony of "four morally upright Muslim men." Traditionally, if a Muslim woman became pregnant outside of marriage and was unable to prove rape, she could be charged with adultery and killed. In addition to these difficulties, the mores of a particular religious tradition may make it taboo to talk about rape.

The common denominator through history and across traditions, from the rape of Tamar (2 Sam. 13) to the abduction of Lucretia, is the absence of the voices of victims in the discussion of rape. Obscuring women's understanding of rape as an act of profound violation and terror is the foundation upon which religious understandings of rape have been built. For example, where religious laws have been put forward, these laws often deal with rape from the point of view of the father or husband of the victim, who are assumed to be the injured parties. In Deuteronomy 22:28 the rapist pays 50 shekels of silver to the victim's father. The rapist may be forced to marry the victim and is prohibited from divorcing her "because he violated her." In Assyrian law, under the *lex talionis,* the father of a raped virgin was permitted to violate the wife of the rapist.

Traditionally, Christianity has focused not only on women as male property but also on women's inherent evil tendencies. The misogynist tendencies of the tradition, which have been well documented, culminated in the *Malleus Mallificarum (The Hammer of Witches),* a book published in 1586 that became a basic text of the Inquisition. In *Sexual Violence: The Unmentionable Sin* (1983), Maria Fortune comments: "The text describes women as evil, subject to carnal lust, weak, impressionable, defective, impulsive, and liars by nature" (p. 61). This view justified the persecution of women and allowed victims to be blamed for rape.

In the Muslim tradition, women are viewed as the embodiment of the honor of their male kinsmen. In an example from the Afghan tribal clan system, Sima Wali reports in *Faith and Freedom: Women's Human Rights in the Muslim World* (1995) that rape is viewed "not so

Saint Agnes gave up her life rather than lose her virginity (Historical Picture Archive/Corbis).

much as violence against the woman, but as a direct challenge to the honor of the men of her clan" (p. 175). In day-to-day life Muslim women are typically protected from rape by the severity of the punishment for violating a woman and undermining the honor of her male kinsmen (the death of the perpetrator and many of his kinsmen is almost certain). However, during times of warfare and feuding, the violation of women who are without their usual male protection is widespread. Shahla Haeri, in another essay in *Faith and Freedom,* points to rape of women as a political act of humiliation and shame aimed not at a particular woman but at a political rival or enemy.

In *Beyond Purdah? Women in Bengal, 1890–1939* (1996), Dagmar Engels argues that, in the Hindu society of that period, "it was the loss of honour, rather than physical pain or psychic damage, which was considered to be the main aspect of rape" (p. 109). Rape within marriage, no matter how young the bride, was incomprehensible.

The profound emotional, physical, and psychological impact of rape on all women has historically not been a concern of organized religious communities. However, this situation has begun to change in the contemporary setting as women organize within their own traditions. Sara Mitter (1991) describes the efforts of women working in India "to tackle questions of rape, traffic in women . . . and all the myriad forms of oppression fostered by the family structure and codified in family law. . . ." Christian and Jewish women, too, have taken up the struggle to be heard.

BIBLIOGRAPHY

Adams, Carol J, and Marie Fortune, eds. *Violence Against Women and Children: A Christian Theological Sourcebook.* 1995.

Brown, Joanne Carlson, and Carole R. Bohn, eds. *Christianity, Patriarchy, and Abuse.* 1989.

Brownmiller, Susan. *Against Our Will: Men, Women, and Rape.* 1975.

Dhruvarajan, Vanaja. *Hindu Women and the Power of Ideology.* 1989.

Engels, Dagmar. *Beyond Purdah? Women in Bengal, 1890–1939.* 1996.

Fortune, Marie M. *Sexual Violence: The Unmentionable Sin.* 1983.

Haeri, Shahla. "The Politics of Dishonor: Rape and Power in Pakistan." In *Faith and Freedom: Women's Human Rights in the Muslim World.* Edited by Mahnaz Afkhami. 1995.

Jalal, Ayesha. "The Convenience of Subservience: Women and the State of Pakistan." In *Women, Islam, and the State.* Edited by Deniz Kandiyoti. 1991.

Mitter, Sara S. *Dharma's Daughters: Contemporary Indian Women and Hindu Culture.* 1991.

Plaskow, Judith. *Standing Again at Sinai: Judaism from a Feminist Perspective.* 1990.

Rozario, Santi. *Purity and Communal Boundaries.* 1992.

Wali, Sima. "Muslim Refugee, Returnee, and Displaced Women: Challenges and Dilemmas." In *Faith and Freedom: Women's Human Rights in the Muslim World.* Edited by Mahnaz Afkhami. 1995.

See also **Violence**.

ANNE MARIE HUNTER

Rationality

The pioneering work of anthropologists E. B. Tylor, Sir James George Frazer, and Lucien Levy-Bruhl focused the discussion of rationality on purported differences between "primitive" peoples and modern Westerners. Philosophers and theologians have also taken up the question, often using E. E. Evans-Pritchard's work among the African Azande as a touchstone. The evolutionary approach embraced by Tylor and Frazer has generally been abandoned, but several major issues remain contested. While some scholars insist on a single, universal form of rationality, others, often influenced by Ludwig Wittgenstein's thinking about "language games" and "forms of life," emphasize that rationality should be gauged by criteria specific to individual cultures. The unresolved debate between "unifiers" and "relativizers" has multiple consequences for the comparison of cultures and religions. Its implications for understanding women's religious experiences in diverse cultures, however, have not been carefully investigated by the major participants in the discussion.

Attempts to differentiate specific modes of reasoning and experience, such as Carol Gilligan's identification of a female "morality of responsibility" and a male "morality of rights" in the contemporary United States, and Sudhir Kakar's effort to identify a distinctively Indian, as opposed to Western, process of ego development, might fruitfully be brought to bear on the question of rationality. Such work suggests that the analytical strategies of those who recognize multiple rationalities may be better suited to the recovery, description, and interpretation of women's religious experience. Adoption of that perspective, however, also demands abandoning a single criterion of rationality.

The broader discussion of rationality should inform the analysis of instances when women are portrayed as being deficient in rationality, as they are by Thomas Aquinas, following Aristotle, or when women's religious actions are portrayed as irrational. The maenads, enthusiastic female devotees of Dionysus, for example, were described by Euripides as "stung in madness from their homes" and "dwell[ing] on the mountain stricken in their wits." But Euripides' dim view of the maenads' rationality was hardly dispassionate. By painting the worship of Dionysus as alien, irrational, and female, he was simultaneously defending a preferred ordering of society, religion, and gender. In such situations, however, the participation of women and other outsiders in ecstatic religion can alternatively be interpreted as offering them access to both temporary and long-term increases in power and prestige. For example, Haitian *manbos* (priestesses), for whom the apparently irrational possession by the *loa* (spirits) is the central religious experience, provide the healing wisdom that unifies their communities and are rewarded not simply with gratitude but also with social status.

Perhaps a thornier example is the practice of sati in India. Mary Daly (1990) has unequivocally condemned suttee as an example of patriarchal religion, which demands female sacrifices. Implicitly appealing to a single standard of rationality, she encourages feminists to overcome fears of criticizing another culture. Ashis Nandy (1994), however, setting the practice of sati squarely within the ongoing discussion of rationality, identifies a calculating, economic rationality in contemporary instances of sati. Daly's and Nandy's different interpretations of sati clearly show how theoretical orientations to rationality have important consequences. They suggest, moreover, that a sustained consideration of questions relating to rationality should be central to the analysis of women's religious experience.

BIBLIOGRAPHY

Daly, Mary. *Gynecology: The Metaphysics of Radical Feminism.* Rev. ed. 1990.

Gilligan, Carol. *In a Different Voice.* 1993.

Hawley, John Stratton, ed., *Sati: The Blessing and the Curse.* 1994.

Nandy, Ashis. "Sati As Profit Versus Sati As a Spectacle: The Public Debate on Ruop Kanwar's Death." In *Sati, the Blessing and the Curse: The Burning of Wives in India.* Edited by John Stratton Hawley. 1994.

Stein, Edward. *Without Good Reason: The Rationality Debate in Philosophy and Cognitive Science.* 1996.

Tambiah, Stanley Jeyaraja. *Magic, Science, Religion, and the Scope of Rationality.* 1990.

Wilson, Bryan R., ed. *Rationality.* 1970.

See also Irrationality; Philosophy of Religion; Possession.

EUGENE V. GALLAGHER

Religion

Religion is fundamental to human experience, history, and culture, but it is difficult to define. No single, universally valid definition applicable across all cultures can be given, although many have been attempted. Religion is studied across a wide range of disciplines, from history to sociology, anthropology, psychology, philosophy, theology, and religious studies. Each discipline has developed its own definitions, methods, and theories in its approach to religion; yet it is important to recognize that the category itself arose historically within the specific sociocultural context of the West: the conceptual structures and leading ideas of the modern study of religion have been derived from Christianity and Judaism, and Western philosophy and theology, which have been heavily text-oriented rather than experience-based. This makes it often problematic to apply current scholarly concepts and methods to the study of non-Western religions. The notion of religion is further rendered problematic because of the undue reification of religion in modern Western culture, where it has been largely understood in terms of objective religious beliefs and practices rather than as people's religiousness and faith. Furthermore, the understanding of religion has come under radical critique because of its embeddedness in a pervasive patriarchal and androcentric framework. For more than a hundred years, scholars have written about the essence and manifestation of religion (beginning with the German Protestant theologian Otto Pfleiderer, *Die Religion, ihr Wesen und ihre Geschichte,* 1869) while remaining almost completely gender-blind. Some late-twentieth-century definitions of religion are semantically thoroughly androcentric (as is evident from Winston King's entry on "Religion" in *The Encyclopedia of Religion,* 1987, vol. 12, where it is still only "man" who "is uncurably religious in one way or another").

The contemporary development of women's studies and feminist theory has raised so many new questions that the notion of religion has now become radically problematic. Women's research in religion is causing a paradigm shift and raising new issues at the level of definition, data-gathering, analysis, and explanation in the history and comparative study of religions.

Definitions of religion can be either exclusive or inclusive, substantive or functional. Substantive definitions relate to a specific content of religion and are therefore more exclusive. For example, many scholars define religion as the recognition of and response to a superhuman power, especially a personal God, together with the effect of this recognition on mental attitudes, beliefs, and conduct. Others connect religion with the positing of a sacred cosmos. A functional definition tends to be wider and more inclusive, since it focuses on what religion does or how it functions. The function of religion is often considered as giving meaning, direction, and value to human life, or to alleviate suffering; it can also be seen as leading to self-integration through self-transcendence. From the perspective of the humanities rather than the theological perspective of a particular faith, religion is a humanly constructed universe of meaning created through language, symbols, concepts, and rituals. Religion shapes personal and social experience and creates human solidarity and community. For some scholars, the understanding of religion is so inclusive that everything human is also religious, so that any human experience can potentially open a door to spiritual insight that profoundly transforms and transfigures ordinary, day-to-day life.

From the perspective of women, much of traditional religion needs to be deconstructed and radically reformed so as to overcome its exclusive, one-sided maleness and be genuinely inclusive of women's experience. Fundamental theoretical problems with religion arise for women on several counts. All historical religions are characterized by a profound dualism, which includes a hierarchized gender dualism between men and women and an asymmetry in social relations, power, authority, and representation. The leadership, institutions, and teachings of almost all religions have been almost exclusively shaped by men, so that the oppressive forces of patriarchy are more visible in religion than anywhere else. Dualism and androcentrism have also determined the construction of religious language and symbolism, especially in the understanding of transcendence versus immanence, of spirit as opposed to body, corporeality, and matter. Spiritualized notions of ultimate transcendence, especially in the male constructions of classical monotheism, include many features oppressive to women and their experience of embodiment.

Studying religion from a critical gender perspective opens up several clusters of new research orientations. If one looks at the external and internal aspects of religion systematically and comparatively from the perspective of women, overlapping areas of concern can be mapped out. First is the question of women's role and status in various religious traditions and institutions. Second is a group of questions concerning the participation or nonparticipation of women in shaping religious language and thought, the absence or presence of the experiences and voices of women, the images and symbols used for the representation of women by either men or women themselves. Third is a concern with women's own religious definition and agency, with the occurrence, nature, description, and shaping of women's religious experience, their spiritual authority and religious creativity. These three newly developed research trajectories are displacing some of the old paths in the study of religion, creating new theoretical insights and problems for further research, and reshaping religious beliefs and practices.

In *Feminism and Religion* (1996) Rita Gross has made an ardent plea for developing a more gender-balanced and gender-inclusive scholarship in the study of religion. This must include a description and analysis of the religious lives of ordinary women as well as the study of extraordinary women. Such scholarship shows how religions contain oppressive as well as liberating elements for women; how they can be compelling as well as disruptive of the social order by pulling women away from their traditional social activities into more unusual roles of nuns, spiritual leaders, mystics, shamans, and founders of new movements; and how they can empower women to develop strategies of resistance. Presenting feminism as both an academic method and a

social vision which aims at transforming the existing social order through abolishing patriarchy, Gross and other scholars raise the crucial question of how much of the religious past, even when reformed and reconstructed, is still usable for women and whether a post-patriarchal transformation of religions can be envisaged in the future. For this it will be important to move away from a Western-centered model of religion to a more inclusive one, drawing on wider comparative data within a global context.

BIBLIOGRAPHY

Annual Review of Women in World Religions. 1987–.

Buchanan, Constance H. "Women's Studies." In *The Encyclopedia of Religion*, vol. 15. 1987. Edited by Mircea Eliade. Pp. 433–440. Discusses the impact of women's studies on the study of religion.

Christ, Carol. "Feminist Studies in Religion and Literature: A Methodological Reflection." In *Journal of the American Academy of Religion* 2 (1976): 317–325.

Gross, Rita, ed. *Beyond Androcentrism: New Essays on Women and Religion.* 1977. A series of insightful, often-quoted essays that broke new ground in the reorientation of the study of religion.

———. *Feminism and Religion: An Introduction.* 1996. Chap. 1, "Defining Feminism, Religion, and the Study of Religion," and chap. 2, "Feminism's Impact on Religion and Religious Studies: A Brief History," set out in considerable detail how the study of religion is radically being changed through the inclusion of women and the integration of feminist perspectives.

———. "Methodological Remarks on the Study of Women in Religion: Review, Criticism and Redefinition." In *Women and Religion.* Edited by J. Plaskow and J. A. Romero. 1974. One of the earliest surveys on the decisive and profound impact of women's studies on the methodological orientation of religious studies.

———. "Women's Studies in Religion: The State of the Art." In *Traditions in Contact and Change: Selected Proceedings of the XIVth Congress of the International Association for the History of Religions.* Edited by P. Slater and D. Wiebe. 1983.

Journal of Feminist Studies in Religion. 1985–.

Joy, Morny, and Eva K. Neumaier-Dargyay, eds. *Gender, Genre and Religion: Feminist Reflections.* 1995. Shows how feminist discourse structures important themes for religious studies and how gendered perspectives can be fruitfully applied to a wide range of questions in and across religious traditions.

King, Ursula, ed. *Religion and Gender.* 1995. Theoretical reflections and empirical investigations provide evidence of the wide-ranging significance of feminist research in the study of religion.

See also **Feminisms**.

URSULA KING

Religious Experience

Feminist work in religion began with the assertion that "theology begins in experience." Extended to all thinking about religion, this insight means that experience is a source of religious knowledge and authority, and also that there is no objective point of view in either religion or scholarship. Excluded from the creating of tradition and authority, women understand that all traditions arise from experience. Ignored or dismissed in traditional histories of religion, women recognize that the history that has been told reflects particular and partial points of view. Women's insights are corroborated in philosophies (such as Marxism, hermeneutical theory, and deconstructionism) which assert that all thought is a product of the experiences, standpoints, and interests of its creators.

Religious experience is often viewed as a threat to tradition and authority. Members of religious groups are frequently told to follow tradition or obey authority no matter what their own experience or conscience tells them. Not surprisingly women saints, mystics, and visionaries often find themselves at odds with the gatekeepers of religious traditions. Religious authorities claim that tradition (scripture, law, custom, etc.) is "given by God" and thus is independent of experience. Feminist theory tells us that this view is a way of mystifying authority so that it cannot be challenged. Feminists (and others) assert that scripture, law, and custom (even if inspired by a divine power) are transmitted through the experiences of individuals and cultures.

In 1960 Valerie Saiving argued that women's religious experience must be considered in the study of religion. Because male experience has explicitly or implicitly been taken as the norm, the resulting theory is incomplete and distorted. At the insistence of women of color, it is now recognized that there is no one universal female experience: ethnicity, race, culture, sexual preference, history, and other variables shape the experience of women.

When women's religious experience is taken seriously, it is immediately recognized that women have been excluded from the sources of power and authority in all the major religious traditions of the world. Many early studies documented male bias in Christianity, Judaism, Islam, Confucianism, Hinduism, and Buddhism. While this work is important, it tells us little about women's religious experience. Though their roles may be restricted, women participate in various ways in each of these religions. Rita M. Gross proposed the model of "exclusion and participation" for studying women's religious lives. While often excluded from leadership positions, in most religions women have specific roles from which men are excluded. For example, in Judaism, women light the Sabbath candles and prepare the Sabbath meal. There also are many religious situations where women participate with men as part of the religious community; for example, the Catholic mass. All areas of exclusion and participation must be studied if we are to have a complete picture of women's religious experience.

Recognizing the exclusion of women within all of the so-called great religious traditions, many have asked if there are any religions in which women are free to express their religious experience without restriction. Paula Gunn Allen (1986) believes that women were not subordinate in Native American religion. Anthropologist Peggy Reeves Sanday (1981) concluded that in cultures and religions traditions organized around symbols of "female power," women are not subordinate, but neither are they dominant, because women mix freely with men and share their power with them. Anthropologist of religion Susan Starr Sered (1994) studied twelve religious groups created and led by women; in the religious contexts they shaped, women's experiences of motherhood and caring for children played primary roles in shaping women's religious understanding.

Location in a female body may cause women to be more aware of religious experiences associated with the body and nature. Some have called attention to the spiritual dimensions of childbirth; others have written about rituals associated with the onset of menstruation. Carol P. Christ (1980) found that women's mystical experiences seemed to be more physical or embodied than men's. Whereas theory defines mystical experience as union with a transcendent (nonphysical) power, women often describe mystical experiences in nature, in sexuality, and in community. Christ argued that rather than dismissing these experiences as "lower" or "lesser" forms of mysticism, we ought to expand our definition of mysticism. Many other ideas about the nature of religion will need to be altered when women's experience is taken into consideration.

The recognition that religious experience is a source of theory has led many feminist writers in religion to challenge the objective voice adopted by theologians and historians of religion. If there is no universal religious experience and no universal standpoint from which to analyze it, then it makes sense to develop new ways of thinking and writing about religion. Feminists are experimenting with genres that combine scholarship with personal experience. Christine Downing (1981) has integrated reflection on her own dreams of the goddesses with careful analysis of the symbol of the Goddess in myth and literature. While studying the life of a Haitian priestess of Vodou, Karen McCarthy Brown (1991) discarded the model of the anthropologist of religion as detached observer, writing about her own increasing involvement with Vodou. From the point of view of traditional notions of objectivity these scholars and others like them have "retreated into subjectivity." They say they are creating new models of embodied scholarship, rooted in experience.

BIBLIOGRAPHY

Since the recognition of the importance of women's religious experience is foundational in almost all research on women and religion, the following list is suggestive rather than inclusive.

Allen, Paula Gunn. *The Sacred Hoop: Recovering the Feminine in American Indian Traditions.* 1986.

Brown, Karen McCarthy. *Mama Lola: A Vodou Priestess in Brooklyn.* 1991.

Christ, Carol P. *Diving Deep and Surfacing: Women Writers on Spiritual Quest.* 1980, 1986, 1995.

Christ, Carol P., and Judith Plaskow, eds. *Womanspirit Rising: A Feminist Reader in Religion.* 1979, 1992.

Downing, Christine. *The Goddess: Mythological Images of the Feminine.* 1981.

Gross, Rita M. *Feminism and Religion: An Introduction.* 1996.

Gross, Rita M., and Nancy Auer Falk. *Unspoken Worlds: Women's Religious Lives.* 1980.

Plaskow, Judith, and Carol P. Christ, eds. *Weaving the Visions: New Patterns in Feminist Spirituality.* 1989.

Saiving, Valerie. "The Human Situation: A Feminine View." In *Womanspirit Rising: A Feminist Reader in Religion.* Edited by Carol P. Christ and Judith Plaskow. 1979, 1992.

Sanday, Peggy Reeves. *Female Power and Male Dominance: On the Origins of Sexual Inequality.* 1981.

Sered, Susan Starr. *Priestess, Mother, Sacred Sister: Religions Dominated by Women.* 1994.

CAROL P. CHRIST

Revelation

Revelation usually refers to the disclosure of truth by a divine source to an individual human being, often by means of an angelic or other subordinate heavenly intermediary. Thus, it essentially means communication from the divine to the human world. Various forms of such communication have been widespread in so-called primal societies of all eras and certainly not limited to either gender. With the appearance of writing and the growth of scriptural religions, such divine communications became more precisely defined. Messages for others beside the self came to be considered prophecy, which was carefully regulated by official religions, while personal revelations are covered by the modern rubric of mysticism. However, any distinction between public and personal revelations must have many shadings, for women have often been spiritual guides for others through their purely personal revelations.

In the ancient Near East, religion was mediated through large-scale, mainly male priesthoods in Egypt and Iraq. However, women continued to play an important role in Egypt, where the positions of High Priestess and God's Wife of Amun were highly esteemed and implied an intimate contact with the divine. In ancient Greece priestesses served as vehicles of ecstatic revelation at the various oracles, including the great Oracle of Apollo at Delphi, the most important of all the Greek religious institutions.

The ancient Judaic tradition shared a general acknowledgment that the divine spoke to women as well as men. In the Hebrew Bible, Miriam (Exod. 15:20), Deborah (Judg. 4:4), Huldah (2 Kings 22:14, 2 Chron. 34:22), and Noadiah (Neh. 6:14) are all spoken of as prophetesses; Eve also is spoken to by God (Gen. 3:13, 16). That this tradition did not die out early is shown by Anna, the daughter of Phanuel, who is mentioned as a Jewish prophetess (Luke 2:36–38). However, with the establishment of the rabbinical form of Judaism in the Talmudic period, prescriptive or normative revelations from God were definitely ended for both genders. Nevertheless, the possibility of a kind of individual revelation continued to be available through mysticism, in which women continued to seek direct personal contact with and inspiration from God despite discouragement by the official religion.

Meanwhile, Christianity somewhat kept the door of revelation open by emphasizing that prophecy has not been cut off, a claim for which Joel 2:28–29, already cited in Acts 2:17–18, is used as proof. These verses specifically mention the prophethood of women as well as men. The exaltation of the Virgin Mary as well as the prophesying daughters of the apostle Philip (Acts 21:8–9) added further authority to the concept of continuing revelation through women. On the other hand, a masculinized countertrend also existed, expressed in the prohibition against women speaking in church attributed to the apostle Paul (1 Cor. 14:34–36; 1 Tim. 2:11–14).

Still, although not commonplace, divine communications are attested for a large number of Christian women across the centuries. Outstanding premodern examples include Christina of Markyate (b.d. 1096–98), Hildegard of Bingen (1098–1179); Mechthild of Magdeburg (1210–1297), Birgitta of Sweden (1303–1373), Julian of Norwich (1343–1413), Catherine of Siena (1347–1380), Joan of Arc (1412–1431), Catherine of Genoa (1447–1510), and Maria Maddalena de' Pazzi (1566–1607). All of these women experienced ecstatic visions or direct divine revelations that were accompanied by prescriptive instructions, and most were involved in a mysticism that sought union with or annihilation in God through absolute, selfless love. In most cases their spirituality and writings were accommodated by the church. Later revelations include the visions of the Virgin at Lourdes by Bernadette Soubirous (1844–1879).

In Protestantism an effort was made to preempt such new revelations by limiting all divine communications to the Bible alone. Under these conditions women receiving divine revelations often founded new sects either outside of Christianity or marginal to it. Such women included Jane Lead (1624–1704), who organized the Philadelphian Society; Mother Ann Lee (1736–1784), founder of the Shakers; Mary Baker Eddy (1821–1910), who established Christian Science; and Ellen Gould White (1827–1915), who became the principal leader of the Seventh-Day Adventists. Each of these women regarded her revelations as divinely inspired, although White subordinated hers to the Bible. A significant number of women received divine revelations in the context of the Holiness movement, including Jarena Lee (b. 1783) and Phoebe Worrall Palmer (1807–1874), both Methodists, who quoted Joel 2:28 in justification of women prophesying.

In Islam several women in the Qur'an are spoken to by God: Abraham's wife, the mother of Moses, and the Virgin Mary. The famous Spanish Muslim scholar Ibn Ḥazm considered this proof that each had received divine revelation and thus deserved the title of prophet. To these, relying on an extra-Qur'anic tradition, he added the wife of the Pharaoh of Joseph. Eve, too, is addressed by God in the Qur'an. But Islam regards further prophecy and revelation as having ended with Muhammad in the seventh century C.E. Thus, as in Judaism, revelation has been cut off for both genders and is continued only in mystical inspirations (*futūḥāt*). Such personal revelations, though not regarded as prescriptive, clearly have some influence. One of the most famous women mystics in Islam was Rābi'ah al-'Adawiyyah (d. 801), who first established the doctrine of divine love.

Generally, for all the women mentioned, revelation meant an ecstatic direct contact with the divine that provided them with reassurance, guidance, and sanctity in an uncertain and often oppressive world. Claim-

An illustrated portrait of Bernadette Soubirous. She claimed to have had visions of the Virgin Mary at Lourdes, France (Harper's Weekly/Corbis).

ing exclusive right to religious interpretations, male-dominated official religious structures often responded by prohibiting or restricting such female spirituality, but they were unable to exclude it altogether and sometimes partially accommodated it.

BIBLIOGRAPHY

Crook, Margaret Brackenbury. *Women and Religion.* 1964. A pioneering and iconoclastic work with many references to divine revelations to women of the Judaic and Christian traditions found in ancient classical sources.

Herodotus. *The Histories.* Translated by A. de Selincourt. 1954. Rev. ed. by A. R. Burn. 1972. Impressive for its emphasis on the centrality of the oracle at Delphi and its female conduit of divine revelation, the Pythia. In this case, there is nothing like the original source.

Ibn Ḥazm, 'Alī. *Al-Faṣl fī al-Milal wa-al-Niḥal.* [1347]. 1928. This Arabic work contains a vitally important discussion of divine revelation to women prophets from a Muslim point of view. (See esp. vol. 5, pp. 12–14).

Matter, E. Ann, and John Coakley, eds. *Creative Women in Medieval and Early Modern Italy: A Religious and Artistic Renaissance.* 1994. Articles by Beonio-Brocchieri, Mooney, Scott, and Riccardi are especially relevant to the question of divine revelations to women.

Oden, Amy, ed. *In Her Words: Women's Writings in the History of Christian Thought.* 1994. An anthology of excerpts, often abridged, from women's writings, with brief introductions about each author. Shows that most claimed some kind of divine sanction, often that of revelation, for their works.

Ruether, Rosemary Radford, and Eleanor McLaughlin, eds. *Women of Spirit: Female Leadership in the Jewish and Christian Traditions.* 1979. Despite the title, this work is mainly focused on Christianity. The articles by Schüssler Fiorenza, McLaughlin, Smith, Zikmund, and Hardesty, Dayton, and Dayton are particularly informative about divine revelations to women in the Christian tradition.

Schimmel, Annemarie. *My Soul Is a Woman: The Feminine in Islam.* Translated by Susan H. Ray. 1997. Many stories about Muslim women in the Sufi tradition.

See also **Prophecy**.

KHALID YAHYA BLANKINSHIP

Riddle

A riddle is a concise expression that, like the proverb, predates the ancient sacred texts in which it often appears. The related terms *riddle* (from Old English *rædan*) and *enigma* (from Greek *ainigma*) are associated with interpreting words, implying that riddles were both a source of wisdom and a means of testing it.

In Greek mythology the women who spoke on Apollo's behalf at the Oracle of Delphi often posed their answers as enigmas; success or failure depended on one's ability to see more than one possible solution. The riddling contest between Oedipus and the Sphinx, a divine avenger sent by Hera to punish Thebes, was more than a battle of words, since the Sphinx destroyed all who could not identify what walked on four legs in the morning, two at midday, and three in the evening. We find echoes of this story in folktales in which a princess commands the execution of would-be suitors who fail to solve her riddles.

The Sphinx's challenge exemplifies the form and the content of many old traditional riddles as clever metaphors that suggest connections between seemingly unlike things, often related to the natural world. In this case the passage of time in a single day correlates to the ages of human life.

Often the metaphoric connection is based on wordplay, as in the query, what falls ever and breaks never? (Night.) Other riddles depend on imagery: the red deer on the hill you cannot kill (the sun); the silver maiden who walks at night (the moon).

It is possible that some nature-related riddles might have been part of initiation rites in which older women asked riddles that tested the knowledge of initiates. For example, one might be expected to know "old one in the fur coat" or "honey-eater" (bears), or "the maidens who change their dress each season" (trees).

Riddles have often been used in seasonal celebration and in rites of passage (birth, initiation, marriage, death). Young women in central Asia could challenge their prospective husbands to riddle contests and could castigate those who failed to answer correctly; Bantu women engaged in rain-bringing rites in southern Africa posed difficult riddles to any men who intruded on their ceremonies. The passage of seasons is such a powerful time of sacred riddling in many parts of the world that it has occasional faint echoes today, even in places where oral riddling is now rare. For example, an old English tradition of riddling during family Christmas festivities, where women played a more central role than in formal church ceremonies, may be related to riddling contests held during the Roman Saturnalia, a time of sacred licentiousness.

In oral societies that value verbal acuity, riddles are still used to educate children and to test adults, particularly in religious contexts. Riddles abound in sacred and secular texts around the world. The Biblical stories of Samson and Delilah and Solomon and the Queen of Sheba feature riddles as tests. Islamic, Buddhist, and Hindu writing (particularly the Upanishads) contain enigmatic passages that encourage mental acuity. The Zen koans in particular are now so widely known that "the sound of one hand clapping" has become a popular expression.

BIBLIOGRAPHY

There are a number of detailed studies of traditional oral riddles, mostly centered on contemporary secular uses. Good general definitions of *riddle* appear in two folklore reference works: Charles Potter's lengthy entry in *Funk and Wagnalls Standard Dictionary of Folklore, Mythology, and Legend* (1949, 1972) is methodologically outdated but offers valuable examples of riddles used in ceremonial contexts; Danielle Roemer's recent contribution to *American Folklore: An Encyclopedia* (1996) focuses on modern secular riddles. A classic work by Archer Taylor, *English Riddles from Oral Tradition* (1951), offers numerous examples and explanations of riddles. A challenging theoretical article, "Riddles," by Roger Abrahams and Alan Dundes, appears in the anthology *Folklore and Folklife* (1972), edited by Richard M. Dorson.

KAY F. STONE

Rites of Passage

Rites of passage are rituals that are meant to bring about a change in social or religious status at important points in a person's life. Arnold van Gennep, who coined the term (in French) in 1909, distinguished three phases of such rituals, in which the subject 1) is separated from the community, 2) remains temporarily in a liminal status, and 3) is reaggregated into the community in a new status. The process is often represented as a (death and) rebirth, or as a passage through a doorway (across a threshold—Latin *limen*). Victor Turner further developed this model in the 1960s.

Broadly speaking, such rituals cluster around birth, childhood, and adolescence, culminating in marriage. During this period of rapid growth and change, the rites are variously understood to protect, purify, and prepare the subject for a new role in society. The funeral, marking the passage from life into death, also figures as a rite of passage emphasizing the element of separation from the living and integration into some afterlife condition. Rites of passage serve to construct the emerging person religiously and socially. Natural, physical changes—birth, puberty, copulation, pregnancy, death—are not in themselves considered sufficient markers of personal development and social identity. Rituals effect transformations of status that are associated often only loosely with such physical facts.

The most common types of rites of passage for women relate to their sexual and reproductive roles. Prepuberty childhood rites, where practiced, tend to be identical to or adaptations of those for male children. Thus Brahmanical Hindu authorities prescribe the rites to be performed for girls in the same manner as for boys, but with the Vedic formulas omitted. Similarly, Reform Jews have developed a rite for girls called *berit ha-hayyim* (covenant of life) that parallels the covenant of circumcision performed for boys, but omitting the surgery.

Initiation, a class of rites marking the onset of adulthood or religious responsibility, may or may not be performed for girls depending on the central purpose envisioned. In traditions in which it commences a period of religious study, apprenticeship, or full participation in religious practice, women are often excluded. For instance, classical Hindu doctrine regards marriage as

the girl's initiation, with the groom taking the paternalistic role of the religious teacher, and domestic duties of the bride equated to the devoted and obedient service a male initiate renders to his teacher. Some Jews, again, nowadays perform a bat mitzvah rite to confirm a girl as a "daughter of the commandment" on the analogy of the traditional bar mitzvah for boys.

On the other hand, where the initiation is more specifically correlated to sexual maturity, indicating full membership in a peer or sex group and eligibility for marriage, rites for girls are likely to be regular and important. Several African societies have special initiations for girls that involve genital mutilation (e.g., excision of the clitoris, intended to suppress sexuality), or other forms of bodily marking (tatoos, scarification) as a mark of maturity and preparation for marriage. Turner's study (1969) of Ndembu girls' initiation (in Zambia)

A Dorze girl has her hair arranged before a coming-of-age ceremony. The ceremony entails applying butter, a rare and precious commodity in the tribe, to the girl's head as a symbol of her femininity and sexuality (Jim Sugar Photography/Corbis).

stresses the new woman's place in the matriliny as future mother.

Marriage figures prominently in all traditions as creating a union of a woman and a man as a basic social unit. Specific social and religious roles often become incumbent on a woman (or man) only at marriage, and it is generally regarded as the prerequisite to parenthood.

In recent decades, some have sought to adapt traditional rites of passage to a modern, largely secular context, arguing for their value in psychological development and social cohesion. At the same time, the new rites for women are meant to express a more positive view of women's bodies and to inculcate a greater sense of self-worth and self-determination than traditional rites (as part of male-oriented theologies) have been seen to do. Often such new rites explicitly embody a feminist theology.

BIBLIOGRAPHY

Fried, Martha N., and Morton M. Fried. *Transitions: Four Rituals in Eight Cultures.* 1980.

Gennep, Arnold van. *Les rites de passage.* Paris, 1909. Translated by Monika B. Vizedom and Gabrielle L. Caffee as *The Rites of Passage.* 1960.

Gluckman, Max. "Les Rites de Passage." In *Essays on the Ritual of Social Relations.* Edited by Max Gluckman. 1962. Pp. 1–52.

Golding, W. *Rites of Passage.* 1980.

Holm, Jean, with John Bowker, eds. *Rites of Passage.* 1994.

Lincoln, Bruce. *Emerging from the Chrysalis: Studies in Rituals of Women's Initiation.* 1981.

Mahdi, Louise Carus, Steven Foster, and Meredith Little, eds. *Betwixt and Between: Patterns of Masculine and Feminine Initiation.* 1987.

Mead, Margaret. *Coming of Age in Samoa.* 1928.

Turner, Victor. *The Ritual Process: Structure and Anti-Structure.* 1969.

Walker, Barbara G. *Women's Rituals: A Sourcebook.* 1990.

See also **Birth and Rebirth; Death; Mutilation, Genital; Initiation; Marriage and Singleness; Menarche; Menstruation.**

TIMOTHY LUBIN

Ritual

Rituals are repeated ceremonial acts, usually performed by a group, that invoke or celebrate the divine or core cultural values. A ritual may include objects and actions symbolizing participants' beliefs and attitudes. Women's participation in or exclusion from male rituals reflects the construction of female gender roles and women's role as social actors. When women are incorporated in ritual, it is often as symbolic figures, and such symbolization shapes societal ideas about women. Women may have their own rituals and thus be able to develop symbolic behavior more in keeping with their own worldviews and existential conditions, although still not entirely independent from male viewpoints. Ritual is dynamic: it can be affected by social change and undergo innovations in practice and meaning. Thus, ritual gender roles and boundaries evolve over time.

When humans were hunters and foragers, spirituality was not compartmentalized from the rest of human life, and religious practitioners were not singled out as specialists. No formal barriers existed against women's participation in spiritual life or ritual leadership. Some ten to fifteen thousand years ago, human life became compartmentalized, with division of labor and the separation into spheres of spiritual and earthly concerns. From this point forward, men were more likely to be the leaders of formally organized public rituals. Such rituals thus represent male concerns and life-styles and male-dominant theologies and symbolic systems. Women's ritual lives are often limited to audience and support roles for male rituals or sex-segregated, often home-based rituals.

Rituals are set aside in time and space but draw upon the resources of quotidian life; it is often women who provide this foundation. Although their contributions have not always been recognized, women have been instrumental in male-dominated ritual life. They work behind the scenes preparing and administering. In Christian traditions women manage music, flowers and decorations, hospitality, food and drink, teaching and socializing children, and cleaning religious spaces. Whether as nuns, laywomen, or the wives of clergymen, women play significant supportive roles, handling the practical, emotional, and connective aspects of ritual work necessary to provide public ritual platforms for male ritual specialists. Women's support enables male specialists to study and perform public ritual activities.

Ritual cannot arise from a vacuum: women maintain social networks and inculcate religious and cultural attitudes from which ritual may periodically flower. This is true of both Jewish tradition—with the pious wife running the household to free her husband for Torah study—and Islamic tradition. Patricia Jeffrey (1989), writing of women in India, describes how the shrine-keepers' womenfolk, although invisible to pilgrims, prepare food and drapes for the shrine, house and feed visiting devotees, and, of course, bear the sons who will one day become shrine-keepers.

In Christian traditions, Mary is a prime example of how ritual gender symbolism dramatically conveys beliefs and expectations about women. For Mexican-American women, Our Lady of Guadalupe embodies compassion, self-sacrifice, and nurturing. She is seen as the ideal human being—life-giving and affiliating. Mexican-American women identify with Our Lady's decision to mother humanity and gain strength for their overwhelming tasks from her endurance. In Oglala Lakota (Sioux) tradition, the mythical White Buffalo Calf Woman, demanding respect for her virginity, presented the symbolic pipe as well as buffalo to her starving people, thereby giving them life. Hindu Indian women who perform rituals for the longevity of their husbands epitomize the ideal wife, both chaste and self-sacrificing.

Women's rituals may commemorate biological or social changes, such as engagement, pregnancy, birth, initiation, scarification, menarche, clitoridectomy, or mourning. They may involve healing, seeking assistance for themselves or family members, or gaining connection with holy figures or spiritual power through home-based ceremonies or shrine visitation. Women may gather to narrate tales of suffering, maintain connections, and celebrate through feasting. Some women's rituals are segregated parallels of public male calendrical rituals.

Settings for women's rituals are generally more informal than those for men. Often they are in homes or shrines. When they take place in public buildings, the presence of children and different approaches to religious gatherings often make them noisier and less orderly. Women's rituals encourage people to interrupt, discuss ritual order or content, and switch back and forth from worship to conversational mode. Women's rituals are less hierarchical, less rigid in format and content, and more emotionally expressive, with women taking turns as leader and some or all of those present actively participating. Arrangement of worshipers is less structured, stiff, and stationary. Often, ritual worship includes a personalized relationship with the divine. As women's rituals are often in a home setting where hospitality is offered to guests, food and drink are commonly included. Informal verbal exchange and socializing are important components of women's rituals, as neighbors, friends, and relatives catch up on news, talk about problems, and commiserate about personal sorrows and family difficulties.

With modernization, higher levels of female education, and more women working outside of the home, women have been chipping away at ritual gender boundaries. Such boundaries seem particularly shaky in the United States at the end of the twentieth century.

Two women help adjust a costume for a first birth ceremony in Belau, Caroline Islands (Richard A. Cooke/ Corbis).

With less gender division of labor, men sometimes help prepare for and participate in home-based celebrations, such as those marking marriage and birth. With secularization in industrialized societies, male-dominated public religious rituals are declining, leaving the female-run home celebrations as the main holiday festivities. The women's movement, together with the small numbers of men going into the Christian priesthood and clergy, has led to more women becoming ritual specialists as ministers and filling priestly roles in the Catholic Church. Women in many religious traditions are rethinking the portrayal of women in ritual and religious texts. In Islamic societies, increasing numbers of women are coming to mosques and study groups. Some are questioning traditional male exegesis of the Qur'an as to women's place in Islam. Perhaps ironically, emerging fundamentalisms have presented new opportunities for women's ritual involvement as ritual specialists, especially in sex-segregated societies, and for ritual activism appreciated by men and women alike who are interested in seeing the flourishing of their movements.

BIBLIOGRAPHY

Allen, Paula Gunn. *Recovering the Feminine in American Indian Traditions.* 1992.

Balzer, Marjorie Mandelstam. "Ritual of Gender Identity: Markers of Siberian Khanty Ethnicity, Status, and Belief." *American Anthropologist* 83, no. 4 (1981):850–867.

Bell, Catherine. *Ritual: Perspectives and Dimensions.* 1997.

Betteridge, Anne H. "The Controversial Vows of Urban Muslim Women in Iran." In *Unspoken Worlds: Women's Religious Lives.* Edited by Nancy Auer Falk and Rita M. Gross. 1989.

Brink, Judy, and Joan Mencher, eds. *Mixed Blessings: Gender and Religious Fundamentalism Cross Culturally.* 1997.

Buitelaar, Marjo. *Fasting and Feasting in Morocco: Women's Participation in Ramadan.* 1993.

Cattell, Maria. "Praise the Lord and Say No to Men: Older Women Empowering Themselves in Samia, Kenya." *Journal of Cross-Cultural Gerontology* 7, no. 4 (1992): 307–330.

Crain, Mary M. "Poetics and Politics in the Ecuadorean Andes: Women's Narratives of Death and Devil Possession." In *The Other Fifty Percent: Multicultural Perspectives on Gender Relations.* Edited by Mari Womack and Judith Marti. 1993.

de Leonardo, Micaela. "The Female World of Cards and Holidays: Women, Families, and the Work of Kinship." *Signs: Journal of Women in Culture and Society* 12, no. 3 (1987):440–453.

Edwards, Walter. *Modern Japan Though Its Weddings: Gender, Person, and Society in Ritual Portrayal.* 1989.

Falk, Nancy A., and Rita M. Gross. *Unspoken Worlds: Women's Religious Lives in Non-Western Cultures.* 1989.

Fruzzetti, Lina M. *The Gift of a Virgin: Women, Marriage, and Ritual in a Bengali Society.* 1982.

Hegland, Mary Elaine. "Flagellation and Fundamentalism: (Trans)forming Meaning, Identity, and Gender through Pakistani Women's Rituals of Mourning." *American Ethnologist.* Forthcoming.

Holland, Dorothy. "Contested Ritual, Contested Femininities: (Re)forming Self and Society in a Nepali Women's Festival. *American Ethnologist* 22, no. 2 (1995):279–306.

Jeffrey, Patricia. *Frogs in a Well: Indian Women in Purdah.* 1989.

Kendall, Laurel. *Shamans, Housewives, and Other Restless Spirits: Women in Korean Ritual Life.* 1985.

Lawless, Elaine J. *Handmaidens of the Lord: Pentecostal Women Preachers and Traditional Religion.* 1988.

Leslie, Julia, ed. *Roles and Rituals for Hindu Women.* 1991.

Myerhoff, Barbara. *Number Our Days.* 1980.

Narayan, Kirin. "First Sour, Then Sweet: Women's Ritual Story Telling in the Himalayan Foothills." *Women and Language* 19, no. 1 (1996):9–14.

Pearson, Anne Mackenzie. *Because It Gives Me Peace of Mind: Ritual Fasts in the Religious Lives of Hindu Women.* 1996.

Powers, Marla N. *Oglala Women: Myth, Ritual, and Reality.* 1986.

Rodriguez, Jeanette. *Our Lady of Guadalupe: Faith and Empowerment among Mexican-American Women.* 1994.

Tapper, Nancy. "Gender and Religion in a Turkish Town: A Comparison of Two Types of Formal Women's Gatherings." In *Women's Religious Experience.* Edited by P. Holden. 1983.

Wallace, Ruth A. *They Call Her Pastor: A New Role for Catholic Women.* 1992.

Wessinger, Catherine, ed. *Religious Institutions and Women's Leadership: New Roles Inside the Mainstream.* 1996.

MARY ELAINE HEGLAND

Ritual Studies

Ritual studies is a relatively new addition to the range of academic disciplines that fall within the field of religion. The study of ritual has long been established by practitioners of ritual themselves ("indigenous" or "insider" reflection), and more recently by "outside observers" during nineteenth- and early-twentieth-century ethnographic investigations of preindustrial societies. Academics in the fields of anthropology and sociology were quick to establish theoretical methods to assess and interpret the ritual practices that were being recorded from various cultural traditions.

The most significant theory to emerge during this early period of investigation comes from Émile Durkheim (*The Elementary Forms of Religious Life* [1915], 1965), who understood ritual as a symbolic enactment of existing social structures and a means to maintain and buttress the social order of the respective culture; in this functionalist account the "purpose" of ritual is to facilitate social integration and group cohesion. Durkheim also established the beginnings of a binary logic, which separated such spheres as "the sacred" and "the profane" in the study of ritual. Continuing Durkheim's work, A. R. Radcliffe-Brown, Bronislaw Malinowski, and other structural functionalists further theorized the importance of ritual for maintaining social organization.

A competing view (formalist view) was proposed by Arnold van Gennep (*The Rites of Passage* [1909], 1960), who fashioned his study of ritual after a cross-cultural investigation of the "initiation rite." Van Gennep coined the term "rites of passage" to denote those formal practices that mark the movement from one period of life to another and, in the process, confer new social status on an individual. He sketched a threefold configuration of rites of passage: separation (removal from original identity and social position), transition (an ambiguous "liminal" state that affords transformation), and incorporation (the beginnings of a new identity in the social group).

The 1960s and 1970s saw a revitalization of the study of ritual with the work of Victor Turner (*Forest of Symbols*, 1967; *The Ritual Process*, 1969). Building on van Gennep, Turner questions Durkeim's analysis of ritual as a practice that reinforces cultural roles, and structures. Instead, Turner explores ritual as a potential creative and transformative practice on many levels (individual, group, social structural), presenting a more dynamic and processual view of ritual than Durkheim's stagnant paradigm previously afforded. Turner further critiques Durkheim by developing van Gennep's notion of liminality to address the ways in which ritual activities transgress standard social regulations and transcend hierarchically informed social organization, and thus celebrate an egalitarian bond between individuals in a community. Turner's model sparked a new era in the study of ritual, opening the field to radically new readings and interpretations of ritual performance.

Ritual studies as an independent field emerged in the 1970s, marked by an interdisciplinary proliferation of studies from departments in the social sciences and humanities, and the founding of the first *Journal of Ritual Studies* (by Ronald L. Grimes). Although this renewed vigor in the study of ritual is typically attributed to the influence of Turner—whose impact cannot be overestimated—it is not likely incidental that during this same period there was an increased participation by women in the field; and new hermeneutical models, such as feminist criticism, equally opened the discipline to fresh challenges and perspectives.

Women's participation in ritual studies has transformed the field significantly. The most evident contribution from women scholars has been a rapid increase in the study of women's ritual practice. Previously, there was a dearth of information in the area of women and ritual, with two possible explanations: 1) male observers, because of their gender, were excluded from knowledge of female ritual by the practitioners; and 2) women's rituals were deemed peripheral and unimportant to the social order of the culture. Recent investigations in ritual criticism have demonstrated that previous theoretical paradigms for examining ritual, including Turner's, have been based on a male model that functions to exclude women's ritual practice as necessarily marginal or nonexistent (see Bynum, Laird, Lutkehaus, and D. Bell). Women's rituals, which are frequently on a smaller and less elaborate scale than men's practices and celebrate the passage of individual women rather than large social groups, often do not meet the established analytical criterion for "ritual," and, as such, have been excluded from literature. Further, cultural biases by early anthropologists (most often from patriarchal Europe or North America) assumed that male contributions in all cultural traditions are fundamental to social and religious organization, whereas women's roles concerned the less important, domestic sphere. Thus, when women's rites were examined at all they were considered in relation to male rituals, and the logic by which they operate was left unacknowledged and unexamined.

The contribution of feminist hermeneutical methodologies has further augmented the range of what qualifies as ritual by rejecting the rigid binary classifications that structured previous ritual criticism—such as sacred–profane, mind–body, culture–nature, social–domestic, active–passive, male–female—which implicitly value one term (male, sacred) at the expense of the other (female, domestic). Feminist analysis too has demonstrated that ritual not only functions to maintain an existing social structure (Durkheim), it can also actively conceal the social hierarchy and power relations that configure any society—thus, in the case of women, veiling the very structures that enforce their subordination. Ritual is also now being examined as a site for the social construction and perpetuation of gender and gender relations, sometimes celebrating women's power, while at other times reinforcing their subordinate role.

Women have brought to ritual studies self-reflexive questions that challenge the discipline from within. Diane Bell (1993) asks the following of ethnography and ritual studies: "What do we do? How do we do it? Should we do it? Who should do it? Why do we do it? What does it mean to do it?" (p. 273). In addressing such demanding questions, ritologists can no longer claim an objective stance but must acknowledge their own implicit value-laden perspective. Such questions have also prompted ritologists to look closer to home. Ritual is no longer considered simply to be discovered "out there," a practice of "the other," "primitive" cultures; rather, ritual criticism can be equally employed to examine the observer's own tradition (see Davis-Floyd). Similarly, "participation in" and "study of" ritual, previously two distinct categories (practice and observation) have merged, as ritologists begin more often to contribute through active participation in the very rites that they profess to examine, producing an important new space ("insider-outsider") from which to conduct their analysis (Grimes, 1996).

While these recent advancements in ritual studies have not been put forth solely by women and feminist scholars of ritual, they have nevertheless fueled the intense reconstruction of the field.

BIBLIOGRAPHY

The bibliography for women and ritual studies while sparse only twenty years ago has since the mid-1980s begun to flourish. It could be divided into two categories—theory and practice—yet more often these two elements are entwined in the same source. Caroline Walker Bynum, "Women's Stories, Women's Symbols," in *Anthropology and the Study of Religion*, edited by Robert L. Moore and Frank E. Reynolds (1984), compares the religious narratives and symbols of medieval European men and women and also offers a cogent critique of Victor Turner's theory of liminality. Such works as Diane Bell, *Daughters of the Dreaming* (1983; rev. ed. 1993), an account of her experiences with aboriginal women in Australia, and M. E. Combs-Schilling, *Sacred Performances: Islam, Sexuality, and Sacrifice* (1989), an examination of Islamic ritual and its relation to the Moroccan monarchy, offer new ethnographic material and analysis; their work also contributes greatly to the theoretical foundations of ritual studies itself, enriching, critiquing, or rejecting existing paradigms in order to accommodate the ritual and lived experiences of women.

An early contribution to women and ritual studies, Mary Douglas, *Purity and Danger* (1966), is instrumental in demonstrating that ritual practice constructs and enforces epistemic categories and situates women at the site of ambiguous signification (the source of power and danger). New contributions to the field of women and ritual studies include investigations of previously overlooked ritual practice, such as childbirth and menstruation, and studies have emerged in which ritologists examine ritual productions from within their own cultures. Robbie Davis-Floyd's groundbreaking *Birth as an American Rite of Passage* (1992) demonstrates that uniform hospital medical procedures for childbirth constitute a rite of passage that both institutes and sustains the technocratic value system of American culture. Her edited volume, with Joseph Dumit, *Cyborg Babies: From Techno-Sex to Techno-Tots* (1998), also offers essays that examine the rituals of childbirth in a Western technological society. Thérèse Blanchet, *Meanings and Rituals of Birth in Rural Bangladesh: Women, Pollution, and Marginality* (1984), provides an analysis of the cultural values of rural Bangladesh society as they are manifested in birthing rituals. Karen Ericksen Paige and Jeffery M. Paige, *The Politics of Reproductive Ritual* (1981), a cross-cultural study of women's ritual experiences, investigates menarcheal rites, birthing rituals, and the practice of sex segregation. Important studies of midwifery such as Lois Paul, "Careers of Midwives in a Mayan Community," and Molly C. Dougherty, "Southern Lay Midwives as Ritual Specialists," along with other women's ritual practices, can be found in *Women in Ritual and Symbolic Roles*, edited by Judith Hoch-Smith and Anita Spring (1978). Claire R. Farrer examines girls' puberty rituals of the Mescalero Apaches in *Thunder Rides a Black Horse: Mescalero Apaches and the Mythic Present* (1994) and *Living Life's Circle: Mescalero Apache Cosmovision* (1991). Nancy C. Lutkehaus and Paul B. Roscoe, eds., *Gender Rituals: Female Initiation in Melanesia*, shows that female initiation rituals have been largely overlooked or treated as a footnote in studies on male initiation, and questions the assumption that women's ritual practices are rare and less important for social organization than their male equivalents. Joan Laird, *Rituals in Families and Family Therapy* (1988), employs a feminist use of ritual in a therapeutic setting.

An important but dense and difficult theoretical text that continues to inform ritual criticism is Catherine Bell, *Ritual Theory, Ritual Practice* (1992). Barbara Myerhoff, *Remembered Lives* (1992), blurs the polar oppositional logic of the "sacred" and "profane" ritual domains in her investigation of aging, death, and dying. Ronald L. Grimes, ed., *Readings in Ritual Studies* (1996), an anthology of the most important theoretical writing and practical applications in the field, offers a comprehensive compilation of essays on "Women in Ritual." Finally, a comprehensive analysis of women's ritual in traditional and alternative religious communities in North American can be found in Lesley A. Northrup's *Ritualizing Women* (1997).

See also: **Domestic Rites; Menarche; Menstruation; Mourning and Death Rites; Rites of Passage; and articles on religious rites and practices for Buddhism, Christianity, East Asian Religions, Hinduism, Islam, and Judaism.**

KATHLEEN O'GRADY

Roman Catholicism

Roman Catholicism as defined at the Council of Trent (1545–1563) onward is Catholicism as a world religion, spread throughout the world among diverse cultures on every continent. Discovery, conquest, and colonialism imported Christianity—often violently—to the Americas, sub-Saharan Africa, Asia, the Pacific Islands, and Australia. When the conquerors were Catholic, so too was the brand of Christianity, which often combined with indigenous religion even as it tried to suppress it (as, for instance, in Mexico, Cuba, and Brazil). Today the center of gravity of the more than 900 million-member Roman Catholic Church has shifted to the Southern Hemisphere. Catholic women are Filipina, Brazilian, Peruvian, Mexican, Nigerian, South African, and Australian as well as Polish, Irish, and American. The majority of Catholic women, men, and children today are poor and living in former colonies; much of the vitality of the church today comes from these people and regions.

It has often been easier to identify and study the lives of women religious (sisters or nuns) than those of the majority of Catholic women, who are not members of vowed religious communities and thus do not benefit from institutional records and archives. Both, however, merit attention. In studying the history and contemporary lives of Roman Catholic women, it is important to distinguish between statements about these women and statements by them. In the late twentieth century, scholarship has focused increasingly on the worldviews, theologies, daily concerns, and self-understanding of Catholic women through ethnographies, historical studies, or works by Catholic women themselves. The Roman Catholic Church is centralized and hierarchical, but it is also a complex, international, multicultural reality with strong life and leadership at the grass roots, and it has never been a monolith.

HISTORICAL GUIDEPOSTS AND TURNING POINTS

The Reformation brought forth a paradoxical situation for women in the Christian West: on the one hand, it broadened the understanding of Christian vocation, made the Biblical texts available in the vernacular, and began opening education to women outside the confines of vowed religious communities. On the other hand, it took away from women what had been—and continued to be for Catholic women—the option of a celibate life lived in the community, which offered an enclave for women to develop a life of the mind, avoid death in childbirth, and bypass subjection to husbands and fathers. Catholicism retained, even privileged, a celibate life of prayer or service in addition to married life for women: the church circumscribed women's lives, but more than one option was available to women for holiness. Persecution of women, however, did not know confessional boundaries: both Catholic and Protestant church authorities perpetuated the witch-hunts begun in Europe in the fourteenth century, which continued till the eighteenth century and disproportionally affected women.

The sixteenth century was a time of vigorous reform in Western Christianity. Chief among women leaders of the Catholic reformation were Teresa of Avila (1515–1582), the Spanish reformer of the Carmelite order and mystic, and Catherine of Siena (1347–1380), mystic, church diplomat, and caretaker of the poor. Rose of Lima (1586–1617), the first canonized saint of the Americas, now patron of both South America and the Philippines, followed a more traditional path than Teresa as a near-recluse, embracing a spirituality of mortification, caring for the poor, and nursing the sick in her home. Catholic women, especially nuns, continued to take on both prayer and care for the needy of society as their path to holiness.

After the founding of the Company of Jesus or Jesuits, who took their first vows in 1534, various groups of women attempted to form counterparts, among them the Company of St. Ursula (Ursulines) founded in 1525 by Angela Merici (1474–1540) in what is now Northern Italy; it received approval for its rule, the first written for women by a woman, in 1534. The Council of Trent imposed enclosure on all nuns. The Daughters of Charity, formed by Vincent de Paul (1580–1660) and Louise de Marillac (1591–1660), managed to remain free from interference from the bishops by avoiding being classified as nuns. Devoted to nursing the sick, helping the poor, and teaching, they organized as a secular congregation with no religious dress or public vows.

In an era when education was not yet available to girls and women, Sor Juana Inés de la Cruz, a Mexican nun (~1648–1695), philosopher and poet, read widely in Spanish, Portuguese, and Latin. When religious orders began educating girls and young women, they attended to their intellectual development, even in eras—such as that of Napoleon—when they were expected to serve as little more than finishing schools for wives-to-be.

The era of revolution in the eighteenth century brought suppression of religious orders but for women ushered in a period of growing emancipation, often criticized and opposed by church authorities. With the industrial revolution of the nineteenth century came public education for women and the beginnings of women's involvement in modern labor. A wave of founding of religious orders was the largest since the reforming days of the sixteenth and seventeenth centuries. Some orders were begun in direct response to the needs of the working class for education and health care, and, in the United States, to the social and religious needs of African-Americans, such as the Holy Family Sisters founded by two free women of color, Jenriette Delille and Juliette Gaudin.

Catholic women continued to lead in the works of mercy in the twentieth century, with the forms of service broadening and marked by innovation. Dorothy Day (1897–1980), founder with Peter Maurin of the Catholic Worker movement, combined Christian anarchism and pacifism and intellectual acumen with relentless hospitality in both farms and urban centers. Mother Teresa of Calcutta (1910–1997) set out to serve "the poorest of the poor," including those dying on the streets, in whom she and her sisters saw the real presence of Christ.

Catholic women also entered the public realm in unprecedented numbers. An American Catholic nurse, Margaret Higgins Sanger (1883–1966), became nationally prominent by the time of World War I as a challenger of nineteenth-century laws making birth control information illegal; she founded in 1929 the organization that became the Planned Parenthood Federation in 1942 and urged a new attitude toward sexuality and romantic love. The influence of Catholic education and Catholic values on women involved in public life is evident in the careers of the first women president of the Philippines, Corazon Aquino, who rose to power with both popular and church support; former prime minister of Portugal, Maria de Lourdes Pintasilgo, who is a member of the Grail, an international movement of lay Catholic women founded in the Netherlands in 1921; Geraldine Ferraro, a United States congresswoman whose run for vice president was marked by public opposition by bishops; and Mary Robinson, former president of Ireland.

WOMEN'S ROLES AND THE CHURCH

Modern and contemporary official church statements about women have increasingly stressed the dignity of women and the equality of women and men. In 1945, Pius XII states: "As children of God, man and woman have a dignity in which they are absolutely equal." Statements on women by Pope John Paul II, such as his 1988 letter on the dignity and vocation of women *Mulieris Dignitatem*, reaffirm the dignity of women but also emphasize "complementarity," a controversial notion involving women's "special gifts," which some in the church applaud as honoring women and others criticize as veiled subordination.

Today both laywomen and vowed sisters minister in increasing numbers in the Roman Catholic Church,

Dorothy Day (1897–1980) founded the Catholic Worker movement (UPI/Corbis-Bettmann).

though without benefit of ordination. In Latin American countries like Brazil and El Salvador, they are often the leaders of base communities, units within parishes, or parishes themselves. At the end of the millennium, globalization creates new opportunities for Catholic women to meet on their own terms. At the 1985 United Nations Conference for Women in Nairobi, an international group of Catholic women issued a statement noting the church's encouragement to women "to take their place in the world but not in the Church" and its ongoing discrimination against women. "We concur," the group said, "that the failure of the Roman Catholic Church to uphold the human rights of women within its own structures and practices undermines the call of the Church for justice in our world." At the 1995 UN Conference held in Beijing, a U.S. Catholic woman, legal scholar Mary Ann Glengon, led the Vatican delegation. Pope John Paul II wrote in a "Letter to Women" on the occasion of the conference an apology for the persistence of sexism throughout human societies, including the sexism to which the Catholic Church had contributed, and recognized in the women's movement a positive contribution to human and social well-being. Still, the document reflects a sense of security and certainty about who women are.

Catholic women worldwide form the majority of church worshipers and volunteers. In the fall of 1987, a group celebrated the Eucharist on a public square in Oakland, California. Similar celebrations followed in Chicago and other cities, the public manifestation of a decade or two of eucharistic celebrations held by women in private homes. Schismatic in some eyes, prophetic in others, unknown or unimportant to many more, these celebrations mark another step in the growing self-definition of Catholic women.

BIBLIOGRAPHY

Brotherton, Anne, S.F.C.C., ed. *The Voice of the Turtle-dove: New Catholic Women in Europe.* 1992. Western European Catholic women from eight countries speak of church practices and church attendance, theological education, and movements for renewal and change.

Brubaker, Pamela K. "Economic Justice for Whom? Women Enter the Dialogue." In *Religion and Economic Justice.* Edited by Michael Zweig. 1991.

Cunneen, Sally. *Sex: Female. Religion: Catholic.* 1968. Catholic women immediately after Vatican II speak about church life, parish, family, love and sex, education, communication, and ministry. Based on extensive questionnaires and interviews nationwide.

Fabella, Virginia, M.M., and Mercy Amba Oduyoye, eds. *With Passion and Compassion: Third World Women Doing Theology.* 1994.

Fiorenza, Elisabeth Schüssler. *In Memory of Her: A Feminist Theological Reconstruction of Christian Origins.* 1983. Ground-breaking work in Biblical interpretation.

Gebara, Ivone, and Maria Clara Bingemer. *Mary, Mother of God, Mother of the Poor.* 1989. A reexamination of Mary by two Latin American Catholic women theologians.

King, Ursula, ed. *Feminist Theology from the Third World: A Reader.* 1994.

LaCugna, Catherine Mowry. ed. *Freeing Theology: The Essentials of Theology in Feminist Perspective.* 1993. A collection of essays by U.S. theologians (women and one man) on the major themes in Catholic systematic theology. LaCugna is also author of the acclaimed *God for Us: The Trinity and Christian Life* (1991).

Latin American Documentation/LADOC. "Reflections of Peruvian Women on the Occasion of the Visit of Pope John Paul II." In *Women in the Church.* Lima, 1986.

McEnroy, Carmel. *Guests in Their Own House: The Women of Vatican II.* 1996. The first full account of women observers at the Second Vatican Council.

McGrath, Albertus Magnus, O.P. *Women and the Church.* 1976. More thorough and detailed work has followed in the two succeeding decades, but this small book is an early classic, spanning twenty centuries.

McNamara, Jo Ann Kay. *Sisters in Arms: Catholic Nuns Through Two Millennia.* 1996. An outstanding, comprehensive historical study of Catholic women religious.

Neal, Marie Augusta Neal, S.N.D. de N. *From Nuns to Sisters: An Expanding Vocation.* 1990. Changes in the collective self-understanding of Catholic sisters after Vatican II by a leading sociologist of religion.

Oduyoye, Mercy Amba and Musimbi Kanyoro, ed. and intro. *Talitha, Qumi: Proceedings of the Convocation of African Women Theologians.* 1990.

Orsi, Robert A. *Thank You, St. Jude: Women's Devotion to the Patron Saint of Hopeless Causes.* 1992. Sensitive, well-researched study of one aspect of popular religion.

Puleo, Mev. *The Struggle is One: Voices and Visions of Liberation.* 1994. Interviews and photographs providing a compelling and informative look at Brazilian men and women, mostly but not exclusively Catholic, including poor residents of slums (mostly women), bishops, and theologians (including one woman). As the title indicates, the book has a liberation bent.

Redmont, Jane. *Generous Lives: American Catholic Women Today.* 1992. An examination of Catholic women in the United States, including but no limited to women in the church, based on interviews with women of diverse ages, races, cultures, sexual orientations, and socioeconomic situations.

Ruether, Rosemary Radford. *Women-Church: Theology and Practice of Feminist Liturgical Communities.* 1985. A re-examination of liturgy and ecclesiology by one of the most prolific Catholic feminist theologians.

Scheper-Hughes, Nancy. *Death Without Weeping: The Violence of Everyday Life in Brazil.* 1992.

Wallace, Ruth. *They Call Her Pastor: A New Role for Catholic Women.* 1992. Catholic women may not be ordained, but many serve in full-time church ministry, and some function as "pastoral administrators"—pastors in charge of entire parishes. Half the women in this U.S.-based study are women religious, the other laywomen.

Weaver, Mary Jo. *New Catholic Women: A Contemporary Challenge to Traditional Religious Authority.* 1985. See esp. chap. 1, "Who *Can* Find A Valiant

Woman? American Catholic Women in Historical Perspective," for excellent historiography. The book as a whole provides a lively examination of the interaction of feminism and Catholicism at a particular point in the late twentieth-century United States.

See also **Catherine of Siena; Christianity: Apostolic Religious Orders and Communities; Day, Dorothy; Juana Inés de la Cruz; Monasticism: In the West; Mother Teresa; Ordination; Teresa of Avila; Thérèse of Lisieux.**

JANE C. REDMONT

Romanticism

Romanticism was an aesthetic movement and intellectual orientation that can be defined as a reaction against eighteenth-century neoclassicism and the rationalism and physical materialism of the European Enlightenment. Cut off from its historical context, it is a term that has been applied to such a broad and diverse set of ideas that, as early as 1948, Arthur O. Lovejoy wrote that we can no longer speak about a singular Romanticism but must discriminate among a plurality of Romanticisms, which may signify distinct, even contradictory, thought-complexes. However, even if we restrict our definition of Romanticism to a historical movement, it is not without ambiguity. It is, for example, still unclear whether Romanticism was a new orientation radically different from the Enlightenment or, as Northrop Frye and others have suggested, a late, rebellious phase of the Enlightenment itself. And, it is unclear what, if any, direct causal ties can be drawn between Romanticism and the momentous events of this period: the American Revolution, the French Revolution, Napoleonic Wars, and the Industrial Revolution.

We do know that in the fifty years between 1780 and 1830 dramatic changes in science, technology, commerce, and warfare, as well as in political and social structures, occurred. These social and political upheavals gnawed at the pristine, geometrical order of neoclassicism, which had viewed humanity as an abstract part, within known limits, of a mechanistic whole. And, it was Romanticism that became one of the dominant voices of this revolutionary age, finding expression in religion and philosophical thought as well as literature, music, and painting throughout America and Europe.

This link between Revolution and Romanticism is already visible in a principal forerunner of the Romantic movement: Jean-Jacques Rousseau, who rejected the abstract, rational notion of humanity and proposed, in-stead, one of "natural" beings—uncorrupted by society and the abuses of reason—who act primarily on impulse and emotion. In the Romantic narrative, exemplified by the works of Blake, Byron, Coleridge, Keats, Shelley, and Wordsworth, we often encounter the quest by the autonomous hero, driven by a yearning for the Sublime, or that lost experience of emotional self-fulfillment from which the hero has been tragically separated. The hero, lost in a fallen universe, strives to capture that ultimate object of desire, which will make this Promethean-type hero into a completed whole. And the only key to this coveted object of desire is the capacity to imagine. Even if this internalized quest, this yearning for what cannot be achieved or obtained, leads to defeat, the quest itself is deemed to be of infinite value.

The religious implications of such a movement were many. The perceived abstraction and sterility of deism, atheism, and materialism, which had been fashionable in the eighteenth century, were confronted with a religious revivalism in the form of a nostalgia for the religious fervor of the Middle Ages, a return to Catholicism, and an embracing of mysticism. The solitary and wholly subjective religious experience replaces religious dogma. Love becomes the definitive, often overburdened term for religious sensibility, for the individual's ultimate desire—the sublime fulfillment.

The legacy of Romanticism for women and religion is immensely complicated. Clearly, the central themes of this movement—individualism, freedom, an appreciation of internal and external dissonance, and an attraction to the occult, the unclean, and uncommon—have been vital for many feminist religious thinkers. It is, however, also the case that the rationalism of the Enlightenment, which Romanticism opposed so vehemently, had given rise to the essential notion of an equality among humans as intellectual beings. Romanticism shunned this notion of equality and, in its stead, immortalized a radically dualistic image of men and women. Except for an elite few, women were deemed to be the emotional and mental antitheses to men; the rational, intellectual areas of similarity between the sexes—which had played such an important political role for women—were sacrificed to this notion of fundamental difference. And, finally, the supreme value that Romanticism placed on individuation, on the centrality of the withdrawn, internalized quest for fulfillment, became both restorative escape into the imagined as well as shallow pacification.

BIBLIOGRAPHY

Barzun, Jacques. *Classic, Romantic and Modern.* 1943, 1961.

Bloom, Harold, and Lionel Trilling, eds. *Romantic Poetry and Prose.* 1973.

de Man, Paul. *Romanticism and Contemporary Criticism.* 1993.

Lovejoy, Arthur O. *Essays in the History of Ideas.* 1948.

Pirie, David B., ed. *The Romantic Period.* Vol. 5 of *Penquin History of Literature.* 1994.

MARY EDWARDSEN

Ruth

According to the Biblical book named for her, Ruth is a young Moabite woman who, after being widowed by an Israelite sojourner in Moab, abandons her homeland for Israel and there marries her dead husband's kinsman, Boaz. Their child, Obed, is the grandfather of King David.

The overall point of Ruth's story is to proclaim a doctrine of inclusiveness by showing that even Israel's great King David was of foreign descent. Yet the narrative is also remarkable for the detailed depictions it provides of women's lives, even though the Biblical tradition is more typically interested in men. The careful descriptions of how Ruth gleans the grain left behind by reapers in the fields, for example, demonstrates both the fiscal vulnerability of widows, bereft of their husbands' support, and the resourcefulness those like Ruth can employ to secure provender. Ruth's resourcefulness, along with that of her mother-in-law Naomi, also widowed in Moab, is further demonstrated by the way the two women work together to arrange Ruth's marriage. By having Ruth come secretly to Boaz in the night, Naomi incites him to fulfill his obligations to his deceased kinsman and take Ruth as his wife. Even after Ruth's marriage, moreover, Naomi and Ruth remain allied, as the loyalty and love Ruth showed by determining to leave her homeland rather than be separated from her mother-in-law reappears when the son Ruth bears to Boaz is laid in Naomi's arms to nurse, and when Ruth is said to mean more to Naomi than seven sons (Ruth 4:15–16).

An engraving of Boaz and Ruth by French printmaker Gustave Doré (Chris Hellier/Corbis).

BIBLIOGRAPHY

Darr, Katheryn P. " 'More than Seven Sons': Critical, Rabbinical, and Feminist Perspectives on Ruth." In her *Far More Precious Than Jewels: Perspectives on Biblical Women.* 1991.

Levine, Amy-Jill. "Ruth." In *The Women's Bible Commentary.* Edited by C. A. Newsom and S. H. Ringe, 1992.

Trible, Phyllis. "A Human Comedy." In her *God and the Rhetoric of Sexuality.* Overtures to Biblical Theology 2. 1978.

SUSAN ACKERMAN

Sacred Literature

"Scripture" can be defined as a sacred text, transmitted in oral or written form, that has been canonized or otherwise officially recognized as sacrosanct and authoritative for a particular religious community. Scripture is a relational category that refers not simply to a text but to a text in its relationship to a religious community for whom it is sacred and authoritative. The study of scripture as a relational category involves a number of important issues, including a consideration of (1) the mechanisms of canon formation by means of which a corpus of texts is circumscribed and set apart as authoritative for a particular religious community; (2) the modes of transmission of the scriptural tradition, whether oral or written; (3) the history of interpretations of the sacred text in the cumulative histories of the various communities that cherish the text as scripture; (4) the multiple reception histories of the sacred text among various groups in various historical periods, cultural contexts, and social locations; and (5) the variety of cultural forms in which the scripture has found expression—in ritual performances, in sermons and testimonies, in drama and dance, in music, literature, and the visual arts, and in political movements and social reforms.

The "human propensity to scripturalize," as Wilfred Cantwell Smith terms it, appears to be almost universal among the world's literate religious traditions. Jews, Christians, Muslims, Hindus, Jains, Sikhs, Parsis, Buddhists, Confucians, and Taoists all have their sacred texts. Nonliterate traditions, such as Native American and African traditions, also generally have a circumscribed corpus of oral lore that is set apart as sacrosanct and authoritative for the community. The Torah, the Christian Bible, the Qur'an, and the Veda are examples of sacred texts that have assumed central roles in their respective religious communities. Of particular interest here is the extent to which women have had access to these sacred texts in the classical formulations of these scriptural traditions prior to the modern period.

TORAH

The Jewish conception of scripture centers on the Torah, which functions within the classical rabbinic tradition as a category that is simultaneously delimited and potentially unlimited. The term is used in its narrow sense to refer to the Pentateuch, the Five Books of Moses or Sefer Torah (Book of the Torah). The term is subsequently extended to refer to the entire Hebrew Bible, the Tanakh, comprising the Pentateuch together with the Nevi'im (Prophets) and Ketuvim (Writings). In rabbinic Judaism the term is expanded further to include not only the Hebrew Bible (the Written Torah) but also the Mishnah, Talmud, and Midrash, which contain the authoritative rabbinic teachings that constitute the Oral Torah. Finally, Torah functions as an encompassing category that includes potentially all of the laws, teachings, and practices of the rabbinic tradition.

The scriptural authority of the Torah is ascribed to its sacred status as the Word of God that was revealed at Mount Sinai. Although rabbinic sources provide a variety of representations of *mattan tôrāh*, the giving of the Torah, they generally take as their starting point the Biblical account that depicts the Sinai revelation as occurring in two main phases. In the first phase God declared directly to the people of Israel the Ten Commandments. In the second phase the prophet Moses assumed the role of the covenant mediator to whom God imparted the detailed teachings of the Torah.

In the classical rabbinic period, access to the Torah was circumscribed by the rabbinic elite, who were responsible for preserving the Written Torah through elaborate scribal traditions, for codifying the authoritative interpretations of its teachings that constitute the Oral Torah, for elaborating a system of law based on the commandments of the Torah, and for regulating the public reading of the Torah in the synagogue liturgy. The majority of Jews—and women in particular—were excluded from the rabbinic academies and from formal study of the Torah. The prevailing rabbinic perspective appears to have been that women were not permitted to study Torah. Through fulfilling their domestic duties, women supported Torah study indirectly by ensuring that their husbands were able to study in the academies and that their sons were properly trained as well. Despite such restrictions, we do find evidence of a number of women scholars in the rabbinic period.

In rabbinic law women were classified in a separate category, along with children and slaves, as exempt from performing certain commandments—in particular those that had to be fulfilled within a certain period. Women were thus excluded from full participation in the way of Torah. Although women could engage the Torah aurally in the synagogue liturgy, through listening to its recitation and to its exposition in the sermon, they were not allowed to recite, study, or interpret the Torah themselves. In the late twentieth century the Orthodox movement continues to uphold the classical rabbinic perspective and to restrict women's access to the Torah. However, in recent decades the Reform, Reconstructionist, and Conservative movements have introduced important reforms to open the way of Torah to women, including counting women in a minyan, the quorum of ten required for the Torah reading, allowing them to be called to the pulpit to read the Torah, and, most significantly, ordaining women as rabbis.

CHRISTIAN BIBLE

The canon of Christian scriptures consists of two parts, the Old Testament and the New Testament, which together constitute the Christian Bible. The process of canon formation was gradual, taking place over several centuries. The authoritative scriptures for the early Christian community were the Hebrew scriptures, which were eventually incorporated into the Christian canon as the "Old Testament." By the middle of the second century the formal public reading of scripture constituted a fundamental part of Christian worship and included readings not only from the Hebrew scriptures but also from the Gospels and the letters of Paul, which formed the basis of the still fluid corpus of "New Testament" writings. The boundaries of the New Testament canon were debated until the fourth century, culminat-

ing in the first official list of the twenty-seven books of the New Testament in the Easter Letter of Athanasius in 367.

The canonical authority of the Old Testament and New Testament writings is held to derive from their sacrosanct status as divinely inspired writings. God's central revelation to Christians is in the person of Jesus Christ himself, who is celebrated as the Word of God incarnate. The Christian Bible, and particularly the New Testament, is revered as the record of the revelation and hence is also ascribed the status of the Word of God.

Alongside the category of "scripture," the Roman Catholic Church upholds a second category, "tradition," comprising the official creeds, dogmas, doctrines, and practices sanctioned by the hierarchy of church authorities headed by the pope. Like the Jewish category of Oral Torah, the category of tradition serves as a means of interpreting, applying, and extending the teachings of the Bible. In the ancient and medieval periods the study, interpretation, and teaching of the Bible were largely the prerogative of male priests, monks, and scholars, who alone had access to advanced education. Women were not allowed to attend cathedral schools and universities and therefore generally did not receive formal training in the scriptures. Excluded from direct access to the Bible as holy writ, women adopted alternative modes of appropriating the scriptures. They encountered the Bible aurally, through hearing, reciting, and singing the words of scripture in the church liturgy and through popular storytelling and dramatic performances of Biblical narratives. They also appropriated the Biblical teachings visually, through the murals, stained-glass windows, and sculptures of the churches as well as through illuminated and illustrated manuscripts and popular art forms. While the majority of laywomen in the medieval period were illiterate, nuns and other female religious generally received a religious education in the convents. The convents produced a number of eminent women interpreters of the Bible, although their scriptural exegeses seldom received the official sanction of church authorities.

The Protestant Reformation in Europe sought to counter the Roman Catholic Church's emphasis on the authority of ecclesiastical tradition and to establish scripture alone—*sola scriptura*—as the source of authority for the church. Over against the hierarchy of priests founded on the ideal of celibacy, Luther, Calvin, and the other reformers championed the "priesthood of all believers" founded on the ideal of holy matrimony. In attempting to close the gap between the clergy and the laity, they placed new emphasis on lay education, on the oral proclamation of the Word of God through preaching and teaching, and on making the scriptures accessible to the general populace through vernacular

A miniature painting of Jesus raising Lazarus illustrates a rare tenth-century synaxarium, a collection of brief lives of saints, portions of which are read during services of the Eastern Orthodox Church (Dean Conger/Corbis).

translations. However, women were excluded from the public ministry of preaching and teaching the Bible and from assuming official positions of religious leadership. Their primary focus became the domestic ministry, in which they were responsible for teaching the Bible to their children and servants. The Quakers were the first Protestant denomination to give women a prominent role in the public preaching of the Word of God in the seventeenth century, followed by the Methodists in the eighteenth century. Other Protestant denominations in the United States began opening the pulpit to women after the mid-nineteenth century, with the majority of denominations allowing the ordination of women by the mid-twentieth century.

QUR'AN

Islam has been characterized as preeminently a "religion of the book," which centers on the Qur'an as the

quintessential scripture. The Qur'an is celebrated as the eternal, uncreated Word of God. This eternal Word entered into history in the form of an "Arabic recitation" (*qur'ān*), which was directly revealed by God through the agency of the prophet Muhammad. Islamic notions of the Qur'an are embedded in a broader conception of successive divine revelations, in which each nation has a prophet or apostle who transmits the revelation in the form of a scripture. Thus God has sent down not one but multiple scriptural revelations, including the Torah of Moses and the Gospel of Jesus. The Qur'an is ascribed the unique status of the final, culminating scriptural revelation that authenticates and completes all earlier revelations. The revelations to Muhammad were compiled in book form during and immediately after his prophetic career and were invested from the outset with the authoritative status of scripture.

In both classical and modern Islam the principal mode of appropriating the Qur'an has been through recitation, which is understood as a means of directly encountering the divine presence. The technical science of Qur'an recitation (*qirā'ah*) is the preserve of the *'ulamā'* (singular, *'ālim*), the male religious scholars who are the custodians of the religious sciences. However, every Muslim, irrespective of gender, literacy level, education, or social status, is expected to master the fundamentals of Qur'an recitation, as such recitation forms an integral part of Muslim ritual and devotional life. Qur'an schools, which teach young children to recite the Qur'an by heart, have traditionally formed the foundation of Islamic education. Prior to the modern period girls generally did not participate in formal training in Qur'an schools, but they commonly were instructed in Qur'an recitation at home.

Although potentially every Muslim, male or female, can attain the cherished status of a *ḥāfiẓ*, one who has learned the entire Qur'an by heart, only men with advanced religious education can attain the status of an *'ālim*, an accomplished religious scholar. Women have generally been excluded from advanced training in the religious sciences, including the science of Qur'an exegesis (*tafsīr*) and the science of jurisprudence (*fiqh*). In medieval Islam women from elite, wealthy families at times assumed prominent roles in founding and administering institutions of higher religious education, but women were not allowed to participate in these institutions as students or teachers. However, women from scholarly or patrician families sometimes had access to less formal venues of religious education, including instruction at home by their male relatives or in private learning circles. Through such avenues women could acquire basic training in the Qur'an and in the fundamentals of jurisprudence, with more advanced training focused almost exclusively on the hadith, the collections of traditions ascribed to the prophet Muhammad. Thus, a number of women in medieval Islam achieved prominence as transmitters of the hadith. However, up to the present women continue to be excluded from positions of religious leadership as *'ulamā'*, who alone are recognized as authoritative interpreters of the Qur'an and *fiqh*.

VEDA

The Veda is revered in Hindu traditions as the paradigmatic scripture, which provides a legitimating source of authority for later sacred texts and teachings. Like the Jewish conception of Torah, the Veda functions in the brahminical Hindu tradition as a category that is simultaneously bounded and open-ended. The term is used in its narrow sense to designate the four Saṃhitās, collections of *mantras*—the Ṛg-Veda, Yajur-Veda, Sāma-Veda, and Atharva-Veda. The term is subsequently extended to include the Brāhmaṇas, sacrificial manuals; the Āraṇyakas, "forest books" that reflect on the inner meaning of the sacrificial rituals; and the Upanishads, the latest speculative portions of the Vedas. In post-Vedic speculations the term is at times extended even further to include the Itihāsas, or epics, and the Puranas, which are respectively designated as the "fifth Veda." Finally, Veda functions as an encompassing category within which can be subsumed potentially all brahminical texts, teachings, and practices.

The Vedic texts are traditionally understood to have been directly cognized by enlightened seers (*ṛṣis*) and are thus designated as *śruti*, "that which was heard." The formal schools of Vedic exegesis, Pūrva-Mīmāṃsā and Vedānta, maintain that the *śruti* texts are eternal, infinite, and uncreated. All other sacred texts are relegated to a secondary status as *smṛti*, "that which was remembered," for they are held to have been composed by authors. On the basis of this criterion the Itihāsas and Puranas are classified as *smṛti* texts, even though they may assimilate themselves to *śruti* by claiming the status of the fifth Veda.

The Vedic Saṃhitās have been preserved in an unbroken chain of oral transmission (*sampradāya*) for over three thousand years. The preservation of the Vedic recitative tradition, along with the performance of the Vedic sacrificial rituals, has remained the exclusive prerogative of male brahmin priests from the Vedic period to the present time. The male members of the other two "twice-born" social classes (*varṇas*), the *kṣatriyas* (rulers and warriors) and *vaiśyas* (merchants, agriculturalists, and artisans), have traditionally been expected to undertake a limited period of Vedic study. However, brahminical ideology provides no paradigm of Vedic study and practice for the larger community who are excluded from the ranks of the twice-born—in particular, women, *śūdras* (servants), and "outcastes" who are beyond the pale of the *varna* system. Indeed, women and *śūdras* are forbidden in the Dharma-Śāstras (brahminical legal codes) from even hearing the Vedic *mantras* recited, let alone reciting them. Although women have been excluded from direct access to the core *śruti* texts, they can participate indirectly in the eternal reality of Veda through appropriating certain *smṛti* texts that are ascribed the status of the fifth Veda, such as the epics and Puranas. In contrast to the highly circumscribed Vedic tradition, these popular devotional texts—both in their original Sanskrit versions and in their multiple vernacular retellings—are intended to inspire and edify the general populace and thus provide an alternative means for women, *śūdras*, and others at the bottom of the social hierarchy to encounter the sacred power of scripture.

BIBLIOGRAPHY

The study of scripture since the nineteenth century has been almost exclusively the domain of biblical and orientalist scholars, who have focused on the historical-critical study of particular sacred texts and canons. In recent years a number of scholars have begun to reflect more generally on the concept of scripture as a cross-cultural category in the history of religions. Following is a list of comparative works and edited collections that treat the category of scripture from a cross-cultural perspective. However, very few of these sources provide substantial treatments of the role of women in relation to sacred texts. Such issues constitute a vital aspect of the relational approach to the study of scripture and remain to be more fully explored in future studies. For sources on feminist and womanist hermeneutics, *see* "Hermeneutics: Feminist Hermeneutics."

Bruce, F. F., and E. G. Rupp, eds. *Holy Book and Holy Tradition.* 1968.

Coward, Harold. *Sacred Word and Sacred Text: Scripture in World Religions.* 1988.

Denny, Frederick M., and Rodney L. Taylor, eds. *The Holy Book in Comparative Perspective.* 1985.

Graham, William A. *Beyond the Written Word: Oral Aspects of Scripture in the History of Religion.* 1987.

———. "Scripture." In *The Encyclopedia of Religion.* Edited by Mircea Eliade. 1987.

Holdrege, Barbara A. *Veda and Torah: Transcending the Textuality of Scripture.* 1996.

Lanczkowski, Günter. *Heilige Schriften. Inhalt, Textgestalt und Überlieferung.* 1956.

Leipoldt, Johannes, and Siegfried Morenz. *Heilige Schriften. Betrachtungen zur Religionsgeschichte der antiken Mittelmeerwelt.* 1953.

Levering, Miriam, ed. *Rethinking Scripture: Essays from a Comparative Perspective.* 1989.

O'Flaherty, Wendy Doniger, ed. *The Critical Study of Sacred Texts.* 1979.

Smith, Jonathan Z. "Sacred Persistence: Toward a Redescription of Canon." Chapter 3 of his *Imagining Religion: From Babylon to Jonestown.* 1982.

Smith, Wilfred Cantwell. "The Study of Religion and the Study of the Bible." *Journal of the American Academy of Religion* 39, no. 2 (1971): 131–140.

———. *What is Scripture? A Comparative Approach.* 1993.

BARBARA A. HOLDREGE

Sacred Marriage

The Greek term *hieros gamos* has long been used in religious studies scholarship to refer to mythical or ritual marriages of a sacred character. The union is in most cases an explicitly sexual one, but the symbolism of sacred marriage generally expands beyond physical sexuality to encompass any fundamental joining of cosmic opposites—female and male, earth and sky, night and day, moon and sun, and so forth. Out of this joining of opposites the *hieros gamos* creates new life. It stimulates fertility, procreation, and renewal at many different levels. Put differently, any effort to bring new vitality into the world requires a sacred marriage.

The earliest manifestations of sacred marriage symbolism appeared with the advent of agriculture. Archaeological evidence indicates that many prehistoric cultures saw the earth as a feminine power and the work of farming as a sexual union of human (male) activity with the earth's (female) generative potential. From an agricultural perspective, the growth of new crops can only occur by means of a sacred marriage of human and divine elements. In some cultures people attempt to promote the greater fertility of the coming year's crops by engaging in ritual sexual activities out in the fields. For instance, in the Ukraine on St. George's Day (23 April) a community's young married couples are asked to go out to the fields and, with the blessings of the priests, roll about together in the first green sproutings that have emerged from the soil.

Sacred marriage symbolism appears in the cosmogonic myths of many different cultures, where the creation of life itself is envisioned as the product of a union of divine opposites. Hesiod's *Theogony* describes the many children born of the sexual union of Gaia, the earth goddess, and Ouranos, the god of the sky. The book of Genesis presents Adam and Eve, the first man and the first woman, as the parents of all humankind.

Another common expression of *hieros gamos* imagery comes in the context of social and political rituals such as royal consecrations and New Year celebrations. These rituals are usually patterned directly on cosmogonic myths: just as the divine opposites came together to produce the world, humans must regularly repeat that primordial union in order to renew the created order. Particularly abundant evidence for such rituals exists from Babylonian and Sumerian cultures, where a city-state's king and a priestess from the temple of the city's goddess would annually join in a marriage ritual intended to praise the goddess, legitimate the king's rule, and preserve the peace and prosperity of the community.

The ecstatic practices of many cultures have been conceived in terms of a marriage between humans and their divine guides. For instance, Catholic nuns have oriented their prayer and liturgical activities toward the goal of becoming "brides of Christ." These unions between human aspirants and divine patrons have their chief procreative yield in the form of sacred knowledge and a heightened presence of sacred power in the human world.

Finally, the nearly universal social institution of marriage is frequently modeled on the religious imagery of the *hieros gamos.* Many elements of marriage rites sym-

A Roman Catholic nun prostrates herself as she takes her vows to become a bride of Christ, London, England, 1965 (Hulton-Deutsch Collection/Corbis).

bolically locate the joining of a particular man and woman within broader contexts: socially, in the marriage's contribution to moral order, economic stability, and generational continuity; and religiously, in its affirmation of divine law and sanctification of procreation.

As these examples indicate, the myths and rites of sacred marriage may be considered typologically according to the partners in the union (e.g., divinity–divinity, divinity–human, human–human) and according to the products of the union (e.g., the world, crops, social order, children). Underlying all these manifestations is the recognition of an essential equality of male and female elements in the creation of life—these myths and rites affirm that nothing may be created without the participation of both male and female energies. Nevertheless, the symbolism of the sacred marriage has often been used as a religious justification for restricting women to the performance of strictly limited social roles patterned after the passively receptive character of the female element in many cosmogonies of the *hieros gamos* type.

BIBLIOGRAPHY

The best source for Sumerian myths and rites of *hieros gamos* is Samuel Noah Kramer's *The Sacred Marriage Rite* (1969). General reference to sacred marriage symbolism include Mircea Eliade's *Patterns in Comparative Religion* (1958), James Frazer's *The Golden Bough* (1959), and Marija Giumbutas's *The Goddesses and Gods of Old Europe, 6500–3500 B.C.: Myths and Cult Images* (1982). Edward Westermarck's *The History of Human Marriage* (1971) gives an overview of marriage rites in various cultures. More detailed studies on marriage are *African Systems of Kinship and Marriage*, edited by A. R. Radcliffe-Browne and Daryll Forde (1962), *Sexual Life in Ancient India*, 2 vols. (1930), by J. J. Meyer, and *Kinship and Marriage in Burma: A Cultural and Psychodynamic Analysis*, by Melford E. Spiro (1977).

KELLY BULKELEY

Sacred, The

The sacred is a category used by comparative religionists to speak collectively about that to which religion points, without imputing to this specific confessional connotations. Depending on specific traditions being addressed, "the sacred" can designate anything from supreme powers and beings, to saints and local or ancestral spirits, to telic destinations, to the aura that surrounds a venerated place or time. Thus, for example,

discussions of "the Christian sacred" might include such concepts as God, Christ, Holy Spirit, Heaven, salvation, saints, angels, Holy City, feast and fast days.

In normal English usage, *sacred* is an adjective, derived from French *sacre* and Latin *sacer,* and meaning "consecrated, set apart by and for the gods or God." Its transformation into a noun and a religionist's tool began with the work of French sociologist Émile Durkheim (1858–1917). In his pathbreaking *Les Formes élémentaires de la vie religieuse* (1912), Durkheim pointed out that all religions share in common their division of existence into two mutually exclusive realms, the first consisting of things that are designated sacred, the second of things called profane. This tendency to distinguish sacred from profane was, for Durkheim, the central problem needing explanation by scholars who wished to understand religion as a form of human social behavior.

Durkheim's distinction between the sacred and the profane was later taken up by Mircea Eliade (1907–1988), a Romanian-born writer and comparative religionist who, after World War II, lived in Paris and the United States. For Eliade, Durkheim's separate realms of "sacred and profane things" became, more simply "the sacred and the profane." (See Eliade's 1957 book by this title.) Eliade was influenced not only by Durkheim, but by German theologian Rudolph Otto, whose book *Das Heilige* (1917) had claimed that religion is based on a unique kind of experience. This was an experience of a *mysterium* (mystery) that is at the same time *tremendum* (frightening) and *fascinans* (alluring). In Eliade's reworking, Otto's "experience of the Holy" became the heirophany, "showing of the sacred," an experience common to human beings of recognizing, in certain concrete manifestations, the presence of an order of reality not belonging to the human realm. Eliade set out to show how humans perceive, appropriate, and respond to such "sacred showings," paying special attention to structures of sacred space, sacred time, and "cosmic" symbolism, and to religious attempts at transcending time and history. Eliade's output was prodigious, and he was very widely read. Hence his language and ideas had a widespread influence.

Scholars of religion nonetheless differ in assessments of Eliade's intent and importance. Some charge that his talk of "the sacred" is a covert ontology, treating the sacred as a reality transcending its varied appearances. This suggests, in effect, that his work constructs a meta-religion, in which "the sacred" is a source underlying all divine forms, and existing religions become alternate modes of its realization. Eliade himself denied such intent, but many of his readers indeed came to think and talk of "the sacred" as his critics suggest. This had the peculiar effect of validating culturally a wide range of religious projects of the 1960s and others that developed later outside the framework of established religions, such as various types of New Age movements. Religious experiments, in effect, assembled mix-and-match religions from the world's religious heritage, expecting that any attractive route could take a practitioner to the final sacred reality.

What has all this meant for women? One by-product of Durkheim's initial work, based on aboriginal Australian materials, was a premise that, among sacred and profane things, women and women's activities commonly classify as "profane." In a Ph.D. dissertation completed in 1974, Eliade student Rita Gross refuted this claim, showing that women's apparent "profaneness" was a product of scholarly bias, not of Australian cultural presuppositions. Australian women, in fact, had a sacred realm of their own, distinct from that of men, and based on experience of their own life-giving powers.

In developing this thesis, Gross herself was influenced by Eliade's own descriptions of a complex of "sacred showings" usually gendered as female that has appeared in many small-scale and ancient societies. This links the earth herself, perceived as mother, with tales of human ascent from caves and underground lands of the dead, and sometimes with lunar goddesses, snakes and dragons, myths about primal waters, spirits of vegetation, and women's capacities for birthing and nurture. When compared with parallel findings by disciples of Swiss psychologist C. G. Jung, these suggest that humans have a deep-set predisposition to acknowledge a mode of sacredness special to women. Knowing what to look for, Gross found traces of such a complex in Australia and hence raised the possibility that it or other woman-centered configurations of the sacred might be lying hidden in other cultures as well.

Moreover, as we have noted, one person's description is easily made another's new religion. Just as "the sacred" has been reified by many Eliade readers and made into a base for new religious explorations, so the idea of a distinctly feminine sacred has been embraced by many women. Declaring fervently that "women need the Goddess," they have taken up female symbols of the sacred and woven them into a women's spirituality movement.

BIBLIOGRAPHY

Émile Durkheim's distinction between the sacred and the profane can be read in translation in *Elementary Forms of the Religious Life* (1995). Otto's *Das Heilige* was translated as *Idea of the Holy* in 1923. Eliade's reflections on the sacred are best approached via *The Sacred and the Profane* (trans., 1959) and *Patterns in Comparative Religion* (trans., 1958); the latter includes the richest development in his work of the "feminine sacred" complex. Brian S. Rennie's *Reconstructing Eliade: Making Sense of Religion* (1996) has a very perceptive analysis of Eliade's use of "the sacred," as well as a useful survey of the controversies surrounding it. Rita Gross's important dissertation is *Exclusion and Participation: The Role of Women in Aboriginal Australian Religion* (1974); an excellent summary of her central argument is found in her "Menstruation and Childbirth as Ritual and Religious Experience among Native Australians," in *Unspoken Worlds: Women's Religious Lives,* edited by Nancy A. Falk and Rita M. Gross (1989). For appropriations of the feminine sacred by the women's spirituality movement, the most revealing piece is Carol P. Christ's "Why Women Need the Goddess: Phenomenological, Psychological, and Political Reflections," in *Womanspirit Rising: A Feminist Reader in Religion,* edited by Carol P. Christ and Judith Plaskow (1979); see also essays by Washbourn, Starhawk, and Z. Budapest in the same volume.

See also **Eliade, Mircea; Jung, Carl; Goddess; Places, Sacred; Time, Sacred; Women and Religion.**

NANCY AUER FALK

Sacrifice

Sacrifice is among the most prominent of human rituals—practiced in Vedic India, ancient Greece, Rome, Israel, Iran, pre-Islamic Arabia, Africa, Meso-America, Andean South America, Hawaii—and is central to Christianity. Historians of religions and anthropologists have studied sacrifice extensively, theorizing it as a gift presented to the gods so that they will give back, as a communal meal harmonizing relations among people and between gods and humanity, as a ritual re-enactment of primordial events, and as a cathartic venting, upon an outsider, of the human propensity for violence that would otherwise destroy social order.

Women's participation in sacrifice is restricted; they are excluded from the role of sacrificer in virtually every society. The common religious logic justifying this exclusion is that women are contaminated by menstruation. Although premenarchal and postmenopausal women may have a larger role in rituals of sacrifice, still their role is always more restricted than men's. Sacrifice functions to pronounce the political power and status of the sacrificer; women are more commonly sacrificed than sacrificer, thus marked as nonplayers in the

The sacrifice of Iphigenia is depicted in a Roman fresco painted before 79 C.E. (Mimmo Jodice/Corbis).

political arena, as semi- or noncitizens, and as expendable to the cause of male ambition and divine demand.

Sacrifice is a system of ritual and discourse in which entities involved in sustaining human life—foodstuffs (grain, dairy products, animals, etc.), work animals, living human flesh and body parts, money, property, and sexuality—and human life itself are used, in religiously sanctioned acts of killing or usurping, for the benefit of and to prove the power of other humans, their principles, and their deities. Religious doctrines of sacrifice offer elegant and persuasive justifications of the asymmetrical power of the sacrificer over the sacrificed, portraying sacrifice as the primordial event from which cosmos and human society were originally created, whose ritual reenactment is crucial to regenerating cosmic order and human society. The ritualized violence of sacrifice celebrates and reproduces the primordial violence of cosmos and society's systemic violence of the strong upon the weak.

WOMEN'S ROLE IN SACRIFICE

Women sponsor animal sacrifice for the sake of healing illnesses in West and East Africa, often at the prompting of a divination ceremony. Women choose the animal, purchase it from an auspicious source, and hire an appropriate priest to perform the sacrificial ritual. Women in east Africa and Haiti who participate in spirit possession cults attribute their illnesses and in-

fertilities to particular spirits possessing them. These spirits, they believe, make women's illnesses continually worse and must be appeased by animal sacrifice. In urban Haitian Vodou, women priestesses themselves sacrifice small animals, such as chickens, but require a male priest to sacrifice large animals such as goats. The Greek Thesmophoria was an elite women's sacrificial festival celebrating Demeter, from which men were excluded. In this festival, women hurled piglets off a cliff; the animals fell and disappeared into the bowels of the earth, as did Persephone. They hired a male *mageiros* (butcher-sacrificer-cook) who killed other sacrificial animals and then left immediately; women then cooked and ate the meat.

SACRIFICE AND FOOD PRODUCTION

Sacrifice transforms animals into food; meat is thereby consecrated and defined as the product of religious devotion rather than crude violence. Historically, most, if not all, the meat consumed by Jews, Hindus, Muslims, and the ancient Greeks and Romans was the product of animal sacrifice. The meat most esteemed by historic Hawaiians and contemporary Alaskan Koyukon—pig and bear respectively—could be killed and eaten only in ritual context, although other animals would be eaten without elaborate ceremony. Through their histories, Greek, Roman, Hindu, Muslim, and Jewish women were allowed, with various restrictions, to eat sacrificial meat; Koyukon women may eat only specific (and least desired, according to Koyukon women) parts of the bear brought home after the male-only forest ritual-feast, and Hawaiian women were barred entirely from sacrificial ritual and were never to eat pork. In many historic as well as contemporary traditions, sacrificed animals are dismembered according to religious evaluation of their body parts; the most valued cuts of meat are generally given to the most prestigious men. The distribution of sacrificial meat is a performance, reenacting the gender and class dynamics of society.

Women are barred from killing animals in almost every society, requiring men to slaughter, but in many societies only women cook. In her ethnography of Bedouin Muslim women, Lila Abu-Lughod explains that "when no man can be found, a postmenopausal woman is permitted to sacrifice the animal, but only if she places the knife in the hand of a circumcised boy. She grasps his hand in hers as she actually slits the neck, but it is the boy who must utter the religious formula" (1986, p. 132). Women's exclusion from killing animals in sacrifice, hunting, or domestic butchery is a systematic, quotidian mode of subordination—women are denied access to control over the production of a significant food group, barred from performing the act of power (killing) by which adult men define themselves, and barred from full participation in religious practice.

SACRIFICE AND POLITICAL CONQUEST

The most prominent sacrifice of Vedic India, the horse sacrifice, was held to establish the king as universal monarch. The king's to-be-sacrificed stallion "wanders" (assisted by an invading army) throughout India for a year, marking every territory it enters as the king's. The stallion's body symbolizes the cosmos and the king. During the ritual sacrifice, after the horse is killed, the chief queens copulate with it; it is then dismembered, cooked, and eaten (*satapatha Brāhmana* 13.5.2.1–10). The final conquest of the horse—the final territory entered by the horse—is the sexualized body of woman. Military conquest is celebrated with and symbolized through sexual conquest, which is enacted as the ultimate religious rite.

The Aztecs' ultimate religious rite was also a celebration of military conquest: men and women who were captured during war were sacrificed to the sun gods and cannibalized by the priests and captors. The Incas celebrated political ascension with human sacrifice; upon the coronation of a new ruler, villages sent gifts of virgin girls to be sacrificed to the gods by live burial. In the Greek myths of Iphigenia and the biblical story of Jephthah's daughter, both girls were sacrificed for the sake of military victory. Iphigenia's father, Agamemnon, promised to sacrifice her to Artemis so as to gain favorable weather for his warships sailing into battle; in Euripides' play, she becomes a willing victim, sacrificing herself for the sake of Greece. Upon going to war against the Ammonites, Jephthah vows that if he defeats them, he will sacrifice "whoever comes forth from the doors to meet me when I return" (Judges 11:31). His daughter, who was the first to greet him, became his sacrificial victim: he "did with her according to the vow which he had made" (11:39). Unlike Isaac, she was not saved by intercession but was killed, with biblical sanction, to ensure victory in war.

SELF-SACRIFICE AS AN IDEAL FOR WOMEN

Societies idealize women who disable themselves for the sake of marriage, religion, and social approval. Cosmetic surgery, high-heeled shoes, clothing fashions that constrict movement (and disable escape from attack), anorexia, genital mutilation, foot-binding, and veiling are modes of self-sacrifice by which women trade parts of the self for acceptance and survival. The religious practice offered as an alternative to sacrifice for Hindu and Christian women is fasting. Married Hindu women are prescribed to perform ritual fasts to purify themselves, ameliorate their husbands' sins, and enhance their household's auspiciousness. The ultimate piety of medieval nuns was subsistence on only the Eucharist, consuming the diseased effluvia of the sick, and reenacting the suffering of Jesus upon themselves through self-mutilation. Society celebrates men who sacrifice others and women who sacrifice themselves.

BIBLIOGRAPHY

Abu-Lughod, Lila. *Veiled Sentiments: Honor and Poetry in a Bedouin Society.* 1986. An ethnography of Bedouin Egyptian women's social and religious life, with analysis of women's relation to ritual killing.

Boddy, Janice. *Wombs and Alien Spirits: Women, Men, and the Zar Cult in Northern Sudan.* 1989. An ethnography of women in an Islamic village where women practice genital mutilation, participate in a spirit possession cult, and use sacrifice of self and animals for healing and fertility.

Brown, Karen McCarthy. *Mama Lola: A Vodou Priestess in Brooklyn.* 1991. A complex but accessible ethnography of a woman as ritual specialist and sacrificial sponsor.

Brundage, Burr C. *The Fifth Sun: Aztec Gods, Aztec World.* 1979. Chapter 9, "The Nuclear Cult: War, Sacrifice, and Cannibalism," gives some information specific to the treatment of women as sacrificial victims.

Bynum, Caroline W. *Holy Feast and Holy Fast: The Religious Significance of Food to Medieval Women.* 1987. Now the classic study of medieval women's fasting.

Detienne, Marcel. "The Violence of Wellborn Ladies: Women in the Thesmophoria." In *The Cuisine of Sacrifice among the Greeks.* Edited by Marcel Detienne and Jean-Pierre Vernant, et al. 1989. Analyzes the Thesmophoria and the gender politics of sacrifice in ancient Greece.

Jay, Nancy. *Throughout Your Generations Forever: Sacrifice, Religion, and Paternity.* 1992. Comparatively analyzes women's role and symbolism in sacrifice, arguing that sacrifice is men's response to women's menstruation, as their attempt to usurp control of reproduction from women.

Lincoln, Bruce. *Death, War, and Sacrifice.* 1991. Chapter 16, "Debreasting, Disarming, Beheading: Some Sacrificial Myths of the Scyths and Amazons," analyzes the gendered discourse of sacrificial violence.

Loraux, Nicole. *Tragic Ways of Killing a Woman.* 1987. Analyzes how women are killed in Greek drama, with some focus on sacrifice of women.

O'Flaherty, Wendy Doniger. *Women, Androgynes, and Other Mythical Beasts.* 1980. Gives a structuralist analysis of women's and men's roles in Indo-European horse sacrifices.

Randall, Robert. "The Mythstory of Kuri Qoyllur: Sex, Seqes, and Sacrifice in Inka Agricultural Festivals." Journal of Latin American Lore 16, no. 1 (1990): 3–45. Discusses Inca history and myth of human sacrifice of women.

Valeri, Valerio. Kingship and Sacrifice: Ritual and Society in Ancient Hawaii. 1985. Gives a structuralist analysis of sexual symbolism in Hawaiian sacrifice; useful but not a feminist resource.

See also Celibacy; Genital Mutilation; Ritual.

KAREN LEE ANDERSON

Egyptian scholar and women's rights activist Nawal al-Sa'dawi (Robert Maass/Corbis).

Sa'dawi, Nawal al-

Physician, writer, political activist, and feminist Nawal al-Sa'dawi was born in Egypt in 1931. Aware as a young child of the inequities Egyptian society visited on women, and rejecting assurances that apparent injustices are the will of God, she has devoted herself for over half a century to speaking boldly on issues of women's rights.

Al-Sa'dawi graduated from the Faculty of Medicine in Cairo in 1955, and has practiced gynecology, family medicine, psychiatry, and thoracic surgery and served as Director General of Health Education in Egypt. At the same time she has devoted herself to writing novels and short stories as well as nonfiction, chronicling her early experiences in semiautobiographical form in Memoirs of a Female Physician (1960). She sees her activities as balancing and linking science and art in the ongoing effort to expose the relationship between gender and power. Her best known work in the West is The Hidden Face of Eve (1980), in which she exposes practices such as clitoridectomy.

Nawal al-Sa'dawi has always been considered dangerously progressive by those in authority in Egypt. She suffered as a socialist feminist under the regime of Anwar Sadat and in 1972 was forced to resign from the Ministry of Health. Her works have been censored and banned, she has been blacklisted from television and radio, and in 1981 she was imprisoned for writing candidly about female sexuality. From this experience she began a series of prison memoirs, including Woman at Zero Point (1975). Released from jail by President Hosni Mubarak, she has remained on what she calls the "grey list" for her freedom of expression in writing and in action. Founder of the international Arab Women's Solidarity Association, she sees the liberation of women as inextricably tied to the liberation of all people from the oppression of patriarchal class systems.

A Muslim by birth and by choice, al-Sa'dawi is a supporter of Islam while a critic of the patriarchy she sees as endemic to all religions. She has little patience with women who veil, affirming that Islam is a religion that frees rather than restricts. Al-Sa'dawi currently resides and works in the United States.

BIBLIOGRAPHY

Sa'dawi, Nawal al-. "Growing up Female in Egypt." In Women and the Family in the Middle East: New Voices of Change. Edited by Elizabeth W. Fernea. 1985.

Malti-Douglas, Fedwa. Women's Body, Woman's Word: Gender and Discourse in Arabo-Islamic Writing. 1991.

Malti-Douglas, Fedwa, and Allen Douglas. "Reflection of a Feminist." In Opening the Gates: A Century of Arab Feminist Writing. Edited by Margot Badran and Miriam Cooke. 1990.

JANE I. SMITH

Saints

The word saint comes from the Latin adjective sanctus, meaning "holy." The term implies that something has been devoted to the gods and set apart from the ordinary world. It was applied by Christians to an exceptionally holy person, who was called *Sanctus* ("holy man") or *Sancta* ("holy woman"). "Saint" is, therefore, a Western and Christian term, but of course there are holy men and women in all religious traditions, so it is permissible to speak of them as saints, as long as one respects the different conception of holiness in each tradition and remembers that non-Western religions developed very sophisticated ideals of sainthood long before Christianity came into existence.

The Western tradition includes two very unusual features. On the one hand, Catholicism has an official list of saints and a rigid legal procedure for determining precisely who should become a saint, a procedure that can last several centuries. On the other hand, most Protestant churches completely reject the very notion of sainthood, partly in reaction to Catholic sainthood, and partly because an officially recognized saint, rather than pointing people toward the divine, might tend instead to block their view of it (a concern also found in Judaism, Islam, and Sikhism). Sainthood is therefore a serious problem for Christian unity, but not for the study of world religions.

HINDUISM

In Vedic and epic India, we find both male and female seers (*rshis* and *rshikas*) and ascetics (*yogis, yoginīs*), but it is the bhakti movement, which began in the middle of the first millennium C.E. that provided India with the saints that still command the love of its people.

These bhakti saints are men and women who transcend the normal precepts of dharma, devote themselves wholly to the divine, and achieve an exhilarating union with the ultimate. In their love for Vishnu, Śiva, and Devī, they reject the normal bonds of caste, class, and gender and offer liberation to women and the lower castes. Antal, Mahadevi, Lalla, and Mirabai are some famous bhakti women saints who escaped the confines of society and defined themselves in relation to the Divine. They composed passionate poetry expressing their spontaneous love for their transcendent Lover. Through the centuries their hymns were sung in Hindu homes and continue to offer a path of liberation for their reciters and hearers as well.

JUDAISM

On the whole, Judaism is uncomfortable with the notion of saints, as indeed with anything that might detract from the transcendent majesty of God. The patriarchs and prophets are in effect saints, in that they have a special calling, are closer to God than the average person, and often have miraculous powers. But they are seen as representatives of the Chosen People rather than chosen individuals, and they do not exercise any

powers beyond the grave. Graves of matriarchs, such as Sarah, are honored by Jewish women. Hasidic Judaism is a partial exception, because the Besht (acronym for the Ba'al Shem Tou) and his successors are seen as exceptionally holy men, in effect as saints. A curious feature of these saints is that they form a school or lineage, a feature also found in Islam.

The Hasidic tradition focuses on male teachers and their male students, but in Biblical Judaism, God calls upon men and women alike. Most of the prophets and religious reformers were men, but Hannah and Deborah are equally important.

CHRISTIANITY

The Catholic and Orthodox traditions are marked by a strong sense of communion with the saints of the past and a belief in their continuing intercession in the present. Churches are usually dedicated to saints, and the saints are also honored by having their statues (in Catholicism) or icons (in Orthodoxy) displayed in religious and secular buildings; these images represent the community of ordinary Christians with the saints of the past.

The Christian saint Teresa of Avila is depicted in a stained-glass window with eyes cast upward and a halo around her head, symbol of her sainthood. She holds an opened book and quill pen, for the many written works that record her visions (The Crosiers).

Women and men become saints for roughly the same reasons, though we often find an emphasis on a woman's role as virgin or mother (the two being combined in the special case of Mary, mother of Jesus). In the case of women martyrs their virginity is often emphasized, and sometimes women seem to have become saints because they were good mothers (Monica, who inspired her son Augustine, to become a Christian). We find women mystics and visionaries (Mechtild of Magdeburg), founders of religious organizations (Clare, who was the friend of Francis and founded a parallel order for women, the Poor Clares), and royal saints (like Queen Margaret of Scotland). Two famous examples of women who managed to break stereotypes are Catherine of Siena (who wrote mystical works but also commanded popes and emperors) and Joan of Arc (who overcame the prejudices against her peasant background and gender and was probably the first nonroyal woman to lead a national army in battle). Last, but not least, is the exceptional case of Mary. Medieval piety revered her as highly as Christ himself, giving her the title Our Lady (Notre Dame) just as he was Our Lord, and proclaiming her Queen of Heaven beside Christ the King, though her main role is that of intercessor.

ISLAM

Islam, like Judaism and Protestantism, is reluctant to acknowledge that particular persons might have a special relationship with God. Nevertheless, in a curious parallel to Hasidic Judaism, the Sufi mystic who seeks union with God is recognized as a saint (*walī*), and there are schools of such saints. Visits to their tombs are a popular if not quite orthodox practice.

Muslim women who may be excluded from public worship in mosques are frequent visitors to the tombs of saints. There are even shrines of women saints from which men are barred. The shrines of their saints provide Muslim women with a religious and social space outside of their homes. Sufis were usually organized into brotherhoods, but we do find some women saints such as the great Rabi'a, whose holiness is based on the same quest for union with God.

SIKHISM

Sikhism rejects the veneration of particular persons as saints; it accepts the potential sainthood of every person, male and female. The Sikh paradigmatic figure lives freely in the world without any bonds or limitations. Such a person may be variously known as a *sant* (a good person, saint), *jivanmukt* (free in life), or *brahmgyani* (enlightened), but she or he invariably enjoys serving others. The company of good men and women (*sangat*) is highly esteemed as a path to personal liberation.

BIBLIOGRAPHY

Abbott, Justin. *Bahina Bai: A Translation of Her Autobiography and Verses.* 1985.

Dehejia, Vidya. *Antal and Her Path of Love.* 1990.

Futehally, Shama. *Songs of Meera: In the Dark of the Heart.* 1994.

Hawley, Jack Stratton, ed. *Saints and Virtues.* 1987.

Johnsen, Linda. *Daughters of the Goddess: The Women Saints of India.* 1994.

Kieckhefer, Richard, and George D. Bond, eds. *Sainthood: Its Manifestations in World Religions.* 1988.

Ramanujan, A, K. "On Women Saints." In *The Divine Consort: Radha and the Goddesses of India.* Edited by John Stratton Hawley and Donna Marie Wulff. 1986.

Women Saints: East and West. Editorial Advisers: Swami Ghanananda and Sir John Steward-Wallace. 1955.

See also **Buddhas, Bodhisattvas, and Arhats; Hagiography.**

NIKKY-GUNINDER KAUR SINGH

HENRY J. WALKER

Salvation

The world's major religious traditions have developed to address a wide variety of human needs and problems. It is fair to say that no concern is greater than the eradication of evil as it is created and perpetuated in the world and, concomitantly, alleviating the suffering that humans experience, often as a result of evil. The term that perhaps best captures this ultimate religious goal of transcending evil and suffering is *salvation,* derived from the Latin verb *salvāre,* meaning "to save." Scholars of comparative religions have sought to understand the practically universal spiritual aspiration to be saved by approaching religions in terms of their core function as soteriologies. A soteriology is a "way of salvation"—in Greek, *sōter,* the word Christians have most frequently used in the sense of "savior."

These root meanings of the terms *salvation* and *soteriology* have important implications. First, there is something from which people need to be saved, such as the imperfect or limited condition(s) of human life in this world (sometimes seen in terms of its attendant evil and suffering), and second, there is something people need to achieve. In the latter sense, the word *salvation* carries the etymological connotation of "making whole," which suggests that it be understood as a state in which human well-being is fulfilled or restored. Thus, the terms imply that some kind of divine being or power exists who can bring about this ultimate state. Indeed, many of the world's religions share the belief in the existence of a savior God or gods who can actively intervene to ensure the welfare of humanity. Yet there are also prevalent religious traditions that focus instead on the potential of human efforts and actions to effect salvation. In Japan, for instance, it is allowed that there are some religious ways based on "other-power" (*tariki*) and some based on "self-power" (*jiriki*). In many religions the two approaches coincide. For example, in the monotheistic traditions of Judaism, Christianity, and Islam, salvation is usually a matter of both divine "grace" and human "works."

The world's religions tend to speak of salvation in terms of both salvation in this world and salvation in the afterlife. In the monotheisms, salvation is typically described in terms of redemption from sin here in this world, receiving deliverance from sin's consequences hereafter in a heavenly world of eternal coexistence with God, and the eventual establishment of the Kingdom of God on earth. Religions of Indian origin aim at *mokṣa*, a state of ultimate liberation from samsara, the potentially endless cycle of rebirth, in worldly conditions of suffering. In Hinduism those pursuing the path of knowledge (*jñāna*) endeavor to discover their identity with the universal source of everlasting being, consciousness, and bliss called *brahman*, and those following the path of devotion (bhakti) seek communion with a personal God. Buddhists aim to transcend suffering by realizing enlightenment (*bodhi*), which involves gaining insight (*prajñā*) into the true nature of reality and living according to the compassion (*karuṇā*) which that insight engenders. The Chinese-based religions are more concerned with the achievement of harmony in this life here on earth, whether the kind of social harmony aimed at by Confucians or a union with nature sought by Taoists.

SOTERIOLOGICAL THEMES AND WOMEN

Many religions have advanced doctrines about inherent female characteristics that have led their cultures to develop structures, institutions, and values that have been socially oppressive to women. Yet they have also seen women as possessing qualities that make them equal or sometimes even superior to men from the point of view of salvation and have treated women accordingly in this respect. In Islam, for example, men and women are seen as having significant biological and psychic differences, corresponding to different cosmic prototypes. Consequently, Islam views it as entirely natural that men and women should play different roles in society. However, with regard to the ultimate judgment of a person's spiritual worth, Islam views men and women as equal in the sight of God. According to the Qur'an, men and women identically possess the essential part of a person's being (*nafs*), which is the entity that encounters God in this life in order to know, love, and obey Him and that experiences the passage into the eternal blessings of Paradise or torments of Hell in the afterlife. Correspondingly, with respect to the sacerdotal rites that serve to connect the person to God, women are seen as having the capacity to perform them all, although precedence is given to men in the performance of public, as opposed to private, rites, such as communal prayer. Thus the Qur'an speaks of "pious and believing women" (*mu'mināt; muslimāt*) in the same context as pious and believing men, and it expects them to perform the same religious duties that bring about salvation as do men. The Qur'an is explicit that recompense in the hereafter is acquired through actions: "And whoever does good deeds, whether male or female, and is a believer, these shall enter Paradise" (sura 4:124).

Furthermore, in Islamic mysticism there is a tendency, also found in certain Christian and Hindu forms, to see the essential spiritual entity of the soul as female and as a woman, who in her longing expresses the highest kind of loving devotion to God. Traditions with this view have often engaged in what is called bridal mysticism, in which the male practitioners have dressed up as or otherwise taken on the persona of a woman in order more truly to commune with the saving God.

There have also been traditions that, on the one hand, have been rightly credited with introducing institutions and values into their cultures that provide women with greater opportunities for social and religious freedom, but on the other hand have been seriously divided over the issue of whether women even possess the capacities to attain spiritual liberation. Two such traditions are the Indian-born Buddhism and Jainism. Although both, in the early period of their formations in the middle of the first millennium B.C.E., radically broke down barriers against women in their society by admitting women into their monastic communities, many influential individuals and groups in these communities were heavily invested in questioning and denigrating the women's potential to attain final salvation as defined in their traditions. Diana Paul, in her groundbreaking *Women in Buddhism* (1979), has shown how the Mahayana tradition, renowned for its supposed greater inclusivity and acceptance of a wide variety of practical means for achieving the goal of liberation, often constructed an image of women as lacking the necessary moral fortitude to progress toward enlightenment. In the case of Jainism, P. S. Jaini (1991) has examined how a major sect, known as the Digambara, argued not only that women lack the physical strength to endure the harsh ascetic practices required to become liberated but that they are intellectually and ethically inferior as well.

The writings of feminist liberation theologians (e.g., Ellis, 1973 and King, 1991) reveal contemporary Christian and Jewish efforts to bring about the greater social and religious freedom of women. Their work is soteriological in the sense that it endeavors to restore the full humanity of women through the project of critiquing and reconstructing traditional theologies.

BIBLIOGRAPHY

Asani, Ali S. "Bridal Symbolism in the Ismaili *ginan* Literature." In *Mystics of the Book.* Edited by R. Herrera and Ruth L. Salinger. 1993.

Brandon, S. G. F., ed. *The Saviour God: Comparative Studies in the Concept of Salvation.* 1980.

Ellis, Marc H. *Towards a Jewish Theology of Liberation.* 2d ed, 1989.

Jaini, P. S. *Gender and Salvation: Jaina Debates on the Spiritual Liberation of Women.* 1991.

King, Ursula. *Liberating Women: New Theological Directions.* 1991.

Leclerq, Jean. *Women and St. Bernard of Clairvaux.* Translated by Marie-Bernard Saïd. 1990.

Leeuw, Gerardus van der. *Religion in Essence and Manifestation: A Study in Phenomenology.* 1963.

McGinn, Bernard. *The Presence of God: A History of Western Christian Mysticism.* 1994.

Morgan, Kenneth W. *Reaching for the Moon: On Asian Religious Paths.* 1990.

Olivelle, Patrick. *Renunciation in Hinduism: A Medieval Debate.* 1986.

Schimmel, Annemarie. *My Soul Is a Woman: The Feminine in Islam.* 1997.

Turner, Denys. *Eros and Allegory: Medieval Exegesis of the Song of Songs.* 1995.

Wadud-Muhsin, Amina. *Qur'an and Woman.* 1992.

BRADLEY S. CLOUGH

Sanghamittā

According to the fourth- and fifth-century chronicles of Sri Lanka, the *Dīpavaṃsa* and the *Mahāvaṃsa,* Sànghamittā was the Buddhist nun who, with the proper quorum of ten nuns, introduced the nuns' lineage to Sri Lanka in the third century B.C.E. Tradition alleges that she was the daughter of India's king Ashoka, and that when she was invited to establish the nuns' order in Sri Lanka, she took with her a branch of the sacred Bo Tree, the tree under which the Buddha was enlight-ened. The tree continues to flourish though her order disappeared mysteriously in approximately the eleventh century. Since that time, the order of nuns has been defunct in Sri Lanka. Despite the disappearance of the order of nuns, tradition credits Sànghamittā and her brother, the monk Mahinda, with firmly establishing Buddhism in the island.

The conservative Theravada Buddhist tradition contends that today it is impossible to ordain a woman into the monastic order because it is impossible to convene the proper quorum of ten. Nonetheless, women assume the monastic life-style without changing formal status and become lay-nuns. In the late nineteenth century an American, Miranda de Souza Canavarro, traveled to Sri Lanka with the hope of reestablishing the lineage. There, she became known as Sister Sànghamittā because she saw herself in the role of the Indian nun Sànghamittā, who, more than two thousand years earlier, had opened the monastic order to women. Though the nineteenth-century Sister Sànghamittā failed, many women have opted for the life-style similar to hers. Today, because of the long history associated with Sànghamittā, the name is one of the most popular among the approximately five thousand who have entered lay-nunneries in Sri Lanka.

BIBLIOGRAPHY

Bartholomeusz, Tessa. *Women under the Bō Tree: Buddhist Nuns in Sri Lanka.* 1994.

Gunawardena, R. A. L. H. "Subtle Silks of Ferrous Firmness: Buddhist Nuns in Ancient and Early Medieval Sri Lanka and Their Role in the Propagation of Buddhism." *The Sri Lankan Journal of the Humanities* 14, nos. 1 and 2 (1988): 1–59.

TESSA BARTHOLOMEUSZ

Sappho

Known in antiquity as one of the greatest of the lyric poets, Sappho, born c. 620 B.C.E. in Lesbos, was called the tenth Muse by Plato. Her words, composed to be accompanied by the seven-stringed lyre, were widely admired and collected in nine books in the great library of Alexandria. In the Christian era Sappho's work was condemned by popes and bishops and purposely destroyed (not "lost," as is often reported). Today it survives primarily in lines quoted by Greek and Roman writers to illustrate elements of style and as reconstructed from fragments of papyrus.

Sappho wrote of love and longing and the beauty of nature. Many of the poems express tender feelings for

Sappho. Undated engraving (Corbis-Bettmann).

young women who (apparently) studied with her; others were composed for weddings. Several depict ritual scenes or are addressed to goddesses, including Aphrodite and Hera. Even in fragmentary form, Sappho's work offers the rare opportunity to study a woman's view of myth and ritual and her relation to the goddesses and other women. In one of her poems Sappho attacks the Homeric ethos, arguing "the finest sight on dark earth" is not "cavalry corps" or "infantry" but "whatever one loves." Praising Helen for following her heart, she is reminded of a woman named Anactoria who moves her more than "glitter of Lydian horse." In others she evokes a ritual where girls dance "around an/ altar of love," and asks Aphrodite to "Fill our gold cups with love/ stirred into clear nectar," not to "cow my heart with grief." In these and other poems we glimpse images of women and goddesses very different than those depicted by Homer and Hesiod. Sappho urges us

to make love not war; views the goddesses as the inspiration of love and beauty, the great gifts of bounteous earth; and celebrates women's love for each other. How different our view of the origins of religion and culture would be if Sappho's work were studied alongside Homer's as one of the foundations of civilization.

BIBLIOGRAPHY

Greek Lyric I: Sappho Alcaeus. Translated by David A. Campbell. 1982. Contains the original words of Sappho in the Aeolian dialect in which she wrote and the ancient commentaries on her life and work.

Malroy, David, ed. and trans. *Early Greek Lyric Poetry.* 1992.

Sappho: A New Translation. Translated by Mary Barnard. Foreword by Dudley Fitts. 1958. Remains the most lyrical translation of Sappho's words and is the source of the quotations in this essay.

CAROL P. CHRIST

Sarah

In the biblical book of Genesis, Sarah is the wife of Abraham and mother of Isaac. Before Genesis 17:15, she is called Sarai; her name is subsequently changed to Sarah as a sign of God's covenant with Abraham (previously Abram).

Immediately after her name is changed, God promises that Sarah, although ninety years of age, barren, and, according to Genesis 18:11, postmenopausal, will bear a son. The narrative that follows is similar in many respects to the stories of the Bible's other barren women (Rebekah, Rachel, Manoah's wife, Hannah, and the Shunammite woman). Each begins with an indication of barrenness, followed by a divinely given promise that the barrenness will be ended, and concluding with the birth of the promised son. Sarah's story also, like the stories of Rachel and Hannah, features the presence of a fertile rival (Sarah's maidservant Hagar), and, like the story of Manoah's wife, describes the barren couple's doubts that the divine promise can really be fulfilled.

Another episode in the Sarah story describes how Abraham, at two different points when he takes his household to sojourn in a foreign land, passes Sarah off as his sister rather than claiming her as his wife (Gen. 12:10–20 and 20:1–18). Isaac is described as doing the same thing with his wife Rebekah in Genesis 26. This thrice-told tale, like the six similar versions of the barren woman's narrative, demonstrates that much of the Sarah cycle of stories is comprised of traditional folk motifs.

Sarah. This painting by Charles Brochart was published in The Woman's Bible in 1876 (Photo Disc, Inc.)

BIBLIOGRAPHY

Exum, J. Cheryl. "The (M)other's Place" and "Who's Afraid of the 'Endangered Ancestress'?" In her *Fragmented Women: Feminist (Sub)versions of Biblical Narratives.* 1993.

Jeansonne, Sharon. *The Women of Genesis: From Sarah to Potiphar's Wife.* 1990.

Niditch, Susan. "Genesis." In *The Women's Bible Commentary.* Edited by C. A. Newsom and S. H. Ringe. 1992.

SUSAN ACKERMAN

dresses Sarasvatī, whose name means "abounding in pools," with two epithets, "best of rivers" and "best of goddesses." The Sarasvatī, the greatest river of Vedic India, was probably an important site for sacrificial activities. She is also conceived in the *Ṛg* and *Yajur* Vedas as a form of the sacrificial fire who is one of Indra's three consorts, and as the spouse of Agni, the god of fire. She first assumes the characteristics of Vāc (sacred speech), in the *Yajurveda* (*Vājasaneyi Saṃhitā* 19.12), where her powers to purify and to bestow material and spiritual gains appear to parallel the cleansing and fertilizing powers of the river goddess. In the *Ṛg* and *Atharva* Vedas the goddess Vāc represents not only skill in debate and rhetoric, but also magical efficacy of sacred sound in ritual recitation. According to *Ṛgveda* 1.164, Vāc creates syllabic sound, the instrument by which the chaotic matter of the universe is organized, anticipating her role as consort of Brahmā, the prime creator in classical Hinduism.

In classical sources Sarasvatī's vehicle is a swan, a symbol of spiritual transcendence, appropriate to her cerebral, sometimes ascetic nature. Her shining white complexion and garments reflect serene purity. Sculptural representations of the goddess commonly show her with four arms in which she may hold a rosary, a book, a receptacle for ritual water, a white lotus, or a *vīnā*, a stringed instrument. As the patron of culture and learning she is associated with the brahmin class and wears the sacred thread. Sarasvatī is worshiped in libraries and institutions of learning, especially during Sarasvatī Pūjā, the fifth day of the month of Māgha (January–February), when teachers are honored, and books, musical instruments, or the tools of craft are placed at her shrine.

BIBLIOGRAPHY

Secondary sources include *Śrī Sarasvatī in Indian Art and Literature,* by Niranjan Ghosh (Delhi, 1984), which treats the iconography of the goddess and contrasts brahminical, Buddhist, and Jain conceptions, and *Sarasvatī in Sanskrit Literature,* by Mohammad Israil Khan (Ghaziabad, 1978), a more comprehensive and scholarly study.

NADINE BERARDI

Sarasvatī

Sarasvatī, goddess of speech, learning, and wisdom in classical Hinduism, is also patron of literature, music, and the dramatic arts. The goddess first appears in the *Ṛgveda* (c. 1200–900 B.C.E.), India's earliest work of sacred literature. An early *Ṛg* Vedic hymn (2.41.16) ad-

Scandinavian Religions

Goddess mythology and women's ritual practices were part of the active worldview of the Viking and pre-Viking periods, dating back to 1600 B.C.E. and continuing into the Christian era, and different ritual practices themselves became part of the oral tradition. Symbols of the goddesses and gods had a living function in the cult rituals. Understanding these rituals requires knowledge of the mythic universe and goddess functions.

There is more information about the mythology of the Norse goddesses than of either the specific folk rituals to these goddesses or the rituals and cult practices of women during this period. Speculation about the lack of written information and archeological evidence concerning these specific ritual practices is varied. There seems to be agreement among scholars that goddess rituals were more clandestine than the public ceremonies that honored the gods. Inscriptions and drawings etched on rock formations primarily relate to male deities and ritual practices. The scanty record of goddess worship may be due to the secrecy with which the goddesses and their followers exercised their special powers and magic in nocturnal ceremonies.

THE NORSE MYTHOLOGICAL UNIVERSE

In the Scandinavian, North Teutonic traditions, the universe was imaged as a tricentric-layered structure, with Yggdrasil, the ashen world tree, as its vertical axis. The structure consisted of three levels and nine worlds: the first level was Asgard (*Asgård*), the world of the Aesir (*Asar*), the warrior gods, the most dominant group of gods in the pre-Christian Nordic traditions. The Asynjur (*Asynjor*) were the corresponding goddesses in Asgard. The number of goddesses varied from 13, 19, 24, to 52, depending on the source.

The second level was Midgard (*Midgård*), surrounded by an immense ocean and inhabited by the world of humans. The giants' world, Jotunheim, was also on this level, as was Nidavellir (*Nidafjällen*), the dwarfs' world. The dark elves lived below them in Svartalfheim (*Svartalvaheim*). A flaming rainbow bridge, Bilfrost (*Bifrost*), connected Asgard and Midgard. The third level, Niflheim (*Nifelheim*), was the world of the dead.

GODDESSES AND OTHER FEMALE SUPERNATURAL CREATURES

A selective sampling of the Asynjur can begin with the two primary figures of Freyja and Frigga. Freyja (*Freja, Fröja*) represented an ideal that included and transcended the wife and mother. She was, in addition, the goddess of love and sensuality, leader of the Valkyries (*Valkyrior*) and one of the Vanir (*Vaner*) fertility gods. She was known for her sexual appetite and partnering with all the gods in Asgard. She was credited with originating the *sedir*, the divination ceremony. Freyja was the mother of Hnoss, the representation of infatuation. A second primary figure was Frigga (*Frigg*), the queen of Asgard. She was one of Odin's wives, mother of Balder, Hermod, Hoder, and perhaps Ty. She was associated with sexuality, family issues, and guardianship.

Frigga, the supreme Norse goddess of Asgard, depicted as a huntress (Corbis-Bettmann).

Analysis of myths and legends as well as scholarly interpretation provide evidence that perhaps these deities represent two aspects of the same goddess: lover, Freyja; conjugal fertility, Frigga. In general, the goddesses have been portrayed as wives of the gods, but the myths also reveal different pairings as well as liaisons with other creatures and spirits.

Other Asynjur inhabited Asgard as well. Sif (*Siv*), a goddess of fertility, love, and beauty, was known for her golden hair, which represented grain or the autumn grass. With Thor, her second husband, she was mother of the goddess Thurd, associated with weather, but often imaged as a storm or cloud deity. Nanna, goddess of purity, blossoms, and vegetation was married to Balder. This pair, devoted and faithful to one another, represented a rare stable partnership among the Norse gods. Jord, personification of the unpopulated and uncultivated earth, was another of Odin's wives and the mother of Frigga. Gerda (*Gerd*) was the daughter born of a union between a giant and mortal. She was associated with beauty, magic, and fire and was married to Freyr. While the powers and functions of the gods and goddesses overlapped in some areas, the goddesses had their own domains. For example, the Asynjur functioned collectively as a judicial council that decided policy and settled disputes.

The Norse pantheon also included other goddesses such as Hel, the Danish goddess of death, also the name of the realm of the dead (Niefhelheim); Hertha, goddess of the earth, who in medieval times was the patron of witches; and Dis, an ancestral goddess of heredity who determined individual talents and defects. She was worshiped in ritual services called *disabolt* during a midwinter festival honoring ancestors. The term *dis* served also as a generic reference for any female deity, and *disir* (plural form) was a general term for female deities, including the Valkyries and fate spirits, the souls of deceased mothers. Although the *disir* formed a collective in different accounts, competition and antagonism were not infrequent.

Another general term, *Vätter*, referred to all supernatural female creatures. This group included the Valkyries, who decide which warriors would die in battle and then return with their bodies to Valhalla, the hall in Asgard where all awaited *Ragnarök*, the final battle between the gods and the forces of evil. Hild, representing immortality and war, was chief of the Valkyries. The Norns, Skuld, Urd, and Verdandi presided over the destinies of humans and gods by deciding the length of life by a process of spinning thread and tearing it off. The Norns had a special status and were not subject to the gods. According to some sources, the Valkyries were subject to them. The Vana Mothers, also referred to as the wave maidens, were the nine daughters of Ran, goddess of the sea, and Aegir. They were custodians of the World Mill. The mill, situated at the bottom of the sea, ground out fertility, seasonal changes, and universal harmony. There were also the Norse prophetic spirits, represented as trolls or sibyls such as Heid, who was often portrayed as a patron of evil women.

The living were the main focus of the Norse; an afterlife was not a dominant part of the functioning cosmology or cosmogony. Archeological evidence, however, shows that especially at the higher levels of society, wives and female slaves were voluntarily killed so that they could be with their departed partner or master. There was a common belief that such self-sacrifice secured a better status in the next world.

WOMEN'S RITUAL PRACTICES

Strong parallels existed between the functions of the goddesses and those of women in the Viking culture. Two common and dominant themes included a connection with nature and natural forces, and responsibility for life cycle events, both biological and social. Women's ritual can be classified both as religious (invoking powers for guidance and assistance) and magical (attempting to gain power).

The best documented of these practices is a Nordic form of shamanistic divination ceremony (*sejd*), which was almost exclusively associated with women and female powers and considered foreign to male nature. The female shaman (*völva*), wore a special animal fur headdress and staff and sat on a high platform which literally and symbolically raised her to the incantation level for communication with divine powers. The occult revelations gained through the trance state were then converted into advice and prophecy or were used in the location of lost objects. Such rituals could also be used for evil purposes to cause injury, illness, or death. From the evidence available, this ritual practice appears to have been used consciously for empowerment purposes.

Other empowering ritual practices related to pregnancy, birthing, and child naming. Physical and spiritual health-related rituals, both preventive and interventive, were primarily women's responsibilities. Groups of women made house visits to bring good luck and to foretell children's futures. In each of these ritual practices different goddesses were called upon to provide direct knowledge, applied wisdom, or special guidance.

Another tradition, which remains active today in parts of northern Scandinavia, that of the indigenous nomadic Saami people, should be mentioned as well. Their religion, which had eight primary goddesses, has had a rich array of subterranean female deities.

Whether the contemporary reader is interested in the historical Viking tradition or that of the historical and current Saami tradition, there is a legacy of knowledge and wisdom here which may serve not only as a base for understanding the Scandinavian past more accurately but also for contributing to the shaping of its future with the renewed interest in goddess mythology and women's ritual practices.

BIBLIOGRAPHY

WORKS IN SWEDISH:

Grönbech, Vilhelm. *Nordiska myter.* 1926.

Holtsmark, Anne. *Fornnordisk mytologi.* Translated by H. Williams. 1992.

Ohlmarks, Åke. *Fornnordiskt Lexikon.* 1983.

Ström, Folke. *Nordisk hedendom.* 3d ed. 1985.

WORKS IN ENGLISH:

Ann, Martha, and Dorothy Myers Imel. *Goddesses in World Mythology.* 1993.

Bonnerjea, Biren. *A Dictionary of Superstitions and Mythology.* 1927.

Crossley-Holland, Kevin. *The Norse Myths.* 1980.

Davidson, Hilda Roderick Ellis. *Scandinavian Mythology.* 1969.

———. *Gods and Myths of the Viking Age.* 1964.

Durdin-Richardson, Lawrence. *The Goddesses of Chaldaea, Syria and Egypt.* 1975.

Jobes, Gertrude. *Dictionary of Mythology, Folklore and Symbols.* 1962.

Leach, Marjorie. *Guide to the Gods.* 1972.

Monaghan, Patricia. *Book of Goddesses and Heroines.* Rev. ed. 1990.

Senior, Michael. *Illustrated Who's Who in Mythology.* 1985.

Sykes, Egerton. *Everyman's Dictionary of Non-classical Mythology.* 1968.

PRIMARY TEXT TRANSLATIONS:

Poems of the Elder Edda. Translated by Patricia Terry. 1990.

Sturluson, Snorri [1179–1241]. *The Prose Edda: Tales from Norse Mythology.* Selected Translations by Jean I. Young. 1964.

VALERIE DEMARINIS

Schurman, Anna Maria van

See van Schurman, Anna Maria.

Science, Religion, and Women

Current scholarship examining science, religion, and women takes a variety of forms. This article addresses the categories of research on science and women and research on women and the integration of science and religion. Research on women and science is analogous to research on women and religion that examines women's professional participation in the academy and religious communities, criticizes gender bias in interpretation of sacred texts, traditions, and religious language, and constructs alternative languages and traditions from women's experience.

Scholarship on science and women considers, first, participation of women in the science professions. Beginning with pedagogical, curricular factors influencing young women's entrance into science professions, studies on women in the sciences track the historical and contemporary professional status of women. Although data show the increasing presence of women in science professions and their significant contributions to Western science, research also discloses gender discrimination in salaries, appointments, and recognition, including crediting others with women's scientific work and minimizing the importance of their discoveries.

Second, scholarship on science and women evaluates traditional forms of Western science. Feminist historical critique queries scientific method and epistemology, experimental design and data interpretation, organization of knowledge and theory building, presuppositions entailed in language and values, and depictions of women and nature. For example, feminist critique observes the metaphor of marriage in biological theories of the relationships of sperm to egg and cell nucleus to cytoplasm. The metaphor attributes courtship language to descriptions of the behavior of gametes. Nucleus and cytoplasm are analogous to husband and wife, in fact reflecting different models of the marriage relationship in competing theories. Although contemporary biologists are aware that nucleus and cytoplasm are interactive, the power of the metaphor continues to influence portrayals of the nucleus as the controller of cell processes.

Third, the study of women and science considers feminist science and feminist theories of science. Feminists have engaged in constructive exploration of the uniqueness of women's science in contrast to male-dominated approaches to science. The question of whether women undertake scientific research differently than men is particularly debatable on grounds of biological essentialism, but some authors consider that the history, status, and socialization of women may affect both women's approaches to research and the reception of their work in the scientific community. Feminist theories of science question the role of gender, race, class, sexuality, values, objectivity and subjectivity, dualism and hierarchy, cultural standpoint, politics and economics, and sociology of knowledge in scientific method and theories. For example, in contrast to traditional androcentric epistemologies, feminist empiricists argue that strict adherence to traditional methods of scientific inquiry can avoid cultural biases in research, and feminist standpoint theorists argue that women's experience forms a base for more trustworthy knowledge claims than men's experience. A further example is Evelyn Fox Keller's theory of the personal and social dynamics of science, particularly in terms of the role of language in mediation and limitation of scientific methods, models, and aims.

Interdisciplinary scholarship on women, science, and religion is particularly rewarding in identifying how dominant, comprehensive systems of thought have supported the inferiority and oppression of women. Nancy Tuana's *The Less Noble Sex: Scientific, Religious, and Philosophical Conceptions* (1993) demonstrates that historical Western paradigms have collectively defined woman as less perfect, rationally inferior, morally defective, and less evolved than her male counterpart and, therefore, more in need of control. The value of Tuana's book is its sufficient evidence for the claim that science, religion, and philosophy have been influenced by presuppositions of women's inferiority and have reinforced the inferiority of women's nature in their historical development, even when data and reason would require contrary explanations of and conclusions about women's nature.

Significant historical claims about women's inferiority in soul and mind make up part of Tuana's analysis of science, religion, and philosophy. Hesiod's *Theogony*, a Greek creation myth, and Plato's *Timaeus* established that women's character is immoral and that her soul and rational capacities are incapable of controlling her body, sensations, and emotions. Hesiod and Plato each envisioned an original world without woman; woman was introduced as punishment to man and was placed in the world's hierarchical order lower than man but above animals. Aristotle and alchemists constructed descriptions of biological processes that corroborated women's innate physical inferiority, not by the weight of empirical evidence but as an assumption guiding theories of physiological and psychological differences in male and female. Aristotle's theory of heat asserted that because woman was defective in heat, her soul was less perfect than man's soul and mind, which were generated by more perfect heat. Influenced by Aristotle's biology, Platonic conceptions of the soul, and the Genesis account of creation and the fall, theologians argued three positions: that woman has no soul and is not the image of God; that woman is only the image of God when she becomes like man; and that woman is an inferior soul and is a lesser image of God.

Modern science continued to develop under historical assumptions of women's inferiority, contending, for example, that woman is mindless or that woman is intellectually inferior by virtue of natural selection, arrested development, or the nature of germ plasm. The embedded cultural assumption of women's inferiority influenced Darwin's theory of sexual selection, which concluded that only males evolve. Darwin's proposal that both women and non-European men were less evolved humans led to comparative research programs on cranial capacity and brain size. Laced with sexism and racism, conclusions, often from flawed observational methods, pointed toward the superiority of European males and compared the less-evolved female skulls to those of gorillas, children, and "savages." The body of theological, philosophical, and scientific literature denigrating women's minds and souls had social and political consequences in arguments against women's right to vote and on the futility of women's education. However, Tuana's book concludes that if we can recognize how the denigration of the nature of women pervades science and culture, then we are in a position to reject the patterns that perpetuate the notion of women's inferiority.

What Tuana accomplishes by analysis of the biological sciences, philosophy, and religion, Margaret Wertheim undertakes with regard to physics, religion, and philosophy in *Pythagoras' Trousers: God, Physics, and the Gender Wars* (1995). Wertheim's analysis generates an analogy between physics and Christianity: that physics is the Roman Catholic Church of science. Arguing that physics is the science with roots most connected with religion, she traces the historical foundations of Mathematical Man's dominance in science that limited women's access to education and professional participation in research and scientific societies. From Pythagorean pursuit of mathematics, belonging to the male psychic sphere, to the contemporary search for the mind of God or Theory of Everything in physics, religious undercurrents in physics have established the physical cosmologist as priest, who interprets the book of nature as the Roman Catholic priest interprets Scripture.

Carolyn Merchant's *The Death of Nature: Women, Ecology and the Scientific Revolution* (1980) traces the history of attitudes toward women and nature in a study that includes science and religion, as well as art, literature, politics, commerce, and philosophy, in an integrative analysis of metaphors connecting women and nature during the rise of the Scientific Revolution. Merchant shows that the pervasive metaphor of nature as nurturing mother corresponded with organic models of nature and limited manipulation of nature; with the rise of science and a mechanistic worldview, the equally powerful metaphor of nature as wild woman became the dominant metaphor for nature, allowing for manipulation and control of inert matter (nature). The atomistic, mechanical view of nature literally signified the death of nature and supported domination of women by male authority in the social sphere. Merchant's ecofeminist perspective advocates return to ecological holism as a step toward ending the subjugation of women and nature.

Women's integrative scholarship on science and religion is most prolific in the political and activist perspective known as ecofeminism. So called Third World ecofeminists criticize reductive forms of Western science and open different perspectives on science and religion. Vandana Shiva, an Indian physicist and ecofeminist activist, condemns Western science and neocolonial development projects for deforestation, famine, and drought in India. Shiva's *Staying Alive: Women, Ecology and Development* (1989) uses the science of ecology to profile the state of agriculture, forest management, and water management since the British colonial period. Shiva proposes that the future of India depends on recovery of the feminine and creative principle, shakti, and the role of women as food producers working within the ecosystem. Shiva's work retrieves the cultural integration of Indian religion and ethnoscience as a model for survival.

BIBLIOGRAPHY

For reading in feminism and science, consult Donna Haraway's *Primate Visions: Gender, Race, and Nature in the World of Modern Science* (1989), a critique of primatology from a feminist perspective; Sandra Harding's *The Science Question in Feminism* (1986), on science and feminist epistemology; Evelyn Fox Keller's *Reflections on Gender and Science* (1985) and *Secrets of Life, Secrets of Death: Essays on Language, Gender and Science* (1992), a feminist theory of science, and her *A Feeling for the Organism: The Life and Work of Barbara McClintock* (1983), an examination of one woman's approach to science. For an overview, see Nancy Tuana's edited work *Feminism and Science* (1989). For reading on the integration of science and religion in women's scholarship, consult the writing of Mary Midgley: her two books, *Evolution as a Religion: Strange Hopes and Strange Fears* (1985) and *Science as Salvation: A Modern Myth and Its Meaning* (1992), explore the religious character of science. (*Science as Salvation* is the publication of Midgley's 1990 Gifford Lectures.) Ecofeminism integrates science and religion in the interest of justice toward nature and women: see Rosemary Radford Ruether's edited volume *Women Healing Earth: Third World Women on Ecology, Feminism, and Religion* (1996), which includes essays by Latin American, Asian, and African women from different religious perspectives. Two Christian theologies of nature are Sallie McFague's *The Body of God: An Ecological Theology* (1993) and Ruether's *Gaia and God: An Ecofeminist Theology of Earth Healing* (1992).

See also **Education: Education and Literacy; Environmentalism.**

NANCY R. HOWELL

Seclusion

Gender differentiation is a common organizing principle in human societies. What varies from one culture to another is the totality of gender segregation and its correspondence to hierarchic gender ideologies, as well as the degree to which religion justifies and facilitates the practice. Segregation—the physical separation of persons from each other based on identity categories—is intensified in the phenomenon of seclusion, in which all contact between designated groups is avoided. In large-scale urban societies, the seclusion of women can be constructed to encompass all aspects of their lives, whereas in small-scale societies, seclusion tends to occur in discrete events such as menstruation and childbirth. Types of gender segregation are inflected by factors including age, reproductive status, sexual purity, menstruation, labor, education, and class.

Feminist scholarship has revealed a contradiction at the heart of gender segregation. Although the exclusion of women from culturally valued spheres functions as a major prop for patriarchy, all-female settings are also locations for women's resistance and creativity. When seclusion is all-encompassing, women have a great deal of latitude within their own sphere into which male authority may not extend.

COSMOLOGICAL JUSTIFICATIONS

Among traditional Pacific Islander societies, strict systems of taboo—prohibitions concerning contact with sacred power—structure many interactions between men and women. In the Solomon Islands male and female seclusion areas are located on opposite sides of the village. During childbirth and menstruation women reside in their area, which is designated by men as ritually polluted. But because men avoid the area, women use it as a refuge from male authority and demands. Women cannot enter the male seclusion area, guarded by priestly authority, which contains sacred objects, altars, and skull pits. An interesting symmetry emerges: all men are born within the female seclusion area—which they never enter again—and women enter the male seclusion area only after dying, when their remains are added to the skull pit.

In Hawaii women could not participate in male rituals or visit *heiaus* (male ritual locations). Certain foods, including pork and banana, were reserved exclusively for men. The cosmology that governed this complex system stressed separation along two lines: commoner and chief, female and male. This separation further reflected two cosmogonies: the separation of earth from heaven, and the mythology of Wākea and his wife Papa. Wākea, so as to hide an incestuous relationship from Papa, instituted the *kapu* (taboo) restrictions, which are rife with gender tensions and power struggles.

Islam inherited sexual seclusion from surrounding cultures, preeminently Byzantine Christianity. The Qur'anic passage used to justify sexual segregation, Sura 33:53–59, actually applies to the Prophet's wives and the necessary modesty that should surround these "Mothers of the Believers." Male authorities, however, extended restrictions to all women; this was concretized in architecture and women's dress (Sura 24:30–31). The nearly parallel societies of men and women does not arise primarily from religious ideology, and it is being challenged and altered by Muslims in many places today.

Sexual seclusion can lead to religious creativity, as in the Iranian Muslim *sofreh*, a ritual display of foods and votive offerings. This practice, derived from Zoroas-

Men and women speak over a partition at the Western Wall in Jerusalem, where the two sexes must pray separately (Annie Griffiths-Belt/Corbis).

trian roots, is frowned on by local Muslim male religious authorities. Rural women exploit the mechanism of sexual separation to maintain and elaborate the *sofreh,* even in distinctly syncretic and unorthodox ways, compensating for their exclusion from public religious observances.

RITUAL

Ritual often highlights gender distinctions. Male scholars of Australian aboriginal culture assumed that women's seclusion at menstruation and exclusion from male rituals revealed a cultural male bias. But feminist researchers uncovered a genuine complementarity, complete with checks and balances, between men and women. Women's ritual activity is complex, time-consuming, socially necessary, and an honored responsibility.

Prohibitions on women's creativity among the Sepik of New Guinea are asymmetrical and severe. Men's initiation ceremonies, cult buildings, and artwork are strictly forbidden to women, who have no counterpart set of complex rituals. But male anxiety about the dangers women pose to their virility cultivates a dominance more symbolic than tangible, since women perform most of the labor necessary for sustenance.

Citing the principle of avoiding sexual temptation, the Talmud has been invoked to justify the physical separation of men and women at worship (Tractate Sukkah 51b). In Orthodox Jewish synagogues this is sometimes actualized in a physical barrier (*mechitsa*). Nineteenth-century Reform Judaism made the introduction of "family seating" a hallmark of its modernity; conversely, Orthodox Judaism and most Muslim mosques still maintain strict sexual separation at worship.

MENSTRUAL SECLUSION

Seclusion of menstruating women, often in small shelters at a distance from settlements, is found in myriad traditions. Ritual seclusions are often more elaborate at the onset of menses. Western male scholars interpreted menstrual taboos as markers of female pollution and inferiority, but listening to women's voices has revealed greater complexity. Among native North American peoples, women's menstrual seclusion is likened to male sweat lodges: both men and women need a monthly time of seclusion to purify the power of their distinctive medicines. Among the tribes of the Pacific Northwest, menstrual seclusion forms the basis for female secret societies. Such practices are based on the inherent power of menstrual blood, considered to be positive yet powerful enough to be dangerous. The origins of these seclusions may be connected to predatory animals' strong reactions to blood: it is common for menstruating women to avoid not only men but animals on which the tribe depends, and to abstain from food preparation duties.

SEXUALITY, SPIRITUALITY, AND SECLUSION

Strict gender seclusion necessarily regulates heterosexual activity, while simultaneously creating homosocial environments. Among the celibate Shakers, men and women had separate dwellings, distinct divisions of labor, and were prohibited from physical contact with each other. Gender difference was valorized as sacred while gender hierarchy was condemned, thus providing opportunities for female leadership.

Within Christianity and Buddhism, strict gender separation of those devoted to monastic life is maintained, ostensibly to reduce sexual temptation. The explicitly patriarchal organization of the Roman Catholic Church has ensured that women's convent lives are closely regulated. Justifying this history in 1950, Pope Pius XII remarked that "the Church, like a Mother, bent lovingly over these virgins who, choosing the better part, separated themselves entirely from the world so as to embrace within the monastery the fullness of Christian perfection, joining to virginity a strict poverty and an absolute obedience" (*States of Perfection,* pp. 384–385). Despite recurring tension between women's secluded spiritual lives and male authority, monastic settings enabled women to flourish creatively. In England in the thirteenth century, women outnumbered men by about five to one in choosing to become anchorites, solitary recluses enclosed in small cells attached to village churches. The anchorite was both solitary and a social resource: villagers believed that her pious Christian prayers aided them. The women anchorites came from all social classes, adopting this strict discipline as a form of spiritual individualism. Enterprising Christian female monastics have been active up to the present day.

Contemporary lesbian separatism sometimes justifies its self-segregation from men on spiritual grounds. Mary Daly defines separatism as "paring away from the Self all that is alienating and confining" (1978, p. 381). Dianic covens, such as Z. Budapest's Susan B. Anthony Coven, launched in 1971, are feminist-separatist forms of neopaganism. These movements combine political and spiritual insights, as evidenced by their presence at Greenham Common (an extended antinuclear protest in the United Kingdom in the 1980s) and in ecofeminist movements.

BIBLIOGRAPHY

Feminist anthropologists have dealt extensively with categories of gender ideology, differentiation, and segregation. In *Female Power and Male Dominance* (1981), Peggy Reeves Sanday theorizes that sexual segregation is a necessary condition for the development of male dominance. The collection *Women United, Women Divided*, edited by Patricia Caplan and Janet Burja (1978), concerns female solidarity and divisions within situations of sexual segregation. Mary Douglas's work, especially the classic *Purity and Danger* (1966), is crucial to structuralist understandings of taboo and pollution.

For general overviews on the topic, readers can consult the articles in *Gender and Anthropology: Critical Reviews for Research and Teaching*, edited by Sandra Morgen (1989), or draw on the textbook approach of Martha Ward's *A World Full of Women* (1996). Exaggerated male and Eurocentric biases mar the few surveys that cover gender seclusions systematically. Sir James Frazer devotes an extensive chapter to female puberty seclusion in volume 10 of *The Golden Bough* (1913), and Webster Hutton's *Taboo: A Sociological Study* (1942) allocates a substantial section to gender separations; however, these studies are dated and untrustworthy in both data and interpretation.

Concerning menstrual seclusion, Judy Grahn's *Blood, Bread, and Roses: How Menstruation Created the World* (1993) is a feminist spiritual and speculative work based on the logic that women originated menstrual seclusion themselves as an ascetic discipline and meditation on the cosmological creativity of women's blood. More scholarly is the collection *Blood Magic: The Anthropology of Menstruation*, edited by Thomas Buckley and Alma Gottlieb (1988). Concerning native North American cultures, two especially valuable works are Marla Powers's "Menstruation and Reproduction: An Oglala Case" (*Signs* 6, no. 1 [1981]: 54–65) and Buck-

ley's "Menstruation and the Power of Yurok Women" (*American Ethnologist* 9, no. 1 [1982]: 47–60).

Gender separation as a central category in Pacific Islander religions is highlighted in Jocelyn Linnekin's study of Hawaii, *Sacred Queens and Women of Consequence* (1990). Elli Köngäs Maranda's article "Lua Malaita: 'A Woman Is an Alien Spirit,'" in *Many Sisters: Women in Cross-Cultural Perspective*, edited by Carolyn J. Matthiason (1974), examines the Solomon Islands, and Sherry Ortner's "Gender and Sexuality in Hierarchical Societies: The Case of Polynesia and Some Comparative Implications," in *Sexual Meanings: The Cultural Construction of Gender and Sexuality*, edited by Sherry Ortner and Harriet Whitehead (1981), examines the status and prestige issues involved in isolating young marriageable women.

Diana Bell's *Daughters of the Dreaming* (1983) compellingly presents the dynamics of gender complementarity in Australian aboriginal culture. Annette Weiner's similar discovery of women's central role in mortuary ritual among the Trobrianders is detailed in *The Trobrianders of Papua New Guinea* (1988). Richard Anderson summarizes the dynamics of Sepik culture, and gives a thorough bibliography, in *Calliope's Sisters: A Comparative Study of Philosophies of Art* (1990).

Jewish gender seclusion is critically analyzed by Judith Baskin in "The Separation of Women in Rabbinic Judaism," in *Women, Religion and Social Change*, edited by Yvonne Yazbeck Haddad and Ellison Banks Findly (1985). Jonathan Sarna traces the U.S. history of the split between Orthodox and Reform over gendered seating arrangements in "The Debate over Mixed Seating in the American Synagogue," in *Religion and American Culture: A Reader*, edited by David Hackett (1995).

The controversial effects of gender seclusion on women in Islam has generated much anti-Muslim propaganda. Responsible works on the topic include Leila Ahmed's *Women and Gender in Islam* (1992); Fatima Mernissi's *Doing Daily Battle: Interviews with Moroccan Women* (1989); Sherri Deaver's "The Contemporary Saudi Woman," in *A World of Women*, edited by Erika Bourguignon (1980); Daisy Hilse Dwyer's *Images and Self-Images: Male and Female in Morocco* (1978); Janice Boddy's *Wombs and Alien Spirits: Women, Men and the Zār Cult in Northern Sudan* (1989); and Laal Jamzedeh and Margaret Mills's "Iranian *Sofreh*: From Collective to Female Ritual," in *Gender and Religion: On the Complexity of Symbols*, edited by Caroline Walker Bynum, Stevan Harrell, and Paula Richman (1986).

Papal writings on monasticism collected in *States of Perfection*, selected and arranged by the Benedictine monks of Solesmes and translated by Mother E. O'Gorman (1967), are a good primary source on Christian monasticism. Jo Ann McNamara's *Sisters in Arms: Catholic Nuns Through Two Millennia* (1996) sets a new scholarly standard. Cloistering and anchorites can be studied in Ann Warren's *Anchorites and Their Patrons in Medieval England* (1985), Linda Georgianna's *The Solitary Self: Individuality in the* Ancrene Wisse (1981), and Grace Jantzen's biography of the most famous female anchorite, *Julian of Norwich: Mystic and Theologian* (1988).

Lesbian separatism and Dianic Wicca are discussed in Cynthia Eller's *Living in the Lap of the Goddess* (1995) and Margot Adler's *Drawing Down the Moon* (1986, repr. 1997). Primary sources include Mary Daly's *Gyn-Ecology* (1978), Z. Budapest's *The Feminist Book of Lights and Shadows* (1976), and Nell Hart's *Spiritual Lesbians* (1989).

See also **Menstruation; Monasticism; Ritual.**

JENNIFER RYCENGA

Secret Societies

Secret societies are voluntary organizations that require potential members to undergo a rite of initiation and to take an oath not to reveal their secret teachings and rituals to nonmembers. Beyond these simple criteria, it is difficult to cite further shared characteristics of the many groups scholars have included in this category. Appearing throughout history and in many cultures, secret societies have been concerned with an array of religious, political, and social interests. They have assumed distinct stances in relation to the larger culture and its prescribed gender relationships; some groups seek to maintain a culture's values, while others have specifically sought to subvert or even transcend those standards.

Secret societies that have dedicated themselves to preserving and conveying a body of occult knowledge have often denounced prevailing social norms, including gender roles, as elements of an inferior order of existence. Accordingly, they have sought to embody an alternative social order within their own doctrines and practices. Ancient secret associations such as the Greco-Roman Eleusinian mystery cult (approximately sixth century B.C.E. to fourth century C.E.) are believed to have abolished distinctions of both class and gender in initiating members. The gnostic movement that flourished in the early Christian church likewise admitted both sexes into its membership and its secrets.

Other secret societies concerned with mystical knowledge have merely upheld the prevailing gender inequalities of their cultures. Many seventeenth- and eighteenth-century European traditions, including Freemasonry and the Order of the Holy Cross (Rosicrucians), historically have followed their culture's lead and excluded women from their membership. Freemasonry, in particular, which has emphasized both an esoteric body of knowledge and a profound sense of the value of fraternalism, has often sought to reinforce the distinctions and social divisions between women and men. Throughout the nineteenth century Masons fought proposals by women, most notably their own wives, to include them in their orders. Only begrudgingly did Freemasonry (unofficially) acknowledge the formation of the Order of the Eastern Star in 1876, an auxiliary organization that was open to Masons as well as their immediate female relatives (wife, daughter, sister). Even then, the Masons denied the Eastern Star the autonomy to run meetings without the supervision of its male membership.

Many secret societies in Africa have also served to uphold social orders in which the roles and tasks of each sex are sharply distinguished from one another. Among the more than one hundred secret societies known to have existed in West Africa at least since the eighteenth century are the Sande and Poro societies of the Kpelle of Liberia. Like their counterparts in other African cultures, these women's and men's societies, respectively, have been responsible for indoctrinating youths into the culture's values and beliefs through extended initiation rites for girls and boys. Initiations for young girls have traditionally taken place over a period of several weeks or more, during which the girls and members of the women's society remain away from the village out in the bush. Prevalent initiation practices include religious and moral training, in which girls are taught cultural mythology and customs, as well as practical information concerning marriage, sexuality, and childbirth. The initiation of both girls and boys has also customarily involved circumcision as a rite of passage.

In addition to these functions, African men's and women's secret societies generally have been charged with enforcing community laws and maintaining control over local protective medicines or magic. Although the Sande has had to rely on the Poro to discipline husbands or other men who have mistreated a woman, the groups otherwise have been autonomous in their actions and have shared responsibility for managing the community, each overseeing the tasks delegated to its members. However, throughout many African cultures, including that of the Kpelle, intertribal concerns, such as warfare, have most often been the sole domain of the

The Daughters of the Universal Chapter of the Order of the Eastern Star, a charitable women's society, hold a parade in New Orleans, Louisiana, c. 1950 (Bradley Smith/Corbis).

male societies. And typically only the men's societies have participated in the advisory councils to local and regional political leaders.

In contrast to these civic-minded organizations, the secret societies of China, possibly numbering in the thousands, provide many examples of subversive groups dedicated not to upholding existing regimes but to replacing them. In their revolutionary efforts these groups, whose members have been mostly peasants and laborers, have frequently dispensed with the gender roles of their culture. Although dominated by men, the records of groups such as the Triad Society, an organization founded in the 1670s to overthrow the ruling dynasty, as well as the Red Beards, a group of Chinese living in northern Manchuria without state approval in the latter half of the nineteenth century, contain many references to women of valor, savagery, and power who led their armies against the enemy. Women are also portrayed in these histories as working alongside men in establishing and governing settlements in inhospitable regions. So common was the acceptance of women's abilities to contribute to revolutionary aims that even groups for young men, such as the Boxers (Fists of Righteous Harmony), supported auxiliary units for girls. It is perhaps worth noting that the mythology of many of these revolutionary groups often spoke of a divine female, the Eternal Mother, who would return one day and transform the earth into a paradise for all of her children.

BIBLIOGRAPHY

Most sources on secret societies, including works from the disciplines of sociology, anthropology, and theology, present their material only from a male perspective, or merely allude to differences in the experiences of women and men in these associations. Information on women's involvement in many groups, therefore, must be carefully gleaned. Works that do treat issues of gender in secret societies are mostly concerned with the mystical or fraternal (or sororal) secret societies of nineteenth- and twentieth-century Europe and the United States.

Burkert, Walter. *Ancient Mystery Cults.* 1987.

Butt-Thompson, F. W. *West African Secret Societies.* 1929. Reprint, 1970.

Carnes, Mark C. *Secret Ritual and Manhood in Victorian America.* 1989.

Chesneaux, Jean, ed. *Popular Movements and Secret Societies in China 1840–1950.* 1972.

———. *Secret Societies in China in the Nineteenth and Twentieth Centuries.* 1965 (French); 1971 (English).

Clawson, Mary Ann. *Constructing Brotherhood: Class, Gender and Fraternalism.* 1989.

Coquery-Vidrovitch, Catherine. *African Women: A Modern History.* 1994 (French); 1997 (English).

Murphy, Robert F. "Social Structure and Sex Antagonism." *Journal of Anthropological Research* 43, no. 3 (1986): 407–416.

Pagels, Elaine H. *The Gnostic Gospels.* 1989.

Parrinder, Geoffrey. *West African Religion: A Study of the Beliefs and Practices of Akan, Ewe, Yoruba, Ibo and Kindred Peoples.* 1961.

Tefft, Stanton K. *The Dialectics of Secret Society Power in States.* 1992.

JULIA WINDEN FEY

Secularization

Because the processes associated with secularization provoke diverse religious reactions, its impact on women is varied. Counter-secular movements may offer women the opportunity to remove themselves from the patriarchal domination of established religious organizations and construct satisfying religious lives unencumbered by others' expectations. More often, however, women will be called upon to embody doctrinal purity and idealized traditional values; they may perceive that responsibility as either a boon or a burden. In addition, their understanding of their own behavior may differ sharply from outsiders' evaluations. Women may also seize upon opportunities to subvert the expectations placed upon them while fulfilling their outward form, as when they exercise religious leadership in culturally acknowledged "feminine" forms. In general, an understanding of the various theoretical options for construing the origins, directions, extent, geographical dispersion, and future of secularization is crucial to assessing its impact on women's religious lives.

Representing the prevailing sociological understanding of secularization, Peter Berger defines it as the process "by which sectors of society and culture are removed from the domination of religious institutions and symbols" (1969, p. 107). Although he sees the most widespread impact of secularization in the modern Western world, Berger finds the roots of that process as far back as ancient Israel where, following Weber, he locates the beginnings of the "disenchantment of the world." In the late nineteenth and early twentieth centuries, theorists like Freud and Durkheim also tended to see secularization as unidirectional and inevitable. Freud in particular welcomed the prospect of a religionless future as a positive development. The expected demise of religion, however, has not yet occurred. A more persuasive understanding of secularization as an inherently self-limiting phenomenon within any "religious economy" has been proposed by Rodney Stark and William Sims Bainbridge (1985) as part of their general theory of religion. They argue that, as secularization advances in some sectors of a society, a countervailing intensification of religion through the processes of revival and innovation will develop in others. As a result, the amount of religion in any society remains relatively constant while its forms are constantly shifting.

Many theoretical statements about secularization have focused on the dominant actors and classes in a given society and ignored its impact on those who participate neither in the public realm nor the upper classes. Insufficient attention, therefore, has been devoted to discerning the differing impact of secularizing forces, such as modernization, urbanization, industrialization, capitalism, and various political and economic ideologies on religious observances in the home and other less easily regulated areas of social life. Recent efforts to recover women's religious lives still need to be integrated with theoretical models of secularization that have not incorporated gender as a significant analytical factor.

Secularization, however, cannot be seen as having an unvarying impact on women's religion. Sectarian religious movements that react to a parent group's perceived accommodation to dominant social norms may emphasize patriarchal values along with a return to doctrinal purity; yet they may also offer multiple opportunities for women's religious participation, and even leadership in the home, in sexually segregated groups and in sectarian groups themselves. For example, many Christian sects in the United States, contemporary evangelical Protestant groups in South America, and new sectarian religions in Japan have combined an emphasis on the restoration of an idealized "traditional" family with a broad, if sometimes uneasy, acceptance of women in positions of power. Similarly, new religious groups do not necessarily promise either continued subjugation to patriarchy or liberation for their female members. In the United States, for example, neopagan and New Age groups typically welcome women's leadership, while groups like the Unification Church and the International Society for Krishna Consciousness tend to reinforce patriarchal models of social organization.

Theories of secularization have been developed largely out of analysis of Western and Christian data, but more attention has recently been devoted to the processes and consequences of secularization in non-Western cultures. Throughout the Muslim world, for example, dilemmas of accommodation and resistance to secularization have figured prominently in religious discourse in the latter part of the twentieth century. The impact on women's religious lives of those discussions has been varied and complex. In Iran the Ayatollah Khomeini condemned attempts by reformers of the 1950s and 1960s to adapt elements of Western family law to an Islamic context and also imposed extensive religiously legitimated restrictions on Iranian women's public and private lives. But the anti-Shah revolution had nonetheless encouraged the participation of some women, which in turn raised their expectations for involvement in public life in the Islamic Republic. The resulting tensions continue to echo through Iranian society.

From any theoretical perspective secularization will continue to be a major factor in contemporary religious life; that alone suggests its importance for women's religion.

BIBLIOGRAPHY

Berger, Peter. *The Sacred Canopy: Elements of a Sociological Theory of Religion.* 1969.

Fenn, Richard K. *Toward a Theory of Secularization.* 1978.

Haeri, Shahla. "Obedience versus Autonomy: Women and Fundamentalism in Iran and Pakistan." In *Fundamentalisms and Society: Reclaiming the Sciences, the Family, and Education.* Edited by Martin E. Marty and R. Scott Appleby. 1993.

Maldonado, Jorge E. "Building 'Fundamentalism' from the Family in Latin America." In *Fundamentalisms and Society.* Edited by Martin E. Marty and R. Scott Appleby. 1993.

Martin, David. *A General Theory of Secularization.* 1978.

Stark, Rodney, and William Sims Bainbridge. *The Future of Religion: Secularization, Revival, and Cult Formation.* 1985.

See also Neopaganism; New Religions.

EUGENE V. GALLAGHER

Seidel, Anna

Anna Katharina Seidel (1938–1991) was one of the most influential and gifted scholars of Chinese religions, especially religious Taoism and Buddhism. Born in Berlin, Seidel read Sinology at Munich and Hamburg from 1958 to 1961 and then continued her training in the study of the ancient religions of China, especially Taoism, in Paris. In 1969 Seidel was elected to the Japanese branch of the École Française d'Extrême-Orient in Kyoto, where she lived and worked for twenty-two years.

Seidel's contributions to the field include a range of important works on Taoism, which she regarded as a messianic religion permeating Chinese culture and society rather than a degenerate form of philosophy. Her influential works span her scholarly career, from her doctoral thesis "La divinisation de Lao-tseu dans le taoïsm des Han" (1969), to the booklet *Taoismus: die inoffizielle Hochreligion Chinas,* published just before her untimely death in 1991. Other works of particular import include the article "Taoism" in the fifteenth edition of the *Encyclopaedia Britannica,* the volume *Facets of Taoism* (1979, coedited with Holmes Welch), and "Chronicle of Taoist Studies in the West 1950–1990" (1990).

At the École Française, Seidel focused in large part on writing and editing the *Hobogirin,* a monumental encyclopedic dictionary of Sino-Japanese Buddhism. She guided the highly regarded bilingual journal *Cahiers d'Extrême-Asie,* which she founded in 1985. Seidel's work is noteworthy not only for its scrupulous scholarly care, but for her ability to relate ancient texts and traditions to modern religious phenomena. Her career is significant not only for her profound influence on the study of Chinese religions but also for her role as mentor and teacher to young scholars.

BIBLIOGRAPHY

Other encyclopedia articles by Anna Seidel include "Henri Maspero," "T'ai-p'ing," "Yü," and "Yü-huang" in *The Encyclopedia of Religion,* edited by Mircea Eli-

ade (1987). A number of Seidel's articles on Taoism will be available in *The Selected Papers of Anna Seidel* (forthcoming). For a comprehensive list of Anna Seidel's works, see *Cahiers d'Extrême-Asie* 8 (1995): xix–xxi; and *Taoist Resources* 3, no. 2 (May 1992): 68–70.

JENNIFER OLDSTONE-MOORE

Self

Full understanding of any culture's view of self requires deep familiarity with its literature, rituals, art, family systems, history, ethical codes, legal institutions, commercial practices, medical techniques, bodily representations, metaphysical beliefs, parenting styles, work distribution inside and outside the home, and oral communication patterns and contents, as well as folkways. In most cultures, these categories are governed by religious beliefs in subtle but formative ways.

Terms such as *self, soul, person,* and *human,* though considered inclusive, are often taken to refer to male persons, which can render females invisible to language. However, in virtually all cultures, female and male selfhood are constructed in fundamentally different ways, with the most valued activities or characteristics associated with males and maleness.

MONOTHEISTIC TRADITIONS

Central questions asked about self in the monotheistic traditions (Judaism, Christianity, Islam) have to do with a person's relationship to the divine, along with the ethics and purification that will facilitate this relationship. These religions understand all persons to have been created by one God.

Biblical Traditions

The Genesis theory of Eve has given rise to two divergent interpretations of her, and by extension, two varying views of women. In the first, Eve's creation from Adam's rib suggests woman's dependence on man and her responsibility because of her sins for all that he suffers as well as for the pain of childbirth.

In the second interpretation, while Adam, "the earth creature," like his animals and the garden, are all created from earth, Eve is created of flesh, of life. This makes her unique in all creation. Moreover, she is Adam's "companion" (*ezer*), a word that is often translated as "helper," and which arguably indicates an equal, one who alleviates isolation. Indeed, in the Hebrew scriptures this term can refer to a superior, notably God, to whom one turns for help (e.g., Ps. 121: 1–2). Further, Adam is identified as male only after

Eve's creation, hence the genders arise simultaneously, not sequentially. Moreover, though Eve has been widely characterized as perpetrator of the Fall, the term *Fall* does not occur in the Hebrew scriptures in relation to the Adam-Eve narrative. Its *locus classicus* is Plato's *Phaedrus*, which enters Christianity through Orphic thought. Thus, Eve's precipation of the Fall, like other interpretations of the narrative pejorative to women, is not found in the original story but in post–second-century interpretative material.

Some feminists see the figure of the Virgin Mary as valorizing the power of motherhood and female relationship to the divine. Others find that birthgiving through divine rather than corporal intervention degrades women and their bodily labors and valorizes bodily transcendence to the point that Simone de Beauvoir (1974) observes, "it is not in giving life but in risking life that man is raised above the animal; that is why superiority has been accorded to humanity, not to the sex that brings forth but to that which kills." [need page #]. Moreover, motherhood has been inextricably linked with women's "nature"; only in the early nineteenth century was motherhood recognized as an institution shaped by culture and religion. Contemporary conservative claims that domesticity reflects true womanhood are also traceable to biblical characterizations of Mary as pious and pure. Mary Daly (1984) signaled a turning point in feminist biblical reflection when she called Mary a "totaled" woman, modeling submission and dependence for all womankind.

Overall, feminist interpreters of both the Hebrew and Christian scriptures argue that the ideal figure of personhood is modeled by God—autonomous, self-made, powerful, and in control. At the same time, the righteous Christian is portrayed in terms often culturally associated with women: pious, meek, providing selfless service to others. These patterns in turn reflect basic hierarchical dualisms traceable to the Platonic religious heritage of classical Christianity, including mind–body, subjective self–objective world, spirit–nature. From these flow the vast array of binary constructions allying the female with the passive, fertile, receptive, emotional, relational, nurturing, and natural, and the male with the active, heroic, intellectual, autonomous, and cultural.

Islam

In Islamic society, conservative elements use interpretations of the Qu'ran and of the family law based on this to regulate the lives of women inside and outside the home. Contemporary Muslim feminists are putting forward equally viable interpretations of the Qu'ran in support of women's comparative autonomy.

Feminist Islamic writings point to similarities in Islamic-Christian treatment of women. These in turn are understood to shape how women themselves are culturally constructed to identify their sense of self. In Islam, Mary (Maryam) becomes a platform on which to image Fāṭimah, daughter of the prophet. Mary gives birth to Jesus from her right thigh; Fāṭimah gives birth from her left. A significant difference, however, is that Fāṭimah does not conceive without intercourse, for that would subvert the paternal line. For Sunnis, and even more so for Shiites, Mary becomes significant for her miraculous intercessions which, though not mentioned in earlier scriptures, grows more prominent over time. She is even sent to help Fāṭimah in childbirth. The eleventh-century mystic at al-Baqli praises her as a bearer of the Word and light of the Spirit. This, together with the unbroken emphasis on paternal lineage, strongly implies a female self primarily—if not exclusively—defined by her relation to males, who carry names and hence cultural memory.

BUDDHISM AND HINDUISM

Central to Buddhism and Hinduism is a person's ability to plumb the depths of his or her mental, physical, or spiritual capacities. These traditions do not regard the world or its inhabitants as created by a creator deity. According to the theory of karma (the cause and effect of actions) all persons and their environments are produced from that person's own previous intentions as well as verbal and physical actions.

Dependent arising (*pratītyasamutpāda*) is an important principle within Buddhism. When Buddhists speak of the "self" (atman) as dependent on causes and conditions, they reflect primarily on the physical conditions of mind and body, and the way a child's survival depends on factors such as warmth, nourishment, and parental care. It has not, in traditional contexts, been applied in any systematic or extensive manner to the psychological, interpersonal, social, or political arenas.

The introspection for which Buddhist and other contemplative traditions are famous means something quite different in ancient Asian and modern Western contexts. Individualism and an increasing affinity for psychological self-narratives mean that Westerners use introspection to better understand their personal stories, their unique contributions and possibilities. Traditional Buddhist practice emphasizes examination of the self's structure rather than its story.

Thus, the "self" denied in Buddhist doctrines of selflessness is something very specific. This is a self regarded, however, subtly, as independent from the mind and body, instead of, more properly, as merely dependently arisen due to these, which are themselves of course dependent arisings. *Self* is thus a philosophical term in Buddhism that does not mean simply "you" or "me." Nor does it simply mean "ego" in any technical or popular sense. Thus, the self so vigorously denied in Buddhist philosophy must not be confused with an integrated sense of self-worth, or the ability to act with intention and decision.

Traditional Buddhist and Hindu cultures are powerfully familial. Their paths to liberation are also paths to greater individuality than other avenues in those cultures provide. Here, as in other traditional contexts, persons are constructed as inextricably linked with their wider social, geographical, and historical context, which, instead of their unique personal qualities, form the core of their identity. Characteristics such as nurturing and domesticity, often regarded as infelicitous in view of the individuated self valorized in modern Western construction, take on a different meaning. In many Asian cultures the bulk of hard physical labor—planting and harvesting, carrying water—is done by women. Thus, a woman's self-image as well as her actual contributions in labor are intimately linked with the creative forces of nature and the satisfaction of bodily needs.

INDIGENOUS TRADITIONS

Indigenous religious cultures in North America are, by their own description, nonpatriarchal. Women are encouraged to see themselves as powerful leaders, socially, spiritually, militarily, and, most recently, politically. Women see their own image in the sacred. For example, Changing Woman is inseparable from creation of the Navajo world, though she is not a cosmic creator. She is related to the White Painted Lady of the Apache, where she is also known as White Beaded Lady, who is time and life together. In other contexts, natural forces are understood as female; the lava coast of the Big Island is often decorated with offerings to Pele, the volcanic energy that created the islands of Hawaii. Among the Lakota, Mother Earth is respected as an elemental force of nature, giving birth to and nurturing life. Such images mean that a woman is encouraged to see herself and her own activities (birthing, for example) as participatory and reflective of the forces of nature, and, like them, powerful and valued.

Understanding the world to be maintained by male and female energies, women of the Blackfoot-related Bloods of Montana were partners with their husbands in all things, including holy rituals, some of which are no longer performed. To this day the entire tribe regards all its older women as their own grandmothers. The work of nurturing is deeply honored and actively fused with a woman's identity. A Blood woman does not say "I have five children," but rather, "I am mother to four sons and a daughter." In other words, she takes her role as mother to be a role that she animates through her own vitality. She is, by her own expression, subject, not object of her role as mother.

BIBLIOGRAPHY

Atkinson, Clarissa. *The Oldest Vocation: Christian Motherhood in the Middle Ages.* 1991. Outstanding analysis of the historical roots of many current debates.

Atkinson, Clarissa W., Constance H. Buchanan, and Margaret R. Miles, eds. *Immaculate and Powerful: The Female in Sacred Image and Social Reality.* 1985. Pathbreaking essays spanning a variety of religious traditions.

Buchanan, Constance. *Choosing to Lead: Women and the Crisis of American Values.* 1996. Outstanding and innovative reflection on the historical, religious, and political context of women's perspectives on current debates regarding values in American life.

Bynum, Caroline Walker, Stevan Harrell, and Paula Richman, eds. *Gender and Religion: On the Complexity of Symbols.* 1986. Extremely useful introduction, with essays drawn from most major religious traditions.

Daly, Mary. *Pure Lust: Elemental Feminist Philosophy.* 1984.

de Beauvoir, Simone. *The Second Sex.* 1974.

Deloria, Vine, Jr. *God is Red.* 1973. Highly recommended by Native Americans as a source for their own religious experience.

Falk, Nancy, and Rita Gross, eds. *Unspoken Worlds: Women's Religious Lives in Non-Western Cultures.* 1979. Outstanding collection of hard-to-find information on women and religion.

Flax, Jane. *Thinking Fragments: Psychoanalysis, Feminism, and Postmodernism in the Contemporary West.* 1990. Brilliant, complex analysis of the perspectives and limitations of the view of selfhood presented in these three contemporary discourses.

Gross, Rita. *Buddhism After Patriarchy.* 1993. Summary of major Buddhist characterizations of women and a proposal for the future.

Hawley, John S., and Donna M. Wulff, eds. *Devi: Goddesses of India.* 1996. An excellent introduction to non-consort goddesses of India.

Hirsch, Maryanne, and Evelyn Fox Keller, eds. *Conflicts in Feminism.* 1990. Top quality essays offering superb insights into the developing feminist debate on the construction of womanhood.

Jaimes, M. Annette, with Theresa Halsy. "American Indian Women: At the Center of Indigenous Resistance in Contemporary North America." In *The State of Native America.* Edited by M. Annette Jaimes. 1992.

Klein, Anne C. *Meeting the Great Bliss Queen: Buddhists, Feminists, and the Art of the Self.* 1995. A conversation between traditional Buddhist and contemporary feminist perspectives and an introduction to Buddhist ways of cultivating crucial aspects of selfhood, especially chapters 2 and 5.

———. "Primordial Purity and Everyday Life: Exalted Female Symbols and the Women of Tibet." In *Immaculate and Powerful: The Female in Sacred Image and Social Reality.* Edited by Atkinson, Buchanan, and Miles. 1985. Survey of certain major female symbols and the lives of Tibetan women.

Marglin, Frederique Apffel. *Wives of the God-King: The Rituals of the Devadasis of Puri.* 1985. Exemplary analysis of an important construction of the feminine in India.

Meyers, Carol. *Discovering Eve: Ancient Isaelite Women in Context.* 1988. Builds on Phyllis Trible's work, disentangling the earliest conceptions of Eve from post-second century commentaries which color current understanding.

McAuliffe, Jane Dammen. "Chosen of All Women: Mary and Fāṭimah in Qur'anic Exegesis." *Islamochristiana* 7 (1981): 19–28. Important resource on this topic.

Nicholson, Linda J., ed. *Feminism/Postmodernism.* 1990. Pathmaking essays on feminist reflections on identity.

Plaskow, Judith. *Sex, Sin and Grace: Women's Experience in the Theologies of Reinhold Nibuhr and Paul Tillich.* 1989. Incisive, innovative reading of classic views of sin and their different relationship to women.

Plaskow, Judith, and Carol P. Christ, eds. *Womanspirit Rising.* 1979. Classic collection of essays on a variety of issues in relation to women and religion.

Shaw, Miranda. *Passionate Enlightenment: Women in Tantric Buddhism.* 1994. A search to uncover the role of women in late Indian Buddhist practice traditions.

Spellberg, Denise A. "Writing the Unwritten Life of the Islamic Eve: Menstruation and the Demonization of Motherhood." *International Journal of Middle Eastern Studies* 28 (1966): 305–324. Succinct discussion of Eve's portrayal in the Qu'ran and changes in her characterization in post-Qu'ranic glosses.

Smith, Jane, and Haddad, Yvonne. "Eve: Islamic Image of Woman." In *Women's Studies International Forum* 5, no. 2 (1982): 135–144. The breakthrough article on this topic.

Sponberg, Alan. "Attitudes toward Women and the Feminine in Early Buddhism." In *Buddhism, Sexuality, and Gender.* Edited by José Ignacio Cabezón. 1992. Outstanding survey of diverse views of women.

Trible, Phyllis. *God and the Rhetoric of Sexuality.* 1978. Brilliant rereading of the Bible's story of creation and its significance for Christian views on female selfhood.

Wolf, Beverly Hungry. *The Ways of My Grandmothers.* 1980. A Native American's account of the ways of her elders, several of whom were the last women to perform traditional ritual practices.

See also **Identity**; **Philosophy**.

ANNE C. KLEIN

Semiotics

Although semiotics has been used as a hermeneutical tool to approach religious texts, particularly by Roland Barthes and Paul Ricoeur, its conceptual frame originates with the structuralist revolution that involved linguistics, anthropology, psychology, and Russian Formalism. It is a discipline that presupposes the centrality of language in the creation of texts, even if the notion of text is not bound to a mere linguistic structure. Not only literary formations but also rituals, protocols, and inconographic and multimedial representations constitute the object of semiotic studies. The signification of systems of signs, rather than the study of the meaning of specific signs, is the disciplinary object that involves semiotics with cultural formations and communicative concerns such as textual reception.

The relatively few women who have contributed to the development of semiotics and religious studies include Julia Kristeva, Mary Daly, and Phyllis Trible. Technically, Kristeva is the only feminist who, as a trained semiotician, has systematically applied semiotics to a variety of disciplines: literary analysis, psychoanalysis, feminist theory, and religion. All of her works relate to the Christian tradition and Christian thought. Daly's *Wickedary* is undoubtedly the most semiotic of her intellectual projects, developing a post-Christian feminist philosophy. The idea of renaming the world without subscribing to a patriarchal symbolic order amounts to a systemic endeavor of re-signification. Trible's *Texts of Terror* is often classified as rhetorical criticism, but her demystifying interest against hermeneutical objectivity, and her implication of storytelling as a feminist signifying practice, warrant her inclusion in the broader frame of textual semiotics.

BIBLIOGRAPHY

Barthes, Roland. "The Struggle with the Angel" (1971). In *Image, Music, Text.* Translated by Stephen Heath. 1977. Pp. 125–141.

Daly, Mary, with Jane Caputi. *Webster's First New Intergalactic Wickedary of the English Language.* 1987.

Kristeva, Julia. *In the Beginning Was Love: Psycho-analysis and Faith* (1985). Translated by Arthur Goldhammer. 1987.

———. *Polylogue.* Paris, 1977.

Ricoeur, Paul. *Essays on Biblical Interpretation.* Edited by Lewis S. Mudge. 1980.

———. *Figuring the Sacred: Religion, Narrative, and Imagination.* Translated by David Pellauer. Edited by Mark I. Wallace. 1995.

Trible, Phyllis. *Texts of Terror: Literary-Feminist Readings of Biblical Narratives.* 1984.

CARLA LOCATELLI

Seton, Elizabeth Ann

Elizabeth Ann Bayley Seton (1774–1821) was the first American-born Roman Catholic saint and founder of the Sisters of Charity. Born in New York City of a wealthy Anglican family, she married William Magee Seton, a successful merchant, in 1794. They had five children. Elizabeth Seton was active in social causes, establishing in 1797 the Society for the Relief of Poor Widows with Small Children. In 1803 Seton took her tubercular husband to Tuscany for a rest cure, where he died within three months. Delays caused her to remain in Italy until June 1804. During this period she was deeply impressed by the kindness of an Italian family and influenced by their expression of Roman Catholicism.

Upon her return to New York and after considerable thought and prayer, Seton converted to Catholicism, formally entering the church on 14 March 1805. In June 1808 she left New York City for Baltimore, where she took her first vows as a Sister of Charity of Saint Joseph in 1809, later moving her school and community to Emmitsburg, Maryland. Archbishop John Carroll of Baltimore worked with Seton to form a sisterhood relevant to the American context. Based on a modified version of the rule of St. Vincent de Paul's Daughters of Charity, Seton's community, which worked outside of convents where needed among the people, was the first active sisterhood in the United States. It was in Baltimore that they first wore their habit, the simple black garb of a widow, including a bonnet to cover the hair. Seton began a school for girls that would later expand to Saint Joseph Academy and then Saint Joseph College. Her work to establish Catholic schools has been noted as the foundation for the U.S. parochial school system.

The rule of the American Sisters of Charity was approved by Archbishop Carroll in 1812. Mother Seton's order spread throughout the United States, Canada, South America, and Italy; the sisters taught and administered schools and orphanages, and served as nurses in hospitals and during periods of epidemic and war.

Elizabeth Ann Seton, canonized as the first American Roman Catholic saint, is pictured here dressed in the simple costume of the Sisters of Charity (Corbis-Bettmann).

Seton's spirituality developed within the context of the religiously pluralistic environment of the eighteenth- and early-nineteenth-century United States. This spirituality applied a Protestant emphasis on the authority and preaching of scripture to a Catholic interest in the sacraments, especially the Eucharist. One of the most influential American Catholic women of the nineteenth century, Saint Elizabeth Ann Seton was canonized as the first native-born American saint by Pope Paul VI on 14 September 1975.

BIBLIOGRAPHY

Dirvin, Joseph I. *Mrs. Seton: Foundress of the American Sisters of Charity.* 1962.

Kelly, Elin, and Annabelle Melville. *Elizabeth Seton: Selected Writings.* 1987. Selections from her letters, journals, meditations, and prayers with a consideration of her life and spirituality.

Melville, Annabelle M. *Elizabeth Bayley Seton, 1774–1821.* 1985. Republished in the wake of Seton's canonization, this book presents a history of her life and activities.

Vincentian Heritage 14(2). Papers from the Symposium, "Elizabeth Seton in Dialogue with Her Time and Ours." 1992.

LEONARD NORMAN PRIMIANO

Sex Change

Sex change is a rare but intriguing event in religious literature. In the Mahāyāna Buddhist text *The Lotus Sutra,* for instance, a young girl known as the Dragon Princess spontaneously becomes a man just before entering buddhahood. During the final days before her martyrdom, the second-century Christian Perpetua sees a vision of herself as a male warrior who bests his opponent with superior strength and skill. What do these and other examples of sex change in scripture, hagiography, and spiritual autobiography indicate about religious importance of sexual identity?

Feminist theory has distinguished "gender," a culturally constructed identity, from "sex," which is purely a function of biology. In order to understand particular textual examples of transitional sexuality, it is important to ascertain how gender roles and biological sex limit or augment religious achievement. The answers depend in part on culturally specific views about the nature of sexual identity. In traditional China, male and female sex were considered points on a continuum. Chinese women were dominated by dark cool yin while Chinese men had a predominance of bright hot yang. Since the essence of yin and yang is change, yang might easily give way to yin, man becoming woman. However, Chinese society enforced strict gender roles, including codes of dress, behavior, hierarchy in family life, access to property and political power. Contrary to what modern Western people might expect, rigid gender provided structural support for fluid sex, rather than the other way around. Medieval European thought also defined sex less strictly than gender. Such culturally specific understandings of sex and gender, and their role in cosmology and salvation, form the landscape in which religiously inspired sex change takes place.

One example of sex change occurs in the concluding passage of the apocryphal Gospel of Thomas. Here, Simon Peter challenges Mary Magdalene's presence among the disciples and Jesus replies, "See, I shall lead her, so that I will make her male, that she too may become a living spirit, resembling you males." A gnostic text, the Gospel of Thomas uses the idea of Mary's transformation to express the triumph of the masculine spirit over the feminine flesh in salvation. In doing so, the idea of male spiritual superiority is also reinforced,

Teresa of Avila, a sixteenth-century mystic who described a graphic vision of Jesus as mother, is depicted in a 1613 engraving (Library of Congress/Corbis).

for masculine spirit and male person are not distinguished by the language of the text. Similarly, the story of the Dragon Princess defies social constrictions on women by depicting the spiritual ascendancy of a young girl. Buddahood necessitates overcoming thought habits plagued by conventional dualities such as distinguishing male from female. Paradoxically, a male body is still a prerequisite for buddhahood, even if assumed by the Princess for only the brief moment prior to her ultimate awakening.

Another Mahāyāna scripture, *The Holy Teaching of Vimalakīrti*, is less ambivalent. In it, a conservative monk, Śāriputra, questions a goddess who happens to be an advanced bodhisattva. Why, he asks, does she, who has so many powers, not transform herself out of the female state? She replies, "Although I have sought my 'female state' for these twelve years, I have not found it." Sexual identity is a temporary and changeable state that has no ultimacy. To prove her point, she magically transforms Śāriputra into herself and herself into Śāriputra.

Turning to medieval Spain, in her *Conceptions of Love of God*, the sixteenth-century mystic Teresa of Avila describes a graphic vision of Jesus as mother. She experiences him drawing her close to his "Divine breasts" that are "sweeter than wine" and sustaining her with "Divine milk." Here, Teresa ascribes the physical qualities of a woman to Jesus not to make a statement about the fluid nature or ultimate insignificance of Jesus' maleness, but as a sign of her intense closeness to him. God and beloved interpenetrate as nursing mother and baby.

Examples of sex change through mutilation, castration, ascetic power, or the decree of the gods abound in Hindu mythology. The thousand eyes of Indra turn into a thousand vaginas when he is cursed by a powerful ascetic whom he has cuckolded. Finding it necessary to hide, the hero of the Mahābhārata epic, Arjuna, disguises himself as a eunuch and is convincing enough (he would have to demonstrate impotence) to get a job as dancing master in a harem. The Gujarati goddess, Bahuchara, patron deity of the caste of transvestite eunuchs called the *hijras,* cuts off her own breasts and presents them to a gang of bandits in exchange for her virtue. The *hijras* imitate her mythic self-mutilation with their own actual self-castration. The focus of sex change stories in the Indian context is usually not the sex change itself, but the demonstration of ascetic power and moral resolve necessary to produce such an alteration of core identity.

BIBLIOGRAPHY

For background on the history of scientific ideas about sex in Europe see Thomas Laqueur, *Making Sex: Body and Gender from the Greeks to Freud* (1990). For China, see Charlotte Furth, "Androgynous Males and Deficient Females: Biology and Gender Boundaries in Sixteenth- and Seventeenth-Century China," *Late Imperial China* 9, no. 2 (December 1988): 1–31. For a discussion of sexual identity and its relationship to religious thought and practice in Christianity, Hinduism, and Buddhism, see José Ignacio Cabezón, ed., *Buddhism, Sexuality, and Gender* (1992); Caroline Walker Bynum, *Fragmentation and Redemption: Essays on Gender and the Human Body in Medieval Religion* (1992); and Wendy Doniger O'Flaherty, *Women, Androgynes, and Other Mythical Beasts* (1980).

For an overview of gender roles and examples of sex change in world religions, see Priscilla Rachun Linn, "Gender Roles," in *The Encyclopedia of Religion,* edited by Mircea Eliade (1987). For a readable discussion of the modern *hijra* community in India, see Zia Jaffrey, *The Invisibles: A Tale of the Eunuchs of India* (1996).

See also **Androgyny; Cross-dressing; Gender Conflict; Yin/Yang Polarity.**

AMY PARIS LANGENBERG

Sexism

The term *sexism* entered the popular vocabulary in the late 1960s. In general, the word refers to social and economic domination of one sex by the other, predominantly through access to power, resources, and cultural and intellectual control. Most commonly, sexism refers to the domination of women by men. Although the word itself is relatively new, the practice might be said to be as old as Adam and Eve. In the Jewish and Christian communities, biblical stories have shaped the way society is structured. The patriarchal structure of ancient Palestine as interpreted in the Scriptures of that time and place have provided a rationale for sexist practices. In other religions as well, sexism is often rooted in religious beliefs. Sometimes when a male deity is worshiped the intensity of the sexism present is increased. For instance, in both Judaism, Christianity, and Islam the association of the Father God with the social construct of paternal right gives credence to a patriarchal culture with its attendant sexist behavior. Yet the Holy Scriptures of these three major religions assert that all humankind arose in a condition of equality. The opening lines of sura (verse) An-Nisa in the Qur'an read, "O Mankind! Be careful of your duty to your Lord who created you from a single soul." Although portions of the Scriptures espouse equality of the sexes, other passages are patriarchal. Unfortunately for both women and men, the more patriarchal readings have become dominant and reinforced the sexism of the secular world.

Because of the sexism of society, the record of the presence of women in history is diminished and sometimes seems nonexistent. The absence of women as important leaders of the faith leads to the assumption that the significant personages of faith were all male. Feminist scholars must search more diligently to uncover sometimes oblique references to women, carefully examine names to ascertain whether *Julia* has become *Junia* through a deliberate act by male translators, and remove diminutives ascribed to women: *deaconess* to *deacon, prophetess* to *prophet.*

Because so many mothers of the faiths of the world remain unnamed and thus invisible, women are less likely to imagine themselves in such a role, or to imagine others in that position. Women who counter this assumption are often criticized by women as well as by men. Women who challenge the patriarchal strictures of religion are sometimes branded as witches or heretics. Even when a religious tradition permits women to assume positions of leadership, many adherents continue to resist leadership by women.

Not only does sexism affect the historical record of women, but also the more recent role of women in religion is compromised. Sexist interpretations of holy writings and sexist theological formulations together have kept women from participation in significant roles within the major religious organizations. Religious interpretations of and pronouncements about the role of women have also circumscribed the lives of women in society in general as well as within a religious context. Freedom of movement is curtailed in certain countries because women are prohibited from driving a vehicle. In November 1990, fourteen Saudi Arabian women drove a short distance in Riyadh to protest the prohibition against female drivers. All were arrested and most lost their jobs. Their passports were not returned until a year later. Even bicycle riding is prohibited for women. Although women's feet are no longer bound as they once were in China, forbidding access to cars and even, in some countries, bicycles, has a very limiting effect on women in modern society.

Sexism in language has been and remains another obstacle for women. Whether or not a language has pronouns with gender, sexist aspects of language operate to discriminate against women. Those who follow a sociolinguistic interpretation of language assert that grammar, as well as vocabulary, maintains sexism in society. A language wherein the masculine pronoun is deemed "generic" leads people to envision the presence of males but not females. That this is so is evident in the different reaction experienced when only the feminine pronoun is used. In English, *men* is also considered a grammatical generic. However, in a study described by J. S. Clarkson, when asked to draw cavemen, most children and adults depict only males, whereas when the prompt is *cavepeople,* both males and females are drawn. Our very imagination is shaped by our language, thus the words we use can have as limiting an effect on us as might the words and strictures of a sexist society.

One of the first works to consider the matter of sexism in religion was *The Church and the Second Sex* (1968) by Mary Daly. Others followed, including the work of Rosemary Radford Ruether, who edited *Religion and Sexism* (1974). In the secular arena, Simone de Beauvoir's *The Second Sex* (1953) and, later, *Politics of Reality: Essays in Feminist Theory* (1983) by Marilyn Frye challenged sexist assumptions. Frye notes a truth that probably may be generalized to issues of racism and heterosexism, that explaining the phenomenon, no matter how logically the argument is construed, cannot ensure that the hearers will understand the concept if they are not willing to entertain the possibility of the condition. The task, then, is not only to expose the sexism in religion, but to interpret its presence for those with "ears to hear."

BIBLIOGRAPHY

Ahmed, L. *Women and Gender in Islam: Historical Roots of a Modern Debate.* 1992.

Clarkson, J. S. *In the Beginning Was the Word: Implications of Inclusive Language for Religious Education.* 1989.

Gross, Rita M. *Buddhism after Patriarchy: A Feminist History, Analysis and Reconstruction of Buddhism.* 1993.

Ruether, Rosemary Radford. *New Woman, New Earth: Sexist Ideologies and Human Liberation.* 1975. Reprint, 1995.

———. *Sexism and God-Talk: Toward a Feminist Theology.* 1983. Reprint, 1993.

Stowasser, B. F. *Women in the Qur'an: Traditions and Interpretation.* 1994.

See also **Classism; Heterosexism; Patriarchy; Racism.**

J. SHANNON CLARKSON

Sexuality

Sexuality may be defined as the complex of socially and culturally constructed attitudes, behaviors, and practices that engage and incite erotic desire. Erotic desire, whether it stimulates the heart, the mind, or the genitals, is characterized by a heightened arousal of the senses. The discourse that encompasses this complex operates within an elaborate and often discrete structure of power relations designed to protect and promote the system of morals upheld by the dominant segment of a particular society. Given the patriarchal model of authority that governs the vast majority of the world's religious traditions, women are rarely allowed to explore and express their sexuality freely and openly without fear of reprimand, restrictions, overt physical and psychological controls, or exhaustive prohibitions.

In most of the world's religious traditions, women are alleged to be the "naturally" inferior gender—physically, intellectually, and spiritually weaker than men. Often associated with the flesh, women are purported to be inherently unsuited to the soteriological goals of many religious paths. Two examples of this conviction may be found in the Catholic and Buddhist traditions. Catholicism has a strict prohibition against women priests due to the religious dogma that women are unable to perform the strictest duties of the priestly office. Buddhist sutras authoritative for both Theravada and certain Mahayana traditions claim that women are unable to achieve the ultimate state of nirvana because of the allegedly inherent impurity of a woman's body.

Despite women's alleged weakness, many religious traditions portray women's sexuality as a powerful and often dangerous force designed to tempt and distract men from their exclusively religious duties. Several of these traditions take this potential threat so seriously that they devote a great many writings and sermons to detailing often exhaustive prescriptions as to what sorts of sexual behavior are acceptable for women. These religious interdictions of women's sexual attitudes and behaviors usually restrict, regulate, or denigrate sexual activity and the uses women make of their bodies. Even in those traditions, such as tantric Hinduism and Buddhism, that depict female sexuality symbolically in a glorified light, there is little evidence that women are treated with such high regard in their real lives outside the rarefied atmosphere of the religious ritual.

FEMALE SEXUALITY AS THREATENING AND POLLUTING

Scripture and other authoritative texts exhibit many of the negative views about women's sexuality that are prevalent in the major religious traditions. These pronouncements tend to rest on one of two essential beliefs about women: 1) Women's sexual drives are insatiable, and therefore women's very presence is too seductive for even the most disciplined man to resist. 2) Women are inherently unclean or impure, and thus their activities are contrary to what is held to be divine or holy. The Hebrew Bible combines these two attitudes in the story of Eve's insatiable curiosity compelling her to eat of the fruit from the tree of knowledge (Gen. 3:6). This act then introduces shame into the garden, which suggests to Adam and Eve that their bodies are inherently different and in need of covering. The church fathers take this idea of shame much further in their writings about the sinful nature of all physical pleasure, especially that derived from sexual relations. Augustine is exceptionally vehement in his denial of pleasure and only with great reservations allows for sexual intercourse for the sole purpose of procreation (*The City of God*, XIV, 23–26).

Islamic law operates under an active theory of women's sexuality that holds that Muslim society struggles to contain women's supposedly destructive, all-absorbing sexual power. Women, therefore, must be controlled to prevent men from being distracted from their social and religious duties (Al-Ghazali, *The Revivification of the Religious Sciences*, vol. 2, chapter on marriage). These beliefs are concretized in Islamic legal prescriptions permitting polygamy, repudiation (where men may receive a divorce simply by stating that desire three times), *idda* (the Muslim guarantee of paternity), and the practice of veiling.

The more severe restrictions placed on women's sexuality involve surveillance and separation of all women

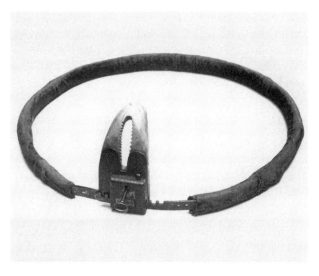

A seventeenth-century chastity belt used for prevention of sexual intercourse on the part of the woman wearing it (Corbis/Bettmann).

from the public eye. South Asian cultures, both Muslim and Hindu, enforce their views of women as potentially threatening and destructive through the institution of purdah. Literally "curtain," purdah refers to the system of secluding women and enforcing stringent standards of female modesty over every possible aspect of women's behavior, attitudes, and actions. Veiling is the most overt manifestation of this system of surveillance; women are expected to remain secluded from public view and when in public must cover more than ninety percent of their flesh. Veiling is meant to protect men from the lustful temptation women allegedly embody, and also to protect women from potentially abusive, invasive attention from men. Purdah also involves elaborate rules restricting the free expression of emotion, physical touching, and laughter, and an insistence on chaperonage for all women.

The many branches of the Hindu faith adhere strongly to rules concerning potential pollution by women's bodies and sexuality. Most Hindu traditions in India dictate conservative norms for women including virginal brides, arranged marriages, and strict regulations concerning when women may engage in sexual relations. The view that women have insatiable sexual appetites is portrayed iconographically in Hindu scripture in the image of the sexually aggressive goddess. Certain Hindu and Buddhist tantric texts, usually designed to be visualized and sometimes mimicked in actual ritual practice, represent female sexuality in an ostensibly positive light through the figure of the consort, who is depicted as engaging in a variety of sexual activities and postures free from male dominance or even participation. In reality, if women were used in these ritual practices their behavior was carefully regulated by priests or practitioners; rarely were they afforded such freedoms outside of the ritual.

PROCREATION

Procreation is the most sanctioned use of sexuality in every religious tradition. Every religion holds, to varying degrees, that women should engage in sexual intercourse for the purpose of propagating the human race. Frequently, this is the only form of sexual activity that is accepted by the tradition. Although there is quite a bit of resistance in the writings of the church fathers to the idea that sexuality can be sanctified even if only for procreation, it is the stance of the Catholic Church to condone sexual relations solely for procreation. In keeping with this injunction, Catholicism absolutely forbids any artificial method of birth control. Transgressors to this imperative may face excommunication from the church.

In many societies, the birth of a male child is far preferred to that of a female child. Often, the birth of a female child is met not only with disappointment, but occasionally with the murder or abandonment of the child. Islamic male autonomy and honor are further substantiated by the institution of polygamy whereby a man may father many children from different wives. A woman has no right to select her own sexual partners, or even to ensure that her husband will remain faithful to her throughout their marriage.

The Jewish tradition, standing as one of the less restrictive of women's sexuality, has a mitzvah or commandment that declares sexual relations between married partners to be a joyous event when practiced on the Jewish Sabbath. In addition, there are passages in the Talmud that proclaim that a married woman is entitled to a certain number of sexual relations with her husband during the week, precluding the week of and five days succeeding her menstrual period. Other passages describe a rather wide range of accepted sexual activities (Talmud, Tractate on marriage). Although the Orthodox Jewish traditions consider procreative sex to be a commandment, there is some discussion among Conservative and Reform Jews as to whether it is better understood as a blessing rather than as a requirement for all couples.

WOMEN'S SUBVERSIVE STRATEGIES

Although negative prescriptions for women's sexuality seem pervasive among most religious traditions, women in many of these traditions have devised subversive strategies to counter the dogmatic suppression of erotic desire. Muslim women have stated publicly that the institution of veiling provides them with a symbolic shelter wherein they feel safe. The songs sung by North Indian Hindu women speak of the veil as both the epitome of female modesty (and thus a neutralizer of sexuality), and also as a subtle enhancer of female charms enticing a woman to feel her own sexual nature. Some women-dominated religious traditions allow women to explore their sexuality outside of the male authoritative space. For example, in the Afro-Brazilian religion of Candomble, in which female cult leaders far outnumber male, women experience a trance state of possession involving certain sexual movements that transgress the male norm of misogynist, abusive treatment of women. Certain spirit cults in northern Thailand also afford women dominant positions in which they are in control of their own fertility and sexuality.

Another strategy women have adopted as a means to control their own sexuality in a number of traditions from Christianity to Buddhism is voluntary celibacy. Both Buddhist and Christian nuns take vows of celibacy that, although required by the male-authored traditions, nevertheless necessitate the woman's taking control of her own body and its sexual impulses. A celibate woman is not necessarily denying her own erotic desire; some celibate women speak of their ability to channel this form of desire into a more spiritually edifying path. The Christian mystics of medieval Europe, for example, discovered ways of deepening their faith through the denial of bodily pleasure in an attempt to feel a closer connection to the divine.

Regardless of the strategy chosen by religious women to assert their sexual and emotional autonomy over men, these choices inevitably entail tension and conflict. It is essential to analyze the actual lived realities of women in all religious traditions as compared with the sometimes ambiguous rhetoric of some religious texts. This attention to reality is particularly important in examining women's roles in tantric rituals where there seems to be the suggestion of liberated sexual activity for both men and women. Unfortunately, the actual evidence for such equality remains to be found. Although the majority of religious pronouncements about women's sexuality are negative, there are traditions that affirm a woman's right to sexual pleasure as divine blessing, and others that afford women control over their bodies and their fertility. As more women assume positions of leadership and authority in various traditions, the more likely it is that sexual behavior and attitudes will start to reflect women's own desires, neither regulated nor denigrated by male prescriptions, nor subject to abuse or invasion.

BIBLIOGRAPHY

O'Flaherty, Wendy Doniger. *Women, Androgynes, and Other Mythical Beasts.* 1980.

Papenek, Hanna, and Gail Minaul. *Separate Worlds: Studies of Purdah in South Asia.* 1982.

Paul, Diana Y. *Women in Buddhism: Images of the Feminine in Mahayana Buddhism.* 1985.

Raheja, Gloria Goodwin, and Ann Grodzins Gold. *Listen to the Heron's Words: Reimagining Gender and Kinship in North India.* 1994.

Ranke-Heinemann, Uta. *Women, Sexuality, and the Catholic Church.* 1990.

Sears, Laurie J., ed. *Fantasizing the Feminine in Indonesia.* 1996.

Sered, Susan Starr. *Priestess, Mother, Sacred Sister: Religions Dominated by Women.* 1994.

AMY LAVINE

Shafiq, Durriyah (Doria)

Durriyah (Doria) Shafiq (1908–1975) was an Egyptian feminist and suffragist leader, poet, and journalist. The daughter of Ahmad Shafiq, an engineer, and Ratiba Nassif, she was born in Tanta, where she attended Notre Dames des Apôtres. She continued her schooling at St. Vincent de Paul in Alexandria and then enrolled at the French Lycée (for boys), there preparing privately for the baccalaureate and finishing second in a nationwide examination in 1924. She went on to the Sorbonne, where she became the first Egyptian woman to earn a Doctorat d'État. In 1937 she married Nur al-Din Ragai, a lawyer, and had two daughters, Aziza and Jehan. In 1945 she became the editor of *La Femme Nouvelle* and the same year founded *Majallat Bint al-Nil* (The Daughter of the Nile Magazine). As founder of the Bint al-Nil Union in 1948 she led a feminist movement focused on women's suffrage and female literacy. Shafiq later organized a women's march to the Parliament and sit-in to demand the vote. In 1952, after the revolution, she published *al-Kitab al-Abyad lil-Huquq al-Mar'a al-Misriyyah* (The White Paper on the Rights of the Egyptian Woman), a compendium of debates on women's suffrage and Islamic argumentation, and was further active in mounting a hunger strike at the Press Syndicate in continued protest against women's exclusion from political life. In 1956 the state issued a new constitution granting women the vote and concurrently outlawed all independent political organizations. The following year, after she conducted a hunger strike protesting the dictatorship in Egypt, Shafiq was placed under house arrest. When she died by her own hand she was widely eulogized for her struggle for women's rights.

BIBLIOGRAPHY

WORKS BY SHAFIQ

L'art pour l'art dans l'Egypte antique. Paris, 1940.

Avec Dante aux enfers. Paris, 1979.

La Femme et le droit religieux de l'Egypte contemporaine. Paris, 1940.

La Femme Nouvelle en Egypte. Cairo, 1944.

al-Kitab al-Abyad lil-Huquq al-Mar'a al-Misriyyah (The White Paper on the Rights of the Egyptian Woman). Cairo, 1952.

Larmes d'Isis (Tears of Isis). Paris, 1979.

al-Mar'a al-Misriyyah min al-Fara'ina ila al-Yaum (with Ibrahim Abduh). (The Egyptian Woman from the Pharaohs until Today). Cairo, 1955.

Rihlati hawla al-'Alam (My Trip Around the World). Cairo, n.d.

Tatawwur al-Nahdah al-Nisa'yyah fi Misr (with Ibrahim Abduh). (The Development of the Renaissance of Women in Egypt). Cairo, 1954.

WORK ON SHAFIQ

Nelson, Cynthia. *Doria Shafiq, Egyptian Feminist: A Woman Apart.* 1996.

MARGOT BADRAN

Shaktism

The term *shaktism* refers to forms of Hinduism involving the Goddess (Devī), especially her manifestations as the dynamic power (shakti) of the cosmos. Followers of the Goddess, known as Shāktas, may worship her in various forms, ranging from the soothing consorts of major Hindu gods to malevolent village goddesses to male and female mediums possessed during festivals. One of the dominant forms of contemporary popular Hinduism, Shaktism has also produced elaborate philosophies, literature, and ritual systems.

Goddess worship seems to be quite ancient in South Asia, although female divinities in the earliest Sanskrit texts have subordinate status to male deities. With the formation of classical Hinduism late in the first millennium B.C.E., popular worship of goddesses was assimilated by religious elites. Texts glorifying the Goddess, such as the *Devīmāhātmya*, appear by the fifth century C.E. The development of distinctive Goddess traditions, regarding her as an absolute creatrix, is reflected in later texts, such as the *Devībhāgavata Purāṇa*. The pan-Asian traditions known as tantra emerged by this time, emphasizing that liberation may be achieved only through the realization and unification of both male and female cosmic powers. Tantra thus rejected the misogyny prevalent in other contemporary Indian traditions. These trends helped to further establish and enhance the worship of the Goddess throughout India, with diverse Shākta schools developing in subsequent centuries up to the present.

Elaborate speculative and ritual traditions were developed by tantric schools including Kashmiri Śaivism, which worshiped Shakti in relation to Śiva, and the South Indian Śrīvidyā tradition, which extolls her in the form of Lakṣmī/Śrī. Through yogic practices, she can appear as kundalini, a cosmic energy that rises along the spinal column, creating bliss as she emerges with Siva. She is also worshiped at important pilgrimage sites, such as Calcutta and Madurai, and in geometric designs called *yantras*.

The Goddess develops as a complex, ambiguous figure. As Sarasvatī, Pārvatī, and Lakṣmī, she becomes the beneficent, if subordinate, consort of the gods Brahmā, Siva, and Vishnu. But more independent forms appear as well. Durgā, for example, is celebrated for her battlefield victory over a buffalo-demon and army whom the male gods could not subdue. The Goddess is also worshiped in her wrathful forms such as Kālī, Cāmuṇḍā, and a group of ferocious yet protective deities called the "seven mothers" (*sapta-mātṛkās*). These figures, as well as the smallpox goddess Śītalā and the snake goddess Manasā, present models of the divine feminine as both life-giver and destroyer. Some wrathful goddesses are depicted as decapitating and drinking the blood of their victims, and goats and other animals may be sacrificed to them by the faithful even today. Such expressions illustrate the ambiguity and tensions regarding independent women and gender constructions in traditional India, and stand opposed to more passive forms such as Pārvatī and Lakṣmī (who embody more mainstream "wifely" virtues). Although Shaktism idealizes the supremacy of the feminine, and women are said to best embody shakti, the social realities of traditional India have not generally reflected these beliefs.

BIBLIOGRAPHY

Bhattacharyya, Narendra Nath. *History of the Śākta Religion.* 2d ed. 1996.

Brooks, Douglas Renfrew. *Auspicious Wisdom: The Texts and Traditions of Śrīvidyā Śākta Tantrism in South India.* 1992.

———. *The Secret of the Three Cities: An Introduction to Hindu Śākta Tantrism.* 1990.

Coburn, Thomas B. *Encountering the Goddess: A Translation of the Devī-Māhātmya and a Study of Its Interpretation.* 1991.

Hawley, John Stratton, and Donna Marie Wulff, eds. *The Divine Consort: Rādhā and the Goddesses of India.* 1982.

Kinsley, David. *Hindu Goddesses: Visions of the Divine Feminine in the Hindu Religious Tradition.* 1986.

McDermott, Rachel Fell. "Bengali Songs to Kālī." In *Religions of India in Practice.* Edited by Donald S. Lopez. 1995.

O'Flaherty, Wendy Doniger. *Women, Androgynes, and Other Mythical Beasts.* 1980.

Stewart, Tony K. "Encountering the Smallpox Goddess: The Auspicious Song of Śītala." In *Religions of India in Practice.* Edited by Donald S. Lopez. 1995.

See also **Goddess**; **Tantra**.

GLEN ALEXANDER HAYES

Shamans

The first descriptions of shamans are found in the reports of eighteenth-century travelers who saw among the native peoples of Siberia men and women who entered trance states through frenzied drumming and dancing and who claimed extraordinary powers through intimate knowledge of the spirits (Flaherty, 1992). The word *shaman*, borrowed from a Siberian language, is now widely used by anthropologists to describe equivalent phenomena throughout Asia and the Americas (Vitebsky, 1995). Shamans are empowered beings who invoke, manipulate, or coerce the spirits for socially recognized ends, both good and ill (Lebra, cited in Harvey, 1979). Masters of the spirits, they are movers and shakers, as distinguished from mediums, who are the spirits' passive vessels (Lewis, 1969).

Shaman and *medium* have not been used with any consistency. Jane Atkinson (1992) notes that while anthropologists favor localized studies embedded in local histories and understandings, much of the writing on shamans, both scholarly and popular, plucks practitioners out of context to construct homogenized theories of shamanism. Mircea Eliade's (1964) portrayal of soul flight as the defining attribute of a shaman is favored by some writers and by North American and European neo-shamans who use techniques of drumming and visualization to experience shamanic "journeys." Ethnographers sometimes gloss as "mediums" practitioners who could also be considered "shamans" for their ability to summon powerful spirits to assist their mediation between the realms of human and spirit (see, e.g., Steedly, 1993).

Confusions of terminology obscure both the number of shamanic traditions perpetuated by women and the importance of women's activities in localized popular religions. Indeed, the terms *shaman* and *medium* have come to us with heavily gendered connotations—the former evoking the heroic warrior figure of early Siberian ethnography, the latter recalling Victorian spiritualists who saw women's docile nature as receptive to possession by spirits.

A particularly well-known gendered treatment of shamans and spirit possession is I. M. Lewis's *Ecstatic Religion* (1969). Lewis offers a global generalization that male shamans are the central figures in "main morality possession religions" (his primary examples being from Siberia), whereas female mediums participate in "peripheral possession cults" (his primary examples being from north Africa and the African diaspora). As possession-cult mediums, women and other oppressed groups use the spirits' complaints and demands as an "oblique redressive strategy" where "men hold a secure monopoly of the major power positions and deny their partners effective jural rights" (Lewis, 1966, pp. 321–322; 1969, p. 89).

According to Lewis, when state bureaucracies and doctrinal religions undermine the shaman's authority, the officially discredited ancient faith is left to the women in compensation for their own "peripheral" social status (Lewis, 1969). The possessed woman is not a master of the spirits; her claims are legitimate only insofar as she is seen as the spirit's unwilling victim—a patient, not a practitioner.

Lewis's work is valuable for its gendered insight into certain types of possession phenomena and its attempt at a comprehensive gendered synthesis of scattered ethnographic material. But it fails to account for the many predominantly female shamanic traditions that are found throughout Asia and also among the Mapuche of Chile (Degarrod, 1995). Indeed, if female shamans are so numerous, might we simply shift Lewis's terminology, suggesting that women become "shamans" in state societies where shamanic activities are "peripheral" to the political authority of the state and the moral authority of established religions? By Lewis's definition, is this not still a "feminist cult," where women invoke the spirits to their own ends?

A strict dichotomy—male shamans have power and authority, female shamans are marginalized—will not hold. Ethnographies from Siberia and the Americas suggest that men are most often the potent shamanic figures where masculine activities such as hunting and warfare are essential survival skills (Hamayon, 1990),

but formidable female shamans have emerged, from time to time, among the spirit masters of Siberia and Mongolia (Balzer, 1997; Humphrey, 1996). When shamans abide within state societies and in the shadow of doctrinal religions, gendered relations with the spirits are highly variable. Male shamans predominate among Malays, Tamang in Nepal, and Han Chinese in Fujian Province, on Taiwan, and in Singapore. Lewis allows that "low status" men might be involved in spirit possession which would support his assertion that "deprivation" is a primary motive for embracing the spirits in state societies.

Some scholars do explain female shamanship in these terms. The Burmese "*nat* wives" described by Melford Spiro (1967) provide Lewis with a rare Asian example of a feminine possession cult, although Spiro, with admitted ambivalence, calls these women shamans. By Spiro's interpretation, Burmese women enter into marriages with *nat* spirits either in response to sexual constraints enforced during puberty or as compensation for the sexual deprivations they experience during menopause. Analyzing the life stories of six Korean shamans, Youngsook Kim Harvey (1979) describes her subjects as highly conscious of the gendered injustices they experienced in their early lives. By assuming the shaman role, these women claim power and authority within their own families that would otherwise be denied them. Margery Wolf (1973) suggests that Chinese daughters, less favored than their brothers, become canny at reading family situations and obliquely furthering their own interests. She speculates that highly developed perceptual skills serve Chinese women in good stead when circumstances force them to become shamans.

Although the notion of deprivation might explain why some women become shamans, it is undermined by the very question it raises: why is it, assuming, as Lewis does, that women are universally oppressed, that so many others do not? The mustering of generalized conditions to explain particularities becomes even more unsatisfactory when the focus shifts from possession cults to shamanship. Lewis describes the north African *zar* and *bori* possession cults as mass phenomena, sometimes reaching epidemic proportions when women respond to the constraints imposed by recent Islamization. Shamanship, by contrast, is a restricted professional specialization. In many shamanic traditions, both male and female, a special and dramatic seizure by the spirits is the requisite of a sincere and genuine calling, a mark of the shaman's difference that must subsequently be validated through a successful initiation.

Whereas spirit-cult adherents seek their own healing and re-creation, shamans are empowered to minister to

Jostinah Rhadebe, an Ndebele *sangoma* (traditional shaman), performs a dance with a goat's tail in her right hand and a wooden dagger in her left to drive away evil spirits, Gemsbok Village, South Africa, 1997 (Earl Kowall/Corbis).

the needs of others. In Korea, for example, shamans purify households and villages, exorcise the afflicted, and ease the souls of the dead along the path from hell to paradise. Clients seek shamanic healing not only for physical afflictions, but for a gamut of domestic troubles that might include delinquent children, adulterous husbands, and failing businesses. Any of these troubles may be symptomatic of a problematic relationship between the living family and their household gods and ancestors. When the shaman manifests these spirits, they air histories of family suffering and grievance. All of the participants—both human and spirit—vent anger, tears, and laughter in a ritual process that purges the household of the ominous forces of affliction (Kendall, 1985).

Do women find a place in shamanic practice only after ancient traditions are officially discredited? Mar-

jorie Mandelstam Balzer (1996) finds evidence that among the Sakha (Yakut), shamans with low profile, particularly women, continued to practice quietly in remote villages during the Soviet period despite the draconian suppression of Siberian shamanship. What is striking here, and in the following examples, is not that women became shamans after suppression—they were involved before the fact—but that specific historical circumstances caused them to become the primary custodians of shamanic traditions.

Cultural historians of Korea, in unknowing agreement with Lewis, sometimes see present-day female shamanship as the degenerate survival of an indigenous spirituality practiced in ancient days by men. Although this historiography is questionable, female shamanship persisted under a cloud of official disapprobation during the Chosŏn period (1392–1910). Confucian officialdom circumscribed the shamans' activities and in some instances banned them as improper or even false. But the predominance of female shamans and clients in Korea may be less a consequence of Confucian ideological disdain than of a particularly Confucian gendering of social and moral space. Men inhabited the "outside" (*woe*), the realm of propriety and face, and women the "inside" (*nae*), the realm of informality and pragmatism. As "inside mistress," a woman in Confucian Korea dealt with all matters pertaining to the health, harmony, and prosperity of the household, concerns articulated in the range of rituals, great and small, that housewives enacted with shamans. In a gender-segregated society, women's ritual specialists were most appropriately women (or, rarely, cross-dressed temporary women). In women's informal realm, embarrassing, shameful, and emotional family matters could be aired amid the play of shamans and spirits. Sometimes the ritual became a theater for the particular grievances of mother-in-law, daughter-in-law, or wife, but it would be a stretch to characterize these outpourings as (again quoting Lewis) an "oblique redressive strategy" or a "peripheral practice." Rather, they complemented other aspects of Korean popular religion in the pursuit of essentially Confucian aspirations for both women and men (Kendall).

While the feminization of Korean shamans is a matter of speculative historiography, the Mapuche Indians of southern Chile provide a well-documented example. When the Mapuche were forced onto reservations a century ago, a variety of healing roles were performed by both men and women. Since the Mapuche's incorporation into the Chilean state, most shamanic healers, or *machis*, have been women (with a few cross-dressed men, as in Korea). This transformation was a consequence of the forced assimilation of Mapuche men into the dominant culture which denigrated indigenous practices. Among the Mapuche themselves, the practices of *machi* women took on new significance as acts of cultural resistance. Lydia Nakashima Degarrod (1995) suggests that where chiefs lost their political power, female shamans actually took on more authority as the authentic voices of Mapuche tradition.

These examples imply that a tension exists in many places between the official denigration of shamanship and the tenacious significance of many local practices, whether the shamans be male or female. For example, V. N. Basilov (1990) describes the vitality of a range of shamanic traditions in (now former) Soviet Central Asia despite Islamization and the best efforts of the Soviet state. Ironically, these descriptions appear in a chapter headed, "The Twilight of Shamanism." Scholars and New Agers have been unduly burdened by the assumption that "real" shamans are "survivals" of a primordial spirituality, and that where shamans transmit the motifs of Buddhist or Islamic societies, they are debased from this "pure" form. By these assumptions, the practices of most female shamans, drawing upon the idioms of complex social and religious milieus, appear debased.

Insofar as the shaman's authority is derived from fluid visions and inspiration, not fixed in doctrinal texts and ritual manuals, we might expect that these are highly innovative practices, even though romantics persist in casting shamans as the "shock absorbers of history," in Michael Taussig's (1987, p. 237) apt phrase. Several studies from the 1990s acknowledge the inherently transformative potential of shamans who appear "chameleon-like," in diverse historical, political, and religious milieus (Vitebsky, 1995).

Anna Lownehaupt Tsing (1993) offers portraits of two highly innovative Meratus Dayak women shamans. One, Induan Hiling, an eccentric in the male-dominated role of public shaman, fashions her own understandings "in the gaps and margins of male-dominated signification" (p. 244). Uma Adang, an eclectic, "flirts with those powerful 'modern' discourses that are available in South Kalimantan . . . creating new forms of speech and new local and global "histories" (p. 254). Other examples of creative shamans can be retrieved from the ethnographic record; future ethnographies will undoubtedly bring us more.

BIBLIOGRAPHY

Atkinson, Jane Monnig. "Shamanisms Today." *Annual Review of Anthropology* 21 (1992): 307–330.

Balzer, Marjorie Mandelstam. "Changing Images of the Shaman: Folklore and Politics in the Sakha Republic (Yakutia)." *Shaman* 4, no. 1–2 (1996): 5–16.

———. "Sacred Genders in Siberia: Shamans, Bear Festivals, and Androgyny." In *Gender Reversals and Gender Cultures.* Edited by Sabrena Petra Ramet. 1997.

Basilov, V. N. "Chosen by the Spirits." In *Shamanism: Soviet Studies of Traditional Religion in Siberia and Central Asia.* Edited by M. M. Balzer. 1990.

Degarrod, Lydia Nakashima. "Mapuche: Dream Interpretation and Ethnic Consciousness." In *Portraits of Culture.* Edited by C. Ember and D. Levine. 1995.

Eliade, Mircea. *Shamanism: Archaic Techniques of Ecstasy.* 1964.

Flaherty, Gloria. *Shamanism and the Eighteenth Century.* 1992.

Hamayon, Roberte. *La chasse à l'âme: Esquisse d'une théorie du chamanisme Sibérian.* Nanterre, 1990.

Harvey, Youngsook Kim. *Six Korean Women: The Socialization of Shamans.* 1979.

Humphrey, Caroline, with Urunge Onon. *Shamans and Elders: Experience, Knowledge, and Power among the Daur Mongols.* 1996.

Kendall, Laurel. *Shamans, Housewives, and Other Restless Spirits: Women in Korean Ritual Life.* 1985.

Lebra, William P. *Okinawan Religion: Belief, Ritual, and Social Structure.* 1966.

Lewis, I. M. *Ecstatic Religion: An Anthropological Study of Spirit Possession and Shamanism.* 1969.

———. "Spirit Possession and Deprivation Cults." *Man,* n.s. 1, no. 3 (1966): 307–329.

Spiro, Melford E. *Burmese Supernaturalism: A Study in the Explanation and Reduction of Suffering.* 1967.

Steedly, Mary Margaret. *Hanging Without a Rope: Narrative Experience in Colonial and Postcolonial Karoland.* 1993.

Taussig, Michael. *Shamanism, Colonialism, and the Wild Man: A Study in Terror and Healing.* 1987.

Tsing, Anna Lowenhaupt. *In the Realm of the Diamon Queen: Marginality in an Out-of-the-Way Place.* 1993.

Vitebsky, Piers. *Dialogues with the Dead: the Discussion of Mortality among the Sora of Eastern India.* 1993.

———. *The Shaman.* 1995.

Wolf, Margery. "Chinese Women: Old Skills in a New Context." In *Women, Culture, and Society.* Edited by M. Z. Rosaldo and L. Lamphere. 1973.

See also **Possession Cults; Spirits; Witchcraft.**

LAUREL KENDALL

Shape-Shifting

Shape-shifting is the ability of a being (divine, demonic, human, animal, and so on) to change form or—closely related—is a metamorphosis undergone by a being as a result of divine or magical action. The shape-shifting motif is found in mythology and folk literature worldwide. Stories of female shape-shifters (who include goddesses, tricksters, and witches) and of females whose forms are changed by the action of others (e.g., Lot's wife; Daphne) abound, as do tales of female beings capable of changing others' shape or appearance, for good or evil ends (Cinderella's fairy godmother; Circe; the Gorgons). Also found are stories of male beings who assume female form for specific purposes (posing, for example, as seductresses to waylay a hero) and tales of men who are involuntarily changed into female form (e.g., Tiresias).

Animal transformers, some of whom are female, constitute an important subset of shape-shifters. Robert Graves (1966) offers an especially dizzying example, taken from a Welsh romance—the pursuit by Queen Cerridwen of her cauldron-stirring assistant, Gwion (also a shape-shifter), who flees from her service when he discovers that she intends to kill him:

> [Gwion]changed himself into a hare; [Cerridwen] changed herself into a greyhound. He plunged into a river and became a fish; she changed herself into an otter. He flew up into the air like a bird; she changed herself into a hawk. He became a grain of winnowed wheat on the floor of a barn; she changed herself into a black hen, scratched the wheat over with her feet, found him and swallowed him. . . . (p. 28)

Shape-shifting involves the trespass of or communication across the fundamental boundaries—of spirit, society, geography, species, or gender—that structure a world. Thus, in the inquisitorial records of the European witch craze, witches (mostly though not exclusively women) are reported to assume the shape of animals such as cats, wolves, hares, or mice to transport themselves great distances or into a transmundane realm to participate in the orgiastic rituals of the witches' sabbath. This transformation and transportation denote multiple violations of the established order: ecclesiastical, sexual, territorial, and so on. Shape-shifting is thus not simply expressive of witches' power; it *is* their power.

As a comprehensive, distinct category, however, shape-shifting proves as elusive as shape-shifters themselves. The impossibility of identifying an "essential" meaning of shape-shifting may have to do precisely with its protean character, always undecidably double and contradictory. Thus, folk tales (from China, the Arctic, and elsewhere) of celestial wives who temporarily come to the rescue of human husbands, or of animal-girls who are captured by men and impressed into wifely roles but who finally escape that servitude (see, e.g., "The Seal's Skin," in Yolen, ed., 1986, 310ff.), seem both to affirm the benefits (at least to men) of the institution of marriage and to betray an abiding (male) insecurity about hierarchically structured gender relations and to raise questions that are both amusing and frightening about which sex, ultimately, wields the greater power.

More generally, shape-shifting appears to mark an inescapable ontological ambivalence in human being itself—mixing fear of the transitoriness of form with wonder at the ongoing transformations of creation. Thus, the shape-shifting White Goddess identified by Graves (1966) as the Great Mother of prepatriarchal pan-European tradition inspires both terror and devotion: she is not only the origin of death (that is, of *disappearance*) but also the source of all making—the muse who speaks through all "true" poets, who, through the transformations of metaphor, participate in her creation. Stories of shape-shifting are unsettling because, even as they seem to imply the existence of something (soul, self, personality) that perdures beyond or inside the impermanences of form (including gendered form), they also seem anxiously or transgressively to assert the radical emptiness of interchangeable appearance. The shape-shifter's message may be that form is nothing other than, to borrow Carlo Ginzburg's provocative phrase, an "elaboration of absence."

BIBLIOGRAPHY

Stories involving shape-shifters can be found in almost any collection of folk or fairy tales; an excellent anthology that includes a section devoted specifically to shape-shifters is Jane Yolen, ed., *Favorite Folk Tales from around the World* (1986). Good comparative overviews of shape-shifting are provided by James P. Carse, "Shape Shifting," in *The Encyclopedia of Religion*, edited by Mircea Eliade (1987), and by R. D. Jameson, "Shapeshifting," in *Funk and Wagnalls Standard Dictionary of Folklore, Mythology and Legend*, edited by Maria Leach and Jerome Fried (repr. 1972). The Carse essay, which proposes a taxonomy of shape-shifters, is especially helpful.

Carlo Ginzburg's brilliant (if dense) *Ecstasies: Deciphering the Witches' Sabbath*, translated by Raymond Rosenthal (1991), traces several components of the witches' sabbath, including animal metamorphosis, to ancient Central Asian and Siberian shamanic beliefs and practices. Robert Graves's egomaniacal and virtually unreadable *The White Goddess: A Historical Grammar of Poetic Myth* (amended and enl. ed., 1966) is nevertheless useful for the inextricable connection it reveals between shape-shifting and artistic creativity. Marjorie Garber's wry exposition of the Tiresias myth in *Vice Versa: Bisexuality and the Eroticism of Everyday Life* (1995), chap. 6, is essential background for any exploration of shape-shifting that would take account of gender.

The inchoate horror—or horror of the inchoate—inspired by the female shape-shifter's trangressive power is a constant of popular culture, as may be glimpsed in films as diverse as Alfred Hitchcock's *Vertigo*, Walt Disney's *Sleeping Beauty*, the original (1942) and remake (1982) versions of *Cat People*, and horror films such as *Species* (1995). Whether their power derives from magic or makeup, Hollywood's boundary-defying, shape-shifting women are by the final moments of the last reel almost always brought into line—or eliminated—and the order of the world restored.

For insight into the meaning of shape-shifting it may be wise occasionally to turn away from the investigations of folklorists and scholars of myth—often too concerned with classification—and toward the work of poets. Informing the remarks here are the observations on resemblance and "the symbolic language of metamorphosis" articulated by Wallace Stevens in his essays "Three Academic Pieces," in his *The Necessary Angel: Essays on Reality and the Imagination* (1951), as well as the delicate demurrals from fixed meaning contained in Wisława Szymborska's lovely and scary poem "Lot's Wife," in *View with a Grain of Sand*, translated by Stanislaw Barańczak and Clare Cavanaugh (1995).

See also Animals; Cross-dressing; Graves, Robert Ranke.

JAMES C. WALLER

Sha'rawi, Huda

Pioneering Egyptian feminist leader Huda Sha'rawi (1879–1947) was the daughter of Sultan Pasha, a prosperous landowner and provincial administrator, and Iqbal Hanim, a young Circassian woman. She was born in Minya in Upper Egypt and raised in Cairo. Tutored privately, she memorized the Qur'an. She married her paternal cousin and guardian 'Ali Sha'rawi at thirteen. In the 1890s she attended a women's salon where, exposed to currents in the recent Islamic reformist debates, she discovered that veiling the face was un-Islamic. She helped found the first Egyptian women's secular philanthropy (1909) as well as two women's literary societies (1914). She was active in the national independence movement from 1919 to 1922 as the president of the Wafdist Women's Central Committee. In 1923, the year after national independence, she founded the Egyptian Feminist Union. Shortly after that, returning from an international women's conference in Rome, she publicly removed the veil from her face. She led a feminist movement that included both Muslims and Christians and that remained within a framework of religious reform. A Muslim feminist, she advocated reinterpreting the Shari'a in order to change the Islamic Personal Status Code. As EFU president Sha'rawi hosted the Women's Conference for the Defense of Palestine in 1938 and the first Pan-Arab Feminist Conference in 1944. She became president of the Pan-Arab Feminist Union, created in 1945. Sha'rawi was a Muslim whose feminism constituted a modernist project compatible with a refigured Islam. Shortly before her death in 1947 she received the highest state decoration for service to the nation.

BIBLIOGRAPHY

WORKS BY HUDA SHA'RAWI

"Assas al-Nahda al-Nisa'iyyah wa Tatawwuratiha fi Misr" (The Foundation of the Feminist Renaissance and Its Evolution in Egypt"). *Majallat al-Shu'un al-Ijtima'iyyah* (Cairo, Aug. 1941): 16–24.

Harem Years: The Memoirs of an Egyptian Feminist. Translated, edited, and introduced by Margot Badran. London, 1986.

Mudhakirrat Ra'idah al-'Arabiyyah al-Hadithah Huda Sha'rawi (The Memoirs of the Modern Arab Pioneer Huda Sha'rawi). Introduced by Amina al-Sa'id. Cairo, 1981.

WORKS ON HUDA SHA'RAWI

Badran, Margot. *Feminists, Islam, and Nation: Gender and the Making of Modern Egypt.* 1994.

————. "From Consciousness to Activism: Feminist Politics in Early Twentieth-Century Egypt." In *Problems of the Middle East in Historical Perspective*, edited by John Spagnolo. London, 1992.

al-Subki, Amal. *al-Harakah al-Nisa'iyyah fi Misr bain al-Thawratain 1919 wa 1952* (The Feminist Movement in Egypt between the Revolutions of 1919 and 1952). Cairo, n.d.

MARGOT BADRAN

Shiism

Shiite Islam emerged as a consequence of a major shift in the early Islamic society of Arabia during the seventh century C.E. over the basis and nature of Islamic political leadership. Following the death of Prophet Muhammad in 632, his cousin and son-in-law, 'Ali b. Ali Talib, advanced his claims to be the rightful successor and believed he was clearly designated to lead the Islamic community after him. The supporters of 'Ali's claims came to be known as his Shia, the party of 'Ali whom the ruling Sunni (mainstream Islam) elite succeeded in suppressing.

It was the martyrdom of Imam Ḥusayn (d. 680), son of ʿAlī, that actually transformed the controversy into a mass religious movement marked by distinct ritual and symbolisms. Imam Ḥusayn was killed in the battle of Karbala in modern-day Iraq, in 680 by the Umayyad caliph Yazid b. Muʿawiya. Yazid, like his father, was seen by the Shia as a usurper of the rights of Imam ʿAlī in the political and religious leadership of the Islamic community. Along with ninety of his family members and followers, Ḥusayn marched to the plains of Karbala to challenge Yazid's sovereignty, only to meet his death and the massacre of all his companions. Ḥusayn's death became the locus for oral and written devotional literature and practices.

The annual commemoration of the death of Imam Ḥusayn in a drama of mourning rituals forms a distinct paradigm of Shiite devotionalism in the Muslim world. Shiite men and women of Iraq, Iran, Bahrain, Lebanon, Pakistan, Afghanistan, India, and South Asia manifest varied dimensions of the Karbala complex and search for its meaning in their present history. Ḥusayn's martyrdom is sacralized in pious historical accounts that embellish his memory as a redeemer and rebel against falsehood and corrupt Islamic practices. Integral to the yearly observance of Karbala are the men's self-flagellation where the flagellants wound themselves and spill blood as a symbolic reminder of the tyranny of Yazid and the illegitimacy of his caliphate. The cosmogonic significance of the awaited imam combines features of chiliasm and millenarian expectations that are at once a reversal of present history.

MOURNING RITUALS AND WOMEN'S PERFORMANCE

Mourning occupies a core position in the Shiite tradition of popular piety. Pious Shiites believe that at the end of time, Fatima, the daughter of the Prophet and mother of Ḥusayn, will gather in her apron all the tears shed on the Karbala martyrs, condemning those who have not wept and rewarding those who have. Whether in the spiritual symbolisms of redemption, sacrifice, or miracle, Fatima is a key figure and an exemplary model for devoted Shiite women. Due to the dearth of scholarship on women's interpretation and contributions to the Karbala rituals in Arab societies, we are confined to the area of Iran, Pakistan, and South Asia about which a number of valuable studies have emerged.

After the triumph of the Islamic revolution in Iran in 1979–1980, Shiite women in urban cities like Tehran became more active in organizing religious gatherings for Qurʾan recitation, prayers for the House of the Prophet and his progeny, chanting, and above all mourning rituals. Although these circles fall in the same category of traditional commemorative assemblies of Karbala, they circumscribe a wide spectrum of women's social activities and manifest the spiritual and cathartic facets of mourning rituals. In a typical circle, which may include women from upper and upper-middle classes, one or more Qurʾan reciters read sections of a designated Qurʾanic verse. The women in the audience are usually handed copies of the verse to follow with the readers. The Qurʾan reciter interrupts the verse with mourning chants recollecting the martyrdom of Ḥusayn, at which point the audience is driven into weeping and spiritual retreat. When the verse ends, the chanting turns into joyful hymns and dancing joined by young, single women. A special kind of soup is served alongside sweets, cucumbers, and pomegranates. The women then break up into smaller circles for conversation and social exchange.

Within the context of the postrevolutionary Islamic society, the specialized male religious elite exerted close and meticulous control of the interpretation of revelation and religious texts. The religious circles provided a great social outlet for women and balanced the dominance of the male element in the formal Karbala drama. Socializing, marriage matchmaking, and Qurʾanic literacy are creatively interwoven in the function of these circles.

In India and Pakistan, a rich and distinct vocabulary of Shiite symbolisms and practices is also evident. The earliest signs of Shiism in India (Pakistan included) were during the Bahmani Kingdom of Delhi. But it was at the age of Mughal ascendancy in the sixteenth and seventeenth centuries that Islam built lasting roots in South Asia. Embedded in South Asian religious tradition are strong millennial forces, Sufi traits, belief in redemption for past sins and life after death, and mourning. *Azadari* or ceremonies and public performances of mourning for the martyrs of Karbala fall into four primary categories:

(1) *Majlis* (lamentation assembly) takes place on the first ten days of the month of Muharram in the Islamic calendar. A Shiite holy center is often the site of a Ḥusayniyya, a place where devotional objects are displayed, including models of the martyr's tombs and replicas of the cradle of Imam Ḥusayn's son, ʿAlī Asghar. Whereas much of the Karbala processions are generally conducted by men, the Ḥusayniyya is closely associated with women's experiences of Muharram as the women martyrs of Karbala are invoked and remembered.

(2) *Julus* are ritual processions of mourning in which sacred objects and banners connected to Imam Ḥusayn and his family are carried through the streets.

This activity is connected exclusively with male worshipers.

(3) *Ziyarat* is the visitation of sacred shrines or objects, utterance of Arabic salutations, and reading from the Qur'an. Within the context of Muharram ceremonies, *ziyarat* refers to visitations of the Ḥusayniyyas as symbolic trips to the graves of the family of Imam ʿAlī in the form of chants and funerary rites. This seems the only public vehicle of ritual in the Karbala drama where women have a visible role.

(4) *Matam* are funereal rituals for the martyrs of Karbala. The *matam* circumscribes men's religious performance involving beating the chest while invoking the names of ʿAlī and Ḥusayn. Other controversial features of a *matam* are acts of self-flagellation or drawing blood from a flagellant through the use of knives, striking oneself on the head with the flat or the edge of a sword, or even walking over red hot coals. The myriad of religious topics chosen every year by the men's and women's community leaders reflect the changing interpretations of the Karbala paradigm due to the historical forces shaping the lives of the performers.

Mary Hegland (1995) has argued that among the Shiite women of northwest Pakistan, mourning rites organized by women create a space that defies their subordinate position in the patriarchal social structure. As makers, watchers, and enactors of ritual, they challenge notions of passive reception and quietism. The religious symbolisms, though shared with the larger male society, take different form as they validate a female ritual experience. They subvert Shiite mourning ceremonies that involve chanting, self-flagellation, and male primacy to exert a control over gender politics and provide "a realm of contention and negotiation" that extends to society at large. Comparing the Pakistani women to rural Shiite women in Iran, Hegland was surprised by the former's indulgence in the dramatic mourning on the first day of Muharram. Pakistani women were exposed to a rigorous system of sex segregation that made their religious experiences at the *majālis* even more noteworthy. They upheld a Shiite interpretation of history and refrained from severing any bonds with family and religion. Instead of openly protesting male dominance in an otherwise human spiritual heritage, women authorized ritual performances that exposed their competence, zeal, and devotion to Shiism. As such, women opened new avenues for creative "agency."

Aside from the women's *majālis*, which are similar in form and content to those of men, the recitations of *muʾjizat Kahanis* (miracle stories) furnish an integral part of popular piety for Shiite men and women. As Vernon Schubel (1995) explains, to initiate a story-

An Iranian woman mourns at Bhesht-Zahra Cemetery of Martyrs of the Revolution near Tehran, Iran, 1984 (Francoise de Mulder/Corbis).

telling, a male or female believer asks a favor from a notable man of religion. Once a favor is fulfilled, the believer must read a particular story and serve sweets. The narratives, whether authentic or fictional, reveal important facets of women's religious power and social situations. Often they focus on Fatima, the infallible mother of all the imams who is presented as modest and scrupulous yet self-motivated and forceful. The narratives are not only powerful lessons in Shiite verities but advance an assertive salvational role for women. Thus, women take part in the manifestation of loyalism to ʿAlī; their own readings and reactions to the narratives become part and parcel of the story's structure and significance.

BIBLIOGRAPHY

Ayoub, Mahmoud. *Redemptive Suffering in Islam: A Study of the Devotional Aspects of ʿAshura in Twelver Shiism*. 1978.

Benjamin, Mary Laurie. "Shiʿi Rituals of Mourning in South Asia: The Heritage of Muharram." M. A. thesis, University of Wisconsin-Madison, 1996.

Denny, Frederick Mathewson. *An Introduction to Islam*. 1985.

Hegland, Mary Elaine. "Shiʿa Women of Northwest Pakistan and Agency Through Practice: Ritual, Resistance, Resilience." *Political and Legal Anthropology Review* 18, no. 2 (1995): 65–79.

Jafri, S. Husain. *Origins and Early Development of Shiʿa Islam*. 1979.

Mahdevi-Khazeni, Shireen. "Women, the ʿUlama, and the State in Iran: A Study in Shiʿi Ideology." M.A. thesis, University of Utah, 1982.

Momen, Moojan. *An Introduction to Shiʿi Islam*. 1985.

Riggio, Milla C., ed. *Ta'ziyeh: Ritual and Popular Belief in Iran.* 1988.

Schubel, Vernon James. *Religious Performance in Contemporary Islam.* 1993.

RULA JURDI ABISAAB

Shintoism

The word *Shinto* refers to Japan's indigenous religion, but it has an unstable history and thus requires some preliminary explanation. In its earliest documented uses, the term signaled a disparate set of phenomena, all of which distinguished Shinto from some more orthodox or systematic set of ideas, practices, or perspectives. More specifically, *Shinto* referred to local or popular religious beliefs and customs as distinct from, for example, Buddhist or Confucian ones, whether in Japan or on the continent. This distinction was theological as well as practical, for popular beliefs were manifested in cults to various local *kami*, which included tutelary deities and ancestors as well as the awesome forces of the natural world. In the aristocratic circles of sixth- and seventh-century Japan, each territory and clan had its distinctive cults, with the imperial clan's mythic ancestor, the sun goddess Amaterasu, occupying a particularly important place in the emerging liturgical state. Beginning in the eighth century, these ideas, practices, and institutions crystallized into a distinct religious system in dynamic interaction with Buddhism and other continental religious and philosophical systems.

The earliest historical records to document Japanese religious attitudes and behavior are ethnographic accounts in Chinese dynastic histories dating from the third and fourth centuries C.E. There one reads of the ancient shamanistic queen Pimiko (c. 201–269 C.E.), "[who] occupied herself with magic and sorcery, bewitching the people. Though mature in age, she remained unmarried. She had a younger brother who assisted her in ruling the country. After she became the ruler, there were few who saw her. She had one thousand women as attendants, but only one man. He served her food and drink and acted as a medium of communication. . . ." (Tsunoda, 1958, p. 6). Following her death, we are told, a period of disorder under male political leadership ensued, until "a relative of Pimiko named Iyo, a girl of thirteen, was made queen and order was restored" (Tsunoda, p. 6). It is unclear from either the terse Chinese accounts or later Japanese records whether priestesses such as these preceded the establishment of male priestly functions or coexisted with them. See, for example, the stories of the female chieftains Kamu-natsuso-hime (or Kamu-nashi-hime) and Hayatsu-hime in the mythic record of Emperor Keikō's conquests (Aston, 1972, pp. 192–94). What is clear is that rulership implied priesthood, and that priestly power in the archaic ruling classes involved a cooperative male-female relationship in which the woman had direct contact with the *kami* and announced the divine will to the male attendant, who was in turn responsible for carrying out the divine directives in society. When this arrangement was not followed, calamity or tragedy ensued, as we can see in the Pimiko story and in later accounts in the Japanese sacred histories of such characters as Tamayori-hime and Okinaga-tarashi-hime (the empress Jingū).

In these same Japanese chronicles, Amaterasu appears in various guises: as an androgynous solar deity associated with agriculture and fertility; as a consort or priestess of the solar deity; and finally, as mentioned above, as the female solar deity and ancestor of the Yamato clan. There is no scholarly consensus on the development of cults to Amaterasu, nor on the precise date of her particular association with the imperial court.

With the gradual centralization of authority around the Yamato (imperial) clan, however, and the subsequent rationalization of political administration in the sixth and seventh centuries, the role of women shifted from divine intermediary to imperial representative, particularly at the Grand Shrines at Ise where Amaterasu was enshrined. With the establishment of a Department of Shinto Affairs (Jingikan) within the imperial court in 701 C.E., routine ritual interaction with the *kami* of heaven and earth was formalized, with official priestly functions carried out in the main not by charismatic religious specialists but by bureaucratic (and hereditary) functionaries both at court and in the provinces.

The rationalization of religious functions associated with the establishment of the Yamato liturgical state followed Chinese models in which male roles in public life (including civil religious functions) were dominant and women were understood to be unreliable, both biologically and psychologically, for important political and religious responsibilities. Still, at the local level and outside of organized religious spheres, charismatic women continued to play important mantic roles, often in cooperation with male ritual specialists. Literature, from imperially sponsored collections to popular folklore, recounts the accomplishments and adventures of such women, but relatively little literary or historical exegesis has yet been done to illuminate the contexts or significance of these stories, particularly for the medieval period.

Under a succession of feudal regimes from the thirteenth to the seventeenth centuries, official Shinto fell under the sway of Buddhist ideological and institutional hegemony; with the decline of imperial fortunes the shrines at Ise were opened to pilgrims from all walks of life and became the focus of a wide range of popular devotion. It was not until the Meiji revolution in the mid-nineteenth century, in fact, that Ise was reconstituted as the ritual center of the imperial cult, but by then Amaterasu's influence was no longer limited to imperial Shinto. A succession of so-called New Religions assimilated Amaterasu into their distinctive theologies, sometimes in ways that explicitly challenged the new imperial mythology.

In the early modern period (seventeenth to nineteenth centuries) especially, religiously gifted women appear in diverse sources and in numerous roles. Some who were unwilling or unable to live ordinary lives as daughters or housewives, or who were born into families associated with such performing arts as dancing and puppetry, struggled to survive in the unsettled world of entertainment. Others (*miko*) carried on traditional roles as seers and healers, often under duress from civil authorities, or worked as ritual assistants at local shrines. Still others began new religious movements, which typically began as the result of possessions by powerful new (or newly understood) deities.

Among the charismatic founders of New Religions, three women stand out for their courage and resourcefulness as prophetic religious leaders (see Nakamura, 1983; Wohr, 1989). Nakayama Miki (1798–1887) founded what came to be known as Tenri-kyō; Deguchi Nao (1837–1918) founded Ōmoto-kyō in 1892; and Kitamura Sayō (1900–1967) founded Tenshō-kōtai-jingū-kyō shortly after World War II. They each provide signal examples of both the trials and the triumphs of women's extraordinary religious experiences in modern Japan.

Shinto itself was reconstituted in the postwar period and (aside from the imperial family religion and the cult of the imperial war dead) has assumed a place as primarily a local phenomenon. Venerable older shrines of national reknown, including Ise, remain centers of popular pilgrimage, and there female attendants (*miko*) continue to perform danced rituals and assist priests in worship services. There have also been steady efforts to initiate women into the official Shinto clergy; there are at present more than a thousand ordained female priests in Japan. Finally, it must be noted that women are the primary actors in the religious rituals of daily life, both within the household and in local cultic practices outside the formal shrine system (Martinez, 1995).

Scholarship on women in Shinto remains a fledgling enterprise, particularly outside of Japan. On the face of it this is not surprising, for the study of Shinto, either in its institutional or its popular forms, continues to be of secondary interest to students of Japanese religions.

A female Shinto monk wearing an elaborate headdress holds a gold fan in a temple at Mount Haguro, Japan, 1990 (Chris Rainier/Corbis).

Earlier generations found the topic interesting only for its peripheral value in framing the dominant (male-oriented) religious history, or as evidence of Japan's quaint and exotic past. It has only been since the early 1980s that sustained and critical ethnographic and archival research has begun, and that research has often focused primarily on the New Religions. Practically, this kind of research is complicated owing to the nature and availability of evidence, especially for the premodern period; but, thanks to growing attention to women's history worldwide, the study of women in Japanese religion, including Shinto, has emerged as a respectable field of endeavor.

BIBLIOGRAPHY

Aston, G. W., trans. *Nihongi: Chronicles of Japan from the Earliest Times to A.D. 697*. Tokyo, 1896. Reprint, 1972.

Blacker, Carmen. *The Catalpa Bow*. London, 1975.

Ellwood, Robert S. "The Sujin Religious Revolution," *Japanese Journal of Religious Studies* 17, nos. 2–3 (1990): 199–217.

Martinez, D. P. "Women and Ritual." In *Ceremony and Ritual in Japan: Religious Practices in an Industrialised Society.* Edited by Jan van Bremen and D. P. Martinez. 1995.

Nakamura, Kyoko Motomochi. "No Women's Liberation: The Heritage of a Woman Prophet in Modern Japan." In *Unspoken Worlds: Women's Religious Lives in Non-Western Cultures.* Edited by Nancy A. Falk and Rita M. Gross. 1980.

———. "The Significance of Amaterasu in Japanese Religious History." In *The Book of the Goddess Past and Present.* Edited by Carl Olson. 1983.

Okano, Haruko. *Die Stellung der Frau im Shinto.* Wiesbaden, 1976.

———. "Women and Sexism in Shinto," *The Japan Christian Review* 59 (1993): 27–31.

Ooms, Emily Groszos. *Women and Millenarian Protest in Meiji Japan: Deguchi Nao and Omotokyo.* 1993.

Tenrikyō honbu, comp. *The Life of Oyasama, Foundress of Tenrikyo.* 3d ed. Tenri, Japan, 1996.

Tenshō-kōtai-jingū-kyō, comp. *The Prophet of Tabuse.* Tabuse, Japan, 1954.

Tsunoda, Ryusaku, et al., comps. *Sources of Japanese Tradition.* Vol. 1. 1958.

Wohr, Ulrike. *Frauen und neue Religionen: die Religionsgrunderinnen Nakayama Miki und Deguchi Nao.* Vienna, 1989.

Yusa, Michiko. "Women in Shinto: Images Remembered." In *Religion and Women.* Edited by Arvind Sharma. 1994.

See also **Amaterasu; New Religions: In East Asia.**

EDMUND T. GILDAY

Shrines

The word *shrine* comes from the Latin *scrinium*, originally meaning a box or container in which sacred objects were placed. Some shrines are fixed places including natural formations, such as caves, springs, and mountains; others are human-made, such as altars, chapels dedicated to holy people or to deities and containing sacred statues or objects, or tombs. Both shrines and temples function as places of worship; however, a shrine is usually smaller than a temple and sometimes part of a temple complex.

There are numerous examples of shrines from both the ancient world and the contemporary period. Ancient Is-raelites carried with them the Ark of the Covenant, a sacred chest. Portable shrines usually contain a sacred image, an object blessed by a spiritual person or power, or relics. By the fifth century B.C.E., each year the Ethiopians carried a statue of Isis, the Egyptian savior goddess and great healer, to lower Nubia to ensure prosperity for the following year. During the Greco-Roman period (330 B.C.E.–400 C.E.) her fame spread from Egypt to Greece and Europe, with temple ruins found as far away as Frauenberg, Austria, and Szombathely, Hungary. Tibetan Buddhists carry personal shrines usually containing blessed images and prayers; like the ancient Israelites, Tibetans who carry shrines are able to worship anywhere and feel protected from adversities.

Today, larger portable shrines usually enclosing a statue of a deity are carried in Hindu, Buddhist, Shinto, and Christian annual processions. These shrines are thought to protect the area and provide blessings for their viewers. In Vila Italia, Brazil, every afternoon women carry a small shrine of Norsa Señhora do Rosario de Fatima from one neighbor's home to the next. In each house families and friends gather to pray; the women are in charge of the shrine. In Sarnath, India, where the Buddha first taught more than 2,500 years ago, every spring a reliquary containing tiny pieces of the Buddha's bones is carried by an elephant. The procession circles the town before arriving at the temple where devotees show reverence to the relics. In many Catholic areas, annual processions of reliquaries containing a saint's relics or objects touched by Jesus or a saint are common.

As early as the Neolithic age in France and Spain, caves and rock shelters served as shrines where rites were performed for plentiful food. Goddesses are frequently associated with caves since they represent a womb or place of creation. The ancient Mixtec of central Mexico worshiped the Mother Goddess in caves. Today Indians go on pilgrimage to Kāmakhya temple in northeast India and worship Kālī's womb in the cave complex. In Mesoamerica, gods connected with rain, growth, and fertility were venerated in caves. Oztoteol (god of caves) was venerated in a holy cave at Chalma, two days' walk from Mexico City. Later, Jesus Christ was also identified with this holy place and worshiped in a church built nearby.

A similar superimposition occurred in Lindos, on the island of Rhodes in Greece. In the tenth or ninth century B.C.E., a cave with a shrine known as Voukopion, perhaps dedicated to a Mycenaean goddess, existed there. By the sixth century B.C.E., a temple to Athena was superimposed on the earlier shrine. This superimposition over an older site by the deities of the newer religion is a common characteristic of shrine sites. Many shrines dedicated to Mary are found in sites distant from human habitation, indicating a rural, pre-Christian notion of sacred landscape or the transformation of a non-Christian sacred site into a Christian one. The annual festival of a deity may be adapted by the new religion. The famous temple of the Roman goddess Diana on the north side of Lake Nemi (southwest of Rome) had its primary festival on the ides of August (August 15); later this day became known as the Assumption of the Virgin Mary.

Shrines by a lake or springs frequently are associated with healing or providing sufficient water for the area. In Lourdes, France, where the Virgin Mary made eighteen appearances to Bernadette Soubirous in 1858, millions of people come to bathe in the sacred water, drink from the divine spring, and take some of the water, known for its miraculous curative powers. The Marian shrine of Copacabana, established in 1583 on the southern shores of Lake Titicaca, Peru, attracts primarily a local population who ask the Virgin Mary to heal them or to prevent a drought.

The great Ise shrine in Japan, dedicated to the Sun Goddess, Amaterasu, attracts adherents who come to experience the serenity of its surroundings. The Japanese emperor continues to visit the Ise shrine to perform the annual secret ritual to ensure a plentiful harvest and prosperity for his people. Thousands of Chinese flock to Putou Island off the coast of southeast China to seek the blessings of the Buddhist Bodhisattva, Kuan Yin, on her birthday. They seek her blessings for children, and for the health and prosperity of their families. Many older women sing praises to Kuan Yin in an all-night vigil. Kuan Yin, a model of a female celibate who is compassionate to all beings, provides inspiration to women who prefer to renounce married life and dedicate their lives to helping others.

Both women and men visit these shrines and participate in various rituals; however, the frequency of attendance often depends on the place and the occasion. In some Islamic countries men frequent mosques on a regular daily or weekly schedule; women may come only for special days, such as the birthday of the prophet Muhammad. An exception is in China, where many mosques (or prayer halls) exist for women alone; these mosques are attended by women, and their trained teachers are women. Both men and women come in great numbers to participate in the obligatory pilgrimage, or hajj, to Mecca, which begins on the eighth day of the twelfth month (*Dhu'l Hijja*) of the Muslim lunar year. In certain places (India and Bali, Indonesia), especially where Indian Brahmanical culture prevails, menstruating women cannot enter Hindu temples. This prohibition also applies to Buddhist tem-

Roadside shrine, Koya-san, Japan, 1996 (Michael Freeman/Corbis).

ples in Thailand. The *nat* (spirit) shrines in Burma and the shaman altars in Korea are much more frequented by women than men.

More often than men, women frequent shrines associated with specific individuals, deities, or spirits because, scholars suggest, women are more involved than men with interpersonal relationships. Usually it is the wife or mother in the family who is in charge of matters within the home. At these shrines, women develop a long-term rapport or connection with a particular saint, deity, or spirit to seek supernatural help and blessings for their families.

Although in many religions women have limited access to public leadership, in certain locales women maintain control of shrines. In Burma, primarily women maintain the *nat* shrines, women attend the ceremonies, and the shamans possessed by *nats* are women. In Egyptian Nubia women maintain the Muslim shrines of saints, and a female functionary (*nakiba*) is present when women pray and make promises, or take vows at the shrines. In Korea, the majority of shamans are women, who in front of their altars perform rituals attended primarily by women. In rare cases when men are the shamans, they usually dress as women when performing shaman rituals.

Throughout the world one encounters women asking saints, deities, or spirits to help them. Among the Zapotec in southern Mexico, women are the primary link between the household and the local pantheon of saints and virgins. They tell the saints their family troubles and petition them to heal the sick, for example, or to find a lost child or animal. At Muslim shrines women ask saints to help them find and marry a good husband, conceive a child, protect them during childbirth, and ensure a family's health and prosperity. The Koreans also ask the shamans to enlist the help of their protective spirits, such as Water Grandmother of the well, Mountain God of the summit, and the Official, so their families have good health, long life, children, prosperity, and a happy and peaceful family life.

Although women and men seek protection and help from spirits, deities, and holy people connected with shrines throughout the world, the holy people to whom shrines are dedicated also serve as models to emulate. Buddhist stupas, shrines containing relics of the Buddha, serve as a reminder for adherents to strive for liberation from cyclic existence. Islamic tombs of holy people or shrines remind Muslims to behave according to Islamic law so they may be rewarded with eternal paradise. Thus shrines are places of refuge, protection, healing, and general aid but also serve as models or reminders in achieving the ultimate goal of a particular religion.

BIBLIOGRAPHY

Betteridge, Anne H. "Specialists in Miraculous Action: Some Shrines in Shiraz." In *Sacred Journeys: The Anthropology of Pilgrimage.* Edited by A. Morinis. 1992. A discussion of the ways in which different shrines meet different needs of pilgrims, including the particular needs of female pilgrims.

Delaney, Carol. "The *Hajj:* Sacred and Secular," *American Ethnologist* 17, no. 4 (August 1990): 513–530. Contains a discussion of women's roles in the pilgrimage to Mecca from a Turkish village.

Dubisch, Jill. *In a Different Place: Pilgrimage, Gender and Politics at a Greek Island Shrine.* 1995. A study of pilgrimage at a major Greek Orthodox site, with particular attention to Greek women's religious roles.

Eck, Diana L. *Banaras: City of Light.* 1982.

Gold, Ann Grodzins. *Fruitful Journeys: The Ways of Rajasthani Pilgrims.* 1988. Although not focused on women and pilgrimage, this book contains rich observations on Hindu pilgrimage from the village perspective and includes much information on women.

Kendall, Laurel. *Shamans, Housewives, and Other Restless Spirits: Women in Korean Ritual Life.* 1985. A fascinating examination of the ritual world of women in a Korean town, including the rituals of pilgrimage.

McDonnell, Mary Byrne. "Patterns of Muslim Pilgrimage from Malaysia, 1885–1985." In *Muslim Travellers: Pilgrimage, Migration, and the Religious Imagination.* Edited by D. Eikelman and J. Pescatori. 1990. Contains information on changing patterns of male and female pilgrimage from Malaysia.

Mernissi, Fatima. "Women, Saints, and Sanctuaries," *Signs* 3, no. 2 (1977): 101–112. An evocative description and analysis of women's pilgrimage to saints' tombs in North Africa.

Naquin, Susan, and Yu Chun-fang, eds. *Pilgrims and Sacred Sites in China.* 1992.

Ross, Ellen. "The Diversities of Divine Presence: Women's Geography in the Christian Tradition." In *Sacred Places and Profane Spaces.* Edited by J. Scott and P. Simpson-Housley. 1991.

Sax, William S. *Mountain Goddess: Gender and Politics in Himalayan Pilgrimage.* 1991. An excellent ethnography of Hindu pilgrimage in the Himalayas, with particular attention to gender and kinship.

Sered, Susan Starr. "Rachel's Tomb and the Milk Grotto of the Virgin Mary: Two Women's Shrines in Bethlehem," *Journal of Feminist Studies in Religion* 2, no. 2 (1986): 7–22; and "The Domestication of Religion: The Spiritual Guardianship of Jewish Women," *Man* 23 (1988): 506–521. The first article examines two shrines of particular interest to women; the second develops the concept of "domestication of religion," which has applications to women's pilgrimage.

Tapper, Nancy. "*Ziyaret:* Gender, Movement, and Exchange in a Turkish Community." In *Muslim Travellers: Pilgrimage, Migration, and the Religious Imagination.* Edited by D. Eikelman and J. Pescatori. 1990. A good discussion of the different kinds of "going out" in a Turkish community (including visits to saints' tombs) and their significance for women.

Turner, Victor, and Edith Turner. *Image and Pilgrimage in Christian Culture.* 1978.

See also **Saints; Space, Sacred.**

ELISABETH BENARD

Sikhism

The origins of Sikhism can be traced to the vision of Guru Nanak. He was born on 15 April 1469, in Talwandi, a small village in the north of India, which is now part of Pakistan, and was named after his older sister, Nanaki. His father was an accountant for the local Muslim landlord. His mother, Tripta, is remembered in Sikh history as a pious woman. Nanak was born in an upper-caste Hindu family, but from a young age he refused to go through any of the traditional rituals associated with his caste. He grew up in a philosophically and culturally vibrant milieu, one in which he freely met and conversed with Hindus, Muslims, Buddhists, and Jains.

ONE REALITY: NO GENDER

In this diverse and pluralistic context Nanak had a revelation of the One Reality. He articulated his experience of the infinite and singular reality as *Ikk Oan Kar,* which is the quintessential formula of Sikh metaphysics and ethics. In *Ikk Oan Kar* (meaning One Be-ing Is), *Ikk* or *I,* literally stands for the numeral one; there is no specification of gender, and it cannot be incarnated in any form. *Oan* or *Om,* from the Sanskrit *Aum,* refers to the ultimate unity. Kar (is) celebrates the existence of the one. This insight into the divine marked the beginning of Guru Nanak's mission. For twenty-four years Guru Nanak traveled throughout India and beyond spreading his message of absolute unity. Nanak's teaching drew people from different religious, cultural, and social backgrounds. Wherever Guru Nanak went, people began to follow him, calling themselves Sikhs, a Punjabi word that means disciple. "Sikh" can be traced to the Sanskrit *shishya* or the Pali *sekka.*

MEN AND WOMEN: COPARTNERS IN THE COMMUNITY AT KARTARPUR

At the end of his travels, Guru Nanak settled in Kartarpur, a Punjabi village he had founded on the bank of the river Ravi. A community of disciples grew around him. The community was not a monastic order but a fellowship of men and women engaged in the ordinary occupations of life. The daily routine and the moral ideals fostered in this first Sikh community constitute the core of Sikh life. Men and women shared equally in the Sikh institutions of *seva* (voluntary labor), *langar* (community kitchen), and *sangat* (congregation). Together they listened and recited the sacred hymns, together they cooked and ate *langar,* together they formed a democratic congregation without priests or ordained ministers.

Guru Nanak was deeply conscious of the victimization of women that was prevalent in his society. Customs like sati (a widow immolating herself on the funeral pyre of her husband) or purdah (veiling), and such beliefs as menstrual pollution, which denigrated women, were denounced. His close association with his older sister Nanaki may have made him sensitive to the low status of women.

GURU GRANTH: AVENUE TO THE TRANSCENDENT

Before he died in 1539, Guru Nanak appointed Angad, his disciple, as his successor, and bequeathed his inspired poetry to him. Guru Angad carried on the tradition of sacred poetry, which he felt was important for the beauty it brought to human life as well as for the knowledge it transmitted. The transference of Guruship from Nanak to Angad was repeated successfully through the installation of the Tenth Guru, Gobind Singh, in 1675. For the Sikhs the same light was re-

Siri Ram Kaur demonstrates the technique of turban wrapping as traditionally practiced by Sikh women (Shelley Gazin/Corbis).

flected in ten different bodies, and the same voice speaks through all ten. Before his death in 1708, the Tenth Guru ended the line of personal gurus by passing the succession not to another person but the Guru Granth, the holy book of the Sikhs. It was compiled by Guru Arjan (Nanak V) and installed in the Golden Temple in Amritsar in 1604. The Guru Granth opens with *Ikk Oan Kar,* and its 1,430 pages can be read as a poetic and sublime commentary on Guru Nanak's initial statement. Thus the message and the mission begun by Guru Nanak continued through nine more gurus and reached culmination in the Guru Granth.

Guru Granth is the sole visual and aural icon for the Sikhs. It contains the poetic verses of the Sikh Gurus as well as those of Hindu and Muslim saints. It is the center of all Sikh rites and ceremonies. In a verse from the Guru Granth, "the Book represents the Infinite One." Its metaphysical and esthetic poetry is inspiring to both male and female devotees. There is no priesthood in Sikhism, so all can directly approach their holy text. To lead in worship, Sikhs choose people from within the *sangat,* or congregation. These leaders may be either men or women, as members of both sexes are regarded to be equally endowed with moral and spiritual faculties. Both have their heads covered in the presence of the Guru Granth, and both are equally free to read and recite the sacred verse at home or in public. Both can perform *kirtan,* the singing of hymns. Both can officiate at any ceremony. In a Sikh wedding, instead of taking vows, the bride and the groom bow in front of the holy book. Their foreheads touching the ground together articulates their acceptance of each other.

THE MATERNAL DIMENSION OF THE ULTIMATE

The Guru Granth acknowledges the absolute transcendence of the ultimate reality. In order to grasp the One, the text uses a variety of images. For example, the One is both father and mother. Although traditional exegetes and translators have underscored the masculine dimension, the feminine is powerfully present in the Guru Granth. The mother's gender and her feminine qualities are exalted. Her natural processes are celebrated. Again and again, we are reminded that we are created from the mother's blood, we are lodged in her womb, and we are first nurtured by her milk. Guru Nanak reprimands those who stigmatize menstrual blood. He poignantly questions: "Why call her inferior from whom all great ones are born?" (Guru Granth, p. 473). The imagery of conception, gestation, giving birth, and lactation is vigorously present in the Sikh sacred book.

WOMAN AND THE DIVINE

All the poets of the Guru Granth are men but they adopt a female tone and imagery in their quest for the divine. They envision woman being physically, psychologically, and spiritually more refined than man. Throughout the Guru Granth women's bodies, activities, dressing up, tenacity, and longing are prized. Woman is the model in forging a sensual and palpable union with the Transcendent.

GURU GOBIND SINGH: AN INCLUSIVE KHALSAHOOD

In 1699 Guru Gobind Singh inaugurated the Khalsa, the Order of the Pure. Chanting verses from the Guru Granth, Guru Gobind Singh began initiation into the Khalsa by churning water, poured into a steel bowl, with a double-edged sword. His wife, Mata Sahib Kaur, came forward and dropped sugar crystals into the vessel. Sweetness through the feminine hand was thus mingled with the alchemy of iron. The occasion marked a dramatic departure from the past.

The *amrita* (drink) initiation is open to both men and women, and both must wear the emblems of the Khalsa, popularly known as the five K's:

1. *kesha* or uncut hair—denoting the way of nature;
2. *kangha,* a comb tucked into the kesha to keep it tidy;
3. *kara,* a steel bracelet worn on the right arm;
4. *kaccha,* short breeches; and
5. *kirpan,* a sword symbolizing self-defense and the fight against injustice.

The *amrita* is sipped from the same bowl, sealing the pledge of equality and faithfulness. Men are given the surname of Singh, meaning lion, and the women, Kaur, meaning princess. Their rebirth into the Order represents an annihilation of their family (caste) lineage, of their confinement to a hereditary occupation, of all their old stifling beliefs and rituals. Women are liberated from tracing their lineage to their father or adopting a husband's name after marriage. As Singh and Kaur, Sikh men and women are enjoined to help the weak and fight the oppressor.

WOMEN IN SIKH HISTORY

Although little is known about the women in Guru Nanak's life, Sikhs believe that his sister, Nanaki, his mother, Tripta, and his wife, Sulakhni, were influential in raising Guru Nanak's consciousness about the tragic plight of women. Of special importance was Nanaki, who was five years older than her brother. Sikh paintings depict the two of them as children, walking lovingly together.

Other Sikh women, too, have been important to the Sikh faith.

Mata Khivi (died 1582), wife of Angad, the second Guru, is praised in the scripture for the warmth and generosity that she brought to the institution of *langar* (community kitchen) and remembered as a wise advisor to her sons on spiritual and social matters.

Mai Bhago (died 1705) was a courageous woman who heroically took part in the battle with Guru Gobind Singh at Muktsar.

Mata Gujri (died 1705) was the wife of Guru Tegh Bahadur. She was imprisoned in Sirhind with her two younger grandchildren, and all three died there as martyrs to the Sikh faith. Sikhs remember her especially for strengthening the faith of the young boys, who were sealed alive behind a brick wall and chose to die there rather than renounce Sikhism.

Sada Kaur (died 1832) was the mother-in-law of Maharaja Ranjit Singh, the first Sikh emperor. Her counsel enabled the young Ranjit Singh to unify the Punjab and create a Sikh state.

Maharani Jindan (died 1863), wife of Maharaja Ranjit Singh, was famous for her keen intelligence. After the death of the Maharaja, she became a regent of the Sikh empire on behalf of her six-year-old son Dilip Singh. When the British occupied the Sikhs' territory, Dilip Singh was taken to England and converted to Christianity, and the Maharani was imprisoned. However, she continued to write powerful letters from prison and later went to England and convinced her son to return to Sikhism.

RULES REGARDING WOMEN

Sikh Rahit Maryada, the Sikh code of conduct, was published by the Shiromani Gurdwara Prabandhak Committee in 1950. It attempted to formalize the message of the Gurus and developed several rules that would combat female oppression. The *Sikh Rahit Maryada* twice makes the point that Sikh women should not veil their faces. It prohibits infanticide, and even association with people who would practice it. It allows for widows to remarry, and it underscores that the ceremony be the same as that of the first marriage—a marked difference from the custom where a widow was shamefully wrapped in a sheet and carried away to a brother of the dead husband. Sikhs should be free of all superstitions and not refuse to eat at the home of their married daughter. The principle underlying this injunction most likely is that a daughter should not be treated like property passed away to her husband and his family. Dowry is prohibited. Neither a girl nor a boy should be married for money. Child marriages are not permitted. A girl should marry only when she has attained physical and mental maturity. There is no prohibition against abortion.

Sikh scripture and its ethical code uphold gender equality. But they need to be reaffirmed against the ancient patriarchal values that have dominated India for so long.

BIBLIOGRAPHY

Cole, W. O., and P. S. Sambhi. *The Sikhs, Their Beliefs, and Practices.* 1978.

Kaur, Upinder Jit. *Sikh Religion and Economic Development.* 1990.

Macauliffe, M. A. *The Sikh Religion.* 1909. 3 vols. Reprint, 1985.

McLeod, W. H. *Guru Nanak and the Sikh Religion.* 1968.

Singh, Harbans. *Heritage of the Sikhs.* 1994.

Singh, Nikky-Guninder Kaur. *The Feminine Principle in the Sikh Vision of the Transcendent.* 1993.

———. *The Name of My Beloved: Verses of the Sikh Gurus.* 1995.

NIKKY-GUNINDER KAUR SINGH

Silence

Silence is highly lauded in religious studies because of its centrality to religious austerities, ritual, initiation, and mysticism. Feminism, by contrast, is skeptical of the phenomenon, because of the forced silencing of women by religious authorities. Both attitudes converge in women's intentional use of silence, which produces the paradox of mystical silence occasioning women's enhanced visibility.

The pivot for understanding silence lies between choice and compulsion. Religious enforcement of women's silence has been a consistently high priority for the patriarchal order. Male religious authorities, in almost all the literate traditions, have commanded women to be silent, exemplified in such infamous Christian New Testament injunctions as "I suffer not a woman to teach, nor to usurp authority over the man, but to be in silence" (1 Tim. 2:8–15; 1 Cor. 14:34–35). Historically, such commands have justified systemic silencings, such as prohibitions against women's ritual participation. Aquinas determines that "addressing the whole Church is not permitted to women, lest men's minds be enticed to lust" (*Summa Theologica* 2a2Æ.177, 2). These regulations dovetailed with sexist mythology concerning women's garrulous, intellectually bankrupt nature; as the Talmud suggests, "Ten measures of speech descended to the world, and women took nine of them" (B. Kiddushin 49b).

However, silence is an honored form of asceticism cross-culturally. *Mysticism* is etymologically related to the Greek word for closing the mouth, and *ineffability* implies both that which is beyond the descriptive power of words and that which should remain a secret. Silence, understood as a state of fullness and contact with the divine, easily slides into the esoteric: its lack of definite content opens an infinite realm of possibility.

Women employed silent contemplative methods as prestigious ways to gain voice and to promulgate ideas that challenged religious and societal norms. Lal Dev of Kashmir (1320–1392), venerated by both Muslims and Hindus, combined mystic silence with a transgressive public life, which included leaving her marriage and wandering naked. Hagiographic accounts state that she withstood taunts in silence so as to answer them later with philosophic finality. In a *vakh* (aphoristic poem) critiquing the hypocrisy of external religious practice, she writes, "Let your worship song be silence." But she also interprets her guru's precept—"withdraw your gaze within"—as warrant for nudity and ecstatic singing.

Seventeenth-century English Quakers likewise embodied the paradox of silence enabling speech for women. Quakers encouraged both men and women to await the Inner Light at meetings. This silence represented suppression of one's own voice in the hopes that the spirit would speak instead; such actualized spiritual equality between the genders enabled women to preach. While George Fox, the Quakers' founder, was adamant in his support of women's voices, maintaining that Paul could not prevent the Lord from speaking through women, his wife, Margaret Fell, addressed the issue more directly. Her 1666 essay, "Womens [*sic*] Speaking Justified," argued that because God had placed enmity between women and the serpent, silencing women gives free reign to Satan: "if the Seed of the Woman speak not, the Seed of the Serpent speaks." Furthermore, because Scripture describes the Church as a woman, "those that speak against the womans speaking, speak against the Church of Christ."

Myrtle Fillmore, cofounder of the Unity School of Christianity in 1890, articulated a similar theology in her *Healing Letters:* "When you start to go into the silence, you should breathe evenly, in the happy feeling that you are taking in great drafts of God's pure life-sustaining air. . . . God gives freely; it is up to us to keep the receiving channels open, to keep attuned to the realities so that our intellect does not take us out among the limited ideas of the world."

These examples reveal numerous assumptions about religious silence: that it is always chosen, that its spirituality is superior to the "carnal" world, and that gender is immaterial to the experience. Feminist theorists have critiqued such assumptions. Inspired by Tillie Olsen's landmark lectures (1963, 1971) on "unnatural" artistic silences—those created by oppression and censorship—and Virginia Woolf's speculative evocation of Shakespeare's muted sister in *A Room of One's Own* (1929), feminists have adopted silence and silencing as categories. Audre Lorde's essay, "The Transformation of Silence into Language and Action," is often cited for its pithy formulations on this topic, such as "Your silence will not protect you" (1984, p. 41).

Lorde's call to break silences has had a lasting impact on women's structural exclusion from religion. Likewise, women's breaking into rabbinical and ministerial positions, and holding religious organizations accountable for sexual abuse, owes much to the notion of ending silence. Feminist thinkers in religion have wanted to expand the resonance of this image; for instance, Mary Daly suggests that "the new sounds of free silence" (1973, p. 150) of women's spiritual self-development will be inaudible to patriarchal authority. Poststructuralist feminists explore how silence can be an active form of resistance, as well as underlining silence's ubiquity. Similarly, lesbian and gay thinkers highlight the complex silences of the closet, as in the slogan "Silence = Death."

BIBLIOGRAPHY

The full-length cross-cultural studies of the topic—Max Picard's *The World of Silence* (1952) and Alice Greene's *The Philosophy of Silence* (1940)—are outdated and lack any gender analysis, a flaw of Bernard Dauenhauer's *Silence: The Phenomenon and Its Ontological Significance* (1980). The article by Elizabeth McCumsey in *The Encyclopedia of Religion* (1987, vol. 13, pp. 321–324) is similarly notable for its lack of gendered dimensions and its entirely laudatory account of the religious uses of silence, but it provides adequate religious typologies.

For an exploration of mystical quiet and contemplation, see chapter 6 of Underhill's monumental volume, *Mysticism* (1910). For a summary of Lal Dev's life, see "A Second Rabia: Lal Ded of Kashmir," *Manushi* 50–52 (January–June 1989). A contemporary translation of her *vakh* has been made by Coleman Barks in *Naked Song* (1992). On Quaker silence, see Richard Bauman, *Let Your Words Be Few* (1983). For a useful (despite its Christian apologetics) survey of regulations concerning silencing of women within Western traditions, see Alvin Schmidt's *Veiled and Silenced: How Culture Shaped Sexist Theology* (1989).

The classic feminist works on silence, in addition to Woolf, are Tillie Olsen's *Silences* (1978), Audre Lorde's *Sister Outsider* (1984), and Adrienne Rich's *On Lies, Secrets and Silences* (1979). *Listening to Silences* (1994), edited by Elaine Hedges and Shelly Fisher Fishkin, explores the impact of Olsen's *Silences* in feminist thought.

The metaphor of breaking silence is addressed in numerous works; the introduction to Alice Hageman's *Sexist Religion and Women in the Church: No More Silence* (1974) is a historic marker. Mary Daly's *Beyond God the Father* (1973) contains explicit dialectics around silence and silencing. Gerda Lerner's *The Creation of Feminist Consciousness* (1993) suggests that mysticism—from the European Middle Ages to the African-American abolitionist movement—was an avenue women avidly traveled to legitimate their thoughts and gain voice. Grace Jantzen's *Power, Gender and Christian Mysticism* (1995) brilliantly analyzes ineffability and gender. Antoinette Goodwin's use of Julia Kristeva's thought in her article, "The Right to Remain Silent," *Pastoral Psychology* 41 (July 1993): 359–376, explores the subversive use women can make of silence. The central work for understanding the dynamics of gay silence is Eve Sedgwick's *Epistemology of the Closet* (1990).

See also **Asceticism; Initiation; Mysticism; Ritual; Voice.**

JENNIFER RYCENGA

Sin

Sin is culpable violation of the moral order imposed by a transcendent God. Related notions such as impurity, egocentricity, and illusion appear in Buddhism, Hinduism, and other traditions, but sin as such figures prominently only in religions based on ethical monotheism—Judaism, Christianity, and Islam. The social functions of the idea of sin are double-sided: it can legitimate the existing social order, but also call society to reform. Because it traces suffering at least partially to fault, the notion of sin can lead variously to appropriate self-critique or to victim-blaming, to the denunciation of injustice or to the deflection of personal responsibility onto social oppression. Theologically, too, doctrines of sin are often paradoxical. They attempt to explain evil as resulting from human moral failure, but, in accounting for the origins of moral failure, again may be driven to posit an evil or flaw that preexisted sin.

In each of these complex dimensions, ideas of sin have had profound consequences for women. Traditionally, women have been associated with evil—for example, as rebel against social order, primal sinner, or weak link in the chain that connects creatures with the Creator. In Judaism and especially in Christianity, the myths of origin within the biblical book of Genesis have been deployed to rationalize these associations. In Genesis 2, the first woman is made from the side of the original earth creature. Then, in Genesis 3, she is tempted by the serpent to eat the forbidden fruit, which she also gives to the man. The punishments meted out to the man (work and death) belong to human nature as such, but for the woman sexuality itself becomes accursed: she will suffer the pain of childbirth and be subject to sexual desire for the very male who dominates her. For both Judaism and Christianity, the punishment of Eve would obtain for all women, prescribing their permanent sexual subordination.

In Judaism, sins are correctable violations of community and of relationship to God, and the subordination of women is rooted in a patriarchal model of social order rather than in a negative view of sex as such. However, the encoding of patriarchalism in myth, law, and rabbinic literature did effect in Judaism particular associations between women, social disorder, and the morally dangerous aspects of sex. Examples include the mythology of Lilith, the image of the *yetzer hara* (the "evil impulse," or simply "desire"), and halachah (laws) concerning sex. Lilith, the rebellious first wife of Adam, imaginatively deduced by the rabbis from Genesis 1, became in the medieval kabbalist tradition a sexual trickster of demonic proportions. The *yetzer hara*, often associated with sexual desire, was praised as necessary

for the continuation of life, yet subjected to constant moral suspicion. Although the *yetzer hara* was imaged as male, both the Palestinian and Babylonian rabbinic traditions attributed a special "light-headedness" to women in regard to sexual temptation (Michael Satlow, *Tasting the Dish: Rabbinic Rhetorics of Sexuality*, 1995, p. 158). Judaism's numerous sexual regulations, although expressing much appreciation of sex, also associated women as a group with the need for sexual control, illustrated by the title of a primary source of sexual regulations: the Mishnah's "Order of Women."

Jewish feminists have analyzed and revised each of these traditions connecting women and sin. In a founding moment for Jewish feminism, the story of Lilith was creatively recast as a parable of women's liberation (Judith Plaskow et al., "The Coming of Lilith," in *Religion and Sexism*, edited by Rosemary Ruether, 1974). The construction of Eve as primal sinner and female archetype within some rabbinic literature has been subjected to critique, along with the prescription of "modesty" (i.e., seclusion from public life) as women's punishment (Bronner, 1994). The notion of the *yetzer hara* is being shorn of its androcentric and anti-sexual aspects by extending the rabbinic description of *yetzer hara* as "desire" or "hunger" and observing that women, too, are tempted to feed on innocent others. (Zoloth Dorfman, "Into the Woods: Killer Mothers, Feminist Ethics and the Problem of Evil," 1995). Finally, because halachah and attitudes regarding sexuality have been part of women's subordination in Judaism, feminists are proposing revisions and reinterpretations, sometimes quite radical, of these as well (Judith Plaskow, *Standing Again at Sinai: Judaism from a Feminist Perspective*, 1990, pp. 170–210; Rachel Adler, *Engendering Judaism: An Inclusive Theology and Ethics*, 1998, pp. 21–60).

In the New Testament, Paul assumes the derivative creation of the first woman (1 Cor. 11:8–9) and this, together with her supposed sin, is later invoked to legitimate subordinate roles for women in the family and in the wider Christian community (1 Tim. 2:11–15). By the fifth century, Augustine had elaborated a notion of "original," inherited sinfulness that reflected his personal mistrust of sexuality. The doctrine of a fallen world became the distinctive worldview of imperial Christianity, legitimating its hierarchical order and establishing celibacy as a spiritually superior life style (Pagels, 1988). From the Middle Ages to the present day, authoritative Christian thinkers such as Thomas Aquinas (d. 1274), Martin Luther (d. 1546), and Karl Barth (d. 1968) have continued to justify male supremacy by woman's supposedly derivative or inferior creation, God's just punishment for her sin, or a divinely covenanted social order.

The critique of Christian doctrines of sin was a founding impulse of feminist theologies in the United States (Saiving in Christ and Plaskow, 1979; Plaskow, 1980). Feminists thoroughly analyze and reject the identification of sin with women via the figure of Eve (Schuller, 1995) and the association of sin with self-love. Inverting the traditional negativism concerning sex and mortality, they attribute sin to the rejection of embodied, relational existence. Sexism rather than sex becomes a paradigm for original sin (Daly, 1982; Ruether, 1983), and blame is placed on beneficiaries of injustice rather than on their victims. Even traditional "deadly sins" such as lust and anger have been rehabilitated as liberating for women (e.g., Harrison, 1985), and the traditional ideal of self-sacrifice has been rejected in favor of an ethic of survival and liberation, especially among womanist theologians and women theologians of the Third World. Led by scholars of color, feminists have nuanced their social critique in terms of racial, economic, and political factors for which women may share responsibility. Sin has been redescribed in historically specific ways, for example, as the "defilement" of African American women and nature by white supremacist structures and practices (Williams, 1993). And the assumptions of racial privilege have been exposed in Eurocentric Christian notions of freedom and other ethical concepts (Cannon, 1995).

In Islam, as feminist scholars have shown, the association of women with sin is more a product of tradition than of scripture. In the Qur'an, the wife of Adam is unnamed, and details of her creation are not given. Both the man and woman are commanded not to eat fruit, and both are tempted by Iblis (Satan); both then view their nakedness with shame and are expelled from the garden. Women have fared worse in the subsequent Muslim tradition, however, as a result of the influence of several controverted hadith (purported sayings of the Prophet Muhammad), in particular one hadith that refers to woman as "the crooked rib." For many commentators, this saying testifies to women's inferior capacity to walk the "straight path" of Islam. In their interpretations Hawwa' (Eve) becomes the temptress of Adam, in some versions employing wine to weaken his powerful reasoning ability. The first sin becomes closely associated with sexuality and, as in Genesis 3, Eve's sexuality and that of all women is seen as accursed by monthly bleeding and forced, painful childbirth. The implications of this sexualized and gendered view of sin are far-reaching. For example, the term *awra*, which for men refers only to the genitals, for women encompasses the entire body and thus supports extremely broad mandates for female modesty or seclusion (Fedwa Malti-Douglas, "Faces of Sin: Corporeal Geographies in Contemporary Islamic Discourse" in *Religious Reflection on the Body,* edited by Jane Marie Law, 1995).

Feminist scholars contend that the sexist elements of Muslim views of sin are based largely on a small number of controverted hadith. Although purported sayings and actions of the Prophet are highly authoritative for Islam, the authenticity of individual sayings can be questioned, particularly if they appear to conflict with the Qur'an. Noting that several Qur'anic passages offer righteousness to men and women in explicitly parallel terms, feminists are questioning the authenticity of the "crooked rib" and similar traditions. Moreover, they are critically analyzing the effects of the Bible and Christian theology on the Islamic view of sin. For example, in Islam women cannot properly be blamed for "original sin" and the fallen world, since for Muslims there is no fall as such; death does not result from fault, and humans are not born into a state of sin (Hassan, 1991; Smith and Haddad, 1982).

Despite a clear consensus among feminist scholars of religion that the symbolic associations among sin, sex, and women need to be broken, much further discussion among religious believers is needed, entailing reexamination of the basic meaning and utility of the idea of sin. Can the notions of moral fault and freedom be applied to women and other oppressed groups without blaming the victims? How can women conceive themselves both as oppressed and as sometimes participating in the oppression of others? More generally, how can moral wrong be understood in both its personal and social dimensions? What are the human consequences of conceiving of moral law as transcendent in origin? How must the notions of moral law and moral freedom be interpreted or changed in order to allow for the reasoned, informed analysis of human suffering, its causes and solutions? Through these and related questions, women's religious reflection can further enrich contemporary moral discourse.

BIBLIOGRAPHY

Bronner, Leila Leah. *From Eve to Esther: Rabbinic Reconstructions of Biblical Women.* 1994. A comparison of biblical and rabbinic texts, arguing that the rabbis' interpretation of Eve's sin as one of sexual temptation underlay their norm of female "modesty," which effectively blocked women from public life.

Cannon, Katie Geneva. *Katie's Canon: Womanism and the Soul of the Black Community.* 1995. A collection of essays by a leading womanist ethicist, including several that explore the moral wisdom of African American women and explicate their ethic of survival.

Daly, Mary. *Beyond God the Father.* 1982. One of the first and most influential feminist theologies, astutely exposing the identification of women with evil as the original and enduring sin of patriarchal Christianity.

Harrison, Beverly. "The Power of Anger in the Work of Love: Christian Ethics for Women and Other Strangers." In *Making the Connections: Essays in Feminist Social Ethics.* Edited by Carol Robb. 1995. An eloquent argument for anger as a source of moral information, outlining a Christian feminist ethic based on activity, embodiment, and relationship rather than on self-sacrifice.

Hassan, Riffat. "Muslim Women and Post-Patriarchal Islam." In *After Patriarchy: Feminist Transformations of World Religions.* Edited by Paula Cooey, William Eakin, and Jay McDaniel. 1991. An argument for the inauthenticity of the purported sayings of the Prophet (Muhammad) on which are based the Muslim association of women, sex, and sin via Eve.

Pagels, Elaine. *Adam, Eve and the Serpent.* 1988. A critique of Augustine's theology of sin, with its sexist and antiworldly implications, contending that his view gained ascendancy because it lent ideological support to the hierarchical order of imperial Christianity.

Plaskow, Judith. *Sex, Sin and Grace: Women's Experience and the Theologies of Reinhold Niebuhr and Paul Tillich.* 1980. A feminist assessment of two influential twentieth-century Protestant theologies in view of experiences of sin that belong distinctively, if not universally, to women.

Ruether, Rosemary Radford. *Sexism and God-Talk: Toward a Feminist Theology.* 1983. A Christian feminist theology, in which the idea of a fallen world refers to social sin in all its dimensions, none of which are accepted as natural or inevitable.

Saiving, Valerie. "The Human Situation: A Feminine View." In *Womanspirit Rising: A Feminist Reader in Religion.* Edited by Carol P. Christ and Judith Plaskow. 1979. A critique of the definitions of sin as excessive self-regard in the theologies of Reinhold Niebuhr and Anders Nygren, contending that the characteristic sin of women is the under-development of self.

Schuller, Eileen. "Feminism and Biblical Hermeneutics: Genesis 1–2 as a Test Case." In *Gender, Genre and Religion.* Edited by Morny Joy and Eva Neumaier Dargyay. 1995. An examination of Eve as a theme that divides recent feminist hermeneutics into two stages, the first attempting a feminist rehabilitation of the Bible and the second questioning whether the Bible in its patriarchalism can be authoritative for women.

Smith, Jane, and Yvonne Haddad. "Eve: Islamic Image of Woman." *Women's Studies International Forum* 5, no. 2 (1982): 135–144. A comparison of Qur'anic account of creation, sin, and punishment with later traditions, demonstrating that notions about women's moral inferiority are products of the latter.

Williams, Delores. "A Womanist Perspective on Sin." In *A Troubling in My Soul: Womanist Perspectives on Evil and Suffering.* Edited by Emilie Townes. 1993. A historical examination of sin in African-American Christianity, describing African American women's experience of sin as "defilement," a desecration of body and soul.

———. "Sin, Nature and Black Women's Bodies." In *Ecofeminism and the Sacred.* Edited by Carol Adams. 1993. Parallel analyses of the defilement of nature and of black women, both images of God, by white American culture.

See also Evil; Lilith; Sexuality.

KATHLEEN M. SANDS

Sister

Sibling relationships are not widely discussed cross-culturally in the context of world religions. In one of the few studies of the myths and meanings of sisterhood, Christine Downing notes that unlike the overwhelming relationship between mother and child, the relationship between sisters is on a human rather than a divine scale (*Psyche's Sisters,* 1988). Downing also observes, however, that there is a religious, transpersonal dimension of sisterhood that highlights themes of complementarity and polarity. Sometimes a sister is the one most like oneself, sometimes the other over against whom a woman defines herself. A sister may be the most loyal and loving of friends and helpers or the most dangerous of shadow-figures. Another aspect of the sister bond underscores mortality and the encounter with death. Because coming to love the sister means letting go of the mother bond, it is associated with the experience of loss and mourning.

Sister-sister relationships are ambivalent and volatile. Psyche's sisters in Apuleius's myth of Psyche and Amor are jealous, devious, and cruel, but they are also the mediums of revelation who push her toward a higher level of self-understanding and a more mature approach to love. The Sumerian myth cycle of Inanna is also rich with the dynamics of sibling relationships. Inanna's encounter with her sister, Ereskigal, queen of the underworld, is a crucial aspect of her soul journey through which she simultaneously confronts her own shadow-self and undergoes the transformative process of death and rebirth. Isis's relationship with her sister, Nepthys, on the other hand, demonstrates a deep bond of loyalty and collaboration.

In Greek myth there are many accounts of brother-sister relationships such as that between Artemis and Apollo. These relationships are models of equality, self-containment, and mutual support.

Among the Hebrews, the term sister is used for female offspring of natural relations between the same father and mother and for children of the same father, or the same mother. It is also sometimes used for near relations. Mosaic law forbids marrying the sister of a wife or two sisters. The word is also used to express resemblance of conditions or inclinations. This use of the term also appears in the New Testament. For example, Christ calls those who keep the commandments brothers and sisters.

Even in traditions that place great emphasis on family relationships, sisters are not accorded the same status as brothers, and their influence is often indirect. In Confucianism, for example, elder sisters typically have the responsibility for caring for the household and the younger children.

The term also applies to female members of religious orders and is a mode of address in many Protestant churches for lay women as well as for those in ministry. In Roman Catholicism, sisterhood is a religious ideal in religious communities bound together by religious vows and devoted to mutual pursuit of moral perfection and helping others, especially the suffering and the poor.

As a feminist ideal, sisterhood has been a key metaphor for mutual support and empowerment, encouraging women to develop alternative models to the hierarchical and competitive structures of patriarchy. Feminist philosophers such as Jan Raymond and Mary Daly and feminist theologians like Mary Hunt and Carter Heyward discuss sisterhood as a model for female friendships. In *Pure Lust* (1984), Mary Daly places sisterhood at the core of her comprehensive vision of women's spirituality. Others critique the sisterhood model for its failure to take into account differences in women's status and experience, especially as reinforced through racism, classism, and other forms of oppression; bell hooks suggests that motives for solidarity differ among communities of women. She argues that white women experience sisterhood in the context of common victimization while black women focus on shared strengths, resources, and political commitment.

Sisterhood may also serve as an important ecofeminist model, viewing earth as sister and thereby affirming a mutual relationship, a shared mortality, and interconnectedness.

BIBLIOGRAPHY

For a detailed discussion of the psychological implications of the sister relationship in the myths of Inanna, see Diane Wolkstein and Samuel Noah Kramer's *Inanna, Queen of Heaven and Earth* (1983). Renita J. Weems's *Just a Sister Away* (1988) contains some very interesting discussions of sister and sister-in-law relationships in biblical narratives; the relational power of the sisterhood model may be found in Mary Hunt's *Fierce Tenderness* (1991), Janice G. Raymond's *A Passion for Friends* (1986), and Carter Heyward's *Touching Our Strength* (1989). Ann Matter's article "My Sister, My Spouse" in *Weaving the Visions* (1989), edited by Judith Plaskow and Carol P. Christ, takes an interesting look at love among women in medieval monastic life. For earth as sister, see Susan Griffin's "This Earth Is My Sister" in the same volume.

See also **Friendship**.

L. J. "TESS" TESSIER

Sītā

Sītā, princess of Videha and later queen of Ayodhya, is the heroine of one of Asia's most popular and enduring story-cycles, commonly referred to by the Sanskrit name Rāmāyaṇa ("the acts of Rāma") and transmitted through hundreds of literary works in most of the languages of the Indian subcontinent and Southeast Asia. Although Sītā is often cited as the epitome of Indian womanhood and the paragon of devoted Hindu wives, her portrayal across a spectrum of texts ranging from the Sanskrit epic attributed to Vālmīki (c. fifth century B.C.E.) through scores of later works in regional languages, to contemporary fiction, folksongs, comic books, and a 1987 Indian television serial in 104 installments, in fact reveals a rich diversity of interpretations.

Her name means "furrow" in Sanskrit, and her miraculous birth from freshly plowed soil links her to the earth goddess. Adopted by a king, she is married to Prince Rāma of Ayodhya, an incarnation of the celestial savior-god Vishnu. The couple's domestic life is interrupted by Rāma's unjust fourteen-year exile, in which Sītā elects to accompany him into the wilderness. There she is kidnapped by the lustful demon-king Rāvaṇa and taken to his island, where she maintains her virtue amid temptations and torments, while her husband mounts an invasion to rescue her. Following Rāma's victory, Sītā is subjected by him to the further ordeal of a fiery test of her purity before being permitted to rejoin him as queen of Ayodhya. In many versions of the story, lingering doubts about her faithfulness result in her eventual re-exile to the forest, where she gives birth to Rāma's twin sons. Bringing the grown boys to Rāma years later, Sītā rejects his invitation to return to him and calls on her mother to witness to her purity, descending into the earth enthroned beside a green-clad goddess.

Whereas most Sanskrit retellings emphasize Sītā's human qualities of endurance, chastity, and longing for an absent beloved (*viraha,* an anguish that Rāma fully shares), later vernacular versions stress the divinity of both hero and heroine, who become the supreme dyad Sītā-Rāma worshiped in countless temples. Sītā is understood to be an embodiment of primordial feminine power (*śakti*) and the Mother of the universe; in some accounts, it is only through her power that Rāma is able to conquer his enemy. In northern India during the seventeenth and eighteenth centuries, a tradition of mystical-erotic devotion (*rasika bhakti*), influenced by the worship of Krishna and his consort Rādhā, gave special importance to Sītā, even inspiring a Sītāyaṇa and other Sītā-centered retellings of the story. Extensive women's folklore (only recently noticed by scholars) draws on both classical and devotional versions but may subvert and challenge patriarchal themes by empathizing with Sītā's experience of, and resistance to, familial and gender-based injustice.

BIBLIOGRAPHY

For Sītā's portrayal in the Sanskrit epic, see the published volumes of *The Rāmāyaṇa of Vālmīki,* edited by Robert P. Goldman (1984–1996). For examples of later interpretations, see the essays by Philip Lutgendorf, Narayana Rao, and David Shulman in *Many Rāmāyaṇas,* edited by Paula Richman (1991).

PHILIP LUTGENDORF

Social Action

Movements for social change often derive from a group's feelings of deprivation, exclusion, or oppression. Collective mobilization of resources enables people to effect change and remedy the situation they feel is unacceptable. When women engage in social action it is partly because such action is true to their spiritual or religious beliefs. Many social movements specifically encourage women to reinterpret patriarchal religious ideologies that contribute to their oppression. When religion has been used as a tool to justify the oppression of women, or of a group with whom women identify, women have responded by joining forces and speaking out.

The Abolitionist movement of the nineteenth century is one example of a social movement in which women were very much involved based on strong religious conviction. Women's struggle for equality within the Abolitionist movement and in American society led to the Women's Suffrage movement in 1848. Religious arguments denying women citizenship rights were countered with reinterpretations of the Bible demonstrating the need for women's influence in the public sphere as a tenet of Christian spirituality. Elizabeth Cady Stanton and other supporters of women's rights wrote *The Woman's Bible,* essentially a commentary focusing on women in the Bible and the importance of their participation in the church and society.

However, in the nineteenth century women's roles, particularly for white, middle-class women, were increasingly defined as wife and mother within the domestic sphere. But women's demands for and justification of religious and spiritual equality found an outlet in the religious revival of the nineteenth century, and in some cases the opportunity to lead the revival. Women's identification with spirituality and religion sometimes made it possible for them to exercise authority and leadership. Women became the founders of new religions such as the Christian Scientists and the Shakers. Women were also particularly active in the Utopian movements of that century.

Influenced by the Civil Rights Movement and the revitalized women's movement of the 1960s, many women questioned their second-class status in male-dominated churches and denominations. Women started to demand ordination and official recognition of their contributions. Feminist theologians critiqued religious traditions. A variety of perspectives emerged along with various feminist strategies for social change. Some feminists concluded that male-dominated religious traditions were beyond reform and called for women to reject them in favor of a feminist spirituality: by recovering goddess worship from the past and combining it with radical feminist theories for social change, women could redefine faith in their own terms. Others such as Rosemary Radford Ruether (1992) and Charlene Spretnak (1990) linked the transformation of patriarchal religion with the environmentalist movement. Male-dominated religious ideologies were identified with aspects of modern industrial capitalism that valued material growth over preserving the environment. However, many feminists maintained that the strong egalitarian roots underlying some religious traditions can be rescued from the hands of patriarchal interpretations and male dominance.

Analyses implicating male-dominated religions in larger male-dominated social institutions influenced the general feminist movement by pointing out how ideol-

Wangari Maathal is the leader of the Green Belt movement in Kenya and an advocate of environmental and women's issues (Adrian Arbib/Corbis).

ogy and belief systems saturate the society. The secular feminist movement offered alternative models of organization to women within religious traditions who wanted to challenge male leadership and hierarchy, or to create altogether separate feminist religious organizations, such as Women-Church. This sharing of theories and strategies has not yet exhausted the possibilities for radical social change (Lorber, 1994).

Conservative social movements and women's religious experiences also influence each other. In the United States, the religious right (embodying fundamentalist, evangelical, and conservative perspectives within large churches and denominations) supports a return to more traditional roles for women and men based on their interpretations of the Bible. Women on the religious right are more likely to be involved in social movements that espouse conservative political beliefs, such as efforts to ban abortion, limit pornography, and suppress gay rights.

Israel, various Islamic countries, and some newly emergent African nations are struggling with resurgent traditional religious ideologies. In some cases, women are returning to traditional social roles as fundamentalist religious ideologies influence the construction of national and individual identities. As anthropologist Susan Starr Sered (1994) has pointed out, a variety of social forces—including urbanization, national econ-

omies, and the global economy—along with religion affect women both as individuals and as cultural symbols. Women strike a "patriarchal bargain," attempting to make the best lives for themselves and their children within a male-dominated society even as that society changes from one form of patriarchy to another (Kandiyoti, 1988).

Religion and women's spirituality are still being redefined and renegotiated. Researching women's religions (those religions, sects, and cults in which women form the majority of participants and leaders and are independent from larger male-dominated organizations), Sered has devised a typology for understanding how religion affects women's choices for organizing for social changes and advantages. She divides them into two models: The first model embodies religions that focus on individuals and seem to obtain only short-term help for women (e.g., Christian Science); they do not aspire to any large, structural social change. The second model embodies religions based on ongoing and collective interests that organize for social structural change—for example, the nineteenth-century Shakers and the contemporary Feminist Spirituality movement. Sered's models include examples of women's religions from many cultures around the world.

Although there is a relationship between religious ideologies and social change, it may not be consistent or as simple and formulaic as equating male-dominated religion with traditionalism and female-dominated religion with radicalism. For example, Hinduism has many powerful female deities, but Hindu society offers little equality for women. Latin American liberation theology, which is based on Christianity, a patriarchal religion, challenges unjust social structures including women's oppression and has laid the foundation for a variety of revolutionary movements. Explaining the many contradictions while illuminating the connections presents a challenge for sociologists of religion and social movements as well as feminists and theologians studying women's religious experiences.

BIBLIOGRAPHY

It seems that every work related to women and religion, especially when discussing ordination, involves a critiquing and reenvisioning of women's spiritual experiences in relation to the feminist movement. The works listed here highlight the connections with feminism or other social movements such as environmentalism, neoconservatism, and fundamentalism.

Ahmed, Leila. *Women and Gender in Islam: The Historical Roots of a Modern Debate.* 1992.

Cottle, Charles, Patricia Searles, Ronald Berger, and Beth Ann Pierce. "Conflicting Ideologies and the

Politics of Pornography." *Gender and Society* 3 (1989): 303–333.

Farrell, Susan A. "Women-Church and Egalitarianism: In Christ There Are No More Distinctions Between Male and Female." In *The Power of Gender in Religion.* Edited by G. A. Weatherby and S. A. Farrell. 1996.

Kandiyoti, Deniz. "Bargaining with Patriarchy." *Gender and Society* 2 (1988): 274–290.

Lorber, Judith. *Paradoxes of Gender.* 1994. In the chapter "Dismantling Noah's Ark," the author discusses various strategies for transforming society and makes connections with various religious and cultural ideologies and feminism.

Luker, Kristen. *Abortion and the Politics of Motherhood.* 1984.

Ruether, Rosemary Radford. *Gaia and God: An Ecofeminist Theology of Earth Healing.* 1992.

Ruether, Rosemary Radford, and Rosemary Skinner Keller, eds. *Women and Religion in America.* Vol. 1. 1981. This volume includes selections from primary sources as well as an excellent commentary on the connections between nineteenth-century social movements and women's religious experiences.

Sered, Susan Starr. *Priestess, Mother, Sacred Sister: Religions Dominated by Women.* 1994.

Spretnak, Charlene. "Ecofeminism: Our Roots and Flowering." In *Reweaving the World: The Emergence of Ecofeminism.* Edited by Irene Diamond and Gloria Femon Orenstein. 1990.

———. *The Politics of Women's Spirituality.* 1982.

Stanton, Elizabeth Cady. *The Woman's Bible* [1895]. 1974.

SOME ADDITIONAL SOCIOLOGICAL PERSPECTIVES

Briggs, Sheila. "Women and Religion." In *Analyzing Gender: A Handbook of Social Science Research.* Edited by B. B. Hess and M. M. Ferree. 1987.

Davidman, Lynn. *Tradition in a Rootless World: Women Turn to Orthodox Judaism.* 1991.

Katzenstein, Mary Fainsod. "Discursive Politics and Feminist Activism in the Catholic Church." In *Feminist Organizations: Harvest of the New Women's Movement.* Edited by M. M. Ferree and P. Y. Martin. 1995.

Palmer, Susan J. *Moon Sisters, Krishna Mothers, Rajneesh Lovers: Women's Roles in New Religions.* 1994.

See also **Environmentalism; Liberation Theologies; Women's Contemporary Spirituality Movement; Women's Suffrage Movement.**

SUSAN A. FARRELL

Social Change

Scholarship in the field of women and religion recognizes that the status of women is inextricably linked to both religious and social contexts. Feminist analysis examines how these two streams of influence intertwine and diverge, especially in light of social change, which women from diverse religious backgrounds have both encouraged and resisted. Religious sentiment continues to determine much of women's experience of marriage, reproduction, law, politics, education, and economics. Advancement as well as deterioration in women's lives within various traditions have rendered imperative ongoing examinations of social change vis-à-vis women and world religions.

During the 1980s two international conferences were held to investigate the significance of religious and social movements for women. The published conference proceedings demonstrate that despite evident cultural variations, researchers identified three key points underpinning their investigations. First, regarding the role that religion plays in shaping women's lives, beyond women's positive and negative experiences within particular traditions are the overarching implications that religious movements have for all women. Recognizing how religious ideologies permeate even so-called secular society, scholars of this approach reveal how virtually all political and cultural attitudes toward women are significantly influenced by religious thought (Eck and Jain). Second, regarding the ambivalent relationship between religious and other social ideals, although religions have often been powerful agents of social change, they have also worked to conserve traditional attitudes and beliefs during periods of social transition. The strong ideological and ritualistic overtones of many social revolutions have even led some scholars to challenge the distinction made between religious and secular endeavors to transform society (Falk, in Haddad and Findly, 1985). Third, women have a significant role in both confronting and maintaining social norms. Women throughout the world are increasingly involved with feminist efforts to improve their lives, yet they also play a strong role as transmitters of heritage (Haddad and Findly).

The integrative study of women, religion, and social change investigates the influence of these three components as they interact together in culture. Throughout history, women have participated in social change either in accordance with or in opposition to religious sentiment and values. In Latin American societies, women have been instrumental in bringing about social change through the religious initiatives of liberation theology and base communities (Turner). Women of tribal traditions, including those in North America, look to women-centered mythology and heritage to heal and grow beyond oppressive regimes (Allen).

Although religious movements have often been vehicles for confronting social injustice, they have also tended to inhibit more progressive social notions regarding women (Eck and Jain). Early Western feminist endeavors were partly encouraged by religious affiliation with churches that provided women with leadership roles outside the home. However, these same institutions were reluctant to approve women's ordination (Ruether, 1984). Although Christian churches and clergy were powerful forces in the American civil rights movement, their focus on male participation spurred feminist demands for both social and religious change (Ruether, 1994).

Highlighting how patriarchal notions such as the inherent maleness of the divinity have served to justify hierarchical structures that oppress women, several feminist scholars challenge traditional religious ideologies and beliefs. Some, such as Rosemary Ruether and Judith Plaskow, suggest that reinterpretations of biblical texts and traditions could favorably alter religious and social views on women. Others, such as Mary Daly and Naomi Goldenberg, are more skeptical, rejecting all forms of patriarchal religiosity as inherently misogynist; they argue that traditional Western religions are incapable of providing the sort of women-centered spirituality demanded by the feminist movement. Their suggestion that women turn to more inspiring female religious symbolism has been affirmed in the goddess movement and witchcraft. Arguing that conceptions of a male deity who exists apart from the material world have had a devastating impact on Western societies and the physical world, Carol Christ and Starhawk assert that an immanent female deity empowers women and can reverse harmful social trends.

Some feminists emphasize what they consider the intrinsic spiritual dimensions of the women's movement. Spirituality that is women-oriented emphasizes the sacrality of women's experience in the world and in relation to others. Although many activists fear that religious involvement detracts from political endeavors, others involved in the women's spirituality movement have taken action against pollution, nuclear arms, and violence (Spretnak). Recognizing the origin of social tensions in religious ideologies, these scholars believe that social change can occur by altering the underlying myths of culture (Starhawk, 1982). In the process of social transformation, negative patriarchal images are replaced by life-affirming symbols that reshape cultures and expand the significance of spirituality in Western women's lives (King).

Despite efforts to incorporate non-Western perspectives in Western discourse on women, religion, and social change, information on women's experience in Eastern and developing countries remains scarce. Although the impact of religion on women's social status varies among cultures, global patterns are nevertheless evident. Throughout history, periods of social upheaval have been characterized by women's increased involvement in either established religions or in the development of new movements. As religions mature, women's spiritual and social functions tend to diminish (Falk). Women's global efforts to enact change therefore demand a return to more egalitarian original religious practices or the creation of more appropriate dogma that values female participation in religious and other social spheres (Carroll, Young). Ironically, advancement in women's status initially occurred more quickly in developing countries, whose hierarchies were criticized by the more resistant, technologically advanced nations (Young). However, in those nations where feminism is associated with Western imperialism and secularization, religious fundamentalism restricting women's behavior may be regarded as a necessary strategy to preserve cultural identity (Young).

Feminist analysis of religion and society challenges earlier understandings about the relationship between these spheres. Topics once discussed under the separate rubrics of religion and social change are now more often situated in discourse that regards religion and culture as continually intertwined and in flux.

BIBLIOGRAPHY

The two most comprehensive texts on topics discussed here are *Women, Religion, and Social Change*, edited by Yvonne Yazbeck Haddad and Ellison Banks Findly (1985), introduction by Nancy Falk; and *Speaking of Faith: Cross Cultural Perspectives on Women, Religion and Social Change*, edited by Diana L. Eck and Devaki Jain (1986). Both collections incorporate the work of researchers from many countries and address several historic periods. The impact of world religions on women and social progress is also addressed in Theodora Foster Carroll, *Women, Religion, and Development in the Third World* (1983).

Katherine Young, in her introduction to *Today's Woman in World Religions*, edited by Arvind Sharma (1994), discusses the influence of Western feminism on religious cultures, including those where it is regarded as a threat to social identity. Also in that volume, Rosemary Ruether, in "Christianity and Women in the Modern World," outlines patterns of women's experience and leadership in Christian churches. The essays in *Gender, Genre, and Religion*, edited by Morny Joy and Eva K. Neumaier-Dargyay (1995), explore the challenges posed by women's demand for increased participation in social and religious spheres. Robert Wuthrow and William Lehrman, "Religion: Inhibitor or Facilitator of Political Involvement Among Women," in *Women, Politics, and Change*, edited by Louise A. Tilly and Patricia Gurin (1990), offer statistical data and discussion of the relationship between religious involvement and the tendency toward political activity among American women.

Women's involvement in liberation theology is examined in *Through Her Eyes: Women's Theology From Latin America*, edited by Elsa Tamez (1989), and in Maria Clara Bingemer's article "Women in the Future of the Theology of Liberation" in *Expanding the View*, edited by Marc H. Ellis and Otto Maduro (1990). Also see Pauline Turner's "Religious Aspects of Women's Role in Nicaraguan Revolution" in *Women, Religion, and Social Change* (Haddad and Findly). Delores S. Williams' *Sisters in the Wilderness: The Challenge of Womanist God-Talk* (1993) explores issues pertaining to black liberation theology. *Mujerista* approaches to liberation and justice are addressed in Ada María Isasi-Díaz's *Mujerista Theology* (1996). Paula Gunn Allen's *The Sacred Hoop: Recovering the Feminine in American Indian Traditions* (1986) highlights the importance of traditional women-centered mythology in tribal women's efforts to improve their lives.

For feminist analyses of Western traditions and the significance of goddess spirituality and witchcraft in North America, see *Womanspirit Rising*, edited by Judith Plaskow and Carol P. Christ (1979), esp. Christ, "Why Women Need the Goddess: Phenomenological, Psychological and Political Reflections." See also Carol Christ, *Rebirth of the Goddess: Finding Meaning in Feminist Spirituality* (1997). Marymay Downing, "For Her, or Against Her? The Power of Religious Metaphor," in *Limited Edition: Voices of Women, Voices of Feminism*, edited by Geraldine Finn (1993), discusses the positive and negative effects of religious imagery on women working for change in their personal and social lives. Martha Reineke, "Out of Order: A Critical Perspective on Women and Religion," in *Women: A Feminist Perspective*, 4th ed., edited by Jo Freeman (1989), examines the link between religious ideologies focused on the female body and women's lower social status.

Feminist criticism and rejection of patriarchal religions is strongly articulated in Mary Daly, *Beyond God the Father: Toward a Philosophy of Women's Liberation* (1973), and in Naomi Goldenberg, *Changing of the Gods* (1979), which argues that, if feminism succeeds, patriarchal religions will no longer be needed.

Susan Starr Sered, *Priestess, Mother, Sacred Sister: Religions Dominated by Women* (1994), identifies the social circumstances in which women-dominated religions are likely to develop. The spiritual dimensions of women's connection to the earth and social justice are explored in Starhawk, "Power, Authority, and Mystery: Ecofeminism and Earth-Based Spirituality," in *Free Spirits: Feminist Philosophers on Culture*, edited by Kate Mehurm and Gray Percepe (1995). Rosemary Ruether explores the connections of Western religion to social and environmental oppression in *New Woman/New Earth* (1975); and in her edited volume, *Women Healing Earth: Third World Women on Ecology, Feminism, and Religion* (1996).

The articles in *The Politics of Women's Spirituality: Essays on the Rise of Spiritual Power Within the Feminist Movement*, edited by Charlene Spretnak (1982), examine the intrinsic connection between spiritual power and efforts to effect change. Starhawk's article in this collection, "Witchcraft as Goddess Religion," examines how women's spirituality can evoke social change once underlying cultural symbols have also changed. In *Women and Spirituality: Voices of Protest and Promise* (1989), Ursula King discusses how social change can usher in a new spirituality based on the power of women.

BIBLIOGRAPHY

FILMS

Adam's World. Directed by Donna Read. 1992.

The Best of Their Service: African American Women, Religion, and Social Change. Directed by Cheryl Townsend Gilkes. Produced by Wesley Theological Seminary. 1993.

In Women's Hands: The Changing Roles of Women. Episode 5 of *The Americas.* Produced by WGBH Educational Foundation. 1993.

Women in Religion. Produced by the Division of Continuing Studies, University of Victoria. This series examines Hinduism, Christianity, Buddhism, Wicca, Native American religious traditions, Islam, and Judaism through interviews with leading scholars of women in religion. 1994.

Women, Religion, and Social Change. Produced by the John F. Kennedy School of Government. Sponsored by the Harvard Institute of Politics and the Center for the Study of World Religions. 1983.

Women and Social Action. Part 14 on Religion. Produced and directed by Cheryl Lambert. 1994.

PEGGY SCHMEISER

Sociology

Sociology, the science of human society, as defined by Anthony Giddens has "as its main focus the study of the social institutions brought into being by the industrial transformations of the past two or three centuries" (1987, p. 9). The nineteenth-century social philosopher Auguste Comte introduced the term *sociology* in 1839, and the field finds its origins in the nineteenth- and twentieth-century writings of Karl Marx, Emile Durkheim, and Max Weber. Several competing and interacting perspectives or paradigms guide questions addressed through research and theory: conflict, structural functionalism, and symbolic interactionism. The theoretical and philosophical foundations address the impact of the Industrial Revolution, democratic political revolutions, the sovereignty of the nation-state, and the emergence of capitalism as the dominant political economic force in modern life.

The changing role of religion as a mediator of economic relationships, an arbiter of political legitimacy, and a moral force for social cohesion forms a significant area of attention. Marx's analysis of capitalism and its exploitative class relations included a critique of religion as "the opiate of the people," as an ideology that deflected the energy of the oppressed away from the material world to spiritual rewards in an afterlife, thus dampening the revolutionary action that should follow from the experience of exploitation. Durkheim and Weber answered Marx's critique and wrote extensively on religion. Durkheim focused primarily on the "elementary forms" or basic elements of the human religious experience in order to explore the sources of solidarity in various types of society. Weber examined the role of ideas in shaping social life through extensive studies of various world religions and an analysis of the role of Calvinist ideas in shaping a particularly successful form of capitalism.

Although sociology defines itself in terms of its founding fathers or its "masters" of sociological thought and theory, feminist perspectives are prompting the recovery of significant women shapers of sociological thought. Calling her "the mother of sociology," Margaret Andersen (1997) points out that British feminist Harriet Martineau not only translated Comte's *Positive Philosophy* but also wrote about society in the United States and offered a treatise on sociological field methods. The contradictions between democracy and slavery and between democracy and the political exclusion of women were contained in her critical feminist sociology. Max Weber's widow, Marianne Schnitger Weber, is rarely considered a sociologist and theorist in her own right. Yet, in addition to the biography of her husband, she left a substantial body of critical writings on women's issues, Marxist and socialist theory, and social problems such as war, marriage, and higher education. Her contributions remained unappreciated until the late twentieth century.

Sociology grew as an empirical social science largely in the United States through the work of the department of sociology at the University of Chicago, commonly called the Chicago school. The Chicago school's empirical work coincided with the important periods of urbanization, European immigration, African-American internal migration, the woman suffrage movement, and the antilynching movement. The emergence of American sociology and the Progressive Era occurred simultaneously with the rise to prominence of powerful women reformers, such as Chicagoan Jane Addams, who played an important role in the direction of the new discipline of sociology and the new profession of social work; Addams was a founding member of the American Sociological Society and active in the profession throughout her entire career at Hull House. Charlotte Perkins Gilman, Ida B. Wells Barnett, Florence Kelley, and Anna Julia Cooper were involved in various social movements and wrote extensively about social problems and women's issues. Although generally unacknowledged as sociological founders or foremothers, these women contributed to the public discourses about social problems that fueled the demand for sociological research and for social workers.

The first African-American sociologist, W. E. B. Du Bois, completed the first empirical community study in the United States and developed a comprehensive research program at Atlanta University that focused on how the structures of oppression governed the everyday lives of black people, of whom over ninety percent lived and worked in the South until World War I. The "great migration" of African-Americans northward, especially to the Chicago area, turned the attention of Chicago sociologists to issues of race relations and social change. Race and ethnicity remained a particularly prominent part of "Chicago sociology," and several African-American sociologists from that department, particularly E. Franklin Frazier and Oliver Cromwell Cox, gained prominence because of the empirical questions they raised concerning the roles of black women in urban family life. Acknowledging the importance of race in the matrix of domination, feminist sociologists later put forth parallels between race-ethnicity and gender to highlight the centrality of power to shaping the society's gender system.

The sociologists of the Chicago school fostered the use of fieldwork and participant observation, generated links with anthropologists, and accomplished broad-based community studies using multiple methods and many kinds of data to study urban life and social problems. Their work connected with the social philosophy of pragmatist George Herbert Mead and expanded the interpretive aspects of Max Weber's and Georg Simmel's sociological thought. Other departments rose to challenge the dominance of the Chicago school in the United States, with a structural-functionalist perspective rooted in the work of Emile Durkheim shaping many of the questions that sociological researchers explored. The structural-functionalist emphasis on roles and statuses in a consensus-bound society meant that women's roles were explored largely with reference to the family. The family and its domestic sphere were expected to be dependent on the public sphere of men's work. When women participated in the labor force, especially black women, they were usually viewed as deviant. The growth to dominance of the middle class and the post–World War II baby boom reinforced the family-centered focus on sex roles even though women's participation in the labor force grew steadily. In the mid-twentieth-century atmosphere of prosperity and anticommunism, attention to social inequality, especially in terms of Marxist thought, became muted as the differential rewards of the occupational structure were explained as the logical outcome of hierarchies of education, technological training, and social need.

The civil rights, black power, and women's movements of the 1960s and 1970s prompted sociologists to rediscover the problems of inequality from a critical perspective and to pay more attention to the ways in which class, race, and gender intersected, interacted, and were socially reproduced in modern societies. The changing relationship of minorities to American institutions and the increased demands for women's labor raised new questions that in turn changed the contours of sociology. Although Judith Stacey and Barrie Thorne pointed to the lack of a feminist revolution in sociology, primarily because of the distraction created by the traditional focus on sex roles, new theoretical perspectives grew at a tremendous rate. These perspectives were enriched by what Shulamit Reinharz identified as the diversity, interactivity, and transdisciplinarity necessary for truly feminist social research methods.

Informed by feminist concerns about the origins and operations of patriarchy in modern society, emerging feminist perspectives in sociology stress the importance of the interstructuring, intersection, or dynamic interactions between gender, race, and class. According to Ruth Wallace, the works of Canadian sociologist Dorothy Smith and African-American sociologist Patricia Hill Collins represent important new theoretical directions for sociology. Collins's work stresses the importance of standpoint as a source of knowledge, and she underscores the importance of many diverse types of knowledge as the primary sources for feminist theory. Collins demonstrates that the roles of black women as "outsiders" within an oppressive society generate a

Ida B. Wells-Barnett (1862–1931) was a journalist and activist who published the names of men in a lynch mob and subsequently compiled statistics on the actual extent of lynchings (Schomburg Center for Research in Black Culture).

specialized knowledge that is both critical of the dominant society and empowering as a source of consciousness and resistance. In a similar vein, Dorothy Smith points to women's everyday lives as the most important source of data. That importance, however, is diminished because of what Smith identifies as the "conceptual practices of power." She points to two interlinked difficulties that make a new sociology necessary for understanding women's lives: first, sociological knowledge is generated in "the male social universe." Second, the worlds of women and the new perspectives developed from women's standpoint are subordinated to the standpoint of men. The interaction between these difficulties operates "to compel women to think their world in the concepts and terms in which men think theirs. Hence the established social forms of consciousness alienate women from their own experiences" (1990, p. 13).

Overall, sociology has been shaped by and benefited from its interaction with progressive social movements in the nineteenth and twentieth centuries. The feminist movement of the late twentieth century challenged sociologists not only to undo the erasure of their fore-mothers from the history of the discipline but also to rethink their own language, their understandings of the sources of social inequality, and the role of gender in structuring occupational segregation, social institutions, and the differential access of men and women to the options and limits of a complex society. The rethinking of gender relations in religious and family life has been important to the deconstruction of difference that Judith Lorber points to as a critical process making it possible to undermine the social construction of gender inequality. As she sees it, "if the construction of categories and the social process of gender inequality are made visible (deconstructed), they might eventually be altered by individuals, groups, and whole societies" (1998, p. 195). Ultimately, sociology is the science of human activity both shaping and shaped by structures and organizations external to the individual. Observing the transformation of sociology through the feminist revolution compels a vision of future equality.

BIBLIOGRAPHY

Andersen, Margaret L. *Thinking About Women: Sociological Perspectives on Sex and Gender.* 1997.

Collins, Patricia Hill. *Black Feminist Theory: Knowledge, Consciousness, and the Politics of Empowerment.* 1990.

Coser, Lewis. *Masters of Sociological Thought: Ideas in Historical and Social Context.* 1971.

Du Bois, W. E. B. *The Philadelphia Negro.* 1899.

Durkheim, Emile. *The Elementary Forms of Religious Life.* Translated by Karen E. Fields. 1995.

Giddens, Anthony. *Sociology: A Brief but Critical Introduction.* 1987.

Lengermann, Patricia Madoo, and Jill Niebrugge-Brantley. *The Women Founders: Sociology and Sociological Theory, 1830–1930.* 1998.

Lorber, Judith. *Gender Inequality: Feminist Theories and Politics.* 1998.

Reinharz, Shulamit. *Feminist Methods in Social Research.* 1992.

Smith, Dorothy E. *The Conceptual Practices of Power: A Feminist Sociology of Knowledge.* 1990.

———. *The Everyday World as Problematic: A Feminist Sociology.* 1987.

Stacey, Judith, and Barrie Thorne. "The Missing Feminist Revolution in Sociology." *Social Problems* 32 (1985): 301–316.

Wallace, Ruth A. "Feminist Theory in North America: New Insights for the Sociology of Religion." *Social Compass* 43, no. 4 (1996): 467–479.

Wallace, Ruth A., and Alison Wolf. *Contemporary Sociological Theory: Continuing the Classical Tradition.* 1995.

Weber, Max. *The Protestant Ethic and the Spirit of Capitalism.* 1958.

Zeitlin, Irving. *Ideology and the Development of Sociological Theory.* 1968.

See also Sociology of Religion.

CHERYL TOWNSEND GILKES

Sociology of Religion

Sociology of religion emerged in the nineteenth century as a part of a larger attempt by European scholars and theoreticians to offer systematic, "scientific" explanations of social life. To these early scholars, religion was an apt starting point for the examination of human society. Religion, or at least certain forms of it, was thought to be a basic feature of human social life, present even among "primitive" groups. The data of ethnographic research into "primitive," non-European cultures, including especially the religious ideas and practices of these groups, was understood as evidence of the evolutionary character of religion and society. Human beings advance through "primitive" religious beliefs to advanced belief systems or even beyond religion to social and moral systems based on reason alone.

Auguste Comte (1798–1857) considered religious ideas and rituals to be characteristic of the first level of human knowledge. "Theological" knowledge, he argued, is surpassed progressively by metaphysics and finally by scientific knowledge as human reason develops. His science of society, called social physics, set out to describe human societies according to these developmental categories. Similarly, the leading nineteenth-century social Darwinist Herbert Spencer found in religion a handy category for tracing the evolutionary tendencies of human societies from simple to more complex forms. Primitive societies with primitive religious beliefs exhibit homogeneous, incoherent belief systems whereas more developed societies demonstrate more heterogeneous, coherent religious ideas. Religion, Spencer claimed, begins as simple ancestor worship and progresses from beliefs about ghosts to beliefs about demigods and, finally, to the recognition of one supreme God over all the others.

Considering evolutionary approaches to be biased and reductionistic, some later sociologists objected to developmental studies of religion and society. Émile Durkheim, one of the founders of sociology and the author of the highly influential *Elementary Forms of Religious Life* (1912), was an early critic of a purely evolutionary approach. Spencer erred, Durkheim argued, in viewing religion as merely a collection of beliefs conjured up by the imagination, beliefs that can then be traced through particular developmental moments in human history. Durkheim was more interested in the social function of religious ideas and symbols than in the evolutionary trajectory of particular religious ideas. Religion should constitute a central topic of the scientific study of human society since, as he famously stated, God is society. An understanding of the meaning and function of religious symbols, ideas, and rituals within a given human group therefore provides essential information about the way in which that group operates. Durkheim assumed that though particular religious symbols and practices may change, religion is a universal characteristic of human social life which works in similar ways across time and place. Both in its simple, primitive forms and in advanced societies, religion functions to provide order by legitimating the structures of society and integrating individual members of society into a collective ideal.

Durkheim's suggestion that religion serves primarily to support and maintain social groups has had lasting influence. The anthropologist Mary Douglas (1966, 1970), building on Durkheim, explored the social meaning of symbols, especially those related to the body. The sociologists Peter Berger and Talcott Parsons were also interested in religion's ability to maintain cultures and societies. Berger (1967) in particular argued that religion is a type of "symbolic universe" that integrates meaning and imposes order on what is felt by the individual to be a chaotic and unpredictable world.

This emphasis on the supportive function of religion led later scholars to accuse Durkheim and many of his followers, the structural functionalists, of adopting a fundamental interest in stability and the maintenance of the status quo. Structural functionalist sociologists of religion are interested in the function of religion as a support to the structures of social arrangements and social life. Feminist scholars such as Kandal (1988) and Lehmann (1994) have particularly challenged this aspect of functionalism. The status quo that Durkheim seems to want to maintain includes a theory that the proper place for women, whose essential nature is nonsocial, is in the home. Though Durkheim's work on religion avoids explicit mention of women, sexuality, and gender, his earlier sociological analyses assume an essential difference between women and men. For example, in a study of suicide published in 1897, Durkheim argued that women are creatures of instinct. Women therefore function most properly when in the home, supporting the more complex social life of men who have greater capacity for intellectual development. Since suicide is linked to levels of knowledge and the ability to reason, women are less likely than men to commit suicide. Interestingly, religious persons are also less likely to commit suicide but for different reasons. Since religion serves to integrate persons into society, it may also serve to prevent suicide, which results, Durkheim theorized, from a felt lack of integration. Responding to the view that women are particularly pious and the preservers of family morality, Durkheim counters that feminine sentiments (modesty and love) are not religious per se, but indirectly associated with religion. Thus, given a proper education by her husband, a woman may come to a scientific rather than a religiously based morality, a reasoned morality that would continue to uphold her status as a humble nurturer ("Guyau—L'Irreligion de l'avenir étude de sociologie," 1887).

Karl Marx (1818–1883) also concluded that religion tends to stabilize and maintain society and, for this reason, must be overcome. Religion is an illusory comfort that prevents the seeking of real, material happiness while expressing real, material oppressions ("Contribution to the Critique of Hegel's Philosophy of Right," 1884). As in his treatment of religion, Marx called for the abolition of the "bourgeois family," founded as it is on private capital and the status of women as mere instruments of production. The coming emancipation of the proletariat requires both freedom from religion and the emancipation of women from the bourgeois household. In contrast to Durkheim, however, Marx is considered to be a conflict theorist, since he asserted the positive, creative features of conflict within and among societies, especially as manifest in the tensions between economic classes. Marx was interested in making protest, specifically the protest of the proletariat, possible. Since religion as Marx understood it prevents protest, it must be overcome.

Disagreeing with what he considered to be Marx's overly materialist approach to history and society, but sympathetic to Marx in the creative possibilities of conflict, Max Weber (1864–1920) argued that ideas, including religious ideas, can and do have a profound effect on human social systems, particularly economics. Drawing this connection, Weber's *Protestant Ethic and the Spirit of Capitalism* (1904) posited that a Calvinistic conception of predestination combined with a Lutheran emphasis on calling enabled capitalism to succeed in the modern West. Differences in the economic success of Catholics and Protestants in industrialized Europe and America were explained not in terms of historical or political factors but by reference to the character of their religious beliefs. Weber's later work *Economy and Society* (1921–22) included a lengthy section on the influence of religious ideas on economic and political structures. Unhindered, religion develops along an evolutionary path, which leads to an ever broadening rational systematization of the idea of God. Such a process can be traced through the "routinization of charisma." When charismatic religious figures succeed, over time their followers develop systems and institutions that bureaucratize the doctrines and teachings of the original leader. An interest in group maintenance becomes the focus of the group and the original focus on the charismatic leader is lost.

Weber's focus on the relationship between ideas and societies continues to be influential in the study of religion and society. Weber has been criticized, however, for defining religion as a set of internalized values without explaining why particular religious ideas become influential in a given society at a given time. In this light, Robert Wuthnow (1992) called for a reinterpretation of the Weberian approach that would more adequately account for the institutional contexts of ideas while paying close attention to the role of types of discursive practice. Weber has been faulted by feminists such as Millman and Kanter (1975) for his emphasis on rationality. Valuing reason over emotion, Weber associated the influence of women with an intensification of the emotional or "hysterical" aspects of religion, though such aspects are possible without women's participation. Women, together with members of the "disprivileged strata," are particularly attracted to salvation religions, which offer psychic relief for their lack of status. Noting the relative religious equality of women in religions associated with the "disprivileged strata," Weber hypothesized that women are given more active roles in religious groups that stress pacifism. On the other hand, women commonly have less active roles in groups that glorify a "warlike spirit." Women were regarded by Weber as pacific by nature, yet emotional and less capable of reason.

Sociology of religion as a subfield of sociology in general is remarkably silent on issues of women, gender, and sexuality. This is surprising given the interest of the sociologists in "the woman question"—the nature of women's proper or improper social subordination and "role" as daughter, wife, mother and homemaker—when making arguments about the division of labor, economics, evolution, and family life. Feminists have argued that sociology, including the sociology of religion, is primarily a male study of male society (see, for example, Ollenburger and Moore, 1992). Women are a special problem to be considered only as they relate to the functioning of "society" which, it is assumed, is to

be examined in its public, official, visible forms which often do not include women. Yet, as even Weber noted, religion often does involve women in profound and interesting ways.

Some feminist sociologists of religion, such as Millman and Kanter (1975) and Laslett and Thorne (1997), have attempted to correct for the relative silence on women, sexuality, and gender in their field, while criticizing the often extreme bias present in the discussions of women that do exist. Jennifer Lehmann (1994) suggests that Durkheim and Marx can be critically appropriated by feminism to examine the social structures of patriarchy. Other feminist scholars of religion have made contributions to the attempt to reclaim the historical experiences of women within particular religious traditions, sometimes employing the theories and methods of sociology of religion (see, for example, Antoinette Clark Wire, *Corinthian Women Prophets*, 1990; or Susannah Elm, *Virgins of God*, 1994).

Other feminist sociologists have seriously challenged the very character of sociology of religion as it has been defined and practiced. Dorothy Smith (1974), for example, has challenged the viability of the discipline of sociology, arguing that the assumptions, methods, and foundations of the field as it is presently construed are incompatible with feminism. As feminist scholars have attempted to transform a field that historically assumed away the experiences of women and supported structures that excluded them, they have wondered whether abandoning the project altogether might not better serve their interests.

Robert Bellah, a twentieth-century proponent of a reconsidered evolutionary approach to religion, noted that the evolutionary tendency implicit in nineteenth-century philosophy and historiography had a profound influence on the emergence of sociology of religion (*Beyond Belief*, 1970). A central feature of this philosophy was the proposition that the one who knows and who reasons is the one who recedes from the world, recognizing that the world is external to oneself. This all-knowing, rational observer can then objectively recognize the relationships between phenomena. The sociology of religion was founded on the proposition that the "scientist" of religion possesses just this type of "objectivity." For feminists, the very idea of objectivity is a problem. The objective observer of nineteenth-century and, in some cases, even contemporary sociology of religion devalued or discounted the views of women and, it might be added, those people previously defined as primitive, other, or different. In the process, social theory and studies of religion have in many cases re-articulated power relationships to the disadvantage of those observed. Thus, though the work of redefining the terms, of reclaiming society and religion for and by women continues, feminist scholars often come to approach sociology of religion with skepticism.

BIBLIOGRAPHY

Useful collections of early work on the sociology of religion include Norman Birnbaum and Gertrud Lenzer, eds., *Sociology and Religion: A Book of Readings* (1969); W. S. F. Pickering, ed., *Durkheim on Religion* (1975); and Saul K. Padover, ed., *Karl Marx on Religion* (1974).

Influential contributions to the sociology of religion that discuss and build on the early theorists include: Peter Berger, *The Sacred Canopy* (1967); N. J. Demerath III and Phillip E. Hammond, *Religion in Social Context* (1969); Mary Douglas, *Purity and Danger* (1966) and *Natural Symbols* (1970; rev. ed., 1982); Clifford Geertz, "Religion as a Cultural System" and "Thick Description," both reprinted in *The Interpretation of Cultures* (1973); Charles Glock and Philip Hammond, eds., *Beyond the Classics* (1973); Wolfgang Schluchter, *Rationalism, Religion, and Domination* (1989); and Robert Wuthnow, *Rediscovering the Sacred* (1992).

Bryan S. Turner, "Recent Developments in the Theory of the Body," in *The Body: Social Process and Cultural Theory,* edited by M. Featherstone, M. Hepworth, and B. S. Turner (1991); and Talal Asad, "The Construction of Religion as an Anthropological Category," in *Genealogies of Religion* (1993), offer two interesting reappraisals of Mary Douglas and Clifford Geertz respectively.

Feminist critiques of sociology abound. Two early critiques have been collected in Sandra Harding, ed., *Feminism and Methodology* (1987). These are Dorothy E. Smith, "Women's Perspective as a Radical Critique of Sociology" (orig. pub. 1974), and Marcia Millman and Rosabeth Moss Kanter, "Introduction" to *Another Voice: Feminist Perspectives on Social Life and Social Science* (orig. pub. 1975). Other contributions include: Terry R. Kandal, *The Woman Question in Classical Sociological Theory* (1988); Barbara Laslett and Barrie Thorne, eds., *Feminist Sociology: Life Histories of a Movement* (1997); Jennifer Lehmann, *Durkheim and Women* (1994); Jane Ollenburger and Helen Moore, *A Sociology of Women: The Intersection of Patriarchy, Capitalism and Colonialization* (1992); and R. A. Sydie, *Natural Women, Cultured Men: A Feminist Perspective on Sociological Theory* (1987).

See also Authority; Charisma; Leadership; Marxism; Weber, Max.

JENNIFER WRIGHT KNUST

Solitude

Solitude refers to inward or outward seclusion from others which, even if not chosen, is nonetheless embraced. It encompasses being or living alone; cultivating a private place or space; and withdrawing from types of human interaction.

A close reading of history reveals women in nearly every age and culture choosing solitude for purposes ranging from escaping slavery (Linda Brent), persecution (Anne Frank), or imposed marriage and/or childbirth (Christina of Markyate, Laksminkara); to attaining divine union (Julian of Norwich), inward travel (Teresa of Avila), or genderless sanctity under male-dominated religions (Rabi'ah al-'Adawiyyah). Alone, through events such as widowhood (Golda Meir), illness (Mary Baker Eddy), or imprisonment (Nawal el Sa'adawi, Nien Cheng), other women exploited their solitude.

Under patriarchal religions, spiritual quests often require social withdrawal. In many societies valuing such solitude, the negative or ambivalent regard for women and the demands of their subordinate roles as caregivers preclude or limit women's solitude.

Throughout Christian history, some women, usually virgins and widows without dependent children, lived in solitude under church auspices to pursue sanctity, avoid marriage, or live in a family of women. While desert hermits have waned, single missionaries and orders of celibates persist. In Catholicism particularly, women in active or contemplative orders combine commitment to solitude with careers in teaching, nursing, or social work. Examples of solitary Christians include mystic Catherine of Siena, missionary Sophia Hume, foundress Baroness de Hueck, and Benedictine sister Joan Chittister.

Buddhism has a history of wandering groups of ascetic women trained in spiritual solitude. Mendicants flourish in China, Japan, Korea, Vietnam, and Taiwan and are spreading to other countries. Some laywomen are adopting the practice of mindful solitude in their homes. Solitary Buddhist women include Japan's itinerant poet, Lady Nijo; and Tibetan A-Yu Khadro, an accomplished tantric whose life-threatening illness released her from her marriage.

Islam has no Qur'anic tradition of women in solitude. During the eighth to tenth centuries, a few solitary Sufi female saints and mystics lived alone or in convents. First among these is the never-married, celibate mystic Rabi'ah al-'Adawiyya. Others include India's spiritual guide Bibi Jamal Khatun, and North Africa's legendary Lalla Mimunah.

A Carmelite nun lies on a bed in her cell, France, 1904 (Hulton-Deutsch Collection/Corbis).

Hinduism values solitude but denies it to women because of their obligations as daughters, wives, mothers, and sisters in male-dominated, family-centered culture. Although history records several solitary women saints, few women have undergone swami initiations. The solitary lives of mystic Antal, Swami Shivananda Rahda, and Satguru Swami Shri Jnanananda are atypical and do not indicate acceptance of women in solitude.

Judaism has a limited tradition of women in solitude. Inner solitude, recommended by some Cabalists and mystics, is not widely valued. Community and its women's support system is essential for safeguarding spiritual pursuits, such as the Torah. Emphasis on family and procreation make women's quest for solitude nearly impossible.

Solitude, a state most often connected with pious religious quests under patriarchal religious or with the harsh conditions imposed on societal outcasts, is being reclaimed by differing types of feminists for new purposes.

Some feminist women have seized solitude's opportunities either for brief periods or as a permanent lifestyle to confront self-doubt or fear (Charlotte Perkins Gilman); to find respite (Tillie Olsen); to foster women-centered autonomy (Elizabeth Cady Stanton); to appreciate nature (Anne LaBastille, Jane Goodall); to provide an intensive opportunity for artistic creation (Georgia O'Keefe); or to advance women's philosophical perspectives (Mary Daly).

Although critical of those ascetical practices that reject or punish female bodies, or restrict women's self-development—and of misogynist religions that demean women and sabotage their pursuits of sanctity or liberation—spiritual feminists have rediscovered solitude through the process of revaluing women's religious history in the reconstruction of the female engendered wholeness. Whereas Valerie Saiving identified the failure to develop and value a centered female self as women's greatest evil or sin, solitude is being claimed as an essential element in women's recovery and liberation.

Spiritual feminism, then, supports the creative use of solitude for spiritual, psychological, physical, political, and other purposes. Periods of solitude provide women with healing from abuse and from overextension in their roles as daughters, wives, mothers, partners, and workers; occasions for self-discovery, self-development, and self-reliance; opportunities to reflect on the value and meaning of their lives; the centering necessary to reconnect with nature, with undeveloped talents, and with one another; and awareness of their ultimate reality.

BIBLIOGRAPHY

Useful works by or about women choosing solitude include Tsultrim Allione's *Women of Wisdom* (1986), Buddhist; Baroness Catherine de Hueck Doherty's *Poustinia: Christian Spirituality of the East for Western Man* (1974), Eastern Catholic; Julian of Norwich's *Revelations of Divine Love* (1961), Christian; and Margaret Smith's *Rabia the Mystic and Her Fellow Saints in Islam* (1928), Muslim.

Autobiographical accounts of enforced, but exploited, solitude include: Linda Brent's *Incidents in the Life of a Slave Girl* (1861), African American; Nawal El Sa'adawi's *Letters from Prison* (1975), Egyptian; and Nien Cheng's *Life and Death in Shanghai* (1986), Chinese.

Formative for the contemporary discussion of solitude by spiritual feminists are works such as Tillie Olsen's *Silences* (1978); May Sarton's *Journal of a Solitude* (1973); Elizabeth Cady Stanton's "The Solitude of the Self" (1892); and Virginia Woolf's *A Room of One's Own* (1929).

Other useful general works include: *The Center of the Web: Women and Solitude*, edited by Delese Wear (1993); *Today's Woman in World Religions*, edited by Arvind Sharma (1994); and *Unspoken Worlds: Women's Religious Lives in Non-Western Cultures*, edited by Nancy Aver Falk and Rita M. Gross (1980).

See also **Asceticism; Monasticism.**

LORINE M. GETZ

Sophia

Sophia (Greek, "Wisdom") emerges most prominently in the biblical book of Proverbs 1–9 as a personified female figure who is God's friend, lover, daughter, and co-creator of the world. As God's energetic spirit, Sophia is later transmuted into the Christian Holy Spirit, with associations to the Virgin Mary as well. Thus, to a monotheistic, patriarchal tradition Sophia congeals into an archetypal, complex female whose autonomy appears potentially threatening. Echoing back to ancient Near Eastern goddesses, Sophia achieves prominence in Hellenistic Judaism, early Christianity, and Gnosticism. Church fathers reverently invoke her as an abstract philosophical principle, the Jewish allegorist Philo pairs her with the male Logos (Word), while Gnosticism fully develops a number of "fallen Sophia" myths. In Gnostic systems Sophia, the last of the spirits in the preexistent heavenly worlds, passionately and—ironically—ignorantly, seeks the unknowable God. So, as Folly, Sophia falters, sinks, and is finally rescued by merging with a male consort, though in some myths she remains less dependent on a male. When she is depicted as overly emotional, sexual imagery prevails, while at other times serene, asexual sobriety characterizes her. As children of God, Jesus and the Sophia figure may be interchangeable as siblings, rivals, or partners. In the New Testament Gospel of Luke 7:35, Jesus defends his own and John the Baptist's behavior by invoking Wisdom as their mother, "Yet Wisdom is justified by all her children."

The most famous concrete symbol of Sophia is the sixth-century church (later a mosque), the Hagia Sophia, "Holy Wisdom," in Constantinople (Istanbul).

BIBLIOGRAPHY

Two feminist works are revised doctoral dissertations, *Wisdom and the Feminine in the Book of Proverbs* (1985), by Claudia V. Camp, and Deirdre J. Good's *Reconstructing the Tradition of Sophia in Gnostic Literature* (1987).

JORUNN JACOBSEN BUCKLEY

Sorcery

Despite repeated efforts, no substantive universal differentiation of sorcery from witchcraft and magic can be sustained. Most beliefs about sorcery are culture-specific, such as the separation of sorcery and witchcraft among the African Azande, Lobedu, and Nyakyusa. Although some societies, such as the Gusii of southwestern Kenya, the Dobu of the western Pacific, and the Abelam of New Guinea, maintain a gendered distinction between female witches and male sorcerers, in others the practice of sorcery has no specific associations with gender. Native systems of classification, however, vary significantly and often include finer dis-

tinctions between subtypes of activities and practitioners. Nonetheless, some generalizations are possible. In practice, sorcery often involves ritual manipulation of herbs, medicines, and other natural items in order to bring unseen forces to bear upon nature or human life, for what are widely perceived as antisocial purposes. In contrast to many forms of witchcraft, sorcery is typically a learned art, rather than an inherent or inherited ability, and is theoretically available to anyone.

In most instances, a sorcerer's expressed aims will be quite specific. But the broader social dramas of accusations and confessions of sorcery can reveal significant patterns of stress in interpersonal relations, particularly in situations of illness and misfortune. They also serve as a means of clarifying social roles and expectations. Those outside of legitimate power structures, including women in many social systems, are particularly susceptible to being accused of seeking power through sorcery and therefore to being subjected to social stigmatization, political control, legal regulation, and divine opprobrium.

BIBLIOGRAPHY

Douglas, Mary, ed. *Witchcraft Confessions and Accusations.* 1970.
Marwick, Max, ed. *Witchcraft and Sorcery: Selected Readings.* 1970.
Watson, C. W., and Roy Ellen, eds. *Understanding Witchcraft and Sorcery in Southeast Asia.* 1993.

EUGENE V. GALLAGHER

Soul

Some notion of the idea of the soul can be recognized in all religious traditions, cultures, and societies, from prehistoric to modern times. The idea or concept of the soul suggests a fundamental animating principle in men and women, often thought to be the essential self-identity of the individual. But even though the idea of the soul is found universally, the differences in interpretation, expression, belief, and thinking in religious traditions remain vast.

Modern assumptions and habits of thought have done much to obscure the traditional understanding of the idea or belief of the soul. With the rise of post-Cartesian and post-Enlightenment thought, modern Western thought has adopted intellectual attitudes that regard the soul as immaterial and disembodied; the mind and mental activity has increasingly become identified as the essential human quality, while the body has become increasingly devalued as a mere extension of the mind, as a mechanism or tool of the thinking self. Thus, the traditional understanding of an organic and dynamic soul as an embodied form, relating and mediating worlds of different energies and materialities, has been lost. But as Caroline Walker Bynum (1991) points out, many modern philosophical discussions are returning to the idea that it is almost impossible to envision a soul or personal survival without some kind of material continuity. Attitudes of antimaterialism with regard to the soul are reflected in numerous examples from modern thought, not the least of which is the recasting of Freud's thought in the English translations of his work. As demonstrated by Bettelheim (1983), many of Freud's central concepts and his essential concerns for the soul of humanity were obscured by rendering terms such as *psyche* and *Seelenleben* as "mind" and "mental life," thus rendering the project of psychoanalysis a mental exercise and denying the dynamic and energetic world of the soul with its mostly unconscious actions, forces, and drives that Freud sought to investigate and call our attention to.

In Greek thought the idea of the psyche emerged in the Homeric period but was refined and altered in Socratic thought where we find the psyche composed of three parts and functions: the intellectual, the passionate, and the appetitive (see Plato's *Republic*, 434d–441c). Mental activity was thus only one aspect of a triadic structure. Furthermore, according to Socrates, the work or activity of the philosopher was the "practice of death," which suggests the repeated attempt in this life to separate the soul (psyche) from the body; thus we are told that the philosopher must "habituate it [the soul] to assemble and gather itself together from every region of the body" (*Phaedo* 67c), resisting the dispersion of the psyche in the multitudinous pulls, impulses, and desires that arise in the body and from life.

The Platonic view of the soul was altered slightly but largely embraced by early Christianity, particularly by the Greek Christian Fathers. In the New Testament, Paul and John (e.g. John 3:5–8) indicate the antinomy of flesh (*sarx*) and spirit (*pneuma*), but both principles are contained within the sphere of embodiment that seems to suggest a neutral form, often translated as body (*soma*). Paul makes explicit the view (Phil. 3:21) that via the power of Christ's resurrection, each man and woman of the Christian way has the possibility of rising with Christ in a body that will be like Christ's "glorious" body (*tô sômati tês doxês autou*): for early Christianity the soul was clearly an embodied phenomena. The triadic structure of human nature and the soul was discussed in various religious forms, but most often in the triad of spirit, soul, and body, referring not only to different functions of the human organism but also to different materialities.

But in all early traditions the materiality of the soul was indisputable. Semitic concepts in Judaism and Islam express the idea that the *ruah* (breath, spirit, *spiritus*, *pneuma*) was breathed into the soul (*nafs*) which was then further embodied in a human form. Nevertheless, from the traditional point of view, knowledge of the distinction between spirit and soul is essential but precarious. Needleman (1980) suggests that the soul is the intermediate principle in human nature *par excellence*, between the spirit and the body, but he also maintains that ideas regarding these distinctions and knowledge of the gradations of being of men and women are historically difficult to maintain and are distorted or disappear altogether from teachings and traditions. In Western philosophy, the last great proponents of the idea of the soul as an intermediate principle can be found in Neoplatonists of the fourth century. For Neoplatonists, the dynamics of the purified soul reflected the "rhythmic weaving" of the cosmos, maintaining that the soul's function was to unify the energies of the gods and thereby assist in the preservation of the cosmos.

Qustâ ibn Lûqâ, a Syrian Christian of the ninth century, wrote the earliest treatise on the soul that reflects the transmission of this idea to the mystic-physicians and Islamic philosophers of the Middle Ages. We are told that the spirit spreads through the heart, forming a subtle body (the soul proper), which controls the functions of the organic body. The idea of the soul as a form of subtle embodiment that is in some sense intermediate and mediating spirit and matter, consciousness and substance, makes Eastern notions of the soul more accessible. Thus, Buddhism maintains doctrines that no-self or no-soul (*anātman*) ultimately exists, but we find numerous ideas and discussions in Buddhism of subtle bodies that have unique powers and functions; these subtle bodies are in large part the result of yogic practices and reflect or measure the transformation of the individual. Furthermore, early Buddhist texts suggest that "bodies made from attention" and developed in yogic practice are related to the process of rebirth in some extraordinary way, suggesting some element of freedom that is otherwise absent.

Vedic ideas of the soul in pre-Buddhist India provide further evidence of the idea of the soul as an embodied form. Hymns in the *Ṛig veda* suggest that it is possible to be joined with a glorious body (*tanû*) after death (*RV.* 10.14) and that exemplary yogins develop a refined body within themselves that is capable of gathering the "power-to-do" (*kratum*) that issues from the gods (*RV.*

10.56). *Ātman,* the well-known Sanskrit term normally translated as "self," must frequently be translated as "body," especially in pre-Upanishadic literature. Thus, in the *Satapathabrāhmaṇa* the recurring term *daivāt-man* ought to be rendered "divine body," suggesting the production or elaboration of a subtle body "built up" from ritual action and sacred work (karma).

The aspect of the feminine enters into discussions of the soul in numerous ways. Annemarie Schimmel (1975) points out that the *nafs,* or lower soul in Islam, is compared to a woman who uses her charms to ensnare the spirit and to lure him down into worldly life. In Kabbalistic writings of medieval Judaism the feminine Shekhinah is personification of God's indwelling, "the unspecified presence of the Divine in the world" (Scholem, 1991). Ultimately, the Shekinah must be redeemed in the soul and reunited with God in a version of "sacred marriage" (*hieros gamos*). The dynamics of the soul, the play of energies and functions, is often paralleled in cosmic dramas, as in the symbiosis of Wisdom (Sophia) and God in Judaism and Gnostic Christianity, or the union of Siva and Shakti in Hindu tantra. One of the best known representations of feminine symbolism in the dynamics of the soul is the portrayal of the soul as the bride who is united with the bridegroom, Christ, who is sent by God (see Wehr, 1990). The drama of the separation and union of these energies and beings can be seen as macrocosmic myths whose meaning can be rediscovered in the play of consciousness, energies, and materiality that takes place in the individual soul of the contemplative adept.

BIBLIOGRAPHY

Bettelheim, Bruno. *Freud and Man's Soul.* 1983.

Bynum, Caroline Walker. *Fragmentation and Redemption: Essays on Gender and the Human Body in Medieval Religion.* 1991.

Collins, Steven. *Selfless Persons: Imagery and Thought in Theravâda Buddhism.* 1982.

Needleman, Jacob. *Lost Christianity.* 1980.

Schimmel, Annemarie. *Mystical Dimensions of Islam.* 1975.

Shaw, Gregory. *Theurgy and the Soul: The Neoplatonism of Iamblichus.* 1995.

Scholem, Gershom. *On the Mystical Shape of the Godhead: Basic Concepts in the Kabbalah.* 1991.

Smithers, Stuart. "Lost Buddhism." *Material for Thought* 14 (1995).

Wehr, Gerhard. *The Mystical Marriage: Symbol and Meaning of the Human Experience.* Translated by Jill Sutcliffe. 1990.

STUART SMITHERS

South American Religions

In the Andes

When the Incas consolidated their power over South America's Andean spine stretching from southern Colombia to northwest Argentina, they attempted to impose an imperial religion on conquered populations. This religion held the goddesses and gods of Cusco, the empire's capital, to be supreme. Nevertheless, Inca religious beliefs and practices resonated with those of the other Andean polities they dominated. This resonance was, in part, tied to a common understanding of gendered principles structuring human, natural, and supernatural worlds. These principles were reflected in dialectical perceptions of female and male sacred powers. They also shaped a significant pattern organizing Andean religious life. While women and men adored the sacred divinities of Andean cosmologies regardless of divine gender, nevertheless women held responsibility for the worship of goddesses and men bore similar obligations for gods.

Many Andeans, regardless of their ethnic and political affiliations, envisioned the natural and supernatural universe to be inhabited by sacred beings, female and male. Goddesses and gods were often paired as complementary forces dominating overlapping supernatural and natural spheres. In contrast to the goddesses of the earth, mountain gods or thunder-lightning (Illapa or Santiago) commanded the skies or "the upper world." Illapa was worshiped throughout the Andes as a provider of beneficial rains and of devastating hailstorms. Illapa was also known as an embodiment of political power, called a god of conquest, and symbolically framed social hierarchies ranking political relations between, and within, Andean polities.

The earth mother, Pachamama, was the premier female deity in local Andean religious pantheons. She was said to govern the earth's fertility, and, in the Andes, where much of life's sustenance was based on agricultural production, her powers were revered by all. While the Pachamama commanded the fecundity of nature, her "daughters" embodied specific products of human labor vital to Andean life. Goddesses like the Saramama (corn mother), Axamama (potato mother), and Cocamama (coca mother), worshiped as the Pachamama's offspring, were pivotal deities in Andean cosmology. Other female divinities of great importance in local religion included Cochamama (mother of all waters) and Moon mother, or Mamaquilla.

Although the Incas conceived the moon to be the leading goddess of imperial religion, she also exerted

A trio of highlanders conduct a Pachamama (Mother Earth) offering at Huilloc, Peru, 1994 (Jeremy Horner/Corbis).

powerful influences over non-Inca Andean peoples. According to local lore, the moon was intimately tied to the success of women's principal endeavors, whether as weavers or as child-bearers. It was said that during lunar eclipses, spinning staffs, the premier symbol of women's labor, would turn into vipers; similarly, women giving birth prayed especially to the moon to bring about a successful result.

Conceptualizations of gender parallelism structured much of local Andean religious thought. Gender parallelism incorporated the principal of gender complementarity as evidenced in local cosmologies; it also shaped the bond between women and female deities and directed the organization of ritual life. Although adored by men and women, women invoked the Pachamama during the most critical periods of the agricultural cycle: when seeds were placed in the earth and when the harvest was reaped. Her "daughters," the mothers of potatoes and corn, were similarly venerated by their gender counterparts as female officiants led celebrations. Chronicler accounts and judicial records suggest that parallel women's and men's organizations were at the heart of ritual life in many Andean communities. It is even possible that some organizations incorporated women from several ethnic polities. In the north-central Andes of Peru, groups of women from various villages came together at a central plaza to worship the moon.

Inca religious organization was built, in part, on the gender parallelism present in local communities. The Incas allowed conquered groups to maintain their traditional religious practices as long as Cusco's divinities were recognized as premier. While the sun, who represented the conquering empire, stood as the dominant male god of the Andes, the moon, as the leading female deity, was called the sacred mother of all women. Inca theology envisioned the sun and the moon as the ancestors of a line of divinities split by gender. The sun, for example, was called the father of Venus of the Morning, grandfather of Pachacamac (lord of the world), and great-grandfather of mortal man. The female gender line of sacred forces, in like fashion, extended from the moon, to Venus of the Afternoon, to Cochamama, the mother of all waters, and finally, to mortal woman.

Inca imperial beliefs also embodied a political ideology that legitimated the power hierarchies of Inca rule. Inca and Coya enjoyed a privileged relationship with the gendered progenitors of humanity. The Inca was called the son of the solar god; the queen, or Coya, was considered the daughter of the moon. Since Andean lore placed the provincial headmen or chiefs as the direct descendants of Venus, it made them the structural equivalents of the Incas' children. As the children of the Incas, local chiefs (*curacas*)—women and men—assumed a position of structural inferiority to the rulers of Cusco. Similarly, peasant men and women were conceptualized as the children of local chiefs. Inca cosmology thus sanctioned a hierarchy of rule, patterned on gender parallelism, that stretched from Cusco's gods—the sun and the moon—to the Incas, to local chiefs, and finally, to commoners.

The moon, as preeminent imperial goddess, oversaw the activities of all female divinities and all female mortals. She was at the same time the mother of all women (in a general sense) and the progenitrix of the Andean queen. The moon's powers were manifest in religious practices. After conquering Andean populations and territory, the Incas imposed a division of local lands to support imperial government and religious organization. Within the domain of "lands of the Sun," designated to underwrite imperial religion, were specific tracts set aside for the worship of the moon.

As the commanding female deity in the imperial pantheon, the moon took on some of the powers that Andeans had traditionally bestowed to local female deities. Village divinities, like the Pachamama and moon, had been revered for their abilities to facilitate birth and propagation. Now the Inca moon assumed these functions. In similar imperial fashion, the Incas declared that one of the founding members of their dynasty was responsible for maize cultivation. According to Inca accounts, Mama Huaco, who, along with her siblings, first settled the valley of Cusco, introduced maize seeds and the necessary techniques for its cultivation to the Andes. Mama Huaco's powers superseded those customarily associated with both the Pachamama and her daughter, the Saramama.

The chronicler narratives about Inca religion depict ritual practices that followed norms of gender parallelism. Women, it seems, were responsible for and directed the worship of the empire's goddesses. For example, descriptions of the imperial festivals to the moon talk of groups of women carrying the moon's image on their shoulders. Women had similar roles in lunar celebrations in Cusco as well as in the "Island of the Moon," located in Lake Titicaca. Significantly, the queen was said to pray and consult the moon, the mother of all women, in the principal lunar shrine in Cusco. There the queen was accompanied by "priestesses" who officiated in ways that paralleled how the Inca king, attended by priests, would worship the sun.

The queen and noblewomen probably enjoyed the independent access to lands and its produce necessary to underwrite a women's religious structure devoted to imperial goddesses. In the precise descriptions of Inca land-tenure systems found in census reports and cadastres, we find listings of royal areas designated to support the queen, noblewomen, and imperial goddesses like the moon and Mama Huaco. Inca political and religious organization was, in part, built around the ability of the privileged to make use of the produce of royal lands and herds to underwrite celebrations and support strategic alliances. Since female gods and mortals could make these claims, they would have been materially able to sustain their own political and religious networks. Actual accounts of these organizations, compared to men's, are scarce: Spanish chroniclers tended to see only men as the legitimate holders of public office and therefore to rely on their accounts to describe imperial secular and religious governance. Also, Inca men were relatively ignorant of women's doings. As a priest noted in a report to his bishop, "even the Incas know little about Mama Huaco and other matters related to women, since that was women's business."

These descriptions of gender parallelism and its role in Inca religion should not be taken as evidence of equality or even parity. We do not know and cannot estimate the relative size or scope of women's religious activities in relation to men's. Moreover, an assessment of gendered attributes of Inca cosmology as well as of women's participation in Andean religious and political life must also bear in mind notable differences. Conquest was still the overriding domain of men and of male gods. Men had positions of authority in imperial armies and administration that women of equivalent social standing could not attain. These differences were also expressed in terms of marriage: men, usually as a reward granted by the Inca, could have more than one spouse. No woman, not even the queen, enjoyed similar privileges. An institution of chosen women, the *aclla*, embodied the fusion of Inca conquest and the ability of Inca men to engage in secondary marriages. Known as "wives of the Inca" or "wives of the sun," they, too, had significant roles in imperial religion. The *aclla*, however, exemplified how conquest of Andean peoples and control over conquered women were also integral to imperial religious and political life.

BIBLIOGRAPHY

The published ethnohistorical material used to reconstruct the Inca past includes chronicles (narrative histories of Inca society), administrative documents, judicial records (both ecclesiastical and secular), and guides to colonization and evangelization. Students of Inca society recognize that this material must be critically evaluated when used to write pre-Columbian Andean history. Precautions are doubly warranted when one tries to reconstruct the role of women in the Andean world, since the andromyopia of the Spanish often blinded them to the profoundly different structures that governed Andean gender relations. Moreover, in spite of the fact that we find significant references to women, much of the secondary literature on the Inca empire does not seriously incorporate women's participation in the Andean world.

Secondary sources that analyze gender and women as critical to understanding Inca history and culture include:

Classen, Constance. *Inca Cosmology and the Human Body.* 1993.

Patterson, Thomas. *The Inca Empire.* 1991.

Rostworowski de Diez Canseco, Maria. *Estructuras Andinas del Poder.* Lima, 1983.

Silverblatt, Irene. *Moon, Sun, and Witches: Gender Ideologies and Class in Inca and Colonial Peru.* 1987.

OTHER IMPORTANT AND INFORMATIVE SECONDARY SOURCES

Duviols, Pierre. *La lutte contre les religions autochtones dans le Pérou colonial: L'extirpation de l'idôlatrie entre 1532 et 1660.* Lima and Paris, 1971.

Murra, John Victor. *The Economic Organization of the Inca State.* 1980.

Zuidema, R. Tom. *Inca Civilization in Cuzco.* 1990.

PRIMARY SOURCES THAT OFFER INSIGHT INTO GENDER AND WOMEN

de Arriaga, Father Pablo Jose. *The Extirpation of Idolatry in Peru* [1621]. Translated by L. Clark Keating. 1968.

de Betanzos, Juan. *Narrative of the Incas.* Translated and edited by Roland Hamilton and Dana Buchanan. 1996.

Cobo, Bernabe. *History of the Inca Empire* [1653]. Translated by Roland Hamilton. 1979.

Duviols, Pierre. *Cultura andina y represion: Procesos y visitas de idolatrias y hechicerias. Cajatambo. Siglo XVII.* Cusco, 1986.

Felipe Guaman Poma de Ayala, El Primer nueva cronica y buen gobierno [1631?]. Edited by John Victor Murra and Rolena Adorno. Mexico, 1980.

The *Huarochiri Manuscript.* Translated by Frank Salomon and George L. Urioste; annotations and introductory essay by Frank Salomon. 1991.

de Molina, Cristobal. *Relacion de las fabulas y ritos de los Incas* [1573]. Lima, 1943.

de Murua, Martin. *Historia del origen y geneologia real de los Incas* [1590]. Madrid, 1946.

IRENE SILVERBLATT

In the Lowlands

A great diversity of native peoples, each with a distinct religious tradition, inhabit the vast lowland regions of South America, which include the tropical forests and savannahs drained by the Amazon River and its tributaries, the Orinoco River system to the north, and the plains that extend from southern Brazil and Paraguay to the continent's southern tip at Tierra del Fuego. Hundreds of different ethnic groups and about two hundred native languages survive today in communities that differ in their environmental situations, social organization, and past and present relations to non-Indians and national societies. Before the spread of Western-style education, the lowland societies had no writing systems, so that spiritual beliefs and practices have been based not on texts but on oral traditions, thereby reinforcing religious diversity.

Most of what outsiders know about native religious life comes from anthropological field studies. This literature is weighted toward masculine perspectives since until recently most ethnographers were males, and many got their information mostly from native men. Although the number of women studying native cultures has grown, few scholars of either sex have made gender their main research focus. Consequently, there is a great deal we do not know about the religious lives of native women, and many issues remain to be explored.

Female deities, culture heroes, and mythological beings appear in many groups' cosmologies, although, like their male counterparts, such figures are not worshiped. Female creators are common in origin myths. Speakers of Tupian and Carib languages attribute the origin of the universe or human beings to a primordial female who gave birth to twin brothers who became the sun and moon. Many groups trace the origins of key cultural elements such as fire, festivals, fermented beverages, body ornaments, and subsistence foods and technologies to a primordial pregnant or menstruating woman or female culture hero. Especially in the Northwest Amazon, the Guianas, and among Tupian speakers, there is a widespread concept of "owners" of wild animals who punish those who engage in wanton killing of their species. Some of these owners are female. Robert Murphy's *Mundurucu Religions* (1958) describes annual ceremonies in which the Mundurucu of central Brazil propitiated the supreme "mother of game" and secondary "mothers" of individual animal species, as well as "mothers" of maize and manioc.

Gardening, typically the domain of women, is the basis of subsistence in almost all these lowland societies. Female supernatural beings often are linked to plant fertility, especially primary food crops such as manioc and maize. East of the Andes in Ecuador and Peru, the Canelos Quichua and Jivaroan peoples revere an earth spirit named Nunghui. Michael Brown's *Tsewa's Gift* (1986) and Philippe Descolas's *In the Society of Nature* (1994) describe how, while planting and tending her garden, a Jivaro woman sings to Nunghui to attract her to the garden. At major life transitions such as puberty and marriage, Jivaro women drink hallucinogenic brews and tobacco juice to seek visions of Nunghi that bring enhanced spiritual knowledge and effectiveness in one's actions. The growth of crops is explicitly linked to human women's sexuality. When women gather to plant manioc shoots for a tobacco feast for an honored woman, the gardener takes the first manioc cutting (painted red), places it against her vagina, and sits on a manioc tuber. After the fields are planted, women dance for five nights to attract Nunghui. Norman Whitten's *Sacha Runa* (1976) explains that Nunghui is also the spirit of pottery making who sends dreams from which Canelos Quichua women obtain designs for pots and songs that keep pots from breaking when fired.

Shamans are the primary religious specialists in lowland South America. Typically only men become shamans, but women do so in a few societies, including the Jivaro, Siona of eastern Colombia, Kamaiura of central Brazil, and Warao of Venezuela's Orinoco delta. Louis Faron's *Hawks of the Sun* (1964) describes the unique all-female shamanism of the Mapuche of Chile. In the past shamans were bisexual or transvestite men, but women displaced them. Mapuche shamans beat a flat skin drum to enter ecstatic trances and communicate with the spirits in order to heal illness; they develop their powers through a lengthy period of seclusion and training. In "The Body of the Guajiro Shaman" (in *Portals of Power: Shamanism in South America*, edited by Jean Langdon and Gerhard Baer [1992]), Michel Perrin reports that among the Guajiro of Venezuela, 80 percent of shamans are women. Guajiro shamanism is closely linked to images of female sexuality, pregnancy, and birth. In her initiation the novice drinks tobacco juice (symbolically associated with fertilization) and experiences a transformation that shamans compare to the bodily experience of childbirth as her power grows and "ripens" in her belly.

So pervasive are spiritual concerns in nearly every aspect of the lives of native South Americans that it is impossible to treat religion as a separate topic or domain of experience. Daily activities—such as producing and preparing food, making pottery, weaving, bearing and raising children—are widely seen as expressions of cosmic forces. The close connection between human experience and phenomena such as weather and the fertility of crops and wild plants and animals is a fundamental principle in native religious thought. Ideas about female physiology and women's moral behavior are central to this connection, as Lawrence Sullivan emphasizes in *Icanchu's Drum* (1988). Many peoples view menstruation as the quintessential sign of how human existence embodies cosmic periodicity. In *The Origin of Table Manners* (1978), the social anthropologist Claude Lévi-Strauss (whose theories of symbolic structures have had an enduring influence on interpretations of South American religions) highlights the salience of native beliefs that morality and culture are based on the control of periodicity (proper action at the proper time) and that various periodic "codes" in South American myths are linked to menstrual cycles, especially menarche.

Much ritual life revolves around efforts to regulate and attune human and cosmic rhythms, to enhance the reproduction and regeneration of persons and groups, seasons, plants, and animals. Often this is enacted through the symbolic control and disciplining of the human body. Some societies have elaborate ceremonies of female initiation or ritual seclusion at puberty or menarche that aim to identify a young woman with sacred powers and enhance her physical and moral development. Menstruation and childbirth also are symbolic templates for some men's initiation rites and the ritual seclusion of warriors after killing an enemy. In a number of societies, men say that they menstruate, or equate to menstruation bleeding from piercing their ears or cutting their skin, or control or enhance their blood with practices of seclusion, fasting, and sexual abstinence that parallel the practices of menstruating or pregnant women.

In some societies women and children of both sexes are barred from witnessing certain aspects of men's rituals—especially in the exclusively male ritual cults of the Mundurucu and Mehinaku of central Brazil, Tukanoans of northwestern Amazonia, and the now extinct Selk'nam (Yahgan) of Tierra del Fuego. These men's cults are associated with a set of common elements: myths of a primordial matriarchy in which women ruled

A rock surface is covered with ancient paintings c. 2800 B.C.E. in the Shelter of Rezar, Januaria, Gerais, Brazil (Pierre Colombel/Corbis).

until overthrown by men; a men's clubhouse that is off-limits to women; and sacred flutes (and in some cases, bullroarers and masks) that cannot be seen by women, with violations punished by death, gang rape, or beatings. These exclusive men's rituals have received various interpretations. Joan Baumberger's "The Myth of Matriarchy: Why Men Rule in Primitive Societies" (in Michele Rosaldo and Louise Lamphere's *Woman, Culture, and Society* [1981]) examines how these myths contribute to male dominance. Robert Murphy's *Mundurucu Religions* (1958) and Thomas Gregor's *Anxious Pleasures* (1985) examine how the rituals express insecurities in masculine identities and reinforce sexual antagonism and male dominance. In *Women of the Forest* (1974), Yolanda Murphy and Robert Murphy revise this interpretation with greater attention to the perspectives of Mundurucu women, who do not completely identify with or feel constrained by the assertions of male superiority encoded in myths and men's rituals. These authors emphasize that women's separate experiences almost amount to two separate female and male cultures within Mundurucu society. This question of the distinct religious experiences and spirituality of women remains to be explored more broadly in indigenous South American societies.

BIBLIOGRAPHY

Lawrence Sullivan's *Icanchu's Drum: An Orientation to Meaning in South American Religions* (1988) offers an invaluable overview, with provocative insights into themes related to women and native religions. Peter Roe's *The Cosmic Zygote: Cosmology in the Amazon Basin* (1982) proposes a complex, quirky model of how the dualistic symbolic oppositions that pervade indigenous myths and cosmologies are rooted in the sexual division of labor and tensions between male–female competition and cooperation. *Pre-Columbian Religions,* by Walter Krickeberg, Hermann Trimborn, Werner Muller, and Otto Zerries (1968), describes numerous female deities and mythological figures. The best sources on menstrual imagery in rituals and myths are Bruce Albert's "Temps du Sang, Temps de Cendre" (Ph.D. diss., University of Paris X, 1985), on the Yano-mami, and Stephen Hugh-Jones's *The Palm and the Pleiades* (1979), a study of Barasana (Tukanoan) boys' initiation rites. Christine Hugh-Jones's *From the Milk River* (1979) is an excellent analysis of related Barasana cultural ideas about the body and human life-cycle reflecting more female perspectives. Anne Chapman's *Drama and Power in a Hunting Society* (1982) presents a nuanced view of how Selk'nam women both resisted and were constrained by the ideology of male superiority projected in the men's cult rituals.

BETH A. CONKLIN

Southeast Asian Religions

Southeast Asia is geographically, politically, linguistically, and culturally diverse, with all the world religions and thousands of indigenous traditions represented within its mainland and island borders. Southeast Asia includes the countries of Myanmar (Burma), Thailand, Laos, Cambodia, Vietnam, Brunei, Malaysia, Singapore, Indonesia, and the Philippines. The world religions entered Southeast Asia with traders, missionaries, and colonizers; wherever they entered, they were transformed by the Southeast Asian societies they encountered.

Southeast Asia as a region is a postcolonial construction. The term came into use in World War II to define Lord Mountbatten's theater of operations in Burma and Malaysia. Its boundaries were further solidified by American foreign policy (e.g., SEATO, Southeast Asia Treaty Organization) in the fifties, the development of ASEAN (Association of Southeast Asian Nations) in the sixties, and by Asia Pacific trading relationships in the nineties.

Among the nations of Southeast Asia, Thailand was the only country to remain free of colonial rule. Coincidentally, it is over 90 percent Theravada Buddhist and has experienced the least missionizing from other religions, although the populations of the four southern provinces are overwhelmingly Muslim. Myanmar, Laos, and Cambodia are predominantly Theravada Buddhist, but under British and French colonization some minority groups were converted to Christianity. Malaysia, Brunei, and Indonesia are Islamic states, with British and Dutch colonial histories. Vietnam has a more heterogeneous religious history, with Confucianism, Tao-ism, and Mahayana Buddhism coexisting with substantial conversions to Catholicism before and during French rule. The Philippines emerged from Spanish and U.S. control as the most Christian country in Southeast Asia, with over 90 percent of the country professing Christianity.

Southeast Asia has been characterized as an area of gender complementarity, which stresses the high status of women, particularly in comparison with the position of women in South and East Asia. Yet there are many contexts in which women are subordinated, oppressed, and exploited. Patriarchal religious traditions and hierarchies, particularly when combined with patrilineal, patrilocal kinship systems, served as means to control women. However, when these traditions encountered strong bilateral and even matrilineal forms of social organization, male bias in the world religions was less pronounced. Throughout Southeast Asia women are active participants in the rituals of their households and communities. But it is impossible to generalize across the incredible diversity of religious traditions in the region. A balanced and deeper understanding of women and religion requires consideration of the historical specificity and cultural context of each tradition, a task beyond the scope of this essay.

Before the entry of the world religions into Southeast Asia, guardian spirits and locality spirits figured prominently in animist practices. Nature was imbued with power and humans were to live in harmony with it. The interdependence between women and nature can be seen today in everyday practices by which women nurture the land and children. Certain household rituals, such as burying the placenta, make the land more valuable and strengthen the unity of the community. Feasting, animal sacrifice, and, in the past, headhunting were all part of the complexes of power and prestige dominated by men. Women were often incorporated in these complexes through marriage alliances. Yet women, as participants in the indigenous religious traditions of the past and present, may possess great knowledge of the spirit world, including how to summon the souls of the ancestors to cure sicknesses.

In both mainland and island Southeast Asia, the upland minority peoples of Myanmar, Thailand, Laos, and Vietnam were more likely to resist the dominant tradition of the colonizers and the lowland majorities. Animist practices reflecting the importance of spirits of localities and life forms exist independently of or in combination with world religions, often Christianity or Buddhism. For example, the Cordillera region of northern Luzon, the most mountainous region in the Philippines, is home to about a million indigenous peoples with distinct cultural traditions. Kalingas and Ifugaos have priestesses, but the majority of practitioners are men. Ancestors remain responsible for the well-being of their lineages and are cared for by male or female elders, depending on each group's kinship pattern. Women often officiate as mediums at their own rites.

Gender ambiguity and reversals dominate the ritual traditions in many parts of Southeast Asia, as evidenced by the popularity of masking and shadow plays. In fact, religious practice as performance or spectacle is characteristic of Southeast Asia.

THERAVADA BUDDHISM

Theravada Buddhism, the predominant branch of Buddhism in Southeast Asia, spread throughout the mainland between the ninth and thirteenth centuries C.E. Hinduism and Buddhism entered together, intertwined with each other in myth and ritual, and strengthened cults of royalty in both island and mainland Indianized kingdoms. Buddhism provides guidelines for moral behavior through the five precepts for the laity—refrain from taking life, stealing, illicit sexual activity, speaking falsely, and consuming inebriating substances. In text and practice, women are regarded as lower in religious status than men. However, women in rural and urban communities are the primary supporters of religious institutions by providing food and money to temples and by having their sons ordained as monks or novices for varying periods of time. Most men become monks or novices for some period of time during their life, and parents and wives obtain the merit from their ordination. The ordination tradition is denied to women, leaving them with less valued religious roles as "nuns," who are essentially pious laywomen.

In addition to monks, mainland Southeast Asian Buddhist communities may have brahmans (men), who carry out life-cycle rituals; healers who are concerned with spirit affliction (men and women); and spirit mediums (men and women). Women mediums may be possessed by male spirits, often of powerful princes. Matrilineal ancestor cults in Burma and Thailand coexist with Buddhist practice and in fact draw ancestors and spirits into the service of Buddhism.

ISLAM

The entry of Islam into Malaysia and the islands of Indonesia began with thirteenth-century traders who demanded conversion to Islam as the price of doing business. Yet the progress of Islam in Southeast Asia was largely peaceful and rapid. (The ease of conversion is also true of Buddhism in Southeast Asia.)

Although the five pillars of Muslim faith remain at the core of religious life, Southeast Asian Muslims emphasize rituals more than strict regulations characteristic of other Islamic states. Muslim practice in Southeast Asia is often syncretic with the Hindu-Buddhist and animist ritual heritage specific to each locality. Nevertheless, governments of Malaysia, Brunei, and Indonesia could be said to have Islamic outlooks on morality and gender.

Historically, Southeast Asia Muslim women have never been secluded or veiled and have been free to work in the public domain, often as market traders. Traditional Malay and Indonesian dress is modest, with women not required to wear full veils but only head scarves. Nevertheless, Islam stresses women's primary roles as wives and mothers and segregation of the sexes. Polygyny is permitted and Islamic law governs divorce. Islamic revival movements are growing in some parts of Southeast Asia, but commitment to fundamentalism is moderated by Southeast Asian gender complementarity and tolerance for religious plurality.

CHRISTIANITY

Christianity is the most rapidly growing religion in Southeast Asia, particularly in Singapore. Many evangelical Christian groups have established congregations in the urban centers throughout Southeast Asia. Minority peoples in mainland Southeast Asia were exposed to missionizing and often converted to Christianity to distinguish themselves from Buddhist lowland majorities.

The Philippines under Spanish control from the sixteenth to the end of the nineteenth century underwent massive conversion to Catholicism. Many upland groups such as the Ifugao of the mountain provinces of the Philippines combine ancestor cults with Catholicism. Other groups were missionized since 1900 but resisted conversion. Efforts were made to Christianize indigenous practices rather than eliminate them. But female religious practitioners and men who dressed as women were banished by Spanish colonizers, who accused them of devil worship.

WOMEN'S ROLE

Although women across the region may be excluded from the most valued religious roles, they are by no means excluded from religious practice and can reach the salvational goals of their respective religions in spite of the androcentric biases of religious institutions. Where they are denied access to esoteric textual knowledge, their knowledge of core teachings and practices may be expressed through artistic performance or, in the case of Theravada Buddhism, through food offerings. Women's roles as fortune tellers, mediums, and healers are integral parts of their religious lives. Women have also emerged in Theravada countries as meditation teachers, bypassing the religious hierarchy of the male monkhood.

The scholarly study of women in these religious traditions is not far advanced, owing in part to the biases of colonial scholarship and the paucity of textual materials on women. Perhaps because religion is closely connected with nationalism and politics, gender analysis has not been prominent.

Nevertheless, women have been active in organizing and advocating for change, both for themselves and for peace and justice for the general population. The radical Christian nuns in the Philippines, for example, have been instrumental in bringing attention to problems of child labor and prostitution. Buddhist women are advocating for the reestablishment of the ordination tradition for women. Newsletters such as NIBWA (*Newsletter on International Buddhist Women's Activities*) and *In God's Image* put Southeast Asia women in contact with each other and with fellow believers in other parts of the world.

BIBLIOGRAPHY

Cabezón, José Ignacio. *Buddhism, Sexuality and Gender.* 1992.

Chatsumarn, Kabilsingh. *Thai Women in Buddhism.* 1991.

Geertz, Clifford. *The Religion of Java.* 1960.

Gross, Rita. *Buddhism after Patriarchy.* 1993.

Mulder, Niels. *Inside Southeast Asia: Thai, Javanese and Filipino Interpretations of Everyday Life.* 1992.

Ong, Aihwa. "State Versus Islam: Malay Families, Women's Bodies, and the Body Politic in Malaysia." *American Ethnologist* 17, no. 2 (1990): 259–275.

Ong, Aihwa, and Michael G. Peletz, eds. *Bewitching Women, Pious Men: Gender and Body Politics in Southeast Asia.* 1995.

Parker, A., M. Russo, D. Sommer, and P. Yaeger, eds. *Nationalisms and Sexualities.* 1992.

Russell, Susan, ed. *Ritual, Power and Economy: Upland-Lowland Contrasts in Mainland Southeast Asia.* 1989.

Van Esterik, Penny. *Women of Southeast Asia.* 2d ed. 1996.

PENNY VAN ESTERIK

Space, Sacred

Three fundamental features of religion are sacred word, sacred act, and sacred space. Creation myths tell how a relatively featureless space became the world as we know it. They mark off sacred space from ordinary space at places where power manifests itself (van der Leeuw). A sacred place is the "intersection" of divine and earthly realms that together make up the world (Eliade). A sacred place serves as a "focusing lens" for communication between humans and the divine (J. Z. Smith). Simply put, sacred space is localized as a "power center" where spirits reside (Medicine Grizzly Bear Lake).

Academicians may categorize space as either sacred or profane, but myths often present a more complex world where spirit realms interact with each other and the human realm. No one can predict where or in what form the power of spirit will break through into ordinary space. Religious observance focuses one's attention on ultimate reality by orienting members to the place where sacred and human spaces intersect. This is why a Muslim inclines in prayer toward Mecca and a Jew recites, "Next year in Jerusalem!" at Passover.

According to New Zealand Maori creation stories, in the beginning mother earth and father sky wrapped themselves in a fecund embrace that produced male offspring, one of whom, Tane, stood on his head and pushed his parents apart, so as to create a "world of light" for human beings. Earth and sky powers intersected the human realm at designated places, such as the village latrine and sweet potato storehouse. Had Tane not delineated *noa* (all that is female) from *tapu* (all that is male), human beings would not know how to behave in an orderly fashion. *Tapu* violations can be neutralized only by *noa* rites. The balanced complementarity of the male and female powers of sky and earth maintains the life force of the people.

Ultimate power emanates from spirit realms at particular places where it is dispensed to human beings through mediators. Power can be dangerous as well as beneficial. Thus, while male and female powers complete one another, they are also antagonistic. The womb symbolizes both life and mortality in Maori religion. Like the moon it waxes and wanes in the course of a month. A menstruating Sioux shaman cannot approach a sacred place and a menstruating Jew or Muslim may not engage in marital sex.

Power centers dedicated to the female realm of earth emerged independent of one another in early cultures. Both the Romans and the Chinese erected central temples to the spirit of earth. The presence of the Roman goddess, Vesta, was symbolized by sacred fire in her circular temple, and the square Chinese Altar of Earth was dedicated to yin, the universal female principle. Earth worshipers in ancient Crete conducted rites for a cult of the dead in natural crevices that may have provided a model for the Labyrinth that was constructed later at Knossos.

Worship is gendered in various religions. In ancient Palestine sky deities were enshrined with their female consorts (*asherah*), represented by sacred groves or pillars at "high places" dedicated to Yahweh. After monotheism developed in Arabia, references to the consorts of Allah were removed from the Qur'an. In pre-Christian Europe women spoke for the earth spirits at

Cumae and Delphi, but priests controlled the interpretation of oracles and their application to affairs of state. As female deities were supplanted by one high god at power centers in the Mediterranean world, the roles of women as oracles and priestesses at sacred sites disappeared.

In Judaism, Christianity, and Islam, sacred space has been variously marked off in temples, mosques, and churches that historically were maintained by male clergy and overwhelmingly dedicated to gods. Yet, within these male-administered precincts evidence of female spirits persists in noticeable ways. Statues of the Virgin Mary occupy a niche second only to the crucified savior in Catholic churches. Hagar, the ancestress of the Arab tribes, is buried beside the holy Kaaba in Mecca and memorialized in the *dawar* rite. The Indian Sikh gurus built temples at sacred springs and pools, healing symbols of the female earth that wash away sin and bestow immortality.

The relegation of female space to a subordinate place in religion is as problematic as the confinement of women in monotheism to household roles. In Judaism and Islam, whose supreme God jealously prohibits the worship of rival deities, most women's religious roles are largely confined to cooking, housekeeping, and childbearing. Women prepare food for the ritual meals of rabbinic Judaism, but men preside over the Passover and Shabbat banquets. Muslim and Jewish women must keep household space ritually pure. After it is thus domesticated, female power can serve, without endangering, male potency. Only recently has feminist exegesis begun to re-present Jewish and Christian traditions in ways that have allowed women to be ordained as rabbis, priests, and ministers. In Islam the holy task of interpretation is still restricted to male scholars, despite the fact that the Prophet Muhammad discussed his visions with Khadija, his first wife and convert.

Nevertheless, the female spirit as the Great [earth] Mother is still worshiped in Indian temples, and the national shrine of Mexico is dedicated to the Virgin of Guadalupe. Millions of Catholic pilgrims have sought healing from the mother of God at Lourdes, France, and Medjugorje, Croatia, where Mary has appeared to visionary children. The twentieth-century phenomenon of Marian devotion has restored a degree of gender complementarity to Christianity.

Rarely have women in religion transcended the gender barrier to attain a position equal to men. Notable exceptions include great mystics, such as the Sufi divine, Rabi'a, whose love of God caused her master to release her from servitude. Muslim women gather in public adoration at her mausoleum. Mary Magdalene was the first witness of the empty tomb of the risen Christ, but her testimony was discounted by the apostles. In the Gospel of Thomas, she is invited to make herself male and enter into the elite circle of religious adepts. The unbridled spiritual woman was not welcomed into the ranks of Buddhist or Christian monastics. However, the female ecstatics of African and Caribbean religions may dance until the body itself becomes a power center possessed by a spirit.

The Temple of Vesta in the Forum in Rome, where the vestal virgins guarded the sacred fire. Vesta, goddess of the hearth, protected the fire, which symbolized the perpetuity of the state (Angelo Hornak/Corbis).

Whether power manifests itself at a natural cave or a constructed temple, at a house or a gravesite, a banquet table or in an entranced devotee, that place is where ordinary space and sacred space intersect. It is there, only at that singular meeting place, that worshipers may encounter the ultimate reality that extends beyond the visible human realm.

BIBLIOGRAPHY

Bolle, Kees W. "The Great Goddess." In Mariam Robbins Dexter and Edgar C. Polomé, eds. *Varia on the Indo-European Past: Papers in Memory of Marija Gimbutas.* 1997.

Brown, Karen McCarthy. *Mama Lola: A Vodou Priestess in Brooklyn.* 1991.

Christ, Carol P. *Odyssey with the Goddess: A Spiritual Journey in Crete.* 1995.

Eliade, Mircea. *The Sacred and the Profane.* 1959.

"The Gospel of Thomas." In *The Five Gospels.* Translated by Robert W. Funk, Roy W. Hoover, and the Jesus Seminar. 1993.

Hirschfelder, Arlene, and Paulette Molin, eds. *The Encyclopedia of Native American Religions.* 1992.

Peters, F. E. *The Hajj.* 1994.

Salmond, Anne. "Te Ao Tawhito: A Semantic Approach to the Traditional Maori Cosmos," *Journal of the Polynesian Society* 87, no. 1 (March 1978): 5–28.

Schimmel, Annemarie. *Islam, An Introduction.* 1992.

Smith, Jonathan Z. *Imagining Religion.* 1982.

Swan, James A., ed. *The Power of Place.* 1991.

Van der Leeuw, Gerardus. *Religion in Essence and Manifestation.* 1986.

Van der Toorn, Karel. *From Her Cradle to Her Grave: The Role of Religion in the Life of the Israelite and the Babylonian Woman.* Translated by Sara J. Denning-Bolle. 1994.

Walther, Wiebke. *Women in Islam from Medieval to Modern Times.* 1995.

Young, Serinity, ed. *An Anthology of Texts by and about Women.* 1994.

JEAN E. ROSENFELD

Speech

Two attributes of religious utterance must be kept in mind when considering women's religious speech. First, much religiously significant speech is, in the influential phrase of the philosopher J. L. Austin, "performative utterance"; that is, it does something. This indelible feature of much religious speech—that it is not "mere saying" but instead action, accomplishment, performance—is crucial to an understanding of the religious speech of women, whose words have often represented acts of defiance against male-constituted authority "merely" through having been spoken.

Second, much religious speech evidences or establishes a relationship between the human speaker and a transhuman reality. In forms such as prophecy, oracle, and glossolalia and other ecstatic speech, a transmundane being is speaking through the human speaker, who is a vessel or medium for the transmission. Ambivalence about who is speaking is therefore inherent in such speech, and this has profound, if often repressed, implications regarding gender. For example, one may ask whether the pronouncements of the Pythia—the priestess of Apollo who presided over the oracle at Delphi and who, in trance, delivered the god's dicta—are better characterized as the female speech of the (female) human speaker or the male speech of the masculine deity who spoke through her (or of the male priests who interpreted the messages).

WOMEN'S SPEECH VERSUS MALE POWER

Such questions gather particular force when applied to theistic traditions in which the deity who is speaking or being spoken to is masculine, the culture is structured heterosexually, and religious authority is (mostly) vested in male speakers. If, as happens in such traditions, inspiration is sometimes imaged as insemination, one may, following Eilberg-Schwartz (1994), ask whether the male prophet or preacher is not "feminized" by his reception of the (male) divine word. Such traditions have typically questioned the authority of strong female speakers: one thinks, for example, of the trial and execution of Joan of Arc. On the one hand, suppression of female speech may betray male anxiety about male speakers' own, heterosexually dubious, relation to the godhead. On the other, the association between preaching and inseminating (the hearers) may itself render women's religious speech suspect, almost as if the female speaker were laying false claim to a biological capability her sex forbids her.

Curiously, the legitimacy of women's speech has been questioned even in the erotically charged realm of devotional poetry addressed to a male deity who is figured as lover. Female devotional poets of superb skill are found in several traditions—Mahādēviyakka in the bhakti tradition of medieval India; the Sufi poet-saint Rabiʻa in Islam—but these women achieved their vocations against the odds. In their male-dominated cultures, even the "feminine" role of enraptured worshiper has mostly belonged to men.

Many traditions have prescribed occasions on which women may legitimately speak. For example, the "speech" of mourning (often wordless, though sometimes highly formalized, lamentation) has across many cultures been assigned to women. In the main, however, women who would speak have been required to assume a mantle of authority ordinarily denied them. This assumption has often been viewed as renegade or insubordinate, and strong women speakers have been called on to defend their speech in courts of opinion and law. In Christian history outspoken women such as Margery Kempe and Anne Hutchinson were subjected to ecclesiastical trials for their preaching (Cahill, 1996).

CREATION SPEECH

The deep, undivorceable connection between speaking and acting is attested in the creation stories of many traditions, where the spoken or, sometimes, sung word brings the world—and living things, including human beings—into existence. Some cultures' myths give this creative voice to a female figure. One often-cited example comes from Hopi mythology, in which Spider Woman, though herself a created being, is accorded the task of animating the previously lifeless world. This she accomplishes by mixing her spit with earth and from this recipe fashioning the first humans, whom she brings to life by singing over them.

The major religions of the West, however, have for the most part traditionally understood the vocal creator of the world to be unequivocally male. In the biblical creation account of Genesis 1, an apparently masculine God says the universe into being; in the second creation account, given in Genesis 2, there is an echo of God's creative speech-acts in the first man's naming of the animals (Gen. 2:19–20).

By contrast with the creative and order-giving speech acts of the ostensibly masculine deity and his male creature, the first words spoken by the first woman represent rote repetition of instruction (Gen. 2:2–3), fatally irresponsible seduction (implicit in Gen. 2:6), and disingenuous blaming (Gen. 2:13). Significantly, the first reason God gives for punishing Adam is not that he had disobeyed God's command but rather that he has "listened to the voice of [his] wife" (Gen. 2:17, NRSV).

That women's speech is fundamentally flawed—intellectually weak, disruptive, disordering, and morally suspect—is thus constitutive of Judaism and the other scriptural traditions (Christian, Muslim). In Christianity, what has traditionally been considered the Pauline prohibition of women's speaking in church (e.g., in 1 Cor. 14:34) stoutly seconds the divinity's opinion of the worthlessness and recklessness of women's speech. (As some scholars now contend, the words prohibiting women from preaching may not be Paul's own but rather a later addition to the text of his letters. This exegetical revisionism certainly has value for Christian feminists intent on reclaiming what they see as the earliest, nonmisogynistic core of the faith and practice of Jesus and his followers. It does not, however, undo the fact that for nearly two millennia of Christian history the prohibition has been—and in many quarters of Christianity still is—identified with the authority of the apostle and therefore stands as a centrally important ideological tool for the silencing of women.)

By itself, however, this rendition of Western traditions as erasing or derogating women's speech is unnuanced and inaccurately monolithic. There are countertendencies at work. For one, the Hebrew scriptures contain a number of tales of women who, through their speech, prove powerful agents of God's will. The judge Deborah (Judg. 4–5) is a compelling military commander and gifted psalmist; the prophet Judith is a persuasive orator and also a seductress who uses her feminine wiles—including rhetorical wiles—to save the people

An engraving shows Judith holding a sword and the severed head of Holofernes (Historical Picture Archive/ Corbis).

of Israel. Moreover, some of the Hebrew Bible's most moving testimony concerning the nature of human love—and, by extension, divine love—issues from women speakers (e.g., Ruth's speech to Naomi in Ruth 1:16–17; the rhapsodic poetry of the female speaker in the Song of Songs). (It is a telling sidenote, however, that many of the biblical writings with strong female actors and speakers—Esther, Song of Songs, Judith, and so on—have historically been among the most contested regarding their suitability for inclusion in the canon.)

The New Testament, too, contains passages that undermine the view that the Bible wholly ignores or invalidates the speech of women. In the Gospel record, Jesus is remarkable (measured against the mores of his time) in his willingness to speak to women and to pay attention to what they have to say. In one of the most important instances of this interaction, in Mark 7:24–30 (see also Matt. 15:22–28), Jesus is confronted by a Gentile (Syrophoenician or Canaanite) woman who wittily castigates him for his initial refusal to heal her daughter because she is not a Jew. Jesus hears her, and he changes his mind.

At a more elementary level, the Hebrew scriptures contain some evidence that weighs against interpreting the deity as either singular or singularly male. In the Wisdom of Solomon, Wisdom is portrayed and praised as the feminine persona or hypostasis of God; indeed, there are passages (esp. in chaps. 7–8) in which she is credited as the creatrix (or at least cocreatrix) of the world. Wisdom is, moreover, closely identified with divine speech: she "passes into holy souls and makes them . . . prophets" (Wis. 7:27, NRSV). Adding to this ambiguity regarding the gender and number of the creator is the first creation account itself: in Genesis 1:26, God speaks of "himself" in the plural and creates human beings—male and female—in "his" image. Mother Ann Lee, the founder of the Shakers, employed this image of God as a plural, male-and-female speaker in her defense—contra the Pauline tradition—of women's right to preach (Cahill, 1996).

These alternative conceptions of the deity, generally ignored or suppressed during the histories of the Western traditions, have since the 1970s been resurrected and renewed by Jewish and Christian feminists. That female speech, divine or human, continues, however, to be regarded as dangerous and unseemly, even within ostensibly profeminist mainline Protestantism, can be seen in the punitive reaction that followed an interdenominational women's conference, "Re-Imagining," in 1993. Participants in that gathering—which, among other sins, had celebrated the life-giving, creative power of Sophia (i.e., Wisdom)—were afterward harshly rebuked by their denominations for "heresy." Despite enormous gains in the numbers of officially legitimized women speakers (rabbis, ministers "of the word") in liberal Jewish and Christian groups, women's speech that challenges the masculinity of the divine word continues to be viewed as offensively subversive of the ordained order.

BIBLIOGRAPHY

Two recent anthologies comprehensively present the "speaking parts" that women have played in religious traditions large and small. Serinity Young, *An Anthology of Sacred Texts by and About Women* (1993), is the more thorough; although Susan Cahill, *Wise Women: Over Two Thousand Years of Spiritual Writing by Women* (1996), is slimmer and reproduces much material already found in the Young volume, it does provide a good helping of nineteenth- and twentieth-century material not found in Young. Both anthologies contain original source material and editorial commentary about all the strong women speakers mentioned above. For more on Wisdom/Sophia, see Elizabeth A. Johnson, *She Who Is: The Mystery of God in Feminist Discourse* (1993), and for an excellent historical summary of Wisdom/Sophia's place in Christian traditions, see Leo D. Lefebure, "The Wisdom of God: Sophia and Christian Theology," *The Christian Century* (October 19, 1994): 951–956. On women's preaching in premodern America, see Mark Chaves, *Ordaining Women: Culture and Conflict in Religious Organizations* (1997), pp. 66–75.

British "ordinary language" philosopher J. L. Austin's *How to Do Things with Words* (1962) has been a touchstone for much subsequent thinking about all sorts of speech, including religious speech. Howard Eilberg-Schwartz, *God's Phallus and Other Problems for Men and Monotheism* (1994), is an insightful study of sexual ambivalence at the core of Judaism, but the questions it raises are widely applicable across theistic traditions.

See also **Mahādēviyakka**; **Joan of Arc**; **Kempe, Margery**; **Lee, Ann**; **Rabʻia**; **Silence**; **Voice**.

JAMES C. WALLER

Spirits

The category of spirits encompasses a wide variety of positive and neutral supernatural mediators, such as nymphs, *apsārases*, fairies, jinns, *yakṣas*, and *nāgas*. However, the terms *positive* and *neutral* do not exist as discrete objective categories, but must be judged in relation to particular religious systems. Although some of these spirits come in both male and female forms, this discussion focuses on female spirits, always keeping in mind that the various conceptualizations of the female character are a direct result of the manner in which and degree to which a larger concept of the feminine is incorporated within a particular divine hierarchy.

APSĀRASES AND NYMPHS

Apsārases and nymphs are female spirits who embody the same function within two distinct mythological traditions, those of India and Greece. Both traditions can be said to be founded upon patriarchal ideologies, and both are polytheistic.

Though often translated as "nymph," *apsāras* derives from the Sanskrit word for waters—*ap*, and the verb $\sqrt{sr}$, meaning to flow or to move. Thus, an *apsāras* is literally one who moves in the waters or who flows through the cloudy vapors of the celestial spheres. Nymphs are associated with the natural fecundity of the earth and were widely worshiped throughout antiquity not only as personifications of nature's bounty but also for their prayer-granting and prophetic abilities.

Both nymphs and *apsāras*es are perceived as embodying unrestrained feminine sexuality, and as Hesiod reports, to "have charge of young men over all the earth." In Hindu mythology, these young men are usually overly dedicated ascetics, who become threatening to the gods as their ascetic practices make them too powerful. The *apsāras*es are sent in with their alluring looks and their erotic dances to entice these ascetics into spilling their seed, which always leads to a reduction of the ascetic's powers.

The sexual function of *apsāras*es (as well as many other feminine spirits) rarely extends to motherhood. The incompatibility of these roles is evinced in the word used to describe these beautiful dancing women, "graspers"—uncontrollable demonesses who steal human embryos. Nymphs, on the other hand, are sometimes credited with producing offspring to found dynastic lineages, or to create children with divine powers such as the prophetic Sybils; but they are characterized as quick to abandon their maternal duties. Reeled in from the sidelines to play a specific role within these divine hierarchies, these female spirits are not allowed full expression. Rather, the role of sexual enticer is kept distinctly segregated from the role of mother as an attempt is made to contain the uncontainable power of feminine sexuality within the divine realm. This is hardly surprising given the fact that, to paraphrase the anthropologist Clifford Geertz, divine figures provide a reflection of and a model for society. Seen in this light, these spirits mirror the marginalized, bifurcated roles often required of women in patriarchal societies. The fact that the divine realm is often made to contain those feminine characteristics deemed too dangerous for the social realm leads to the following result: this divine reflection, conforming to all mirror images, is a reversal of that found on the social level, where the socially constructive maternal role is prescribed while the sexual is denied. These funhouse mirrors have severe social consequences: not only is a woman's sexuality fragmented from the whole to be objectified and commodified within the dominant discourse but also a woman is blocked from looking toward her spiritual double as an affirming figure. Thus, the explicit union of a woman with a sexual nature results in such pejorative labels as "nymphomaniac," a term still in common usage.

FAIRIES AND JINN

Signifying a descriptive category rather than a discrete figure, the word *fairy* covers a wide assortment of creatures encountered throughout the British Isles, Europe, and Scandinavia. Jinn, part of a pre-Islamic Arabian heritage, are earth-dwelling spirits created from fire. Though having a long literary history, both are creatures of folklore and do not belong to any organized religious system. Both fairies and jinn represent a divine feminine that has been made peripheral in relation to the patriarchal ideologies of the Jewish, Christian, and Islamic traditions, thus providing a reflection of the unacknowledged position of women within these traditions. This fact is further exemplified as angels are uniformly presented as male throughout these traditions. Although restricted from the ranks of the dominant ideology, both fairies and jinn have remained within the popular milieu for centuries; the social fact of the feminine will demand its divine reflection.

Given that neither fairies nor jinn can be contained within the parameters of a dominant religio-ethical order, they are usually presented as terrifically ambivalent creatures: they will help friend or foe alike and are as often malevolent as benevolent. When benevolent, fairies often attach themselves to families: brownies help with household chores, banshees warn of impending death, and tutelary fairies offer protection during feuds. Both fairies and jinn are great lovers of music; the best pipers are thought to be fairy-taught, and stories abound of jinn irresistibly drawn by the power of certain ragas. Their malevolent reputations are never long forgotten, however, and while incorporated spirits such as angels and nymphs are thought to lead one closer to the divine, these ungoverned spirits are thought to lead one both morally and spiritually astray. In fact, the word *jinn* as well as the Arabic word for madness, *junun*, derive from the same root.

As independent female spirits, fairies and jinn are considered dangerous both for their sexual and maternal aspects. Fairly lovers are often described as succubi—she-demons who cause men to ejaculate while they sleep and in so doing draw their life-force from them—or selkies—seal-women who cast spells of enchantment upon their mortal lovers. Beautiful and alluring jinn must be mastered before they allow their lovers access to their cache of riches. This sexual recreation must not lead to procreation, for fairies, restricted from motherhood like nymphs and *apsāras*es, are portrayed as having to kidnap human children to replenish their population—unbaptized babies being their specialty. Whereas jinn are able to reproduce, the ferocious desert-roaming variety are believed to ensnare unwary humans by calling out in the soothing tones of a mother to her child. The figure of the sinister fairy godmother, such as the one portrayed in the tale of Sleeping Beauty, further elaborates this theme, and as Marie-Louise von Franz (1972) has noted, mirrors a culturally inspired fear of the powerful yet disenfranchised female who refuses to accept her marginalized position.

YAKṢAS AND NĀGAS

Yakṣas, most often associated with trees, and nāgas, anthropomorphic snake figures, are both indigenous fertility deities of pre-Aryan India. Their worship predates the arrival of the Aryan tribes responsible for the Vedas, the books of sacred revelation upon which Hinduism is based. Going beyond the association of spirits with natural elements and the simple personification of nature's bounty, *yakṣas* and *nāgas* represent the terrific power and ambivalent forces of nature upon which human beings are so dependent. Perceived as local spirits having mastery over rain, vegetation, the riches of the earth, and human fertility, *nāgas* and *yakṣas* embody Mother Nature's desire to gratify herself in procreation, as well as her need to destroy in the endless process of re-creation. Their worship thus represents a form of religious practice that sacralizes and propitiates those beings whose mysterious powers are thought to exceed human control.

Yakṣas are usually portrayed iconographically as voluptuous feminine figures intertwined with trees in full bloom. Benevolent and beautiful, *yakṣas* are believed to confer fertility on those wishing to become pregnant; yet, emblematic of the full expression of natural forces, they devour as well as nurture. *Nāgas* are female serpent deities. Though sometimes presented in human form, they are always equipped with a hood to mark their association with the cobra, as the worship of these snakes is widespread throughout India and Southeast Asia. *Nāgas* are depicted as both sexual and sensual; the inhabitants of spectacular oceanic palaces, they, along with their consorts, have mastery over all of the life-giving waters on the earth. Equipped with a priceless jewel in the center of their foreheads to mark their association with the earth's riches, they are often the keepers and dispensers of magical weapons.

We come to know *nāgas* and *yakṣas* most readily through Hindu and Buddhist texts, which often attempt to incorporate them as guardians of higher-ranking spirits. The preestablished position of *nāgas* and *yakṣas* as objects of worship, however, precludes the possibility of either isolating them, as with jinn and fairies, or incorporating them into narrowly contained roles, as with nymphs and *apsāras*es. As such, these full-bodied female spirits, embodied alternatives to a dominant ideology, provide a more accurate reflection of and model for women—as women intrinsically embody an alternative to patriarchal structures of order.

This second-century C.E. sculpture on a rail-post depicts Yaksas, a female earth spirit commonly portrayed as the voluptuous woman. It was found in Uttar Pradesh, India (Angelo Hornak/Corbis).

BIBLIOGRAPHY

Bottigheimer, Ruth B. *Fairy Tales and Society.* 1986.

Briggs, K. M. *The Fairies in Tradition and Literature.* 1967.

Brown, Karen McCarthy. *Mama Lola: A Vodou Priestess in Brooklyn.* 1991.

Coomaraswamy, Ananda K. *Yakṣas: Essays in the Water Cosmology.* 1993.

Franz, Marie-Louise von. *Problems of the Feminine in Fairy Tales.* 1972.

Geertz, Clifford. *The Interpretation of Cultures.* 1973.

Neuman, Daniel M. *The Life of Music in North India.* 1980.

O'Flaherty, Wendy D. *Women, Androgynes, and Other Mythical Beasts.* 1980.

Schafer, Edward H. *The Divine Woman.* 1973.

Sutherland, Gail H. *The Disguises of the Demon.* 1991.

Vogel, J. Ph. *Indian Serpent-Lore.* 1926.

LAURIE COZAD

Spiritualism

The term *spiritualism* is used to describe a variety of nineteenth- and twentieth-century religious movements that share the beliefs that the human personality survives beyond death and that the spirits of the dead can communicate with the living through mediums. Spiritualism resists formal organization and usually does not demand exclusive participation. Thus, there is no agreement on orthodox beliefs, no central authority, and no clear sense of membership. Spiritualist organizations can be found in over forty countries, where they provide important avenues for women's religious leadership.

The term *spiritualism* is frequently associated with the movement begun in 1848 in western New York State by Margaret and Kate Fox, who heard spirits tapping in order to communicate with them. From there it spread rapidly throughout the United States and to other countries. Because of its belief in the equality of all, it particularly appealed to many of the leading social reformers of the day and was closely associated with movements concerned with equality, especially women's rights, abolition, and marriage reform. In England (where it was even more popular) and Europe, spiritualism was similarly allied with social reform movements. By challenging the religious orthodoxy of the day, spiritualism created space to challenge political, economic, medical, and gender assumptions and provided a "third way" between science and religion. By promoting women's religious leadership (more than other contemporary religious groups), it encouraged women to challenge expected social roles. Yet it also reinforced Victorian notions of women's nature as passive and intuitive, which were viewed as characteristics of the ideal spirit medium. By the turn of the century, spiritualism in the United States had lost most of its reform inclinations, but it continues as a religious movement. In England and Europe spiritualism gained in numbers during World War I and was particularly attractive to the great many who had lost a loved one in the war.

Despite spiritualism's support of abolition and its obvious relation to many African-derived religious traditions such as Vodou, African-American participation in spiritualism per se was limited until early in the twentieth century. African Americans adapted spiritualism to their own experience and formed a variety of Spiritual churches (usually founded by women, such as Mother Leafy Anderson) in Chicago and New Orleans, which continue to be spiritualistist centers. Although highly independent, Spiritualist churches incorporate aspects of black Protestantism, Catholicism, or Vodou. In Mexico, where spiritualism started in the 1860s, spiritualist temples are usually anti-Catholic and see themselves as a separate and total religion. This differentiates Mexican spiritualists from spiritists, who remain affiliated with Christian churches. In contrast to earlier spiritualist movements, African-American and Latina spiritualism puts more emphasis on healing and explicitly discourages political activism. Although spiritualism thus maintains the status quo by encouraging women to adapt to their social situation, it is transformational at the personal level. It also promotes alternative gender roles by empowering women and encouraging men to refrain from drinking and abuse. Spiritualism is one of the fastest-growing religious movements in Mexico, with temples in all major cities. In the United States, spiritualism is active in cities such as Los Angeles and among the Puerto Rican community in New York and elsewhere.

In addition to specific spiritualist organizations, contemporary interest in psychic phenomena, channeling, the Course of Miracles, and other New Age movements reflects the influence of spiritualism.

BIBLIOGRAPHY

Baer, Hans. *The Black Spiritual Movement: A Religious Response to Racism.* 1984.

———. "The Limited Empowerment of Women in Black Spiritual Churches: An Alternative Vehicle to Religious Leadership." *Sociology of Religion* 54 (1993): 65–82.

Braude, Ann. *Radical Spirits: Spiritualism and Women's Rights in Nineteenth-Century America.* 1989. The best work on spiritualism and women.

Finkler, Kaja. *Spiritualist Healers in Mexico: Success and Failures of Alternative Therapeutics.* 1984. Based on a medical anthropological field study of the healing aspects of spiritualism in particular.

Haygood, Carol L. "The Authority and Empowerment of Women among Spiritualist Groups." *Journal for the Scientific Study of Religion* 22 (1983): 157–166. Based on field study of contemporary spiritualist groups.

Moore, R. Laurence. *In Search of White Crows: Spiritualism, Parapsychology, and American Culture.* 1977. Covers nineteenth-century spiritualism and related twentieth-century movements.

Nelson, Geoffrey. *Spiritualism and Society.* 1969. A good source on spiritualism in England.

LAUREL D. KEARNS

Spirituality

Historically and etymologically, the word *spirituality* is rooted in the history of Christian theology and praxis. Today the word is widely used beyond its original matrix and applied cross-culturally in various religious and nonreligious contexts. Spirituality often refers now to a general human search for meaning, wholeness, self-transcendence, and connectedness with others. From a historical and comparative perspective, there exists no single permanent spirituality, but only different spiritualities linked to particular times, places, and cultures. Spirituality must therefore be examined within a wider cross-cultural context, where one has to ask what spirituality means, what kind of teachings and disciplines are connected with spiritual practice, and how these are best studied.

Spirituality is first a lived experience and praxis; second, it is related to the teachings that grow out of such praxis (for example, counsels on holiness and perfection, on leading a good life, or on finding liberation or salvation as taught by different religions); third, as understood today, it is also concerned with a fast-growing new field of study that deals in a systematic, comparative, and critical way with specific spiritual experiences and teachings of various religions or groups, including women's spirituality and a global spirituality based on the spiritual heritage of the whole of humankind.

All faiths contain spiritual insights and directions, but although the languages of many religions do not even contain a word that corresponds exactly to the term *spirituality*, the term is today used as a universal code word across traditions. Spirituality is no longer primarily approached from an a priori theological standpoint tied to particular doctrines, but is mainly understood anthropologically as the search for or an exploration of what is involved in becoming fully human, in finding self-transcendence. Thus, spirituality is seen as intrinsic to the human subject as such. Much experimentation is taking place in spirituality within and across religious traditions and outside religions altogether.

Evelyn Underhill has said that the spiritual life is "the heart of all real religion," but also that spirituality is "that full and real life for which humanity is made." Today the comparative, cross-cultural, and global significance of spirituality is well documented by the groundbreaking studies in the series *World Spirituality: An Encyclopedic History of the Religious Quest* (25 vols., edited by Ewert Cousins, 1985– , including vol. 21, *Modern Esoteric Spirituality* and vol. 22, *Spirituality and the Secular Quest*).

In the past, much of spirituality was developed by particular social and religious elites (ascetics, monastics, yogis, pirs, holy men and women) who possessed the necessary leisure and aptitude for spiritual pursuits. Two main models of spiritual practice can be distinguished cross-culturally: the ascetic or monastic model of renunciation spirituality, setting the seeker apart from society, and a "householder spirituality," or "spirituality-of-being-in-the-world," practiced within the context of living one's ordinary life.

Although ultimately gender-transcendent, spiritual ideals are not gender-neutral. Comparative investigations provide abundant evidence of deeply embedded patriarchal structures and a predominantly androcentric framework that have shaped traditional spiritual practices and teachings. While spiritual advice seems to be addressed to apparently asexual spiritual seekers, on closer examination it often turns out to be antibody, antiwoman, and antiworld. Male models of holiness often imply not only a contempt for the body in general, but especially for women's bodies. The worldwide history of renunciation and asceticism, which still remains to be written, is certainly responsible for a great deal of misogyny and sexism. Past spirituality has often been deeply dualistic in dividing men from women, men from each other and the world, and in too sharply separating the experience of the body, work, and matter from that of the spirit. In spite of the most difficult conditions and numerous social obstacles, women have struggled throughout the ages to follow their own spiritual quest within the world's religions. Yet few spiritual ideals of the past hold much attraction for contemporary women and their spiritual quest. Feminist insights critically call into question and reject many traditional forms of spirituality, and countless women today seek alternative patterns of an embodied and immanent spirituality that is more attuned to their own experience.

Of the many creative developments in the contemporary understanding of spirituality, one of the most important is the worldwide growth in women's spirituality. Others concern the lively interest in native spiritual traditions and the spiritual heritage of indigenous peoples and cultures, praised for their inherent reverence for life and nature. These new understandings capture the dynamic, transformative quality of spirituality as lived experience, as the struggle for the fullness of human life in justice and peace, free from violence and oppression, and as a great adventure of body, mind, and soul, seeking the graciousness, goodness, and abundance of life—a life healed and whole, sustained and nurtured by the ever-present power of the spirit.

The explicit interest in spirituality among contemporary women is referred to as the womanspirit movement, or spiritual and metaphysical feminism. It draws on both traditional and nontraditional religious sources but is often linked to the worship of the goddess and described as goddess spirituality. The rediscovery of the goddess has produced a vibrant goddess thealogy, in strong contrast to traditional male-centered theology. The great goddess, manifest in myriad historical and cultural forms, is seen as immanent rather than transcendent and is strongly connected with body and earth. Thus, she can be experienced within ourselves, within other human beings, and within nature.

Feminist spirituality, though multiform and diverse, shares numerous common themes. These include women's new awareness of their own empowerment from within to effect personal, social, and political changes; the discovery of the self and its agency; women's experience of bonding and power-sharing; the creative re-imaging and renaming of the sacred; and enhanced sensitivity to the interdependent connectedness and sacredness of all forms of life. Many of these themes are reflected in contemporary women's literature, which, through poetry and fiction, explores different aspects of women's spiritual needs and quest, themes of loss and pain, of oppression and freedom, of intimacy and mutuality, of the connections between sexuality and spirituality. Women are also discovering a rich spiritual heritage in the women saints and mystics of the past and in the female imagery and symbolism present in many religions of the world.

BIBLIOGRAPHY

Astell, Ann W., ed. *Divine Representations: Postmodernism and Spirituality.* 1994. A helpful volume for exploring the affinities between contemporary searches in spirituality and perspectives of postmodernism. Deals with representations of God and self, of spirit, and of the social. Contains some reflections on feminism and spirituality.

Cahill, Susan, ed. *Wise Women: Over Two Thousand Years of Spiritual Writing by Women.* 1996. Sourcebook for texts by women from various religions from ancient cultures to the Middle Ages, early modern period, and the nineteenth and twentieth centuries.

Christ, Carol. *Rebirth of the Goddess: Finding Meaning in Feminist Spirituality.* 1997. Summing up much of Christ's well-known earlier work and developing it further, this volume provides a fine guide to the goddess spirituality movement and its influential thealogy, presented by one of its leading figures.

Conn, Joann Wolski, ed. *Women's Spirituality: Resources for Christian Development.* 1986; 2d ed., 1996. A widely used anthology. Its second, enlarged edition covers a wide range of authors and issues in women's spirituality, with special emphasis on classical and contemporary texts relating to Christianity.

Eller, Cynthia. *Living in the Lap of the Goddess: The Feminist Spirituality Movement in America.* 1995. Based on personal interviews, a wide range of literature, a study of rituals and workshops, this comprehensive study provides an excellent introduction to the goddess traditions and feminist spirituality movement in the United States from the critical perspective of an outsider.

King, Ursula. "Spirituality." In *A New Handbook of Living Religions.* Edited by John R. Hinnells. 1998. A comparative survey of contemporary approaches to spirituality relative to world religions. Provides an introduction to the field.

———. *Women and Spirituality: Voices of Protest and Promise.* 1989; 2d ed., 1993. A helpful textbook providing a critical introduction to the feminist challenge of religion, feminist theology, and spirituality, including comparative material from several religions. Argues that besides the explicit development of women's spirituality, the feminist movement also contains an implicit spirituality because the feminist aims of liberation from oppression and the realization of the full humanity of women are ultimately not only social, economic, and political, but also spiritual.

Plaskow, Judith, and Carol P. Christ, eds. *Weaving the Visions: New Patterns in Feminist Spirituality.* 1989. Wonderfully rich set of essays on many aspects of feminist spirituality; excellent sequel to the earlier, influential *Womanspirit Rising,* edited by Carol P. Christ and Judith Plaskow (1979; 2d ed., 1992).

Salomonsen, Jone. " 'I am a witch—a healer and a bender': An Expression of Women's Religiosity in Contemporary USA." Ph.D. diss., University of Oslo, 1997. An outstanding and exceptionally detailed study of the Reclaiming Collective in San Francisco, founded in 1979 by Starhawk. The author uses historical, anthropological, phenomenological, and theological approaches in presenting her analysis of a new religious movement.

Schneiders, Sandra M. "Feminist Spirituality." In *New Dictionary of Catholic Spirituality.* Edited by M. Downey. 1993. Comprehensive and informative survey dealing with the basic terminology, phenomenology, and major characteristics of contemporary feminist spirituality, connecting them with the development of Catholic feminist spirituality. See also her "Feminist Spirituality: Christian Alternative or Alternative to Christianity," in *Women's Spirituality: Resources for Christian Development,* edited by Joann Wolski (1996).

Spretnak, Charlene, ed. *The Politics of Women's Spirituality: Essays by Founding Mothers of the Movement.* 1982; 2d ed., 1994. Women's search for wholeness and integration is closely tied to radically transforming traditional patriarchal attitudes to gender, sexuality, work, and society; this profoundly empowering spirituality has important political implications, as is evident from many inspiring essays in this influential book.

Starhawk. *The Spiral Dance: A Rebirth of the Ancient Religion of the Great Goddess.* 1979; 2d ed., 1989. A classic of the contemporary feminist spirituality movement. Starhawk, sometimes described as the high priestess of the modern witchcraft movement, has influenced many women and some men. The most thorough analysis of Starhawk's work is found in Salomonsen above.

Tomm, Winnie. *Bodied Mindfulness: Women's Spirits, Bodies and Places.* 1995. Drawing on Buddhist, shamanist, and feminist resources, this book explores important topics on the self as spiritual, spirituality and the body, and the integral relation of spirituality and social change with regard to ethics, politics, and the environment.

Umansky, Ellen M., and Dianne Ashton, eds. *Four Centuries of Jewish Women's Spirituality: A Sourcebook.* 1992. An invaluable resource for reclaiming the voices of Jewish women; describes their spiritually significant experiences from 1560 onward, with a large number of modern contributions from 1960 to 1990.

Zappone, Katherine. *The Hope for Wholeness: A Spirituality for Feminists.* 1991. An engaging book that clearly maps out the pluralism of spiritual paths, explores the origins and future directions of feminist spirituality, and highlights the importance of rituals for the ordinary and extraordinary experiences of women's lives.

URSULA KING

Stanton, Elizabeth Cady

See Woman's Bible, The.

Structuralism

The term *structuralism* dates to mid-century. It denotes a method the anthropologist Claude Lévi-Strauss devised to study scientifically a wide range of cultural products. In the structural linguistics of Ferdinand de Saussure and Roman Jakobson, Lévi-Strauss found a promising antedote to what he perceived as the regnant existentialism's dangerous and defeatist exaltation of subjectivity. Throughout his career, Lévi-Strauss sought to demonstrate that kinship systems, myths, and totemic classifications all exhibit a logic reflecting universal structures of the human mind. He believed that the mind, at the most fundamental level, works by means of binary oppositions. The opposition between nature and culture figures most prominently in Lévi-Strauss's reconstructions of human psychology.

Myth functions in his view as an unconscious attempt to mediate contradictions generated by the oppositions. The basic plot elements of a myth, perspicuously arranged into categories, reveal an underlying algebraic structure. One can read the meaning of a myth from the basic formula. Although few any longer follow Lévi-Strauss's ambition to isolate universal, mathematically figured structures in myth, many have made fruitful use of structuralism to interpret discrete, local groups of myths. Wendy Doniger O'Flaherty, for example, selectively applies structuralist techniques to the Hindu Puranas. The methodological insight that the individual characters or events in a myth disclose their full significance for a culture only when viewed in their relation to a larger system has proven especially powerful. The contradictory attributes of the Hindu god, Siva, for instance, only make sense against the background of the Indian householder–ascetic opposition which he mediates.

Short of embracing structuralism, some feminists—for example Gayle Rubin, Sherry Ortner, and Catherine Clément—have found Lévi-Strauss's claims about women and the nature–culture opposition suggestive in trying to account for the oppression of women. Like Freud, Lévi-Strauss places the incest prohibition at the origin of culture. He locates the origin of both symbolic thought (which separates human culture from merely animal nature) and society in exogamy. This exchange of women constitutes the primary form of communication, and through it families create alliances and form societies. The women exchanged symbolize the relationship forged and represent two cultural categories of women: wives and sisters.

Lévi-Strauss argues that these human symbols are endowed with value for the men who communicate with them. Words once had value too but have become devalued because of their autonomy from their referents: signs become common, shared by many. Early language, imbued with value, was poetic, affective; words eventually became debased, tokens suitable for ratiocination. Lévi-Strauss claims that women, conversely, sustain the value and mystery present at the origin of culture. In this feature women represent an intermediary between nature and culture. Their menstrual flow, close to nature according to Lévi-Strauss, also situates women as anomalously intermediate between nature and culture. Ortner argues that this perceived proximity to nature explains women's pancultural secondary status. Lévi-Strauss, moreover, endorses Marcel Mauss's theory that societies invest cultural anomalies with extraordinary power. Clément focuses on this transgressive power in her analysis of the sorceress and the hysteric as archetypal images of women. Most feminists who employ Lévi-Strauss's theories supplement them with psychoanalysis to explain the gender distinctions presupposed by kinship systems and cultural gender hierarchies.

BIBLIOGRAPHY

Cixous, Hélène, and Catherine Clément. *The Newly Born Woman.* Translated by Betsy Wing. 1986.

Lévi-Strauss, Claude. *The Elementary Structures of Kinship.* Translated by James Harle Bell, John Richard von Sturmer, and Rodney Needham. 1969.

O'Flaherty, Wendy Doniger. *Women, Androgynes and Other Mythical Beasts.* 1980.

Ortner, Sherry B. "Is Female to Male as Nature Is to Culture?" In *Woman, Culture, and Society.* Edited by Michelle Zimbalist Rosaldo and Louise Lamphere. 1974.

Rubin, Gayle. "The Traffic in Women: Notes on the 'Political Economy' of Sex." In *Toward an Anthropology of Women.* Edited by Rayna Rapp Reiter. 1975.

MATTHEW C. BAGGER

Suffering

While pain is a physical sensation, suffering is a psychological experience combining emotional anguish and despairing cognition. Simone Weil (1909–1943), a French philosopher and theologian, spoke of "affliction," in which physical, psychological, and social suffering are combined. Affliction, she argued, requires the isolation and rejection of the sufferer.

Suffering is a ubiquitous feature on the landscape of human experience. In religion it poses a challenge to religious faith and understanding, and it serves as a vehicle for spiritual growth. Where the suffering of women differs from that of men, that difference has two roots. First, women bear children and have primary responsibility for their care and nurture. Thus women suffer the physical pain of childbirth and psychological anguish should harm befall a child. Second, in most cultures, men are entitled to exercise power over women, and women are expected to be submissive to men. Women are far more likely to be beaten and raped, to be subjected to domestic torture. Men, on the other hand, suffer from loss of power, status, and possessions and from humiliation.

Religion is a key agent in the social construction of reality. Religious myths and doctrines tell us why we suffer and what to do about our suffering. Religions may also legitimize cultural inequities that cause suffering. Since the major religions are all grounded in patriarchal cultures, the stories that explain suffering often justify patriarchy. It must be noted that feminist scholars working within a religious tradition may insist on a distinction between the truths of the religion and cultural practice, and would thus see the portrayal of woman as source of suffering as a cultural deviation from religious truth.

The dialectic of suffering contrasts deserved with undeserved suffering and meaningful suffering with meaningless suffering. The most intolerable suffering is that which is experienced as capricious or without purpose. The perception of suffering as undeserved is a particularly difficult challenge to belief in a benevolent, omnipotent diety. This is one aspect of the problem of theodicy, which struggles to reconcile the notion of a good, loving, all-powerful God with the existence of evil in the world. Making all or most suffering deserved resolves this dilemma.

ORIGINAL SIN IN THE JUDAIC AND CHRISTIAN TRADITIONS

In the Judaic and Christian traditions, the entry of both sin and suffering into a paradisal creation is explained by the myth of the Fall. In this story, the wily serpent persuades Eve that she will not die from eating the fruit of the tree of knowledge, as threatened by Yahweh. Eve eats the fruit and gives Adam some, which he eats. Yahweh appears and expels Adam and Eve from the Garden of Eden. God condemns Adam, who is Everyman, to a life of labor and frustration. To Eve, Everywoman, God says:

> I will increase your labor and your groaning,
> and in labor you shall bear children.
> You shall be eager for your husband,
> and he shall be your master.
> (New English Bible, Gen. 3:16)

While this canonical account makes curiosity Eve's crime, the non-canonical Pseudepigraphical, Apocryphal, and rabbinical literature shifts her crime to that of lust and seduction. Through her lust, woman allows herself to be seduced by the Devil and, in turn, seduces man. In the works of early Christian church fathers Clement, Tertullian, and Augustine, woman becomes the ultimate culprit whose dangerous sexuality corrupts men and contaminates the innocent newborn with original sin. In this view, woman not only deserves both suffering and domination but is also responsible for men's suffering. In contrast, Islam's interpretation of this legend holds Adam and Eve to be equally responsible for succumbing to temptation and does not equate sin, suffering, and sexuality. The Muslim concern with women's sexuality, evidenced in veiling and female circumcision traditions, is not rooted in the core metaphor of Eve the Temptress.

KARMA IN THE HINDU AND BUDDHIST TRADITIONS

In the Eastern religious traditions of Hinduism and Buddhism, the cosmic law of karma (or kamma) ensures that suffering obeys laws of cause and effect. Wrongful action creates negative karma or a karmic debt. Thus, that individual soul must pay that debt through both suffering and good deeds whose positive karma cancels the karmic debt. Suffering is seen as a natural part of worldly existence, inevitable as long as the soul is bound to the wheel of birth and rebirth. It is both karmic penalty and a way to purify the soul through penance. For example, wife abuse is seen as wrong action on the part of the husband. It causes suffering for his wife and generates negative karma for him. However, to some degree, that abuse indicates a karmic debt incurred by the wife in this or a previous existence.

In Buddhism, however, feminine sexuality and sensuality are linked directly to samsara, the continuous cycle of suffering and rebirth. Life is suffering, and suffering is caused by desire and attachment. Not only is a woman at a disadvantage in achieving liberation from suffering, but she is also an obstacle to men's spiritual growth and liberation. This is particularly true in the Theravadin Buddhist tradition, where Buddhist monks are forbidden to touch or to be touched by a woman or to accept anything from the hand of one.

THE LIBERATION THEOLOGY VIEW OF SUFFERING

The causal association of women's sexuality and suffering clearly originates in a male perspective. Male sexual passion puts men in jeopardy, as the Hebrew Bible story of Samson and Delilah shows. When women address the problem of suffering, a very different sort of account emerges. Liberation theology, for example, links suffering with oppression. Dorothee Sölle, Marxist liberation theologian, rejects what she calls masochistic suffering, either as punishment for our sinful nature or in penance. This, she argues, makes God a sadist. For Sölle, God is the symbol of our unending capacity to love. The significant distinction, Sölle argues, is between meaningful and meaningless suffering. When out of our love for reality we throw ourselves into the battle against oppression, we suffer meaningfully. The proper metaphor for such suffering, Sölle says, is labor pains, not carnality. That still leaves the problem of innocent suffering. The only response, Sölle concludes, is to stand with sufferers empathically, to share their pain, and to ease the isolation of affliction.

BIBLIOGRAPHY

Allen, M., and S. N. Mukherjee, eds. *Women in India and Nepal.* ANU Monographs on S. Asia, no. 8, 1982.

Jootla, Susan E. "Inspiration from Enlightened Nuns." Wheel Publication no. 349–350. Buddhist Publication Society. Using the poems and writings of nuns from the time of the Buddha, Jootla shows how giving up attachment specifically affects women. This paper and many other works are available electronically from DharmaNet International. Their World Wide Web address is hhttp://www.dharmanet.org

Paul, Diana Y. *Women in Buddhism.* 1979. This book describes the range of ways in which women are viewed in Buddhist traditions. Paul's arguments are well documented by selections from Buddhist texts.

Prusek, Bernard P. "Woman: Seductive Siren and Source of Sin?" In *Religion and Sexism.* Edited by Rosemary Reuther. 1974.

Ricoeur, Paul. *The Symbolism of Evil.* 1967. Although certainly not written from a feminist perspective, Ricoeur's excellent work sets forth the problem suffering presents to the religious consciousness and discusses the mythical responses of the Judaic and Christian traditions.

Reuther, Rosemary. "Misogyny and Virginal Feminism in the Fathers of the Church." In *Religion and Sexism*. Edited by Rosemary Reuther. 1974. Reuther and Prusek's essays in this excellent collection explore the origins of the attribution of suffering to women's sexuality.

Soelle (Sölle), Dorothee. *Suffering.* Translated by Everett R. Kalin. 1973.

Weil, Simone. *Waiting for God.* Translated by Emma Craufurd. 1951.

Whyte, Susan R. "Men, Women, and Misfortune in Bunyole." In *Women's Religious Experience.* Edited by Pat Holden. 1983. African traditions attribute suffering to the actions of ghosts and spirits. In this account the author shows how gender politics play out in the Nyole explanations of misfortune and suffering.

See also **Karma**.

SUSAN L. ANDREWS

Suicide

Suicide and self-sacrifice both result in self-destruction, but the impulses that lead to a self-induced death either reduce the death to the sin of suicide or elevate it to the heroic act of self-sacrifice. The distinction is significant: in general, suicide is deplored, but self-sacrifice is glorified. For example, in Christian cultures suicide was perceived to be a rejection of God's grace. Female suicides became symbols for the moral weakness of women. Christian society did, however, honor religious martyrdom, which, even if eagerly sought, was perceived not to be the sin of suicide, but the saintly virtue of self-sacrifice. Many women joined the ranks of early church martyrs. Just as society justifies killing in warfare or by judicial execution, self-destruction is condoned when it is an act of self-sacrifice.

Not all societies rejected suicide, especially when it was done to preserve one's honor. The Roman patrician class, for example, viewed suicide as an honorable end to a life that had reached crisis. Perhaps the most famous suicides in the Roman world were those of the Egyptian Ptolemy queen Cleopatra and her Roman lover, Mark Antony. After years of unsuccessful intrigue and political maneuvering, Cleopatra killed herself rather than face disgrace at the hands of the Roman armies. Some women committed suicide to accompany their husbands; for instance, Arria Paeta, when her husband, Caecina Paetus, was commanded to die by his own

Cleopatra VII (69–30 B.C.E.), the most famous female suicide of ancient times, took her own life probably with poison (legend says with the bite of an asp, a poisonous snake) rather than be captured by her Roman enemies (Corbis-Bettmann).

hand, stabbed herself first, then handed the dagger to her husband saying, "It does not hurt" (Martial, I, 14).

In China a suicide could bring curses to bear against perceived wrongdoers. Suicide therefore became a woman's tool for aggression in a patriarchal society. Chinese literature is full of references to desperate and aggrieved women who jumped down wells or swallowed jade hairpins in reaction to a loss of position as wives or concubines. (See, for example, the popular Ch'ing novel *Dream of the Red Chamber.*) Japanese women of the samurai class, like their men, performed sanctioned suicide because of slights to honor, or to signal disagreement with a liege lord.

Other societies made exceptions to the opprobrium against female suicide if it conformed to the societal norms of female self-abnegation and self-sacrifice. Widow self-destruction was known particularly throughout the Indo-European world. Indians, Scythians, Teutons, ancient Slavs, and Scandinavians practiced widow self-immolation. It was also honored among some Greeks and Romans. Seneca was reported to have pressured his wife to promise to commit suicide upon his death.

India especially revered the sati, the "virtuous woman" who burned herself on her husband's funeral pyre. (A woman who commits to fire is a sati, but the rite itself is usually referred to by the Anglo-Indian term *suttee*.) A Hindu woman who died as a sati displayed the ideal of wifely love and self-abnegation. Her death secured remission of her own sins and cleansed her husband of sin as well. It relieved her in-laws of the burden of a widow, and her chastity was assured. The sati was considered a reincarnation of the goddess Satī, a predecessor of the goddess Pārvatī, consort to the god Siva. The sati's blessing given on the way to death was highly valued, and her curses brought destruction and ruin.

Sati memorial stones usually display an upright arm decorated with bracelets. The first act of a widow's grief was the destruction of her bangles. She had failed as a *pativrata*, an ideal wife, by "allowing" her husband to die before her and had lost her right to personal adornment. The decorated arm signifies that the sati was not a widow, but a wife joining her husband in death. She was a *sahagamani*, "one who accompanies." A sati stone would often become the focus of a cult, some of which continue to be influential.

The origins are vague. It may have been a practice brought into India by the Scythians, who consigned the widows of their chiefs to the pyre. It is mentioned in the Indian epic that centers on a great ancient war, the Mahabharata (although in late passages). Mādrī burned herself on the pyre of Pāṇḍu; and the disconsolate widows of Krishna immolated themselves. The earliest historical record dates to 316 B.C.E. The rite was performed by a wife of the Hindu general Keteus, who died while fighting Antigonos in Iran. Suttee was most commonly performed by *kṣatriya*, or warrior caste women. There have always been those who deplore the practice. In the nineteenth century Rammohun Roy and Lord Bentinck worked successfully nearly to eradicate it.

Jauhar was a type of mass self-destruction sanctioned by medieval Indian Rajput society under the duress of the Muslim invasions. *Jauhar* and suttee share some similarities but are quite different in purpose and intent. *Jauhar* did not emphasize the intense personal identification of wife to husband, but like the rite of suttee, it emphasized the purification of death by fire.

A protest against the horrors of war, and the ultimate expression of a military scorched earth policy, *jauhar* insured that if the enemy prevailed, he would have no spoils of war: no plunder and no rape. Rajput women watched the outcome of battle and, if it was evident that their husbands would be defeated or that their own capture was inevitable, they would commit *jauhar* to avoid the violation of rape and the possibility of a dishonored bloodline. Dressed in their wedding finery,

with their children and all their valuables, they immolated themselves on a great pyre. At times thousands of women and children died en masse to avoid capture. Like satis, the participants of a *jauhar* were honored as divinities in their family shrines.

But Indian women, like men, also participated in religious rituals involving voluntary abandonment of the body. These forms of religious suicide included the Jain rite of *sallekhanā* or fasting unto death, or the Hindu custom of drowning at the confluence of the Yamunā and Gaṅga rivers, or certain pilgrimages that were exhausting unto death. In medieval India some men and women voluntarily cut off their own heads as offerings to Durgā or Siva Bhairava. These were highly unusual events and the performers were memorialized with "hero stones," which, like sati memorials, often became the focus of a cult.

BIBLIOGRAPHY

Bassein, Beth Ann. *Women and Death: Linkages in Western Thought and Literature.* 1984.

Headley, Lee A., ed. *Suicide in Asia and the Near East.* 1983.

Hawley, John Stratton, ed. *Sati: The Blessing and the Curse: The Burning of Wives in India.* 1994.

Ide, Arthur Frederick. *Martyrdom of Women: A Study of Death Psychology in the Early Christian Church to 301 C.E.* 1985.

Kinsley, David. *Hindu Goddesses.* 1988.

Morris, Ivan. *Nobility of Failure: Tragic Heroes in the History of Japan.* 1975.

Sewell, Robert George. "The Theme of Suicide: A Study of Human Values in Japanese and Western Literature." Ph.D. diss., University of Illinois, 1976.

Sharma, Arvind, with Ajit Ray, Alaka Hejib, and Katherine K. Young. *Sati: Historical and Phenomenological Essays.* Delhi, 1988.

Sreenivasachar, P. A. "A Note on Medieval Sculpture in Hyderabad Museum Depicting Self-Immolation." *Andhra Pradesh Archaeological Series*, no. 15 (Hyderabad). *The Archaeological Bulletin* 2 (1963).

Thakur, Upendra. *The History of Suicide in India: An Introduction.* Delhi, 1963.

Tod, James. *Annals and Antiquities of Rajasthan, 1829–32.* Delhi, 1983.

MARY STORM

Sun

Within most Western literature about mythology—particularly, as Patricia Monaghan points out, in psychological and especially Jungian interpretations—the sun is considered a masculine symbol while the moon is seen as feminine. Sun and daylight symbolize renewed life, truth, and logic; the rising and falling of the sun is associated with man, empires, and war. The night, or moonlight, symbolizes mystery, death, and danger; the cycles of the moon are associated with woman, nature, and fertility.

Within many cultures, however, the sun is a feminine symbol. Amaterasu, the highest *kami* (deity or force) of Japan's Shinto pantheon and the most popular figure on family and public shrines, is a female sun goddess whose symbol and *shintai* (body on earth) is the mirror. Her brother, unimportant in the mythology, is the moon *kami.* Many (particularly older) Japanese worship Amaterasu by showing reverence to the sun itself. Both in cities and in rural areas, the Japanese go outside early in the morning to clap their hands at the rising sun. New Year's Day sunrise is the most auspicious time for this ceremony. Notably, in Japan the sun is female and also the symbol of the empire, for the Japanese flag is a rising sun. Siberian mythology also speaks of a feminine sun embodied in the toli, a mirror used by shamans for divining. In Korea the sun is understood to have been a girl, Hae-Soon, who was raised into the heavens after being killed by a tiger.

The Celts had a sun goddess called Sulis, from Suil, which means both eye and sun. The sun goddess Sul, Sol, or Sulis was also worshiped in Britain at the Avebury complex of megalithic monuments now known as Silbury Hill, where she was said to give birth to each new aeon. The hot springs at her shrine at Bath were believed to be warmed when the sun passed below the earth at night. In Germany this same goddess was Sunna; in Norway she was Sol; in the Scandinavian Eddas she was Glory-of-Elves, who will give birth to a daughter at the end of time, when the Fenris Wolf, the wolf of darkness who perpetually pursues the sun, finally catches the goddess and devours her. The daughter born at that moment will become the sun of the next creation.

Saule, the sun goddess of the Balts, discovered that her husband, the moon god, had raped their daughter Meness. Saule slashed her husband's face with a sword, leaving marks that are still visible, and refused to be in the same part of the sky with him from then on. Cherokee mythology relates how the young female sun was raped by a stranger. By marking his face with coal, the sun discovered that her rapist was her brother. A similar story appears among the Inuit, as well as among various cultures of the Pacific Rim.

Ancient Arabs worshiped the sun goddess Atthar, sometimes called the torch of the gods. For the Dogon, the sun is female. In Amerindian, Maori, Teutonic, and Oceanic myth systems, the sun is female and the moon male.

The sun and moon together frequently symbolize fertility. In Oceanic mythology, the sun is the mother of all, the moon is father, and the stars are children. This relationship is often symbolized by eyes. For the Maori, the sun and moon are the eyes of heaven. In some versions of Shinto mythology, Amaterasu is born from the right eye of Izanagi (the male creator god, whose consort is Izanami), while her brother, the moon, is born from Izanagi's left eye.

BIBLIOGRAPHY

Cooper, J. C. *An Illustrated Encyclopedia of Traditional Symbols.* 1978.
Eliade, Mircea, ed. *The Encyclopedia of Religion.* 1987.
Gimbutas, Marija. *The Language of the Goddess.* 1989.
Kinsley, David. *The Goddess' Mirror.* 1989.
Monaghan, Patricia. *O Mother Sun: A New View of the Cosmic Feminine.* 1993.
———. *The New Book of Goddesses and Heroines.* 1997.
Walker, Barbara. *Woman's Encyclopedia of Myths and Secrets.* 1983.

JENNIFER DUMPERT

Superstition

Superstition indicates beliefs and practices whose fundamental premises are mistaken or false, irrational insofar as they cannot be proven through the logic of empirical science. Calling something "superstition" or someone "superstitious" is necessarily a negative judgment, an assertion of distance between the presumably enlightened speaker and the allegedly backward subject: a member of an exotic culture, a peasant, one's own grandmother. The term has global coinage; it appears in multiple translations, everywhere cast as modernity's dark alter ego, a quality of "traditional" life and thought that must be overcome if progress is to take place. The concept of superstition, like that of modernity, has had tremendous salience in the construction of both metropolitan and local worldviews, defining acceptable and unacceptable religious practices and practitioners. Students of religion and gender ought, therefore, to carefully examine this term, both as it is used by those they study and as it has been used within the traditions of scholarship. Superstition, the inscription rather than the beliefs and practices so inscribed, merits a critical reevaluation.

Within the traditionally relativist discipline of anthropology, the word is almost never used. Since Malinowski's (1954) ground-breaking original writing in the 1920s, anthropologists' informants have practiced "religion" or utilized the techniques of "magic," sacrificing buffaloes or holding long conversations with the dead because these things make sense by the logic of their own cosmologies and social systems. Ethnographers note in passing that missionaries, colonial officials, religious reformers, and all manner of nationalist movements have denigrated these same activities as superstition, often with little attention to the consequences of that denigration for those who are the subjects of study (some exceptions are cited in this essay). Anthropologists and other students of religion consider the term prejudicial and therefore wrong, and thus tend not to take it seriously when it crops up in local discourse. If, in common parlance, superstition is something that ignorant people (who are often women) practice, for scholars of comparative religion, superstition is a term that ignorant people use. When such people impinge upon the subjects of scholars' studies, either by hurling invective or by making religious policy, they should be included in the frame of these studies as ethnographic subjects themselves. The vehement iconoclasm of the Reformation is easily forgotten; indeed, contemporary Euro-American superstitions—knocking on wood, the pinch of spilled salt tossed over the shoulder—seem so inconsequential that it is difficult to imagine the mid-twentieth-century antisuperstition campaigns in China and the former Soviet Union that mustered the full power of the modern state to destroy sacred sites, ban ritual practices, and bring shamans and seers to account.

The term *superstition* has enjoyed a long currency in the West. With subtle shifts in meaning over time and space, it originally connoted improper, transgressive, or false beliefs in contrast to better, more orthodox religious ideas and practices. Orthodoxy has, in most places, been defined by male religious authorities. With the Enlightenment, superstition acquired its modern meaning as not merely bad religion but bad science, "misplaced assumptions about causality stemming from a faulty understanding of nature" (O'Neil, 1987, p. 165). In Michel de Certeau's (1984) terms, superstition became the residual category of an all-defining modernity; science would conquer this irrational hinterland of the imagination by assimilating it to the texts of anthropology, folklore, and history. De Certeau thus turns the tables upon a relativistic social science by casting it as a technique of domination, imposing its own alien understandings upon things otherwise strange and incomprehensible.

For eighteenth- and nineteenth-century European folklorists, who found their subjects close to home, the space between city and countryside signified the distance between the present and the past, between self and other just as ethnographers, who ventured farther afield, would characterize their subjects as "still" living in harmony with the dictates of age-old traditions (Fabian, 1983). Social historian Peter Burke (1978) writes that French intellectuals easily turned their interest from early accounts of Tahiti and the Iroquois to studies of their own peasants, "scarcely less distant from them (they thought) in beliefs and style of life. Interest did not necessarily imply sympathy, as the frequent use of terms like 'prejudice' or 'superstition' [applied to the peasants] make abundantly clear" (p. 14). Folklore studies followed in the wake of new nationalisms in colonial and postcolonial settings, promising the retrieval and preservation of ancient national traditions. The pervasive past tense of folklore fostered profound ambivalence toward its subjects, sources of both nostalgia and embarrassment. Distinctions between quaint custom and backward superstition were made with a glance over the shoulder toward the perceived expectations and attainments of the modern West. Writing of late-nineteenth- and early-twentieth-century Japan, Marilyn Ivy (1995) describes how "in the Meiji drive to incorporate diversity under state supervision, marginal sites and events were selectively either held up as paragons of Japanese culture—such as kabuki—or stigmatized, such as 'folk' practices associated with a backward countryside . . . [and] at odds with western mores and morality" (p. 33). Early-twentieth-century folklorists in China and Korea saw themselves as sifting the significant stuff of national culture from the chaff of dangerous superstition (Janelli, 1986; Linke, 1990; Hung, 1985).

Policy makers have been less ambivalent in their adversarial stance toward superstition. In Siberia in Soviet times, shamans were hunted down, imprisoned, and in many cases executed (Balzer, 1993, 1996; Vitebsky, 1995). The government of the People's Republic of China permits the practice of "feudal religion," meaning world religions and organized Taoism, but prohibits "feudal superstition," a term that by the Chinese state's definition embraces much of popular religion (Anagnost, 1987; Luo, 1991). Although this abhorrence is consistent with Marxist materialism, antisuperstition has been a consistent tenet of East Asian modernity as defined by new elites from both sides of the political spectrum (Cohen, 1991). Maoist excesses were preceded by the New Life Movement of Republican China, which countenanced attacks on local temples and on all manner of ritual specialists (Duara, 1991). In

Korea antisuperstition campaigns were carried out in the twilight years of the Chosôn Kingdom by the Japanese colonial government, which annexed it, and by regimes of the right and the left that came to govern the two halves of the peninsula after 1945 (Kendall, forthcoming). A similar story could be told in Vietnam (Luong, 1992; Malarney, 1993).

Religious organizations and movements have attempted to reform their practices along what they regard as modern and scientific lines. For Buddhist reformers in Thailand (Keyes, 1989) and Sri Lanka (Obeyesekere, 1991; Swearer, 1991), this has meant an emphasis on doctrine and a denigration of many ritual and divinatory practices as superstitious. Clifford Geertz (1973) describes the young Balinese of a generation past, engaged in discussions that would distill the sacred essence of their Hinduism from "customs performed out of blind habit and tradition" (p. 184). Years later, Jane Atkinson (1983) describes how, in response to the Indonesian state's stringent definition of modern, progressive, and legally permitted religion, the Wana of Sulawesi struggle to justify "pagan" practices that fall outside the state's definition of acceptability.

New middle classes, self-consciously modern as they define themselves against a recently abandoned rural way of life, often assume antisuperstition as an attribute of class identity. In urban India middle-class households adopt new "rationalized" devotional practices that dissociate them from rural "superstition" (Babb, 1990). In rural Nepal those whose occupations define them as agents of "development" are most likely to reject superstitious practices in order to assert their own claims to modernity (Pigg, 1996). From Cyprus (Argyrou, 1993) to Sri Lanka (Kapferer, 1983), the middle class's identification with science or with more rational-seeming religious practices has been interpreted as a means of asserting and naturalizing class domination.

Superstition is often gendered. Gillian Bennet (1987) notes the commonsense assumption that folklore is perpetuated by grannies steeped in quaint, nonsensical, and wrong-headed beliefs. Susan Sered (1990) provides examples from her own fieldwork among elderly Jews in Israel and her broad reading of comparative ethnography. In Korean discourse women's enthusiasm for shamanic activities is commonly attributed to their "backward" nature or relative "lack of education" (Kendall, 1985). The duplicitous female shaman is a common villain in works of modern Chinese fiction set in rural villages. Bennet argues that precisely because certain beliefs are stigmatized as irrational, it is difficult to know how prevalent they are. Conducting research in a London suburb among women who were neither badly educated nor geographically isolated nor eccentric, she found that belief in the supernatural was both pervasive and consistent with the women's gendered understandings of themselves and their society.

Like modernity, superstition has been a potent concept. That women's religious activities have so often been labeled as "superstitious" contributes to the notion that women are the backward elements of modernizing societies. But the values with which this term is invested are neither consistent nor immutable. Despite official disapprobation and past persecution, "superstitious" practices have emerged in post-Mao China as a dodge on the uncertainty of the marketplace. Shamans have become icons of ethnic identity in post-Soviet Siberia. In the Republic of Korea, where shamanic practices were long denigrated as superstition, they are now increasingly celebrated as "national culture." These processes also merit our attention insofar as women are often in the thick of them.

BIBLIOGRAPHY

Anagnost, Ann S. "Politics and Magic in Contemporary China." *Modern China* 13 (January 1987): 40–42.

Argyrou, Vassos. "Under a Spell: The Strategic Use of Magic in Greek Cypriot Society." *American Ethnologist* 20, no. 2 (1993): 256–271.

Atkinson, Jane Monnig. "Religions in Dialogue: The Construction of an Indonesian Minority Religion." *American Ethnologist* 10, no. 4 (1983): 684–696.

Babb, Allan. "New Media and Religious Change." *Items* 44, no. 4 (1990): 72–76.

Balzer, Marjorie Mandelstam. "Dilemmas of the Spirit: Religion and Atheism in the Yakut-Sakha Republic." In *Religious Policy in the Soviet Union.* Edited by S. Ramet. 1993.

———. "Flights of the Sacred: Symbolism and Theory in Siberian Shamanism." *American Anthropologist* 98, no. 2 (1996): 305–318.

Bennet, Gillian. *Traditions of Belief: Women and the Supernatural.* 1987.

Burke, Peter. *Popular Culture in Early Modern Europe.* 1978.

Certeau, Michel de. *The Practice of Everyday Life.* 1984.

Cohen, Myron L. "Being Chinese: The Peripheralization of Traditional Identity." *Daedalus* 120, no. 2 (1991): 113–134.

Duara, Prasenjit. "Knowledge and Power in the Discourse of Modernity: The Campaigns Against Popular Religion in Early Twentieth-Century China." *Journal of Asian Studies* 50, no. 1 (February 1991): 67–83.

Fabian, Johannes. *Time and the Other: How Anthropology Makes Its Object.* 1983.

Geertz, Clifford. *The Interpretation of Cultures: Selected Essays by Clifford Geertz.* 1973.

Hung, Chang-tai. *Going to the People: Chinese Intellectuals and Folk Literature 1918–1937.* 1985.

Ivy, Marilyn. *Discourses of the Vanishing: Modernity Phantasm Japan.* 1995.

Janelli, Roger L. "The Origins of Korean Folklore Scholarship." *Journal of American Folklore* 99, no. 391 (1986): 24–49.

Kapferer, Bruce. *A Celebration of Demons: Exorcism and the Aesthetics of Healing in Sri Lanka.* 1983.

Kendall, Laurel. *Shamans, Housewives, and Other Restless Spirits: Women in Korean Ritual Life.* 1985.

———. "Who Speaks for Korean Shamans When Shamans Speak of the Nation." In *Configuring Minority and Making Majorities: Composing the Nation in Japan, China, Korea, Fiji, Malaysia, Turkey, and the United States.* Edited by D. Gladney. Forthcoming.

Keyes, Charles F. "Buddhist Politics and Their Revolutionary Origins in Thailand." *International Political Science Review* 10, no. 2 (1989): 126.

Linke, Uli. "Folklore, Anthropology, and the Government of Social Life." *Comparative Studies of Society and History* 32, no. 1 (1990): 117–148.

Luo, Zhufeng, ed. *Religion under Socialism in China.* Translated by D. E. MacInnis and Zheng Xi'an. 1991.

Luong, Hy V. *Revolution in the Village: Tradition and Transformation in North Vietnam, 1925–1988.* 1992.

Malarney, Shaun Kingsley. "Ritual and Revolution in Vietnam." Ph.D. diss., University of Michigan, 1993.

Malinowski, Bronislaw. *Magic, Science and Religion: And Other Essays.* 1948. Reprint, 1954.

Obeyesekere, Gananath. "Buddhism and Conscience: An Exploratory Essay." *Daedalus* 120, no. 3 (Summer 1991): 219–239.

O'Neil, Mary R. "Superstition." In *The Encyclopedia of Religion.* Edited by M. Eliade. 1987.

Pigg, Stacy Leigh. "The Credible and the Credulous: The Question of 'Villagers' Beliefs' in Nepal." *Cultural Anthropology* 11, no. 2 (1996): 160–201.

Sered, Susan Starr. "Women, Religion, and Modernization: Tradition and Transformation among Elderly Jews in Israel." *American Anthropologist* 92 (1990): 306–318.

Swearer, Donald K. "Fundamentalistic Movements in Theravada Buddhism." In *Fundamentalists Observed.* Edited by Martin E. Marty and R. Scott Appleby. 1991.

Vitebsky, Piers. "From Cosmology to Environmentalism: Shamanism as Local Knowledge in a Global Setting." In *Counterworks: Managing the Diversity of Knowledge.* Edited by R. Fardon. 1995.

LAUREL KENDALL

Susanna

According to additions to the book of Daniel found in Greek translations of the Hebrew Bible, Susanna is a young Jewish woman of Babylon, the wife of Joakim. When she is falsely accused of adultery by two elders in the Jewish community, she is defended by the seer Daniel.

The story of Susanna begins by praising her beauty and her devotion to the biblical law of Moses. The former attribute engenders the initial crisis in the story: her beauty so attracts the two elders that they lust after her, even to the point of concealing themselves in her garden one day as she prepares to bathe. Once they reveal themselves, they require her to lie with them and threaten that if she refuses, they will bring a false accusation of adultery. Susanna's fidelity to Mosaic law determines her response to the elders: she refuses to violate the commandment requiring marital fidelity, even though she knows that if their false accusation holds, the punishment is death.

The descriptions of Susanna's trial again stress her piety, as she lifts her voice in prayer, after being found guilty, to ask God to deliver her. God responds by inciting the spirit of Daniel, who, although only a youth, earns the respect of the community. Daniel exposes the lie the accusing elders have told by questioning them separately about the kind of tree under which Susanna and her lover allegedly lay; when they give different responses, Susanna is vindicated and they are put to death.

BIBLIOGRAPHY

Moore, Carey A. *Daniel, Esther, and Jeremiah: The Additions.* Anchor Bible 44. 1977.

Susanna, depicted in an engraving c. 1802 (Historical Picture Archive/Corbis).

Nickelsburg, George W. E. "Susanna." In *Jewish Writings of the Second Temple Period: Apocrypha, Pseudepigrapha, Qumran Sectarian Writings, Philo, Josephus.* Compendia Rerum Iudaicarum ad Novum Testamentum 2. Edited by M. E. Stone. 1984.

———. "Susanna." In his *Jewish Literature Between the Bible and the Mishnah: A Historical and Literary Introduction.* 1981.

SUSAN ACKERMAN

Szold, Henrietta

Henrietta Szold (1860–1945), founder of Hadassah, was one of eight daughters of a prominent Baltimore Reform rabbi. After receiving an excellent Jewish as well as secular high school education, she became a teacher in a private high school, contributing her salary to her family like many other single, middle-class Jewish and non-Jewish women of her era.

Brilliant, erudite, and scholarly, Szold contributed articles to American Jewish publications, many of which were not taken seriously because she was female. She began her literary career as a volunteer on the editorial board of the Jewish Publication Society of America. After 1893 Szold served for twenty-three years as the paid literary secretary to the society, editing the American Jewish Yearbook and serving as proofreader, translator, and unacknowledged editor of many of the society's most distinguished publications. At the same time, Szold maintained her Zionist sympathies and her concern for Eastern European Jewish refugees.

Szold became the first woman to attend classes at the Jewish Theological Seminary in New York on condition she not request rabbinic ordination. There, she assumed editing tasks for Louis Ginzberg, a distinguished rabbinic scholar and professor at the seminary. The two shared a close friendship and working relationship for several years, which for Szold turned into a profound romantic attachment. When Ginzberg became engaged to a young woman he met in Europe, Szold broke off the relationship and went into a severe depression.

She recovered partly as a result of a trip to Israel in 1909. Appalled at the conditions suffered by the pioneers, when Szold returned to the United States she reorganized Hadassah Circle, a literary Zionist women's society. Under her direction, in 1912 Hadassah focused on meeting the health needs of Jewish settlers in Palestine; she oversaw much of the work herself. Eventually, the modest medical facilities expanded into Hadassah Hospital in Jerusalem.

In 1919 Szold accepted an invitation from the International Zionist commission to assume leadership of its medical unit in Palestine, though they refused to grant her a seat on the commission itself because she was female. Painfully aware of being snubbed by the Jewish leadership in Palestine because she was a woman, she boycotted the 1921 Zionist Congress when it became clear the leadership wanted to incorporate Hadassah's medical unit into another group so as to merge her position out of existence. Szold managed to keep her position.

Under Szold's leadership, Hadassah became one of the preeminent women's organizations in the United States. Hadassah harnessed the combined appeal to Jewish women of service, support of the Jewish people, and personal independence through a women's organization that was socially acceptable in American Jewish society.

As World War II loomed on the horizon, Szold organized Youth Aliyah to take refugee children to Israel and safety. After the war Youth Aliyah became the central vehicle for bringing child survivors of the Holocaust to a new life in Israel.

In these later years Szold was careful to maintain her independence as a woman. When her mother died, Szold rejected a male friend's offer to recite kaddish, the traditional memorial prayer, on Szold's behalf, as a woman, Szold was exempted from doing so. Szold asserted that Jewish law did not free women from positive duties when they were able to perform them.

BIBLIOGRAPHY

Baum, Charlotte, Paul Human, and Sonya Michel. *The Jewish Woman in America.* 1976.

Dash, Joan. *Summoned to Jerusalem: The Life of Henrietta Szold.* 1979.

Kuzmack, Linda Gordon. *Woman's Cause: The Jewish Woman's Movement in England and the United States, 1881–1933.* 1990.

LINDA GORDON KUZMACK

Taboos

Taboo is a means of instituting and maintaining a particular social order through appeal to supernatural sanction. Generally defined as a prohibition whose infringement results in a state of defilement or danger, taboo is often understood as a dynamic of purity and pollution. Its power is said to be mitigated through religious rites and "correct" observance. Etymologically, the term derives from the Tongan *tabu*, a local variant of the more general Polynesian *tapu*. It was introduced into English by Captain James Cook (1777) and subsequently was adopted by theorists, from Sigmund Freud to Émile Durkheim, to describe the fear or awe-inspired prohibitions that characterize "primitive" life, the unconscious mind, or the religious mentality.

The most prominent taboos affecting women can be categorized into those that establish kin units; those that surround life passage events, especially childbirth and death; and those that focus on bodily fluids. Kin relation taboos restrict social contact between kinspeople brought into contact through marriage. The incest taboo is the most prominent of this type of taboo.

Life passage taboos include prohibitions on using the name of the deceased; seclusion; restrictions on washing and dress; as well as prohibitions on subsistence or pleasurable activities during mourning. Postpartum women are often viewed as particularly polluted and are the focus of taboos necessitating ritual seclusion or ritual immersion before they can be reincorporated into society.

Bodily fluids are another predominant source of taboos. Menstruation often occasions seclusion, avoidance of certain activities and persons, and extensive rites of purification. Breast milk, sexual fluids, urine, and feces may also be the focus of similar purity rituals.

In the comparative study of religion and culture, the concept of taboo traditionally has been applied to certain classes of persons, objects, or activities invested with a power that is at once sacred, dangerous, and contagious. Some taboo items are held to be sacred (shrines, priests, gods, rulers), others ritually impure (menstrual blood, saliva, urine, feces), and others transitional and highly dangerous (childbirth, death, puberty). Thus, in many societies, menstruating women are believed to be highly polluting and are prohibited from contact with men and male property, as well as being excluded from religious rituals and spaces. Among rural Muslims, for example, a menstruating woman may not touch the Qur'an, enter a mosque, or participate in religious observances such as the fast of Ramadan, nor can she engage in sexual relations.

The work of Mary Douglas (1966) suggests that taboo is a social construct rather than a fundamental category of religious experience. Within a culturally specific symbolic order, taboos mark boundaries and determine limits. They function to identify the anomalous, defining and protecting the social order from the threat constituted by those things that do not fit in. In this way they serve to maintain the status quo and are significant in the construction and maintenance of gendered systems. This approach helps explain, for example, the elaborate linguistic taboos that affect Mongolian women, who are forbidden to use the names of their husbands' older male kin. In patrilineal Mongolian culture, this taboo effectively marks the daughter-in-law as anomalous, a part of her husband's lineage through marriage, but not really of it.

Recent feminist scholarship demonstrates the need for close attention to local context, and indicates that the predominant approach to menstrual taboos has relied upon a male-dominated view of society, obtained by and from male anthropologists and informants, which sees women as passive and that obscures the potential ambivalence of taboo. For example, menstrual blood may not be coded as impure in all societies, as, for instance, among certain Native American groups, who believed its flow purified a woman's womb. Alternatively, women excluded from some activities during menstruation may utilize this opportunity to develop women's community or break from the demands of daily life.

BIBLIOGRAPHY

Although there are very few book-length works dealing exclusively with the subject of women and taboo, many anthropologists, area specialists, and historians of religion have considered taboo as part of larger religious and cultural systems that construct norms for women's bodies, roles, capabilities, activities, and privileges within society. In addition to the works cited below, Carol Delaney's *The Seed and the Soil: Gender and Cosmology in Turkish Village Society* (1991) and Janice Boddy's *Wombs and Alien Spirits: Women, Men and the Zar Cult in Northern Sudan* (1989) furnish detailed, culturally specific, and theoretically sophisticated accounts of the influence of religion, including taboo beliefs, on gender and sexuality in the context of women's lives.

Buckley, Thomas, and Alma Gottlieb, eds. *Blood Magic: The Anthropology of Menstruation.* 1988. A rich compilation of ethnographically detailed essays dealing with menstrual taboos in various religions and cultures. The editors have written a thoughtful introductory chapter that critiques traditional approaches to taboo and explores the significance of menstruation both in women's lives and in anthropological theory.

Cook, James, and J. King. *A Voyage to the Pacific Ocean, 1776–80.* 1784. Cook's account is interesting for the light it sheds on the origins of taboo theory, as well as for the role it played as a source for much early anthropological work on so-called primitive peoples.

Culpepper, Emily. "Zorastrian Menstruation Taboos: A Women's Studies Perspective." In *Women and Religion.* Edited by Judith Plaskow and Joan Arnold. Rev. ed., 1974. A concise, invaluable account of Zoroastrian menstrual taboos.

Douglas, Mary. *Purity and Danger.* 1966. A seminal work on purity and pollution beliefs as both mechanisms and symbols of social order. Douglas's theoretical insights into the role of anomaly and ambiguity have been important for feminist scholars concerned with the marginalization of women.

Durkheim, Émile. *The Elementary Forms of the Religious Life.* 1915. In this classic work, Durkheim locates taboo within a larger group of rites whose function is to separate the realm of the sacred from that of the profane. This and other insights proved very important for later social theory, including the work of Mary Douglas.

Humphrey, Caroline. "Women, Taboo and the Suppression of Attention." In *Defining Females: The Nature of Women in Society.* Edited by Shirley Ardener. Rev. ed., 1993. Humphrey documents and analyzes linguistic taboos in Mongolia, focusing on those that pertain to daughters-in-law and demonstrating that they function to mark these women as ambiguous in Mongolian patrilineal society.

See also **Blood; Body; Menstruation.**

KELLY E. HAYES

Tantra

The term *tantra* refers to a wide range of religious paths that developed mainly in northwestern (Kashmir) and northeastern (Bengal) India, perhaps as early as the third century C.E. among Buddhists, Hindus, and Jains, though it took several centuries to achieve widespread influence. Although its earliest history is unclear, we do know that tantra drew extensively on preexisting traditions such as yoga and Vedic sacrifice, among others. In addition to conferring divine or magical powers on its adepts, it is described as a fast path to enlightenment (in a single lifetime), and one of its essential features is an abundance of female symbolism. These include divine females such as Shakti, Kālī, Tārā, Vajrayoginī, and various *ḍākinīs* and *yoginīs* usually depicted in their fierce forms, as well as an emphasis on the *piṭhas* (centers of goddess worship) created when pieces of the goddess Sati's dead body fell off as Siva, dancing madly in his grief, carried her on his head (Sircar, 1972). Additionally, there is the symbolic or actual use of menstrual blood (and semen) in rituals and the valorization of female-identified substances such as primal matter (*prakriti*), attributes such as wisdom (*prajñā*), and cosmic energy (*shakti*). These last two are also the terms used for goddesses who are worshiped as the consort (Hindu: *shakti*; Buddhist: *prajñā*) of a male god or celestial Buddha.

Tantra spread throughout South, Southeast, Central, and East Asia and survives today among Buddhists in the Himalayan countries of Tibet, Nepal, and Bhutan;

in Japan in the Shingon and Tendai schools of Buddhism; among exiled Tibetans everywhere; and among Hindu groups, especially in the Indian states of Bengal, Orissa, and Kerala, as well as in Nepal and Indonesia. In the Hindu context there are three main branches: Śaiva, Vaiṣṇava, and Śākta, focusing respectively on Śiva, Vishnu/Krishna, and the Goddess (Devī) under various names. The tantric Bāuls of India and Bangladesh respectively emphasize Hindu and Muslim forms of devotion. Today both Buddhist and Hindu tantric practices are flourishing in North America and Europe.

Both texts (the Tantras) and practices (*sādhanas*) are difficult to access, let alone understand, because these teachings are kept secret and require complete dependence on a guru for preliminary training followed by initiation, typically by conferring a mantra. Tantric practice utilizes the human body—indeed valorizes it as the means to salvation, especially through mastery of a secondary bodily system, often termed the "subtle body." The importance of visualization in tantric practice has fostered a rich legacy of tantric art, including the geometrical designs of mandalas and *yantras* and the temples of major sites such as Khajuraho in India, well known for its highly erotic elements.

Central to tantric ritual are the "five m's" (*pāncamakāra*): wine, meat, fish, parched grain, and sexual union (respectively, in Sanskrit, *madya*, *māṃsa*, *matsya*, mudra, and *maithuna*). The first four are described as aphrodisiacs and lead up to the fifth, actual or symbolic sexual union. Theoretically, the right-handed path (*dakṣiṇācār*) uses substitutes for the first four and visualizes the fifth, sexual union, while the left-handed path (*vāmācār*) imbibes these substances and involves ritual sexual intercourse. In point of fact, though, left-handed practice also frequently uses substitutes and visualization.

The five m's are forbidden to orthodox Hindus because they are polluting, but the tantric practitioner, Buddhist or Hindu, ritually uses these forbidden substances to get beyond the concepts of good and evil, forbidden and allowed, and to achieve an experience of the ultimate union of all opposites, even of female and male. In both Hindu and Buddhist Tantra, reality is one, but it is understood through a process of conceptual and intuitive polarization, or duality, symbolized in terms of gender. For instance, in Hinduism Śiva is conceptualized as passive intelligence while *shakti* (energy) is active primal matter; from these two everything else in the universe arises, yet they are really one. In Buddhism the gender is reversed into passive feminine *prajñā* (wisdom) and active male *upāya* (skillful means).

A tantric painting depicts Lha-Mo, protector of the faith, riding her mule. She wears a necklace of bones and is seen devouring brains. **Gompa de Spituk, Ladakh, India** (Charles & Josette Lenars/Corbis).

In both traditions, though, these poles merge philosophically: through the doctrine of the oneness of the universe, experientially through ritual practices (*sādhanas*), and visually through representations of divine sexual union. Through visualization practices during rituals or meditation the adept seeks to merge with the deities, or the Buddhas, and their consorts. So tantric practice can be theistic and nondualistic, and it stresses the essential divinity of humanity.

The distinction of a left-handed and right-handed path indicates that sexuality and ritual intercourse are central yet often absent. Such is also the case with women's participation. The vast majority of practitioners were and remain men; the Tantras specifically address men as the active ritual participants, referring to women solely as consorts to men. Ritually, women participants are often only passive partners for male adepts when not actually excluded from parts of the ritual (Bharati, 1975), or completely absent, as in many right-handed practices where the female is only visualized. In many texts, when ritual sex does occur, the man is instructed not to ejaculate; instead the goal is to reverse the flow of semen and in some cases to absorb the female's sexual fluids, thus enhancing the male's spiritual powers and denying the female any share of the spiritual power thought to be contained in his semen (Hayes, 1995). In other words, ritually speaking, actual women are frequently passive, secondary, or absent, whereas symbolic women (e.g., goddesses), although they may be temperamentally active, will ultimately be absorbed back into the Absolute. Tantra is essentially a theoretical valorization of the feminine, and as such has had very little impact on the lives of the vast majority of Buddhist and Hindu women.

Recent feminist appropriations of Tantra, especially those of Miranda Shaw and Rita Gross, suggest it is a liberating spiritual path for Western women; this may very well be, especially for women who are comfortable with vivid heterosexual imagery. However, although some exceptional women have achieved prominence in various tantric traditions, theoretical egalitarianism in terms of caste and sex has rarely escaped into social reality. Whether this will be changed by Western converts remains to be seen.

BIBLIOGRAPHY

Beyer, Stephan. *The Cult of Tārā: Magic and Ritual in Tibet.* 1978.

Bharati, Agehananda. *The Tantric Tradition.* 1965. Reprint, 1975. Chap. 9 has a detailed outline of a left-handed practice.

Dasgupta, S. *Obscure Religious Cults.* Calcutta, 1969.

Desai, Devangana. *Erotic Sculptures of India: A Socio-Cultural Study.* New Delhi, 1979.

Dimock, E. C. *The Place of the Hidden Moon: Erotic Mysticism in Vaiṣṇava Sahajiyā Cult of Bengal.* 1966. A good introduction to an important form of Hindu Tantra, including some discussion of women.

Eliade, Mircea. *Yoga: Immortality and Freedom.* 1954; 2d ed., 1969. See esp. chaps. 6, 7, and 8.

Gellner, David N. *Monk, Householder and Tantric Priest: Newar Buddhism and Its Hierarchy of Ritual.* 1992. A useful and rich study of tantric Buddhism in Nepal. See esp. pp. 273–281 for a detailed outline of the initiation ceremony of female and male lay practitioners led by a guru and his wife.

Gross, Rita. *Buddhism After Patriarchy: A Feminist History, Analysis, and Reconstruction of Buddhism.* 1993.

Hayes, Glen A. "The Vaiṣṇava Sahajiyā Traditions of Medieval Bengal." In *Religions of India in Practice.* Edited by Donald S. Lopez Jr. 1995.

Jhavery, Mohanlal B. *Comparative and Critical Study of Mantraśāstra.* Ahmedabad, 1944. A study of Jain Tantra.

Klein, Anne Carolyn. *Meeting the Great Bliss Queen: Buddhists, Feminists and the Art of the Self.* 1995. Discusses feminist issues in relation to tantric Buddhism.

Lauf, Detlef Ingo. *Tibetan Sacred Art: The Heritage of Tantra.* 1976.

Lopez Jr., Donald S., ed. *Religions of Tibet in Practice.* 1997. See pp. 14–18 for an accessible introduction to tantric Buddhist visualization practices.

McDaniel, June. *The Madness of the Saints: Ecstatic Religion in Bengal.* 1989.

Mookerjee, Ajit. *Tantra Art.* Basel, 1972.

Nālandā Translation Committee. "The Life of Tilopa." In *Religions of Tibet in Practice.* Edited by Donald S. Lopez Jr. Particularly noteworthy for its exposition of Vajrayoginī and other female divinities, as well as tantric Buddhist practices.

Sircar, D. C. *Śakta Pithas.* New Delhi, 1972. Contains a list of the centers of goddess worship.

Salomon, Carol. "Bāul Songs." In *Religions of India in Practice.* Edited by Donald S. Lopez Jr.

Shaw, Miranda. *Passionate Enlightenment: Women in Tantric Buddhism.* 1994.

TEXTS ON WOMEN AND TANTRA

Biographies of important Tibetan Buddhist female practitioners are *Sky Dancer: The Secret Life and Songs of the Lady Yeshe Tsogyel*, translated by Keith Dowman (1984); Jérôme Edou, *Machig Labdrön and the Foundations of Chöd* (1996); Tsultrim Alione, *Women of Wisdom* (1984); Reginald Ray, "Accomplished Women in Tantric Buddhism of Medieval India and Tibet," in *Unspoken Worlds: Women's Religious Lives in Non-Western Cultures*, edited by Nancy A. Falk and Rita M. Gross (1980). Life stories of Indian Buddhist women are contained in Shaw, *Passionate Enlightenment*, and in James B. Robinson, trans., *Buddha's Lions: The Lives of the Eighty-Four Siddhas* (1979) (four of the eighty-four siddhas are women); those of Hindu tantric women are in McDaniel. Sanjukta Gupta, "Women in the Śaiva/Śākta Ethos," in *Roles and Rituals for Hindu Women*, edited by Julia Leslie (1991), discusses tantric elements in the lives of six Hindu women saints usually defined as Bhaktis. This essay is also notable for distinguishing Shakti in Śaiva and Vaiṣṇava contexts. Tsang Nyön Heruka, *The Life of Marpa the Translator*, translated by the Nālandā Translation Committee (1982), especially the India sections, describes a few Buddhist female practitioners and teachers.

Michael R. Allen, *The Cult of Kumari: Virgin Worship in Nepal* (Kathmandu, 1992), concentrates on the "living goddesses," premenstrual girls who are often the focus of both Hindu and Buddhist tantric rites; Lynn Bennett, *Dangerous Wives and Sacred Sisters: The Social and Symbolic Roles of High-Caste Women in Nepal* (1983), has a particularly revealing chapter on gender differences in Hindu goddess worship in tantric and nontantric rites. David Kinsley, *Tantric Visions of the Divine Feminine: The Ten Mahāvidyās* (1997), focuses on ten important tantric Hindu goddess. James H. Sanford, "The Abominable Tachikawa Skull Ritual," *Monumenta Nipponica* 46, no. 1 (Spring 1991): 1–20, describes a Japanese Buddhist tantric rite that brings out some of the actual and symbolic appropriations of women. David Gordon White, *The Alchemical Body: Siddha Traditions in Medieval India* (1996), extensively treats the sexual symbolism of Tantra and the rise of the feminine.

SERINITY YOUNG

Taoism

An Overview

Taoism is a complex component of traditional Chinese civilization. Formed from many strands originating in various regions, periods, and social contexts, Taoism developed into a rich mixture of religious ideals and practices. Westerners, influenced by Confucian informants hostile to Taoism, have usually deeply misunderstood it. Many, for instance, have dismissed it as antithetical to the Enlightenment mentality—that is, as a ritualistic, priestly religion embodying all the abhorred elements of Catholicism and offering little to the "enlightened" intellectual in search of "Truth." Protestant missionaries valued only two ancient texts—the *Daode jing* (*Tao te ching*, also called the *Laozi* or *Lao-tzu*) and the *Zhuangzi* (*Chuang-tzu*)—and persuaded virtually all subsequent Westerners that later elements of Taoism were degenerate superstition. In the process, moderns—Western and Asian alike—were generally denied accurate knowledge of a fascinating religious tradition, in which women often played significant roles.

To appreciate Taoism, one must recognize carefully the historical phases and segments of the religion. In some, women not only played active roles but were officially welcomed into leadership roles. In others, women's roles were quite limited, although the pertinent practices remained fully accessible. Unfortunately, it is only for the last generation or two that scholars, Asian or Western, have taken Taoism seriously enough to do the necessary historical or textual research; much remains unknown, and the following assessment may be radically affected by future discoveries.

CLASSICAL TAOISM

It is helpful to distinguish three major phases in the evolution of Taoism: 1) Classical Taoism (fl. fourth–first century B.C.E.), 2) Traditional Taoism (fl. second–tenth century C.E.), and 3) New Taoism (fl. tenth century–present). "Classical Taoism" refers to the ideas found in several ancient texts. Recent research suggests that there may have been local groups engaged in "bio-spiritual" practices, for example, the cultivation of an ambient life-energy called *qi* (*ch'i*). Such practices are outlined in a little-known text called the *Neiye* (fourth–century B.C.E.) and obliquely mentioned in the *Laozi* and *Zhuangzi*. These practices, which endured in Taoism down to present times, are clearly accessible to both genders, though the sparse records of classical times mention no women practitioners.

The *Zhuangzi* originated in the musings of Zhuang Zhou, a fourth-century B.C.E. intellectual, and was expanded and edited by many later hands. In its present form (edited 300 C.E.), it deemphasizes the practices commended in the *Neiye*. Instead, it works to stimulate new perspectives on reality by undermining common assumptions and playfully twisting the intellect.

The third text of Classical Taoism, the celebrated *Daode jing*, may have originated in local traditions of the southern nation of Chu (Ch'u). Apparently, the original oral teachings of the elders (*laozi / lao-tzu*) of Chu urged a return to "feminine" behaviors—that is, to a quiet and unassertive life of selfless beneficence. Several passages characterize such ideals in motherly images. Sometime around 300 B.C.E., an unknown writer (presumably male) brought the traditions of his land's elders (*laozi*) to the northern cities where intellectuals were debating social and political issues. Apparently inspired by the *Neiye*, he wove the oral traditions of his ancestors together with novel teachings to create an ambiguous text that presented ideas designed to compete with the teachings of Confucianism and other schools. Though anonymous, it was soon read as the product of a man named "Laozi," and became one of the most widely read texts of Chinese civilization.

TRADITIONAL TAOISM

After the disappearance of the community that produced the *Neiye*, the cultivation of *qi* reappeared as an ideal in a text called the *Taiping jing* (second century

A fourteenth-century painting depicts the Chinese philosophers Laozi (left) and Confucius nurturing the infant Sakayumi, the future Buddha (The British Museum).

C.E. with later additions). Compiled from many different traditions, it envisioned a utopian society of Grand Tranquility, in which people of all elements of society, led by a Heavenly Master (*tianshi*), would cooperate to restore the harmonious life attributed to the halcyon days of legendary kings. These ideas helped inspire new popular movements, including one led by a man who claimed to be that Heavenly Master. His Tianshi (T'ien-shih) movement became the starting point for what later became so-called organized Taoism.

The Tianshi priesthood included women on a basis that was explicitly equal with men and reserved the highest offices for married persons. One fifth-century Tianshi text outlines the religious roles and responsibilities for laywomen in five specific life-situations: 1) unmarried daughters who live at home, 2) unmarried daughters who leave home (i.e., young women who wish to enter the religious life rather than marry), 3) married women, 4) single women, and 5) daughters who return to live at home. (The latter two categories included widows and estranged wives.) In each situation, the Taoist woman vows to be conscientious and to take a religious teacher, who could be either male or female (though male masters who lived alone were not permitted to accept female disciples). Under some circumstances, a married woman could take a different teacher from her husband's, but each was to take a religious surname (i.e., relinquish their family surname).

It is not yet known how much leadership women provided in the Tianshi organization. But one Tianshi woman cleric, Wei Huacun (Wei Hua-ts'un, 251–334), gained posthumous fame in a new movement of the fourth century called Shangqing Taoism. Revelations from Lady Wei and other male and female Perfected Ones told of a heavenly realm known as Shangqing. They taught mortals how to purify themselves through visualizational meditation, including the projection of one's own *qi*-energy into a visualized goddess, such as the Mysterious Woman of the Nine Heavens. Some Shangqing leaders also incorporated the alien practice of alchemy and transformed it from a pursuit of physical transmutation into a process of spiritual purification. In other periods, historical texts mention a few women as "alchemists," though their relationship to Taoist organizations is very dubious.

It is also unclear whether any women took part in the slightly later movement called Lingbao, which taught that a saving deity provided the opportunity for mortals to assimilate themselves to the cosmic reality called Tao through recitation of powerful scriptures. Though the Lingbao founders, like the Shangqing leaders, were well-educated aristocrats, their ideal was a universal salvation. They therefore developed formal liturgies to be performed by priests on behalf of all members of society. The Lingbao ideal of inclusiveness led one leader, Lu Xiujing (Lu Hsiu-ching, fifth century), to assemble a collection of all the writings of Shangqing, Lingbao, and other related traditions. It became the forerunner of the *Daozang* (*Tao-tsang*), the 5,305-volume "Taoist Canon" compiled in the fifteenth century. Through the efforts of people like Lu, a sense of Taoist identity began to develop, resulting in an ecumenical organization called *Daojiao* (*Tao-chiao*)—the term Taoists use for their own tradition.

For the next five hundred years or so, male and female priests (*daoshi* / *tao-shih*), based at abbeys (*guan* /

kuan), lived the spiritual life through self-cultivation and liturgy, and enjoyed the respect and sponsorship of emperors, aristocrats, and cultural elite. During the high Tang dynasty (c. 700), imperial princesses underwent ordination as priestesses, and women clerics of more obscure origin sometimes earned the admiration of local and imperial officials by activities such as restoring lost shrines. During the same period, poets pondered the meaning of the goddess Xiwangmu (Hsi Wang Mu—the Queen Mother of the West), whom Taoists conceived as the deity who controls access to "transcendence"—the spiritual state that transcends life in the mortal world. Though honored by men and women alike, Xiwangmu played a special role as patron of women who renounced the traditional roles of wife and mother. Medieval women often felt free to disregard social convention and pursue the religious life, both as Buddhist nuns and as Taoist priestesses. Also, some pursued, and reportedly achieved, the supreme goal of transcendence, through a variety of practices, such as meditating, ingesting supernal essences, and performing altruistic deeds.

The culmination of Traditional Taoism came in the writings of the court historian Du Guangting (Tu Kuang-t'ing, 850–933). Among his works is a collection of accounts of Taoist goddesses and exemplary women, the *Yongcheng jixian lu* / *Yung-ch'eng chi-hsien lu* ("Records of the Assembled Transcendents of the Fortified Walled City.") But political and social change during the subsequent Sung dynasty led to the eclipse of the broad-based Daojiao, and a consequent diminution of women's roles.

NEW TAOISM

Beginning around the tenth century C.E., a series of historical developments led to several new movements. Some scholars have begun to refer to these new movements collectively as New Taoism, though actually they fall into two broad groups. Among the new liturgical traditions was Qingwei Taoism, founded by a little-known young woman, Zu Shu (Tsu Shu), around 900. Its "thunder rites" (*lei-fa*) empower a priest to heal, banish evil influences, and bless children.

In the fourteenth century invading Mongol emperors gave formal jurisdiction over all Taoists to another new liturgical organization called Zhengyi (Cheng-i), which claimed (baselessly, it now seems) to continue the earlier Tianshi organization. Nineteenth-century Protestant interpreters became obsessed with the notion that Zhengyi leaders represented "Taoist popes," thereby equating Taoist religion with the alleged evils of Catholicism. Zhengyi priests preserve many of the earlier liturgies and provide public service through healing

rituals and exorcism. Their "Southern Taoism" remains strong in Taiwan, and a few Western men have been ordained as Zhengyi priests. Women are banned from the sacred space ritually created by the priest and play a very marginal role in the tradition.

Other new movements of the early modern era preserve the other side of Taoist religious life—the personal pursuit of spiritual perfection. These movements arose in North China, attracted followers from all levels of society, and stressed the harmony of the Three Teachings—Confucianism, Buddhism, and Taoism—especially their common interest in self-perfection through morality, meditation, and spiritual insight. One such movement was Quanzhen / Ch'üan-chen (Integral Perfection) Taoism, founded by a twelfth-century scholar named Wang Zhe / Wang Che (also called Wang Chongyang / Wang Ch'ung-yang). Wang's seven famous disciples included a woman, Sun Buer (Sun Pu-erh). Though it allows for individual variation, Quanzhen Taoism, a monastic tradition, assumes the value of commitment to moral and spiritual discipline in pursuit of spiritual perfection. Though it is generally unknown to Westerners, Quanzhen Taoism (sometimes called Northern Taoism) endures today, based at the White Cloud Abbey in Beijing. Women remain active in Quanzhen practice.

WOMEN IN TAOISM

The foregoing data demonstrates that women had a notable presence in the Taoist tradition, but generally became more marginalized in later ages. We know nothing for certain about women's participation in Classical Taoism; we know only that they were never explicitly excluded, and that the ideals and practices involved would seem to have been accessible to members of either gender. In Traditional Taoism, on the other hand, women were from the outset assumed to be equal participants, though few are known to have participated in the Shangqing or Lingbao movements. Once Taoism came to take on a sense of common unity in the fifth century, women clerics officially held the same title as men's, though they apparently took part in fewer numbers. Not only are there relatively few Taoist priestesses known by name, but women's religious establishments were fewer. In 739, for instance, there were reportedly 550 abbeys for women, compared to 1,137 for men. Assuredly, women entered the religious life in smaller numbers because society expected them to confine themselves to domestic roles. But the acceptance of exceptional women was apparently far greater in medieval times, when Traditional Taoism flourished, than in later centuries. Over time, the number of women Taoists declined sharply. In the year 1077, for instance, there were only some 700 ordained Taoist women, compared to 18,500 men. By the year 1677 there were no women recognized as priests, and reports of life in the White Cloud Abbey from the mid-twentieth century mention no women at all. In the 1980s, however, travelers reported having met women practitioners at temples in Sichuan and throughout the Chinese countryside, sometimes in positions of monastic authority.

The reason for the diminishing roles of women had to do not with any attitudinal changes among Taoists but rather with the broader social changes in late imperial and modern China: after the Mongol conquest, the government became more authoritarian and utilized Neo-Confucian ideology to indoctrinate society with an ethos of obedience to authority. Women throughout Chinese society were subjected to increasing restrictions, and eventually those changes left little of the opportunity that Taoism had provided for women of earlier ages.

ACCESSIBILITY OF THE SPIRITUAL LIFE

Taoist concepts of the spiritual goal, and of the processes that lead to its achievement, contain little that is gender-specific, in any segment of the tradition. In general, the goal of the Taoist life is to ascend to a more exalted spiritual state called "transcendence" (often misleadingly called "immortality"). Taoist texts, and Chinese literature more generally, are replete with accounts of both female and male transcendents (*xian, hsein*), demonstrating to both genders that the goal of the religious life can be achieved by dedicated women as well as by men. Also, texts of Traditional Taoism featured female divinities (including mortal women who had ascended) as teachers and coparticipants in the processes of self-cultivation.

There is no practice shared by all forms of Taoism. In fact, the revealing seventeenth-century novel *Qizhen zhuan* (*Ch'i-chen chuan*) teaches a variety of methods of self-cultivation, never attempting to establish any as inherently preferable. Most are methods of meditation, particularly in terms of what Westerners call Inner Alchemy. This was actually a system of spiritual refinement through meditation, a pursuit of reunion with the Tao that was sometimes expressed in metaphors drawn from the ancient teaching of operative alchemy ("External Alchemy"). In the *Qizhen zhuan*, such practices were sometimes expressed in Neo-Confucian terms—that is, as cultivating the true heart/mind (*hsin*) or the "original nature" (*hsing*). More often, they were expressed in terms of the ancient practice of cultivating

qi, working to preserve and replenish one's inherent store of "vital essence" (*jing*) to achieve "spiritual consciousness" (*shen*).

Some moderns have become obsessed with the notion that such processes involved sexuality, because in imperial China the concern with preserving "vital essence" was appropriated by some non-Taoist writers concerned with enhancing healthy sexuality: they simplistically identified the "vital essence" with semen. If such had indeed been Taoist practice, it would naturally have been inaccessible to women. But in fact, classical Taoist texts show no trace of sexual ideas, and texts from all later segments of Taoism occasionally warned against seeing self-cultivation in sexual terms: all authentic Taoist practices actually involve the refinement of biospiritual energies and the elevation of personal awareness. Though men apparently participated in much greater numbers, Taoists always seem to have assumed that the religious life is essentially the same for women and men alike.

BIBLIOGRAPHY

The serious study of Taoism did not get under way until the 1970s, so little published before 1978 is reliable. The following works are generally sound.

Benn, Charles D. *The Cavern-Mystery Transmission: A Taoist Ordination Rite of* A.D. *711.* 1991. A study of the rituals of investiture employed in Taoism's heyday, the Tang dynasty, focusing on the ordination of two imperial princesses.

Berling, Judith A. *The Syncretic Religion of Lin Chao-en.* 1980. Focuses on a sixteenth-century "syncretist"; incudes a comprehensible exposition of the methods and symbols of the Inner Alchemy meditative system.

Boltz, Judith M. *A Survey of Taoist Literature: Tenth to Seventeenth Centuries.* 1987. An expert analysis of the texts of many forms of New Taoism, including rare information on women leaders like Zu Shu and Sun Buer.

Cahill, Suzanne. "Marriages Made in Heaven." *T'ang Studies* 10–11 (1992–1993): 111–122. A translation of twelve medieval Taoist songs that celebrate marriage and give that institution "a Taoist meaning and purpose" for both partners.

———. "Practice Makes Perfect: Paths to Transcendence for Women in Medieval China." *Taoist Resources* 2, no. 2 (1990): 23–42. An indispensable study of selected materials from Du Guangting's *Yongcheng jixian lu.*

———. *Transcendence and Divine Passion: The Queen Mother of the West in Medieval China.* 1993. A definitive exploration of centuries of literary and religious traditions about the goddess Xiwangmu. Bibliography lists many important studies of related topics by Cahill and others.

Graham, A. C., trans. *Chuang-tzu: The Seven Inner Chapters and Other Writings from the Book of Chuang-tzu.* 1981. The best available translation of a well-known text of classical Taoism.

Henricks, Robert G., trans. *Lao-zu Te-Tao Ching.* 1989. The best available translation of the most famous Taoist text, based on the manuscripts discovered at Mawangdui in the late 1970s.

Kirkland, Russell. "Huang Ling-wei: A Taoist Priestess in T'ang China." *Journal of Chinese Religions* 19 (1991): 47–73. A thorough analysis of two medieval texts on a little-known woman cleric (c. 700), who won renown by restoring a shrine to Lady Wei.

Kohn, Livia. *The Taoist Experience: An Anthology.* 1993. A good collection of texts heretofore accessible only to specialists. One (#28) is attributed to a female Perfected One. In another (#35) the Queen Mother instructs in achieving union with a divine Jade Maiden; note that the interaction there, though presented in mildly erotic terms, is a meditative process of visualizing an exchange of energies, not a physical act involving a human couple.

Kroll, Paul W. "Seduction Songs of One of the Perfected." In *Religions of China in Practice* (1996). Edited by Donald S. Lopez Jr. Nine poems by Lady Youying, one of the celestial Perfected Ones who revealed the sacred materials of Shangqing Taoism. Youying's poems "aim to lure [the recipient] on to a mystical union with her."

Overmyer, Daniel. "Women in Chinese Religion: Submission, Struggle, Transcendence." In *From Benares to Beijing: Essays on Buddhism and Chinese Religion in Honour of Prof. Jan Yün-hua.* Edited by Koichi Shinohara and Gregory Schopen. 1991. A thorough and well-documented study by a leading expert in Chinese religions. Includes extracts from several Tianshi texts concerning women. Highly recommended.

Robinet, Isabelle. *Taoism: Growth of a Religion.* 1997. The most thorough historical introduction to Taoism by a well-informed specialist. Unfortunately, it has little to say about Taoism after about the twelfth century.

———. *Taoist Meditation.* Translated by Julian Pas and Norman Girardot. 1993. An exploration of themes in Later Taoism, focusing on Shangqing texts.

Roth, Harold . "The Inner Cultivation Tradition of Early Daoism." In *Religions of China in Practice* (1996). Edited by Donald S. Lopez Jr.

———. "Psychology and Self-Cultivation in Early Taoistic Thought." *Harvard Journal of Asiatic Studies* 51 (1991): 599–650. These two studies introduce the self-cultivation practices of Classical Taoism, as presented in long-neglected texts like the *Neiye.* Vital for correcting overemphasis on *Lao-tzu* and *Chuang-tzu.*

Schafer, Edward H. "The Capeline Cantos: Verses on the Divine Loves of Taoist Priestesses." *Asiatische Studien* 32 (1978): 5–65. Schafer pioneered the study of women and goddesses in Taoism through meticulous analysis of long-neglected texts in the *Daozang.* In addition, both he and his successor, Suzanne Cahill, have translated numerous poems by medieval women Taoists. Since few other texts were composed by women, such verses give us our most direct glimpse into their lives.

———. "The Jade Woman of Greatest Mystery." *History of Religions* 17 (1978): 387–398. A reliable exposition of another Shangqing text on a meditative technique for a "mystical marriage" between a male practitioner and a female celestial being.

Schipper, Kristofer. *The Taoist Body.* Translated by Karen C. Duval. 1994. A misleadingly titled story of themes in Taoist history, by a respected scholar who is also a Zhengyi priest. Not updated since its 1982 French publication, so now fairly outdated.

Seidel, Anna. "Taoism: The Unofficial High Religion of China." *Taoist Resources* 7, no. 2 (1997): 39–72. The final word by one of the scholars who established the modern study of Taoism.

Sivin, Nathan. "On the Word 'Taoist' as a Source of Perplexity." *History of Religions* 17 (1978): 303–331. An essential discussion of the concept of "Taoism," vital for distinguishing elements of authentic Taoism from other phenomena that have mistakenly been associated with it in the popular mind, in both Asia and the West.

Wong, Eva, trans. *Seven Taoist Masters: A Folk Novel of China.* 1991. A nonscholarly translation of the *Qizhen zhuan* ("Accounts of the Seven Perfected Ones"), about the exploits of Wang Zhe and his seven disciples. The woman disciple Sun Buer plays a prominent role. Though fictionalized (e.g., there is no evidence that Sun really disfigured herself), the novel introduces many of the concepts and values of the later Taoist tradition, including Inner Alchemy and the ascent to "immortality" through spiritual self-discipline.

———. *The Shambhala Guide to Taoism.* 1997. A useful though sometimes inaccurate exposition of some of the many forms of Taoism through the ages, intended for a non-scholarly audience. Wong is a Taoist practitioner trained in Northern School traditions.

See also **Miaoshan; Queen Mother of the West.**

RUSSELL KIRKLAND

Images of the Tao

One of the central conceptions of ancient Chinese philosophy is the Tao, or Dao. The term means "road" or "way," and by extension "method," "principle," "order," "morality," "good government," and so on. Confucius used the word mainly in its ethico-political sense, declaring that the Tao had prevailed in the world only in the past under the utopian rule of certain sage kings, now thought to be mostly legendary. If the ethical and ritual ways of the sage kings were revived, especially among those in power, thought Confucius, the Tao would again prevail. In Taoist writings, however, Tao mainly refers to an infinite and ineffable reality that precedes, produces, and underlies all phenomena. Therefore, no particular ethics, ritual, or language can adequately embody or express it. It is even beyond the polarities of yin (negative, passive, feminine, etc.) and yang (positive, active, masculine, etc.). Nevertheless, when pressed to speak of the nature of the Tao, the Taoists frequently used images of femininity. Maternal metaphors were especially frequent. For example, in the *Tao te ching* [Dao de jing], "The Scripture of the Way and Its Power," by Lao Tzu [Lao Zi], a shadowy figure of the fourth or third century B.C.E., the Tao is called "the mother of all things" (Chap. 1), and as such "it gives birth to them, supports them, makes them grow, rears them, corrects them, punishes them, feeds them, and protects them" (Chap. 51).

The images were not always from the human world, however, as in Chapter 6, one of the most beautiful and mysterious of the *Tao te ching*, "The goddess of the valley never dies. She is called the Mysterious Doe. The Pass to the Mysterious Doe is called the root of Heaven and Earth." Here the image is of a theriomorphic divinity (one having an animal form), as was common in Chinese shamanism. There is also no distinction made here between the goddess and the valley where she resides, since the word for a female animal (*pin*, translated here as "doe") can also be used for valleys.

In the ancient Chinese view, valleys and ravines were considered yin, complementing mountains and hills, yang. Association with the generative power of the womb made such empty spaces, and receptacles in general, perfect images of the Tao. Emptiness is thus not merely negativity or absence; it is infinite potential.

"We knead clay to make a vessel, but where it is empty there the usefulness of the vessel resides" (Chap. 11).

Being empty, the Tao does nothing yet creates infinitely without will, purpose, or attachment. This creative inactivity of the Tao is known in Chinese as *wu wei* (literally, "possessing no action") and is best understood by observation of the spontaneity of nature. To act with that kind of spontaneity one must free oneself of the preconceptions that education and acculturation, the mainstays of Confucianism, engender. The Taoists recommend this yin mode of acting without acting not only for spiritual adepts but even for "men of action." "The best commander is not warlike. The best warrior is not wrathful. The best victor never meets the enemy" (Chap. 68).

Such passages do not advocate elimination of the virile, active yang mode of action. They simply recognize the feminine mode as more effective. "Know the masculine, but practice the feminine: be the valley stream of the world. Once you are the valley stream of the world, the Power of the eternal will never leave you" (Chap. 28).

This is counsel meant especially for rulers of states. According to it, even if one occupies the rulership, that most yang of positions, one should act as if one were in the most yin of positions symbolized by the valley. For through it flows that most yin, yet most powerful, of elements: water.

Water is a metaphor for the Tao because it produces and sustains life while adapting to all conditions. "For the highest good, be like water. Water benefits everything in the world without contention. It occupies places despised by everyone, and is thus close to the Tao" (Chap. 8). But water, being not always placid and beneficent, is the image of yet another aspect of the Tao: "Nothing in the world is softer or weaker than water, but when it comes to destroying the hard and the strong, nothing can surpass it" (Chap. 78). Rocks worn smooth by the flow of streams and the periodic catastrophe of Yellow River floods, which often led to the fall of dynasties, cannot have been far from the author's mind.

BIBLIOGRAPHY

DeWoskin, Kenneth J., trans. *Doctors, Diviners, and Magicians of Ancient China: Biographies of Fang-shih.* 1983.

Kaltenmark, Max. *Lao Tzu and Taoism.* Translated by Roger Greaves. 1969.

Kohn, Livia. *The Taoist Experience: An Anthology.* 1993.

Lau, D.C. *Lao Tzu, Tao Te Ching.* 1963.

Robinet, Isabelle. *Taoism: Growth of a Religion.* Translated by Phyllis Brooks. 1997.

Waley, Arthur, *The Way and Its Power.* 1958.

Watson, Burton. *The Complete Works of Chuang Tzu.* 1968.

GOPAL SUKHU

Neumaier-Dargyay, Eva K. "Buddhist Thought from a Feminist Perspective." In *Gender, Genre and Religion: Feminist Reflections.* Edited by M. Joy and E. K. Neumaier-Dargyay. 1995.

Sangren, P. Steven. "Female Gender in Chinese Religious Symbols: Kuan-Yin, Ma-tsu, and the Eternal Mother." *Signs* 9, no. 1 (1983): 4–25.

EVA K. NEUMAIER-DARGYAY

Tārā

The symbolization of the feminine in Tibetan Buddhist culture is ambiguous at best. On the one hand, there is the myth of the Tibetan land personified as an ogress in need of harsh disciplining and the tradition that the female ancestor of the Tibetans was a fierce cannibalistic demoness. On the other hand is the enduring devotion to Tārā, whom Tibetans call mother in more than one sense. The worship of Tārā, a female bodhisattva (a Buddha to-be) who is closely linked with the male bodhisattva Avalokiteśvara, is historically documented in India and Southeast Asia from the seventh century on. Legend has it that the ancestral demoness was in reality Tārā, thus becoming truly the mother of all Tibetans, and that Tārā was embodied in the Chinese wife of Emperor Songtsen Gampo (reigned 618–641), a marriage that marked the introduction of Buddhism to Tibet. Although some texts praising Tārā were translated into Tibetan and stored in the imperial library by the late eighth century, her worship became popular only after Atisha, a Buddhist scholar-monk from India, had arrived in Tibet in 1042. The cult quickly spread in Tibet among the monastic centers as well as among the laity, in part because of Atisha's personal devotion to Tārā (she was his guiding personal deity throughout his life). Evocation prayers celebrate her as "mother of all Buddhas" and protectress of all her devotees. She embodies the loving compassion so essential for a bodhisattva. These feelings of pious love and devotion were often expressed by the literate elite in poetry; popular songs and playwrights also celebrated her. Among the twenty-one forms of Tārā, the Green Tārā and the White Tārā are the most popular ones.

BIBLIOGRAPHY

Beyer, Stephan. *The Cult of Tārā: Magic and Ritual in Tibet.* 1973.

Dīpaṃkaraśrījñāna (Atisha). *Ārya-tārā-sādhana* (text no. 4511). In *Tibetan Tripitaka, Peking Edition.* Vol. 81, fol. 94.5.5–95.2.1. 1962.

Galland, China. *Longing for Darkness: Tārā and the Black Madonna.* 1990.

Temptation and Seduction

From the original Latin word *temptare*, which means to try or to test, the later usage of the term *temptation* by some Christians is significantly narrowed to mean enticing to do evil. To seduce is to lead aside or away in Latin, but the word has evolved to mean leading away from what is right. Therefore in both concepts the meaning is similar in its specialized pattern: two separate figures, one leading or enticing another from what is perceived as good to what is perceived as evil.

While in secular life men are often seen as the seducers that tempt innocent women, in religious belief it is more often the women who tempt the purer men to do evil. A common view reasons that in Western tradition the patriarchy, in order to keep kinship lines clear, upholds the chaste wife and condemns the sexual temptress. In religious life dichotomy dominates: spirit and body, mind and emotion, male and female. Good and bad values were imposed on women based on their sexual behavior. Especially promoted by the three monotheistic traditions, the condemnation of sexually aggressive women is a reaction in part to the Greco-Roman world of powerful goddesses and priestesses. However, the "myth of feminine evil," grandly entitled, is well entrenched in the Jewish, Christian, and Greco-Roman traditions.

Eastern traditions also associate evil temptation with women. The Buddha is portrayed as having judged that a woman's heart is haunted by sensuality. This follows the classical Indian stereotype of the female as a sexual aggressor who cannot control her passions. During his final meditation under the Bo Tree of Enlightenment, the Buddha was tempted from his path by Mara's three daughters. Sexuality, a foundation of the Indian householder's existence, is an instrument to tempt both men and women from the path of the renunciate. Written from a male viewpoint, however, the texts tend to identify the female as the sole symbol of seduction. Monks are warned in the Buddhist text *Anguttaranikaya* (IV. 8. 80) that "a woman even when going along will stop to ensnare the heart of a man." The Buddha states that

Temptation and seduction remain common themes in modern culture. The serpent offers two apples, to a smiling Eve and a more hesitant Adam, in a 1995 cartoon by Mischa Richter and Harald Bakken (Mischa Richter and Harald Bakken).

nothing is so alluring and so tempting as the form of a woman, and "verily, one may say of womanhood that it is wholly a snare of Mara" (V.6.5). Stories abound of women trying to seduce monks.

The archetypal temptation in the Jewish, Christian, and Muslim context is Eve's seduction of Adam into the knowledge of worldly ways. The biblical parable served as a model for subsequent imagery of the female as evil-doer tempting the male away from God. The early church father Tertullian equates all women with Eve, who as the gate of the Devil enticed Adam, the man the Devil dared not approach. By introducing evil to humankind, women bore responsibility for the death of Christ. By the Middle Ages, writers such as Marbode, an eleventh-century bishop of Rennes, saw woman, with her vicious fount of honey and poison, as a seducing prostitute and the Devil's worst snare.

Genesis 6:1–4 recasts women as seductresses in the ancient tale of the union of the sons of god and the daughters of men. A divine and human union is now seen to be a seduction, and monstrous births follow. The daughters of men are seen presented as a gateway of evil, and sexual segregation becomes the solution. From Lilith, created equally with Adam according to the biblical commentary *Alphabet of Ben Sira* (seventh to tenth centuries C.E.), to Delilah, tempting Sampson from God in Judges 16, to Jezebel, foreign queen (I Kings 16–21; 2 Kings 9), the power and evil ways of some outstanding women are feared and attested. The overall tradition views women, for example Judith and Esther, as quite beneficial to the group and positive as role models. However, once cast as "evil temptress" no positive values accrue to the women so described.

In the *Malleus Maleficarum,* a 1486 handbook for inquisitors, witches are said to be natural seductresses. While men study to please God, women in their vanity study to seduce men. All witchcrafts are said to come from carnal lust and the Devil-inspired desire to entrap the male.

Even in seduction the female is often assigned an extraneously catalytic role as agent of evil; she relinquishes independent power as in Shakespeare's often-quoted phrase "Frailty, thy name is woman" (*Hamlet* I,ii,146). In the Letter of James (1:14), man is lured and enticed by his own desire. Augustine believes temptation to be a heritage of sin from Adam that demonstrates itself in an inner passionate inclination or weakness. Rabbinic literature discusses the ambivalent impulses and inclinations (*yester*) assigned to Adam, explaining away his capacity for being tempted. The initiative to tempt is found in the serpent, who is pitted against rationality; the serpent represents chaos to the theologian Paul Ricoeur and ambiguity to the theologian Dietrich Bonhoeffer. Saint Paul firmly establishes the body-soul dichotomy by describing the struggle in our lower bodily nature to overcome temptations. The challenge for the paradoxical nature of the human person, says philosopher Immanuel Kant, is to live one's life in freedom purely for goodness. The guilt from yielding to temptation cannot be reduced by blaming the temptress or projecting onto her the source of the problem.

Sometimes it is the goddess herself that seduces in a pleasurable temptation that is without guilt. Both gods and men are seduced by the African goddess Osun, whose extraordinary beauty comes from her source in the river waters. When this Yoruba belief reached Cuba and Brazil through the filter of Catholic morality, Osun had become the divine whore. The early Christian church fathers did much the same to Mary Magdalene by misrepresenting her in various texts and displacing her from the position as church leader and faithful follower of Jesus into a converted prostitute. Rādhā's divine seduction of Krishna in Hindu mythology and ritual demonstrates the holy nature of erotic love and represents the cosmic union. In ritual representation of this relationship, Hindu male devotees sometimes take on female characteristics, in imitation of Rādhā in order to tempt the god Krishna into spiritual union with them.

While women are seen in the history of religions as both positive and negative, once labeled temptress or seductress, the negative pattern overwhelmingly holds. Sexual seduction is mostly seen in the negative to men and community. The gender dichotomy is rigidly held. The religious man is often enticed from good to evil; the woman is then a temptress.

BIBLIOGRAPHY

Borgarucci, P. "Della contemplatione anatomica sopra tutte le parti del corpo humano." Venice, 1564. In *Not in God's Image: Women in History from Greeks to Victorians.* Edited by Julia O'Faolain and Lauro Martines. 1973. This text connects the nature of woman as temptress to her physical body. The whole collection of essays in this volume are valuable.

Church, Cornelia Dimmitt. "Temptress, Housewife, Nun: Women's Role in Early Buddhism." *Anima: An Experiential Journal* 1, no. 2 (1975): 53–58. Presents fundamental translations of temptress materials in Buddhism.

Clark, Elizabeth, and Herbert Richardson. *Women and Religion: A Feminist Sourcebook of Christian Thought.* 1977. Contains Western images of women in all historical periods. Temptresses and seductresses are common and carefully delineated.

Dijkstra, Bram. *Evil Sisters: The Threat of Female Sexuality and the Cult of Manhood.* 1996. A study of nineteenth-century attitudes toward female sexuality, based on Mendel's genetics (the spurious notions of male dominance and female receptivity) and Darwinism. This encouraged the notion that men would lose brainpower if seduced by women, who all had a basic instinct that made them predators, witches, and vampires who stole men's sperm and life.

Falk, Nancy Auer. "An Image of Woman in Old Buddhist Literature: The Daughters of Mara." In *Women and Religion.* Edited by Judith Plaskow and Joan Arnold Romero. Rev. ed., 1974. Falk is an expert in this field and the whole volume is valuable.

Hays, H. R. *The Dangerous Sex: The Myth of Feminine Evil.* 1964. Elucidates the negative qualities projected onto the female and the value judgments that followed.

Murphy, Joseph M. "Oshun the Dancer." In *The Book of the Goddess Past and Present.* Edited by Carl Olson. 1994. This excellent cross-cultural study of goddesses also contains materials on Rādhā as divine seductress. Materials from cultures throughout history on various goddesses are presented.

O'Flaherty, Wendy Doniger. *Asceticism and Eroticism in the Mythology of Siva.* 1973. Explores temptation and renunciation in the Hindu context.

Paul, Diana Y. *Women in Buddhism: Images of the Feminine in Mahayana Tradition.* 1979. A classic in the field.

Prusak, Bernard P. "Women: Seductive Siren and Source of Sin?" In *Religion and Sexism: Images of Women in the Jewish and Christian Traditions.* Edited by Rosemary Radford Ruether. 1974. This book contains many images portraying women in negative ways such as temptress.

Tertullian. "De cultu feminarum." In *Patrologia Latina,* vol. 1. Edited by J. P. Migne. 1879. The classic work that sets the stage for women as evil.

See also Osun; Rādhā.

LINDA L. LAM-EASTON

Teresa of Avila

A Spanish mystic, writer, and monastic reformer, Teresa of Avila (born Teresa de Ahumada y Cepeda, 1515–1582), had a comfortable childhood and entered Avila's Carmelite convent of the Incarnation in 1535, at the age of twenty. This decision, Teresa later admitted, was motivated more by the "servile fear" of hell than by the love of God.

Teresa of Avila described her visions as like an arrow piercing her heart, depicted in the sculpture *The Ecstasy of Saint Teresa* by Gian Lorenzo Bernini, Santa Maria Della Vittoria, Rome, Italy, 1645–1652 (Gianni Dagli Orti/Corbis).

The transformation of the rather pampered Doña Teresa de Ahumada to the ascetic Teresa of Jesus occurred gradually, over a period of nearly twenty years. Searching for a meaningful life of prayer, she scoured the abundant devotional literature of her day. Finally, when she was about forty, Teresa began to have frequent and powerful spiritual experiences—seeing visions, hearing voices, and even achieving the coveted state of mystical union with the Divine. She at last found the strength to cut her ties to worldly things and commit herself totally to the service of God.

In August 1562 Teresa opened the first reformed or Discalced (unshod, a sign of humility) Carmelite house of St. Joseph in Avila. Here, in contrast to her first convent, she and a few hand-picked nuns would reside in strict poverty and strict enclosure, with the quiet and autonomy necessary for the contemplative life as she understood it. In a genuinely egalitarian atmosphere, where even sisters from aristocratic families adopted religious names and did the manual chores of the convent, Teresa urged her nuns to pray unceasingly for the missionary priests working among the "heretics" and "heathens." Through this women's apostolate of prayer, she reminded her sisters, they would be doing God's work "although [they] are very cloistered."

During the last seventeen years of her life, Teresa not only founded fourteen more convents but composed four major works (*The Book of Her Life, The Way of Perfection, The Interior Castle,* and *The Book of Her Foundations*), as well as minor works and some five hundred extant letters. She is regarded as one of the greatest writers of Spain's Golden Age and a peerless teacher of the Christian spiritual life. She was beatified in 1614, canonized in 1622, and declared Doctor (teacher) of the Church in 1970.

BIBLIOGRAPHY

Santa Teresa de Jesús, Obras completas, edited by Efrén de la Madre de Dios Montsalva and Otger Steggink (Madrid, 1977), is a one-volume critical edition of Teresa's complete works, including her letters. The best English translation of Teresa's own writings is *The Collected Works of St. Teresa of Avila,* translated by Kieran Kavanaugh and Otilio Rodríguez, 3 vols. (1976–1985). Unfortunately, these scholars have not yet translated Teresa's letters, for which see *The Letters of Saint Teresa of Jesus,* translated by E. Allison Peers, 2 vols. (London, 1951).

Stephen Clissold, *St. Teresa of Avila* (1982) is a well-written short biography in English. Also helpful for historical context is Teófanes Egido, "The Historical Setting of St. Teresa's Life," *Carmelite Studies* 1 (1980): 122–182, and "The Economic Concerns of Madre Teresa," *Carmelite Studies* 4 (1987): 151–172.

Teresa of Avila is the subject of a number of studies by feminist historians, literary scholars, and theologians: Gillian Ahlgren, *Teresa of Avila and the Politics of Sanctity* (1996); Jodi Bilinkoff, *The Avila of Saint Teresa: Religious Reform in a Sixteenth-Century City* (1989); J. Mary Luti, *Teresa of Avila's Way* (1991); Carole Slade, *St. Teresa of Avila: Author of a Heroic Life* (1995); and Alison Weber, *Teresa of Avila and the Rhetoric of Femininity* (1990).

JODI BILINKOFF

Thealogy

From *thea*, goddess, and *logos*, meaning, the word *thealogy* was coined by twentieth-century feminists to remind us that the traditional discipline of theology (from *theos* or god) is reflection on the meaning of an implicitly or explicitly male deity. Contemporary Goddess thealogy is reflection on the meaning of life from the perspective provided by the image of the Goddess in the Goddess movement. Whereas traditional theology elevates God and man as rulers of woman and nature, Goddess thealogy honors women and nature, providing a mythic basis for feminism and ecological renewal. Thealogy is implicit in works concerned with Goddess ritual, magic, history, and ethics, most of them written by women.

Traditional theology considers the following topics: authority; history; divinity; nature; humanity; and ethics. This entry will look at these topics from the perspective of contemporary Goddess thealogy.

Authority

While the source and norm for traditional theology is revealed tradition and rational thought, Goddess thealogy, like feminist theology more generally, begins in experience. Contemporary experiences of the Goddess in dreams, meditations, and rituals are taken as authoritative. Goddess history, especially ancient images of the Goddess, is cited as inspiration and to some extent validation for contemporary experience. But Goddess history never becomes (as the Bible often does in Christian theology) the final authority. Because experience is privileged, Goddess thealogy is likely to be plural and suggestive, rather than unified and definitive.

History

A myth of beginnings has emerged in the Goddess movement. It goes something like this. In the beginning humankind worshiped the Goddess as the animating force within nature. Human beings understood themselves as part of the web of life and lived in harmony with each other and all beings. Modern culture, with its emphasis on the domination of women and nature, hierarchy, greed, consumption, warfare, and destruction of the ecosystem, is a result of a disruption of this initial harmony. By remembering the Goddess, human beings can learn again to live in harmony with the universe. No single text or tradition is cited as the source of this new myth. It has emerged through a combination of intuition and historical research.

Divinity

Goddess thealogy rejects the "God out there" who is traditionally pictured as an old white man sitting on a throne in the sky ruling his subjects and defined philosophically as transcendent. In contrast the Goddess is seen as a power inherent in nature and humanity. The Goddess as giver, taker, and renewer of life is reflected in the cycles of birth, death, and regeneration; darkness is valued equally with light.

Nature

In Goddess thealogy, neither humanity nor divinity is radically distinguished (as in traditional theology) from nature. All beings are understood as interconnected in the web of life. All life forms are animated by the Goddess. All participate in the cycles of birth, death, and regeneration.

Humanity

Humanity is part of the web of life, not higher or better than rocks, plants, other animals. The body, sexuality, and birth are sacred, reflecting the creative powers of the Goddess as giver of life. This contrasts with traditional theology's depiction of the naked Eve as the source of sin and death. Human intuition (as reflected in dreams, visions, and mystical experience) is valued as the source of human knowledge of deep connection to all beings in the web of life. Death is part of the cycle of life and will be followed by rebirth or regeneration.

Ethics

Ethical behavior is based on recognizing that all beings are interconnected in the web of life. Patterns of hierarchical domination, unrestrained greed, warfare, sexism, racism, heterosexism, and ecological destruction stem from failing to recognize that humans are part of the web of life and that what harms one, harms all. Goddess ethics is about repairing the web. Human beings can learn again to live in harmony with each other and all beings in the web of life. Those who nurture life, including mothers, would be honored.

The critique of God as a dominating other, and many of the constructive proposals of Goddess thealogy—including focus on experience, critique of hierarchical dualism, and positive evaluation of the body and nature—are also found in Christian and Jewish feminist theologies.

BIBLIOGRAPHY

Budapest, Zsuzsanna E. *The Holy Book of Women's Mysteries.* 1989. Based on her manifesto of contemporary Goddess worship, *The Feminist Book of Lights and Shadows.* 1975.

Christ, Carol P. *Rebirth of the Goddess: Finding Meaning in Feminist Spirituality.* 1997. The first systematic Goddess thealogy.

———. "Why Women Need the Goddess." In *Womanspirit Rising: A Feminist Reader in Religion.* Edited by Carol P. Christ and Judith Plaskow. 1979. Reprint, 1992. A widely reprinted essay.

Daly, Mary. *Beyond God the Father: Toward a Philosophy of Women's Liberation.* 1973. In documenting the sexism of Christian theology, Daly cleared the way for Goddess thealogy.

Gimbutas, Marija. *The Language of the Goddess.* 1989. Gimbutas is often cited as validation of thealogy's myth of origins.

Goldenberg, Naomi R. *Changing of the Gods: Feminism and the End of Traditional Religion.* 1979. Goldenberg is often credited with inventing the word *thealogy,* defined in this book.

Griffin, Susan. *Woman and Nature: The Roaring Inside Her.* 1978. Articulates the intuition of the connection of women and nature, central to the development of Goddess thealogy.

Gross, Rita M. "Hindu Female Deities as a Resource for the Contemporary Rediscovery of the Goddess." *Journal of the American Academy of Religion* 46, no. 3 (1978). Proposes that Goddess thealogy not focus exclusively on Western sources.

Starhawk [Miriam Simos]. *Dreaming the Dark: Magic, Sex, and Politics.* 1982. Shows the connection of Goddess spirituality and ethics and defines the Goddess as immanence.

———. *The Spiral Dance.* 1979. Rev. ed., 1989. A classic work.

Stone, Merlin. *When God Was a Woman.* 1976. Influential in the development of Goddess thealogy's myth of origins.

Teish, Luisah. *Jambalaya.* 1985. Roots Goddess thealogy in African and African-American tradition.

See also **Environmentalism; Goddess; Nature; Theology.**

CAROL P. CHRIST

Theism

In Western philosophical and theological traditions, theism and atheism refer to debate about the existence of God and the coherence of belief in God. Theism and atheism take on new significance in light of gender analysis that deconstructs masculine concepts of God. Women's scholarship, rather than focus on the existence of God, is concerned with the meaning of "God," the presence of God in women's lives, and activism evoked by God-language.

The problem of monotheism for Jewish and Christian feminists is the hegemonic interpretation of theism in patriarchal, misogynist terms that marginalize women's experience and participation within the traditions and that limit concepts of God to masculine attributes and metaphors. Responses to theism reflect diversity among feminist, womanist, and *mujerista* perspectives, but three integrated methodological approaches to theism dominate: rejection of traditional theism; retrieval of traditional, though marginal, female-inclusive theistic metaphors; and construction of feminist alternative theism.

Jewish and Christian feminists reject traditional theism associated with the male Warrior-Judge-King of the Hebrew Bible, God the Father, and the male Savior of the Christian New Testament, as well as the omnipotent, transcendent God derived from Greek philosophy. Mary Daly's *Beyond God the Father* (1973) explored how, with the realization that Father God legitimated patriarchal society and the oppression of women, the death of God the Father was emerging in women's consciousness. Daly argued that a radical transformation of collective imagination would be necessary to eradicate the masculine God and to spark new language for God (such as Daly's God the Verb) arising out of women's experiential context. In *Changing of the Gods: Feminism and the End of Traditional Religions* (1979), Naomi Goldenberg made the visionary observation that the feminist movement in the West would bring about the demise of God, "the slow execution of Christ and Yahweh." Women's abandonment of Judaism, Christianity, Christ, and Bible would obviate the need for an external deity in favor of interior psychic understandings of goddesses and gods.

For women who reject traditional patriarchal theism, one methodological option is the retrieval of submerged or marginalized female-identified theist alternatives from within one's tradition or from other traditions. Some Jewish feminist scholarship advocates the retrieval of female imagery for God in the Jewish mystical tradition and the reunification of God and Shekhinah, the alienated female aspect of God. Among Christian womanist scholars, Elisabeth Schüssler Fiorenza

The deity is imaged as God the Father in a fifteenth-century Romanesque church fresco (LinMarc Garanger/Corbis).

(1983) recalls Sophia from the biblical wisdom tradition. Delores Williams draws from black women's experience and the black church the image of God as Way Maker, the one who assists black women in making a way out of no way, in distinction to God the Liberator. Latin American *mujerista* theologians have not systematically addressed the question of God images but do retrieve, in la Virgen de Guadalupe, the goddess Coatlalopueh, a female deity submerged by male-dominated culture and the Christian church after the Spanish conquest. For women who abandon Christianity and Judaism, goddess spirituality and religions provide an alternative religious experience. While polytheist traditions balance male and female deities, Lina Gupta demonstrates that goddess mythology must be extracted from patriarchal appropriation for the purpose of sanctioning women's unequal treatment. To that end, Gupta recovers Kālī, mother and destroyer, as a Hindu model of women's inherent power. Native North American women who have benefited from the spiritual power of female deities, such as 'Isanaklesh, Thought Woman, Corn Woman, and Old Spider Woman, in cultures that value women's leadership, spirituality, and experience, retrieve these images from cultural invisibility and assimilation for the benefit of non-native women.

Deeply embedded masculine God-language is met with constructive feminist alternatives. Feminist theology counters idolatrous patriarchal metaphors with metaphors for God that arise from women's experience. The first step in this constructive work is to establish that metaphors for God cannot be literal and always fall short of adequate descriptions of God—a point typologically symbolized in Rosemary Radford Ruether's "God/ess" and Schüssler Fiorenza's "G-d" and "G*d." While feminists have become more reluctant to propose androgynous metaphors, which perpetuate gender stereotypes, theologians employ a range of metaphors particular to women's identity, including God as Mother and God-She; to women's relationships, such as God as Erotic Power, Lover, and Friend, and God as "community-in-relationship" in Asian women's theology; and to women's experience of divine immanence, for example, Asian women's God "who weeps with our pain." Some feminists draw upon process theism to inform contemporary metaphors, note especially Rita Nakashima Brock's Christa/Community as a relational interpretation of Christ, Sallie McFague's panentheistic interpretation of the world as God's body, and Ruether's Gaia as creative matrix.

BIBLIOGRAPHY

For general knowledge about the importance of theism in women's scholarship, refer to Carol P. Christ and Judith Plaskow's anthologies, *Womanspirit Rising: A Feminist Reader in Religion* (1979) and *Weaving the Visions: New Patterns in Feminist Spirituality* (1989); Paula M. Cooey, William B. Eakin, and Jay B. McDaniel's anthology, *After Patriarchy: Feminist Transformations of the World Religions* (1993); Maura O'Neill's *Women Speaking, Women Listening: Women in Interreligious Dialogue* (1990), especially chapter 4. Within the Christian tradition, Sallie McFague's work has articulated a feminist method for metaphorical theology in *Metaphorical Theology: Models of God in Religious Language* (1982) and *Models of God: Theology for an Ecological, Nuclear Age* (1987). On goddess spirituality, refer to Cynthia Eller's *Living in the Lap of the Goddess: The Feminist Spirituality Movement in America* (1993).

Women's efforts to explore the naming of deity appear in a number of sources. This article refers especially to Rita Nakashima Brock's *Journeys by Heart: A Christology of Erotic Power* (1988), Lina Gupta's "Kali, the Savior" in *After Patriarchy* (1993), Sallie McFague's *The Body of God: An Ecological Theology* (1993), Rosemary Radford Ruether's *Gaia and God: An Ecofeminist Theology of Earth Healing* (1992), Elisabeth Schüssler Fiorenza's *In Memory of Her: A Feminist Theological Reconstruction of Christian Origins* (1983) and *But She Said: Feminist Practices of Biblical Interpretation* (1992), and Delores S. Williams' *Sisters in the Wilderness: The Challenge of Womanist God-Talk* (1993).

See also **Goddess: Contemporary Goddess Movement, History of Study; Hebrew Bible: God in the Hebrew Bible; Liberation Theologies; Mujerista Tradition; Theology.**

NANCY R. HOWELL

Theology

An Overview

The concept of theology has had a variety of uses and references and has undergone significant changes throughout its history. The term derives from the Greek *theos,* meaning god, and *logos,* referring to discourse or speech about God or the gods. The notion first appears with Greek thinkers who often refer to myths or narratives about the gods. For Aristotle the term designates mythological portrayals of reality and, in his *Metaphysics,* names first or highest philosophy what would come to be identified as metaphysical reflection and argument.

While *theologia* had its conceptual beginnings in Greek thought, it developed as a concept and into a discipline within the Western theistic traditions, especially Christianity. During the first centuries of the Christian era the term appeared most often in the writings of Eastern Christians. Despite the absence of theology as an explicit concept in the West, the notion of knowledge of God became widespread as Christianity developed as a religious movement. Such knowledge of or discourse about God was, in early Christianity, understood as a spiritual pursuit of faithful believers. Theology in this mode is, thus, a form of salvific knowledge.

Theology, as salvific knowledge and as a faithful practice or habit of the soul, was pursued primarily through interpretation of and commentary on the Scriptures and later through the creedal and dogmatic expressions of the church. Creedal formulations carried particular stature in the early church because of their presumed revelatory origins and assumed proximity to the apostolic witness of the original Christian community. Orthodoxy and connection with the apostolic witness thus became the twin norms for assessing theological validity.

Early Christian theology was, for the most part, neither systematic nor comprehensive. It reflected the church's struggles to define orthodox Christian belief and practice, to draw the boundaries of the community, and especially to resolve conflicts concerning such issues as the nature of Jesus and his relation to God and humanity.

In the West, Christian theology as a specific intellectual discipline or science began to emerge in the medieval period (beginning in the late fifth century C.E.). At the end of this era there had occurred the appropriation of an Aristotelian emphasis on reason, the pursuit of knowledge as theoretical science, and the rise of the great medieval universities. While theology as personal and communal knowledge of God remained, and reflec-

Traditional Christian theology is enacted in a Catholic Palm Sunday service held at the Stone of Anointing, where Jesus is said to have been anointed after death, Church of the Holy Sepulchre, Jerusalem, 1968 (Ted Spiegel/Corbis).

tion and commentary on the Scriptures continued, increasingly there was a distinction between spiritual reflection and the form of knowledge derived through rational analysis and argument. Moreover, an institutional shift took place during this period as theology, now understood as a scientific discipline, was located by some thinkers in the university. Thus contrasts emerged, though not yet total separation, between theology as a habit of the soul and theology as a rational discipline, between faith and reason, and between the church and the university or school. While Christian thinkers espoused each of these emphases as the means toward salvific knowledge, not as contradictory pursuits, divergent paths nonetheless began to take shape.

Beginning in the late Middle Ages and intensifying during the Protestant Reformation and the early modern period, many social, cultural, and intellectual developments took place that drastically altered the nature and prospects of Christian theology in the West. In particular, as older forms of authority and societal consensus broke down reason, especially in its scientific form, came to the fore as the source of secure knowledge and the provider of criteria through which differences might be adjudicated.

The drive for certitude, now no longer grounded in appeals to religious authorities or traditions but based on reason, found its fullest expression in Western Christianity in the Enlightenment. As rationality extended to all arenas of human activity, religion and theology both received critical analysis. Enlightenment thinkers challenged traditional claims to knowledge of God, God's nature and character, and God's relation to humanity.

Some theology sought to defend its assertions by appeal to the canons of scientific reason. However, much theology, especially Protestant theology following the nineteenth-century thinker Friedrich Schleiermacher, turned its attention to religious experience assumed to be beyond the reach of empirical reason. Western Christian theology thus became preoccupied with exploring the depths of human subjectivity. Still other theological thinkers turned to the developing historical disciplines and critical Biblical studies, seeking to uncover firm ground in the originating events and texts of the early Christian period.

The turn to human subjectivity and religious experience and the return to historical origins have, in the twentieth century, also proven problematic. Theological movements such as neo-orthodoxy simultaneously accepted the limits on reason proposed by early modernity and denounced the appeal to human experience, denying its adequacy as a vehicle for knowledge of God. In turn, neo-orthodoxy's own assertions of true knowledge based on radical revelation were called into question as they increasingly appeared to be a new form of special pleading. Moreover, historical-critical Biblical studies steadily undermined any easy or normative return to the sources of Christianity. Progressively, appeals to reason, experience, and revelation all were called into question.

By the late 1960s other critical challenges were directed at Christian theology. In particular, liberation movements around the globe raised questions about Christianity's and Christian theology's role in a variety of forms of oppression. Liberation theology in developing countries, Black theology, and feminist theology all focused attention on the ways in which religion and theology were complicit in inequitable distribution of power and resources, including religious resources. Many proponents of liberation perspectives advocated leaving religious traditions such as Christianity while others sought to reformulate both theology and religious beliefs and practices in ways more supportive of efforts for the full humanization of marginalized and oppressed groups.

The result of all of these changes and challenges is that Western Christian theology has been in a process of crisis and reformulation throughout the last decades of the twentieth century. No one perspective dominates and there are varied schools of thought presenting themselves as possible alternatives. Such alternatives run the gamut from a variety of liberation perspectives to a resurgence of conservative, evangelical, and fundamentalist perspectives to postmodern forms of reflection that stand in opposition to modern assumptions and projects.

Women, as theological thinkers and as objects of theological reflection, have had differing roles in the varied Christian tradition. Generally, however, it can be said that until recently women have been markedly absent as recognized and valued contributors to the theological enterprise. While women have been religious practitioners and the transmitters of religious beliefs and practices, historically they have not been identified as theologians who might legitimately reflect on and contribute to their traditions. Moreover, often male lives and experiences have provided the central data for reflection upon the ultimate; women's lives and experiences have been understood as derivative or as deviant and therefore as not providing distinctive or central material for theological analysis. Nonetheless, women have been both the topics of theological claims and have been affected by theological assertions even when they have not been mentioned. For example, Christian theology in the West, on the level of church proclamation and in individual theologies, has explicitly made normative pronouncements on a wide variety of realities including the nature of marriage, sexuality, and the relation of men and women and children. Or again, it has offered understandings of evil that have identified or connected evil with sexuality and sexuality with femaleness. It has likewise justified women's exclusion, until recently, from central religious roles such as priests or ministers. These have had direct impact upon women. But Christian theological assertions have also affected women more obliquely by leaving women out or making males, often unconsciously, normative. Male language for God, interpretations of Jesus as the Son of God, of the soul as male, of the priesthood as the province of those who are like Jesus, of sin as pride and salvation as self-abnegation all are examples of Christian developments that have had impact upon women even when women are not the explicit topic of analysis.

This entry has focused on the development of Western Christian theology. Eastern Christian theology has continued, for the most part, in the mode of Scriptural commentary and reflection on the tradition as forms of spiritual practice. Analogues to both Western and Eastern Christian theology also occur in the theistic traditions of Judaism and Islam, though in both there is a far greater delineation of practice and the interpretation of religious law.

In Judaism religious reflection has been centered on the Torah or the five books of Moses; the Talmud, which consists of the ancient rabbinic teachings that have been the authoritative foundation for much of religious Judaism; and halakah, which forms the legal part of the Talmudic tradition and articulates the specific ways of living a Jewish life. Jewish reflection has had

less of the systematic or dogmatic interests evidenced in Christian theology but has historically instead focused on exegesis, law, practice, and ritual. Moreover, in post-Biblical Judaism, Jewish reflection has for the most part taken place in a wider environment where Jews were in the minority and hence were continually interpreting Jewish identity and relations and boundaries with an often hostile non-Jewish world. Much traditional Jewish thought has continued reflection on Jewish identity and practice through halakic interpretation even on the contemporary scene. However, since the Enlightenment, with the emergence of Reform and Reconstructionist Judaism, non-Orthodox Jewish religious reflection has focused attention beyond legal interpretation.

Religious reflection about women has taken place both within and in response to halakic interpretation and, more recently, in relation to other dimensions of Jewish history and tradition. Because traditionally Jewish law has been considered authoritative not only in terms of legal pronouncements but as the articulation of authentic Jewish identity, debates around the nature and role of women have often been centered on the law. As with traditional Christian theology and Islamic law, women in Jewish law are both shaped by what is explicitly said about them and by that from which they are excluded. As with other religious reflection, ideals of women as wives and mothers, as compassionate and pious, and as important transmitters of the tradition are held in high esteem. But so too are strictures on women's social, political, and religious status. Women are often excluded from religious practices, denied participation in central communal prayers, relegated to subordinate positions in relation to men, deemed unclean, and subjected to multiple strictures. Importantly, authentic Jewishness is often defined in ways that women cannot fulfill by virtue of their femaleness.

Contemporary Jewish reflection, especially feminist thought, has concerned itself with the reinterpretation of Jewish law in relation to women, with women from all branches of Judaism engaging not only in reformulating particular teachings about women but also the nature of Jewish law itself. Some Jewish thinkers, most notably from the Reform movement, have increasingly pressed the debates beyond consideration of the law. In particular, they have called for reconsidering and reconstructing central categories that have shaped Jewish history and identity for centuries, most notably the categories of God, Israel, and Torah. In so doing they have suggested a more decisive and self-conscious move beyond interpretation of an assumed-to-be-authoritative tradition to the more self-conscious reconstruction of the Jewish tradition and the reclaiming of counter-traditions of women within Jewish history. Central to these efforts have been the concern to maintain Jewish identity while simultaneously rethinking women's identities and roles.

Islam, too, has traditions of reflection that are both parallel to Christian theological thought and Jewish religious reflection and also quite distinctive. Islamic religious reflection has had, since the seventh century C.E., several authoritative sources that have formed the foundations for Islamic thought and law. The first of these is the Qur'an. The Qur'an, the collection of revelations given to Muhammad by God, historically has been considered God's word, eternal in nature and unmatched by any other revelations or human words. A second source for Islamic reflection is the hadith, sayings of the Prophet Muhammad that were collected and compiled by his followers. While not as authoritative as the Qur'an such sayings have also played a central role in the development of Islamic law and traditions. Out of reflection on these sources emerged Shari'a or Islamic law. Islamic law, articulated and interpreted by ulema, scholars of the law, has covered all aspects of Islamic life, including centrally the family and family relations.

In each of these sources, the Qur'an, hadith, and Shari'a, there has been explicit attention to the situation and role of women. The Qur'an explicitly asserts the religious equality of women and men, calling both to witness to the one God, outlaws female infanticide, asserts the right of women to contract marriages and to control dowers and to receive inheritance. It also limits the number of wives men can have and insists upon the responsibility of men to support their wives and children. Later Islamic law detailed more on the role of women, emphasizing their role in the family and enumerating legal positions, often far more restrictive than in the Qur'an itself, on marriage, divorce, inheritance, dress, especially veiling, the seclusion of women from public life, and religious practice. Islamic family law has been the central means of defining the role of women in Muslim society and, though modified in different historical times and places, has remained remarkably stable over the centuries.

In the nineteenth and twentieth centuries a number of factors have raised questions for Islamic thought and especially for the interpretation of Islamic law. Modernity, both embraced and resisted by Islamic societies, has greatly affected Islamic self-interpretation. The worldwide emergence of consciousness about women and the development of feminist movements have also raised questions in Muslim societies, as elsewhere, about everything from divorce laws to proper dress for women in public. Economic changes have placed many women in the public workplace, functionally altering the role of women in society. In particular, there has emerged an intense reconsideration of Islam and its role in society as the Muslim world redefines its identity in a post-colonial world. Significantly, there has taken shape a major call for the re-Islamization of Muslim societies and the repudiation of westernization and Western values and ways of life. Family law and gender issues have come to the fore in these debates. As in Christianity and Judaism, there are many positions being articulated concerning the nature and role of women, ranging from calls for modernization to women reclaiming traditional interpretations of women, including reveiling, as a way of affirming Islam and its distinctive history and identity.

In each of these traditions men have historically been the theological interpreters, including defining women, their roles, and natures. While each tradition includes resources that positively portray women, they all also restrict, negatively evaluate, and ignore women's lives. Increasingly, women are becoming self-interpreters and interpreters of their religious traditions. There is certainly no consensus within or across Christianity, Judaism, or Islam about what theological directions should be pursued. It is clear, however, that women, both as the topic of theological thought and as theological thinkers themselves, are changing the character of their traditions and of reflection on these traditions.

BIBLIOGRAPHY

Adler, Rachel. *Engendering Judaism: An Inclusive Theology and Ethics.* 1998.

Briggs, Sheila. "A History of Our Own: What Would a Feminist History of Theology Look Like?" In *Horizons in Feminist Theology: Identity, Traditions, and Norms.* Edited by Rebecca S. Chopp and Sheila Greeve Davaney. 1997.

Conger, Yves M. J. *A History of Theology.* 1968.

Fernea, Elizabeth Warnock, and Basima Qattan Bezirgan, eds. *Middle Eastern Muslim Women Speak.* 1977.

Haddad, Yvonne Yazbeck, and John L. Esposito, eds. *Islam, Gender, and Social Change.* 1997.

Haddad, Yvonne Yazbeck, and Ellison Banks Findly, eds. *Women, Religions and Social Change.* 1985.

Hodgson, Peter C., and Robert H. King. *Christian Theology: An Introduction to Its Traditions and Tasks.* 1985.

Johnson, Elizabeth A. *She Who Is: The Mystery of God in Feminist Theological Discourse.* 1992.

Peskowitz, Miriam, and Laura Levitt, eds. *Judaism Since Gender.* 1997.

Plaskow, Judith. *Standing Again at Sinai: Judaism from a Feminist Perspective.* 1990.

Ruether, Rosemary Radford. *Sexism and God-talk: Toward a Feminist Theology.* 1983.

Stowasser, Barbara Freyer. *Women in the Qur'an, Traditions, and Interpretation.* 1994.

SHEILA DAVANEY

Feminist Theology

Feminist theology began and remains primarily a Christian discourse concerned with the subordination of women in various Christian traditions and practices. Feminist theology offers a systemic critique of gendered power relationships. It has been taken up by different groups of feminist scholars who have challenged it from within as well as from outside of particular Christian traditions. Given this, feminist theology has been marked by a series of ambivalences around the limits of its critique of these traditions.

Changes in female roles in European society after the Enlightenment elicited the involvement of women in religious studies scholarship. In the nineteenth century women scholars looked to Biblical texts as a site for their feminist critique of the subordination of women. So, for example, a critique of ecclesiastical complicity in female subordination begun by U.S. suffragists at Seneca Falls in 1848 culminated in the publication of *The Woman's Bible* by Elizabeth Cady Stanton and others in 1895. This text may be viewed as a precursor to the work of more recent feminist theologians in its commitment to rereading canonical texts for liberatory ends. Moreover, in response to the absence of opportunities for theological training for U.S. Catholic women, Sister M. Madaleva, the president of St. Mary's College, South Bend, Indiana, established a School of Sacred Theology for women there in 1944. In the 1950s, Mary Daly, one of the founders of contemporary feminist theology, earned a doctorate in theology in that program, the first of her several advanced degrees.

Though Daly's first book, *The Church and the Second Sex* (1968), showed the influence of Betty Friedan and other secular feminists, feminist theological discourse per se began with the publication of her *Beyond God the Father* in 1973. During the decade following the publication of *Beyond God the Father*, Christian women, concerned primarily with questions of faith, enhanced their own power in seminaries, universities, and schools of theology by appropriating and transforming classical and critical modern Christian theological discourse.

This initial period of development among Christian feminist theologians culminated in 1983 in the publication of two of the classics of Christian feminist theology: *Sexism and God Talk,* by Rosemary Radford Ruether and *In Memory of Her* by Elisabeth Schüssler

Elizabeth Cady Stanton (1815–1902), women's rights activist, reformer, and editor of *The Woman's Bible*, was an early proponent of feminist theology (National Portrait Gallery, Washington, D.C.).

Fiorenza. Ruether uses a philosophically based feminist anthropology to revise the standard topics of Christian systematic theology, while Schüssler Fiorenza offers a feminist-theological reconstruction of Christian origins.

The discourses constructed by Daly, Ruether, Schüssler Fiorenza and others set the terms for subsequent feminist theology. Their work opened up a space for women of other religious traditions to do feminist theology. These efforts have included systemic critiques of the subordination of women within, for example, Jewish and Islamic traditions.

The Jewish feminist theologian Judith Plaskow got her training at Yale University in Religious Studies. Plaskow honed her skills by reading Christian theological texts, and her first book offered a feminist critique of two Christian theologians (Plaskow, 1980). In this way Christian theological discourse helped shape Jewish feminist theological discourse. More recently, this pattern has been repeated by Muslim feminist theologians such as Riffat Hassan and Ghazala Anwar.

The pioneering contributions of Christian feminists have been offset somewhat by certain universalizing tendencies within Christian feminist theology. Claims for and about "all women" belie the presence of a liberal-inclusive framework in many Christian feminist theologies, one inadequate to the incommensurability of religious traditions, races, sexualities, and ethnicities.

Nonetheless, some non-Christian feminist theologians like Plaskow have managed to accept the invitation extended by Christian feminist theology while sidestepping the triumphalism sometimes implicit in it. The anthology *Womanspirit Rising* (1979, 1991), edited by Carol P. Christ, a theologian and practitioner of goddess spirituality, and Judith Plaskow, inaugurated this opening of feminist theological discourse even before the publication of the Christian feminist classics of 1983. This work was fostered by the even earlier collective efforts of many of these same women to create the Women's Section of the American Academy of Religion, the chief professional organization for scholars of religion. In 1984, Plaskow, with Elisabeth Schüssler Fiorenza, founded the influential *Journal of Feminist Studies in Religion,* and in 1989 Plaskow and Christ revisited issues of differences among and between various feminist thea/theologies in *Weaving the Visions: New Patterns in Feminist Spirituality.*

By the mid-1980s, a wide range of feminist discussions was fostered by the Women's Section of the American Academy of Religion. Classic feminist theological initiatives echoed across a range of distinct ethnic and religious traditions. Women-based theologies by an increasing number of African-American and Latina scholars began to appear, including work by Delores S. Williams and Ada-María Isasi-Díaz. Jewish feminists—including Rachel Adler, Marcia Falk, Susannah Heschel, Judith Plaskow, and Ellen Umansky—likewise initiated critical reflections on their tradition. Plaskow's *Standing Again at Sinai: Judaism from a Feminist Perspective* (1990) became the most widely read feminist theology outside the Christian orbit. Muslim feminist theologians, following the lead of many Christian feminist theologians, began to argue for some of Islam's inherently liberating effects for women, offering a critique of historically masculinist traditions of interpretation of Islamic texts and practices. A small group of Muslim scholars, including Riffat Hassan and Ghazala Anwar, are currently extending these critiques, working within the United States to produce a more systematic feminist interpretation of Islam.

A significant development is the incipient critique of the liberal and liberationist tradition that marks much classic feminist theological discourse coming out of the Enlightenment. These more recent efforts continue Daly's legacy of radical, structural critique by questioning on the one hand the legacy of the first generation of feminist theologians and on the other feminist theorists outside the field of religion who themselves continue to perpetuate Enlightenment notions of religion. These feminist theological critiques draw on secular feminist, literary-critical, and poststructuralist theory but also offer a critique of those theories in relation to questions of religious discursive practices. These efforts were launched by the publication of Sharon D. Welch's *Communities of Resistance and Solidarity* in 1985. For Welch, the fundamental crisis of the twentieth century includes the shattering of women's experience as a self-evident unified category that had previously served as the foundation of Christian feminist theology. Welch turned to the philosophical works of Michel Paul Foucault to shift the discourse of feminist theology to account for these complexities better.

Rebecca S. Chopp extends this feminist-postmodernist theological trajectory in *The Power to Speak: Feminism, Language, God* (1989). Using rhetoric, poetics, and semiotics, Chopp displays the power of women's discourses as emerging from God, the "Perfectly Open Sign," to enable the transformation of the social-symbolic order of the late twentieth century. Finally, in *Changing the Subject: Women's Discourses and Feminist Theology* (1994), Mary McClintock Fulkerson replaces the feminist theological appeal to women's experience with an "analytic of women's discourses," interrogating specific social locations in which gender issues have been enacted. Fulkerson's close readings of discursive performances by three Christian women's groups, each in a different socioeconomic location, has furthered the feminist-poststructuralist critique of liberal Christian feminist theology.

In the 1990s a new generation of feminist theologians emerged. While clearly indebted to the first generation of feminist theologians, these feminist scholars of religion employ an increasingly wide range of interdisciplinary methods—feminist, womanist, *mujerista,* queer, postcolonial, literary—to problematize and extend the feminist theological discourses they have inherited.

Such critiques are especially evident among a dynamic generation of Christian womanist, *mujerista,* and Asian feminist theologians including Rita Nakashima Brock and Kwok Pui Lan as well as among queer Christian scholars. The latter use Foucault and poststructuralism to raise questions about the efficacy of theology as a means of resisting heteronormativity in Christian scholarship and communal practice.

Beginning in the 1980s with the initial publications of Beck's *Nice Jewish Girls: A Lesbian Anthology*, Heschel's *On Being a Jewish Feminist: A Reader*, and Klepfisz and Kaye/Kantrowitz's *Tribe of Dina: A Jewish Women's Anthology*, Jewish feminists have also raised questions about the efficacy of theology as the central discourse for Jewish feminist critique. More recently these efforts have expanded into a more explicit critique of Jewish liberalism (Levitt, 1997) and the legacy of the Enlightenment for Jewish scholarship (Peskowitz and Levitt, 1997). These Jewish feminist works go so far as to challenge the notion that Jewishness is necessarily and exclusively a religion (as defined in theological terms) in order to validate Jewish feminist works that would otherwise not be considered part of a Jewish feminist corpus.

Critique and resistance to the structural legacy of masculinist religious traditions remains at the contested center of feminist theological discourses at the present time. What is striking about this legacy is the way in which feminist scholars have been able both to build on and also critique the centrality of Christian theological categories in shaping this feminist critical practice.

BIBLIOGRAPHY

Adler, Rachel. *Engendering Judaism: A New Theology and Ethics.* 1997.

Anwar, Ghazala. "Muslim Feminist Discourses." In *Women in World Religions.* Edited by Elisabeth Schüssler Fiorenza. *Concilium.* 1996.

Beck, Evelyn, ed. *Nice Jewish Girls: A Lesbian Anthology.* 1982. Rev. ed., 1989.

Brock, Rita Nikashima. *Journeys by Heart: A Christology of Erotic Power.* 1991.

Brock, Rita Nakashima, Claudia Camp, and Serene Jones, eds. *Setting the Table: Women in Theological Conversation.* 1995.

Chopp, Rebecca S. *The Power to Speak: Feminism, Language, God.* 1989.

Chopp, Rebecca S., and Sheila Greeve Davaney, eds. *Horizons in Feminist Theology.* 1997.

Christ, Carol P. "Embodied Thinking: Reflections on Feminist Theological Method." *Journal of Feminist Studies in Religion* 5 (1989): 7–15.

Christ, Carol P., and Judith Plaskow, eds. *Womanspirit Rising: A Feminist Reader in Religion.* 1979.

Daly, Mary. *Beyond God the Father: Toward a Philosophy of Women's Liberation.* 1973, 1985.

Davaney, Sheila Greeve. "Problems with Feminist Theory: Historicity and the Search for Sure Foundations." In *Embodied Love: Sensuality and Relationship As Feminist Values.* Edited by Sharon Farmer et al. 1987.

Falk, Marcia. *The Book of Blessings.* 1996.

Fulkerson, Mary McClintock. *Changing the Subject: Women's Discourses and Feminist Theology.* 1994.

Gross, Rita M. *Feminism and Religion: An Introduction.* 1996.

Hassan, Riffat. "The Development of Feminist Theology as a Means of Combating Injustice Towards Women in Muslim Communities/Culture." *European Judaism* 28, no. 2 (1995): 80–90.

Heschel, Susannah, ed. *On Being a Jewish Feminist: A Reader.* 1983, 1995.

Isasi-Díaz, Ada-María. *An La Lucha/In the Struggle: A Hispanic Women's Liberation Theology.* 1993.

Klepfisz, Irena, and Melanie Kaye/Kantrowitz, eds. *The Tribe of Dina: A Jewish Women's Anthology.* 1986, 1989.

Levitt, Laura. *Jews and Feminism: The Ambivalent Search for Home.* 1997.

Peskowitz, Miriam, and Laura Levitt, eds. *Judaism Since Gender.* 1997.

Plaskow, Judith. *Sex, Sin, and Grace: Women's Experience and the Theologies of Reinhold Niebuhr and Paul Tillich.* 1980.

———. *Standing Again at Sinai.* 1990.

Plaskow, Judith, and Carol P. Christ, eds. *Weaving the Visions: New Patterns in Feminist Spirituality.* 1989.

Ruether, Rosemary Radford. *Sexism and God-Talk: Toward a Feminist Theology.* 1983.

Russell, Letty M., and L. Shannon Clarkson, eds. *Dictionary of Feminist Theologies.* 1996.

Fiorenza, Elisabeth Schüssler. "The Ethics of Interpretation: De-Centering Biblical Scholarship." *Journal of Biblical Literature* 107, no. 1 (1988): 3–17.

———. *In Memory of Her: A Feminist Theological Reconstruction of Christian Origins.* 1983.

———. *Jesus: Miriam's Child, Sofia's Prophet; Critical Issues in Feminist Christology.* 1994.

Umansky, Ellen. "Creating a Jewish Feminist Theology." In *Weaving the Vision.* Edited by Judith Plaskow and Carole Christ. 1989.

———. "Jewish Feminist Theology." In *Choices in Modern Jewish Thought: A Partisan Guide.* Edited by Eugene Borowitz. 1995.

Umansky, Ellen, and Dianne Ashton, eds. *Four Centuries of Jewish Women's Spirituality: A Sourcebook.* 1992.

Welch, Sharon D. *Communities of Resistance and Solidarity: A Feminist Theology of Liberation.* 1985.

Williams, Delores S. *Sisters in the Wilderness: The Challenge of Womanist God-Talk.* 1993.

See also: **Mujerista Tradition; Queer Theory; Womanist Traditions.**

MARIAN RONAN

LAURA LEVITT

Women-Centered Theology

Feminist theology has not been able to avoid becoming a sort of metanarrative that privileges the experiences of some women while silencing differences. Some also believe that it has fallen into an essentialism that ignores or minimizes the experiences of so-called minority and marginalized women, and women of developing countries. To counter these tendencies theologies coming from different women's groups have created their own identities and names (womanist, *mujerista*, eco-feminist, lesbian), or have had to add their own specificity to "feminist": Asian feminist, Asian-American feminist, Latin American feminist. "Women-centered theologies" or "women's liberation theologies" could be umbrella terms that include all of these different theologies without placing in the center the understandings and practices of feminist theology, which has been elaborated mostly by Euro-American women, and without reducing or transforming differences into opposition.

Women-centered or women's liberation theologies have as their source and locus the experiences of women, which are understood as social processes that include actions, evaluations, ethical value judgments, tendencies, and perspectives of the subject-agent within social, economic, political, and cultural frameworks. These experiences are valued because they reveal and validate different comprehensive ways of self-interpretation, of seeing and understanding the world, and of constructing self and society. Instead of attempting to identify attributes, define identity, or homogenize women's experiences, women-centered or women's liberation theologies highlight the material effects of their enterprise. Women-centered or women's liberation theologies consider as intrinsic elements the struggle for subjectivity and self-identity of all women and their liberation from various oppressions, including, but not limited to, racial, gendered, economic, and political.

The belief that it is not possible for anyone to be fully liberated until all are liberated makes terms such as women-centered or women's liberation theologies necessary for three reasons. First, women's theologies must not only acknowledge the problem of differences but they must do so in an interactive way. In other words, the understandings and struggles of women's groups other than one's own must be taken into consideration in each and every woman's theological elaboration and praxis. Second, because of their emphasis on liberation, women's theologies are praxical, that is to say, they are not only about elaborating analytical categories and understandings but also are about producing effective strategies that contribute to women's liberation. Thus women-centered or women's liberation theologies fa-cilitate the coming together of women's theologies to elaborate strategies that are beneficial to all women's groups. Third, liberation is not possible without effective solidarity among oppressed people and between oppressed people and privileged persons who are committed to the liberation of all persons. Women-centered or women's liberation theologies facilitate this process of solidarity by helping women's theologies' practitioners implement understandings of mutuality and accountability—intrinsic elements of solidarity—without being reduced to one feminist theological understanding and practice. Women-centered or women's liberation theologies seem to be more important to marginalized women's groups in Europe and the United States. This is in part because when such groups share their context with white Euro-American women through the elaboration of such theologies, the latter experience more keenly the oppressive nature of the essentializing and metanarrative tendencies of feminist theology. However, it is important to notice that African women refer to their theological work as African women-centered theology. They have found this term to be the one that best gathers the variety of theological insights based on the multiplicity of cultures and religious practices in the African continent.

BIBLIOGRAPHY

Cannon, Katie G., Ada María Isasi-Díaz, Kwok Pui-Lan, and Letty M. Russell. *Inheriting Our Mothers' Gardens: Feminist Theology in a Third World Perspective.* 1988.

Davaney, Sheila Greeve. "The Limits of the Appeal to Women's Experiences." In *Shaping New Visions.* Edited by Clarissa W. Atkinson, Constance H. Buchanan, and Margaret M. Miles. 1987.

Haddad, Beverly G. "Constructing Theologies of Survival in the South African Context: the Necessity of Critical Engagements Between Postmodernism and Liberation Theology." A presentation at the American Academy of Religion Conference, New Orleans, Louisiana, November, 1996.

hooks, bell. *Feminist Theory: From Margin to Center.* 1984.

Lugones, Maria C. "On the Logic of Pluralist Feminism." In *Feminist Ethics.* Edited by Claudia Card. 1991.

Mohanty, Chandra Talpade. "Feminist Encounters: Locating the Politics of Experience." In *Social Postmodernism: Beyond Identity Politics.* Edited by Linda Nicholson and Steven Seidman. 1995.

Welch, Sharon. "Sporting Power: American Feminism, French Feminism, and an Ethic of Conflict." In *Transfigurations: Theology and the French Feminists.*

Edited by C. W. Maggie Kim, Susan M. St. Ville, and Susan M. Simonaitis. 1993.

Young, Iris Marion. "Gender as Seriality: Thinking About Women as a Social Collective." In *Social Postmodernism: Beyond Identity Politics.* Edited by Linda Nicholson and Steven Seidman. 1995.

See also Liberation Theologies; Mujerista Tradition; Theology: Feminist Theology; Womanist Traditions.

ADA MARÍA ISASI-DÍAZ

Theosophy

Theosophy was articulated by Helena Petrovna Blavatsky (1831–1891), a Russian aristocrat, world traveler, and adventuress who, with a native of the United States, Col. Henry Steel Olcott (1832–1907), cofounded the Theosophical Society in 1875 in New York City. Blavatsky's two major works are *Isis Unveiled* (1877) and *The Secret Doctrine* (1888). Blavatsky claimed to have gained her knowledge by studying with mysterious Masters of the Wisdom, men with advanced spiritual understanding who communicated with her via occult means. Blavatsky and Olcott established the international headquarters of the Theosophical Society at Adyar, Madras, India, in 1882. Theosophy became an international movement, attracting liberals, freethinkers, socialists, and feminists in the West, where it popularized Eastern religious concepts, and sparked revitalization and nationalist movements among Hindus in India and Buddhists in Ceylon. Theosophical concepts continue to be important today in various New Age movements.

Theosophy teaches that the material universe was emanated from an impersonal, unmanifest source that can be metaphorically described in either feminine or masculine terms. The human soul has no sex and will be born variously into male and female bodies and in all races. One's life is best dedicated to service of all living beings, because all contain the spark of divinity. Spiritual disciplines and meditation should be practiced to develop wisdom. Theosophy is a monistic philosophy; higher consciousness is the awareness that all are one. Though Theosophy aims at awareness of higher planes of consciousness expressed in subtle matter, it values gross physical life because it is rooted in the divine source. The Theosophical Society (Adyar) formulated its goals in "Three Objects": 1) To form a nucleus of the universal brotherhood of humanity, without distinction of race, creed, sex, caste, or color. 2) To encourage the comparative study of religion, philosophy, and science. 3) To investigate unexplained laws of nature and the powers latent in humanity.

Madame Blavatsky struggled mightily to escape nineteenth-century restrictions on women, and early Theosophy attracted numerous feminists and social activists. Englishwoman Annie Besant (1847–1933), was the second president of the Theosophical Society (Adyar): in her speaking and writing she worked for the rights of women and the oppressed in England and India. She founded a Hindu educational system, agitated for Indian home rule, and promoted J. Krishnamurti as the next World-Teacher. Irishwoman Margaret Cousins (1878–1954) worked in Ireland and India for women's suffrage and in India founded the first two national women's organizations. Katherine Tingley (1847–1929) founded the Point Loma community in California, noted for its alternative school system, creative architecture, pageants and plays, and orchestra. Tingley and her core followers engaged in extensive social service with poor children and mothers in the United States

British feminist speaker and writer Annie Besant (1847–1933) was the second president of the Theosophical Society (Hulton-Deutsch Collection/Corbis).

and Cuba and with U.S. soldiers returning from the Spanish–American War.

In the early twentieth century, Theosophy was closely associated with the Russian women's movement. Theosophists have had varied understandings of gender roles, but the majority have affirmed the equality of women and men. Based upon Blavatsky's teachings many believe that, through male and female incarnations, the spiritually mature personality will develop an androgynous balance of feminine and masculine qualities. Tingley stressed that men and women have different characteristics and duties, and she opposed women's suffrage. Tingley's participation in public social service was seen as an extension of the role of mother. After 1928 Annie Besant and others promoted the World Mother movement, which asserted that motherhood was the defining experience and primary spiritual initiation of a woman's life. Although Theosophists' understandings of gender have usually reflected those of their cultural milieus, the initial relativizing of embodied femaleness by the doctrine of reincarnation was a distinctly feminist and countercultural position in the late nineteenth and early twentieth centuries.

Theosophical doctrines adopted from Hinduism are much in evidence in contemporary feminist spirituality. Feminist spirituality has been open to alternative forms of healing such as Therapeutic Touch, developed by contemporary Theosophists Dora Kunz and Delores Krieger. The definition of magic given by feminist wiccan thealogian Starhawk, as "the art of changing consciousness at will," is indebted to the theosophical belief that thought manifests in subtle matter as forms and colors, and that thought has the power to effect changes in gross physical matter. Contemporary feminist spirituality shares with Theosophy a concern to recover the wisdom of ancient traditions so as to create a better world, and an effort to create meaningful syntheses of the world's religions.

BIBLIOGRAPHY

Anderson, Nancy Fix. "Annie Besant as Champion of Women's Rights." *The American Theosophist* 82, no. 7 (1994): 3–5.

Ashcraft, William Michael. "The Dawn of the New Cycle: Point Loma Theosophists and American Culture." Ph.D. diss., University of Virginia, 1995.

Candy, Catherine Monica. "The Occult Feminism of Margaret Cousins in Modern Ireland and India, 1878–1954." Ph.D. diss., Loyola University of Chicago, 1996.

Carlson, Maria. *"No Religion Higher Than Truth": A History of the Theosophical Movement in Russia, 1875–1922.* 1993.

Cranston, Sylvia. *HPB: The Extraordinary Life and Influence of Helena Blavatsky, Founder of the Modern Theosophical Movement.* 1993.

Dixon, Joy. "Gender, Politics, and Culture in the New Age: Theosophy in England, 1880–1935." Ph.D. diss., Rutgers University, 1993.

Ellwood, Robert, and Catherine Wessinger. "The Feminism of 'Universal Brotherhood': Women in the Theosophical Movement." In *Women's Leadership in Marginal Religions: Explorations Outside the Mainstream.* Edited by Catherine Wessinger. 1993.

Kirkley, Evelyn A. " 'Equality of the Sexes, But . . .': Women in Point Loma Theosophy, 1899–1942." *Nova Religio* 1, no. 2 (1998): 272–288.

Waterstone, Penny Brown. "Domesticating Universal Brotherhood: Feminine Values and the Construction of Utopia, Point Loma Homestead, 1897–1920." Ph.D. diss., University of Arizona, 1995.

CATHERINE WESSINGER

Thérèse of Lisieux

Popular saint of the Catholic tradition and Doctor of the Church, Thérèse Martin (1873–1897) is widely seen as having remained a sentimental child throughout her short life. In truth, her autobiography, *Story of a Soul,* and the two volumes of her *Collected Letters* reveal her struggle for a spiritual maturity that integrated both independence and close relationships.

Thérèse's holiness was shaped by her family, late nineteenth-century French Catholicism, and most of all by her attraction to contemplative life in a Carmelite monastery. (The original Carmelites were inspired by Israelite and Christian hermits on Palestine's Mount Carmel.) Although her community included three of her four older sisters, she gradually differentiated herself from their views and even became a spiritual mentor to them. In contrast to Catholics who stressed a just God's desired reparation for the evils of the Franco-Prussian War and for Republican secularism and restriction of religion, Thérèse focused on a merciful God's compassion for the weak; she voiced her own desire to support all who struggled with religious doubt and needed assurance of God's love and goodness. Her Carmelite vocation inspired her to fashion a unique and modern image of holiness—an elevator. The spiritual journey is not an arduous human effort to ascend Mount Carmel, but a resting in the elevator of God's maternal arms, a Little Way of confidence and love. While tuberculosis decimated her physically, her desire to be generative love at the heart of the church vitalized her spiritually.

BIBLIOGRAPHY

Conn, Joann Wolski. "A Feminist View of Thérèse." In *Experiencing Saint Thérèse Today.* Edited by John Sullivan. 1990. Also included in *Women's Spirituality.* Edited by Joann Wolski Conn. 1996.

Martin, Thérèse. (Sainte Thérèse de l'Enfant-Jesus et de la Sainte-Face). *Manuscrits autobiographics.* Translated by François de Sainte-Marie. Lisieux, 1957.

Six, Jean-François. *Thérèse de Lisieux au Carmel.* Paris, 1973.

JOANN WOLSKI CONN

Time, Sacred

The term *sacred time* denotes the idea that certain moments, days, events, and intervals render sacred and powerful realities or alternative realities accessible to humans. Usually linked to notions of sacred space, which allows for connections and movements between the human and the divine, sacred time is a useful category for understanding important aspects of world religions. The many observances of sacred time can be divided into periodic or calendrical sacred times (such as sabbaths, holidays, and renewal rites) and occasional or noncalendrical sacred times (such as rites of passage, war, and crisis).

Ideas of sacred time are based on models provided by mythology and cosmology, so that notions of the origins and process of time are interwoven with views of creation, divinity, and the underlying structures of reality. Most notions of sacred time as cyclical have been based on the archaic observations of the passing of the seasons, planting and harvesting, the migration of animals, the movements of celestial bodies, solstices, and equinoxes. Contemporary secular notions of time as basically linear and irreversible—with a past, present, and future—are the result of complex historical interactions between religion, science, and culture. The idea of time moving independently of the seasons may be traced in part to mainstream interpretations of Judaism, Christianity, and Islam, and their basic beliefs in a singular creation (which occurred in the "past"), an ongoing sacred history revealing the presence of divinity, and a final Judgment or Apocalypse and paradisal age, which awaits in the "future." However, it would be simplistic to reduce Judeo-Christian-Islamic ideas to only linear time, as important elements of cyclical time

Muslim women in traditional dress pray at the Dome of the Rock during the holy month of Ramadan, Jerusalem, 1987 (Richard T. Nowitz/Corbis).

endure. In Judaism, for example, the festivals of Shavuot and Sukkot are related to the spring and fall agricultural seasons, and some Christian celebrations of Easter incorporate symbols of spring and fertility such as eggs, flowers, and rabbits. Both cyclical and linear models of time allow for the use of ritual as a means of engaging and renewing the sacred, ranging from seasonal planting and harvest festivals to Christian celebrations of the Eucharist and Muslim observances of Ramadan.

Although sacred time may be observed daily, as in Islamic prayers (*salat*) to Allah or Hindu devotions (*puja*) to Durgā or Krishna, it is also marked weekly in the Jewish Sabbath and annually in many "New Year" or renewal rites. Calendrical rites are often based on the idea that the presence of the sacred in the world "wears down" during the year and must be restored or renewed at special times. These widespread festivals of regeneration may involve activities such as fasting, purification, gift-giving, sacrifice, settling debts, and kindling new fires; they often require narrating or reenacting the cosmogonic myth, bringing to life the mythic time of creation, "origins," and ancestors. Such festivals in agricultural societies revive the fertility of soil and plants; in hunting societies restore the souls of game animals; and in city-states reestablish the sacred king and social order. There are underlying themes of rebirth; in ancient India, for example, the coronation of a king involved use of symbolic wombs, embryos, and birth fluids. Sacred time may thus celebrate the rise to earthly power of a male being, but this is often contingent on the blessing and support of a goddess or the agreement of ancestors and spirits.

Sacred time is also connected to ideas of cosmic order and chaos. While recitation of the cosmogonic myth serves to renew the basic structures of reality, chaos itself is recognized during special times of ritual license, disorder, and unconventional sexuality. For example, in Hinduism the springtime ritual of Holi allows for temporary role reversals and rowdiness; Roman Saturnalia had masters temporarily serving slaves; the pre-Christian harvest festival of Samhain (later Halloween) acknowledged the visit of disruptive departed spirits; and the Christian Lenten season is preceded by the licentious atmosphere of Mardi Gras and Carnival. Such times of license are especially sacred—if dangerous—because they represent the primal, uncontrolled forces of nature, the excesses that are balanced out by the conventions in place throughout most of the year.

Gender is recognized and reinforced during rites of passage, which mark stages of life including gestation, birth, naming, puberty, marriage, and death. In Hinduism, for example, a ritual performed during the third month of pregnancy is believed to result in the generation of a male fetus. Among the Navajo and Apache peoples of North America, the onset of menses is traditionally a time of celebration, identifying a young woman with the creatrix Changing Woman. Such rituals bring the individual and community into a special sacred time during which new identities are created and established. The correlation between a woman's menstrual cycle and the changing phases of the moon has led to notions of sacred time as renewable and lifegiving. Ancient artifacts represent these sacred lunar times using crescent, full, and new moons; some found in or near graves suggest the hope for the rebirth of the deceased. Cyclical time is not always viewed positively; in Buddhism the idea of the wheel of time and death (samsara) is often opposed to the experience of enlightenment (nirvana), the "extinction" of time.

At the close of the twentieth century, many views of sacred time are evident. Especially prevalent are apocalyptic notions that historical time will end with a final divine judgment, destruction of the old world, resurrection of the faithful, and the beginning of a paradisal age. Based on ideas found traditionally in Judaism, Christianity, and Islam, some interpretations of the coming end time envision an approaching cataclysm restoring the cosmos to its state at creation, before the Fall, with others hewing to themes of resurrection and paradise. Still others add intriguing dashes of alien beings, flying saucers, science fiction, and prophecy to the mix. Concepts and observances of sacred time will continue to change as society changes, providing scholars with windows into human values, attitudes, and institutions.

BIBLIOGRAPHY

Eliade, Mircea. *Myth and Reality.* 1990.

Lewis, James R., ed. *The Gods Have Landed: New Religions from Other Worlds.* 1995.

Paden, William E. *Religious Worlds: The Comparative Study of Religion.* 1994.

Russell, Jeffrey Burton. *A History of Heaven: The Singing Silence.* 1997.

Sproul, Barbara. *Primal Myths: Creation Myths Around the World.* 1992.

See also: **Geography, Sacred**; **Space, Sacred**.

GLEN ALEXANDER HAYES

Torah

In Judaism, the Torah is more than the base text of scriptural revelation; it functions as the living personification of the divine word in the physical world of space and time. This attitude is clearly reflected in the traditional laws and practices pertaining to the Torah scroll in the liturgical community of Israel. In the mythic imagination of the rabbis, which has provided the conceptual and practical framework within which the religious sensibility of Judaism in all of its diverse manifestations has evolved in the course of the last two thousand years, the Torah assumes the role of the instrument through which God created the world (Gen. Rabbah 1:1).

According to a Talmudic legend, R. Ishmael warned a particular scribe that he had to be very careful with respect to his professional activity since his work was the labor of God (*mele'khet shamayim*), and that if he added or subtracted one letter from the Torah, he could destroy the entire world (Babylonian Talmud, ʿEruvin 13a; Sotah 20a). This story underscores the supreme significance that rabbinic tradition places on the letters of Torah as instruments of divine creativity. By means of the Torah—that is, by means of the Hebrew letters, which are the subatomic particles of being—God created. It is in the Jewish mystical literature, however, that this rabbinic orientation is most fully embellished. Indeed, one of the ground concepts that has informed the various currents of Jewish esotericism is the belief that the letters reveal deep mysteries about the nature of being manifest in the divine, human, and cosmic spheres. In the ultimate sense, the letters are the divine form insofar as the spiritual energy of the divine light is concretized in the orthographic shape of the letters. From this perspective, as kabbalists themselves express the matter, the Torah symbolizes the female garment in which the masculine body of God is concurrently cloaked and revealed. Just as a garment hides and discloses the body over which it is draped, so the literal meaning of the scriptural text, which is closely linked to the material shape of the letters, functions as the cloak that conceals and reveals the spiritual sense. The profound paradox of the kabbalistic hermeneutics lies in the awareness that the concealment is itself the modality of disclosure.

The kabbalistic conception is an elaborate expansion of the feminine status attributed to the Torah already in the rabbinic sources. One may assume that the rabbinic depiction is itself based on earlier conceptions of the feminine wisdom (*sophia*) characteristic of apocryphal texts from the Hellenistic period. In the classical works from the formative period of rabbinic Judaism, there are several female images applied to the Torah: the Torah is depicted as the daughter of God, the bride of God or of Israel (and, in some cases, of Moses), or as the mother of Israel or of the sage more particularly. One of the most daring formulations regarding the erotic nature of the feminine Torah vis-à-vis the masculine deity is found in the aggadic statement attributed to R. Joshua ben Levi wherein Moses is portrayed as describing the Torah as the "hidden treasure" with which God takes delight each day. Here we encounter an interesting disjuncture between the social plane and the realm of symbolic discourse. That is, the ideal Torah society constructed by the rabbis is a thoroughly androcentric one in which the woman is accorded a respectful but ultimately secondary socioreligious status. There may be some exceptions, but the preponderance of evidence indicates that in the world of the rabbis the female is there to fulfill the domestic role that comple-

A rabbi studies a Torah scroll, Jerusalem, 1990 (Richard T. Nowitz/Corbis).

ments the task of the man to become a Torah scholar. The idealization of Torah as the female persona reinforced the androcentrism of rabbinic society.

Within the axiological framework of rabbinic culture, the feminine portrayal of Torah engendered a culture of desire centered on learning as an erotic activity. Perhaps this is most dramatically represented by the tradition regarding the second-century Palestinian sage, Ben Azzai, who was criticized by his colleagues for adopting a life of celibacy, which made it impossible for him to fulfill the biblical injunction to procreate (Gen. 1:28). In his own defense, Ben Azzai reportedly said, "What can I do? My soul lusts for the Torah; the world can be sustained by others" (Babylonian Talmud 63b). The Torah functions as Ben Azzai's feminine mate, and his passionate cleaving to her replaces his marrying an earthly woman with whom he would be engaged in procreative sex. Although this figure is clearly presented as the exception, from the extreme case one can learn something about the norm.

The spiritual lust that informs the texture of rabbinic culture is most fully developed in the medieval kabbalistic tradition. Thus, for instance, according to the Zohar—the major work that surfaced in the latter part of the thirteenth century—the propitious time for the conjugal act is midnight, which is the hour when God is said to visit the souls of the righteous in the Garden of Eden so as to take delight in them. In almost every instance, the delight that is attributed to God is related to the study of Torah on the part of the kabbalists. Hence, at the very moment that most Jewish males engage in marital sex, the mystical elite renounce physical sexuality in favor of a spiritualized relationship with God that is consummated through midrashic activity of an intensely erotic nature. The Torah has been transformed, therefore, into the textual body of the divine feminine, the Shekhinah, which is the object of the male mystic's erotic desire on the spiritual plane. The model of the abstinent mystic was Moses, who, according to rabbinic sources, separated from his wife after having received the Torah. The primary means by which the kabbalist emulates Moses and is united with the Shekhinah is study of Torah, a spiritually erotic experience that presupposes the negation of physical eros.

BIBLIOGRAPHY

Boyarin, Daniel. *Carnal Israel: Reading Sex in Talmudic Literature.* 1993.

———. *Intertextuality and the Reading of Midrash.* 1990.

Fishbane, Michael. *The Garments of Torah: Essays in Biblical Hermeneutics.* 1989.

Fraade, Steven D. *From Tradition to Commentary: Torah and Its Interpretation in the Midrash Sifre to Deuteronomy.* 1991.

Goldberg, Harvey E. "Torah and Children: Some Symbolic Aspects of the Reproduction of Jews and Judaism." In *Judaism Viewed from Within and from Without: Anthropological Studies.* Edited by Harvey E. Goldberg. 1987.

Idel, Moshe. "Infinities of Torah in Kabbalah." In *Midrash and Literature.* Edited by Geoffrey Hartman and Sanford Budick. 1986.

Neusner, Jacob. *Torah: From Scroll to Symbol in Formative Judaism.* 1985.

Scholem, Gershom. "The Meaning of Torah in Jewish Mysticism." In *On the Kabbalah and Its Symbolism.* Translated by Ralph Manheim. 1965.

Stern, David. *Parables in Midrash: Narrative and Exegesis in Rabbinic Literature.* 1991.

Wolfson, Elliot R. "Female Imaging of the Torah: From Literary Metaphor to Religious Symbol." In *Circle in the Square: Studies in the Use of Gender in Kabbalistic Symbolism.* 1995.

ELLIOT R. WOLFSON

Transcendentalism

Transcendentalism was a religious, philosophical, literary, and social reform movement. Emerging in the United States in the 1820s and lasting about forty years, it peaked in the 1840s with the formation of the "Transcendental Club" (1836–1840), the publication of its literary journal, *The Dial* (1840–1844), and the establishment of two utopian communities, Brook Farm (1841–1847) and Fruitlands (1843–1844). Among the figures most strongly associated with Transcendentalism are Ralph Waldo Emerson, whose *Nature* (1836) was considered the Transcendentalist bible; Margaret Fuller (*Woman in the Nineteenth Century* and first editor of *The Dial*); Henry David Thoreau (*Walden* [1854]); George Ripley (*Discourses on the Philosophy of Religion* [1836] and founder of Brook Farm); Sophia Ripley; social activist Orestes Brownson (*New Views of Christianity, Society, and the Church* [1836]); Bronson Alcott (founder of Fruitlands); Elizabeth Peabody (founder of the Peabody School); and several practicing ministers—Frederic Henry Hedge, James Freeman Clarke, Theodore Parker, and William Ellery Channing.

Transcendentalism grew out of Unitarianism. Some would say it was a break from, others that it was a reform of Unitarianism. It raised a general challenge to the Lockean empiricism of the day, claiming that evidence of miracles in the Bible was unnecessary for a belief in Christianity. Rather, Transcendentalists believed in the direct perception of God. They believed that the truth that transcended sensory experience could be known intuitively, and any woman or man could grasp the truth by searching within their own soul.

Transcendentalists believed in an all-encompassing unity variously referred to as the Oversoul, the Universal Spirit, or God, that surrounded and pervaded all. Transcendentalists were not so much pantheist as panentheist—believing that the divine was expressed and revealed in all of creation. They particularly embraced nature as revealing the divine spirit and found in nature a source of moral and spiritual meaning, joy, and wonder.

Transcendentalists regarded the individual soul both as a unique expression of the individual and as an ex-ing up more possibilities for women. Third, the fact that this experience of the divine was available to all, male and female, and that the divine was in all, male and female, led to a particular appreciation of the equality of the sexes. Fourth, inasmuch as females are historically and culturally associated with nature, Transcendentalism through its appreciation of nature brought a positive perspective to conceptions of womanhood. Finally, Transcendentalism encouraged women to discover their own special genius, free from sexual stereotypes and expectations, a theme that is especially developed in Margaret Fuller's *Woman in the Nineteenth Century*. The Transcendentalist movement helped to lay an intellectual foundation for the women's rights movement that was to develop in the United States in the late 1840s.

BIBLIOGRAPHY

Some of the most important primary works, as mentioned above, include:

Brownson, Orestes. *New Views of Christianity, Society, and the Church.* 1836.

Emerson, Edward Waldo, ed. *The Complete Works of Ralph Waldo Emerson.* 12 vols. 1903–1904. Reprint, 1968.

Fuller, Margaret. *Woman in the Nineteenth Century.* 1845. Facsimile repr. with intro. by Madeleine B. Stern and textual note by Joel Myerson. 1980.

Harding, Walter, et al. *The Writings of Henry D. Thoreau.* 1971.

Ripley, George. *Discourses on the Philosophy of Religion. Addressed to Doubters Who Wish to Believe.* 1836.

Thoreau, Henry David. *Walden: Or Life in the Woods.* Unabridged ed. 1995.

Among the most useful overviews of the Transcendentalist movement are:

Boller, Paul F. *American Transcendentalism, 1830–1860.* 1974.

Koster, Donald N. *Transcendentalism in America.* 1975.

Rose, Anne C. *Transcendentalism as a Social Movement, 1830–1850.* 1981.

Though somewhat dated, a thorough compilation of primary and secondary sources, as well as critical research, is:

Myerson, Joel, ed. *The Transcendentalists: A Review of Research and Criticism.* 1984.

Of particular interest are the more recent feminist biographies of Margaret Fuller. These include:

Bartlett, Elizabeth Ann. *Liberty, Equality, Sorority: The Origins and Interpretation of American Feminist*

Poet and essayist Ralph Waldo Emerson (1803–1882) was a central figure of the Transcendentalism movement (Library of Congress/Corbis).

pression of the Universal Soul and sought the mystical experience of the union, or reunion, of the individual soul and the Universal Soul. This strong belief in the uniqueness of the individual soul was the foundation for accompanying beliefs in self-reliance, independence, and the gifts of one's own special genius. Yet this individualism was not isolationism, but rather a linking of all through the Universal Soul.

That Transcendentalism was open to the idea of the equality of the sexes is apparent in the inclusion and leadership of women in the movement. Several aspects of Transcendentalism rendered it more inclusive of women than contemporary religious sects. First, Transcendentalists regarded God not so much as a Creator-Father as a universal spirit. Rather than a male figure, this spirit was generally perceived as genderless. Second, the fact that Transcendentalists believed that religious truths were discovered through immediate perception eliminated reliance on male-translated and written texts and the male-dominated ministry, open-

Thought: Frances Wright, Sarah Grimké, and Margaret Fuller. 1994.

Stern, Madeline B. *Life of Margaret Fuller.* Rev. ed., 1990.

Von Mehren, Joan. *Minerva and the Muse: A Life of Margaret Fuller.* 1994.

See also Nature.

ELIZABETH ANN BARTLETT

Tricksters

The figure of a trickster, in any story, is intended to provide both entertainment and education. Trickster conveys the sense that the creation of the world is a continual process. Trickster can appear as man, woman, animal, or as a natural or supernatural force. Traditions that have the figure of trickster frequently contain one or more of the following elements: deception, disguise, sexuality, seduction, gender, transvestism, substitution, the birth of twins or siblings, younger sibling displacing an older sibling, reversals, reconciliation following deception, and subversion of authority. Because tricksters characteristically undermine normative roles within the social order, stories with trickster point to the ways in which human beings remember and reconcile themselves to the way life unfolds: inevitably contrary and difficult to evaluate. Life is often many things at once, both and neither at the same time, tragic and hilarious. Trickster motifs underscore the way humor acts as a tool to survive the tragic limits of human beings and the consequences of attempting to defy those limits. Trickster figures themselves often defy boundaries and play against the limits of human beings (whether they take human form or not), the social order, and the multiple manifestations of the sacred.

Tricksters are best known as figures in indigenous storytelling. The name *trickster* was developed regarding Native North American religious traditions. However, as a being and as a motif generally, the trickster is prevalent in and as various as many religious traditions. There are certain characteristics that most tricksters share, and by comparing trickster as it appears in several cultural traditions, one can more fully understand its complexities and nuances.

Language, as it is understood in many indigenous traditions, as well as in text-based religions, brings the world into being. The figure of trickster is often closely associated with language, its genesis, use, and misuse. In the Lakota tradition, Iktome is a trickster in the form of a female spider and is associated with the creation of

the alphabet and the beginning of speech. The relationship between trickster and language is not exclusive to the American Indian tradition. The ancient Greeks credited Hermes with the discovery of the character *delta*. Hermes, the messenger god who was also the patron of thieves, rogues, and troubadours, had an association with language that persisted. Renaissance mystics devoted to alchemy related Hermes to the Egyptian figure of Thoth, the Egyptian god of wisdom and originator of language. Though the origin of language and its relationship to trickster is inevitably gendered, the figure is implicated in the origin of both speech and writing.

Though tricksters are mostly male there are some female trickster figures. The Cree, located in Alberta, Canada, have an extremely flexible trickster figure. Sometimes appearing as a female animal, often a coyote, she will disguise herself as a man in order to seduce another female animal, often a fox (who is also a tricky seducer). Once the coyote is discovered in her ruse, there is initial astonishment followed by reconciliation between the two. More common are stories where women are duped into having sex with tricksters who disguise themselves in order to seduce the innocent women. For instance, one version of a common Sioux motif contains a young maiden at a river; the trickster will send his enormous penis across the water which the (innocent) maiden will feel only as a water snake between her legs. Another recurrent theme involves mothers assisting their child, usually male, to disguise himself to thwart his rival, often a sibling. Understanding the gender implications of trickster must include not only the figure itself but also who assists the trickster and who is tricked. The transgression of normative sexual, social, and gender boundaries is often operating at several levels.

One helpful way to interpret trickster is to compare various portrayals. The book of Genesis has been read by Susan Niditch as a series of trickster folktales where wives, sisters, brothers, and even sacrifices are switched repeatedly, confounding those struggling to come into relation with God. In the Christian tradition, there are several early, non-canonical gospels that depict Jesus as a young boy who does not understand his power. Numerous indigenous accounts show how trickster comes to understand his or her own power through its misuse. Jesus as a speaker of parables also mirrors the figure of trickster as one who confuses and confounds through language, revealing multiple and contradictory levels of truth about human relationship to the sacred and the profane. Krishna, in the Hindu tradition, is depicted as a little boy who steals butter and is called the "Butterstealer," though in an affectionate and indulgent way. Thievery is a common theme throughout trickster sto-

The Greek Hermes is a divine messenger, trickster, and thief. He carries the caduceus, serpents twined about a winged staff, symbol of his mission as herald of the gods, in a sculpture by Giovanni Bologna, 1580 (Art Resource, New York).

"liberate[s] the mind." This liberation happens when trickster reverses or subverts the social order and erupts into life, the most important story of all, as thief, liar, seducer, lover, and clown.

BIBLIOGRAPHY

Basso, Keith H. *Portraits of the "Whiteman": Linguistic Play and Cultural Symbols among the Western Apache.* 1979, 1995.

Cooper-Oakley, Elizabeth. *Masonry & Medieval Mysticism: Traces of a Hidden Tradition.* 1900, 1977.

Cunningham, Keith. *American Indians' Kitchen-Table Stories.* 1992.

Dimmitt, Cornelia, and J. A. B. van Buitenen, eds. and trans. *Classical Hindu Mythology: A Reader in the Sanskrit Puranas.* 1978.

Erdoes, Richard, and Alfonso Ortiz. *American Indian Myths and Legends.* 1984.

Frankfort, Henri, ed. *The Intellectual Adventure of Ancient Man: An Essay on Speculative Thought in the Ancient Near East.* 1946, 1977.

Niditch, Susan. *Underdogs and Tricksters: A Prelude to Biblical Folklore.* 1987.

O'Flaherty, Wendy Doniger. *Women, Androgynes, and Other Mythical Beasts.* 1987.

Radin, Paul. *The Trickster: A Study in American Indian Mythology.* 1972, 1978.

Scott, James C. *Domination and The Arts of Resistance: Hidden Transcripts.* 1990.

Sullivan, Lawrence E. *Icanchu's Drum: An Orientation to Meaning in South American Religions.* 1988.

Vizenor, Gerald. *Shadow Distance: A Gerald Vizenor Reader.* 1994.

CATHERINE MCHALE

ries. Krishna as a young man is also capable of making love to several thousand women at once, like many trickster figures in the Americas and West Africa. The stories involving the Buddha and his propensity for teaching through the use of riddle also reflect a trickster sensibility. Each tradition offers a variety of lenses through which people perceive their culture; some views destabilize the sacred through irreverence whereas others subvert the social order. Many trickster stories do both things at once.

Of the many layers within trickster motifs, some point to profound theological understandings regarding how human beings locate themselves in the world. This sense of place, when understood or remembered through a trickster motif or the figure of trickster with all of the accompanying reversals, has both serious and humorous implications. Trickster motifs enable us to see ourselves as embedded in the social order but also able, to varying degrees, to defy the limits of social constraints. Gerald Vizenor observes that trickster motifs

Truth

Truth has been personified as female in several religious traditions. The ancient Egyptian goddess of truth, Ma'at, daughter of the sun god Re, was an important figure in funerary rituals, where she was depicted as weighing the hearts of the departed. Her name referred also to the concept of cosmic order, represented on a national level by the pharaoh and on an individual level by principles of honesty and harmony.

Personifications of Wisdom similar in some ways to Ma'at occur in the religions of the Ancient Near East, especially in the figure of Wisdom (Ḥokhmah) as described in the Wisdom books of the Bible. Under the Greek name of Sophia she undergoes further developments in the Hellenistic traditions of both Jewish and Christian theology, and most strikingly in gnostic thought, with its elaborate descriptions of successive emanations from the Absolute. In the most influential school of gnosticism, that of the second-century Egyptian philosopher Valentinus, prominence is given not only to Wisdom or Sophia but also to Truth or Aletheia. Aletheia is the female half of a paired emanation, which becomes the source of Logos (the Word) and Zoe (Life) and, in a later emanation, of Christ and the Holy Spirit.

In ancient Greek and Roman culture direct personifications of truth such as Aletheia in Greece and Veritas in Rome were probably more literary than religious, but closely related goddesses were of considerable religious importance. In Rome the temple of Fides, the goddess of honesty and trustworthiness, had an active place in official diplomatic and legislative matters, and in Greece the cult of Themis, goddess of justice, was widespread. Themis was connected with truth not only because of her judicial aspect but also because of her role as the giver of oracles; she was considered the original owner of the oracle at Delphi, which later became Apollo's. Like Ma'at in Egypt, Themis was depicted as holding scales; she survives in modern form in the figure of Blind Justice still associated with the American legal system.

In South Asia cosmic order was considered impersonal, just as it was in Chinese Taoism and in many other traditions, but aspects of wisdom were personified in the form of female deities associated with insight and knowledge, most richly so in tantric forms of religion, both Hindu and Buddhist. Of greatest general importance is the goddess of speech, often called Sarasvatī, who is worshiped across a wide spectrum of South Asian religious traditions and who is associated with a range of matters connected with speech, including insight, education, literature, and judicial testimony.

Rules for judicial testimony in religiously based systems of law have much to say about women. Despite general remarks on the wickedness of women, specific rules are usually based less on moral assessments than on issues of cognitive disposition and access to information. In Jewish law the Talmud rejects the testimony of women in general on the grounds of their lightheadedness. In Islamic law two women's testimony is necessary to equal that of one man; women's testimony is valued in connection with crimes committed in the interior of the house and is essential in disputes involving matters such as breastfeeding. Hindu law is similar. The best-known Hindu treatise, the Laws of Manu, allows both men and women to testify falsely if the truth would cause grave harm but requires the witness to make expiatory offerings to the goddess Sarasvatī. Manu re-

marks in general on the crookedness of women, equates them with falsehood itself, and says that where one good man is acceptable as witness even a hundred pure women are not; but the text allows the testimony of women on crimes committed in the interior of a home and recommends women as witnesses for women.

Questions of marital fidelity involve special rules of testimony. In the Laws of Manu, lust is cited as an excuse both for accepting false oaths from men and for rejecting true pleas from women. As a necessity of life in a polygamous society, a man is expressly allowed to swear to each wife that he loves her more than the others and to swear to a bride that he will take no other wives. But a woman suspected of marital infidelity is not allowed to claim innocence and must be subjected to an ordeal, as in Mosaic law (Numbers 5:11).

Such ordeals are central in India's most popular story, that of Rama's treatment of his wife Sītā and her reliance on the truth, as told in the epic Rāmāyaṇa. Elsewhere in Indian religious literature the theme of the woman who clings to the truth as her only defense against male-dominated institutions of power is conspicuous in every period, from the Vedic texts (such as the tale of Jabālā and her sidestepping of the paternity issue, Chāndogya Upanishad 3.4.1–4), through the old Mahābhārata epic (such as the story of Draupadī in the court, told in the second book, and of Damayantī at her groom-choosing, told in the third book), to medieval and modern literature (as in many of the *vratakathā* stories told in the performance of votive observances).

Recourse to an utterance of the truth was ritualized in ancient India in the practice called the Act of Truth (Sanskrit *satya-kriyā*, Pali *sacca-kiriyā*), in which a person publicly proclaimed some personal truth, usually one not openly known, and then formally called upon the power of the truth she had released in order to bring about a particular result. Often the truth that is revealed is an embarrassing one or one that is in ironic contrast to the result being sought; for example, a woman may save her husband's life by revealing that she has never loved him. The ritual is found in both Hindu and Buddhist texts from the Vedic period onward. Although both men and women are on record as having performed the Act of Truth, it was particularly important for women because of its frequent portrayal as their only means of access to power.

BIBLIOGRAPHY

Brown, W. Norman. "Duty as Truth in Ancient India." *Proceedings of the American Philosophical Society* 116 (1972): 252–268.

Bryce, Glendon E. *A Legacy of Wisdom: The Egyptian Contribution to the Wisdom of Israel.* 1979.

Burlingame, Eugene Watson. "The Act of Truth (Saccakiriya): A Hindu Spell and Its Employment as a Psychic Motif in Hindu Fiction." *Journal of the Royal Asiatic Society* (1917): 429–467.

Buitenen, J.A.B. van, trans. *The Mahābhārata.* Vol. 2: Book 2 (The Book of the Assembly Hall) and Book 3 (The Book of the Forest). 1975.

Doniger, Wendy, and Brian K. Smith, trans. *The Laws of Manu.* 1991.

Olivelle, Patrick, trans. *Upaniṣads.* 1996.

Rudolph, Kurt. "Wisdom." Translated from the German by Matthew J. O'Connell. In *The Encyclopedia of Religion.* Edited by Mircea Eliade. 1987.

Venkatesananda, Swami. *The Concise Rāmāyaṇa of Vālmīki.* 1988.

Wayman, Alex. "The Hindu-Buddhist Rite of Truth: An Interpretation." In *Studies in Indian Linguistics.* Edited by Bhadriraju Krishnamurti. 1968.

Würthwein, Ernst. "Egyptian Wisdom and the Old Testament." In *Studies in Ancient Israelite Wisdom.* Edited by James L. Crenshaw. 1976.

See also **Draupadī**; **Sarasvatī**; **Wisdom**.

GARY A. TUBB

Twelve-Step Programs

The genesis of the recovery movement can be found in the Alcoholics Anonymous (AA) program, which began in 1935 with the recognition that one alcoholic sharing with another can be a source of healing. Although the membership was initially restricted to men, Lois Wilson and Anne Smith, the wives of the founders, began their own support group for relatives of alcoholics known by 1951 as Al-Anon. While women now too join AA, they remain the majority in Al-Anon groups. The core of the recovery system of AA and Al-Anon is codified in the Twelve Steps, which, according to AA, delineate the process of achieving sobriety.

While there is much to be supportive of, the popularity and positive aspects of Twelve-Step recovery programs need to be understood in terms of their implications for women's healing. Whether these communities truly are sites of transformation and whether they actively support the radical altering of the oppressive conditions of many women's lives must be addressed.

It may be that the desire to be related to others in meaningful and mutually empowering ways is at the heart of our "disorders."

Many women entering a Twelve-Step group are burdened by the uniquely female "sin" of self-negation and of hiding (see Dunfee, 1982). Too often, women's strivings for "more self" and more life-giving relationships become pathologized as diseases and are then internalized as being sick and shameful. It is of concern that, within the recovery movement, the realities of women's lives may tend to be obscured by the metaphors of addiction.

By turning to contemporary feminist thought in religion and in psychology, we may search for new mythologies as sources of different kinds of knowledge and power for women and for men. If Twelve Step and other recovery programs are to be truly transformative for women, then women and men will be challenged to move from the denial of eros to living truthfully our erotic connection to all of life; from alienation in our relationships to an awareness of our interconnectedness; from inauthenticity in our communities to active responsibility for changing cultural oppressions. Perhaps then the split in consciousness that is our religious and cultural heritage, born by women and inscribed on our bodies and in our lives, may eventually be healed.

BIBLIOGRAPHY

Alcoholics Anonymous World Services, Inc. *Twelve Steps and Twelve Traditions.* 1975.

Bepko, Claudia. "Disorders of Power: Women and Addiction in the Family." In *Women in Families.* Edited by Monica McGoldrick, Carol M. Anderson, and Froma Walsh. 1989.

Brown, Laura. "What's Addiction Got to Do with It: A Feminist Critique of Codependence." *Psychology of Women* 17, no. 1 (1990): 1–4.

Clemmons, Peggy. "Feminists, Spirituality, and the Twelve Steps of Alcoholics Anonymous." *Women and Therapy* 11, no. 2 (1991): 97–109.

Driscoll, Ellen. "The Politics of Recovery." In *Consuming Passions: Feminist Approaches to Weight Preoccupation and Eating Disorders.* Edited by Catrina Brown and Karin Jasper. 1993.

Dunfee, Susan. "The Sin of Hiding: A Feminist Critique of Reinhold Niebuhr's Account of the Sin of Pride." *Soundings* 65, no. 3 (1982): 316–327.

Goldenberg, Naomi. *Returning Words to Flesh: Feminism, Psychoanalysis, and the Resurrection of the Body.* 1990.

Haaken, Janice. "A Critical Analysis of the Codependency Construct." *Psychiatry* 53, no. 4 (1990): 396–406.

Heyward, Carter. *Touching Our Strength: The Erotic as Power and the Love of God.* 1989.

hooks, bell. *Sisters of the Yam: Black Women and Self-Recovery.* 1993.

Tallen, Bette. "Twelve Step Programs: A Lesbian Feminist Critique." *NWSA Journal* 2, no. 3 (1990): 390–407.

Van Den Bergh, Nan. "Having Bitten the Apple: A Feminist Perspective on Addictions." In *Feminist Perspectives on Addictions.* Edited by Nan Van Den Berg. 1991.

ELLEN M. DRISCOLL

Underhill, Evelyn

Evelyn Underhill (1875–1941), English author and spiritual director, is best known for her book *Mysticism* (1911), a monumental phenomenological study that charts an influential landscape of the spiritual life through successive stages. She wrote at least ten other books on the spiritual life (the best known is *Worship*, 1936), several novels, and a book of poetry. She also assisted Rabindranath Tagore in the translation of Bengali poetry attributed to Kabir and (often with Lucy Menzies) edited or introduced modern English translations of medieval Christian mystics.

Underhill grew up in a nonreligious but loosely Anglican home. She was one of the first women at King's College, London, where she studied history, languages, botany, art, and philosophy. In 1907 she decided to convert to Roman Catholicism, but the papal condemnation of modernism created such deep intellectual obstacles that she stayed instead in the Anglican communion. Also in that year she married Hubert Stuart Moore, who encouraged her literary life but shared none of her religious convictions.

Renowned as a retreat leader, Underhill served as spiritual director for several women but always sought male guidance for herself—notably, from the English Catholic and modernist Baron Friedrich von Hügel. Her understanding of religious life was highly schematic and ahistorical, deeply influenced by the French philosopher of vitalism, Henri Bergson. Although her works take other religions into account, she is essentially a Christian author. Late in life she became an ardent pacifist, but she was no feminist, arguing against women's ordination to the priesthood for fear of further separating Anglicans and Roman Catholics. Nevertheless, she was responsible for bringing attention to such medieval women mystics as Julian of Norwich, Angela of Foligno, and Teresa of Avila.

BIBLIOGRAPHY

The major works by Underhill still easily available include *Mysticism: A Study in the Nature and Development of Man's Spiritual Consciousness* (1911); *Practical Mysticism: A Little Book for Normal People* (1914); *Worship* (1936); *The Essentials of Mysticism and Other Essays* (1960); and *The Letters of Evelyn Underhill*, edited by Charles Williams (1943). Biographies of Underhill are Christopher Armstrong, *Evelyn Underhill* (1975) and Dana Greene, *Evelyn Underhill: Artist of the Infinite Life* (1990).

E. ANN MATTER

Utopian Communities

The term *utopia*, which Thomas More coined for the title of his book in 1516, carries an ironic double meaning from the Greek. The "good place" (*eu-topos*) is also "no place" (*ou-topos*). Utopia may be broadly used to refer to an ideal primordial past, such as the Garden of Eden in Genesis or Hesiod's vision of a Golden Age, or to a heaven or other idyllic world, such as the Muslim visions of paradise, the Greco-Roman Isles of the Blessed, and the Buddhist Pure Land. Any utopian vision will present influential models of ideal gender roles, as the story of Adam and Eve shows. Utopian communities can be more narrowly conceived as

A dance at a Shaker meeting house, New Lebanon, New York (Library of Congress/Corbis)

vividly imagined and hopefully implemented blueprints for an ideal society, which also inevitably include guidelines for the proper conduct and relationships of women and men.

As ideas and as social experiments, utopias are explicitly conceived as alternatives to a flawed status quo. They critique existing practices and propose a better way. For example, in the early fifteenth-century French allegory *The Book of the City of Ladies,* the author, Christine de Pizan, is commissioned by the female figures of Reason, Rectitude, and Justice to construct an ideal city that will display the many virtues of women and refute the calumnies spoken against them by men. In practice, however, utopian communities face unrelenting internal and external pressures to compromise or abandon their ideals and conform to existing social norms. In Rosabeth Moss Kanter's words, "reality modifies the dream." But even when they remain wholly in the realm of ideas, utopias can have a powerful critical force. For example, toward the end of Charlotte Perkins Gilman's feminist utopian novel *Herland* (1915) the male narrator remarks, "I began to see both ways more keenly than I had before; to see the painful defects of my own land, the marvelous gains of this."

Many religious communities start out as utopian ventures. Often responding to the message proclaimed by a charismatic leader, devout followers assemble in order to make the new religious vision a social reality. The utopian enclave can differentiate itself from its host society by implementing dramatic changes in the organization of work, the distribution of wealth, social relations, education, government, law, politics, and other areas that it understands as definitive of human life. Re-imaginings of gender roles and of practices such as marriage and child-rearing often play a prominent role in utopian visions. For example, child-rearing and education in the all-female society of *Herland* are both communal rather than familial responsibilities. But whenever they have occurred, departures from conventional gender roles and sexual practice have also been a source of turmoil within utopian groups and a flashpoint for conflict between utopian communities and the outside world, as the difficulties both provoked and encountered by the male visitors to the fictional *Herland* suggest. Similar turmoil occurs when independent women such as Māhādeviyakka and Mirabai visit utopian communities.

Utopia remains very much in the eye of the beholder, and the roles of women within utopian communities vary significantly. In the nineteenth-century United States, the Shakers, Mormons, and the Oneida community all attempted to implement utopian visions of the family, marriage, and sexual relations. Their strikingly different sexual arrangements ranged from the Shakers' evenhanded demand for strict male and female celibacy through the Mormons' androcentric polygamy to the Oneida Perfectionists' complex group marriage. Late twentieth-century religious movements such as the Family (formerly the Children of God), the Unification Church, and the Branch Davidians have also tried to put into practice their own visions of an ideal society. For a time the Family encouraged the use of female sexuality in recruiting new members (through "flirty fishing") and advocated complete sexual freedom within the community; the Unification Church continues to promote interracial marriages of couples "matched" by the Reverend Sun Myung Moon himself; David Koresh imposed celibacy on his followers while claiming all Branch Davidian women as his potential mates in the effort to sire a group of holy children who would reign in the world to come. Those three examples demonstrate forcefully that utopian experiments need not necessarily move in the direction of greater freedom and equality for women.

As the double meaning of utopia suggests, and as practical experience abundantly confirms, the path from idea to experiment to continuing way of life progressively leads any utopian community into persistent tension and conflict with the intransigent realities of social life and history. Attempts to make a utopia come alive and stay alive face many obstacles. As a result, utopian communities typically face the difficult dilemma of softening their commitments to their original ideals or putting their very existence in peril. Part of a compromise may involve delaying the full accomplishment of the utopian ideals until an indefinite future, but it may also involve other adjustments to the original utopian vision.

The present situation of the Shakers suggests some of the potential costs of remaining strictly faithful to utopian ideals. Inspired by the accounts of primitive Christian communism in Acts 2:44–45, Mother Ann Lee's United Society of Believers in Christ's Second Appearing formed celibate communities that practiced communal ownership of goods and thoroughgoing sexual equality and understood God as being both Mother and Father. The ability of Shaker communities to attract converts, however, has consistently and dramatically declined since the mid-nineteenth century. Today, only a handful of the faithful remain. Joseph Smith's Church of Jesus Christ of Latter-day Saints presents a different example. The Mormons' original espousal of plural marriage was one of the primary causes of tension with non-Mormon society. The 1890 Manifesto that announced that the Mormon Church had terminated the practice of plural marriage significantly lessened the tensions between Mormons and their fellow citizens and also paved the way for Utah's admission into the Union. In an effort to return to the purity of Mormon origins, however, some contemporary dissidents have reintroduced the practice of polygamy, indicating the persistence of the utopian ideal and disturbing Mormon feminists in the process. Economic factors, including both prosperity and poverty, can also disturb the fragile stability of utopian communities. The Farm, a contemporary communal group located in southern Tennessee and given to wide-ranging spiritual experimentation, suffered a severe decrease in membership because of economic difficulties in the early 1980s and no longer insists on holding all goods in common.

In some cases a utopian vision can be projected onto a hoped-for future. For example, in his letter to a group of fellow believers in ancient Galatia, the Christian missionary Paul of Tarsus wrote that "there is neither Jew nor Greek, there is neither slave nor free, there is neither male nor female; for you are all one in Christ Jesus" (Gal. 3:28). Other information from his correspondence, however, shows that such a total undoing of social conventions, including gender roles, was beyond Paul's practical grasp. There was, in his world, literally no place where such a utopian vision could be put into practice. He seems, however, to have envisioned that such an unfettered existence would finally become possible at the imminent end of the world, a transformation for which he so eagerly hoped.

Utopian experiments, in both thought and action, must always be seen in relationship to their host societies. Perceived unfaithfulness, injustices or inequalities in the status quo provide their inspiration, but utopian communities often focus selectively on the ills that they seek to remedy. As a result, utopian communities may simply replicate the pre-existing gender dynamics of their host societies, especially if the attention of the leadership and most members is concentrated elsewhere. Not every utopia is a Herland, and gender-based tensions can threaten the stability of utopian communities. Whatever form they take, the society from which they spring exerts on utopian communities tremendous pressure to conform, whether through the force of public opinion, formal legal mechanisms, or even the exercise of violence. Utopian dreams and visions, however, remain remarkably resilient and sometimes provide the primary vehicle for efforts to establish a good, just, and equal society.

BIBLIOGRAPHY

Burridge, Kenelm. *New Heaven, New Earth: A Study of Millenarian Activities.* 1969.

de Pizan, Christine. *The Book of the City of Ladies.* Translated by Earl Jeffrey Richards. 1982.

Fiorenza, Elisabeth Schüssler. *In Memory of Her: A Feminist Theological Reconstruction of Christian Origins.* 1983.

Foster, Lawrence. *Women, Family, and Utopia: Communal Experiments of the Shakers, the Oneida Community, and the Mormons.* 1991.

Kanter, Rosabeth Moss. *Commitment and Community: Communes and Utopias in Sociological Perspective.* 1972.

Kolmerten, Carol A. *Women in Utopia: The Ideology of Gender in the American Owenite Communities.* 1990.

McCord, William Maxwell. *Voyages to Utopia: From Monastery to Commune: The Search for the Perfect Society in Modern Times.* 1989.

Rohrlich, Ruby, and Elaine Hoffman Baruch, eds. *Women in Search of Utopia: Mavericks and Mythmakers.* 1984.

EUGENE V. GALLAGHER

Vagina

From ancient times and all around the world the vagina was and is a symbol associated with women's divine and creative power. While patriarchal scholarship tends to denigrate goddesses rich in vagina or vulvic imagery, such as the Sumerian goddess Inanna (second millennium B.C.E.) as merely governing human and crop fertility, the feminine critique of religion has reaffirmed the importance of female genital imagery as symbolic of women's multifaceted divine powers. An examination of the literature on Inanna indicates that she possessed or dispensed the usually male-defined powers of kingship, priesthood, culture, and heroism for her city of Uruk.

The use of the word *vagina* as symbol can be likened to the word *phallus*, which implies both the external genitalia and the reproductive functions in reference to this gendered power base. Natural resemblances to various parts of the female anatomy such as cave openings, canyons, cracks in rocks, cowrie shells, figs, pomegranates, almonds, and the lotus are but a few examples of genital imagery celebrated or revered in different parts of the world. In iconography, the vagina is represented by an elongated pointed oval, also associated with the Sanskrit term *yoni,* and by a slit at the bottom vertex of the inverted triangle, the most ancient symbol for woman. The oval shape is also referred to as the *vesica piscis* because of the ancient belief that women's genital odors smelled fishy. Ovate-shaped fish goddesses from the sixth millennium B.C.E. with well-defined vulvas are common to the Lepenski Vir region of the Danube River basin. Other well-known goddess figures such as Kālī from India, Kuan Yin from China, Isis from Egypt, and Artemis from Greece are sometimes depicted with or as fish.

As the gateway to the mysteries of the cosmos associated with the birth-death-rebirth cycle, the vagina was both feared and revered. When revered, men thought of sexual intercourse as connection with women's energy. Such is the belief in tantric Hinduism, which views women's orgasm as a cosmic force. The vaginal birth hole has also been seen as the passageway to and from the spiritual world. Numerous examples of carvings depicting a woman with legs spread apart over doorways to ritual lodges are found in Micronesia and elsewhere. Interestingly, women were sometimes not admitted to these structures in spite of the invocation of this power site.

The Lotus Goddess from India was often depicted as a horizontal sculpture with legs drawn up in a birth position displaying her pubic area. Instead of a human head, the neck is crowned with a lotus bud, itself a yoni symbol, thus proclaiming her as the genetrix of cosmic consciousness.

Power also engenders fear, and the orgasmic capacities of women have alienated as well as attracted men. The Latin phrase *vagina dentata* (toothed vagina) proclaims the widespread and ancient belief that the vagina is a mouth which can eat or bite off the penis. From India, Native American, and Maori traditions come stories of rituals designed to tame women by breaking the vaginal teeth before men can safely have intercourse. Even in apocryphal biblical literature there is a veiled reference to this dangerous site (see Raitt, 1980): the Book of Tobit (3:7–17, 6:10–17, 7:9–8:19) contains the story of the woman possessed by a demon whose seven bridegrooms did not survive their wedding night. Contemporary psychoanalytic literature confirms that the fear of the devouring vagina has not disappeared.

The power of the vaginal or genital display is multifarious. The horseshoe, a vaginal image known to Druids, Hindus, and Arabs, is hung over doorways to bring good luck, and touching the yoni of Siva when entering a Hindu temple imparts a blessing. The Bakweri women of West Africa overcome insults to women's genitals by displaying, with rude gestures, the parts that have been insulted. Irish mythology tells of warrior women using the display to vanquish the legendary prowess of the Celtic hero, Cù Chulainn. The genital display of *Sheila-na-gig* sculptures, still found on churches and castles in Ireland and Britain, is said to be apotropaic, scaring away evil or enemies. However, its placement near doorways and windows overlooking church cemeteries reminds us that the birth hole can also be the passageway to regeneration in the next world. Interpretation of these sculptures is conflicted because Christianity readily identifies sexuality with sin and personifies it with images of lewd women, whereas Celtic culture celebrated women's sexuality.

The most compelling evidence for the persistence of the veneration of female generative powers is the widespread use of the *vesica piscis* in Christian iconography. Church preference for the alternate term, *mandorla* (almond shape), substitutes but another referent to the vagina. This shape appears as early as the sixth century in Coptic frescoes and was widely used in illuminated manuscripts of medieval times. It is most often found around the imposing figure of Christ triumphant on tympanums over the main portals of cathedrals or monasteries—the gateways from the secular into the sacred world. Even if the mandorla refers to Christ's incarnation, Mary becomes, like Isis, the Gate of Heaven, the conduit for divine power into and out of our material existence.

That the vaginal symbolism of the mandorla was understood is evident in devotional images. An example from a fourteenth century Psalter shows the sacred side wound of Christ's crucifixion rendered as a vagina and displayed vertically within a mandorla. The analogy was to show that Christ gave birth to his church through this death wound. The sexual referent suggests that the birth was effected symbolically by the phallic thrust of the lance.

BIBLIOGRAPHY

Erich Neumann's *The Great Mother* (1963; repr. 1974) is still remarkably useful for its extensive collection of prehistoric female imagery and his discussion of its symbolism. Joseph Campbell is equally important for his comprehensive exploration of mythology: *The Masks of God: Oriental Mythology* (1962), *The Mythic Image* (1974), and many other works. *The Language of the Goddess* (1989) and *The Goddesses and Gods of Old Europe 6500–3500: Myths and Cult Images* (1982), by Marija Gimbutas, are invaluable in reevaluating goddess iconography, particularly in abstracted or coded formats. In *Innana, Queen of Heaven and Earth: Her Stories and Hymns from Sumer* (1983), Diane Wolkstein and Samuel Noah Kramer collaborated on this new translation of the ancient texts that extoll the multifaceted benefits of the sexual energy of this goddess.

For anthropological evidence, see Shirley Ardener, "Sexual Insult and Female Militancy," in *Man* 8, no. 3 (1973): 422–440; "A Note on Gender Iconography: The Vagina" in *The Cultural Construction of Sexuality*, edited by Pat Caplan (1987); and Douglas Fraser, "The Heraldic Woman," in *The Many Faces of Primitive Art*, edited by D. Fraser (1966).

Jill Raitt examines both the fear of the *vagina dentata* and how the Christian church tried to counterbalance this threat in "The Vagina Dentata and the Immaculate Uterus Divini Fontis," in the *Journal of the American Academy of Religion* 48, no. 3 (1980): 415–431. An essential reference for the psychoanalytic approach to this phenomena is provided by Otero Solimar, "Fearing Our Mothers: An Overview of the Psychoanalytic Theories Concerning the *Vagina Dentata* Motif F547.1.1" in *The American Journal of Psychoanalysis* 56, no. 3 (1996): 269–288.

Both Anne Ross, *Pagan Celtic Britain: Studies in Iconography and Tradition* (1967), and Miranda Green, *The Celtic Goddesses: Warriors, Virgins and Mothers*, (1996), affirm the symbolism of women's sexual powers and imagery in Celtic culture. Vaginal images from the Indian *yoni* tradition are discussed by Ajiit Mookerjee, *Kali: the Feminine Force* (1988), and Rufus C. Camphausen, *The Yoni: Sacred Symbol of Female Creative Power* (1996).

No one is more influential in her use of genital imagery in contemporary art than Judy Chicago with her two megaprojects, well documented in book form: *The Dinner Party: A Symbol of Our Heritage* (1979) and *The Birth Project* (1985).

A compelling examination of *Sheila-na-gig* sculptures can be found in Jorgen Andersen's book, *The Witch on the Wall: Medieval Erotic Sculpture in the British Isles* (1977), although he is more inclined to categorize them as medieval grotesques warning against the sin of *luxuria*.

References for the significance of the *vesica piscis* or the mandorla as the persistence of vaginal iconography are scarce. Of importance is Jeffrey Hamburger's study of *The Rothschild Canticles: Art and Mysticism in Flanders and the Rhineland circa 1300* (1990). Other references to vaginal imagery and symbolism must be gleaned from occasional comments in both historical and contemporary works.

E. ANN PEARSON

Vajrayogini

Vajrayogini is the chief goddess of the tantric Buddhist pantheon. Her name means Adamantine Yogini: *yogini* denotes a female who derives her power from yoga, while *adamantine* refers to the supreme spiritual state that she has attained. Vajrayogini is featured in some of the earliest tantric scriptures in India and appears to date to the origins of the tantric movement (seventh–eighth centuries C.E.). She remained important in India through the demise of Buddhism there in the twelfth century and is a prominent deity in the living traditions of Tibet and Nepal.

Vajrayogini is a fully enlightened being, or female Buddha. She has attained perfect wisdom and supreme bliss, the two aspects of enlightenment. Like all Buddhas, Vajrayogini has three levels of embodiment. Her ultimate body is a formless "truth body," the aspect of her being which is one with all of reality. She also manifests an "enjoyment body," in which she appears as a deity to express her spiritual realizations and provide a model that others may emulate as they aspire to the same goal. Third is the "emanation body," in which she appears in the human realm, manifesting her presence through female adepts (*dākinīs*) and indeed in all women throughout the world. Vajrayogini presides over a Buddha-land known as Khecara, to which an advanced yogi or yogini may ascent at death in a trail of rainbow light.

Vajrayogini is bright red in color, bespeaking the heat of her yogic fire. She has an intensely focused yet rapturous expression as her piercing gaze penetrates the depths of reality. Vajrayogini appears in dynamic lunging, leaping, and soaring poses with her long hair swirling around her, naked except for delicate bone ornaments. The goddess cups in her left hand a skull-bowl that contains the nectar of bliss that she distills from every experience. In her right hand she brandishes a curved knife that she uses to sever all illusion and duality at the root. The crook of her left arm supports a staff that signifies that she has integrated her eroticism into her spiritual path. It is said of Vajrayogini that her "very essence is passion" (*Sādhanamālā*, p. 456); she manifests a state of wholeness in which all the passions are freely flowly, refined of their self-referential content and capacity to cause suffering, available as pure energy to be directed to enlightened ends.

Vajrayogini has several major forms. Her earliest documented sculptures from the tenth and eleventh centuries portray the form known as Sarvabuddha-ḍākinī. She lunges to her left and raises her skull-bowl above her head, pouring its contents into her mouth, and holds her knife in a taut, outstretched arm. In Nepal this form is important as a deity of the fivefold Yoginī Mandala of the Kathmandu Valley. In Tibet this form became known as Naro Khachöma, because several of her practice lineages are traced to the Indian adept Naropa. The female adept Lakṣmīṅkarā (c. eighth century) introduced a distinctive form known as Chinnamundā, who waves aloft her own severed head and nourishes herself and others with the blood that flows forth. Another major form is Vajravārāhī, the Adamantine Sow, characterized by a dancing pose and the head of a wild boar that emerges behind her right ear or above her topknot. This form is prominent in Tibet and is the supreme deity of Nepalese Buddhism.

Vajrayogini arose in a lay, noncelibate movement in which men and women together performed pilgrimage, cremation-ground feasting, ritual, and sexual yoga. Authority rested in the hands of individual gurus, both male and female. The practices centering upon Vajrayogingini were highly esoteric, intended for advanced practitioners. For women, meditation upon their identity with Vajrayogini was an important method for discovering their innate divinity. A woman also envisioned herself as Vajrayogini in the context of sexual yoga and ritual worship, while her male partner was enjoined to recognize her as a living embodiment of Vajrayogini and to render her the homage and offering due to a Buddha.

Vajrayogini practice in Nepal falls within the purview of the Vajrācārya priestly caste. Her initiation rituals and feasts must be led by a married couple acting in concert. When a ritual calls for the bodily presence of the goddess, one or more of the women present typically perform this role. Vajrācāryas also have a practice in which the meditator dances as Vajrayogini as part of the yoga of transforming into a deity. Several temples (Bijeśvarī, Śankhu, and Parphing) dedicated to the goddess in the Kathmandu Valley are major sites of tantric meditation, daily devotions, pilgrimage, and periodic large-scale rituals.

In Tibet the practice of Vajrayogini was adapted to a monastic context. Literary sources emanating from this sector tend to sever her connection to human women and pursue an abstract line of doctrinal interpretation in order to render the goddess more relevant to celibate males. However, in the noncelibate, yogic context she remains vitally important for female practitioners, as well as for laywomen who perform Vajrayogini meditation retreats after their familial obligations have been fulfilled. The traditional affinity between women and their divine prototype is still recognized in Tibet today, where a woman who attains enlightenment is customarily recognized as an embodiment of Vajrayoginī.

BIBLIOGRAPHY

Primary sources on Vajrayoginī include the *Cakrasamvara-* and *Candamahārosana-tantras* (the latter has been partially translated by Christopher George, 1974) and meditation manuals in the *Sādhananmālā* (edited by Benoytosh Bhattacharyya), Nepalese *cārya* songs used in meditation and dance, and extensive Tibetan commentarial literature. On the original practice of Vajrayoginī in the Indian context, see Miranda Shaw, *Passionate Enlightenment: Women in Tantric Buddhism* (1994). David Gellner, *Monk, Householder, Tantric Priest* (1992) provides information on Vajravārāhī rituals in Nepal. Useful Tibetan-style commentaries written in English include Geshe Kelsang Gyatso, *Guide to Dakini Land* (1991), and Chogyam Trungpa Rinpoche, "Sacred Outlook," in *Silk Route and the Diamond Path* (1982). The only scholarly monograph devoted to a form of Vajrayoginī is Elisabeth Benard, *Chinnamastā* (1994). For feminist psychoanalytic analysis of the male monastic expropriation of Vajrayoginī in Tibet, see June Campbell, *Traveller in Space* (1996). An overview of the historical development and iconographic forms of the goddess may be found in Miranda Shaw, *Her Waves of Bliss*, q.v. "Vajrayoginī" (forthcoming).

MIRANDA SHAW

van Schurman, Anna Maria

Anna Maria van Schurman (1607–1678), Dutch linguist, philosopher, and theologian, was educated in the humanities by her father, Frederik van Schurman (d. 1623). Van Schurman debated and corresponded with other learned women and men all over Europe, including Princess Elizabeth of the Palatinate (1616–1680), René Descartes (1596–1650), and Batsua Makin (1600–after 1673). She achieved international renown for her *Dissertatio* (1641), a defense of a woman's right to engage in scholarly pursuits. According to van Schurman, by studying, women would be serving God as well as striving for the salvation of their souls.

Initially van Schurman endorsed the Pietist movement of the so-called further reformation (*nadere reformatie*) within the Dutch Reformed Church, a movement intended to couple religious doctrine with a thoroughly pious life. Gradually, however, she became

convinced that the efforts of the further reformation had failed. In 1669 she therefore joined the sectarian community of Jean de Labadie (1610–1674), a converted Catholic and former Reformed minister. He had turned his back on the Reformed Church because in his eyes it had wholly departed from its original and intended state. Van Schurman was publicly denounced for leaving the Reformed Church. She defended her decision in her *Eukleria* (1673), in which she also tried to demonstrate that de Labadie's community represented the church made up of true purified Christians as it was described in the New Testament. In the *Eukleria*, moreover, she presented herself as a theologian who adhered to strict Calvinist principles with regard to predestination and redemption. Van Schurman remained in the Labadist community until her death.

BIBLIOGRAPHY

de Baar, Mirjam, Machteld Löwensteyn, Marit Monteiro, and A. Agnes Sneller, eds. *Choosing the Better Part: Anna Maria van Schurman (1607–1678).* 1996. The contributions of Rang, de Baar, and Scheenstra in this collection of essays deal with van Schurman as a scholar and theologian. The bibliography contains further references to primary sources and secondary literature. For a list of printed works and manuscripts, see pp. 155–157.

Irwin, Joyce. "Anna Maria van Schurman and Antoinette Bourignon: Contrasting Examples of Seventeenth-Century Pietism." *Church History* 60 (September 1991): 301–315.

Saxby, Trevor. *The Quest for the New Jerusalem: Jean de Labadie and the Labadists.* 1987.

van Schurman, Anna Maria. *De vitae termino.* 1639.

———. *Dissertatio, de Ingenii Mulierbris ad Doctrinam, et meliores Litteras aptitudine.* 1641.

———. *Eukleria seu melioris Partis Electio.* 1673. Reprint, 1782.

———. *Opuscola Hebreae, Graeca, Latina, Gallica: prosaica adque metrica* (1648 and 1650). Contains letters and poems to and from van Schurman in Latin, Greek, Hebrew, and French.

MARIT MONTEIRO

Vegetarianism

Vegetarianism, a diet of grains, vegetables, fruits, nuts, and seeds, with or without eggs and dairy products, rejects dead animal bodies as a source of food. Some religious traditions—for example, Christianity and Judaism, citing Genesis 1:29—hold that paradise was vegetarian. Vegetarian elements run through many of the world's religions, arising from any of a variety of influences: asceticism; the belief in reincarnation; respect for all beings; the belief that meat eating contributes to "heaviness" in the body, impeding one's spirituality; health concerns associated with meat eating; nonviolent ethics. Hinduism, Buddhism, and Jainism all promulgate the doctrine of ahimsa—noninjury to sentient beings—and have strong vegetarian traditions. Only Jainism requires it as a practice.

Making flesh-food abstinence obligatory has prompted controversy in various sects. Within Christianity, John Wesley, founder of Methodism; William Booth, founder of the Salvation Army; and Ellen Gould White, cofounder of the Seventh-day Adventists, were vegetarians. However, only Seventh-day Adventists advocate vegetarianism. Some have argued that Jesus was a vegetarian, while within Buddhism there is a debate as to whether the Buddha, regarded as a vegetarian, died of poisoning by eating contaminated pork or a mushroom. Within Judaism, those who practice vegetarianism do so for several reasons—as a spiritual discipline; to reintroduce the Garden of Eden and hasten the coming of the Messiah; to show compassion for animals as intrinsic to God's creation; to enact environmental awareness.

Religious groups have often advocated both celibacy and vegetarianism. This emphasis on controlling appetites, also associated in patriarchal religions with women as sexual temptation, results in confusion: does vegetarianism represent a repressive role for religion? What is the relationship between flesh foods and the "sins of the flesh" associated with sexuality?

In the past one hundred years, a variety of religious movements have been allied with vegetarianism, often advocated by women leaders. In the nineteenth century, Annie Besant, a Theosophist, promoted vegetarianism; toward the end of the twentieth century, both New Age and feminist spirituality movements have evidenced vegetarian connections. Here vegetarianism represents a spirituality committed to enhancing the individual and the world, including the natural world, rather than legislating individual abstinence. Ecofeminism posits a connection between the oppression of women and the oppression of the rest of nature. Ecofeminist analyses of how world religions have fostered or inhibited environmental consciousness have only begun; such analyses could promote nonpatriarchal attitudes toward animals' well-being. Sally Abbott (1990) speculates that ritual and religion evolved in response to the killing of animals for food, while Carol Adams (1994) argues that a patriarchal cosmology recalls itself symbolically through meat eating.

Traditional histories of vegetarianism often reflect an elite Western male perspective. However, vegetarianism can be a rejection of patriarchal attitudes. Because of the association of vegetarianism with many of the world religions, women's vegetarianism—and the question of how gender influences it—has not been fully considered. As the main food preparers in most cultures, women who became vegetarians may have done so for reasons unrelated to traditional religious doctrine, among them a body-affirming spirituality, the extension of an ethic of care to animals, Goddess spirituality, and a recognition of the interlocking oppressions of women and animals.

BIBLIOGRAPHY

Abbott, Sally. "The Origins of God in the Blood of the Lamb." In *Reweaving the World: The Emergence of Ecofeminism.* Edited by Irene Diamond and Gloria Feman Orenstein. 1990.
Adams, Carol J., ed. *Ecofeminism and the Sacred.* 1993.
———. *Neither Man nor Beast: Feminism and the Defense of Animals.* 1994.
Chapple, Christopher Key. *Nonviolence to Animals, Earth, and Self in Asian Traditions.* 1992.
Gottlieb, Roger S. *This Sacred Earth: Religion, Nature, Environment.* 1996.
Rosen, Steven. *Food for the Spirit: Vegetarianism and the World Religions.* 1987.

See also **Environmentalism**.

CAROL J. ADAMS

Venkamamba, Tarigonda

Tarigonda Venkamamba (c. 1800–1866) was a poet, lyricist, author, and composer of folk songs in the Telugu language of Andhra Pradesh, South India. Venkamamba is known for her unorthodox behavior. She refused to do housework, saying she would only work for God. When her husband died young, she apparently refused to shave her head and dress in a mode that befits a high-caste widow. According to a well-known legend, when a religious head ordered her to dress and behave like a widow, she is said to have miraculously set his pontifical seat on fire. The pontiff retracted his command.

Venkamamba is said to have written more than eighteen major works and hundreds of folk songs, some of which are now lost. Her best-known work is *Dwipada Bhagavatam,* a Telugu poem capturing the essence of the Sanskrit work Bhagavata Purana, which primarily describes, in couplets, the life of Lord Krishna. Venkamamba also wrote several devotional poems to Lord Venkateśvara (a form of the God Vishnu) and considered herself to be his bride. Written with striking imagery and forceful language, her poems are at once sensuous and spiritual.

BIBLIOGRAPHY

"Tarigonda Venkamamba." In *Women Writing in India.* Edited by Susie Tharu and K. Lalita. 1991.

VASUDHA NARAYANAN

Venus

See Aphrodite (Venus).

Vesta

See Hestia and Vesta.

Violence

Although the call for peace is well established in the world's religious traditions, most if not all of the major religions also perpetuate violence. Women and children are common targets, enduring the consequences of scriptures, theologies, religious rituals, and institutions that nurture the alienation in which such violence breeds and grows.

Violence is traditionally associated with physical force that produces injury or harm, and violence against women may include physical assault, mutilation, murder, infanticide, sexual violation, and neglect. It may also take more covert forms. The power inequalities perpetuated through sexism, racism, and classism support institutional violence because they exercise coercive restraint. Oppression may take the form of exclusion of women from leadership roles in religious institutions, theological support for patriarchal social structures, and religious leaders' emphasis on gender-specific virtues for women such as submissiveness, self-sacrifice, and obedience. The more unequal the organization of power, the more violent the system. When power is defended by control, overt physical force may be used to maintain it.

Western patriarchal religious traditions promote alienation of the spiritual, associated with the male, from the physical, sexual, and erotic, associated with the female. The tendency to denigrate the physical, bodily, and sexual is present in the dominant traditions of all of the monotheistic religions. Males assume supremacy through identification with a male God and view women as male property. Traditions that suppress the physical and erotic often treat women and nature with horror and contempt. Hebrew scripture treats rape as a property crime and describes numerous acts of violence and repression against women, including the rape, torture, murder, and dismemberment of the unnamed concubine in Judges 19, the rape of Dinah, the sacrifice of Jephthah's daughter, and the incestuous abuse of Tamar. Susan Thistlethwaite notes the interweaving of Christian scriptures with the history of belief systems that view women as scapegoats and cites denial of the severity of the problem of violence against women by religious institutions as a significant contributor to the continuing abuse of women ("Every Two Minutes," in *Feminist Interpretations of the Bible*, edited by Letty M. Russell [1985]).

In addition to the prioritizing of male over female and spirit over nature, Margaret Miles cites two other traditional Christian views that contribute to a religious culture of violence: the support of patriarchal order as the right ordering of society, reflecting the God-ordained cosmic order, and the glorification of suffering as the path to transcendence and salvation. Support for these views is drawn from scriptural and theological interpretations and perpetuated through verbal and visual imagery ("Violence against Women in the Historical Christian West and in North American Secular Culture," in *Shaping New Vision: Gender and Values in American Culture*, edited by Clarissa W. Atkinson et al. [1987]).

Glorification of suffering, in turn, supports the Christian churches' failure to address domestic violence. Women are told in many Christian congregations to suffer and be still, although one out of three women in the United States can expect to be beaten by her husband, and more than half of violent crimes against women are committed by male family members. Patriarchal culture stresses the view that women's ability to endure suffering is a test of faith, and their appropriate role is to exemplify the perfect prayerful humility and self-sacrifice of the ideal Christian. Violence against women is therefore imbedded in the ways that patriarchal cultures construct power. Religious rhetoric may deplore violence, but theological interpretations and the silence of denial continue to support the gender oppression that leads to victimization of women.

Violence against women is also overtly practiced in many religious traditions. One of the most dramatic historical examples of such institutionalized violence is the witch-hunts in Europe during the fifteenth and seventeenth centuries. The *Malleus Maleficarum*, published in 1484 as a manual for witch-hunters, concluded that persecution and execution of witches was ordained by God. It justified violence against women through theological arguments for their inferiority, holding that women were feebler in mind and body, less understanding of spiritual things, more carnal and deceptive.

Certain patriarchal values in Eastern religious traditions also perpetuate the alienation and degradation of women, fostering a cultural climate conducive to antifemale violence. The association of women with sensual pleasure and desire, as well as with the household and childbirth—that is, with the world of attachment—may lead to the view that women are barriers to salvation. Degradation of the natural world may also result in a view of women as belonging to the realm of deceit and illusion. From the twelfth century until the early twentieth century, the binding of women's feet was common in China. Genital mutilation affects several million women in more than thirty countries. In India widow burning (sati) was commonly practiced until the early nineteenth century and still occurs. The dowry system in India, supported by tradition, mythology, and religion, has resulted in an epidemic of "dowry deaths"—the murder or forced suicide of women whose families cannot meet the demand for larger dowries. In countries where Islamic fundamentalism is growing, patriarchal forces may oppose women who challenge Islamic traditions through means ranging from legal prosecution to physical attack.

Sex-determination technology throughout the world causes the deaths of more and more female fetuses, reflecting the often religiously supported prioritizing of male children. Meanwhile, the mortality rate for female children is often much higher than that of males in many parts of the world, due in part to the failure to provide female children with sufficient medical care, food, and social services. It is a painful reality that many of these forms of violence against women are practiced and perpetuated by women as they supervise or conduct these misogynistic rituals and give priority to their male over their female children.

Japanese journalist and scholar Yayori Matsui has argued that, in developing nations, patriarchal culture, religion, and tradition have institutionalized violence against women, while fundamentalism and communal tension perpetuate or aggravate it. Those who oppose, criticize, and resist violence against women often suffer imprisonment, sexual torture, and even execution ("Violence Against Women in Development, Militarism, and Culture," in *Feminist Theology from the Third World*, edited by Ursula King [1994]).

Two Berber men bring a woman accused of adultery before the village leader for judgment. In many religious traditions, women are more often tried and treated more severely than men and face violent punishment by flogging, stoning even death, Bord; Okriss, Algeria, 1960 (Marc Garanger/Corbis).

In many religious traditions, sex is linked to temptation and sin, and female sexuality is understood to be the property of men. These views also perpetuate an atmosphere conducive to sexual violence against women. Where access to the workforce is closed to women, their economic survival may depend on prostitution. The sex industry in Thailand, the Philippines, Sri Lanka, and Indonesia exploits women and children, and prostitution is growing among Taiwanese, Korean, and Malaysian women.

Other forms of sexual violence are perpetuated by theologies that endorse sacrifice and by the patriarchal tendency to blame the victim. Joanne Carlson Brown critiques ways in which the Christian doctrine of atonement has been used to glorify abuse by assigning women the role of suffering servant ("Divine Child Abuse?" *Daughters of Sarah* [Summer 1992]: 24–28). If God intended the created order, then God created victims and victimizers. Religion conspires with other aspects of culture in requiring women to accept abuse. Societies do exist, however, in which sexual violence does not occur. In *Female Power and Male Dominance* (1981) Peggy Reeves Sanday notes that in 40 percent of the cultures she studied, rape is absent or rare. Beryl Lieff Benderly indicates that in these cultures, women are respected, share power equally, and participate fully in religious leadership. Sexual violence is viewed as unnatural ("Rape Free or Rape Prone" *Science* [October 1982]). If the divine is understood to support the vulnerable and judge those who use power to harm, the ethical norm for human relationships must be shared power and responsibility.

BIBLIOGRAPHY
Mary Daly has examined several forms of religiously supported violence against women in *Gyn/Ecology* (1978; repr. 1990). Phyllis Trible, *Texts of Terror* (1984), examines acts of violence against women in Hebrew scripture. A number of sources consider Christianity and violence against women, including Joanne Carlson Brown and Carole R. Bohn, eds., *Christianity, Patriarchy, and Abuse* (1989); James Alsdorf and Phyllis Alsdorf, *Battered into Submission: The Tragedy of Wife Abuse in the Christian Home* (1989); Marla Selvidge, *Women, Violence, and the Bible* (1996); and Mary Pellauer, "Violence Against Women: The Theological Dimension," in *Christianity and Crisis* 43, no. 9 (1983): 206–212. Marie Marshall Fortune focuses more specifically on sexual violence in *Sexual Violence, the Unmentionable Sin* (1983). David Blumenthal, *Facing the Abusing God: A Theology of Protest* (1993), is an interesting consideration of women survivors of childhood sexual abuse from the perspective of Jewish thought. The prostitution industry in Asia and other forms of violence against women in the Third World are discussed by several authors in Ursula King, ed., *Feminist Theology from the Third World* (1994). Religious violence against women is also considered from a global perspective in Wim Beuken and Karl-Joseph Kuschel, *Religion as a Source of Violence* (1997), pp. 55–70. For information about female genocide, infanticide, and the disproportionate ratio of men to women, see Amartya Sen, "More than 100 Million Women are Missing," *The New York Review of Books* 37, no. 20 (December 1990): 61–63. Wanda Teays examines dowry murders in "The Burning Bride," *Journal of Feminist Studies in Religion* 7, no. 2 (Fall 1991): 29–52. An excellent anthology is *Violence against Women*, edited by Elisabeth Schüssler Fiorenza and Shawn Copeland (1994).

L. J. "TESS" TESSIER

Virginity

The state of virginity appears frequently in the history of religions as an indication of being set apart from others or from the human condition in general. Whereas virginity is a natural feature of the lives of prepubescent children, adults who are capable of sexual intercourse but choose to avoid it set themselves apart from their peers. The adult virgin's nonparticipation in the sexual acts that foster the perpetuation of human society marks her or him as a special being with a special relationship to the social world.

Being disengaged from the network of social ties that come with sexuality and marriage, the adult virgin is often depicted as a being who is more at home in the natural world than in the social world of humans. In the Babylonian *Epic of Gilgamesh,* dating to around 1600 B.C.E., the virginal Enkidu wanders naked, living among the animals as a man of nature until seduced by a courtesan. After his seduction, Enkidu's animal companions flee from him, and he finds he has lost his former agility and speed. Having been humanized through his introduction to sexuality, Enkidu becomes the companion of King Gilgamesh.

VIRGINITY AS A TEMPORARY STATE

Temporary sexual renunciation appears commonly in the history of religions as a means of consecration to be undergone by women and men when moving from the profane to the sacred (before entering a temple, for example, or performing a religious ritual). Likewise, virginity is often a prerequisite for contact with the sacred. Thus virginity was required of the priestesses of many of the cults of Greco-Roman antiquity. Virginity played a central role in the Roman cult of Vesta, goddess of the hearth, whose undying flame symbolized the continuity of the Roman family and the state. As Sara Pomeroy (1975) has noted, the Vestal Virgins belonged to no man and thus to everyone, thereby instantiating the collective.

The *Kumāris,* or living virgin goddesses, of Nepal perform today a sacred role similar to that once played by the Vestal Virgins. Young girls chosen from among the Newar population of the Kathmandu Valley are formally installed in office as living incarnations of the Hindu goddess Durgā. The *Kumāris* are venerated until signs of impurity (such as menstruation or loss of teeth) indicate that the goddess has departed. Like the Vestal Virgin, the *Kumari* is free to marry after leaving office; most, however, remain single (Allen, 1975). Although the majority of the living goddesses of Nepal are worshiped only at the local level, one *Kumari* is the center of a national cult. Living in seclusion in a special building close to the old palace in Kathmandu, the royal *Kumari* of Kathmandu is venerated as a source of royal power by the king of Nepal, government officials, and the nation at large. The Nepalese cult of the living virgin goddess has its roots in the Hindu custom of venerating prepubescent girls as temporary incarnations of the divine. During the annual festival of Durgā-Pūjā in October and occasionally at other times, young girls are worshiped by Hindu families throughout India and Nepal as living forms of the goddess.

Like prepubescent Hindu girls, unmarried Muslim women who make their virginity conspicuous are commonly exalted as maintainers of family honor. Most Islamic scriptural sources deem sexual desire "natural" for both women and men; permanent virginity is there-

In Kathmandu, Nepal, young girls are chosen to become *Kumāris* (living virgin goddesses). This young girl is considered to be the living incarnation of the goddess Durgā (Alison Wright/Corbis).

fore rare in Islamic cultures. Thus, while Muslim brides should be virgins, virgins should (in due time) be brides.

VIRGINITY AS A PERMANENT CONDITION

One of the remarkable developments in the history of women in late antiquity is the enthusiastic pursuit of sexual asceticism by large numbers of early Christian women vowed to permanent virginity. Feminist scholars suggested that virginity allowed women the opportunity to escape narrowly conceived social roles and exercise forms of autonomy and power otherwise unavailable to them (Clark, 1981; Fiorenza, 1983; McNamara, 1976; Rouselle, 1988; Ruether, 1979). Through sexual abstinence, women were able to control wealth, obtain education, and exercise leadership in their communities. Virginal women were said to become "male" or even transcend gender distinctions altogether; the

abolition of a female nature considered inferior to that of men was a major motive for women who practiced sexual abstinence (Castelli, 1991; Harrison, 1990; Meyer, 1985).

Although the New Testament contains the roots of an ascetic ideology supportive of virginity as a lifelong practice (for example, Paul's exhortations to early Christian communities to follow his example in leading a celibate life), it was not until the Christianizing of the Roman Empire in the fourth century of the common era that the image of virginity as the ideal Christian life became widespread. Asceticism replaced martyrdom as a means of achieving Christian perfection. Serving an important ecclesiastical function as symbols of the true church and an economic function as patrons who built monasteries and supported ascetic communities, virginal women of the fourth and fifth centuries won considerable admiration for their sexual abstinence. Church fathers dedicated both treatises and personal letters to the task of praising female virgins and convincing women to renounce marriage. Fourth-century encomiums on virginity promise women liberation from the burdens of marriage and motherhood. Instead, the virgin is offered a sublime erotic fulfillment in the form of a celestial union with Christ as the divine bridegroom (Castelli, 1986). In this celestial union, virginal women were said to possess a spiritual fecundity resembling that of Mary, the virginal mother of Jesus.

VIRGIN BIRTH

Some of the oldest references to virginity are to be found in accounts of the birth of culture heroes and deities. The exceptional nature of such figures is often signaled by the unusual circumstances of their conception and birth. Conceived by their mothers through a variety of nonsexual means such as the ingestion of certain foods, contact with water, wind, and rays of the sun, or simply by means of a wish, heroes and deities enter into the world in an extraordinary manner that corresponds to their extraordinary qualities. The Greek hero Perseus, for example, was conceived when Zeus visited his mother Danae in the form of a shower of gold. The mother of the Hottentot ancestor-god Heitsi-Eibib conceived through the ingestion of a certain sap-filled grass. The Aztec god Quetzalcoatl, according to one legend about his birth, came into being when his mother swallowed a precious stone. According to another legend, it was the breath of an Aztec god upon his mother's body that led to Quetzalcoatl's conception. These few examples indicate the variety of forms that supernatural conception can take.

BIBLIOGRAPHY

Ahmed, Leila. *Women and Gender in Islam.* 1991.

Allen, Michael. *The Cult of the Kumari: Virgin Worship in Nepal.* 1975.

Bauer, Janet. "Sexuality and the Moral 'Construction' of Women in Islamic Society." *Anthropological Quarterly* 58, no. 3 (1985): 120–130.

Brown, Peter. *The Body and Society: Men, Women, and Sexual Renunciation in Early Christianity.* 1988.

Burrus, Virginia. "Word and Flesh: The Bodies and Sexuality of Ascetic Women in Christian Antiquity." *Journal of Feminist Studies in Religion* 10 (Spring 1994): 27–51.

Castelli, Elizabeth. "'I Will Make Mary Male': Pieties of the Body and Gender Transformation of Christian Women in Late Antiquity." In *Body Guards: The Cultural Politics of Ambiguity.* Edited by Julia Epstein and Kristina Straub. 1991.

———. "Virginity and Its Meaning for Women's Sexuality in Early Christianity." *Journal of Feminist Studies in Religion* 2, no. 1 (Spring 1986): 61–88.

Clark, Elizabeth. "Ascetic Renunciation and Feminine Advancement: A Paradox of Late Ancient Christianity." *Anglican Theological Review* 63 (1981): 240–257.

Elm, Susanna. *"Virgins of God": The Making of Asceticism in Late Antiquity.* 1994.

Fiorenza, Elisabeth Schüssler. *In Memory of Her: A Feminist Theological Reconstruction of Christian Origins.* 1983.

Harrison, Verma E. F. "Male and Female in Cappadocian Theology." *Journal of Theological Studies* 41 (1990): 441–471.

Hartland, Edwin Sidney. *The Legend of Perseus: A Study of Tradition in Story, Custom, and Belief.* 1894.

———. *Primitive Paternity: The Myth of Supernatural Birth in Relation to the History of the Family.* 1909.

Jacobsen, Thorkild. *Treasures of Darkness: A History of Mesopotamian Religion.* 1976.

Kraemer, Ross. "The Conversion of Women to Ascetic Forms of Christianity." *Signs* 6 (1980–81): 298–307.

McNamara, Jo Ann. "Sexual Equality and the Cult of Virginity in Early Christian Thought." *Feminist Studies* 3 (1976): 145–158.

Meyer, Michael W. "Making Mary Male: The Categories 'Male' and 'Female' in the Gospel of Thomas." *New Testament Studies* 31 (1985): 554–570.

Moran, William L. "Ovid's Blanda Voluptas and the Humanization of Enkidu." *Journal of Near Eastern Studies* 50 (April 1991): 121–127.

Pomeroy, Sara. *Goddesses, Whores, Wives, and Slaves: Women in Classical Antiquity.* 1975.

Rousselle, Aline. *Porneia: On Desire and the Body in Antiquity.* Translated by F. Pheasant. 1988.

Ruether, Rosemary Radford. "Mothers of the Church: Ascetic Women in the Late Patristic Age." In *Women of Spirit: Female Leaders in the Jewish and Christian Traditions.* Edited by Rosemary R. Ruether and Eleanor McLaughlin. 1979.

Schulenburg, Jane Tibbetts. "The Heroics of Virginity: Brides of Christ and Sacrificial Mutilation." In *Women in the Middle Ages and the Renaissance.* Edited by M. B. Rose. 1986.

Tigay, Jeffrey H. *The Evolution of the Gilgamesh Epic.* 1982.

Warner, Marina. *Alone of All Her Sex: The Myth and the Cult of the Virgin Mary.* 1983.

See also **Birth and Rebirth; Celibacy; Chastity; Durgā and Kālī; Saints; Sexuality; Virgin Mary.**

LIZ WILSON

Virgin Mary

The Virgin Mary is the principal symbol of female holiness and power in the Christian tradition. Very briefly mentioned in the New Testament as the mother of Jesus and witness to his death, the contours of the symbol of Mary have been filled in by generations of popular devotion, theological speculation, and political and pastoral manipulation. The Apocryphal Gospel of James (mid-second century) contributed some of the most enduring legends about her, including stories about her Davidic lineage, her childhood dedication to virginity, her marriage to a widower with sons, the trial by which she and Joseph proved that they never had sexual relations, and the doubt of Salome whose hand fell off after touching Mary's virginal, postpartum womb. Even though this text was condemned in the Western church, its emphasis on the perpetual virginity of Mary and its attribution to Mary of many characteristics associated with Jesus would be echoed in later developments.

Although the cult of the Virgin has served the interests of ruling constituencies, as when the empress Augusta Pulcheria (399–453) promoted veneration of Mary as Theotokos (Mother of God) as part of her program of institutionalizing her imperial power, popular veneration of Mary can be traced to as early as the third century, including some practices that suggest the syncretization of the Marian piety with the worship of the pagan goddesses. From the mid-eleventh century, veneration of the Virgin exploded in new forms of prayer, scriptural exegesis, song, art, pilgrimage, drama, church dedication, and social organization (in confraternities dedicated to Mary), all of which were marked by new emotional expression of personal intimacy with the mother of God. Hundreds of stories circulated in oral and written forms celebrating Mary's miraculous intervention in the lives of her devotees, stories in which themes of divine punishment of sinners gave way to themes of Mary's maternal compassion toward sinners and those in need who sang her praises. The delight, both popular and learned, in praising Mary's pure body, coupled with the representation of Mary as exemplary Christian, also rendered her a powerful symbol in the construction of the perceived enemies of such faith and purity. Thus devotion to the Virgin was sometimes harnessed to anti-heretical and anti-Jewish preaching campaigns. Some of the most visible effects can be seen in the razing of synagogues, such as that of Nürnberg in 1349, which were replaced by shrines dedicated to the Virgin.

In the modern age, devotion to Mary continues within the Catholic and Orthodox traditions of Christianity. The modern cult of the Virgin is strongly shaped by frequent and widespread claims of Marian apparitions. The seers of these apparitions have usually been uneducated members of geographically isolated communities, and most strikingly, usually female and often very young. These apparitions have then been subject to many levels of intervention, from the reactions and interpretations of immediate family and community, to the investigations by clerical officials. Most of these devotional centers continue the medieval tradition of attributing miracles to Mary's maternal care. Sandra Zimdars-Swartz (1991) has noted the prevalence of a generalized apocalyptic theology in which Marian apparitions are read as signs of her maternal intervention in this final stage of history. Official church approbation has contributed to the success of a few of these cults as clerical leaders have tried to channel the fervor of these popular devotions, but official neglect or even rejection of most apparition cults has not always squelched the power they have exerted over popular devotion. In these apparitions and their subsequent interpretations, the maternal symbol of Mary is sometimes linked to conservative pastoral and political programs, such as condemnation of failed devotion, critiques of secularization, or warnings against imminent Communist takeover.

The cult of the Virgin has been variously interpreted as offering women a liberating image of female divinity and as devaluing women by the exaltation of such a suprahuman female symbol. The difficulty in adjudicating this matter lies primarily in the fact that until the modern era there is much less information about women's actual participation in the cult than about images and practices that have been offered to women for their devotion. But even in the modern age, the complexity of women's roles in Marian apparitions—as visionaries who experience the benevolence of the Virgin Mother who addresses their own personal suffering and as women whose religiously satisfying practices of devotion to Mary are often closely allied with politically conservative goals of the clergy—points to the ambigu-

The Virgin Mary is depicted in a stone carving located in a nature preserve, Lokrum Island, Croatia (Jonathan Blair/Corbis).

ity and power of the symbol of Mary in the Christian tradition.

BIBLIOGRAPHY

Blackbourn, David. *Marpingen: Apparitions of the Virgin Mary in Nineteenth-Century Germany.* 1994. A fascinating examination of one modern Marian apparition cult that embeds religious practice within cultural conflicts. The introduction also provides a good overview of modern developments in devotion to Mary.

Graef, Hilda. *Mary: A History of Doctrine and Devotion.* 1963. Reprint, 1965. Still the most accessible and comprehensive history of theological developments about Mary.

Hale, Rosemary. "*Imitatio Mariae:* Motherhood Motifs in Devotional Memoirs." *Mystics Quarterly* 16 (1990): 193–203. Very important for its examination of how women related to Mary by adapting images of her motherhood in their mystical experience.

Limberis, Vasiliki. *Divine Heiress: The Virgin Mary and the History of Christian Constantinople.* 1994. An examination of the theological, political, and devotional dynamics in the evaluation of Mary as patron of Constantinople.

Warner, Marina. *Alone of All Her Sex: The Myth and the Cult of the Virgin Mary.* 1976. A very influential and comprehensive analysis; its strength lies in its examination of the rich repertoire of images offered to women for their devotion.

Zimdars-Swartz, Sandra L. *Encountering Mary: From La Salette to Medjugorje.* 1991. Focuses on the theological and devotional aspects of a wide range of modern apparition cults with a somewhat apologetic cast.

The Marian Library at the University of Dayton has an ever-expanding collection with more than 90,000 books and pamphlets spanning five centuries in more than fifty languages.

See also **Maryam (Mary).**

ANNE L. CLARK

Virtue

At root, the English word *virtue* refers to strength or power, defined in terms of "manliness"; by extension, the term broadly connotes the innate quality, or the inherent power, of any subject or object. Religious definitions of virtue—which in some traditions is understood to be innate and in others to be acquired—focus on attitudes, dispositions, tendencies, and actions that further human good; moreover, religious virtues may be moral, intellectual, theological, or practical, but all require the exercise of judgment, including the choosing of virtue for its own sake. Frequently, the exercise of virtue is tied to the application of self-control; thus traditions that philosophically maintain the opposition of rationality to emotion (as is generally the case in Western monotheistic traditions), and that also identify rationality with maleness and emotion with femaleness, exhibit strong tendencies to denigrate women's abilities to cultivate virtues such as temperance and justice.

The association of the word *virtue* with particularly masculinist forms of potency and power is manifest from its definition alone. In examining concepts comparable to *virtue* as applied to women in many of the world's religious traditions, two tendencies predominate. The first posits universal virtue(s) but nonetheless valorizes attitudes and behaviors deemed "masculine," such as courage or filiality; in this instance, the virtuous woman is defined by the degree to which she successfully instantiates masculine ideals. The second offers differential definitions of "masculine" and "feminine" virtue(s); these dualistic typologies generally define masculine virtues as active and dominant and feminine virtues as passive and submissive; moreover, masculine virtues are frequently enacted in the public sphere, whereas feminine virtues are observable in the domestic realm. These several polarities reveal the construction of feminine or "womanly" virtues as "separate but equal" in theory, but in reality acting to buttress patriarchal control of female sexuality and social initiative—with the not infrequent result of women's social and even legal infantilization.

These two tendencies—the positing of universal virtues, and the construction of distinctly masculine and feminine virtues—can coexist, further complicating the view of feminine virtue. For example, in the case of traditional Confucianism, the highest or truest virtue, *de* (often translated as "benevolence" or "humanity"), understood to be psychologically and morally compelling, carried no gender restrictions. A ruler's *de*-virtue effortlessly commands the loyalty of the people, and any individual's *de*-virtue influences the actions and attitudes of those surrounding him or her. Liu Xiang (77–6 B.C.E.) compiled the *Lienu zhuan* (biographies of exemplary women) out of his conviction that the fortunes of the empire had long been heavily influenced by the actions of women; however, chief among a woman's virtues were those demonstrated through the fulfillment of her maternal and spousal roles. Ideals of female propriety were cast in terms of obedience, submissiveness, and the "ability to yield"; these virtues were to be both the guidelines and hallmarks of women's lives. Therefore, the constraint on womanly virtue was a function of its confinement to the domestic environment: women were idealized for the exercise of virtue in dealings with spouse, children, and in-laws, and in ways specifically conducive to the auspicious maintenance of the family.

Historically, the content and purpose of women's education in appropriate virtue (as well as education for men regarding appropriate virtues for women) has been conveyed through a variety of mutually reinforcing media, both religious and secular. Scriptural or quasi-scriptural sources, whether laudatory or hortatory, are increasingly subject to scholarly investigation and popular reinterpretation. The Biblical Fall of Adam and Eve and the story of Lot's wife can be read prescriptively as underscoring the need for women's obedience, or descriptively as sad yet brave commentary on the consequences of women's exercise of intellect and free will. While it remains true that Islam places an

Hanuman finds Sītā (right) in a scene from the Rāmāyaṇa, in which Sītā embodies self-sacrificing yet ultimately powerful feminine virtue, painting c. 1750 (Philadelphia Museum of Art/Corbis).

extremely high premium on a woman's virtue, understood mainly in terms of sexual purity, Qur'anic statements concerning female modesty and propriety (e.g., veiling and seclusion) are variously read as narrowly prescriptive or as descriptive and open to interpretation in practical application. In Hinduism, the story of Sītā, celebrated in the Rāmāyaṇa, confirms a self-sacrificing model of Hindu wifely devotion but also provides a glimpse of the ultimate power of feminine energy, or *shakti*. The Talmudic tale of the learned Beruriah, among other tales of virtuous women, exalts the virtue of an intellectual orientation coupled with faith—while simultaneously reinforcing her complementary yet subordinate position as the famed Rabbi Meir's wife. Finally, the tens of thousands of biographies of exemplary women (*lienu*) found in dynastic histories, local gazetteers, and independent biographical

compendia in China and Korea offer endless cameos of submissive patience and suffering, yet are testament to the feminine appropriation of masculinist virtues such as courage, loyalty, and filial devotion to one's parents (as opposed to the filial devotion to in-laws expected of a woman).

Such exemplary texts often reveal the tension between virtues required for the pursuit of religious goals and the ordinary social parameters of female virtue. Conflicts over chastity are evident in hagiographical accounts of many female saints, in the case of songs and life stories of Tibetan Buddhist female adepts, and in the traditions surrounding Hindu female devotional poets, such as Mirabai—all of whom defy conventional social expectations for virtuous women and resist marriage and childbearing.

In reconsidering theories of virtue, contemporary feminists are divided as to approach and outcome. Some Christian thealogians, such as Katie Cannon, Delores Williams, and Ada Maria Isasi-Diaz, urge an explicitly woman-centered redefinition of virtue that is not confined to traditional and universalist maternal ideals but situated in the particularities of womanist, mujerista, or Asian feminist theory; others, such as Nel Noddings, advocate a shift away from prizing individual virtue to valuing relational or communitarian virtues such as "reciprocity"—although, as the classical Confucian tradition demonstrates, even when reciprocity (*shu*) is a "universal" cardinal virtue, reciprocal relations are not easily freed from a welter of hierarchical authority and power issues. In every case and in every tradition, the interface between religious and secular constructions of virtue is being addressed, and less vaunted but no less influential channels for the inculcation of virtue, such as traditional primers, popular didactic literature, and even oral rhyme and doggerel, are also under examination.

BIBLIOGRAPHY

Atkinson, Clarissa W. " 'Your Servant, My Mother': The Figure of Saint Monica in the Ideology of Christian Motherhood." In *Immaculate and Powerful: The Female in Sacred Image and Social Reality.* Edited by C. W. Atkinson, Constance H. Buchanan, and Margaret R. Miles. 1985.

Hawley, John Stratton, ed. *Fundamentalism and Gender.* 1994. Discussion across religious traditions of fundamentalist religion as idealizing a conservative typology of women's virtue. Case studies drawn from American Christian, Indian Islam, Hindu, and Japanese New Religions traditions.

Klein, Anne C. "Primordial Purity and Everyday Life: Exalted Female Symbols and the Women of Tibet."

In *Immaculate and Powerful: The Female in Sacred Image and Social Reality.* Edited by Clarissa W. Atkinson, Constance H. Buchanan, and Margaret R. Miles. 1985.

Lee, Lily Xiao Hung. "Ban Zhao (c. 48–c. 120): Her Role in the Formulation of Controls Imposed Upon Women in Traditional China." In *The Virtue of Yin: Studies on Chinese Women.* 1994.

Mitter, Sara S. *Dharma's Daughters: Contemporary Indian Women and Hindu Culture.* 1991. An investigation into the lives of Bombay women, whose choices are colored by traditional patriarchal expectations of behavior, even in a modern urban society. Examines the roles that Goddess mythology and normative models such as Sita play in shaping the experience of these contemporary women.

Noddings, Nel. *Caring: A Feminine Approach to Ethics and Moral Education.* 1984.

Sharma, Arvind, ed. *Women in World Religions.* 1987. Recommended for concise overview of ideas about women and the feminine, offering insight into typologies of virtue in major world religious traditions.

Williams, Delores S. "Black Women's Surrogacy Experience and the Christian Notion of Redemption." In *After Patriarchy: Feminist Transformations of the World Religions.* Edited by Paula M. Cooey, William R. Eakin, and Jay B. McDaniel. 1991.

See also: **Mujerista Tradition; Womanist Traditions.**

VIVIAN-LEE NYITRAY

Visionaries in Medieval Europe

Visionary experience, either by way of the appearance in the human realm of otherworldly figures or by transfer of the seer to another world, was important in Christianity from its origins. In the early fifth century the North African bishop Augustine divided visions produced by divine action into three categories of ascending importance: corporeal visions of actual bodies; spiritual (i.e., imaginative) visions that involve images given to the mind; and intellectual visions, which are the infallible grasp of incorporeal realities without images. Both of the latter types imply ecstasy (latin *extasis, excessus mentis*) in which the mind is carried away from the bodily senses (see *Literal Commentary on Genesis* 12). Augustine's division provided a touchstone for theological evaluation of visions throughout the Middle Ages, though in practice many descriptions of visionary experience intermingle the spiritual and the intellectual types.

The characteristic form of vision in the early Middle Ages (c. 500–1200 C.E.) was an unexpected transport to heaven and hell in which the seer (usually a man) underwent a vivid tour of some duration whose effect was designed to produce a conversion to a more serious life on the visionary's part, as well as in the lives of his audience. Beginning in the twelfth century a new form of vision became evident, one in which women played a much larger, even a preponderant, role. These visions, which flourished throughout the remainder of the Middle Ages and well beyond in Catholic Christianity, involved repeatable brief experiences, often consciously prepared for by the visionary. Celestial figures (God, angels, saints) appeared to the seer, who at times also ascended into the heavenly world. Negative visions were also found, mostly in the form of attacks by demons. This second form of vision generally served more to confirm the sanctity and spiritual authority of the visionary than to induce conversion. Hence, it is not surprising that women, who had so little access to other avenues of spiritual power in medieval Christianity, were the most frequent recipients of such showings.

Many of these visions can be described as mystical in the sense that they center on an intense and direct encounter with God, most often Christ the God-man, seen as the Divine Lover or as the Crucified Redeemer. Such visions often took place within a eucharistic context in which the visionary beheld Christ in the Host. Other visions did not involve a personal and emotional contact with God but rather were more prophetic and doctrinal in character. From the thirteenth century on, one can discern an increasingly "excessive" strand in many visionaries, especially women, in terms of the frequency, the descriptive intensity, and the physical effects, especially on the bodies of the mystical visionaries.

The list of famous female visionaries begins in the twelfth century with Hildegard of Bingen (d. 1179) and Elisabeth of Schönau (d. 1165). Hildegard is among the most distinctive of all medieval visionaries, since her experience of two forms of vision—"the shadow of living brightness," in which she sees and hears complex allegorical images, and "the living light," in which she has a direct and indescribable contact with God—do not fit into standard categories. Elisabeth's multiple visions of a variety of heavenly figures who give her mostly practical and doctrinal messages are more typical of many late medieval seers, such as Birgitta of Sweden (d. 1373).

The female mystical visionaries of the thirteenth through fifteenth centuries comprise a lengthy list. Many of these women are known to us primarily through the hagiographical accounts penned by their male confessors and admirers. Among these are Marie d'Oignies (d. 1211), the first Beguine; Margaret of Cortona (d.

The visionary Catherine of Siena is depicted in a stone statue, Rome, Italy (Karen Tweedy-Holmes/Corbis).

1297), a member of the Franciscan Third Order; Christina of Stommeln (d. 1312), who was closely associated with the Dominicans; and the married seer Dorothy of Montau (d. 1394). The most interesting examples, however, are the women who have left us accounts of their often extraordinary mystical visions and the theological insights these visions brought to them. In the thirteenth century we find examples in the Dutch Beguine Hadewijch (c. 1250), the German Beguine Mechtild of Magdeburg (d. c. 1290), two Cistercian nuns of Helfta, Mechtild of Hackborn (d. 1298) and Gertrude the Great (d. 1302), as well as the Italian Third Order Franciscan, Angela of Foligno (d. 1309). The fourteenth century witnessed an outpouring of visionary texts among German Dominican nuns. The most noted visionaries, however, are the Italian Third Order Dominican Catherine of Siena (d. 1380), and English anchoress Julian of Norwich (d. c. 1416), whose *Showings* (Revelations) of Christ's passion are among

the best known of all medieval mystical texts. The fifteenth century produced the married ecstatic Margery Kempe (d. c. 1439) in England, as well as Magdalena Beutlerin (d. 1458) in Germany, and Catherine Vigri (d. 1463) in Italy. This is just a partial listing of the many women visionaries who enriched mystical literature during the later Middle Ages.

BIBLIOGRAPHY

New translations and commentaries of the texts of many medieval women visionaries have been published in the Classics of Western Spirituality Series (1978–). A useful anthology is Elizabeth Alvida Petroff, *Medieval Women's Visionary Literature* (1986). A key work for the investigation of the role of women in late medieval religion is Herbert Grundmann, *Religious Movements in the Middle Ages* (1995). For detailed accounts of medieval visions, see Peter Dinzelbacher, *Vision und Visionsliteratur im Mittelalter* (Stuttgart, 1981); and *Revelationes* (Typologie des Sources du Moyen Age Occidental, fasc. 57; Turnhout, 1991). Aspects of the spirituality of late medieval female visionaries have been treated in Richard Kieckhefer, *Unquiet Souls: Fourteenth-Century Saints and Their Religious Milieu* (1984); and Caroline Walker Bynum, *Holy Feast and Holy Fast: The Religious Significance of Food to Medieval Women* (1987).

See also Angela of Foligno; Catherine of Siena; Elisabeth of Schönau; Hadewijch of Brabant; Hildegard of Bingen; Julian of Norwich; Kempe, Margery; Mechtild of Magdeburg.

BERNARD McGINN

Visions

Visionary experience is part of a spectrum of extraordinary states of consciousness characterized by sensory perceptions without external stimuli. Visions are related to and can be part of hallucinations, dreams, illusions, spirit possessions, delirious states, ecstasies, oracle trances, and near-death experiences. Perceived to be religiously meaningful, objectively true, and of positive value to the visionary (and oftentimes to her community), visions constitute a phenomenologically distinct and often complex body of knowledge that can be transmitted ritually, textually, and orally. Although accounts of visions can be found in all religious traditions, their relevance, cultural functions, and interpretive frameworks vary widely among religions and even within the historical, geographical, and social parameters of a single religious tradition. Because visions are a type of religious knowledge that claims direct communication with divine or demonic beings, visionary women have historically either (1) confirmed and elaborated dominant religious teachings and supported religious or secular ruling elites or the community as a whole, (2) challenged, innovated, or subverted dominant belief systems and the claims to power of their representatives, or (3) operated nominally within a dominant system, yet have pursued separate and often secretive goals.

Certain techniques, such as drumming, fasting, dancing, or sensory stimulus deprivation, can be used to induce visionary experience, but visions may also occur spontaneously or as the result of brain injury, of the ingestion of hallucinogenic substances (such as peyote), or of mental illness. Although historically both men and women visionaries have suffered from persecution, male visionary technologies, teaching, and the memory of male visionary figures have on the whole survived far more intact than women's legacies.

Within a patriarchal religious culture, four distinct types of female visionary activity predominate. (1) In times of large-scale crises (whether political, military, or ecological), exceptional women visionaries are called on to explore alternative modes of knowledge that might generate a crisis-resolution or predictions about the future, or disclose the will of a divinity (e.g., the classical Sybilline traditions in Roman, Jewish, and Christian circles; Joan of Arc in medieval France). (2) Within the separate sphere of women's lives under patriarchy, especially in premodern Western and traditional non-Western societies, a distinct gynocentric religiosity may develop (often in the form of domestically oriented values) that includes a sophisticated, institutionalized use of female visions for the well-being of the community and can have roots in prepatriarchal women's spirituality (e.g., Burmese *Nat* religion). (3) Small-scale religious dissent may arise in the form of heretical or sectarian, often mystical groups, during which some women visionaries may gain temporary leadership as founders or supporters of the movement (e.g., Maximilla and Priscilla, Montanist prophetesses from the second to third centuries C.E. in Phrygia [modern west-central Turkey]). (4) Syncretistic spiritual activity may arise around female visionary leadership with an emphasis on healing trances, the safeguarding and development of indigenous religious knowledge and practices, and strong community ties (e.g., Mexican *espiritualismo* with its emphasis on healing, *videncia*, spiritual sight, and *alta luz*, spiritual communication with the divine). The first and third types of visionary women's social contributions gravitate toward political, cosmological, and apocalyptic teachings; the second and fourth types tend to be more shamanic in character and focus on healing and intimate relationship, whether among the living or the dead.

The boundaries between these four visionary modes can be fluid; for example, political figures such as Joan of Arc were also approached as healers.

In Eastern patriarchal religions such as Buddhism and Confucianism, women's visionary activities could survive and flourish best where preceding ancient local traditions encouraged religious leadership roles for women. Most female visionaries in the East today operate in the context of localized domestic religiosity as shamanic healers and oracles. Historically, only few women visionaries, however, have been remembered in or contributed to the textual, oral, and ritual traditions of mainstream Eastern religions. In Tibetan Buddhism, for example, the mystic Yeshe Tsogyel (eighth century C.E.) is the only woman teacher recognized by all Tibetan teaching lineages. Another renowned Tibetan visionary teacher is Machig Labdron (eleventh century C.E.), who introduced the Cöd (cutting) meditation practice, which is still used today. In Chinese Taoism, dream vision, shamanic trances, and other visionary technologies were also practiced by women. Among female Taoist adepts are Zhou Xuanjing (twelfth century C.E.) and her famous contemporary, the teacher and poet Sun Bu-er. An exceptional female visionary of the Hindu bhakti movement is Mirabai (c. 1500–1550), a devotee of the Hindu god Krishna and a widely revered teacher, composer, and poet.

In indigenous religious traditions, as in syncretistic traditions such as Black Carib religions, female visionary activity is frequently fully institutionalized (e.g., as a women's secret society) and therefore less dependent on unpredictable factors—such as individual strength and talent and favorable historical circumstance—that often decided the fate of women visionaries in the transnational, literacy-based world religions. Indigenous women tend to use visions for the purpose of healing, communication with ancestor spirits, and the well-being of the community. Female visionaries may function as respected shamans (as in aboriginal Australia), medicine women and community elders (as with Native Americans), or enjoy only secondary status in their respective societies (as in the *zār* cult in Islamic African nations such as Sudan).

The Catholic Church has acknowledged numerous women visionaries, especially from the European Middle Ages, as saints. Three of these saints achieved the rare status of *doctor ecclesiae:* Teresa of Avila (1515–1582), Catherine of Siena (1347–1380), and Thérèse of Lisieux (1872–1897). The first recorded visions by a Christian woman, Vibia Perpetua, date from the beginning of the third century C.E. in North Africa. In the Orthodox churches, male visionary traditions are well documented and researched, but this is not the case for female spirituality. In the institutions of female monasteries and hermitages, however, visionary women were not unusual. Well-known Russian visionaries are the peasant hermit Anastasiia Logacheva (1809–1875) and Abbess Taisiia (1840–1915), a member of the St. Petersburg nobility. Among Protestant churches women's visionaries have flourished in revivalist, spiritualist, and charismatic groups, especially in non-European communities, where indigenous visionary practices have fused with Westernized Christian traditions. A remarkable African-American visionary is the Shaker Eldress Rebecca Jackson (1795–1871), who founded a predominantly African-American Shaker sisterhood in Philadelphia.

In biblical Israel, as in other Near Eastern cultures, women appear to have played a significant religious role either negatively as spirit mediums or positively as "wise women" and prophetic visionaries who mediated political conflicts though oracles and visions (see, e.g., I Sam. 28:7; 2 Sam.; Isa. 8:3; Neh. 6:14); women prophets mentioned by name include Miriam (Exodus 15:20) and Hulda (2 Kings 22: 14–20). In late antiquity the Jewish contemplative monastic community of the Therapeutae might have encouraged visions among both men and women. During the Middle Ages, female Jewish visionaries emerged in times of social upheaval, as during a period of Jewish revival among *conversos* in late-fifteenth- and early-sixteenth-century Spain. The visionaries Marie Gomez of Chillon and Ines, the twelve-year-old daughter of Juan Esteban of Herrera, were persecuted by the Inquisition because of their messianic prophecies; Ines was burned at the stake in 1500. In Hasidic Judaism, the most famous female visionary is Hannah Rachel (1805–1892), also called the Maid of Ludomir, who became a Torah scholar and revered teacher in her own right. Visions form an integral part of contemporary Middle Eastern Jewish women's domestic religion.

Not unlike women in other male-dominated world religions, women in Islam have developed two settings for visionary activity: that of localized domestic religion, often centered on the cult of a saint's grave, and a more tenuous hold in the Islamic mystical traditions of Sufism. The singularly most famous Sufi visionary and mystic is Rabi'ah al-'Adawiyyah (d. 801 C.E.), whose contribution to early Sufism is her emphasis on radical love of God and mystical union. Many of her teachings survive in the form of memorable parables and biographical stories. Whereas Rabi'a lived in great poverty, the revered Indian poet and visionary Fātima Jahānārā Begum Ṣāḥib (seventeenth century C.E.) was the daughter of a Mogul emperor.

BIBLIOGRAPHY

Baskin, Judith R. *Jewish Women in Historical Perspective.* 1991.

Cleary, Thomas. *Immortal Sisters: Secrets of Taoist Women.* 1989.

Humez, Jean McMahon. *Gifts of Power: The Writings of Rebecca Jackson, Black Visionary, Shaker Eldress.* 1981.

Kraemer, Ross S. *Maenads, Martyrs, Matrons, Monastics: A Sourcebook on Women's Religions in the Greco-Roman World.* 1988.

Petroff, Elizabeth Alvilda. *Medieval Women's Visionary Literature.* 1986.

Ruether, Rosemary Radford, and Rosemary Skinner Keller. *In Our Own Voices: Four Centuries of American Women's Writing.* 1995.

Sered, Susan Starr. *Priestess, Mother, Sacred Sister: Religions Dominated by Women.* 1994.

Shostak, Marjorie. *Nisa: The Life and Words of a !Kung Woman.* 1983.

Wessinger, Catherine. *Women's Leadership in Marginal Religions: Explorations Outside the Mainstream.* 1993.

Young, Serinity. *An Anthology of Sacred Texts By and About Women.* 1993.

See also **Catherine of Siena; Hebrew Bible: Prophets and Judges; Hulda; Machig Labdron; Mirabai; Miriam; Perpetua and Felicity; Rabi'a; Teresa of Avila; Thérèse of Lisieux.**

ULRIKE WIETHAUS

Visual Arts

The material expression of religious beliefs through the visual arts is a practice all religions share. Even those that disallow any form of imagery inside or on their holy sites construct a type of visual expression through the style of architecture and materials used in their place of worship. Women, typically excluded from authorship of sacred texts, play a key role in the history of the visual arts and religion as subject matter and, more important, as the creators of objects whose purpose is the expression and transmission of religious ideas.

The history of women's role in the visual arts and religion is an old one, but the interdisciplinary study and documentation of these relationships is new. As more and more histories of women in art and craft are published, it becomes clear that women have always designed and created art for religious purposes, much of it, to the bane of historians, for ritual use and then discarded. Specifically, the 1970s saw an explosion of books on ritual art and women, many of which focused on the recovery of goddess or "prehistoric" religions within the Western tradition. The archaeologist Marija Gimbutas was the first widely recognized scholar to challenge the received academic interpretation of female artifacts as simply emblems of fertility cults. Her exhaustive analysis of material remains from approximately 3,000 excavation sites in southeastern Europe sparked the realization that women's early religious histories had been completely overlooked by previous scholarship. The argument that material remains from the age before writing are too problematic for reconstructing a history of women in religions cannot be brooked when one considers, for example, the amount of research funding that goes into reconstructing the history of dinosaurs. Research on women, art, and religion using visual art as testimony to women's history is contributing to a new and inclusive world history of religions across different academic disciplines.

WOMEN AS OBJECTS OF REPRESENTATION

As an object of religious representation, the female form has served as an allegory for moral ideals and as the embodiment of otherworldly life-forms. From the Queen of Heaven and Mother of Earth to the evil, stick-riding hag, representations of superhuman and subhuman women have borne little relation to the actual lives of female believers. The female form has frequently been employed as a stand-in for abstract moral concepts such as good and evil, plenitude, piety, and vice. H. Diane Russell has shown, for example, that representations of mythical female figures such as Fortune in sixteenth-century Northern Renaissance prints, which circulated widely in their day, served the Christian cause by providing models of female behavior against which actual women were expected to gauge themselves.

Women appear as representations of religious ideas in almost every religion. However, from the angry black Kālī of Hinduism to the voluptuous Venus of Roman religions, from the erotic *Sheila-na-gig* of Celtic origin to the holy *vesica piscis* of medieval Christianity, it is women's sexuality that is the primary metaphor informing stories of creation and destruction, sin and rebirth. As the seducer or the seduced, the repertoire of female visual roles is weighted in favor of physical functions and less in favor of intellectual capacities. As Diane Apostolos-Cappadona has stated, in religious art in which women are the objects of representation, we must ask ourselves why and where such imagery was produced, by whom, and for whom. For example, the philosophy of aesthetics or the contemplation of what is beautiful in art has been used as a justification for the salacious representation of females (Berger, 1972). Women imaged as witches in sixteenth-century Europe consistently identified evil with women (Miles, 1991).

Visual art, like written texts, puts forth a point of view. Challenging the history of rhetorical images of women created by patriarchal religions and offering new images of the female divine has been one of the great aims of twentieth-century feminist artists.

WOMEN AS IMAGE-MAKERS

Equally as damaging to the history of women, the philosophy of aesthetics has been used historically against female artists as a device to classify objects made by women as falling outside of the exalted boundaries of "serious" art. Serious or fine art in the Western tradition has been identified as oil painting and sculpture. In the West, conceptual frames of painters and sculptors, however, have been quite narrow. Thanks to movies, plays, operas, books of art history, and coffee-table tomes, Western culture has successfully created the mythos of the heroic artist as male, young, and, typically, a substance-abuser. The scarcity of women artists in traditional histories of art, amongst other issues, has triggered an attack on this stereotype and a rethinking by feminist scholars of philosophical concepts such as timelessness and universality.

There is a different consensus that serious art is as much a cultural artifact as, say, an aboriginal tribal mask. Like cultural artifacts, serious art is produced on an interactive basis with life experience, incorporating both physical and imaginative realities. Given that experience is culturally encoded, products of culture such as art will also be encoded with the values and beliefs, including gender ideologies, specific to a particular time and place. Art produced by women will to some degree fall within the scope of values and beliefs esteemed within their specific milieu.

In some parts of the world, women are considered to be artists by making images through the production of children. Any other type of artistic production during childbearing years, therefore, is thought to put women's fertility at risk. In West Africa, this is a widespread belief, based on the cultural connection between procreation and making pottery. This link is a symbiotic one. For example, female fertility may be adversely affected if the artist who makes pots is still able to have children. Conversely, firing pots when a pubescent girl is close by may cause the containers to break (Barley, 1994).

It is sometimes believed that women who make ritual art may be harmful to others. Among the Dowayos of Cameroon, potters are believed to cause diseases, to be steeped in witchcraft, and to be sexually perverted (Barley, 1994). This perception may be due in part to the artist's contact with blood (a charged substance) in her other functions as midwife, healer, and female circumciser. Or it may be due in part to the pots' function as vessels of spiritual essences, or it may be due to the potter's handling of the clay, which is seen as a conductor of spirit presences. Regardless of how the belief arises, religious art and artifacts, even in the Christian world, have been considered at one time or another to be miraculous cure-enhancing vehicles. It is a short stretch to consider the maker of such artifacts as also possessing supernatural powers.

Art made by women in a religious context can be grouped into four categories, all relating to environments: 1) forest environment; 2) urban environment; 3) bodily environment; and 4) dwelling environment. It is important to note that there may be works of art by women that due to their ritual nature do not fit neatly into any of the above categories or that might cross more than one type. Generally speaking, however, each of these types may be understood as an expression of the female maker's task of sanctifying a particular site (including the human form) as part of her ritual practice.

Forest environment describes the creation of art to honor and communicate with the forest. It may incorporate the idea of movement as an element of the presentation (Meurant and Thompson, 1995). Mbuti women of the Ituri Forest in central West Africa are best known for their rhythmic paintings on pounded inner bark. Each barkcloth or *pongo* is a painting of an event experienced by the artist; each woman may be an expert in drawing a particular design or motif. However, the final authorship of the multipatterned paintings is usually communal, since they are made while the women sing to the forest as a seated group. Visual expressions of gratitude to the forest for abundance and for permission to enter its domain, *pongos* are typically abandoned after they have served their ritual purpose. Thus only a handful of these exquisite records of forest worship have been preserved.

The term *urban environment* deals with art that responds to broad religious ideas in a public setting and tends to be exhibited as a permanent or semi-permanent installation. Issues such as racial and class conflict, the state of the environment, indifference to social ills, and national memorials are just some of the topics addressed in this kind of art. Intervention in the landscape may take the form of violent graffiti on subways, apocalyptic texts or images on billboards, outdoor wall murals, or sacred earthworks, to name just a few examples. The U.S. artist Jenny Holzer's confrontational public invectives such as "ANY SURPLUS IS AMORAL" writ large on outdoor spectacolor boards in the middle of Manhattan are a call to New Yorkers to act morally in their role as citizens of the world. Minority communi-

A detail of the Vietnam Veterans' Memorial wall (1982), designed by Maya Lin, which has become a near-sacred site (Joseph Sohm; ChromoSohm Inc./Corbis).

ties have found expression in large scale mural paintings. Chinese artist Hui-Xiang Xiao's "Golden Phoenix Is Flying" in Los Angeles (1992) combines imagery and symbols from traditional and modern Chinese painting with visual elements of pre-Columbian Mexico. The aim of this particular mural is to reduce tensions between hostile Chinese and Latino neighbors through a public acknowledgment of the mutually rich heritage of mythical symbols.

One of the most interesting artists to emerge in this category in the last half of the twentieth century is Ohio-born Maya Ying Lin, best known for her Vietnam Veterans Memorial (1982) in Washington, D.C. Lin, a sculptor and architect of great vision, created this elegant earthwork made of black polished stone while still an architecture student at Yale. Despite the initial controversy over her nontraditional design, the war memorial has become a major pilgrimage site in the United States. Here loved ones, friends, and relatives of the 58,000 men and women killed or declared missing in action gather to grieve and to heal, leaving behind votive objects such as candles, flowers, baseball gloves, baby pictures, and love letters for those named on the reflective surface. In her construction of two triangular walls that meet on the shortest sides, set deep into the earth, Lin has managed to transform the private act of mourning, an action that historically took place on consecrated ground outside the city, into a public ritual where national and personal loss can be reconciled.

Curiously, like many religious icons of the past, some of Lin's work has evoked an iconoclastic response. A 1993 sculptural landscape entitled "Groundswell," consisting of 43 tons of shattered safety glass was made for the exterior of Ohio State University's Wexner Center, was vandalized a week after its installation by someone who poured red paint into the section of the work with the greatest public access (Stein, 1994).

Bodily environment refers to the process of marking the body through painting, tattooing, scarification, and cicatrization (the making of raised scars). In a ritual context, these marks are acknowledged indicators of religious identity. Markings may be temporary or permanent and may refer to status change (especially with regard to the reproductive cycle in women), group affiliation or cosmological matters. Bodily markings may also convey beauty or the sexual availability of a woman or the virility of a man. In some cultures, such as the Ga'anda of Nigeria in West Africa, beautiful body scars on women are a sign of spiritual approval by the guardian spirits of their community; a botched job signals the spiritual disgrace of the recipient (Elder, 1996).

Dwelling environment descries art such as frescoes or wall murals that are painted directly onto a surface in the devotee's house or place of worship. These works may memorialize and honor a deity or bring protection, wealth, or fertility to those who dwell inside. On the occasion of weddings or religious festivals, the Hindu women of Mithila, a province in northeastern India, make visually complex devotional paintings of the deities of Hinduism. Before a wedding, for example, murals are painted on the courtyard walls of the village and especially in the room of the house where the bride will receive her husband. The murals, which depict colorful male and female figures, animals, birds, and abstract designs, typically represent familiar episodes, many of them sexual, in the lives of the Hindu deities. The murals, outlined in ink and filled in with flat color, are visual prayers, invoking the supernatural beings addressed in the images to bless and protect the newly married couple.

As the care of the home has traditionally been the job of women, the task of sanctifying its space has also fallen to females. Women everywhere sanctify space within and without their homes by creating restorative areas in gardens, by installing protective "guardians" over transitional or vulnerable places such as doorways and children's sleeping quarters, and by cooking and serving festive meals on religious holidays. Domestic space may also be extended to the burial ground, the dwelling place of one's ancestors. Here women and their families bring prepared food and wine to share with their deceased relations. Another way space is sanctified in the home is through the construction and maintenance of domestic altars and shrines. Devotional objects may include images or carvings of god(s) or goddesses, incense, photographs, jewelry, perfume, fruit, flowers, and candles. The shrine may have an altar which is hidden or veiled in some way. These private installations, emphasizing the senses and the body, are, in patriarchal religions, inversions of formal religious hierarchies in which male priests preside.

CONCLUSION

As image-makers, women throughout the world have participated and continue to participate in an artistic-ritual heritage that has been handed down from mother to daughter over many generations. As an object of representation the image of woman has typically been used, especially in Western culture, to reinvent and update the personifications of good and evil. In art mediated by men it may be argued that there are no images of woman, only significations of male desire (Pollock, 1990). The visual arts therefore, are an important graphic record of how gender ideology is used by different cultures to portray and transmit religious beliefs through material form.

BIBLIOGRAPHY

Anderson, Janet A. *Women in the Fine Arts: A Bibliography and Illustration Guide.* 1991.

Apostolos-Cappadona, Diane. *Encyclopedia of Women in Religious Art.* 1996.

Barley, Nigel. *Smashing Pots: Works of Clay from Africa.* 1994.

Berger, John. *Ways of Seeing.* 1972.

Bachmann, Donna G., and Sherry Piland. *Women Artists: An Historical, Contemporary and Feminist Bibliography.* 1978.

Elder, George R. *An Encyclopedia of Archetypal Symbolism: The Body.* 1996.

Ergas, G. Aimee. "Maya Lin." In *Artists: From Michelangelo to Maya Lin.* 1995.

Fister, Patricia. *Japanese Women Artists, 1600–1900.* 1988.

Gimbutas, Marija A. *The Gods and Goddesses of Old Europe, 6500–3500 B.C.: Myths and Cult Images.* 1974.

———. *The Language of the Goddess.* 1989.

Heartney, Eleanor. "Recontextualizing African Altars." *Art in America* (December, 1994) 58–64.

Hedges, Elaine, and Ingrid Wendt. *In Her Own Image: Women Working in the Arts.* 1980.

Huyler, Stephen P. *Painted Prayers: Women's Art in Village India.* 1994.

Korp, Maureen. *Sacred Art of the Earth: Ancient and Contemporary Earthworks.* 1997.

Korsmeyer, Carolyn. "Pleasure: Reflection on Aesthetics and Feminism." *The Journal of Aesthetics and Art Criticism* 51, no. 2 (Spring, 1993): 199–206.

Kramrisch, Stella. "The Ritual Arts of India." In *Aditi: The Living Arts of India.* Edited by Rajeev Sethi. 1986.

Lauter, Estella. *Women as Mythmakers: Poetry and Visual Art by Twentieth-Century Women.* 1984.

Link, Howard A., with Sanna Saks Deutsch. *The Feminine Image: Women of Japan.* 1985.

Lippard, Lucy. *Overlay: Contemporary Art and the Art of Prehistory.* 1983.

Lobell, Mimi. "The Buried Treasure: Women's Ancient Architectural Heritage." *Architecture: A Place for Women.* Edited by E. P. Berkeley. 1989.

Meurant, Georges, and Robert Farris Thompson. *Mbuti Design: Paintings by Pygmy Women of the Ituri Forest.* 1995.

Miles, Margaret R. *Carnal Knowing: Female Nakedness and Religious Meaning in the Christian West.* 1991.

Pollack, Rachel. *The Body of the Goddess: Sacred Wisdom in Myth, Landscape and Culture.* 1997.

Pollock, Griselda. "Missing Women: Rethinking Early Thoughts on Images of Women." In *The Critical Image: Essays on Contemporary Photography.* Edited by Carol Squires. 1990.

Russell, H. Diane. *Eve/Ave: Women in Renaissance and Baroque Prints.* 1990.

Sethi, Rajeev, ed. *Aditi: The Living Arts of India.* 1986.

Slatkin, Wendy. *Women Artists in History: From Antiquity to the 20th Century.* 1990.

Stein, Judith E. "Space and Place" *Art in America.* (December 1994): 67–71, 117.

Turner, Victor. "Bodily Marks." In *The Encyclopedia of Religion*, vol. 2. Edited by Mircea Eliade. 1987.

Vequaud, Yves, *The Women Painters of Mithila.* 1977.

JANET HELEN TULLOCH

Voice

The voice has been perceived by religious traditions both as an instrument of devotion and as a medium of seduction. According to the view that the voice of song heightens spiritual concentration and experience of the divine, a tremendous variety of chants, recitations, and vocal music has been composed for liturgical purposes by religious cultures throughout the world. The voices of women, however, have particularly been associated with the invocation of sensuality and distraction from religious pursuits. Reconciling themselves to the spiritual value of vocalization, authority structures of religious institutions have suppressed women's public devotional and speaking voices. The silencing of women's voices is a pervasive feature of many religious societies.

Contrasting attitudes are articulated by the following uncomfortable couplet:

> Let me hear your voice for it is arousing.
> (Song of Songs 2:14)
>
> A woman's voice is a lascivious distraction.
> (Babylonian Talmud, Tractate Berachot, 24a)

In the biblical context, the desire for arousal by the woman's voice is understood metaphorically to be an invocation of the love relationship between God and the people. The contradictory Talmudic utterance presumes a male universe in which proper devotional conduct must exclude the voice of a woman at the peak moment of religious concentration, during the recitation of *Shema*, the emblematic prayer of Judaism. A woman's voice, sought in the symbolically erotic and spontaneous relationship between lovers, is often considered to be a distraction within the confines of institutional practice. The author of the Book of Revelation (2:18–29) admonishes the church at Thyatira for following the voice of Jezebel, who is accused of teaching Christians to practice sexual immorality and to eat food sacrificed to pagan deities. Jezebel's voice, according to the text, exhorts to impious bodily acts.

Though many texts dating from early periods of religious traditions attest to inclusivity of the genders, subsequent institutionalization has tended toward subjugation of women's voices. The Buddha himself presented no barrier to women who sought his path, became arhats, saints, chanted and preached. The *Therīgatha*, poems of early Buddhist nuns, depict bold and outspoken women's voices on the quest for enlightenment. Concerning the question of perpetuating religious authority, however, social custom asserted itself against women's public voices. Three times the Buddha's aunt Pajapati repeated her request for women to be allowed to become nuns. Only when Ananda, the Buddha's personal (male) attendant, articulated the plea in his voice did the Buddha accept the women, severely subjugating them to the monks. According to the Christian New Testament, Mary Magdalene first apprehended the resurrection of Jesus and Jesus appeared first to women. (Luke 7; John 20) In spite of these significant initial revelatory experiences, women's voices were swiftly stifled in the early church.

Sacred authorities of many traditions have exercised divine privilege to repress women's voices in prayer, ritual, interpretation, and decision-making, both explicitly and subtly. Buddhist tantric works describe night time feast assemblies of yoginīs in the forest playing cymbals, bells, and tambourines, dancing within a halo of light and a cloud of incense. From this celebration, the women's voices are conspicuously absent; it is the aroma that arouses the narrator. The women are silent in the text.

Historically, both Jewish and Muslim religious authorities have attempted to distinguish between cantillation of scripture and liturgy, usually undertaken by men in pubic sacred space, and nonsacred music performed in secular settings, sometimes by women. Outside the formal structures, the voices of women have been heard in religious societies performing significant roles in community rituals. The prayer-song at the sea led by Miriam after the Israelites' redemption from slavery is a prototype of women's public vocal celebration (Exodus 15:1–21). The thrilling ululations of women from Arab lands at celebration rites are an uncanonized form of "alleluia." Professional women mourners have been well known throughout the Levant since the earliest written records. The wails and cries of the mourners for Jerusalem, twice destroyed, echo the cries of Rachel in the biblical and early Christian texts. Though these public women's roles give voice to intense affective community religious experiences, they are nonetheless dissociated from the center of sacred space, authority, and leadership.

Varieties of women's folk music culture have flourished continuously, parallel to male-dominated institutions in religious societies. A song was composed by Hindu Laksminkara (eighth century C.E.) to celebrate the daily possibility of transcendent ecstasy. Professional *karinat* (singing-girls) performed folk songs for tribes, in wine shops and at private family gatherings, from the pre-Islamic period through the Orthodox Caliphal period while opposition to vocal music peaked in the Islamic world. In the contemporary generation, new folk compositions and liturgies articulate women's will to assert their public voices in religious communities and to experiment with feminist imagery of the divine. Poetry, theater, and music that is written, practiced, and performed by women ennobles the experiences of women whose stories have been untold by male voices. During the latter part of the twentieth century, women's voices have become more accepted in the metaphoric chorus of religious music through the proliferation of women in the clergy of many Protestant Christian denominations, where they assert the role of women's voices in ritual and public discourse. Nevertheless, powerful resistance remains in some sacred settings. The decade-long struggle by "Women of the Wall" to affirm the rights of Jewish women to sound their voices in prayer and celebration at the Western Wall in Jerusalem has been countered with violence.

In contemporary religious life, women are becoming more vocal participants. The passion of women's voices is being summoned for religious purposes. Perseverance in public prayer, song, and teaching irrevocably reckons women's voices among the polyphony of religious experience.

BIBLIOGRAPHY

No systematic study of women's voices in world religions has been undertaken. The citations here include only works that consider the issue of voice explicitly, or critically assemble primary sources that are useful for research on the subject.

Concerning early Christian texts and their attitudes toward women, see Ross Shepard Kraemer, *Her Share of the Blessings* (1992).

For a compilation of sources about women in Buddhist cultures, see José Ignacio Cabezón, *Buddhism, Sexuality and Gender* (1992); Miranda Shaw has undertaken an intensive study with feminist self-consciousness, *Passionate Enlightenment: Women in Tantric Buddhism* (1994).

Recordings by Gila Razyl Raphael, Linda Hirschorn, Shefa Gold, Debbie Friedman, Hannah Tiferet Siegel, and Margot Stein Azen exemplify women's music experiments in the contemporary Jewish world. Lynn Gottlieb has written some of the stories and rituals that she performs in *She Who Dwells Within* (1995).

For an example of an activist posture toward the transformation of the role of women's voices in Judaism, see Bonna Devora Haberman, "Nashot hakotel: Women in Jerusalem celebrate Rosh Chodesh," in *Celebrating the New Moon: A Rosh Chodesh Anthology*, edited by Susan Berrin (1995).

For feminist interpretations of Miriam's song see, for example, Phyllis Trible, "Bringing Miriam out of the Shadows," *Biblical Review* 5, no. 18 (1989): 14–25, 34; and Gerald J. Janzen, "Song of Moses, Song of Miriam: Who Is Seconding whom?" *Catholic Biblical Quarterly* 54, no. 2 (1992): 210–220.

See also **Mourning and Death Rites.**

BONNA DEVORA HABERMAN

Vows

Most world religions have some kind of activity that corresponds roughly to the English word *vow*. In general terms, a vow is a commitment made either to a particular type of lifestyle or to the accomplishment of a particular deed. Most major religions assume a kind of initial vow taken on the part of the participant, such as a basic fidelity to its faith or fundamental outlook. These may be considered implicit vows. In addition to these common commitments, religions may also include the option of taking various types of voluntary, or super-erogatory, vows. This article will be concerned solely with voluntary vows. These can be classed under two rubrics: 1) those vows that are undertaken to implore a particular favor from the deity and 2) general lifestyle vows that aim to increase the spiritual stature of the practitioner.

Among the vows of type 1—those that seek a particular boon—one may again identify two varieties: those that are fulfilled before the fact and those fulfilled after. Vows fulfilled before the fact include such practices as the Hindu *vrata* or the ancient Hebrew vow of the Nazirite, in which the aspirant first performs various penitential acts or avoids ritual pollution, anticipating the fulfillment of his or her desires (most typically the birth of a son) upon successful completion of the regimen. An example of those fulfilled after the fact are the vows made by Roman Catholics to St. Jude, patron saint of "lost causes," in which the aspirant vows to perform a work of merit (for instance, building a shrine) upon the fulfillment of his or her wish.

Vows of type 2—those meant to increase spiritual stature—include commitment to the maintenance of certain precepts with regard to lifestyle and behavior. Most common of these vows are the monastic precepts followed in many traditions. These usually demand strict chastity and obedience to a monastic hierarchy. In most traditions, the monastic order of nuns is compelled to follow a more restrictive set of precepts than that of the monks. In Jaina and Buddhist traditions, nuns are compelled to show greater deference to monks than to fellow nuns. In the Christian monastic tradition also, nuns are generally subordinated to monks.

Other types of vows focus less on avoiding non-virtue than on performing virtue. For instance, the Buddhist tradition of the Unexcelled Yoga Tantra requires its practitioners to pledge to maintain certain positive qualities of mind at all times. Interestingly, these vows also include a precept that seems to have unique importance to the issue of gender equality in religious practice. This discipline demands that the practitioner never disparage women and always regard them as emanations of the divine. This vow is perhaps unique among world traditions and has been seen by some as a result of the prominent role played by women in establishing the tradition. Critics, however, cite the frequent disparity between such religious precepts and actual practice. Unfortunately, sound

A Roman Catholic priest blesses two nuns who are taking their final vows, Huyton, Merseyside, England, 1967 (Hulton-Deutsch Collection/Corbis).

research has not yet been undertaken to explore this issue in depth.

In terms of gender dynamics and power, vows are an area where it is important to maintain a nuanced view. As seen briefly above, a wide variety of vows are undertaken for similarly diverse reasons that satisfy a range of religious and social impulses. While it is undoubtedly true that vows have often been employed to shore up patriarchal social structures, vows have often been empowering to women and have served them as liberating instruments of religious and social endeavor.

Consider, for instance, the issue of the subordination of women within monastic hierarchies. While undoubtedly not a model of egalitarian social planning, the very possibility of a monastic vocation was, historically speaking, a clear advance for women. This can be seen in both the Buddhist and the Christian monastic traditions. The ordination of Buddhist nuns was a revolutionary advance that Indian women long struggled for—liberating them from compulsory service to their male family members. This was also the experience of Christian nuns, for whom the religious life of chastity was the only option to the life of domestic subservience. For these reasons, female monasticism has been viewed with suspicion by many groups interested in the perpetuation of male dominance.

Within the typology of vows, then, one should pay close attention to the dialectics of bondage and liberation, and restriction and freedom, implicit in them. One can then begin to look in a sophisticated way at what the taking and keeping of vows means for women and the societies in which they live.

BIBLIOGRAPHY

Cartledge, Tony W. *Vows in the Hebrew Bible and the Ancient Near East.* 1992.

Doorn-Harder, Pieternella van. *Contemporary Coptic Nuns.* 1995.

Horner, I. B. *Women Under Primitive Buddhism.* 1930. Reprint, 1989.

Shaw, Miranda. *Passionate Enlightenment.* 1994.

CHRISTIAN WEDEMEYER

War

What is war? A traditional, masculinist definition might evoke two or more male contenders for hegemony over a territory who declare their intention to fight because they say they have been deprived of their political, economic, or social rights, and the rules of conduct for that fight. Wars, according to such a definition, involve combatants only, and combatants are necessarily men. This definition has never been absolutely true, as all wars have involved nurses and the nurses have almost always been women. Hidden between the lines of world history books are the countless stories of these women's unacknowledged bravery as they faced enemy fire to save the lives of their wounded.

One nurse who did achieve recognition was Clara Barton (1821–1912), known as the "Angel of the Battlefield" of the U.S. Civil War, who later founded the American Red Cross.

In the twentieth century women became, more than ever before, a part of war. This is so partly because strategic planning involves civilians as combatants as well as official military targets. Women's articulations of their experiences of war challenge the war-versus-peace dichotomy—front versus home front; friend versus foe; victory versus defeat; male combatants versus female noncombatants—and link the experiences of civil wars, guerrilla wars, and twentieth-century total wars, which target the spaces and actors said to be outside the conflict, with violence not usually associated with war. Removing violence from the category of combat reveals that the deliberate and officially sanctioned inflicting of injury is not necessarily in the service of some higher cause such as just war. As weapons of mass destruction proliferate, feminists have been arguing with each other over the role of women in their countries' militaries. Some advocate the opening up of opportunities for women in the military as corollary to their demand for greater participation by women in civilian life. They make the connection between military service, and its assumption of preparedness to die for one's country and one's god, and rights of full citizenship. Other feminists absolutely reject any interaction with the military.

War has often been declared in the name of religion, a god or gods. Some religions seem to be predisposed to warlike behavior; others merely excuse it. The Hindu Bhagavad Gita justifies killing in the pursuit of justice. The Hindu social system includes the *Kṣatriya*, or warrior, caste whose men and women are expected to kill if necessary. They, like the Sumero-Babylonian Akkadians, associate war with a goddess: the Hindus have Kālī, whose ornaments are severed heads and arms, and the Akkadians Ishtar. Even the Buddhists, whose moral ideal is ahimsa (generally translated as nonviolence), have justified war in self-defense. In the early states of the three Abrahamic religions, war was the means for the spread of the new faith. Although evidence is scant, historical fragments indicate that women participated in these wars not only as nurses but also as warriors. The prophet Muhammad is quoted as having commended the bravery of Nusayba, a woman combatant, and his wife Aisha led one faction of Muslims against another in Islam's first civil war (658). In the West the best-known female martyr is Joan of Arc, the fifteenth-century French woman who fought during the Hundred Years War and who was burned at the stake for heresy and witchcraft.

As religions took root in various cultures, wars were explained spiritually. In some cases, jurists and theologians developed the notion of "just war" to indicate that the faithful were doing their god's will as they fought reactively to defend the faith and to defeat its enemies. Those who died while killing in the name of their god(s) were supposed to be especially blessed; they were called martyrs, their salvation assured. In the 1980s in Iran, young men went to the Iraqi front wearing bandannas decorated with the words "God is Great!" and carrying their coffins on their shoulders. However, critics of war in the latter part of the twentieth century, especially feminists, have been arguing that the line between defensive and aggressive action is often hard to situate and that religions have in fact been invoked to initiate violence.

From the fifteenth century on, Christian Europe started to colonize—some say to civilize, and others say to feminize—parts of South America, Asia, and Africa. The vanguard of these colonizing troops were usually men. Later, when the European system was in place, women joined their men. They saw themselves as providing models of piety and development to indigenous women. It was against just such models that many colonized men and women rebelled. In cases like Algeria, colonized by the French between 1830 and 1962, women withdrew from colonial spaces. This withdrawal symbolized their utter otherness, which was expressed as a religious difference. To be Algerian was to be Muslim. By the middle of the twentieth century, African and Asian countries launched wars of independence against their European occupiers, often in the name of the religion the Europeans had originally come to fight. Women guerrilla fighters played important roles in these liberation struggles. To mobilize women in segregated societies into the quintessentially masculine space of war symbolized the total commitment of the people to fight their oppressors. The euphoria of victory did not last long, nor did the recognition of the women who had contributed to the nationalist successes. Though women in decolonizing societies are continuing to participate militarily, they are aware that, as women who have not been expected to participate in war, they may have a special and more effective role by resisting differently. Frantz Fanon, the Martinican psychiatrist and analyst of the racialization of colonial relations, had already praised the Algerian women for their *stratégie-femme;* Palestinian women are continuing the tradition. After Israel seized land back from Jordan in the 1967 war, Muslim and Christian Palestinian women under occupation evolved a stone-throwing and tire-burning strategy that other nationalists like the Irish Protestants emulated. Women's consciousness everywhere has been raised, and many are warning of postbellum disempowerment, particularly in regions where religious extremism is on the rise.

In the late twentieth century, postcoloniality and the failure of modernization and secular nationalism have provoked a global religious response sometimes called fundamentalism. Fundamentalists, or antimodernists, present themselves as warriors for the establishment of a true religious—Christian, Jewish, Muslim, Hindu, or Sikh—state on the ruins of bankrupt Westernized values, foremost among which is the promotion of women's rights. The recent emergence of women in decision-making positions has been linked to the breakdown in what has been called "family values." In Egypt, Sudan, Israel, Iran, and even in the United States some militant extremists call for war on behalf of the religiously sound state, which, they announce, will be structured according to the model of the ideal family where the father goes out to earn income and the mother stays at home to tend the family. In such a system mother and father have different but equal, or complementary, roles. Ironically, these religious zealots, who at home call for moral reform, when they are engaged in fighting may sexually abuse their enemy's women to demoralize and humiliate the men. The contradiction between this kind of behavior and their radically patriarchal views is never acknowledged. Some women are trying to find a visible space for themselves in this system. In 1935, the Egyptian Zaynab al-Ghazali founded a women-only Islamist group and then set herself up as the model pious woman; she demonstrated that she could play both domestic and political roles by engaging herself in jihad (an Arabic term often translated as "holy war" but which means struggle for spiritual improvement at the individual as well as communal levels). Other women are beginning to counter neotraditionalist tendencies by producing feminist interpretations of religious texts that have been used as the basis for such an exclusionary ideology.

War would not be war without its story to confirm the details, such as who won and who lost. Traditionally, the war story was written by official participants. Combat experience was deemed to be so intense and immediate that it defied the imagination. Experience conferred the right to relay to noncombatants the awe and honor of having been prepared to die for a cause or a country. Just as in the twentieth century journalists (increasing numbers of whom are women) are expected to be at the front, so throughout history military leaders recruited male artists and writers to record the battles they were about to wage. Although absent from official records, it is likely that women have always written about wars because, however physically distant they may have been, these wars disturbed their lives. It was not until World War I, however, that women who ventured to describe the experience of war, an experience they were said not to have had, dared to call themselves women war story writers. Their stories refused to follow the abstract justifications and neat structure of the traditional war story tailored to men's experiences. During the Lebanese civil war (1975–1992), women's fiction and journalism mocked the political analyses that emphasized Christian–Muslim discord and declared it casus belli. Bosnian women have echoed this sentiment, writing that, like the Lebanese war, the Bosnian conflict of the 1990s, said to be waged between Muslims, Orthodox Christians, and Catholics, was not about religion but about competing nationalisms. Women in many places have been saying just that throughout history: war is never just, is never for the good of the people, and always about politics and the power of the few.

BIBLIOGRAPHY

Beauvoir, Simone de, and Giselle Halimi. *Djamila Bouphacha: The Story of the Torture of a Young Algerian Girl which Shocked Liberal French Opinion.* 1962.

Cleaver, Tessa, and Marion Wallace. *Namibia Women in War.* 1990.

Cooke, Miriam. *Women and the War Story.* 1996.

Elshtain, Jean Bethke, and Sheila Tobias, eds. *Women, Militarism, and War: Essays in History, Politics, and Social Theory.* 1990.

Ghazali, Zaynab al-. *Ayyām min ḥayātī* (Days from My Life). Cairo, 1966.

Hélie-Lucas, Marie-Aimée. "Women, Nationalism, and Religion in the Algerian Struggle." In *Opening the Gates: A Century of Arab Feminist Writing.* Edited by Margot Badran and Miriam Cooke. 1990.

Peteet, Julie M. *Gender in Crisis: Women and the Palestinian Resistance Movement.* 1991.

Reeves, Minou. *Female Warriors of Allah: Women and the Islamic Revolution.* 1989.

Ruddick, Sara. *Maternal Thinking: Towards a Politics of Peace.* 1989.

Stiehm, Judith, ed. *It's OUR Military, Too! Women and the U.S. Military.* 1996.

Stiglmayer, Alexandra, ed. *Mass Rape: The War against Women in Bosnia-Herzegovina.* 1994.

See also Amazons; Violence; Warriors.

MIRIAM COOKE

Warriors

The existence of ancient women warriors can be reconstructed from mythological settings in the Indo-European epics and from references in the later Greek and Roman historians. Although Hippocrates fostered the interpretation that Amazon meant "without a breast" (Greek *a mazos*), the name seems to be derived from the Indo-European root *magh*, meaning "to be able" or "to have power," or secondarily "to fight." Old Iranian **ha-maz-an*, "the warrior," is possibly loaned into Greek as *Amazon.* Amazons have always been associated with the worship of a goddess, the riding and taming of horses, and skill in the use of the bow and labrys (double axe). During the third or second millennium B.C.E, the chariot-driving dawn goddess, Uṣas, came into India with the bands of Indo-European peoples who called themselves Aryans. Uṣas was celebrated in twenty-one hymns and hundreds of verses of the *Ṛgveda.* She is said to "drive away evil" from the priest-poets and their patrons (*RV* 5.80.5; 7.77.1,4; 7.78.2). However, the independence of the horse-driving Uṣas, her position as an overseer of the moral order, and her fabled wealth attracted the violence of the warrior god, Indra. He attacked Uṣas, smashed her chariot (*RV* 2.15.6; 4.30.8– 11), and used his ultimate weapon (*vajra*, diamond) (10.138.5) to send her fleeing.

The reappearance of the warrior goddess as Kālī in the Sanskrit text *Devīmāhātmya* dates to the fifth or sixth century C.E. The text marks an attempt of the Hindu tradition to balance the spiritual and psychological losses of patriarchy. Like Uṣas, Kālī is a creation of male text composers, but unlike Uṣas, Kālī escaped the confines of the text tradition to enter, or reemerge from, the popular imagination as Kālī-Mā, the saving Mother.

Kālī/Durgā is the fighting face of the Goddess in India. She is found at battlefields and cemeteries. Whereas patriarchal cultures shun death as gruesome and frightful, the inner reality of Kālī is her intense relationship to the cycle of life, death, and rebirth, which is the pervasive theme in Stone Age iconography, both in India and Old Europe. Indo-European text traditions have transmogrified the powerful female energies associated with death into avenging Furies, predatory Harpies, or the skull-wreathed Kālī, but in Norse mythology the Valkyries still retain the gracefulness of the Stone Age bird goddesses as they hover over battlefields to take the souls of dead warriors to Valhalla. Bird imagery was also retained by the elder tantric priestesses (*ḍākinīs*) in India, Nepal, and Tibet, where they were revered as "Skywalkers," and were thought to embody the spirit of Kālī-Mā as the angel of death. Both Valkyries and Skywalkers have fierce warrior capabilities.

Many warrior women of high spiritual energy have chosen death in the face of foreign conquerors. After the Chinese annexed Vietnam in 111 B.C.E., the first major revolt (39 C.E.) was led by two sisters, Trung Trac and Trung Nhi. The Vietnamese had resisted Chinese religious and ethical practices and had increased their own solidarity through continued worship of the spirits found in natural forces. When Trung Trac's husband was killed by the Chinese, she and her sister were able to turn the resistance of their people into a rout of the Chinese. The sisters ruled as joint queens of Vietnam for three years, until the Chinese sent a powerful army to defeat them. They threw themselves into the river rather than be captured. Two hundred years later, Trieu An led another uprising. She wore golden armor and rode an elephant into battle at the head of 1,000 men. Within a year (249 C.E.) she was defeated but chose "not to resign myself to the lot of women who bow their heads as concubines" (Bergman, 1974, pp. 31). Like the Trungs, she threw herself into a river and drowned.

Boudicca, queen of the Iceni in Britain, consciously became the Celtic warrior goddess while she harangued her soldiers on the values of independence and freedom from slavery under the Romans. But when her army, 80,000 strong, was finally defeated in 61 C.E., according to Tacitus she took poison. The Romans had scourged Boudicca, and raped her daughters before the revolt began. Like the Vietnamese, the Celtic Iceni developed their resistance to the conqueror on the path of the old religion. The Celts, Indo-Europeans who had been moving across Europe over several millennia, worshiped the Goddess and recognized women as warriors. Medb was another Celtic warrior queen, whose tale is told in the Irish epic *Táin Bó Cuailnge*. Because of deception involving the stealing of a prize bull, she had to face the hero Cú Chulainn. The sister warriors, Scáthech and Aife of Scotland, had trained him in superhuman feats that were possible only through asceticism and deep concentration. Although the text centers on the hero, the translator, Thomas Kinsella (1983), comments on the women of the epic: "It may be as goddess-figures, ultimately, that these women have their power; it is certainly they, under all the violence, who remain most real in the memory" (Intro. xv).

The same interplay of visionary power and strong warrior involvement is glimpsed briefly in the Book of Judges 4:1–24 and 5:1–31. Deborah is a warrior who is also a "judge" and a "prophetess." She is called a "mother in Israel" and has the power to summon armies. She possesses the mystical skills of inspired speech and action, which presuppose spiritual discipline. Jael is mentioned in the same set of verses known as Deborah's Song. Jael's murder of Sisera, like Judith's beheading of Holofernes, helped her people escape tyranny. Of all women warriors, Joan of Arc is most famous for being rooted in spiritual understanding.

Not all women warriors have had to choose death. Harriet Tubman returned to Maryland eighteen times after her own escape from slavery to rescue another

BOADICEA, QUEEN *of the* ICENI, *Animating the* BRITONS *to Recover their* LIBERTY.

An eighteenth-century engraving depicts Queen Boudicca of the Iceni addressing her army of Britons before a battle against the forces of Rome (Michael Nicholson/Corbis).

three hundred slaves. She carried a gun, and threatened to kill anyone who tried to turn back. She never lost a slave, nor was she ever caught. Lozen, an Apache medicine woman and warrior, fought against invaders of the sacred Apache lands in the nineteenth century. During times of peace, she worked as a healer. As a rule, Apache women were not expected to fight, but rather to pray during battles to keep evil away from the men.

The twentieth century has seen its share of fighting women. In Russia during both world wars, women often escaped abusive family situations to fight fiercely for the homeland. The Jhansi ki Rani women's regiment of the Indian National Army fought against the British in World War II. The name of the regiment was a tribute to Lakṣmi Bai, the Rani of Jhansi, who in 1858 lost her life battling the British at Gwalior, after the sack of Jhansi. In Israel, women's military and training service were part of the attempt to secure a homeland, as well as a particular response to the Holocaust. In Central America, women of Guatemala, El Salvador, and Nicaragua fought against oppressive regimes and formed guerrilla groups to protect their families and their people. Some of these groups took shape in the gospel reflection work of liberation theology. In Guatemala, Rigoberta Menchú and her family marshaled their traditional Indian beliefs about the earth and freedom into a fierce resistance.

BIBLIOGRAPHY

A Dream Compels Us: Voices of Salvadoran Women. Edited by New Americas Press. 1989.

Barstow, Anne Llewellyn. *Joan of Arc: Heretic, Mystic, Shaman.* 1985. Allows an outstanding woman warrior to appear in the light of her considerable spiritual development.

Bergman, Arlene Eisen. *Women of Viet Nam.* 1974.

Daly, Mary. *Beyond God the Father.* 1973.

du Bois, Page. *Centaurs and Amazons: Women and the Pre-History of the Great Chain of Being.* 1982.

Eliade, Mircea. *Rites and Symbols of Initiation.* 1958. Chapter 5, "Heroic and Shamanic Initiations," is a primary text for understanding the spiritual genesis of a warrior.

Fraser, Antonia. *Boadicea's Chariot: The Warrior Queens.* 1988.

Kinsella, Thomas, trans. *The Tain.* 1983.

Lebra, Joyce. *The Rānī of Jhansi.* 1986.

Lerner, Gerda. *The Creation of Patriarchy.* 1986. Focus on Mesopotamia.

Markale, Jean. *Women of the Celts.* 1986.

Menchú, Rigoberta. *I, Rigoberta Menchú: An Indian Woman in Guatemala.* 1984.

Newark, Tim. *Women Warlords: An Illustrated Military History of Female Warriors.* 1989. Famous female warriors; sound scholarship; sensitivity to issues.

Plaskow, Judith. "Jewish Memory from a Feminist Perspective." In *Weaving the Visions: New Patterns in Feminist Spirituality.* Edited by Judith Plaskow and Carol P. Christ. 1989. Proposes a feminist midrashic reading of the "normative" texts, which have always "reflected the views of the historical winners."

Randall, Margaret. *Sandino's Daughters.* 1981.

Salmonson, Jessica Amanda. *The Encyclopedia of Amazons: Women Warriors from Antiquity to the Modern Era.* 1991. An attempt to list every woman who has gained notice for fighting. Includes warrior goddesses "to indicate the religious underpinnings that spawned actual and mythic Amazons."

Sheldon, Walter J. *Tigers in the Rice: The Story of Vietnam from Ancient Past to Uncertain Future.* 1969.

Smith, Mary Carroll. "Dawn and Darkness: The Faces of the Goddess in India." In *Mother Goddesses and Other Goddesses in the Indic Religious Tradition.* Forthcoming. The juxtaposition of Uṣas and Kālī allows a new psychological and spiritual analysis of the goddess in India.

———. *The Warrior's Code of India's Sacred Song.* 1992. Spiritual realities of Indic warriorhood that are lost in the Greek and Roman epic traditions.

Stockel, H. Henrietta. *Women of the Apache Nation: Voices of Truth.* 1991.

Truby, J. David. *Women at War: A Deadly Species.* 1977. Vitriolic; portrays fighting women as evil.

Wheelwright, Julie. *Amazons and Military Maids: Women Who Dressed as Men in the Pursuit of Life, Liberty and Happiness.* 1989. Sprightly narrative; political analysis of military cross-dressing.

See also **Amazons**; **Furies**; **Joan of Arc**; **Liberation Theologies**; **Menchú, Rigoberta**.

MARY CARROLL SMITH

Weather

The religions of the world are rich in meteorological divinities, and religious experts, be they priestesses or shamans, are expected to exercise control over the weather by propitiating these deities, mastering the elements through their spiritual powers, or at least being able to foretell the weather or use the weather to foretell the future. Such beliefs are grounded in a worldview in which human beings, nature, and the divine all interact, for good or ill. Animals are given both human and divine characteristics, while humans assume the characteristics of certain animals in order to participate in their powers, especially powers of fertility for the land, people, and animals. For instance, in many cultures bulls were linked with thunder (because of the noise they make when running) as well as with rain, which in turn was connected to sexual prowess, since rain is linked with semen. Somewhat like bulls, who are perceived as great but hard-to-control sources of power, divinities who control the weather are believed to be sources of both fertility (the right amount of rain at the right time) and destruction (through flooding or drought), and many male divinities are identified with bulls (Indra, Siva, Zeus, Baal). Weather is a vivid, all-encompassing, and often spontaneous manifestation of these ideas. Humans attempt to enter into the powers of controlling divinities—whose meteorological powers frequently also manifest in purely mythical animals such as dragons (particularly in East Asia) and thunder-birds (among Native Americans)—through understanding, propitiating, or threatening them. In this intensely charged and symbolically rich worldview, humans achieve a sense of being part of a larger whole; they transcend their mundane concerns and attempt to arbitrate their fates.

Annual celebrations of a sacred marriage between a goddess and god at the New Year, when the crops are sown, go back to ancient Mesopotamia and Egypt, and possibly even earlier people. These ceremonies were often accompanied by a ritual enactment of the divine marriage to assure the fertility of the fields; the ritual aimed at making rain plentiful but not excessive in the coming year, the sun equally moderate, and storms mild. Seasonal rituals are attempts to harness cosmic energies in order to get what is needed from them without being overwhelmed by them. The sacred marriage of the goddess and god was sometimes enacted by their human devotees through a general orgy that took place in the freshly planted fields. Human sexual activity was believed to stimulate the divine marriage so that the earth (female) is productively related to the sky (male) in the form of rain (semen). Such rituals were performed in Europe into the twentieth century in ancient Greece and Rome, and among innumerable tribal people.

Similar ideas are found among the Australian aborigines, who believe their ceremonies cause clouds to release rain. Male rainmakers are bled and their blood sprinkled over the rest of the men of the tribe. Significantly, it is male, not female, blood that is used, and male participants must avoid contact with their wives until the rains come. Similar beliefs existed among the Javanese and ancient Babylonians. The association of rain with maleness continues, for instance, among the Australian aborigines, who attribute rain-giving powers to the foreskins that are removed during circumcision and preserved, carefully out of the sight of women, in the event of drought. Given rain's association with semen, male chastity is recommended as a way of avoiding unwanted rain; women play a role in the bringing of rain by stimulating male desire by appearing nude before or singing ribald songs to male rain gods (ancient Europe, India, and Africa). Occasionally, young women were sacrificed (Rhodesia, Mozambique). In parts of Europe, when rain was desired, water was sprinkled over people of both sexes dressed in leaves (representing the crops that depend on rain).

The rainbow is an almost universal sign of a bridge linking this world and the divine world. Shamans from all parts of the world are believed to climb up to heaven on it to commune with the deities and to change the weather (Polynesia, Australia, Japan, Native American, Buryat). The rainbow represents the calm after the storm that indicates the gods are once again at peace with humankind. In the Hebrew Bible, Yahweh created the rainbow to be a reminder of his covenant with Noah and the rest of humankind that never again would there be total destruction through flood (Gen. 9:13–17). Among the ancient Greeks the rainbow is the goddess Iris, a messenger of the gods. In China it is a dragon, a symbol of the ubiquitous rain goddesses, especially Yao Chi; and rainbows are associated with the feminine, with yin. The ancient Chinese saw dragons-rainbows-women-rain-fertility-moon-death on the same continuum. Their water goddesses were great seductresses, much like the Lorelei of German Legend, and the subject of many erotic tales. In ancient times the rain goddesses were ritually married to the king in order to have their fertility channeled. In Tibet rainbows are always perceived to be an auspicious sign, and they are particularly associated with *ḍākinīs*, divine women who confer spiritual power and act as guides to enlightenment.

The ancient Hebrews believed Yahweh spoke and acted through thunder and lightning, and Psalms 147 and 148 praise his timely sending of rain, snow, hail, frost, wind, and sun. Jesus was also believed to have these abilities, as when he calmed the winds and a stormy sea (Matt. 8:23–27, Mark 4:35–41, Luke 8:22–25). Christian saints also share in this divine power, such as St. Genovefa (423–502), whose prayers, when rain threatened as she and her neighbors were harvesting their crops, succeeded in keeping her part of the field dry. Saints Radegund (525–587) and Gertrude of Nivelles (628–658) calmed stormy seas, as did the Virgin Mary, who became the protector of sailors. Muslim saints also participate in controlling the weather and other natural forces, such as Habib al-Ajami (c. ninth to tenth centuries), who calmed winds and walked on water. In general, Muslim saints are believed to be so close to Allah that they have access to his mercy and are therefore able to make the rains fall. Villagers in Turkey and Iran evoke this belief in their word for rain, *raḥmat*, mercy. The obverse of these examples are witches who are believed to raise storms so as to spread sickness and destruction.

BIBLIOGRAPHY

Chemery, Peter C. "Meteorological Beings." In *The Encyclopedia of Religion*. Edited by Mircea Eliade. 1987.

Dumézil, Georges. *Gods of the Ancient Northmen*. 1959. Reprint, 1977.

Elaide, Mircea. *Patterns in Comparative Religion.* 1958. Reprint, 1974.

———. *Shamanism: Archaic Techniques of Ecstasy.* 1951. Reprint, 1972.

Frankfort, Henri, et al. *Before Philosophy: The Intellectual Adventure of Ancient Man.* 1946. Reprint, 1949.

Frazier, Sir James. *The Golden Bough.* 1922. Reprint, 1963.

Gaster, Theodor H. *Thespis: Ritual, Myth, and Drama in the Ancient Near East.* 1950. Reprint, 1977.

James, E. O. *The Worship of the Sky God.* 1963.

Leach, Maria, ed. *Funk and Wagnalls Standard Dictionary of Folklore, Mythology, and Legend.* 1972.

Schafer, Edward H. *The Divine Woman: Dragon Ladies and Rain Maidens.* 1973. Reprint, 1980.

SERINITY YOUNG

Weaving

Weaving is the construction of cloth by interlacing horizontal weft threads at right angles with vertical warp threads. Generally, weaving is a women's domain, although in some cultures only men or both men and women weave. Weaving is seen universally as a metaphor for life—a length of time crossed with experience. Requiring the mathematical organization of loose threads, weaving also provides a paradigm for bringing order out of chaos. Religious language and mythology are rich in references to weaving and the auxiliary craft of spinning. For example, the Hindu and Buddhist terms *sutra* and *tantra,* respectively mean "thread" and "loom" in Sanskrit. Many mythologies include the image of a woven net as an archetypal construct. In an old Chinese myth, for example, a Spinning Maiden wove the net of the constellations. Pre-Columbian Andeans regarded weaving as the structural equivalent of the created world.

In *Patterns in Comparative Religion* (1972), Mircea Eliade combines elements from many myths in a reference to the moon, envisioned as an enormous spider, as the weaver of destinies: "To weave is not merely to predestine, and to join together different realities, but also to create, to make something of one's own substance as the spider does in spinning the web" (p. 181).

Marija Gimbutas, in *The Language of the Goddess* (1989), speculates that the notion of Fate as a goddess who weaves or spins the duration and quality of life originated in Neolithic times. The goddess evolved into a triad which, through many transmutations, became the Greek Moirae—Clotho, Lachesis, and Atropos—described as either weavers or spinners who dole out,

A close-up of a traditional Ikat weaving depicting a man in a village on Sumba Island, Indonesia (Wolfgang Kaehler/Corbis)

measure, and cut the days of life. European folklore echoes the Fates in tales (like *Sleeping Beauty*) wherein fairy godmothers or other mentors use implements of weaving and spinning to cast women's destinies.

In some creation myths, weaving is an essential skill bestowed on humankind by a deity. As the ancient Greek patroness of artisans, Athena taught weaving to Pandora, the first woman. (Barbara G. Walker in *A Woman's Encyclopedia of Myths and Secrets* [1983] writes that Athena proceeded from the goddess Neith, who gave weaving to the Egyptians.) As weaver par excellence, Athena created elaborate tapestry cloaks for Hera and herself. Arachne, a mortal, challenged Athena's superiority at the loom, and a contest ensued. Paraphrasing Ovid, Elizabeth Wayland Barber in *Women's Work: The First 20,000 Years* (1994) vividly describes Arachne's woven depiction of Zeus' amorous affairs and deceptions; conversely, Athena wove stories of mortals who were punished after losing contests with the gods.

Athena angrily destroyed Arachne's work and changed her into a spider. Arachne's punishment often is attributed to Athena's jealousy, but it also has been interpreted as Athena's protectiveness toward the reputation of her father, Zeus. Jungian analyst Jean Shinoda Bolen in *Goddesses in Everywoman* (1985) states that the goddess's rage was aroused not as much by Arachne's challenge to Athena's weaving skills as by her audacious use of weaving to expose Zeus.

In the *Odyssey* weaving is portrayed as a domestic occupation that defines women's realms, a female complement to the sailing skills of men. During the absence of her husband, Odysseus, Penelope promised to choose from numerous suitors when she finished weaving a shroud for Laertes, father of Odysseus. By unraveling at night what she wove during the day, she held off the suitors. Meanwhile, Calypso, a nymph residing on the island of Ogygia, wove with a golden shuttle while she kept Odysseus with her for seven years.

For some peoples, including the Navajo, weaving remains a living tradition rooted in myth. Different versions of Navajo mythology agree that Spider Woman, sometimes accompanied by Spider Man, is the source of weaving. Residing in the Second World of a layered cosmology, Spider Woman belongs to a colorful theophany that includes Coyote and Warrior Twins. Spider Woman weaves webs both to trap and to rescue. A ritual chant recorded by Gladys Reichard, a pioneering anthropologist, tells of a web that captured Water Monster's baby, probably during a great primordial Flood. In another ritual chant, Spider Woman helps a hero through a test by stringing webs across a path of flints, allowing him safe passage over them. Among the Hopi, for whom baskets are a primary textile, the creation myths refer to basketry.

High status has been accorded weaving where it has been incorporated into myth and ritual. Textile historian Rebecca Stone-Miller states that textile structure influenced other early Andean art forms, including architectural design. In one version of an Andian creation myth, a husband and wife created weaving as well as the natural environment, architecture, and agriculture. Textile tools discovered in graves of pre-Columbian women in Peru indicate that women participated in this weaving tradition still renowned for technological sophistication. Stone-Miller states that the "killing" of textiles by ritual burning as sacrifices to the sun cemented the integral relationship of Andean textiles to cosmic forces. Athena and Spider Woman also required textiles as offerings.

In some cultures the notion of weaving as a divinely given gift established symmetry between gender-specific roles. In *Splendid Symbols* (1979), Mattiebelle Gittinger cites an Iban myth from Kalimantan, Indonesia,

recorded at the turn of the twentieth century, in which Singalang Burdang, the major god's daughter who had married a mortal, wanted to return to heaven. Before leaving her husband and son, she wove them "jackets of the birds." Wearing his, the son followed her to heaven, where knowledge he gained to take back to earth included how to avenge the dead by taking a head and placing it in a great blanket. This myth names the major Iban textiles. Sharing a mythical source with the male prerogative of headhunting qualified textiles for ceremonial use. Paul Michael Taylor and Lorraine V. Aragon, in *Beyond the Java Sea* (1991) named Kumang as the deity who taught women to weave and who teaches new designs to weavers in their dreams.

Weaving was placed on an equal level with other civilizing technologies in a myth from the Indonesian island of Flores, recorded by anthropologist Michael P. Visher. Therein, the first settlers, wearing only bark cloth, were given knowledge of weaving, fire, and metal from a second group of settlers in exchange for territory.

Sometimes the sacred source of weaving presented women with identity, as well as technical knowledge. For example, among the Maya of Chiapas, Mexico, each town's costume identifies the people as descendants of patron saints who taught them to weave. Walter F. Morris, Jr., in *Living Maya* (1987), charts a mythology, reconstructed from contemporary woven patterns, in which Christian saints are allies of the ancient ancestors. One myth tells of Mary Magdalene, founder of the community of Magdalenas, climbing into a cedar tree, setting up her loom, and starting to weave a *huipile* in the brocade patterns still worn by women of the town.

Dyeing may be incorporated into myth and ritual where it is integral to a weaving tradition.

BIBLIOGRAPHY

For in-depth discussion of weaving and related rituals in ancient Greece, see Sue Blundell's *Women in Ancient Greece* (1995). The chapter "Behind the Myths," in Elizabeth Wayland Barber's work cited above, offers a fresh and original interpretation of the relationship of Greek goddesses to textiles. For detailed research on the religious significance of textile production in Southeast Asia, see *Gift of the Cotton Maiden: Textiles of Flores and the Solor Islands*, edited by Roy W. Hamilton (1994) and *Textiles and the Tai Experience in Southeast Asia* by Mattiebelle Gittinger and Leedom H. Lefferts, Jr. (1992). Gladys A. Reichard's extensive documentation of Navajo myths is compiled in *Navajo Religion: A Study of Symbolism* (1970), while contemporary Navajo knowledge of myths is recorded in *Weaving a World: Textiles and the Navajo Way of Seeing*, by Roseann S. Willink and Paul G. Zolbrod (1996). A broad survey of textiles of the Americas, including their religious aspects, is found in *Textile Traditions of Mesoamerica and the Andes*, edited by Margo Blum Schevill, Janet Catherine Berlo, and Edward B. Dwyer (1991; repr. 1996), while the essays in *To Weave for the Sun* (1992), edited by Rebecca Stone-Miller, draw on recent and authoritative research on Andean textiles. Most of the essays in *Cloth and Human Experience*, edited by Annette B. Weiner and Jane Schneider (1989), have a sociopolitical rather than a religious thrust but include Patricia Darish's "Dressing for the Next Life" on the ritual function of textiles among the Kuba of Africa.

PATRICIA MALARCHER

Weber, Max

A highly influential social scientist, Max Weber (1864–1920) was a founder of the historical sociology of religion. After a brief career as professor of commercial law (Berlin) and political economy (Freiburg, Heidelberg), and as an active member of the Protestant social reform movement *(Evangelisch-sozialer Kongress)*, a psychosomatic breakdown after 1898 freed Weber for a life of private scholarship unrestrained by disciplinary boundaries. He made basic contributions to the methodology of the social sciences from a neo-Kantian position and to the sociologies of law, domination, and culture (including music), but all his major writings remained unfinished.

Weber's theory of modern society is centered on a juxtaposition of autonomous value and institutional spheres, in which religion no longer provides an over-arching integration. He interpreted the world religions as long-range processes of intellectualization and rationalization. The "rise of the West" is explained in terms of an accidental constellation of factors, in which Protestant inner-worldly asceticism inadvertently contributed to the rationalized and secularized structure of the modern world. Reformed (Calvinist) Protestantism is seen as the religious culmination point of a long "dis-enchantment of the world" through the substitution of magic by ethics.

Weber's major contributions to the history of religious developments—in opposition to older evolutionism and ahistorical theories of religion—are found in *The Protestant Ethic and the Spirit of Capitalism* (1905; rev. 1920), which he called "an essay on cultural history,"; *The Economic Ethics of the World Religions* (1915–1921), of which only three volumes were finished: "Confucianism and Taoism," "Hinduism and Buddhism," and "Ancient Judaism"; and the chapters on religion and hierocracy in *Economy and Society* (1921f.). Weber's famous speech "Science as a Voca-

tion" (1917–1919) explores the radical difference between modern science and the religious search for transcendent meaning.

Women appear in Weber's writings in his treatment of early forms of the gender division of labor and his critique of the "mother-right" theories of Johann Jakob Bachofen, Lewis Morgan, and Friedrich Engels. Matriarchy is interpreted as evidence of the military segregation of males from the household, with no real transfer of power. Weber believed that the Protestant sects encouraged some equality for women (through the priesthood of all believers). He supported the feminist career of his wife, Marianne Weber (1870–1954), president of the Union of German Women Associations, and guided her in the composition of her influential book *Wife and Mother in Legal Development* (1907; repr. 1971), a historical survey from the earliest stages to the latest demands of the women's movement.

BIBLIOGRAPHY

The complete edition of Weber's work is *Max Weber Gesamtausgabe*, 1984–, 22 vols., and 10 volumes of correspondence. See especially Part 1, vol. 17, *Wissenschaft als Beruf* (1992); Part 1, vol. 19, *Konfuzianismus und Taoismus* (1989); Part 1, vol. 20, *Hinduismus und Buddhismus* (1996).

The most up-to-date treatment of Weber's analysis of the world religions is Wolfgang Schluchter, *Rationalism, Religion, and Domination: A Weberian Perspective* (1989), and his *Paradoxes of Modernity. Culture and Conduct in the Theory of Max Weber* (1996).

On the perennially controversial theory of the religious origins of modernity, see Hartmut Lehmann and Guenther Roth, eds., *Weber's Protestant Ethic: Origins, Evidence, Contexts* (1993).

For a critical feminist treatment see Roslyn W. Bologh, *Love or Greatness: Max Weber and Masculine Thinking, A Feminist Inquiry* (1990), and Rosalind Ann Sydie, *Natural Women, Cultured Men: A Feminist Perspective on Sociological Theory* (1987).

GUENTHER ROTH

Weil, Simone

Simone Adolphine Weil (1909–1943) was a French social critic, political activist, and religious thinker. Although Weil was the child of Jewish parents, her family was nonobservant and she considered herself an heir to French Catholic culture. Her religious writings present a mystical Christian faith marked by an extreme sensitivity to human suffering and an unrelenting analysis of its meaning.

On their surface, the events of Weil's brief life seem a series of misadventures punctuated by failure. Though sickly, Weil was a brilliant student. After university, she taught philosophy at girls' high schools at various locations in France during the 1930s, but was several times dismissed from these posts because of her unorthodox teaching methods or her leftist political activity. Her early enthusiasm for the workers' rights movement led her from 1934 to 1935 to take a series of factory jobs, each of which she left, physically exhausted, after a few months. Her participation as a volunteer for the Republican forces during the Spanish Civil War in 1936 was cut short by a cooking accident that scalded her severely. These experiences, however, provided the background for her intensely felt meditations on the purpose of education, the nature of power, the spiritually deforming effects of war on all combatants, the insufficiency of materialist ideology to explain or alleviate the woes of the oppressed, and the threat to the individual posed by the collectivization and mechanization of modern society.

After 1938—when, at Eastertime, she had a mystical experience of the presence of Jesus Christ—her writing took a decidedly religious turn. Despite her conversion, however, Weil resisted baptism, a refusal she maintained to the end of her life. Rejecting the church's cultural parochialism and as distrustful of religious organizations, as she had come to be of any other human collectivity, she insisted that her vocation lay "at the intersection of Christianity and everything that is not Christianity" (Panichas, 1977, 21). Weil's obsessive focus on the crucified Christ's abandonment by God is coincident with her distaste for the "consolations" of religion and with her paradoxical assertions to the effect that creaturely existence most perfectly expresses divine love exactly when it is most unbearably painful.

A victim of the displacements suffered by French Jews after the outbreak of World War II, Weil eventually ended up in London, intent on working for the Free French government-in-exile there. Her writings from this, the final period of her life, express the ethical dilemma endured by someone deeply suspicious of the rhetoric of patriotism—and, in fact, of the liberative potential of any collective political action—yet urgently compelled by circumstance to join with others to fight the indisputable evils of fascism.

As a gesture of solidarity with the people of occupied France, Weil began refusing food in early 1943; her self-starvation, complicated by tuberculosis, led to her death in the summer of that year. Weil's status as a twentieth-century "saint"—the result of her passionate involvement in the events of her time and of her self-styled martyrdom—probably overshadows the influence of her written work, whose theoretical

sophistication, unrelieved attention to the ethically and metaphysically revelatory power of affliction (*malheur*), and profound political pessimism render it difficult in all senses of the word.

BIBLIOGRAPHY

Weil's only full-length work, *L'Enracinement*, a historical and philosophical exploration of the problems of national reconstruction that would face postwar France, dates from her last months. It was first published in France in 1949 (Eng. ed., *The Need for Roots: Prelude to a Declaration of Duties toward Mankind*, translated by Arthur Wills with a preface by T. S. Eliot, 1953). Numerous collections of her essays (mostly unpublished during her lifetime) as well as of her aphorisms, letters, poems, and notebook entries have appeared in English; the most comprehensive of these anthologies is George Panichas, ed., *The Simone Weil Reader* (1977), which contains Weil's best-known essays, including "Sketch of Contemporary Life," "Reflections on the Right Use of School Studies with a View to the Love of God," "The *Iliad*, Poem of Might," and "The Love of God and Affliction." There are several full-length biographical studies, including Simone Petrement's *Simone Weil: A Life* (Eng. trans. by Raymond Rosenthal, 1976). Janet Patricia Little's *Simone Weil: A Bibliography* (1973) and a supplement published in 1979 are helpful research tools. A brief though insightful examination of the theme of suffering in Weil's work can be found in Dorothee Soelle's *Suffering* (1975), chap. 6, "The Religion of Slaves."

JAMES C. WALLER

Wicca

The word *wicca*, familiar today as an appellation for the practice of certain groups that worship the Goddess, is used with several meanings. Its etymology has been traced to the Middle English *wicche* (witch), from Old English *wicce* (f.) or *wicca* (m.), meaning a practitioner of magic. These terms are based on an Indo-European root *wic*, meaning to bend, twist, shape, or turn; and some say they are related to the Anglo-Saxon *witan*, to see or know and, by extension, to be wise. Although there appears to be less historical basis for the latter connection, the meanings of both bending and wisdom are used to support aspects of the Wiccan religion.

Among groups who use the word *wicca*, neopagan groups such as Gerald Gardner's British witchcraft movement worship the Goddess and sometimes the horned god as well. They use the Anglo-Saxon *wicca* to indicate that they have revived the ancient northern

European nature religion. These groups are not necessarily feminist.

In the United States all feminist spirituality groups give a female name to the divine, respect nature, and create a space where women's experience is honored. Wiccan groups or covens can be distinguished from the other feminist spirituality groups by their belief in the power of magic and their use of magic through the channeling of energy. They may use the word *wicca* interchangeably with *witchcraft.*

One finds extracted meanings for the word *wicca.* For example, from "bend"—to have a flexible, nonauthoritarian religion (Margot Adler); from "twist"—to weave, "weaving a context in which women can Realize our Self-transforming participation in Be-ing" (Mary Daly); from "witan"—to be a wise woman (Naomi Goldenberg); from "turn"—"When evil comes upon you, turn it around, make it work for you" (Z. Budapest); and from "shape"—"to shape the unseen to our will" (Starhawk).

Although the word is in constant use, it has not been much written about nor has it been clearly defined. Its meanings are in flux, as befits this religion of bending and changing.

BIBLIOGRAPHY

Adler, Margot. *Drawing Down the Moon.* 1986. Rev. ed., 1997.

Budapest, Z. *The Grandmother of Time: A Woman's Book of Celebrations, Spells, and Sacred Objects for Every Month of the Year.* 1989.

Daly, Mary. *Gyn/Ecology.* 1981.

"The Goddess Remembered" (1990) and "Full Circle" (1993). Directed by Donna Read. National Film Board of Canada. Distributed by Direct Cinema Ltd., Santa Monica, CA.

Goldenberg, Naomi. *Changing of the Gods: Feminism and the End of Traditional Religions.* 1979.

Starhawk. *The Spiral Dance: A Rebirth of the Ancient Religion of the Great Goddess.* 1979. Rev. ed., 1989.

See also **Goddess**; **Witchcraft**.

ANNE LLEWELLYN BARSTOW

Widows

The English word *widow* is related to a Latin root meaning "to place apart." This etymological meaning bespeaks the place of widows in religions all over the world, since widows are often treated as distinct from married women. Two aspects of widowhood are especially responsible for this special treatment: socio-economic position and sexual ambivalence. Widows were—and are—often left in destitute circumstances. In Islamic and Jewish tradition God pitied them in their poverty, and thus widows' prayers were thought to be especially effective. The Hebrew Bible says that God will surely hear the "cry" of the widow or the orphan (Exod. 22:22–23). The same tradition is still in evidence in the New Testament, where it is said of the "real widow" that "she continues in supplications and prayers night and day" (1 Tim. 5:5). In fact, widows were so important in the early Christian church that there existed a separate order of widows (*ordo viduarum*). Widows over sixty who had married only once acted as official advisers to other women and, as a sign of their dignity, were allowed to sit in the front of the church, next to the bishop and other church dignitaries. When the Christian faith became the official religion of the Roman Empire, the male clergy soon abolished this order, which is not heard of after 400 C.E.

In various religious traditions widows are not allowed to inherit their husband's property or choose a new husband by themselves; rather, they are forced to marry their deceased husband's brother, who will thus also appropriate the inheritance. This institution, the so-called levirate (from Latin *levir*, husband's brother), has given us the fascinating scenes in the Hebrew Bible of Tamar seducing her father-in-law in order to force him to give her his son as second husband (Gen. 38), and Ruth seducing her relative Boaz in order to remind him of his duty (Ruth 2–3). The levirate was also prevalent in pre-Islamic traditions, but Muhammed denounced its enforcement: "Believers, it is unlawful for you to inherit the women of your deceased kinsmen against their will, or bar them from re-marrying" (sura 4:19). In ongoing practice, however, the words of the Prophet

A Danis widow shows her severed fingers. The custom is for one finger to be cut off for each family bereavement, Baliem Valley, Irian Jaya, Indonesia, 1992 (Charles & Josette Lenars/Corbis).

are not always followed, and in some Muslim countries (e.g., Morocco) women marry their late husband's brother. In Hindu society the levirate (*niyoga*) is typical for lower castes, especially with a young widow, whereas in the highest castes widows remain unmarried or practice sati (discussed below).

THE DESEXUALIZATION OF WIDOWS

Having had sexual experience, widows often become a source of cultural anxiety. Various religious traditions therefore stress the chastity of widows and hold them up as role models, as were Judith, the heroine of the eponymous book of the Hebrew Bible, and Fāṭimah, Muhammad's only daughter, who in popular Shiite imagery is totally devoid of sexuality. Another approach is the attempt to desexualize the appearance of widows, such as by shaving their heads, as in various brahmin castes, or by making them wear unattractive clothes, as happened in earlier Christian mourning customs.

One of the most drastic kinds of desexualization of widows is the withdrawal from the world altogether. In addition to monkhood, Buddhism and Christianity also have female orders. Unfortunately, the recruitment of widows as nuns in these orders is still a very much underresearched aspect of widows' lives. Some early Christian wealthy widows withdrew to their houses in the country and gathered a kind of monastic community around them, as we know from the correspondence of the Church Father Jerome (c. 400 C.E.). In the Middle Ages in Europe, the large estates and commercial activities of many monasteries provided poor widows with the kind of safe haven the outside world could or would not give them. On the other hand, many an aristocratic or royal widow ended her life as abbess of a nunnery, such as the Anglo-Saxon Cynethruth, the widow of King Offa of Mercia, who became the abbess of Cookham. In fact, the shapeless habit of many widows had already likened them, to a certain extent, to nuns.

The most intriguing and, to an outsider, most abhorrent ritual concerning widows is undoubtedly sati, the Hindu rite of a widow burning herself on the funeral pyre of her deceased husband. The term, used nowadays both for the practice and for the wife who commits it, means "a truly virtuous wife": it is believed that by following her husband on the funeral pyre the wife achieves his well-being in the hereafter. In Hindu tradition widow-burning was uncommon, and it was controversial among broad strata of the population. Over time it was acknowledged by brahminical authorities and sanctioned when specific legal rules were met. The authorities determined that the immolation had beneficial religious effects only when it was performed volun-

tarily by an adult wife who had not used intoxicating drugs, who was not pregnant, and who did not have small children to care for. The wife concerned was regarded not as a widow but as a bride who followed her husband on the pyre to the hereafter. This belief was expressed in the ritual by dressing the wife in her bridal costume with all her ornaments. Although under British rule the ritual was prohibited, sati still takes place in modern India, even if sporadically.

BIBLIOGRAPHY

Blom, Ida. "The History of Widowhood: A Bibliographic Overview." *Journal of Family History* 16 (1991): 191–210.

Bremmer, Jan N., and L. P. van den Bosch. *Between Poverty and the Pyre: Moments in the History of Widowhood.* 1995. In addition to a comprehensive bibliography, this volume contains several studies relevant to the religious life of widows, among them those on widows in the Hebrew Bible and ancient Near East, in early Christianity, in Islam, and in Hinduism, all with extensive literature.

Hawley, Juliah S., ed. *Sati, the Blessing and the Curse: The Burning of Wives in India.* 1994.

Mirror, L. *Upon My Husband's Death: Widows in the Literature and Histories of Medieval Europe.* 1992.

Willis, Janice D. "Tibetan Ani-s. The Nun's Life in Tibet." *The Tibet Journal* 9 (1984): 14–32.

See also **Marriage and Singleness; Monasticism.**

JAN N. BREMMER
LOURENS P. VAN DEN BOSCH

Wisdom

An Overview

Wisdom, the personification of human or divine knowledge, appears in many world religions as a goddess. This is a curious feature of patriarchal religions, which usually hold up the male as the possessor of reason and the proper subject of salvific disciplines while simultaneously excluding women from full education and denigrating their specialized knowledge as old wives' tales. Although some scholars have tried to posit a submerged "matriarchal" history of great goddesses whose power and wisdom were coopted by later patriarchal systems, there is controversy as to whether such a golden era ever existed. Further, the appearances of goddesses in a culture do not necessarily correlate with positive, egalitarian social positions for women. The term *wisdom* may occur in the feminine gender in certain languages (e.g., Sanskrit, Hebrew, Greek), but one should be wary of relating this feature to some sort of ontological female essence that all women exemplify. Nevertheless, the preponderance of wisdom goddesses throughout wide-ranging religious systems raises critical questions about the source and meaning of such traditions.

MESOPOTAMIAN GODDESSES

From the earliest Sumerian period through the neo-Babylonian period two millennia later, the goddess Inanna-Ishtar figures heavily in cult and text. A fertility goddess also associated with the morning star and the arts of war, Inanna-Ishtar becomes mistress of "right counsel" by winning a drinking contest with Enki, god of wisdom, and moving the *mē*, the ordinances and arts of civilization, from his city to her own. Human kings became her consorts in order to secure rulership over their city-states or empires, thereby acquiring wisdom and the means to govern. The goddess Nisaba was the patron deity of the scribal guilds; she appeared to King Gudea in a dream (Gudea Cylinder A), holding a stylus and clay tablet with which she shows him how to build his proposed temple. The goddess Gula, often imaged as a hound, also appears with strong ties to the magico-ritual wisdom tradition in her aspect of goddess of healing. In her hymn of self-praise, she says she carries life-giving incantations, texts, and herbs, makes decisions, gives commands, enriches the poor, and gives life to her followers (Foster, 1995).

It seems likely that such portraits may stem from women's roles as health-care providers, agriculturalists, teachers of very young children, and household managers in charge of food and clothing production. As such, women were crucial to the survival of any household and are often portrayed as counselors to husbands or clients (like Siduri of *The Gilgamesh Epic*), and their trickery is able to thwart the will of the gods (witness Eve's theft of wisdom from the Tree of Life in Eden).

ANCIENT EGYPT AND THE BIBLE

In Egypt the goddess Ma'at (order, justice, wisdom) functioned in ways similar to Nisaba. She was viewed as both the first creation of the creator Ptah or Amon-Ra, and as the world-plan he used. In the *Book of the Dead*, the lives of the newly dead are judged in the Hall of Double Ma'at; there the deceased recites the Negative Confession (Chapter 125) while her or his heart is weighted on a scale counterbalanced by an ostrich feather, the symbol of Ma'at. Although no extant mythological narratives are associated with this goddess, her name and symbols appear on seals worn by professional scribes and her name is incorporated by Queen Hatshepsut as an element in her throne name: Ma'at-ka'-Re' (Wisdom-is-the-Image-of-God). Attributes of goddesses Isis and Hathor were also important in shaping the notion of female wisdom in Egypt.

In biblical wisdom materials, most of which were edited if not composed during the postexilic period (sixth–third centuries B.C.E.), the term *wisdom* is grammatically feminine; a female personification of wisdom (Hokmah) is given center stage and a considerable amount of dialogue in Proverbs 1–9. These poems rely heavily on Egyptian influence, but give a specific Israelite twist: fear of the Lord is the beginning and end of wisdom, and this scribal goddess is wholly assimilated to Israelite patriarchal theology. She is mother, prophet, beloved wife or partner, a tree of life, the first creation of God, and the source of all human authority. The iconography of Isis, Hathor, Ma'at, and the fertility and scribal goddesses of Mesopotamia has clearly had impact on the shaping of this portrait. Hokmah's followers find wealth and a path to salvation, understood as a prosperous and long life. In apocryphal texts by later Jewish writers, she is identified both with Torah and Greek philosophy. This survival of a "Hebrew" goddess, if you will, finds her way into gnostic speculations as Sophia, who mediates between the hidden and material worlds and conveys salvation on those who know her. The New Testament speaks of Hokmah (Greek, Sophia) as one who sent Jesus of Nazareth and other prophets, and Jesus as the Christ is later identified outright as "the Sophia of God" (1 Cor. 1:24). This may be due to gnostic philosophical speculation as well as the Jewish tradition of the redemptive work of Hokmah in delivering the people from Egypt and giving the Torah (the Teaching). In Byzantine Christianity, Hagia Sophia (Saint Wisdom) was a focus of great devotion and may have assimilated features of the great goddess cults of the region. Hokmah is also an emanation of the hidden eternal Source in the Tree of Life on the Jewish Kabbalistic traditions of medieval mystics.

CLASSICAL MYTHOLOGY

Greco-Roman mythology contains goddesses of wisdom who bestow their benefits on heroes, kings, and communities. Metis, (Prudent Counsel), a Titan goddess, was pivotal in helping Zeus overthrow the cannibal god Kronos, but was later swallowed by Zeus, who feared that their child would be greater than he. That child, Athena, was then born from the head of her father Zeus fully grown and armored. Patron of Athens, credited with the invention of the implements and techniques of civilization (agriculture, industry, shipbuilding, military arts, etc.), her symbols were the owl, serpent, cock, crow, and aegis (breastplate). Her Roman counterpart Minerva shared similar features, and both goddesses were fully allied with supporting the patriarchal states that revered them. Their cults also assimilated elements from the Egyptian Isis, Vedic Ushās, and Persian Anāhita.

ASIA AND THE AMERICAS

In Persia, the great mother goddess of the Iranians was called Anāhita. She is described as the high, powerful, and undefiled one, and was associated with all of the gifts of a wise and well-ordered life. She maintained all good things for humanity, sustained fertility, rescued women in childbirth, and came to all to heal them of severe illnesses. Like Athena, she was also imaged as a war goddess, whose good favor grants victory to her followers.

The Sanskrit word *prajñā* (feminine for *wisdom*), finds its way into both Hinduism and the various strands of Buddhism. In the Vedas, *prajñā* is the ideal unified wisdom of atman, the eternal soul of all; it is wisdom that sustains creation. This concept may be associated with the figure of the Lady of the Spheres, who illuminates the universe and is associated with the sun. Golden-skinned and emitting flashes of light, she is the mother and creatrix of cosmic space and hidden secrets. In Buddhism, *prajñā* is the goal of human enlightenment achieved through right thought and right action. In the Prajñā-pāramitā (Perfection of Wisdom) Sūtras, Mahayana Buddhism identifies this wisdom with that possessed by all bodhisattvas and as one of the dimensions of the Eight-Fold Path to be achieved through meditation. In tantric Buddhism, *prajñā* is the female principle that mates with the male *upāya* to produce the undifferentiated "great bliss," the goal of salvation. In Chinese appropriations of Buddhism, the practices and achievement of *prajñā* are interpreted and merged with the goals of Confucianism.

In North America the figure of Old Woman in the hero tales of Plains Indians plays a role similar to that of Athena in her guise of advisor to heroes, and probably represents a personification of the roles played by women in tribal society. The hero's title is usually Old Woman's Grandchild, and she is his tutor; she provides him with all he needs to know and possess in order to be successful on his hero-quest. Old Woman often appears in animal form (as a moose in the tale of Mudjiki-wis, from the Eastern Woodlands tale cycle), filling roles similar to other animal helper-donors in native tales. When Old Woman's Grandchild is transformed into the north or morning star by his grandmother's teachings, she in turn becomes associated with the moon, giving her light to her male offspring. This motif

recalls the figure of the witch in early modern Europe, who was wise in unearthly knowledge, often transmitted to younger members of her circle during moon rituals.

Some final summary features should be highlighted. The wisdom goddess, while usually embodying the household roles of able mother or grandmother, operates in the cosmic realm as well as the human. Though often associated with fertility, in her old-woman guise sexuality is usually not a particularly prominent feature of her résumé. The transfer of her wisdom to a male divinity or human hero is a prerequisite for his success or salvation, and she is often thought of as the repository of the deepest and most important teachings of her culture. That this takes place in contexts that often limit or forbid education to women, maintain rigid gender ideologies, or which characterize women as representing flesh (matter) rather than spirit (reason) is a caution against presuming that the presence of such goddesses necessarily affects the status of women in a positive way. Although difficult to substantiate historically, the pattern of a cosmically wise female who willingly gives her knowledge and power into the hands of the male establishment of wise men does suggest an ancient and foundational role for women's knowledge—whether given willingly or grudgingly—in the development of patriarchal thought systems. The most likely explanation for this is that preindustrial cultures extrapolated wisdom's role from the gynocentric, agrarian household that could not survive without the technical expertise of women, orally passed from mothers to daughters, and then transposed it into the cosmic realm in the form of a goddess of wisdom.

BIBLIOGRAPHY

Baring, Anne, and Jules Cashford. *The Myth of the Goddess: Evolution of an Image*. 1993.

Bhattacharyya, N. N. *A Glossary of Indian Religious Terms and Concepts*. 1990.

Camp, Claudia V. *Wisdom and the Feminine in the Book of Proverbs*. 1985.

Fontaine, Carole R. "The Social Roles of Women in the World of Wisdom." In *A Feminist Companion to Wisdom Literature*. Edited by Athalya Brenner. 1995.

Foster, Benjamin R. *From Distant Days: Myths, Tales and Poetry of Ancient Mesopotamia*. 1995.

Goddard, Dwight, ed. *A Buddhist Bible*. 1938.

Knipe, David M. "Hinduism: Experiments in the Sacred." In *Religious Traditions of the World*. Edited by H. Byron Earhart. 1993.

Larrington, Carolyne, ed. *The Feminist Companion to Mythology*. 1992.

Lester, Robert C. "Buddhism: The Path to Nirvana." In *Religious Traditions of the World.* Edited by H. Byron Earhart. 1993.

Matt, Daniel C. *The Essential Kabbalah: The Heart of Jewish Mysticism.* 1996.

Matthews, Caitlin. *Sophia, Goddess of Wisdom: The Divine Feminine from Black Goddess to World-Soul.* 1991.

Patai, Raphael. *The Hebrew Goddess.* 1978.

Perkins, Pheme. "Sophia and the Mother-Father: The Gnostic Goddess." In *The Book of the Goddess: Past and Present.* Edited by Carl Olson. 1985.

See also Sophia.

CAROLE R. FONTAINE

In the Ancient Near East and Israelite Religion

Originally the literature and worldview created by the male scribes of the great temples of Mesopotamia and Egypt for training their members, wisdom literature covers a variety of literary genres: proverbs and sayings; "instructions" from a father to his son (or sage to student); onomastica (encyclopedic lists); disputes and debates; numerical sayings, acrostic poems, hymns to wisdom, and speculative literature (e.g., *Job; Ecclesiastes*). In Mesopotamia and Egypt, the tradition was also connected to magical and incantational texts (e.g., *The Book of the Dead*). Scribal schools very often had a female deity who served as the patron of the sages' arts. Nisaba played this role in Sumer, Ma'at in Egypt; Lady Wisdom of Proverbs 1–9 may be a biblical literary remnant of this tradition.

Since women seldom received specialized scribal training, few appear as major figures in wisdom schools, though some female scribes did exist, and other noble women were known for their canonical literary compositions (see *Enheduanna of Sumer*). Women's participation in wisdom was typically at the oral level of "performance" of proverbs, settling disputes, and the giving of wise counsel. The wise women of 2 Samuel show such women acting as ritual experts at the oral, traditional stage of the wisdom movement; the MI.ŠU.GI (old woman; mother goddesses) of the Late Bronze Age Hittite empire (modern Turkey) left a variety of ritual texts where the use of proverbs serves as a format for rites of healing.

Beyond their divine role as patrons and their informal roles as wise women, the topic of women forms a major area of interest where the sages give guidance to their young pupils. While wisdom literature grew up in the public domain of ancient patriarchal states, its informal beginnings at the village level where proverbs summarized group teachings and values still makes itself felt in the texts of the elite. The values of the home pervade much of wisdom's teaching, whether it be concerning agriculture, family management, or problem solving (cf. Prov. 31:10–31). Men are directed to establish stable households through the choice of a good wife and the avoidance of prostitutes and adulteresses. The wickedness of women forms a major concern: in Israel men are directed toward fidelity to their wives, and to the exalted (metaphorical?) figure of Lady Wisdom as their behavioral model. Nagging wives, prostitutes, foolish women, foreign temptresses, concerned mothers, and household maids all appear in wisdom teachings. The idealized woman appears as the good wife (or better, strong woman) in Proverbs 31:10–31, where her indefatigable acts on behalf of her household earn her a paean of patriarchal praise.

The New Testament connects Lady Wisdom of Israel with the new figure of the Jesus, who is the Sophia of God (1 Cor. 1:24), and Gnostic materials from Nag Hammadi also testify to the potency of this female figure as a model for the role and person of Jesus of Nazareth confessed as "the Christ." In modern Christian feminist reinterpretation of the biblical tradition, personified Wisdom has also been revived as a feminized Christological symbol.

BIBLIOGRAPHY

Camp, Claudia V. "The Female Sage in Ancient Israel and in the Biblical Wisdom Literature." In *The Sage in Israel and the Ancient Near East.* Edited by John G. Gammie and Leo G. Perdue. 1990.

————. "What's So Strange About the Strange Woman?" In *The Bible and the Politics of Exegesis.* Edited by David Joblin, Peggy L. Day, and Gerald T. Sheppard. 1991.

————. *Wisdom and the Feminine in the Book of Proverbs.* 1985.

Fontaine, Carole R. "The Sage in Family and Tribe." In *The Sage in Israel and the Ancient Near East.* Edited by John G. Gammie and Leo G. Perdue. 1990.

————. "The Social Roles of Women in the World of Wisdom." In *A Feminist Companion to Wisdom Literature.* Edited by Athalya Brenner. 1995.

Maier, Christl. *Die "fremde Frau" in Proverbien 1–9: Eine exegetische und sozialgeschichtliche Studie.* Orbis Biblicus et Orientalis, 144. Göttingen, 1995.

Yee, Gale A. "'I Have Perfumed My Bed with Myrrh': The Foreign Woman ('iššā zārâ) in Proverbs 1–9." In *A Feminist Companion to Wisdom Literature.* Edited by Athalya Brenner. 1995.

Washington, Harold C. "The Strange Woman (אשה זרה/נכריה) of Proverbs 1–9 and Post-

Exilic Judean Society." In *A Feminist Companion to Wisdom Literature.* Edited by Athalya Brenner. 1995.

Westermann, Claus. *Wurzeln der Weisheit: Die ältesten Sprüche Israels und anderer Völker.* 1990.

See also Education: Teaching Women and World Religions.

CAROLE R. FONTAINE

Prajñā and Prajñāpāramitā

Prajñāpāramitā, alternatively translated as "wisdom gone beyond," "transcendent wisdom," or, most commonly, "perfection of wisdom," is simultaneously a collection of classic texts, an iconographical representation of the wisdom (*prajñā*) to which these texts point, and an expression of what Mahayana Buddhist traditions consider to be the changeless and womblike nature of reality. When wisdom of this reality is perfected, one is born as a Buddha, and thus the female embodiment of emptiness, the divinity called Prajñāpāramitā, or Perfect Wisdom, is known as the mother of all Buddhas. "The basis of all coming and going is this,/ And all that exists arises from here,/ The womb of the mother-consort" (attributed to Padmasambhava, eighth century). (The verse translations in this essay are my own or adaptations from uncopyrighted Tibetan sources.)

According to Mahayana Buddhist traditions, Perfection of Wisdom texts record words of the Buddha too esoteric to be understood in his own time; forty years after he spoke them they disappeared from land and were preserved under the sea by the snakelike Nagas. Five hundred years later, they were retrieved by the great systemizer of the Middle Way, Nagarjuna, whose 800-line version is among the most ancient of the Mahayana wisdom literature. There also exist Perfection of Wisdom sutras in 8,000, 10,000, 18,000, 25,000, and 100,000 lines. According to the Tibetan historian Buston, all these were spoken simultaneously by the Buddha. The shortest Perfection of Wisdom sutra, recited regularly by Mahayana monastics throughout Asia, is the Heart Sutra, dated variously from the second and fourth centuries C.E. in India, although scholarship by Jan Nattier (1992) argues that the Heart Sutra originated in seventh-century China and thus—against all traditional understanding of its origins—was translated from Chinese into Sanskrit rather than from Sanskrit to Chinese.

The emptiness realized by perfect wisdom is variously referred to as the sphere of reality (*dharma dhātu*) and, in some contexts, as the womb of the Buddhas (*tathāgata-garbha*). This wisdom is embodied by the female divinity known as the Perfection of Wisdom. Hers

A **Cambodian sculpture from the Angkor period (twelfth to thirteenth centuries C.E.) shows the kneeling figure of Prajñāpāramitā, the Perfection of Wisdom** (Kevin Morris/© Corbis).

is a womb from which (unlike Freudian characterizations of human development) one never seeks to emerge but which one only wishes to recognize. The 8,000-line sutra states that just as children concern themselves when their mother is ill, so also Buddhas in all ten directions "bring to mind this perfection of wisdom as their mother" (XII.1–2). Bringing her to mind births one as a Buddha and is also the activity of all Buddhas for, the sutra continues, "She reveals the thoughts and actions of other beings."

The fruitional qualities of emptiness are also articulated in commentarial literature. Nagarjuna expresses the quintessence of the Perfect Wisdom's understanding in his *Root Verses of the Middle Way* (*Mūlamadhyamakakārikā,* 24:14):

> For whom emptiness is possible
> Everything is possible
> For whom emptiness is impossible
> Nothing is possible

Sutra traditions characterize this wisdom as a quality developed through cultivation; other traditions, such as Ch'an (Zen), Dzogchen, and much of Tantra, regard wisdom as already present, needing only to be discovered. However, this crucial difference between "sudden" and "gradual" paths is a difference in emphasis only, for both elements are vital in virtually all traditions.

In her four-armed manifestation, Prajñāpāramitā raises two hands in gestures of teaching and protection;

two other hands hold a text and a *vajra,* a diamond, symbol of the indestructible nature of wisdom and its indissoluble union with compassion. In a verse often quoted in Buddhist texts (from *sgra can 'dzin gyis stod pa*) she is praised thus:

> Inexpressible, inconceivable, indescribable perfect wisdom,
> Unborn, unceasing, essence of space itself
> Womanly domain of my own naturally knowing wisdom,
> Homage to you, mother of Conquerors past, present, and future.

Prajñāpāramitā is also connected with other female figures. In a late twelfth-century painting of Alchi Monastery, Ladakh, a six-armed Prajñāpāramitā takes the form of the green Tārā, thereby uniting wisdom and compassion in a single portrait. The liturgy of Yeshe Tsogyal, the partly mythic Tibetan queen of Trisong Daytsen (*Khri-srong-sde-btsan*) and consort of Padmasambhava, describes her womb and her vulva as conveying the expanse and oneness of wisdom. In this way she too is united with Prajñāpāramitā. The natural and ubiquitous presence of wisdom is also sometimes symbolized by the letter *Ah,* considered the life-giving sound of all letters and the ultimate condensation of perfect wisdom. Yeshe Tsogyal herself is queen of the *ḍākinīs,* "wisdom women who travel the sky." This sky is suffused by the wisdom *ḍākinīs'* own compassionate activities. In metaphor as in painted image, wisdom and compassion are one.

Emptiness, the Heart Sutra famously states, is not other than form. And Prajñāpāramitā the great mother is also not other than her children. She is simultaneously path and goal; she is the possibility of reaching the goal and the utter lack of any need to do so.

> Amazing, stunning, marvelous teaching
> Secret of all the perfect Buddhas
> That everything is born from the birthless
> When that very birth is unborn.
> —*Secret Essence (gSang Snying, Guhyagarbha)*

BIBLIOGRAPHY

Conze, Edward, trans. *The Large Sutra on Perfect Wisdom.* 1975. The most complete translation of this text, from Sanskrit.

———, trans. *The Perfection of Wisdom in Eight Thousand Lines.* 1973.

Hixon, Lex. *Mother of the Buddhas: Meditation on the Prajnaparamita Sutra.* 1993. A poetic reflection on and translation of selections from the 8,000-line Perfection of Wisdom sutra by a highly respected contemplative.

Inada, Kenneth, trans. *Nagarjuna: A Translation of His "Mulamadhyamikakarika" with an Introductory Essay.* Tokyo, 1970. A major scholar's translation of a crucial text.

Klein, Anne C., ed., comp., and trans. *Path to the Middle: Oral Mādhyamika in Tibet, the Spoken Scholarship of Kensur Yeshey Tupden.* 1995. One of the last great Tibetan scholars to complete his training in Tibet, Loling Kensur Rinpoche, comments on the opening portion of Tsongkhapa's *Illumination of the Thought,* itself a classic commentary on Candrakīrti's work *Entering the Middle Way,* a classic Buddhist supplement to Nagarjuna's *Treatise on the Middle Way.*

Lindtner, Christian. *Nagarjuniana: Studies in the Writings and Philosophy of Nāgārjuna.* Delhi, 1987. The classic anthology of works attributed to Nagarjuna.

Lopez, Donald S., Jr. *Elaborations of Emptiness: Uses of the Heart Sutra.* 1996. Essays on important elements of the Heart Sutra alternate with translations from the Tibetan of eight Indian commentaries on the sutra.

Macy, Joanna. "Perfection of Wisdom: Mother of All Buddhas." In *Beyond Androcentrism: New Essays on Women and Religion.* Edited by Rita Gross. 1977. Analysis of the female characteristics of the Goddess.

Napper, Elizabeth. *Dependent Arising and Emptiness: A Tibetan Buddhist Interpretation of Mādhyamika.* 1989. Detailed and clear presentation of a major school of Mādhyamika thought; includes translation of a four-fold annotation to Tsongkhapa's discussion of emptiness in his Great Exposition of the Stages of the Path (*Lam rim chen mo*).

Nattier, Jan. "The *Heart Sutra:* A Chinese Apocryphal Text." *Journal of the International Association of Buddhist Studies* 15, no. 2 (1992): 153–223.

Ruegg, David S. *The Literature of the Mādhyamika School of Philosophy in India.* Wiesbaden, 1981. An impeccable historical analysis.

Silk, Jonathan. *The Heart Sutra in Tibetan: A Critical Edition of Recension A and Recension B of the Kanjur Text.* Vienna, 1994.

ANNE C. KLEIN

Witchcraft

An Overview

To anthropologists, witchcraft is a cultural belief in the antisocial use of occult power by a human agent to harm other persons. The British anthropologist Edward Evans-Pritchard's pioneering 1937 study of witchcraft among the Azande of central Africa distinguished between witchcraft, as the antisocial use of an inherent mystical power, and sorcery, an antisocial act requiring the use of learned magical techniques. The Azande make this distinction, which is also recorded from cultures in East Africa, West Africa, and New Guinea. However, in many cultures all unsocial users of occult power are believed to use magical techniques, and some anthropologists prefer to term all such beliefs *witchcraft* (Douglas, 1970). Most cultures reserve a particular odium for persons believed to cause mystical harm out of malice, and most anthropologists would probably reserve the term *witch* for such persons. Other antisocial mystical practitioners may be motivated by more rational considerations, such as personal gain or revenge for a wrong. Witches are believed to act out of envy, hatred, and malice.

Historians generally focus upon the late medieval and early modern European idea of witchcraft as devil-worship and regard witchcraft as a phenomenon of European history (Russell, 1981). Self-styled "witches" of contemporary Europe and North America see themselves as followers of a pre-Christian fertility religion (Luhrmann, 1989; Russell, 1981), although historians such as Russell reject their claim to any connection with the witches of European history. Some covens of contemporary "witches" identify with feminism, but feminist "witches" have had little or no influence on the feminist movement.

THE IDEA OF THE WITCH
Witchcraft beliefs, as anthropologically defined, are common in preindustrial societies, but they are not accorded the same importance in all cultures. Witchcraft is associated particularly with stable, farming communities, where life is lived within small groups whose members interact constantly and intimately, and have many kinds of relationships with each other. When quarrels and ill-feelings arise, people must continue interacting. Among nomadic peoples, geographical mobility enables persons who do not get on together to live apart, so witchcraft is not usually accorded much importance (Baxter, 1972).

Witchcraft often explains personal misfortunes that appear undeserved and have a random character. It explains why they strike one individual rather than another. A Pondo schoolteacher in South Africa, accepting that typhus may be carried by lice, asked, ". . . who sent the infected louse? Why did it bite one man and not another?" Witchcraft provides the answer (Wilson, 1970). In sixteenth- and seventeenth-century England, unidentifiable and inexplicable illnesses among people and domestic animals (for example, stroke and epilepsy) were particularly likely to be attributed to witchcraft (Macfarlane, 1970).

The nature of these misfortunes has created a culturally widespread image of witches as the epitome of evil. In contrast to other occult wrongdoers, their lives are believed to be a perversion of the whole moral order. They kill and cannibalize their relatives and commit acts of incest and bestiality. They operate at night, in association with animals identified with darkness and evil. Among the Navajo Indians of Arizona and New Mexico, witches kill close relatives in order to be initiated into witchcraft, use magical powder made from dead children, and commit necrophilia. They turn themselves into wolves and coyotes. Witches among the Shona of Zimbabwe have owls and snakes as familiars. Witches usually have their own local organization, which is a perversion of normal human society. Navajo and Shona witches meet at night to plan evil and eat their dead victims (Kluckhohn, 1967; Mair, 1969).

WITCHCRAFT SUSPECTS
Because witchcraft is associated with malice, persons suffering misfortunes usually examine their personal relationships to discover anyone with a grievance toward them. Accusations of witchcraft often occur in relationships where the parties have conflicting interests but where there is no formal outlet for the tensions this generates. In polygynous families two wives of the same man may accuse each other; and anthropological studies in central Africa have noted the prevalence of witchcraft accusations between kinsmen competing for the office of village headman (Marwick, 1965; Turner, 1957).

Accusations are often regarded as a private matter between families or small kinship groups, and attempts may be made to reconcile the parties involved. Punishment is usually demanded only when a suspect comes to be regarded as a public menace by the community. This usually requires a gradual build-up of suspicions and accusations over a long period. The accused witch may then be killed or driven from the community. A reputation for witchcraft is most likely to be acquired if an accused shows characteristics culturally associated with malice or is believed to have a disaffected position within the community. Unsocial persons are associated with witchcraft. In many cultures any kind of strange behaviour may be suspect. Other suspects may occupy ambiguous or marginalized social positions, as often do the elderly and the poor. Women, who are usually marginalized as a gender, appear more commonly branded witches than men. Where men provide most suspects there is usually an ideological reason, as among the contemporary Western Apache of Arizona, where men's mystical power is believed stronger than that of women (Basso, 1969). These characteristics are often mutually reinforcing. An accused may be a woman who is old and eccentric and has demonstrated mystical power by practicing as a curer.

CONFIRMING WITCHCRAFT

Witches are often identified by oracles or by human diviners. A famous oracle is the Azande poison oracle, where poison is fed to a chicken in the name of a suspect (Evans-Pritchard, 1937). Diviners possess mystical power enabling them to detect witches, and their diagnoses are usually influenced by public opinion regarding the cause of a misfortune. As power intended for good may be subverted and used for evil, diviners themselves may be accused of witchcraft. The witches of the simplest human societies, hunter-gatherer bands, were shamans accused of misusing their powers.

Accused persons might be subjected to ordeals. In much of precolonial Africa they might be made to drink poison. If they vomited they were innocent. In sixteenth- and seventeenth-century England a suspect might be floated on water. If she sank she was innocent, as water rejected a witch.

WITCHCRAFT AND POWER

When accusations occur within a situation of marked power inequalities the treatment of witchcraft changes. The witch is punished and is often accused of causing communal misfortunes. Witchcraft against a king is always a public offence. In medieval Europe, political competition between powerful institutions and individuals led the intellectual classes to formulate the idea of a heretical sect of Devil-worshipers, and they incorporated the witch of the local community into this conception. Witchcraft became a public wrong, requiring punishment. Being a witch became an offence, whereas in the traditional situation the offence is causing misfortune by witchcraft. Among the common people the traditional pattern of beliefs was retained, and persons denounced to the public authorities were usually those who had gradually become labeled as witches over a long period (Sanders, 1995). Some historians argue that in Western Europe, the devil-worshiping witch replaced marginal groups such as lepers and Jews as a scapegoat for widespread misfortunes; once witchcraft became associated with heresy, the witch was imagined as an apostate Christian (Ginzburg, 1992). However, scapegoats continued to be drawn from among socially marginalized persons, such as poor, elderly women. Today in developing countries, tensions created by social change and disruption may promote new antiwitchcraft movements. These demand public confession for witchcraft and may also advocate punishment.

BIBLIOGRAPHY

Basso, Keith H. *Western Apache Witchcraft.* 1969.

Baxter, Paul T. W. "Absence Makes the Heart Grow Fonder: Some Suggestions Why Witchcraft Accusations Are Rare among East African Pastoralists." In *The Allocation of Responsibility.* Edited by Max Gluckman. 1972.

Douglas, Mary. "Thirty Years After Witchcraft, Oracles and Magic." In *Witchcraft Confessions and Accusations.* Edited by Mary Douglas. 1970.

Evans-Pritchard, Edward Evan. *Witchcraft, Oracles and Magic Among the Azande.* 1937. Abr. ed., 1976.

Ginzburg, Carlo. *Ecstasies: Deciphering the Witches' "Sabbath."* Translated by Raymond Rosenthal. 1992.

Kluckhohn, Clyde. *Navaho Witchcraft.* 1967.

Luhrmann, Tanya R. *Persuasions of the Witch's Craft: Ritual Magic and Witchcraft in Present-day England.* 1989.

Macfarlane, Alan. *Witchcraft in Tudor and Stuart England: A Regional and Comparative Study.* 1970.

Mair, Lucy. *Witchcraft.* 1969.

Marwick, Max G. *Sorcery in Its Social Setting: A Study of the Northern Rhodesian Cewa.* 1965.

Russell, Jeffrey B. *A History of Witchcraft: Sorcerers, Heretics and Pagans.* 1981.

Sanders, Andrew. *A Deed without a Name: The Witch in Society and History.* 1995.

Turner, Victor W. *Schism and Continuity in an African Society: A Study of Ndembu Village Life.* 1957.

Wilson, Monica. "Witch-beliefs and Social Structure." In *Witchcraft and Sorcery.* Edited by Max Marwick. 1970.

See also **Magic**; **Shamans**; **Wicca**.

ANDREW SANDERS

Witchcraft and Magic in the Ancient Near East and the Bible

The peoples of the ancient Near East recognized many types of supernatural beings: gods, ghosts, demons, and the spirits of trees, stones, or medicinally valuable plants. Gods and goddesses were treated as a divine ruling class kept happy by the avoidance of certain foods and unclean practices, daily sacrifices, the washing and clothing of a statue in which the deity resided, and periodic festivals. In Mesopotamia and Hatti, divinities were also addressed humbly in prayer. The Egyptians were noticeably less polite; Old Kingdom kings sought to achieve afterlife immortality by literally eating gods for breakfast (and lunch and dinner).

Ghosts of the dead expected to receive offerings from the living and to be treated with respect on their periodic visits to the upper world. Unfortunately, ghosts without surviving relatives fell between the cracks of this ancient welfare system and were dangerous sources of illness and disease. This was equally true of demons or demonesses, disagreeable and often extremely unattractive spirits who, when not being used by the gods as a sort of rough-and-ready police force, were distressingly prone to freelancing. They were not regularly worshiped but could, like beggars, expect handouts and a kind word. They were also expected to put up with curses and occasional threats of violence. Lower-order spirits were less troublesome, but still not to be crossed.

Formal religious practices not only avoided the angry god(s) problem but also set the stage for what we might call magic (Mesopotamian *āšipūtu;* Egyptian *heka*): bargains with god(s) or spirits designed to achieve specific practical ends. Ancient Near Eastern magical rituals were used inter alia to increase the effectiveness of herbal remedies, boost the morale of defeated armies, determine the guilt or innocence of an accused party in a legal case, ensure the success of crops and business ventures, recover runaway slaves, soothe family quarrels, and to quiet crying babies. Magic was also used to ensure the proper foundation of temples and other houses, to ensoul divine statues, to mollify angry gods, to enforce oaths, and, conversely, to loosen curses (as in the Mesopotamian magical series *Šurpu*). In Egypt magic could also be used without embarrassment to ensure that an overburden of evil deeds did not bar the deceased from a desired afterlife.

To ensure that a god or spirit understood what was wanted, the practitioner might "translate" the spoken part of a spell into divine language or act out the desired result in a sort of pantomime. One could, for example, encourage a recalcitrant vine to produce abundant clusters of grapes by showing it one of a large litter of piglets. The importance of the communicative aspects of magic is particularly stressed in Egypt, where the sounds of the words (and even the shapes of the hieroglyphs used to write them) were considered to be imbued with numinous power. Depending on the circumstances, the objective of this pantomime might be apotropaic (to keep a spirit at a safe distance), exorcistic (to drive him out), or propitiatory (to buy him off). Some form of pleading, self-abasement (wearing sackcloth and ashes, fasting, blood letting), flattery, offerings before or after the granting of a wish, or threats were also part and parcel of a successful bargain. Also common was the invocation with offerings of gods not directly involved in the proceedings as guarantors that a spirit did what was required of him or her.

Some of these rituals were designed to be performed in the patient's house or in a place cleared in the steppe; some required visits to the "house" of the divinity whose help was being solicited. The temple of the goddess Gula in ancient Mesopotamian Isin was packed with miniature figurines of her animal, the dog, as well as ex-votos in the form of human patients gripping (formerly) afflicted body parts. Ishtar, the irresistible but grim liminal goddess of uncontrolled sexuality and war, received presents of miniature penises from Mesopotamian men she had previously inflicted with impotence and venereal disease. New Kingdom Egyptian temples often contained stelae showing Horus standing on a crocodile, which were doused by petitioners desiring to use the resulting "charm water" to cure snake and scorpion bites. Another method of enlisting divine medical assistance through a temple was to dedicate a child to the service of a god, as in the case of the future Hittite king Hattušili III (compare the boyhood of the prophet Samuel).

Even in ancient Israel (where interactions with spirits other than Yahweh were forbidden), bargains of this sort were considered fully legitimate. (Note Jephthah's vow, resulting in the sacrifice to Yahweh of his only daughter [Judg. 11:29–40], and Gen. 30:31–43, where Jacob cheats Laban by ensuring that an undue percentage of his flock are born speckled by the rather unorthodox method of causing the animals to view striped rods as they are mating.) Equally remarkable is the use of what is clearly a magical ordeal (complete with written curses dissolved in water!) to determine the innocence of an accused adulteress in Numbers 5:11–31. Even Israelite prophets did not flinch from purely practical miracles, such as making jars overflow and recovering lost axes (1 Kings 17; 2 Kings 4, 6) or from curing skin diseases by instructing patients to bathe seven times in a particular river (2 Kings 5).

Some rites, such as the rituals ensuring military victory, involved exclusively male participants (e.g., the Hittite soldiers asked to march between thornbushes, fires, and halved puppies to cleanse them of a defeat). Rites such as childbirth and wet-nursing rituals involved exclusively female participants (even the husband was not welcome in the birth room). Most magical rites, however, were potentially beneficial to either sex and were consequently patronized by both, sometimes simultaneously (as in the Mesopotamian impotence rituals, wherein female sexual partners of affected males were called upon to help with the rubbing on of salves and the reciting of erotic spells).

Magical rites were generally presided over by male magical experts associated with temples (Mesopotamia: *āšipū;* Egypt: *hry-tb,* lector-priest). This is hardly surprising considering that all polytheistic ancient Near Eastern cultures attributed magic's invention to gods (Ea for Mesopotamians and Hittites; Thoth for Egyptians). The Hittites are unusual for the prominent (though by no means exclusive) role given to female magical experts, the ḫašawa-women, and to rituals composed by these and other women. Elsewhere there were female magical experts, but these seem to have addressed themselves chiefly to feminine concerns.

Divination (communication with the gods via signs such as the lumps and bumps on the liver of a sacrificial sheep or the arrangement of stars in the heavens) was a respectable science in most of the ancient Near East and, apart from the Hittite ḫašawa-women, largely a male preserve. With the notable exception of the Biblical prophets, ecstatics (persons claiming to speak for "supernatural" beings by virtue of inspiration rather than formal education), although still perfectly legal, tended to be women rather than men (e.g., Mesopotamian dream interpretesses and Egyptian "wise women"). Necromancy (seeking advice or knowledge of the future from ghosts) typically involved "letters to the dead" (in Egypt), male practitioners playing special musical instruments or smearing on magical salves (in Mesopotamia), or practitioners of the ecstatic type (in Biblical lands). Such activities were anathema to Yahwists in Israel. Yahweh spoke to his people via (male) prophets; those people (either male or female) who claimed foreknowledge on the basis of access to spirits other than Yahweh were thereby seen as challenging the authority of Israel's god. Even so, unlike later Christian readers, the authors of the Hebrew Bible did not consider dealers in spirits, such as the woman of Endor illegally consulted by Saul, to be witches.

Practices seeking to harm other persons without just cause (Mesopotamian *kišpu;* Hittite *alwanzatar;* Hebrew *kešep*) were indeed witchcraft (except in Egypt, where literally anything went). Falling into a gray area between legitimate practice and witchcraft were a set of Mesopotamian rites purporting to allow a man with a weak case to bind his opponent so thoroughly that he was rendered not only speechless but unable to pass gas. A similar ambiguity surrounded rituals to seduce a woman. It was hard to argue when such love magic was employed to ensure the success of an arranged marriage. It was less appreciated when a man used the same magic to seduce another man's wife. Note that the practitioner of such spells was assumed to be male; in sharp contrast with seventeenth-century Europe, hostile magic or witchcraft was equally open to both sexes.

In the ancient Near East, the witch or sorcerer was a person whose envy and hatred of other people led him or her to attempt the destruction of his victims by such means as sticking pins in figurines and collecting semen to lay in the laps of corpses. Some rites were for witches only and were forbidden by law on pain of death. In addition to the direct infliction of illness,

witchcraft was also used to deprive a victim of the protection of her or his own personal god and goddess.

The Mesopotamian good magical expert encouraged his or her clients to turn the witch's own tricks against him or her, sticking figurines full of pins or feeding them to dogs (an entire magical series, *Maqlû,* is devoted to such spells). Egyptian lector-priests also understandably took the attitude that the best defense was a good offense (e.g., the execration rituals in which potential rebels, male and female, were, figuratively speaking, smashed). Hittite ḫašawa-women preferred less aggressive purification rituals involving the "unraveling" of spells with the help of bits of colored yarn, passage through gates of hawthorn, and creative use of scapegoats, scapepuppies, and even scapemice. Such rituals sought to transfer the evil to an object or animal that could then be harmlessly disposed of. A Mesopotamian ghost could also be asked to carry a witch away to the netherworld.

Again in contrast to the situation in early modern Europe, the official approach to witchcraft (despite the presence of death penalties for certain practices) actively discouraged actual accusations. Occasionally in Egypt those who used their skills against the Pharaoh were tried (as, for example, the men and women of the harem who tried to murder Ramses III by magic).

Elsewhere in the ancient Near East, there was a concept of witchcraft but no judicial torture, and false accusers routinely received the same penalty as the defendant would have received, if convicted. This encouraged putative victims, whatever their actual suspicions, to trust in a higher form of justice overseen by the god(s). The putative witch is never named in ancient Mesopotamian antiwitchcraft rituals, only indicated by means of pairs of figurines (male and female). In theory, the magical rite would find and punish the witch, avoiding the difficulties of perversion of justice for which witches were curiously infamous even in Europe, and without any danger of having mistakenly accused the wrong person.

BIBLIOGRAPHY

Allen, T. G. *The Book of the Dead.* Studies in Ancient Oriental Civilizations 37. 1974.

Beckman, G. *Hittite Birth Rituals.* Studien zu den Boğazköy Texten 29. Wiesbaden, 1983.

Biggs, R. ŠÀ.ZI.GA. *Ancient Mesopotamian Potency Incantations.* 1967.

Bourghouts, J. F. *The Ancient Egyptian Magical Texts.* NISABA 9. Leiden, 1978.

Dietrich, M., and O. Loretz. "Ugaritische Rituale und Beschwörungen." In *Religiose Texte: Texte aus der Umwelt des Alten Testaments* 2/3. Edited by C. Butterweck et al. Gütersloh, 1988..

Engelhard, D. H. "Hittite Magical Practices: An Analysis." Ph.D. diss., Brandeis University. 1970.

Farber, W. *Beschwörungsrituale an Ištar und Dumuzi.* Wiesbaden, 1977.

———. *Schlaf, Kindschen, schlaf!: Mesopotamische Baby-Beschwörungen und Rituale.* 1989.

Finkel, I. "Necromancy in Ancient Mesopotamia." *Archiv für Orientforschungen* 29/30 (1983–1984): 1–17.

Meier, G. *Die assyrische Beschwörungssammlung Maqlu.* Archiv für Orientforschungen Beiheft 2. Berlin, 1937.

Meyer, M., and P. Mirecki, eds. *Ancient Magic and Ritual Power.* Leiden, 1995.

Oppenheim, A. L. *The Interpretation of Dreams in the Ancient Near East.* Transactions of the American Philosophical Society 46, no. 3 (1956).

Reiner, E. *Šurpu, A Collection of Sumerian and Akkadian Incantations.* Archiv für Orientforschung Beiheft 11. Graz, 1958.

Ritner, R. *The Mechanics of Ancient Egyptian Magical Practice.* Studies in Ancient Oriental Civilizations 54. 1993, 1995.

Sasson, J., ed. *Civilizations of the Ancient Near East.* 1995. See vol. 3, part 8.

Scurlock, J. A. "Baby-Snatching Demons, Restless Souls and the Dangers of Childbirth: Medico-Magical Means of Dealing with Some of the Perils of Motherhood in Ancient Mesopotamia." *Incognita* 2 (1991): 137–185.

———. "Magical Means of Dealing with Ghosts in Ancient Mesopotamia." Ph.D. diss., University of Chicago. 1988.

———. "Was There a 'Love-hungry' Ēntu-priestess Named Eṭirtum?" *Archiv für Orientforschung* 36/37 (1989/1990 [1992]): 107–112.

Scurlock, J. A. and J. K. Kuemmerlin-McLean. "Magic." In *Anchor Bible Dictionary.* Edited by D. N. Freedman. 1992. Vol. 4, cols. 464–471 (with further bibliography).

Tropper, J. *Nekromantie: Totenbefragung im Alten Orient und im Alten Testament.* Alter Orient und Altes Testament 223. Neukirchen-Vluyn, 1989.

Wiggermann, F. A. M. *Babylonian Prophylactic Figures: The Ritual Texts.* Amsterdam, 1986.

JO ANN SCURLOCK

In European Traditions

In traditional European folk cultures, witch beliefs formed part of a broader system of magical beliefs and practices, including remedies against the kinds of harm (*maleficium*) attributed to witches. In anthropological terms, *witchcraft* refers to magical harm inflicted by a hostile human being through occult means. Belief in the possibility of witchcraft serves most clearly to explain misfortune; an injured person's question, "Why me, but not my neighbor?" is answered by personifying the source of harm in the ill will of a potentially identifiable witch, who could then be pursued for relief, reparations, or revenge.

Although analogous belief systems are common among traditional cultures studied by anthropologists, a tension between learned and popular levels of belief lends European witch traditions a distinctive character. The successive conversions to Christianity of indigenous cultures, whether Greco-Roman, Celtic, Germanic, or Slavic, meant that European witch beliefs drew from multiple cultural sources. Diverse traditions were fused during the late medieval period into the image of a (usually) female, evil-doing demon worshiper. Forged from deeply rooted popular beliefs as well as from newer clerical theories, it was this composite image that led to the witch hunts of the sixteenth and seventeenth centuries.

In the early fifth century, the Christian theologian Augustine condemned the worship of multiple "false gods" in the Roman Empire as idolatrous. He further asserted that the idols themselves were demonic, so that pagan devotees were automatically guilty of demon worship. The prescribed remedy for such "demonolatry" was the Christian initiation rite of baptism, which included an exorcism, cleansing newly won souls of the demonic allegiance implicit in their previous state of original sin. This Christian interpretation of the many gods and goddesses of antiquity as so many personifications of evil spirits formed the theoretical basis for the learned culture's demonization of preexisting magical and witch beliefs.

European folk cultures did indeed attribute magical powers both to human witches and to a range of supernatural beings, including fairies, elves, and trolls, as well as superseded deities or demigoddesses, such as Diana and Circe. The boundaries between natural and spiritual worlds were porous, each inhabited by ambiguous beings whose preternatural powers could be used for good or for ill. Metamorphosis or shape-shifting, for example, consisted of the magical ability to change from one kind of being into another, usually an animal. But the early medieval church, engaged in the project of converting pagan Europe to Christianity, rejected the very possibility of these transformations, attributing them instead to demonic illusion. Such beliefs were categorized as "turning back to the errors of the pagans, by believing there is anything of a power except the one God." This phrase comes from the canon

Episcopi, a tenth-century church council's condemnation of the belief of "some wicked women" that they went flying at night with the goddess Diana on generally beneficent errands, "worshipping her as their mistress."

Early medieval law codes and church councils identified a range of such paganizing errors that "Christian minds should not believe," thus providing the earliest historical sources concerning popular witch beliefs. In addition to Diana and her retinue, the *strix* or *striga* formed a different, more menacing strand of popular witch belief. Described in late Roman literary sources such as Apuleius's *The Golden Ass*, this shape-shifting, predatory creature was an old woman by day, transformed at night into a flesh-eating screech owl, flying into open windows to "devour living men from within" as they slept. Night flying with Diana and the *striga* represent distinct, even opposed beliefs, for Diana and her "ladies of the night" rewarded those households who left out food or drink for them, whereas the *striga* was a wholly maleficent, deadly being with a special taste for infant flesh. But these separate traditions shared crucial elements—shape-shifting and night flying by women—which contributed to their eventual fusion in European witch imagery. Later sources testify to the survival of similar pre-Christian beliefs, such as Frau Holda in Germany, or the *donne de fuori* ("ladies from outside") in Sicily. These were benevolent female spirits, goddesses, or fairies, whose human followers accompanied their leader "in spirit" at night, feasting and in some cases dancing. It was these preexisting beliefs that formed the popular substratum onto which the theologically elaborated image of a devil-worshiping Sabbath was grafted in the later Middle Ages.

Between the thirteenth and the fifteenth centuries, the church's attitude toward such beliefs changed drastically. Scholastic theology developed a systematic explanation of the nature of the universe and the various creatures it contained—from angels and human beings to the plants and animals of the natural world. The earlier view, that "Christian minds should not believe" in the reality of supernatural powers attributed to beings other than "the one God," was undermined by the newly developed theory of the diabolical pact. Speculating on the widespread belief that magical effects could be achieved by witches and sorcerers (literate male magicians), scholastic theologians argued that such effects could occur only with the aid of the devil, whose limited and largely illusory powers were permitted by God to test humankind. Magic was thus defined as necessarily depending on a prior diabolical pact, in which guilty parties renounced God and pledged their souls to the devil in return for suprahuman magical powers.

A remarkably lifelike wax figure depicts a witch condemned to burn at the stake. She is chained, white paint or chalk covers her face, and her shaved head is covered with a conical cap denoting heresy, Visegrad Citadel museum, Hungary (Dave Bartruff/Corbis).

The well-known witch-hunting manual of 1486, *Malleus Maleficarum*, rejected the earlier view that activities such as night flying were illusory, declaring on the contrary that "*not* to believe in witchcraft is the greatest of heresies." Written by two Dominican Inquisitors, Heinrich Kramer and Jacob Sprenger, this systematization of witch beliefs drew on the scholastic theory of the diabolical pact to explain that "three things are necessary for witchcraft; the devil, a witch, and divine permission." The third element was necessary in order to preserve the role of God as the ultimate or final cause of all created phenomena, including evil. The biblical source for this crucial point was the Book of Job, but theologians from Augustine through the scholastics had always stressed that God permitted evil to test human beings and ultimately to bring good out of the struggle against evil.

The *Malleus Maleficarum* is perhaps most famous, or rather infamous, for the misogynist attitude announced in the title's use of the female *malefica* to indicate that witches were overwhelmingly women. A long section, "Why it is that chiefly women are addicted to evil superstitions," drew on both classical and early Christian sources for an authoritative, exhaustive documentation of the many defects of women that inclined them toward witchery. Among these were avarice, envy, hostility, and intellectual weak-mindedness, but above all, the authors concluded, "witchcraft comes from carnal lust, which in women is insatiable." Women were seen as sexually voracious to the point that they would do literally anything to satisfy their boundless appetites, including copulate with demons. Celibate male clerics like Kramer and Sprenger, for whom sexuality itself was unacceptable, can be understood as projecting repressed and demonized sexual feelings onto women, who became the cause of sexual temptation. However, men too could make pacts with the devil, and theologians never ruled out the possibility of male witches; it was just far less likely. Kramer and Sprenger attributed their heightened immunity against becoming witches to Christ's incarnation as a man, by virtue of which men were spared many pitfalls awaiting women.

If clerical misogyny goes a long way toward explaining learned theories of "why witches are women," this question is far more complicated on the level of popular witch beliefs. In some areas, most notably eastern Europe, the ratio was reversed and men were more likely than women to be seen as witches. In the early witch trials of fifteenth-century France and Switzerland, male defendants were at least as frequent as women. These were areas with large numbers of Cathar and Waldensian sectarians, where the medieval Inquisition conducted the bulk of its heresy trials in the 1200s and 1300s. Since heretical groups included both male and female members, it is possible that this gender-neutral pattern was carried over into subsequent witchcraft prosecutions.

On the other hand, there were areas, especially England, New England, and some parts of Germany, where the overwhelming majority (over 80 percent) of accused witches were women. Local variations of this sort are the focus of historians' study, as they attempt to sort out the many different factors that led up to the identification of specific individuals as witches. The English "beggar witch" described by Keith Thomas (1971) provides a striking example of the social context in which ordinary accusations arose. Known to all as she tramped from house to house begging for food or money, the beggar's marginality, resentment, and hostility made her the prime suspect when misfortune struck those who had refused her requests. Poor, older women with no surviving family occupied the lowest rungs of the social ladder, and it was precisely their lack of power, along with hostility, that made them suspect. Neighbors feared witchcraft, "the revenge of the weak," only from those from whom they feared nothing else.

Another role occupied by women that generated many witchcraft accusations was that of village healer or "cunning folk" who knew how to cure the effects of *maleficium* by removing spells from those harmed by witches. The suspicions generated by this kind of magical activity are expressed by an Italian proverb, "Who knows how to heal, knows how to harm," quoted in denunciations of healers for witchcraft. The universe of magical remedies against witches was readily accessible, as every village had its own magical healers; but they often fell prey to the suspicion that they had themselves caused the harm they were called in to heal. (By contrast, research on midwives has rejected the older theory that they were especially likely to be accused of witchcraft.)

There was, then, a clear gap between learned and popular witch beliefs in the Middle Ages; theologians pondered philosophical issues about the powers permitted by God to the devil, while peasants persisted in the traditional practice of attributing misfortunes of everyday life—sickness, bad weather, crop failures—to the hostility of witches. The fusion of these distinct levels produced the "witch panic" whose very intensity paradoxically undermined the credibility of witch-hunting procedures. Governments withdrew from witch trials by the late seventeenth century, but scattered episodes of vigilante actions against witches at the local level demonstrated the persistence of perceptions of witchcraft among the peasantry. The marginalization of traditional witch beliefs in modern Europe is visible in the twentieth-century French psychiatric category of "delusions of witchcraft persecution," a diagnosis that provided the anthropologist Jeanne Favret-Saada with the starting point for her important research on surviving witch beliefs in a remote area of rural France (1980).

BIBLIOGRAPHY

Ankarloo, Bengt, and Gustav Henningsen, eds. *European Witchcraft: Centres and Peripheries.* 1989. Articles on the wide range of fairy and spirit beliefs eventually absorbed into the witch belief system, in outlying areas of Europe, from Scandinavia to the Mediterranean.

Barstow, Anne. *Witchcraze.* 1993. Perceptive study of role of women as targets of witch hunting.

Boyer, Paul, and Steven Nissenbaum. *Salem Possessed: The Social Origins of Witchcraft.* 1974. The best book on Salem witch trials, made possible by the survival of Massachusetts records for a half-century preceding 1692.

Briggs, Robin. *Witches and Neighbors: The Social and Cultural Context of European Witchcraft.* 1996. Based on important archival research in Lorraine; argues that in France, men were as likely as women to be accused of witchcraft; includes an up-to-date bibliographical essay.

Clark, Stuart. *Thinking with Demons: The Idea of Witchcraft in Early Modern Europe.* 1997. A major work of intellectual history showing the penetration of learned disciplines of law, theology, medicine, and natural philosophy by witch theory through the seventeenth century.

Cohn, Norman. *Europe's Inner Demons: An Enquiry Inspired by the Great Witch-Hunt.* 1975. The basic study on medieval witch beliefs, including a definitive critique of Margaret Murray's theory of witchcraft as an underground "fertility cult."

Demos, John. *Entertaining Satan: Witchcraft and the Culture of Colonial New England.* 1982. Psychological interpretation of New England outbreaks; focuses on adolescent girls' responses to religious repression.

Favret-Saada, Jeanne. *Deadly Words: Witchcraft in the Bocage.* 1980. Study of surviving witch belief systems in twentieth-century western France.

Ginzburg, Carlo. *Ecstasies: Deciphering the Witches' Sabbath.* 1991. Translation of *Storia Notturna,* 1990. Argues that folkloric myths about night flying and nocturnal meetings influenced theological views of Sabbath.

———. *The Night Battles: Witchcraft and Agrarian Cults in the Sixteenth and Seventeenth Centuries.* 1983. English translation of *I benandanti: culti agrari e stregoneria fra '500–'600,* 1966. A unique series of Roman Inquisition trials against an organized group, not of witches, but of counter-witches, men and women whose role was to fight off witches in order to protect the crops against their attacks.

Karlsen, Carol. *The Devil in the Shape of a Woman: Witchcraft in Colonial New England.* 1987. Well-done feminist analysis of competing Puritan images of women as handmaidens either of the Lord or the devil; identifies a measurable pattern of witchcraft accusations against recent widows with no brothers and no sons, or "anomalous property inheritors."

Larner, Christina. *Enemies of God: The Witch-Hunt in Scotland.* 1981. Sociological analysis of Scottish cases; along with infanticide, witchcraft emerges as the dominant female crime in Europe.

Levack, Brian. *The Witch-Hunt in Early Modern Europe.* 1987. 2d ed., 1995. The best one-volume introduction to the topic, including issue of women.

Midelfort, H. C. Erik. *Witch Hunting in South Western Germany, 1562–1584.* 1972. Important work on the German witch panic, the largest of all witch hunts; argues that a demographic surplus of older women contributed to sixteenth- and seventeenth-century witch hunting.

Roper, Lyndal. *Oedipus and the Devil: Witchcraft, Sexuality and Religion in Early Modern Europe.* 1994. Well-argued feminist psychological analysis of German witchcraft accusations, drawing on Melanie Klein's theories to interpret postpartum witchcraft accusations against "lying-in maids."

Sharpe, James A. *Instruments of Darkness: Witchcraft in Early Modern England.* 1997. Important study of the English witch-hunting experience.

Thomas, Keith. *Religion and the Decline of Magic.* 1971. A pioneering study that identified the pattern of "English beggar witch" both at the village level and in the Reformation context.

See also **Shape-Shifting.**

MARY R. O'NEIL

Witchcraft in Africa

Studies of African witchcraft have been conducted primarily by anthropologists. Students of African religions increasingly regard discussions of attitudes about witchcraft as essential to their understanding. Historians have also turned to the study of witchcraft, seeing it as an integral part of the social upheavals that have marked African history from the fifteenth to the twentieth centuries. Witchcraft has also become an important theme of African novels in the postcolonial era.

In the context of African societies, witchcraft is often distinguished from sorcery by its emphasis on spiritual forms of attack rather than a reliance on medicines and amulets to harm others. Witches are usually described as having souls that are capable of leaving the body and traveling in the night, consuming the life force of other humans or of material goods—leaving the afflicted with potentially fatal illness or with material goods in an advanced state of decay. Although the contrast with sorcery may not be as absolute as some have suggested, sorcerers tend to be masters of medicines and herbs and can use their power for beneficial as well as harmful purposes. In many African societies, however, there are people who have the same power as do witches but

Women witch doctors in bright traditional dress tell fortunes by divination through the throwing of bones, Gemsbokspruit, South Africa, 1997 (Nazima Kowall/ Corbis).

who use their powers to protect their community rather than attack it. In most societies, there is no material evidence of witchcraft.

Witchcraft is usually seen as working most effectively against close relatives or neighbors and rarely against strangers. This is not because of physical distance— African witches are considered quite capable of attacking African immigrants in Europe or America—but rather reflects the lack of motivation for an attack against strangers. The anthropologist Mary Douglas has emphasized the importance of witchcraft in societies where the expression of resentment or anger against close kin or neighbors is considered improper. Accusations of witchcraft often are accompanied by a public airing of these resentments, which are seen as evidence of motivation for witch attacks.

Despite similarities in the way that witches harm others, African attitudes about witches differ considerably. In most societies witches can either be male or female, but there are some in which witches are drawn exclusively from one gender. The Igbo of southeastern Nigeria stress women's witchcraft, whereas the Lugbara of Uganda see witchcraft as the exclusive preserve of men. Among the Yoruba of southwestern Nigeria and Benin, witches are described as "our mothers" and are exclusively women. Among some Yoruba groups, male initiates of the Gelede cult perform dances in which they wear costumes and masks of "our mothers" to "cool" the power of witches and enhance the life-enriching power of *ase*. Yoruba witches can cause the sterility of co-wives and the deaths of fetuses and newborns; they can steal the sexual organs of their husbands (rendering them impotent) in order to have sex with other women, including their husband's co-wives. Cases of genital theft reported in newspapers in the 1990s may be a sign that Yoruba witches have found a way to operate by day, stealing the life force of male strangers whom they encounter in the large urban areas of Nigeria.

Functionalist anthropologists, such as Mary Douglas and Max Marwick, emphasize the correlation between areas of stress in a particular society and its gender relations. When women are seen as a source of conflict or their activities a source of anxiety for men and for other women, witchcraft is often a primarily female activity. For example, in polygynous societies, problems of infertility and infant mortality are often attributed to witchcraft arising from competition among co-wives. When men are seen as the primary source of witchcraft, conflicts over access to land, cattle, or the resources needed to enter into marriage are often seen as the motivating factor for witchcraft attacks.

Historians have examined the impact of the slave trade and the ensuing expansion of commercial relations in the European-dominated world trade system as the source of increasingly frequent witchcraft accusations. Especially in stateless societies, new slave trading elites became the object of witchcraft accusations because their hoarding of wealth contradicted social norms that obligated them to share. The destruction and uncertainty brought on by the colonial conquest in the late nineteenth and early twentieth centuries generated a crisis of confidence in many African social systems. The pervasiveness of witchcraft became a powerful explanation both for the relative weakness of the conquered peoples and the strength of the European conquerors, who were seen as a powerful scourge that would generate movements to eliminate witchcraft from African societies. Indeed, from Senegal to South Africa, witch-finding movements became increasingly important in the wake of the colonial conquest. The most famous of these, the Xhosa cattle-killing movement of 1857, arose in the wake of a series of devastating military defeats. A young Xhosa woman named Nongqawuse had visions in which she learned that the cause of the Xhosa's defeats was the excessive use of witchcraft in their communities. In order to purify the land and demonstrate their determination to purge this nefarious activity from their communities, the Xhosa, she prophesied, had to destroy all their crops and cattle. Then the ancestors would return, the people would be blessed with more grain and cattle than they had ever had, and the Europeans would leave their lands. The prophecy did not come true and the Xhosa lost their lands, but the linkage of witchcraft and colonial subjugation was firmly established.

In the colonial and postcolonial eras, the wealth of successful women traders has often spurred jealousy and witchcraft accusations. In some cases their success was attributed to their use of witchcraft to garner more than their fair share of wealth. The economic success of childless women or those who had few children was often seen as coming at the expense of their primary obligation of motherhood.

Usually witches are identified only after someone has fallen ill or died. Many societies require a ritual form of inquiry into the causes of each death. In many societies of the Upper Guinea Coast, from southern Senegal to Sierra Leone, the deceased, whose corpse rests on a stretcher, responds to a series of questions about the cause of death by compelling the pallbearers and the bier to move in certain ways. One question usually asked is whether the person died of witchcraft. In some cases the questioning continues until a specific person is identified as responsible. The identity of witches is often revealed by diviners using a variety of techniques, including poison ordeals. Most of these forms of witchcraft accusations are controlled by men, and most of the accused are women. In other communities, such as the Diola of Senegal, Gambia, and Guinea-Bissau, divinatory shrines controlled by both women and men are an important supplement to the primary mode of identifying witches by seeing them in dreams.

Witchcraft accusations have a particularly corrosive effect on community solidarity. Wives and husbands who have shared the same bed for years might begin to suspect one another once accusations have been made. Wives in patrilocal societies are particularly suspect because they are strangers in their husbands' compounds and have loyalties elsewhere. The apparently cordial behavior of relatives and neighbors toward one another also becomes suspect once witchcraft accusations are made. The solidarity of families and neighborhoods often falls victim to the pervasive suspicions associated with a witchcraft scare. In periods of rapid social change, such as the slave trade era and the colonial conquest, the intensity and frequency of witchcraft accusations increased.

BIBLIOGRAPHY

Baum, Robert M. *Shrines of the Slave Trade: Diola Religion and Society in Precolonial Senegambia.* Forthcoming.

Comaroff, Jean, and John Comaroff, eds. *Modernity and Its Malcontents: Ritual and Power in Postcolonial Africa.* 1993.

Douglas, M., ed. *Witchcraft Accusations and Confessions.* London, 1970.

Drewal, Henry J., and Margaret Drewal. *Gelede: Art and Female Power among the Yoruba.* 1983.

Evans-Pritchard, E. E. *Witchcraft, Oracles, and Magic among the Azande.* 1937.

Fissy, Cyprian, and Peter Geschiere. "Witchcraft, Violence and Identity: Different Trajectories in Postcolonial Cameroon." In *Postcolonial Identities in Africa.* Edited by Richard Werbner and Terence Ranger. London, 1996.

Mair, Lucy. *Witchcraft.* 1969. Reprint, 1976.

Marwick, Max, ed. *Witchcraft and Sorcery.* 1970.

Middleton, John, and E. H. Winter, eds. *Witchcraft and Sorcery in East Africa.* 1963. Repr. 1969.

Mulaisho, Dominic. *The Tongue of the Dumb.* 1971.

ROBERT M. BAUM

Witchcraft in Asia

A witch, in what is now accepted anthropological discourse about Asia, is intrinsically evil, with innate powers, capable even unknowingly and unintentionally of bringing misfortune or death upon anyone in her or his vicinity. By contrast, a sorcerer intentionally learns how to make evil and may or may not have intrinsic propensities for sorcery. The lived reality often does not correspond neatly to such methodological distinctions; however, being a witch is almost never a self-proclaimed identity, as being a sorcerer often is. Conventionally, people accuse as witches those whom they dislike or resent and use that charge to justify persecuting or killing those accused—most often, the socially marginalized or exceptional, including old, unmarried, widowed, or powerful women.

In China the role of *wu*, shaman or shamaness is considered predominantly a female or transgender realm. Shamanism gradually declined from its apex during the Shang Dynasty (second millennium B.C.E.). During the Zhou (Chou) Dynasty (traditionally, 1122–256 B.C.E.), male shamans increasingly came to the forefront of religious practice. Women who were successful shamanesses earned the respect and power of many, thus threatening the male-dominated ruling classes. This gender change also reflected a shift in the intentions of shamanism. As greater respect came to be vested in (male-dominated) knowledge of the hierarchical positions or status of the deities, and the proper performance of religious ceremonies, the magical power of shamanism came to be held as secondary, even demonized as witchcraft, and not supported by the state cult. Since the Han period, Confucian orthodoxy in cult matters came to be increasingly important, and quite often, small unorthodox shrines and estates of the shamanesses who did not enjoy the protection of the court were targeted for destruction in the name of "public morality" (Schaefer, *The Divine Woman*, 1980). Certain practices were curtailed, including the ritual nudity of shamanesses and human sacrifice. The combination of all these factors contributed to the gradually diminishing importance of women in Chinese shamanism.

The tasks of *wu* include both healing and serving as spirit mediums; in more remote areas, *qigong* practitioners even today perform acts akin to psychic surgery. *Wu* has been applied to indigenous healers in a manner comparable to *witch doctor* or *witch*, resulting in persecution, as in the tenth and eleventh centuries in southern China. In Chinese popular religion, fear of foreigners, marginalized people, and outsiders fueled rampant panics of "soul stealing" (*chiao-hun*) in 1768, 1810, and 1876. Soul stealers had the power to "call" a person's soul from his body; social outcasts, such as beggars, were perceived as so polluted or unlucky that they could commit magical terrorism by mere contagion. Miao (an ethnic minority) women are said to know a particular type of poison that forces men to remain in their border area against their will. Among southern Chinese, the minor-marriage bride, reared as a "sister" to her future husband and treated as a virtual slave within the family while she is growing up, is often accused of sorcery against the husband, the manifestation of which is his impotence.

In Japan witchcraft is closely associated with animals. Families who have reputedly kept foxes, snakes, or dogs in their homes attain levels of wealth and prestige others cannot; further, they can set their creatures upon their enemies. The stigma of association with witch animals can be caught merely by living in a house occupied by a former fox owner, for example; it is also a hereditary pollution, transmitted largely in the female line. Thus, the fox owner is intrinsically a witch simultaneously capable of bringing misfortune even unintentionally by contagion and capable of deliberate sorcery. This same set of symbols once had a much more positive valence. Foxes, dogs, and snakes were considered household guardians, who would behave benevolently if kindly treated. They have since evolved into uncanny, often frightful instruments of evil, so that spirits understood to have benefited one family are now seen as primarily harmful to others.

Southeast Asian Lisu highlands of Northern Thailand believe shamans and incantation masters can only be men; medicine women can only be women. By contrast, the witch or were-animals—persons so transformed that they may be forced, as though predators, to consume human flesh—can be of either gender. The killer of a witch becomes a witch, and people may catch the witchcraft (*phyiphea*) or the were-animal (*phwu swi*) spirit by contagion. Once infected, a person cannot be rid of it. For the Nage of Indonesia, witches (*polo,*

ata polo) are humans possessed of a special soul called *wa*, which can leave the body and travel in animal or human form in search of victims (Watson and Roy, 1975).

Turning to South Asia, witchcraft accusation is a form of scapegoating, motivated primarily by envy or fear. In particular, accusations of the "evil eye" are based on perceived envy or jealousy, emotions most often attributed to women. In some verses of the Sanskrit texts (c. 1500 B.C.E.) called the Vedas, women in particular were noted for the negative consequences of their envy, and their ability to cause harm to others. Incantations and spells were provided to offset the evil such women could occasion. Those with the most to envy are the most likely to occasion the evil eye or dabble in witchcraft; thus, the extremely low status of the high-caste Hindu widow makes her a natural object of suspicion. Tantric practice—conjurational techniques drawing on natural substances, invocations, and magical gestures— is often understood as witchcraft. In anthropological scholarship on Sri Lanka, the Sinhala term *huniyam* (Tamil, *suniyam*) is usually translated as "sorcery" rather than "witchcraft," yet it, too, conveys contagion; because it is often occasioned by poisonous or malicious talk, it is closely linked with South Asian cultural belief in the evil eye, mouth, and thought. *Huniyam* exorcists often place responsibility for an illness not merely on demons or ghosts but on other human beings who act in the immediate environment of the patient.

BIBLIOGRAPHY

Asian sources to date have focused on women and witchcraft only briefly within more general works or in journal articles. Philip Kuhn, *Soulstealers: The Chinese Sorcery Scare of 1768* (1990), brings to life in impressive detail and depth a time period of rampant witchcraft accusations against numerous marginalized people. Carmen Blacker, *The Catalpa Bow: A Study of Shamanastic Practices in Japan* (1975), focuses on the Japanese context and amply investigates women and gender issues. C. W. Watson and Roy Ellen, eds., *Understanding Witchcraft and Sorcery in Southeast Asia* (1993), is a collection of excellent essays and a useful introduction to a great diversity of practices. Among South Asian sources, F. G. Bailey, *The Witch-Hunt; or, The Triumph of Morality* (1994), is an interesting personal retrospective detailing events that unfolded subsequent to a young girl's death in Orissa, India, attributed to possible witchcraft. In *Ghosts: Life and Death in North India* (1993), Ruth S. Freed and Stanley A. Freed provide an enormously rich ethnography offering insights into the lives of numerous North Indian men and women regarding death, sorcery, and imputations of witchcraft. Bruce Kapferer, *A Celebration of Demons: Exorcism and the Aesthetics of Healing in Sri Lanka* (1983), examines from a thematic perspective webs of related concepts of sorcery, possession, and witchcraft; in a chapter on exorcisms and the symbolic identity of women the author delineates components within Sri Lankan women's cultural typification that serve to place them in a special and significant relation to the demonic.

CYNTHIA ANN HUMES

Witchcraft in Native America

Native American traditions of witchcraft are complex and vary widely from tribe to tribe. Therefore, it is difficult to generalize about such a diverse subject. What one can safely assert is that the standard European fantasy of the old hag riding a broomstick deviates strongly from the supernatural phantoms who haunt the indigenous imagination. In addition, the popular belief that witches congregate into satanic covens bound by a pact with the devil is not very widespread among Native American groups. It is a notion largely confined to the folklore of the southwestern United States and Mesoamerica.

A defining characteristic of the Native American witch is that it can change its shape into a variety of physical forms: a ball of fire, a predatory bird, a wolf, a lizard, or an insect. This ability to metamorphose is a cardinal trait of the Native American witch. In the folklore of the Navajo there are many tales about the *yenatho'si* (shape-shifter). Among the Cherokee, the perceived similarity between the nocturnal activities of malevolent beings and necrotic birds of prey led to the creation of the generic term, *tsi:sgili*, which can mean both witch and owl. Because the witch can assume any guise (human, animal, or other) it follows that accusations of witchcraft can be leveled at any individual, male or female, young or old in a community who exhibits suspicious behavior.

Native American witches might be regarded as genderless creatures who enjoy a parasitic relationship with human beings: they need our life force to survive. As a result, it is a widely held fear that witches hover about deathbeds and hospitals hoping to gain entrance and to feed themselves on the heart and entrails of the weak and the dying.

Unlike Glenda, the good witch who befriends Dorothy in *The Wizard of Oz*, Native American witches are thought to be inherently evil. Because of this dangerous predisposition, most Native American groups (with the notable exception of the Minominee) believe "the only good witch is a dead witch." Therefore, if their nefarious activities are exposed, Indian witches are swiftly put to death.

The Native American witch has the ability to cause harm in a variety of ways. First, witches have the power to magically cripple or kill a victim by projecting their thoughts or focusing their gaze. This fear of the "evil eye" is widespread throughout the Americas and is thought by some scholars to have originated in the ancient Near East.

Another means of transmitting harmful magic is to induce soul loss in the victim. The belief that the human body houses a multiplicity of souls or vital energies exists among various Indian groups such as the Aztecs in central Mexico, the Lakota Sioux in the Plains, and the Huron of the Great Lakes. Folk wisdom holds that this life-nurturing force can be snatched from the body by some menacing outside agent, particularly during periods of unconsciousness, with the result that the victim will weaken and die.

Through their wizardry, Native American witches are also thought to be able to magically implant objects into a victim's body. There is an astounding range of these intrusive substances enumerated in the ethnographic literature: buffalo hair, stones, lizards, splinters of wood, crystal fragments, feathers, and even yards of yarn. Again, this concern about object intrusion is not confined to the indigenous folklore of North America but has an almost universal distribution throughout Africa, Asia, Australia, and Europe.

Like the Afro-Caribbean vodou traditions, Native American witches are also thought to be capable of making human effigies or dolls and, by torturing this smaller image, to transfer the actual pain to its human counterpart. This use of imitative magic is a well-documented feature among the Minominee, the Iroquois, the Seminoles, and certain Pueblo cultures.

In Native American communities, there is a corresponding belief that witches collect human hair, fingernails, urine, or spittle and use these personal parts against their intended victim. This use of contagious magic is widely noted in the ethnohistorical writings of sixteenth-century European missionaries in Mexico, who relate how the Aztec sorcerers highly prized the severed left forearms of women who had died in childbirth and would use these captured limbs to cripple, paralyze, and otherwise harm their intended victims.

A witches magical powers can be counteracted by various techniques such as ringing a house with a protective layer of ceremonial smoke or by placing sharp objects in their path. The most effective means is to employ the services of a conjuror who, unlike the witch, must learn their arcane craft. Conjurers have the acquired power to dispatch these destructive creatures through certain magical rites.

BIBLIOGRAPHY

Kilpatrick, Alan. *The Night Has a Naked Soul: Witchcraft and Sorcery among the Western Cherokee.* 1997.

Kluckhohn, Clyde. *Navajo Witchcraft.* 1944.

Mair, Lucy. *Witchcraft.* 1969.

Nutini, Hugo G., and John M. Roberts. *Bloodsucking Witchcraft: An Epistemological Study of Anthropomorphic Supernaturalism in Rural Tlaxcala.* 1993.

Walker, Deward E., Jr., ed. *Witchcraft and Sorcery of the American Native Peoples.* 1989.

ALAN KILPATRICK

Contemporary Witchcraft Movement

While some neopagans object to the term *witchcraft,* many others refer to themselves as witches in an attempt to reclaim positive permutations of the word. Although the belief systems and practices of modern witches vary widely from group to group, there are generally consistent qualities: a female principle is deified, equal to or greater than a male principle; body and soul are interdependent; nature is sacred; individual will is sacred and powerful; time is cyclical; sexuality, spontaneity, imagination, and play are sacred and often incorporated into ritual; and the experience of pleasure is sacred—a positive life force. Worship can be monotheistic, polytheistic, or pantheistic.

Modern witchcraft movements, what many call "the Craft," frequently place themselves within the lineage of Western occultism. Some also claim witchcraft as a religion whose history dates back to Paleolithic times, a universal religion that worshiped the goddess of fertility and perhaps also the horned god (Adler, 1987; Starhawk, 1989). According to this myth-history, Christianity rose and persecuted the old religion, forcing it underground where small groups, families, and secret lineages maintained old practices and traditions until 1951, when the Witchcraft Laws in England were repealed and the old religion began to surface again.

Few now insist on the truth of this myth-history, though it was instrumental to the formation of the movement. Charles Leland's *Aradia, or the Gospel of the Witches* (1899) claimed discovery of a Diana-worshiping tradition in Italy that had survived from ancient times, passed down through a succession of female cult leaders. Margaret Murray's *The Witch-Cult in Western Europe* (1921), one of the earliest books in the canon of modern witches, popularized the idea of witchcraft as the surviving pre-Christian religion of Europe. Gerald B. Gardner, to whom can be traced many of the practices and rituals still used today (many witches, or Wiccans, are "Gardne-

rians"), claimed to have been initiated into a cult in England that had persisted from antiquity. For the purpose of preserving the knowledge of the cult, he published some of the knowledge he had supposedly learned in the form of a novel, *High Magic's Aid* (1949). After the repeal of the English Witchcraft Laws, he published *Witchcraft Today* (1954) and *The Meaning of Witchcraft* (1959), both important texts for those who took up the practice and belief of the Craft. Many have come to doubt the veracity of Gardner's claims, but his importance to the development of modern witchcraft movements is undeniable.

Much of the language of modern witchcraft comes from Gardner, such as the "Wiccan Rede": "An' it harm none, do what thou wilt." Doreen Valiente, initiated into the Craft by Gardner in 1953, authored several important texts, including *Where Witchcraft Lives* (1962) and *The Rebirth of Witchcraft* (1989), and is also credited with writing many of the creeds of modern witches, such as "The Charge of the Goddess" and "The Witches Creed." In 1974, a group calling themselves the Council of American Witches composed a list of fourteen principles titled the "Principles of Wiccan Belief" that has been widely circulated and cited since. Few witches, however, attribute great importance to individual authorship of such phrases and terminology. Craft language, much of which emulates ancient esoteric language, generally takes on the air of anonymous sayings containing wisdom of old.

Gardner's form of Wicca, the greatest influence for early Craft practitioners, depended upon a balance between male and female principles—god and goddess. Gardnerian ritual is led by a priest and priestess together. In the early 1970s, however, woman-centered practices and covens and the idea of the supremacy of a female principle—the Goddess—began to gain popularity. Women politically invested in feminism, such as the Hungarian-born Zusanna Budapest, who claims a family heritage of Craft and whose Los Angeles–based Susan B. Anthony Coven #1 (of which she is high priestess) stood as model for groups in the United States, and Starhawk, whose *The Spiral Dance* (1979) provided instructions for rituals and practices and was one of the first widely read books about the Craft, saw witchcraft as a religious haven for women. Offering women community, rituals, songs, female deity or deities, and positions of leadership, "spiritual feminism" empowered women by giving them prominence within the traditionally male-governed realm of religion.

For some groups or covens, the feminist dimension is expressed through separatism. In *The Holy Book of Women's Mysteries, Part 2* (1980), Budapest insists that "women have a greater spiritual need than men. Yet men capitalize on this instinct and set themselves up to govern women through religion. When we break the stronghold of men on women in religion, we can consider the revolution of women won" (p. 162). The manifesto of the Susan B. Anthony Coven #1 states that its members are opposed to teaching their magic and craft to men until the equality of the sexes becomes a reality. For others, the feminist spirit manifests in the celebration of freely expressed eros and sexuality, regardless of gender, sexual orientation, or body type; the wide range of modern witchcraft includes Dianic lesbian covens, queer faeries (mostly gay men), and eco-feminists.

Some feminists, however, argue that spiritual feminism is a religious movement, not a political one capable of achieving equal rights for women. According to such arguments, witchcraft—far outside mainstream culture—gives participants a false sense of having achieved feminist goals by giving them power in their own little world. Furthermore, the Craft, which deifies and worships the feminine, can be seen as biological essentialism by supporters of cultural determinism—the idea that sex and gender categories are artificial in and of themselves.

Modern witchcraft further allies itself with feminism by claiming a lineage of historical religious persecution of women. Witches identify with women who were tortured and killed by the Inquisition, burned at the stake in Salem, Massachusetts, or otherwise victimized by patriarchal religious leaders attempting to eradicate "women's magic"—ranging from the production of herbal remedies to the celebration of menstrual rituals to the working of esoteric magic. Modern witches also sometimes fear persecution themselves. Wary of the potential for harassment, hostility, and discrimination, many contemporary witches are closeted or underground. In the mid 1970s, the Aquarian Anti-Defamation League, founded by Isaac Bonewits and a number of other occultists, battled cases of discrimination on behalf of neopagans, witches, and other occultists. In some areas, however, the Craft has become more familiar and has thus achieved a greater degree of acceptability.

Ritual is of primary importance to modern witches. Margot Adler, whose *Drawing Down the Moon* (1979) stands as a definitive work on neopaganism, said in an interview posted on the "Voices of Women" website that "the primary purpose of ritual is to return us to our sense of attunement with the universe, to reconnect us with who we really are." Witches connect to the cycles of the earth through rituals that mark the rhythms of nature. The most important ritual days are the eight days of the year called Sabbats and the thirteen full moons, the Esbats. The Sabbats (Yule, Imbolg, Ostara, Beltane, Litha, Lughnasadh, Mabon, and Samhain), spaced evenly throughout the "Wheel of the Year," are divided into the quarters—the solstices and equinoxes—and the cross-quarters—marked by traditional festivals.

Members of the "Red Hoods" sect worship using the skulls of persons who have died in the Tiber River. Here they kneel before a skull they call "L'Avvocato," (the lawyer), Italy, 1956 (UPI/Corbis).

Sabbats and Esbats are the most powerful and auspicious days for working magic—ranging from producing personal experiences of transcendance to scrying to obtaining a lover's devotion. Some witches understand magic metaphorically; others are more literal-minded. The vast majority agree, however, that magic must result from a combination of energy and will. Ritual usually consists of raising energy, such as joy, sexual energy, or excitement. Physical activity, such as the popular spiral dance or dancing around a maypole, as well as theatrical devices, which invoke enthusiasm and emotion, can be used to energize ritual participants or, in the case of solitary practitioners, the person performing the ritual.

Raised energy channeled by will to certain effects is magic. Dion Fortune, a prominent figure in the history of contemporary witchcraft, called the techniques of magic "the art of changing consciousness at will" (Starhawk, p. 7). Starhawk, in *The Spiral Dance*, sees the "subtle, unseen forces that flow through the world" (p. 27) as malleable; one may sense and shape these forces by accessing deeper levels of consciousness beyond the rational. She defines a spell as "a symbolic act done in an altered state of consciousness, in order to cause a desired change. To cast a spell is to project energy through a symbol" (p. 124). Learning this art, according to Starhawk as well as to most witches, requires long, disciplined learning. Starhawk believes one must undergo a process of neurological repatterning, opening the gate between the conscious and unconscious mind, to learn magic. All witches agree that the ability to control and focus individual will is no easy matter; one must train one's mind to achieve this goal.

Contemporary witchcraft encompasses a widely diverse set of beliefs and practices, influenced by a great number of ideals and traditions. Attempting to rewrite, reconstruct, and remember a rich tradition of personal relationship to the divine, nature worship, and feminine power by piecing together bits of history and inventing the rest, witchcraft derives its power from play, eros, and imagination.

BIBLIOGRAPHY

Adler, Margot. *Drawing Down the Moon: Witches, Druids, Goddess-Worshippers, and Other Pagans in America.* 1979; 2d ed., 1987.

Bonewits, Philip Emmons Isaac. *Real Magic: An Introductory Treatise on the Basic Principles of Yellow Magic.* 1971.

Budapest, Zsuzanna. *The Feminist Book of Lights and Shadows.* 1976.

————. *The Holy Book of Women's Mysteries, Part 2.* 1980.

Clifton, Chas S., ed. *Witchcraft and Shamanism: Witchcraft Today, Book Three.* 1994.

Fortune, Dion. *Sane Occultism.* 1967.

Gardner, Gerald Brosseau. *The Meaning of Witchcraft.* 1959.

————. *Witchcraft Today.* 1954. Reprint, 1968.

Leland, Charles. *Aradia, or the Gospel of the Witches.* 1899. Reprint, 1974.

Luhrmann, T. M. *Persuasions of the Witch's Craft: Ritual Magic in Contemporary England.* 1991.

Murray, Margaret. *Witchcraft in Western Europe.* 1967.

Starhawk. *The Spiral Dance: A Rebirth of the Ancient Religion of the Goddess.* 1979. 10th anniversary ed. 1989.

Valiente, Doreen. *The Rebirth of Witchcraft.* 1989.

ON-LINE RESOURCES

Australian IRC#Witchcraft home page.
<http://fl.net.au/~jasmine/witchcraft.html>

Cauldrons & Broomsticks [U.S. on-line magazine].
<http://www.geocites.com/Athens/3038/cauldron.html>

Voices of Women website. <http://www.voiceofwomen.com/articles/margot.html>

White Dragon [U.K. on-line magazine].
<http://www.whitedragon.demon.co.uk/>

See also **Magic**; **Shamans**; **Wicca**.

JENNIFER DUMPERT

History of Study

Using a variety of interpretive models, anthropologists, historians, and historians of religion have made important contributions to the study of witchcraft and the overlapping phenomena of sorcery and magic. Feminist scholars, concentrating largely on the history of witchcraft in Europe, have skillfully uncovered the frequently overlooked gender dynamics of the practice of witchcraft, accusations lodged against purported practitioners, and the broader social, political, legal, and religious contexts.

Important studies of witchcraft have been done in several different cultural areas. Focusing on African tribal societies, anthropologists such as Mary Douglas, E. E. Evans-Pritchard, and Victor Turner have shown that witchcraft and sorcery beliefs are part of a broader social drama that includes attempts to explain illness and misfortune, to redress felt grievances, and to shift the balance of power within a social system. Detailed anthropological case studies, predominantly from Africa, demonstrate the variety of roles women play in witchcraft beliefs and practices. The diversity of witchcraft beliefs within individual cultures serves as a check against unwarranted generalizations about both witchcraft in general and about women's roles in witchcraft. Douglas and others have shown how crucial it is to understand the native beliefs about witchcraft within their specific local systems of classification. Recent case studies from Southeast Asia have added a wealth of data and also provoked a reinvestigation of the theoretical consensus formed in the 1970s on the basis of African examples, as did Max Marwick in his comparative studies of witchcraft in Africa and in Oceania. Explicit analysis of the dynamics of gender in cases discussed by anthropologists, however, is not as fully developed as feminist analysis of other examples of witchcraft.

Witchcraft and related phenomena in Ancient Near Eastern, classical Greek, and particularly Greco-Roman sources have received ample scholarly attention, for example in the broad surveys of Jeffrey Burton Russell and in focused, narrow studies such as those of Peter Brown. But the most important historical work for understanding women and witchcraft has focused on the European "witchcraze" of the sixteenth through eighteenth centuries. Although historians like Norman

Cohn, Hugh Trevor-Roper, and Keith Thomas have made successful use of analytical perspectives from the social sciences and psychology and have at least inadvertently documented the importance of gender in witchcraft beliefs, they have not employed gender as a primary interpretive category. Recent feminist scholarship, however, has brought to light new sources and proposed a number of striking reinterpretations. In her history of the European witch-hunts, for example, Anne Llewellyn Barstow identifies the European witchcraze as a "persecution by gender." She focuses on the violence, usually of a sexual nature, done to accused witches and observes that "having a female body was the factor most likely to render one vulnerable to being called a witch" (Barstow, 1994, p. 16). Although Barstow effectively links the European witch-hunts to the broader issue of violence against women, it remains to be seen whether that linkage can be sustained in cross-cultural analyses.

The contemporary revival of Wicca has also led some within the Craft to investigate its origins. Renewed interest has been directed to Margaret Murray's controversial argument that modern witchcraft represents the revival of pre-Christian nature religion. Opinion remains divided, however, about whether Murray's thesis represents likely fact, an open question, or, more likely, mythmaking in the guise of scholarship. Questions also remain about how important historical continuity is and should be to contemporary Wicca. Participants in the modern revival of witchcraft have contributed a number of important studies, notably Margot Adler's *Drawing Down the Moon* and Starhawk's several books, that document both ancient and contemporary practices. Some works produced by practitioners, however, display an uncritical credulity toward dubious historical claims. On the other hand, many neopagan thinkers acknowledge that contemporary witchcraft is a modern invention, and some praise such inventiveness for the creative freedom it affords. A few within the modern Craft movement have subjected their own tradition to rigorous scholarly scrutiny. Aidan Kelly, for example, has identified some of the material from which modern witchcraft has been constructed through careful investigation of founding figures, such as Gerald Gardner.

The study of witchcraft offers a diverse set of examples of women's religious experience. Though it includes ample evidence of atrocities from "the burning times," it also presents counterbalancing evidence of how women in many different societies have used witchcraft beliefs to assert their own power, critique oppressive social systems, provide tangible and spiritual benefits for themselves and their communities, and fashion alternative and empowering religious traditions.

BIBLIOGRAPHY

Adler, Margot. *Drawing Down the Moon: Witches, Druids, Goddess-Worshippers, and Other Pagans in America Today.* 1986. Rev. and exp. ed., 1997.

Barstow, Anne Llewellyn. *Witchcraze: A New History of the European Witch Hunts.* 1994.

Douglas, Mary, ed. *Witchcraft Confessions and Accusations.* 1970.

Kephart, M. J. "Rationalists vs. Romantics Among Scholars of Witchcraft." In *Witchcraft and Sorcery: Selected Readings.* Edited by Max Marwick. 1982. 2d ed., 1990.

Lewis, James R., ed. *Magical Religion and Modern Witchcraft.* 1996.

Marwick, Max, ed. Introduction to *Witchcraft and Sorcery: Selected Readings.* 1982.

Roper, Lyndal. *Oedipus and the Devil: Witchcraft, Sexuality, and Religion in Early Modern Europe.* 1994.

Russell, Jeffrey Burton. *A History of Witchcraft: Sorcerers, Heretics, and Pagans.* 1980.

Watson, C. W., and Roy Ellen, eds. *Understanding Witchcraft and Sorcery in Southeast Asia.* 1993.

EUGENE V. GALLAGHER

Wives

The role of wife has both provided women with status and entailed their subordination; it has served both to protect women and to legitimate their abuse. Because woman's role of wife is further complicated by her role as mother and guardian of home and family, no simple portrait can be drawn of the relationship so central to the lives of heterosexual women around the world.

Traditional religious understandings of the duties and obligations of wives sometimes have their origins in creation myths, sacred histories that narrate, in part, the creation of women and men and their purpose and place in the created order. Christians, for example, may look to the biblical creation myth in the book of Genesis and find in Adam and Eve the model of the first marriage. Traditionally, scholars and theologians such as Augustine, Thomas Aquinas, and Martin Luther focused on the second creation account (Gen. 2:4–3:24), arguing that woman was made both from man and for man. Eve is created out of Adam, and God gives Adam authority over her. Thus, her subordination is both natural (she is a derivative creature) and divinely ordained. Contemporary religious conservatives, such as

Jerry Falwell, continue this interpretation. However other scholars, such as Phyllis Trible, focus on the first creation account (Gen. 1:1–2:3), in which the creation of man and woman is simultaneous, and neither is described as having authority over the other.

In addition to creation myths, religious tradition, ritual, and legal codes have all served to shape the role of wife. Within traditional Judaism the goal of a woman is to become a wife and the rabbinic tradition has primarily defined a wife's duties and obligations. In Islam the hadith literature (sayings attributed to the Prophet Muhammad) has much to say about husband-wife relationships, for the most part tending to promote the subordination of women. Feminist Islamic scholars, such as Fatima Mernissi, also point to the fact that within the Qur'an itself, men are described as guardians of, sometimes interpreted as superior to, women. Within Chinese traditions most views of wives are from classical Confucian sources that subordinate women to their husbands. In Hinduism a wife's role is addressed in the Dharmashastras (sacred law books) in which negative comments about women outweigh positive ones; women are told they cannot do anything independently of a man and are instructed to serve their husbands like gods. Yet these and other textual statements about women were often ignored and are certainly not the whole story. For instance, Hindu wives are viewed as highly auspicious beings who bring prosperity to their husbands' home through fertility and their ritual activities for the benefit of their families.

Christianity is particularly problematic in relation to wives, since for a large part of its history Christianity tended to see marriage as a second-best choice; the spiritual ideal for both men and women was celibacy, though nuns were described as brides of Christ and the church. Within marriage, husbands (who held a superior position both by nature and divine ordinance) were exhorted to control their wives. Augustine, for example, claimed that a husband's authority was instituted by God, and that wives were obliged to obey. Martin Luther continued this argument in the sixteenth century, introducing demands for wifely obedience to Protestant theology.

Religious arguments such as these require wifely submission, and have led feminist scholars, such as Marie Fortune, to claim that male privilege has legitimated spousal abuse throughout the centuries. However others, like Riffat Hassan, point to the fact that religious tradition has also served to protect women within marriage. The marriage contract in both Judaism (*ketubah*) and Islam (*nikah*), for example, while it gives authority to the husband, also makes explicit the man's obligations to his wife. These include sexual pleasure, food, clothing, and monetary compensation to her if he predeceases or divorces her.

Because in all religious traditions procreation is seen as one of the primary purposes of marriage, the role and status of wife must be understood in relationship to the role of mother. It is in her role as mother (particularly of sons) that a wife is often accorded honor and respect. Within Islamic tradition children are understood as the wealth and future of the Muslim *ummah* (community), and thus women's role as childbearer is of particular importance. An oft-quoted saying from the hadith states that "Heaven lies under the feet of mothers." Chinese traditions honor the wife because she assures descendants for ancestor rites and family continuity. Within Christianity, with its historical preference for celibacy, procreation served to legitimate both sexuality and marriage. Martin Luther declared that procreation is a divine command for all persons, thus elevating woman's role as childbearer from its second-best status. Judaism does not share Christianity's negative attitude toward sex, instead maintaining that sexuality, marriage, and children are all good gifts from God; this emphasis on procreation is all the more important because of the historical experience of Jewish persecution. Hindu legal codes state that, in her role as mother, a wife brings the highest good for herself, her husband, and society; a Hindu woman at the time of her marriage may be offered the blessing, "May you have a hundred sons." Thus, insofar as wives are also mothers, they are accorded a degree of honor; women carry within their bodies the future of the religious community.

Despite a wife's status as subordinate, her role is also an essential one. So, for example, in Hebrew scripture the "excellent wife" is valued above jewels (Prov. 31); she manages all aspects of her husband's household, providing food, shelter, clothing, medical care, and economic resources. Her husband and children, we are told, bless her and praise her. Within Hinduism the *pativrata* (ideal wife) is typified in the epic literature, such as the *Rāmāyaṇa*, in which she is personified in the character of Sītā, the devoted wife of Rāma, the epic's hero.

Contemporary feminist theologians and scholars, such as Judith Plaskow, Fatima Mernissi, and Phyllis Trible, argue that the requirement of female subordination in marriage is the product of male-dominated tradition and exegesis, and offer an understanding of text and tradition that is more in keeping with modern commitments to equality, human rights, and female empowerment. Phyllis Trible, for example, argues that the Genesis 1 creation story provides evidence that an egalitarian tradition may be found in biblical literature that should serve as a paradigm for human relationship. Fatima Mernissi claims that demands for female subordination within Islam were the production of a "male elite," which perverted the egalitarian thrust of the Qur'an. Judith Plaskow challenges the hierarchical structure of traditional Judaism, which privileges men over women, and calls for a transformation of Judaism that begins with a feminist commitment to "the liberation of all women and all people."

BIBLIOGRAPHY

Ahmed, Leila. *Women and Gender in Islam: Historical Roots of a Modern Debate.* 1992.

Bumiller, Elisabeth. *May You Be the Mother of a Hundred Sons.* 1990.

Boyarin, Daniel. *Carnal Israel: Reading Sex in Talmudic Culture.* 1993.

Clark, Elizabeth A., and Herbert Richardson, eds. *Women and Religion: The Original Sourcebook of Women in Christian Thought,* Rev. ed. 1996.

Fiorenza, Elisabeth Schüssler. *In Memory of Her: A Feminist Theological Reconstruction of Christian Origins.* 1983.

Fortune, Marie M. *Sexual Violence: The Unmentionable Sin.* 1983.

Hassan, Riffat. "Muslim Women and Post-Patriarchal Islam." In *After Patriarchy: Feminist Transformations of the World Religions.* Edited by Paula M. Cooey, William R. Eakin, and Jay. B. McDaniel. 1991.

Keddie, Nikki, and Beth Baron. *Women in Middle Eastern History: Shifting Boundaries in Sex and Gender.* 1991.

Kinney, Anne Behnke, ed. *Chinese Views of Childhood.* 1995.

Leslie, Julia. ed. *Roles and Rituals for Hindu Women.* 1991.

Mernissi, Fatima. *The Veil and the Male Elite: A Feminist Interpretation of Women's Rights in Islam.* 1991.

Meyers, Carol. *Discovering Eve: Ancient Israelite Women in Context.* 1988.

Plaskow, Judith. *Standing Again At Sinai: Judaism from a Feminist Perspective.* 1990.

Stafford, Charles. *The Roads of Chinese Childhood.* 1995.

Trible, Phyllis. *God and the Rhetoric of Sexuality.* 1978.

Wegner, Judith Romney. *Chattel or Person? The Status of Women in the Mishnah.* 1988.

See also **Domestic Rites.**

ELIZABETH A. SAY

Womanist Traditions

Emerging first in the United States in the 1980s, *womanist,* a term coined by African-American poet and novelist Alice Walker, is the name given to that branch of the feminist movement addressing the issues of African-American women or other women of color.

Walker points to female traditions from the African-American community that have, through the ages, been made invisible in the progression and dominance of black and white male history. Some of the traditions she invokes are women's resistance and liberation traditions; female traditions of parenting girl children; the girl child's thirst for knowledge; women's way of appreciating nature, hospitality, women's culture, and women's emotional flexibility; and women's concern for the survival of an entire people, male and female. These womanist traditions are energized by women's love of spirit, of the folk, and of themselves.

Christian womanist ethicists, theologians, and biblical scholars have identified issues that must be addressed if black Christian theology is to include more than male experience and if feminist Christian theology is to include more than white women's experience. Thus, among ethicists, Katie Cannon emphasizes the historical and moral agency of African-American women in both the liberation struggles of African-Americans and the community building in both the larger society and in the church. Emilie Townes addresses the spirituality of black American women that has been absolutely essential in these women's work for social change. Marcia Riggs directs attention to the African-American women's organizations that have served as catalysts in the black liberation struggle. Among womanist theologians, Jacqueline Grant critiques the exclusivity of white feminist Christology while she explores the nature of black women's understanding of deity through the person of Jesus. As a corrective, she portrays Christ as a black woman. Kelly Brown Douglas has related Christ to black women, but she maintains that Christ can be seen in the face of black women involved in liberation struggle. However, Brown Douglas's Christology suggests that Christ can be seen in the face of anyone involved in the liberation struggle. The work of Delores S. Williams focuses on the issues of survival and quality of life. Informed by the womanist tradition of caring about the survival of a people (female and male), Williams gives attention to the themes of African-American women's surrogacy experience, the genocide history of black Americans, the anatomy of racism, and Christian theories of atonement. Karen Baker-Fletcher shows how a black foremother's biography yields material necessary for the construction of theology. Cheryl Kirk-Duggan is concerned to demonstrate how certain deposits of African-American religious culture (e.g., the spiritual songs) reflect the community's understanding of evil.

The discipline of biblical studies has also experienced the introduction of womanist ideas and methods. Womanist scholars have provided reinterpretations of biblical stories that take seriously black Christian women's experiences and traditions. Biblical scholar Renita Weems focuses on and reinterprets biblical stories so that the necessity of sisterhood is appreciated across cultural differences. Weems has also shown how domestic violence against women can be supported by the language in the Hebrew Bible book of Hosea. Clarice Martin interprets the household codes in the Christian scriptures so that the sexism in the domestic allusions in the story is clearly revealed to black women, many of whom are domestic workers.

These womanist scholars in ethics, theology, and biblical studies have found in Alice Walker's definition the building blocks they need to construct Christian theology compatible with the life experience and history of African-American women. As black women's traditions, these building blocks reflect images and ideas of resistance, liberation, praise and celebration, female power and authority, as well as love and spiritual commitment. Womanist scholars in religious and theological studies will undoubtedly continue to produce significant ideas informed, in large measure, by black women's traditions now emerging from the underside of history.

BIBLIOGRAPHY

Baker-Fletcher, Karen. *A Singing Something: Womanist Reflections on Anna Julia Cooper.* 1994.

Cannon, Katie. *Black Womanist Ethics.* 1988.

Douglas, Kelly Brown. *The Black Christ.* 1994.

Grant, Jacqueline. *White Women's Christ and Black Women's Jesus: Feminist Christology and Womanist Response.* 1989.

Kirk-Duggan, Cheryl. *Exorcizing Evil: A Womanist Perspective on the Spirituals.* 1996.

Riggs, Marcia. *Arise, Awake, and Act: A Womanist Call for Black Liberation.* 1994.

Townes, Emilie. *In a Blaze of Glory: Womanist Spirituality as Social Witness.* 1995.

Walker, Alice. *In Search of Our Mothers' Gardens: Womanist Prose.* 1983.

Weems, Renita. *Battered Love: Marriage, Sex, and Violence in the Hebrew Prophets.* 1995.

———. *Just a Sister Away: A Womanist Vision of Women's Relationships in the Bible.* 1988.

William, Delores S. *Sisters in the Wilderness: The Challenge of Womanist God-Talk.* 1993.

DELORES S. WILLIAMS

Woman's Bible, The

In 1886 Elizabeth Cady Stanton, already well established as a leading feminist reformer of nineteenth-century North America, launched a project to revise and comment on the parts of the Bible that dealt with women. Her original plan was very ambitious, involving three committees of women scholars. The first subcommittee was to work on more accurate and inclusive translations of the Greek and Hebrew; the second was charged with commenting on the historical and literary background of the text; and the third, largest, committee was to comment on the "plain English" versions of the Old and New Testaments. To Stanton's great disappointment, her enthusiasm for the revision of the Bible was not shared by other women reformers of her day, and this grand scheme never unfolded as she had envisioned it. Some of the most learned and prominent women approached by Stanton (Julia Ward Howe, Antoinette Brown Blackwell) declined her repeated invitations to participate. Twentieth-century historians have suggested that this was mostly the result of fear, since even famous women did not want to be seen associated with a project as radical as revision of the Bible. The project went forward, but with a smaller, less expert, and somewhat uneasy coalition of authors, with Stanton herself taking responsibility for much of the end result.

The first part of *The Woman's Bible*, comments on the passages of the Pentateuch dealing most clearly with women, was published serially in 1895 in the periodical *Woman's Tribune*. It attracted immediate attention of the most acrimonious sort from all corners, including from Stanton's fellow feminists. The book version of Part I followed in the same year in an edition by the European Publishing Company in New York. Part II, covering selected books of the Bible from Joshua to Revelation as well as an essay on the Kabbalah and an Appendix of letters pertaining to the project, appeared in 1898. Like Part I, it was organized in the form of comments on selected passages of scripture that dealt most evidently with women's experience or images of women. *The Woman's Bible* Parts I and II was an instant bestseller, running through seven printings in six months; then it sank into obscurity. Historian Kathi Kern has demonstrated that *The Woman's Bible* was pivotal in opening up questions of religious liberty to feminist inquiry, but the impact was delayed by almost a century. In fact, in Stanton's own time the project was ultimately understood as a failure and was directly responsible for ending Stanton's career as a leader in the feminist movement.

With the rise of the second wave of feminism in the twentieth century, *The Woman's Bible* once again attracted the attention of reformers and critics of the patriarchy. Two reprintings with original introductions appeared in 1974, and yet another edition was published in 1993. The irony is that *The Woman's Bible* has been in print longer in the late twentieth century than it was in the late nineteenth century.

Indeed, the centennial of the original publication of *The Woman's Bible* inspired two multiauthored publications continuing Stanton's project of commenting on the Bible from a feminist point of view. Carol Newsome and Sharon Ringe's *The Woman's Bible Commentary* (1992) does what Stanton was unable to do in that it brings together leading women scholars with the linguistic skills to offer expert commentaries on each book of the Bible from the point of view of feminism. This work also contains essays on the daily life and religious context of women in various periods of Jewish and Christian history, as well as some attention to noncanonical works. Elisabeth Schüssler Fiorenza's *Searching the Scriptures: A Feminist Commentary* (2 vols., 1993–1994) rethinks and transforms *The Woman's Bible.* In the first volume, a series of essays considers the theoretical implications of race, class, and ethnicity and the difficulty of auto critique; in the second volume, the commentaries transgress canonical boundaries by including a number of gnostic and other extracanonical texts and are organized according to their relationship to Sophia, the female manifestation of wisdom. These twentieth-century projects, both of which include the participation of Jewish feminists, honor *The Woman's Bible* as an idea ahead of its time.

BIBLIOGRAPHY

The Woman's Bible has been reprinted at least three times since 1974: Elizabeth Cady Stanton, *The (Original) Feminist Attack on the Bible (The Woman's Bible)*, introduction by Barbara Welter (1974); from the Coalition on Women and Religion: Elizabeth Cady Stanton and the Revising Committee, *The Woman's Bible: Part I The Pentateuch, Part II Judges, Kings, Prophets and Apostles* (1974), with comments by members of the Coalition; Elizabeth Cady Stanton, *The Woman's Bible*, foreward by Maureen Fitzgerald (1993).

Late-twentieth-century commentary projects inspired by *The Woman's Bible* are: *The Woman's Bible Commentary*, edited by Carol A. Newsome and Sharon H. Ringe (1992); and *Searching the Scriptures:* Vol. 1., *A Feminist Introduction;* Vol. 2., *A Feminist Commentary*, edited by Elisabeth Schüssler Fiorenza with the assistance of Shelly Matthews (1993–1994).

The only book-length study of *The Woman's Bible* is Kathi Lynn Kern, *The Woman's Bible: Gender, Religion and Ideology in the Work of Elizabeth Cady Stanton, 1854–1902*, Ph.d. diss., University of Pennsylvania (1991).

E. ANN MATTER

Womb

The term *womb* (synonymous with the Latin term *uterus*) derives from the Old High German word for belly (*wamba*) and is thus associated with hidden growth, birth, and the inner creativity of the female. The womb becomes a religious symbol when it conveys the creative power of the divine as hidden, mysterious, inner, and involving process or growth. Womb symbolism is found in a great variety of religious expression: in myth, ritual, religious art, and architecture. Three related themes are commonly associated with womb symbolism: the creation of life, the rebirth of the dead through burial, and transformation involving the death of the old and emergence of a new self.

CREATION

In religious art and myths alike the womb is a common symbol for the origin of life, found in the oldest extant creation myths as well as in the tales of nonliterate cultures of the modern period. In the *Ṛgveda*, oldest of the sacred texts of India, a primordial act of incest between the unnamed father and his daughter results in an embryo that the father places in the womb that exists in the space between heaven and earth. The Dogon of Africa tell how creation began when God had intercourse with his wife: water, the divine semen, penetrated the womb of the earth and twins were created.

Creation is not always regarded as a sexual act, however. The Barasan of South America relate how the ancestors were created in the womb of Romi Kumu (Vagina Woman), a Supreme Being who is identified with the sky and who has no male partner. A common theme in North American mythology is the "emergence myth"—which locates the primordial womb within the body of the earth.

DEATH AND REBIRTH

Death is often regarded as a return to the primordial womb. For the Desana of South America, Ahpikondiá, the cosmic womb, is the third and lowest zone of the universe. The invisible Sun emerged from this womb so as to fashion the world, and he returned there after finishing his creation. The souls of the dead likewise journey to this paradise, whose name means "river of milk." The seafaring Warao, also of South America, see life as a gradual process of dying, or journeying back to the womb of the goddess Dauarani.

Rituals that are based on the view of death as a return to the womb include the Krahó (South American) pilgrimage to the maternal village, undertaken so as to die in the maternal matrix. Most common, however, is burial of the corpse in a grave that is clearly modeled on the womb. For example, the so-called passage graves of prehistoric western Europe are constructed with stones to represent a long narrow passage that ends in a womb-shaped central chamber.

TRANSFORMATION

Sometimes the womb as symbolic source of the universe points to the ongoing transformation of the cosmos as a whole. In tantric Buddhism the so-called womb mandala, based on the *Mahāvairocana Sūtra*, is a graphic representation of the cosmic processes of transformation, with Vairocana, the Great Sun Buddha, at the center. Self-realization, the birth or liberation of the transcendent self, is the goal of many who practice spiritual disciplines. In such practices the symbolic womb may be one component of a spiritual body. For example, the *tathāgata-garbha* in Yogācāra Buddhism is the womb of Buddhahood that exists in all sentient beings. In addition to the seeds generated by past actions, the *tathāgata-garbha* contains the ungenerated seed of the enlightened self, something like the potential to become a Buddha. Similarly, in Chinese alchemy, self-realization involves conceiving and nourishing an immortal fetus within the womblike cavities of the spiritual body. In the gnostic Christian homily "Exegesis on the Soul" from the Hellenistic period, the immortal soul has a womb, which through desire for cosmic experience becomes externalized, like the male genitalia. Having lost its natural receptivity to the divine, the womb compels the soul to search in vain for fulfillment in the world. Only after it is reestablished within does the womb provide a receptacle for the divine seed, which unites with the soul in order to restore her to her original immortal nature.

BIBLIOGRAPHY

Aubert, Jean-Jacques. "Threatened Wombs: Aspects of Ancient Uterine Magic." *Greek, Roman, and Byzantine Studies* 30 (Autumn 1989): 421–449.

Eliade, Mircea. *Rites and Symbols of Initiation: The Mysteries of Birth and Rebirth.* (Originally, *Birth and Rebirth.*) 1958.

Gimbutas, Marija. *The Language of the Goddess.* 1989.

Ritner, Robert K. "A Uterine Amulet in the Oriental Institute Collection." *Journal of Near Eastern Studies* 43 (July 1984): 209–221.

Sullivan, Lawrence E. *Icanchu's Drum: An Orientation to Meaning in South American Religions.* 1988.

BEVERLY MOON

Women and Religion

Monotheistic Traditions and Orientalism

Orientalism is a Western field of study that posits the existence of essential differences between the Occident (West) and the Orient (East) that are crucial for the understanding of each. Orientalism has deeply influenced the historical understanding of monotheistic religious traditions and also has important implications for understanding the role of women in those traditions.

In its discussion of these differences, Orientalism maintains a "flexible positional superiority" (Said, 1979, p. 7) that places the West in a series of relations with the Orient without ever losing its relative upper hand. In the modernization theories of Daniel Lerner and Manfred Halpern, the Occident is presented as building modern, secular societies that are less dependent on religion and therefore able to move closer to gender equality. In contrast, the Orient is represented as maintaining traditional societies that continue to uphold and emphasize religion and hence greater acceptance of gender inequality. Whereas Christianity is compatible with rationality and egalitarianism, Eastern religions fall short on both counts. They are either prone to violence, fanaticism, or irrationality, as is thought to be the case with Islam, or to the mystical, as is thought to be the case with Southeast Asian religions. Both tendencies are seen as contributing to obstacles that undermine the ability of these societies to equalize gender roles.

However, Judaism, Christianity, and Islam all trace their regional and historical roots to the Middle East. Despite their distinct beliefs, rituals, and narratives, they share an overlapping set of male and female religious figures and tales. The histories of these three dominant monotheistic traditions are also very much intertwined. They share a long history of religious competition and political rivalry. Christianity replaced Judaism and was itself replaced in the seventh and eighth centuries by Islam as the religion of the majority in the Middle East.

Geographers suggest that the reason Judaism and Christianity are categorized as Western religions has less to do with where they emerged and more to do with where they historically spread: to Europe and North and South America. In contrast, Islam, which has spread largely to Asia and to a lesser extent to Africa, is understandably categorized as an Oriental or non-European religion. But the geography of these religions has changed over time and no longer provides accurate bases for West–East dichotomies. During the

1980s and the 1990s, Islam's geographic stretch turned westward with the settlement in Europe and North America of large numbers of Muslim immigrants from Asia, the Middle East, and Africa. Indeed, Islam is the fastest growing religion in the United States, a fact that supports Islam's Western social credentials.

Until the last quarter of the nineteenth century, Judaism was treated as a religious and cultural "other" in Christian Europe. The rise of Zionism, as a modern nationalist movement that emerged and gathered support in Europe for the goal of building a homeland and eventually a state for the Jews outside of Europe, contributed to the redefinition of the old antagonistic relationship. Zionist mobilization in Europe stressed the religious and the cultural affinities between Christianity and Judaism in a new representation, that is, the Judeo-Christian tradition. Christian guilt over the Holocaust in the United States led to the wide use of and cultural reference to the Judeo-Christian tradition as a basis for the management of past and present religious and cultural tensions between the two religions. This term has fallen into disfavor because of the way it subordinates Judaism to Christianity as the more dominant monotheistic religion.

In contrast, Orientalist representations of Islam stressed its dubious status as a monotheistic religion and its essential opposition to the two other monotheistic religions. This particular negative definition of a monotheistic Islam became an integral part of the historical discussions of what defined Western religious traditions. It justified the inclusion of Islam in the discussion of Western religious traditions as an oppositional other. Most discussions of Islam have internalized these attacks by a Christian West and feel obliged to spend considerable time addressing these views (Esposito, 1992).

There is considerable literature produced first by Christian missionary women and later by U.S. feminists, such as Robin Morgan and Letty Cottin Pogrebin, that makes comparisons between Christian and to a lesser extent Jewish women on the one hand and Muslim women on the other. The benevolent character of the former religions and societies is contrasted to the oppressiveness and intolerance of the latter. Sarah Johnson, a nineteenth-century Christian missionary woman, emphasized the fact that Christian men and women were spiritual equals in their possession of a soul, whereas she believed Muslim women were considered religiously inferior to Muslim men. Because menstruation undermined Muslim women's ability to perform certain religious rituals, it provided a basis for their religious inequality. Johnson wrote that Islamic tolerance of abortion and varied forms of contraception revealed a measure of the religion's lack of respect for human life and the licentiousness of its women. In Johnson's view, Christian and Jewish women were considered socially privileged because the monogamous marital bond was defined as holy. This was said to contribute to the stability of Christian and Jewish families. In contrast, Muslim women were represented as the victims of polygamous families with high divorce rates, which produced unstable Muslim families full of discord.

When divorce laws were liberalized in many Western societies in the 1970s, with U.S. divorce rates reaching very high levels, Nikki Keddie and Lois Beck (1978) interpreted these social changes as a measure of the new marital freedom enjoyed by Christian women in the family. They saw Muslim women as less liberated because personal status laws denied women the equal right to divorce. The importance of a stable family unit was no longer a staple of discussion.

Finally, when abortion was legalized in some Western societies, reproductive rights emerged in U.S. feminist discourse as the standard by which the superiority of Western societies and religions and the inferiority of Islamic ones could be reasserted. Muslim women's lack of legal access to abortion was used in international conferences such as the Cairo population conference (1994) as evidence of their continued subordination in Islamic societies.

As majority-Christian and Jewish societies claimed the mantle of modernity, the discussion of the religious rights of women became increasingly supplemented with that of the civil and political rights of women. Keddie and Beck used women's increased participation in the economic and political arenas as a new measure of Muslim women's continued subordination in modernizing society. In the case of Israel, public political discourse gave symbolic importance to the fact that Golda Meir became prime minister of Israel in the 1970s and that Israeli women were required to serve in the army alongside men.

In contrast, the Western media tended to highlight the restrictiveness of Islamic societies and their definitions of women's roles within the family and outside it. A great deal of space was devoted to purdah. The fact that Saudi women were prevented by law from driving provided anecdotal evidence of the overly patriarchal character of Islamic law.

In Israeli public debates on development the binary opposition between West and East was internalized in discussion about the Palestinians (whether Muslim or Christian) and Mizrahi Jews from North Africa and the Middle East. These groups' subordination in modern

Israeli society was explained by their origins in "primitive," "backward," "underdeveloped," and "premodern" societies, that is, societies of the East. Their cultures were specifically described as sexist and reactionary, forcing women to have large families.

The Orientalist representation of gender in Judaism, Christianity, and Islam must continue to be problematized. Its normative and ahistorical discussions of the relationship between religion and society must be replaced by historically grounded studies of how religious rules and interpretations have changed over time and left their imprint on the status of women. Rather than set Islam and Muslim women as "separate" in this discussion, one must simultaneously discuss what Islam shares with other monotheistic religions as well as its differences from them. In this new discourse, one must accommodate the perspectives of various groups of women, the clergy, and public figures as they struggle to shape the spiritual and social aspects of gender within the family and the society at large.

BIBLIOGRAPHY

Esposito, John L. *The Islamic Threat: Myth or Reality?* 1992.

Halpern, Manfred. *The Politics of Social Change in the Middle East and North Africa.* 1963.

Hatem, Mervat. "Secularist and Islamist Discourses on Modernity in Egypt and the Evolution of the Postcolonial Nation-State." In *Islam, Gender and Social Change.* Edited by Yvonne Yazbeck Haddad and John L. Esposito. 1998.

Johnson, Sarah Barclay. *Hadji in Syria.* 1858.

Kadi, Joanna, ed. *Food for our Grandmothers.* 1994.

Keddie, Nikki, and Lois Beck. "Introduction." In *Women in the Muslim World.* Edited by Lois Beck and Nikki Keddie. 1978.

Lerner, Daniel. *The Passing of Traditional Society: Modernizing the Middle East.* 1958.

Morgan, Robin. *Sisterhood Is Global.* 1984.

Pogrebin, Letty Cottin. "Antisemitism in the Women's Movement." *Ms. Magazine* (June 1982): 45ff.

Said, Edward. *Orientalism.* 1978.

Sharoni, Simona. "Motherhood and the Politics of Women's Resistance." In *Politics of Motherhood: Activist Visions from Left to Right.* Edited by Alexis Jetter. 1997.

Shohat, Ella, "The Narrative of the Nation and the Discourse of Modernization: The Case of the Mizrahim." *Critique* (1997): 3–18.

———. "Sepharadim in Israel: Zionism from the Standpoint of its Jewish Victims." *Social Text* 19–20 (1988): 1–36.

Spellberg, D. A. "Writing the Unwritten Life of the Islamic Eve: Menstruation and the Demonization of Motherhood." *International Journal of Middle East Studies* 28 (1996): 305–324.

See also Education: Teaching Women and World Religions; History of Religions; Orientalism.

MERVAT F. HATEM

In The East

Throughout the history of Eastern religions the first approach to their study occurred with insiders (Hindus, say, or Buddhists) discussing with other insiders doctrines, rituals, and so forth in what was largely a male-to-male discussion. The second approach entailed discussions between outsiders occurring during the colonial period. Westerners living in colonized countries wrote about Eastern religions—sometimes critically, sometimes romantically—for other Westerners back home. They were influential in introducing the study of Eastern religions, languages, and cultures into European universities. Like the insider-to-insider phase, this one was also largely androcentric. The third approach, with outsiders addressing insiders, began with first-wave Western feminists criticizing Asian religions for their subordination and disenfranchisement of women.

In India this proceeded directly via missionary women (some of whom were first-wave feminists who had gone abroad searching for greater freedom), via British suffragists who were linked to Indian women's organizations, and via authors such as Katherine Mayo (who argued in her 1927 book *Mother India* that male dominance in India has been responsible for all its problems—disease, poverty, illiteracy, etc.). First-wave feminism also influenced India indirectly via the British Raj. Even though between 1772 and 1947 the British (with the collaboration of Indian reformers) introduced laws forbidding female infanticide, sati, and child marriage as well as raising the age of marriage, permitting the remarriage of widows, and giving women better inheritance rights, they refused women the vote. This was partly because British women themselves did not gain it until 1928 and partly because the traditional subordination of women was a major justification for the need for British rule itself.

The colonial period in China witnessed growing poverty and loss of morale. Colonial rulers and Chinese reformers alike blamed Confucianism for societal problems, especially those strictures related to women, such as female seclusion, footbinding, infanticide, slavery, and marital constraints. (Because both Hinduism and

Confucianism were family-based religions and used their authority to promote gender norms, the critique of marriage by outsiders and their native collaborators amounted to a devastating critique of the religion itself.) Another Western source for feminist influence on Asian religions is Marxism (China under Mao, but also Marxist movements in Vietnam, Indonesia, Sri Lanka, and India) or its socialist offshoots (India under Nehru), both of which inspired more legal and political reforms. Whereas the spirit of reform in Hinduism has led to some stunning reversals—male gurus, for instance, began passing on their spiritual mantles to female disciples; women began studying and chanting the Vedas; menstrual taboos disappeared; and restrictions that had prevented women from pursuing spiritual paths were removed—the change in women's status in Chinese religions has been slower, mainly because the Communists made the religions themselves nonviable (closing monasteries, for instance, and promoting atheism). Women played a major, underground role to help their religions survive during the Cultural Revolution; yet even after 1979, when the legitimacy of religions was recognized again, they did not achieve equality in religious institutions, thanks to lack of male support, Communist focus on class rather than gender analysis, and a conservative reassertion of the Confucian family system in the 1990s.

The status of women in Japan has also been indirectly influenced by the West on account of the Allied occupation after Japan's defeat in World War II. One Japanese response to the profound identity crisis and dislocation that ensued was the development of the "new religions." Many of these were founded by charismatic Japanese women who became possessed or had special powers by which they could help people in trouble. Their leadership roles have sometimes been taken over by men; nevertheless, the new religions have remained popular with women. Western capitalism and secularism have also had an impact on the lives of Japanese women, though their move into the realm of public work has occurred slowly.

The impact of outsider on insider has also occurred in the West, because Asian students have taken courses on Asian religions in Western universities, especially after the economic diaspora from East to West. Gradually since the 1970s, Western female scholars trained mainly as historians of religions have begun to teach Asian religions. With this demographic change in the professorate (a development parallel to the second wave of feminism from the 1960s, which encouraged the education and professionalism of women), the interest in Asian women's religion grew enormously.

With their knowledge of scriptural and classical languages, these scholars have been combing the primary sources for mention of women through all periods of history. They have also been reading between the lines for further clues to penetrate women's "silent" history.

Research on women and religion has included not only the scriptural and religio-legal norms for domestic space (daughter, wife and mother, widow) but also alternative female roles in public space, which, depending on the religion, can be poetess, philosopher, teacher, saint, heroine, temple dancer, musician, patron, courtesan, adept on spiritual paths, reformer, novice, nun, or abbottess. Scholars have translated and interpreted texts written by women and biographies, hagiographies, inscriptions, or other sources about them, and examined the historical contexts of women's lives, including the vicissitudes of temple or monastery life. They have also studied women's religious status: can they achieve the higher stages of the spiritual path, salvation in this life, leadership, and the religious, ideal person? Divine female figures—Hindu goddesses, Buddhist female bodhisattvas, and Taoist female celestials—have also been of considerable interest, especially as they pertain to the question of whether they can be correlated with a higher social status for women.

Whereas postmodernism in the West has encouraged the study of unofficial religion (vernacular, experiential, folk, noncanonical) over official religion (classical or literary, reason-oriented, institutional, canonical), the study of Eastern religions hews to the "classical" approach. Nevertheless, the meager information about women in the historical record and the desire for more positive models have inspired some to turn their attention to the anthropology of religion to document the religious lives and agency of real women (vows; folk songs; stories; rituals for fertility, husband's longevity, and children's welfare; purification and decoration of ritual space; preparation of ritual and festival food; asceticism; states of possession; and manipulation of the androcentric religion and its politics for their own ends), thus supporting the idea of women "naming their own reality." And the feminist call to support minorities has encouraged anthropological study of rural, low-class and low-caste or tribal women.

In general, scholars of religion take a phenomenological approach: they bracket out cultural, religious, and even feminist values in order to provide nuanced descriptions based on emic (insider) categories. Still, research questions and methods are usually informed by the larger context of women's studies and feminism, and there are the occasional methodological comments, critical reflections, or comparisons with Western examples. Occasionally, Western feminist interests such as immanence over transcendence, human relationships over ascetic isolation, ecological concern over technological advance, and embodied concepts over disembodied, abstract ones have inspired the choice of research topics and informed scholarly analysis.

The fourth approach to the study of Eastern religions is that of insider to outsider (and via outsiders sometimes back to insiders). Debates over religion by insider men with other men, apologetic or polemic (for instance, Buddhists with Hindus, Confucianists, Taoists, and Shintoists), have been common in the history of Asian religions. Asian men and women have studied, in token numbers, at Western universities since the 1960s (partly because religion was not a recognized academic discipline in Asian countries). Only in the 1990s did second-generation, immigrant Asian women begin to enter the field or related ones in greater numbers, contributing to the interdisciplinary forum on women and Asian religions. Asian female scholars have criticized the excesses of colonialism's religious and cultural critiques, which did not take responsibility for their own role in the economic exploitation of Asian countries and the cultural havoc and identity crisis left in colonialism's wake. They have pointed out problems of anachronism and cross-cultural biases that involve superimposing modern, Western categories such as equality and rights on ancient and alien cultures. Finding inspiration in Edward Said's criticism of Orientalism (*Orientalism,* 1978) but also in the womanist and Mujerista critiques of white, middle-class feminism, they have criticized the views of some Western, female scholars as colonial, Orientalist, or Eurocentric, that is, lacking an understanding of the complexity of Eastern religions and perpetuating colonial stereotypes (though their own critiques are sometimes based on those of Western scholars). They have also used their scholarly credentials to speak to members of their own religious communities, pressing for reforms, especially more opportunities for religious education and leadership positions in the public world still dominated by men. The issue of insider status is made more complex today because many people who claim insider status are, in fact, not religious but secular, and because some are Western converts to Asian religions. Using the rhetoric of pluralism and syncretism, some Western women have been looking to Asian symbolism, especially that of goddesses and androgyny, to enhance Western spirituality movements such as neopaganism.

BIBLIOGRAPHY

No single published work explicitly focuses on the methodologies used to study women and religion, though one is forthcoming: Arvind Sharma, ed., *The Interface between Women's Studies and Methodology in the Study of Religion.* For overviews of methodological issues, see Serene Jones, "'Women's Experience' Between a Rock and a Hard Place: Feminist, Womanist and *Mujerista* Theologies in North America," *Religious Studies Review* 21 (1995): 19–25. Rita Gross, *Feminism and Religion: An Introduction* (1996) discusses a number of methodological debates on the topic inclusive of reflections on the study of women in Asian religions. Also helpful are methodological discussions in the introductions to important studies of women and world religions: Caroline Walker Bynum, Stevan Harrell, and Paula Richman, eds., *Gender and Religion: On the Complexity of Symbols* (1986); Ursula King, ed., *Religion and Gender* (1995); Nancy Auer Falk and Rita M. Gross, eds., *Unspoken Worlds: Women's Religious Lives in Non-Western Cultures* (1980); Carol P. Christ and Judith Plaskow, eds., *Womanspirit Rising: A Feminist Reader in Religion* (1979); and Serinity Young, ed., *An Anthropology of Sacred Texts By and About Women* (1993).

See also Colonialism and Postcolonialism; Feminisms; Mujerista Tradition; New Religions: In East Asia; Orientalism; Womanist Traditions; Women and Religion: Monotheistic Traditions and Orientalism.

KATHERINE K. YOUNG

Women as Heroines

Heroines can be divided broadly into those the (patriarchal) culture presents as models of heroic female virtues and those selected by women themselves as exemplars of liberating behavior. The two categories are not necessarily exclusive. Joan of Arc of France (1412–1431); the Trung sisters of Vietnam, warrior maidens and corulers who defended their country against the Chinese (c. 39–42 C.E.); Queen Boudica of Britain, who led her people in battle against the Roman invaders (c. 25–62 C.E.): all represent heroines who simultaneously serve the interests of society and offer tantalizing glimpses into a life beyond gender limitation.

Women took inspiration from certain goddess and mythical figures. In Western culture inspiring figures were in particular Diana, perceived as independent and free-spirited; Athena, who as goddess of wisdom affirmed women's intellects; and the Amazons, whose very existence proved that women could live autonomously. But by and large, heroines exhibit few of the sacred elements common to their male counterparts. Heroes characteristically represent the apotheosis of male value and thus are essentially a conservative force. Both ancient Greek and Shakespearean tragic heroes suffer and even die to restore balance in a universe that is the projection of patriarchy. Their deeds tend to confirm conventional definitions of masculinity; whereas the "woman hero is an image of antithesis. . . . [As] Western culture's opposing self, the woman hero uncovers fractures in the surface of reality, contradictions in its structure, gaps in its social ideology" (Edwards, 1984, p. 4).

Heroines or heroes produced by oppression are often revolutionary—they subvert or overthrow and thus fulfil Joseph Campbell's definition that the hero slays the dragon or monster of the status quo (Campbell, 1957). An important part of the heroic journey for women is to escape "from the limiting assumptions about appropriate female and male behavior . . . in defining [a]truly human—and truly humane—pattern of heroic action" (Pearson and Pope, 1981, p. 5). Sojourner Truth's (c. 1797–1883) deeds and words confront those who would relegate women to weakness and passivity; Judith (fourth century B.C.E.) saves the Hebrews from conquest by cutting off the head of the enemy general Holofernes. Lakshmi Bai, the rani of Jhansi, leads her troops against the British forces sent to seize her kingdom on the pretext of mismanagement. She died in battle at the age of 28 (1858).

Quite commonly, the mythic hero dies after having lived a short life of exemplary virtue. Often the warrior heroine is prodded by extreme circumstances into a burst of gender-defying activity, which subsides when the crisis has passed. In the absence of able-bodied men, fourteen-year-old Madeleine de Verchères of Quebec organized the defense of her village in 1692 against an Iroquois attack. The warrior maiden Hua Mulan (c. 581–618) adopted male clothing and fought valiantly for the emperor in her father's place. She refused a court appointment to high office to return home. When her former comrades-in-arms visited, they were amazed to discover she was a woman. Her name has long been synonymous with heroine in China. During World War II, Odette Churchill, who liked to describe herself as a humble housewife, was one of Britain's most effective agents in France. She was awarded the George Cross for bravery having kept her silence under torture and imprisonment. After the war, she was content to return to her private life at home.

In the early years of Christianity, numerous women died heroic deaths as martyrs to the new faith. Gender was not a factor in mass executions. Particular tales of heroism such as those of saints Catherine of Alexandria,

The fourth-century martyr Catherine of Alexandria is depicted before the Roman emperor Maxentius after she converted his wife to Christianity. Legend tells that Catherine heroically retained her faith despite being sentenced to death (Paul Almasy/© Corbis).

Agatha, and Felicity and Perpetua have provided inspirational reading during mealtime for centuries of female and male religious communities. Thousands of anonymous women suffered and died for their faith as Albigensians or other "heretics" or as members of the many Protestant congregations that emerged following the Reformation. In fact, women of all faiths and cultures have died courageously for their beliefs. However, in their everyday existence, the predominant role models for women almost universally emphasized the feminine virtues of obedience and passivity. In the Catholic tradition, these virtues are glorified as heroic in the life of Mary. It is believed that she accepted to be the mother of Jesus in the foreknowledge of all the pain and suffering it would entail. The deaths of most heroines are not attended by extraordinary signs, but at the end of her life Mary is granted the hero's apotheosis.

All heroism involves both doing and knowing. The hero's knowledge is a growth in self-consciousness that allows him or her to act independently with imagination, strength, and courage (Edwards, p. 11). Thus, many founders of religious communities are heroines because they broke through the conventions of their times in working among the poor and the oppressed, in enduring hardship to bring education and medical services to distant lands, or simply in making higher education available to women. But even from the earlier monastic period, the reputations of Brigit of Ireland, Hildegard of Bingen, and Theresa of Avila for wisdom, learning, and sanctity persist today.

Through the work of feminist scholars, we have come to know more about Mary Magdalene, Phoebe, and Thecla, all important in the early Christian church when the "prophetic" voice spoke through both women and men. By the third and fourth centuries, however, the Church Fathers reacted against female leadership by imposing religious authority over individual interpretation of the Bible (Ruether and McLaughlin, 1979). Centuries later, this prophetic voice reemerged in women like Anne Hutchinson with the Protestant revival of the belief that each person could interact with God directly. Between 1634 and 1638 large numbers of educated people in Boston, including the then governor of the colony, participated in her Bible discussion groups. Her interpretation of scripture favored the "covenant of grace," unlike the predominant preaching elsewhere in the town. When she was ultimately brought before the General Court, she successfully rebutted all the charges against her except the one that earned her and her family exile: that as a woman, she should not teach or preach. A statue honoring her as a "courageous exponent of civil liberty and religious toleration" stands on Boston Common.

Female heroes in Judaism and Islam are also more easily found before patriarchy enforced the institutional primacy of males. Thus we have the well-known heroines of the Hebrew scriptures, Miriam, Deborah, Judith, Rachel, and Esther, but then centuries pass before Jewish women are officially allowed access to religious learning and leadership. In 1972 Sally Preisand was the first woman admitted to the Reform rabbinate. Previously there were exceptions such as Hannah Rachel in the late nineteenth century, known as the maid of Ludomir, who "became a religious authority because her father had no sons to educate and succeed him" (Ruether and McLaughlin, 1979, p. 337).

From the early days of Islam we have Kadedija, Mohammed's first wife, an independent and successful businesswoman, fourteen years his senior, who actually proposed the marriage. Through this union, the orphaned Mohammed achieved status as well as the physical and moral support that allowed him to pursue his spiritual goals. Both 'A'ishah, the child bride of his later years, and his favorite daughter Fāṭimah became involved in the armed conflicts following the death of the Prophet, but it is through Fāṭimah's children that Mohammed's line of succession is established. Both 'A'ishah and Umm Salam, another of the Prophet's wives, were heavily consulted in compiling the hadiths

or sayings of Mohammed (Minai, 1981). Many Islamic women were known for their learning and their writings. Most notable is Rabi'a, an eighth-century poet and mystic, who is considered a Sufi saint.

Along with their religious sisters, secular women of all persuasions organized against social injustices. Writers, educators, philosophers, and political activists campaigned against slavery and other social evils, particularly those that restricted women's civil rights, access to education and the professions, and control over their own bodies. Whether we classify Christine de Pizan (fifteenth century), Mary Wollstonecraft (eighteenth century), Simone de Beauvoir and Virginia Woolf (twentieth century) as heroines, trail blazers, or simply as role models, all women benefited from their writings. On their visions rest the work of activists such as the American Margaret Sanger (1883–1966), a militant advocate of birth control as a woman's right, or Emmeline, Sylvia, and Christobel Pankhurst, who suffered frequent imprisonment during their struggle to obtain women's right to vote. They were among the first to use the hunger strike as a tool of resistance. The constitutional amendment extending the vote to women in the United States was named the Anthony Amendment in honor of Susan B. Anthony, who devoted her life to the women's suffrage movement. Her coworker of fifty-two years, Elizabeth Cady Stanton, crowned her life's achievement by directing the work on *The Woman's Bible* (1895–1898), to provide a feminist reading of the scriptures, which had been used so long to legitimize the oppression of women (Clark and Richardson, 1977). As late as 1929, Nelly McClung and Emily Murphy of Canada led the appeal to the British high court to overthrow the Canadian Parliament's declaration that women were not persons.

Popular culture has played a significant role in making known the exploits of women of achievement who might otherwise have remained obscure. Without the *Reader's Digest* condensation of Alan Burgess' book *The Inn of the Sixth Happiness* and the subsequent film version, how many would know about the extraordinary accomplishments of Gladys Aylward, missionary to China in the 1930s and 1940s. As a working-class candidate, she had trouble meeting the qualifications of the London China Mission Centre. Nevertheless, she responded to the call of 73-year-old Jeannie Lawson and paid her own way to China on the Trans-Siberian Railway. Not only did she save the lives of more than one hundred children during the Japanese invasion of China, but having earned the respect and trust of the local mandarin, she became his official "foot-inspector" to encourage the population to respect the governmental decree to end the practice of binding women's feet.

The list of heroines could address every field of human experience and endeavor, including the academy (Mary McLeod Bethune, M. Carey Thomas) and art (Judy Chicago, Artemisia Gentileschi); philosophy (Mary Daly, Hypatia) and medicine (Florence Nightingale, Barbara McClintock); society and politics (Indira Gandhi, Golda Meir, Rigoberta Menchú, Eleanor Roosevelt, Sarah Winnemucca); adventure (Amelia Earhart, Sally Ryde); and athletics ("Babe" Didrikson Zaharias, Wilma Rudolph). The achievements of women such as these allow us "to move with confidence into a newly constituted world, and inevitably, to dream beyond the borders of any momentary knowledge" (Edwards, p. 16).

BIBLIOGRAPHY

Anderson, Bonnie S., and Judith P. Zinsser. *A History of Their Own: Women in Europe from Prehistory to the Present.* 2 vols. 1989.

Ashby, Ruth, and Deborah Gore Ohrn. *Herstory: Women Who Changed the World.* 1995.

Brown, Pat, ed. *Heroines of Popular Culture.* 1987.

Campbell, Joseph. *The Hero with A Thousand Faces.* 1957.

Clarke, Elizabeth, and Herbert Richardson. *Women and Religion: A Feminist Sourcebook of Christian Thought.* 1977.

Coffin, Tristram Potter. *The Female Hero in Folklore and Legend.* 1981.

Chicago, Judy. *The Dinner Party: A Symbol of Our Heritage.* 1979.

———. *Embroidering Our Heritage: The Dinner Party Needlework.* 1980.

Edwards, Lee R. *Psyche as Hero: Female Heroism and the Fictional Form.* 1984.

Klein, Yvonne M. *Beyond the Home Front: Women's Autobiographical Writings from the Two World Wars.* 1997.

Lichtman, Susan A. *Life Stages of Women's Heroic Journey.* 1996.

Minai, Naila. *Women in Islam: Tradition and Transition in the Middle East.* 1981.

Noble, Kathleen. *The Sound of the Silver Horn: Reclaiming Heroism in Contemporary Women's Lives.* 1994.

Pearson, Carol, and Katherine Pope. *The Female Hero in American and British Literature.* 1981.

Ruether, Rosemary Radford. *Womanguides: Readings toward a Feminist Theology.* 1985.

Ruether, Rosemary and Eleanor McLaughlan. *Women of Spirit: Female Leadership in the Jewish and Christian Traditions.* 1979.

Information on heroines from all traditions can be found on numerous Internet sites.

See also 'A'isha; Amazons; Artemis (Diana); Athena (Minerva); Deborah; Esther; Fāṭimah; Mary Magdalene; Miriam; Seton, Elizabeth Ann; Virgin Mary; Woman's Bible, The; Women's Suffrage Movement.

E. ANN PEARSON

Women's Contemporary Spirituality Movement

Contemporary women's spirituality is based upon a gender-egalitarian theology that seeks to create communities in which women struggle actively to resist oppression and to affirm their spiritual agency by participating in creative political, social, and spiritual acts that are liberatory and transformational.

Concomitant with the feminist critique of sexism and the patriarchal structures prevalent in mainstream religious institutions, some contemporary women of faith, informed by the political and social issues raised by the women's movement, voice their dissatisfaction with traditional religious ceremonies, which do not meet their spiritual needs. They contrast the concept of spirituality (which for them includes the emotional, psychological, clairvoyant, aesthetic, and ethical dimensions of a woman-centered connection to the spiritual) with the concept of religious practice, which they believe is based solely upon androcentric liturgy and patriarchal theology, responsible for excluding women from agency and leadership roles in all forms of worship.

Thus, some contemporary women from traditional religions have created their own rituals, both within and outside of their religious institutions, in order to reclaim their ancient powers as wise women and priestesses within their own sacred spaces. These rituals have been recovered via feminist historical research, and inspired by Native American spirituality. In addition to the creation of new rituals, women today are exploring the arts of channeling and divination and have written many books on spiritual practices from a female perspective. Feminist tarot, feminist perspectives on the I Ching, and feminist astrology serve as prime examples of an emerging feminist spirituality. Numerous women of spiritual vision have become mediums, setting up their own mystery schools. One example is The Healing Light Center Church first located in Glendale, now in Sierra Madre, California. The church was founded by clairvoyant Rosalyn Bruyere, a specialist in energy healing within diverse spiritual traditions. Other women whose clairvoyant faculties have been recognized have opened personal practices, teaching the shamanic arts and providing counseling and trance

Cocoon ceremony, a segment from "Great Lakes Great Circle Continuous Ritual Tranceformation Cycle," Lake Margarethe, Michigan, July 1978 (Donna Henes)

channeling (often of female personae such as Athena or Mary) in order to provide woman-centered spiritual guidance to all spiritual seekers.

Women who develop their psychic gifts do not always affiliate themselves with the feminist movement. Some who have answered a spiritual calling have established ministries in which they present various teachings. Marianne Williamson presents "A Course in Miracles"; channeled materials transmitted by Barbara Hand Claw (from the Pleiades) or by Jane Roberts (the Seth material) address the spiritual needs of both traditional and new age women and men.

While some feminist spiritual practices began to filter into mainstream religious practice once women entered the ministry (e.g., naming ceremonies for females as forms of entry into the covenant, akin to male circumcision in Judaism), other forms of women's spiritual practice flourished outside traditional patriarchal spaces.

In these feminist Jewish and Christian spaces, women perform services written in nonsexist language that seek to heal the wounds inflicted by patriarchal exclusionary and discriminatory practices. Women create prayers that call upon their female ancestors, that speak of God not simply as Father, but as lover, friend, companion, mother, God(dess)—or of a mother-father god, who is nurturing and compassionate. These rituals have been produced by communities of women worshipers, not by experts in theology. They explore and celebrate women's direct relationship with deity, and while they often remain on the margins, they still maintain their affiliation with the patriarchal religion of their origin. These women strive to enlarge and diversify their own religion's worship practices. They create ceremonies that do not discriminate against lesbians and gays, that refuse to conceive of female sexuality as evil, that are gender-egalitarian, and that transform their traditions. Many of these innovations are often institutionalized. Thus, many prayerbooks are now written in nonsexist language; some even include poetry by women writers.

Storytelling has become an important way to legitimize women's voices in womanist (Afro-American), *mujerista* (Hispanic), and Jewish feminist creations. Formerly inaudible voices have been carried by the oral tradition, in contrast to the written texts that represented androcentric, exclusionary gender biases. Songwriters (such as Debbie Friedman in Jewish tradition) set prayers to their own music and compose songs expressing women's spiritual empowerment, liberation, and solidarity. Afro-American women reclaim their female foremothers and sisters through rituals that include ancestor worship, gospel music with singing and clapping, and the telling of personal stories—all enacted around an altar made by women, bearing symbols of womanist, activist spiritual significance. An important feature of women's spiritual practice is the "breaking of bread" in community, and the sharing of food in sacred space. Most women's spiritual groups feature potlucks and feasts, with libations and offerings to God and to the ancestors. Many women's spirituality groups incorporate moments of silence, lamentation, grieving, and mourning into their services. They take the time to offer special prayers for healing in which women are named who are in need of spiritual blessing. The political aspect of these rituals often includes prayers for women's political struggles for liberation worldwide. Another aspect of women's spiritual practice is working with crystals to energize and balance the subtle energy centers of the human body. Spiritual women in the West have learned from Native Americans how to create a sacred circle, how to call upon the powers of the directions, and how to perform crystal healings.

The practice of Midrash, or the retelling of Bible stories from a woman's perspective, often plays an important role in these new rituals. Contemporary women identify with biblical women, both in their visibility and their invisibility, and by "reading between the lines" of scripture, they fill in the gaps, restoring these biblical women to the fullness of their experiences. Creative rituals in women's spiritual practice often present feminist research on women in the Bible and the ancient world in order to recover the agency and womanpower of their foremothers and ancestors. In these ceremonies, women take leadership roles. There is no intermediary of a male priesthood in feminist spiritual worship.

BIBLIOGRAPHY

Christ, Carol P., and Judith Plaskow, eds. *Weaving The Visions: Patterns In Feminist Spirituality*. 1989.

Daly, Mary. *Gyn/Ecology: The Metaethics of Radical Feminism*. 1978.

Gunn Allen, Paula. *Grandmothers of the Light: A Medicine Woman's Sourcebook*. 1991.

———. *The Sacred Hoop: Recovering the Feminine in American Indian Traditions*. 1986. Reprint, 1992.

King, Ursula, ed. *Feminist Theology from the Third World: A Reader*. 1994.

Ruether, Rosemary Radford. *Gaia and God: An Ecofeminist Theology of Earth Healing*. 1992.

———. *Sexism and God-Talk: Toward a Feminist Theology*. 1983.

———. *Women-Church: Theology and Practice of Feminist Liturgical Communities*. 1985.

Russell, Letty, et al. *Inheriting Our Mothers' Gardens: Feminist Theology in Third World Perspective*. 1988.

Schüssler Fiorenza, Elisabeth. *But She Said: Feminist Practices of Biblical Interpretation*. 1992.

———. *Bread Not Stone: The Challenge of Feminist Biblical Interpretation*. 1984.

———. *In Memory of Her: Feminist Theological Reconstruction of Christian Origins*. 1983.

Teisch, Luisah. *Jambalaya: The Natural Woman's Book of Personal Charms and Practical Rituals*. 1985.

Thistlethwaite, Susan Brooks. *Sex, Race, and God: Christian Feminism in Black and White*. 1988.

FILMOGRAPHY

Goddess Remembered. Women and Spirituality series. Directed by Donna Read. Distributed by the National Film Board of Canada. 1989.

Harmony and Balance. Faithful Women series. Directed by Kathleen Shannon. Distributed by the National Film Board of Canada. 1990. Addresses issues relating to women and religion.

I'll Never Forget You. Faithful Women series. Directed by Kathleen Shannon. Distributed by the National Film Board of Canada. 1990.

Priorities and Perspectives. Faithful Women series. Directed by Kathleen Shannon. Distributed by the National Film Board of Canada. 1990.

See also Goddess: Contemporary Goddess Movement; Women and Religion.

GLORIA F. ORENSTEIN

Women's Religions

The term *women's religions* entered scholarly discourse only recently, most probably because research predating the surge of interest in women's studies paid little attention to women's lives, and then the first wave of writing about women and religion focused primarily upon the status of women within male-dominated contexts. The earliest book to look seriously at women's own religious experiences, *Unspoken Worlds: Women's Religious Lives in Non-Western Cultures* (1980), did not utilize women's religions as an analytic category, but rather organized a wide range of women's ritual activities into groupings such as "ritualized rebellion for women," "rituals for housewives and mothers," and "women in male dominated systems." Subsequent authors did not refine or expand upon this typology, but rather concentrated their attention upon particular religious phenomena. Ross Shepard Kraemer, in a study of women and religion in the Greco-Roman world, used the term women's religions to include "whatever women themselves do and think in religious contexts" (p. 3). Kraemer's work served to shift discussion of women's religiosity in the ancient world from prehistorical speculation to textually oriented scholarship, and to prove that under some circumstances women are religiously active.

SOCIAL CONTEXTS

Priestess, Mother, Sacred Sister: Religions Dominated by Women (1994) set out to develop a typology in which women's religions could be treated as a well-defined conceptual category, the bounding off of which would make it possible to explore both the social contexts in which women enjoy religious autonomy and the fruits of that autonomy. The definition of women's religions in *Priestess, Mother, Sacred Sister* is religions, religious sects, religious situations, and religious movements dominated by women—in which women have been the leaders and the majority of participants, in which women's concerns have been central, and in which there is some sort of recognition that this religious group is independent from a larger, male-dominated institutional context. The number of known women's religions, according to this narrower definition, is small; most religions reasonably well-documented in ethnographic or historical sources have been dominated by men. Among the known women's religions are ancestral cults of Black Caribs in contemporary Belize, the Zar cult of northern Africa, the Sande secret society of Sierra Leone, matrilineal spirit cults in northern Thailand, Korean shamanism, Christian Science, Shakerism, Afro-Brazilian religions, nineteenth-century Spiritualism, the indigenous *nat* cultus of Burma, the feminist spirituality movement in the twentieth-century United States, and the indigenous religion of the Ryukyu Islands. The last example is the only one in which the women's religion is the main or official religion of the entire society.

Although (or perhaps because) women's religions are rare, it is possible to identify certain circumstances in which they are more likely to occur. First, when a new and powerful religion conquers a tribal or village-level society, women may gain control of what used to be a religious system in which both men and women participated. This model is true, for example, of Korean shamanism. A second model concerns male migration and resulting matrifocality: when men are absent a great deal of the time (for a variety of possible reasons such as war or economic necessity), women become more independent in terms of a range of social interactions, including religious ones. This model is relevant, for example, to the Zar cult and the religion of the Black Caribs. In other cultural situations a male-dominated mainstream religion does not provide adequate explanations of and solutions to problems that are particularly acute for women. If the society tolerates alternate religious choices, women may become involved with "fringe" cults. For example, some scholars explain women's dominance in nineteenth-century North American Spiritualism as an outgrowth of women's dissatisfaction with Calvinist belief that their dead babies were going to hell rather than heaven.

Given the wide geographical spread of women's religions, it is not surprising that there is no particular pattern, theme, belief, or ritual practice that characterizes all women's religions. Just as male-dominated religions vary, so do women's religions. On the other hand, there are certain emphases that can be seen in most (not all) women's religions. Some of these emphases can be explained by the fact that almost all women's religions are, within their particular cultural contexts, secondary to a male-dominated religion such as Buddhism or Christianity. Other emphases can be understood in terms of women's concern with issues of motherhood, whether the concern is to avoid motherhood or seek it, keep one's children alive, or preserve relations with a dead child.

Women's religions are more likely to occur in societies that are matrilineal, matrilocal, or matrifocal than in societies that are not. In matrifocal societies women's identity as mother (an active identity) is emphasized more than their identities as wives or daughters (passive identities), and women as mothers control significant cultural and economic resources. In matrilocal societies women tend to be freer to meet together with other women. In matrilineal societies women are more likely to control their own fertility. All of these factors foster the emergence of women's religions.

SALIENT CHARACTERISTICS

Social aspects of motherhood are highly salient to women's religions; biological aspects are not. Fertility rituals and myths of mother goddesses who give birth to the world are almost totally absent from women's religions. What do receive attention and elaboration in these religions are women's social roles as nurturers and healers, women's rights and responsibilities as primary providers of child care, women's emotional experiences of pain at the illness and death of children, and women's social ties with other mothers. Very few women are able simply to pack up and leave their families in order to pursue ascetic or other extraordinary religious paths. Women's religions tend to encourage women to seek out the divine within the profane "real" world of relationships and nature.

No known women's religion worships a single, all-powerful, male deity. The two most common theological stances are polydeism and belief in a mother-father deity. The deities of women's religions are immanent. Women in these religions are willing to meet their gods and goddesses face to face and even to share their bodies with divinities (in spirit possession).

None of these religions teaches that women are inherently either inferior or superior. Many of them explain why women are more suited for religious leadership (they understand suffering better, their souls are softer, and so on). Women's religions teach that men and women are different, and that although both male and female are necessary in this world, the two are often in tension. No women's religion engages in any sort of jihad or holy war. Although most of the religions welcome new members, none carries out any sort of forcible conversion.

Women's religions exhibit an ease with and affinity for interpersonal relationships. This is manifested, for example, in an emphasis on food rituals, ancestor rituals, and initiation rituals, all of which function to strengthen communal bonds. Women's religions tend to be internally hierarchical within the individual chapters or congregations although displaying an aversion to centralization and institutionalized doctrine. Women's religions serve women's secular interests, sometimes obtaining permanent, collective benefits for women as a group, and sometimes providing individual women with short-term support vis-à-vis specific men.

In short, current studies suggest that women's religions both reflect and enhance a relatively strong position for women in society. This does seem to be in contrast to women's religious activity in male-dominated religions, which often seems to reflect and encourage women's exclusion from significant arenas of cultural power (see, for example, I. M. Lewis).

BIBLIOGRAPHY

WOMEN'S RELIGIONS IN GENERAL

Bednarowski, Mary Farrell. "Outside the Mainstream: Women's Religion and Women Religious Leaders in Nineteenth-Century America." *Journal of the American Academy of Religion* 48 (1980): 207–231.

Falk, Nancy A., and Rita M. Gross, eds. *Unspoken Worlds: Women's Religious Lives in Non-Western Cultures.* 1980.

Kraemer, Ross Shephard. *Her Share of the Blessings: Women's Religions among Pagans, Jews, and Christians in the Greco-Roman World.* 1992.

Lewis, I. M. *Ecstatic Religion.* 1975.

Sered, Susan Starr. *Priestess, Mother, Sacred Sister: Religions Dominated by Women.* 1994.

SPECIFIC WOMEN'S RELIGIONS

Boddy, Janice. *Wombs and Alien Spirits: Women, Men, and the Zar Cult in Northern Sudan.* 1989.

Braude, Ann. *Radical Spirits: Spiritualism and Women's Rights in Nineteenth-Century America.* 1989.

Eller, Cynthia. *Living in the Lap of the Goddess: The Feminist Spirituality Movement in America.* 1995.

Kendall, Laurel. *Shamans, Housewives, and Other Restless Spirits: Women in Korean Ritual Life.* 1985.

Kerns, Virginia. *Women and the Ancestors: Black Carib Kinship and Ritual.* 1983.

Leacock, Seth, and Ruth Leacock. *Spirits of the Deep: A Study of an Afro-Brazilian Cult.* 1972.

Lebra, William P. *Okinawan Religion.* 1966.

MacCormack, Carol. "Sande: The Public Face of a Secret Society." In *The New Religions of Africa.* Edited by Bennetta Jules-Rosette. 1979.

Spiro, Melford. *Burmese Supernaturalism.* 1967.

Wijeyewardene, Gehan. *Place and Emotion in Northern Thai Ritual Behaviour.* 1986.

SUSAN STARR SERED

Women's Studies

Women's studies, an interdisciplinary field originating in the late 1960s with the purpose of exposure and redress of women's oppression, began to exert an influence on religious studies in the early 1970s. The discipline of women's studies continues to have a tremendous impact on the field of religious studies in at least three areas: critique, construction, and diversity. Women's studies in religion has enabled greater understanding of the relationship between religion and sexism in the wider culture; provided tools for rooting out this sexism and working for constructive change; and supplied the impetus for the field of gender studies, a discipline whose agenda includes both the liberation of men and women from patriarchy and an analysis of the constructed nature of gender and sexuality. Although the focus of this article is primarily theology, women's studies has equally influenced other areas of the multidisciplinary field of religious studies.

CRITIQUE

According to Constance Buchanan (1987), women's studies in religion developed in large part as a response to increasing numbers of women seeking preparation for religious leadership in Jewish and Christian traditions, and to women's growing frustrations with the explicit and implicit barriers to that leadership. Inquiry into the exclusion of women from religious leadership led to a recognition of the male-centeredness of major Western religious traditions and instigated the deeper question of the role of gender in religious life and thought. The result of these queries has been a major shift in assumptions in the field of religious studies: what previously was thought to be an objective perspective is in fact a male point of view. This shift in assumptions necessitates deconstructing the "ethos of objectivity" in the academy and offering instead an "ethos of eros and empathy" as a model for scholarship (Christ, 1987).

Feminist scholars such as Rosemary Radford Ruether and Mary Daly address androcentric biases in the methodological frameworks of theology. In *Sexism and God-Talk: Toward a Feminist Theology* (1983) Ruether attacks male-biased theology imputing that women are weak, sinful, and less than full representatives of humanity. She elucidates the origins of this patriarchal anthropology in the views of Augustine, who used the Genesis story of the creation of Adam and Eve to promote a view of female inferiority. Ruether explains the ways in which this story was interpreted by later male theologians such as Thomas Aquinas, Martin Luther, and Karl Barth to justify women's subordination and submission to men. Daly focuses on the significance of religious symbols. As long as the church worships a male deity and a male savior, for Daly, women will always be excluded from symbolic representation of God and of humanity. Daly writes in *Beyond God the Father: Toward a Philosophy of Women's Liberation* (1973) that symbol systems generated by patriarchy not only fail to reflect the experiences of women, but they undercut women's self-concept and render those experiences false. In exposing androcentric thinking, these scholars and many others help to expose and undermine misogynist doctrines and attitudes that have functioned to suppress women's leadership in Jewish and Christian traditions.

CONSTRUCTION

Critique of the male point of view led scholars in women and religion in three directions: reconstruction, reform within the tradition, and revision outside the tradition. Reconstruction is closely linked with the reformist task of working for women's liberation within sexist traditions. For example, feminist New Testament scholar Elisabeth Schüssler Fiorenza, in *In Memory of Her: A Feminist Theological Reconstruction of Christian Origins* (1988), sets out to reconstruct early Christian history to include the experiences of women, and in doing so to reclaim this history from its androcentric grasp. Schüssler Fiorenza attempts to show that, contrary to the work of many male authors, the early Christian movement was inclusive of women's leadership and was therefore egalitarian. This movement, she argues, became patriarchalized largely for political reasons, as recorded, for example, in the pastoral epistles of Titus and I Timothy. Schüssler Fiorenza's work has been used to refute Vatican arguments prohibiting Catholic women's ordination.

Proponents of the third position posit that the Jewish and Christian traditions are inherently patriarchal and incapable of sufficient reform to permit gender equality. For example, Naomi Goldenberg suggests, in *Changing of the Gods: Feminism and the End of Traditional Religions* (1979), that Judaism essentially concerns the relationship between a male god and his sons. According to Goldenberg, if Jewish women become leaders in their tradition, the religion will be so altered it will no longer appropriately be called Judaism. Gold-

enberg favors embracing Goddess spirituality, for in her view it is the only Western religion that recognizes woman as a divinity in her own right. Similarly, Carol Christ (1982) argues that patriarchal religion has devalued and denigrated female power, the female will, the female body, and female bonds. Goddess spirituality in her view enables women to revalue these dimensions of themselves and their history.

DIVERSITY

The bedrock of women's studies in religion has been a focus on women's experience as the starting point for theology. This focus has in turn led to criticisms of essentialism—the notion that "womanhood" is biological and inherent—and to the recognition that there is no universal women's experience. Women's studies has introduced the theoretical perspectives of psychoanalysis and poststructuralism to religious studies. In addition, the growing significance of the awareness of race and class has led women of color to distinguish their endeavors from feminist theology, that is, theology developed by white women. In the 1980s a number of theologies began to emerge from women's differing social locations, among them mujerista theology, womanist theology, Asian women's theology, and lesbian theology. Mujerista theologian Maria Pilar Aquino suggests that while all feminist theoretical models are concerned with women's liberation from oppression, the models must be more accountable to the interaction of race, culture, class, and religiosity; that more sophisticated strategies must be developed to counter patriarchal power; and that the relationship between feminist thought, society, and social change must be made more explicit. These are the future tasks of women's studies in religion.

BIBLIOGRAPHY

Aquino, Maria Pilar. "Roundtable Discussion: What's in a Name? Exploring the Dimensions of What 'Feminist Studies in Religion' Means." *Journal of Feminist Studies in Religion* 11 (1995): 111–136.

Brekus, Catherine A. "Studying Women and Religion: Problems and Possibilities." *Criterion* 32 (1993): 24–28.

Buchanan, Constance. "Women's Studies." In *The Encyclopedia of Religion*. Edited by Mircea Eliade. 1987.

Christ, Carol. "Feminists—Sojourners in the Field of Religious Studies." In *The Knowledge Explosion: Generations of Feminist Scholarship*. Edited by Cheris Kramarae and Dale Spender. 1992.

———. "Toward a Paradigm Shift in the Academy and in Religious Studies." In *The Impact of Feminist Re-*

search in the Academy. Edited by Christie Farnham. 1987.

————. "Why Women Need the Goddess: Phenomenological, Psychological, and Political Reflections." In *The Politics of Women's Spirituality: Essays on the Rise of Spiritual Power Within the Feminist Movement.* Edited by Charlene Spretnak. 1982.

Driver, Anne Barstow. "Religion." *Signs: Journal of Women in Culture and Society* 2 (1976): 434–442.

King, Ursula. "Voices of Protest and Promise: Women's Studies in Religion, the Impact of the Feminist Critique on the Study of Religion." *Studies in Religion* 23 (1994): 315–329.

Madsen, Catherine. "A God of One's Own: Recent Work by and About Women in Religion." *Signs: Journal of Women in Culture and Society* 19 (1994): 480–498.

Plaskow, Judith. "We Are Also Your Sisters: The Development of Women's Studies in Religion." *Women's Studies Quarterly* 1 and 2 (1993): 9–21.

Ruether, Rosemary Radford. "The Feminist Critique in Religious Studies." In *A Feminist Perspective in the Academy: The Difference It Makes.* Edited by Elizabeth Langland and Walter Gove. 1981.

Yates, Gayle Graham. "Spirituality and the American Feminist Experience." *Signs: Journal of Women in Culture and Society* 9 (1983): 59–72.

See also **Feminisms; Gender Studies; Liberation Theologies; Mujerista Tradition; Patriarchy; Womanist Traditions.**

KELLEY ANN RAAB

Women's Suffrage Movement

Women's suffrage refers to women's right to vote. Traditional patriarchal societies throughout history denied women the vote on the grounds that women as daughters, wives, and mothers were inherently dependent on the male head of family, who, in public political transactions, represented himself, his family, and the servants under his rule. Thus the patriarch or male head of family was both an autonomous person in his own right and a collective person or "head" of a corporate body of persons dependent on him. Women, on the other hand, were inherently incapable of being either autonomous persons in their own right or rulers over others.

Although there were some exceptions to this general rule, such as the occasional ruling queen in the absence of a male heir to a throne, and independent, single, propertied women, this exclusion of women from vot-

ing and holding political office was based on a general view of social order as being determined either by God or natural law and of female inferiority. Classical Christianity believed that God's divinely ordained order of creation decreed that women, though spiritually equal to man in soul and hence redeemable to eternal life, were put under male dominion in society. This condition had been deepened through sin and the Fall, for which women were deemed primarily responsible. Hence women were doubly dependent on men in family and society—both by nature and as punishment for sin.

Islamic law has generally followed a similar line. Women are seen as inherently weaker, created by God with lesser judgment and thus incapable of making political decisions. For women to vote and participate in public life is seen as violating women's modesty and opening the way for sexual immorality, a view that has been echoed by antisuffrage Protestants and Catholics in the late nineteenth and early twentieth centuries. American Protestant theologian Horace Bushnell argued in his book, *Women's Suffrage: The Reform Against*

A woman is arrested during an October 1913 suffrage demonstration, London, England (Library of Congress/Corbis).

Nature (1869), that women were more Christlike than men, but this "natural" piety and goodness were delicate and could be preserved only by keeping women out of the corrupt sphere of male public life.

In the United States the fight for women's suffrage began with the First Women's Rights Convention called by Lucretia Mott and Elizabeth Cady Stanton in Seneca Falls, New York, in 1848. Among the resolutions passed at the convention was the demand for women's right to vote. It was the only resolution that did not receive a consensus vote, owing to the principles of radical abolitionists, like Mott, who believed that no one should vote under a Constitution that condoned slavery. Later she conceded that if it was moral for men to vote, it was equally moral for women to vote.

The Fourteenth Amendment to the Constitution gave the freedman the vote, but restricted the franchise to men, using the word "male" as a qualification for voting. This caused a split in the women's suffrage movement in 1869. Elizabeth Cady Stanton and Susan B. Anthony formed the National Women's Suffrage Association, arguing that the amendment should not be passed until it included women, while moderates, led by Lucy Stone and Henry Ward Beecher, formed the American Women's Suffrage Movement, which accepted the priority of the vote for black men over women. These two movements reunited in 1890 as more radical leaders, like Susan B. Anthony, accepted strategies to win the vote which privileged white women, rather than demanding radical equality for all.

The suffrage movement in the United States sought to win the vote for women both through state-by-state reforms and a federal amendment. Beginning with Wyoming in 1869, successive territories and states gave women the vote; the final victory was won by the passage in 1920 of the Nineteenth Amendment to the Constitution. Other Western democratic countries, such as Great Britain, granted women the vote during the period between World War I and World War II. Women also gained the vote in Russia and other communist states who enacted revolutionary new constitutions in this period.

Emerging developing countries generally gave women the vote after World War II as part of new constitutions developed after national liberation. Today women vote in all countries where there are elections, but this has not brought them equal political power. Even in the United States, women in Congress remain a small minority. In some Muslim countries women vote, but only for men. For example, in Morocco, women are 48.5 percent of the electorate, but only men are present in the legislature. The vote is an important step, but by itself is insufficient to overcome women's historic subjugation by patriarchy.

BIBLIOGRAPHY

Bushnell, Horace. *Women's Suffrage: The Reform Against Nature.* 1869.

Daley, Caroline, and Melanie Nolan. *Suffrage and Beyond: International Feminist Perspectives.* 1994.

Flexner, Eleanor. *Century of Struggle: The Women's Rights Movement in the United States.* 1970.

Kraditor, Aileen. *The Ideas of the Woman Suffrage Movement, 1890–1920.* 1971.

Liddington, Jill. *One Hand Tied Behind Us: The Rise of the Women's Suffrage Movement.* 1978.

"Shoulder to Shoulder: A Documentary." Directed by Midge MacKenzie. 1975.

Stanton, Elizabeth Cady, Susan B. Anthony, and Matilda Joslyn Gage. *The History of Woman Suffrage.* 1889.

See also **Patriarchy**; **Social Action**; **Social Change**.

ROSEMARY RADFORD RUETHER

Worship

Worship signifies the act of affirming, renewing, celebrating, and expressing an individual's relationship with a spiritually supreme being. A Jewish and Christian term, it may or may not have cognates in other religious traditions. The content and form of the act of worship depends on how the relationship to the divine is understood.

In the Abrahamic traditions, the act of worship affirms human dependency on a creator God, acknowledges gratitude toward God, and renews and celebrates the relationship between human and divine. Recognizing that worship both individual and communal does not simply affirm and determine one's relationship with God but also with oneself, one's community, and one's society, Jewish and Christian feminists are developing forms of worship that include and honor women. They are rethinking the concept of God, rewriting liturgies, and enacting gynocentric rituals. They call for inclusive language for liturgy, a vocabulary for God that is not exclusively male, and equal participation of women in the ritual leadership of the worshiping community (which for many denominations includes the ordination of women). Jewish and Christian women are creating worship services intended to be nonhierarchical and egalitarian and that correspond to the lived experience of participants. These services enact empowering relational patterns that continue to operate outside the ritual context. Some Jewish and Christian women have left their congregations but continue to identify with their tradition; others no longer do so and have joined worshiping communities such as the feminist religion known as Wicca.

Although the issues raised by Jewish and Christian feminists with regard to worship are pertinent in the case of Islam, Muslim feminists have chosen to focus their attention on other issues. In Islam, the required acts of worship—ritual prayer (*salāt*), fasting (*ramaḍān*), almsgiving (*zakāt*), and pilgrimage (hajj)—are equally obligatory for women and men. The requisite state of ritual purity (*tahara*) for the performance of all these rituals (except almsgiving) precludes women from participation during menstruation and postpartum discharge. This keeps them from full participation in the worshiping community and consequently from exercising leadership roles within it. Some Muslim feminists are beginning to question the exclusion of women from the ritual leadership of the community in the mosque; yet the linking of menstruation and postpartum discharge with ritual impurity remains largely unquestioned within Islam. Historically, the understanding of menstruation as a ritually impure state that precludes women from various forms of worship has been shared by patriarchal religions, including Judaism, Christianity, and Hinduism. However, significant parts of the Jewish and Christian communities have moved away from this concept.

In various parts of the Muslim world, Muslim women participate in forms of ritual that are considered either harmless or undesirable by the male religious elite; these rituals are neither a substitute for nor as meritorious as the obligatory forms of worship. The communal observance of these popular rituals may be more prevalent among certain groups of women than the practice of the obligatory prayers. The *mawlid*, birth celebration of the Prophet Muhammad, is one such gathering of Muslim women. In recounting Aminah's experience of carrying and giving birth to the Prophet, women honor and celebrate their own powers of giving birth and nurturing. The *mawlid* is also celebrated in male gatherings, with greater emphasis on the person of the Prophet.

The telling of the story of Fāṭimah is strictly a women's ritual. Muslim women gather informally to tell and listen to the story of the Prophet's daughter, in which on several occasions Fāṭimah is saved through divine intervention from suffering at the hands of a cruel world. At these gatherings women bring petitions for the resolution of an undesirable situation and vow to tell the story of Fāṭimah to another woman should the situation improve. Fāṭimah, the submissive and virtuous daughter, symbolizes their own virtue as well as their circumscribed and compromised circumstance in life. She also functions as the saint whose remembrance invokes divine intervention in their own lives. Both the *mawlid*s and the telling of the story of Fāṭimah are egalitarian gatherings that provide important occasions for bonding, support, and networking among women.

Worship in Hinduism takes two major forms: *pūjā* and *upasana*. *Pūjā* is the adoration of a personal deity, to whom ritual offerings of incense, flowers, food, drink, and devotional words are made in the home or the temple. Unlike temple worship, household worship does not require a brahmin (officiating male priest). Women may engage in *pūjā* individually or with their families. Occasionally the widow of a brahmin may take over the performance of the rituals after the death of her husband. Aside from the performance of *pūjā* and other rites, brahmins usually do not function as leaders in the community.

Upasana, reverence of, devotion to, and constant attendance upon a chosen deity, is undertaken to achieve spiritual realization and a mystical experience of the divine. *Upasana* involves repetition of a divine name (*japam*) and meditation (*dhyāna*). Though best exemplified in the life of the renunciant, it may be undertaken with or without a life of renunciation and is open to all regardless of their caste or gender, as is renunciation itself. Renunciants, perceived as having achieved a certain intimacy with the divine, are more likely to be considered leaders by their community, even though they do not perform the ritual worship or *pūjā*.

Hindu women, regionally, have developed their own rituals around the dreams, visions, and mystical experience of individual women. Women who claim to have attained spiritual realization—or are recognized as having done so—act as teachers, healers, and spiritual guides of other women and men.

BIBLIOGRAPHY

Anderson, Elizabeth. "Contemplative Life and Worship." *Daughters of Sarah* 21 (Fall 1995): 1–80.

Berger, Teresa. "The Classical Liturgical Movement in Germany and Austria: Moved by Women?" *Worship* 66 (May 1992): 231–251.

———. "Women and Worship: A Bibliography." *Studia Liturgica* 19, no. 1 (1989): 96–110.

———. "Women and Worship: A Bibliography Continued." *Studia Liturgica* 25, no. 1 (1995): 103–117.

Berry, Jan. "Liberating Worship—Pastoral Liturgy and the Empowering of Women." In *Life Cycles: Women and Pastoral Care*. Edited by Elaine Graham and Margaret Halsey. 1993.

Bolin, Nona R., and Gene G. James. "Ritual in the World's Religions." *Dialogue and Alliance* 4 (Spring 1990): 1–117.

Bradshaw, Paul F., and Lawrence A. Hoffman, eds. *Life Cycles in Jewish and Christian Worship.* 1996.

Butler, Sara. "The Priest as Sacrament of Christ the Bridegroom." *Worship* 66 (November 1992): 498–517. See reply by E.J. Picken, *Worship* 67 (May 1993): 269–270.

Challinor, Lori. "The Worth of Woman-Created Worship." *Daughters of Sarah* 21 (Fall 1995): 30–33.

Chauvet, Louis-Marie, and François Kabasele Lumbala, eds. *Liturgy and the Body.* 1995.

Emswiler, Sharon N., and Thomas N. Emswiler. "Women and Worship: A Guide to Non-Sexist Hymns, Prayers and Liturgies." *Review and Expositor* 84 (Summer 1987): 552.

Gilkes, Cheryl Townsend. "Some Mother's Son and Some Father's Daughter: Gender and Biblical Language in Afro-Christian Worship Tradition. In *Shaping New Vision: Gender and Values in American Culture.* Edited by Clarissa W. Atkinson, Constance H. Buchanan, and Margaret R. Miles. 1987.

Hitchcock, Helen Hull, ed. *The Politics of Prayer: Feminist Language and the Worship of God.* 1992.

Holden, Pat. *Women's Religious Experience: A Cross Cultural Perspective.* 1983.

Kendall, Laurel. "Korean Shamanism: Women's Rites and a Chinese Comparison." In *Religion and the Family in East Asia.* Edited by George De Vos and Takao Sofue. 1986.

Mitra, Kana. "Women and the Hindu Tradition." In *Women's and Men's Liberation: Testimonies of Spirit.* Edited by Leonard Grob, Riffat Hassan, and Haim Gordon. 1991.

Plaskow, Judith, and Elisabeth Schüssler Fiorenza. "Feminist Scholarship in Religion: Reformist or Revolutionary?" *Journal of Feminist Studies in Religion* 5 (Spring 1989): 7–142.

Procter-Smith, Marjorie, and Janet R. Walton, eds. *Women at Worship: Interpretations of North American Diversity.* 1993.

Winter, Miriam Therese, Adair Lummis, and Allison Stokes, eds. *Defecting in Place: Women Claiming Responsibility for Their Own Spiritual Lives.* 1994.

See also **Liturgy.**

GHAZALA ANWAR

Yates, Frances A.

Yates, Dame Frances A. (1899–1981) was a Renaissance historian whose work on occult philosophy, the Hermetic tradition, and neo-Platonism transformed religious studies of the Renaissance. Born in England in 1899, Yates was schooled only intermittently in her early years. In 1925 she moved with her family to Surrey, where she lived in the family house until her death; she never married.

Yates' part-time studies at University College, London, eventually led to a degree in French (1924), which was followed by an M.A. on sixteenth-century French theatre. Her studies reflected the passions of her family, who were avid Shakespearians and Francophiles. Yates worked as a private scholar for some fifteen years, modestly supported by her family. Her first book, *John Florio: The Life of an Italian in Shakespeare's England* (1934) and *A Study of Love's Labour's Lost* (1947), gained her academic recognition and established her reputation as a serious scholar of the Renaissance. In 1941 Yates joined the staff of the Warburg Institute, becoming lecturer in 1944 when the Institute was incorporated by the University of London.

Yates' seminal work on Bruno and Lull, *Giordano Bruno and the Hermetic Tradition* (1964), continued her multilayered study of Renaissance themes, examining religious, political, and intellectual history. She devoted much of her late study work to the examination of Shakespeare, insisting on the relevance of alchemical and hermetic thought in his work. *The Occult Philosophy in the Elizabethan Age* (1979) draws together most of the main concerns and interests of her late studies.

Yates won several academic prizes and was recipient of many honorary degrees. Although she is said to have lived a quiet life, she was passionate about her studies and vigorously defended her unique views. Frances Yates is remembered by J. Trapp in *Dictionary of National Biography, 1981–1985* as possessing a "magisterial presence" that was offset by "charm and a sort of grand dishevelment." Yates died in 1981, leaving most of her estate to the Warburg Institute for scholarships. Her papers and books are also housed at the Institute.

BIBLIOGRAPHY

Yates, Frances A. *The Art of Memory.* 1966.
———. *The French Academies of the Sixteenth Century.* 1947.
———. *Ideas and Ideals in the North European Renaissance.* 1984.
———. *Lull and Bruno.* 1982.
———. *Shakespeare's Last Plays: A New Approach.* 1975.
———. *Theatre of the World.* 1969.
———. *The Valois Tapestries.* 1969. 2d ed., 1975.

STUART SMITHERS

Yemaya

Among the cultural consequences of the Atlantic slave trade that forcibly displaced millions of Africans was the diffusion of the Yoruba mother and sea goddess, Yemaya, throughout the new world. Yemaya now appears in several religions that incorporate elements of African traditions, Christianity, and local beliefs. In the Afro-Cuban religion of Santeria a complex pattern of associations reverberates throughout the myths and rituals that involve Yemaya. She is associated with the patron saint of Havana's port, Our Lady of Regla; the days of Friday and Saturday; the colors white, crystal, and blue; the number seven; sea shells and stones found by the sea; and specific sacrificial animals (lambs, ducks, roosters, turtles, goats, fish, and pigeons) and herbs (indigo, purple basil, chayote fruit). When Yemaya mounts a devotee in spirit possession, her movements can be as calm and regular as the waves of a placid sea or as violent as those of a hurricane-ravaged ocean.

In Santeria some traditional tales relate that after Obatala, the father of the gods and creator of humans, created Chango, the *orisha* (deity) of fire, thunder, and lightning, Yemaya raised him as her own child. Eventually she also tried to teach her hot-blooded and impetuous stepson, Chango, more respect for women by demonstrating her fearsome command of the sea. Yemaya's strong connection with female devotees also occurs in many ritual contexts, particularly those associated with fertility.

By some estimates Yemaya has one hundred million worshipers in the family of African-derived religions that has spread through northern South America (particularly in Brazilian Macumba, Candomble, and Umbanda), Latin America, the Caribbean, and North America. Beyond the boundaries of those traditions she also finds devotees among those who revere "the goddess" as a single figure with manifold culturally-specific manifestations.

BIBLIOGRAPHY

Brandon, George. *The Dead Sell Memories: Santeria From Africa to the New World.* 1993.

Drewal, Henry John, and Margaret Thompson Drewal. *Gelede: Art and Female Power among the Yoruba.* 1983.

Gonzalez-Wippler, Migene. *Santeria: The Religion.* 1989.

Murphy, Joseph M. *Santeria: An African Religion in America.* 1993.

Wafer, Jim. *The Taste of Blood: Spirit Possession in Brazilian Candomble.* 1991.

See also **Afro-Atlantic Religions**.

EUGENE V. GALLAGHER

Yin/Yang Polarity

Traditional Chinese religious and philosophical systems understand the cosmos as continually in flux. Every instant is the product of the interplay of the two forces of yin and yang, as well as of their combined interaction with the Five Phases or Elements (wood, earth, metal, water, and fire), the hexagrams of the *I Ching* (Book of Changes), and other processes of change. The earliest extant texts in which the terms appear date to the early fourth century B.C.E., although evidence from the Shang dynasty suggests awareness of these fundamental polarities in the mid-second millennium B.C.E.

The terms do not exist in absolute binary opposition. Yin and yang are complementary rather than antagonistic, and together they form a dynamic, positive whole. As a formal system, yin/yang theory acknowledges the internal contradictions of things, while at the same time viewing the cosmos as an organic whole. The two terms originally referred to the shaded (yin) and sunlit (yang) sides of a mountain or a river, the orientation for each of which differed: yang indicated the south side of a mountain, the side that receives sunlight, but connoted the north side of a river, as the light on China's major eastward-flowing rivers is reflected to that side. These concepts were extended gradually by association from light and shadow to include other observable complementary forces or tendencies, for example, warmth and cold, dryness and moisture, growth and decay, strength and weakness, health and illness, and so forth. In general, the tendency toward positive, auspicious, or life-sustaining states was designated as the yang aspect of the pair of concepts. It is important to note, however, that neither yin nor yang was understood as static; yang tendencies might be preferable, but the emphasis was on context and necessary processes of change.

During the Han dynasty (second century B.C.E.–second century C.E.), as part of a syncretic and systematic move to establish state ritual and Confucian intellectual orthodoxy, the brace of terms came to correlate everything from seasons, numbers, colors, tastes, temperatures, and locations to gods, ghosts, and social and military ranks. In terms of the individual self, the unified human heart-mind was described as the locus of both yang rationality and yin emotionality, but the latter was seen to cause inconstancy, confusion, and error; yang was thus more highly regarded and, ultimately, seen as morally superior. This linkage of morality with general notions of yang superiority contributed to an increasingly hierarchical appreciation of yang's value over that of yin, with the result that things and persons associated with yin were increasingly vulnerable to essentialist definition as inferior and even dangerous to the maintenance of preferred yang conditions. Yin could never be eliminated, nor should it be, but its potentially destructive or inauspicious aspects ideally could be forestalled, contained, or otherwise held at bay.

To appreciate the broad understanding of yin/yang relationality, an example can be drawn from the positioned siting of graves, houses, and even furniture according to the principles of traditional geomancy or *feng-shui:* the necessary presence of yin elements in the landscape is acknowledged, but the task of the geomancer is to maximize the beneficial effects of yang forces, often with a goal of achieving a three-fifths to two-fifths positive ratio between them.

This weighting of an appropriate yin/yang balance is present also in the traditional classification of foods, in which yin and yang are associated with "cold" and "hot" foods, respectively. The human body requires both kinds of foods, but their necessary balance will vary by season (one eats fewer hot foods in summer and fewer cold foods in winter), by health circumstances (one may need more of either kind to combat illness caused by imbalance of hot and cold), and by individual tolerance and proclivity. Hot yang foods, thought to be more nutritious, tend to be animal-based, oily, and sticky; cold yin foods tend to be vegetable-based, watery, and free-flowing. It is significant that a surfeit of yang foods can lead to obstructions in the body's natural pathways and thus cause illness, and that although yin foods are often eaten to "wash away" perceived poisons, they are not harmful in and of themselves. Neither type of food is inherently auspicious or beneficial; what is crucial is their overall ratio.

In the patriarchal context of the traditional Chinese kinship system, pre-Confucian notions of patrilineality and patrilocality combined with the Confucian educational imperative to control the self, so that the application of yin/yang terminology to kinship and social roles produced a gendered dual standard. An adult man existed in both yin and yang context simultaneously: he stood in yang relationship to his wives and children but in yin relationship to his parents, elders, and ruler; among his friends or peers, the balance of yin/yang relationality shifted according to circumstance. In contrast, a woman rarely escaped the ascription of yin-associated traits, remaining bound by the rules of "thrice-following" (*san cong*)—following her father in the natal home, following her husband after marriage, and following her son in widowhood—although she typically maintained a yang stance toward her children and, especially, her daughter(s)-in-law. Outside the home, in religious or business communities, older women might move beyond the confines of yin essentialism to assume visible leadership roles; however, it is unclear whether such authority was possible because the postmenopausal woman became less yin and thus perhaps "not-woman." Specifics of social class, historical period, and regional custom allowed significant variation in the application of yin/yang relationality to women's roles; it was never the case that women were perceived as incapable of attaining either virtue or knowledge, although the essentializing tendency to associate them with yin always carried the potential to undermine their accomplishments and to suggest that even their strengths and talents might be inauspicious.

The dual vulnerability and danger of yin-associated beings extends beyond this life to the afterworld. Gods and male ancestors (women were generally venerated as adjuncts of their husbands), all of whom are generally thought to be responsible for cosmic order, inhabit a yang realm; spirits of the unhappy dead (those without heirs to mourn them, or those whose bodies were unrecovered and who were thus deprived of requisite funerary rites) inhabit a yin realm of disorder and misery. In this scheme, goddesses are anomalous, problematic for their female (and therefore yin) presence in a yang realm. Anthropologist P. Steven Sangren has suggested that for their devotees, goddesses' "outsider" status often renders them more individually powerful than the gods, and thus the faithful often approach them with personal requests that others might see as subversive of the perceived cosmic order. Whether or not one accepts this interpretation, the goddesses' ambiguity provides a clear reminder that the intersections between yin and yang and other conceptual binary systems of male and female, auspicious and inauspicious, and purity and pollution are multiple and subtle and demand careful analysis.

BIBLIOGRAPHY

Ahern, Emily M. "Sacred and Secular Medicine in a Taiwan Village: A Study of Cosmological Disorders." In *Medicine in Chinese Cultures: Comparative Studies of Health Care in Chinese and Other Societies.* Edited by Arthur Kleinman. 1975. Especially useful for her detailed discussion of yin/yang within both the human body and human social groups.

Lee, Lily Xiao Hong. *The Virtue of Yin: Studies on Chinese Women.* 1994. A collection of articles about the ways in which yin-indentification has defined women's roles in Chinese culture, and of attempts both historical and contemporary to remedy the problem.

Pao, Chia-lin. "Yin-yang Thought and the Status of Women." In *Confucian-Christian Encounters in Historical and Contemporary Perspective.* Edited by Peter K. H. Lee. 1991. A historical overview of the textual sources for the negative association of women and yin in traditional Chinese Confucian culture.

Sangren, P. Steven. *History and Magical Power in a Chinese Community.* 1987. See esp. chap. 7, "*Yin and Yang:* Disorder and Order," for a provocative schematic appreciation of Chinese deities in yin and yang terms.

VIVIAN-LEE NYITRAY

Yoga

In Indian tradition, the word *yoga* has a variety of meanings. Etymologically, *yoga* derives from the Sanskrit verbal root *yuj*, meaning to yoke, unite, or join. By extension, yoga has come to designate any of the psycho-physical and philosophical systems that facilitate the attainment of higher states of consciousness. Traditionally, yoga refers to the classical system articulated by Patañjali in the *Yoga* sutra and its various commentaries such as *Yogasūtra-bhaṣya* of Vyāsa and *Tattvavaiśāradī* of Vācaspatimiśra. This system, which is one of the six orthodox schools of Indian philosophy known as *darśanas*, closely resembles the earlier Sāṃkhya (Discrimination) school, from which it borrows much of its philosophical material. Other Indian traditions of yoga, such as medieval hatha and tantra, the three

Relief at a Hindu temple depicts several figures performing yoga exercises (Abbie Enock; Travel Ink/Corbis).

yoga-*mārgas* (paths of yoga)—that is, *karma* (action, *jñāna* (knowledge), and *bhakti* (devotion)—promulgated in the Bhagavadgītā, and even the early teachings of the Buddha, exhibit commonality with this classical tradition by their inclusion of *samādhi* (absorption, union, etc.) as the goal of yoga practice.

Few works, however, have been written specifically on yoga and women. Indeed, classical yoga texts treat the male practitioner (*yogin*) as the normative model; rarely do they specify practices for the female practitioner (*yoginī*). Still, the yogic path is open to women. Within Indian tradition there have been paradigmatic illustrations to confirm that although yoga is not considered the norm for women, since their duty (dharma) is reserved for the role of wife and mother, women have certainly gained access to, and knowledge of, yoga. For example, in the Upanishads there is reference to Maitreyī, the wife of philosopher Yajñavalkya, who, it is said, attained liberation through the practice of yoga. In addition, Kausalyā, the mother of Rāma; Sulabhā, the daughter of King Pradhān; Madālasā, the wife of King Ṛtvdhvaja; Lallā, the fourteenth-century Kashmirī Shaivite poet-saint; Shāradā Devī, the wife of Rāmakrishna Paramahansa; and others have gained liberation through the practice of yoga. Another important precedent in Indian tradition is set by the Hindu goddess Pārvatī, whose practice of yoga-*tapas* (asceticism) secures for her marriage with Siva, the Lord of yoga. As a result, the principal texts of the hatha yoga tradition, such as the *Haṭhayogapradīpikā* (Lamp of Yoga), are considered divine revelation passed on from Siva to Pārvatī in the style of oral transmission; through her the esoteric process of hatha yoga is imparted to the lineage of *siddhas* (accomplished ones) and Nāthayogis.

In medieval Hindu and Buddhist tantric yoga the role of women is elevated. The esoteric and coded aspects of these traditions, however, have seriously limited scholars' access to information as well as to a comprehensive understanding of the role that women have played in these traditions. Current studies such as that of Miranda Shaw indicate that women did play central roles as accomplished practitioners, gurus (teachers), and creators of discourse in the Hindu and Buddhist tantric traditions. Perhaps the expressed realization within tantric yoga traditions of the fundamental unity of existence conceived in gendered terms as male and female, the valorization of feminine symbolism and imagery in its philosophical presuppositions, the primacy of the body, and the perceived necessity of a ritual partner, to name just a few examples, provided an avenue of accessibility to women that other types of yoga denied.

The benefits of classical yoga practice are becoming more readily available to women both in India and the West. The eight stages (*aṣṭāṅgas*) of classical yoga are *yama* (five restraints), including ahimsa (nonviolence), *satya* (restraint from falsehood), *asteya* (nonstealing), *brahmacarya* (restraint from sexuality), and *aparigraha* (restraint from avarice); *niyama* (five disciplines), including cleanliness, contentment, asceticism, study, and surrender to Īśvara (god); *āsana* (postures); *prāṇāyamā* (breathing techniques); *pratyāhāra* (withdrawal of the senses); *dhāraṇā* (concentration); *dhyāna* (meditation); and *samādhi* (absorption). Although the male body was considered the norm in classical yoga treatises, and men, for the most part, held positions of authority and power within most of its schools, these elements are not gender- or sex-specific and can be practiced by both men and women. It is important to point out that generally the third, fourth, and sixth stages—postures, breathing techniques, and *dhyāna* (meditation)—are emphasized, particularly for their physical and mental health benefits, such as reducing stress and back pain, overcoming fatigue, and calming the mind. In yoga centers in India and elsewhere both men and women are learning and teaching this system of yoga.

BIBLIOGRAPHY

Dasgupta, Shashibhusan. *Obscure Religious Cults*. 1974.
Dasgupta, Surendranath. *A History of Indian Philosophy*. Vol. 2. 1922.
Eliade, Mircea. *Yoga: Immortality and Freedom*. 1969.
Feuerstein, Georg. *Yoga: The Technology of Ecstasy*. 1989.
Shaw, Miranda. *Women in Tantric Buddhism*. 1994.
Woods, James H. *The Yoga System of Patañjali*. Delhi, 1966.

See also **Buddhism: Religious Rites and Practices; Hinduism: Religious Rites and Practices; Pārvatī; Tantra; Yoginīs.**

ELLEN GOLDBERG

Yoginīs

A *yoginī* is a female adept of yoga. Yoga, developed in India, has many interrelated forms, such as hatha yoga, which makes the body supple enough to endure lengthy meditative sessions, and *jñāna* yoga, which helps one to develop wisdom and realize ultimate reality. Most ascetic techniques, such as restraining the breath and meditations, that develop spiritual discipline and applications are classified under the definition of yoga. The Sanskrit word for yoga is *yuj*, and its English cognate "to yoke" indicates the action of yoking, joining, attaching, harnessing, being diligent or zealous, to bring under control one's body and mind. Patañjali, a fourth-century Indian author, begins his treatise the *Yoga* sutra by noting, "yoga is the restraint of the mental processes (*yogah cittavṛtti nirodhaḥ*)." Patañjali's mother, Gonika, was herself an accomplished *yoginī* who gained great wisdom by applying yogic techniques.

Both in Hinduism and Buddhism, *yoginīs* can be practitioners of yoga, partners for sexual yoga, endowed with magical powers, or goddesses and therefore can represent many aspects of spiritual life for both Buddhists and Hindus. In both traditions, a great *yoginī* understands ultimate reality. In Hinduism this is a joining or transcending of the individual self (atman) with all-encompassing reality. A famous example is Mirabai (1516–1546), the Indian Rajasthani princess, who through her divine love for the great Hindu god Krishna, dissolved herself within him and realized universal reality. In Tibetan Buddhism, the eleventh-century *yoginī* Ma Chig Lab Dun achieved enlightenment when she realized the inherent voidness of all phenomena.

Sometimes yogic practices involving sexual union between a woman and a man are utilized to achieve these realizations. In tantric Hinduism, the female practitioner is referred to as a *yoginī* or Shakti, a woman of great power or a goddess; the man is known as a yogin or Siva, a great Hindu god. In tantric Buddhism, the woman is known as the mother (Tibetan, *yum*) symbolizing wisdom and the man as the father (Tibetan, *yab*) symbolizing skillful means. Both traditions stress the need to combine female and male attributes to achieve realization of ultimate reality.

Many *yoginīs* are described as goddesses, though the two terms are not interchangeable. In Hindu tantric treatises that describe the body as a microcosm of the universe, the goddesses within the body are called *yoginīs*. A practitioner seeks their help or tries to become them. When found in groups of eight, they are called sources or mothers (Sanskrit, *mātṛkā*). Another popular grouping is sixty-four *yoginīs*. In the eastern Indian state of Orissa, many circular roofless temples are dedicated to the sixty-four *yoginīs*. In Tibetan Buddhism one of the most famous goddesses is Vajrayoginī (adamantine or indestructible yoginī). Her practitioners, both women and men, aspire to become great spiritual adepts or perfected human beings.

BIBLIOGRAPHY

Benard, Elisabeth. *Chinnamastā: The Aweful Buddhist and Hindu Tantric Goddess*. 1994.

Shaw, Miranda. *Passionate Enlightenment: Women in Tantric Buddhism.* 1994.

See also **Mirabai.**

ELISABETH BENARD

Yoni

Yoni is a Sanskrit word referring to the female sexual organ (vulva, vagina, or sometimes womb). In Hindu cosmology it is the symbol of divine procreation and origin of the universe, along with its male counterpart, the *liṅga.* The two are identified with the goddess Shakti and the god Siva as Mother and Father of the universe, represented in iconography as a stone or marble aniconic image consisting of a shaft or pillar (lingam) set into a curved base with a spout (yoni). This image is commonly found in temples to Siva, where it is worshiped with offerings such as perfumed water, sandalwood paste, and incense.

The yoni is also worshiped independently in a ritual called the *yonipūjā,* particularly in the context of Shākta Tantrism, a highly esoteric Hindu religious movement that entails the quest for spiritual liberation through identification with or union with Shakti, the female principle. Schematically, the yoni is represented as a downturned triangle. This worship is associated with the goddess Kāmākhyā, whose temple is located at Kāmarūpa on the outskirts of Gauhati, Assam. This is the place of power, *shakti pīṭha,* where, according to Hindu mythology, the *yoni* of the goddess Satī fell when her body was dismembered by the gods after she immolated herself in the sacrificial fire. The main sanctum of the temple is a round stone depression within a cave through which a river runs. During the Hindu month of Sravana (July–August), the goddess menstruates; the water that oozes from this stone becomes reddish in color. A festival follows this event, and pilgrims gather on the site to receive bits of cloth stained by the menstrual flow of the goddess. These are believed to have curative powers.

This author asked a senior priest and tantric practitioner at the Kāmākhyā temple how he reconciled the worship of the yoni with the general Hindu devaluation of women's sexuality and reproductive powers. He replied that the general attitude is one of ignorance and that the yoni is sacred because it is the creative force of the Mother, from whom all life proceeds. His answer reflects the many different levels of understanding and ambiguities found within the diverse traditions of Hinduism.

BIBLIOGRAPHY

Kakati, Bani Kanta. *The Mother Goddess Kamakhya: Or Studies in the Fusion of Aryan and Primitive Beliefs in Assam.* 1948.

Khanna, Madhu. *Yantra.* 1979.

Kinsely, David. *Tantric Visions of the Divine Feminine: The Ten Mahavidyas.* 1997.

Mookerjee, Ajit, and Madhu Khanna. *The Tantric Way.* 1977.

Yonitantra. Edited with an introduction by J. A. Schoterman. 1980.

See also **Shaktism.**

KATHLEEN M. ERNDL

Synoptic Outline

The outline of contents presented here is intended to provide a general view of the conceptual scheme of this encyclopedia.

RELIGIOUS TRADITIONS

Prehistoric Religions
Principal Articles
    Pre-agricultural Peoples
    Agriculturalists

Religions of Microhistorical Societies
Principal Articles
  African Religions
  Afro-Atlantic Religions
  Caribbean Religions
  Mesoamerican Religions
  Native American Religions
  Oceanic Religions
    Polynesia and Micronesia
    Australia
  South American Religions
    In the Andes
    In the Lowlands
Theographies and Legendary Figures
  Ala
  Hina
  Mammy Wata
  Osun
  Pele
  Yemaya
Biographies
  Alinesitoué
  Dona Beatriz
  Lenshina, Alice

Ancient Near Eastern Religions and Israelite Religion
Principal Articles
  Ancient Egyptian Religions
  Canaan-Phoenicia, Religions of
  Hebrew Bible
    God in the Hebrew Bible
    Prophets and Judges

Israelite Religion: Pre-Monarchical
  Israelite Religion and Ancient
  Israel under the Monarchs,
  Prophets, and Priests
  Mesopotamian Religions
  Queens, Biblical
  Wisdom
    In Ancient Near East and
      Israelite Religion
  Witchcraft
    Witchcraft and Magic in the
      Ancient Near East and the
      Bible
Theographies and Biblical Figures
  Asherah
  Deborah
  Esther
  Eve
  Hagar
  Hannah
  Hulda
  Inanna
  Ishtar and Anat
  Miriam
  Ruth
  Sarah
  Susanna

Indo-European Religions
Principal Articles
  Celtic Religions
  Etruscan and Roman Religion
  Gnosticism
  Greek Religion
  Indo-European Religions
  Iranian Religions
  Mandaean Religion
  Minoan (Cretan) Religion
  Mystery Religions
  Scandinavian Religions

Supporting Articles
  Amazons
  Delphi
  Furies
  Maenads
Theographies or Legendary Figures
  Aphrodite (Venus)
  Artemis (Diana)
  Awthena (Minerva)
  Cybele
  Demeter and Persephone
  Freyja
  Hecate
  Hera
  Hestia and Vesta
  Isis
  Juno
  Psyche
  Sophia
Biographies
  Diotima
  Hypatia
  Sappho

South Asian Religions
Principal Articles
  Hinduism
    An Overview
    Religious Rites and Practices
    Modern Movements
    In the West
    History of Study
  Jainism
  Shaktism
  Sikhism
  Southeast Asian Religions
Supporting Articles
  Apsāras
  Bhakti
  Devadāsīs

Dharma
Kāma
Karma
Kuṇḍalinī
Maya
Prakriti
Tantra
Yoga
Yoginis
Yoni
Theographies
Draupadī
Durgā and Kālī
Lakṣmī
Pārvatī
Rādhā
Sarasvatī
Sītā
Biographies
Ānandamayī Mā (Ananda Ma)
Antal
Kāraikkāl Ammaiyār
Mahādēviyakka
Mirabai
Venkamamba, Tarigonda

**Northern Eurasian, Arctic, and
Central and Inner Asian Religions**
Arctic Religions
In Asia
In North America
Himalayan Religions
Inner Asian Religions of Nomadic
Peoples

East Asian Religions
Principal Articles
Confucianism
An Overview
Modern Movements
Politics and Authority in the
Confucian System
East Asian Religions
An Overview
Religious Rites and Practices
New Buddhist Movements
History of Study
Shintoism
Taoism
An Overview
Images of the Tao
Supporting Articles
Body: Female Body as Text in
Imperial China
Yin/Yang Polarity
Theographies
Amaterasu
Benten
Mazu (Tianhou)

Miaoshan
Nugua
Queen Mother of the West
Biographies
Mugai Nyodai
Pan Ch'ao
Seidel, Anna

Buddhism
Principal Articles
Buddhism
An Overview
Religious Rites and Practices
Himalyan Buddhism
East Asian Buddhism
Southeast Asian Buddhism
Modern Movements
Buddhism in the West
History of Study
Supporting Articles
Buddhas, Bodhisattvas, and Arhats
Compassion
Ḍākinīs
Emptiness
Ordination
In Buddhism
Wisdom
Prajñā and Prajñāpāramitā
Theographies
Hāritī
Kuan Yin (Kannon)
Tārā
Vajrayoginī
Biographies
Machig Labdron
Mahāprajāpatī
Saṅghamittā

Judaism
Principal Articles
Judaism
An Overview
Religious Rites and Practices
From the Babylonian Exile
Through the Second Temple
Roman, Byzantine, and Sassanian
Judaism
In the Middle Ages
Early Modern Era (1492–1789)
Modern Era
The Holocaust
Contemporary Jewish Life
Modern Movements
History of Study
Supporting Articles
Antisemitism and Jewish Identity
Divinity
In Judaism

Images of Women
In the Hebrew Bible
Ordination
In Judaism
Torah
Legendary Figure
Lilith
Biographies
Gluckl of Hameln
Jonas, Regina
Pappenheim, Bertha

Christianity
Principal Articles
Christianity
Historical Overview from 300 to
1800
Religious Rites and Practices
New Testament Canon
Paul and the Pauline Tradition
Apocrypha
Gnostic Writings
In Africa
In Asia
In Europe
In Latin America and the
Caribbean
In North America
Canada
United States
American Protestant Women's
Foreign Missionary Activity
Apostolic Religious Orders and
Communities
History of Study
Supporting Articles
African American Churches
Eucharist
Evangelical, Holiness, Pentecostal,
and Fundamentalist
Christianity
Images of Women
In the New Testament
In the Apocrypha
Liberation Theologies
Ministry
Ordination
In Christianity
Orthodox Christianity
Protestantism
Roman Catholicism
Visionaries in Medieval Europe
Biographies
Angela of Foligno
Blackwell, Antoinette Louisa
Cabrini, Frances Xavier
Catherine of Genoa
Catherine of Siena

Clare of Assisi
Day, Dorothy
Eddy, Mary Baker
Elisabeth of Schönau
Elizabeth of Hungary
Goretti, Maria
Guyon, Jeanne Marie Bouvier de la
    Motte
Hadewijch of Brabant
Heloise
Hildegard of Bingen
Jackson, Rebecca Cox
Joan of Arc
Juana Inés de la Cruz
Julian of Norwich
Kempe, Margery
Lee, Ann
Manfreda, Sister
María de Santo Domingo
Mary and Martha
Mary Magdalene
McPherson, Aimee Semple
Mechtild of Magdeburg
Menchú, Rigoberta
Mother Divine
Mother Teresa
Pazzi, Maria Maddalena de'
Perpetua and Felicity
Porete, Marguerite
Seton, Elizabeth Ann
Teresa of Avila
Thérèse of Lisieux
van Schurman, Anna Maria
Virgin Mary

Islam
Principal Articles
  Islam
      An Overview
      Religious Rites and Practices
      In the Arab Middle East
      In Iran and Turkey
      In Africa
      In Asia
      In Europe
      In North America
      Islamist Modern Movements
      History of Study
Supporting Articles
  Islamic Law
  Qur'an and Hadith
  Shiism
Qur'anic Figures
  Hawwa' (Eve)
  Maryam (Mary)
Biographies
  'A'ishah
  Fāṭimah

Ghazali, Zaynab al-
Khadija
Hawwa' (Eve)
Rabi'a
Sa'dawi, Nawal al-
Sha'rawi, Huda
Shafiq, Durriyah (Doria)

New Religions
Principal Articles
  New Religions
      An Overview
      In Europe and the United
          States
      In East Asia
      In Southeast Asia
      In Native American Traditions
      In Mexico
      In South America
Supporting Articles
  Cults
  Esotericism
  Mormons
  Neopaganism
  Occultism
  Spiritualism
  Theosophy
  Transcendentalism
  Twelve-Step Programs
  Wicca
  Witchcraft
      Contemporary Witchcraft
          Movement
  Women's Contemporary Spirituality
      Movement

**TRANSRELIGIONAL
PHENOMENA**
Topical Articles
  Abortion
  Adultery
  Afterlife
  Agricultural Rituals
  Alchemy
  Almsgiving
  Amulets
  Ancestor Worship
  Androgyny
  Animals
  Anonymous
  Asceticism
  Astrology
  Athletics
  Auspicious and Inauspicious
  Authority
  Birth and Rebirth
  Blood
  Body Postures and Trance

Body
    Microhistorical Societies
    In the East
    In the West
Boundaries
Breasts
Castration
Celibacy
Charisma
Chastity
Circle
Clothing
Community
Confession and Penitence
Contraception
Conversion
Couples
Couvade
Creation and Recreation
Cross-dressing
Crossroads
Death
Desire
Disciples
Divination
Divine Child
Divinity
    Divinity and Humanity
Divorce
Doctrine
Domestic Rites
Dreams
Dualism
Earth
Education
    Education and Literacy
Egg
Emotion
Epistemology
Evil
Family
Fasting
Fate
Female Personifications
Femininity
Fertility and Barrenness
Festivals
Folklore
Food
Founders
Friendship
Gender Conflict
Gender Roles
Geography, Sacred
Ghosts
Goddess
    Prehistoric Goddesses
    Historical Goddesses

Goddess (*continued*)
  Contemporary Goddess
    Movement
  History of Study
Hair
Hermaphrodite
Heterodoxy and Orthodoxy
Hierarchy
Home
Hospitality
Humor
Identity
Images of Women
  Myths and Symbols
Immanence and Transcendence
Incest
Infanticide
Initiation
Inspiration
Intoxicants and Hallucinogens
Inversion
Irrationality
Knowledge
Laity
Lands, Mythic
Language
Law
Leadership
Lesbianism
  A Classical View
  In the West
  In Asia
  In Microhistorical Traditions
Liturgy
Love
Lying and Dissimulation
Magic
Marriage and Singleness
  An Overview
  In Microhistorical Traditions
  In Asian Religions
  In Judaism, Christianity, and
    Islam
Martyrdom
Meditation in Asian Traditions
Memory
Menarche
Menopause
Menstruation
Misogyny
Monasticism
  In the East
  In the West
Monotheism
Moon
Motherhood and Grandmotherhood
Mourning and Death Rites
Muses
Mutilation

Mutilation, Genital
Nature
Nudity
Ordination
  An Overview
Ornamentation
Pacifism and Nonviolence
Paradise
Patriarchy
Patronage
Pilgrimage
Places, Sacred
Polytheism
Possession
Possession Cults
Prayer
Pregnancy
Priestess
Prophecy
Prostitution
Purification
Purity and Pollution
Rape
Rationality
Revelation
Riddle
Rites of Passage
Ritual
Sacred Marriage
Sacrifice
Saints
Salvation
Seclusion
Secret Societies
Self
Sex Change
Sexuality
Shamans
Shape-Shifting
Shrines
Silence
Sin
Sister
Solitude
Sorcery
Soul
Space, Sacred
Speech
Spirits
Spirituality
Suffering
Suicide
Sun
Superstition
Taboos
Temptation and Seduction
Theism
Time, Sacred
Tricksters

Truth
Utopian Communities
Vagina
Vegetarianism
Violence
Virginity
Virtue
Visions
Voice
Vows
War
Warriors
Weather
Weaving
Widows
Wisdom
  An Overview
Witchcraft
  An Overview
  Witchcraft in European
    Traditions
  Witchcraft in Africa
  Witchcraft in Asia
  Witchcraft in Native America
  History of Study
Wives
Womb
Women as Heroines
Women's Religions
Worship

**METHODS AND THEORIES IN
THE STUDY OF WOMEN AND
RELIGION**
Topical Articles
Androcentrism
Anthropology
Anthropology of Religion
Archaeology
Asian and Asian-American
  Traditions
Classism
Colonialism and Postcolonialism
Comparative Religion
Critical Theory
Cultural Studies
Deconstruction
Economics
Education
  Teaching Women and World
    Religions
Environmentalism
Essentialism
Ethics
  An Overview
  Feminist Ethics
Ethnicity
Feminine, The
Feminisms

Folklore Studies
Fundamentalism
Gender Studies
Hermeneutics
    An Overview
      Feminist Hermeneutics
Heterosexism
History
History of Religions
Ideology
Interreligious Dialogue
Lesbian Studies
Literary Theory and Criticism
Marxism
Material Culture
Matriarchy
Men's Spirituality Movement
Morality
Mujerista Tradition
Mysticism
Mythology
    An Overview
      Feminist Uses of Mythology
        about Goddesses
Oral Tradition
Orientalism
Performance Theory
Periodization
Phenomenology of Religion
Philosophy
    In the East
    In the West
Philosophy of Religion
Political Science
Postmodernism
Psychology of Religion
Queer Theory
Racism
Religion
Religious Experience
Ritual Studies
Romanticism
Sacred, The

Secularization
Semiotics
Sexism
Social Action
Social Change
Sociology
Sociology of Religion
Structuralism
Thealogy
Theology
    An Overview
      Feminist Theology
      Women-Centered Theology
Womanist Traditions
Woman's Bible, The
Women and Religion
      Monotheistic Traditions and
        Orientalism
      In the East
Women's Studies
Women's Suffrage Movement
Biographies
    Beauvoir, Simone de
    Benedict, Ruth
    Eliade, Mircea
    Freud, Sigmund
    Gage, Matilda Joslyn
    Gimbutas, Marija
    Graves, Robert Ranke
    Harrison, Jane Ellen
    Hurston, Zora Neale
    Jung, Carl
    Mead, Margaret
    Myerhoff, Barbara
    Seidel, Anna
    Underhill, Evelyn
    Weber, Max
    Weil, Simone
    Yates, Frances A.

RELIGION AND CULTURE
Topical Articles
    Architecture

    Overview
      Nomadic or Seasonal
Art
Autobiography and Biography
    An Overview
    In Asian Religions
    In Monotheistic Traditions
Bible as Literature, The
Craft
    An Overview
    In Microhistorical Traditions
    In Asian Traditions
    In Monotheistic Traditions
Dance and Drama
    An Overview
    In Microhistorical Traditions
    In Asian Traditions
    In Monotheistic Traditions
Film and Video
    Documentary Films and Videos
    Feature Films and Videos
Genre and Gender
Hagiography
Iconography
    In the East
    In the West
Images of Women
    Literary Images of Human and
      Divine Women
    Visual Images of Human and
      Divine Women
Literature
    In the East
    In the West
Media and Religion
Music
    An Overview
    Instruments and Voices
Sacred Literature
Performance Art
Photography
Science, Religion, and Women
Visual Arts

Index

Note: Page numbers in **boldface** indicate main article on subject. Those in *italics* indicate illustrations.

A

Aaron, 397, 516, 665
Abbott, Nabia, 511
Abbott, Sally, 999
'Abduh, Muhammad, 492, 496
Abel, 319
Abelam (people), 925
Abelard, Peter, 400–401
Abhidhamma (Buddhist text), 128
Abigail, 397, 756
Able-Peterson, Trudee, 810
Abnaki (people), 329
Abolitionists, 756, 832, 913, 1022
Abortion, **1–3**, 472
   Christian fundamentalism and, 354
   of female fetuses, 41, 97, 418, 1001
   Hinduism and, 203
   Islam and, 2, 507
   Japanese Buddhism and, 2, 115, 337
   Roman Catholicism and, 1–2, 165,
      681
   Sikhism and, 907
Abosom, 7
Abraham, 387–388, 394, 398, 488, 490,
     494, 869
Abram, David, 237
Abravanel, Benvenida, 541
Abstraction, 457
Abu Bakr, 21
Abu-Khalid, Fowziyya, 82
Abu-Lughod, Lila, 739, 862
Accidental Napalm Attack (Hung Cong
     Ut), 778
Achan Naeb, 128, 723
Achan Pongsak, 723
Achan Suchim, 128, 723
Ackerman, Susan, 553
Acoma (people), 687
Actaeon, 66, 332

Act of Abolition of 1829 (India), 431
Act of Truth, 988
Acts of the Martyrs of Lyons, 628
Acts of Paul and Thecla, 628
Adam, 207, 319–320, 332, 347, 362, 371,
     393, *410*
   as androgynous being, 36
   authority over Eve, 618, 1051, 1068,
     1069
   disobedience of God, 243
   and Eve's creation, 136, 221, 265,
     319, 881–882
   Eve's temptation of, 249, 273, 320,
     485, 490, 491, *675*, 712, 718, 946,
     966
   as humankind parent, 859
   and Lilith, 273, 593, 966
   Orthodox Christian view of, 752
Adams, Carol, 999
Adams, Evangeline, 70–71
Adang, Uma, 895
Adawiyah, Rabi'ah al-. *See* Rabi'a
Addams, Jane, 170, *171*, 918
Addu-guppi, 138
Adler, Margot, 1029, 1049, 1051
Adler, Rachel, 47, 312, 527, 976
Adonesia, 338, 339
Adonis, 48
Adorno, Theodor W., 46, 222
Adultery, **3–4**, 148, 183, *1001*
   Islam and, 4, 835
   Judaism and, 148, 288, 390, 461
   mutilation as female punishment, 694
   Susanna and the elders, 952
Advaita Vedanta, 772, 791
Aegir, 872
Aeneas, 48, 403
Aeneid (Virgil), 315, 403, 557, 563
Aeschylus, 27, 71, 299, 356, 452

Aesir, 871
Aesthetics, 852, 1012
Afek, 213
Affinity (organization), 583
Afghanistan, 504, 513
Africa. *See* African religions; *specific
     peoples*
African American churches, **4–6**, 170,
     241
   feminist revisionism, 434
   founding leaders, 349–350
   ghosts, 368
   Mother and Father Divine, 678–
     679
   music genres, 688–689
   ordination of women, 742
   Shaker community, 519, 1011
   spiritualism-based, 941
   womanist traditions, 1053–1054
   See also Nation of Islam
African American feminism. *See*
     Womanist traditions
African American writers, 444–445, 599,
     600–601
African Methodist Episcopal Church, 5,
     170, 742
African religions, **6–12**, 614–615
   Alinesitoué, 24
   ancestor worship, 31
   body portrayals, **95–96**
   Christianity, **160–162**, 1020
   circle symbolism, 179–180
   crafting in, 214, 1012–1013
   creation myths, 8–9, 222, 1055
   dance and drama, 233, 236–237
   divorce, 266
   female genital mutilation, 695–697
   fertility cults and rituals, 10, 337
   gelede rite, 9–10, 96, 338, 339

African religions (*continued*)
  goddesses, 7, 11, 22, 377, 604,
    614–615, 706, 754, 966
  Independent Churches, 161
  Islam, **500–502**
  lesbianism, 587
  liberation theologies, 592
  Lumpa Church, 578–579
  Mammy Wata, 614–615
  menarche ritual, 645
  moon representation, 674
  mourning and death rites, 684
  older women's status, 680
  polygyny, 618
  prehistoric humans, 795, 796
  purity and pollution, 817, 818,
    819–820
  sacrifice rituals, 861, 862
  secret societies, 9, 11, 233, 878–879
  spirit possession, 787, 788
  witchcraft, 9, 10, 1035–1036,
    1043–1045, 1050
  women's religions, 1066
Afro-Atlantic religions, **12–17**, 717,
  1073–1074; *See also* Santeria;
  Vodou
Afro-Brazilian religions, 16, 241, 442,
  1066, 1074; *See also* Candomble;
  Umbanda
Afterlife, **17–19**
  Islamic, 102, 630
  Norse, 872
  paradise, **758–759**
  psykhē and soul, 813, 814
  reincarnation, 14, 18, 110
  salvation, 867
  spiritualism, 941
  yin and yang polarity, 1075
  See also Resurrection
After Patriarchy (Cooey, Eakin, and
  McDaniel eds.), 760
Agamemnon, 333, 356, 863
Agape, 149
Agatha, 82, 382, 1061
Aggadah, 807
Agia, 464
Agnes, Saint, 82, 834, *835*
Agnes of Prague, 180
Agni, 819, 870
Agnosticism, 371, 785
Agricultural rituals, **19–21**
  blood's significance, 94
  geographic sacredness, 366
  Indian nudity symbols, 729
  menarche, 645
  prehistoric, 800–804
  sacred marriage, 21, 859
  sacred time, 981

  in South American religions, 930
  weather and, 1024
  See also Fertility and barrenness
Agunah, 530
Agunot, 625
Ahab, 396
Ahalyā, 771
Ahasuerus, 307, 308
Ahern, Emily Martin, 282–283
Ahimsa (nonharming), 25, 253, 261, 606,
  667, 755, 818, 999, 1019, 1077
Ahl al-bayt, 328
Ahmad, Hakim Niaz, 21
Ahmed, Leila, 766, 827
Ahmose-Nefertari, 34
Ahoe-Komy dance, 7
Ahpikondiá, 1055
Ahra Mainyu, 321
Ahriman (Angra Manyu), 484
Ahura Mazda (Ohrmazd), 483–484
AIDS, 681, 764, 825
Aife, 1022
Ainu (people), 94
'A'ishah, **21–22**, 208, 256, 477, 1019,
  1062
Ājīvikas, 109
Akan (people), 7, 8, 9, 645, 674, 684
Akhenaten, 34
Akinssowon, Christiana, 161
Akkadians, 373, 656, 657, 658, 1019
Akkā Mahādevī, 422
Akpafu (people), 684
Ala, 7, **22**
Alchemy, **22–24**, 874
  nature alignment, 712
  occultism and, 733, 734
  in Taoism, 23, 960, 962
  trickster figure and, 986
  womb symbolism, 1056
Alchi Monastery, 1035
Alcmene, 402
Alcoholics Anonymous (AA), 41, 989
Alcott, Bronson, 984
Aldura Churches, 161
Ale. *See* Ala
Aleotti, Raffaella, 688
Aletheia, 988
Aleuts, 59
Alevi, 498
Alexander V, pope, 142
Alexander, Priscilla, 810
Alexander the Great, 532, 656
Alexandra Salome, 533
Algeria, 497, 507, 508, 509, 834, 1020
'Ali Asghar, 898
'Alī ibn Alī Ṭālib, 21, 256, 328, 440,
  897–898, 899
Alinesitoué, **24**

Allah, 488, 604, 793, 794, 827, 1024
Allen, Paula Gunn, 704, 725, 839
All India Women's Conference, 426, 431
Allione, Tsultrim, 131, 191, 679
Alloula, Malek, 749
Almáguer, Tomas, 825
Almsgiving, **24–26**, 568
  Buddhism and, 667, 25
  cenobitic mendicancy, 667–668
  Hinduism and, 25, 421, 424
  Islam and, 25, 344, 494, 513
  Jainism and, 25, 520–521
  by laypersons, 567
Alourdes, 789
Alpert, Rachel, 582
Alphabet of Ben Sira, 593, 966
Alphonsus Ligori, Saint, 260
Altars, 902, 903
  domestic, 152–153, 269, 1014
Altekar, A. S., 771
Altered states. *See* Possession; Trance
Alternative religions. *See* New religions
Al Waqwāq (mythic island), 570
Ama'Ashtart, 138
Amadioha, 22
Amara-Singham, Lorna Rhodes, 330,
  666
Amar Das, 254
Amaterasu, **26**, 54, 217, 239, 279, 330,
  607, 687, 703, 900, 901, 903, 949
Amazons, **26–27**, 27, 39, 474, 569, *570*,
  580, 634, 694, 1021, 1060
Ambapālī, 810
Ambedkar, B. R., 128, 129, 746
Ambela (Oli), fast of, 325
Ambikā, 522
Ambree, Mary, 223
Ambrose, 241
Amenemhet III, queen of Egypt, 714
Amenirdis, 34
Ame no Uzumi, 239, 687
Ameretat, 484
American Academy of Religion, 294,
  364, 437, 976
American Lutheran Church, 742
American Museum of Natural History,
  637
American (Northern) Baptist
  Convention, 318
American Red Cross, 1019
American Sociological Society, 918
American Spiritualism, 603
American Woman Suffrage Association,
  93
American Women's Suffrage Movement,
  1070
Amesha Spenta, 483–484
Amida Buddha, 217

Amin, Qasim, 492, 496
Aminah, 1071
Amish, 183
Amitabha, 115, 123, 759
Amma, 6, 7, 8, 9
Amon-Ra. *See* Amun Re
Amorites, 136
Amos, 396
Amrita, 906
Amritanandamayi, Ma, 429
Amsas, 41
Amulets, **27–29**, 211
    Arctic religions, 57
    Egyptian religions, 33
    Islamic, 28, 495
    Jewish, 28, 593
    as ornamentation, 750
    Orthodox Christian, 153
Amun Re (Ptah), 32–33, 34, 273, 1031
An (god), 467
Anabaptists, 151
Anactoria, 869
Anagarika (Buddhist lay nuns), 67, 124,
    125–127, 128, 669, 744–745, 868
Anahita, 374, 483, 484, 1032
Analytic psychology. *See* Psychology of
    religion
Ānandamayī Mā (Ananda Ma), **29**, 67,
    97, 362, 614, 1015
Anastasia, 223
Anat. *See* Ishtar and Anat
Anatbethel, 517
Anātman, 108, 263, 300, 301, 926
Anatyahu, 517
Ancestor worship, **29–32**
    African religions, 6–7, 8, 31, 684
    Afro-Atlantic religions, 14
    in Canaan-Phoenicia, 137
    Confucianism, 30, 201, 280, 624
    East Asian religions, 74, 282, 283,
        284, 323
    ghosts and, 30, 368, 369
    Hinduism, 30–31, 424
    Native American religions, 724
    nomadic religions, 475
    Oceanic religions, 735–736
    Santeria, 324
    Southeast Asian religions, 933
    spirits, 262
    visions and, 1010
Anchorites, 876–877
Ancient Egyptian religions, **32–35**
    animal imagery, 39
    dance and drama, 233
    death portrayals, 243
    desert monasteries, 671
    female personifications, 329, 987
    female priesthood, 840

goddesses, 373, 486, 714–715, 987
goddess of wisdom, 1031, 1033
henge, 798
magical rituals, 1037–1039
music mythology, 691
mythological incest, 468
occultism, 733
pyramids, 32, 439
pyramid texts, 323, 487
serpent imagery, 38
shrines and temples, 605, 903
trickster figure, 986
zar ceremony, 409
Ancient Greece. *See* Greek religion
Ancient Israelite religion. *See* Israelite
    religion
Ancient Rome. *See* Etruscan and
    Roman religion
Āṇḍāl, 771
Andaman Islanders, 325
Andean culture, 1026
Andersen, Margaret, 918
Anderson, Mother Leafy, 576, 941
Andreas-Salomé, Lou, 815
Andreini, Isabella, 240
Andrews, Lynn, 708
Androcentrism, **35–36**
    African religions, 11
    in anthropological study, 42
    in comparative religion studies,
        187–188
    East Asian religions, 36, 282–284
    and Eliade's works, 36, 297–298
    in Freudian psychology, 815
    genre and gender, 365
    as hermeneutic, 406, 436
    in history of religion, 435–436, 839
    in interreligious dialogue, 478
    language and, 571
    literary criticism of, 594
    monotheism seen as, 673, 785
    postmodernism and, 791
    pregnancy and, 795
    in religion definition, 837–838
    religious symbolism, 769
    in ritual studies, 847
    in scientific study, 873–874
    social activism against, 913–914
    spirituality and, 942
    women's studies and, 1067–1068
    See also Sexism
Androgyny, **36–37**
    Afro-Atlantic religions, 15
    Arctic peoples, 60
    in humanity models, 35
    India, 403
    Jainism, 522
Angad, 905

Angela of Foligno, **38**, 82, 193, 317, 991,
    1009
Angela Merici, 176, 348, 849
Angelico, Fra, *583*
Angelou, Maya, 607
Angkatan Belia Islam Malaysia, 722
Angkor Wat temple, 238, *419*
Anglicanism (Episcopalianism), 151,
    168
    on contraception, 203
    Eucharist, 316
    government, 813
    and homosexuality, 583
    liturgy, 602
    Mead's affiliation, 638
    monasticism, 144
    ordination of women, 153, 661, 740,
        742
    Puritan reaction against, 812
    in United States, 170
    vestment making, 220
Angra Manyu (Ahriman), 484
Anguttaranikaya, 965–966
Ani. *See* Ala
Anima, 37, 300, 331, 458, 556, 815
Animals, **38–40**
    craftwork utilizing, 214
    dance ritual portrayals, 235
    goddess iconography, 38, 374, 456
    Native American personifications,
        1032
    in nomadic religions, 475
    prehistory imagery, 797
    sacrificial rites, 93, 94, 428, 494, 862,
        932
    serpent imagery, 38, 179, 319, 491,
        564–565, 755, 940, 966
    shape-shifting and, 896
    in South American religions, 930
    weather linkages, 1023
    witchcraft and, 1036, 1046, 1047
    See also Vegetarianism
Anima Mundi (World Soul), 733
Animism, 238, 475, 932
    divinity and, 262
    Native American, 708–709
    prehistoric Korea, 803
Animus, 37, 300, 458, 556, 815
Ani ohev otakh, Rosa (film), 343
Anishnaabeg (people), 709
Anishnabe (people), 645
Ankh, 33
Ankhnesneferibre, 34–35
Anna, 325, 464, 807, 840
Anna O. (case study), 334, 757
Annapurna Bhavani, 53
Anne, Saint, 455
Annulment, 266

Annunciation, 808
Annunuitum, 466
Anonyma Network, 41
Anonymous, **40–41**, 63
Anorexia. *See* "Holy anorexia"
Antal, **41**, 87, 361, 422, 692, 865, 924
Anthanasia, 223
*Anthology of Sacred Texts by and about
    Women* (Young), 76
Anthony, Saint, 270
Anthony, Susan B., 359, 1062, 1070
Anthony of Egypt (monk), 67
Anthropology, **42–45**, 77, 950
    Benedict, Ruth, 42, 85–86
    ethnographic films, 340
    feminist, 42–44, 621
    Mead, Margaret, 637–638
    microhistorial marriage traditions,
        620–621
    misrepresentations, 778
    oral tradition research, 739–740
Anthropology of religion, 43, **45–46**
    matriarchists, 634, 635
    on ritual, 765, 846
    weaving myths, 1026
    witchcraft, 1035–1037, 1040,
        1042–1046, 1050
Anthropomorphism, 263, 264
Antichrist, 612
Antifemale cultural bias. *See*
    Androcentrism; Misogyny; Sexism
Antigone, 243, 342, 452, 774
Antigone (Sophocles), 683
Antigoni (film), 342
Antiochus IV Epiphanes, 464, 627
Antiope (Hippolyta), 27
Antisemitism and Jewish identity,
    46–47, 312, 545, 815, 1005; *See
    also* Holocaust
Anubis, *18*
Anwar, Ghazala, 976
Anzaldua, Gloria, 225, 313
Aoko, Guadencia, 161
Apache (people), 883
    dance ritual, 234–235
    hair-cutting ritual, 390
    menarche ritual, 645
    puberty rites, 52, 94, *708*, 710, 982
    ritual complex, 710
    woman warrior, 1022
Apame, 464
Apartheid, 161, 592
Aphrodite (Venus), **47–48**, 314, 315,
    332, 384, 403, 487, 581, 604
    as archetype, 457
    depictions of, 1012
    dove as symbol, 39

literary images, 452
    Psyche association, 813
    in Sappho's poetry, 869
    temples to, 53
Apocalypse, 19, 982
Apocrypha, 159, 360, 464, 627, 1004
Apocryphon of John, 371–372, 671
Apollinaris, 223
Apollo, 66, 260, 333, 356, 384, 912
    Delphic oracle, 246–247, 787,
        805–806, 806, 988
    Muses accompanying, 687
    priestess, 805
Apostasy, 492
Apostolos-Cappadona, Diane, 1012
Apparel. *See* Clothing
Apphia, 158
Appleby, J. Scott, 116
Apple symbolism, 458–459
Applewhite, Marshal, 227
Apsāras, **48–49**, 938–939
Apuleius, 383, 488, 699, 813, 911, 1041
Aquarian Anti-Defamation League,
    1049
Aquila, 155, 158
Aquino, Corazon, 850
Aquino, Maria Pilar, 1068
Arabic language, 793
Arab Women's Solidarity Association,
    864
Arachne, 72, 1025–1026
Aragon, Lorraine V., 1026
Arai, Lucy, 213
Aranda (people), 587
Āraṇyakas, 858
Aratta, 467
Arcadia, of the Gospel of the Witches
    (Leland), 1048
Archaeology, **50–51**
    comparative religion studies, 187
    goddess religions, 705
    magic practices, 611
    material culture, 633–634
    Mesoamerican religions, 653–654
    Minoan (Cretan) religion, 663
    Native American religions, 707
    nudity representations, 633, 729
    prehistoric, 800–804
Archetypes
    Jungian, 300, 380, 457–458, 555, 556,
        702, 815
    men's spirituality movement, 648
    weaving, 1025
Architecture, 27, **51–57**, 1011
    Christian women's patronage, 761
    nomadic or seasonal, **55–57**
    overview, **51–55**

Arctic religions, **57–61**
    in Asia, **57–59**
    in North America, 18, 39, **59–61**, 329
Ardèche region (France), 797
Ardvi Sura Anahita. *See* Anahita
Arens, W., 467
Ares, 27, 48, 384
Arete, 452
Arhats. *See* Buddhas, bodhisattvas, and
    arhats
Ariadne, 774
Arianrhod, 145
Aristobulus II, 535
Aristophanes, 385, 755
Aristotle, 70, 687, 971
    friendship view, 352
    on menstruation as polluting,
        650–651
    on natural law, 203
    political theory, 288, 784
    virtue theory, 309
    on women as imperfect men, 299,
        485, 773, 836, 874
Arjan, 905
Arjuna, 887
Ark of the Covenant, 902
Arles monastery (France), 671
Armaiti, 484
Arria Paeta, 947
Arsinoë, 464
Art, **61–65**
    anonymous artists, 40, 63
    apple symbolism, 458–459
    apsārases depictions, 49
    body posture utilization, 103
    breast representations, 106, 454
    in Confucianism, 216
    emotional expression and, 300
    goddess depictions, 373–374,
        377–378, 381, 447, 569, 794, 813,
        995
    Greek afterlife symbols, 813
    hermaphrodites as subject, 403
    in Hinduism, 216–217
    images of women, 63, 454–457,
        1012
    performance art, 763–764
    performance theory, 764–765
    photography, 777–778
    pregnancy depictions, 362, 794
    prehistoric, 796–797, 802, 803
    Protestant view of, 813
    symbolism, 458–459, 729
    tantric, 957
    vagina imagery, 454, 995, 996, 1078
    Venus figures, 796–797
    visual arts, **1011–1015**

See also Architecture; Craft; Iconography; Music
Artemis (Diana), **65–66**, 314, 332, 384, 399, 400, 485, 581
  Atalanta and, 72
  continued worship of, 1048
  depictions of, 39, 995
  as heroine inspiration, 1060
  Iphigenia's sacrifice to, *862*, 863
  medieval view of, 1041
  priestesses of, 66, 805
  as sister, 912
  temples to, 53, 247, 903
Artha, 559, 622
Arthur, King, 329
Arya Mahila Samaj, 426
Aryans (people), 106, 469, 1021
Arya Samaj, 292, 426
Asase Ya, 22
Ascarelli, Debora, 541
Ascended Masters, 808
Asceticism, **66–68**
  almsgiving and, 25
  Basilian Plan, 348
  body's denigration and, 102
  Buddhist, 66, 67, 109, 281, 923
  Christian, 66, 67, 149–150, 408, 1003
  Confucian, 197
  as family renunciation, 66, 324
  Hindu *sannyasi*, 66, 105, 421
  Indian Buddhist nuns, 772
  Jainist, 521, 730
  Jewish practices, 541
  laypersons and, 567
  self-mutilation, 694
  silence and, 907
  spirituality and, 942
  Thai Buddhist new religion, 723
  virginity and, 1003
  See also Celibacy; Meditation in Asian traditions; Monasticism
Asch, Timothy and Patsy, 340
Asdzáá Nádleehé. *See* Changing Woman
Aseneth, 699
Asgard, 871
Ashanti (people), 6, 95–96, 266, 455
Asherah, 51, **68–69**, 137, 395–397, 486, 515, 516–517, 553
Ashkenazi, Jacob, 571
Ashram, 667
Ashrama, 252
Ash-Shabib, Ruqayya, 82
Ashtart, 487
Ashtoret, 486
Ashvaghosha, 361
Asian American traditions, **69**, 592

Asian religions. *See* East Asian religions; Inner Asian religions of nomadic peoples; Meditation in Asian traditions; Southeast Asian religions
Asiatic Society of Bengal, 430
Asma'u, Nana, 502
Aspasia, 255, 810
Assemblies of God, 318, 728
Assembly of the United Church of Canada, 583
Association for the Advancement of Women, 93
Association of Islamic Students, 722
Association of Muslim Ladies, 367–368
Assumption, 164, 325, 332, 556, 903
Astarte, 39, 137, 138, 333, 486, 805
Astrology, **69–71**, 75
Asynjur, 871
Atabeira, 140
Atalanta, 72
Atar, 484
Athabascan-speaking tradition, 18, 645, 710
Athaliah, 397
Athanasius, 856
Atharva-Veda, 858, 870
Atheism, 775, 785, 970
Athena (Minerva), **71–72**, 314, 332, 333, 356, 373, 374, 384, 390, 703, 774
  Anat and, 486
  as inspiration, 477, 1060
  literary images, 452
  and musical instrument, 692
  Neith linked with, 714
  owl symbolism, 39
  priestesses of, 66, 805
  temples to, 53, 247, 902
  weaving and, 1025–1026
  wisdom and, 1031–1032
Athena Polios, 805
Athletics, **72–73**
Athtar and Athtari, 137
Atisha, 965
Atkinson, Clarissa, 77, 561, 769
Atkinson, Jane, 892, 951
Atlanta University, 918
Ātman, 262, 263, 466, 882, 927, 1077
Atonement, 192, 1001
Atoni (people), 52
Ātreyī, 771
Atropos, 327, 1025
Attar, 79, 949
Augustine, 314, 321, 582, 966, 1008
  autobiography, 77
  celibacy, 143, 144
  contraception rejection, 203

conversion of, 204, *205*
desire typologies, 249
on good vs. evil, 1041
menstruation taboos, 650
Original Sin doctrine, 320, 909, 946
on pagan idolatry, 1040
and personal identity, 449
rape perspectives, 834–835
sexual pleasure rejection, 889
on visions, 1008
on wifely subordination, 1051, 1052, 1068
on women's resurrection, 17–18
Aulos, 693
Aung San Suu Kyi, 191
Auspicious and inauspicious, **73–75**, 250
Austin, J. L., 936
Australian Aborigines
  birth rituals, 91, 794–795
  female genital mutilation, 695
  folklore, 344, 736
  hallucinogen use, 479
  menarche ritual, 645
  menstruation beliefs, 820
  religion, **736–737**
  scholarly study, 298, 861
  seclusion practices, 876
  separate holy spaces, 783
  weather rituals, 1024
Authority, **75–76**
  Confucian, 201–202
  religious experience and, 839
  in thealogy, 968
  See also Hierarchy; Patriarchy
Autobiography and biography, **76–83**
  in Asia, **79–81**
  hagiography, 78–79, 80–81, 82, **389**, 432, 502
  monotheistic traditions, **81–83**
  overview, **76–79**
Auto sacramental, 525
Avalokiteśvara, 190–191, 261, 281, 285, 286, 448, 564, 965; *See also* Kuan Yin
Aveling, Eleanor Marx, 629
Avesta, 483
Axamama, 927
Ayahuasca, 480, 728
Ayia Triada, 663
Aylestock, Addie, 169
Aylward, Gladys, 1062
Aymara (people), 587
Ayse, 499
Ayu Khandro (A-yu Khadro), 81, 118
Azadari, 898–899
Azande (people), 75, 467, 587, 588, 620, 836, 925, 1035–1037

Aztec culture, *167*, 725, 1003, 1047
    childbirth, 655
        dance rituals, 235
        goddess, *653*
        human sacrifice, 20, 94, 863
        religion, 18, 652, 653, 655

B
Baal, 137, 338, 394–395, 397, 486, 514,
    515, 516
Baalat, 138
Baal Shamem, 138
Ba'al Shem Tov (Besht), 542, 865
Baal-Zebyl (Beelzebub), 138
Babata, 537
Babylonia, 323, *324*, 360, 366–367
    agricultural rituals, 21
    circle symbolism, 179
    Goddess creator, 755
    goddesses, 656, 657
    sacred marriage, 859
    temple prostitutes, 805, 809
Babylonian exile, 537
Bacchae (Euripides), 610
Bacchantes, 315
Bacchus. *See* Dionysus
Bachelor cult, 620
Bachofen, J. J., 188, 370, 380–382, 634,
    705, 800, 1027
Baeck, Leo, 524
Baha'i faith, 183
Bahiṇābāī, 87, 422
Bahuchara, 141, 887
Bai, Laksmi, 1023
Bainbridge, William Sims, 880
Baker-Fletcher, Karen, 1053
Baking, 209
Bakken, Harald, *966*
Bakongo (people), 13
Bakweri (people), 996
Bal, Mieke, 406, 594
Balabanoff, Angelica, 629
Balasaraswati, 692
Balder, 871
Baldwin, Margaret A., 810
Bali, 233, 236, 238, *339*, 788
    Mead fieldwork, 637, 638
    purification ceremony, *818*
Balts (people), 459, 949
Baluba (people), 179, 180
Balzer. Marjorie Mandelstam, 894
Bambara (people), 95
Bambara, Toni Cade, 600, 601
Bambuti (people), 52
Baneth, Eduard, 524
Bangladesh, 504, 834
Banks, Mirra, 40, 41
Banna, Hasan al-, 367

Bano, Shah, 354–355
Banshee, 368, 939
Bantu (people), 842
Ban Zhao. *See* Pan Ch'ao
Baozhang, 121
Baptism, 69
    Mandaean, 616
    naked, 730
    as rebirth, 91, 92
    removing Original Sin, 320
    as ritual cleansing, 817
Baptist churches, 318, 602, 742–743
    African American conventions, 5
    black music, 689
    women ministers, 153
Baraita de Niddah, 540
Barak, 245, 398, 515
Barasan (people), 1055
Barat, Madeleine Sophie, 176
Barbara, Saint, 15, 82, 449
Barbēlo, 371–372
Barber, Elizabeth Wayland, 210, 1025
Barbour, John D., 206
Bar mitzvah, 531, 843
Barnes, Nancy, 723
Baron, Dvorah, 552
Baron Samedi, 225
Barot, Madeleine, 164
Barrenness. *See* Fertility and barrenness
Barrett, Ellen, 583
Barry, Kathleen, 810
Barstow, Anne Llewellyn, 633, 1051
Barth, Karl, 164, 465, 909, 1068
Barthes, Roland, 778, 884
Barton, Clara, 1019
Basava, 605
Basavanna, 306
Basic Christian Community, 724
Basil of Caesarea, 671
Basilov, V. N., 895
Basket dance, 710
Bast, 39
Basu, Amrita, 355
Basu, N. K., 809
Batammaliba (people), 52
Bathing. *See* Water
Bathsheba, 824
Bat mitzvah, 531, 843
Baumberger, Joan, 931
Beach, Amy (Mrs. H. A. A.), 689
Beach, Frank A., 587, 588
Beard, Mary, 432
Bear Mother, 39
Bears, 39, 57–58, 235, 862
Beata de Piedrahita. *See* María de Santo
    Domingo
Beatas, 151
Beatrijs of Nazareth, 700

Beatriz. *See* Dona Beatriz
Beauvoir, Simone de, **85**, 164, 331, 334,
    643, 700, 774, 882, 888, 1062
Bebel, August, 629
Beck, Charlotte Joko, 131
Beck, Lois, 1057
Beckford, William, 510
Bednarowski, Mary Farrell, 718
Bedouin, 55, 500, 739, 862
    mourning and death rites, 684
    polygyny, 618
Beecher, Catharine, 170–171
Beecher, Henry Ward, 1070
Bee imagery, 39
Beers, William, 816
Beguines, 387, 448, 638, 1008
    Porete, Marguerite, 150–151, 193,
    293, **786**
Belenky, Mary Field, 300
Bell, Diane, 344, 620, 736, 783, 847
Bell, Gertrude, 510
Bell, Rudolph, 317
Bellah, Robert, 922
Bellerophon, 27
Beltum of Qatna (Mishrife), 136–137
Bemba (people), 10, 96, 323
Bembo, Bonifacio, *330*
Ben, Susila, *427*
Ben Azzai, 983
Benderly, Beryl Lieff, 1001
Benedict, Ruth, 42, **85–86**, 436, 638
Benedictine Rule, 672
Benedict of Aniane, 672
Benefaction. *See* Patronage
Benevolence, 196, 197, 301, 939
Beng (people), 20
Benhabib, Selya, 310
Bennet, Gillian, 951
Benten, **86–87**, 691
Bentinck, Lord, 948
Beowulf (epic), 333
Berbers, *1001*
Berdaches, 620
Bereavement. *See* Mourning and death
    rites
Berger, Peter, 880, 921
Berger, Theresa, 603
Bergounioux, Frédéric, 801
Bergson, Henri, 481, 991
Berit ha-hayyim, 843
Berkowitz, Michael, 545, 554
Berlin Conference (1884–1885), 161
Berndt, Catherine, 736
Bernini, Gian Lorenzo, 966
Berns, Marla, 214
Bernstein, Deborah, 551
Bertha, 150
Berthier, Brigitte, 279

Beruriah, 256, 1007
Bes, 33, 691
Besant, Annie, 979, 980, 999
Besht. *See* Ba'al Shem Tov
Betancourt, Ana, 686
Beth Chayim Chadashim (Los Angeles), 582
Beth Simcha Torah (New York City), 582
Bethune, Mary McLeod, 1063
Beutlerian, Magdalena, 1009
Beyond God the Father (Daly), 1068
Beyond the Java Sea (Taylor and Aragon), 1026
Bez Straha (film), 343
Bhagavadgītā, 87, 253, 257, 1019
Bhago, Mai, 906
Bhaisajyaguru, 286
Bhakti, **87–89**, 257, 422, 425
    gender and, 87–88, 105, 408
    paradise, 759
    poetry, 80, 87, 88–89, 408, 865, 936
    salvation, 642, 867
    women musicians, 688
    women saints, 80, 87–89, 771–772, 865
Bharata, 300
Bharata Mahila Parishad, 426
Bharata Muni, 238
Bharatanāṭyam (dance), 239, *250*, 251
Bharati, Uma, 355, 427
Bharatiya Janata Party, 355, 427
Bhārat Mātā, 53, 418
Bhārat Stree Mahamandal, 426
Bhesht-Zahra Cemetery of Martyrs of the Revolution (Iran), *899*
Bhikkhu Buddhadasa, 723
Bhikkhuni Ta Tao. *See* Voramai Kabilsingh
Bhikshunis, 668–669
Bhikṣuṇī Lakṣmī (Gelongma Pamo), 118
Bhṛkuti, 117
Bhudevi, 41
Bhutan, 415, 669
Bhutto, Benazir, 513
Bhutto, Zulfikar Ali, 493
Bia, 7
Biale, David, 553, 554
Biale, Rachel, 582
Bianchi, Ugo, 436
Bible
    authority of, 75
    barren women in, 336, 625, 794
    Christian fundamentalism and, 318
    concubinage in, 625
    contemporary women's retelling, 1065
    female access to, 291, 571

female heroines in, 6, 104, 1022, 1061, 1062
female peacemakers in, 756
feminist critiques of, 434
gender-inclusive language, 571–572, 813
hermeneutics, 404, 405–406, 594, 916
on homosexuality, 158, 581, 581–582
law and, 573
magical rites in, 1038, 1039
Pentecostalism and, 727
possession references, 787
prophets, 397–399, 441–442, 527, 806–807, 1038, 1039
Protestant emphasis on, 153, 811, 812
queens in, 461, **823–825**
as revelation source, 841
riddle tests, 842
as sacred literature, 856–857
self concept and, 881–882
serpent in, 38
study of, 104
temptress portrayals, 966
throne imagery, 455
vagina imagery, 995
vernacular translation, 811, 812
warfare in, 1019
on widowhood, 1029
on wifely duties, 1051
wisdom literature, 1033
wisdom personifications, 1031
witchcraft in, 400, 807, **1037–1040**
womanist study constructs, 1053–1054
Woman's Bible, 1054–1055
women warrior portrayals, 1022
See also Apocrypha; God; Hebrew Bible; New Testament
Bible as literature, **89–91**
Bibliander, 510
Bilfrost, 871
Bilhah, 387
Bilum, 213
Binding ritual, 97–98
    footbinding, 100, 197, 666, 694–695, 863, 1001
Bint al-Nil Union, 891
Biographies of Exemplary Women (*Lienu Zhuan*), 196
Biography. *See* Autobiography and biography
"Biography of Lilith, A" (film), 340–341
Bi-qiu-ni-zhuan (Lives of Nuns), 121
Bird imagery, 38–39
Birgitta of Sweden, 77, 841, 1008
Birth and rebirth, **91–93**
    amulet wearing, 28
    Arctic religions, 57

auspiciousness and inauspiciousness, 74
Buddhism, 18, 111, 120, 143
Chinese view of, 282–283
couvade, 208–209
fasting, 325–326
festivals, 338
Greek goddess of, 384
Hinduism, 18, 252, 418
Jainism, 521
Korean view of, 283
Lilith as demon of, 593
Mesoamerican religions, 655
in mystery religions, 698–699
Orthodox Christianity, 753
pain as punishment for Fall, 319, 650, 795
peyote as painkiller, 725
pollution beliefs, 91, 283, 321, 819, 820
reincarnation, 14, 18, 110, 771
ritualization, 91, 794–795
seclusion practices, 875
in South American religions, 931
spiritual dimensions, 839
taboos, 955
in thealogy, 969
vagina imagery, 995, 1078
virgin birth, 1003
womb symbolism, 1055–1056
See also Enlightenment; Fertility and Barrenness; Resurrection; Salvation
Birth control. *See* Abortion; Contraception; Infanticide
Bivia, 225
Black Caribs (people), 338, 442, 647, 680, 820, 1010, 1066
Black churches. *See* African American churches
Black Elk, 708, 709
Black Fast, 326
Blackfoot (people), 222, 710
Black Theology of Liberation, 161
Blackwell, Antoinette Louisa, **93**, 170, 740, 742, 1054
Blackwood, Evelyn, 587
Blavatsky, Helena Petrovna, 130, 147, 226, 268, 306, 362, 576
    Theosophy movement, *717*, 979, 980
Blind Justice (figure), 988
Blood, **93–95**, 115, 321, 540
    African rituals, 8, 10
    menarche ritual, 645–646
    powers of menstrual, 650
    ritual purification, 818
    sacrificial, 8, 10, 94, 95, 244, 654
    tantric rituals, 956
    See also Menopause; Menstruation

Blood (people), 883
Blood libel, 46
Blood money, 491
Blood sacrifice, 8, 10, 94, 95, 244, 654
Bloody Bowl Sutra, 74, 115
Blue Angel, The (film), 332
Blue Corn Woman, 347
Blues (music), 689
Blunt, Anne, 510
Bly, Robert, 648
Boas, Franz, 42, 45, 85
Boas, Franziska, 242
Boaz, 853, 1029
Boddy, Janice, 789
Bode, Mabel, 132
Bodh Gāya, 109
Bodhi, 867
Bodhisattvas. *See* Buddhas,
    bodhisattvas, and arhats
Bodily fluids
    Islamic beliefs, 491
    taboos, 955
    See also Blood; Semen
Body, **95–103**
    athleticism, 73
    in the East, **97–99**, 106–107, 418, 771,
        772
    exploitation of female, 778
    female body as text in Imperial
        China, **99–101**
    female impurity, 730, 774
    of God, 264, 265
    maternal, 816
    Mesoamerican ritualization, 654
    microhistorical societies, 8, 9, **95–97**
    musical instrument symbolism,
        692–693
    mutilation, 693–695
    nudity, 729–730
    ornamentation, 750–751, 1014
    performance theory, 764, 765
    Platonic view of, 773
    prehistoric female figurines, 796–797,
        803
    purification rituals, 818
    soul vs., 926–927
    in tantra, 957
    visual imagery, 454–456
    in the West, **101–103**, 107, 240
    women's relationship with nature
        and, 712–713
    yin/yang polarity and, 1075
    See also Breasts; Hair; Penis; Vagina
Body painting, 750
Body piercing, 751
Body postures and trance, **103–104**
Boehme, Jacob, 371
Boesak, Allan, 161, 592

Boff, Leonardo, 591
Bogomils, 371
Bojaxhiu, Agnes Gonxha. *See* Mother
    Teresa
Bole Maru Dreamers, 725
Bolen, Jean Shinoda, 1026
Boleyn, Anne, 691
Bolger, Diane, 633
Bologna, Giovanni, *987*
Bolshevik Revolution (1917), 543
Bona Dea, 315
Bonaparte, Marie, 351, 815
Bonewits, Isaac, 1049
Bonhoeffer, Dietrich, 966
Bonpo, 667
Book of Rites (Chinese text), 757, 771
Book of Rites (*Liji*), 78, 80, 195, 325
Book of the Dead, The (Egyptian text),
    1031, 1033
Book of the Law, The (Crowley), 612
Book of Wisdom or Folly, The
    (Crowley), 612
Booth, Catherine, 318
Booth, Evangeline, 318
Booth, William, 318, 999
Bora, Katherine von, 151, 207
Bori cult, 893
Borneo, 274, 750
Bororo (people), 326
Borra (people), *480*
Bosnia, 834, 1021
Bossuet, Bishop, 385
Boswell, John, 619
Bo Tree, 868
Boucher, Sandy, 131
Boudicca, queen of the Iceni, 145, 1022,
    1060
Boulanvilles, Henri, 510
Boundaries, 60, **104–106**, 844, 845
    hierarchical, 412–413
    Orthodox Jewish worship, 876
    taboos and, 955
Bourguignon, Erika, 788, 790
Bourke-White, Margaret, 778
Boxers (Chinese society), 879
Boxer Uprising (1900), 163
Boyarin, Daniel, 553, 826
Bracetti, Mariana, 686
Brahma, 75, 221, 238, 262, 321, 791,
    870, 892
Brahmacāriṇī, 421
Brahmacarya, 585
Brahman, 867
Brāhmaṇas, 109, 263, 759, 858, 933
Brahmavādinīs, 421, 771
Brahmin caste, 431, 559
    ancestor worship, 30–31
    foods and ritual, 346

karma, 560, 561
    widow desexualization, 1030
Brahmo Samaj, 292, 426
Branch Davidians, 227, 324, 992
Braude, Ann, 268
Brazil, 728, 902
    prehistoric figurine finds, 803
    See also Afro-Brazilian religions
Bread making, 209
Breaking the Waves (film), 342
Breasts, **106–107**, 454
    Amazon self-mutilation, 27, 694
Bresson, Robert, 341
Breton, Raymond, 139
Breuer, Josef, 757
Breuill, Abbé Henri, 796
Brid (goddess), 477
Bridal mysticism, 387, 867
Bride-price, 512, 530
Bridget of Sweden, 151, 561
Brigge, Mabel, 326
Brigit (Bridgid) of Ireland, 477, 691,
    1062
Brihadāraṇyaka Upanishad, 306
Brink, Judy, 354
British East India Company, 430
British Methodist Episcopal Church,
    169
Brochart, Charles, *870*
Brock, Rita Nakashima, 810, 971, 976
Broner, E. M., 47
Bronze Age, 663, 755
Brook Farm, 984
Brooten, Bernadette, 295, 537, 553,
    581
Brothel (Ephesus), *810*
Brother A., 38
Brothers and Sisters of the Free Spirit,
    241
Brothers Second, 680
Brown, Antoinette. *See* Blackwell,
    Antoinette Louisa
Brown, Joanne Carlson, 1001
Brown, Judith C., 582
Brown, Karen McCarthy, 77, 605, 706,
    739, 789, 840
Brown, Michael, 930
Brown, Peter, 102
Brown Douglas, Kelly, 1053
Brownies, 939
Browning, Elizabeth Barrett, 453
Brownmiller, Susan, 834
Brownson, Orestes, 984
Brunei, 932, 933
Bruyere, Rosalyn, 1063
Buber, Martin, 352
Bucer, Martin, 811
Buchanan, Constance, 769, 1067

Budapest, Zsuzsanna E., 226, 242, 379, 380, 877, 1048–1049
Buddha. *See* Siddhārtha Gautama
Buddhas, bodhisattvas, and arhats, **107–108**
  bodhisattvas, 111–112
  compassion and, 190, 191, 301, 331
  emptiness and, 263, 302
  female attainment of dharma, 772
  female status, 759
  gender boundaries, 105
  gendered sun imagery, 703
  in goddess tradition, 377
  Himalayan Buddhist, 117
  iconography, 447–448
  Mazu, 636–637
  paradise and, 759
  prajñā, 1032, 1034
  womb symbolism, 1056
  See also specific names
Buddhism, **108–133**
  on abortion, 2
  adultery punishments, 4
  afterlife, 18
  alchemy, 23
  almsgiving, 25, 667
  amulet wearing, 27
  ancestor worship, 323
  asceticism, 66, 67, 109, 281, 923
  astrology, 69
  biographical writings, 80–81
  birth and rebirth images, 92
  body's significance, 97
  breast symbolism, 106–107
  caste, 109, 569, 5591
  celibacy, 107, 111, 117, 120, 121, 122, 143–144, 149, 285, 585–586, 666
  compassion, 189–191, 301, 331, 606
  confession and penitence, 192
  creation stories, 112, 115
  dharma, 253
  disciple designation, 257
  divinity concept, 263
  documentary films, 340
  dreams, 272
  East Asian, 106–107, **119–124**, 197, 278, 283, 900, 901
  economic issues, 290
  emptiness, 189, 263, 301–302, **301–302**, 964, 1034, 1035
  enlightenment as goal. *See* Enlightenment
  esotericism, 305, 306
  fasting, 192, 325
  female emotionality, 300–301
  female impurity, 771
  female literacy and education, 292
  female patrons, 762

female sexuality, 321, 888, 965–966
female status, 770, 771
female voice, 1015–1016
feminine aspect, 331
feminine images, 333
fertility issues, 337, 794
friendship concept, 353
gender boundaries, 105, 112
gender roles, 675, 720, 721, 771
goddess of music, 687
goddess tradition, 377, 391–392
heterodoxy and, 408, 419
Himalayan, **116–119**, 415, 416–417, 609, 772
history of study, **131–133**, 839
homosexuality and, 585–586
hospitality, 441
Hungary Ghosts festival, 369
iconography, 447–448
initiation rites, 92
inspiration, 476
karma, 125, 192, 560–561, 882, 946
laity, 111, 118, 120, 124–127, 285, 286, 567, 744–745
legal systems, 573
literary traditions, 596, 598
as liturgy, 602
Machig Labdron, 609
Mahāyāna. *See* Mahāyāna Buddhism
marriage, 121, 124
maya concept, 635
meditation, 111, 117, 118, 125, 129, 189–190, 191, 563, 641–642, 668, 723, 1010
memory, 644
menstrual pollution, 651
misogyny, 666
modern movements, **128–130**, 264, **284–287**, 721, 722, 723
monasticism, 67, 98, 105, 106, 110, 111, 112, 114, 115, 118, 120–126, 128, 143–144, 186, 191, 253, 281, 284–285, 286, 575, 744
moral precepts and gender inequities, 675
Mugai Nyodai, 685
nonharming teaching, 755
ordination. *See under* Ordination
overview, **108–114**
paradise concept, 758, 759
pilgrim, *780*
possession beliefs, 787
prajñā (wisdom), 1032
prostitute conversions, 810
Pure Land, 123, 758, 759, 991
religious order founders, 348
religious patronage, 568

religious rites and practices, **114–116**, 118; *See also* Ordination
riddle tests, 842
saints, 109–110
salvation concept, 867; *See also* Enlightenment
samsara, 92, 327, 421, 573, 867, 946, 982
scholarly study, 287, 881
self concept, 882–883
sex-change aspects, 107, 109, 115, 302, 886
shrines, 109–110, 783, 902, 904
sin concept, 909
soul. *See* Anātman
Southeast Asian, **124–128**, 932, 933, 934
Theravada. *See* Theravada Buddhism
time-related beliefs, 982
vegetarianism, 120, 999
visionary activity, 1010
wandering mendicancy, 667
war justification, 1019
weaving, 217
in the West, **130–131**
widowhood, 1030
womb mandala, 1056
Zen. *See* Zen Buddhism
See also Tantra
Buddhism after Patriarchy (Gross), 769
Buddhist Compassion, Relief, Love and Mercy Foundation, 122, 285
Bührig, Marga, 164
Bulabay (people), 214
Bulls, 1023, 1024
Burgess, Alan, 1062
Burgos-Debray, Elisabeth, 646
Burial. *See* Mourning and death rites
Burial mounds. *See* Grave mounds
Buriats (people), 794
Burke, Kenneth, 481
Burke, Peter, 950
Burma
  Buddhism, 125, 127, 741, 745, 932, 933
  Engaged Buddhist movement, 723
  marriage, 622
  Nat religion, 127, 903, 1066
  polyandry, 619
  sacred performance, 238
  spirit worship, 603
Burqa, 723
Burroughs, Nannie Helen, 5
Bushido, 198
Bushnell, Horace, 1069–1070
Bu-ston, 131
Butalia, Urvashi, 355
Butler, Josephine, 810

Butler, Judith, 332, 364, 590, 765, 773, 825
Butler, Octavia, 601
Bwiti cult, *473*
Bynum, Caroline Walker, 76, 102, 178, 317, 413, 433, 434, 482, 766–767, 769, 926
Byzantine Christianity. *See* Orthodox Christianity

C
Cabezón, José, 191
Cabrini, Frances Xavier, **135–136**, 348
Caecina Paetus, 947
Cahill, Suzanne, 100
Cahokia, 708
Cain, 319
Caitanya, 105
Cakrasaṁvara, 37, 117, 232
Cakreśvarī, 522
Calligraphy, 216
Calliope, 687
Callisto, 66
Calvin, John, 616, 811, 856
Calypso, 452, 1026
Cambodia, 932
    Buddhism, 125, 746, 932, *1034*
    dance and drama, 239
    Engaged Buddhist movement, 723
    lay Buddhist nuns, 669
Cameron, Julia Margaret, 777–778
Campbell, Joseph, 648, 702, 801, 1061
Campbell, Lucie E., 689
Cāmuṇḍa, 244, 892
Canaan-Phoenicia, religions of, **136–139**, 394, 397, 514–517
Canada, 168–169, 220, 340, 583
Canadian Girls in Training, 169
"Can a Sexist Model Liberate Us?" (Hackett), 801
Candomble, 8, 13, 14, 16, 241, *300*, 890, 1074
Canelos Quicha (people), 930
Cankam poems (Tamil), *692*
Cannon, Katie, 312, 676, 832, 1007, 1053
Canonesses, 672
Cantarella, Eva, 581
Cao Ngoc Phuong, 191
Capps, W. H., 188
Caracalla, emperor of Rome, 537
Caribbean religions, 16, **139–140**
    Christianity, **166–167**
Caring. *See* Compassion
Carmelite order, 151, 762–763, 968
Carnality. *See* Temptation and seduction; Sexuality
Carnival, 443, 982

Caro, Joseph, 541–542
Caroline Islands, 735–736
Carpocrates, 371
Carr, Anne, 268, 769
Carreto, Leonor, 525
Carroll, John, 885
Carson, Rachel, 303
Cartesianism. *See* Descartes, René
Carthage, 767
Carthusians, 387
Carus, Paul, 129
Case, Sue-Ellen, 240, 765
Cassandra, 485, 562, *807*
Castaneda, Carlos, 708
Caste, 109, 291–292, 425, 429
    Brahmin, 346, 431, 559, 560, 561
    dharma, 251
    hierarchical structure, 413, 858
Castor, 207
Castration, **140–141**
    eunuchs, 361, 403, 887
    Freudian anxiety theory, 815
    male *castrati* opera singers, 688
Cataldo Mission (Idaho), *219*
Çatal Hütük excavations, 801, 802
Cathari, 371
Cathar sect, 76, 1042
Catherine of Alexandria, 82, 104, 525, 1061
Catherine of Genoa, **141–142**, 317, 841
Catherine of Siena, 82, **142**, 144, 151, 256, 317, 325, 841, 849, 866, 923, 1009, 1010
Catholicism. *See* Roman Catholicism
Catholics for a Free Choice, 1
Catholic Women's Suffrage Society, 164
Catholic Worker Houses of Hospitality, 243, 440
Catholic Worker movement, 242–243, 756, 850, 1028
Cat imagery, 39
Catullus, 699
Cavani, Liliana, 342
Cave paintings, 373, 374, 797
Cecilia, Saint, 82, 687, 691
Celibacy, **143–145**
    Buddhist, 107, 111, 117, 120, 121, 122, 143–144, 149, 285, 585–586
    Christian, 144, 149, 671, 923, 1042, 1052
    in cult religions, 227
    Eastern monastics, 666, 670
    Essene community, 671
    Hindu, 143, 420–421, 585
    Islamic disfavor, 149, 626
    Judaic disfavor, 149, 625
    New Testament, 619, 626
    Roman Catholic, 144, 626, 742, 849

Shaker, 227, 577–578, 992, 993
Sikh, 254
voluntary, 890, 923
woman as temptress and, 249
See also Chastity; Virginity
Celtic religions, **145–146**
    banshees, 368, 939
    goddesses, 39, 145, 146, 377, 477, 949
    myths, 145, 146, 459, 477, 701
    symbolism, 39, 459
    vagina imagery, 996
    woman warrior, 1022
    women's lamentations, 682, 683
Cemeteries, 782
Cenobitic mendicancy. *See* Community
Central America. *See* Mesoamerican religions; *specific countries and peoples*
Central Committee for the United Study of Foreign Missions, 173
Ceremonial Magic, 733
Ceres, 53, 314
Cerridwen, 896
Certeau, Michel de, 950
Ceylon. *See* Sri Lanka
Cézanne, Paul, 459
Chadhurani, Saraladevi, 426
Chador. *See* Veiling
Chaiyaboon Sitthiphon, 723
Chakras, 98, *252*, 565
Ch'an Buddhism, 121
Chando-gwan, 720
Chandogya Upanishad, 296
Changing of the Gods, The (Goldenberg), 815, 1068
Changing Woman, 222, 710, 883, 982
Chango, 1074
Chân Không, 123, 128, 723
Channing, William Ellery, 984
Chanting
    ancient Egypt, 32–33
    Jaina, 521
    Native American, 234–235
    neopagan feminist, 716
Chaos, 459–460, 492
Charcot, Jean-Martin, 787
Charisma, 111, **146–147**
    authority and, 75–76
    of cult leaders, 226
    as leadership factor, 15, 147, 348, 349, 575, 576, 577, 900, 901
    Mexican new religions and, 726, 727
    possession and, 787–788
    sociological view, 922
    of utopians, 992
Charismatic movements, 171, 318
Charitine, 159

Charity, 25, 344, 440, 567; *See also* Almsgiving
Charles, dauphin of French, 523
Charles I, king of England, 808
Chastity, **147–149**
  celibacy vs., 143
  Chinese view of, 100, 121
  Confucianism and, 280
  femininity and, 332
  self-mutilation to preserve, 694
  Vestal Virgins, 315, 407, 806, 1002
  as virtue, 676, 1007
  widow, 1030
  See also Adultery; Celibacy; Virginity
Chastity belts, *889*
Chat'an ka, 598
Chatsumarn Kabilsingh, 128, 723
Chatterjee, Partha, 749
Chaucer, Geoffrey, 606
Chaza, Mai, 161
Chen Duxiu, 199, 200
Cheng (scroll painter), 216
Cheng, Nien, 923
Cheng Yen, 122, 285
Ch'en Shu, 216
Chera. *See* Hera
Cherokee (people), 329, 710, 949, 1047
Cherokee movement, 724
Chessler, Phyllis, 485
Chestnutt, Charles Waddell, 600
Chewa (people), 10
Cheyenne (people), 620
Chiang Kai-shek, 200
Chiaravalle monastery, 616
Chicago, Judy, 1063
Chicago school, 918–919
Chichén Itzá, 653
Chidvilasānanda, 257
Childbirth. *See* Birth and rebirth
Child labor, 934
Childlessness. *See* Fertility and barrenness
Child marriage, 431, 666, 771, 907
Children
  communal rearing practices, 680
  divorce and, 266, 267
  goddesses of, 391–392, 400, 721
  home's importance, 439–440
  love and, 605
  sacrifice of, 136, 138
  in utopian communities, 992
  violence against, 468, 1001
  See also Family; Infanticide; Motherhood and grandmotherhood
Children of God. *See* Family, The
Childs, Lydia Maria, 810
Chimalma (Teomama), 654
Chimera, 237

China
  almsgiving, 25
  amulet use, 28
  antifemale cultural bias, 97, 888
  antisuperstition campaigns, 950
  astrology, 70
  biographical writings, 78–79, 80
  birth control, 624
  Buddhism, 106, 115, 120–122, 124, 191, 197, 281, 283–285, 325, 448
  Buddhist monasticism, 348, 670, 745
  Christianity, 163, 334, 1062
  Communist government, 121, 200, 284–285, 624
  dance and drama, 236, 239, 765
  divorce, 266
  earth's significance, 277
  emotionality of women, 300
  family, 99, 282, 289–290, 323, 721
  fasting, 325
  female body as Imperial-era text, **99–100**
  female personifications, 329, 330
  fertility beliefs, 337
  folk religions, 278–279, 795, 934
  footbinding, 100, 197, 666, 694–695, 863, 1001
  gender roles, 765, 886, 1052
  heroines, 1061
  infanticide, 472
  laity, 567
  literary tradition, 596, 598
  marriage, 622, 623–624
  Mazu deity, 636–637
  mosques, 903
  mourning and death rites, 683
  new religions, 720–721
  nomadic religions, 475
  Nugua mythological figure, 730–731
  philosophical status of women, 770–771
  prehistoric humans and sites, 795, 803
  religious architecture, 53–54
  religious patronage, 568
  religious traditions study, 287, 288
  rituals and practices, 91, 282–283, 325
  secret societies, 879
  shamans, 348, 893, 1045–1046
  suicide view, 947
  superstition, 950, 951
  weather symbols, 1024
  wifely subordination, 1052
  witchcraft, 1046
  women and religion, 1059
  women's movements, 334
  See also Confucianism; Taiwan; Taoism

Chineke, 22
Chinese opera, 765
Ching Chien, 348
Chinmaya mission, 429
Chinnamastā, 244, 622
Chinnamundā, 997
Chinul, 122
Chione, 149
Chiricahua (people), 587
Chisungu, 10, 96
Chittister, Joan, 923
Chloe, 158
Chloia, 247
Chö, 117, 118
Chodron, Pema, 131
Chogyam Trungpa, 131
Chogye Order (Korea), 122, 285
Chokwe (people), 9
Chopp, Rebecca S., 976
Chosbrŏn dynasty, 279, 280, 281, 894, 951
Christ. *See* Jesus of Nazareth
Christ, Carol, 370, 379, 408, 443, 594, 598, 700, 705–706, 769, 783, 839, 916, 976, 1068
Christa/Community, 971
Christian, William, 267
Christian and Missionary Alliance, 318
Christianity, **149–179**
  on abortion, 1–2
  in Africa, **160–162**
  African American women, 1053–1054
  Afro-Atlantic, 12–13
  almsgiving, 25
  American Protestant women's missions, **172–174**
  animal symbolism, 39
  antisemitism, 46–47, 1005
  Apocrypha, **159–160**, 360, 464, 1004
  apostolic religious orders and communities, **174–177**; *See also* Community; Monasticism
  asceticism, 66, 67, 149–150, 408, 1003
  in Asia, **162–164**, 284, 286, 292, 334, 425, 426, 932, 933
  athletics and, 72–73
  autobiographical and biographical writings, 81–82
  blood's significance, 94
  body's significance, 101–102
  in Canada, **168–169**
  canonical New Testament, 90
  castration opposition, 140–141
  celibate life, 144, 149, 671, 923, 1042, 1052
  circle symbolism, 179
  confession and penitence, 192–194

Christianity (continued)
contraceptive practices, 203
crafts and, 219–220, 448
creation stories, 221–223, 277
dance and drama, 240–242
demonic possession, 787
disciple designation, 255, 256
divinity concept, 263
divorce, 266
early ecstatic prophecy, 807
early mourning and death rites, 683
economics, 288–289
egg's significance, 297
environmental issues, 303
esotericism, 305
in Europe, **164–166**
Eve's portrayal, 319–322, 332, 758,
946, 966
on evil's origins, 321–322
family's significance, 324
fasting, 289, 325, 347, 863
female attire, 183
female inclusion in early movement,
1068
female knowledge, 563–564
female literacy and education, 293
female martyrs, 767–768, 628, 1061
female nudity symbolism, 729–730
female personifications, 329
female prophets, 807, 808
feminine images, 332–333, 452–453,
462–463
feminist neopaganism, 716
feminist revisionism, 1064
food and, 347, 998–999
friendship concept, 352
gender boundaries, 104
gender conflict, 360
gnostic writings, 159, **160**; See also
Gnosticism
hair symbolism, 390
heroic women, 1061
heterodox movements, 408–409
heterosexism and, 411
historical overview from 300 to 1800,
149–152
history of study, **177–179**, 432, 433,
839
Holocaust response, 548
homosexuality and, 158, 581, 582
hospitality and, 440
immanence vs. transcendence
debate, 465, 466
Incarnation, 102
incest prohibitions, 468
indigenous style, 621
inspiration and, 476, 477
Islam and, 488

Judaic tradition and, 535–536, 1057
laity, 567
language and, 571
in Latin America and the Caribbean,
166–168, 318
lesbianism and, 158, 353
liberation theologies, 167, 591, 592,
914, 972
literary traditions, 598–599
marriage, 621, 625–626
Marxist, 629
Mary Magdalene, 631–632
medieval same-sex unions, 619
menstruation view, 645–646, 650, 651
ministry, 576, 661–662
monasticism, 67, 144, 150, 174–177,
186, 575, 876
monogamy, 621
monotheism, 673, 785, 1056–1057
moral precepts and gender
inequities, 675
mourning, 1030
new religions, 717
New Testament canon, 90, **155–157**;
See also New Testament
in North America, **168–174**
ordination. See Ordination
paradise concept, 758, 759
patriarchy, 760, 765
Paul and the Pauline tradition,
157–159; See also as separate
listing
pilgrimages and shrines, 780–781
polytheistic aspects, 785
possession, 787–788
prayer, 152, 449, 792–793
pregnancy, 795
prostitute conversions, 809–810
racism, 832
rape perspectives, 834–835, 836
religious architecture, 53
religious conversion, 204–205
religious patronage, 149, 448–449,
568, 761
religious rites and practices, **152–155**,
844, 845, 1070–1071
Resurrection, 101, 102, 926
revelation acceptance, 840–841
rosary praying, 152, 449
sacred space, 935
sacrifice rituals, 861
saints, 575, 865–866
salvation concept, 867
separation from Judaism, 535–536
serpent symbolism, 755
shrines, 902
sin and suffering, 945–946, 909–910
soul, 814, 926

suicide rejection, 947
theistic portrayals, 970
theological discourse, 971–973, 975
Trinity, 673, 785
in United States, **169–172**, 318,
349–350
vagina imagery, 996
vegetarianism, 998–999
and violence against women, 1000,
1001
virginity valuation, 671, 1003
visionaries, 82, 150–151, 841,
1008–1009, 1010
votive offerings, 211
weather and, 1024
widow status, 1029, 1030
wifely duties and status, 618,
1051–1052
witchcraft beliefs, 1041–1042
women's history, 766–767, 774
women's public speaking
prohibitions, 146, 156, 158, 563,
857, 907, 937, 1015
women's stories, 643
worship, 1070–1071
See also Evangelical, Holiness,
Fundamentalist, Pentecostal
Christianity; Orthodox
Christianity; Protestantism; Roman
Catholicism; specific sects
Christian Science, 170, 226, 268, 409,
913
Eddy leadership, **290**, 349, 362, 576,
717, 719
Mother Church, 719
as new religion, 717, 719, 720
as women's religion, 1066
Christian Science Monitor, 290
Christians for Biblical Equality, 319
Christina of Markyate, 841, 923
Christina of Stommeln, 1009
Chronicles of Sri Lanka, 124, 131
Ch'üan-chen Taoism, 961
Chuang-tzu, 221, 771, 959
Chughtai, Ismat, 586
Chu Hsi. See Zhu Xi
Chūjōhime, 217
Chukchee (people), 587
Chukchi (people), 58
Chukwu, 7, 22
Ch'un-ch'iu (Lü Pu-wei), 691
Chün-fang Yü, 100
Chung Hyun Kyung, 313
Church and the Second Sex, The (Daly),
85, 888
Church building. See Architecture
Churchill, Caryl, 241
Churchill, Odette, 1061

Church Missionary Society, 161
Church of Christ, Scientist. *See*
    Christian Science
Church of England. *See* Anglicanism
Church of God in Christ, 5, 153, 318
Church of Jesus Christ of Latter-day
    Saints. *See* Mormons
Church of North India, 163
Church of San Francisco (Ecuador), *153*
Church of Scientology. *See* Scientology
Church of South India, 163
Church of the Nazarene, 318
Church Universal and Triumphant, 226,
    350, 808
Churel, 368
Cicatrization, 750, 1014
Cicero, 259–260, 315
Cilappatikāram (Tamil epic), 692
Cimbri (people), 145
Cinamwali, 10
Circe, 243, 452, 611, 896
Circle, **179–180**, 457
Circle of Concerned African Women
    Theologians, 162
Circumambulation, 180, 266
Circumcision
    as anti-Semitic issue, 46–47
    Australian Aborigine beliefs, 1024
    female genital mutilation vs., 695
    as initiation rite, 10, 96, 878
    in Judaism, 531, 533, 843
    See also Mutilation, genital
Cisneros, Cardinal, 617
Cistercian order, 150, 616
Civil rights movement, U.S., 913, 916,
    919
Civil War, U.S., 1019
Ci Xi, empress dowager of China, 202
Cixous, Hélène, 607
Clare of Assisi, 150, **180–181**, 317, 361,
    866
Clarke, James Freeman, 984
Clarkson, J. S., 888
Classism, **181**
    in hierarchical societies, 413
    Marxism on, 629
    sociological view, 919
    as violence factor, 1000
    See also Caste
Cleanliness. *See* Purity and pollution
Clement VII, pope, 142
Clément, Catherine, 944, 945
Clement of Alexandria, 183, 946
Cleopatra, 464, 534, 733, 947
Clergy. *See* Ministry; Ordination
Clio, 687
Clitoridectomy. *See* Mutilation, genital
Clothild, 150

Clothing, **181–184**, 211
    Christian widow mourning, 1030
    costumes, 233, 235
    gender inversion, 481, 482
    head coverings, 104, 155, 158, 183,
        390, 418, 421, 750, 753
    Indian saris, 97
    Islamic bride, *623*
    Islamic *hijab*, 390, 723
    Jewish prayer garments, 792
    Lakota ghost skirts, 724
    married Hindu woman, 623
    Orthodox Christian, 753
    vestments and textiles, 219, 220
    weaving, 1026
    See also Cross-dressing; Masks;
        Nudity; Veiling
Clotho, 327, 1025
Cluacina, 314
Cluniacs, 672
Clytemnestra, 333, 356, 452, 774
Coatlalopueh, 970
Cobras, 940
Cochamama, 927, 928
Coconut woman, 94
Cöd meditation, 1010
Cohambee River Collective, 410
Cohen, Aaron I., 690, 691
Cohen, Shaye, 537
Cohen, Ze'eva, 241
Cohn, Norman, 1051
Coitus interruptus, 202, 203
Collective unconscious, 457–458, 702,
    815
Collins, Patricia Hill, 919
Colonialism and postcolonialism, 24, 73,
    184–185
    in Africa, 161–162, 497
    in Asia, 163, 236, 932
    comparative religion studies, 187
    in India, 236, 250–251, 425, 426–427,
        430–431
    Islam and, 492, 497, 503
    magic and, 611
    patriarchy and, 760
    racism and, 832
    Roman Catholicism and, 848
    warfare, 1020
    witchcraft and, 1044–1045
Combs-Schilling, Elaine, 765
Coming of Age in Samoa (Mead), 637
Commitment ceremonies, 582
Communion. *See* Eucharist
Communism, 546
    in China, 121, 200, 284–285, 721
    Chinese marriage reform, 624
    Jewish adherents, 545
    in Vietnam, 123

    woman suffrage, 1070
    See also Marxism
Communist Manifesto (Marx and
    Engels), 620
Communitarianism, 784
Community, **185–186**, 352, 440
    Christian, 150, 151, 174–177,
        849–850
    cloistered, 175–176, 348
    of early Christian virgins, 671
    as family, 324
    identity and, 449
    initiation as rebirth, 91–92
    monastic, 667–668
    Paraclete, 401
    Sikh, 906
    sisterhood concept, 912
    solitude and, 923
    Vestal Virgins, 53, 183, 315, 407, 413,
        935, 1002
    See also Founders; Leadership;
        specific orders
Company of Saint Ursula. *See* Ursuline
    order
Comparable worth, 289
Comparative religion, **186–189**, 435,
    860, 866, 950
Compassion, **189–191**, 301, 331, 606
    as religious order goal, 440
    women linked with, 676
Comstock, Gary L., 76
Comte, Auguste, 918, 920
Conception. *See* Pregnancy
Concubinage, 625, 626
Confession and penitence, **192–194**, 632
Confessions of Lady Nijo, 324
Confucian Classics, 280
Confucianism, 97, **194–202**, 215, 216,
    278, 290, 573
    ancestor worship, 30, 201, 280, 624
    biographical writings, 78–79, 80
    body's significance, 99–100
    divorce and, 266
    on emotionality of women, 301
    family and, 201–202, 280, 323
    female literacy and education, 292
    female status, 770–771
    filial piety, 196, 280, 301
    friendship concept, 353
    gender roles, 361, 675, 720, 722,
        1052, 1058–1059
    love's importance, 605–606
    marriage, 623–624, 770–771, 1059
    modern movements, **199–201**
    overview, **194–199**, 280–281
    politics and authority, **201–202**
    pregnancy and birth, 794
    religious traditions study, 287, 839

Confucianism (continued)
  salvation concept, 867
  shamanism curtailments, 1045–1046
  sisters' role, 912
  Taoist reaction to, 771
  virtue and, 1006, 1007
  visionaries, 1010
  wifely subordination, 1052
  See also Yin/yang polarity; specific
    countries
Confucius, 194, 195, 196, 960, 964
Congregationalism, 153, 170, 740, 742
Conjurers, 1047–1048
Connor, Linda, 340
Conrad of Marburg, 298, 299
Consequentialism, 309
Conservative Judaism. See Judaism
Constantine, 150
Contraception, 202–204, 507, 1062
  Chinese "one child" dictum, 624
  Islamic view, 203, 507
  Jewish practices, 202–203, 527, 540
  religious prohibitions, 795
  Roman Catholic opposition, 165, 203,
    890
Convent of Perpetual Adoration, 672
Conversion, 204–207
  to Islam, 501
  modern Buddhist movements, 128,
    129, 746
  visionary experiences and, 1008
  See also Missionary activity
Conversos, 1011
Cooey, Paula M., 760
Cook, James, 955
Coons, Ellen, 416
Cooper, Anna Julia, 918
Copacabana shrine (Peru), 903
Copán (Maya site), 653
Coptic Church, 325, 326, 751
Corn ceremonies, 710
Cornell, Drucilla, 222
Corn Maiden, 94
Corn Mother (Corn Woman), 329, 970
Corpse. See Mourning and death rites
Corpus Christi Cycle, 234, 317
Corpus Domini, 175
Correspondences principle, 733
Cosmetics, 750–751
Cosmogenic myth. See Creation and
    recreation
Costumes. See Clothing
Council of American Witches, 1048
Council of Chalcedon (451), 149
Council of Constance (1417), 786
Council of Elvira (306), 241
Council of Nicaea (325), 140
Council of Nicaea (787), 150

Council of Orange (529), 320
Council of Trent (1545–1563), 176, 688,
    849
Council of Vienne (1311), 786
Council on Biblical Manhood and
    Womanhood, 319
Counterculture (1960s), 715
Counter-Reformation, 151, 433
Couples, 207–208; See also Marriage
    and singleness
Course of Miracles, 941
Cousins, Margaret Gillespie, 431, 979
Couvade, 208–209
Covenant of Unitarian Universalist
    Pagans, 380
Cover, Mrs. (Pawnee visonary), 724
"Covered: The Hejab in Cairo, Egypt"
    (film), 341
Coward, Rosalind, 801
Cowgill, George, 800
Cow imagery, 39, 261
Cox, Oliver Cromwell, 181, 918
Coya (people), 928
Coyote (mythic), 1026
Craft, 209–221
  anonymity of crafters, 40
  art vs., 63
  Asian traditions, 215–219
  iconography, 448
  maya concept, 635
  microhistorical traditions, 212–215,
    1012–1013
  monotheistic traditions, 219–221
  overview, 209–212
Craft, the. See Witchcraft,
    contemporary witchcraft
    movement
Creation and recreation, 221–222
  Adam and Eve relationship, 618,
    1051–1052, 1053
  African myth, 8–9, 222
  Babylonian myth, 323, 324, 366–367
  birth-related myths, 91
  Buddhist belief, 112, 115
  Chinese Nugua figure, 730
  Christian belief, 221–223, 277
  crossroads imagery, 225
  dualistic views, 273–274
  earth's significance, 277
  egg symbolism, 221, 273, 296–297
  Egyptian goddess Neith, 714
  geographic sacredness, 366–367
  Gnostic belief, 371–372
  Goddess-Mother figures, 755
  Hindu belief, 91, 221
  Islamic belief, 277, 651
  Japanese myths, 91, 277
  Judaic belief, 221–222, 277

as legal system factor, 573
  maya, 635–636
  music mythology, 687
  Native American belief, 724, 1026
  sacred spaces, 934
  sacred time, 982
  serpent imagery, 38
  South American belief, 930
  theistic view of, 775
  weaving myth, 1025
  womb symbolism, 1055, 1056
  women's speech and, 936–937
Cree (people), 986
Creon (king), 243
Cretan religion. See Minoan (Cretan)
    religion
Crispina, 149
Critias (Plato), 303
Critical theory, 222–223
Cro-Magnon culture, 796–797, 797–798
Crone, 39, 333
Cronus, 686
Cross-Cultural Study of Women, The
    (Dudley and Edwards eds.), 769
Cross-dressing, 223–224
  Arctic peoples, 60
  bridal mysticism, 867
  dramatic performances, 240
  feminine images and, 333–334
  hermaphrodites and, 403
  role inversion and, 481
  by shamans, 894
Crossroads, 224–226
Crow (people), 587
Crowley, Aleister, 612, 734
Crowley, Rose, 612
Crucifixion, 631
Cruikshank, Margaret, 589
Cruz, Sor Juana Inés de la. See Juana
    Inés de la Cruz
Crypto-Jews, 541
Cuba, 335
CUC (Committee for Peasant Unity),
    646
Cù Chulainn, 996, 1022
Cullavagga X, 108
Cult Awareness Network, 226
Cultic prostitution. See Temple
    prostitutes
Cults, 226–227
  Asherah, 516–517
  Bhārat Mātā, 418
  Bwiti, 473
  Dionysus, 315, 610, 698
  Draupadī, 270–271
  Fātima, 272, 328
  fertility, 337, 352, 801
  goddess, 783–784

khita, 10
Mesopotamian, 804–805
mystery religions, 698–699
Nat, 127, 348, *349*, 442
Neith, 714
new religions vs., 716
possession, 348–349, 788–790
Sacred Heart, 94
secret societies, 878
South American native, 931
territorial, 20–21
UFO, 346
vampire, 94
Vesta, 407, 934
Virgin Mary, 1005
Wiccan, 1048
See also Zar cult
Cultural relativism, 42
Cultural Revolution (China), 121, 285,
1059
Cultural studies, **227–228**
feminism, 335
Native American traditions, 708–
709
structuralism, 944–945
See also Anthropology; Women's
studies
Cuneiform, 656
Cuntarar, 559, 560
Curb, Rosemary, 740
Curie, Marie, 164
"Curse" (menstruation), 650
Cutting teaching (Tibetan Buddhism),
609
Cybele, 27, 53, **228–229**, 315, 456, 698,
699, 806
Cynethruth, abbess of Cookham, 1030
Cyril, bishop of Alexandria, 445
Cyrus, king of Persia, 474, 531–532

D
Dada, 763
Dagan (Dagon), 136, 137, 138
Dahomey (people), 587, 588
Dainas (folksongs), 702
Dākinīs, 116–117, 191, **231–232**, 272,
390, 563, 570, 611, 956, 1024, 1035
Daksha, 759
Dakwah movement, 722–723
Dalai Lama, 129, 131, 191, *640*, 745
Dalit theology, 591
Daly, Mary, 41, 206, 225, 267, 352, 376,
405, 443, 449–450, 573, 583, 590,
705, 924, 970, 975, 976, 1063
on androcentric theological bias,
1067, 1068
on Catholic women's symbols, 765
feminist philosophy of religion, 776

on misogyny-based religious customs,
85, 666, 888
rejection of silence, 908
on religion's patriarchal roots, 774,
916
on sati suicide practice, 836–837
semiotics development, 884
separatism definition, 877
sisterhood concept, 912
Virgin Mary characterization, 882
on wicca, 1029
Damayanti, 426, 988
Dambalah-Wedo, 15
Damiana, 727
Dan (divinity), 179
Danae, 1003
Dance and drama, **232–242**
in Asian traditions, *20*, **237–239**, 429,
765, 901, 933
feminine images, 452
festivals and, 339
gendered portrayals, 774
in microhistorical traditions, 7,
234–237, *736*, 788
in monotheistic traditions, **239–242**
Muses, 686–687
mystery plays, 32
Native American, 710, 724, 725
overview, **232–234**
performance theory, **764–765**
possession, 788
visions accompanying, 1010
See also Devadāsīs
Dandiya raas dance, 429
Daniel, 271, 808, 952
Danis (people), *1029*
Dante Alighieri, 19, *244*, 452–453
Danza Azteca, 235
Daode jing. See Tao-te ching
Daojiao. See Tao-chiao
Daozang. See Tao-tsang
Daphne, 896
Darby, John Nelson, 318
Darśanas, 1076
Darul Arquam, 723
Darwin, Charles, 712, 874
Dauarani, 1055
Daughters of Bilitis, 582
Daughters of Charity, 151, 176, 348, 849
David, 241, 756, 824, 853
David, Nicholas, 214
David-Neel, Alexandra, 132, 133, 306
Davie, Jody, 344
Davies, Lady Eleanor, 808
Davis, Angela, 689
Dawar, 935
Day, Dorothy, **242–243**, 440, 756, 850
Day of Atonement. *See* Yom Kippur

Day of Judgment, 807, 808
De, 1006
Deaconesses, 153, 169, 477
Dead Sea Scrolls, 75, 398, 533, 671
Dean, Laura, 242
Death, **243–245**
female personifications, 329
martyrdom, 627–628
paradise as reward, 758–759
purification rituals, 818
in thealogy, 969
warrior goddesses, 1021
widowhood, 1029–1030
witchcraft and, 1045, 1047
as womb return, 1055–1056
See also Afterlife; Birth and rebirth;
Mourning and death rites; Suicide
"Death of a Princess" (television
documentary), 641
deBary, W. T., 200
de Beauvoir, Simone. *See* Beauvoir,
Simone de
DeBerg, Betty, 354
Deborah, **245**, 295, 397, 398–399, 441,
464, 515, 516, 865, 937
as prophet, 806, 807
as warrior, 1022
Deconstruction, **246**, 459, 481, 837–839
"Deconversion," 206
Deer imagery, 39
Defilement. *See* Purity and pollution
Degarrod, Lydia Nakashima, 895
Deguchi Nao, 576, 717, 901
Deities
crossroads, 225
divine couple, 207
divinity beliefs, 252–265
Etruscan and Roman, 314–315
Greek, 314, 384–385
Himalayan Buddhism, 116–117, 563
Hindu, 642
household, 282, 283
immanent and transcendent views of,
465–466
Jaina, 521–522
Japanese, 86–87
Mesoamerican, 654
Mesopotamian, 657–658
Orixas, *300*
of women's religions, 1066
See also God; Goddess; *specific
deities*
Delacoste, Frédérique, 810
de Lauretis, Teresa, 341, 342, 343, 481,
773, 825
Delcourt, Marie, 36
Delilah, 332, 390, 606, 842, 946, 966
Delille, Jenriette, 850

Delog Dawa Drolma, 118
Delphi, **246–247**, *259, 260, 787,*
    805–806, 840, 842, 935, 936, 988
Delta Sigma Theta, Inc., 5
Demeter and Persephone, 53, 207,
    247–248, 304, 333, 384–385, 399,
    457, 472, 581, 698, 774, 805, 862
Demiurge (Ialdabaoth), 371, 372
Demons, 433
    characteristics, 1038
    ghosts vs., 368
    Lilith and, 593
    medieval Christian, 1041
    Mesopotamian, 659
    possession by, 787
    in visionary experiences, 1008
    witchcraft linked with, 1037, 1042
Denison, Ruth, 131
Deontological ethics, 309
De Periculoso (1298), 672
de Pizan, Christine, 63, 524, 599, 992,
    1062
Deren, Maya, 789
Derrida, Jacques, 246, 331–332, 404
Dervishes, 241
Desana (people), 1055
Descartes, René, 485, 562, 774, 998
    mind-body dichotomy, 704
    sex-gender distinction, 773
Descola, Philippe, 930
de Silva, Mapuana, *736*
Desire, **248–249**, 254–255, 559; *See also*
    Temptation and seduction
des Roches, Catherine and Madeleine,
    599
Destutt de Tracy, Comte, 451
Determinism, 712
Deuchler, Martina, 280
Deuteronomy, Book of, 792
Deutsch, Helene, 815
Dev, Lal, 907
Devadasi Act of 1947 (India), 251
Devadāsīs, 74, 236, 238–239, **250–251**,
    337, 338, 422, 425, 431, 688, 692,
    809
Devaki, 472
Devāra Dāsimayya, 306
"Development monks" (Thai Buddhist),
    723
Devendra, Kusuma, 128
Devi (film), 342, 422
Devī (goddess), 53, 262, *263*, 373, 374,
    416, 636, 891
Devi, Basanti, 426
Devi, Satyavati, 427
Devi Bhagavata Purāna, 253, 891
Devil. *See* Satan
Devil dances, 236

Devotio Moderna, 387
Dhamma, 129
Dhammapada, 361, 606
Dhammavati, Anagarika, 128
Dhanammal, Veena, 692
Dhanvatiī, 762
Dharma, **251–254**, 418, 559, 573, 585,
    614, 622, 772, 1052
Dharmagupta (*Ssu-fen*) Buddhism, 120
Dharmajinaree Wittya (Thai nunnery),
    128
Dharmakirti Vihara (Nepal nunnery),
    126, 128
Dharmaśāstras, 251, 292, 559, 585, 858
Dhouda, 82, 150
Dhruvarajan, Vanaja, 834
Diakonos, 155
Dial, The, 984
Diana. *See* Artemis
Diatta, Aline Sitoué. *See* Alinesitoué
Dickens, Charles, 453
Dickerson, Glenda, 242
Dickinson, Emily, 607
Diderot, Denis, 510
"Did Women Have a Renaissance?"
    (Kelly), 766
Didyma shrine, 806
Dienemann, Max, 524
Diesing, Freda, 212
Dietary laws. *See* Food
Dietrich, Marlene, 332
Digambaras (Jain sect), 67, 520, 521,
    522, 667, 730, 867–868
Digital camera, 778
Dignity (organization), 583
Dīksā, 92
Dilthey, Wilhelm, 404
Dinah, 553, 1000
Dinesen, Isak, 40, 482
Dinka (people), 7, 9
Dinocrates, 767
Diodorus Siculus, 26, 27
Diola (people), 24, 1045
Dionysus (Bacchus), 330, 390, 452, 836
    cult and rite of, 315, 610, 698
    maenads, 609–610
    priestess, 805
Diotima, **254–255**, 306, 563
Dīpavamsa (chronicle), 124
Dirge singers, 683, 684
Dis, 872
Discalced Carmelites, 968
Disciples, **255–258**, 463
Disciples of Christ, 153
Disir, 872
Dissimulation. *See* Lying and
    dissimulation

Divali (festival), 338
Divination, **258–260**, 733
    African religions, 8, 9, 862
    Afro-Atlantic religions, 14
    ancient Near East, 1039
    biblical prophets, 397
    intoxicant and hallucinogen use, 479
    possession and, 787, 788
    sacrifice rituals, 862
    by nomadic peoples, 475
    Scandinavian religions, 872
    witchcraft and, 1037, *1044*, 1045
Divin dine'é (Navajo mythic founders),
    710
Divine, Reverend Major J. *See* Father
    Divine
Divine Child, **260–262**, 472
Divine Comedy (Dante), 19
Divine couples, 207
Divine Votaress, 34
Divinity, **262–265**
    in African religions, 6–8
    in Afro-Atlantic religions, 15–16
    as authority factor, 75
    female models, 776, 785
    and humanity, **262–264**
    immanence and transcendence,
        465–466
    in Judaism, **264–265**
    literary images, 451–453
    masculinity linked with, 712
    Mesoamerican duality, 654
    in mystery religions, 698–699
    and nature, 712
    nonmasculine principle of, 718
    prehistoric and ancient female
        creators, 755
    revelation experiences, 840–841
    shrines for female figures, 780
    in Sikhism, 906
    in thealogy, 969
    Transcendental view of, 984, 985
Divorce, **265–267**, 1057
    gender inequality, 675
    Hinduism, 623
    Islam, 266, 489, 492, 496, 507, 512,
        627, 827, 889, 933
    Judaism, 266, 390, 527, 529, 530, 532,
        537, 539, 541, 625
    legal perspectives, 573
    Orthodox Christianity, 266, 626, 752
    Protestant remarriage, 626
    Roman Catholic ban, 625
Diwali festival, 429
Dix, Dorothea, 171
Dixon, Jane Hart Holmes, 742
Djilagons, 212
Dobu (people), 925

Doctrine, **267–268**
  heterodoxy and orthodoxy, 408–409
  sin-related, 909
  See also Original Sin
Dog imagery, 39
Dogon (people), 6–7, 8, 95, 96, 949,
    1055
Dolls, 57
Doll's House, A (Ibsen), 771
Dolni Vestonice Venus, 797
Domestic rites, **268–270**, 845
  architecture and, 52–53, 55–56
  Arctic religions, 57
  Christianity, 152–153
  East Asian religions, 282, 282–284,
    283
  Egyptian religions, 33
  Hinduism, 421, 424–425, 429
  Islam, 494, 499, 935
  Jainism, 520–521
  Judaism, 347, 529, 531, 935
  men as head of, 712
  motherhood and, 679–680
  Orthodox Christianity, 152, 753
  Southeast Asian religions, 932
Domestic violence, 311, 427, 540, 541,
    1000, 1052, 1054
Dominguez, Manuela, 727
Dominican order, 150, 1009
Dona Beatriz, **270**
Donations. *See* Patronage
Dong Zhongshu, 196
Doni-Su, 415
Donley-Reid, Linda, 802
Donne, John, 600
Dorotheus, 223
Dorothy of Montau, 1009
Dorsey, Thomas, 689
Dorze (people), *843*
Douglas, Ann, 433
Douglas, Mary, 819, 820, 921, 955,
    1044, 1050
Dowayos (people), 1012–1013
Downing, Christine, 583, 706, 839–840,
    911
Dowry, 25, 421, 489, 907
"Dowry death," 420, 1001
Drama. *See* Dance and drama;
    Performance theory
Draupadī, **270–271**, 390, 420, 426, 988
Drawing Down the Moon (Adler), 1049,
    1051
Dream Drum of Peace, 687
Dreams, **271–273**
  biblical prophets and, 397
  Jungian archetypes, 458, 555, 556,
    815
  as Native American influence, 725

  premonitory, 259–269
  prophecies through, 397, 808
Dreamtime, 736, 737
Dream Yoga, 272
Dress. *See* Clothing
Drewal, Margaret, 233
Dreyer, Carl Theodore, 341, 524
Drower, Lady Ethel S., 616
Drugs. *See* Intoxicants and
    hallucinogens
Drum Dance, 237
Drumming, 716, 1010
Druze, 683–684
Du'ā', 793
Dualism, **273–274**
  astrological, 69–70
  compassion and, 190
  esotericism and, 305–306
  Gnostic, 615
  Mandaean, 615–616
  Mesoamerican religions, 654
  misogynistic beliefs and, 666
  moon-sun hierarchies, 703, 704
  in religion definition, 838
  Taíno, 140
  virtue and, 1006
  Zoroastrian, 483
  See also Yin/yang polarity
Dubisch, Jill, 782
Du Bois, W. E. B., 4, 918
Duce, Ivy O., 242
Dudley, Margot I., 769
Du Guangting (Tu Kuang-t'ing), 669,
    961
Dumézil, Georges, 470
Dumont, Louis, 45, 413
Dumuzi, 333, 467, 487, 516
Duncan, Isadora, 241
Dunham, Katherine, 242
Duppies, 368
Duran, Khalid, 582, 583
Durgā and Kālī, 53, 221, 244, 253, 262,
    274–275, 329, 362, 390, 420, 422,
    428, 622, 956
  depictions of, 38, 244, *378*, 447, 456,
    995, 1012
  Kālī as warrior goddess, 1019, 1021
  linguistic descriptions, 572
  living goddesses of, 1002
  shaktism and, 892
  temples to, 902
  theistic reinterpretation and, 485, 970
Durgā-Pūjā festival, 1002
Durkheim, Émile, 45, 801, 846–847,
    860, 880, 918, 919, 920–921, 922,
    955
Dworkin, Andrea, 810
Dybbuk, 368

Dyer, Mary, 756
Dzogchen Buddhism, 1034

E
Ea (Mesopotamian god), 1038
Eakin, William R., 760
Earhart, Amelia, 1063
Earth, **277–278**
Earth Mother, 222, 277, 645; *See also*
    Mother Earth
East Asian religions, **278–288**
  body portrayals, 97–98
  breast symbolism, 106–107
  Christian colonialism and, 1020
  history of study, **287–288**
  new Buddhist movements, 264,
    284–287
  new religions, 717, **720–722**
  nonviolence teachings, 755
  overview, **278–282**
  religious rites and practices, **282–284**
  three major philosophies, **770–772**
  See also Buddhism; Confucianism;
    Taoism
Easter, 297, 981
Easter Letter (346), 856
Eastern Christianity. *See* Orthodox
    Christianity
Eastern Star, 5
Eaubonne, Françoise d', 303
Ebba, Saint, 694
Eberhard, Isabelle, 510
Ebner, Margaret and Christine, 352
Ebrey, Patricia, 99, 288
Echols, Alice, 335
Eckhart, Meister, 263
Ecofeminism. *See* Environmentalism
*Economic Ethics of the World Religions,
    The* (Weber), 1027
Economics, 43, **288–290**
  commercial prostitution, 809,
    810–811
  Hinduism, 290, 421
  Judaism, 288, 539
  liberation theology and, 591–592
  Marxism, 629
  sociological view, 921–922
  in utopian communities, 993
  of widowhood, 1029
Economy and Society (Weber), 1027
Ecstatic religions. *See* Evangelical,
    Holiness, Pentecostal, and
    Fundamental Christianity
Ecumenism, 661, 812
Edda, 351, 352, 949
Eddy, Mary Baker, 147, 170, 226, 268,
    290–291, 349, 362, 465, 576, 717,
    719, 841, 923

Education, **291–296**
　　Buddhist nuns, 118, 121, 122, 128
　　European Christian women, 164
　　gender equality, 774
　　Hindu women, 419, 426, 505
　　Islamic women, 497, 502, 508
　　Jaina women, 520
　　Jewish traditions, 531, 539, 541, 543,
　　　549–550
　　literacy, **291–294**, 497, 502, 596,
　　　738–739
　　Protestant Sunday School, 661
　　scriptural study, 104
　　teaching women and world religions,
　　　294–296
　　See also Women's studies
Edwards, Mary I., 769
Eger, Susan, 214
Egg, 91, 221, 273, **296–297**
Egypt (modern)
　　feminist leaders, 891, 897
　　Ghazal, Zaynab al-, 367–368,
　　　492–493, 508, 511
　　Islam, 492–493, 497–498, 507, 508
　　See also Ancient Egyptian religions
Egyptian Feminist Union, 897
Eidetic vision, 768
Eighteen Verses (Ts'ai Yen), 691
Eight-Fold Path, 1032
"Eight Honorable Ways of Conduct"
　　(print), *333*
Eilberg, Amy, 546, 740
Eilberg-Schwartz, Howard, 102
Eileithyia, 384, 805
Einstein, Albert, 712
Eipo (people), 213
Eisenstein, Zillah, 335
Eisler, Riane, 370
Ekajaṭī, 116
El (deity), 68, 136, 137, 394–395, 486,
　　514, 516–517
Elam, Diane, 246
Eland Dance, 237
Elbogen, Ismar, 524
Eleusinian mysteries, 248, 385, 698,
　　805, 878
Eliade, Mircea, 36, **297–298**, 334, 435,
　　703, 768, 801, 860–861, 892, 1025
Elijah, 256, 399, 440
Eliot, George, 40
Elisabeth of Schönau, 82, 178, **298**, 414,
　　1008
Elisha, 256, 396, 399
Elizabeth (New Testament), 336, 448,
　　462, 463
Elizabeth, Palatinate princess, 998
Elizabeth I, queen of England, 151
Elizabethan Settlement, 151

Elizabethan theater, 765
Elizabeth of Hungary, 82, **298–299**, 561
El-Or, Tamar, 543
Elves, 1040
El Zapotal (Mexico), 653
Emar, 338
Embroidery, 209, 210, 213, 219, 220,
　　448
Emergence Myth, 687
Emerson, Ralph Waldo, 984, 985
Emilia, 671
Emitai, 24
Emotion, **299–301**, 1006
Empiricism, 776
Emptiness, 189, 263, **301–302**, 964,
　　1034, 1035
*Encyclopedia of Feminist Literary
　　Theory*, 594
Encyclopedia of Religion, The, 435–436
Endogamy, 413, 625, 627
Endowments. *See* Patronage
Engaged Buddhism, 264, 723
Engels, Dagmar, 835
Engels, Friedrich, 381, 629, 635, 809,
　　1027; *See also* Marxism
England. *See* Great Britain
Englesman, Joan Chamberlain, 815
Enheduanna, 467, 656, 658
Enki, 103, 373, 467, 656, 657
Enkidu, 182, 1002
Enlightenment (Buddhist spiritual), 18,
　　107, 108, 109, 110–112, 117
　　compassion's importance to, 302
　　emptiness and, 189, 263, 302
　　Mahayana tradition, 759
　　prajñā (wisdom) as goal, 1032
　　as salvation concept, 867
　　women's capacity for, 666, 675, 759,
　　　770, 771, 810
Enlightenment (European eighteenth-
　　century), 77, 178, 228, 408, 485,
　　510, 554, 573, 852, 950, 972, 812
Enlil, 467
Enmerkar, 467
Ennius, 315
Ennoia, 160
Entu, 805
Enuma Elish (Babylonian epic), 274,
　　323, 360, 366, 657
Environmentalism, **303–304**, 874, 913
　　ecofeminism, 874, 877, 912
　　Goddess movement and, 379
　　vegetarianism as, 999
Epiphanius, 141, 371, 752
Episcopal Church. *See* Anglicanism
Episteme, 304
Epistemology, **304–305**, 771, 776
Epitaphios Logos, 683

Epona, 39, 145
Equal Rights Amendment, 354, 355
Equicola, Mario, 617
Equinox celebration, 715
Erato, 687
Erdrich, Louise, 453
Ereshkigal, 373, 467, 657, 911
Erichthonios, 72
Erickson, John H., 752
Erinyes. *See* Furies
Eris, 458, 459
Ermentrude of Bruges, 180
Eros, 48, 254–255, 813
Esbats. *See* Sabbats and esbats
Eschatology, 432
Eshin-ni, 123
Eshmun, 138
Eshu, 180
Eshu-Elegba, 15
Eskenazi, Tamara Cohn, 527, 532
Eskimos. *See* Inuit/Eskimos
Esoteric Buddhism. *See* Tantra
Esotericism, 70, **305–307**, 733
Espirituales, 563
Espiritualismo, 13, 1010
Espiritualismo Trinitario Mariano,
　　726–727
Essenes, 306, 527, 533, 671
Essentialism, **307**, 331
Esteban, Ines, 1011
Estefan, Gloria, 686
Esther, 78, *90*, 104, 240, 256, **307–308**,
　　325, 397, 461, 464, 966, 1062
Eternal Mother, 879
Ethical God, 263–264
Ethical wills, 370
Ethics, **308–313**
　　Confucian, 197
　　feminist, **310–313**
　　morality and, 675–676
　　overview, **308–310**
　　Sikh, 907
　　in thealogy, 969
Ethiopia, 17, 902
Ethnicity, 312, **313–314**, 543; *See also*
　　Asian American traditions;
　　Mujerista tradition; Womanist
　　traditions
Etruscan and Roman religion, **314–316**
　　Bacchanalian rites, 610
　　Christian martyrs, 671
　　Christian women celibates, 671
　　cosmetics use, 750–751
　　death and mourning rites, 243
　　divination, 258
　　female attire, 182–183
　　female literary portrayals, 563
　　female patrons, 761, 806

female personifications, 329, 330, 988
Jewish history and, 533, 535, 536, 537
mystery religions, 698
nature conceptualization, 712
as pagan, 715
priestesses, 805, 806
sacrifice rituals, 861, 862
Saturnalia festival, 842, 982
suicide acceptance, 947
sun imagery, 703
Vesta cult, 407, 934
Vestal Virgins, 53, 183, 315, 407, 413, 806, 935, 1002
See also specific deities
Eucharist, 104, 154, **316–317**, 347, 602, 981
communion wafers, 448
divorced persons and, 266
gendered symbolism of, 816
"holy anorexia," 317, 325, 863
Orthodox Christian prohibitions, 753
transubstantiation, 288, 316
Euclid, 457
Eudoxia, 149
Eugenia, 223
Euhemerus, 315, 703
Eumenides (Aeschylus), 299, 356
Eunuchs, 361, 403, 887
Euodia, 158
Euphrosyne, 223
Euripides, 247, 452, 610, 836, 863
Eusebius of Caesarea, 178, 432, 487
Eustochium, 671
Euterpe, 687
Evangelical and Ecumenical Women's Caucus, 319
Evangelical, Holiness, Fundamentalist, and Pentecostal Christianity, **317–319**
as charismatic, 76, 146, 171
counter-cult movement, 716
founding leaders, 349–350, 637
fundamentalism connotations, 354, 356, 914
leadership, 153, 171, 576
men's movement, 648
Mexican form, 727
as new religions, 717, 718, 727
oral traditions, 739
patriarchical values, 719
possession, 787, 789
revelation experiences, 841
South American form, 728
See also Fundamentalism
Evangelical Lutheran Church in America, 742
Evangelical Marian Sisterhood, 176
Evangelicals Concerned, 583

Evans, Sir Arthur, 633
Evans-Pritchard, E. E., 45, 588, 801, 836
witchcraft study, 1035–1036, 1050
Eve, 207, **319–320**, 322, 332, 347, 362, *410*, 969
apple symbolism, 458, 459
before the Fall, 758
Christian Science on, 719
creation of, 136, 221, 265, 319, 881–882
death, sorrow, and suffering linked with, 243, 909, 946
gnosticism and, 371, 372
God's speaking to, 840
hermeneutical study of, 405
as humankind parent, 859
Lilith as "first," 593
and nudity symbolism, 729
Orthodox Christian view, 752
prehistoric "hypothetical" maternal ancestor, 796
as prototypical female seductress, 676, 729, 774
self concept and, 881–882
shame and, 889
temptation of Adam, 249, 273, 485, 490, 491, *675*, 712, 718, 946, 966
theft of wisdom by, 1031
wifely subordination to Adam, 618, 1051, 1068, 1069
women's punishments for sins of, 650
See also Hawwa'
Evil, **320–322**
as consequence of free will, 775, 776
as God's test, 1041
salvation from, 866
serpent as symbol, 319, 755
temptation and, 965
witches epitomizing, 1036, 1042, 1045, 1047
women as, 311, 835, 909, 965, 1012, 1042
Evil eye, 1046, 1047
Evodia, 155
Evolutionary polytheism, 785
Evolution theory, 796, 874
Ewe (people), 8
Existentialism, 404, 700, 774
Exodus, 644, 665, 806, 807
Exorcism, *103*, 283, 416, 443, 631, 787, 788, 808
Exum, Cheryl, 553
Ezekiel, 232, 399, 807
Ezili-Danto, 15, 16
Ezili-Freda, 14, 15, 16
Ezra, 532

F
Fackenheim, Emil, 548
Fairies, 939–940, 1040
Faith, 811, 816
Faith healing, 318
Faivre, Antoine, 305
Falk, Marcia, 976
Falk, Nancy, 45, 189, 436, 1065
Fall, The. *See* Eve; Original Sin; Temptation and seduction
False Face maskers, 818
Falwell, Jerry, 318, 1052
Family, **323–324**
Buddhism, 114–115
in China, 99, 282, 289–290, 323, 721
Christian hierarchy, 676
Confucianism, 201–202, 280, 323, 770
divine, 323
emotional expression, 301
festivals, 338
foods and ritual, 346–347, 782
fundamentalist view of, 1020
gender-differentiated moral rules, 675, 676
importance to community, 186
Islam, 186, 289, 507, 626
in Japan, 284
in Korea, 283–284
male economic control, 288, 289
Mormonism, 677
sisters, 911–912
sociological view, 919, 921
Unificationist theology of, 718–719, 722
in utopian communities, 992
witchcraft within, 1044
yin/yang polarity and, 1075
See also Ancestor worship; Incest; Marriage and singleness; Motherhood and grandmotherhood; Wives
Family, The (formerly Children of God), 226, 324, 717, 992
Family planning. *See* Contraception
Family Ritual of Master Zhu, The, 280
Fa Mu Lan, 223
Fang (people), 52, 693
Fanon, Frantz, 749, 1020
Farley, Margaret, 312
Farm, The (community), 993
Faron, Louis, 930
Farrakhan, Louis, 649
Fasting, **324–327**, 338
asceticism, 66
Christianity, 289, 325, 347, 863
Himalayan Buddhism, 118
Hinduism, 253, 325, *326*, 338, 422, 424, 863

Fasting *(continued)*
  in initiation rites, 473
  Islam, 325, 494, 513, 827
  Jainism, 325, 521, 948
  Native American religions, 645
  Orthodox Christianity, 753
  as penitential practice, 192
  as suicide means, 948
  as vision inducer, 1010
Fasti (Ovid), 315
Fate, 14, **327**, 1025
Fates (mythic), 39, 327, 333, 1025
Father Divine, 678, 679
Fāṭimah (Zahra), 21, 53, 256–257, 272,
    325, **328**, 440, 477, 499, 502, 808,
    882, 1030, 1062
  Maryam and, 630
  persecution of, 627
  Shiist view, 898, 899
  storytelling ritual, 1071
Favret-Saada, Jeanne, 1042
Fecundity. *See* Fertility and barrenness
Fedelma, 145
Fee, Elizabeth, 801
Feldhaus, Anne, 820
Felicity. *See* Perpetua and Felicity
Fell, Margaret, 151, 908
Female personifications, **329–331**
  Maharashtra (India) rivers, 820
  nature, 329–330, 711–712
  truth, 988
  wisdom, 329, 987–988, 1030–1032,
    1033, 1034–1035
  See also Images of women
Female pope, 616–617
Feminine, The, **331–332**, 556
  androcentric view of, 35
  artistic depictions, 62
  as Asian meditative imagery, 642
  goddesses and, 380, 382
  Jungian archetype, 331, 457, 458,
    459, 815
  mythological representations,
    569–570
  as salvation's path, 98
  soul and, 927
  sun as force of, 703–704
  Taoist philosophy, 642, 770
  See also Female personifications;
    Images of women
Feminine Dimension of the Divine, The
    (Chamberlain), 815
Femininity, **332–334**, 360–362, 433
"Feminino Sagrado" (video), 341
Feminisms, **334–336**
  African American. *See* Womanist
    traditions
  anonymity issues, 40–41

anthropology, 42–44, 621
and art, 62, 63
in Christian America, 171–172
Christian Marxism, 629
comparative religion studies,
    188–189
contemporary spirituality movement,
    1063–1064
critical theory, 222–223
crossroads symbolism, 225
cultural studies, 228
deconstructionism, 246, 839
documentary films, 340–341
Eastern religions studies, 1058–1060
education, 293, 294–295
emotions, 301
environmentalism, 303, 874, 877, 912
epistemology, 304–305
essentialism, 307
ethics, **310–312**, 1053
evilness interpretation, 322
friendship concept, 352–353
gender role criticism, 361
gender studies, 363–364
goddess myths usage, 377, 383, 703,
    704, **705–706**
on Hebraic monotheism, 673
hermeneutics, **405–406**, 436, 774,
    839, 847, 916
heterodoxy views, 408
heterosexism issue, 410
humor and sacred meanings, 442
identity image needs, 449–450
in India, 335, 1058
Jewish-German movement, 757–758
Judaic, 47, 433, 527–528, 533, 549,
    551, 572, 650, 973
knowledge theory, 562–563
language reexamination, 571–572
Latina. *See Mujerista* tradition
legal system critiques, 573, 574
lesbian, 589–590
liberation theology, 335, 629
Lilith and, 593
literary criticism and theory, 594–595
literary writings, 85
liturgical issues, 603
Marxist, 335, 451, 629, 839
men's movements and, 648, 649
modern magic, 612
on moral reasoning styles, 675–676
mysticism, 700–701
mythologies usage, 703, 704, **705–706**
neopaganism, 715–716
new religions, 718, 720
orientalism, 749
patriarchical social construct, 760
performance art, 764

performance theory, 764–766
philosophy of religion, 775–777
pilgrimages to goddess shrines, 783
political theorists, 784–785
polytheistic leanings, 673, 785
postmodernism, 790–791
psychology of religion, 814, 816
racism issues, 832
religion definition issues, 837–838
religious experience inclusion,
    839–840
religious revisionism, 164, 167, 376,
    382, 432–434, 436, 577, 592, 913,
    972, 975–977
ritual studies, 847–848
scientific scholarship, 873–874
seclusion practice, 875, 924
self concept, 882
semiotic study, 884
sex vs. gender distinction, 363–364,
    773, 774
silence view, 907, 908
sin theory rejection, 909, 910
sisterhood concept, 912
social change perspectives, 915–916
sociology, 918, 919–920, 922–923
spirituality, 466, 577, 715–716, 777,
    914, 942–943, 980, 999
structuralism, 944–945
Thai Buddhist, 723
thealogy, 376, 968–969
theism reinterpreation, 970
wicca, 1029
on wifely subordination, 1052–1053
witchcraft movement, 1048–1049,
    1051
Woman's Bible, 1054–1055
women's studies, 1067–1069
worship concerns, 1070–1071
  See also Gender; Gender conflict;
    Gender roles; Goddess
"Feminization of poverty," 289
Fénelon, Archbishop, 385
Feng-shui, 1075
Fenris Wolf, 949
Ferdinand, king of Aragon, 617
Fernández de Santa Cruz, Manuel, 525
Fernea, Elizabeth, 42
Ferraro, Geraldine, 850
Fertility and barrenness, **336–338**
  African religions, 10
  animal symbolism, 39
  art creation, 1012
  Buddhism, 115
  Chinese goddesses, 721
  economic valuation, 288, 289
  egg symbolism, 297
  female nudity symbolism, 729

fertility cults, 337, 352, 801
food symbolism, 347
goddesses, 279, 337, 711, 796–797, 800, 801, 1024
Greek festivals, 325, 338
Hannah's story, 391
Hebrew Bible, 336, 625, 794
Hinduism, 361, 424–425, 771
Islam, 1052
Judaism, 288, 625
marital procreation emphasis, 625, 890, 1052
menarche ritual, 645
menopause, 647–648, 794
Mesopotamian rites, 659
nature personification, 711, 712, 713
nomadic group rituals, 475
prehistoric images, 796–797, 798–799, 800, 803
ritual practices, 96, 325, 338, 361
sacred marriage, 859
Sarah's story, 869
shame of childlessness, 794
twins' significance, 95–96
weather ceremonies, 1024
See also Birth and rebirth; Motherhood and grandmotherhood; Pregnancy
Festival of the First Fruits, 217
Festivals, **338–340**
ancient Egyptian, 33
ancient Greek, 325, 338, 339, 384, 385, 580
carnival, 443, 982
Etruscan and Roman, 314–315
Hindu, 253, 275, 338, 429, 442, 569, 982, 1002, 1078
music making, 391
riddle use, 842
sacred times, 981–982
Thesmophoria, 39, 247, 325, 338, 339, 385, 580, 862
transgressive behavior, 339
See also Ritual
Fetch, 368
Fetus, 1–2, 18
Feuerbach, Ludwig, 263, 776
Fides, 988
Filial piety, 99–100
ancestor worship and, 30
Buddhism, 120, 121
Confucianism, 196, 280, 301
East Asian folk religions, 279
Fillmore, Myrtle, 147, 908
Film and video, **340–343**
documentary films, **340–341**
feature films, **341–343**, 422, 443, 505, 524

feminine images, 332, 333
Islamic stereotypes, 641
Finley, Karen, 764
Fiorenza, Elisabeth Schüssler. *See* Schüssler Fiorenza, Elisabeth
Fiqh, 491, 857, 858
Fire, 329, 475, 818–819, 820
First Man, 222
Fishbane, Simcha, 611
Fish imagery, 39
Fisk Jubilee Singers, 688
Five Long Life Sisters, 116
Five Mountains system, 123
Five Scriptures, 195
Flagellants, 241, 898, 899
Flamel, Nicolla and Pernella, 733
Flaminica, 315
Flood (mythic), 1024, 1026
Flora, 160
Florentine Codex (Sahagán), 652, 655
Flower friendships, 588
Flowing Light of the Godhead, The (Mechtild of Magdeburg), 639
Fludd, Robert, 733
Flutes, 691–692
Foley, Helene, 377
Folklore, **343–345**
Australian Aborigines, 344, 736
cross-dressing tales, 223–224
fairies and jinn, 939–940
genre and gender, 365
ghosts, 368
lying and deception in, 606
myth survival, 702
shape-shifting, 895–896
sun goddesses, 703
superstitions, 950
Taoist, 771
weaving symbols, 1025
witchcraft, 1040–1042, 1047
See also Mythology; Oral tradition
Folklore studies, **345–346**, 950
Folk music, 739, 1016
Folk religions
East Asian, 278–279, 281, 288, 605, 721, 934
folklore and, 343–344, 346
nomadic peoples, 474–475
pregnancy beliefs, 795
See also New religions
Fon (people), 7, 8, 13
Food, **346–348**, 875
in ancestor worship, 30, 31
Hindu rituals, 424, 862
in initiation rites, 473–474
Jaina rules, 520, 521
Judaic rules, 531, 782, 818, 819, 862
male fears of women poisoners, 611

sacrifice rituals, 862–863
vegetarianism, 120, 818, 998–999
yin/yang balance, 1075
See also Fasting
Footbinding, 100, 197, 666, 694–695, 863, 1001
Ford, Clellan S., 587, 588
"Forest preservation monks, 723
Formes élémentaires de la vie religieuse, Les (Durkheim), 801
Fortes, Meyer, 31
Fortune, Dion, 612, 733–734, 1048
Fortune, Marie, 835, 1052
Fortune-telling. *See* Divination
Foster, Hal, 790
Foucault, Michel, 304, 332, 748, 825, 976
Founders, **348–350**
charisma and, 147, 348, 349
Christian Science, 290, 349, 362, 576, 717
Discalced Carmelites, 968
Espiritualismo Trinitario Mariano, 726–727
historians of, 767
new religions, 717–718, 721, 726–727, 767, 913
Paraclete, 400, 401
Poor Clares, 180
Shakers, 349, 362, 576, 577–578, 717, 787
spiritual possession of, 787–788
Foursquare Gospel, 349, 728
Fourteenth Amendment, 1070
Fox, George, 352, 908
Fox, Margaret and Kate, 226, 941
Fragrant Mountain (Hebei), 661
Franciscan order, 180
Francis de Sales, Saint, 176, 193
Frank, Anne, 552, 923
Frankfurt school. *See* Critical theory
Franklin, Aretha, 689
Franz, Marie-Louise von, 556, 940
Frazer, Sir James George, 346, 658, 659, 801, 836
Frazier, E. Franklin, 4, 918
Frederick II, Holy Roman emperor, 299
Freedman, Maurice, 282
Freedom (Taoist), 771
Free love, 629
Freemasonry, 734, 878
Free will, 775, 776
French Revolution, 543
Freud, Amalie, 815
Freud, Anna, 351
Freud, Sigmund, 45, **350–351**, 485, 555, 607, 757, 774, 955
feminine concept, 331

Freud, Sigmund (continued)
  Greek mythology use, 702
  and Jewish self-hatred, 46
  psychology of religion, 350–351,
    814–815
  religious myth, 468
  secularization view, 880
  soul theories, 926
Freud on Femininity and Faith (Van
    Herik), 815
Freud, Race, and Gender (Gilman), 815
Freyja, **351–352**, 374, 871
Frideswide, Saint, 348
Friedan, Betty, 975
Friedländer, Saul, 546
Friedman, Debbie, 1064
Friends of God, 352
Friends of the Western Buddhist Order,
    352, 746
Friendship, **352–353**, 588
Frigga, 352, 871
Fruit Bowl, Glass and Apples (Cézanne
    painting), 459
Fruitlands, 984
Frye, Marilyn, 311, 888
Frye, Northrop, 852
Fuchs, Esther, 553, 554
Fulani (people), 55
Fulkerson, Mary McClintock, 976
Fuller, Margaret, 984, 985
Funado, 225
Functionalism, 42, 45
Functional polytheism, 785
Fundamentalism, **354–356**
  Christian, 171, 203, 317–319, 354,
    356, 914
  Confucian, 200
  Islamic, 354–355, 500, 1001
  Jain, 521
  as political force, 148, 784
  postcolonialism and, 916, 1020
Fundamentalism Project, 354
Fundamentals, The (pamphlets), 318,
    354
Funerary practices. See Mourning and
    death rites
Furies, 299, 329, **356–357**, 452, 1021
Furies (lesbian feminist group), 410
Future of an Illusion, The (Freud), 814
Futurism, 763
Fuxi, 730

G
Ga (people), 684
Ga'anda (people), 1014
Gabra (people), 56
Gabriel, angel, 630, 827
Gadamer, Hans-Georg, 404

Gage, Matilda Joslyn, 267, **359**, 434,
    634–635
Gaia, 247, 304, 384, 459, 468, 859, 971
Gaiwiio, 725
Galas, Diamanda, 764
Galland, Antoine, 510
Galli, 140, 229
Gandhi, Indira, 29, 275, 1063
Gandhi, Mohandas K., 203, 264, 426,
    427
Ganeśa, 262
Garber, Marjorie, 223
Garbha (dance), 429
Garbha-adhana (womb-placing ritual),
    795
Gardner, Gerald, 380, 715, 716,
    1028–1029, 1048, 1051
Gardner, Kay, 689
Gargani, Maria, 194
Gargī, 78, 251, 771
Gārgī Vācaknavī, 419, 421
Garhwal Himalayas, 782
Garifuna. See Black Caribs
Garments. See Clothing
Garvey, Marcus, 17
Gatens, Moira, 773
Gates, Henry Louis, 594
Gathering of All the Secrets of the
    Dakinis, The (Buddhist text), 117
Gatumdug, 657
Gaudin, Juliette, 850
Gaur, Albertine, 291
Gautama. See Siddhārtha Gautama
Gavua, Kodzo, 214
Gayatri, E., 692
Gechak Tekchenling, 118
Gede (trickster), 225, 443
Geertz, Clifford, 36, 45, 267, 939, 951
Gegu (flesh-cutting practice), 100
Gelede (Yoruba rite), 9–10, 96, 338, 339,
    1044
Geller, Joy, 102, 815
Geluk (Buddist sect), 117
Gemara, 530
Gender
  in Afro-Atlantic religions, 15
  architectural interpretations, 52
  art and, 61–62
  astrology and, 69–70
  deconstructed definition of religion
    and, 838
  as divination factor, 259–260
  dualism and, 273–274
  emptiness concept, 302
  feminist ethics, 310–311
  genre and, 365
  of ghosts, 368–369
  heterodoxical views, 408

Jaina views, 521, 522
  magic associations, 610–612
  Mandaean symbolic balance, 615–616
  Mesoamerican primordial duality,
    654
  moon representations, 674
  moral development and, 675–676,
    815
  of musical instruments, 691, 692
  neopaganism and, 715, 716
  nudity as symbol, 729–730
  origination of, 882
  Orthodox Christian view, 752
  possession and, 787, 788–790
  prakriti concept, 791
  queer theory, 825–826
  sacred places and, 782
  in science scholarship, 873–874
  sex change and, 886
  sex vs., 363–364, 773, 774
  Sikh rejection of, 905
  social hierarchy and, 413
  of sun, 703–704
  weather rituals, 1024
  of witches, 1042, 1044, 1045, 1046,
    1050
  See also Feminisms
Gender conflict, **360**; See also
    Misogyny; Sexism
Gender-inclusive language, 268,
    571–572, 603, 748, 813, 1064, 1070
Gender roles, **360–363**
  academic study, 363–364
  African religions, 9
  anthropological studies of, 42–44,
    637–638
  bhakti spiritual equality, 772
  biological differences and, 712–713
  boundaries, 60, 104–105, 112, 844,
    845
  in Buddhism, 720, 771
  in Christian ministry and missions,
    661–662
  in Christian scripture. See Pauline
    tradition
  in Christian traditional family, 676
  comparative religion study, 188
  in Confucianism, 196–197, 201–202,
    675, 720, 770–771
  couvade practice, 208–109
  in cult religions, 226–227
  feminine images and personifications,
    332–334, 1030
  feminist movements, 334–336
  festival participation, 338–339
  fundamentalist religions on, 354–355,
    914, 1020
  grace as equalizer, 812–813

hagiography and, 389
in Hinduism, 251–253, 362, 771, 772
inversion of, 481–482
in Islam, 361, 508, 512–513
in Jainism, 730
in Judaism, 362, 461, 819, 983
karma factor, 125
leadership and, 575, 603, 887–888
liturgical mandates, 603
magical rituals, 1038–1039
Marxism on, 629
men's movement, 648–649
new religions, 717–720, 722–723, 727
in Pauline tradition, 155–156, 158,
    361, 463, 618, 700, 807–808, 812
pilgrimages and, 781
politics and, 784–785
prophecy and, 808
in Protestantism, 811–813, 1027
purity and pollution, 819–820
in ritual activity, 844
in Roman Catholicism, 164–165, 743,
    850–851
sacred sites control, 782–783
secret societies, 878
shamanism, 1045
social activism, 913, 914
sociological views of, 919, 920, 921,
    922
in Taoism, 675, 771
in utopian communities, 992
weaving, 1025, 1026
in Western Buddhism, 130–131
in Western philosophy, 772–774
wifely duties, 361, 362, 1051–1053
witchcraft and, 1044–1045
in women's religions, 1066
women's suffrage, 1069–1070
See also Feminisms; Hierarchy;
    Misogyny; Patriarchism; Sexism
Gender studies, **363–365**; *See also*
    Lesbian studies; Women's studies
Generation of Animals (Aristotle), 299,
    650–651
Genesis, 319–320, 624, 650, 1051, 1052,
    1068
Genitalia. *See* Vagina; Penis
Genital mutilation. *See* Mutilation,
    genital
Gennep, Arnold van, 91, 843, 847
Genocide, 707
Genovefa, Saint, 1024
Genre and gender, **365–366**
Gentileschi, Artemisia, 63, 1063
Gentlemen Prefer Blondes (film), 443
Geography, sacred, **366–367**, 475
    monotheistic tradition, 1056–1057
    mythic lands, 569–571

See also Crossroads; Pilgrimages;
    Places, sacred
Geomancy, 475, 1075
Georgianna, Linda, 193
Gerda, 871
German Romanticism, 299–300
Gershom, Rabbi, 530, 539, 625
Gertrude of Nivelles, Saint, 1024
Gertrude the Great, 150, 639, 1009
Geshtinanna, 271, 467
Ghana, 28, 645, 674, 684
Ghazali, Zaynab al-, **367–368**, 492–493,
    497, 508, 511, 1020
Ghosh, Latika, 426–427
Ghost Dance, 724, 725
Ghosts, 30, **368–370**, 425, 1037–1038,
    1039
Ghouls, 368
Gibbon, Edward, 178
Giddens, Anthony, 917–918
Gilgamesh (epic), 182, 658, 1002, 1031
Gilgamesh (Uruk ruler), 271, 467, 1002
Gillen, F. J., 736
Gilligan, Carol, 206, 300, 311, 675–676,
    836
Gilman, Charlotte Perkins, 918, 924,
    992
Gilman, Sander, 46, 102, 545, 553, 815
Gimbutas, Marija, 103, 188, 207, 360,
    370, 459, 704
    on ancient goddess religion, 376–377,
        380, 434, 705
    on archaeological sites, 801, 802
    on fate as spinning and weaving, 1025
    on female figurines, 633
    on goddess worship, 1011–1012
    Indo-European construct, 469–470
Ginsberg, Ruth Bader, 551
Ginzberg, Louis, 953
Ginzburg, Carlo, 896
Giobbe, Evelina, 810
Giraffe Dance, 237
Gittinger, Mattiebelle, 1026
Glazer, Myra, 545
Gleason, Judith, 706
Glengon, Mary Ann, 850
Glenn, Susan, 552
Global Ethic, A (1993), 478
Glory-of-Elves, 949
Glossolalia. *See* Speaking in tongues
Gluck, Carol, 287
Gluckl of Hameln, **370–371**, 541, 552,
    554, 758
"(G)nos(e)ology" (Geller), 815
Gnosis, 698
Gnosticism, 144, **371–372**, 408, 878, 927
    esotericism, 306
    hermaphrodite depictions, 403

Jesus images, 107
Mandaeans as sole survivors, 615
Nag Hammadi writings, 159, 160
sex (biological) superiority, 886
Sophia myths, 160, 371, 372, 925, 988
truth personifications, 988
wisdom personification, 987–988,
    1031, 1033
womb symbolism, 1056
on women celibates, 671
Gobineau, Comte de, 469
God
    alternative religious views of, 226
    as androgynous, 718, 719
    biblical images, 90, 394–396,
        461–462, 464
    and creation, 277; *See also* Eve
    divinity of, 263, 264–265, 452
    and evil, 775, 776, 1041
    existence proof, 775
    as giver of grace, 812
    Goddess vs., 379
    as immanent vs. transcendent,
        465–466, 984, 985
    incorporality of, 264
    Judaic, **264–265**, 461–462, 526, 529
    liturgical language on, 603
    and love, 604
    as masculine, 263, 264–265, 712, 774,
        776, 1068, 937, 938
    and monotheism, **673**, 785
    and new religions, 718–719
    prayer to, 792–793
    pregnancy linked with, 794
    as savior, 867
    theistic concept of, 775, 776, 970–971
    theological discourse on, 971–972
    in visionary experiences, 1008
    weather and, 1024
    wisdom stemming from, 1031
    women as image of, 874
    worship of, 1070–1071
    See also Allah; Goddess; Yahweh
Godard, Jean-Luc, 342
Goddess, **373–382**
    African, 706
    animal imagery, 38–39
    apparel, 182
    Aztec, 653
    Celtic, 39, 145, 146, 377, 477
    Chinese, 636–637, 721, 1024
    comparative religion studies, 188
    contemporary Goddess movement,
        226, 242, 264, 304, 370, **379–381**,
        383, 434, 612, 705–706, 716, 861,
        913, 916, 943, 1011–1012, 1068
    of contemporary witchcraft
        movement, 1048

Goddess (continued)
  death, 243–244
  divine couples, 207
  East Asian, 279
  Egyptian, 32, 33, 34, 39, 714–15
  Etruscan and Roman, 314–15
  fate, 1025
  as female personifications and
    images, 329, 332, 333, 452,
    454–457, 705–706, 987–988, 1012
  and feminist theory, 377, 383,
    705–706, 776
  fertility, 337, 711, 794, 801
  friendship, 353
  gender conflict and roles, 360, 362
  Greek, 813–814, 1025
  Hawaiian, 763
  as heroine inspirations, 1060
  Himalayan Buddhist, 116–117, 780,
    782
  Hindu, 377, 420, 422, 425, 622, 706,
    759–760, 791, 833, 891–892, 1019
  historical goddesses, **376–379**
  history of study, 370, 376–377, 380,
    381–382, 434, 702–703, 705–706,
    1011–1012
  iconography, 447–448
  incestuous pairings, 468
  Indian traditions, 88, 112, 377, 378,
    391–392
  Indo-European, 471
  Iranian religions, 483
  Israelite religion, 515, 553
  Jaina, 522
  life-affirming, 755
  love, 604, 605
  Mahayana Buddhist, 1034–1035
  Mesoamerican, *653*, 654
  Mesopotamian, 333, 373, 604, 656,
    657–658, 805, 1031
  Minoan, 633
  moon, 674
  music, 687
  neopagan, 715, 716
  nomadic religions, 475
  Oceanic religions, 735, 736
  as photographic muse, 778
  prehistoric goddesses, **373–376**, 794,
    796–797, 802
  priestesses, 805, 806
  sacred sites, 367, 783–784
  in Sappho's poetry, 869
  Scandinavian religions, 871–872
  shrines and pilgrimages, 780, 782,
    902, 783
  South American, 927–929, 930
  sun, 703
  symbolic imagery, 995

  Taoist, 771
  temple architecture, 53
  temptation by, 965, 966
  thealogy, 376, 968–969, 970
  truth, 987–988
  Venus figurines, 633, 796–797
  war, 1019, 1021, 1022, 1032
  weather, 1024
  weaving, 1025–1026
  wicca, 1028–1029
  wisdom, 1030–1032
  yin/yang polarity, 1075
  See also specific goddesses
Goddesses in Everywoman (Shinoda),
  1026
Goddess Temple (China), 803
Godfrey of Fontaine, 786
Godfrey of Viterbo, 510
Godiva, Lady, 39
God the Mother, 380
God She, 380
God's Wife, 34, 840
Goffman, Erving, 764
Goitein, S. D., 553–554, 807
Gold, Ann Grodzins, 739
Goldberg, Vicki, 778
Golden Ass, The (Apuleius), 699, 1041
Goldenberg, Naomi, 312, 765, 815, 916,
  970, 1029, 1068
Golden Bough, The (Frazer), 658, 659,
  801
Golden Embryo Hiranyagarbha, 296
Golden Mother of the Turquoise Pond,
  823
Golden Orchid Association, 586
Goldenweiser, Alexander, 42
Goldie, Rosemary, 165
Goldziher, Ignaz, 510
Gomez, Marie, 1011
Gonika, 1077
Goodale, Jane, 736
Goodall, Jane, 924
Goodeagle, Mrs., 724
Goodison, Lucy, 704
Goodman, Felicitas, 788–789, 790
Gopi Chand, 611
Gopīs, 105
Goretti, Maria, **382–383**
Gorgons, 896
Gospel, 689
Gospel of Mary (gnostic text), 159, 160,
  372
Gospel of Philip (gnostic text), 160, 372
Gospel of Thomas (gnostic text), 372,
  886, 935
Gotami, 80–81
Gotamī-apadāna, 614
Gottlieb, Alma, 20

Göttner-Abendroth, Heide, 612
Gough, E. Kathleen, 31
Govindadāsa, 88
Grace, Protestant, 811, 812–813, 1062
Graham, Billy, 319
Graham, Martha, 241
Graham, William, 343
Grahn, Judy, 225
Grail (lay group), 850
Grajales, Mariana, 686
Grandchamp ecumenical communities,
  176
Grandmotherhood. *See* Motherhood
  and grandmotherhood
Grant, Jacquelyn, 434, 1053
Grassroots theology, 163
Grave mounds, 798, 802
Graves, Robert Ranke, 380, 382,
  383–384, 702, 896
Grave-tending, 682
Great Awakening, 151
Great Britain
  anchorites, 876–877
  athletics, 73
  grey ladies, 368
  Hinduism, 428
  Indian colonialism, 236, 250, 425,
    426–427, 430–431, 1058
  Judaism in, 550
  magical order, 612
  peace movement, 756, 877
  Protestant and Catholic queens, 151
  Puritanism, 812
  spiritualism, 941
  witchcraft laws repeal, 715, 1048
  witchcraft movement, 1028–1029
  women's suffrage movement, *1069*,
    1070
  women warriors, 1022
Great Compassion Dharani, 564
Great Goddess, 207, 243, 329, 333, 391,
  705, 802
Great Moon Mother, 794
Great Mother, 9–11, 329, 815, 896, 935;
  See also Mother Earth
Great Spirit, 818
Greek philosophy, 772–773, 813–814
Greek religion, **384–385**
  astrology, 70
  athletic competition, 72
  cosmetics use, 750
  dance and drama, 232
  death and mourning, 243
  Delphic Oracle, 246–247, *259*, 260,
    787, 840, 842, 935, 936
  divine family, 323
  environmentalism, 303
  fasting, 325

fate, 327, 333
female attire, 182
female patrons, 806
female personifications, 329, 988
femininity representations, 332, 569, 570
festivals, 39, 247, 325, 338, 339, 384, 385, 580, 862
goddess shrines, 783
Harrison's historical studies, 392–393
homosexuality, 255, 580–581
inspirational deities, 477
literary images, 452, 563, 755
maenads, 609–610
Minoan (Cretan) religion, 663
Moirae, 1025
mourning and death rites, 682–683, 688
Muses, 686–687
mystery religions, 698–699
nature conceptualization, 712
as pagan, 715
priestesses, 805–806
rationality standard, 485
sacrifice rituals, 861, 862
serpent imagery, 38
temptresses, 332
theology origins, 971
trickster figure, 986
virtue theory, 309
weather symbols, 1024
weaving, 1025–1026
women's status, 765, 773
See also Goddess; Mythology; Orthodox Christianity
Green belt movement, 914
Greenham Common (England), 756, 877
Gregor, Thomas, 931
Gregory I (the Great), pope, 631–632
Gregory IX, pope, 299
Gregory XI, pope, 142
Gregory of Nyssa, 82, 671, 752
Grey ladies, 368
Grhajstya, 622
Griffiths, Paul J., 267
Grima, Benedicte, 739
Grimes, Ronald L., 847
Grimké, Sarah and Angelina, 171, 334, 434, 756
Grimm brothers, 702
Grinquist, Hilma, 511
Gross, Rita, 36, 37, 45, 131, 133, 189, 191, 295, 436, 706, 769, 838, 839, 861, 958, 1065
Grosz, Elizabeth, 773
Group marriage, 620, 992
Growing Up in New Guinea (Mead), 637–638

Gruchy, Lydia, 169
Gryson, Roger, 408
Guabancex, 140
Guabonito, 139
Guajiro (people), 930–931
Guan Daosheng, 216
Guardian spirit, 86
Guatemala, 646–647, 653, 1023
Guayahona, 139
Gudea, king of Mesopotamia, 1031
Gudorf, Christine, 312
Guénon, René, 305
Guerrilla warfare, 1020, 1023
Guglielma of Bohemia, 616
Guilt, temptation and, 966
Gujri, Mata, 906
Gula, 657, 658, 1031, 1038
Gumerman, George, 800
Gunn, Janet Varner, 77
Gupta, Lina, 572, 970
Guru Granth (sacred text), 905–906
Gurung (people), 416
Gurus, 429–430, 667, 904–907, 957, 1076
Gusii (people), 925
Gutierrez, Gustavo, 591
Guttmann, Julius, 524
Guyon, Jeanne Marie Bouvier de la Motte, 385–386
Gwion, 896
Gylany, 377
Gypsies, 546, 548

H
Habbaba, 691
Habermas, Jürgen, 404
Habiba, 28
Habir, 203
Haci, 499
Hackett, Jo Ann, 515, 801
Hackett, Rosalind, 674
Hadassah, 544, 551, 552, 953
Haddad, Yvonne, 511
Hadda ([H]Adad; H[A]ddu), 136
Hades, 248, 384, 385, 472
Hadewijch of Brabant, 387, 1009
Hadith. See Qur'an and Hadith
Hadrian, emperor of Rome, 330, 537
Haeri, Shahla, 835
Hae-Soon, 949
Hagar, 53, 387–388, 460, 463, 464, 490, 553, 869, 935
Hagia Sophia, 925, 1031
Hagiography, 78–79, 80–81, 82, 389, 432, 502
Haida (Foam Woman), 330
Haida (people), 39, 212
Hair, 389–391

African religions, 10
Buddhist nuns, 123, 143, 390
as female sexual symbol, 615
funeral practices, 74
in Hinduism, 418, 623, 1030
See also Head coverings; Veiling
Haiti, 587, 784, 862; See also Vodou
Haji, 499
Hajj, 180, 323, 387, 490, 494, 501, 513, 651, 827, 903
meaning to women, 779–780, 781, 782
Halakah, 47, 325, 747, 909, 973
Hall, Stuart, 228
Hallucinogens. See Intoxicants and hallucinogens
Haloa, 247, 339
Halpern, Manfred, 1056
Halprin, Anna, 241
Hamamoto Sōshun, 217
Haman, 308, 325
Hand Claw, Barbara, 1064
Handmaids of the Most Pure Heart of Mary, 348
Handsome Lake (Seneca chief), 725
Han dynasty, 99, 195–197, 279, 695, 757, 1045, 1074
Hannah, 391, 397, 460, 865, 869
Hanuman, 729, 1007
Han Xiaoling, 195
Han Yu, 197
Haoma, 484
Harappan cemeteries, 802
Hardacre, Helen, 287, 288
Harding, M. Esther, 380, 556, 705
Harding, Sandra, 607
Hare Krishnas, 226, 227, 429, 717, 880
Haribhadrasuri, 772
Hāritī, 244, 337, 391–392
Harlan, Lindsey, 766
Harnack, Adolph von, 178
Harpies, 1021
Harrell, Stevan, 368
Harris, Barbara, 742, 743
Harris, Elizabeth, 783
Harrison, Beverly Wildung, 312, 629
Harrison, Jane Ellen, 187, 380, 381–382, 392–393, 436, 705
Harry, Martha, 59
Hart, C. W. M., 737
Harvey, Youngsook Kim, 893
Hasan ibn ʿAli, 328, 586
Hasidim, 241, 256, 542, 865, 1011
Hassan, Riffat, 511, 572, 976, 1052
Hathayogapradīpikā, 1076
Hathor, 32, 33, 34, 39, 243, 373, 485, 487, 687, 714, 1031

Hatshepsut, queen of Egypt, 34, 54, 63, 1031
Hattušili III, king of Hittites, 1038
Haudenosaunee (people), 621
Hauerwas, Stanley, 309
Hauptman, Judith, 553
Haurvatat, 484
Hausa (people), 787
Hawaii, 236, 413, 735
    goddess Pele, 763
    sacrifice rituals, 861, 862
    seclusion practices, 875
Hawkes, Jacquette, 377
Hawley, John, 261, 354
Hawwa' (Eve), 320, **393–394**, 491, 841, 910, 946
Hayatsu-hime, 900
Hayles, Katherine, 459, 460
Hazal (film), 343
Head coverings
    Christian women in church, 104, 155, 158, 390, 807
    Orthodox Christian women, 753
    Orthodox Jewish women, 104, 183
    Sikh turban, *905*
    See also Veiling
Healing, 10, 146, 153, 237
    faith, 318
    folk practices, 712
    hallucinogen use, 479
    Islamic, 495
    Japanese new religions, 721–22, 728
    motherhood and, 679–80
    Native American, 1022
    Pentecostal, 728
    possession beliefs, 787, 788, 819–820
    purification rites, 818
    sacrificial rites, 862
    by postmenopausal women, 647
    shrines and, 903
    sorcery and, 1043
    Southeast Asian religions, 933
    spiritualism and, 941
    visions and, 1010
    witchcraft and, 1042, *1043*
Healing Light Center Church, 1063
Hearth, 57, 406–407
Heart Sutra, 1034, 1035
Heath, Shirley, 738
Heaven. *See* Paradise
Heaven's Gate community, 227
Hebrew Bible, 78, 232, 241, **394–400**, 526, 532, 856
    Anat/Ishtar portrayals, 486, 487
    Apocrypha, 627
    as archaeological resource, 50, 51
    Asherah references, 68

on barren women's plight, 336, 625, 794
    Deborah portrayal, 245
    Eve portrayal, 319–320, 624
    female sexuality portrayal, 889
    folklore studies, 345–346
    gender conflict, 360
    gender roles, 361
    ghosts, 369
    God in the, **394–397**, 673; *See also* God
    hermeneutics, 404, 406
    heroines, 90, 104, 1061, 1062
    on homosexuality, 581
    images of women, 90, 104, **460–462**, 463
    Israelite religion, **514–517**
    lying and deception in, 606
    magical rites, 1038, 1039
    matriarchal fertility, 336
    on menstruation, 650, 651
    Miriam portrayal, 665, 688
    modern scholarship, 553
    moon significance, 674
    prophets and judges, **397–400**, 461, 516, 840, 1011
    on rainbow, 1024
    as sacred literature, 855
    on uncleanliness, 321, 818
    violence against women, 835, 1000
    on widow status, 1029, 1030
    on wifely value, 1052
    wisdom personifications, 1031, 1033
    witchcraft in, 400, 807, **1037–1040**
    women musicians, 665, 688
    women prophets, 441–442, 806–807
    Women's Bible commentary, 1054
    women's speech, 937–938
    See also Apocrypha; Queens, biblical; Torah; *specific figures*
Hebrew language, 571, 792
Hecate, 225, 333, **400**
Heck, Barbara, 812
Hecuba, 452
Hedge, Frederic Henry, 984
Hefferman, Thomas, 77
Hegel, G. W. F., 222, 430–431, 481, 699–700, 774, 776
Hegland, Mary, 899
Heidegger, Martin, 246, 404
Heinzelmann, Gertrud, 165
Heisenberg, Werner, 712
Heitsi-Eibib, 1003
Hekman, Susan, 246
Hel, 871
Helena, queen of Adiabene, 527
Helena, Saint, 149, *150*
Helen of Troy, 48, 402–403, 869

Hell, 18–19
Heloise, 82, **400–402**
Heners, 32–33
Henge monuments, 798, 802–803
Henna, 750
Henotheism, 673, 785
Hephaestus, 48, 402
Hephaistos, 384
Hera, 72, 314, 384, **402–403**, 457, 459, 468, 472, 557, *702*, 805, 842, 1025
Heraclitus, 814
Herbert, Mary, 599–600
Hercules (Heracles), 27, 315, 402, 569
Heresy, 150–151, 160, 408
    Christian women's public speech as, 808
    Marguerite Porete, 786
    Sister Manfreda, 616–617
    witchcraft as, 1041, 1042
Heresy of the Free Spirit (papal decree), 786
Hermaphrodite, 36, **403–404**
Hermeneutics, **404–406**, 594, 884
    feminist, **405–406**, 436, 774, 839, 847, 916
    object-relations theory, 815–816
    overview, **404–405**
    phenomenological, 768–769
Hermes, 225, 384, 403, 404, 986, *987*
Hermod, 871
Herod, 472, 535
Herodias, 463
Herodotus, 332, 432, 474, 483
Heroic monomyth, 702
Heroines. *See* Women as heroines
Herskovits, Melville J., 588
Hertha, 871–872
Heschel, Susannah, 312, 976
Hesiod, 36, 277, 323, 356, 384, 392, 400, 402, 459, 468, 607, 686, 859, 869, 874, 939, 991
Hesperides, 459
Hester Street (film), 342
Hestia and Vesta, 53, 247, 314, 384, **406–408**, 472, 934, *935*, 1002
Hetepheres I, queen of Egypt, 32, 714
Heterodoxy and orthodoxy, **408–409**
Heterosexism, **409–412**
    in Judaic concept of God, 265
    Lesbianism and, 589
    liberation theologies and, 592
Hevajra, 232
Hewitt, Marsha Aileen, 222
Heyward, Carter, 268, 311–312, 583, 590, 666, 912
Hibri, Aziza al-, 511
"Hidden Faces" (film), 341

Hierarchy, **412–414**
  African religions, 6–8
  Christian family, 676
  divinities, 262
  Islamic, 827
  misogynistic, 666
  Roman Catholic, 413, 742
  solar imagery, 703–704
  See also Dualism
Hieros gamos (sacred marriage), 402,
    859, 927
Higginbotham, Evelyn Brooks, 4
High Magic's Aid (Gardner), 1048
Highwater, Jamake, 708
Hi'iaka, 763
Hijab, 183, 390, 723
Hijras, 141, 887
Hildegard of Bingen, 78, 82, 144, 150,
    178, 234, 240, 293, 361, **414–415**,
    433, 519, 688, 691, 703, 841, 1008,
    1062
Hiling, Induan, 895
Hilkiah, 441
Hill, Renee, 313
Hillesum, Etty, 600
Hillman, James, 648
Hiltebeitel, Alf, 271
Himalayan religions, **415–417**
  polyandry, 619
  shrines and pilgrimages, 780, 782
  virginity's importance, 97
  See also Buddhism, Himalayan
Himiko, Fujita, 279
Himmler, Heinrich, 548
Himpunan Mahasiswa Islam, 722
Hina, **417–418**, 735
Hindu Code Bill, 427
Hinduism, 362, **418–432**
  on abortion, 203
  adultery prohibitions, 3, 4
  afterlife, 18
  alchemy, 23
  almsgiving, 25, 421, 424
  ancestor worship, 30–31, 424
  animal imagery, 39
  arts, 216, 1014
  asceticism, 66, *67*
  astrology, 69
  auspiciousness and inauspiciousness,
    73–74, 250
  bhakti sects. *See* Bhakti
  birth and rebirth images, 92
  body's significance, 97, 418
  celibacy, 143, 420–421, 585
  chastity's importance, 148
  circle symbolism, 457
  confession and penitence, 192
  contraceptive practices, 203

creation stories, 91, 221
cross-dressing by males, 334
dance and drama, 233, 236, 238–239;
    See also Devadāsīs
death portrayals, 244
dharma, 251–253
disciple designation, 257
divine couples, 207
divinity concept, 262–263
divorce, 266
dualism in, 274
economic life, 290, 421
esotericism, 305
fasting, 253, 325, *326*, 338, 422, 424,
    863
female personifications, 329
female possession, 787
female sexuality, 143, 321
feminine aspect, 331
feminine ideal, 332
fertility-related, 361
festivals, 253, 275, 338, 429, 442, 569,
    982, 1002, 1078
foods and ritual, 346
friendship concept, 353
fundamentalism, 355
gender boundaries, 105
gender conflict, 360
gender roles, 251–253, 362, 1052,
    1058–1059
goddess Pārvatī, 325, 420, 422, 559,
    759–760
goddess tradition, 88, 112, 377, 378,
    706, 791, 1019
hair symbolism, 390
Himalayan, 415–417
history of study, **430–432**, 839
homosexuality and, 585
hospitality, 421, 424, 441
iconography, 447
identity images, 450
infanticide, 418, 425
inspiration, 476
kāma, 559
karma, 946
kuṇḍalinī, 564, 565, 892
laity, 567
language reexamination, 572
law books, 105, 559
leadership, 575–576
levirate, 420, 1030
liberation theologies and, 591
literary tradition, 596
love, *605*, 606
marriage, 97–98, 148, 253, 418,
    419–421, 424–425, 429, 618,
    622–623, 843, 988, 1030, 1059
maya concept, 635–636

meditation, 642
menstruation, 97, 650, 903
modern movements, **425–428**
monasticism, 667
motherhood valuation, 1052
music goddess, 687
nonharming tradition, 755
oral tradition, 739
overview, **418–424**
paradise concept, 759
polygyny, 618
possession beliefs, 787
pottery, 218
prakriti, 635–636, 772, **791**
pregnancy, 795
purification rituals, 818, 819
rape victim treatment, 834, 835
religious architecture, 53
religious patronage, 568
religious rites and practices, 421–422,
    424–425, 429, 845
riddle tests, 842
rites of passage, 843
sacred literature, 858
saints, 87–89, 105, 422, 559–560, 560,
    575, 865
salvation concept, 867
samsara, 92, 327, 421, 867
self concept, 882, 883
sex change aspects, 887
sexual intercourse, 559, 995
shrines and pilgrimages, 780, 902
sin concept, 909
social inequality, 914
solitude, 923
son valuation, 418
temptation portrayal, 966
vagina (yoni) imagery, 995, 996, 1078
vegetarianism, 818, 999
veiling, 183, 421, 889, 890
virginity, 1002
virtue, 1007
visionary activity, 1010
vow narratives, 344
wandering mendicancy, 667
war justifications, 1019
in the West, **428–430**
widowhood, 98, 253, 1030; *See also*
    Sati
wifely duties, 618, 642, 666, 1052
women authors, 361
women dancers and singers. *See*
    Devadāsīs
women's literacy and education, 291
women's philosophical status,
    771–772
women's status gains, 1059
women's truthfulness, 988

Hinduism *(continued)*
  worship, 1071
  yoga, 421, 1076, 1077
  See also Shaktism; Tantra
Hippocrates, 1021
Hippodameia, 402
Hippolyta, 27
Hippolytus, 371
Hippomenes, 72
Hirata Atsutan, 703
*Historia de los Mexicanos por sus
    Pinturas* (Olmos), 654
Histories (Herodotus), 332
History, **432–435**
  memory and, 642–644
  periodization, 766–767
  political activism, 784–785
  sexism and, 887–888
  in thealogy, 968–969
  on women philosophers, 779
  women's history, 432–433
History of religions, 432, **435–438**
  feminist reconstruction, 1068
  historians of women's roles, 766–767
Hitler, Adolf, 546, 547
Hittites, 1038–1039
Hobbes, Thomas, 675, 784
Hobby horse possession trancers, 788
Hodder, Ian, 802
Hoffman, Dustin, 334
Hofriyati (people), 439
Hokhmah, 476–477, 987, 1031
Holden, Pat, 436
Holi festival, 429, 442, 982
Holiness Christianity. *See* Evangelical,
    Holiness, Fundamentalist, and
    Pentecostal Christianity
Holmberg, David, 416
Holocaust, 46, 469, 545, 546–549, 550,
    1023, 1057
  women's survival traits, *643*, 644
Holofernes, *937*, 1022, 1061
"Holy anorexia," 317, 325, 863
Holy Book of Women's Mysteries, Part 1
    (Budapest), 1048–1049
Holy Family Sisters, 850
"Holy Fool," 443
Holy Ghost. *See* Holy Spirit
Holy Mother Wisdom, 563, 578
"Holy people" (Navajo), 709
Holy sites. *See* Places, sacred
Holy Spirit, 4, 5, 616, 728
  Christian prayer emphasis on, 792
  Christian prophecy through, 807, 808
  dove as symbol, 39
  Roman Catholic terminology, 369
  Sophia and, 455, 477, 925
Holy Teaching of Vimalakirti, 302

Holy Virgin of Saut D'Eau (Haiti),
    784
Holy war, 1020
Holzer, Jenny, 1013
Home, **438–440**, 447
  Greek patron goddess, 406–407
  Orthodox Christian practices, 753
  sanctification of, 1014
  yin/yang balance, 1075
  See also Domestic rites; Hospitality
Homeland theology, 163
Homer, 26, 27, 72, 356, 384, 402, 439,
    452, 563, 686, 688, *807*, 869, 1026
Homo erectus, 795, 796, 798
Homophobia, 410, 411, 582, 583, 586,
    589, 592
Homo religiosus, 297
Homo sapiens, 795, 796
Homosexuality, 70, 265, 361, 403
  ancient Greece, 255, 580–581
  Holocaust treatment of, 546
  Jewish perspectives, 543, 581, 582
  microhistorical traditions, 620
  ordination and, 582–583, 740
  scriptural views, 158, 581–582
  See also Homophobia; Lesbianism;
    Queer theory
Honen, 123
Hong, Lady, 597
Hong Kong, 74, 683, 745, 746
Honor, 329
hooks, bell, 40, 450, 773, 777, 912
Hopi (people), 222, 362, 377, 937
  creation myth, 1026
  elevation of women, 645
  harvest festival, 710
  kachina doll, *709*
  purification rites, 818
  ritual societies, 710
Hopkins, Emma Curtis, 465, 717
Hopper, Edward, 459
Horai (Seasons), 402
Horkheimer, Max, 46, 222
Horner, I. B., 132, 187
Horodezky, Samuel A., 542
Horses, 39, 863
Horus, 32, 261, 468, 487, 488, 605, 714,
    1038
Hosea, 68, 396, 605, 1054
Hospitality, 25, 406–407, 421, 424,
    440–441, 845
Hospital Sisters of Saint Augustine, 440
Howe, Julia Ward, 1054
Hroswitha, 688
Hrotsvitha of Gandersheim, 150, 234,
    240
Hsi Wang Mu. *See* Queen Mother of the
    West

Hua (people), 645
Huainanzi (Taoist text), 730
Hua Mulan, 1061
Hua-yen Buddhism, 121
Hubbard, L. Ron, 719
Hueck, Baroness de, 923
Huehuetlatolli, 655
Huerta, Dolores, 686
Hügel, Friedrich von, 991
Huichol (people), 210, *211*, 214, 725
Hui-Xiang Xiao, 1013
Hula dance, *736*
Hulda, 399, **441–442**, 516, 806–807,
    840, 1011
Huli (people), 620
Hull House, 918
Humanae Vitae (encyclical), 203
Humanism, 187, 335, 776
Humanity, 35, 262–264, 969
Human origins, 795–796
Human potential religions, 717
Human rights
  documentary films, 340
  feminism and, 335
  genital mutilation, 695
  legal aspects, 574
  Menchú activism, 646–647
  See also Liberation theologies
Human sacrifice. *See* Sacrifice
Hume, David, 299, 301
Hume, Sophia, 923
Humor, **442–444**, 986
Humphrey, Doris, 241
Hungary Ghosts festival, *369*
Hung Cong Ut, 778
Hunter-gatherers, 645
Hunt, Mary E., 352–353, 583, 912
Hur (maidens of paradise), 759
Huron (people), 329, 1047
Hürrem Sultan, 54
Hurston, Zora Neale, **444–445**, 600
Husayn, Imam, 328, 494, 898, 899
Husbands. *See* Marriage and singleness;
    Wives
Hu Shi, 200
Hus, Jan, 811
Hussain, Khalida, 586
Husserl, Edmund, 768
Hutchinson, Anne, 151, 170, 808, 812,
    936, 2062
Hwaom Buddhism, 122
Hyman, Paula, 544, 554
Hymn singing, 521, 683
Hypatia, **445–446**, 1063
Hypergamy, 413
Hypogeum, 455
Hyrcanus II, 535
Hysteria, 787, 808

I

Ialdabaoth. *See* Demiurge
Iblis, 321
Ibn (people), 1026
Ibn al-Jawzi, 82
Ibn Arabi, 79, 263
Ibn Ḥazm, ʿAlī, 841
Ibrahim. *See* Abraham
Ibsen, Henrik, 771
Icaiñāiyār, 559, 560
I Cannibali (film), 342
Ice Age, 796
Ice Queen, 485
I Ching, 333, 716, 1074
Iconography, **447–449**
  African religions, 6, 11
  Celtic, 145–146
  circle symbolism, 179
  Eastern, **447–448**
  goddesses, 373–374, 377–378,
    447–448
  Jaina, 522
  Jesus as divine child, 260
  Orthodox Christian, 753
  in religious art, 62
  vagina imagery, 454, 995, 996, 1078
  Western, **448–449**
  See also Images of women
Icons, 153
Idda, 889
Iddin-Dagan of Isin, 467
Iddindagan, king of Ur, 658
Identity, 313, **449–451**, 776, 777
Ideology, **451**, 466
Ie, 284
Ifa divination system, 8
Ifugaos (people), 932, 933
Igbo (people), 7, 8, 22, 1044
Ijesa kingdom, 754
Ikat (people), *217*
Ikk Oan Kar, 905
Iktome, 986
Ila (people), 20
Ilamatlatolli, 655
Ilan, Tal, 527, 533
Iliad (Homer), 27, 72, 356, 402, 452,
  562, 563, 686, 688, *807*
Illapa, 927
Images of women, **451–465**
  in Apocrypha, **464–465**
  in Hebrew Bible, 90, 104, **460–462**,
    463
  literary images, 451–454, 563
  myths and symbols, **457–460**
  in New Testament, 90, 336, **462–464**
  self-sacrificial elements, 863, 910
  visual images, 63, **454–457**, 1012
Immaculate Conception, 164, 267

Immanence and transcendence, 262,
  452, **465–466**, 673, 838, 906, 961,
  962
Impurity. *See* Purity and pollution
In a Different Voice (Gilligan), 311
Inanna 373, **466–467**, 485, 487, 656,
  657, 658, 659, 911–912, 995, 1031;,
  See also Ishtar
Inauspicious. *See* Auspicious and
  inauspicious
Inca culture, 863, 927–929
Incarnation, 102, 263
Incest, 2, 333, **467–469**, 817, 945, 955
Inculturation theology, 162
Independence movements, 1020
Independent Association of Bible
  Churches, 318
Independent Churches, 161
India, 749, 982
  ancestor worship, 30–31
  androgyne representations, 36, 403
  animal imagery, 38, 39
  animal sacrifice, 94
  antifemale cultural bias, 97
  astrology, 70
  bhakti sects, 87–89, 865
  birth control policy, 203
  birth rituals, 91
  breast representations, 106
  British colonialism, 236, 250–251,
    425, 426–427, 430–431
  castration practices, 141
  child marriage, 431, 771
  Christianity, 162, 163, 292, 425, 426,
    681
  creation mythology, 221, 296, 1055
  dance and drama, 236, 238–239; *See
    also* Devadāsīs
  death portrayals, 243–244
  dharma concept, 251–254
  divorce, 266
  emotionality of women, 300
  female literacy and education,
    291–292
  female monastics as patrons, 762
  female nudity as fertility symbol,
    729
  female possession, 787
  feminist movements, 335, 1058
  festivals, 338, 1002
  foods and ritual, 346
  fundamentalists, 354–355
  ghosts, 368
  infanticide, 471
  lesbianism, 588
  liberation theologies, 591
  marriage, 88, 97–98, 346, 622–623
  midwives, 563

  modern Buddhist movements, 128,
    129
  Mother Teresa, 681
  mourning and burial practices, 297
  music, 692, 738–739; *See also*
    Devadāsīs
  mythology, 706
  patriarchism, 88
  philosophical status of women,
    771–772
  pilgrimage sites, 367
  polyandry, 619, 620
  prostitution, 809
  purity and pollution, 818, 820
  religious architecture, 53
  religious patronage, 568
  sacrifice rituals, 94, 861, 863
  samsara, 327, 867
  Shiism, 898
  shrines and temples, 367, 902,
    1078
  superstition, 951
  suttee. *See* Sati
  wedding rituals, 442
  witchcraft, 1046
  women and religion, 1059
  women musicians, 692
  women's movement, 426–427, 431
  women's religious status, 1058
  women's truthfulness, 988
  women warriors, 1021, 1023
  See also Buddhism; Caste; Hinduism;
    Islam; Jainism; Sikhism; Yoga
Indian First Nations, 168
Indian National Army, 1023
Indian Shakers, 725
Indo-European religions, **469–471**,
  818–819
Indology, 430–431
Indonesia, 951
  birth rituals, 91, 820
  festivals, 339
  Islam, 504, 508, 932, 933
  Islamic new religion, 722–723
  sex industry, 1001
  weaving myth, 1026
  widowhood, *1029*
  witchcraft, 1046
Indra, 48, 321, 441, 870, 887
Infanticide, **471–473**, 890
  Canaan-Phoenicia, 136, 138
  Hinduism, 418, 425
  Islamic condemnation, 489
  Sikh rejection, 907
Infant of Prague, 260
Infertility. *See* Fertility and barrenness
Infidelity. *See* Adultery
"In Her Own Time" (film), 340

Initiation, **473–474**
African religions, 8, 10, 237
ancient Greece, 384
Arctic peoples, 60
body cutting, 96, 843
dance rituals, 237
documentary works, 340
Eliade's theories, 298
fasting, 325
festivals, 338
food and, 347
genital mutilation as, 10, 96, 474, 843
intoxicant and hallucinogen use, *473*, 479
maenadic rites, 610
masquerades, 233
Native American, 52, 94, 645, *708*, 709, 710, 982
purification rites, 817, *818*, 819
rebirth rituals, 91–92
riddle tests, 842
as rite of passage, 843–844
secret societies, 878
Sikh practices, 906
South American religions, 930–931, 931
trances, 104
See also Menarche; Ordination
In Memory of Her (Schüssler Fiorenza), 433, 1068
Innana, 333
Inner Asian religions of nomadic peoples, **474–476**, 499
Innocent II, pope, 401
Inn of the Sixth Happiness, The (Burgess), 1062
Inquisition, 193, *539*, 541, 554, 1011
execution of Sister Manfreda, 616
witchcraft trials, 1041, 1042
Insect imagery, 39
Insight meditation, 125, 129
Inspiration, **476–477**
Institute of the Blessed Virgin Mary, 176, 348
Institute of the Missionary Sisters of the Sacred Heart of Jesus, 135
Instructions for Women (*Nujie*), 196–197
Instructions for Women (Pan Ch'ao), 292, 361, 757
Instrumentalists, 691–693
Instruments, 690–693
Integrity (organization), 583
Intercourse. *See* Sexuality
Interfaith movement. *See* Interreligious dialogue
Intermarriage, 532, 543

International Alliance for Women's Suffrage, 492
International Association for the History of Religions, 435, 437
International Association of Buddhist Women. *See* Sakyadhita
International Church of the Foursquare Gospel, 318, 637
International Encyclopedia of Women Composers, 690, 691
International Peace Mission Movement, 678
International Sakyadhita Conference (1997), 129
International Society for Krishna Consciousness. *See* Hare Krishnas
Internet, 429–430
Interreligious dialogue, **477–479**
In the Hall of the Goddesses (photograph), 778
Intoxicants and hallucinogens, **479–481**
African religions, 8
initiation rites, *473*, 479
peyotism, 725
South American religions, 480, 728, 930
as vision inducer, 1010
Inuit/Eskimos (people), 18, 39, 56, 59–60, 211, 329, 739, 949
Inupiat (people), 346
Inversion, **481–482**
Io, 273
Iphigenia, 66, *862*, 863
Iqshati, Bula, 541
Iranian religions, **483–484**
homosexuality prohibitions, 586
Islam, 493, **498–499**, 513, 898
just war, 1020
Mandaeism, 615, 616
sacrifice rituals, 861
secularization opposition, 880
wisdom and mother goddess, 1032
See also Zoroastrianism
Iraq, 409, 615, 616; *See also* Mesopotamian religions
Ireland. *See* Celtic religions
Irenaeus, 160, 320, 371
Irene, 149, 150
Irigaray, Luce, 331, 481, 485, 700, 774, 776
I, Rigoberta Menchú (Menchú and Burgos-Debray), 646
Iris, 1024
Irony, 443
Iroquois Confederacy, 359, 621, 725, 818, 1047
Irrationality, **484–486**
Isaac, 388, 394, 606, 863, 869

Isaiah, 516, 674, 807, 832
'Isanaklesh, 970
Isasi-Díaz, Ada María, 312, 313, 976, 1007
Isbahani, Abul Farraj al-, 586
Ise shrine (Japan), 26, 54, 217, 279, 900, 901, 903
"Is Female to Male as Nature Is to Culture?" (Ortner), 712
Ishkhara, 136
Ishmael (Isma'il), 53, 387–388, 490
Ishtar and Anat, 48, 136, 137, 209, 245, 333, 373, 466, 483, **486–487**, 515, 517, 604, 805, 1019, 1031, 1038
Isis, 32, 34, 315, 329, 390, **487–488**, 604, 605, 733
cult of, 698, 699
depictions of, 455, 456, 995
and Osiris, 243, 249, 390, 468, 487, 488
priestesses of, 66, 806
sisterly relationship, 912
temples to, 53, 902
wisdom attribute, 1031, 1032
Islam, 443, **488–511**, 749
on abortion, 2, 507
in Africa, **500–503**
afterlife, 18–19, 102
almsgiving and patronage, 25, 494, 513
amulet use, 28, 495
animal imagery, 39
apocalyptic vision, 19
in Arab Middle East, **496–498**
asceticism, 67–68
in Asia, 427, **503–505**, 932, 933
Asian new religions, 722–723
autobiography and biography, 82
body's significance, 101–102, 750
chastity's importance, 148
contraceptive practices, 203, 507
crafts, 220
creation stories, 277
dance and drama, 238, 240–242
disciple designation, 256–257
divinity concept, 263
divorce, 266, 489, 492, 496, 507, 512, 827, 889, 933
documentary films, 341
domestic architecture, 52
economic issues, 289
in Europe, **505–506**
Eve (Hawwa') portrayal, 319, 320, 322, **393**, 946, 966
fasting, 325, 494, 513, 827
female voice, 1016
feminist ethics, 312
feminists, 1057

feminist theology, 882, 976
fertility, 336
festivals, 338
friendship concept, 353
fundamentalism, 354–355, 500, 1001
gender boundaries, 104, 845
gender conflict, 360
gender roles, 361, 508, 512–513, 675, 1069
geographic distribution, 1056, 1057
ghouls, 368
gnosticism, 371 l, 387, 388
Hagar portrayal, 387, 388
history of study, **509–511**, 839
hospitality's importance, 440–441
identity images, 450
incest prohibitions, 468
inspiration, 477
in Iran and Turkey, 257, 493, **498–500**, 513, 898
language and, 572
leadership, 576
liturgy, 602
male control of holy sites, 782
marriage and marital obligations, 208, 489, 491–492, 496, 512–513, 622, *623*, 626–627, 827–828, 1051–1053
Maryam (Mary) portrayal, 490, **630**, 828, 882
media coverage of, 640–641
menopause benefits, 647
menstruation practices, 491, 645–646, 651, 934, 955
modern movements, 492–493, 497, **507–509**
monotheism, 673, 785, 1056–1057
moral precepts and gender inequities, 675
mosques and shrines, 903, 904
mourning and death rites, 683–684
in North America, **506–507**
overview, **488–494**
paradise concept, 758, 759
patriarchism, 512, 760
pilgrimages and shrines, 779–780, 781, 782; *See also* Hajj
polygyny, 289, 618, *619*, 627, 827, 1057
possession beliefs, 787
prayer, 793–794
pregnancy and, 794, 795
purification, 102, 491, 494
Ramadan, 325, 494, 827, 981
rape victim treatment, 834, 835
religious architecture, 53, 54
religious conversion, 205–206
religious patronage, 568

religious rites and practices, 323, **494–496**, 499, 844
revelation experiences, 841
riddle tests, 842
ritual purity, 817–818
sacred space, 935
sacrificial meat consumption, 862
saints, 494, 495, 502, 576, 831, 866
salvation concept, 867
seclusion requirements, 183, 490, 496, 513, 875–876
self concept, 882
sexuality as property belief, 289
sin concept, 909, 910
solitude, 923
soul concept, 814, 926, 927
taboos, 955
theological discourse, 974
virginity valuation, 1002–1003
virtue, 1006–1007, 1007
visionary activity, 841, 1011
vow narratives, 344
weather control, 1024
widow status, 1029–1030
women architectural patrons, 761–762
women heroines, 1062
women peacemaker, 756
women prophets, 808
women's literacy and education, 291, 293
women's religious status, 1057
women's veiling. *See* Veiling
women's worship, 1071
women warriors, 1019
See also Fāṭima ; Khadija; Muhammad; Qur'an and Hadith; Shiism; Sufism; Sunni Islam; Veiling
Islamic law, 491–492, 503, **512–514**, 582, 828
on adultery, 4, 835
homosexuality prohibitions, 581–582, 583, 586
Qur'an, Hadith, and, 496, 512–513, 573, 827–829, 974
women's rights, 723
women's sexuality, 889
women's truthfulness, 491, 988
Isles of the Blessed, 991
Isma'il. *See* Ishmael
Ismāʿīlīyah sect (Islam), 371
Israel (modern), 544, 549–550, 1057–1058
male control of holy sites, 783
warfare, 1020
women's military service, 1023
Israel ben Eliezer (Ba'al Shem Tov), 542, 865

Israelite religion, **514–518**
archaeological studies, 50–51
Ark of the Covenant, 902
Babylonian exile through Second Temple, 527, **531–534**
biblical portrayals, 90, 394–399, 514–517, 823–824
henotheism, 673, 785
martyrdom, 627
nature perception, 712
polygyny, 618
sacrifice rituals, 861
visionary activity, 1011
wisdom personifications, 1031, 1033
women prophets, 806–807
See also Hebrew Bible
Isserles, Moses, 541
Īśvara, 1077
Iti, 691
Itihāsās, 858
Ivy, Marilyn, 950
Ixion, 402
Iyanala, 9
Iyo, 900
Izanagi and Izanami, 26, 225, 277, *458*, *459*–460, 949

J
Jabālā, 988
Jackson, Mahalia, 689
Jackson, Rebecca Cox, **519**, 1011
Jacob, 323, 794, 1038
Jacobi, Jolande, 556
Jacobs, Janet, 206
Jade Emperor of Heaven, 282
Jade Woman, 98
Jael, 78, 398, 515, 1022
Jaganmātā, 244
Jagannāth Temple, 218
Jaggar, Alison M., 335
Jahānārā Begum Ṣāhib, Fāṭima, 1011
Jaini, P. S., 867
Jainism, 109, **519–523**
almsgiving, 25, 520–521
asceticism, 66–67, 521, 730
confession, 192
dharma, 253
fasting, 325, 521, 948
heterodoxy, 408, 419
karma, 192, 561
laity, 520, 567
monasticism, 66–67, 253, 520, 667, 772, 1017
nonviolence, 755
nudity, 521, 730
nuns, 253, 520, 1017
salvation concept, 521, 867–868
samsara, 327, 867

Jainism (continued)
  vegetarianism, 999
  wandering mendicancy, 667
  women's philosophical status, 772
Jai Santoshi Ma (film), 422
Jakata stories, 239
Jakobson, Roman, 944
Jallot, Nicolas, 180
Jamaica, 368
James, E. O., 382
Jamieson, Penelope Ann Bansall, 742
Jamison, Judith, 241
Jane Frances de Chantal, Saint, 176
Janelli, Dawnhee Yim and Roger, 30
Japan
  abortion, 2, 115, 337
  amulet use, 28
  ancestor worship, 284
  animal sacrifice, 94
  antifemale cultural bias, 97
  Buddhism, 107, 115, 120, 123, 217,
      278, 281, 286–287, 323, 745–746,
      758, 759, 900, 901
  Christianity, 163
  Confucianism, 198–199, 199, 280
  creation myths, 91, 277
  dance and drama, 232, 239
  deities of luck or happiness, 86–87
  embroidery work, 213
  family's importance, 323–324
  female personifications, 330, 333
  fertility beliefs, 337
  food's significance, 347
  infanticide, 472
  Ise shrine, 26, 54, 217, 279, 900, 901,
      903
  Korea as colony, 122, 285
  literary tradition, 596–597
  monasticism, 669
  money washing, 87
  Mugai Nyodai, 685
  new religions. See Japanese New
      Religions
  prehistoric excavations, 803
  religious patronage, 568
  religious traditions study, 287
  rituals and practices, 284
  sacred places, 783
  salvation concept, 867
  samurai suicide, 947
  superstition, 950
  tea ceremony, 217–218
  weaving, 217
  witchcraft, 1046
  See also Shintoism
Japanese New Religions, 284, 286–287,
    323
  characteristics, 721–722

  founding leaders, 349, 717
  menstruation view, 820
  scholarly study, 288
  in South America, 728
  women's status, 1059
Jarā, 244
Jātakas, 4, 111
Jauhar, 948
Java, 236
Jay, Nancy, 413
Jayadeva, 418, 604
Jayarajadevi, 454
Jeffrey, Patricia, 844
Jehoiachin, 824
Jehovah's Witnesses, 546, 547, 717
Jehu, 396
Jelinek, Estelle, 77
Jen, 605–606
Jephthah, 863, 1038
Jepsen, Maria, 742
Jeremiah, 36, 67, 256, 399, 807
Jericho excavations, 801
Jerome, 149, 159, 160, 271, 290, 671,
    761, 1030
"Jero on Jero" (film), 340
Jero Tapakan, 340
Jerusalem
  holy sites, 264, 780, 783
  Jewish prayer directed toward, 792
Jesuits, 287, 849
Jesus of Nazareth (the Christ), 156–157,
    241, 575, 605, 857, 886, 937
  almsgiving, 25
  as charismatic leader, 147
  and Christian antisemitism, 46–47
  disciples, 160, 255, 256, 257, 463
  as divine child, 260–261, 262
  as divine incarnation, 263
  escape from Herod, 472
  and Eucharist, 316–317
  on family, 324, 333
  grace derived from, 812
  and Holy Spirit, 477
  and hospitality, 440
  as identity image, 449
  Jewish movements, 533–534,
      535–536
  and Mary and Martha, 630–631
  and Mary Magdalene, 631–632, 935,
      1015
  as mothering figure, 107, 886
  Pietà imagery, 448
  and prophecy, 808
  and prostitutes, 809–810
  recognition as Messiah, 807
  shrines to, 902
  as Sophia of God, 159, 925, 1031,
      1033

  and soul concept, 927
  Spiritual marriage with, 700
  as trickster figure, 986
  Unification Church view of, 718–719
  vagina imagery and, 996
  weather and, 1024
  womanist portrayal of, 1053
Je Tsong-kha-pa, 190
Je vous salue Marie (film), 342
Jewish Theological Seminary, 545, 546,
    549, 740–741, 953
Jewish Women's Organization
    (Germany), 545
Jews. See Antisemitism and Jewish
    identity; Hebrew Bible; Israelite
    religion; Judaism
Jezebel, 68, 461, 463, 516, 807, 823,
    824, 966, 1015
Jhansi ki Rani, 1023
Jiang Qing, 202
Jilaliyyat, 409
Jimenez de Rada, Rodrigo, 510
Jimmu, emperor of Japan, 26
Jīmon stages, 803
Jinas (Tīrthaṃkaras), 521–522
Jindan, Maharani, 907
Jingū, 900
Jingvang Mingjing (Buddhist text), 325
Jinn, 939–940
Jiriki, 867
Jīva, 561
Jivaros (people), 930
Jiv Goswami, 664
Jizo (Kṣitigarba), 115
Jñānana, 867
Jnanananda, Shri, 924
Joachim of Fiore, 616
Joan, pope. See Manfreda, Sister
Joan of Arc, 151, 223, 295, 482,
    523–524, 936, 1060
  film depictions, 341–342
  sainthood, 866
  shorn hair, 390
  as visionary, 1010
  as warrior, 1019, 1022
Joanna, 156
Job, 1041
Jocasta, 333
Joel, 159
Johannine community, 535
John, Gospel of, 371, 535, 631
John of Arles, Saint, 671
John the Baptist, 336, 616, 925
John Cassian, 671
John Chrysostom, 149, 159, 241, 752
John Paul II, pope, 165, 640, 743,
    850–851
Johnson, Elizabeth A., 246

Johnson, Penelope, 178
Johnson, Sarah, 1057
Johnson, Sonia, 640
Jomo Menmo, 117
Jonas, Regina, **524–525**, 528, 545–546
Jones, David E., 77
Jones, Eva, 600
Jones, Gail, 600
Jones, William, 430
Jord, 871
Jordan, 497, 509
Jordan, Kay, 431
Joseph (Hebrew Bible), 271
Joseph (husband of Mary), 472, 1004
Joseph and Asenth (Psudepigrapha), 699
Josephus, Flavius, 533–534, 535
Joshi, Rama, 431
Joshua, 256, 747
Joshua ben Levi, 983
Josiah, 68, 399, 441, 806, 807
Jotunheim, 871
Journalism. *See* Media and religion
Journal of Feminist Studies in Religion, 437, 976
Journeys. *See* Pilgrimage
Jowo, 117
Joyce, James, 46
Juana Inés de la Cruz, 151, 234, 240, **525–526**, 686, 849
Judaism, **526–555**
  on abortion, 1
  adultery prohibitions, 3, 148, 288, 390, 461
  afterlife, 18
  almsgiving, 25
  amulet use, 28, 593
  androgyny, 36
  antisemitism, **46–47**, 312, 545, 815, 1005
  asceticism, 67
  autobiography and biography, 81, 82
  Babylonian exile through Second Temple, 527, **531–534**
  birth control practices, 202–203, 527, 540
  body's significance, 101–102
  chastity's importance, 148
  Christian tradition and, 535–535, 1057
  confession and penitence, 194
  contemporary Jewish life, **549–551**
  crafts, 219
  creation belief, 221–222, 277; *See also* Eve
  dance and drama, 240–242
  death rites, 243
  demon beliefs, 368, 593, 787
  dietary laws, 531, 782, 818, 819, 862

disciple designation, 256
divinity concept, 263, **264–265**, 461–462, 526, 529
divorce, 266, 390, 527, 529, 530, 532, 537, 539, 541, 625
domestic rites, 347, 529, 531, 935
economic issues, 288, 539
egg's significance, 297
embroidery, 210
esotericism, 305, 306
Essenes, 306, 527, 533, 671
ethics, 309, 312, 370
Eve's portrayal, 319–320, 322, 758, 946, 966
family's significance, 67, 323
fasting, 325
female personifications, 329
female sexuality, 890
female voice, 1015, 1016
feminine aspect, 331
feminist movements, 549, 551, 757–758
feminist neopaganism, 716
feminist revisionism, 47, 433, 527–528, 553, 572, 909, 973, 1064, 1065, 1068
feminist theology, 976, 977
festivals, 338, 981
friendship, 352
gender boundaries, 104, 973
gender conflict, 360
gender roles, 362, 461, 819, 983, 1052–1053
Hagar's story, 387–388, 553
hair symbolism, 390
Hasidim, 241, 256, 542, 865, 1011
heterosexism, 411
history of study, **553–555**, 839
Holocaust, 46, 469, 545, **546–549**, 550, *643*, 644, 1023, 1057
on homosexuality, 543, 578, 582
hospitality's importance, 440
incest prohibitions, 468
inspiration, 476–477
Islam and, 488
language, 571–572
law. *See* Torah
male control of holy sites, 782, 783
marriage and marital obligations, 67, 530, 539, 624–625, 912, 1052
media coverage of, 640
menstruation taboos, 527, 534, 540, 645–646, 650, 651, 818, 934
in Middle Ages, 264, 265, 527, **538–540**
modern era (1492–1789), **540–543**
modern era (1789–), 528, **543–546**
modern movements, **551–553**

monotheism, 553, 673, 785, 1056–1057
moral precepts and gender inequities, 675
Mosaic law, 532, 912, 988
motherhood, 186, 460–461, 531
mysticism, 409, 540, 541–542, 571–572, 733
ordination. *See under* Ordination
overview, **526–529**
paradise concept, 758–759
Passover, 52, 297
patriarchism, 460, 526, 529–530, 553, 747, 760, 765, 774
prayer, 791, 792
procreation importance, 794, 890
prophets. *See* Prophets, biblical
purification rituals, 527, 544, 549, 818
Purim, 308, 443
on rape, 836
on reincarnation, 18
religious conversion, 205
religious rites and practices, 362, **529–531**, 844
rites of passage, 531, 843
ritual bath, 527, 540, 544
Roman, Byzantine, and Sassanian Judaism, **534–538**
Sabbath observance, 52, 183, 527, 529, 531, 537, 839
sacred space, 935
sacrificial meat consumption, 862
saintly people, 865
salvation concept, 867
sexism, 774
sexuality as property, 288, 1052
on sin and suffering, 909, 945–946
sister relationships, 912
and solitude, 924
soul concept, 814, 926
theistic portrayals, 970
theological discourse, 973, 974
Torah access, 856
vegetarianism, 998–999
visionaries, 1011
vow taking, 1017
widow status, 1029
wifely duties and status, 1052
women as patrons, 761
women heroines, 1062
women prophets, 806–807
women's attire, 183
women's literacy and education, 291, 292–293
women's liturgical participation, 792
women's movement, 334
women's pilgrimages and shrines, 780
women's prayers, 792

Judaism (*continued*)
women's stories, 643
worship, 528, 530, 539, 543, 549–550,
876, 1070–1071
Zionist movement, 542, 543, 545,
551, 554, 1057
See also Hebrew Bible; Israelite
religion; Kabbalah; Ordination;
Jude, Saint, 1017
Judges, Book of, 398–399, 527, 1022
Jüdischer Frauenbund, 334, 552, 758
Judith, 104, 256, 360, 464, 703, 937,
966, 1022, 1030, 1060, 1062
Juergensmeyer, Mark, 354
Julia, 155, 158
Juliana of Mont-Cornillon, 317
Julian of Norwich, 78, 82, 144, 151, 433,
555, 703, 774, 841, 923, 991, 1009
Julus, 898–899
Jung, Carl, 36, 37, 272, 300, **555–557**,
861
archetypes, 380, 457–458, 555, 556
feminine concept, 331, 457, 458, 459
genderized solar symbolism, 703
goddess archetype, 380, 702, 705
as men's spirituality movement
influence, 648
psychology of religion, 555–556, 815
*Jung and Feminism: Liberating
Archetypes* (Wehr), 815
Junia, 155, 157
Juno, 53, 314, 315, 403, **557**
Juok, 277
Justice, 196, *330*, 673, 988
Justin, 140, 320
Just war, 1020
Jyeṣṭhā, 244

K
Kaaba, 180, 793
Kabbalah, 222, 265, 272, 331, 477, 540,
674, 733, 909, 983, 984, 1031
Kaberry, Phyllis, 736
Kabir, 991
Kabuki, 239
Kachina, 709, 710
Kadedija. *See* Khadija
Kadlu, 329
Kagan, Richard L., 271
Kagura dance, 239
Kagyu (Buddhist sect), 117
Kahlo, Frida, 454
Kahn, Miriam, 347
Kairos Document (1985), 161
Kaititja (people), 620
Kakar, Sudhir, 836
Kālacakra, 92
Kalamaia (female ritual), 247

Kalanga (people), 20
Kalash (people), *650*
Kālī. *See* Durgā and Kālī
Kālidāsa, 49
Kālī-Mā, 1021
Kalingas (people), 932
Kalthoum, Om, 342
Kaluli (people), 620, 684
Kāma, 249, **559**, **560**, 585, 622, 759
Kamaiura (people), 930
Kāmākhyā, 1078
Kāmākhyā temple, 367, 902, 1078
Kamasutra, 559, 585
Kami, 97, 279, 900, 949
Kamsa, 472
Kamu-natsuso-hime, 900
Kan, Sergei, 18
Kang Youwei, 200
Kaṅkālī, 443
Kannon. *See* Kuan Yin
Kant, Immanuel, 299, 309, 485, 776,
966
Kanter, Rosabeth Moss, 992
Kanwar, Roop, 355, 420, 628
Kapila, 772
Kaplan, Marion, 544, 554
Kaplan, Mordecai, 543
Kappeler, Susanne, 569
Kāraikkāl Ammaiyār, 87, 88, 98, 361,
422, 447, **559–560**, *560*, 692
Karaites, 538
Kardec, Allan, 13
Karinat, 1016
Karma, 192, **560–561**, 882, 946
female body and, 418, 771
gender boundaries, 105, 125
and paradise, 759
Karmapa, 131
Karuṇā, 189, 606
Karva Chauth, 253
Kasa, 597–598
Kāśakṛtsnās, 771
Kashaya Pomo (people), 725
Kashmiri Śaivism, 892
Kaska (people), 588
Kassia, 688
Katha-Kālī, 765
Katz, Richard, 237
Kauai (Hawaii), 763
Kaur, Mata Sahib, 906
Kaur, Sada, 906
Kaur, Siri Ram, *905*
Kausalyā, 1076
Kay, Herma Hill, 573
Kaye/Kantrowitz, Melanie, 312
Keddie, Nikki, 354, 355, 1057
Keen, Sam, 648
Keeners, 682

Keisei, 281
Keller, Evelyn Fox, 607, 873
Keller, Rosemary, 206, 433
Kelley, Florence, 918
Kelly, Aidan, 1051
Kelly, J. N. D., 617
Kelly, Joan, 434, 766
Kempe, Margery, 75, 77–78, 82, 293,
555, **561–562**, 619, 936, 1009
Kendall, Laurel, 288, 739
Kennedy, Adrienne, 241–242
Kennedy, John F., 171
Kern, Kathi, 1054
Kerr, John, 815
Keteus, 948
Ketubah, 530, 539, 1052
Ketuvim, 855
Khadija, 21, 208, 256, 477, 499, 513,
562, 935, 1062
Khadro, A-Yu, 923
Khalsa, 906
Khanty (people), 57–58
Khare, Ravindra, 346
Khatun, Bibi Jamal, 923
Khecara, 997
Khema, Ayya, 131
Kheper, 273
Khita healing cult, 10
Khivi, Mata, 906
Khleifi, Michel, 342
Khoisa (people), 7
Khomeini, Ayatollah, 880
Khuddakanikāya, 614
Kia, 237
Kilauea volcano, 763
Kiliai (people), 647
Kinaaldé (Navajo rite), 710
King, Sallie, 723
King, Ursula, 769
King, Winston, 837
Kingston, Maxine Hong, 77
Ki no Tsurayuki, 597
Kinsella, Thomas, 1022
Kinsley, David, 330
Kirk-Duggan, Cheryl, 1053
Kirschbaum, Charlotte von, 164
Kirta, 394
Kīrtanīyās, 422, 425
Kish, 467
Kitamura Sayo, 576, 721, 901
Kitchen God, 282
Kivas, 52
Klein, Anne C., 36, 37, 131, 191, 246
Klein, Melanie, 815
Kliun, Ivan, 454
Knight, J. Z., 226
Knossos (Crete), 663
Knott, Kim, 769

Knowledge, **562–564**
  Afro-Atlantic religions, 15
  epistemology, 304–305
  Jainism, 522
  oral tradition, 739
  visions as, 1008, 1009–1011
  wisdom personification, 1030–1032
Koans, 333, 842
Kobayashi Eitaku, *458*
Kohanim, 747
Kohn, Sara, 511
Koita (people), 325
Kojiki, 26, 232, 239, 279
Kondos, Vivienne, 416
Kongo, 270
Kong Zi. *See* Confucius
Koniag Eskimos, 211
Konkomyo-saishookyo (Buddhist text), 86
Kore. *See* Demeter and Persephone
Korea
  ancestor worship, 30, 201
  biography, 80
  Buddhism, 120, 122, 281, 285–286, 745, 746
  Christianity, 163, 284, 286
  Confucianism, 122, 198, 199, 201, 280–281, 722, 894
  divorce, 266
  folk religions, 279, 288
  literary tradition, 596, 597–598
  minjung theology, 591
  new religions, 722
  pilgrimages, 780
  postmenopausal women healers, 647
  prehistoric sites, 803
  prostitution, 1001
  religious traditions study, 287, 288
  rituals and practices, 283–284
  shamanism. *See under* Shamans
  sun mythology, 949
  superstition, 950, 951
  Unification Church, 718–719
  women's lamentations, 683
Koresh, David, 147, 227, 324, 992
Koryaks (people), 56
Koryo dynasty, 122, 198, 280
Kosher, 782, 818, 819
Kosofsky, Eve, 590
Kotani Kimi, 286
Koyama Kosuke, 591
Koyukons (people), 862
Kpelle (people), 878
Kraemer, Ross, 527, 1065
Krahó (people), 1055–1056
Kramer, Heinrich, 1041, 1042
Krieger, Delores, 980
Kris dancers, 788

Krishna, 428, *605*, 1077
  bhakti sects, 88, 105
  breast symbolism and, 106
  as divine child, 261
  escape from murder, 472
  Mirabai and, 665–665
  music metaphor, 693
  paradise of, 759
  and Rādhā, 105, 249, 833, 966
  as trickster figure, 986–987
Krishnamurti, J., 979
Kristeva, Julia, 404, 571, 749, 816, 884
Krondorfer, Gorsline, 648
Kronos, 468, 472, 1031
Ksatriyas, 858, 1019
Kṣhemā, 772
Kuan Yin (Kannon), 97, 98, 100, 115, 120, 281, 285, 286, 362, 563, **564–565**, 636, 965
  depictions of, 191, 216, 448, 456, *721*, 758, 995
  fertility and, 337, 721
  goddess tradition and, 377
  inspiration and, 476
  love and, 604
  Miaoshan as human manifestation, 660–661
  pilgrimages, 285
  temples and shrines, 54, 903
  See also Avalokitésvara; Hāritī
Kubra. *See* Khadija
Kuiye, 52
Kuma (people), 480
Kumang, 1026
Kumarbi, 140
Kumāris, 1002, *1003*
Kumina tradition, 13
Kuṇḍalinī, 38, **565**, 892
!Kung (people), 237
Kunz, Dora, 980
Kurangī, 109
Kuranko (people), 818
Kurgan culture, 469–470
Kush (people), 377
Kutenai (people), 588
Kutiyattam, 238
Kut mudang, 233
Kuts, 30, 238
Kuwait, 508
Kwok Pui Lan, 334, 976
Kyklades Islands, 103
Kyriarchy, 673, 760
Kyubang kasa, 597–598

L
La'a-hana, 735
Labadie, Jean de, 998
Laban, 1038

LaBastille, Anne, 924
Lacan, Jacques, 331, 571
Lachesis, 1025
Lactation, 712
Lady Alchimia, 23
Lady from Balzi Rossi, 797
Lady Leviathan, 116
Lady of the Beasts, 329
Lady of the Lake, 329
Lady of the Plants, 329–330
Lady of the Spheres, 1032
Lady Wisdom, 329, 461, 462, 1033
Lady Xie, 330
Lady Yu, 330
Lady Yuan, 330
Laertes, 1026
Lai (Celtic genre), 598–599
L'ai-l'ai, 459
Laima, 374
Laity, **567–569**
  Buddhism, 111, 118, 120, 124–127, 285, 286, 567, 744–745
  Egyptian religions, 32
  Jainism, 520, 567
  penitential movements, 193
  Roman Catholicism, 567, 845, 850
  Taoism, 567
Lakon (Hopi society), 710
Lakon lueng dances, 239
Lakota Sioux (people), 323, 845, 883, 930, 934, 986
  Black Elk, 708, 709
  Ghost Dance, 724, 725
  goddesses, 377
  menarche ritual, 650
  seven rites, 709
  Sun Dance, 94, 709, 710
  sweat lodge, 341
  trickster figure, 986
  witchcraft, 1047
Lakshmi Bai, 1061
Lakṣmī, 253, 338, 418, 420, 422, 428, 441, **569**
  devadāsīs and, 250
  shaktism and, 892
  shrines and temples, 53
Lakṣmīnkarā, 923, 997, 1016
Lala Aziza, 756
Lalitavistara (Buddhist text), 110
Lallā, 865, 1076
Lalla 'Aisha Manoubia, 502
Lallā Dēd, 422
Lalla Zaynab, 502
Lambeth Conference (1930), 203
Lambton, Ana, 511
Laments, 344, 682–684
Lamphere, Louise, 303
Landes, Ruth, 213–214

Lands, mythic, **569–571**
Lange, Dorothea, 778
Language, **571–572**, 595
  in Afro-Atlantic religions, 15
  biblical, 90
  in Confucianism, 99
  deconstruction of, 246
  gender-inclusive, 268, 571–572, 603,
    748, 813, 1064, 1070
  Indo-European construct, 469,
    470–471
  lying and, 606, 607
  semiotics, 459, 884
  sexist, 888
  theistic issues, 970–971, 973
  tricksters and, 986
  weaving metaphor, 1025
  wisdom as feminine gender,
    1030–1031
  See also Speech
Language of the Goddess, The
    (Gimbutas), 1025
Laos, 125, 932
Lao Tzu, 97, 959, *960*, 964
Lapps (people), 55
Larner, Christina, 433
Larsa, 208
Larson, April Ulring, 742
Lascaux cave paintings, 797
Latimer, Kate, *741*
Latin America. *See* Liberation
    theologies; Mesoamerican
    religions; South American
    religions; *specific countries*
Latin American Bishops' Conference,
    728
Latinas. *See Mujerista* tradition
Latter-day Saints. *See* Mormons
Lauhuki, 735
Laussel, goddess of, 373, 379
Laveaux, Marie, 14
Lave tèt, 390
Law, **572–575**; *See also* Islamic law;
    Laws of Manu; Torah
Lawless, Elaine, 344, 739
Lawrence, Bruce, 354
Laws of Manu, 4, 75, 252–253, 292, 361,
    413, 573, 618, 650, 988
Lawson, Jeannie, 1063
Lay nuns, Buddhist. *See Anagarika*
Lazarus, 857
Lazarus, Moritz, 545
Leacock, Eleanor, 43, 737
Lead, Jane, 841
Leadership, **575–577**
  African American churches, 5
  charisma factor, 15, 575, 576, 577, 992
  Christian male, 676

Christian Science women, 719
Confucian, 201–202
cult religions, 226
liturgical worship and, 603
ministry, 661–662
Native American women, 621
neopagan dominance of women, 715
new religions, 717–718, 722, 726
by women in prehistoric agricultural
    societies, 801
sexism and, 887–888
Sikh, 906
Taíno, 139
See also Founders; Saints
League of Jewish Women (Germany),
    334, 552, 758
Lebacqz, Karen, 312
Lebanon, 507, 1021
Lechesis, 327
Le dynasty, 123
Lee, Ann, 147, 170, 208, 227, 349, 362,
    563, 576, **577–578**, 717, 787, 841,
    938, 993
Lee, Jarena, 519, 841
Lee, William, 578
Lee Kuan-yu, 200
Leeuw, Gerardus van der, 768
Lefferts, Leedom, 128
Left Ginza (Mandaean text), 616
Legba, 9, 225
Lehmann, Jennifer, 922
Leibniz, Gottfried, 510
Leland, Charles, 1048
Lemaire, Ria, 365
Lenshina, Alice, 161, **578–579**
Lent, 325, 982
Leo I, pope, 140
Leo XIII, pope, 135
Leo, Alan, 70
Leon, Lucrecia de, 808
Leonora, duchess of Tuscany, 541
Lepinski Vir excavation, 802
Lernean Hydra, 402
Lerner, Daniel, 1056
Lerner, Gerda, 37, 207, 432, 433, 760,
    809
Lesbianism, 311, **579–589**
  in Asia, **585–587**
  classical view, **579–581**
  contemporary separatism, 877
  feminist movements and, 335
  friendship and, 353
  gender studies and, 364
  heterosexism and, 70, 410, 411
  Judaism and, 543, 581, 582
  in microhistorical traditions, **587–589**
  Paul's condemnation of, 158
  queer theory, 590, 825–826

same-sex unions, 619
Sappho's lyrics, 868–869
shared child-rearing, 680
silence rejection, 908
theology, 1068
video documentary, 340
Western perspectives, **581–585**
Lesbian studies, **589–591**
Lespugne Venus, 796
Lessing, Doris, 594, *595*
Lessing, Theodor, 46
Levinas, Emmanuel, 309, 545, 548
Levine, A. J., 533
Levine, Nancy, 619
Levine, Renée C., 528
Levirate, 420, 1029–1030, *1030*
Lévi-Strauss, Claude, 42, 702, 931,
    944–945
Levi-Tanai, Sara, 241
Levy-Bruhl, Lucien, 836
Lewis, I. M., 45, 76, 610, 789, 893, 894
Lewis, Reina, 749
Lewisohn, Ludwig, 46
Lha-Mo, 957
Liang Qichao, 200
Liang Shuming, 200
Liberal feminism, 335
Liberation theologies, **591–593**, 972
  in Africa, 161, 592
  antiprostitution measures, 810
  feminisms and, 335, 629, 666
  guerrilla forces, 1023
  hermeneutics and, 406
  in Latin America, 167, 591–592,
    915–916
  Marxism and, 629
  in Philippines, 591, 723–724
  Protestant, 812
  racism and, 832
  salvation concept, 868
  social activism, 914
  suffering perspective, 946
  womanist, 1053
  women-centered, 978
Li chi (Confucian text), 770
Lichtenstädter, Ilse, 511
Liddle, Joanna, 431
Lidzbarski, Mark, 616
Lieh Nu, 78
Life-writing, 77
Ligoupup, 736
Liji (Book of Rites), 78, 80, 195, 325
Lilith, 28, 271, 273, 340–341, 377, **593**,
    729, 909, 966
Lin, Maya Ying, 1013
Lincoln, Bruce, 271
Lincoln, C. Eric, 4
Lindbeck, George, 267

Lingbao Taoism, 960, 961
Lingling Weng, 74
Lin Moniang. *See* Mazu
Lin-Shui Furen, 279–280
Li Rong, 730
Literacy, 291–294, 497, 502, 596,
738–739
Literary theory and criticism, 404–406,
593–596, 594
Literati (East Asian elite), 195–198
Literature, **596–602**
anonymous, 40
autobiography and biography, **76–83**
Bible as, **89–91**
convert narratives, 206
in the East, 129, **596–598**
feminist spirituality themes, 943
genre and gender, **365–366**
hagiography, **389**
hermaphrodites as subject, 403
images of human and divine women,
451–453, 563
Jewish authors, 552
Joan of Arc as subject, 524
Mesopotamian, 656, 658
p'ansori novels, 279
playwrights, 234, 240
rabbinic, 530–531
Romanticism, 852
symbolism, 457
in the West, 150, **598–602**
wisdom, 1033
See also Poetry; Sacred literature
Littel, Franklin, 548
Liturgical Movement, 602
Liturgy, **602–604**
musical accompaniment, 688
See also Gender-inclusive language
Liu Hsiang, 78–79
Liu I-Ming, 92
Liu Shu-hsien, 200
Liu Xiang, 80, 99, 196, 1006
Living Maya (Morris), 1026
Livy, 432, 610
Li Yu, 586
Loa, 836
Lobedu (people), 925
Locke, John, 784
Logacheva, Anastasiia, 1011
Logos, 455, 925, 988
Lohi'au, 763
Lollards, 561–562, 811
Lombards, 616
Lonrott, Elias, 702
Lorber, Judith, 920
Lorblanchet, Michel, 797
Lord, Albert, 738
Lorde, Audre, 313, 590, 601, 908

Lord of the Forest, 57
Lorelei, 1024
Loren, Sophia, 333
Lost Goddesses of Early Greece
(Spretnak), 706
Lot's wife, 896
Lotus Goddess, 995
Lotus sutra, 107, 123, 563, 564, 886
emptiness concept, 302
Japanese New Religions, 286
Loudon, possessed nuns of, 787
Louis IX, king of France, 786
Louisiana Spiritual churches, 717
Lourdes Pintasilgo, Maria de, 850
Love, 189, **604–606**, 636, 852
Lovedu (people), 467
Lovejoy, Arthur O., 852
Lovelace, Linda, 810
Love potions, 611
Lowe, Lisa, 749
Lowie, Robert, 801
Lozen, 1022
Lozi (people), 339
Lucius, 699
Lucretia, 835
Lugalbanda, 467
Lugbara (people), 1044
Lugones, Maria, 313
Luiseno (people), 277
Luke, 156, 630, 631, 632
Lull, Raymond, 510
Lumpa Church, 578–579
Lunar renewal rituals. *See* Moon
Lun Yu (Analects of Confucius), 195,
198, 361
Lü Pu-wei, 691
Luria, Isaac, 371
Lust. *See* Desire
Luther, Martin, 151, 207, 582, 626, 811,
856, 909, 1051, 1052, 1068
Lutheranism
civil rights, 582
Eucharist, 316
gift of grace, 812–813
government, 813
liturgy, 602
ordination of women, 153, 740,
742
Lü Tung-pin, 216
Luvedu (people), 20
Luxemburg, Rosa, 629
Lu Xiujing, 960
Lu Xun, 200
Lu Zhi, empress of China, 202
Lwas, 14, 15
Lydia of Thyatira, 463
Lying and dissimulation, **606–608**
Lysistrata (Aristophanes), 755

M
Maacah, 68, 395, 516
Ma'at, 987, 988, 1031, 1033
Maathal, Wangari, *914*
Maccabees, 532–533
Macha, 145
Machig Labdron, 117, 192, **609**, 1010
Ma Chig Lab Dun, 1077
Machig Ongjo, 118
Machis, 894–895
MacKenzie, Maureen Anne, 213
MacKinnon, Catharine, 573, 810
MacLeod, Mary Adelia, 742
Macpherson, Fergus, 579
Macrina, 82, 150, 348, 671
Macuch, Rudolf, 616
Macumba. *See* Umbanda
Macy, Joanna, 131, 723
Madālasā, 1076
Madness, 485
Madonna (religious). *See* Virgin Mary
Madonna (singer), 443, 689
Madrī, 420, 948
Maenads, 390, 580, **609–610**, 836
Mafa (people), 214
Magic, **610–613**, 980
Celtic religions, 145–146
female nudity ritualization, 729
in feminist witchcraft, 380
nature as ally, 712
neopagan, 715
occultism and, 733–734
wicca, 1029
See also Superstition; Witchcraft
Magna Mater, 315, 698, 699, 806
Magnani, Anna, 333
Maguire, Mairead, 755
Magus, 734
Mahābhārata, 233, 321, 419, 948, 988
Mahabodhi temple, 129
Mahādēviyakka, 78, 87, 88–89, 143, 243,
257, 596, **613–614**, 623, 759, 865,
936, 992
Maha Ghosananda, 723
Mahakali Pathshala, 426
Mahāprajāpatī, 67, 106, 111, 115, 295,
348, 614, **614**, 744, 772
Maharashtra (India), 820
Mahāvaṃsa, 124, 131
Mahāvidyas, 447
Mahāvira, 261, 520, 522, 667, 772
Mahāyāna Buddhism, 105, 107, 108,
109, 111–112, 121, 124, 131, 132,
263
compassion, 190
emptiness, 263, 301–302, 1034, 1035
female enlightenment, 759
ordination of nuns, 741

Mahāyāna Buddhism (continued)
  prajñā (wisdom), 1032, 1034
  salvation attainment, 867
Mahayana Yogācāra, 699, 794
Mahikari, 728
Mahinda, 868
Mahiṣa, 275
Mahler, Margaret, 815
Mahmud II, Ottoman sultan, 762
Mahya (Syrian martyr), 729–730
Maia, 315
Maid of Ludomir. See Verbermacher,
    Hannah Rachel
Maimela, Simon, 161
Maimonides, Moses, 25, 540, 582
Maitreyī, 78, 251, 419, 421, 771, 1076
Maitri, 189
Maitrīpa, 306
Majlis, 898, 899
Ma Jñānānanda, 257
Makeup, 750–751
Makin, Batsua, 998
Malabari, Behramji, 426
Malayasia, 749
  Islam, 504, 508, 932, 933
  Islamic new religion, 722–723
  Islamic women's pilgrimage from,
    781
  prostitution, 1001
  shamans, 893
Malchi, Esperanza, 541
Malice, 1036
Malinké (people), 95
Malinowski, Bronislaw, 42, 45, 702, 847,
    950
Malleus Maleficarum, 835, 966, 1001,
    1041, 1042
Malli (Mallinātha), 66–67, 522, 772
Malmgreen, Gail, 433
Malpede, Karen, 241
Mama Huaco, 928, 929
Mamaquilla (Moon mother), 927–928
Mamba Muntu, 615
Mamessi, 605
Mamiya, Lawrence, 4
Mammy Wata, 7–8, 614–615
Manahan, Nancy, 740
Manasā, 38, 244, 892
Manavadharmashastra, 105
Manbos, 226, 836
Mandaean religion, 615–616
Mandalas, 565, 957, 997
Mandate of Heaven (tianming), 196
Mandelbrot, Benoit, 457
Mandell, Jacqueline, 131
Mande (people), 9
Mandorla, 996
Manfreda, Sister, 223, 616–617

Mang Gong, 122
Mani, 371
Mani, Lata, 749
Manimekhalai, 441
Manjushri, 105
Mankaiyarkkaraci, 559, 560
Manoah's wife, 869
Manrique de Lara, María Luisa, 525
Manseong, 122
Mantras, 565, 858, 957
Manu, 75, 249; See also Laws of Manu
Manus (people), 587, 637–638
Manusmrti, 78
Manyōshū, 596
Maori (people), 297, 417, 735, 794, 934,
    949, 995
Mao Zedong, 202
Mapuche (people), 688, 893, 894–895,
    930
Māra, 48, 110, 249, 321, 965
Maraw (Hopi ritual society), 710
Marbode, Bishop of Rennes, 966
Marcela de San Félix, 234
Marcus, 160
Marcuse, Herbert, 222
Mardi Gras, 982
Marduk, 274, 323, 324, 360, 366–367,
    657
Margaret, Saint, 449, 866
Margaret of Cortona, 193, 1008–1009
Marglin, Frédérique Apffel, 74, 431
Mari (Mesopotamia), 659
María de Santo Domingo, 617–618
Maria Goretti, Saint, 835
Maria-José, 790
Maria Lionza cult, 728
Maria Maddalena de'Pazzi, 841
Mariamne, 535
Marianne (French heroine), 107
Maria Prophetissa, 733
Mariatale, 360
Marie de France, 598–599
Marie de l'Incarnation, 168
Marie d'Oignies, 77, 1008
Marie of the Incarnation, 151
Marillac, Louise de, 176, 348, 849
Māriyamman, 422
Mark, 156, 631–632
Mark Antony, 947
Marquesas Islands, 735
Marriage and singleness, 618–627
  Adam and Eve model, 618, 1051
  adultery, 3–4, 148, 183, 288, 390, 835,
    1001
  arranged marriage, 622, 624
  in Asian religions, 622–624; See also
    Wedding ceremonies; specific
    religions

bridal mysticism, 387, 867
bride-price, 512, 530
Chinese Instructions for Women, 757
Chinese inventer and patrons of, 730
Christian spiritual symbolism, 700
couples, 207–208
in cult religions, 227
economic issues, 288–290
gender roles, 361, 362, 1052–1053
Greek goddess of, 402
hair symbolism, 390
in hierarchical societies, 413
intermarriage, 532, 543
in Judaism, Christianity, and Islam,
    624–627, 676; See also Wedding
    ceremonies; under separate
    listings
legal perspectives, 573
levirate marriage, 420, 1029–1030,
    1030
Mandaean advocacy, 616
Mesopotamian ritual, 658
in microhistorical traditions, 620–622
Mormon, 677
overview, 618–620
in patriarchical societies, 618, 760
prenuptial agreements, 530
rape and, 835
as rite of passage, 843, 844
sacred marriage as model, 859–860
same-sex unions, 619, 620
in utopian communities, 992
widowhood, 1029–1030
wives, 1051–1053
See also Celibacy; Child marriage;
    Family; Incest; Polygyny
Marshack, Alexander, 798
Marshall, Paule, 601
Martha. See Mary and Martha
Martin, Clarice, 1054
Martin, Roberta, 689
Martineau, Harriet, 918
Marty, Martin, 354
Martyrdom, 79, 627–628
  Christian virgins, 671
  female nudity symbolism, 729–730
  heroic women, 1061
  iconography, 449
  Joan of Arc, 1019
  just war, 1020
  Perpetua and Felicity, 72, 77, 81–82,
    159, 767–768
  of religious converts, 205
  saints, 866
  self-mutilation as, 694
  suicide vs., 947
Marudevī, 522
Marwick, Max, 1044, 1050

Marx, Karl, 45, 222, *289*, 451, 629, 918, 921, 922
Marxism, **629–630**
    Chinese new religions and, 721
    cultural studies and, 227
    feminisms, 335, 451, 629, 839
    gendered reforms, 1059
    liberation theologies and, 591, 592
    See also Communism; Socialism
Mary (missionary to Romans), 155, 158
Mary, mother of James, 156
Mary, mother of Jesus. *See* Virgin Mary
Maryam (Mary), 490, **630**, 828, 882
Mary and Martha, 156, 160, 347, **630–631**
Mary Magdalene, 81, 156, 193, *257*, 332–333, 630, **631–633**, 966, 1062
    gnosticism and, 371, 372, 886
    Mayan weaving myth on, 1026
    New Testament account, 462, 463
    and prostitution, 632, 809–810
    at Resurrection, 935, 1015
Mary of Clophas, 156
Mary of Oignies, 561
Mary Stuart, queen of Scotland, 151
Mary the Jewess, 23
Mary Theodore, Mother, 348
Mary Tudor, queen of England, 151
Masai (people), *93*
Masculinist ethics, 311
Masculinity ideology, 648–649
Mashhadi, 499
Masks, 10–11, 233, 235, 236, 933
Masons, 734, 878
Maspero, Henri, 287
Masquerades, 233
Massagetae (people), 474
Massim, 326
Mass (rite); *See also* Eucharist
Master Meng, 99, 195, 196
Master of the Forest, 57
Master Xun, 195
Ma'sumeh, 499
Matam, 899
Material culture, 50, 214, **633–634**
Mater Matuta, 315
Matriarchy, **634–635**
    comparative religion studies, 188
    fertility and, 336
    goddess systems and, 373, 376–377, 380, 705, 1030
    Weber interpretation, 1027
    women's religions, 1066
    See also Amazons
Matrilineality/matrilocality, 634
Matriphobia, 816
Mātṛkās, 231, 421, 522
Matsui, Yayori, 1001

Matthew, 156
Matthews, Marjorie, 742
Matu, 674
Māui (trickster), 417
Maurin, Peter, 242, 850
Maurras, Charles, 470
Mauss, Marcel, 945
Mawlid (Muhammad birth), 1071
Mawu, 7, 9, 222
Mawu-Lisa, 7
Maxentius, emperor of Rome, *1061*
Maximilla, 159, 226, 808, 1010
Māyā (Buddha's mother), 106, 110, 115, 272, 361, 447, 614
Maya (Hindu concept), **635–636**
Maya culture, 289, 727
    divination, 258
    human sacrifice, 94
    postmenopausal women healers, 647
    pregnancy and childbirth, 655
    religion, 653, 654
    weaving, 1026
Mayana Sundari, 325
May festival (Tibet), 339
May Fourth Movement (China), 199–200, 771
Mayo, Katherine, 431, 1058
Maziniyya, Nusayba bint Ka`b al-, 367
Mazu (Tianhou), 281, **636–637**, 721
Mbuti Pygmies (people), 339, 587, 674
McAuliffe, Jane Dammen, 511
McClintock, Barbara, 1063
McClung, Nellie, 169, 1062
McDaniel, Jay B., 760
McFague, Sallie, 353, 971
McGinn, Bernard, 178
McIntosh, Peggy, 295
McLaughlin, Eleanor, 766
McLennan, John Ferguson, 381, 634
McNamara, JoAnn, 178, 767
McPherson, Aimee Semple, 318, 349, 576, **637**
McSheffrey, Shannon, 408
Mead, George Herbert, 918
Mead, Margaret, 42, 43, 85, **637–638**
Meade, Michael, 648
Meaning of Witchcraft, The (Gardner), 1048
Mecca
    Islamic prayer toward, 793
    pilgrimage to, 323, 387, 779–780, 781, 782, 827
Mechtild of Hackeborn, 639, 1009
Mechtild of Magdeburg, 82, 144, 150, 605, **638–639**, 774, 841, 866, 1009
Medb of Connacht, 145, 1022
Medea, 485

Media and religion, 335, 430, **639–641**;
    See also Film and video
Medicine bundle, 710
Medicine-lodge ceremony, 710
Medicine Women (*menma*), 116
Médicis, Marie de, 63
Medieval period. *See* Middle Ages
Meditation in Asian traditions, **641–642**
    body's significance, 98
    Buddhist new religions, 723
    "Cutting" visualization, 609
    kuṇḍalinī arousal, 38, 565, 892
    as liturgy, 602
    prayer vs., 791
    tantric practices, 957
    Taoism, 962
    See also under Buddhism
Meditation centers, 125, 128
Mediums, 892–893
    Brazilian new religion, 728
    Buddhism, 127, 933
    Himalayan religions, 416
    Nat religion, 127, 893
    as possessed, 787, 788, 789, 790
    spiritualism, 941
    See also Shamans
Medusa, 390
Mehet-Weret, 714
Meir, Golda, 551, 552, 923, 1057, 1063
Melaart, James, 801
Melanesia, 94, 325
Melania, 671
Melissa, 399
Mellaart, James, 377
Mellon, Mary Conover, 556
Melpomene, 687
Melqart, 138
Melusina, 607
Memory, **642–644**
Menā (Hindu nymph), 759
Menarche, 52, 60, 94, 97, 237, 473–474, **644–646**, 647, 649, 650, 931, 982
Menchú, Petrocinio, 646
Menchú, Rigoberta, 335, **646–647**, 1023, 1063
Menchú, Vicente, 646
Mencius (Master Meng), 99, 195, 196
Mende (people), 820
Mendicancy. *See* Almsgiving
Mendonsa, Eugene, 259
Menelaus, 403
Meness, 949
Meng, Widow, 196
Menopause, **647–648**, 794
Menscher, Joan, 354
Men's spirituality movement, **648–649**
Menstruation, **649–652**
    agricultural rituals, 20

Menstruation *(continued)*
  alchemical practices, 23
  Aristotelian view, 773
  blood interpretations, 93–94, 321,
    540, 876
  Buddhist practices, 115, 120, 903
  Eastern views, 97, 282–283
  end to. *See* Menopause
  exclusionary practices, 338, 861, 1071
  fasting, 325
  and female-dominated religions, 820
  first. *See* Menarche; Puberty rites
  Hindu practices, 73, 252, 425, 429,
    903
  inauspiciousness of, 73–74
  Islamic practices, 491, 934, 955
  Jewish practices, 527, 534, 540, 782,
    818, 934
  moon linked with, 417
  Native American practices, 52, 876,
    934, 956, 982
  nature linked with, 712
  Orthodox Christian practices, 752,
    753
  as polluting, 646, 647, 649–650
  possession beliefs, 819–820
  and ritual purification, 818, 819
  as sacred time, 982
  seclusion practices, 875, 876
  Sikh practices, 905, 906
  South American religions and, 931
  spiritual dimensions, 839
  structuralist view, 945
  taboos, 20, 57, 137, 649, 650, 666,
    876, 903, 934, 955–956
Menzies, Lucy, 991
Meomama (chimalma), 654
Meratus Dayak (people), 895
Merchant, Carolyn, 303, 874
Mercury, 23
Meresankh, 32
Meret-Neith, queen of Egypt, 714
Merici, Angelica, 348
Meritamun, 34
Mermaid, 615
Mernissi, Fatima, 312, 450, 749, 782,
    829, 1052
Me Sai Ban ritual, *424*
Meskell, Lyn, 377
Mesoamerican religions, **652–656**
  female personifications, 329
  human sacrifice, 94, 654
  as Mexicanidad (new religion) basis,
    727
  sacrifice rituals, 94, 861, 863
  shrines and temples, 902
Mesopotamian religions, **656–660**
  clothing, 182

cultic prostitution, 809
dualism, 274
life-affirming Goddess creator, 755
magical beliefs and rituals,
    1037–1039
priestess, 804–805, 809
sacred marriage, 605
warfare, 1019
wisdom goddesses, 1031, 1033
See also Babylonia; Canaan-
    Phoenicia, religions of; Inanna;
    Ishtar
Mestiza theology, 592
Metaethics, 308
Metamorphoses (Apuleius), 813
Metamorphoses (Ovid), 315, 403
Metaphor
  music, 692–693
  nature as, 702, 712
  weaving as, 1025
Metaphysical feminism, 943
Metaphysics (Aristotle), 971
Methodism, 5, 151, 153, 318, 742, 812,
    857
Metis, 71, 1031
Metropolitan Community Church, 583,
    740
Mèt tet, 390
Mevlûd (festival), 338, 339
Mexica. *See* Aztec culture
Mexicanidad, La (new religion), 727
Mexico
  dance rituals, 235–236
  mesoamerican religion, 652–655
  new religions, 725, **726–727**
  prehistoric figurine finds, 803
  rosary praying, 152
  shrines and pilgrimages, 780, 783,
    902, 903
  spiritualism, 941
  weaving, 1026
Meyerhoff, Barbara G., 436
Miaoshan, 281, **660–661**
Micah, 665
Micaiah, 399
Michigan Journal of Law and Gender,
    810
Micronesia, 734, 735–736, 995
Middle Ages
  breast symbolism, 107
  Christianity, 150–151, 863, 890
  Christian matron patrons, 761
  Christian mysticism, 699, 700
  economics, 288–289
  emotionality of women, 299
  eucharistic devotion, 317
  female literacy and education, 293
  feminist revisionism, 433

food's significance, 347
friendship concept, 352
iconography, 448, 455
Judaism, 264, 265, 527, **538–540**, 625
literature, 598–599
masculine vision of sun, 703
monasteries, 672
mystic view of nature, 712
pagan holdovers, 1041
religious authority, 75
same-sex Christian unions, 619
self-mutilation, 694
visionaries, 82, 150–151, 841,
    1008–1009, 1010
widow status, 1030
witchcraft beliefs, 151, 1036, 1037,
    1041–1042
women's communities, 293, 387, 786
women's philosophical status,
    773–774
women's role, 102
Middle Way (Buddhism), 1034
Midgard, 871
Midrash, 36, 536, 855, 1065
Midwives, 461, 527, 563, 647, 655
Migrant Mother (Lange), 778
Míguez Bonino, José, 591
Mihrimah Sultan, 54, 762
Miko, 278, 901
Mikveh, 650, 782, 818
Milarepa, 231, 272
Miles, Margaret, 729, 769, 1000
Milk-debts, 106–107
Mill, James, 425, 430
Millenarian movements, 807, 808
Miller, Patricia Cox, 271
Million Man March, 649
Mills, Patricia Jagentowicz, 222
Milton, John, 332, 618
Mīmāṃsā, 772
Mimi spirit, *332*
Mimunah, Lalla, 923
Minahassa (people), 277
Minerva. *See* Athena
Ming dynasty, 99, 100, 115, 216, 279
Mingyur Paldron, 117
Ministry, **661–663**; *See also* Leadership;
    Ordination
Minjung theology, 163, 591
Minne, 387
Minnich, Elizabeth Kamarck, 311,
    312
Minoan (Cretan) religion, 367, 377,
    663–664, *805*, 934
  prehistoric sites, 801
  snake goddesses, 38, 379
Minominee (people), 1047
Minyan, 186, 530, 748, 856

Mirabai, 78, 80, 87, 88–89, 143, 257,
    361, 389, 422, 450, 596, 619, 623,
    664–665, 691, 771, 865, 992, 1007,
    1010, 1077
Miriam, 233, 241, 397–398, 441, 515,
    516, 644, **665**, 688, 703, 806, 807,
    840, 1011, 1016, 1062
Mirror of Simple Souls, The (Porete),
    786
Miscarriage, 337, 729
Mishnah, 183, 527, 530, 536, 553, 855,
    909
Mishrife, 136–137
Misogyny, 149, 303, **665–666**
    body's denigration and, 102
    Buddhism, 120
    comparative religion studies, 188
    feminist revisionism, 433, 716
    Judaic and Christian theology, 1068
    prakriti interpretation, 791
    theistic portrayals and, 970
    witchcraft and, 1042, 1045, 1051
    See also Sexism
Missionaries of Charity, 681
Missionary activity, 153, 168–169, 173
    in Africa, 161–162, 237, 501
    in Asia, 162–163, 503
    Baptist Church, 743
    in colonial America, 170
    dance prohibitions, 236, 237
    female leadership, 172–174, 576, 661,
        812, 1062
    in India, 425, 426, 681, 1058
    microhistorical traditions and, 621
    Mormon, 677
    postcolonial studies of, 185
    Roman Catholic nuns, 672, 681
Missionary Sisters of the Sacred Heart,
    348
Mississippi culture, 708
Mistress of the Animals, 455, 456
Mistress Sarah Rebecca Rachel Leah,
    81
Mithras, 484, 605, 698, 699
Mitter, Sara, 836
Mitzvot, 526, 536
Mix, Sarah, 318
Mixtecs (people), 902
Mizoguchi Kenji, 598
Mizrahi Jews, 1057–1058
Mnemosyne, 686, 687
Modena, Fioretta (Bat Sheva), 541
Modesty, 730
Mofokeng, Tsakatso, 161
Mohamed, Jan, 825
Mohave (people), 588
Moi, Toril, 595
Moirae (Moirai), 327, 1025

Moksa, 143, 421, 559, 585, 622, 867
Molakata fast, 325
Molimo festival, 339
Molinos, Miguel de, 193
Moloch, 471
Molodowsky, Kadya, 552
Molza, Tarquinia, 691
Monaghan, Patricia, 948
Monasticism, **666–673**
    almsgiving to, 25
    asceticism life, 67
    ashram, 667
    biblical interpretation, 856
    biographical writings, 80–81
    caring and compassion, 440
    celibacy, 143–144, 619, 890, 923
    devotional objects, 448–449
    disciples, 257
    documentary films, 340
    in the East, 443, **666–670**; *See also*
        Buddhism; Jainism; Taoism
    fasting, 863
    friendship between, 352
    gender separation, 876–877
    hair shaving, 123, 143, 390
    hair symbolism, 390
    hierarchy, 413, 1017
    inferior status, 771
    Jewish Therapeutae, 67, 527, 533,
        671, 1011
    liturgical singing, 688
    meditation, 641–642
    missionary activity, 161, 170
    modern era, 284–285, 286
    monastery architectural patrons, 54
    mystics, 762–763
    order founders, 135, 348, 361,
        400–401, 614, 849, 967–968
    ordination, 143, 741, 744–746, 1015
    patronage by, 762
    penitential practices, 192–194
    in Philippines, 934
    possession and, 787
    as sacred marriage, 671, 859, 1052
    seclusion, 672, 876–877
    self-mutilation, 863
    sisterhood concept, 912
    spirituality, 942
    temptation and, 965–966
    Thai new religion, 723
    in United States, 170
    vow taking, 1017–1018
    in the West, 150, **671–673**; *See also*
        Christianity; Orthodox Christianity
    widow recruitment, 1030
    women historians, 767
    women visionaries, 1011
Mone, F. J., 387

Mongolia, 893, 955
Mongols (people), 55, 475
Monica, 204, *205*, 866
Monogamy, 621, 625, 634
Monophysites, 751–752
Monotheism, **673**
    autobiography and biography, 81–83
    divinity concept, 263–265
    feminist issues, 970
    misogyny and, 666
    modern Jewish scholarship, 553
    myth reinterpretations, 702
    neopagan reaction to, 715–716
    orientalism and, 1056–1058
    as patriarchal, 887
    polytheism vs., 784
    and self concept, 881–882
    women's crafts, 291–220
    women's role, 1056–1058
    See also Christianity; Islam; Judaism
Monroe, Marilyn, 443
Montagu, Mary Wortley, 510
Montanists, 159, 226, 408, 807, 808
Montanus, 808
Montesquieu, Baron de, 510
Montgomery, Carrie Judd, 318
Montgomery, Helen Barrett,, 173
Moon, **673–674**
    Artemis as goddess, 66
    in astrology, 70
    as feminine symbol, 703
    Hina's association with, 417
    Incan beliefs, 927–929
    menarche ritual, 645
    pregnancy linked with, 794
    in South American religions,
        927–929, 930
    Sun and, 949
Moon, Meenakshi, 129
Moon, Sun Myung, 226, 324, 718, 719,
    722, 992
Moore, Henrietta, 42, 43
Moore, Robert, 648
Morality, **675–676**, 815; *See also* Ethics;
    Virtue
Moravian fragments, 797
Moravians, 151
Mordecai, 307, 308, 325
More, Thomas, 991
Morgan, Julia, 54
Morgan, Lewis, 634, 1027
Morgan, Robin, 1057
Mormons, **676–678**
    divine couple, 207
    feminist excommunication, 640
    on homosexuality, 583
    as new religion, 717, 718, 720
    paradise concept, 759

Mormons (*continued*)
  as patriarchal, 718
  polygyny, 227, 574, 618, 677, 992, 993
  prophet, 808
  traditional gender roles, 808
  utopianism, 992, 993
Morning Star, 802
Morrigan, 39, 145
Morris, Brian, 45
Morris, Walter F., Jr., 1026
Morrison, Toni, 599, 600, 601
Mosaic law. *See* Torah
Moses, 67, 256, 397, 398, 515, 516, 526,
    537, 747
  escape from Pharoah, 472
  Islamic view of, 490
  sister Miriam, 665
  Torah and, 855, 984
Moses and Monotheism (Freud), 814
Mosques, 761, 762, 903
Mot, 137, 486, 515
Mother Cabrini. *See* Cabrini, Frances
    Xavier
Mother Divine, **678–679**
Mother Earth, 11, 323, 379, 454, 455,
    883; *See also* Earth Mother
Mother-Elk, 58
Mother Goddess, 145, 800, 802, 805,
    806, 902
Motherhood and grandmotherhood,
    679–681
  anthropology and, 43
  in Buddhism, 115, 124, 190, 302
  in Confucianism, 196
  femininity images, 333
  grandmotherhood, 680
  in Hinduism, 420
  home and, 439
  importance to community, 186
  in Judaism, 186, 460–461, 531
  Kristeva theory, 816
  love imagery, 605
  object-relations theory, 815–816
  in Orthodox Christianity, 752–753
  prehistoric, 798
  religious experience and, 839
  Virgin Mary and, 882
  visual imagery, 454–455
  wifely status and, 1052
  as wisdom symbols, 1032, 1034, 1035
  women's religions and, 1066
  See also Family; Fertility and
    barrenness; Matriarchy; Pregnancy
Mother India (Mayo), 431, 1058
Mother Nature, 304, 455, 940
Mother of the World, 833
Mother's Day, 165
Mothers of the Believers, 827–828

Mother Teresa, 440, 640, **681–682**, 850
Mott, Lucretia, 756, 1070
Moulton, Janice, 775
Mountain God, 904
Mountain Wolf Woman, 725
Mountbatten, Lord, 932
Mount Hei center (Japan), 123
Mount Helicon, 686
Mount Koya center (Japan), 123
Mount Sinai Holy Church in America,
    349
Mourning and death rites, 243,
    682–685, 843
  ancient Egyptian, 33–34
  auspiciousness and inauspiciousness,
    74
  burial site importance, 439
  dance and, 233
  egg's significance, 297
  fasting practices, 326
  festivals, 338
  hair-related practices, 390
  Islamic, 495
  Israelite, 397
  Judaic, 531
  Korean, 283
  lamentations, 682–684, 688
  quarantine and purification rituals,
    818
  Shiite, 898–899
  taboos, 955
  wailing and crying, 1016
  widow, *1029*, 1030
  widow suicide. *See* Sati
  womb-like graves, 1056
  See also Ancestor worship
Mou Zongsan, 200
Movies. *See* Film and video
Movimiento Confederado Restaurador
    del Anahuac. *See* Mexicanidad, La
Mu'awiya, Yazid b., 898
Mubarak, Hosni, 864
Mudang, 278, 279
Muesis, 698
Mugai Nyodai, **685**
Muhammad, 102, 104, 488, 575, 808
  and afterlife, 19
  birth celebration, 1071
  celibacy rejection, 626
  as charismatic leader, 147
  and contraceptive practices, 203
  daughter. *See* Fāṭima
  disciples of, 256
  divine revelation to, 263
  female prophets, 808
  and horse imagery, 39
  hospitality's importance, 440–441
  on levirate, 1029–1030

and Qur'an, 263, 826–827, 828, 857
  Western portrayals of, 510
  wives. *See* 'Aisha; Khadija; Zaynab
  and women warriors, 1019
Muhammad, Elijah, 808
Mujerista tradition, **685–686**
  feminism and, 312, 335, 592, 976,
    1060
  storytelling, 1064
  theism and, 970
  women's studies, 1068
Mu'jizat Kahanis, 899
Mukherjea, Charulal, 588
Mukta, Parita, 450
Mu Lian, 115
Müller, Max, 187, 435, 469
Mulungu, 7
Mundurucu (people), 930, 931
Munn, Nancy, 737
Mun Sonmyong. *See* Moon, Sun Myung
Murals, 1013, 1014
Murasaki, Lacy, 596
Murphy, Emily, 1062
Murphy, Robert, 930, 931
Murphy, Yolanda, 931
Murray, Margaret, 1048, 1051
Musaylimah, 808
Muses, 452, 477, **686–687**
Mushrooms, 480
Music, 391, **687–693**
  anonymous artists, 40
  contemporary women's spirituality
    movement, 1064
  Egyptian religions, 32–33
  female voice, 1016
  folk songs, 739
  instruments and voices, **690–693**
  Israelite religion, 397, 515–516, 527,
    807, 1016
  Jaina hymns, 521
  laments and dirge singing, 682, 683
  Mormon Tabernacle Choir, 677
  Muses, 686–687
  overview, **687–690**
  performance theory, 764–765
  Rāmāyaṇa singing groups, 738–739
  women composers, 689, 691
Muslim Brotherhood, 367–368, 493,
    497, 508
Muslims. *See* Islam
Muslim Women's Association, 492,
    497
Mussolini, Benito, 165
Mutiah, Meena, 216
Mutilation, 77, **693–695**
  Confucian practices, 280
  footbinding, 100, 197, 666, 694–695,
    863, 1001

by Miaoshan, 661
  self, 661, 694, 863, 887
Mutilation, genital, 41, 94, **695–697**,
      749, 1001
  as chastity guarantor, 3, 149
  films about, 343
  as initiation rite, 10, 96, 474, 843
  Islamic law, 492, 494
  old women's enforcement of, 680
Muttā, 109
Mutterrecht, Das (Bachofen), 634, 800
Myadpukuche, 57
Mycenaeans, 663
Myerhoff, Barbara, 340, **697–698**
Mygdonia, 159
Mystery plays, 32
Mystery religions, **698–699**; *See also*
      Gnosticism
Mysticism, **699–701**
  academic studies of, 178, 991
  authority and, 76
  bridal, 387, 867
  desire imagery, 249
  divine plan and, 263
  friendship concept, 352
  Hadewijch of Brabant, 387
  Judaic, 409, 540, 541–542, 571–572,
      733
  knowledge and, 564
  María de Santo Domingo, 617
  Mechtild of Magdeburg, 638–639
  medieval, 150–151, 433, 563, 712,
      890
  nature as divine creation, 712
  negative theology, 385
  Pazzi, Maria Maddalena de', 762–763
  religious experience and, 839
  revelation and, 840
  Roman Catholic, 1028
  sacred marriage, 605
  secret societies, 878
  silence practices, 907
  Sufi, 409
  See also Esotericism; Visionaries in
      medieval Europe; Visions
Mythology, **701–706**
  African, 8–9, 95
  Afro-Atlantic, 15
  androgyny in, 36
  authority of, 75
  Babylonian, 323, *324*, 360, 366–367
  birth portrayals, 91
  blood's significance, 94
  breast symbolism, 106
  Celtic, 145, 146, 459, 477, 701
  Chinese, 730–731
  divine family, 323
  dualism in, 273–274

earth in, 277
  Etruscan and Roman, 315–316, 1031,
      1032
  on evil's origins, 321
  fate in, 327, 333
  female knowledge portrayals, 563
  feminine images, 332–333, 457–460,
      569–570, 770, 774
  feminist uses of goddess myths, 377,
      383, 703, 704, **705–706**
  fertility, 336
  on gender conflict, 360
  gendered solar imagery, 703–704
  on gender roles, 362
  geographic sacredness, 366–367
  Greek, 26–27, 39, 384–385, 459, 474,
      477, 569, *570*, 580–581, 686–687,
      692, 702, 703, 705–706, 755,
      1031–1032
  hair symbolism, 390
  Hawaiian, 763
  hermaphrodite depictions, 403
  Hindu, 420, 706, 759–760, 887, 939,
      966
  incestuous pairings, 468
  Jaina, 521–522
  Jungian archetypes, 555, 556, 815
  lands, **569–571**
  as literary influence, 591
  lying and deception in, 607
  on matriarchies, 634
  as men's movement influence, 648
  Muses, 686–687
  of music, 687, 691, 692
  Navajo, 1026
  Norse, 18, 39, 243, 327, 351–352,
      871–872
  orthodoxy and, 408
  overview, **701–705**
  as photographic subjects, 778
  sacred marriage, 859
  sacred spaces, 934
  on sacrificial victims, *862*, 863
  on sexual temptation, 332, 559
  shape-shifting, 895–896
  Sinhalese, 329
  on sister relationships, 911–912
  structuralist view, 944
  sun, 949
  Taíno, 139
  Taoist, 770
  vagina imagery, 995, 996
  weather personifications, 1024
  weaving, 1025–1026
  wisdom personifications, 1030–
      1032
  womb symbolism, 1055
  women warriors, 1021

See also Creation and recreation;
      Goddess; Lands, mythic; *specific*
      figures
Mythopoetic men's movement, 648–649

N

Nabonidus, king of Babylonia, 804
Nader, Laura, 749
Nafisa, 53
Nafs, 926, 927
Nāgadevī, 109
Naganuma Myōkō, 286
Nagarjuna, 1034
Nagas, 940, 1034
Nage (people), 1045
Nag Hammadi, 159, 160
Naguib Al-Atlas, 722
Nahjul Balagha, 498
Nahua Guardians of the Traditions of
      Mexico, 727
Nahuatl language, 727
Naidu, R. Venkata Ratnam, 426
Naidu, Sarojini, 426
Nairātmyā, 116
Nakayama Miki, 349, 576, 621, 717, 901
Nakedness. *See* Nudity
Nakiba, 903
Nama (people), 587
Namkai Norbu, 118
Nanabozho, 709
Nana Buku, 222
Nanak, 254, 904–905, 906
Nanaki, 904, 905, 906
Nanaya, 466
Nandadevi, 780, 782
Nandy, Ashis, 837
Nanea, 464
Nangsa Obum, 118
Nanna, 467, 871
Nanshe, 657
Naomi, 256, 460, 853, 937
Napoleon, emperor of France, 451,
      849
Napoleonic Code (1804), 164–165
Naquin, Susan, 288
Narada, 105
Nara Shrine (Japan), *120*
Narayan, Kirin, 344, 415, 416
Naro Khachöma, 997
Nāropa, 117, 231
Narratology, 594
Nasi, Gracia, 541
Nasser, Gamal Abdel, 367
Natchez (people), 708
Nathan, 399
Nāthayogis, 1076
National Baptist Convention, 5, 689
National Council of Churches, 203

National Council of Jewish Women, 544, 552
National Council of Women in India, 426
National Social Conference (India), 426
National Women's Suffrage Association, 359, 1070
Nation of Islam, 649, 808
Native American Church, 725
Native American/Inuit Photographers' Association of Canada, 778
Native American religions, **707–711**, 845
  afterlife concept, 18
  animal imagery, 39
  archaeological site interpretations, 802
  Arctic region, 59–60
  Benedict's analyses, 86
  berdaches, 620
  cautionary tales, 570
  Christianity and, 168, 170
  circle symbolism, 179, 457
  crafts and, 211, 212, 213–214
  creation stories, 222, 937
  crossroads imagery, 225
  dance and drama, 233, 234–235
  divine couples, 207
  divine family, 323
  divorce, 266–267
  documentary films, 341
  earth's role, 277
  female personifications, 329, 330
  folklore, 344
  food and, 347
  gendered solar imagery, 703–704
  goddesses, 377
  grandmother as moral instructor, 680
  hospitality and, 441
  lesbianism and, 587, 588
  liberation theologies, 592
  liturgy and, 602–603
  menarche ritual, 645, 650
  menstruation and, 52, 876, 934, 956, 982
  misrepresentations, 778
  mythology of music, 687
  new religions, **724–726**
  oral tradition, 235, 707, 708, 855
  personified principles, 208
  polygyny, 618
  puberty rites, 52, 94, 982
  purification rites, 818–819
  religious experience, 839
  sacred times, 982
  self concept, 883
  shamanism, 787
  sun mythology, 949

sweat lodges, 341, 602–603
tepees, 52, 55, 56
theistic reinterpretation, 970
trances, 104
trickster figures, 986
vagina imagery, 995
visionaries, 1010
wisdom personifications, 1032
witchcraft beliefs, 1036, **1047–1048**
women warriors, 1022
See also Mesoamerican religions; *specific peoples*
Nat kadaw (spirit-wives), 238, 893
Nat (spirit) religion, 127, 238, 348, *349*, 442, 893, 903, 1010, 1066
Nattier, Jan, 1034
Natural History (Pliny), 650
Natural law, 203, 852
Natural selection, 712, 874
Nature, **711–713**
  in Arctic religions, 57
  artwork, 1013
  definitions, 711
  environmentalism, 303–304, 874
  female personifications, 329–330, 711–713
  geographic sacredness, 366–367
  neopagan worship of, 715
  in nomadic religions, 475
  in occultism, 733
  in Oceanic religions, 735
  scientific view of, 874
  in South American religions, 931
  in Southeast Asian religions, 932
  spirits associated with, 940
  thealogy, 969
  Transcendentalism and, 984, 985
Nature (Emerson), 984
"Nature mytholopgy" theory, 702
Nātya, 250
Natyasastra, 238
Nautsiti, 687
Navajo (people), 52, 222, 377, *708*, 709, 883, 982
  menarche ritual, 645
  ritual complex, 710
  weaving, 1026
  witchcraft beliefs, 1036, 1047
Navarātrī (Nine Nights) festival, 275, 429, 569
Nayars, 31, 620
Naylor, Gloria, 453, 600
Nayyar, Sheila, *427*
Nazis Germany. *See* Holocaust
Ndebele (people), *894*
Ndembu (people), 96, 347, 818, 819–820, 843–844
Neanderthal culture, 796–798

Necromancy, 1039
Needleman, Jacob, 305
Nefertiti, 34
Negative dialectics, 222
Negative theology, 385
Nehemiah, 399, 532, 534, 807
Neih, 32
Neihardt, John G., 708
Neith, 487, **714–715**, 1025
Neith-hetap, queen of Egypt, 714
Neiye, 959
Nelson, Sarah, 633
Nelson, Vednita, 810
Nemean Lion, 402
Nenets (people), 57
Neoclassicism, 852
Neo-Confucianism, 197, 279, 280, 300, 770
Neolithic period, 801, 802, 803
Neopaganism, 207, 226, 264, **715–716**, 717, 734, 877, 880
  contemporary witchcraft movement, 1048–1050, 1051
  wicca, 1028–1029
Neoplatonism, 926
Neowitchcraft, 734
Nepal, 97, 117, 118, 125, 126, 128, 416–417, 997
  male magicians, 611
  Newar living goddesses, 1002
  polyandry, 620
  superstition, 951
Nephthys, 32, 487, 488, 912
Nero, emperor of Rome, 671
Nesbitt, Paula, 576
Nestorians, 162
Nettles, Bonnie Lu, 227
Neu, Dianne, 603
Neumann, Erich, 243, 380, 382, 801
Neumann, Theresa, 317
Neumark, Martha, 545
Neusner, Jacob, 536
Nevi'im, 855
Neville, Gwen Kennedy, 346
New Age movements, 241, 861
  feminist shamans, 718
  men's spirituality, 648–649
  possessed women, 788
  secularization and, 880
  spiritualism and, 941
  theosophy and, 979
  women's roles, 226, 719–720
Newars (people), 117, 416, 1002
"New Criticism," 593
New Guinea, 39, 213, 480
New Life Movement, 950
New religions, **716–729**
  borderline with old religions,

716–717
divinity concepts, 264
in East Asia, **720–722**; *See also*
Japanese New Religion
environmental aspects, 304
in Europe and United States,
718–720
family's significance, 324
Goddess movement, **379–380**
homosexuality and, 583
humor incorporation, 443–444
media coverage, 640
menstruation view, 820
in Mexico, **726–727**
in Native American traditions,
724–726
neopaganism, **715–716**, 717, 734
occultism and, 734
in Oceania
overview, **716–718**
secularization and, 880
in South America, **728–729**
in Southeast Asia, **722–724**
vegetarianism, 999
women founders, 717–718, 721,
726–727, 767, 913
women's musical expression, 688–
689
Newsome, Carol, 1055
New Testament, 241, 535, 536, 856, 926,
937
on celibacy, 619, 626
as Christian canon, 90, **155–157**
feminist scholarship, 1068
gender roles, 361
heroic women, 90
images of women, 90, 336, **462–463**
Mary Magdalene portrayal, 631–632
Mary and Martha portrayal, 630–631
on menstruation, 651
on ministry, 661
possession references, 787
prostitution references, 809–810
virginity valuation, 626
on weather, 1024
on widow status, 1029
wisdom personifications, 1031, 1033
women prophets, 807
See also God; Jesus of Nazareth; Paul
and the Pauline tradition; Virgin
Mary; *specific figures*
New Thought, 717
New Zealand, 417
Ngaju Dayak (people), 367
Nicaragua, 335
Nicomachean Ethics (Aristotle), 773
Nidaba, 656, 658
Nidavellir, 871

Niditch, Susan, 986
Nietzche, Friedrich, 85, 246, 332, 481
Niflheim, 871
Nigeria, 620, 754
Nightingale, Florence, 1063
Niguma, 117, 272
Nihongi, 91
Nihonshoki, 26, 279
Nijo, Lady, 78, 923
Nikah, 1052
Nikova, Rina, 241
Ni Made Suri, *424*
Nimue (Lady of the Lake), 329
Ninakapansi, 21
Nine Mountains system (Buddhism),
122
Nine Muses. *See* Muses
Nineteenth Amendment, 1070
Ningal, 467, 658
Ninhursag, 657
Ninigi no Mikoto, 26
Ninshatapada, 658
Ninshubur, 373
Ninsu, 657
Ninsud, 657
Ninsun, 271
Nintu, 657
Nirṛti, 225, 243
Nirvana, 121, 124–125, 249, 263, 888,
982
as goal of renunciatory life, 667
women's attainment, 772
Nisaba, 657, 1031, 1033
Nisus, 390
Nitocris, 34–35
Nityasumaṅgalī, 250, 251
Niuheliang excavation (China), 803
Niwano Nikkyō, 286
Njanja (people), 9
Nku, Christina, 161
Nnna, 658
Noa, 735, 934
Noadiah, 397, 399, 441, 516, 807, 840
Noah, 1024
Nobel Peace Prize, 646, 647, 681
Noble, Margaret (Sister Nivedita),
431
Noce en Galilée (film), 342
"No-church" movement (Japan), 163
Noddings, Nel, 1007
Noh drama, 765, 239
Nomads, 55–56, 474–475, 499
Nommos, 6–7
Nonviolence. *See* Pacifism and
nonviolence
Norns, 327, 872
Norsa Senñora do Rosario de Fatima,
902

Norse mythology, 871–872
animal imagery, 39
fate, 327
Freyja, 351–352, 374, 871, 872
heaven, 18
Valkyries, 243, 327, 871, 872, 1021
Nortan, Max, 102
North Africa, 620
colonialism and postcolonialism,
1020
pilgrimages and shrines, 780–781, 782
polygyny, 618
Northern (American) Baptist
Convention, 318
Not Without My Daughter (film), 505
Noyes, John Humphrey, 227
Nryta dance, 236
Nubia, 409
Nudity, 182, **729–730**
bhakti saints, 88
Jaina ascetics, 521, 730
photographic exploitation of women's,
778
Venus figures, 633, 796–797
Nuemaier-Dargyay, Eva, 585
Nuer (people), 7
Nugua, **730–731**
Numa, 407
Numbering systems, 798
Number Our Days (Myerhoff), 697
Numen (journal), 437
Nunghui, 930
Nuns. *See* Monasticism
Nurcholish Majid, 722
Nusayba, 1019
Nuwa/Nuxi. *See* Nugua
Nyakyusa (people), 925
Nyame, 6, 674
Nyāya, 772
Nyeshangba (people), 416
Nyinba (people), 619
Nyingma (Buddhist sect), 117
Nyingwan Mbege, 693
Nympha, 155, 158
Nymphs, 18, 581, 938–939

O

Oakley, Violet, *353*
Obatala, 15, 1074
Obedience, 299, 333, 676, 757, 1006
Obeyesekere, Gananath, 194, 783
Object-relations theory, 815–816
O'Brien, Patricia, 802
Obudua, 222
Occultism, **733–734**, 878
female nudity ritualization, 729
Mead anthropological studies,
637–638

Occultism (*continued*)
  neogpagan affinity, 715
  witchcraft, 1035–1036, 1040, 1048
  See also Mediums
Oceanic religions, **734–738**
  animal imagery, 39
  Australia, **736–738**
  dance and drama, 236, *736*
  Mead fieldwork, 637–638
  Polynesia and Micronesia, 417,
    734–736, 995
  possession trances, 788
  purification ceremony, *818*
  seclusion practices, 875
  sun mythology, 949
Odalan festival, *339*
Odawa (people), 645
Odin, 871
Odiyana, 570
Odomankoma, 8
Oduduwa, 7
Oduyoye, Mercy, 162, 313
Odyssey (Homer), 243, 356, 439, 452,
  562, 563
  Odysseus and Penelope, 439, 452,
    1062
  weaving portrayal, 1026
Oedipus, 333, 842
Oedipus complex, 814–815
Offa, king of Mercia, 1030
Official (spirit), 904
O'Flaherty, Wendy Doniger, 36, 403,
  706, 944
Oglala Lakota. *See* Lakota Sioux
Ogo, 7, 9
Ogun, 15
Ohio State University, 1013–1014
Ohnuki-Tierney, Emiko, 347
Ohrmazd (Ahura Mazda), 483–484
Ojibwa (people), 213–214, 587, 645,
  687, 709
O'Keeffe, Georgia, 924
Okinaga-tarashi-hime, 900
Okinawa, 603, 783
Okuni, 239
Olcott, Henry Steel, 130, 979
Old Europe (Gimbutas construct), 470
"Old Man Hat," 708
Old Spider Woman, 970
Old Testament. *See* Hebrew Bible
Old Woman, 1032
Old Woman's Grandchild, 1032
Oli (Ambela), fast of, 325
Oliveros, Pauline, 689
Olmec culture, 653, 727
Olmos, Andrés de, 654
Olodumare (Olurun), 7
Olokun, 179

Olsen, Tillie, 908, 924
Olympians, 384
Olympias, 159
Olympic Games, 72, 73
Omar (caliph), 627
Omecihuatl and Ometecuhtli (Lady and
  Lord of Duality), 654
Ometeotl, 654
Omo-orishas, 324
Omosupe, Ekua, 825
Omotokyo, 576, 717, 721, 901
Onan, 202
One Great Goddess. *See* Great Goddess
Oneida community, 227, 992
O'Neill, Maura, 478
Ong, Aihwa, 749
Onile, 22
Onondaga (people), 621
Onuris, 32
Onyame, 9
Oomoto (Omotokyo), 576, 717, 721
Open City (film), 333
Opera, 688
Ophites, 371
Oracle at Delphi. *See* Delphi
Oral tradition, **738–740**
  African religions, 6, 855
  Afro-Atlantic religions, 14
  contemporary spirituality movement,
    1064
  East Asian folk religions, 278
  Egyptian religions, 33
  ethnic aspects, 313
  folklore, 343–344, 345
  genre and tradition, 365
  Hinduism, 858
  Islam, 828, 857
  Jainism, 521
  male bias, 109
  mythology, 702, 706
  Native American, 235, 707, 708, 855
  riddles, 842
  Scandinavian religions, 870
  scholarly misrepresentations, 708
  South American religions, 930
  women's wisdom, 1032, 1033
Order of the Eastern Star, 878
Order of the Golden Dawn, 612
Order of the Holy Cross. *See*
  Rosicrucians
Order of the Hospital of Saint John of
  Jerusalem, 175
Order of the Missionaries of Charity,
  681
Ordination, **740–748**
  in Buddhism, 105, 111, 121, 124, 128,
    131, 143, 741, **744–747**, 868, 933,
    1015

  in Christianity, 153, 169, 171, 350,
    576, 603, 740–744, **742–744**, 857
  of homosexuals, 582–583, 740
  in Judaism, 293, 543, 545–546, 549,
    603, 740–741, **747–748**
  in Orthodox Christianity, 165, 317,
    603, 752
  overview, **740–742**
  of women clergy, 524–525, 528,
    545–546, 661–662, 740, 742, 812,
    813
Ordo Templi Orientis, 717, 734
Oresteia (Aeschylus), 356
Orestes, 333, 356
Orientalism, **748–750**, 1060
  and Buddhism, 130, 132
  gender representation, 1056–1058
  and Islam, 510, 1056, 1057, 1058
  media stereotypes, 641
Origen, 140
Original Sin, 319–320, 322, 650, 712,
  733, 909, 910, 945–946
  Eve's initiative, 676, 729
  pain as women's punishment for, 650,
    795
  See also Suffering
Orisha (divinities), 7, 13, 14, 15, 611
Orixas, *300*
Ornamentation, 183, **750–751**, 1014
Ornithomancy, 75
Orochon (people), 57
Orphics, 703
Orthodox Christianity, 67, **751–753**
  contraceptive practices, 203
  divorce, 266, 752
  domestic shrines, 52
  Eucharist, 316, 602
  marriage and divorce, 626, 752
  menstruation taboos, 651
  monasticism, 67, 144, 753
  ordination, 165, 317, 603, 752
  religious architecture, 53
  religious rites and practices, 152, 153
  sacred literatue, 857
  saints, 865–866
  theological discourse, 752, 971, 973
  visionaries, 1010–1011
  wisdom personification, 1031
  women's laments, 682, 683, 688
  women's visits to holy places, 782
Orthodox Judaism. *See* Judaism
Orthodox Presbyterian Church, 318
Orthodoxy. *See* Heterodoxy and
  orthodoxy
Ortiz, Apolonia, 727
Ortner, Sherry, 43, 303, 712, 944, 945
Oshun, 15
Osiris, 243, 249, 390, 468, 487, 488

Osorkon III, 34
Osun, 11, 485, 604, **754**, 966
Otto, Rudolf, 768, 860
Ottoman Empire, 54, 510, 541, 762
Oudil, 256
Ouranos, 48, 384, 859
Our Grandmother (Papoothkwe), 724
Our Lady of Lourdes, 841, 903, 935
Our Lady of Perpetual Help, 260
Ovid, 315, 403

P
Pachacamac, 928
Pachamama, 927, 928
Pacifism and nonviolence, **755–757**,
    818, 922
Packer, Toni, 131
Paden, William E., 187, 188
Padmasaṁbhava (Guru Rinpoche), 116,
    117, 231, 261
Padmāvatī, 522
Padre Pio, 194
Paganism
    defined, 715
    early Christian views, 1040–1041
    mystery religions, 698–699
    as "outsider" practice, 611
    See also Neopaganism
Pagels, Elaine, 408
Pahnke, Donate, 612
Pain. *See* Suffering
Pais. *See* Hera
Paiute (people), 724, 725
Pajapati, 1015
Pakistan, 493, 504, 508, 513, 898, 899
Palenque (Maya site), 653
Paleolithic period, 633, 755, 797, 798
Palestinian nationalism, 1020,
    1057–1058
Pali canon, 109, 124–125, 132, 292
Palmer, Phoebe Worrall, 318, 576, 841
Palmer, Susan, 227, 718
Panageis (all-holy women), 805
Pan-Arab Feminist Union, 897
Pan Ch'ao (Ban Zhao), 80, 99, 196, 292,
    361, 596, 597, **757**
Pāñcika, 392
Pandora, 221, 392, 607, 1025
Pānini, 419
Pankhurst, Emmeline, Sylvia, and
    Cristobel, 1062
Pan Piao, 757
P'ansori novels, 279
Pantheism, 673, 686, 715, 785
Pantoja, Antonia, 686
Pantulu, Virasalingam, 426
Papa, 735, 875
Papa Legba, 15

Papa Ogou, 15
Papoothkwe (Our Grandmother), 724
Pappenheim, Bertha, 334, 371, 552,
    757–758
Papua New Guinea, 337, 620, 621, 637,
    647, 692
Paraclete, 400, 401
Paradise, 18, 196, 630, **758–759**, 991
Paradise Lost (Milton), 332, 618
Paranormal experiences, 369
Parcella, 671
Pardes, Ilana, 553
Parham, Charles, 318
Pari de Bintou, Le (film), 343
Parker, Rozasika, 210
Parker, Theodore, 984
Parrinder, Geoffrey, 468
Parrish, Essie, 725
Parsis, 66, 484
Parsons, Talcott, 921
Parthana Samaj, 426
Parthenogenesis, 277, 468
Parthenon, 53
Particle physics, 712
Pārvatī, 36, 192, 249, 325, 420, 422,
    447, 456, 559, 679, **759–760**, 892,
    1076
Passion de Jeanne d'Arc, La (film), 341,
    524
*Passion of Saints Perpetua and Felicitas,
    The* (anonymous), 767
Passover, 52, 297
Patai, Raphael, 383, 703
Patañjali, 772, 1076, 1077
Paternity, 889
Pather Panchali (film), 333
Pativrata, 332, 948
Patiyoga, 253
Patmore, Coventry, 453
Patriarchy, **760–761**
    ancestor worship, 30–31
    art effects, 61
    charisma and, 146
    chastity emphasis, 148
    in China, 99, 289–290, 323
    in Confucianism, 770–771
    in cult religions, 226–227
    Dakwah movement, 723
    desire and, 249
    educational exclusion and, 291
    environmental issues, 303
    on female inferiority, 1068
    and female personification of wisdom,
        1030–1031
    friendship and, 352
    gender conflict and, 360
    gendered solar imagery, 703–704
    goddess tradition and, 377

hermeneutics and, 404–406, 916
    as incest factor, 468
    in India, 88
    in Islam, 512
    in Judaism, 460, 526, 529–530, 553,
        747, 774
    leadership roles and, 575, 576, 712,
        718
    as legal systems influence, 574
    male identification with God as basis,
        712, 774
    Marxist analysis of, 629
    motherhood and, 679
    new religions and, 718, 719
    philosophical, 773, 774
    possession trance as response to,
        789–790
    purity and pollution systems,
        645–646, 819–820
    in Rastafarian religion, 17
    and religion definition, 837–838
    religious ritualization of, 765
    in ritual studies, 847
    and sacred sites control, 782–783
    secularization and, 880
    sexism and, 887
    sin and, 909
    social activist challenges to, 913–
        914
    social change and, 916
    sociological study of, 922
    in Southeast Asian religions, 932
    spirituality and, 942
    temptress portrayal, 965
    theistic portrayals and, 970
    as violence factor, 1000–1001
    visionary activity and, 1010
    women's silence and, 907
    women's suffrage as challenge to,
        1069–1070
    yin/yang polarity and, 1075
    See also Matriarchy; Misogyny;
        Sexism
Patricia, 223
Patroclus, 72
Patronage, 25, 54, 63, 114–115, 149,
    448–449, **761–762**
    of Protestant reformers, 812
    by Greek and Roman women, 806
    by laypersons, 567–568
Patterns in Comparative Religion
    (Eliade), 1025
Patterns of Culture (Benedict), 85
Pattini, 783
Patton, Cindy, 825
Paul VI, pope, 165, 203, 885
Paul, Diana Y., 131, 132, 867
Paula, 149, 671

Paul and the Pauline tradition, 78,
     157–159, 316, 323, 388, 443, 631
  and asceticism, 67
  celibacy endorsement, 144, 155, 619,
     1003
  on Christian marriage, 618, 619, 625
  on Eve's sin, 909
  on gender roles, 155–156, 158, 361,
     463, 618, 807–808
  separation from Judaism, 535
  on slave obedience, 832
  on soul's resurrection, 926
  on temptation, 966
  as utopianism, 993
  on women's hair covering in church,
     155, 158, 183, 390, 807
  on women's silence in church, 700,
     808, 812
Paulist Press, 178
Pausanius, 72, 402
Pawnee (people), 724, 802
Pazzi, Maria Maddalena de', **762–763**
Peabody, Elizabeth, 984
Peabody, Lucy, 173
Peace People (Northern Ireland), 755
Pearson, Ann, 778
Pedro IV, king of Kongo, 270
Pele, 236, 735, **763**, 883
Pelikan, Jaroslav, 178, 267
Pelops, 402
Pemikiran Pembarua, 722
Penance, 193–194, 632
Penelope, 439, 452, 1026
Peninnah, 391, 678
Penis, 995
  bloodletting, 94
  castration, 140
  circumcision, 10, 46–47, 96, 531,
     533
  Freudian castration anxiety, 815
Penis envy, 331
Penitence. See Confession and
     penitence
Penley, Constance, 343
Pentateuch, 855
Pentecost, 325
Pentecostalism. See Evangelical,
     Holiness, Fundamentalist, and
     Pentecostal Christianity
Perfection of Wisdom. See
     Prajñāpāramitā
Perfection of Wisdom Sutras (Buddhist
     texts), 302
Performance art, **763–764**
Performance theory, **764–766**; See also
     Dance and drama; Music
Periodization, **766–767**
Perot, Rebecca, 519

Perpetua and Felicity, 72–73, 77, 81–82,
     159, 223, 271, 272, 628, **767–768**,
     886, 1010, 1061
Perrin, Michel, 930
Persephone. See Demeter and
     Persephone
Perseus, 1003
Persia. See Iranian religion
Persis, 158
Personhood. See Self
Personifications. See Female
     personifications; Mythology;
     Symbolism
Pertevniyal (wife of Mahmud II), 762
Peru, 728, 1026
Peskowitz, Miriam, 527
Peter, 372, 671, 886
Peter the Venerable, 510
Petition. See Prayer
Peublo (people), 235
Peyotism, 725
Pfeiffer, John, 797
Pfleiderer, Otto, 837
Phadampa Sangye, 609
Phadet Phongasawad, 723
Pharisees, 527, 533, 535
Phenomenology of religion, **768–770**
Pheterson, Gail, 810
Phibionites, 94
Philippines, 932–933
  Christianity, 163, 932, 933
  dance and drama, 236
  earth's significance, 277
  liberation theologies, 591, 723
  sex industry, 934, 1001
Philip the Evangelist, 807
Philo of Alexandria, 67, 361, 533, 814,
     925
Philo Judaeus, 671, 699
Philosophia, 455
Philosophy, **770–775**
  aesthetics, 1012
  afterlife, 813–814
  in the East, **770–772**
  epistemology, 304–305, 771
  ethics, 308, 309
  hermeneutics, 404, 768, 769
  nature and, 712
  pacifism as, 755–756
  phenomenology, 768–769
  rationality vs. irrationality, 485, 836
  semiotics, 459, 884
  soul concept, 926
  and theist precepts, 776
  in the West, **772–775**
  See also Political science
Philosophy of religion, **775–777**
Phoebe, 157, 1062

Phoenicia. See Canaan-Phoenicia,
     religions of
Photography, **777–779**
Phra Dattajivo. See Phadet
     Phongasawad
Phra Dhammajayo. See Chaiyaboon
     Sitthiphon
Phra Khru Pitak, 723
Phra Prachak, 723
Phulan Devi, 223
Physics, 712, 874
Pietà imagery, 448
Pietists, 151, 998
Pigs, 39, 862
Pihsia Yuan-chün, 53
Pilate, Pontius, 535
Pilgrimage, **779–781**
  in Asian American traditions, 69
  Buddhist, 285, 636, 661
  feminist, 783
  Hindu, 425
  Islamic, 180, 323, 387, 490, 494, 499,
     501, 513, 779–780, 782, 827, 903
  sacred geography, 367
  sacred places, 782, 783
  shrine architecture, 53
Pillar of Fire Church, 349
Pilling, Arnold, 737
Pimiko, 900
Pindar, 72
Pisan, Christine de. See de Pizan,
     Christine
Pistis, 371
Pituri, 479
Pius XI, pope, 165, 203
Pius XII, pope, 135, 382, 626, 850, 876
Places, sacred, **782–784**
  pilgrimages, 779–781
  priestesses, 806
  See also Geography, sacred; Space,
     sacred
"Plague Mass" (Galas), 764
Plains Indians, 56, 709, 710
  circle symbolism, 179, 457
  female personifications, 329, 1032
  Ghost Dance, 724
  vision quest, 86, 104
Planned Parenthood Federation, 850
Plaskow, Judith, 295, 312, 352, 409, 582,
     643, 916, 975–976, 1052–1053
Plato, 36, 247–248, 303, 306, 403, 407,
     413, 452, 485, 563, 580, 687, 882
  Diotima and, 254, 255
  on female immorality, 874
  and mystery religions, 699
  on politics, 784
  on psykhē, 814
  on Sappho, 868

on women's laments, 688
on women's status as philosophers, 772–773
Pleroma, 371–372
Pliny, 650, 729
Pliny the Younger, 535
Plural marriage. *See* Polyandry; Polygyny
Poetry, 596, 597
    bhakti, 80, 87, 88–89, 408, 865, 936
    Buddhist, 108–109, 125, 306
    feminine images, 452
    Juan Inés de la Cruz's works, 525
    Muses, 686
    of religious converts, 204
    Sappho's works, 452, 580, 868–869
    Sikh, 905
    Venkamamba's (Tarigonda) works, 999–1000
    and women's speech legitimacy, 936
Pogrebin, Letty Cottin, 1057
Political science, 784–785; *See also* Women's suffrage
Politics of Women's Spirituality, The (Spretnak), 706
Pollock, Griselda, 778
Pollution. *See* Purity and pollution
Pollux, 207
Polyandry, 618, 619, 620
Polygamy. *See* Polygyny; Polyandry
Polygyny, 618–619, 620
    African communities, 266
    biblical queens, 824
    Confucianism, 624
    Islam, 289, 489–490, 492, 493, 496, 512–513, 618, *619*, 627, 827, 889, 890, 933, 1057
    Judaism, 529, 530, 532, 539, 625
    Mormonism, 227, 574, 618, 677, 992, 993
    witchcraft charges, 1044
Polyhymnia, 687
Polynesia, 417, 734–735
Polynices, 243
Polytheism, 785–786
    feminist leanings, 673, 785
    henotheism vs., 785
    incestuous pairings, 468
    love gods and goddesses, 604
    magical rituals, 1038–1039
    neopaganism, 715
    nomadic peoples and, 475
Pomeroy, Sara, 1002
Pompey, 535
Pomponius Mela, 145
Pongos, 1013
Pontifex maximus, 315
Poor Clares, 180, 866

Pope Joan. *See* Manfreda, Sister
Popmyong, 122
Porete, Marguerite, 150–151, 193, 293, **786**
Pork, 862, 875
Poro (secret society), 9, 878
Posals, 286
Poseidon, 72, 138, 384, 390, 472
Possession, **786–788**
    African religions, 8
    Afro-Atlantic religions, 14
    agricultural rituals, 20
    authority and, 76
    charisma and, 146
    dance rituals, 233
    of Delphic priestess, 805, 806
    of early Christian prophets, 807, 808
    in Hinduism, 425, 429
    in Japanese New Religions, 721
    ordination and, 741
    rational aspects, 836
    sacred-comic view of, 442
    and women's reproductive disorders, 819–820
    See also Shamans
Possession cults, 348–349, **788–790**
    bori, 893
    Islam, 495
    leadership of, 575, 893
    maenadic rites, 609–610
    ordination of women, 740
    sacrifice rituals, 862
    See also Zar cult
Postcolonialism. *See* Colonialism and postcolonialism
Postmodernism, **790–791**
    cultural studies, 227, 1059
    deconstruction, 246
    performance art, 764
Poststructuralism, 227, 481, 700, 816, 908
Posture. *See* Body postures and trance
Potowatami (people), 645
Potter, Jack, 680
Pottery, 10, 214, 217–218, 803, 930, 1012–1013
Powamuy, 710
Powers of Horror (Kristeva), 816
Pradhāna, 791
Prajānā, 1032, 1034–1035
Prajapati, 468, 476
Prajñā and *prajñāpāramita*, 116, 189, 377, 476, 867, 1032, **1034–1035**
Prakriti, 635–636, 772, **791**
Prātimoksa, 192
Pratyekabuddha, 190
Prayer, **791–794**
    Christianity, 792–793

fundamentalist (Christian) view, 354
    Islam, 494–495, 496, 502, 513, 793–794, 817–818
    Judaism, 542, 782, 783, 792
    Mesopotamian woman, *657*
    ritual purification before, 817–818
    rosary and, 152, 449
    women's contemporary spirituality movement, 1064
Prayers (Greek deities), 329
Preaching. *See* Ministry; Speech
Pregnancy, **794–795**
    amulet wearing, 28
    artistic representations, 362
    conception dreams, 271–272
    contraception, 795
    emotions and, 300
    fasting and abstinence, 325
    hallucinogens and, 480
    medium possession as parallel, 790
    Mesoamerican religions, 655
    prehistoric figures, 796, 797
    resulting from rape, 835
    See also Birth and rebirth; Fertility and barrenness; Motherhood and grandmotherhood; Womb
Prehistoric religions, **795–804**
    agriculturalists, **800–804**
    goddesses, **373–376**, 633, 755, 794, 796–797, 802
    Marxist theory, 629
    material culture, 633–634
    matriarchy theory, 634
    pre-agricultural peoples, **795–800**
Preiswerk, Emilie and Helene, 556
Prem, 261
Premonstratensian order, 150
Prenuptial agreements, 530
Prepatriarchal hypothesis, 188
Presbyterianism, 318, 574, 602, 742
Presley, Elvis, 346
Pretty Woman (film), 333
Priesand, Sally, 546, 740, 1062
Priestess, **804–806**
    Afro-Atlantic religions, 15
    Anglican, 661
    ascetic practices, 66
    in Canaan-Phoenicia, 137
    Celtic religions, 145
    Egyptian, 32, 840
    Etruscan and Roman, 315, 805, 806
    festival participation, 338
    Greek, 805–806
    Hindu, 425
    Mandaean, 616
    Mesoamerican, 653
    Mesopotamian, 658–659
    Shinto, 362, 900

Priestess *(continued)*
    temple prostitutes, 805, 809, 810–811
    Yoruba, 15, 754
Priestess, Mother, Sacred Sister (Sered), 1065–1066
Priests, 186, 603, 752
    ancient Rome, 806
    sexual abuse by, 193
    Tao, 960, 961
Princeton Seminary, 318
"Principles of Wiccan Belief," 1048
Printing press, 812
Prisca, 155, 157–158
Priscilla, 159, 226, 463, 808, 1010
Priscillianists, 808
Procès de Jeanne d'Arc, Le (film), 341
Procreation. *See* Fertility and barrenness; Pregnancy; Sexuality
Procter-Smith, Marjorie, 603, 717
Proerosia (female ritual), 247
Profane, 860, 861
Prolegomena to the Study of Greek Religion (Harrison), 392
Promise Keepers, 648, 649
Prophecy, **806–809**, 840
    Alinesitoué, 24
    ascetic practices, 66
    biblical, **397–399**, 441–442, 461, 516, 527, 806–807, 840, 865, 1011, 1022, 1038, 1039
    Celtic, 145
    Christian, 155, 159
    Egyptian, 32
    Islamic, 808, 827, 828
    Mormon, 675–676
    Pentecostal, 728
    possessed state, 787
    See also specific prophets
Prophet, Elizabeth Clare Wulf, 147, 226, 350, 576, 808
Prophetess of Mut, 34
Prophetic Theology (South Africa), 161
Prophets. *See* Prophecy
Prostitution, 332–333, 431, **809–811**, 966, 1001
    in ancient Rome, 183
    biblical, 461
    Mary Magdalene association, 632, 809–810
    Mesopotamian patron goddess of, 658
    in Philippines, 934
    temple, 659, 805, 809, 810–811
    traffic in, 810
Protestant Ethic and the Spirit of Capitalism, The (Weber), 1027
Protestantism, 151, 164, 207–208, **811–813**, 849
    abortion views, 1, 2

antisuffrage arguments, 1069–1070
in Canada, 168–169
charismatic renewal, 318
condemnation of celibacy, 626
contraceptive practices, 203
divorce, 266
domestic architecture, 52
Eucharist, 316
evangelical, 318
female voices, 1016
feminist revisionism, 433, 766
food and ritual, 346–347
founding religious leaders, 349–350
French "sleeping" preaching girls, 787
fundamentalism, 354, 356
gender roles, 661, 811–813, 1027
Holocaust and, 547, 548
homosexuality and, 582, 583
identity images, 449
in Latin America, 167
lay ministries, 661, 662
liturgical reform, 602, 603
marriage and divorce, 626
media coverage, 640
missionary activity, 161, 163, **172–174**
new religions, 717
ordination, 153, 169, 171, 576, 603, 740, 742, 743–744, 857
Original Sin doctrine, 320
religious conversion, 205, 206
religious rites and practices, 153, 220
revelation acceptance, 841
sacred literature, 856–857
sacred song, 688
sainthood view, 865
sister as form of address, 912
sociology of religion, 1027
spiritualism and, 941
theological discourse, 972
in United States, 170
visionary activity, 1011
wifely duties, 1052
women's moral purity, 676
women's roles, 661–661
women's speech, 938
See also Reformation; *specific denominations*
Proverbs, Book of, 1031, 1033
Psalm singing, 683
Pseudopolytheism, 785
Psychedelics. *See* Intoxicants and hallucinogens
Psyche (mythological figure), **813–814**, 911
Psyche (soul), 926
Psychoanalysis, 350–351, 814–817, 945
Psychology and Religion (Jung), 815

Psychology of religion, **814–817**
    emotionality and, 300
    Freudian theory, 350–351, 814–815
    Jungian theory, 555–556, 648, 815
    Kristevan theory, 816
    object-relations theory, 815–816
Psychopomp, 272, 278, 280
Psykhē, 813–814
Ptah. *See* Amun-Re
Ptolemy, 70, 160
Puberty rites. *See* Initiation; Rites of passage
Pueblo (people), 708, 709, 710, 1047
Pūjā (Hindu worship), 1071
Pūjāriṇīs, 422
Pulcheria Augusta, 149, 1004
Purāṇas, 48, 91, 569, 858, 944
Purdah, 148–149, 421, 889, 905, 1057; *See also* Veiling
Pure Land Buddhism, 123, 758, 759, 991
Purification, **817–819**
    birth-related, 33, 955
    domestic rites, 269
    in Islam, 102, 491, 494
    Orthodox Christian rites, 753
    See also Purity and pollution
Purim, 308, 443
Puritanism, 77, 170, 183, 240, 439, 808, 812
Purity and pollution, **819–821**
    auspicious and inauspicious, 73–74
    birth rituals, 91
    blood and, 93–94, 321, 818
    in Buddhism, 120, 771
    caste system, 413
    Chinese views, 282–283
    death rituals, 682, 683, 818
    female sexuality as, 889
    in Hinduism, 252, 418, 429, 650, 889
    in Islam, 651, 1071
    Japanese beliefs, 284
    in Judaism, 527, 534, 650, 651, 818
    Korean beliefs, 283
    menstruation, 262, 650–651
    midwives and, 563
    misogyny and, 665–666
    in Orthodox Christianity, 651, 752, 753
    purification rituals, **817–819**
    seclusion practices, 875
    in Sikhism, 254
    See also Taboos
Purūavas, 48–49
Puruṣa, 362
Puruṣārthas, 559
Puruṣsa, 772, 791
Pūrva Mīmāṃsā, 771, 858

Pyramids, 32, 439
Pythagoras, 306
Pythagorean community, 182
Pythia, 66, 246, 247, 260, 936
Pythia at Delphi, 805–806

Q

Qashqa'i, 56, 499
Qasmuna, 691
Qigong practitioners, 1046
Qin dyansty, 195
Qing dynasty, 100, 279
Qinggui (Buddhist regulations), 325
Qingwei Taoism, 961
Qin Shihuangdi, 196
Quadrivia, 225
Quakers, 170, 286, 352, 756, 808, 857,
    907–908
Quanzhen Taoism, 670, 961
Queen Mother of the West, 279, 333,
    771, **823**, 961
Queen of Babylon, 824
Queen of Ethiopia, 824
Queen of Heaven, 487, 516
Queen of Sheba, *611*, 824, 828, 842
Queens, biblical, 461, **823–825**; *See
    also* Esther
Queer Nation, 825
Queer theory, 590, 648, **825–826**
Quest myth, 601
Quetzalcoatl, 1003
Quietism, 193, 385
Quinault (people), 587
Quindecemviri, 260
Quintilla, 159, 808
Quintillianists, 808
Quintus of Smyrna, 27
Qur'an and Hadith, 78, 361, 440,
    488–492, 496–497, 582, **826–829**,
    974, 1062
    afterlife portrayal, 18, 102
    'A'ishah and, 21
    on almsgiving and patronage, 25, 513
    as authoritative source, 75
    celibacy seen as violation of, 626
    on contraception, 203
    on Eve and Adam's transgression,
        320, 393, 490, 491, 910
    female access to, *292, 293*, 857–858
    on female attire, 183
    feminist interpretations, 509, 511
    friendship cautions, 353
    on gender roles, 361
    on homosexuality, 581–582, 586
    on hospitality, 440
    on inspirational women, 477
    on Islamic prayer ritual, 793
    language reexamination, 572

Latin translation of, 510
    and law. *See* Islamic law
    on marriage and marital relationship,
        208, 626, 627, 1052
    on Maryam, mother of Jesus, 630
    on menstrual pollution, 651
    on paradise, 759
    on prophets, 808
    recitation of, 898
    revelation experiences, 263, 841
    as sacred literature, 857–858
    on salvation of women, 867
    sin pronouncements, 910
    Southeast Asian new religion
        emphasis on, 722
    theological discourse and, 974
    virtue requirements, 1007
    on women's rights and roles,
        488–490, 496, 509, 974, 1052
Qustâ ibn Lûqâ, 926
Qutb, Sayyid, 493

R

Rabbis. *See* Judaism; Ordination
Rabi'a, **831**
    aceticism of, 68, 325, 619, 923
    biographies of, 79, 82, 831
    boundary-crossing by, 104, 306, 409
    devotional poetry by, 361, 596, 936
    as disciple, 257
    film documentary on, 342
    hospitality of, 441
    learning of, 1062
    as mystic and saint, 249, 866
    shrines, 935
    as visionary, 841, 1011
Rachel, 336, 460, 606, 794, 869, 1016,
    1062
Rachel's Tomb, 780, 783, 784
Racism, **832–833**
    classism and, 181
    in essentialism theory, 307
    in evolution theory, 874
    feminist ethics and, 312
    feminist spirituality and, 777
    Freudian theory and, 815
    identity and, 450
    Indo-European studies, 469
    liberation theologies, 161, 592
    patriarchy and, 760
    rape and, 834
    sin concept and, 910
    sociological view of, 919
    as violence factor, 1000
    See also Antisemitism
Radcliffe-Brown, Arthur Reginald, 42,
    847
Radegund, Saint, 671, 1024

Rādhā, 418, 422, 604, *605*, 693, **833–834**
    bhakti sects, 88
    and Krishna, 105, 249, 833, 966
    shrines and temples, 53
Radhakrishnan, Sarvepalli, 203
Radical Faeries, 648
Radical feminism, 335
Radin, Paul, 42
Raelian Movement, 718
Rahab, 606
Rahda, Shivananda, 924
Raheja, Gloria Goodwin, 415, 739
Rainbow, 1024
Rainey, Gertrude ("Ma"), 689
Rainmaking, 20, 1024
Raja Samkranti, 650
Rajneesh movement, 717, 718
Rāma, 332, 362, 420, 428, 912–913, 988,
    1052
Ramadan, 325, 494, 827, 981
Ramakrishna Mission, 429
Ramanujan, A. K., 88
Rāmaprasād Sen, 88
Rāmāyaṇa, *207*, 233, 253, 362, 771, 912,
    988, 1052
Rāmāyaṇa singing groups, 738–739
Ramses III, king of Egypt, 1039
Ramshaw, Gail, 571
Ran, 872
Ranande, Mahadev Govind, 426
Ranande, Ramabai, 426
Ranger, Terrence, 20–21
Rankin, Jeanette, 756
Rape, 1, 2, 4, 41, **834–836**, 1000, 1001
Raphael, 687
Rapoport-Alpert, Ada, 528
Rasa, 300
Rashap (Reshep), 136, 137
Rashtra Sevika Samiti, 427
Rashtriya Stree Sangha, 426
Rasika bhakti, 913
Rasmussen, Knud, 59
Rastafarianism, 16–17, 226
Rasulid dynasty, 54
Rationality, **836–837**
    Aristotle on women's lack of, 773
    emotion and, 299–300
    ethical actions and, 308–309
    Harrison's (Jane Ellen) theories, 392
    sociological view, 922
    theological discourse and, 971–972
    virtue and, 1006
    See also Irrationality
Ratté, Lou, 335
Rauschenbach, Emma, 556
Rāvaṇa, 912
Raven, 709
Raven Clan, 330

Ray, Satyajit, 333, 342
Raymond, Janice, 352, 583, 912
Reagon, Bernice Johnson, 689
Reason. *See* Rationality
Reay, Maria, 480
Rebecca (Rebekah), 336, 347, 460, *461*, 869
Rebirth. *See* Birth and rebirth
Rebirth of the Goddess (Christ), 379
Rebirth of Witchcraft, The (Valiente), 1048
Rechungpa, 272
Reconstructionist Judaism, 409, 528, 543, 549, 571, 582, 740, 856
Reconstruction theology, 162
Recreation. *See* Creation and recreation
Red Beards, 879
Red Crown of Lower Egypt, 714
Red King, 23
Redmond, Layne, 689
Red Queen, 653
Reformation, 151, 433, 811, 849, 856; *See also* Protestantism
Reformed Church, 998, 1027
Reform Judaism. *See* Judaism
Reginos (new religion), 727
Reichard, Gladys, 1026
Reign of God movement, 533
Re-Imagining (1993), 640, 938
Reincarnation
    Afro-Atlantic religions, 14
    Buddhism, 110, 771
    gender changes, 18
Reinharz, Shulamit, 919
Reitemeyer, Else, 511
Reiyūkai, 286
Reiyu-kau, 120
Rejang dance, 233
Relativity theory, 712
Religion, **837–839**
    anthropology of, 43, 45–46
    comparative, 186–189, 435, 860, 866, 950
    crafts and, 210–211, 448
    cultural studies of, 228
    doctrine and, 267–268
    ethics and, 308, 309
    founders, 348–350
    heterodoxy and orthodoxy, 408–409
    heterosexism, 410–411
    intergroup dialogue, 477–478
    lesbian studies and, 590
    magic vs., 611, 612
    Marxist view of, 629
    media and, 335, 430, 639–641
    misogyny and, 665–666
    monotheism, 673
    neopaganism, 715–716

    as normalizing sexism, 774, 887–888
    patriarchal elements, 760–761, 887
    phenomenology of, 768–769
    polytheism, 785–786
    psychology of, 714–817
    queer theory and, 826
    science and, 873–874
    secularization and, 879–880
    social change and, 915–916
    sociology of, 918, 920–923
    theism, 775–776, 970–971
    warfare and, 1019–1021
    weather beliefs, 1023–1024
    women's movements and, 334
    See also Liberation theologies; New religions; Philosophy of religion; *specific religions*
Religious Autobiographies (Comstock), 76
Religious experience, **839–840**
Religious orders and community. *See* Community; Monasticism
Renaissance, 599–600, 761, 1073
Renan, Ernest, 469
Renaud, Etienne, 633
Renewal Movement, 722
Renuka, 360
Reproductive functions. *See* Birth and rebirth; Fertility and barrenness; Pregnancy
Republic (Plato), 306, 413, 772–773
Resurrection, 17–18, 101, 102, 631, 632, 926, 935, 1015
Returning Words to Flesh (Goldenberg), 815
Revelation, **840–842**, 856, 857
Revivalism, 151, 318
Reyes Acquino, Francisca, 236
Reymond, Lizelle, 306
Ṛgveda (Hindu text), 420, 771, 1021, 1055
Rhadebe, Jostinah, *894*
Rhea, 229, 468, 472
Rhiannon, 145
Rhys-Davids, C. A. F., 132, 187
Rhys-Davids, T. W., 132
Rhythm method, 203
Rich, Adrienne, 363, 410, 590
Richter, Mischa, *966*
Ricoeur, Paul, 404, 702, 768, 884, 966
Riddle, **842–843**, 987
Riddle of Freud, The (Roith), 815
Ride, Sally, 1063
Rieti, Diana, 541
Rifaat, Alifa, 77
Riggs, Marcia, 1053
Rig Veda, 48, 251, 296, 858, 870, 926
Ringe, Sharon, 1055

Ringelheim, Joan, 644
Ring place, 783
Rinpoche. *See* Padmasaṁbhava
Rinzai Buddhism, 123
Riot girls, 335
Ripley, George and Sophia, 984
Risshō Kōsei-kai, 120, 286
Ritchings, Edna Rose. *See* Mother Divine
Rites of passage, **843–844**, 847
    Arctic peoples, 60
    body cutting and, 96
    circumcision and, 878
    crafts and, 211
    family and, 323
    in Judaism, 531, 843
    menstruation as. *See* Menarche
    in Mesopotamian religion, 659
    riddle tests, 842
    as sacred time, 982
    See also Initiation
Rite of the Water of Bitterness, 3
Rithambara, Sadhvi, 427
Ritual, **844–846**
    abortion-related, 2, 115, 337
    African religions, 6, 8, 9–11, 96, 338, 339
    agricultural, 19–21, 94, 366, 981
    ancestor worship, 30–31, 201
    ancient Near Eastern magic, 1038–1039
    anthropological view of, 45
    binding as element, 97–98, 1001
    birth-related, 91, 794–795
    blood and, 93–94, 95
    body and, 95–96
    body postures and, 103
    Canaan-Phoenician, 136, 137
    Confucianism, 195, 197
    crafts and, 209–220
    dance and drama, 232–242
    Durkheim on, 846–847
    East Asian religions, 280–284
    egg's significance, 297
    emotional aspects, 299
    Etruscan and Roman, 315
    family protection, 447
    fasting and, 325
    fertility, 336, 337, 361, 859
    festivals and, 338, 385
    folklore and, 344
    friendship-related, 353
    Goddess movement, 379
    hair-cutting, 390
    Himalayan, 416, 782
    identity and, 449
    Islamic women and, 1071
    Jaina, 520, 521

Japanese money-washing, 87
Jewish women and, 782, 783
leadership, 575–576, 603
life-cycle, 97–98; *See also* Birth and
   rebirth; Mourning and death rites
liturgy, 602–604
lunar, 674
maenadic rites, 609–610
Mesopotamian, 658
Minoan, 663
modern witchcraft, 1049
music and, 687–688
neopagan, 715
nudity and, 729
Oceanic, 236, 735, 737, 875
oral tradition, 738, 739
orthodoxy and, 408
patriarchal, 765
performing arts vs., 765
photographic misrepresentations, 778
pilgrimage as, 779–780
possession, 787
prayer, 792, 793
priestesses, 805–806
purification, 817–819
riddle tests, 842
sacred-comic traditions, 443
sacred foods, 346–347
sacred places, 782, 783
sacred times, 981–982
Scandinavian, 871–872
seasonal, 1024
seclusion, 876; *See also* Menstruation
South American, 930–931
Southeast Asian, 933
tantric, 642, 957–958
textile use, 1026
weaving, 1025–1026
witchcraft, 1039, 1049
worship, 1070–1071
See also Domestic rites; Healing;
   Initiation; Ordination; Rites of
   passage; Sacraments
Ritual adoption, 680
Ritual bath (Judaic), 782, 650, 815
Ritual studies, **846–848**
River celebrations, 820
Robert of Ketton, 510
Roberts, Jane, 226, 1064
Robinet, Isabel, 287
Robinson, Ida, 349–350
Robinson, Mary, 164, 850
Rock, Judith, 242
Roded, Ruth, 82
Rodríguez de Tío, Lola, 686
Rogers, Susan Carol, 42, 43
Rohiṇī, 421
Roho (Spirit) Churches, 161

Roith, Estelle, 815
Rojas, Roque, 726
Roma, 330
Roman Catholicism, 67, **849–852**
  abortion prohibitions, 1–2, 165
  almsgiving, 25
  in Canada, 168
  Catholic Worker movement, 242–243,
    756, 850, 1028
  celibacy, 144, 742, 849, 923
  charismatic renewal, 318
  confession and penance, 193–194
  contraception opposition, 165, 203,
    890
  craftwork, 220, 448
  dance and drama, 233–234
  divorce prohibition, 266
  domestic shrines, 52
  family's significance, 324
  gender roles, 164–165, 743, 850–851
  Guatemalan human rights, 646
  heaven belief, 759
  heresy, 616, 786
  hierarchical structure, 413, 742
  Holocaust and, 547, 548
  Holy Ghost terminology, 369
  homosexuality and, 583
  interfaith initiatives, 478
  Jesus as divine child, 260–261, 262
  laity, 567, 845, 850
  in Latin America, 167
  lay ministries, 662
  liturgy, 602, 603
  marriage, 625–626
  Mary veneration. *See* Virgin Mary
  media coverage of, 640
  missionary activity, 161, 162–163,
    661, 681
  Mother Teresa, 681
  mujeristas and, 685–686
  music and, 688
  ordination, 165, 317, 603, 740, 742,
    743, 888
  ordination of women movement, 662
  Original Sin doctrine, 320
  in Philippines, 163, 932, 933
  Protestantism as reaction to, 811, 812
  rape perspectives, 834–835
  religious architecture, 53
  religious order founders, 175–176,
    348, 400–401, 967–968
  religious rites and practices, 152–153,
    154; *See also* Eucharist
  sacred literature, 856
  sacred marriage, 859, 671, 1052
  saints, 865–866; *See also specific*
    saints
  shrines, 902, 903

  sisterhood, 912
  and South American new religions,
    728
  spiritualism and, 941
  in United States, 170, 171
  in Vietnam, 932
  visionaries, 82, 150–151, 1008–1009,
    1010, 841
  vow taking, 1017
  Weil's conversion mysticism,
    1027–1028
  women's endeavors, 151, 661,
    850–851
  See also Inquisition; Liberation
    theologies; Martyrdom;
    Monasticism, Christian
Roman Empire. *See* Etruscan and
   Roman religion
Romanticism, 299–300, 712, **852–853**
Romi Kumu (Vagina Woman), 1055
Romulus, 407
Room of One's Own, A (Woolf), 773, 774
Roosevelt, Anna, 803
Roosevelt, Eleanor, 1063
Root Tantric Downfalls, 118
Roper, Lyndal, 433, 766
Rosaldo, Michelle Zimbalist, 303
Rosary, 152, 449
Rosen, Ruth, 810
Rosenblat, Wibrandis, 811
Rose of Lima, Saint, 849
Roshi, 131
Roshi, Maureen Stuart, 131
Rosicrucians, 734, 878
Ross, Cheryl Lynn, 815–816
Ross, Mary Ellen, 815–816
Rossellini, Roberto, 333
Rousseau, Jean-Jacques, 774, 852
Rowbotham, Sheila, 432
Roy, Rammohun, 425, 948
Royal Cambodian Ballet, 239
Rozario, Rita, 810–811
Rubenstein, Richard, 548
Rubin, Gayle, 363, 944
Rudolph, Kurt, 616
Rudolph, Wilma, 1063
Ruether, Rosemary Radford, 206, 295,
   303, 376, 405, 433, 573, 576, 666,
   760, 766, 774, 790, 888, 913, 916,
   970, 971, 975, 1067–1068
Rufinus, 36
Rule of Arles, 671–672
Rule of Benedict, 150, 175
Ruqayya, 53
Ruslaka, 368
Russell, H. Diane, 1012
Russell, Letty, 666
Russell, Pamela, 633

Ruth, 256, 460, **853**, 937, 1029
Ruusbroec, 387
Ryonen Genso, 78
Ryukyu Island, 442

S
Saami (people), 872
Sabbah, Fatna, 312
Sabbath, 183, 527, 529, 531, 537, 792,
    839, 981
Sabbats and esbats, 1049
Sacrae cantiones (Rafaella), 688
Sacred, The, 442, 735, **860–861**
Sacred geography. *See* Geography,
    sacred
Sacred literature, **855–859**
    female access to, 253, 291, 571,
        856–858
    hermeneutics, 404–406, 436, 916
    on homosexuality, 158, 581–582
    Judaic. *See* Torah
    language reexamination, 571–572
    oral tradition and, 738
    religious experience and, 839
    scripture definition, 855
    study of, 104
    See also specific texts
Sacred marriage, 402, 605, **859–860**,
    927
    as agricultural ritual, 21, 859
    androgynous aspects, 36
    brides of Christ, 671, 859, 1052
Sacred places. *See* Places, sacred
Sacred song, 688
Sacrifice, **861–864**
    Afro-Atlantic religions, 14
    animal, *93*, 94, 428, 494, 862, 932
    blood's significance, 8, 10, 94, 95,
        244, 654
    in Canaan-Phoenicia, 138
    Celtic religions, 145
    of children, 136, 138
    Hinduism, 424, 428, 862
    human, 20, 94, 471, 475, 862, 863,
        872
    Mesoamerican religions, 654
    purification rites, 819
Sacy, Silvestre de, 510
Sadat, Anwar, 368, 498
Sa'dawi, Nawal al-, **864**, 923
Sadducees, 527, 533
Sādhanas, 957
Sadhus, 334
Sadiq, Jafar al-, 586
Safrai, Chana, 527
Safrai, Samuel, 553
Sahagamani, 948
Sahagún, Bernardino, 652, 655

Said, Edward W., 641, 748, 749, 1060
Saigyo, 80
St. Denis, Ruth, 241
Saint George's Day, 859
Saint Joan's Social and Political
    Alliance, 164
Saint Mary's College, 975
Saints, **864–866**
    in Afro-Atlantic religions, 15
    autobiographies and biographies,
        77–82
    bhakti, 80, 87–89, 771–772, 865
    Buddhist, 109–110
    as charismatic leaders, 575
    Christian, 632, 763, 767–768, 1024
    churches dedicated to, 53
    cross-dressing by, 223
    hagiography, 78–79, 82, 389
    Hindu, 105, 422, 575, 865
    iconography, 449
    Islamic, 494, 495, 502, 576, 831, 923
    pilgrimages and shrines, 780–781,
        902
    Protestant disavowal of, 813
    Vaiṣṇava, 41, 88, 422, 613
    Vīraśaiva, 613
    virtue and, 1007
    weather control by, 1024
    See also specific saints
Saïs (Egypt), 714
Saiving, Valerie, 839, 924
Sajah, 808
Sakayumi, *960*
Sakha (people), 894
Sakhis, 333, 334
Śakti, 221, 418
Sakya (Buddist sect), 117
Sakyadhita, 128, 129
Śākyamuni, 192
Ṣalat, 793
Salem witch trials, 787
Salian Virgins, 315
Sallekhanā, 948
Salome, 156, 241, 462, 1004
Salome Alexandria, 535
Salvation, **866–868**
    bhakti, 642
    family as central to, 718–719
    Jainist, 521, 730, 867–868
    Mormon, 677
    See also Enlightenment
Salvation Army, 169, 318
Samādhi, 1076
Sama-Veda, 858
Samding Monastery, 118
Samhain, 982
Saṃhitās, 858
Saṃhitās (Vedic text), 771

Sāṃkhya, 772
Samoa, 587, 637, 735
Samsara, 92, 327, 421, 573, 867, 946,
    982
Samskāra, 418
Samson, 332, 390, 842, 946, 966
Samuel, 391
Samurai, 198, 947
Sanctified Church, 4
Sanctuaries. *See* Places, sacred; Shrines
Sand, George, 40
Sanday, Peggy Reeves, 188, 760, 800,
    839, 1001
Sande, 11, 233, 680, 878, 1066
Sandogo, 8
Sanger, Margaret, 850, 1062
Sanger, William, 809
Sangha, 520, 723, 772
Sangha Act of 1962 (Thailand), 723
Sanghamittā, 348, **868**
Sangharakshita, 129
Sangren, P. Steven, 283, 1075
San hyang dedari, 233, 238
Sankovich, Tilde A., 601
Sannyasi, 66, 105, 421
San Pedro (hallucinogen), 479
Sanskrit drama, 238
Sanspoil (people), 587
Santals (people), 588
Santa Maria degli Angeli (convent),
    762–763
Santeria, 13, 16, 324, 362, 603, 604
    divination system, 8
    magical practices, 611
    Yemaya as goddess, 1073–1074
Santiago (god), 927
Santi Asok, 723
Santo Niño de Atocha, El, 260, *261*
San Vito's convent, 688
Sanzu-no-baba, 225
Sapienta, 455
Sappho, 452, 579, 580, **868–869**
Saptāmatṛkās, 244
Sarada Ashram (Michigan), 429
Sarah (biblical), 78, 336, 387–388, 394,
    397, 460, 463, 464, 606, 865,
    869–870
Sarah (desert mother), 150
Saramama, 927, 928
Sarasvatī, 86, 216, 476, 522, 687, 692,
    870, 892, 988
Sarasvatī, Sri Jnananda, 66
Sarasvatī Pūjā, 870
Saraswati, Dayananda and Ramabai, 426
Sargon of Agade (Akkad), 467, 656
Sari (garment), 97
Śāriputra, 108, 886
Sarkar, Tanika, 355

Sarnath Jokhang Temple (Tibet), *252*
Sartre, Jean Paul, 46, 774
Sarvānukramaṇikā (Vedic text), 771
Sarvodaya movement (Buddhism), 128
Sashiko, 213
Sasso, Sandy, 546
Śāstras, 262
Śāstri, Syāma, 692
Satan, 321, 718, 1041
Satī (goddess), 367, 420, 759, 948, 1078
Sati (widow suicide), 41, *148*, 149, 252,
    355, 420, 425, 431, 749, 836–837,
    948, 1001, 1030
  as martyrdom, 627–628
  Sikh opposition to, 905
Satomi Myodo, 78
Saturnalia, 842, 982
"Satya: A Prayer for the Enemy" (film),
    340
Saudi Arabia, 508, 861, 888
Saul, 515–516
Saule, 459, 949
Sauromatians (people), 474
Saussure, Ferdinand de, 246, 459, 944
Sāvitrī, 253, 254, 420
Sawyer, Deborah, 433
Sax, William, 782
Sayo Kitamara, 349
Scandinavian religions, **870–873**; *See
    also* Norse mythology
Scapegoating, 1037, 1046
Scapulimancy, 475
Scarification, 750, 843, 1014
Scáthech, 1022
Schechner, Richard, 765
Schimmel, Annemarie, 306, 511, 927
Schlafly, Phyllis, 355
Schleiermacher, Friedrich, 299–300,
    404, 465, 972
Schneiderman, Rose, 552
Scholasticism, 1041
School of Youth for Social Service
    (Vietnam), 123, 128
Schopenhauer, Arthur, 485
Schreber, Dr. (Freud patient), 350
Schubel, Vernon, 899
Schurman, Anna Maria van. *See* van
    Schurman, Anna Maria
Schüssler Fiorenza, Elisabeth, 37, 406,
    433, 434, 573, 643, 703, 740, 774,
    791, 970, 975, 976
  early Christian history
    reconstruction, 1068
  on kyriarchy, 760
  Woman's Bible commentary, 1055
Schwartz, Howard, 553
Science, Freudian view, 350
Science and Health (Eddy), 290

Science, religion, and women, **873–875**,
    435
  nature and, 712
  superstition and, 950
  theism and epistemology of, 776
  Weber (Max) on, 1027
Scientology, 717, 719
Scott, Joan Wallach, 37, 551
Scripture. *See* Sacred literature
Scroll painting, 216
Sculpture. *See* Art
Scylla, 390
Searching the Scriptures (Schüssler
    Fiorenza), 1055
Seasonal rituals, 1024
Seattle, Chief, 708
Seclusion, **875–878**, 955
  Chinese practices, 197
  Christian monasticism, 672, 876–877
  couvade, 208, 209
  Hindu, 421
  in initiation rites, 473, 474
  Islamic requirements, 183, 490, 496,
    513, 875–876
  menstrual, 875, 876
  purdah, 148–149, 421, 889, 905
  in rites of passage, 843, 931
  solitude and, 923–924
Seclusion Edict (1639), 287
Second Sex, The (Beauvoir), 85, 164,
    334, 643, 774, 888
Second Vatican Council (1963–1965),
    165, 176–177, 220, 369, 602, 723,
    728
Secret societies, 11, 15–16, 876,
    878–879, 1010
Secularization, **879–881**
  conversion movements, 205
  Islam and, 493, 498, 880
  Judaism and, 543–544, 554
  legal systems, 573–574
  ritual celebration and, 845
  women's movements and, 334, 845
Sedazzari, Bernardina, 175
Sedgwick, Eve Kosofsky, 825
Sedir, 871
Seduction. *See* Temptation and
    seduction
Seguin, Seguin de, 523
Seicho-no-ie, 728
Seidel, Anna, 287, **881**
Seidman, Naomi, 554
Seikai Kyusei Kyo, 728
Sejd, 872
Selassie, Haile, 17
Self, 77, **881–884**
  in Afro-Atlantic religions, 15
  ātman, 262, 263, 466, 882, 927, 1077

body and, 101–102
  emptiness and, 189, 263, 301
  identity, 449–450
  as Jungian archetype, 815
  possession and, 789–790
  psykhē as component, 814
Self-flagellation, 241, 898, 899
Self-mutilation, 661, 694, 863, 887
Self-psychology, 816
Self-sacrifice
  Confucianism, 280
  feminist view, 910
  as image of women, 863
  Norse view, 872
  suicide as, 947–948
Selina, countess of Huntington, 812
Selivanov, Kondratij, 141
Selket, 714
Selk'nam (people), 931
Selvidge, Marla, 703
Semen, 94, 773, 956, 958, 1024
Seminoles (people), 1047
Semiotics, 459, 702, 816, **884–885**
Semnai Theai, 356
Sen, Amartya, 472
Sen, Keshub Chandra, 426
Seneca (people), 725
Seneca (Roman), 947
Senufo (people), 8
Separate spheres. *See* Gender roles
Sepik (people), 876
Septuagint, 533
Śerāṅvālī, 422
Sered, Susan Starr, 189, 267–268, 380,
    442, 680, 790, 820, 839, 914, 951,
    1065
Serenelli, Alessandro, 382
Serpent, 38, 179, 319, 491, 564–565,
    755, 940, 966
Serpent Goddesses (*lumo*), 116
Servant social class, 559, 858
Servius, 314
Seth (biblical), 319
Seth (Egyptian god), 488, 714
Seton, Elizabeth Ann, 348, **885–886**
Seven Crows, 724
Seven Eagle Brothers, 724
Seven Mothers, 892
Seventh-Day Adventists, 349, 409, 999
*Sex and Temperament in Three Primitive
    Societies* (Mead), 637
Sex change, **886–887**
  bridal mysticism, 867
  in Buddhism, 107, 109, 115, 302, 886
  shape-shifting, 896
Sexism, 97, **887–888**, 890, 1001
  in Buddhism, 109

Sexism *(continued)*
classism and, 181, 858
in evolution theory, 874
gender conflict and, 360
heterosexism, 409–411
identity images and, 450
Jungian theory and, 556
misogyny and, 665–666
mujeristas as reaction to, 685–686
in neopagan offshoot, 716
new religions and, 718
in Roman Catholicism, 850–851
sin concept and, 910
as violence factor, 1000
in Western philosophy, 773, 774
Sexism and God-Talk (Ruether),
1067–1068
Sex selection, 874
Sexual abuse, 193, 468, 908
Sexuality, **888–891**
in afterlife, 17–18
alchemy and, 23
Aphrodite and, 47–48
ascetic practices and, 66
Celtic religions and, 996
clothing and, 182, 224
cult religions and, 227
erotic dreams, 271
female, 143, 148, 321, 360, 443, 540,
828, 888–890, 965–966
female nudity symbolism, 730
Freudian theory, 815
gender and carnality, 712, 774
gender conflict and, 360
gendered moral standards, 676
heterosexism, 409–411
Hinduism and, 143, 250–251, 559,
995
Islam and, 102
Judaism and, 265, 321, 527, 625, 984,
1052
magic linked with, 611
marriage as domestication of, 618
menstruation prohibitions, 650
Mesopotamian goddess, 656, 657, 658
Mesopotamian sacred marriage, 658
microhistorical marital traditions, 620
misogynism linked with women's, 666
mutilation as woman's punishment,
694
neopagan, 716
in occultism, 733
Orthodox Christianity and, 203, 752
patriarchical control of female, 760
primal dissociation of pregnancy
from, 794
for procreation only, 890, 1052
as property, 288, 289, 1001

prostitution, 809–811
queer theory, 825–826
sacred marriage and, 859
sin and, 909, 910
sociological study of, 922
South American religions and, 930
of spirits, 939
in tantric practice, 642, 957–958
Taoism and, 642, 962
utopian communities and, 992
visual imagery, 1012
widow desexualization, 1030
witchcraft and, 1041, 1044
See also Celibacy; Chastity; Fertility
and barrenness; Homosexuality;
Incest; Lesbianism; Temptation
and seduction; Virginity
Seymour, William, 318
Shabarī, 771
Shadow (Jungian archetype), 815
Shadow plays, 933
Shafi, Doria, *497*
Shafiq, Durriyah (Doria), 312, **891**
Shahsavan, 499
Shakers
African American community, 519,
1011
asceticism, 67
celibacy, 227, 577–578, 913, 914, 992,
993
clothing, 183
dance as worship, 233, 241
equal empowerment of women, 76,
170
gender separation, 876
Holy Mother Wisdom, 563
as new religion, 717, 719, 720
textile making, 220
as utopian community, 170, 992–993
woman founder. *See* Lee, Ann
as women's religion, 913, 914, 1066
Shakers, Native American, 725
Shakespeare, William, 966, 1073
Shākta Tantrism, 1078
Shakti, 244, 262, 362, 456, 891, 892,
927, 956, 957, 1007, 1078
Shaktism, 362, **891–892**, 956, 957, 1007,
1077
divinity and, 262
fertility rituals, 337
magical powers, 611
maya, 636
Pārvatī, 759
prakriti construct, 791
Shakyamuni, 605
Shallum (Hulda's husband), 399, 442
*Shamanism, Archaic Techniques of
Ecstasy* (Eliade), 801

Shamans, **892–895**
Arctic religions, *57, 58, 59, 60, 950*
ascetic practices, 66
charisma and, 146
China, 278–279, 348, 1045
contemporary women's spirituality
movement, 1063–1064
East Asian folk religions, 278–279,
281, 605
female sun figure, 703
Himalayan religions, 416
initiation rites, 92
Japan, 286, 390
Korea, 201, 233, 238, 286, 348, 362,
442, 607, 722, 741, 894, 903–904,
951, 1066
leadership by, 575, 603
music and dance rituals, 687
Native American, 709, 787
New Age feminists, 718
nomadic peoples, 475
Oceanic religions, 735
possession, 787
in sacred performances, 238
Scandinavian religions, 872
South American religions, 893,
894–895, 930–931
Taoism, 279–280
transvestism, 334
visionary activity, 1010
weather rituals, 1024
as witches, 1037, 1045
Shame, 729, 889
Shamgar, 486
Shan Dao, 115
Shang dynasty, 278–279, 330, 1045
Shange, Ntozake, 379, 600, 601
Shango, 7, 13, 15
Shangqing Taoism, 960, 961
Shankara, 772
Shan nu-ren zhuan, 121
Shantideva, 190
Shape-shifting, **895–897**
Shāradā Devī, 1076
Sha'rawi, Huda, **897**
Sha'rawi, Muhammad Metwali al-, 493
Sharecroppers Home (Bourke-White),
778
Shari'a. *See* Islamic law
Shari'ati, 'Ali, 328
Sharma, Arvind, 769
Sharpe, Eric, 436
Shattamkiyazi of Mari, 659
Shavuot, 981
Shaw, George Bernard, 524
Shaw, Miranda, 36, 37, 131, 306, 958,
1076
Shaw, Rosalind, 259, 769

Shawnee Prophet (Tenskwatawa), 724
Sheba, Queen of. *See* Queen of Sheba
Sheila-na-gig sculptures, 996, 1012
Shekhinah, 222, 265, 272, 331, 347, 380, 477, 540, 542, 571, 733, 927, 970, 984
Shema, 1015
Shemoneh 'Esreh, 792
Shepenwepet I, 34
Shepenwepet II, 34
Shih ching (Confucian text), 770
Shih Yung Kai, 129
Shiism, 494, 499, 627, 828, **897–900**
   'A'ishah's portrayal, 21
   Fātima cult, 272, 328, 808
   folklore, 344
   homosexuality and, 586
   in Iran, 498, 898
   Mary's (Maryam) importance, 882
Shilluks (people), 277, 467
Shinn, Thelma J., 601
Shinran, 123
Shintoism, 225, 279, **900–902**
   Amaterasu deity, 26, 54, 279
   ancestor worship, 323
   body's significance, 97
   dance rituals, 239, 901
   money-washing ritual, 87
   moon representation, 674
   music mythology, 687, 691
   new religions and, 721
   priestesses, 362, 900
   religious tradition study, 287
   sun symbolism, 949
   weaving and, 217
Shiptu, 137
Shiromani Gurdwara Prabandhak Committee, 907
Shitala, 53
Shiva, Vandana, 874
Shiv Sena, 427
Shlama, 616
Shoah. *See* Holocaust
Shōnagon, Sei, 596
Shona (people), 1036
Shostak, Marjorie, 77
Showings (Julian of Norwich), 555
Shrines, 52–54, 220, 269, 516, 866, **902–904**, 1014
   pilgrimages to, 780
   priestesses, 806
   segregation vs. equal access to, 783
   See also Space, sacred; *specific shrines*
Shu ching (Confucian text), 770
Shulgi of Ur, 467
Shulhan Arukh, 530, 541
Shun, emperor of China, 195

Shur, Fanchon, 242
Siberia, 57, 214, 605, 949
   shamans, 92, 892, 893, 894, 950
Sibylline Books, 315, 563, 806
Sibyl of Cumae, 315, 563
Sibyl of the Rhine. *See* Hildegard of Bingen
Sibyls, 327, 563, 806
Sicarii, 533
Siddha, 112, 421, 614, 1076
Siddharājñī, 118
Siddhārtha Gautama, 348, 522, 575, 605
   ascetic order, 87
   begging bowl of, 441
   bhūmisparśa image, 110
   as celibate, 143
   as charismatic leader, 147
   compassion emphasis, 189
   enlightenment, 109, 110–111
   foster mother Mahāprajāpatī, 111, 614
   iconography, 447–448
   literary accounts of, 80
   ordination of nuns, 105, 111, 186, 257, 744, 1015
   prophecy, 808
   and prostitutes, 809
   shrines to, 902
   temptation of, 249, 965–966
   as trickster figure, 987
   See also Buddhism
Sidney, Philip, 599–600
Siduri, 1031
Sierra Leone, 818
Sif, 871
Signs (journal), 227
Sikhism, 254, 355, 669, 866, **904–907**, 935
Sikh Rahit Maryada, 907
Silbury Hill (Great Britain), 949
Silence, **907–908**; *See also* Speech; Voice
Silent Spring (Carson), 303
Silla dynasty, 122
Silva, Ranjiini de, 128
Sim Ch'ŏng, 279
Simmel, Georg, 918–919
Simmer-Brown, Judith, 131
Simon, Simone, 333
Simon bar Giora, 533–534
Simon Peter. *See* Peter
Sin, **909–911**
   of Adam and Eve, 319–320
   confession and penitence, 192–194
   as human fall from grace. *See* Original Sin
   redemption from, 867

   temptation and, 966
   women held more vulnerable to, 712
Sinclair, Karen, 769
Singalang Burdang, 1026
Singapore, 202, 893, 932, 933
Singh, Dilip, 907
Singh, Gobind, 905, 906
Singh, Ranjit, 906
Singing. *See* Music
Single-genesis theory, 796
Singleness. *See* Marriage and singleness
Sinha, S. N., 809
Sinhalese mythology, 329
Sinilau (Tinirau), 417, 735
Sioux (people). *See* Lakota Sioux
Sipish, 136
Sirach, 360
Sirens, 332
Sisala (people), 259
Sisera, 245, 398, 443, 1022
Sister, 832, **911–912**
Sisters in Islam, 504, 723
Sisters of Charity, 348, 885
Sisters of Loretto, 352
Sisters of Mercy, 164, 440
Sisters of Saint Dominic of Amityville, 440
Sisters of Saint Paul, 176
Sisyphus Works (Pappenheim), 758
Sītā, *207*, 244, 253, 254, 332, 362, 420, 422, 426, **912–913**
   hospitality and, 441
   as ideal wife, 1052
   truth and, 988
   virtue and, 1007
Sītalā, 422, 892
Śiva, 221, 244, 249, 262, 367, 559, 560, 613, 957
   abode as paradise, 759
   androgynous depictions, 36
   bhakti saints and, 88
   circle symbolism, 179
   depictions of, 456
   as god of dance, 236
   Mahādēviyakka and, 613–614
   maternal imagery, 605
   Shakti and, 892, 927
   structural view, 944
   wife Pārvatī, 679, 759–760
   yoga and, 1076
   yoni symbolism and, 1078
Śivabhakti, 559, 560
Siwan (people), 620
Six Dynasties period (China), 279, 281
Skanda, 262
Skeggjason, Hjalti, 352
Skira (female ritual), 247
Skokomish (people), 720

Skopcy, 141
Skuld, 872
Sky, 277
Skywalkers, 1021
Slavery and slave trade
　sexual, 810
　in United States, 832, 834, 913
　witchcraft and, 1044
Sleeping Beauty, 939–940
Slocum, John, 725
Slocum, Mary, 725
Smith, Amanda Berry, 576
Smith, Anne, 989
Smith, Barbara, 594
Smith, Dorothy, 919, 922
Smith, Hannah Whitall, 318
Smith, Jane I., 19
Smith, Joseph, 676–677, 808, 993
Smith, Mark S., 515
Smith, Wilfred Cantwell, 855
Snakes. *See* Serpent
Snow White, 458
Social action, **913–915**, 918
　Christian justice ministries, 661–662
　German Women's Welfare group,
　　757–758
　Marxist, 629
　nonviolence, 756
　Philippines, 724
　Protestant, 661, 711
　women's suffrage movement,
　　1069–1070
　See also Liberation theologies
Social change, **915–917**
Social Gospel, 812
Socialism, 334, 335, 545
Social physics, 920
Society for the Relief of Poor Widows
　with Small Children, 885
Society of Friends. *See* Quakers
Society of Jesus. *See* Jesuits
Society of the Sacred Heart of Jesus,
　176
Sociology, **917–920**
　ethnographic films, 340
　prostituted women studies, 810–811
　ritual studies, 846
　Weber studies, 1027
　See also Psychology of religion
Sociology of religion, **920–923**
Socrates, 254, 255, 306, 485, 563,
　926
Soelle, Dorothee, 629
Sofreh, 875–876
Sohye, Queen Mother, 597
Soka Gakkai, 717
Sokolow, Anna, 241
Sol (Sul), 949

Sola, Carla de, 242
Solar imgery. *See* Sun
Solitude, **923–924**
Sölle, Dorothee, 946
Solomon, *611*, 618, 824, 842
Solomon Islands, 875
Solstice celebration, 715
Soma, 70, 108, 109
Somé, Malidoma, 648
Son Buddhism, 122
Sondok, 69
Song dynasty, 197, 280
Sophia, **924–925**, 927, 970
　and creation, 222, 371
　and Demiurge, 371, 372
　as gendered Christ, 159, 925
　gnostic portrayals, 160, 371, 372, 925,
　　988
　and Holy Spirit, 455, 477, 925
　occultism and, 733
　wisdom personification, 380,
　　987–988, 1031, 1033, 1055
Sophia-achamoth, 329
Sophia of Jesus Christ, 159, 160
Sophocles, 452, 683
Sorcery, **925**, 1043, 1045
Sorel, Agnes, 454
Sortilege, 75
Soteriology. *See* Salvation
Sōtō Zen Buddhism, 123
Soubirous, Bernadette, 841, 903
Soul, **925–927**
　asceticism and, 66
　body and, 101, 102
　Buddhist *anatman*, 108, 263, 300,
　　301, 926
　female inferiority, 874
　ghosts, 368–369
　Greek concept of, 813–184
　in paradise, 758–759
　Platonic maleness of, 773, 774
　sin and, 320
　Spiritual marriage with Christ, 700
　three Western religions' articulation
　　of, 813
　Transcendental view of, 984–985
　transmigration, 18, 105, 521
　witchcraft and, 1046, 1047
　womb symbolism, 1056
Soul stealers, 1046, 1047
South Africa, 161, 335, 592
South American religions, **927–932**
　in the Andes, **927–930**
　Christianity, **166–167**, 318, 1020
　feminist movements, 335
　hallucinogen use, 479–480
　liberation theologies, 167, 591–592,
　　629, 915–916

in the Lowlands, **930–932**
music rituals, 688
new religions, **728–729**
prehistoric figurine finds, 803
sacrifice rituals, 861
shamans, 893, 894–895, 930–931
womb symbolism, 1055–1056
Southeast Asian religions, **932–934**
new religions, **722–724**
sacrifice myths, 94
witchcraft, 1046, 1050
South Family (Shaker community), 519
South Korea. *See* Korea
Souza Canavarro, Miranda de (Sister
　Sánghamittā), 348, 868
Sovereignty (Celtic goddess), 329
Sowei, 11
Space, sacred, 211, 235, 860, **934–936**
Spain, 539, 541, 554, 563, 798, 1011
Speaking being (Kristeva concept), 816
Speaking in tongues, 318, 727, 728, 936
Speech, **936–938**
possessed, 786
preaching by women, 562, 700, 812
women's public speaking
　prohibitions, 146, 156, 158, 563,
　700, 808, 812, 857, 907, 937, 1015
See also Voice
Spencer, Baldwin, 736
Spencer, Herbert, 485, 920, 921
Sphinx, 842
Spider imagery, 39
Spider Man, 1026
Spider Woman, 222, 362, 937, 1026
Spielberg, Herbert, 769
Spier, Leslie, 42
Spinning, 184, 212, 1025
Spiral Dance, The (Starhawk), 1048,
　1049–1050
Spirit
Christian Science conception, 719
Quaker conception, 808
Scientology conception, 719
Spirit guardians, 31
Spirit intrusion, 787
Spiritism, 728
Spirit possession. *See* Possession;
　Possession cults
Spirits, **938–941**
Afro-Atlantic religions, 14–15
apsārases, 48–49, 938–939
Arctic religions, 57–58
banshees, 368, 939
birth, 282
dance rituals, 233, 234
divinity of, 262
fertility, 337
ghosts, 368–369

guardian, 86
Himalayan religions, 416
Native American, 104
nomadic religions, 475
nymphs, 18, 581, 938–939
possession by, 786, 787, 788
possession cults, 348–349, 442, 788–790
sacred space and, 934
Santeria, 324
soul vs., 926
Southeast Asian religions, 932
See also Animism
Spiritual feminism, 943
Spiritualism, 226, **941–942**
as new religion, 717, 728
as women's religion, 1066
Spirituality, **942–944**
esotericism, 305–306
feminist, 466, 577, 715–716, 777, 914, 942–943, 980, 999
feminist invocation of moon, 674
feminist magic as form of, 612
grace bestowing gender equality, 812–813
lesbian studies and, 590–591
men's movement, 644–645, 648–649
spirit manifestation and, 790
Spirituality movement. *See* Women's contemporary spirituality movement
Spiritual Marriage, 700
Spirit-wives, 238
Spiro, Melford, 893
Spivak, Gayatri Chakravorty, 481, 773
Splendid Symbols (Gittinger), 1026
Sponberg, Alan, 522
Sports. *See* Athletics
Sprenger, Jacob, 1041, 1042
Spretnak, Charlene, 131, 370, 703, 704, 706, 723, 913
Śrāddha, 31
Śramaṇas, 109
Śrāvakas, 190
Śrī, 476
Srí Anirvan, 306
Śrīdevī, 116
Sri Lanka
Buddhism, 124, 125, 126, 127, 128, 130, 443, 741, 744, 746, 868
menarche ritual, 651
polyandry, 620
sex industry, 1001
Sinhalese mythology, 329
witchcraft, 1046
women penitents, 194
Śrīmālā, 107–108
Śrīvidya tradition, 892

Stacey, Judith, 919
Stanhope, Hester, 510
Stanley, Susie C., 742
Stanton, Elizabeth Cady, 434, 634–635, 924
Woman's Bible, 359, 913, 975, **1054–1055**, 1062
woman suffrage, 1070
Starhawk, 242, 379, 380, 603, 612, 916, 980, 1048, 1049–1050, 1051
Stark, Freya, 510
Stark, Rodney, 204, 880
State Theology (South Africa), 161
Stenia (female ritual), 247
Stern, Gertrude, 511
Sterner, Judy, 214
Stigmata, 75
Stoics, 36
Stone, Lucy, 93, 1070
Stone, Merlin, 376, 379, 703, 704, 705
Stone Age cultures, 799, 1021
Stonehenge (England), 798
Stone-Miller, Rebecca, 1026
Stonewall riots (1969), 589
Storm, Hyemeyohsts, 708
Story-telling. *See* Oral tradition
Stowasser, Barbara, 511
Stowe, Harriet Beecher, *365*
Strabo, 145, 483
Strīdhana, 25, 253, 421, 422
Strīdharma, 622, 623
Strīdharmapaddhati (Tryambaka), 418
Striga (Diana's retinue), 1041
Stringed instruments, 691, 692–693
Structural functionalism, 919, 921
Structuralism, 42, 459, **944–945**; *See also* Poststructuralism
Stupas, 109–110, 904
Stuttgart Declaration of Guilt (1946), 548
Subanbali, 223
Subbalakshmi, M. S. (vocalist), 689
Subbalakshmi, "Sister" (teacher), 426
Subjectivity, 776
Sudan, 96, 508, 618
Suddhodhana, king of Kapilavastu, 614
Śūdras, 858
Suffering, **945–947**
Buddhist thinking, 18, 125, 191, 771, 946
childbirth, 319, 650, 795
Christian Science thinking, 719
Christian thinking, 795, 834–835, 1000
evil and, 320, 776, 866
Hindu thinking, 18, 946
as Japanese New Religions' emphasis, 721

martyrdom, 627–628
menstrual pain, 650
self-mutilation, 661, 694, 863, 887
sin as cause, 909, 910, 945–946
theistic justification of, 775, 776
Suffrage. *See* Women's suffrage movement
Sufism, 242, 293, 499
in Africa, 500, 502
ascetic practices, 68
in Asia, 503
biographical writings, 79, 82
circle dances, 179
disciple concept, 257
divine concept, 263
esotericism, 305, 306
fasting, 325
as heterodox movement, 409
on Maryam, 630
religious rites and practices, 494
saintly people, 866, 923
visionary activity, 1011
Suicide, **947–948**
adultery prompting, 4
Confucianism and, 280
crossroad burials, 225
Hindu widow. *See* Sati
rape as cause for, 834
sociological view of, 921
Sujātā, 110
Sukhāvatī paradise, 759
Sukkot, 981
Sulabhā, 1076
Sulakhni, 906
Sulak Sivaraksa, 723
Sulis, 145, 146, 949
Sullam, Sarra Copia, 541
Sullivan, Lawrence, 931
Sulphur, 23
Sul (Sol), 949
Sumedhā, 772
Sumeria, 373, 656–657, 755, 859
Sumerian Bridal Songs, 659
Summer, Toby, 810
Sun, **948–949**
in astrology, 70
gendered imagery of, 703–704
Incan beliefs, 928
in South American religions, 928, 930
Sun Bu-er, 79, 362, 961, 1010
Sun Dance, 94, 179, 709, 710
Sunday School movement, 661
Sung dynasty, 99
Sun-Mother, 58
Sunna, 949
Sunni Islam, 21, 498, 630, 828, 882, 898
Śūnya. See Emptiness

Supernatural. *See* Magic; Occultism;
    Witchcraft
Superstition, 907, **949–952**
Supplication. *See* Prayer
Surabhi, Amrita, 441
Sur Das, 105
Surrealism, 763
Susan B. Anthony Coven, 877, 1048,
    1049
Susanna, 156, 462, 464, **952–953**
Susano, 687
Sutta Piṭaka, 614
Suttee. *See* Sati
Suttee Regulation Act (1829), 420
Svairini, 585
Svartalfheim, 871
Śvetāmbaras (Jain sect), 66–67, 192,
    520, 521, 522, 730
    nun philosophers, 772
    women monastics, 667
Swaminarayan movement, 429
"Sweating Indian Style" (video), 341
Sweat lodges, 341, 602–603, 708, 709,
    818
Sweden, 335, 352
Sweet Angel (Mother Divine), 678–
    679
Sweet Honey in the Rock, 689
Sybil, 485
Sybil of Cumae, 260
Sybils, 939, 1010
Symbolism
    biblical, 90
    circle, 179–180
    cosmic, 860
    egg, 91, 221, 273, 296–297
    Eucharist, 816
    fertility, *803*
    Greek afterlife, 813
    hair, 389–390
    identity and, 449
    images of women, 38, 457–460
    moon, 673–674, 703
    nudity, 729
    patriarchical, 1068
    phenomenology of, 768, 769
    pregnancy, 794
    semiotics, 816, 884
    sociological study of, 921
    sun, 703–704
    Tao, 794
    weather, 1024
    womb, 1055–1056
    See also Mythology
Symposium (Plato), 36, 254, 306, 403,
    563, 580
Synaxarium, 857
Syncletica, 150

Syncretic religions
    African-American, 717
    Korean new religions, 722
    Native American, 725
    Santeria, 611
Synesius, 445
Syntyche, 155, 158
Syria, 338, 373, 507, 671
Syrian Church, 751
Szold, Henrietta, 545, 551–552, 740,
    953

T

Table for Ladies (Hopper painting), 459
Taboos, **955–956**
    ancestor worship, 31
    Arctic religions, 57
    festival participation, 338
    incest, 467, 945
    marital, 620
    menstruation, 20, 57, 137, 649, 650,
        666, 876, 903, 934, 955–956
    seclusion practices, 875
Tacitus, 145, 1022
T'aego Order (Korea), 122, 285–286
T'aesong-am (Korea), 122
Taggart, James, 224
Tagore, Rabindranath, 203, 991
Tahara (ritual purity), 817–818
Tahira. *See* Khadija
Tahtawi, Rifa'ah Rafi' al-, 496
T'ai Chi, 274
Taima Mandala, 217
Táin Bó Cuailnge (Irish epic), 1022
Taíno Intertribal Council, 140
Taínos (people), 139–140
Taiping jing, 959–960
Tairen, 196
Taisiia, Abbess, 1011
Taiwan, 74, 823
    Buddhism, 122, 129, 285, 745, 746
    Christianity, 163
    Confucianism, *200*, 202
    Mazu cult, 636, 637
    new religions, 721
    prostitution, 1001
    shamans, 893
Takara-bune (treasure ship), 86
Tale of Genji (Murasaki), 596, *597*
Tale of Kieu (novel), 598
Taliban, 355
Talismans, 211
Talking cure, 334
Tallensi (people), 31
Tallfeathers Woman, 687
Talmud, 512, 526–530, 536, 538, 550
    adultery prohibitions, 3
    on homosexuality, 582

on menstrual impurity, 650
on moon and sun, 674
on prayer, 792
as sacred literature, 855
sexual activity guidelines, 890
theological discourse and, 973
on virtue, 1007
on women's speaking, 907
on women's truthfulness, 988
Tamang (people), 416, 893
Tamar, 390, 606, 835, 1000, 1029
Tamayori-hime, 900
Tamayowut, 277
Tamez, Elsa, 629
Tamil Nadu, 692
Tammuz. *See* Dumuzi
Tanakh. *See* Hebrew Bible
Tanaquil, 315
Tane, 934
Tang dynasty, 100, 197, 198, 669–670,
    731
Tang Junyi, 200
Tanit, 138
Tanjore painting, 216
Tano, 7
Tantansai, 217
Tantra, 112, 257, 362, **956–959**
    androgyny in, 36–37
    canons, 109
    compassion, 190
    confession and penitence, 192
    dākinīs, 231–232
    emotion as energy, 300–301
    esotericism, 305, 306
    exaltation of women, 118, 772
    female sexuality, 889–890
    female voices, 1015–1016
    goddesses, 988, 997–998
    knowledge and women, 563
    kuṇḍalinī, 38, 565, 892
    prajñā, 1032
    rituals, 94, 956, 997
    shaktism and, 892
    Western practice, 131
    on wisdom, 1034
    witchcraft, 1046
    yoga, 1017, 1076, 1077
Tao, 195, 221, 249, 331, 794, 964–965
Tao-chiao, 960, 961
Taoism, 197, 278, 362, 823, 932,
    959–965
    alchemy, 23, 960, 962
    almsgiving, 25
    androgynous concepts, 36
    birth and rebirth images, 92
    body's significance, 97, 98
    circle symbolism, 179
    creation stories, 221

desire's release, 249
female representation, 770, 771
feminine meditative symbols, 642
gender roles, 675
images of the Tao, **964–965**
laity, 567
Mazu deity, 636–637
monasticism, 279, 667, 669–670
Nugua mythological figure, 730
overview, 279–280, **959–964**
religious tradition study, 287
salvation concept, 867
scholarly study, 881
visionary activity, 1010
yin and yang, 675, 757, 770, 771, 964
See also Yin/yang polarity
Tao-te ching, 221, 959, 964
Tao-tsang, 960
Tapas, 192
Tapaswini, Mataji Maharani, 426
Tapu, 735, 934
Tārā, 448, 956, **965**, 1035
compassion of, 190–191, 377
depictions of, 456
enlightenment of, 116, 117
inspiration and, 476
Tarabotti, Archangela, 619
Taranatha, 131
Tariki, 867
Tarot cards, 716
Tation, 761
Tattooing, 750, 751, 843, 1014
Taussig, Michael, 895
Taweret, 33
Taylor, Leeza, 528
Taylor, Paul Michael, 1026
Tea ceremony, 217–218
Te Atua Fafine, 735
Tea women, 333
Techinot prayers, 792
Tecla, 81
Teer, Barbara Ann, 242
Tefnut, 34
Teish, Luisah, 377
Tekhines, 542
Tekna (people), 56
Teleia. *See* Hera
Temearu, 222
Temiar (people), 688
Temmu, emperor of Japan, 279
Temne (people), 259
Temperance movement, 661
Temple Emanu-El (New York City), 543
Temple of Re (Egypt), 323
Temple of Vesta (Italy), *935*
Temple priestesses, 806
Temple prostitutes, 659, 805, 809, 810–811

Temples. *See* Architecture
Temple wives, 120
Templo de las Inscripciones (Maya), 653
Templo del Medio Día, El (Mexico City), 727
Temptation and seduction, 257, 332–333, **965–967**
Adam and Eve's story, 249, 273, 485, 490, 491, 946, 966
cautionary tales, 570
desire and, 249
female sexuality and, 889
Jewish views, 540
misogynistic beliefs on, 666
water goddesses, 1024
women linked with, 675, 676, 712, 729, 774, 1042
Tengri, 475
Tenochtitlán (Aztec) capital, 652, 654
Tenrikyo, 349, 576, 621, 717, 820, 901
Tensho-kotai-jingu-kyo, 349, 721, 901
Tenskwatawa, 724
Tents, 55–56
Teomama (Chimalma), 654
Teotihuacán (Mesoamerican site), 653
Terāpantha movement (Jainism), 520
Terence, 234
Teresa, Mother. *See* Mother Teresa
Teresa of Avila, 78, 82, 104, 142, 144, 151, 193, 249, 256, 519, 563, 672, 700, 849, 865, 886, 923, **967–968**, 991, 1010, 1062
Terpsichore, 687, 691
Terrible Mother, 243
Territorial cults, 20–21
Terry, Jennifer, 825
Tertullian, 159, 183, 322, 360, 371, 372, 671, 946, 966
Testimony (religious), 153–154
Tetum (people), 91, 820
Teutonic Knights, 175
Tewa (people), 347
Textiles. *See* Clothing; Weaving
Texts of Terror (Trible), 594
Thailand
amulet wearing, 27, 28
Buddhism, 125, 128, 217, 741, 745, 746, 903, 932, 933, 951
Buddhist new religion, 723
kinship religion, 603
lay Buddhist nuns, 669
sex industry, 1001
spirit cults, 442, 890
weaving in, 217
witchcraft, 1046
Thakali (people), 416
Thalia, 687
Thamyris, 686

Thatcher, Margaret, 164
Thealogy, 376, 943, **968–969**
Theater. *See* Dance and drama
Thecla, 159, 390, 671
Theism, 775–776, **970–971**; *See also* Monotheism
Thekla, 688
Themis, 988
Theodora, 150
Theodosius, 72
Theogony (Hesiod), 36, 277, 323, 356, 384, 459, 468, 687, 859, 874
Theology, **971–979**
doctrine and, 267
feminist, 164, 167, 376, 382, 577, 592, 673, 882, 913, 972, **975–977**
Judaic, 545
Orthodox Christian, 752, 971, 973
overview, **971–975**
salvation, 866–868
thealogy vs., 968–969
women-centered, **978–979**
See also Liberation theologies
Theosophical Society, 70, 147, 226, 426
Theosophy, 362, 717, **979–980**
Theotokos, 752, 1004
Therapeutae, 67, 527, 533, 671, 1011
Therapeutic Touch, 980
Theravada Buddhism, 111, 112, 124–127, 131, 132, 932, 933
ascetic practices, 67
desire typologies, 249
divinity, 263
enlightenment, 759
ordination proscriptions, 143, 741, 744, 868, 933
religious order founders, 348, 361
sacred-comic traditions, 443
Theresa of Avila. *See* Teresa of Avila
Thérèse of Lisieux, 604, 672, **980–981**, 1010
Therīgāthā, 67, 77, 81, 108, 109, 111, 128, 144, 192, 257, 292, 596, 614, 1015
Theseus, 27, 562, 569
Thesmophoria, 39, 247, 325, 338, 339, 385, 580, 862
Theurgy, 611
Thich Nhat Hanh, 123, 191, 723
Third Orders, 193
Thistlethwaite, Susan, 810, 1000
Thomas, Apostle and Saint, 162, 371
Thomas, Keith, 1042, 1051
Thomas, M. Carey, 1063
Thomas Aquinas, 101, 309, 317, 562
contraception rejection, 203
on Eve's sin, 909
on female rationality, 485, 836

Thomas Aquinas (continued)
    friendship with God, 352
    homosexuality condemnation, 583
    on subordination of woman, 1051
    on women's philosophic inequality,
        773–774, 1068
    on women's public speaking, 907
Thompson (people), 277
Thoms, William, 345
Thor, 871
Thoreau, Henry David, 984
Thorne, Barrie, 919
Thoth, 32, 986, 1038–1039
Thought Woman, 970
Three Bonds doctrine, 196
"Three obediences" (Buddhism), 107
Throne imagery, 455
Thubten Chöling, 118
Thurd, 871
Tiamat, 221, 274, 323, 324, 360, 367,
        657
Tianhou. See Mazu
Tianshi (T'ien-shih) movement, 960
Tibetan Buddhism, 105, 116, 118, 129,
        131, 300, 306, 416, 997–998
    alchemical traditions, 23
    androgyny concept, 36–37
    authority in, 76
    biographical writings, 81
    compassion depictions, 190–191
    dākinīs, 231
    divinity concept, 263
    documentary films, 340
    dreams and, 272
    festivals, 339
    iconography, 448
    lay Buddhist nuns, 669
    Machig Labdron, 609
    meditation, 641–642
    nuns, 668, 669
    ordination of nuns, 744, 745
    pilgrim, 780
    polyandry, 619, 620
    shrines, 902
    Tārā worship, 965
    virtue, 1007
    visionary activity, 1010
    wisdom personification, 1035
T'ien-t'ai Buddhism, 121
Tiep Hien Order (Vietnam), 123
Tij Brata festival, 326, 416
Tikal (Maya site), 653
Tikopia, 735
Timaeus (Plato), 874
Time, sacred, 860, 981–982
    Mesoamerican measurements, 655
    paradise beliefs, 759
Timothy, 156, 1068

Tingley, Katherine, 979–980
Tinirau (Sinilau), 417, 735
Tiresias, 896
Tīrthaṅkara, 521, 772
Tīrthas, 561
Tirumuṟai (Śaiva canon), 559, 560
Tiruttontar Purāṇam, 560
Titans, 384, 1031
Tithing, 25
Titus, 1068
Tkhines, 81, 371
Tlatilco (Mesoamerican site), 653
Tlingit (people), 18
Tokeiji (Japanese convent), 123
Tokiwa Gozen, 333
Tolbert, Mary Ann, 406
Toltecs (people), 94
Tomoe Gozen, 224
Tomyris, 474
Tonga, 735
T'ongil-gyo. See Unification Church
Tongues. See Speaking in tongues
Tootsie (film), 334
Toradjas (people), 277
Torah, 912, 982–984
    as Judaic law, 526, 529–532, 537, 573,
        636
    as sacred literature, 855–856
    as theological discourse source,
        973
    truth and, 988
    wisdom and, 1031
    women's traditional exclusion from,
        102, 528, 856
Torelli, Louise, 176
Tosefta, 536
Totems, 475, 735–736
Towish, 277
Townes, Emilie, 832, 1053
Tragedy. See Dance and drama
Trajan, emperor of Rome, 535
Trance
    African religions, 7, 8
    body postures, 103–104
    Candomble ceremonies, 300
    dance and drama, 788, 233, 234,
        238
    Mead anthropological studies, 638
    performance art, 764
    possession, 610, 787, 788–789
Transcendence. See Immanence and
    transcendence
Transcendentalism, 262, 984–986
Transcendent One (Ikk Oan), 254
Transcendent Wisdom, 455
Transformations of Myth through Time
    (Campbell), 801
Transforming Grace (Carr), 769

Transitional space (Winnicott concept),
        816
Transmigration
    after life, 18
    gender boundaries, 105
    Jaina, 521
Transsexuals, 60, 361
Transubstantiation, 288, 316
Transvestism, 60, 140, 238, 334
Trapp, J., 1073
Travel, pilgrimages justifying, 779–781
Tree of Life, 367, 1031
Trees Dance, 237
Tree worship, 329–330
Trevor-Roper, Hugh, 1051
Triad Society, 879
Tribal dance, 234–235
Trible, Phyllis, 405–406, 553, 594, 884,
        1052, 1053
Tricksters, 7, 9, 15, 417, 443, 986–987
Trier, Lars von, 342
Trieu An, 1022
Trilok Bauddh Mahasanga Sahayaka
        Gana, 128, 129, 746
Trinity, 673, 785
Tripta, 904, 906
Trismegistus, Hermes, 179
Trivedi, Harshad R., 809, 810
Trivia. See Hecate
Trojan War, 458, 459
Trolls, 1040
Trung Nhi, 1021–1022, 1060
Trung Trac, 1021–1022, 1060
Truth, 77, 491, 607, 840, 987–989
Truth, Sojourner, 334, 756, 1060
Tryambaka, 418
Tryphaena, 155, 158
Tryphosa, 155, 158
Ts'ai, 691
Ts'ai Yen (Lady Wen-chi), 216, 691
Tsenerene, 371
Tsichtinako, 687
Tsing, Anna Lownehaupt, 895
Tsomo, Karma Lekshe, 191, 744
Tsonga (people), 479, 480
Tswana (people), 587
Tuana, Nancy, 873–874
Tuareg (people), 55
Tubman, Harriet, 756, 1022
Tubu (people), 56
Tukanoan (people), 931
Tukārām, 422
Tukomit, 277
Tu Kuang-t'ing, 669, 961
Tukuna (people), 338
Tuli, 459
Tulku, 76, 118
Tulsi, 416

Tum, Juana, 646
Tuna (Eel), 417
Tun Huang caves (China), 115
Tunisia, 507, 508
Turbans, *905*
Turkey, 257, 498–499
Turner, Kay, 152
Turner, Victor, 45, 91, 482, 765, 779,
    843, 847, 1050
Tutilina, 314
Tutu, Desmond, 161, 592
Tu Wei-ming, 200
Twain, Mark, 524
Twelve Steadfast Women (*tenma*), 116
Twelve-step programs, 41, **989–990**
Twentieth-Century Faith (Mead), 638
Twins, 95–96
Ty, 871
Tylor, Edward B., 45, 208, 345, 381, 801,
    836
Typhaon, 402

U
Ubaida, 691
Uchtsiti, 687
UFO cults, 346
Uich'on, 122
Ulanov, Ann, 300
Umā Haimavatī. *See* Pārvatī
Umansky, Ellen, 312, 582, 976
Umay, 475
Umbanda (Macumba), 13, 14, 16, 75,
    790, 1074
Umiliati order, 616
Umm Salam, 1062
Uncertainty principle, 712
Uncleanliness. *See* Purity and pollution
Unconscious (Freudian), 814
Unconscious (Jungian), 300, 457–458,
    459, 702, 815
Underground Railroad, 756, 1022
Underhill, Evelyn, 436, 612, 942, **991**
Uniao do Vegetal, 480
Unification Church, 226, 227, 323,
    717–720, 722, 880, 992
Union of Egyptian Women, 492
Unitarianism
    first female minister, 93, 742
    Goddess movement and, 380
    homosexuality and, 582
    Transcendentalism and, 984
United Church of Canada, 169, 340
United Church of Christ, 742, 812
United Holiness Church in America,
    349
United Methodist Church, 5, 742
United Nations, 646–647, 850
United Presbyterian Church, 742

United Society of Believers. *See*
    Shakers
Unity (organization), 147
Universal Life, 717
Universal Soul, 66, 985
Universal Spirit, 984
University of Chicago, 918–919
Unspoken Worlds (Falk and Gross eds.),
    1065
Upanishads, 78, 143, 203, 251, 252, 296,
    306, 419, 421, 771, 1076
    ashram, 667
    maya concept, 635
    prakriti concept, 791
    riddle tests, 842
    as sacred literature, 858
    on sacred power, 262–263
Upasana (Hindu worship), 1071
Upāya, 1032
Upham, Edward, *321*
Upper Tianzhu Monastery (Hangzhou),
    661
Ur, 658
Urania (Muse of dance), 232, 687
Urania of Worms, 539
Urban IV, pope, 317
Urban VI, pope, 142
Urd, 872
Ursula, Saint, 298
Ursuline order, 151, 168, 176, 348, 849
Urvaśī, 48–49
Usās, 1021
Ushās, 1032
Uterus. *See* Womb
Utopian communities, 170, 913,
    991–993; *See also* Mormons:
    Shakers; *other specific groups*
Utu, 467
Uwaifo, Victor, 615
Uxmal (Maya site), 653

V
Vac, 476, 870
Vācaspatimiśra, 1076
Vagina, 454, 656, 795, **995–997**, 1078
Vagina dentata, 995
Vagina Woman, 1055
Vaglieri, Laura Veccia, 511
Vairochana, 703, 1056
Vaiśeṣika, 772
Vaiṣṇava, 261, 569, 957
    Rādhā's importance, 833
    rituals, 94
    saints, 41, 88, 422
Vaiśyas, 858
Vajrasattva, 192
Vajravārāhī, 117, 232, 997
Vajrayana. *See* Tantra

Vajrayoginī, 36, 37, 117, 231, 232, 956,
    997–998, 1077
Valentinus, 371, 988
Valenzuela, Romana, 727
Valeri, Valerio, 413
Valesians, 140–141
Valhalla, 872, 1021
Valiente, Doreen, 1048
Valkyries, 243, 327, 871, 872, 1021
Valley of the Dawn, 728
Vālmīki, 912
Valone, Carolyn, 761
Vampire cults, 94
Vana Mothers, 872
van der Veer, Peter, 354
Van Esterik, John, 128
Van Herik, Judith, 815
Vanir, 871
van Schurman, Anna Maria, **998**
Varāha Mihira, 70
Varnas, 559, 858
Vashti, 464
Vasudeva, 472
Vatican II. *See* Second Vatican Council
Vatsyāyana, 559
Vätter, 872
Vedānta, 858, 772
Vedanta Temple (San Francisco), 428
Vedas, 75, 92, 109, 236, 430, 870
    breast symbolism, 106
    deity of death and sorrow, 243
    female study of, 291–292, 419
    gender roles, 251, 361, 772
    heaven as Yama, 759
    maya concept, 635
    pollution beliefs, 819
    as sacred literature, 858
    soul concept, 926–927
    wisdom, 1032
    witchcraft, 1046
    women's philosophic status, 771
Vedic tradition. *See* Vedas
Vega, Lope de, 234
Vegetarianism, 120, 818, **998–999**
Vegoia, 315
"Veiled Revolution, A" (film), 341
Veiling
    Hindu, 183, 421, 889, 890
    Islam, 148, *182*, 183–184, 341, 343,
        390, 490, 493, 497–498, 501–502,
        504, 505, 508–509, 512, 513, 574,
        723, 828, 889, 890, 897, 933
    Jewish bride, *751*
    media stereotypes, 641
    as self-sacrifice, 863
    Sikh rejection of, 905, 907
    symbolic meanings, 390
Veleda, 145

Venezuela, 728
Venkamamba, Tarigonda, **999–1000**
Venkateśvara, 428
Venkateśvara Temple (Atlanta), 429
Venus. *See* Aphrodite
Venus figures, 633, 796–797
Venus impudique, 797
Venus of Laussel, 798
Venus of Lespugne, 796
Venus of the Afternoon, 928
Venus of the Morning, 928
Venus of Willendorf, 373, 379, 729, 796–797
Verbermacher, Hannah Rachel (Maid of Ludomir), 528, 542, 747, 1011, 1062
Vercheres, Madeleine de, 1061
Verdandi, 872
Veritas, 988
Vertumnus, 314
Vesica piscis, 995, 996, 1012
Vesta. *See* Hestia and Vesta
Vestal Virgins, 53, 183, 315, 407, 413, 806, *935*, 1002
Vestments, 219–220
Vetali, 232
Vibia Perpetua. *See* Perpetua and Felicity
Video. *See* Film and video
Vidyādevīs, 522
Vidyasagar, Iswar Chandra, 425–426
Vietnam, 932
  Buddhism, 120, 122–123, 125, 128, 746, 932
  Buddhist meditation, *642*
  Confucianism, 123, 198, 199, 932
  Engaged Buddhist movement, 723
  literary tradition, 598
  superstition in, 951
  women warriors, 1021–1022
Vietnam Veterans' Memorial (Washington, D.C.), 1013
Vietnam War, 778
Vieyra, Antonio, 525
Vigri, Catherine, 1009
Vikings. *See* Norse mythology; Scandinavian religions
Vimalā, 810
Vimalakīrtinirdeśa, 306
Vina (musical instrument), 692
Vinaya, 192, 292, 586, 668, 669, 744
Vinaya Piṭaka, 614
Vincent de Paul, 176, 849
Vindication of the Rights of Women, A (Wollstonecraft), 774
Violence, **1000–1002**
  adultery punishments, 3, 4, 148, 835, *1001*

anonymous victims of, 41
"dowry death," 420, 1001
misogyny and, 666
of sacrificial rites, 862–863
sexual abuse, 193, 468, 908
suffering and, 945
war, 1019
See also Domestic violence; Pacifism and nonviolence; Rape
Vīraśaiva tradition, 88, 613–614
Virgil, 315, 403, 557, 563, 699
Virgin birth, 1003
Virginity, 923, **1002–1004**
  Artemis as protector of, 65–66
  celibacy vs., 143
  early Christian communities, 671
  Eastern views of, 97
  femininity and, 332
  goddesses, 705
  hair's symbolism, 390
  Islamic brides, 626
  New Testament valuation of, 626
  priestess, 805, 806
  saints and, 866
  self-mutilation to preserve, 694
  See also Celibacy; Chastity
Virgin Mary, 73, 361, 449, 1003, **1004–1006**
  Annunciation, 808
  assumption of, 164, 325, 332, 556, 903
  breast symbolism, 107
  depictions of, 63, 342, 449, 454, 455, 456
  dichotomy with Eve the temptress, 774
  as feminine essence, 331, 332, 333
  film depictions, 342
  as goddess figure, 377
  heroism of, 1061
  Holy Spirit and, 477
  Immaculate Conception of, 164, 267
  Islamic view of, 630, 808
  as literary influence, 452
  and Mother-Goddess worship tradition, 755
  motherhood and, 882
  in New Testament, 156, 462, 463, 1004
  in Orthodox Christianity, 752
  as Our Lady of Lourdes, 841, 903, 935
  as Our Lady of Perpetual Help, 260
  Pietà imagery, 448
  as prophet, 840
  as queen of heaven, 759
  resurrection of, 298
  as saint, 866

shrines and sacred sites, 53, 367, 780, 783, 784, 903, 935
Sophia and, 925
vagina imagery and, 996
Visitation to Elizabeth, 448
weather-calming abilities, 1024
wisdom and, 329
See also Maryam
Virgin Mary of the Annunciation (Tinos), 780
Virgin of Guadalupe, 53, 235, 269, 780, 783, 784, 845, 935, 970
Virtue, **1006–1008**
  African religions, 11
  chastity as, 676
  in Confucianism, 197
  gender equality in attaining, 774
  theories of, 309
  vow taking and, 1017
Visakha, 54, 124
Visconti, Matteo, duke of Milan, 616
Visher, Michael P., 1026
Vishnu, 41, 105, 216, 262, 428, 569, 759, 892
Vishva Hindu Parishad, 355
Visionaries in medieval Europe, 82, 150–151, 841, **1008–1009**, 1010
  Elisabeth of Schönau, 298, 414
  Hildegard of Bingen, 293, 361, 414–415, 433, 519, 1062
  Julian of Norwich, 433, 555, 774
  Mechtild of Magdeburg, 638–639
Vision quest, 86, 104, 708, 709
  menarche ritual, 645
  purification prior to, 818
Visions, 1008, **1009–1011**
  Christian, 763, 767, 808, 1011
  eidetic, 768
  Native American new religions, 724, 725
  Pentecostal, 728
  trances and, 103
  See also Prophecy
Visitation of Holy Mary, 176
Visitation of Virgin Mary, 448
Visual arts, **1011–1015**
  images of women, 63, **454–457**, 1012
  prehistoric, 373, 374, 797
  See also Art; Iconography
Visualization, 642, 957
Vitalism, 712
Vivekananda, Swami, 429
Vizenor, Gerald, 987
Vocal music. *See* Music
Vodou (Vodun), 13, 14, 16, 362, 706, 1047
  circle symbolism, *180*
  comic performances, 442–443

crossroads imagery, 225
dance rituals, 233
female leadership, 226
hair symbolism, 390
ordination, 741
sacrifice rituals, 862
spirit marriages, 605
spiritualism and, 941
trance, 787, 789
zombies, 368
Voice, **1015–1016**
musical, 690–693, 1016
public speaking prohibitions. *See*
Speech
See also Silence
Volcano creation, 763
Volmar, 414
Voltaire, 510
Voltumna, 314
Voragine, Jacobus de, 79
Voramai Kabilsingh, 128, 723
Voting rights. *See* Women's suffrage
movement
Votive objects, 211
Voukopion shrine (Greece), 902
Vows, **1016–1018**
folklore, 344
Hindu, 192, 344, 422, 424–425, 561,
739, 1017
Islam, 495
See also Marriage and singleness;
Monasticism; Ordination
Vratas, 192, 422, 424–425, 561, 1017
Vrat kathās, 344, 739, 988
Vrindaban (India), 759
Vulva. *See* Vagina
Vyāsa, 1076

W
Wabets, 32
Wach, Joachim, 267, 435
Wadud-Muhsin, Amina, 511, 827
Wafdist Women's Central Committee,
897
Wagner, Richard, 469
Wailing. *See* Laments
Wailing Wall. *See* Western Wall
Waiwai (people), 209
Wākea, 875
Wakefield cycle, *241*
Walbiri (people), 820
Wald, Lillian, 552
Waldenses, 76, 1042
Wales, 145, 146, 896
Wali, 233, 353, 866
Wali, Sima, 835
Walker, Alice, 5, 600–601, 1053, 1054
Walker, Barbara, 459

Walker, Margaret, 600
Wallace, Ruth, 919
Wamirans (people), 347
Wana (people), 951
Wandering mendicancy. *See* Almsgiving
Wang Xizhi, 216
Wang Yangming, 197, 198
Wang Zhe (Wang Che), 961
Waqf (religious endowment), 762
War, **1019–1021**
goddesses of, 1031–1032
mass suicides, 948
rape as instrument of, 834, 835
sacrifice of victims, 863
See also Warriors
Warao (people), 684, 930, 1055
Waraqa bin Nawfal, 562
Ward, Mary, 176, 348
Wardley, Jane and James, 577, 578
Warlpiri (people), 620
Warner, Marina, 704, 766
Warner, Michael, 825
Warner, W. Lloyd, 737
Warring States period (China), 279
Warriors, **1021–1023**
Amazons, 26–27, 39, 474, 569, *570*,
580
Aztec childbearing, 655
biblical women, 245, 515, 1019, 1061
cross-dressing, 223
Dona Beatriz, 270
goddesses, 658, 1019, 1021, 1022
Valkyries, 243, 327, 871, 872, 1021
women heroines, 1060, 1061
Warrior social class, 559, 858, 948
Warrior Twins, 1026
Washing, ritual. *See* Purification
Washington, James Melvin, 4
Washington, Mrs. (Pawnee visonary),
724
Wat Dhammakaya, 723
Water
African deities, 7–8
goddesses, 614–615, 1024
Mandaean symbolism, 616
as Mesopotamian mother-goddess
symbol, 657
as purification agent, 650, 817, 818,
820
as Tao metaphor, 964
See also Baptism
Water Grandmother, 904
Water Monster, 1026
Watson, James, 74
Wat Songdharma Kalyani, 723
Wat Suan Mokkh, 723
Wat Tham Mongkorn Thong
Kanchanburi, *124*

Weather, 329, **1023–1025**
Weaving, 184, 212, 217, **1025–1027**
fate analogy, 327, 1025
Weber, Marianne Schnitger, 918, 1027
Weber, Max, 45, 75, 147, 880, 918,
921–922, **1027**
Webner, Richard, 20
Wedding ceremonies
bridal adornment, 220, 750, 751
commitment vows, 982
Indian rituals, 442, 1014
Jewish tradition, 219, 531, *751*
Korean tradition, 280–281
Sikh tradition, 906
Weems, Renita, 1054
Weerakoon, Abhaya, 128
Wegner, Judith, 527, 536, 553
Wehr, Demaris, 815
Wei Furen (Wei Shuo), 216
Weigle, Marta, 344, 739
Wei Huacan, 960
Weil, Simone, 945, **1027–1028**
Weiner, Annette, 42
Weininger, Otto, 46, 47
Weissler, Chava, 528
Welch, Holmes, 881
Welch, Sharon D., 976
Wells-Barnett, Ida B., 171, 918, *919*
Welter, Barbara, 433
Wen (civility), 99
Wen Chen, princess of China, 117
Wen Cheng, 69
Wensinck, Arendt J., 510
Wepwawet, 32
Wertheim, Margaret, 874
Wesley, John, 318, 999
Wesleyan Methodist Church, 318
Wesleyan movement. *See* Methodism
Wessinger, Catherine, 718
West, Robin, 573, 574
Western Wall (Wailing Wall), *550*, 780,
783
When God Was a Woman (Stone), 379
Where Witchcraft Lives (Valiente), 1048
White, Alma, 349, 576
White, Ellen Gould, 576, 841, 999
White, Ellen Harmon, 349
White, Lynn, Jr., 303
White Buffalo Calf Maiden, 709, 845
White Corn Maiden, 347
White goddess, 702, 896
White Painted Lady (White Bearded
Lady), 52, 883
White Queen, 23
White Tara, *190*, 476
Whiting, John and Beatrice, 43
Whittaker, James, 578
Whitten, Norman, 930

"Why Women Need the Goddess" (Christ), 705–706
Wicca, 226, 377, 378, 380, 734, **1028–1029**
  contemporary witchcraft movement, 1048–1049, 1051
  female leadership, 577, 717
  female ritualized nudity, 729
  friendship concept, 353
  as new religion, 717
  as women's worshipping community, 1071
Widows, **1029–1030**
  as alms recipients, 25
  as biblical prophets' concern, 807
  biblical queens, 824
  brahmin, 31
  as celibates, 144
  Confucian, 280
  as early Christian disciples, 671
  Hindu, 31, 98, 253, 420–421, 623, 627–628; *See also* Sati
  inauspiciousness of, 74, 250
  Islamic, 513
  purification ritual, 818
  Sikh, 905, 907
  solitary life, 923
Wiesel, Elie, 548
Wiesner, Merry, 433
Wife and Mother in Legal Development (Weber), 1027
Wigman, Mary, 241
Wilgefortis, 223
Willard, Frances, 171, *576*
Willendorf, goddess of. *See* Venus of Willendorf
Williams, Delores, 313, 600, 832, 970, 976, 1007
  rejection of term "patriarchy," 760
  and womanist tradition, 1053
Williams, Patricia J., 607
Williams, Raymond, 227
Williams, Walter L., 588
Williamson, Marianne, 1064
Willis, Janice, 36, 131
Wilson, Lois, 989
Winnebago (people), 273, 725
Winnemucca, Sarah, 1063
Winnicott, Donald W., 815, 816
Winterson, Jeanette, 77
Wisdom, 477, 938, **1030–1035**
  in ancient Near East and Israelite religion, **1033–1034**
  in Buddhism, 190, 191
  female personifications, 329, 987–988, 1030–1032
  overview, **1030–1033**

prajña and *prajñaparamita*, 116, 189, 377, 476, 867, **1034–1035**
  riddle tests, 842
  Sophia personification, 380, 987–988, 1031, 1033, 1055
  See also Knowledge
Wise Old Man (Jungian archetype), 815
Witchcraft, **1035–1051**
  in Africa, 9, 10, **1043–1045**, 1050
  in ancient Near East and Bible, 400, 659, 807, **1037–1040**
  in Asia, **1045–1047**, 1050
  contemporary witchcraft movement, 226, 916, 1028–1029, **1048–1050**, 1051
  crossroads symbolism, 225
  emotional aspects, 299
  in European traditions, 151, 1032, 1036, 1037, **1040–1043**, 1050–1051
  female ritual nudity, 729
  hair symbolism, 390
  Hecate as goddess of, 400
  history of study, 433, 644, **1050–1051**
  midwives and, 563
  in Native America, 1036, **1047–1048**
  neopagan, 715, 716
  overview, **1035–1037**
  possession, 787
  shape-shifting, 896
  sorcery vs., 925, 1043, 1045
  temptation and seduction, 966
  visual imagery, 1012
  wicca, 1028–1029
  witch-hunting, 1001, 1051
  women linked with, 1042
  See also Wicca
Witchcraft Today (Gardner), 1048
Witch-Cult in Western Europe, The (Murray), 1048
Wittek, Gabriele, 717
Wittgenstein, Ludwig, 836
Wittig, Monique, 363, 364, 643
Wives, **1051–1053**
  biblical images, 461
  Christian, 618, 625–626, 1051–1052
  Confucian, 196
  gender roles, 361, 362, 1051–1052
  hair symbolism, 390
  Hindu, 419–421, 424–425, 618, 642, 988, 1052
  Islamic, 489–490, 496, 827–828, 1052–1053
  Israelite, 1033
  Jewish, 625
  Mormon, 677
  Protestant activists, 811
  Roman clothing, 183
  submission to husband, 666

  See also Marriage and singleness; Motherhood and grandmotherhood; Widows
Wodziwob, 725
Wo Hok Shep Cemetery (Hong Kong), *30*
Wolf, Margery, 282, 893
Wolff, Toni, 556
Wolfson, Elliot, 572
Wollstonecraft, Mary, 86, 164, *165*, 774, 1062
WomanChurch, 186
Womanist traditions, 335, 434, 592, 976, **1053–1054**, 1060
  African American churches, 5
  communal childrearing, 680
  moral reasoning style, 676
  polytheistic leanings, 785
  racism and, 832
  rejection of patriarchy construct, 760
  sin concept, 910
  storytelling, 1064
  woman's studies, 1068
Woman Question, The (Aveling), 629
Woman's Bible, The, 334, 359, 913, 975, **1054–1055**, 1062
Woman's Bible Commentary, The (Newsome and Ringe), 1055
Woman's Christian Temperance Union, 576
Woman's Encyclopedia of Myths and Secrets, 1025
Woman's National Liberal Union, 359
WomanSpirit (magazine), 379
Womanspirit movement, 943
Woman of the Water's Edge, 279–280
Womb, **1055–1056**
  in African religions, 10, 11
  amulets and, 28
  of Buddhist wisdom, 1034, 1035
  cosmic purpose, 95, 794
  earth as, 277–278
  fundamentalist view, 354
  in Maori religion, 934
  pregnancy, 794–795
  See also Fertility and barrenness
Women Against Fundamentalism, 355
Women and religion, **1056–1060**
  in the East, **1058–1060**
  monotheism and orientalism, **1056–1058**
  theology, 978–979
  See also specific religions
"Women and Religion" (Sinclair), 769
Women and Sacrifice (Beers), 816
Women as heroines, **1060–1063**
  biblical, 90, 104, 1062
  new religions, 717–718

religious martyrs, 627
warfare situations, 1019
Women at the Wall, 550, 1016
Women-Church movement, 466, 577,
743, 914
Women, Culture, and Society (Rosaldo
and Lamphere eds.), 710
Women in Black, 756
Women in the Past, Present, and Future
(Bebel), 629
Women's American ORT, 544
Women's Christian Temperance Union,
163, 168
Women's Conference for the Defense of
Palestine (1938), 897
Women's contemporary spirituality
movement, 466, 861, 914, 916, 943,
1063–1065
leadership roles, 577
lesbian couples' shared child-rearing,
680
lesbian studies and, 590–591
theosophical influences, 980
vegetarianism, 999
wicca, 1029
Women's Day, 5
Women's Exponent (Mormon journal),
677
Women's history. *See* History
Women's Indian Association, 426
Women's International League for
Peace and Freedom, 756
Women's International Zionist
Organization, 551
Women's Ordination Worldwide, 165
Women's religions, **1065–1067**
contemporary spirituality movement,
1063–1065
contemporary witchcraft movement,
1048–1050
feminist, 815
life-cycle rituals, 820
neopaganism, 715–716
priestesses, 804–806
See also Thealogy
Women's Rights Convention (1848),
1070
Women's studies, **1067–1069**
ancient goddess religions, 705–706
gender studies vs., 363
on women philosophers, 779
world religions, 294–295
See also Gender studies; Lesbian
studies
Women's suffrage movement, 93, 164,
169, 359, *497*, 545, 677, 758, 891,
913, 1062, **1069–1070**
Women's Trade Union League, 552

Women's Welfare, 757–758
Women's Work (Barber), 1025
Women's Zionist Organization of
America, 551
Women in World Religions (Sharma), 769
Won pulgyo, 722
Woodson, Carter, 4
Woodworth-Etter, Maria, 318
Woolf, Virginia, 40, 41, 164, 451, *773*,
774, 908, 1062
Word, Protestant emphasis on, 813
World Congregation of Gay and Lesbian
Jewish Organizations, 582
World Council of Churches, 164, 478
World Hindu Council, 335
World Mill, 872
World Mother movement, 980
World Soul (Anima Mundi), 733
World's Parliament of Religions (1893),
130, 478
World War I, 1020–1021
World War II, 1028
Worship, 845, **1070–1072**
dance and drama as, 233, 237–238
Hindu women, 642
Jewish practices, 528, 530, 539, 543,
549–550, 876
liturgy, 571–572, 602–604, 748
See also Ritual; Shrines
Wounding, ritual, 94
Wovoka, 724
Wraith, 368
Wronsky, Siddy, 552
Wu, 278–279, 1045, 1046
Wu-sheng Lao-mu, 605
Wuthnow, Robert, 922
Wu wei, 249, 964
Wuxue Zuyuan, 685
Wu Zetian, empress of China, 202
Wycliffe, John, 811

X
Xerxes, 325
Xhosa (people), 1044
Xia dynasty, 330
Xiangshan Baojuan, 661
Xilonen, 20
Xiong-nu (people), 475
Xiong Shili, 200
Xiwangmu. *See* Queen Mother of the
West
Xochitecatl (Mesoamerican site), 653
Xu Fuguan, 200

Y
Yab-yum, 117, 263
Yael, 443
Yaffa, *13*

Yagel, Abraham, 541
Yahgan (people), 931
Yahweh, 264, 394–396, 514–517, 934,
946, 1024, 1038, 1039
Yājñavalya, 306
Yajur-Veda, 858, 870
Yaka (people), 10, 96
Yākinī, 772
Yakṣas, 940
Yakshi, 278
Yakut (people), 894
Yam, 137
Yama, 759
Yamaga Soku, 198
Yamato clan, 900
Yaminya, 57
Yamm, Prince, 486
Yam Woman, 94
Yangoru Boiken (people), 473–474
Yantras, 565, 892
Yao, emperor of China, 195
Yao (people), 217
Yao Chi, 1024
Yaqui (people), 235
Yashts, 483
Yasoda, 472
Yasodhara, 614
Yates, Frances A., **1073**
Yazatas, 484
Yeats, William Butler, 612
Yemaja, 15
Yemaya, **1073–1074**
Yemoja, 7
Yeshe Tsogyal, 97, 117, 362, 1035
Yeshe Tsogyel, 36, 67, 79, 81, 97, 117,
231, 362, 1010
Yetzer hara, 909
Yggdrasil, 871
YHWH, 264
Yi/Choson dynasty, 122, 198
Yidam, 117
Yiddish, 571, 792
Yin/yang polarity, **1074–1075**
and Chinese woman's traditional role,
757
Confucian law and, 573
dead flesh and bones, 683
earth's significance, 277
emotional aspects, 300
feminine aspect, 331, 333, 823, 886,
964
as male-female dualism, 274
as paired principle, 208
Taoist, 23, 36, 221, 675, 757, 770, 771,
964
Yoder, Don, 346
Yoga, 772, **1076–1077**
as ascetic practice, 66

Yoga (*continued*)
  body's subtlety, 98
  divinity and, 262, 263
  kuṇḍalinī arousal, 38, 565, 892
  sexuality and, 585, 997, 1077
  vow taking, 1017
Yoga sutra, 585, 1076, 1077
Yoginīs, 231, **1077–1078**
  Himalayan Buddhism, 116, 118, 191
  Hinduism, 421
  tantra and, 956, 1015–1016
Yom Kippur, 194, 325
Yoni, 995, 996, **1078**
Yonipūjā, 1078
Yoruba (people), 96, 326, 338, 598, 600,
    604, 754, 966
  circle symbolism, 179–180
  enslavement of, 13
  gelede ritual, 9–10, 96, 338, 339
  masquerades, 233
  menarche ritual, 645
  religious beliefs, 7, 8, 14, 15
  witchcraft, 1044
Yoshikawa Buntaro, 281
Yoshitoshi Taiso, *26*, *333*
Youmans, Letitia, 168
Young, Brigham, 677
Young, Serinity, 76
Young Women's Christian Association,
    163
Youth Aliyah, 953
Yuan dynasty, 100
Yuma (people), 587
Yu Nu, 329

Yupik (people), 235
Yurok (people), 650

Z

Zaharias, Babe Didrikson, 1063
Zahra. *See* Fāṭima
Zaire, 615
Zambia, 579, 819–820
Zapotec culture, 727, 754, 903
Zar cult, 233, 337, 348, 409, 442, 501,
    575, 603, 789, 893, 1010, 1066
Zarephath, widow of, 807
Zaynab, 53, 440, 499
Zayran spirits, 337
Zeitkin, Clara, 629
Zell, Katherine, 151, 811
Zell, Matthias, 811
Zen Buddhism, 123, 131, 198
  feminine images, 333
  koans, 333, 842
  Mugai Nyodai, 685
  pottery and, 217–218
  on wisdom, 1034
Zeresh, 464
Zeus, 36, 472, 609, 1003
  Athena and, 71, 333, 1026, 1031
  defeat of father Kronos, 472
  Demeter and, 248
  feminist view of, 703
  Hera and, 402, 468, *702*
  mountaintop temples to, 367
  Muses and, 686, 687
  as ruler of Olympus, 384
  serpent as power symbol, 755

Zhang Junmai, 200
Zhang Yimou, 598
Zhengyi, 961
Zhou dynasty, 195, 279, 280, 330
Zhou Xuanjing, 1010
Zhuang, king of China, 660–661
Zhuang Zhou, 959
Zhuangzi. See Chuang-tzu
Zhu Xi (Chu Hsi), 121, 197, 198, 280
Zia ul-Haq, 493, 508
Zilpah, 387
Zimdars-Swartz, Sandra, 1005
Zionism, 542, 543, 545, 551, 554, 1057
Zionist and Ethiopian Churches, 161
Zito, Angela, 99
Ziyaret, 781, 899
Zodiac, 70, 179
Zoe, 988
Zohar, 541, 984
Zoloth-Dorfman, Laurie, 312
Zombies, 368
Zoroaster, 271, 483
Zoroastrianism, 18, 19, 221, 483–484,
    819, 875–876
Zosara, 464
Zubayda, 54
Zuesse, Evan, 20
Zulaykha, 828
Zulu (people), 339
Zuni (people), 208
Zuni Mythology (Benedict), 86
Zu Shu, 961
Zwingli, Ulrich, 811
Zwi Werblowsky, R. J., 785